interdisciplinary applied approach"; rather, STEM education is viewed as comprising attributes that are common to the four disciplines, namely, engaging students in "critical thinking, inquiry, problem solving, collaboration, and what is often referred to in engineering as design thinking" (p. 7). This perspective aligns with the recognition by many nations of the importance of these generic skills in advancing students' learning across the STEM disciplines.

An aspect of concern for mathematics education within an integrative STEM approach, however, is the need to maintain a strong presence and role alongside the other disciplines. A balanced distribution of the four discipline areas is essential, otherwise mathematics could very well be in danger of being overshadowed. At present, science seems to dominate many current STEM reports. Indeed, the STEM acronym itself is frequently referred to as simply "science" (e.g., Office of the Chief Scientist, 2014). Many countries also refer to the role of STEM education as one that fosters "broad-based scientific literacy" with a key objective in their school programs being "science for all," reflected in an increased focus on science education in elementary, junior, and middle secondary school curricula (Marginson et al., 2013, p. 70). As Marginson et al. commented, discussions on STEM education rarely adopt the form of "mathematics for all" even though mathematics underpins the other disciplines; they thus argue that "the stage of mathematics for all should be shifted further up the educational scale" (p. 70). Even the rise in engineering education, commencing in the early school years (e.g., Lachapelle & Cunningham, 2014), would appear to be oriented primarily towards the science strand at the expense of mathematics. This concern has been raised by several researchers in engineering education (e.g., English & King, 2015; Honey et al., 2014; Walkington, Nathan, Wolfgram, Alibali, & Srisurichan, 2014).

An interesting way of viewing mathematics within a unified STEM approach is evident in the California State Department (2014), where the integrative nature of each of the four disciplines is defined. Mathematics is viewed in terms of fostering "mathematically literate" students, who not only know how "to analyze, reason, and communicate ideas effectively," but can also "mathematically pose, model, formulate, solve, and interpret questions and solutions in science, technology, and engineering" (p. 11). Although advancing mathematics learning from such a perspective is potentially rich, the discipline nevertheless remains underrepresented in terms of ways to achieve this, with science still appearing to receive considerably greater attention, as Honey et al. (2014) indicated.

One of the underutilized roles of mathematics within STEM lies in providing critical grounding for success beyond school, where skills are needed for making informed decisions on issues that are central to national and international debates on political, economic, environmental, health, and defense issues, to name a few. Together with the exponential rise in digital information within STEM, the ability to handle contradictory and potentially unreliable online data is critical (Lumley & Mendelovits, 2012). Mathematics provides the grist for making evidence-based decisions in dealing with data across disciplines. More recognition needs to be given to this powerful role of mathematics in STEM integration.

In essence, we argue that mathematics as a discipline within the current STEM climate needs to have a stronger voice. Mathematics must maintain equitable discipline representation, especially with the burgeoning of publications devoted to STEM education (e.g., Honey et al., 2014; National Research Council, 2014; Purzer, Stroble, & Cardella, 2014; *International Journal of STEM Education*; www.stemeducationjournal.com/). At the same time, the research conducted across all STEM disciplines needs to reach the classroom and other relevant learning environments. As we indicate in the next section, one of the most enduring challenges for mathematics education, and indeed any field, is linking research with practice.

Linking Research with Practice

The perennial nature of the research into practice challenge is reports, editorials, and articles devoted to ways in which we might

our significant research outcomes so that they directly enhance learning and teaching (e.g., Arbaugh et al., 2010; Burkhardt & Schoenfeld, 2003; Heid, 2012). Indeed, though only Chapter 9 by Michael Fried and Miriam Amit on mathematics education reform was solicited to address this theme, it has been substantively addressed throughout the book, especially in Chapters 2, 4, 5, 7, 10, 18, 19, 20, 21, 22, and 29. Thus a general overview of the research/practice rift in this introductory chapter also serves to orient the reader to a major theme of the *Handbook*.

Policy concerns about the alienation of research from educational practice, and more generally about the efficacy of educational research, are deep-seated and international in scope. As reported in Vanderlinde and van Braak (2010), since the turn of the century there have been major governmental and government-funded reports filed in the UK, France, The Netherlands, and the United States, as well as multinational reports from the OECD's Center for Educational Research and Innovation, and the Commission of the European Communities.

Because funding of educational research is tied to public and political perception of its impact on practice, researchers are necessarily attentive to criticisms that educational research results are little utilized (Onderwijsraad, 2003), of poor quality (Coalition for Evidence-Based Policy (2002), and of limited influence (Burkhardt & Schoenfeld, 2003). Still, there is little consensus as to what role educational research should play, for instance whether production of knowledge or improvement of educational practice should predominate (Mortimore, 2000; Bauer & Fisher, 2007); and whether, in principle, knowledge produced by educational research can directly delineate educational practice, or if its appropriate service is to enrich the conversation about educational possibilities (Bridges, Smeyers, & Smith, 2008; Nuthall, 2004).

To gain some perspective on the range of issues involved in the research/practice split, we turn to the work of Broekkamp and Van Hout-Wolters (2007), which identifies four quite different interpretations of the underlying concern, as summarized in Vanderlinde and van Braak (2010, p. 302):

1.   Educational research yields few conclusive results; or educational research does not provide valid and reliable results that are confirmed through unambiguous and powerful evidence.
2.   Educational research yields few practical results; or educational research is limited in practical use.
3.   Practitioners believe that educational research is not conclusive or practical; or educational research is not meaningful for teachers.
4.   Practitioners make little (appropriate) use of educational research; or practitioners do not have the skills to use educational research results.

Depending on which interpretation one subscribes to, the actions needed to affect positive change will vary widely:

1.   Rethink the kinds of research questions that are pursued and/or the methodologies employed to address those questions (Levin & O'Donnell, 1999); or invest more in high-quality, validated research (Kennedy, 1997).
2.   Design research studies that more effectively address the needs of practitioners (Hammersley, 2002); include practitioners as partners in research (De Vries & Pieters, 2007; Ruthven & Goodchild, 2008).
3.   Do a better job of articulating the linkages of research studies to practice (Gore & Gitlin, 2004); or train teachers in the science of educational research (NRC, 2002).
4.   Disseminate research results more widely (Chafouleas & Riley-Tillman, 2005); or train practitioners in the interpretation and utilization of educational research results (Edwards, Sebba, & Rickinson, 2007).

The critical point offered by Broekkamp and Van Hout-Wolters (2007) is that our current discourse about the research/practice gap is dominated by "monocausal analyses": "When a certain cause has been determined, there is often a plea for the extensive and radical application of a single solution that is supposed to close the gap. Other solutions are then regarded as incompatible" (p. 204). We do well to keep this point in mind as we consider the multifaceted and conflicting interpretations of the research/practice gap, and the need for judicious and inclusive solutions to it.

OVERVIEW OF HANDBOOK CHAPTERS

Section I: Priorities in International Mathematics Education Research

We now turn to highlighting some of the core points raised in the chapters of each section. Those of the first section, following this introductory chapter, provide an exoskeleton for the concerns of mathematics education research with respect to teaching and learning. The starting point is recognition, well established by "almost four decades of significant scholarly work . . . that teachers make a difference in student learning" (Charalambous & Pitta-Pantazi, Chapter 2, p. 44). The challenge undertaken by the authors in this section is to provide perspectives on how to ground the research effort so as to mine this rich connection of learning and teaching for the benefit of teachers and students.

To begin, Charalambos Charalambous and Demetra Pitta-Pantazi (Chapter 2) provide a state-of-the-art review of the literature, focusing on theoretical and methodological advances in research over the past decade on mathematics *teacher knowledge, teaching practice*, and *student learning*. Although these topics are first treated independently, the goal of the chapter is to understand them in mutual relation. Their review documents the extant multifaceted effort to derive insight into the learning/teaching connection for mathematics.

The next two chapters move away from this basic overview in opposite directions, from inward toward the substance of learning and teaching, to outward toward the structure of the supporting disciplines. Susan Gerofsky (Chapter 3) seeks grounding for mathematics learning and teaching in the body, highlighting approaches to embodiment through *metaphor and language, cognitive science, semiotics, cultural studies, feminist materialism*, and *gesture* and *performance studies*. Gerofsky begins by tracing the roots of the current emphasis on embodiment to the encompassing philosophical transition from modernist to postmodernist sensibilities, the mind/body dualism of modernism gradually giving way to "a fully embodied world where mental and physical ways of being are inseparable" (p. 64). Her inclusive overview of the various approaches to embodiment provides a birds-eye view of a sea change in mathematics education thinking that easily can be missed by scholars focusing more locally on personal agendas of research. Gerofsky concludes the chapter by documenting the many touch points in her own Graphs & Gestures Project to the various literatures on embodied learning, thereby illustrating the interdisciplinary potential of this scholarship.

To conclude the opening section, David Kirshner (Chapter 4) addresses the conundrum for educators posed by the presence of multiple branches of psychology (e.g., behavioral, developmental, sociocultural) each providing its own independent vision of learning. Kirshner cautions against adopting any single one of these major theoretical schools to guide educational practice. Likewise he eschews the integrative schools (e.g., situated cognition, social constructivism) that have sprung up in the interstices of the major branches. From a Sociology of Scientific Knowledge perspective, Kirshner argues that adopting any single theorization—either unitary, or integrative—serves psychology's interest in achieving paradigmatic unity, the hallmark of a mature science (Kuhn, 1970). But it denies the current multiparadigmatic reality of psychology, and it subverts education's own interest in achieving coherent theoretical grounding for what, indeed, are separate and discrete notions of learning that motivate educational practice across its broad span.

As an alternative, Kirshner articulates independently coherent *genres* of teaching, each addressing itself to a unique learning goal (knowledge, skills, dispositions; see National Council for Accreditation of Teacher Education [NCATE], 2002), each informed by a theorization of learning specific to that goal. Such a move, he argues, resolves the *conflict* that arises when groups of scholars line up behind different basic notions of learning, and the *confusion* inherent in attempts to stretch a single theorization across incommensurable conceptions of learning.

Section II: Democratic Access to Mathematics Learning

The chapters in the second section address the theme of democratic access to a sound mathematics education throughout schooling. This theme was also addressed in the previous editions of the *Handbook*, where issues related to learners, teachers, and learning contexts were examined. In the current edition, a shifting landscape of learning contexts has emerged as a more sustained focus of research, so we have collected related chapters where the theme of *transformations in learning contexts* is examined. The current section maintains the interest on learners, which we trace through grade-bands from early childhood education through university-level mathematics education, and we have added in a chapter on mathematics education reform as it impacts students' educational experiences in schools. The penultimate chapter turns to a focus on the education of mathematics teachers, and a final chapter has been added on the much-neglected topic of mathematics education doctoral programs to round out the focus on issues related to school learning.

In Chapter 5, Moss, Bruce, and Bobis present a picture of dynamic possibility for mathematics in the early grades to counter the low expectations and limited challenge inherent in many current curricula. Current practice reflects a mélange of influences, including an outmoded perspective of unstructured play as the optimal pathway to concept attainment in the early years, a narrow curricular tradition focused on counting and on sorting and naming of shapes, and a behaviorist focus on repetition and reinforcement as guiding instructional modes. The chapter presents alternatives to all of these influences, centered around a *guided discovery* alternative to unstructured play illustrated through vignettes that demonstrate the depth and sophistication of learning possible for young children. These innovative teaching practices are framed with a special focus on geometry/visualization instruction, which Moss, Bruce, and Bobis highlight as a burgeoning area of current research. An equity thesis enwraps the whole chapter. Early childhood mathematics achievement is the single most significant factor in later academic success (e.g., Watts, Duncan, Siegler, & Davis-Kean, 2014); and guided discovery succeeds equally well with students of all backgrounds. Early mathematics education has a special cultural role to play in narrowing gender, class, and race achievement gaps, and in increasing social mobility.

Progressing to the elementary school years, Carrarher and Schliemann (Chapter 6) target the powerful ideas of functions and relations as an avenue for increasing learning access for elementary school students. The authors view these ideas as facilitating more in-depth learning and understanding of key mathematical content areas, laying the foundation for major long-term developments. Carrarher and Schliemann draw upon four core notions in examining these foundational domains of functions and relations. First, the operations of arithmetic are themselves, functions—the first instances that students encounter. Second, functions and relations are central to the development of students' concept of number beyond natural numbers, and they also underlie variables. Third, these ideas play a uniting role in linking arithmetic, algebra, and geometry, with the abstract nature of functions calling for representation in diverse forms such as tables of data, graphs, diagrams, arithmetic and algebraic expressions, and even as spoken and written language. The final notion builds on the fact that the left- and right-hand sides of equations and inequalities can be viewed as "the comparison of two functions across their domains" (p. 193).

In arguing for greater attention on these core ideas, Carraher and Schliemann provide rich examples of how we might advance students' access to these underrepresented topics in existing curricula. They argue that bringing out early understanding of functions and relations through informal methods can lead to more in-depth and integrated mathematical knowledge, as well as an enhanced ability to draw generalizations. Furthermore, early access to these constructs can lay powerful foundations for the later introduction of formal study of these topics.

In examining access to mathematics in the middle and junior secondary schools, Rojano (Chapter 7) analyzes the role of sense development and meaning assignment as processes that provide access to life-long mathematics learning. Adopting a semiotic perspective, Rojano provides an in-depth analysis of the relationship between these processes and students' mathematics and linguistic experiences, and argues how it is possible to design teaching models that are appropriate for these school levels. In addition, Rojano addresses modes of technology use that have the potential to offer students increased experimental approaches to mathematics, link their learning across domains, and provide an early introduction to advanced mathematics topics. For example, developments in three-dimensional Dynamic Geometry enable students in the junior secondary school to access themes of spatial geometry usually reserved for college or university study.

Rojano also touches upon the rapid growth in interactive materials on the Cloud and through mobile devices, which she views as wielding significant influences over social aspects in fostering long-term mathematics learning (further discussion on these promising technological developments is presented in the last section of this *Handbook*). While welcoming these breakthroughs in technology, Rojano reminds us of the need to work towards closing the gap between research and practice, one of the ever-present challenges we face. We would add that increasing students' access to these new technologies is paramount. It cannot be assumed, of course, that the latest technology is available to all students across all nations, or even in the more affluent ones. Increasing this access is an equally challenging issue that warrants urgent attention.

Moving to tertiary-level mathematics in Chapter 8, Mamona-Downs and Downs discuss ways of increasing students' access to advanced mathematical thinking with respect to mathematical structure, proof, and definition. They adopt the notion of mathematical structure as an avenue to blend intuition and semantics with the abstract and the formal, which enables the authors to investigate ways to enhance the transition period from school study to university. Given that this transition period can be difficult for many students, the authors illustrate how structure has a supportive role in developing understanding of proof and definition. For example in considering their perspective on proof, they maintain that the rules of predicate logic must be respected explicitly, given that proof construction can be a difficult process for many students. For example, students can accept faulty argumentation because they fail to understand the language used and the structure involved.

Fried and Amit (Chapter 9) address challenges facing all nations engaged in the complex endeavor of mathematics education reform—indeed, reform in general. As the authors indicate, such reform targets nearly every component in the field including teaching and learning and the associated environments, curriculum design, assessment, technological developments, national and economic needs, cultural values, and social justice. As such, research that addresses reform in mathematics education needs to be considered holistically, not reduced to any one of these sectors.

In advancing a general framework for addressing reform research in our field, Fried and Amit consider three core interrelated factors: change, communication, and cooperation. At the heart of reform lies change, which is entwined with communication, itself a complex process embracing different populations with varied interests, expertise, and needs. Promoting change through reform research is a significant challenge. Researchers of course must consider how their work on reform effects change and what the anticipated (and unanticipated) responses to change might be. The latter aspect is especially important given that reform movements are not always successful, especially when rapid changes are expected across many sectors. As a final point, Fried and Amit emphasize the importance of reform researchers being cognizant of the role of values in the reform process. The perspectives and values of many other stakeholders need to be taken into consideration including those of other mathematics education researchers, mathematicians, scientists, philosophers, and historians. The importance of cooperation in undertaking reform research is thus emphasized.

In Chapter 10, Pedro da Ponte and Chapman update their review of research on the education of prospective mathematics teachers from the second edition of the *Handbook* to include the period 2006–2013. Their graphic model of the domain includes an inner core of mathematical knowledge intersecting with mathematics teaching knowledge and embedded within the prospective teacher's professional identity, which itself is embedded in the professional community of teachers. Impinging on this from the outside is a wide range of cultural, institutional, and professional factors. The review is centered around the three elements of the inner core, providing continuity with the previous *Handbook* and enabling a coherent analysis of trends in the literature, which occupy the concluding section of the chapter.

These trends include continuing "deficiencies in prospective teachers' knowledge of mathematics and mathematics teaching that require special attention in teacher education," (p. 293), as well as "a variety of instructional approaches [that] can make a difference to the quality of this knowledge such as building on prospective teachers' sense making of mathematics and mathematics learning by involving them in activities that bear on fundamental mathematical ideas at school level and focusing on the learner's thinking" (p. 293). In terms of the infrastructure of research, daPonte and Chapman have noted a paucity of large-scale, objectively oriented research studies (see also Chapter 29 for a discussion of this point).

Section III concludes with Chapter 11 by Kilpatrick and Spangler addressing an underrepresented domain, namely, educating future professors of mathematics education. Given that this education is foundational to the professional growth of future teachers and leaders in schools, universities, education departments, and other institutions, it is surprising that limited research has been devoted to the topic. Kilpatrick and Spangler present an informative and insightful examination of the comparatively recent establishment of doctoral programs for mathematics educators, and their growth in the United States and in other countries. The nature of doctoral programs varies widely, with different emphases placed on course work, dissertations, and field experiences. The authors argue that irrespective of where new professors are eventually employed, they must be prepared in both mathematics and mathematics education. Doctoral programs should provide the foundations for the current and future development of the required mathematical and pedagogical knowledge, skills, and competencies. At the same time, these programs should provide future professors with valuable experience in teaching mathematics and mathematics education.

Kilpatrick and Spangler emphasize that irrespective of how such programs might change over the years, they must engender in these young professors a wide-ranging perspective on the field and proficiencies in critically analyzing reported research. We would reiterate these points, including the importance of a solid knowledge and appreciation of research and developments across a range of mathematics topics, and experience in conducting and critiquing research studies.

Section III: Transformations in Learning Contexts

This third section of the *Handbook* brings together chapters related to the changing contexts of mathematics education, including the different demands of the workplace and the economy wrought by technological innovations, the changing cultural, political, and demographic environment of the schools and the broader societies, and the changing intellectual landscape occasioned by complexity theory.

English and Gainsburg (Chapter 12) open the section with examining problem solving and advancing it beyond the current literature. They set the scene by reviewing briefly how problem-solving research over many years has yielded numerous pendulum-like swings in recommendations for mathematics education. Among the debates are the effectiveness of teaching general heuristics and strategies, the role of mathematical content (as the means versus the learning goal of problem solving), the role and relevance of context, and whether social and affective dimensions should be central concerns of problem-solving education.

English and Gainsburg look beyond these unresolved debates to examine the literature on the demands of modern work and life. They consider some of the drivers of change in the workplace and everyday life, resultant changes in the nature of quantitative problems arising in these changing contexts, and the competencies needed for successful solving of such problems. The authors then return to the long-standing debates that introduced the chapter and suggest possible resolutions responsive to the changing context of 21st century problem solving. They argue that, although we cannot just transport mathematical problems beyond school into the classroom, there are many ways in which "school problems" can be realistically contextualized. The result, English and Gainsburg maintain, should encompass a transition to more cognitively challenging problems where students' curiosity is stimulated, critical thinking and creative solutions are fostered, and multiple entry and exit points are included to facilitate increased access by a range of students.

In Chapter 13, Appelbaum and Stathopoulou address the burgeoning interest in culture that has emerged in mathematics education in recent decades. Because individual psychology has dominated our field historically, there is a tendency to regard the new focus on culture as a unitary alternative. Early in their chapter, Appelbaum and Stathopoulou disabuse us of this premise in the form of a two-dimensional table that crosses five notions of culture with six notions of mathematics/mathematics education, the cells of which reflect distinct interests and orientations "that have become significant in the field, including: mathematics as a culture; funds of knowledge pedagogies; ethnomathematical critiques and approaches to teaching and learning; popular culture studies; public pedagogies; and critical mathematics education" (p. 340). Even though "these are not separate, analytic categories, but mutually informing strands of interwoven discourse" (p. 340), we risk incoherence in our theories and in our educational initiatives if we address mathematics and culture without identifying our particular location within this broad set of discourses. The chapter by Appelbaum and Stathopoulou provides insightful outlines of the major formations in that landscape, as a valuable resource for orienting ourselves—as individual researchers and as a community.

Skovsmose and Penteado (Chapter 14) examine through a philosophical lens the complexities attending to the relation of democratic ideals and mathematics education. This complexity stems in part from the different forms that democracy has taken—for instance, a Rousseauean participatory democracy versus notions of representative democracy conceived in terms of "'competitive struggle' [wherein] people's democratic activity consists solely in casting their votes" (p. 359). However, as these ideals have played out, democratic principles have called into play a variety of associated concepts such as *social justice*, *equality*, and *freedom*, each just as complex and contested as democracy, itself. The result is an "aporetic condition" (p. 361) characterized by tensions, uncertainties, and challenges.

Skovsmose and Penteado explore multiple facets of how notions of democracy have played out in the larger society and in the microcosms of mathematics education practice. These rich portraits do not and cannot cohere; however, "contested concepts might have other functions than providing analytical clarity and proper justifications for particular educational approaches"—particularly, they can fuel "pedagogical imaginations . . . [that] help to reveal that alternative educational practices are possible" (p. 365).

In Chapter 15, Rousseau Anderson and Tate home in on the intricacies of race, class, and equity policies and scholarship to organize a review of the sociology of mathematics education oriented to the U.S. context. The review is structured around a set of four questions: How does mathematics education socialize? What role does mathematics education serve in credentialing? How do various entities in society influence mathematics education? What role does mathematics education play in creating and maintaining inequality? The chapter is introduced through a vignette of teaching in a low socio-economic status–classroom, which is revisited in the course of addressing each of these organizing questions, lending a sense of coherence and intertextuality to the topic.

In common with many of the authors in this *Handbook*, Rousseau Anderson and Tate provide guidance as to how to negotiate the diverse and often contradictory theorizations and approaches encountered in the literature. In particular, race, class, and equity in mathematics education are informed by a broad array of scholarly fields and theoretical endeavors. Rousseau Anderson and Tate suggest the virtues and advantages of organizing mathematics education inquiry as a subdiscipline of the sociology of education, which itself is a subdiscipline of sociology. In addition to providing a broader arena of influence for our scholarship, this move would facilitate access to constructs and perspectives of sociology that we currently are neglecting. For instance a "geospatial perspective would take into account multiple factors at the local level that might be related to educational achievement and attainment. These factors would include . . . employment and other economic indicators [that] . . . are well beyond the scope of traditional mathematics education scholarship. Yet, attention to these factors is necessary to understand the nature of democratic access at a local level and to design interventions that are likely to be successful" (p. 391).

In Chapter 16, de Abreu and Crafter focus on the continuities and discontinuities of mathematics learning in and out of school: "Our major interest resides in examining the implications of these [cultural] processes to the understanding of school mathematical learning. What makes mathematical practices to be experienced as continuous or discontinuous between in school and out of school settings?" (p. 395)

The structure of their chapter reflects historical shifts in the cultural psychology of mathematics education. "Research of the late 1970s and early 1980s tested the plausibility of [a sociocultural] theoretical framework. It . . . focused on a discussion around the relationship between cognition and cognitive tools . . . such as counting systems, and how these were appropriated and used as cognitive tools" (p. 411) within indigenous cultures. In the next period, "the framework was broadened to pay attention to processes of social mediation" (p. 411). This featured a shift in attention of research in "school mathematics . . . from cross-cultural comparisons to social practices within the Western societies" (p. 411). The third turn in this field has focused research in a poststructural direction "on the person as a participant in multiple mathematical practices. In this perspective discontinuity is a starting point, and research explores trajectories of participation, attempting to make sense of the processes that result in a person experiencing discontinuity in practices over time and across practices, and processes that enable change and facilitate continuity" (p. 411). Overall, de Abreu and Crafter regard these shifting foci of research as offering complementary analyses of what contributes to experiencing continuities and discontinuities across different mathematical practices. The new phase does not erase or discredit what came before.

Complementing English and Gainsburg's perspectives on 21st century problem solving, Davis and Simmt (Chapter 17) explore the increasing prevalence and impact of complex systems in our world, and ultimately on mathematics teaching and learning. There is no readily acceptable and unified definition of complexity; rather Davis and Simmt explore it from a variety of viewpoints: historically; mathematically as a digitally enabled, modeling-based branch of mathematics; theoretically as the study of learning systems; and pragmatically as a means to nurture emergent possibility. Mathematics education is richly implicated at the nexus of complex interactions among social conditions, cultural tools, and mathematical content that can enrich the development of curriculum and teaching approaches. Unfortunately, the mathematical affordances of our complex and interlinked world, including availability and rapid communication of large data sources, are often not adequately reflected in today's mathematics curricula.

Davis and Simmt (and others, e.g., Lesh, 2010) provide a vital service in recommending and explicating complexity as a core foundation for curriculum. Complexity arises for mathematics educators not only as an important subject matter of disciplinary mathematics, widely applied in STEM disciplines (science, technology, engineering and mathematics), but increasingly as a source of insight into the functioning of social systems, including the social system of mathematics education research and social systems of classroom mathematics.

As the research of English (e.g., 2008, 2013) has shown, even young learners are capable of dealing with complexity in solving modeling problems. Incorporating complexity and complex systems within the mathematics curriculum remains an issue in need of urgent attention, especially given the increasing demands of complex, data-driven problems in the work place and society in general.

Section IV: Advances in Research Methodologies

We turn in the fourth section to advances in the methods of research, with a particular focus on the relation of theory to method. Thompson (Chapter 18) opens the section with a critical analysis of the construct of "knowledge" as a driver for much of our research into the learning and teaching of mathematics. Knowledge—in the declarative sense of knowing *about*—he argues, is separate from the mental schemes that underlie our actions in the world. As an alternative, he proposes a focus on *meaning* that reflects the inherently subjective constructive process. Consider a boy who has appended a fourth meter stick to three that are lying end-to-end, and then declares that the total length has been increased by a meter: "The child *knows* that he added a meter. But what did it *mean* to him? Did he mean that he added one more stick called 'a meter'? Or did he mean that he added a meter in length that is constituted by centimeters, which in turn are constituted by millimeters, which in turn are constituted by (and so on)" (p. 457). In the chapter, Thompson outlines a method for developing items and instruments that focus on teachers' mathematical meanings for teaching mathematics, and examines how to link research and assessment more intimately than simply using the results of each in the activities of the other.

In Chapter 19, Callingham addresses the challenges of achieving reliable and trustworthy research designs within a heterogeneous theoretical environment. To explore this terrain, she introduces the constructs of *environmental* and *instrumental* context. Environmental context presents the kinds of challenges to generalizability that stem from the diversity of contexts in which mathematics education is practiced, including divisions across national boundaries, cultural settings, social classes, race and gender divisions, etc. Though formidably complex, the nature of these challenges are well understood through the methodological traditions that education inherits from the various supporting sciences. Instrumental context concerns the context of the researcher, including "the influence of prior experiences, previous research understandings, and personal preferences" (p. 467). These challenges are the more daunting in that what we think of as shared terminologies actually are adapted to one's personal constraints. For instance, as Callingham discusses, the notion of Pedagogical Content Knowledge has been operationalized in very different ways in studies in the United States, Australia, and Europe owing to the cultures of research shaping each research team's interpretive frameworks.

In Chapter 20, Cobb, Jackson, and Dunlap make a notable effort toward institutionalization of design research methodology by providing an authoritative guide that gives an account of its essential features, explores two major forms in detail (classroom instructional design and professional development), delineates the research process, and considers limitations. The most serious of such limitations is what Kelly (2004) described as absence of an "argumentative grammar" that explains the logic "link[ing] research questions to data, data to analysis, and analysis to final claims and assertions" (p. 489), the result being that "design studies lack a basis for warrant for their claims" (Kelly, 2004, p. 119). Cobb, Jackson, and Dunlap offer in this chapter some initial steps toward such a grammar.

Cusi and Malara (Chapter 21) take up the challenge of the theory/practice gap indicated by "a widespread prejudice about theory among teachers and practitioners, who often conceive it as irrelevant for practice" (p. 504). After surveying many dimensions of the problem, they settle on the quality of teachers' awareness of their practice as a critical focus point for engaging them in theoretical exploration. Their chapter recounts Cusi and Malara's use of a new tool, Multi-commented Transcripts, for engaging teachers-as-experimenters in serious theoretical co-reflection on their teaching: "The transcripts . . . are sent by experimenters-teachers, together with their own comments and reflections, to mentors-researchers, who make their own comments and send them back to the authors. . . . Often, the authors make further interventions in this cycle, commenting on comments or inserting new ones" (p. 508). This co-reflective process as a kind of apprenticeship in the art of understanding practice through theory is a promising and provocative vehicle for healing the theory/practice split.

Concluding this section, Ruthven and Goodchild (Chapter 22) link the domains of scholarly knowledge and craft knowledge of teaching through a "dialogic cycle of knowledge creation" introduced in Ruthven (2002): "In one phase . . . scholarly knowledge is (re)contextualized and activated within teaching, stimulating (re)construction of craft knowledge. In the complementary phase . . . craft knowledge is elicited and codified through researching, stimulating (re)construction of scholarly knowledge" (p. 528). Their chapter explores various mechanisms—"boundary-spanning didactical apparatus"—to facilitate this mutual engagement, but with the caution that these "approaches tend to privilege particular aspects of knowledge creation and conversion within the dialogic cycle" (p. 537).

Section V: Influences of Advanced Technologies

The final section of the *Handbook* is devoted to the influences of advanced technologies, a theme that was addressed in previous editions. With the evolution of the digital era, numerous technologies are emerging and becoming more ubiquitous in our lives. As Hegedus and Tall (Chapter 23) illustrate, these technologies are affording exciting opportunities for students to be fully immersed in the learning experiences, enabling them to connect with each other, share their ideas and creations, and have ready access to numerous and diverse resources. Yet the common question featured in this section is how such ubiquitous and highly usable technologies can be used in classrooms in mathematically meaningful ways. As Hegedus and Tall stress, the potential of technology as a change agent appears unfulfilled.

In addressing the challenge that mathematics educators face in capitalizing on these technological advances, Hegedus and Tall investigate the potential of multimodal technologies as core foundations for learning mathematics now and in the future. With a focus on the younger grades, the authors describe how recent developments in multimodal learning environments using haptic and multitouch technologies can facilitate greater access to core mathematical ideas and offer rich insights into long-term mathematical learning. In doing so, Hegedus and Tall build on strong theoretical foundations for learning to think mathematically. Specifically, they draw upon the well-established work of Tall (2013) and consider the important role of the fundamental processes of perception, operation, and reason.

Watson and Fitzallen (Chapter 24) consider technological affordances of a different kind, namely, those of computer software that target the learning of statistics. These affordances, which scaffold and support student learning, are determined by the inherent features, capabilities, and flexibility of the software. Using the software program TinkerPlots, the authors illustrate how these affordances can facilitate student learning and assessment across levels, as well as promote teacher learning. The associated constraints are also explored, given that some of the software's features may hinder student learning and therefore need to be taken into account when designing learning experiences. In essence, Watson and Fitzallen move beyond what software applications *promise* to do by highlighting what students *can* learn from using software, in contrast to what they might *not* learn, or not learn as easily, without it. At the same time, the authors consider the associated affordances for teachers as they plan for and subsequently assess student learning.

Adopting a different perspective, Moreno-Armella and Santos-Trigo (Chapter 25) offer suggestions for reconciling traditional and emerging approaches to technology use in mathematics learning. In particular, the mediating influence of the school culture is taken into consideration in efforts to capitalize on the affordances of new digital technologies to enhance students' access to more powerful mathematical ideas. The authors point out the tensions between traditional approaches to learning such as pencil and paper, and the innovative learning opportunities offered by technology. Focusing on ideas from geometry and calculus, Moreno-Armella and Santos-Trigo discuss the design of dynamic teaching models and activities where new forms of reasoning can emerge.

Extending their work from that reported in the second edition of this *Handbook* (English, 2008), Hershkowitz, Tabach, and Dreyfus (Chapter 26) target the research processes that were central to the development and implementation of a large-scale project for a computerized learning environment at the junior high school level. Specifically, the authors targeted open technological tools (graphical tools, spreadsheets, dynamic geometry software, computer algebra systems) with their rich features having the potential to enhance students' learning.

Hershkowitz et al. point out how their research commenced as design studies but ultimately yielded basic questions concerning teaching and learning in a technological environment. They illustrate how computerized environments produce new dilemmas in developing learning experiences in regular mathematical topics, such as linear equations and geometrical proof and proving. One of the issues they address in this regard is the role of students as agents in shifts of knowledge between small groups and the whole class community. Addressing these questions generated a number of broad theoretical and methodological outcomes, such as creating an operational definition of abstraction. This need for such a definition arose from asking in the later stages of the project, "What did students learn and consolidate, and how?" (p. 627)

A different, potentially transformative perspective on how technology can advance mathematical learning is offered by Pepin, Gueudet, Yerushalmy, Trouche, and Chazan in Chapter 27. Exploring how e-textbooks can enhance the teaching and learning of mathematics, the authors initially identify three models: the integrative e-textbook, which is basically a digital version of a paper textbook; the evolving or "living e-textbook," which is continuously developing due to input from several stakeholders; and the interactive e-textbook, which adopts the form of a "toolkit model" based on a set of connecting learning objects (tasks, diagrams, tools) (p. 640). The nature of student-teacher interactions in using these different models is explored, with a particular focus on quality and coherence considered as central to the design of e-textbooks and hence subsequent research.

The authors make the important point that is applicable to most developments in technology for classroom use: their presence alone is not sufficient. The usual expansive expectations of technology for educational advantages have not materialized to produce sustained changes in education. Nevertheless, there are several examples of where modifications to the nature of the technological object have lead to the development of new teaching paradigms. A case in point that the authors provide is the picture album that was transformed into a digital folder, enabling pictures to perform a totally new visual, social, and semiotic role.

The final chapter in the section on advanced technologies explores the increasing opportunities afforded by digital technologies in the early primary school years (K-2). With a particular focus on the two broad content domains of number and geometry, in Chapter 28 Sinclair and Baccaglini-Frank provide an overview of some of the major theoretical developments from research on technology use in these domains. In doing so, they identify affordances of the tools and the tasks that appear to most effectively support young children's mathematical engagement. To better facilitate the identification of these affordances, the authors untangle the range of tools that are broadly categorized as digital technologies including "multipurpose computer-based software programs, web-based applets, virtual manipulatives, programming languages, CD-ROMs, games, calculators, touch-screen applications and interactive white-boards" (p. 662). As Sincalir and Baccaglini-Frank note, the distinction between these various types is not always apparent. By presenting useful distinguishing features of these various technologies, the authors offer a means for teachers to better evaluate and select among them in their mathematics planning.

Despite the vast range of digital tools from which educators and researchers can choose, there is limited information on how particular design choices might impact children's learning, including how they use manipulative materials in the classroom. In considering this issue, Sinclair and Baccaglini-Frank highlight specific themes that they consider likely to emerge as significant areas of research, including the affective dimension of learning, the impact of different types of feedback given by the tools and teachers, and dealing with the constraints these tools present in addition to the affordances. The last issue is a particularly salient one that has been emphasized in several chapters in this section. As Sinclair and Baccaglini-Frank stress, in order to fully appreciate the potential of digital technologies and their impact on students' learning, the nature and consequences of such constraints need to be taken into consideration. This calls for improved communication among technology designers, researchers, and teachers, and, we would add, feedback from the students themselves.

The *Handbook* concludes with a wry reflection by Hugh Burkhardt—winner of the 2013 Excellence in Educational Design prize of the International Society for Design and Development in Education—on why "our [research] work on what happens in classrooms at large usually travels a long path where any causal effect is far from clear" (p. 689). His particular viewpoint highlights the atomization of the research effort, the tendency for there to be an imbalance of too many independent research strands, and not enough sustained, large-scale, multi-researcher programs of research: "Individual researchers, mostly university staff and their graduate students, make autonomous decisions as to what to work on next" (p. 691). The problem, he argues, is *not* the absence of excellent candidate programs that are strong and deep enough to warrant the focus he is calling for. Rather, he traces the paucity of large-scale research initiatives to the infrastructure of research support, the reward system for university-based research, and what he calls, "the academic value system" (p. 692). This is a summative critique of mathematics education research we would do well to reflect on as a community.

REFERENCES

Arbaugh, F., Herbel-Eisenmann, B., Ramirez, N., Knuth, E., Kranendonk, H., & Reed Quander, J. (2010). *Linking research and practice: The NCTM Research Agenda Conference Report.* Reston, VA: National Council of Teachers of Mathematics.

Bauer, K., & Fisher, F. (2007). The education research—practice interface revisited: A scripting perspective. *Educational Research and Evaluation, 13,* 221–236.

Bridges, D., Smeyers, P., & Smith, R. (2008). Educational research and the practical judgment of policy makers. *Journal of Philosophy of Education, 42,* 5–14.

Broekkamp, H., & Van Hout-Wolters, B. (2007). The gap between educational research and practice: A literature review, symposium and questionnaire. *Educational Research and Evaluation, 13,* 203–220. Retrieved from http://dare.uva.nl/document/2/52865.

Burkhardt, H., & Schoenfeld, A.H. (2003) Improving educational research: Toward a more useful, more influential, and better-funded enterprise. *Educational Researcher 32*(9), 3—14.

California State Department (2014). *Science, technology, engineering, & mathematics (STEM) information.* Retrieved from www.cde.ca.gov/PD/ca/sc/stemintrod.asp (December 16, 2014).

Chafouleas, S.M., & Riley-Tillman, T.C. (2005). Accepting the gap: An introduction to the special issue on bridging research and practice. *Psychology in the Schools, 42,* 455–458.

Coalition for Evidence-Based Policy (2002). *Bringing evidence-driven progress to education.* Report for the US Department of Education. Washington, DC, Coalition for Evidence-Based Policy.

De Vries, B., & Pieters, J. (2007). Knowledge sharing at conferences. *Educational Research Evaluation, 13,* 237–247.

Edwards, A., Sebba, J., & Rickinson, M. (2007). Working with users: Some implications for educational research. *British Educational Research Journal, 33*, 647–661.

English, L. D. (Ed.) (2008). *Handbook of international research in mathematics education* (2nd Edition). New York: Routledge.

English, L. D. (2013). Complex modelling in the primary and middle school years: An interdisciplinary approach. In G. Stillman, G. Kaiser, W. Blum, and J. Brown (Eds.), *Mathematical modelling: Connecting to practice—Teaching practice and the practice of applied mathematicians* (pp. 491–505). New York: Springer.

English, L. D., & King, D. (2015). *Integrating STEM Learning through Engineering Design: Fourth-Grade Students' Investigations in Aerospace*. Manuscript submitted for publication.

Gore, J. M., & Gitlin, A. D. (2004). [Re]Visioning the academic–teacher divide: Power and knowledge in the educational community. *Teachers and Teaching, 10*, 35–58.

Hammersley, M. (2002). *Educational research, policy making and practice*. London: Paul Chapman.

Heid, M. K. (2012). Editorial: Some thoughts on the importance of the community and on the challenge of identifying great research challenges in mathematics education. *Journal for Research in Mathematics Education, 43*(5), 502–508.

Honey, M., Pearson, G., & Schweingruber, H. (Eds.). (2014). *STEM integration in K-12 Education: Status, prospects, and an agenda for research*. Washington, DC: National Academies Press.

Kelly, A. E. (2004). Design research in education: Yes, but is it methodological? *Journal of the Learning Sciences, 13*, 115–128.

Kennedy, M. M. (1997). The connection between research and practice. *Educational Researcher, 26*(7), 4–12.

Kuhn, T. S. (1970). *The structure of scientific revolutions* (enlarged edition). Chicago: University of Chicago Press.

Lachapelle, C. P., & Cunningham, C. M. (2014). Engineering in elementary schools. In S. Purzer, J. Stroble, & M. Cardella (Eds.). *Engineering in pre-college settings: Research in synthesizing research, policy, and practices* (pp. 61–88). Lafayette, IN: Purdue University Press.

Lesh, R. (2010). The importance of complex systems in K–12 mathematics education. In B. Sriraman & L. D. English (Eds.), *Theories of mathematics education: seeking new frontiers* (pp. 563–566). Berlin: Springer.

Levin, J. R., & O'Donnell, A. M. (1999). What to do about educational research's credibility gaps? *Issues in Education, 5*(2), 177–229.

Lumley, T., & Mendelovits, J. (2012). How well do young people deal with contradictory and unreliable information on line? What the PISA digital reading assessment tells us. Paper presented at the *Annual Conference of the American Educational Research Association*, Vancouver, WA.

Marginson, S., Tytler, R., Freeman, B., & Roberts, K. (2013). *STEM: Country comparisons: International comparisons of science, technology, engineering and mathematics (STEM) education*. Melbourne: Australian Academy of Learned Academies.

Mortimore, P. (2000). Does educational research matter? *British Educational Research Journal, 26*, 5–24.

National Council for Accreditation of Teacher Education. (2002). *Professional standards for the accreditation of schools, colleges, and departments of education*. Washington DC: Author.

National Research Council. (2002). *Scientific research in education*. Washington, DC: National Academy Press.

National Research Council. (2014). *STEM learning is everywhere: Summary of a convocation on building learning systems*. Washington, DC: The National Academies Press.

National Science and Technology Council (May, 2013). *Federal science, technology, engineering, and mathematics (STEM) education: 5-year strategic plan*. A report from the Committee on STEM Education. Washington, DC: Executive Office of the President of the United States.

Nuthall, G., (2004). Relating classroom teaching to student learning: A critical analysis of why research has failed to bridge the theory-practice gap. *Harvard Educational Review,74*(3), 273–306. Retrieved from http://her.hepg.org/content/e08k1276713824u5/fulltext.pdf.

OECD (2013). PISA 2012 *Results: What students know and can do: Student performance in mathematics, reading and science*. Retrieved from www.oecd.org/pisa/keyfindings/pisa-2012-results.htm.

Office of the Chief Scientist (2013). *Science, technology, engineering and mathematics in the national interest: A strategic approach*. Canberra: Australian Government.

Office of the Chief Scientist (2014). *Benchmarking Australian science, technology, engineering and mathematics*. Canberra: Australian Government.

Onderwijsraad. (2003). *Kennis van onderwijs: Ontwikkeling en benutting* [*Knowledge about education: development and utilization*]. The Hague: Author.

Purzer, S., Stroble, J., & Cardella, M. E. (Eds.). (2014). *Engineering in pre-college settings: Synthesizing research, policy, and practices*. Purdue, IN: Purdue University.

Ruthven, K. (2002). Linking researching with teaching: Towards synergy of scholarly and craft knowledge. In L. English (Ed.), *Handbook of international research in mathematics education* (pp. 581–598). Mahwah, NJ: Lawrence Erlbaum.

Ruthven, K., & Goodchild, S. (2008). Linking researching with teaching: Towards synergy of scholarly and craft knowledge. In L.D. English (Ed.), *Handbook of international research in mathematics education* (2nd Ed.) (pp. 565–592). New York: Routledge.

STEM Task Force Report (2014). *Innovate: A blueprint for science, technology, engineering, and mathematics in California public education.* Dublin, CA: Californians Dedicated to Education Foundation.

Tall, D.O. (2013). *How humans learn to think mathematically: Exploring the three worlds of mathematics.* Cambridge: Cambridge University Press.

Vanderlinde, R., & van Braak, J. (2010). The gap between educational research and practice: Views of teachers, school leaders, intermediaries and researchers. *British Educational Research Journal, 36*(2), 299–316. doi:10.1080/01411920902919257. Retrieved from www.academia.edu/526808/The_gap_between_educational_research_and_practice_views_of_teachers_school_leaders_intermediaries_and_researchers.

Walkington, C., Nathan, M., Wolfgram, M., Alibali, M., & Srisurichan, R. (2014). Bridges and barriers to constructing conceptual cohesion across modalities and temporalities: Challenges of STEM integration in the pre-college engineering classroom. In S. Purzer, J. Strobel, & M. Cardella (Eds.). *Engineering in pre-college settings: Research into practice* (pp. 183—210). West Lafayette, IN: Purdue University Press.

Watts, T., Duncan, G., Siegler, R., & Davis-Kean, P. (2014). What's past is prologue: Relations between early mathematics knowledge and high school achievement. *Educational Researcher, 43*(7), 352–360.

2 Perspectives on Priority Mathematics Education

Unpacking and Understanding a Complex Relationship Linking Teacher Knowledge, Teaching, and Learning

Charalambos Y. Charalambous and Demetra Pitta-Pantazi

University of Cyprus

In the 1960s and early 1970s, two seminal reports (Coleman et al., 1966; Jencks et al., 1972) questioned the contribution of teachers and schools to student learning. Since then, heated debates have ensued, trying to prove that teachers and schools *do* matter for what students learn. Several studies undertaken since the 1970s have repeatedly documented the teachers' role in student learning (Cochran-Smith, 2003; Nye, Konstantopoulos, & Hedges, 2004; Rowan, Correnti, & Miller, 2002). Teacher effects, in particular, have been found to explain a higher percentage of variance in student achievement compared to school-level or system-level effects (see Luyten, 2003; Muijs & Reynolds, 2000; Scheerens & Bosker, 1997). Teacher effects have also been found to be cumulative and to last over a sequence of years (Konstantopoulos & Chung, 2011; Rivers & Sanders, 2002). Attempting to understand what contributes to student learning, several studies over the past four decades have suggested that what matters most is what teachers *do* in the classroom (Brophy & Good, 1986; Gallagher, 2004; Muijs & Reynolds, 2000; Stronge, Ward, & Grant, 2011)—that is teach*ing* per se—rather than different teach*er* attributes, such as their beliefs or job satisfaction (see Borich, 1992; Creemers & Kyriakides, 2008), their background qualifications (Palardy & Rumberger, 2008), or the resources made available to them (Cohen, Raudenbush, & Ball, 2003). Despite these encouraging results, as Hiebert and Grouws (2007) remind us, the core question in educational research lingers: "What is it, exactly, about teaching that influences student learning?" (p. 371).

In this chapter, we engage with this question, attempting to understand what research has suggested about the link between teaching and learning. Broadening our focus, we also add another link to the chain—teacher knowledge—thus, considering *the complex association among teacher knowledge, instructional quality, and student learning*. By adding teacher knowledge to the mix, we do not underestimate several other personal resources that teachers bring to the equation of teaching and learning (see Kennedy, 2010). We, however, consider teacher knowledge not only because of the significant work that has been accrued during the last decade in this arena, but also because Mewborn's (2003) argument about "a complicated relationship [that] exists among teachers' knowledge, their teaching practices, and student learning [and which] research has yet to untangle" (p. 47) is, by and large, still pertinent. In fact, notwithstanding the several advancements that have been made during the last decade in better conceptualizing and measuring the three components of the aforementioned chain, a range of open issues remain to be addressed if we are to better understand how the resources that teachers bring to instruction can inform their practice, and how their practice, in turn, can inform student learning. In doing so, a stronger link between research and practice—a still unfulfilled demand (see Arbaugh et al., 2010; Langrall, 2014)—could be forged.

Developing a better understanding of this relationship is both crucial and timely. In an era of intense economic crisis during which the accountability pressure exercised on teachers is intensified (Koretz, 2008; Papay, 2012) and the role and contribution of teacher education programs is severely debated (Grossman, 2008), unpacking and understanding this relationship can offer significant insights for teacher preparation and ongoing professional development. This becomes even more critical for mathematics, given that during the last decade the mathematics curricula in many countries have undergone notable reforms that impose increased demands on teachers and students alike.

To examine what has been accomplished over the past decade with respect to understanding this complex relationship and sketch priorities for future research, in this chapter we first parse the chain into its three constituent components and examine advancements made with respect to each link. We then bring these three links together and explore connections between and among them. To engage in this work, we started our exploration by first examining review studies in handbook chapters (e.g., *Handbook of Research on Mathematics Teaching and Learning, Handbook of International Research in Mathematics Education, Handbook of Research on Teaching, Handbook of Research on the Psychology of Mathematics Education*, and *The International Handbook of Mathematics Teacher Education*). Reviewing these works helped identify both what has been accomplished in the past and what have been considered as open issues. We then reviewed studies published during the last decade in mathematics education journals (e.g., *Educational Studies in Mathematics, Journal of Mathematical Behavior, Journal for Mathematics Teacher Education, Journal for Research in Mathematics Education, Mathematical Thinking and Learning*, and *ZDM: The International Journal on Mathematics Education*), and teaching education journals (e.g., *American Education Research Journal, Cognition and Instruction, Learning and Instruction*, and *Teaching and Teacher Education*). Our goal in reviewing these works was threefold: first, to identify trends with respect to studying each of the three chain components separately or combinations thereof; second, to explore whether open issues, as highlighted in handbook review chapters, have been addressed; and third, to identify lingering questions and priorities for future studies.

We hasten to note, however, that our review is neither comprehensive nor exhaustive—and it could not be, given that each link in the chain could comprise a review chapter in and of itself. What is reported here should be seen as a Janus-faced approach to look backward—and delineate advancements and trends in the fields of teacher knowledge, teaching, and student learning—and, by looking forward, consider directions for future work. In essence, we present what we consider to be key findings and developments as a basis for discussion, and for further research and development. As happens with any such approach, our approach in reviewing these studies might have constrained both what we have been able to sketch for the past or present and the priorities we offer for the future.

In this context, this chapter is organized into four sections. Each of the first three sections focuses on one link in the chain: teacher knowledge, teaching, and student learning, respectively. Within each of these sections, we first delineate advancements made at both theoretical and methodological fronts. We also examine conceptual and methodological trends observed during the past 10 years, and conclude with open issues. Considering the chain as a unified whole, in the last section we identify trends observed during the last decade with respect to exploring the conglomerate of the three components, and outline priorities for future research.

TEACHER KNOWLEDGE: UNDERSTANDING A KEY TEACHER RESOURCE

That teacher knowledge matters for student learning is neither a novel nor a particularly counterintuitive idea. In fact, thousands of years ago, the philosopher and scientist Aristotle distinguished between someone who just learns and possesses the subject matter—whom he called *a knower*—and the person who does not only know the content, but learns it in such a way so as to be equipped to teach it—whom he called *a master* (see Mason, 2008). The layperson opinion also holds that "you cannot learn from a teacher that does not know." However, during the 20th century, empirical evidence corroborating the role of teacher knowledge in student learning has been mixed at best and inconclusive at worst. For example, in his meta-analysis of studies conducted between 1960 and 1976 examining the effects of teacher knowledge on student performance, Begle (1979) concluded that these effects "seem to be far less powerful than most of us had realized" (p. 54), and urged for a redirection of the research foci away from teachers and their personal characteristics.

Scholarly interest in teachers' knowledge was revitalized after Shulman's (1986) seminal work. Shulman not only called for increased attention to the subject matter itself, but also set the stage for better conceptualizing the knowledge needed for the work of teaching. Whereas most educational production function studies (e.g., Monk, 1994) were concerned solely with exploring proxies of teacher knowledge, such as the courses taken or the credentials held, Shulman talked about teacher knowledge as comprising seven different components. The most crucial among them were Subject-Matter Knowledge (SMK), General Pedagogical Knowledge (PK), and Pedagogical Content Knowledge (PCK)—with the latter component attracting amassed scholarly interest during the last three decades (see Ball, Thames, & Phelps, 2008; Depaepe, Verschaffel, & Kelchtermans, 2013; Graeber & Tirosh, 2008). Capitalizing on or motivated by Shulman's work, scholars during the last decade have made significant advancements in both conceptualizing and measuring the knowledge needed to teach mathematics. In what follows, we consider these advancements while at the same time discuss open issues.

Conceptualizing the Knowledge Needed to Teach Mathematics

Talking about the unresolved problem of teachers' mathematical knowledge, at the dawn of the 21st century, Ball, Lubienski, and Mewborn (2001) called for studying teacher knowledge *in the context of teaching*. They maintained that to better understand this knowledge, we need to explore not only how teachers know the content, but also "what they are able to mobilize mathematically in the course of teaching" (p. 451). It was, therefore, not a coincidence that during the last decade, largely following a practice-based approach (see Ball & Bass, 2003), several scholars have offered different conceptualizations about this knowledge. In this section we review selected conceptualizations that have been advanced and/or refined during the last decade, then engage in a discussion on pressing questions and issues for further elaboration in the years to come.[1]

Analyzing 24 videotaped lessons offered by prospective teachers during their practicum training, and following a grounded-theory approach, Rowland and colleagues (Rowland, 2008a; Rowland, Huckstep, & Thwaites, 2005) developed a four-dimensional framework to capture the knowledge needed to teach mathematics. Identified as *Knowledge Quartet* (KQ), this framework organizes the 17 components that these scholars came up with into four dimensions: *foundations*, which includes knowledge, beliefs, and understanding acquired during preservice teaching; *transformations*, which corresponds to choice and use of examples, representations, and demonstrations; *connections*, that captures the knowledge displayed when teachers draw connections between ideas; and *contingency*, which pertains to the knowledge needed to respond to unanticipated events that occur during instruction. Instead of paying particular emphasis to distinguishing between different knowledge components—as was the case in Shulman's framework and the framework considered next—the developers of KQ gave more attention to instances in which knowledge surfaces during instruction.

Largely analyzing lessons taught by Deborah Ball while teaching a third-grade class for an entire year, scholars at the University of Michigan have advanced the notion of *mathematical knowledge for teaching* (MKT, see Ball et al., 2008). Building on, refining, and extending Shulman's distinction between SMK and PCK, this research group proposed a six-domain framework, with the three former components corresponding to SMK, and the latter three to PCK: *common content knowledge*, which captures mathematical knowledge and skills possessed by professionals outside of teaching; *specialized content knowledge*, which pertains to knowledge and skills unique to teaching mathematics; *horizon knowledge*, which enables teachers to see how the content being taught is situated in and connected to the broader disciplinary territory; *knowledge of content and students*, which requires familiarity with both mathematics and student mathematical thinking and misconceptions; *knowledge of content and teaching*, which requires mathematical knowledge of the design of instruction; and *knowledge of content and the curriculum*, which largely builds on Shulman's knowledge of instructional materials and programs.

While the prior two frameworks might be considered to attend to more personal aspects of knowledge, Davis and colleagues' (Davis & Simmt, 2006) *mathematics for teaching* pays particular attention to the dynamic and collective aspect of teacher knowledge—not only as something to be possessed and held, but also as something to be developed through interacting with other colleagues. More recently, building on Ma's (1999) idea of *profound understanding of fundamental mathematics*, Davis and Renert (2013) coined the term *profound understanding of emergent mathematics* to denote the dynamic, evolving, complex, and distributed character of this knowledge,[2] which is seen as a learnable participatory disposition, rather than as a fixed body of knowledge to be mastered.

Other conceptualizations of teacher knowledge have also been advanced during the last decade, including *mathematics for teaching* (Adler & Davis, 2006; Adler & Huillet, 2008), and *knowledge for teaching mathematics* proposed in the context of the international TEDS-M study (Tatto et al., 2012). Frameworks specifically developed to capture the knowledge needed to teach particular content strands have also been developed (e.g., in algebra, the *Knowledge of Algebra for Teaching* framework proposed by McCrory, Floden, Ferrini-Mundy, Reckase, & Senk, 2012).

The availability of all these different theoretical frameworks is a significant asset not only for studying the nature of teacher knowledge, but also for exploring its relationship with teaching quality and student learning (a topic we consider later). At the same time, however, the existence of several theoretical frameworks and the rate at which such conceptualizations appear to accumulate raise a set of issues that are worth considering in the coming years:

- To what extent and in what particular ways do these frameworks offer different perspectives for studying the knowledge needed for teaching the subject matter effectively? Are these frameworks complementary? If so, how?
- To what extent are they compatible with and synergistic to each other, especially when it comes to frameworks that emphasize either the individual nature or the collective/social aspect of teacher knowledge?
- To what degree could/should these frameworks be combined to offer a better understanding of the knowledge that teachers need to possess and develop to effectively teach mathematics?

Attempts to address such questions have been undertaken by different scholars in several venues and occasions, including a research forum conducted during the 33rd Conference of the International Group for the Psychology of Mathematics Education (see Ball, Charalambous, Thames, & Lewis, 2009; Even, 2009; Neubrand, 2009), a working session in the 8th Congress of European Research in Mathematics Education (e.g., Clivaz, 2013), and a review book chapter that compared and synthesized different theoretical conceptualizations (Petrou & Goulding, 2011). Pointing to similarities across the frameworks proposed and discussing their affordances and limitations, these scholars have suggested that, despite some overlaps, these frameworks are complementary to a certain degree. Nevertheless, much more work is needed to more comprehensively and convincingly address the aforementioned questions, given the limitations of the attempts already undertaken toward this direction (see Ruthven, 2011, pp. 85–86).

Despite the accumulating work related to theorizing and conceptualizing the knowledge needed to teach mathematics, studies *empirically validating* the theoretical constructs or frameworks proposed thus far are relatively scarce. For example, in their review of studies on PCK conducted in mathematics, Depaepe et al. (2013) list only a handful of studies that attempted to validate the distinction between PCK and SMK. Interestingly, one of the few large-scale studies conducted toward this direction (Krauss, Brunner, et al., 2008) showed that PCK and SMK are distinguishable for non-Gymnasium rather than for Gymnasium teachers, thus casting serious doubts about the distinguishability of different components of teacher knowledge. Similarly, empirical studies on MKT yielded mixed results about the extent to which the different MKT components are clearly distinct from each other (Hill, 2007, 2010; Hill, Ball, & Schilling, 2008; Hill, Schilling, & Ball, 2004). These equivocal findings, alongside the lack of studies that empirically support the construct validity of other theoretical frameworks, such as KQ, and the fact that doubts are cast about the multidimensionality of teacher knowledge at both theoretical (see Bednarz & Proulx, 2009; Huillet, 2009) and empirical levels (e.g., Beswick, Callingham, & Watson, 2012), raise another set of pressing questions warranting consideration:

- To what extent is teacher knowledge multidimensional, as suggested by different theoretical frameworks and conceptualizations? Can this multidimensionality be empirically supported?
- If teacher knowledge is multidimensional, how are the different components connected to each other?
- What are the implications of a multidimensional vs. a unidimensional construct of teacher knowledge for teacher initial preparation and teacher ongoing professional development and learning? To echo Graeber and Tirosh (2008), are some components of teacher knowledge more suitable for initial teacher education and others more appropriate for later stages of teachers' professional development?

Closely related to the conceptualization of teacher knowledge are the issues of *applicability* and *transferability*. By applicability, we refer to the extent to which the different conceptualizations generated to capture teacher knowledge also apply to content domains and educational levels beyond those in which they were developed. The reader is reminded that several of the frameworks discussed so far were developed bottom-up by considering teaching mathematics in elementary grades, and mostly with respect to number sense and operations. By transferability, we consider the degree to which these conceptualizations transfer across borders and are applicable to educational settings other than those in which they were initiated. Considering issues of transferability is not trivial, given that most of the frameworks discussed above have been developed and elaborated in Western countries. During the past decade significant advancements have been made at both fronts.

With respect to *applicability*, whereas earlier works were mostly focusing on number sense and operations (e.g., fractions, multiplication, and division), scholars have increasingly attended to other subject strands, including advanced algebra (e.g., Bair & Rich, 2011; McCrory et al., 2012; Yakes & Star, 2011; Zachariades, Christou, & Pitta-Pantazi, 2013); measurement (e.g., Murphy, 2012), geometry (Herbst & Kosko, 2012; Nason, Chalmers, & Yeh, 2012; Yanik, 2011), and statistics (Groth & Bergner, 2006, 2013). Although not all of these works necessarily examine the applicability of the aforementioned frameworks to different content strands, the very fact that researchers have expanded their foci to also include these topics highlights a trend that appears to be beneficial in the future—especially when combined with attempts to explore teacher knowledge in these content strands by employing different theoretical conceptualizations. Another trend pertains to shifting emphasis from merely elementary education to also considering secondary education. Largely missing from the picture are, however, studies that explore teacher knowledge for teaching pre-primary grades or tertiary education, with only some minor exceptions (e.g., Tsamir, Tirosh, Levenson, Tabach, & Barkai, 2014; Wagner, Speer, & Rossa, 2007; Zazkis & Zazkis, 2011). Given that a recent exploration that compared the knowledge needed to teach mathematics to elementary and secondary students (Rowland, 2012) has pointed to different demands imposed on teachers, investigating the applicability of different frameworks and constructs to different educational levels seems inescapable. In this respect, addressing the following questions appears to be consequential:

- How applicable are the theoretical frameworks developed to examine teacher knowledge to different content strands and to various levels of schooling (pre-primary, primary, lower secondary, higher secondary, and tertiary education)?
- To what degree can our insights about the knowledge needed to teach mathematics be broadened by considering less-emphasized topics (such as geometry, statistics, data, and probability) or less-investigated educational levels?

With respect to *transferability*, recently we have witnessed attempts to explore whether different theoretical frameworks (and measurement tools) are applicable to European (Delaney, Ball, Hill, Schilling, & Zopf, 2008; Ng, Mosvold, & Fauskanger, 2012), Asian (Kwon, Thames, & Pang, 2012; Ng, 2012), and African countries (Cole, 2012). These and other studies (e.g., Andrews, 2011; Pepin, 2011; Tatto et al., 2012) have shown the importance of exploring issues of transferability, since differences were found not only in specific items used to measure teacher knowledge, but also with respect to different teaching practices themselves. For example, as Pepin's (2011) work revealed, an apparently global practice—that of listening to student ideas—was manifested in dissimilar ways across educational systems, thus imposing different knowledge demands on teachers across systems. From this respect, the following questions that have started attracting research interest (see Stylianides & Delaney, 2011) should continue engaging scholarly attention:

- To what extent are the theoretical constructs and frameworks discussed earlier generic, in the sense that they travel across different educational settings, systems, and cultures?
- What aspects of them might be more culture-specific and why might this be the case? What might this suggest about the frameworks themselves and what implications could it have for teacher education in particular contexts?

Before departing from issues of theorizing and conceptualizing teacher knowledge, another trend observed during recent years merits discussion. Earlier works on teacher knowledge—especially those conducted in the 1990s (e.g., Cohen, 1990; Wilson, 1990) as well as more recent ones (e.g., Charalambous, Hill, & Mitchell, 2012; Lewis & Blunk, 2012; Lo & Luo, 2012; Rowland et al., 2005; Sleep & Eskelson, 2012)—seem to view teacher knowledge from a more static perspective, examining the knowledge *possessed* by teachers or lack thereof. More recently, there seems to be a tendency toward also examining how teacher knowledge can be enhanced, thus viewing teacher knowledge from a more dynamic perspective, which is more consonant with the idea of ongoing teacher development. Key in these studies is the structuring of an arena that can facilitate the development of teachers' learning, be it in the context of preservice education courses (e.g., Buchholtz & Kaiser, 2013; Nason et al., 2012; Steele, Hillen, & Smith, 2013), in the context of field placement (Philipp et al., 2007), or through teacher professional development that can take different forms and formats, ranging from Japanese "open lessons" (e.g., Miyakawa & Winsløw, 2013), to "problem-solving cycles" (e.g., Koellner et al., 2007), to guided reflection on practice using certain theoretical conceptualizations (Bell, Wilson, Higgins, & McCoach, 2010; Boston, 2013; Turner, 2012), or alternative certification programs (e.g., Lannin et al., 2013). Given recent studies documenting the differential effect that the same course can have on the development of teachers' knowledge (Lannin et al., 2013), but also given the promising results yielded from the aforementioned studies, in the years to come, scholars could devote concerted efforts to address inquiries such as:

- What specific aspects of teacher initial preparation/ongoing education endeavors facilitate (or constrain) the development of teacher knowledge?
- If teacher knowledge is multidimensional, how do the different components (co-)develop? Are some components prerequisites for the development of others?
- How does teacher knowledge evolve? Are there distinct trajectories in the development of teachers' learning and how might these be affected by other teacher personal resources (beliefs, identities, etc.) or other instructional and contextual resources (e.g., curriculum materials)?

The list of these questions is by no means exhaustive. It, however, points to what we regard a fruitful arena for directing research on teacher knowledge, and one that can help link research and practice. With that in mind, we now turn to issues pertaining to measuring teacher knowledge.

Measuring the Knowledge Needed to Teach Mathematics

During the 1990s, a widely employed approach to measure the knowledge needed to teach mathematics was to investigate teachers' practice. By observing teachers' lessons, scholars were drawing inferences about the presence or absence of teacher knowledge. The last decade has seen a movement toward more and more complex approaches for measuring this knowledge (see Hill, Sleep, Lewis, & Ball, 2007).

For example, the Learning Mathematics for Teaching group has developed and validated a set of paper-and-pencil multiple-choice instruments designed to capture different manifestations of teachers' MKT. To a large extent these instruments were found to capture knowledge entailed in teaching the subject matter rather than other personal competencies (see Hill, Ball, Blunk, Goffney, & Rowan, 2007; Schilling, Blunk, & Hill, 2007). Other groups have used open-ended questions describing different scenarios to which teachers are asked to respond (e.g., Baumert et al., 2010; Tatto et al., 2012). For instance, in the context of the Cognitive Activation project (Baumert et al., 2010; Krauss, Baumert, et al., 2008), teacher knowledge was measured by a paper-and-pencil test asking teachers to identify multiple solution paths, recognize student misconceptions, and offer explanations, etc. Using these instruments—either those comprising closed-ended questions or those involving open-ended prompts—has enabled researchers to conduct large-scale studies, which marks a significant departure from the single or multiple case-studies carried out during the 1990s.

Beyond the typical paper-and-pencil tests, during the last decade several other approaches have been employed to gauge teacher knowledge. These include, for instance, using video clips of mathematics lessons as stimuli to elicit teacher knowledge (Kersting, 2008; Kersting et al., 2010); employing simulations of teaching, which invite teachers to comment on the interactions of animated teacher cartoon characters with students (Charalambous, 2008); immersing teachers in post-lesson reflections on their lesson plans and practice (İmre & Akkoç, 2012); and engaging teachers in video-based prediction assessments (Norton et al., 2011).

As has been the case with different conceptualizations of teacher knowledge, attempts have recently been observed to juxtapose these different measurement approaches and examine their relative contribution. For example, Kersting and colleagues (Kersting, Givvin, Thompson, Santagata, & Stigler, 2012) showed that a classroom-video analysis measure of teachers' knowledge, although moderately related to a paper-and-pencil multiple choice test measuring this knowledge ($r = .41$), was more predictive in terms of both instructional quality and student learning. Examining gains in teachers' MKT during a K–8 mathematics content/pedagogy hybrid course and a general mathematics content course, Copur-Gencturk and Lubienski (2013) showed that two different paper-and-pencil tests captured different aspects of the growth in teachers' learning. Whereas the former seemed to be more conducive to gauging growth in teachers' common content *and* specialized content knowledge, the latter lent itself to tapping changes only in teachers' common content knowledge.

Other scholarly attempts have also been directed to examining the extent to which certain measures of teacher knowledge (or items thereof) are culturally sensitive, providing evidence that this is a legitimate concern. For instance, an international comparative study that examined teachers' knowledge across seven countries suggested that differences in the format, content, and the cognitive demands of the items used in the test had an impact on teachers' performance (Blömeke, Suhl, & Döhrmann, 2013).

The work that has been pursued during the last years in the arena of measuring teacher knowledge, as briefly delineated earlier, raises a gamut of questions that are worth considering in the future. Some of these questions have already attracted scholarly interest, but, by and large, remain partly addressed; others have not received the level of attention they deserve:

- What are the affordances and limitations of different approaches in measuring teacher knowledge?
- Given the dynamic character of teacher knowledge, as postulated by different theoretical frameworks, what approaches (or combinations thereof) can better capture teacher knowledge?
- How sensitive are the measures of teacher knowledge to the measurement approaches employed? To what extent are certain measures of teacher knowledge culturally sensitive and what might contribute to this sensitivity?
- If teacher knowledge is multidimensional, can certain aspects of teacher knowledge be captured by certain approaches? Could a combination of approaches help better portray teachers' knowledge, and more importantly changes thereof?
- If teacher knowledge is distributed across teachers, how can this knowledge best be measured (e.g., through collaborative planning, through collectively analyzing and reflecting on instruction, etc.)? What inferences can be drawn from such measurements?

Measuring teacher knowledge is, of course, not a goal in and of itself, since scholarly interest lies in examining the contribution of teacher knowledge to instructional quality and student learning—an issue we elaborate in the last section of this chapter. However, for the time being, it is worth mentioning that such attempts need to take into consideration whether the knowledge measures are aligned with the aspects of instructional quality under consideration and student learning. This is not trivial given recent findings showing teachers' performance in more "local" knowledge items (i.e., items related to the content of instruction) to be more highly associated with teachers' instructional performance, as compared to other items that capture teacher knowledge more holistically (e.g., Hill & Charalambous, 2012). This raises another question that ought to be considered in the years to come, if more progress is to be made in exploring associations between teacher knowledge, instructional quality, and student learning:

- At what level of granularity should we measure teacher knowledge to ensure its predictive validity, but at the same time maintain the generalizability of the inferences that can be drawn from such explorations?

The list of questions with respect to both conceptualizing and measuring teacher knowledge, as discussed earlier, should be considered as sketching venues for future explorations rather than as offering an exhaustive mapping of the terrain. Even so, to echo Askew (2008), "It seems there is plenty to keep researchers in this field going for many more years yet" (p. 32). Keeping that in mind, we now turn to the next link of the chain: teaching and instructional quality.

TEACHING AND INSTRUCTIONAL QUALITY: LOOKING INSIDE ANOTHER COMPLEX TERRAIN

If teacher knowledge is hard to conceptualize and measure, defining, studying, and measuring teaching and its quality is much more complicated. In fact, although there is wide consensus that teachers and teaching do matter for student learning, what comprises teaching—and especially quality teaching—and how it can be measured constitutes one of the biggest conundrums faced by educational researchers (see Cochran-Smith, 2003; Croninger, Valli, & Chambliss, 2012; Franke, Kazemi, & Battey, 2007; Hiebert & Grouws, 2007). As Cochran-Smith (2003) aptly puts it, "Although there is great consensus that teaching quality matters, there is little consensus about most other matters related to teaching quality" (p. 97). In this context, we contemplate two fundamental issues: first, we consider what teaching is (and consequently how we can define and study teaching quality); second, we explore the advancements made in measuring teaching and its quality.

Conceptualizing and Studying Teaching and Teaching Quality

According to Hiebert and Grouws (2007), the first step in exploring any connections of teaching quality to its contributors and outcomes is to *define* teaching. Synthesizing prior definitions, Hiebert and Grouws (2007) delineate teaching as consisting "of classroom interactions among teachers and students around content directed toward facilitating students' achievement of learning goals" (p. 372). To this, we add that these interactions occur in and are shaped by certain contexts.

The two components of this definition—interactions and learning goals—capture the essence of Fenstermacher and Richardson's (2005) conceptualization of quality teaching. For these scholars, quality teaching is the synthesis of *good* and *successful* teaching. When defining *good* teaching, they refer to the teacher-students interactions around the content. They maintain:

> By *good* teaching we mean that the content taught accords with disciplinary standards of adequacy and completeness, and that the methods employed are age appropriate, morally defensible, and undertaken with the intention of enhancing the learner's competence with respect to the content studied.
>
> (p. 192)

The *successful* component accords with the idea of promoting certain learning goals and bringing about specific learning outcomes. Otherwise stated, "successful teaching is the teaching that produces results, it 'leads to learning'" (Fenstermacher & Richardson, 2005, p. 192).

By integrating good and successful teaching, the abovementioned definition could offer a good starting point for studying teaching. However, such a definition in and of itself does not suffice for understanding the complex work of teaching. In contrast, to effectively unpack and understand this work, scholars are in need of theoretical frameworks that decompose teaching into its constituent components and explore the mechanisms through and the conditions under which these components can contribute to student learning. Unfortunately, despite more than a century of research on specifying and studying effective teaching, perhaps with only some exceptions, as a field we still lack specific theories and established theoretical frameworks that stipulate what teaching is, let alone detail how it is connected to student learning (see Ball & Rowan, 2004; Hiebert & Grouws, 2007; Nuthall, 2004).

The role of such theories in improving our ability to understand teaching, predict its determinants and consequences, and through that improve teaching and learning is indisputable

(Gage, 2009). Why, then, is developing such theories and theoretical frameworks so difficult to accomplish? Part of the answer lies in that there is not a single way through which teaching can influence learning. This was revealed by different studies—especially international comparative studies (Hiebert et al., 2003; Stigler & Hiebert, 1999)—that documented different approaches to teaching and showed that the presence or absence of certain instructional aspects alone does not suffice for inducing learning. In this sense, what we need is not theories or frameworks that promote one or the other approach or component, but theoretical tools that will enable us to examine how *constellations* of different components can advance our thinking and understanding of teaching and its effects (see Hiebert et al., 2005). In fact, this is another key challenge that researchers are expected to face in the years to come.

Mapping the terrain of teaching is, according to Grossman and McDonald (2008), a pivotal step for engaging in this work and another way through which theories and theoretical frameworks of teaching can be developed. For, as these scholars opine, despite decades of work and the plethora of research papers that have been produced so far, the field of teaching still comprises an uncharted terrain; it still lacks a common language and analytic tools for parsing and decomposing instruction in ways that could help describe, analyze, and improve teaching. Grossman and McDonald (2008) go on to offer some guidelines for successfully decomposing this terrain. They suggest that our approach be agnostic to the type of instruction; that it be directed to identifying the underlying grammar of the practice of teaching; that it establish common and precise language in describing teaching and its constituent parts; and that it be informed by several research paradigms.

A recent promising line of research and thought that builds on these guidelines pertains to identifying core practices of teaching mathematics (see Ball, Sleep, Boerst, & Bass, 2009; Grossman, Hammerness, & McDonald, 2009; Lampert, 2010; McDonald, Kazemi, & Kavanagh, 2013). Although initially scholars had somewhat different conceptualizations as to what exactly these practices are, during the recent American Educational Research Association (AERA) 2014 conference held in Philadelphia, Pennsylvania, they came up with the following definition:

> Core Practices are identifiable components fundamental to teaching that teachers enact to support learning. [These] practices consist of strategies, routines, and moves that can be unpacked and learned by teachers. Core Practices can include both general and content specific practices.
>
> (Core Practice Consortium, 2014)

Such practices can occur with high frequency in teaching and can be learned and enacted by even novice teachers to support student learning. Thus, a key challenge that lies ahead for researchers in the next decade—and one that was also alluded by Franke et al. (2007)—concerns tackling the following inquires:

- Which practices are core for teaching mathematics? How can these practices be identified? Can consensus be reached on what comprises such practices?
- To what extent are these practices culturally sensitive, given prior works documenting differences across educational systems in the teaching of mathematics?
- What is the underlying grammar of these practices—to use Grossman and McDonald's (2008) words?
- Through which mechanisms and under what conditions can these practices support student learning?

To contribute toward the effort of mapping the terrain of teaching by considering certain practices that resonate with the definition given earlier, in what follows we draw on two broad lines of research, which, by and large, seem to have moved along parallel paths. In doing so, we abide by Grossman and McDonald's (2008) guidelines to capitalize on different research paradigms. Along with their recommendation to be agnostic to the teaching approach considered, in our review we refrain from endorsing certain teaching approaches. Also, because of space limitations, we avoid considering the role of certain curricula or technological tools in shaping instruction, given that these resources in and of themselves are not self-enacting.

The first line of work pertains to teacher effectiveness research (TER). In contrast to TER, which uses mathematics as a content and context for studying effective teaching, the second line of work pertains to research that foregrounds the content of mathematics and the disciplinary demands it imposes on teachers. As such, our review resonates with the last sentence in the Core Practices definition, according to which we need to attend to both generic *and* content-specific practices: the first line of research reviewed reflects more generic practices, while the second is closer to content-specific practices.

Both older (e.g., Brophy & Good, 1986; Creemers, 1994) and more recent (e.g., Klieme, Pauli, & Reusser, 2009; Kyriakides & Creemers, 2008; Pianta, Belsky, Vandergrift, Houts, & Morrison, 2008; Stronge et al., 2011) individual TER studies, but more so, a set of meta-analyses (Hattie, 2009; Kyriakides, Christoforou, & Charalambous, 2013; Kyriakides, Creemers, Antoniou, & Demetriou, 2010; Scheerens & Bosker, 1997; Seidel & Shavelson, 2007) point to a gamut of observable teaching behaviors that have consistently been found to contribute to student learning. These studies, and especially the meta-analyses, have also shown these practices to be more significant determinants of student learning than other teacher background characteristics (see Hattie, 2009; Muijs & Reynolds, 2000). Although stemming from studies focusing on mathematics, these behaviors are *generic* in the sense that they cut across different subject matters; in other words, their applicability transcends the subject matter in which these studies have been conducted. Considering the TER state-of-the-art and synthesizing the results of studies conducted over the past 35 years, in a recent review article, Muijs et al. (2014) catalogue several such generic teaching practices. At the top of the list of those practices are the opportunity to learn and the time students are on task. Structuring of information and soliciting student thinking through effective questioning that consists of both lower- and higher-level questions, as well as giving timely and relevant feedback to students, are also included in the list. Classroom management and creating a positive learning environment through productive student-student, and teacher-student interactions has also been found to contribute significantly to student learning (Bell et al., 2012; Kane, Taylor, Tyler, & Wooten, 2011). Other generic practices include using advanced organizers, employing concept mapping, exposing students to worked examples, and giving students opportunities for practice and application (see Creemers & Kyriakides, 2008; Hattie, 2009).

Absent from the list of the practices is a close scrutiny of the subject matter per se and the demands that teaching mathematics imposes on teachers—a lacunae that Shulman (1986) identified when referring to the missing paradigm of the then-existing body of research. As a result of the increased emphasis given to the content since then, and especially during the last two decades, a wealth of studies have been conducted that focus on (composites of) practices that are more content-specific for mathematics. These practices include, for example, using and linking representations to highlight the meaning of certain mathematical concepts or procedures (e.g., Huang & Cai, 2011; Izsák, Tillema, & Tunç-Pekkan, 2008; Mitchell, Charalambous, & Hill, 2014; Murata, Bofferding, Pothen, Taylor, & Wischnia, 2012); drawing connections between mathematical ideas and real-world situations (e.g., Gainsburg, 2008); engaging in proving and reasoning (e.g., Bieda, 2010; Stylianides, 2007); and identifying patterns and developing generalizations (e.g., Ellis, 2011).

Although applicable to other subject matters beyond mathematics, other practices are particularly pertinent to teaching mathematics, since their enactment can take particular forms and formats because of the disciplinary demands the subject matter imposes. These include, for instance, providing explanations (Charalambous, Hill, & Ball, 2011; Gil & Ben-Zvi, 2011); steering classroom discussions toward the mathematical point that each lesson is designed to make (e.g., Sleep, 2012; see also the concept of directionality in Hill, Blunk, et al., 2008); selecting and using appropriate examples and counterexamples to reinforce student understanding of mathematical concepts and processes (e.g., Mills, 2014; Rowland, 2008b; Zazkis & Chernoff, 2008; Zodik & Zaslavsky, 2008); setting and maintaining the cognitive demand of tasks through student engagement in complex tasks (e.g., Boston & Smith, 2009; Jackson, Garrison, Wilson, Gibbons, & Shahan, 2013; Stein, Smith, Henningsen, & Silver, 2000); carefully monitoring student responses during seatwork, and selecting and purposefully ordering responses to be displayed and shared during whole-group discussions (e.g., Cengiz, Kline, & Grant, 2011; Jackson et al., 2013; Nathan & Kim, 2009; Stein, Engle, Smith, & Hughes, 2008); and, in general, supporting discourse for doing and learning mathematics (see Chapin, O'Connor, & Anderson, 2003; Franke et al., 2007). Following recommendations to not only identify these practices and explore how they play out in teaching, but also to unpack and decompose them into their constituent components, in some of the studies listed earlier scholars have also gone into more depth, identifying the underlying components and grammar of these practices.

To summarize, an increasing body of studies has zoomed in on either generic or content-specific teaching practices. Beyond extending this work to better unpack and understand what is entailed in teaching *mathematics*, the following research inquiries seem to pose productive directions for future research:

- Are the practices considered thus far sufficient for capturing teaching quality in mathematics? If not, what other practices might be important and how can they be identified?
- What manifestations of these practices define teaching quality and what are the underlying mechanisms through which each of these practices contributes to student learning?
- Are these practices equally effective for different student populations? Given that most of these studies have been conducted in primary or secondary grades, are these practices equally effective for pre-primary grades or even tertiary education? More generally, under what conditions and for which student populations are these practices effective in terms of promoting student learning?
- Are these practices equally effective for promoting noncognitive learning outcomes? To what degree are they conducive to promoting higher-order thinking skills?
- Can a hierarchy of practices be developed that rank orders these practices in terms of their relative contribution to teaching quality and student learning? What might the implications of such a hierarchy be for the preparation of prospective teachers and the ongoing development of practicing teachers?

Given the importance of considering constellations of practices, and given that for years researchers in the two aforementioned lines of inquiry have largely been working in parallel, at least an equally productive path of research and a key priority for researchers and practitioners alike during the next decade pertains to searching for synergies between generic and content-specific practices. Exploring such synergies has been underlined by scholars working in either of the two domains (e.g., Brophy, 1986; Grossman & McDonald, 2008; Hamre et al., 2013). A recent study (Charalambous, Komitis, Papacharalambous, & Stefanou, 2014) has also shown that such integration is supported by teachers as well, given that they do not rate the two types of practices as distinctly important or feasible to implement in their instruction. In this respect, the following inquiries also seem important to be considered:

- To what extent can combinations of generic and content-specific teaching practices help better explain student learning?
- Which are these combinations and what is their nature? Do generic and content-specific teaching practices contribute individually to instruction or is their effect synergistic/interactive? To what degree could practices of one type mediate the effect of practices of the other type?

- Are some combinations of such practices prerequisite for others? In other words, does effective enactment of certain combinations of practices set the bedrock for effective engagement in other practices? If so, what implications might this have for teacher education?

Given the complexity of teaching and the difficulties that inhere in studying it, combining different practices and different perspectives seems both a legitimate and a promising way to tackle complexity. Having discussed issues of conceptualizing and studying teaching, we next turn to aspects of measuring teaching quality, which are equally challenging and productive to explore.

Measuring Teaching and Teaching Quality

Writing about measuring teaching and its quality almost three decades ago, Shavelson, Webb, and Burstein (1986) concluded: "The domain of the measurement in research on teaching is enormous [. . .] each topic within this domain is terribly complex" (p. 86). The rapidly accumulating work on measuring teaching (quality) over the past 30 years could not have attested more convincingly to the legitimacy of this argument. Indeed, significant progress has been made both in terms of the approaches pursued and the tools developed to measure instructional quality. This progress notwithstanding, scholars interested in measuring instruction are still faced with several challenges. In reviewing some of these challenges—which, in fact, point to directions for future research in this arena—we also consider different ways advanced to measure instructional quality. We pay particular attention to classroom observation, which has recently attracted a lot of attention.

Taking into account how complex teaching is, the first challenge in measuring its quality concerns determining and defining the aspects of teaching to be measured. Correnti and Martínez (2012) put this very nicely by pointing out that when it comes to teaching, "there are different aspects [. . .] we may choose to measure, and each represents a complex entity that may be defined and described in different ways and with different languages" (p. 55). Part of this challenge resides in the lack of a clear and widely agreed-upon conceptualization as to what comprises teaching quality (see Ball & Hill, 2009; Gage, 2009; Hiebert & Grouws, 2007). Without well-defined theoretical frameworks about teaching and its relationship with learning, attempts to measure instructional quality might not be particularly productive, since explorations might not be guided by sound hypotheses linking teaching to its antecedents and outcomes/consequences.

A second, closely related, challenge pertains to attending to constellations of different aspects of teaching. As discussed earlier, teaching is something more than the summation of its individual components. Although it might be important to examine the quality of, say, the connections that the teacher draws when using representations, or the type of questions she or he poses, much more value resides in investigating and measuring combinations of such practices. The predicament, however, lies in determining what to include and what to exclude, especially taking into consideration the multitude of components assumed to define quality teaching in mathematics. Hopefully, as we explain, when considering classroom observations, videotaping of classroom interactions enables researchers to attend to more components than what would have been feasible to observe through live classroom observations alone.

A third challenge relates to the fact that teaching and learning do not happen in a vacuum, and thus, both are affected by multiple other factors. That makes detecting the effect of teaching—and the effectiveness of different teaching components—hard to identify. Speaking to this idea, Gitomer (2009) argues that although in several cases a signal (i.e., teaching quality) exists, this signal is lost amidst a very noisy environment. He claims,

> [O]ur analytic models are attempting to detect a consistent signal in an exceedingly noisy environment. And the fact that weak signals are often detected does not necessarily mean

that the signal is weak, only that the other noise is so overwhelming. An alarm clock just does not sound as loud in the subway.

(p. 229)

Hence, the real bet for scholars immersed in measuring teaching quality and linking this to student learning lies in figuring out ways to eliminate the noise and better capture the signal. Notable steps are made toward this direction both by using different tools to measure instruction and by combining such tools. That brings us to the last challenge to be discussed in this section.

The fourth challenge relates to developing appropriate instruments to gauge instructional quality and using them to measure this quality at scale (Ball & Hill, 2009; Chester & Zelman, 2009). In their review chapter, Hiebert and Grouws (2007) contend that developing such instruments is harder than developing measures of learning, both because of the complexity of teaching and because of the relatively less attention that teaching has received, compared to learning. Hopefully, during the last decade there seems to be increased attention to teaching and its measurement, as indicated both by the several methods that have been advanced and pursued to study teaching and the ongoing discussions about improving the ways employed to tap instructional quality. Apart from classroom observations—which we consider in more depth later—these methods include teacher (e.g., Kunter & Baumert, 2006; Mayer, 1999) or student ratings (e.g., Fauth, Decristan, Rieser, Klieme, & Büttner, 2014; Kunter & Baumert, 2006); interviews with teachers about their instructional practice (e.g., Murphy, 2012); teacher logs (e.g., Rowan, Harrison, & Hayes, 2004); instructional artifacts, such as assignments and student homework (e.g., Baumert et al., 2010; Boston, 2012; Martínez, Borko, Stecher, Luskin, & Kloser, 2012); and structured classroom vignettes that engage teachers in reflections about how they would react in different teaching situations (e.g. Stecher et al., 2006).

Because all these methods have their own affordances and limitations (see Ball & Rowan, 2004; Croninger, Buese, & Larson, 2012), there is growing consensus about the need of mixing approaches, measures, and tools to better capture and understand teaching quality. During the next decade, attempts should also be directed at detailing the affordances and limitations of different *combinations* of approaches and instruments. Given that different combinations of instruments and approaches might be more cost effective for studying particular aspects of teaching, scholars are encouraged to be more explicit as to which combinations lend themselves better to studying teaching and its association with learning, and the conditions under which this occurs. For example, are classroom observations and student survey ratings equally effective for studying the quality of instruction in teaching second-grade number sense and operations as they might be for studying teaching algebra in eighth grade? Are some combinations of instruments better than others in capturing instructional quality when it comes to more subtle aspects of teaching, such as the level of cognitive demand at which students are asked to work or the quality of the explanations offered by teachers? We envision that the "one-combination-fits-all" approach might be counterproductive to advancing our understanding of teaching quality and its effects. This hypothesis is reinforced by recent findings suggesting that measuring certain aspects of instruction—especially the more content-specific ones—is harder than measuring more generic teaching aspects (e.g., Praetorius, Pauli, Reusser, Rakoczy, & Klieme, 2014).

We close this section by focusing on an approach that has received increased attention and interest, especially during the last decade, partly because of the accountability pressure exercised on teachers (see McClellan, Donoghue, & Park, 2013; Papay, 2012), and partly because of the technological advancements that have reduced the cost of videotaping and analyzing videotaped instruction (see Tomás & Seidel, 2009): classroom observations, be they live or videotaped. Often considered the gold standard of studying instructional quality (Rowan & Correnti, 2009), classroom observations are becoming a key tool for investigating the quality of teaching, despite being a costly method. This is indicated by the fact that during the last decade a rapidly increasing number of observation instruments have been developed and validated, including both more generic instruments, such as the Framework for Teaching (Danielson, 2007), the Dynamic Model of Educational Effectiveness (Creemers & Kyriakides, 2008), and the Classroom Assessment Scoring System, or CLASS (Hamre et al., 2013), as well as more content-specific instruments, such as the Mathematical Quality of Instruction (e.g., Learning Mathematics for Teaching Project, 2011), the UTeach Observation Protocol (see Kane & Staiger, 2012), the Mathematics-Scan (Walkowiak, Berry, Meyer, Rimm-Kaufman, & Ottmar, 2014), and the Reformed Teaching Observation Protocol, or RTOP (Sawada et al., 2002).

The use of classroom observations is, however, not without limitations and complexities. In fact, a growing number of scholarly works published during the last few years point to a conglomerate of challenges that researchers need to tackle if classroom observations are to yield reliable and valid estimates of teaching quality. Talking about these complexities, Hill, Charalambous, and Kraft (2012) referred to teacher observation *systems*, to emphasize that estimates of instructional quality are influenced by a gamut of elements that include the observational instrument itself, the recruitment and training of raters, and the scoring design employed. The scoring design pertains to decisions such as the number and the length of observation to be conducted, the time of the year/school day during which observations are carried out, the number or raters that code each observation, and the sequence in which the observations are rated.

Recent studies have provided empirical evidence suggesting that all these decisions have a significant impact on the estimates yielded for instructional quality. For instance, the choice of observation instrument matters, since different instruments—although seemingly similar—capture different aspects of instructional quality (see McClellan et al., 2013). Studies have also shown that there is more variability in content-specific rather than generic teaching aspects; thus, more classroom observations are needed to capture the former rather than the latter instructional aspects (Praetorius et al., 2014). In contrast, with more generic instruments such as CLASS, even smaller observation lengths might suffice for yielding valid and reliable estimates of instructional quality (Mashburn, Meyer, Allen, & Pianta, 2014). Furthermore, from recent studies we know that different coding methods (e.g., observing lessons on one versus multiple days, attending to whole-class interactions only versus also considering small-group work) cause fluctuations in the characterizations of the instructional quality yielded by using a given observation instrument (Ing & Webb, 2012); that raters might not rate lessons consistently across the year and that their ratings might change as they become more experienced over time (Casabianca et al., 2013); and that even training raters might not suffice for reliably capturing certain aspects of instruction or identifying effective teachers (see Praetorius, Lenske, & Helmke, 2012; Strong, Gargani, & Hacifazlioğlu, 2011). These and other associated findings forcefully suggest that more concerted efforts are needed in the future to better understand the conditions under which reliable and valid estimates of instructional quality can be obtained. Addressing this issue becomes even more consequential given the recent shift from considering teacher observation instruments solely as tools for evaluating teaching to also regarding them as key levers for *improving* teaching quality (see Hill & Grossman, 2013).

STUDENT MATHEMATICAL LEARNING

To explore the priorities regarding student mathematical learning, we felt that categorizing where the emphasis lies by various studies in this domain would lead to a clearer discussion. Thus, studies that fall under this domain were organized into three subsections. The first subsection considers trends and open issues related to conceptualizing student mathematical learning. Zooming in on the components of mathematics and students, in the next two subsections we identify trends with respect to each of these components and discuss additional issues that warrant consideration in the coming years. Like the previous sections, this section closes by contemplating measurement issues regarding student learning.

Conceptualizing Student Mathematical Learning

Just like studying teacher knowledge and the quality of teaching, the issue of theoretical perspectives[3] on students' mathematical learning is crucial and attracted significant scholarly attention. Such perspectives allow researchers to more clearly express hypotheses of how complex phenomena work and communicate their understanding of these phenomena to other scholars. In the past, researchers claimed that there was a lack of theoretical perspectives of mathematics learning, and that mathematics education research needed to build its own theories and research paradigms (see Hiebert & Grouws, 2007). Nowadays, such theoretical conceptualizations are much more prominent in mathematics education. Important steps toward this direction have been, among others, the publication of the book *Theories of Mathematics Education: Seeking New Frontiers* by Sriraman and English (2010) and the establishment of a working group on Theoretical Perspectives and Approaches in Mathematics Education Research, initially set by Artigue, Bartolini-Bussi, Dreyfus, Gray, and Prediger (2005) and run in the context of the European Society for Research in Mathematics Education. As Lesh, Sriraman, and English (2014) recently stated, there is clearly "a shift beyond theory-borrowing toward theory-building in mathematics education; the relevant theories draw on far more than psychology" (p. 615).

Some theoretical perspectives on student learning that have been used quite extensively are rather *global*, since they are applicable to discussing student mathematics thinking and learning about various mathematical concepts (e.g., Biggs & Collis, 1991; Chevallard, 1999; Cobb & Yackel, 1996; Davis & Maher, 1990; Dubinsky, 1992; Freudenthal, 1968; Kruteski, 1976; Lakoff & Nuñez, 2000; Pirie & Kieren, 1989; Presmeg, 1985; Sfard, 1991; Siegler, 2000; Tall, 2013; Tall & Vinner, 1981; Tirosh & Stavy, 1999; Vergnaud, 1990). Given that, as Lesh et al. (2014) note, drawing on Begle (1979), a large part of what was presented as theories in mathematics education was (and still continues to be) dogma, a first research priority pertains to empirically validating these theoretical conceptualizations on student learning. The reader is reminded that this relative scarcity of studies that empirically validate various theories was also an open issue for teacher knowledge, as well.

Carrying out large-scale studies to confirm the results of small-scale studies is also warranted. Some attempts have been made towards this direction, leading either to the confirmation or negation of the proposed theoretical perspectives. On the one hand, Vergnaud's (2009) theory of conceptual fields was used by Griffiths (2013) as well as Caddle and Brizuela (2011) to analyze students' work on the fundamental theorem of arithmetic and linear graphs, respectively. On the other hand, Christou, Pitta-Pantazi, Souyoul, and Zachariades (2005) explored Tall's three-world theory in the context of functions, while Pantziara and Philippou (2012) used Sfard's (1991) theory to assess students' understanding of fractions. These examples are indicative of a trend observed during recent years to empirically explore various concepts based on theoretical frameworks developed in the past—an approach that seems productive to continue pursuing and extending in the future.

Other theories employed over the past years are more *topic specific*, since they deal with particular mathematical concepts such as fractions (Lamon, 1999; Olive, 1999; Post, Cramer, Behr, Lesh & Harel, 1993; Steffe, 2001), number sense (Steffe, Cobb, & von Glaserfeld, 1988; Steffe, von Glasersfeld, Richards, & Cobb, 1983), algebra (Kaput, 1998; Kieran, 1996), functions and limits (Cottrill et al. 1996), or geometry (Battista, 2007; Battista & Clements, 1996; Clements & Sarama, 2007; Fishbein, 1993; Van Hiele, 1985). Studies conducted during the past decade have attempted to empirically test and substantiate such theories. This includes, for example, testing Steffe's claims on fraction schemes (Norton & Wilkins, 2009; Wilkins & Norton, 2011), empirically validating Behr, Lesh, Post, and Silver's (1983) model on different fractional constructs (Charalambous & Pitta-Pantazi, 2007), or examining Steffe et al.'s (1988) model of numerical development (Biddlecomb & Carr, 2011). Building on various theoretical perspectives, other studies have attempted to expand existing theoretical works in various directions. For instance, Van den Heuvel-Panhuizen and colleagues (Kolovou, Van den Heuvel-Panhuizen, & Köller, 2013; Van den Heuvel-Panhuizen, Kolovou, & Robitzsch, 2013) investigated how upper-elementary students worked in an online environment to solve early algebra problem, while Chrysostomou, Pitta-Pantazi, Tsingi, Cleanthous, and Christou (2013) investigated individuals' procedural and conceptual understanding of number sense and algebra by relating this understanding to their cognitive styles.

Besides focusing on different mathematical *topics*, researchers over the past decade have also been increasingly attending to and investigating students' mathematical *processes*. These attempts have been informed by theoretical frameworks and conceptualizations developed in the previous century, such as those pertaining to reasoning or problem solving (Polya, 1954; Schoenfeld, 1992), problem posing (Silver, 1997; Stoyanova & Ellerton, 1996), modeling (Lesh & Zawojewski, 2007), argumentation (Toulmin, 1958), conjecturing and developing generalizations (Burton, 1984), engaging in proof and proving (Harel & Sowder, 1998), and visualization (Battista, 2007). For instance, Levenson (2013) explored the different forms that students' explanations may take at different ages, as well as how students perceive the nature of mathematical explanations under different circumstances. Using Silver's (1997) ideas of problem posing, Cai et al. (2013) investigated how problem posing can contribute to student learning. Along the same lines, but setting off from a different framework, Van Harpen and Presmeg (2013) explored the relationship between students' mathematical problem-posing abilities and their mathematical content knowledge. Similar attempts have been observed with other mathematical processes, such as reasoning and engaging in pattern generalization (e.g., Ellis, 2011; Jurdak & Mouhayar, 2014; Nilssona & Juter, 2011), problem solving (e.g., Muir, Beswick, & Williamson, 2008; Stein & Burchartz, 2006), proving (e.g., Bieda, 2010; Inglis & Alcock, 2012; Stylianides & Stylianides, 2009), and argumentation (Hollebrands, Conner, & Smith, 2010). Interestingly, a number of researchers have also started attending to how gestures can scaffold students' engagement in the processes discussed, and in general, support their thinking and learning (see, for instance, Bjuland, Cestari, & Borgersen, 2008; Kim, Roth, & Thom, 2011; Zurina & Williams, 2011).

Further pursuing and extending the line of thinking advanced in the previous century, during the last decade researchers have continued conceptualizing student learning as more than just student cognitive development. Hence, drawing on theories not necessarily confined to the domain of mathematics, researchers have explored several facets of learning, including student creativity (e.g., Leikin & Pitta-Pantazi, 2013); metacognition (e.g., Kim, Park, Moore, & Varma, 2013; Modestou & Gagatsis, 2010; Schneider & Artelt, 2010; Yang, 2012); and affective aspects such as emotions, attitudes, and beliefs (e.g., Hemmings, Grootemboer, & Kay, 2011; Schorr & Goldin, 2008; Sumpter, 2013).

In sum, during the last decade, scholars have not only tried to better conceptualize student learning and consider its multiple facets, but they have also capitalized on different theoretical frameworks—while empirically validating them—to examine student learning of different topics and engagement in different practices. Still, a lot more needs to be done toward fully unlocking what is involved in student learning. For example, the novelties observed in the mathematics curricula and/or changes in teaching practices that may accompany them, such as the development of STEM programs, or the implementation of more inquiry-based, and modeling-oriented environments (see English, 2013; Ministry of Education of Singapore, 2013) call for the investigation of how we may best combine theories to better understand student learning in such complex settings. Discussing this need, Bikner-Ashbahs and Prediger (2010) coined the term *networking theories* to describe how constellations of theories can support unpacking and better understanding student learning in more complex situations. Such theories could attend to the multiple facets of learning, as discussed earlier. New theories may also need to be developed to address and encompass these complexities, as well as the fact that learning should not be seen from a static perspective, but rather from a more dynamic viewpoint. Thus, questions that may be important to answer in the future include:

- Which theories or combinations thereof may best describe student learning in the environments listed earlier?
- How do different facets of student learning interact with each other and how might changes in one aspect of learning contribute to changes in another?

One of the factors accentuating the complexity of the learning environments, and hence the theoretical perspectives that need to describe them, is the incorporation of new technologies (e.g., Drijvers, Godino, Fornt, & Trouche, 2013). The functionalities, representations, and possibilities offered by new technological tools and media also suggest that scholars need to continue exploring and describing the impact that these tools may have on student thinking and learning processes (e.g., Hollebrands, 2007; Pitta-Pantazi, & Christou, 2009; Tabach, Hershkowitz, & Dreyfus, 2013) and aspects of student affective domain (e.g., Schorr & Goldin 2008). In this context, a number of questions that still, by and large, remain unresolved concern the following:

- What is the impact of technological advances on students' thinking processes, visualization/ communication/and representational skills, abilities to research and solve problems, mathematical understanding, mathematical achievements, self-awareness, and abilities to interact productively with one another, with teachers, and with data?
- What theoretical frameworks are needed to describe and explain the phenomena identified?

Having briefly considered student mathematical learning in general, we now focus on each of its constituent components to identify additional trends within each and suggest priorities for future work.

Mathematics

When referring to the component of mathematics, the literature review we have conducted has revealed that not all mathematical concepts share an equal proportion of scholarly attention. In particular, we are still witnessing a disproportional emphasis of studies on number sense and operations, as well as on algebra, and fewer studies on space and geometry, statistics, measurement, and probabilities. We detected a similar trend during our literature review in the domain of teacher knowledge. For example, although recently there has been an increased attention to statistics (e.g., Lavigne, Salkind, & Yan, 2008; Makar, Bakker, & Ben-Zvi, 2011; Sharma, 2006; Watson, 2007), work in this domain is still negligible compared to studies conducted on numbers and algebra. Some renewed interest has also been observed in geometry, especially due to the use of various technological environments—and this was mainly focused on studies conducted in secondary education (Hollebrands, 2007). Research studies on measurement (e.g., Barrett, Clements, Klanderman, Pennisi, & Polaki, 2006; Kamii & Kysh, 2006; Szilágyi, Clements, & Sarama, 2013) and probability (Rubel, 2007) are still quite sparse. Therefore, the following question seems to provide fruitful ground for further work:

- Can coherent learning trajectories for specific mathematical concepts be identified, especially for content areas that have not been well represented over the past decade? What similarities and differences might trajectories for different content areas have?

A word of caution is, however, in order here. By attempting to consider the aforementioned issues, one should not lose sight of the fact that mathematical concepts are not developed in isolation, but rather co-occur with other concepts in specific contexts. Therefore, the development of mathematical concepts should not only be examined linearly, but also in more complex situations where the development occurs in certain contexts (see Jurdak, 2006; Murata & Kattubadi, 2012) and through social interactions (Dekker, Elshout-Mohr, & Wood, 2006; Wood, Williams, & McNeal, 2006).

Furthermore, we feel that mathematics education researchers need to reexamine which mathematical concepts are currently being taught and therefore deserve being investigated, but foremost which mathematics is *needed* for the 21st century (see English, 2006; English & Gainsburg, Chapter 1 in this volume). This takes us to a different approach as to what mathematics we feel students should learn in school. As Lesh et al. (2014) observe, the national curricula in many countries were written mainly by mathematicians and educators, whereas other groups of experts, such as (social) scientists, economists, and engineers were not consulted. As a result, according to these scholars, the mathematics probably needed by future citizens goes far beyond what is typically presented in these documents. This view offers additional perspectives as to which questions mathematics educators ought to contemplate in the coming years:

- What mathematics do students of the 21st century need for success in life? To what extent do different curricula promote student learning of these types of mathematics?
- Apart from the mathematics content itself, how may we develop, document, and assess higher-order thinking skills needed for the 21st century? Which theories may allow us to best describe or examine students' higher-order thinking skills?
- In what ways does the incorporation of new technologies change the mathematics that contemporary students need to learn in order to adequately function in tomorrow's world?

Students

Our literature review revealed that most of the research in mathematics education investigated student learning in primary and secondary grades. Recently, however, increasing interest has been observed toward studying student learning in early years (Clements, Sarama, Spitler, Lange & Wolfe, 2011; English & Mulligan, 2013; Levenson, Tirosh, & Tsamir, 2011; Papic, Mulligan & Mitchlmore, 2011; Sarama & Clements, 2009). In fact, several researchers are interested in investigating younger students' understanding of various concepts that were often taught at later stages. Examples include introducing kindergarteners to pre-algebra (Carraher, Schliemann, Brizuela, & Earnest, 2006; Papic et al., 2011), fractions (Brizuela, 2006), and even functions (Francisco & Hahkioniemi, 2012). Studies have also investigated the effect of preschool mathematics curricula on children's short-and long-term achievement (e.g., Clements & Sarama, 2007). Research on university students' understanding in tertiary mathematics education and their abilities in various processes is also underrepresented, and ought to receive more attention (Mesa, 2012; Tall, 2013). As the reader might recall, this trend also became apparent among research studies on teacher knowledge. Therefore, some of the questions that need further attention are:

- What are younger students' and university students' understanding and abilities in mathematics?
- Can the focus on specific topics or processes in early years promote (or hinder) students' mathematical thinking and learning later on?
- What can we learn from longitudinal studies about the development of students' mathematical understandings, processes, and affective learning?

Increasingly realizing that one size does *not* fit all, researchers in mathematics education are also steadily attending to the needs, characteristics, and achievements of diverse groups of students (Gilleece, Cosgrove, & Sofroniou, 2010). This includes, for example, students from low socioeconomic backgrounds (e.g., Baker, Street, & Tomlin, 2006; Balfanz, Mac Iver, & Byrnes, 2006; Tirosh, Tsamir, Levenson, Tabach, & Barkai, 2013), students who are struggling with various mathematical constructs (e.g., Yerushalmy, 2006) or with learning disabilities (e.g., Newton, Star, & Lynch, 2010; Peltenburg, Van den Heuvel-Panhuizen, & Robitzsch, 2012), high-achieving students (e.g., Alsawaie, 2012; Leikin & Lev, 2013; Pitta-Pantazi, Christou, Kontoyianni, & Kattou, 2011), or bilingual students (Ambrose & Molina, 2014; Dominguez, LópezLeiva, & Khisty, 2014; Verzosa & Mulligan, 2013). In pursuing this approach, caution should be exercised so that researchers not end up restricting the types of treatments offered to students to those *assumed* to be effective for particular groups of students (see Lesh et al., 2014). In this context, the following questions seem to offer productive paths for further exploration:

- In what ways can we facilitate the learning of diverse groups of students?
- What are the benefits and drawbacks of various instructional approaches for these groups of students?
- What kind of environments and tools are needed to develop and test various groups of students' mathematics learning?

We close this section by briefly considering measurement issues.

Measuring Student Mathematical Learning

Like teaching, which comprises a multifaceted phenomenon, student learning is also multidimensional. Consequently, developing appropriate measurement tools to tap student learning becomes particularly convoluted (see, Lesh et al., 2014), especially when trying to capture different aspects of it. As a case in point, consider the five strands identified in the Adding It Up (Kilpatrick, Swafford, & Findell, 2001) framework to conceptualize proficiency in learning mathematics: conceptual understanding, procedural fluency, strategic competence, adaptive reasoning, and productive disposition. For such a proficiency to be achieved, considerable efforts should be devoted to developing tasks that lend themselves to measuring the integration of these strands, given that measuring each strand separately might yield an inconclusive picture of student learning. Furthermore, measurement approaches and tools that lend themselves to tapping student creative, critical, and complex thinking abilities, as well as collaborative skills in mathematics are needed. Although some attempts have been undertaken toward this direction (e.g. Leikin, 2013; Lesh, 2010), the field still seems to be in a rather nascent state with respect to developing such instruments. In fact, the main means employed to explore student mathematical learning have been tests or questionnaires (e.g., Jurdak & El Mouhayar, 2014; Modestou & Gagatsis, 2010; Norton & Wilkins, 2009; Wilkins & Norton, 2011) or task-based interviews (e.g. Kamii & Kysh, 2006; Muir et al., 2008; Verzosa & Mulligan, 2013). Although combinations of these methods have also been employed (e.g., Hollebrands, 2007; Papic et al., 2011; Van Harpen & Presmeg, 2013), the field does not seem to have reached consensus as to which (combinations of) instruments and/or methods are more appropriate for exploring different types of learning. All these taken into consideration, the following research inquiries seem to suggest productive directions for further research:

- How can we measure mathematical proficiency *as a whole*? How can we measure these outcomes both at micro-level (to understand underlying mechanisms) and at macro-level?
- What instruments and approaches are more conducive to gauging (the development of) student learning, especially when it comes to less frequently explored aspects of it, such as creative, critical, complex thinking processes and collaborative skills in mathematics?
- What are the costs and benefits of combining different measurement tools to explore student learning, conceived of as both processes and final outcomes?

- What methodological advancements are needed to obtain more explicit, valid, and reliable results of student learning?
- How can the field of exploring student learning benefit from the methodological and statistical advancements made in other related fields? (See, e.g., Creemers, Kyriakides, & Sammons, 2010.)

The last question brings to the fore another key area related to measuring student mathematical learning—as a means of determining teacher effectiveness—that has received paramount attention during the past decade: value-added models. Initially developed and introduced by Sanders and colleagues (Sanders & Horn, 1994), value-added models are currently widely used as a way to examine teacher contribution to student learning. Although different ways have been developed to capture this contribution, value-added models are typically based on some variant of calculating the difference between students' end-of-year and beginning-of-year performance and making adjustments to account for differences in student background characteristics and/or school-wide factors. Despite their widespread use, value-added models have both supporters and critics (Baker et al., 2010; Glazerman et al., 2010). Advocates, for example, point out that, although not perfect, value-added models can control for selection bias; they also provide a much better tool for measuring student learning and ultimately teacher effectiveness compared to other more subjective approaches, such as principal ratings (see Harris, 2009). Sceptics, however, point to the instability of value-added estimates across statistical models, years, classes that teachers teach, and different tests (McCaffrey, Sass, Lockwood, & Mihaly, 2009; Newton, Darling-Hammond, Haertel, & Thomas, 2010; Papay, 2011; Sass, 2008). Methodological concerns about the use of these models (e.g., Amrein-Beardsley, 2008) along with more substantive concerns related to factors beyond teachers' control (e.g., out-of-school learning experiences, tutoring, etc.) that can affect student learning (see Baker et al., 2010) have also been raised. Additionally, although observation measures of teaching effectiveness were found to significantly relate to student learning, as captured through value-added models (e.g., Kane et al., 2011), other studies (e.g., Hill, Kapitula, & Umland, 2011) point to noticeable discrepancies between these two measures for a significant proportion of teachers. As the scholarly community increasingly realizes the potentials and limitations of value-added models (Harris, 2011), more work will be needed in the coming years to determine how these models can better capture different manifestations of student learning—as conceptualized and discussed earlier—and to link these types of learning to teacher effectiveness. These attempts, we argue, can greatly benefit from also incorporating considerations of instructional quality, since marrying value-added models with explorations of the quality of teaching can help better understand what aspects of student learning might be easier or harder to measure and how these relate to teachers' actions and interactions with students during instruction.

Finally, our literature review showed that longitudinal studies conducted thus far are quite limited. Hence, longitudinal studies that identify the long-term effects of various conditions on student learning are highly needed. As a field, we are also in need of meta-analyses, which at the moment seem to be rather limited, with only some exceptions (e.g., Gilmore & Papadatou-Pastou, 2009). Both longitudinal studies and meta-analyses will enable drawing causal inferences about what contributes to student learning. This is an issue to which we now turn by juxtaposing all three components of the chain.

AGGRAVATING COMPLEXITY: BRINGING TOGETHER THE THREE COMPONENTS

In the previous three sections, we considered each of the three links of the chain in isolation. Our review has suggested that over the past decades significant progress has been made in all three domains, although in varying degrees and shades. We argue, however, that the real challenge—and, in our view, the core priority of research for the coming years—pertains to considering the chain as a whole. The proverbial Indian story of the blind men each studying a different part of the elephant speaks to this idea. Although exploring different segments of the chain has been both productive and useful—as suggested by our review—we cannot fully fathom the process of teaching and learning, and its relationship to teacher knowledge, unless we bring all constituent components together. Therefore, this last section is devoted to reviewing works undertaken toward this direction. Following the structure of the previous sections, we first consider more conceptual issues when it comes to studying the entire chain and then conclude with methodological advancements and challenges.

Conceptualizing the Entire Chain of Interactions

Although during the past years researchers have mostly been preoccupied with studying parts of the chain, during the last decade the first significant steps toward considering all components of the chain in tandem were witnessed. In what follows, we briefly review works that have considered parts of the associations in this chain, and then we focus on studies that have attended to all associations encompassed in the chain. However, in contrast to previous sections, we start by identifying the two main conceptual challenges in studying the entire chain. We present these challenges first to orient the reader to the work that has been pursued in this domain and the opportunities that lie ahead of us in the coming years.

A close examination of the studies and associated frameworks advanced so far suggests that, as a research field, we lack a comprehensive theoretical framework that brings together all pieces considered so far, let alone explains the underlying mechanisms through which each part of the chain contributes to the others. To clarify: several theoretical frameworks or conceptualizations have been developed to capture teacher knowledge, teaching, or student learning. As the preceding literature suggested, compared to some decades ago, we now have a better understanding of issues related to each of the three components reviewed in this chapter. Lacking, however, is a theoretical framework that brings all three together and examines (i) the particular ways and the conditions under which teacher knowledge contributes to the quality of instruction and through that to student learning, and (ii) how the quality of instruction, in turn, informs student learning. It is also still an open question whether teacher knowledge might have a direct effect on student learning, beyond the indirect effect it is assumed to have through teaching quality. Such a framework needs to consider the chain of associations not only from a static perspective—to capture these associations at a fixed point in time—but also from a more dynamic perspective. This implies that such a framework needs to detail how changes in each of these three components might contribute to changes in the other components of the chain, as well as how (phases of) stagnation in one component might impede progress in the other components.[4] The need of such frameworks is imperative, given that the mixed and inconclusive findings related to the associations discussed herein might be a byproduct of weak theory, not necessarily of weak measurement alone (see Shechtman, Roschelle, Haertel, & Knudsen, 2010). We agree with Sriraman and English (2010), however, that attempts to develop such a framework should not be geared toward generating grand theories, since generating such theories could lead into surface delineations of the complexity inherent in the chain, as captured in the previous three sections.

Developing such a framework would be a particularly arduous task and one that would require concerted efforts from scholars in different domains, probably across different research groups and projects. Several questions need to be addressed when attempting to develop such a framework: Would it apply to different mathematical topics or should it be more centered on particular topics (e.g., geometry or algebra)? Would it be applicable to different educational levels or should it be more pertinent to particular grades (e.g., for kindergarten)? Would it "'travel" across different educational systems or should it mostly be concerned with the educational systems in which it will be given birth? As the reader might recall, these and other related issues were considered when examining each of the links of the chain in isolation. Such issues, however, merit much closer consideration when it comes to considering the entire chain of associations.

The studies we review here were not driven by such a framework, but were based on theoretical considerations that linked different parts of the chain. As such, they can provide insights about the work that has already been pursued in this terrain and sketch areas where more work can be done in the future. In this context, we first briefly review studies that explored two components of this chain and then give more emphasis to studies that investigated the entire chain.

A set of studies have been devoted to exploring the link between teacher knowledge and teaching quality. Although this link was investigated in the 1990s as well, studies conducted during the last decade have approached this inquiry with a renewed emphasis. Instead of (simply) considering this issue from either an affordance or constraint perspective—which was central in the explorations in the early 1990s—scholars in the current decade have also invested in understanding how teacher knowledge can support the work of teaching. As a result, we now know that teacher knowledge[5] can support teachers in planning and implementing their lessons (e.g., Tanase & Wang, 2013); deciding which ideas to pursue when interacting with students during whole-class discussions (e.g., Cengiz et al., 2011); providing instruction that is rich in mathematical connections between different ideas and is based on mathematically appropriate language and notation (e.g., Hill, Blunk, et al., 2008; Hill, Umland, Litke, & Kapitula, 2012); using representations appropriately and capitalizing on student mathematical contributions (Izsák, 2008); maintaining the level of cognitive demands in which students engage by keeping emphasis on the underlying meaning of mathematical procedures (e.g., Charalambous, 2010); cognitively challenging and supporting students during instruction (e.g., Baumert et al., 2010); and appropriately responding to student errors and capitalizing on their work to address their misconceptions (e.g., Bray, 2011; Ding, 2008). In contrast to previous studies that explored the association between teacher knowledge and teaching from a static perspective, other studies—admittedly, much fewer than the previous body of research—explored how *changes* in teachers' knowledge were reflected in the quality of their instruction. These studies have shown, for example, that supporting teachers to enhance their knowledge of comparing and contrasting multiple solutions can help teachers materialize this practice in their teaching (Yakes & Star, 2011) or that engaging teachers with challenging tasks can enhance their PCK, which, in turn, can aid teachers in identifying and comparing multiple student solutions during their practice (Tirosh, Tsamir, Levenson, & Tabach, 2011).

Other studies have investigated the association between teaching quality and student learning. Such studies have suggested, for instance, that different teaching patterns have differential impact on dimensions of students' affective domain (Hugener et al., 2009) or that the total number of distinct mathematics activities in which students engage has significant potential in supporting student cognitive performance (Clements et al., 2011). An experimental study using teacher random assignment to students (Kane, McCaffrey, Miller, & Staiger, 2013) has also empirically corroborated this association by showing several teaching practices to significantly predict student learning.

Large-scale studies have also pointed to moderate associations (at best) between teacher knowledge and student learning. For example, in Rockoff, Jacob, Kane, and Steiger's study (2011), teachers' MKT was the only significant predictor of student performance along with teachers' personal and general efficacy. Similarly, in Hill, Rowan, and Ball's work (2005), students taught by teachers with high levels of MKT experienced gains in their scores equivalent to about two weeks of instruction compared to their counterparts taught by average MKT teachers. Krauss, Baumert, and Blum (2008) also found that ninth grade students taught by teachers with higher PCK scores performed significantly better in mathematics in tenth grade, compared to their counterparts taught by less PCK-knowledgeable teachers.

In sum, the studies considered here paint a more promising and encouraging picture compared to that sketched at the beginning of this century by Ball and colleagues (Ball et al., 2001), who found that only 5% of the 354 papers they reviewed explored how teachers' mathematical understanding affected their practice, and only 2% examined how it affected student learning. Although we have not generated analogous statistics, the studies that we reviewed suggest that significant work has been carried out in this domain during the past decade—yet, Ball and colleagues' plea for more work in this terrain is still pertinent.

What is particularly interesting, however, is that the last few years have also seen studies that bring together all three components under consideration—something largely missing in the 1990s, perhaps with a notable exception (Sowder, Philipp, Armstrong, & Schappelle, 1998). Although focusing on the same chain of associations, these studies have notable differences. First, they differ in the constructs they employ. For example, in terms of teacher knowledge, some studies focused on the distinction between SMK and PCK (Baumert et al., 2010; Kunter et al., 2013); others drew on the MKT or different manifestations of it (Cantrell & Kane, 2013; Shechtman et al., 2010); still others employed author-developed conceptualizations (Tchoshanov, 2011) or used a combination of theoretical perspectives (Kersting et al., 2012). Differences were also observed in the aspects of instructional quality under consideration and the ways in which those were measured, ranging from attending to teachers' instructional *decisions* captured in teacher logs (Shechtman et al., 2010), to considering limited aspects of instruction (e.g., Baumert et al., 2010; Kersting et al., 2012; Kunter et al., 2013), to attending to a conglomerate of instructional aspects included in different observation instruments (Cantrell & Kane, 2013). Most of the studies also focused on student cognitive outcomes, with only one exception (Kunter et al., 2013) that also considered student motivation. Second, these studies differed in scale, with some employing no more than 50 teachers (Kersting et al., 2012) and others recruiting more than 1,300 teachers (Cantrell & Kane, 2013). Third, with only one exception (Shechtman et al., 2010), all other studies examined the focal chain of associations from a static perspective; even the study that comprised the exception, however, limited its attention to only considering changes in the first link of the chain.

These differences notwithstanding, these studies as a whole have yielded promising findings about the association among teacher knowledge, teaching quality, and student learning. With only two exceptions (Cantrell & Kane, 2013; Shechtman, Haertel, Roschelle, Knudsen, & Singleton, 2013), all other studies showed aspects of teacher knowledge to relate to aspects of instructional quality. With no exception, all studies suggested that instructional quality contributes positively to student learning, although the effects of these contributions ranged. Interestingly, more complicated interactions among the three links of the chain were also documented, showing, for instance, instructional quality to mediate the effect of teacher knowledge on student learning (Kersting et al., 2012). As a collective, then, these studies not only suggest that investigating the entire chain *is* feasible, but they also point to the significant benefits that can be accrued by bringing together the three components under consideration. What remains, however, a key challenge for researchers in the years to come is exploring the entire chain of associations from a dynamic perspective and at scale, given that such a dynamic exploration was already undertaken in the 1990s with only four teachers (Sowder et al., 1998). This is not only a conceptual challenge, but also a methodological one that we envision will face researchers in the years to come. We conclude by considering other related methodological challenges.

Methodological Challenges in Considering the Entire Chain of Interactions

Several of the methodological issues inherent in exploring the entire chain of associations have already been discussed in previous sections. Instead of recapitulating these issues, here we briefly consider four additional methodological challenges that become more pertinent when considering all three components of the chain together.

The first issue relates to the design of a study that lends itself to delving deeper into this complex set of associations. Different such designs have been employed to study aspects of this chain, ranging from experimental studies (e.g., Clements et al., 2011; Kane et al., 2013) to more qualitative descriptive explorations (e.g., Izsák et al., 2008; Mitchell et al., 2014). Given how complex each of the three constructs entailed in this association are, and given that studying the entire chain further aggravates complexity, scholars are encouraged to be explicit about the research design they employ, and clearly discuss its affordances and limitations in tackling complexity. Such explicitness is expected to accumulate collective knowledge that is highly needed when it comes to investigating particularly complicated phenomena.

The second methodological consideration pertains to exploring more than linear effects, which have almost exclusively been considered thus far, as our review of the literature suggests. With sufficiently powered studies, future works might point to curvilinear effects as well. From a policy perspective, such effects can offer invaluable guidelines for supporting student learning through inducing changes in certain aspects of teaching quality or dimensions of teacher knowledge. For example, instead of exploring only interactions between the mathematical richness of the environment in which students are engaged and the cognitive level at which students experience the subject matter, as Hiebert and Grouws (2007) suggested, researchers could also determine optimal levels of richness and cognitive complexity through exploring curvilinear effects.

The third and equally critical consideration relates to the optimal level of alignment that needs to be obtained in such studies. Alignment "designates the similarity [and] congruence between the content taught and the assessments of achievement in that content area" (Gage, 2009, p. 59). If we extend this definition to also include teacher-knowledge performance, then, alignment refers to the degree to which the three components examined in this chapter are congruent with each other. Ensuring satisfactory levels of alignment is necessary if the true effects entailed in this chain are to be revealed. For it does not make much sense to measure, say, teacher knowledge in statistics, explore the quality of their instructional approaches in geometry, and gauge student performance in numbers and operations, unless we are convinced that the topic does not really matter—something that is not supported by a number of studies reviewed throughout this chapter. Attending to issues of alignment was a key characteristic of one of the few studies that brought together all three components under consideration. In this study (Kersting et al., 2012), all measures obtained focused on the content of fractions, something that helped minimize the noise introduced by attending to different content areas for different parts of the chain. As a consequence, the effects of teacher knowledge on teaching quality (Cohen's f^2 = .54) and of teaching quality on student learning (Cohen's f^2 = .22) or of teacher knowledge on student learning (Cohen's f^2 = .16) appeared to be stronger than those typically observed in similar studies. Establishing a satisfactory level of alignment appears to be a sine qua non design aspect of studies aiming to shed more light on how the three components considered herein interact with each other. A caveat is, however, in order: Erring too much on the side of alignment can yield results that might have limited generalizability. To bring this idea home, let us consider a hypothetical design that explores teachers' knowledge in teaching a nonconventional whole-number multiplication algorithm to third graders, examines teachers' practices in teaching this content, and explores students' corresponding performance. By securing a high degree of alignment, this study has the potential to further minimize the noise discussed earlier and better capture the signal of the effects. But what is this signal really about? How applicable might the results of such an exploration be to other situations? Although a rather extreme case, this hypothetical scenario suggests another key priority for future research: devoting energy and thought to determine optimal levels of alignment that would help capture the real effects of the associations examined, on the one hand, and on the other, ensure the applicability and generalizability of these findings.

Finally, studies that employ a more dynamic perspective in exploring the associations at hand, as suggested earlier, lend themselves to investigating issues of growth and stability. Writing almost 30 years ago, Shavelson et al. (1986) lamented that scholars are attending to the association between teaching and learning from a static perspective. As they noted, this approach is deficient in the sense that both teachers and students grow and change as they interact with each other and the content throughout the year(s). Although our review in this chapter suggests that some steps have been made toward considering the phenomena at hand from a more dynamic perspective, more work will definitely be needed to engage with such issues and to examine both teacher and student learning trajectories, exploring how these trajectories intersect and inform each other. Such investigations will require longitudinal studies that follow teachers and students for an entire school year at least. Recent measurement and statistical advancements (see Creemers et al., 2010) offer handy machinery that researchers can employ in pursuing such endeavors.

IN LIEU OF CONCLUSION: IN CHALLENGES LIES OPPORTUNITY

We initiated this chapter by pointing out that, after almost four decades of significant scholarly work, we have by now accumulated sufficient empirical evidence suggesting that teachers make a difference in student learning. However, questions regarding the interactions among teacher knowledge, teaching quality, and student learning—as well as the particular ways in which these interactions are manifested—remain open. Our review has suggested that during the past decade significant work has been carried out to understand each of the three components of the chain, and to a much smaller extent, the chain as a whole. As we have discussed, significant advancements have been made at both theoretical and methodological fronts that offer the bedrock for future explorations. However, there still exist a lot of unanswered questions. Fully unpacking and understanding the complex relationship we have sketched in this chapter is neither inconsequential nor easily tractable. To aggravate complexity, it is important to keep in mind that this chain of associations is only partially represented here, given that additional teacher personal resources (e.g., beliefs, identities, etc.), as well as several resources within the instructional milieu (e.g., curricula, technological tools, time and other constraints) might contribute to instructional quality and student learning (see Kennedy, 2010). However, to echo Walter Cole, an American politician of the 19th century, in challenges really lies the opportunity, as long as we are not paralyzed at the thought of challenge that rests in every opportunity. Hopefully, the advancements made so far offer a springboard for moving forward.

We close by considering an issue that has been alluded to in several parts of this chapter—the implications of understanding this complex relationship for policy and practice. Developing a clearer understanding of this relationship, alongside a clear vision of the learning we aspire to for students in the 21st century, can help create those conditions that will maximize the possibilities of securing this learning. By understanding how teaching quality can contribute to student learning, scholars and practitioners can work together to develop teaching interventions that will offer students the opportunities to experience mathematics in ways that lead to powerful learning. At the same time, developing more insights into the mechanisms through which teacher knowledge contributes to instructional quality can help craft preservice teaching education programs and in-service teaching professional development programs that can help teachers develop the knowledge and the skills to effectively enact certain teaching practices that contribute to the desired learning outcomes. In this respect, working on unpacking and understanding this complex relationship creates an arena for forging fruitful and productive collaborations between researchers, policy makers, and practitioners—which comprises a still unfulfilled demand in the field of mathematics education and beyond.

NOTES

1. Because of space constraints and our decision to focus on frameworks offered during the last decade, we omitted other important conceptualizations, e.g., Ma's work (1999) on profound understanding of fundamental mathematics or Fennema and Franke's earlier work (1992) on teacher knowledge.
2. This situated, social, and distributed character of teacher knowledge is also reflected or emphasized in other works, as well (e.g., Askew, 2008; Hodgen, 2011).
3. Although we are aware of the debate between theories, theoretical perspectives, approaches, and models, in this chapter we refrain from entering this discussion; therefore, we simply refer to theoretical perspectives as a matter of convenience.
4. Although some frameworks detailing the development in different components have been proposed (e.g., for teacher knowledge, see Silverman and Thompson, 2008), no frameworks that examine changes in the three components considered herein are available.
5. For the sake of brevity, here we consider teacher knowledge as a unified whole, without getting into discussions about different types of knowledge, as we did in the first section.

REFERENCES

Adler, J., & Davis, Z. (2006). Opening another black box: Researching mathematics for teaching in mathematics teacher education. *Journal for Research in Mathematics Education*, 37(4), 270–296. doi:10.2307/30034851

Adler, J., & Huillet, D. (2008). The social production of mathematics for teaching. In P. Sullivan & T. Wood (Eds.), *Knowledge and beliefs in mathematics teaching and teaching development* (Vol. 1, pp. 195–221). Rotterdam, The Netherlands: Sense Publishers.

Alsawaie, O. N. (2012). Number sense-based strategies used by high-achieving sixth grade students who experienced reform textbooks. *International Journal of Science and Mathematics Education*, 10(5), 1071–1097. doi:10.1007/s10763-011-9315-y

Ambrose, R., & Molina, M. (2014). Spanish/English bilingual students' comprehension of arithmetic story problem texts. *International Journal of Science and Mathematics Education*, 12(6), 1469–1496. doi:10.1007/s10763-013-9472-2

Amrein-Beardsley, A. (2008). Methodological concerns about the education value-added assessment system. *Educational Researcher*, 37(2), 65–75. doi:10.3102/0013189X08316420

Andrews, P. (2011). The cultural location of teachers' mathematical knowledge: Another hidden variable in mathematics education research? In T. Rowland & K. Ruthven (Eds.), *Mathematical knowledge in teaching* (pp. 99–118). New York: Springer. doi:10.1007/978-90-481-9766-8_7

Arbaugh, F., Herbel-Eisenmann, B., Ramirez, N., Knuth, E., Kranendonk, H., & Quander, J. R. (2010). *Linking research and practice: The NCTM research agenda conference report*. Reston, VA: National Council of Teachers of Mathematics.

Artigue, M., Bartolini-Bussi, M., Dreyfus, T., Gray, E., & Prediger, S. (2005). Different theoretical perspectives and approaches in research in mathematics education. In M. Bosch (Ed.), *Proceedings of the Fourth Congress of the European Society for Research in Mathematics Education* (pp. 1239–1244). Barcelona: Fundemi IQS.

Askew, M. (2008). Mathematical discipline knowledge requirements for prospective primary teachers, and the structure and teaching approaches of programs designed to develop that knowledge. In P. Sullivan & T. Wood (Eds.), *Knowledge and beliefs in mathematics teaching and teaching development* (Vol. 1, pp. 13–35). Rotterdam, The Netherlands: Sense Publishers.

Bair, S. L., & Rich, B. S. (2011). Characterizing the development of specialized mathematical content knowledge for teaching in algebraic reasoning and number theory. *Mathematical Thinking and Learning*, 13(4), 292–321. doi:10.1080/10986065.2011.608345

Baker, E. L., Barton, P. E., Darling-Hammond, L., Haertel, E., Ladd, H. F., Linn, R. L., . . . Shepard, L. A. (2010, August). *Problems with the use of student test scores to evaluate teachers* (Briefing Paper No. 278). Washington, DC: Economic Policy Institute.

Baker, D., Street, B., & Tomlin, A. (2006). Navigating schooled numeracies: Explanations for low achievement, in mathematics of UK children from low SES background. *Mathematical Thinking and Learning*, 8(3), 287–307. doi:10.1207/s15327833mtl0803_5

Balfanz, R., Mac Iver, D. J., & Byrnes, V. (2006). The implementation and impact of evidence-based mathematics reforms in high-poverty middle schools: A multi-site, multi-year study. *Journal for Research in Mathematics Education*, 37(1), 33–64. doi:10.2307/30035051

Ball, D. L., & Bass, H. (2003). Toward a practice-based theory of mathematical knowledge for teaching. In E. Simmt and B. Davis (Eds.), *Proceedings of the 2002 Annual Meeting of the Canadian Mathematics Education Study Group* (pp. 3–14). Edmonton, AB: CMESC/GCEDM.

Ball, D. L., Charalambous, C. Y., Thames, M. H., & Lewis, J. (2009). Teacher knowledge and teaching: Viewing a complex relationship from three perspectives. In M. Tzekaki, M. Kaldrimidou, & C. Sakonidis (Eds.), *Proceedings of the 33rd Conference of the International Group for the Psychology of Mathematics Education* (Vol. 1, pp. 121–125). Thessaloniki, Greece: PME.

Ball, D. L., & Hill, H. C. (2009). Measuring teacher quality in practice. In D. H. Gitomer (Ed.), *Measurement issues and assessment for teaching quality* (pp. 80–98). Thousand Oaks, CA: Sage.

Ball, D. L., Lubienski, S. T., & Mewborn, D. S. (2001). Research on teaching mathematics: The unsolved problem of teachers' mathematical knowledge. In V. Richardson (Ed.), *Handbook of research on teaching* (4th ed., pp. 433–456). Washington, DC: American Research Association.

Ball, D. L., & Rowan, B. (2004). Introduction: Measuring instruction. *The Elementary School Journal, 105*(1), 3–10.

Ball, D. L., Sleep, L., Boerst, T. A., & Bass, H. (2009). Combining the development of practice and the practice of development in teacher education. *The Elementary School Journal, 109*(5), 458–474. doi:10.1086/596996

Ball, D. L., Thames, M. H., & Phelps, G. (2008). Content knowledge for teaching: What makes it special? *Journal of Teacher Education, 59*(5), 389–407. doi:10.1177/0022487108324554

Barrett, J. E., Clements, D. H., Klanderman, D., Pennisi, S. J., & Polaki, M. V. (2006). Students' coordination of geometric reasoning and measuring strategies on a fixed perimeter task: Developing mathematical understanding of linear measurement. *Journal for Research in Mathematics Education, 37*(3), 187–221.

Battista, M. T. (2007). The development of geometric and spatial thinking. In F. Lester (Ed.), *Second handbook of research on mathematics teaching and learning* (pp. 843–908). Reston, VA: National Council of Teachers of Mathematics.

Battista, M. T., & Clements, D. H. (1996). Students' understanding of three-dimensional rectangular arrays of cubes. *Journal for Research in Mathematics Education, 27*(3), 258–292. doi:10.2307/749365

Baumert, J., Kunter, M., Blum, W., Brunner, M., Voss, T., Jordan, A., . . . Tsai, Y. M. (2010). Teachers' mathematical knowledge, cognitive activation in the classroom, and student progress. *American Educational Research Journal, 47*(1), 133–180. doi:10.3102/0002831209345157

Bednarz, N., & Proulx, J. (2009). Knowing and using mathematics in teaching: Conceptual and epistemological clarifications. *For the Learning of Mathematics, 29*(3), 11–17.

Begle, E. G. (1979). *Critical variables in mathematics education: Findings from a survey of the empirical literature.* Washington, DC: Mathematical Association of America.

Behr, M., Lesh, R., Post, T., & Silver E. (1983). Rational number concepts. In R. Lesh & M. Landau (Eds.), *Acquisition of mathematics concepts and processes* (pp. 91–125). New York: Academic Press.

Bell, C. A., Wilson, S., Higgins, T., & McCoach, D. B. (2010). Measuring the effects of professional development on teacher knowledge: The case of developing mathematical ideas. *Journal for Research in Mathematics Education, 41*(5), 479–512.

Beswick, K., Callingham, R., & Watson, J. (2012). The nature and development of middle school mathematics teachers' knowledge. *Journal of Mathematics Teacher Education, 15*(2), 131–157. doi:10.1007/s10857-011-9177-9

Biddlecomb, B., & Carr, M. (2011). A longitudinal study of the development of mathematics strategies and underlying counting schemes. *International Journal of Science and Mathematics Education, 9*(1), 1–24. doi:10.1007/s10763-010-9202-y

Bieda, K. N. (2010). Enacting proof-related tasks in middle school mathematics: Challenges and opportunities. *Journal for Research in Mathematics Education, 41*(4), 351–382.

Biggs, J. B., & Collis, K. F. (1991). Multimodal learning and the quality of intelligent behavior. In H.A.H. Rowe (Ed.), *Intelligence: Reconceptualisation and measurement* (pp. 57–75). Hillsdale, NJ: Erlbaum.

Bikner-Ahsbahs, A., & Prediger, S. (2010). Networking of theories —An approach for exploiting the diversity of theoretical approaches. In B. Sriraman & L. English (Eds.), *Theories of mathematics education: Seeking new frontiers* (pp. 483–506). London, UK: Springer.

Bjuland, R., Cestari, M. L., & Borgersen, H. E. (2008). The interplay between gesture and discourse as mediating devices in collaborative mathematical reasoning: A multimodal approach. *Mathematical Thinking and Learning, 10*(3), 271–292. doi:10.1080/10986060802216169

Blömeke, S., Suhl, U., & Döhrmann, M. (2013). Assessing strengths and weaknesses of teacher knowledge in Asia, Eastern Europe, and Western countries: Differential item functioning in TEDS-M. *International Journal of Science and Mathematics Education, 11*(4), 795–817. doi:10.1007/s10763-013-9413-0

Borich, G. D. (1992). *Effective teaching methods* (2nd ed.). New York: Macmillan.

Boston, M. D. (2012). Assessing instructional quality in mathematics. *The Elementary School Journal, 113*(1), 76–104. doi:10.1086/666387

Boston, M.D. (2013). Connecting changes in secondary mathematics teachers' knowledge to their experiences in a professional development workshop. *Journal of Mathematics Teacher Education, 16*(1), 7–31. doi:10.1007/s10857-012-9211-6

Boston, M.D., & Smith, M.S. (2009). Transforming secondary mathematics teaching: Increasing the cognitive demands of instructional tasks used in teachers' classrooms. *Journal for Research in Mathematics Education, 40*(2), 119–156.

Bray, W.S. (2011). A collective case study of the influence of teachers' beliefs and knowledge on error-handling practices during class discussion of mathematics. *Journal for Research in Mathematics Education, 42*(1), 2–38.

Brizuela, B.M. (2006). Young children's notations for fractions. *Educational Studies in Mathematics, 62*(3), 281–305. doi:10.1007/s10649-005-9003-3

Brophy, J. (1986). Teaching and learning mathematics: Where research should be going. *Journal for Research in Mathematics Education, 17*(5), 323–346. doi:10.2307/749326

Brophy, J., & Good, T. (1986). Teacher behavior and student achievement. In M.C. Wittrock (Ed.), *Handbook of research on teaching* (3rd ed., pp. 328–375). New York: Macmillan.

Buchholtz, N., & Kaiser, G. (2013). Improving mathematics teacher education in Germany: Empirical results from a longitudinal evaluation of innovative programs. *International Journal of Science and Mathematics Education, 11*(4), 949–977. doi:10.1007/s10763-013-9427-7

Burton, L. (1984). Mathematical thinking: The struggle for meaning. *Journal for Research in Mathematics Education, 15*(1), 35–49. doi:10.2307/748986

Caddle, M.C., & Brizuela, B.M. (2011). Fifth graders' additive and multiplicative reasoning: Establishing connections across conceptual fields using a graph. *The Journal of Mathematical Behavior, 30*(3), 224–234. doi:10.1016/j.jmathb.2011.04.002

Cai, J., Moyer, J.C., Wang, N., Hwang, S., Nie, B., & Garber, T. (2013). Mathematical problem posing as a measure of curricular effect on students' learning. *Educational Studies in Mathematics, 83*(1), 57–69. doi:10.1007/s10649-012-9429-3

Cantrell, S., & Kane, T.J. (2013). *Ensuring fair and reliable measures of effective teaching: Culminating findings from the MET project's three-year study.* Seattle, WA: Bill & Melinda Gates Foundation. Retrieved from www.metproject.org/reports.php.

Carraher, D.W., Schliemann, A.D., Brizuela, B.M., & Earnest, D. (2006). Arithmetic and algebra in early mathematics education. *Journal for Research in Mathematics Education, 37*(2), 87–115.

Casabianca, J.M., McCaffrey, D.F., Gitomer, D.H., Bell, C.A., Hamre, B.K., & Pianta, R.C. (2013). Effect of observation mode on measures of secondary mathematics teaching. *Educational and Psychological Measurement, 73*(5), 757–783. doi:10.1177/0013164413486987

Cengiz, N., Kline, K., & Grant, T.J. (2011). Extending students' mathematical thinking during whole-group discussions. *Journal of Mathematics Teacher Education, 14*(5), 355–374. doi:10.1007/s10857-011-9179-7

Chapin, S.H., O'Connor, C., & Anderson. N.C. (2003). *Classroom discussions: Using math talk to help students learn.* Sausalito, CA: Math Solutions Publications.

Charalambous, C.Y. (2008). *Preservice teachers' Mathematical Knowledge for Teaching and their performance in selected teaching practices: Exploring a complex relationship.* Unpublished doctoral dissertation, University of Michigan, Ann Arbor.

Charalambous, C.Y. (2010). Mathematical knowledge for teaching and task unfolding: An exploratory study. *The Elementary School Journal, 110*(3), 247–278. doi:10.1086/648978

Charalambous, C.Y., Hill, H.C., & Ball, D.L. (2011). Prospective teachers' learning to provide instructional explanations: How does it look and what might it take? *Journal of Mathematics Teacher Education, 14*(6), 441–463. doi:10.1007/s10857-011-9182-z

Charalambous, C.Y., Hill, H.C., & Mitchell, R.N. (2012). Two negatives don't always make a positive: Exploring how limitations in teacher knowledge and the curriculum contribute to instructional quality. *Journal of Curriculum Studies, 44*(4), 489–513. doi:10.1080/00220272.2012.716974

Charalambous, C.Y., Komitis, A., Papacharalambous, M., & Stefanou, A. (2014). Using generic and content-specific teaching practices in teacher evaluation: An exploratory study of teachers' perceptions. *Teaching and Teacher Education, 41*, 22–33. doi:10.1016/j.tate.2014.03.001

Charalambous, C.Y., & Pitta-Pantazi, D. (2007). Drawing on a theoretical model to study students' understandings of fractions. *Educational Studies in Mathematics, 64*(3), 293–316. doi:10.1007/s10649-006-9036-2

Chester, M., & Zelman, S. (2009). Approximations of teacher quality and effectiveness: View from the state education agency. In D.H. Gitomer (Ed.), *Measurement issues and assessment for teaching quality.* (pp. 131–149). Thousand Oaks, CA: Sage.

Chevallard, Y. (1999). L'analyse des pratiques enseignantes en théorie anthropologique du didactique. *Recherches en Didactique des Mathématiques, 19*(2), 221–265.

Christou, C., Pitta-Pantazi, D., Souyoul, A., & Zachariades, T. (2005). The embodied, proceptual and formal worlds in the context of functions. *Canadian Journal of Science, Mathematics and Technology Education, 5*(2), 241–252. doi:10.1080/14926150509556656

Chrysostomou, M., Pitta-Pantazi, D., Tsingi, C., Cleanthous, E., & Christou, C. (2013). Examining number sense and algebraic reasoning through cognitive styles. *Educational Studies in Mathematics, 83*(2), 205–223. doi:10.1007/s10649-012-9448-0

Clements, D. H., & Sarama, J. (2007). Effects of a preschool mathematics curriculum: Summative research on the building blocks project. *Journal for Research in Mathematics Education, 38*(2), 136–163. doi: 10.2307/30034954

Clements, D. C., Sarama, J., Spitler, M. A., Lange, A. A., & Wolfe, C. B. (2011). Mathematics learned by young children in an intervention based on learning trajectories: A large-scale cluster randomized trial. *Journal for Research in Mathematics Education, 42*(2), 127–166.

Clivaz, S. (2013). Teaching multidigit multiplication: Combining multiple frameworks to analyse a class episode. In B. Ubuz, Ç. Haser, & M. A. Mariotti (Eds.), *Proceedings of the 8th Congress of European Research in Mathematics Education* (pp. 2995–3004). Ankara, Turkey: Middle East Technical University.

Cobb, P., & Yackel, E. (1996). Constructivist, emergent, and sociocultural perspectives in the context of developmental research. *Educational Psychologist, 31*(3–4), 175–190. doi:10.1080/00461520.1996.9653265

Cochran-Smith, M. (2003). Teaching quality matters. *Journal of Teacher Education, 54*(2), 95–98. doi:10.1177/0022487102250283

Cohen, D. K. (1990). A revolution in one classroom: The case of Mrs. Oublier. *Educational Evaluation and Policy Analysis, 12*(3), 311–329. doi:10.3102/01623737012003311

Cohen, D. K., Raudenbush, S. W., & Ball, D. L. (2003). Resources, instruction, and research. *Educational Evaluation and Policy Analysis, 25*(2), 119–142. doi:10.3102/01623737025002119

Cole, Y. (2012). Assessing elemental validity: The transfer and use of mathematical knowledge for teaching measures in Ghana. *ZDM—The International Journal on Mathematics Education, 44*(3), 415–426. doi:10.1007/s11858-012-0380-7

Coleman, J. S., Campbell, E. Q., Hobson, C. J., McPartland, J., Mood, A. M., Weinfeld, F. D., & York, R. L. (1966). *Equality of educational opportunity.* Washington, DC: U.S. Government Printing Office.

Copur-Gencturk, Y., & Lubienski, S. T. (2013). Measuring mathematical knowledge for teaching: A longitudinal study using two measures. *Journal of Mathematics Teacher Education, 16*(3), 211–236. doi:10.1007/s10857-012-9233-0

Core Practice Consortium (2014, April). *Enriching research and innovation through the specification of professional practice.* Paper presented at the annual meeting of the American Educational Research Association, Philadelphia, PA.

Correnti, R., & Martínez, J. F. (2012). Conceptual, methodological, and policy issues in the study of teaching: Implications for improving instructional practice at scale. *Educational Assessment, 17*(2–3), 51–61. doi:10.1080/10627197.2012.717834

Cottrill, J., Dubinsky, E., Nichols, D., Schwingendorf, K., Thomas, K., & Vidakovic, D. (1996). Understanding the limit concept: Beginning with a coordinated process scheme. *The Journal of Mathematical Behavior, 15*(2), 167–192. doi:10.1016/S0732-3123(96)90015-2

Creemers, B.P.M. (1994). *The effective classroom.* London: Cassell.

Creemers, B.P.M., & Kyriakides, L. (2008). *The dynamics of educational effectiveness: A contribution to policy, practice and theory in contemporary schools.* London & New York: Routledge.

Creemers, B.P.M., Kyriakides, L., & Sammons, P. (2010). *Methodological advances in educational effectiveness research.* London & New York: Routledge.

Croninger, R. G., Buese, D., & Larson, J. (2012). A mixed-methods look at teaching quality: Challenges and possibilities from one study. *Teachers College Record, 114*(4), 1–36.

Croninger, R. G., Valli, L., & Chambliss, M. J. (2012). Researching quality in teaching: Enduring and emerging challenges. *Teachers College Record, 114*(4), 1–15.

Danielson, C. (2007). *Enhancing professional practice: A framework for teaching* (2nd ed.). Alexandria, VA: Association for Supervision and Curriculum Development.

Davis, R. B., & Maher, C. A. (1990). What do we do when we "do mathematics"? (Monograph). *Journal for Research in Mathematics Education, 4*, 65–78. doi:10.2307/749913

Davis, B., & Renert, M. (2013). Profound understanding of emergent mathematics: Broadening the construct of teachers' disciplinary knowledge. *Educational Studies in Mathematics, 82*(2), 245–265. doi:10.1007/s10649-012-9424-8

Davis, B., & Simmt, E. (2006). Mathematics-for-teaching: An ongoing investigation of the mathematics that teachers (need to) know. *Educational Studies in Mathematics, 61*(3), 293–319. doi:10.1007/s10649-006-2372-4

Dekker, R., Elshout-Mohr, M., & Wood, T. (2006). How children regulate their own collaborative learning. *Educational Studies in Mathematics, 62*(1), 57–79. doi:10.1007/s10649-006-1688-4

Delaney, S., Ball, D.L., Hill, H.C., Schilling, S.G., & Zopf, D. (2008). "Mathematical knowledge for teaching": Adapting US measures for use in Ireland. *Journal of Mathematics Teacher Education, 11*(3), 171–197. doi:10.1007/s10857-008-9072-1

Depaepe, F., Verschaffel, L., & Kelchtermans, G. (2013). Pedagogical content knowledge: A systematic review of the way in which the concept has pervaded mathematics educational research. *Teaching and Teacher Education, 34,* 12–25. doi:10.1016/j.tate.2013.03.001

Ding, M. (2008). Teacher knowledge necessary to address student errors and difficulties about equivalent fractions. In G. Kulm (Ed.), *Teacher knowledge and practice in middle grades mathematics* (pp. 147–171). Rotterdam, The Netherlands: Sense Publishers.

Dominguez, H., LópezLeiva, C.A., & Khisty, L.L. (2014). Relational engagement: Proportional reasoning with bilingual Latino/a students. *Educational Studies in Mathematics, 85*(1), 143–160. doi:10.1007/s10649-013-9501-7

Drijvers, P., & Godino, J.D., Font, V., & Trouche, L. (2013). One episode, two lenses: A reflective analysis of student learning with computer algebra from instrumental and onto-semiotic perspectives. *Educational Studies in Mathematics, 82*(1), 23–49. doi:10.1007/s10649-012-9416-8

Dubinsky, E. (1992). A learning theory approach to calculus. In Z. Karian (Ed.), *Symbolic computation in undergraduate mathematics education* (MAA Notes No. 24, pp. 48–55). Washington, DC: Mathematical Association of America.

Ellis, A.B. (2011). Generalizing-promoting actions: How classroom collaborations can support students' mathematical generalizations. *Journal for Research in Mathematics Education, 42*(4), 308–345.

English, L.D. (2006). Mathematical modeling in the primary school: Children's construction of a consumer guide. *Educational Studies in Mathematics, 63*(3), 303–323. doi:10.1007/s10649-005-9013-1

English, L.D. (2013). Complex modelling in the primary and middle school years: An interdisciplinary approach. In G.A. Stillman, G. Kaiser, W. Blum, & J.P. Brown (Eds.), *Teaching mathematical modelling: Connecting to research and practice* (Vol. 16, pp. 491–505). Dordrecht: Springer.

English, L.D., & Mulligan, J. (Eds.). (2013). *Reconceptualizing early mathematics learning.* Dordrecht: Springer.

Even, R. (2009). Teacher knowledge and teaching: Considering the connections between perspectives and findings. In M. Tzekaki, M. Kaldrimidou, & H. Sakonidis (Eds.), *Proceedings of the 33rd Conference of the International Group for the Psychology of Mathematics Education* (Vol. 1, pp. 147–148). Thessaloniki, Greece: PME.

Fauth, B., Decristan, J., Rieser, S., Klieme, E., & Büttner, G. (2014). Student ratings of teaching quality in primary school: Dimensions and prediction of student outcomes. *Learning and Instruction, 29,* 1–9. doi:10.1016/j.learninstruc.2013.07.001

Fennema, E., & Franke, M.L. (1992). Teachers' knowledge and its impact. In D.A. Grouws (Ed.), *Handbook of research on mathematics teaching and learning: A project of the National Council of Teachers of Mathematics* (pp. 147–164). Reston, VA: NCTM.

Fenstermacher, G.D., & Richardson, V. (2005). On making determinations of quality in teaching. *Teachers College Record, 107*(1), 186–213.

Fishbein, E. (1993). The theory of figural concepts. *Educational Studies in Mathematics, 24*(2), 139–162. doi:10.1007/BF01273689

Francisco, J.M., & Hähkiöniemi, M. (2012). Students' ways of reasoning about nonlinear functions in guess-my-rule games. *International Journal of Science and Mathematics Education, 10*(5), 1001–1021. doi:10.1007/s10763-011-9310-3

Franke, M.L., Kazemi, E., & Battey, D. (2007). Mathematics teaching and classroom practice. In F.K. Lester (Ed.), *Second handbook of research on mathematics teaching and learning* (pp. 225–256). Charlotte, NC: Information Age Publishers.

Freudenthal, H. (1968). Why to teach mathematics so as to be useful. *Educational Studies in Mathematics, 1*(1–2), 3–8. doi:10.1007/BF00426224

Gage, N.L. (2009). *A conception of teaching.* New York: Springer.

Gainsburg, J. (2008). Real-world connections in secondary mathematics teaching. *Journal of Mathematics Teacher Education, 11*(3), 199–219. doi:10.1007/s10857-007-9070-8

Gallagher, H.A. (2004). Vaughn elementary's innovative teacher evaluation system: Are teacher evaluation scores related to growth in student achievement? *Peabody Journal of Education, 79*(4), 79–107. doi:10.1207/s15327930pje7904_5

Gil, E., & Ben-Zvi, D. (2011). Explanations and context in the emergence of students' informal inferential reasoning. *Mathematical Thinking and Learning, 13*(1–2), 87–108. doi:10.1080/10986065.2011.538295

Gilleece, L., Cosgrove, J., & Sofroniou, N. (2010). Equity in mathematics and science outcomes: Characteristics associated with high and low achievement on PISA 2006 in Ireland. *International Journal of Science and Mathematics Education, 8*(3), 475–496. doi:10.1007/s10763-010-9199-2

Gilmore, C.K., & Papadatou-Pastou, M. (2009). Patterns of individual differences in conceptual understanding and arithmetical skill: A meta-analysis. *Mathematical Thinking and Learning, 11*(1–2), 25–40. doi:10.1080/10986060802583923

Gitomer, D.H. (2009). Crisp measurement and messy context: A clash of assumptions and metaphors—Synthesis of section III. In D.H. Gitomer (Ed.), *Measurement issues and assessment for teaching quality* (pp. 223–233). Thousand Oaks, CA: Sage.

Glazerman, S., Loeb, S., Goldhaber, D., Staiger, D., Raudenbush, S., & Whitehurst, G. (2010). *Evaluating teachers: The important role of value-added* (Report No. 6829). Washington, DC: Brown Center on Education Policy, Brookings.

Graeber, A., & Tirosh, D. (2008). Pedagogical content knowledge: Useful concept or elusive notion? In P. Sullivan & T. Wood (Eds.), *Knowledge and beliefs in mathematics teaching and teaching development* (Vol. 1, pp. 117–132). Rotterdam, The Netherlands: Sense Publishers.

Griffiths, M. (2013). Intuiting the fundamental theorem of arithmetic. *Educational Studies in Mathematics, 82*(1), 75–96. doi:10.1007/s10649-012-9410-1

Grossman, P. (2008). Responding to our critics: From crisis to opportunity in research on teacher education. *Journal of Teacher Education, 59*(1), 10–23. doi:10.1177/0022487107310748

Grossman, P., Hammerness, K., & McDonald, M. (2009). Redefining teaching, re-imagining teacher education. *Teachers and Teaching: Theory and Practice, 15*(2), 273–289. doi:10.1080/13540600902875340

Grossman, P., & McDonald, M. (2008). Back to the future: Directions for research in teaching and teacher education. *American Educational Research Journal, 45*(1), 184–205. doi:10.3102/0002831207312906

Groth, R.E., & Bergner, J.A. (2006). Preservice elementary teachers' conceptual and procedural knowledge of mean, median, and mode. *Mathematical Thinking and Learning, 8*(1), 37–63. doi:10.1207/s15327833mtl0801_3

Groth, R.E., & Bergner, J.A. (2013). Mapping the structure of knowledge for teaching nominal categorical data analysis. *Educational Studies in Mathematics, 83*(2), 247–265. doi:10.1007/s10649-012-9452-4

Hamre, B.K., Pianta, R.C., Downer, J.T., DeCoster, J., Mashburn, A.J., Jones, . . . Hamagami, A. (2013). Teaching through interactions: Testing a developmental framework of teacher effectiveness in over 4,000 classrooms. *The Elementary School Journal, 113*(4), 461–487. doi:10.1086/669616

Harel, G., & Sowder, L. (1998). Students' proof schemes: Results from an exploratory study. In A.H. Schoenfeld, J. Kaput, & E. Dubinsky (Eds.), *Research in collegiate mathematics education* (Vol. 3, pp. 234–283). Providence, RI: American Mathematical Society.

Harris, D.N. (2009). The policy uses and policy validity of value-added and other teacher quality measures. In D.H. Gitomer (Ed.), *Measurement issues and assessment for teaching quality* (pp. 99–130). Thousand Oaks, CA: Sage.

Harris, D.N. (2011). *Value-added measures in education: What every educator needs to know.* Cambridge, MA: Harvard Education Press.

Hattie, J. (2009). *Visible learning. A synthesis of over 800 meta-analyses relating to achievement.* London: Routledge.

Hemmings, B., Grootenboer, P., & Kay, R. (2011). Predicting mathematics achievement: The influence of prior achievement and attitudes. *International Journal of Science and Mathematics Education, 9*(3), 691–705. doi:10.1007/s10763-010-9224-5

Herbst, P., & Kosko, K.W. (2012). Mathematical knowledge for teaching high school geometry. In L.R. Van Zoest, J.J. Lo, & J.L. Kratky (Eds.), *Proceedings of the 34th Annual Meeting of the North American Chapter of the International Group for the Psychology of Mathematics Education* (pp. 438–444). Kalamazoo, MI: Western Michigan University.

Hiebert, J., Gallimore, R., Garnier, H., Givvin, K.B., Hollingsworth, H., Jacobs, J., . . . Stigler, J. (2003). *Teaching mathematics in seven countries: Results from the TIMSS 1999 video study.* Washington, DC: National Center for Education Statistics.

Hiebert, J., & Grouws, D.A. (2007). The effects of classroom mathematics teaching on students' learning. In F.K. Lester (Ed.), *Second handbook of research on mathematics teaching and learning* (pp. 371–404). Charlotte, NC: Information Age Publishers.

Hiebert, J., Stigler, J.W., Jacobs, J.K., Givvin, K.B., Garnier, H., Smith, M., . . . Gallimore, R. (2005). Mathematics teaching in the United States today (and tomorrow): Results from the TIMSS 1999 video study. *Educational Evaluation and Policy Analysis, 27*(2), 111–132. doi:10.3102/01623737027002111

Hill, H.C. (2007). Mathematical knowledge of middle school teachers: Implications for the No Child Left Behind policy initiative. *Educational Evaluation and Policy Analysis, 29*(2), 95–114. doi:10.3102/0162373707301711

Hill, H.C. (2010). The nature and predictors of elementary teachers' mathematical knowledge for teaching. *Journal for Research in Mathematics Education, 41*(5), 513–545.

Hill, H.C., Ball, D.L., Blunk, M., Goffney, I.M., & Rowan, B. (2007). Validating the ecological assumption: The relationship of measure scores to classroom teaching and student learning. *Measurement: Interdisciplinary Research and Perspectives, 5*(2–3), 107–118. doi:10.1080/15366360701487138

Hill, H.C., Ball, D.L., & Schilling, S.G. (2008). Unpacking pedagogical content knowledge: Conceptualizing and measuring teachers' topic-specific knowledge of students. *Journal for Research in Mathematics Education, 39*(4), 372–400.

Hill, H.C., Blunk, M.L., Charalambous, C.Y., Lewis, J.M., Phelps, G.C., Sleep, L., & Ball, D.L. (2008). Mathematical knowledge for teaching and the mathematical quality of instruction: An exploratory study. *Cognition and Instruction, 26*(4), 430–511. doi:10.1080/07370008802177235

Hill, H.C., & Charalambous, C.Y. (2012). Teaching (un)Connected Mathematics: Two teachers' enactment of the Pizza problem. *Journal of Curriculum Studies, 44*(4), 467–487. doi:10.1080/0022027 2.2012.716972

Hill, H.C., Charalambous, C.Y., & Kraft, M.A. (2012). When rater reliability is not enough teacher observation systems and a case for the generalizability study. *Educational Researcher, 41*(2), 56–64. doi:10.3102/0013189X12437203

Hill, H.C., & Grossman, P. (2013). Learning from teacher observations: Challenges and opportunities posed by new teacher evaluation systems. *Harvard Educational Review, 83*(2), 371–384.

Hill, H.C., Kapitula, L., & Umland, K. (2011). A validity argument approach to evaluating teacher value-added scores. *American Educational Research Journal, 48*(3), 794–831. doi:10.3102/0002831210387916

Hill, H.C., Rowan, B., & Ball, D.L. (2005). Effects of teachers' mathematical knowledge for teaching on student achievement. *American Educational Research Journal 42*(2), 371–406. doi:10.3102/00028312042002371

Hill, H.C., Schilling, S.G., & Ball, D.L. (2004). Developing measures of teachers' mathematics knowledge for teaching. *The Elementary School Journal, 105*(1), 11–30. doi:10.1086/428763

Hill, H.C., Sleep, L., Lewis, J.M., & Ball, D.L. (2007). Assessing teachers' mathematical knowledge: What knowledge matters and what evidence counts? In F.K. Lester (Ed.), *Second handbook of research on mathematics teaching and learning* (pp. 111–155). Charlotte, NC: Information Age Publishers.

Hill, H.C., Umland, K., Litke, E., & Kapitula, L.R. (2012). Teacher quality and quality teaching: Examining the relationship of a teacher assessment to practice. *American Journal of Education, 118*(4), 489–519.

Hodgen, J. (2011). Knowing and identity: A situated theory of mathematics knowledge in teaching. In T. Rowland & K. Ruthven (Eds.), *Mathematical knowledge in teaching* (pp. 27–42). London, UK: Springer. doi:10.1007/978-90-481-9766-8_3

Hollebrands, K.F. (2007). The role of a dynamic software program for geometry in the strategies high school mathematics students employ. *Journal for Research in Mathematics Education, 38*(2), 164–192.

Hollebrands., K., Conner, A., & Smith, R.C. (2010). The nature of arguments provided by college geometry students with access to technology while solving problems. *Journal for Research in Mathematics Education, 41*(4), 324–350.

Huang, R., & Cai, J. (2011). Pedagogical representations to teach linear relations in Chinese and US classrooms: Parallel or hierarchical? *The Journal of Mathematical Behavior, 30*(2), 149–165. doi:10.1016/j.jmathb.2011.01.003

Hugener, I., Pauli, C., Reusser, K., Lipowsky, F., Rakoczy, K., & Klieme, E. (2009). Teaching patterns and learning quality in Swiss and German mathematics lessons. *Learning and Instruction, 19*(1), 66–78. doi:10.1016/j.learninstruc.2008.02.001

Huillet, D. (2009). Mathematics for teaching: An anthropological approach and its use in teacher training. *For the Learning of Mathematics, 29*(3), 4–10.

İmre, S.Y., & Akkoç, H. (2012). Investigating the development of prospective mathematics teachers' pedagogical content knowledge of generalising number patterns through school practicum. *Journal of Mathematics Teacher Education, 15*(3), 207–226. doi:10.1007/s10857-012-9203-6

Ing, M., & Webb, N.M. (2012). Characterizing mathematics classroom practice: Impact of observation and coding choices. *Educational Measurement: Issues and Practice, 31*(1), 14–26. doi:10.1111/j.1745-3992.2011.00224.x

Inglis, M., & Alcock, L. (2012). Expert and novice approaches to reading mathematical proofs. *Journal for Research in Mathematics Education, 43*(4), 358–390.

Izsák, A. (2008). Mathematical knowledge for teaching fraction multiplication. *Cognition and Instruction, 26*(1), 95–143. doi:10.1080/07370000701798529

Izsák, A., Tillema, E., & Tunç-Pekkan, Z. (2008). Teaching and learning fraction addition on number lines. *Journal for Research in Mathematics Education, 39*(1), 33–62. doi:10.2307/30034887

Jackson, K., Garrison, A., Wilson, J., Gibbons, L., & Shahan, E. (2013). Exploring relationships between setting up complex tasks and opportunities to learn in concluding whole-class discussions in middle-grades mathematics instruction. *Journal for Research in Mathematics Education, 44*(4), 646–682.

Jencks, C., Smith, M., Acland, H., Bane, M.J., Cohen, D., Gintis, H., . . . Michelson, S. (1972). *Inequality: A reassessment of the effects of family and schooling in America*. New York: Basic Books.

Jurdak, M. E. (2006). Contrasting perspectives and performance of high school students on problem solving in real world situated and school contexts. *Educational Studies in Mathematics, 63*(3), 283–301. doi:10.1007/s10649-005-9008-y

Jurdak, M. E., & El Mouhayar, R. R. (2014). Trends in the development of student level of reasoning in pattern generalization tasks across grade level. *Educational Studies in Mathematics, 85*(1), 75–92. doi:10.1007/s10649-013-9494-2

Kamii, C., & Kysh, J. (2006). The difficulty of "length×width": Is a square the unit of measurement? *The Journal of Mathematical Behavior, 25*(2), 105–115. doi:10.1016/j.jmathb.2006.02.001

Kane, T. J., McCaffrey, D. F., Miller, T., & Staiger, D. O. (2013). *Have we identified effective teachers? Validating measures of effective teaching using random assignment.* Seattle, WA: Bill & Melinda Gates Foundation. Retrieved from www.metproject.org/reports.php.

Kane, T. J., & Staiger, D. O. (2012). *Gathering feedback for teaching: Combining high-quality observations with student surveys and achievement gains.* Seattle, WA: Bill & Melinda Gates Foundation. Retrieved from www.metproject.org/reports.php.

Kane, T. J., Taylor, E. S., Tyler, J. H., & Wooten, A. L. (2011). Identifying effective classroom practices using student achievement data. *Journal of Human Resources, 46*(3), 587–613. doi:10.3386/w15803

Kaput, J. J. (1998). Transforming algebra from an engine of inequity to an engine of mathematical power by "algebrafying" the K–12 curriculum. In S. Fennel (Ed.), *The nature and role of algebra in the K–14 curriculum: Proceedings of a National Symposium* (pp. 25–26). Washington, DC: National Research Council, National Academy Press.

Kennedy, M. M. (2010). Attribution error and the quest for teacher quality. *Educational Researcher, 39*(8), 591–598. doi:10.3102/0013189X10390804

Kersting, N. (2008). Using video clips of mathematics classroom instruction as item prompts to measure teachers' knowledge of teaching mathematics. *Educational and Psychological Measurement, 68*(5), 845–861. doi:10.1177/0013164407313369

Kersting, N. B., Givvin, K. B., Sotelo, F. L., & Stigler, J. W. (2010). Teachers' analyses of classroom video predict student learning of mathematics: Further explorations of a novel measure of teacher knowledge. *Journal of Teacher Education, 61*(1–2), 172–181. doi:10.1177/0022487109347875

Kersting, N. B., Givvin, K. B., Thompson, B. J., Santagata, R., & Stigler, J. W. (2012). Measuring usable knowledge: Teachers' analyses of mathematics classroom videos predict teaching quality and student learning. *American Educational Research Journal, 49*(3), 568–589. doi:10.3102/0002831212437853

Kieran, C. (1996). The changing face of school algebra. In C. Alsina, J. Alvarez, B. Hodgson, C. Laborde, & A. Pérez (Eds.), *8th International Congress on Mathematical Education: Selected lectures* (pp. 271–290). Seville, Spain: S.A.E.M. Thales.

Kilpatrick, J., Swafford, J., & Findell, B. (Eds.). (2001). *Adding it up: Helping children learn mathematics.* Washington, DC: National Academy Press.

Kim, M., Roth, W. M., & Thom, J. (2011). Children's gestures and the embodied knowledge of geometry. *International Journal of Science and Mathematics Education, 9*(1), 207–238. doi:10.1007/s10763-010-9240-5

Kim, Y. R., Park, M. S., Moore, T. J., & Varma, S. (2013). Multiple levels of metacognition and their elicitation through complex problem-solving tasks. *The Journal of Mathematical Behavior, 32*(3), 377–396. doi:10.1016/j.jmathb.2013.04.002

Klieme, E., Pauli, C., & Reusser, K. (2009). The Pythagoras study. In J. Tomás & T. Seidel (Eds.), *The power of video studies in investigating teaching and learning in the classroom* (pp. 137–160). Münster, Germany: Waxmann.

Koellner, K., Jacobs, J., Borko, H., Schneider, C., Pittman, M. E., Eiteljorg, E., . . . Frykholm, J. (2007). The problem-solving cycle: A model to support the development of teachers' professional knowledge. *Mathematical Thinking and Learning, 9*(3), 273–303. doi:10.1080/10986060701360944

Kolovou, A., Van den Heuvel-Panhuizen, M., & Köller, O. (2013). An intervention including an online game to improve grade 6 students' performance in early algebra. *Journal for Research in Mathematics Education, 44*(3), 510–549.

Konstantopoulos, S., & Chung, V. (2011). The persistence of teacher effects in elementary grades. *American Educational Research Journal, 48*(2), 361–386. doi:10.3102/0002831210382888

Koretz, D. (2008). *Measuring up: What educational testing really tells us.* Cambridge, MA: Harvard University Press.

Krauss, S., Baumert, J., & Blum, W. (2008). Secondary mathematics teachers' pedagogical content knowledge and content knowledge: Validation of the COACTIV constructs. *ZDM—The International Journal on Mathematics Education, 40*(5), 873–892. doi:10.1007/s11858-008-0141-9

Krauss, S., Brunner, M., Kunter, M., Baumert, J., Blum, W., Neubrand, M., & Jordan, A. (2008). Pedagogical content knowledge and content knowledge of secondary mathematics teachers. *Journal of Educational Psychology, 100*(3), 716–725. doi:10.1037/0022-0663.100.3.716

Kruteski, V.A. (1976). *The psychology of mathematical abilities in school children*. Chicago, IL: University of Chicago Press

Kunter, M., & Baumert, J. (2006). Who is the expert? Construct and criteria validity of student and teacher ratings of instruction. *Learning Environments Research, 9*(3), 231–251. doi:10.1007/s10984-006-9015-7

Kunter, M., Klusmann, U., Baumert, J., Richter, D., Voss, T., & Hachfeld, A. (2013). Professional competence of teachers: Effects on instructional quality and student development. *Journal of Educational Psychology, 105*(3), 805–820. doi:10.1037/a0032583

Kwon, M., Thames, M.H., & Pang, J. (2012). To change or not to change: Adapting mathematical knowledge for teaching (MKT) measures for use in Korea. *ZDM—The International Journal on Mathematics Education, 44*(3), 371–385. doi:10.1007/s11858-012-0397-y

Kyriakides, L., Christoforou, C., & Charalambous, C.Y. (2013). What matters for student learning outcomes: A meta-analysis of studies exploring factors of effective teaching. *Teaching and Teacher Education, 36*, 143–152. doi:10.1016/j.tate.2013.07.010

Kyriakides, L., & Creemers, B.P.M. (2008). Using a multidimensional approach to measure the impact of classroom level factors upon student achievement: A study testing the validity of the dynamic model. *School Effectiveness and School Improvement, 19*(2), 183–205. doi:10.1080/09243450802047873

Kyriakides, L., Creemers, B., Antoniou, P., & Demetriou, D. (2010). A synthesis of studies searching for school factors: Implications for theory and research. *British Educational Research Journal, 36*(5), 807–830. doi:10.1080/01411920903165603

Lakoff, G., & Nuñez, R. (2000). *Where mathematics comes from: How the embodied mind brings mathematics into being*. New York: Basic Books.

Lamon, S.J. (1999). *Teaching fractions and rations for understanding*. Mahwah, NJ: Lawrence Erlbaum Associates.

Lampert, M. (2010). Learning teaching in, from, and for practice: What do we mean? *Journal of Teacher Education, 61*(1–2), 21–34. doi:10.1177/0022487109347321

Langrall, C.W. (2014). Linking research and practice: Another call to action? *Journal for Research in Mathematics Education, 45*(2), 154–156.

Lannin, J.K., Webb, M., Chval, K., Arbaugh, F., Hicks, S., Taylor, C., & Bruton, R. (2013). The development of beginning mathematics teacher pedagogical content knowledge. *Journal of Mathematics Teacher Education, 16*(6), 403–426. doi:10.1007/s10857-013-9244-5

Lavigne, N.C., Salkind, S.J., & Yan, J. (2008). Exploring college students' mental representations of inferential statistics. *The Journal of Mathematical Behavior, 27*(1), 11–32. doi:10.1016/j.jmathb.2007.10.003

Learning Mathematics for Teaching Project. (2011). Measuring the mathematical quality of instruction. *Journal of Mathematics Teacher Education, 14*(1), 25–47. doi:10.1007/s10857-010-9140-1

Leikin, R. (2013). Evaluating mathematical creativity: The interplay between multiplicity and insight. *Psychological Test and Assessment Modeling, 55*(4), 385–400.

Leikin, R., & Lev, M. (2013). Mathematical creativity in generally gifted and mathematically excelling adolescents: What makes the difference? *ZDM—The International Journal on Mathematics Education, 45*(2), 183–197. doi:10.1007/s11858-012-0460-8

Leikin, R., & Pitta-Pantazi, D. (2013). Creativity and mathematics education: Overview on the state-of-art. *ZDM—The International Journal on Mathematics Education, 45*(2), 159–166. doi:10.1007/s11858-012-0459-1

Lesh, R. (2010). Tools, researchable issues & conjectures for investigating what it means to understand statistics (or other topics) meaningfully. *Journal of Mathematical Modelling and Application, 1*(2), 16–48.

Lesh, R.A., Sriraman, B., & English, L.D. (2014). Theories of learning mathematics. In S. Lerman (Ed.), *Encyclopedia of Mathematics Education* (pp. 615–623). New York: Springer. doi:978-94-007-4978-8.

Lesh, R., & Zawojewski, J. (2007). Problem-solving and modeling. In F. Lester (Ed.), *Second handbook of research on mathematics teaching and learning* (pp. 763–804). Reston, VA: NCTM.

Levenson, E. (2013). Exploring one student's explanations at different ages: The case of Sharon. *Educational Studies in Mathematics, 83*(2), 181–203. doi:10.1007/s10649-012-9447-1

Levenson, E., Tirosh, D., & Tsamir, P. (2011). *Preschool geometry: Theory, research, and practical perspectives*. Rotterdam, The Netherlands: Sense Publishers.

Lewis, J.M., & Blunk, M.L. (2012). Reading between the lines: Teaching linear algebra. *Journal of Curriculum Studies, 44*(4), 515–536. doi:10.1080/00220272.2012.716975

Lo, J.J., & Luo, F. (2012). Prospective elementary teachers' knowledge of fraction division. *Journal of Mathematics Teacher Education, 15*(6), 481–500. doi:10.1007/s10857-012-9221-4

Luyten, H. (2003). The size of school effects compared to teacher effects: An overview of the research literature. *School Effectiveness and School Improvement, 14*(1), 31–51. doi:10.1076/sesi.14.1.31.13865

Ma, L. (1999). *Knowing and teaching elementary mathematics: Teachers' understanding of fundamental mathematics in China and the United States.* Mahwah, NJ: Lawrence Erlbaum Associates.

Makar, K., Bakker, A., & Ben-Zvi, D. (2011). The reasoning behind informal statistical inference. *Mathematical Thinking and Learning, 13*(1–2), 152–173. doi:10.1080/10986065.2011.538301

Martínez, J. F., Borko, H., Stecher, B., Luskin, R., & Kloser, M. (2012). Measuring classroom assessment practice using instructional artifacts: A validation study of the QAS notebook. *Educational Assessment, 17*(2–3), 107–131. doi:10.1080/10627197.2012.715513

Mashburn, A. J., Meyer, J. P., Allen, J. P., & Pianta, R. C. (2014). The effect of observation length and presentation order on the reliability and validity of an observational measure of teaching quality. *Educational and Psychological Measurement, 74*(3), 400–422. doi:10.1177/0013164413515882

Mason, J. (2008). PCK and beyond. In P. Sullivan & T. Wood (Eds.), *Knowledge and beliefs in mathematics teaching and teaching development* (Vol. 1, pp. 301–322). Rotterdam, The Netherlands: Sense Publishers.

Mayer, D. P. (1999). Measuring instructional practice: Can policymakers trust survey data? *Educational Evaluation and Policy Analysis, 21*(1), 29–45. doi:10.3102/01623737021001029

McCaffrey, D. F., Sass, T. R., Lockwood, J. R., & Mihaly, K. (2009). The intertemporal variability of teacher effect estimates. *Education Finance and Policy, 4*(4), 572–606. doi:10.1162/edfp.2009.4.4.572

McClellan, C., Donoghue, J., & Park, Y. S. (2013, April). *Commonality and uniqueness in teaching practice observation.* Paper presented at the annual meeting of the National Council of Measurement in Education, San Francisco, CA.

McCrory, R., Floden, R., Ferrini-Mundy, J., Reckase, M. D., & Senk, S. L. (2012). Knowledge of Algebra for Teaching: A framework of knowledge and practices. *Journal for Research in Mathematics Education, 43*(5), 584–615. doi:10.5951/jresematheduc.43.5.0584

McDonald, M., Kazemi, E., & Kavanagh, S. S. (2013). Core practices and pedagogies of teacher education a call for a common language and collective activity. *Journal of Teacher Education, 64*(5), 378–386. doi:10.1177/0022487113493807

Mesa, V. (2012). Achievement goal orientation of community college mathematics students and the misalignment of instructors' perceptions. *Community College Review, 40*(1), 46–74. doi:10.1177/0091552111435663

Mewborn, D. S. (2003). Teaching, teachers' knowledge and their professional development. In J. Kilpatrick, W. G. Martin, & D. Schifter (Eds.), *A research companion to principles and standards for school mathematics* (pp. 45–52). Reston, VA: NCTM.

Mills, M. (2014). A framework for example usage in proof presentations. *The Journal of Mathematical Behavior, 33,* 106–118. doi:10.1016/j.jmathb.2013.11.001

Ministry of Education of Singapore. (2013). *Primary mathematics teaching and learning syllabus.* Singapore: Curriculum Planning and Development Division. Retrieved from www.moe.gov.sg/education/syllabuses/sciences/.

Mitchell, R., Charalambous, C. Y., & Hill, H. C. (2014). Examining the task and knowledge demands needed to teach with representations. *Journal of Mathematics Teacher Education, 17*(1), 37–60. doi:10.1007/s10857-013-9253-4

Miyakawa, T., & Winsløw, C. (2013). Developing mathematics teacher knowledge: The paradidactic infrastructure of "open lesson" in Japan. *Journal of Mathematics Teacher Education, 16*(3), 185–209. doi:10.1007/s10857-013-9236-5

Modestou, M., & Gagatsis, A. (2010). Cognitive and metacognitive aspects of proportional reasoning. *Mathematical Thinking and Learning, 12*(1), 36–53. doi:10.1080/10986060903465822

Monk, D. H. (1994). Subject area preparation of secondary mathematics and science teachers and student achievement. *Economics of Education Review, 13*(2), 125–145. doi:10.1016/0272-7757(94)90003-5

Muijs, D., Kyriakides, L., van der Werf, G., Creemers, B., Timperley, H., & Earl, L. (2014). State of the art—Teacher effectiveness and professional learning. *School Effectiveness and School Improvement, 25*(2), 231–256. doi:10.1080/09243453.2014.885451

Muijs, D., & Reynolds, D. (2000). School effectiveness and teacher effectiveness in mathematics: Some preliminary findings from the evaluation of the mathematics enhancement programme (primary). *School Effectiveness and School Improvement, 11*(3), 273–303. doi:10.1076/0924-3453

Muir, T., Beswick, K., & Williamson, J. (2008). "I'm not very good at solving problems": An exploration of students' problem solving behaviours. *The Journal of Mathematical Behavior, 27*(3), 228–241. doi:10.1016/j.jmathb.2008.04.003

Murata, A., Bofferding, L., Pothen, B. E., Taylor, M. W., & Wischnia, S. (2012). Making connections among student learning, content, and teaching: Teacher talk paths in elementary mathematics lesson study. *Journal for Research in Mathematics Education, 43*(5), 616–650.

Murata, A., & Kattubadi, S. (2012). Grade 3 students' mathematization through modeling: Situation models and solution models with multi-digit subtraction problem solving. *The Journal of Mathematical Behavior, 31*(1), 15–28. doi:10.1016/j.jmathb.2011.07.004

Murphy, C. (2012). The role of subject knowledge in primary prospective teachers' approaches to teaching the topic of area. *Journal of Mathematics Teacher Education, 15*(3), 187–206. doi:10.1007/s10857-011-9194-8

Nason, R., Chalmers, C., & Yeh, A. (2012). Facilitating growth in prospective teachers' knowledge: Teaching geometry in primary schools. *Journal of Mathematics Teacher Education, 15*(3), 227–249. doi:10.1007/s10857-012-9209-0

Nathan, M. J., & Kim, S. (2009). Regulation of teacher elicitations in the mathematics classroom. *Cognition and Instruction, 27*(2), 91–120. doi:10.1080/07370000902797304

Neubrand, M. (2009). Two lessons—three views—some comments. In M. Tzekaki, M. Kaldrimidou, & H. Sakonidis (Eds.), *Proceedings of the 33rd Conference of the International Group for the Psychology of Mathematics Education* (Vol. 1, pp. 149–150). Thessaloniki, Greece: PME.

Newton, K. J., Star, J. R., & Lynch, K. (2010). Understanding the development of flexibility in struggling algebra students. *Mathematical Thinking and Learning, 12*(4), 282–305. doi:10.1080/10986065.2010.482150

Newton, X. A., Darling-Hammond, L., Haertel, E., & Thomas, E. (2010). Value-added modeling of teacher effectiveness: An exploration of stability across models and contexts. *Education Policy Analysis Archives, 18*(23), 1–27. doi:10.14507/epaa.v18n23.2010

Ng, D. (2012). Using the MKT measures to reveal Indonesian teachers' mathematical knowledge: Challenges and potentials. *ZDM—The International Journal on Mathematics Education, 44*(3), 401–413. doi:10.1007/s11858-011-0375-9

Ng, D., Mosvold, R., & Fauskanger, J. (2012). Translating and adapting the Mathematical Knowledge for Teaching (MKT) measures: The cases of Indonesia and Norway. *Montana Mathematics Enthusiast, 9*(1&2), 149–178.

Nilssona, P., & Juter, K. (2011). Flexibility and coordination among acts of visualization and analysis in a pattern generalization activity. *The Journal of Mathematical Behavior, 30*(3), 194–205. doi:10.1016/j.jmathb.2011.07.002

Norton, A., McCloskey, A., & Hudson, R. A. (2011). Prediction assessments: Using video-based predictions to assess prospective teachers' knowledge of students' mathematical thinking. *Journal of Mathematics Teacher Education, 14*(4), 305–325. doi:10.1007/s10857-011-9181-0

Norton, A., & Wilkins, J. L. M. (2009). A quantitative analysis of children's splitting operations and fraction schemes. *The Journal of Mathematical Behavior, 28*(2–3), 150–161. doi:10.1016/j.jmathb.2009.06.002

Nuthall, N. (2004). Relating classroom teaching to student learning: A critical analysis of why research has failed to bridge the theory-practice gap. *Harvard Educational Review, 74*(3), 273–306.

Nye, B., Konstantopoulos, S., & Hedges, L. V. (2004). How large are teacher effects? *Educational Evaluation and Policy Analysis, 26*(3), 237–257. doi:10.3102/01623737026003237

Olive, J. (1999). From fractions to rational numbers of arithmetic: A reorganization hypothesis. *Mathematical thinking and learning, 1*(4), 279–314. doi:10.1207/s15327833mtl0104_2

Palardy, G. J., & Rumberger, R. W. (2008). Teacher effectiveness in first grade: The importance of background qualifications, attitudes, and instructional practices for student learning. *Educational Evaluation and Policy Analysis, 30*(2), 111–140. doi:10.3102/0162373708317680

Pantziara, M., & Philippou, G. (2012). Levels of students' "conception" of fractions. *Educational Studies in Mathematics, 79*(1), 61–83.doi:10.1007/s10649-011-9338-x

Papay, J. P. (2011). Different tests, different answers: The stability of teacher value-added estimates across outcome measures. *American Educational Research Journal, 48*(1), 163–193. doi:10.3102/0002831210362589

Papay, J. P. (2012). Refocusing the debate: Assessing the purposes and tools of teacher evaluation. *Harvard Educational Review, 82*(1), 123–141.

Papic, M., Mulligan, J. T., & Mitchelmore, M. C. (2011). Assessing the development of preschoolers' mathematical patterning. *Journal for Research in Mathematics Education, 42*(3), 237–268.

Peltenburg, M., Van den Heuvel-Panhuizen, M., & Robitzsch, A. (2012). Special education students' use of indirect addition in solving subtraction problems up to 100: A proof of the didactical potential of an ignored procedure. *Educational Studies in Mathematics, 79*(3), 351–369. doi:10.1007/s10649-011-9351-0

Pepin, B. (2011). How educational systems and cultures mediate teacher knowledge: 'Listening' in English, French, and German classrooms. In T. Rowland & K. Ruthven (Eds.), *Mathematical knowledge in teaching* (pp. 119–137). London & New York: Springer. doi:10.1007/978-90-481-9766-8_8

Petrou, M., & Goulding, M. (2011). Conceptualising teachers' mathematical knowledge in teaching. In T. Rowland & K. Ruthven (Eds.), *Mathematical knowledge in teaching* (pp. 9–25) London & New York: Springer. doi:10.1007/978-90-481-9766-8_2

Philipp, R. A., Ambrose, R., Lamb, L. L., Sowder, J. T., Schappelle, B. P., Sowder, L., . . . Chauvot, J. (2007). Effects of early field experiences on the mathematical content knowledge and beliefs of prospective elementary school teachers: An experimental study. *Journal for Research in Mathematics Education, 38*(5), 438–476. doi:10.2307/30034961

Pianta, R. C., Belsky, J., Vandergrift, N., Houts, R., & Morrison, F. J. (2008). Classroom effects on children's achievement trajectories in elementary school. *American Educational Research Journal, 45*(2), 365–397. doi:10.3102/0002831207308230

Pirie, S., & Kieren, T. (1989). A recursive theory of mathematical understanding. *For the Learning of Mathematics, 9*(3), 7–11.

Pitta-Pantazi, D., & Christou, C. (2009). Cognitive styles, dynamic geometry and measurement performance. *Educational Studies in Mathematics, 70*(1), 5–26. doi:10.1007/s10649-008-9139-z

Pitta-Pantazi, D., Christou, C., Kontoyianni, K., & Kattou, M. (2011). A model of mathematical giftedness: Integrating natural, creative and mathematical abilities. *Canadian Journal of Science, Mathematics and Technology Education, 11*(1), 39–54. doi:10.1080/14926156.2011.548900

Polya, D. (1954). *Induction and analogy in mathematics.* Princeton, NJ: Princeton University Press.

Post, T. R., Cramer, K. A., Behr, M., Lesh, R., & Harel, G. (1993). Curriculum implications of research on the learning, teaching, and assessing of rational number concepts. In T. Carpenter, E. Fennema, & T. Romberg (Eds.), *Rational numbers: An integration of research* (pp. 327–362). Hillsdale, NJ: Erlbaum.

Praetorius, A. K., Lenske, G., & Helmke, A. (2012). Observer ratings of instructional quality: Do they fulfill what they promise? *Learning and Instruction, 22*(6), 387–400. doi:10.1016/j.learninstruc.2012.03.002

Praetorius, A. K., Pauli, C., Reusser, K., Rakoczy, K., & Klieme, E. (2014). One lesson is all you need? Stability of instructional quality across lessons. *Learning and Instruction, 31*, 2–12. doi:10.1016/j.learninstruc.2013.12.002

Presmeg, N. C. (1985). *The role of visually mediated processes in high school mathematics: A classroom investigation.* Unpublished doctoral dissertation, Cambridge University, England.

Rivers, J. C., & Sanders, W. L. (2002). Teacher quality and equity in educational opportunity: Findings and policy implications. In L. T. Izumi & W. M. Evers (Eds.), *Teacher quality* (pp. 13–23). Stanford, CA: Hoover Press.

Rockoff, J. E., Jacob, B. A., Kane, T. J., & Staiger, D. O. (2011). Can you recognize an effective teacher when you recruit one? *Education Finance and Policy, 6*(1), 43–74. doi:10.1162/EDFP_a_00022

Rowan, B., & Correnti, R. (2009). Studying reading instruction with teacher logs: Lessons from the Study of Instructional Improvement. *Educational Researcher, 38*(2), 120–131. doi:10.3102/0013189X09332375

Rowan, B., Correnti, R., & Miller, R. (2002). What large-scale survey research tells us about teacher effects on student achievement: Insights from the Prospects Study of Elementary Schools. *Teachers College Record, 104*(8), 1525–1567.

Rowan, B., Harrison, D. M., & Hayes, A. (2004). Using instructional logs to study mathematics curriculum and teaching in the early grades. *The Elementary School Journal, 105*(1), 103–127. doi:10.1086/428812

Rowland, T. (2008a). Researching teachers' mathematics disciplinary knowledge. In P. Sullivan & T. Wood (Eds.), *Knowledge and beliefs in mathematics teaching and teaching development* (Vol. 1, pp. 273–298). Rotterdam, The Netherlands: Sense Publishers.

Rowland, T. (2008b). The purpose, design and use of examples in the teaching of elementary mathematics. *Educational Studies in Mathematics, 69*(2), 149–163. doi:10.1007/s10649-008-9148-y

Rowland, T. (2012). Contrasting knowledge for elementary and secondary mathematics teaching. *For the Learning of Mathematics, 32*(1), 16–21.

Rowland, T., Huckstep, P., & Thwaites, A. (2005). Elementary teachers' mathematics subject knowledge: The knowledge quartet and the case of Naomi. *Journal of Mathematics Teacher Education, 8*(3), 255–281. doi:10.1007/s10857-005-0853-5

Rubel, L. H. (2007). Middle school and high school students' probabilistic reasoning on coin tasks. *Journal for Research in Mathematics Education, 38*(5), 531–556.

Ruthven, K. (2011). Conceptualising mathematical knowledge in teaching. In T. Rowland & K. Ruthven (Eds.), *Mathematical knowledge in teaching* (pp. 83–96). London & New York: Springer. doi:10.1007/978-90-481-9766-8_6

Sanders, W. L., & Horn, S. P. (1994). The Tennessee value-added assessment system (TVAAS): Mixed-model methodology in educational assessment. *Journal of Personnel Evaluation in Education, 8*(3), 299–311.doi:10.1007/BF00973726

Sarama, J., & Clements, D. H. (2009). *Early childhood mathematics education research: Learning trajectories for young children.* New York: Routledge.

Sass, T. R. (2008). *The stability of value-added measures of teacher quality and implications for teacher compensation policy* (Brief No. 4). Washington, DC: National Center for Analysis of Longitudinal Data in Education Research.

Sawada, D., Piburn, M.D., Judson, E., Turley, J., Falconer, K., Benford, R., & Bloom, I. (2002). Measuring reform practices in science and mathematics classrooms: The reformed teaching observation protocol. *School Science and Mathematics, 102*(6), 245–253. doi:10.1111/j.1949-8594.2002.tb17883.x

Scheerens, J., & Bosker, R.J. (1997). *The foundations of educational effectiveness.* Oxford, UK: Pergamon.

Schilling, S.G., Blunk, M., & Hill, H.C. (2007). Test validation and the MKT measures: Generalizations and conclusions. *Measurement: Interdisciplinary Research and Perspectives, 5*(2–3), 118–128. doi:10.1080/15366360701487146

Schneider, W., & Artelt, C. (2010). Metacognition and mathematics education. *ZDM—The International Journal on Mathematics Education, 42*(2), 149–161. doi:10.1007/s11858-010-0240-2.

Schoenfeld, A.H. (1992). Learning to think mathematically: Problem solving, metacognition, and sense-making in mathematics. In D. Grouws (Ed.), *Handbook for research on mathematics teaching and learning* (pp. 334–370). New York: MacMillan.

Schorr, R.Y., & Goldin, G.A. (2008). Students' expression of affect in an inner-city SimCalc classroom. *Educational Studies in Mathematics, 68*(2), 131–148. doi:10.1007/s10649-008-9117-5

Seidel, T., & Shavelson, R.J. (2007). Teaching effectiveness research in the past decade: The role of theory and research design in disentangling meta-analysis results. *Review of Educational Research, 77*(4), 454–499. doi: 10.3102/0034654307310317

Sfard, A. (1991). On the dual nature of mathematical conceptions: Reflections on processes and objects as different sides of the same coin. *Educational Studies in Mathematics, 22*(1), 1–36. doi:10.1007/BF00302715

Sharma, S.V. (2006). High school students interpreting tables and graphs: Implications for research. *International Journal of Science and Mathematics Education, 4*(2), 241–268. doi:10.1007/s10763-005-9005-8

Shavelson, R.J., Webb, N.M., & Burstein, L. (1986). Measurement of teaching. In M.C. Wittrock (Ed.), *Handbook of research on teaching* (3rd ed., pp. 50–91). New York: MacMillan.

Shechtman, N., Haertel, G., Roschelle, J., Knudsen, J., & Singleton, C. (2013). Development of student and teacher assessments in the scaling up SimCalc Project. In S.J. Hegedus & J. Roschelle (Eds.), *The SimCalc vision and contributions* (pp. 167–181). London & New York: Springer. doi:10.1007/978-94-007-5696-0_10

Shechtman, N., Roschelle, J., Haertel, G., & Knudsen, J. (2010). Investigating links from teacher knowledge, to classroom practice, to student learning in the instructional system of the middle-school mathematics classroom. *Cognition and Instruction, 28*(3), 317–359. doi:10.1080/07370008.2010.487961

Shulman, L.S. (1986). Those who understand: Knowledge growth in teaching. *Educational Researcher, 15*(2), 4–14.

Siegler, R.S. (2000). The rebirth of children's learning. *Child development, 71*(1), 26–35. doi:10.1111/1467-8624.00115

Silver, E.A. (1997). Fostering creativity through instruction rich in mathematical problem solving and problem posing. *ZDM—The International Journal on Mathematics Education, 29*(3), 75–80. doi:10.1007/s11858-997-0003-x

Silverman, J., & Thompson, P.W. (2008). Toward a framework for the development of mathematical knowledge for teaching. *Journal of Mathematics Teacher Education, 11*(6), 499–511. doi:10.1007/s10857-008-9089-5

Sleep, L. (2012). The work of steering instruction toward the mathematical point: A decomposition of teaching practice. *American Educational Research Journal, 49*(5), 935–970. doi:10.3102/0002831212448095

Sleep, L., & Eskelson, S.L. (2012). MKT and curriculum materials are only part of the story: Insights from a lesson on fractions. *Journal of Curriculum Studies, 44*(4), 537–558. doi:10.1080/00220272.2012.716977

Sowder, J.T., Philipp, R.A., Armstrong, B.E., & Schappelle, B.P. (1998). *Middle-grade teachers' mathematical knowledge and its relationship to instruction: A research monograph.* New York: State University of New York Press.

Sriraman, B., & English, L. (2010). *Theories of mathematics education: Seeking new frontiers.* London & New York: Springer.

Stecher, B., Le, V.N., Hamilton, L., Ryan, G., Robyn, A., & Lockwood, J.R. (2006). Using structured classroom vignettes to measure instructional practices in mathematics. *Educational Evaluation and Policy Analysis, 28*(2), 101–130. doi:10.3102/01623737028002101

Steele, M.D., Hillen, A.F., & Smith, M.S. (2013). Developing mathematical knowledge for teaching in a methods course: The case of function. *Journal of Mathematics Teacher Education, 16*(6), 451–482. doi:10.1007/s10857-013-9243-6

Steffe, L.P. (2001). A new hypothesis concerning children's fractional knowledge. *The Journal of Mathematical Behavior, 20*(3), 267–307. doi:10.1016/S0732-3123(02)00075-5

Steffe, L.P., Cobb, P., & von Glaserfeld, E. (1988). *Construction of arithmetical meanings and strategies.* New York: Springer-Verlag.

Steffe, L.P., von Glasersfeld, E., Richards, J., & Cobb, P. (1983). *Children's counting types: Philosophy, theory, and application.* New York: Praeger.

Stein, M., & Burchartz, B. (2006). The invisible wall project: Reasoning and problem solving processes of primary and lower secondary students. *Mathematical Thinking and Learning, 8*(1), 65–90. doi:10.1207/s15327833mtl0801_4

Stein, M.K., Engle, R.A., Smith, M.S., & Hughes, E.K. (2008). Orchestrating productive mathematical discussions: Five practices for helping teachers move beyond show and tell. *Mathematical Thinking and Learning, 10*(4), 313–340. doi:10.1080/10986060802229675

Stein, M.K., Smith, M.S., Henningsen, M.A., & Silver, E.A. (2000). *Implementing standards-based mathematics instruction: A casebook for professional development* (2nd ed.). New York: Teachers College Press.

Stigler, J.W., & Hiebert, J. (1999). *The teaching gap: Best ideas from the world's teachers for improving education in the classroom.* New York: Free Press.

Stoyanova, E., & Ellerton, N.F. (1996). A framework for research into students' problem posing. In P. Clarkson (Ed.), *Technology in Mathematics Education* (pp. 518–525). Melbourne: Mathematics Education Research Group of Australasia.

Strong, M., Gargani, J., & Hacifazlioğlu, Ö. (2011). Do we know a successful teacher when we see one? Experiments in the identification of effective teachers. *Journal of Teacher Education, 62*(4), 367–382. doi:10.1177/0022487110390221

Stronge, J.H., Ward, T.J., & Grant, L.W. (2011). What makes good teachers good? A cross-case analysis of the connection between teacher effectiveness and student achievement. *Journal of Teacher Education, 62*(4), 339–355. doi:10.1177/0022487111404241

Stylianides, A.J. (2007). Proof and proving in school mathematics. *Journal for Research in Mathematics Education, 38*(3), 289–321. doi:10.2307/30034869

Stylianides, A.J., & Delaney, S. (2011). The cultural dimension of teachers' mathematical knowledge. In T. Rowland & K. Ruthven (Eds.), *Mathematical knowledge in teaching* (pp. 179–191). London, UK: Springer. doi:10.1007/978-90-481-9766-8_11

Stylianides, G.J., & Stylianides, A.J. (2009). Facilitating the transition from empirical arguments to proof. *Journal for Research in Mathematics Education, 40*(3), 314–352.

Sumpter, L. (2013). Themes and interplay of beliefs in mathematical reasoning. *International Journal of Science and Mathematics Education, 11*(5), 1115–1135. doi:10.1007/s10763-012-9392-6

Szilágyi, J., Clements, D.H., & Sarama, J. (2013). Young children's understandings of length measurement: Evaluating a learning trajectory. *Journal for Research in Mathematics Education, 44*(3), 581–620.

Tabach, M., Hershkowitz, R., & Dreyfus, T. (2013). Learning beginning algebra in a computer-intensive environment. *ZDM—The International Journal on Mathematics Education, 45*(3), 377–391. doi:10.1007/s11858-012-0458-2.

Tall, D. (2013). *How humans learn to think mathematically: Exploring the three worlds of mathematics.* New York: Cambridge University Press.

Tall, D., & Vinner, S. (1981). Concept image and concept definition in mathematics with particular reference to limits and continuity. *Educational Studies in Mathematics, 12*(2), 151–169. doi:10.1007/BF00305619

Tanase, M., & Wang, J. (2013). Knowing students as mathematics learners and teaching numbers 10–100: A case study of four 1st grade teachers from Romania. *The Journal of Mathematical Behavior, 32*(3), 564–576. doi:10.1016/j.jmathb.2013.06.006

Tatto, M.T., Schwille, J., Senk, S.L., Bankov, K., Rodriguez, M., Reckase, M., Ingvarson, L., Rowley, G., Peck, R., . . . Reckase, M. (2012). *Teacher Education and Development Study in Mathematics (TEDS-M): Policy, practice, and readiness to teach primary and secondary mathematics in 17 countries. Findings from the IEA Study of the mathematics preparation of future teachers.* Amsterdam, The Netherlands: IEA.

Tchoshanov, M.A. (2011). Relationship between teacher knowledge of concepts and connections, teaching practice, and student achievement in middle grades mathematics. *Educational Studies in Mathematics, 76*(2), 141–164. doi:10.1007/s10649-010-9269-y

Tirosh, D., & Stavy, R. (1999). Intuitive rules: A way to explain and predict students' reasoning. *Educational Studies in Mathematics, 38*(1–3), 51–66. doi:10.1023/A:1003436313032

Tirosh, D., Tsamir, P., Levenson, E., & Tabach, M. (2011). From preschool teachers' professional development to children's knowledge: Comparing sets. *Journal of Mathematics Teacher Education, 14*(2),113–131. doi:10.1007/s10857-011-9172-1

Tirosh, D., Tsamir, P., Levenson, E., Tabach, M., & Barkai, R. (2013). Exploring young children's self-efficacy beliefs related to mathematical and nonmathematical tasks performed in kindergarten: Abused and neglected children and their peers. *Educational Studies in Mathematics, 83*(2), 309–322. doi:10.1007/s10649-012-9458-y

Tomás, J., & Seidel, T. (2009). *The power of video studies in investigating teaching and learning in the classroom.* Münster, Germany: Waxmann.

Toulmin, S.E. (1958). *The uses of argument.* Cambridge: Cambridge University Press.

Tsamir, P., Tirosh, D., Levenson, E., Tabach, M., & Barkai, R. (2014). Developing preschool teachers' knowledge of students' number conceptions. *Journal of Mathematics Teacher Education, 17*(1) 61–83. doi:10.1007/s10857-013-9260-5

Turner, F. (2012). Using the Knowledge Quartet to develop mathematics content knowledge: The role of reflection on professional development. *Research in Mathematics Education, 14*(3), 253–271. doi: 10.1080/14794802.2012.734972

Van den Heuvel-Panhuizen, M., Kolovou, A., & Robitzsch, A. (2013). Primary school students' strategies in early algebra problem solving supported by an online game. *Educational Studies in Mathematics, 84*(3), 281–307. doi:10.1007/s10649-013-9483-5

Van Harpen, X.Y., & Presmeg, N.C. (2013). An investigation of relationships between students' mathematical problem-posing abilities and their mathematical content knowledge. *Educational Studies in Mathematics, 83*(1), 117–132. doi:10.1007/s10649-012-9456-0

Van Hiele, P.M. (1985). The child's thought and geometry. In D. Fuys, D. Geddes, & R. Tischer (Eds.), *English translation of selected writings of Dina van Hiele-Geldof and Pierre M. van Hiele* (pp. 243–252). Brooklyn, NY: Brooklyn College.

Vergnaud, G. (1990). La théorie des champs conceptuels. *Recherches en Didactique des Mathématiques, 10*(2–3), 133–170.

Vergnaud, G. (2009). The theory of conceptual fields. *Human development, 52*(2), 83–94. doi:10.1159/000202727

Verzosa, D.B., & Mulligan, J. (2013). Learning to solve addition and subtraction word problems in English as an imported language. *Educational Studies in Mathematics, 82*(2), 223–244. doi:10.1007/s10649-012-9420-z

Wagner, J.F., Speer, N.M., & Rossa, B. (2007). Beyond mathematical content knowledge: A mathematician's knowledge needed for teaching an inquiry-oriented differential equations course. *The Journal of Mathematical Behavior, 26*(3), 247–266. doi:10.1016/j.jmathb.2007.09.002

Walkowiak, T.A., Berry, R.Q., Meyer, J.P., Rimm-Kaufman, S.E., & Ottmar, E.R. (2014). Introducing an observational measure of standards-based mathematics teaching practices: Evidence of validity and score reliability. *Educational Studies in Mathematics, 85*(1), 109–128. doi:10.1007/s10649-013-9499-x

Watson, J.M. (2007). The role of cognitive conflict in developing students' understanding of average. *Educational Studies in Mathematics, 65*(1), 21–47. doi:10.1007/s10649-006-9043-3

Wilkins, J.L.M., & Norton, A. (2011). The splitting loope. *Journal for Research in Mathematics Education, 42*(4), 386–416.

Wilson, S.M. (1990). A conflict of interests: The case of Mark Black. *Educational Evaluation and Policy Analysis, 12*(3), 293–310.

Wood, T., Williams, G., & McNeal, B. (2006). Children's mathematical thinking in different classroom cultures. *Journal for Research in Mathematics Education, 37*(3), 222–255.

Yakes, C., & Star, J.R. (2011). Using comparison to develop flexibility for teaching algebra. *Journal of Mathematics Teacher Education, 14*(3), 175–191. doi:10.1007/s10857-009-9131-2

Yang, K.L. (2012). Structures of cognitive and metacognitive reading strategy use for reading comprehension of geometry proof. *Educational Studies in Mathematics, 80*(3), 307–326. doi:10.1007/s10649-011-9350-1

Yanik, H.B. (2011). Prospective middle school mathematics teachers' preconceptions of geometric translations. *Educational Studies in Mathematics, 78*(2), 231–260. doi:10.1007/s10649-011-9324-3

Yerushalmy, M. (2006). Slower algebra students meet faster tools: Solving algebra word problems with graphing software. *Journal for Research in Mathematics Education, 37*(5), 356–387.

Zachariades, T., Christou, C., & Pitta-Pantazi, D. (2013). Reflective, systemic and analytic thinking in real numbers. *Educational Studies in Mathematics, 82*(1), 5–22. doi:10.1007/s10649-012-9413-y

Zazkis, R., & Chernoff, E.J. (2008). What makes a counterexample exemplary? *Educational Studies in Mathematics, 68*(3), 195–208. doi:10.1007/s10649-007-9110-4

Zazkis, R., & Zazkis, D. (2011). The significance of mathematical knowledge in teaching elementary methods courses: Perspectives of mathematics teacher educators. *Educational Studies in Mathematics, 76*(3), 247–263. doi:10.1007/s10649-010-9268-z

Zodik, I., & Zaslavsky, O. (2008). Characteristics of teachers' choice of examples in and for the mathematics classroom. *Educational Studies in Mathematics, 69*(2), 165–182. doi:10.1007/s10649-008-9140-6

Zurina, H., & Williams, J. (2011). Gesturing for oneself. *Educational Studies in Mathematics, 77*(2–3), 175–188. doi:10.1007/s10649-010-9294-x

3 Approaches to Embodied Learning in Mathematics

Susan Gerofsky

The University of British Columbia

INTRODUCTION

A consideration of mathematics as potentially embodied and the topic of embodied ways of knowing in a more democratized mathematics education immediately raise a number of foundational issues that are both fraught and interesting. Just a few examples follow.

At a theoretical/definitional level: What is meant by "embodiment"? Are theorists in agreement about its meanings and implications? Is it time for mathematics educators to discern and name the contrasts between different senses of the word? Are embodied ways of knowing distinct from other ways of knowing? Is such a distinction possible? How does embodied knowing relate to the senses and to the imagination—for example, to the visualization of mathematical ideas? *Can* mathematical concepts be embodied?

In terms of competing philosophies of mathematics: Starting from an Enlightenment/ Modernist standpoint, what do bodies have to do with the learning of mathematics, since mathematics is often characterized as the most abstract and disembodied of disciplines? Is the process of learning mathematics a matter of adopting increasingly abstract, non-bodily conceptual ways of knowing—creating abstractions of abstractions? The high-Modernist Bourbaki group banned all triangles, diagrams and visual/embodied representations from mathematical texts and discussions in the 1960s; does increasing mathematical sophistication necessarily entail decreased reliance on the realm of actual physical bodies (viewed in the Enlightenment/ Modernist paradigm as "coarse" and "primitive") and the so-called "deceptions" of the sensory world?

To start from a very different, Postmodern standpoint: Does mathematics arise from humans' lived, sensory, experiences of the world? If so, how can our bodies' limitations (in terms of size, flexibility, sensory capacity, etc.) be used to represent and explore the infinitely large, infinitesimally small and subtly nuanced relationships of mathematical entities? Does mathematics arise from, and return to, the physical, embodied world—and if so, does that help to explain the "unreasonable reasonableness" of mathematics as a means for modeling physical phenomena? What might be the relationship between our multisensory, embodied, imaginative encounters with the physical world, our generalizations of those encounters, and the abstract relationships within mathematical systems?

In terms of the history of ideas: It is clear that there has been a tremendous swell of interest and new research in the area of embodied cognition in recent years. Why the increased interest in embodied ways of knowing at this particular time and era of history? What could account for the sudden interest in bodies in terms of cognition in general and mathematics learning in particular in our era?

From a sociopolitical viewpoint: What is meant by "democratic access to mathematics"? How could embodied ways of knowing contribute to democratic access to mathematical ideas? Is this access differential depending upon the particularities of the bodies involved—that is, particularities of race, class, gender, ability, sexuality, age, etc.? Does access depend on power structures within and across cultures, nations, and locations? What can be said generally and particularly about democratic access to mathematics via bodies and embodied knowing?

Each of these questions raises theoretical/conceptual issues that will be addressed in this chapter, under the headings:

1) Abstraction, Mathematics, and Mind/Body
2) Why Embodiment Now? A Postmodern Theoretical Approach
3) Current Approaches to Research on Embodiment in Mathematics Education

The first and second of these sections offer historical and philosophical perspectives on issues of embodiment, mathematics/math education and culture.

The third section offers a "map of the territory" of current approaches to embodied mathematics teaching and learning, with the aim of introducing readers to the range of theoretical groundings for research in this area.

Readers should note that each of these theoretical approaches entails a very different working definition of what is meant by *body* and *embodiment*. There is no one, singular agreed-upon meaning for the term *embodied learning* (just as, in a similar way in studies of the language of mathematics education, there is no singular, agreed-upon meaning for the term *discourse analysis*). Particular researchers take up aspects of the meanings of embodiment from the approaches that suit their work, in a sort of methodological bricolage or pastiche.

Knowing that this is the case, and equipped with a sense of the theoretical discourses at play, readers should have an easier time sorting out the references and sorting out trends and influences. I hope that this will be helpful as new researchers make sense of contemporary work in this area and begin to develop their own research programs. I have also included citations of key works related to each approach, to offer researchers new to this area an entry point to some of the most influential ideas that are animating new work in embodied mathematics education.

In the final section, I will describe the trajectory of my own multiyear research program on embodied learning in mathematics, the Graphs & Gestures Project, to exemplify some of the ways that research in embodied mathematics learning can develop and take new directions. I will try to identify some of the theoretical groundings from the "Current Approaches" section that have been influential in my own work, in order to highlight the interdisciplinary nature of embodied learning research. This section of the chapter will be written in a more informal, narrative tone than the earlier theoretical sections.

As with other topics included in this *Handbook*, there are hundreds of publications in each of the areas touched on in this chapter, and it is not possible to give a complete overview of the whole field. My aim is to highlight some of the important developments in the areas discussed here. The fact that I am a (primarily) English-speaking Canadian mathematics educator will certainly have influenced the publications and authors selected; I encourage readers to look further to build a fuller picture of the flourishing international research scene in the area of embodied mathematics learning.

ABSTRACTION, MATHEMATICS, AND MIND/BODY

Mathematics has had both the privilege and burden over many centuries of being considered the sine qua non exemplar of a purely mental, abstract discipline. In the Western philosophical tradition, from Plato and Descartes and their followers to the height (and perhaps last gasp) of the Enlightenment/Modernist movement in the second half of the 20th century, mathematics and mathematicians were taken to inhabit an otherworldly realm of "pure" thought—disembodied, certain, and eternal.

This realm has been posited to exist beyond our sublunary world here on earth—our familiar wet, messy world of physical bodies subject to birth, life, death, decay and regeneration. The mathematical realm is imagined to be other than this one: a world of clean, crystalline, eternal objects that partake of the qualities of the infinite and even the divine. (See Frye, 1980, for a more detailed discussion of this in terms of Sky Father/Earth Mother mythological traditions.) Mathematical beauty in this paradigm is held to be something ethereal and highly refined, its subtlety accessible only to a small priestly caste of mathematicians with huge and specialized intellects—those who are able to work beyond and outside of the world of the physical and the bodily, grasping abstract objects solely through mental effort.

This Enlightenment/Modernist view dichotomizes the world into a realm of abstract, disembodied mathematical perfection and a realm of physical, bodily experience—and the physical, experiential aspects of life are relegated to the status of base and inferior ways of being. Such philosophies treat physicality, the senses, and even the imagination and imagined sensory experiences as suspect, unreliable, and deceptive. Empirical (scientific and other) investigation, technical skills, bodily enjoyment and anything hands-on and involved in making, growing, and changing are similarly regarded as impermanent, lower functions based on unreliable knowledge. Only that which is seen as mental, eternal, and "perfect" is regarded as being of a high level in a system that has adopted this dichotomous value system.

This division of the world into two realms is also clearly a nonegalitarian philosophical move, one which does *not* promote democratic access to the arcane mysteries of mathematical beauty, and one which has obvious potential for political ramifications in terms of gender, culture, ethnicity, colonialism, and even personality type. For example, anyone who is intimately connected with birth, childrearing, and death (chiefly women), with making and tending things physically (notably working-class people, artists, and craftspeople) or with a deep connection to a particular physical place (for example, Indigenous peoples, farmers, and fishers) is considered unlikely to be a potential participant in the disembodied, exalted, purely mental world of mathematical beauty.

I will begin by exploring some of the roots of this mind/body dichotomy in mathematics and refer readers to other studies that have explored these themes, to set the background for the contemporary Postmodern interest in the embodied learning of mathematics.

Plato and Descartes as Markers for Disembodied Mathematics

It is tempting to blame Plato or Descartes for the Western mind-body split, though it is clearly an exaggeration to credit two individual mathematician/philosophers with single-handedly turning whole civilizations away from an integration of mind-body. Many other people and other influences were certainly involved, including other philosophers and writers, theologians (with the Christian church in its various denominations particularly influential), the effects of technological change (especially literacy, of which more later), and popular reactions to the physical difficulties of life in conditions of injustice, war, disease, and hunger.

That said, it is still meaningful to refer to the influential writings of Plato (in 5th century BCE Greece) and Descartes (in 17th century France) as markers of the move toward a philosophical separation of mind from body and a preference for a disembodied mental faculty over human physical being. Both Plato and Descartes did take a stand in favor of a rarified mental "realm" as opposed to physical life on earth, and their writing deserves attention in this regard.

Plato, working at the time when literacy and the alphabet were being introduced in Greece, spoke vehemently against a preceding culture of oracy, partially improvised epic poetry, and traditional performative arts, especially in his tirade against the poets (Havelock, 1982; Plato, 2004). His allegory of the cave is well known, and speaks to the Platonic dichotomy between the lived, physical world of most people (in which only the shadows of the abstract, glorious

Forms are seen) and the otherworldly realm of these abstract Forms, which is considered more real than the physically present world. Only the chosen few can dwell in this abstract realm, and in *The Republic*, Plato argues for an ascendant meritocratic oligarchy of these philosopher kings, who he feels ought to rule the rest—hardly a democratic vision!

Plato's *Meno* (Plato, 1976) is also well known among mathematicians and mathematics educators. In the dialogue between Socrates and the slave boy, Socrates shows his colleague Meno that even an uneducated young man is capable of reasoning about subtle mathematical relationships (with Socratic guidance, of course). Plato attributes this capability to an inborn human capacity for understanding the Forms, which he posits as arising from our having dwelt in the realm of these Forms before our birth.

The Platonic world view emphasizes the primacy of numinous, "perfect" forms, accessible to humans only through abstract thought, dialectic Socratic discussion and Plato's posited memory of direct access to those forms in an otherworldly life before birth. This Platonic worldview was well suited for adoption by religious authorities, particularly Christian ones, where there was emphasis on another, "perfect" eternal world outside the physicality of human birth, life and death. Resonances of this Platonic ideal echo through mathematics classes in our own time, where roughly sketched circles, dots, and lines on a blackboard are taken as tokens of students' numinous, otherworldly knowledge of the Forms of perfect circles, "points that have no part" and lines that have no thickness (see Euclid, 1956). In most mathematics classes, the use of physical, tangible models and materials are grudgingly allowed at only the lowest levels of mathematical study; at "higher" levels of mathematics, starting in secondary school or earlier, the use of physical manipulatives for learning is generally considered primitive and babyish. A Socratic-style dialectic (with the lecturer playing both roles—viz Gerofsky, 1996) is very often adopted as the preferred teaching modality, one that immediately recalls a Platonic approach to learning.

René Descartes, born in Europe in the era when the printing press was making literacy much more widespread and consequentially revolutionizing all the institutions of society, also wrote about mathematics and a mind-body split. In his *Meditations* (Descartes, 1641/1996), Descartes emphasizes his distrust of his senses and the physical sensations related to his body, treating the sensory, embodied world as one of deception. He takes a stance of radical doubt, finding only the kernel of his own doubting presence and thought as reliable and verifiable proof of his existence—the famous *cogito ergo sum*. Rebuilding his image of the world from this basis, Descartes rejects bodily ways of knowing in favor of pure thought and abstract mental work, particularly exemplified by mathematics.

Although both Descartes and Plato rejected the body and the senses as ways of knowing truth, the mathematics of both of these philosopher/mathematicians was firmly grounded in geometry, along with logic, number, and other areas of mathematics. Indeed, Greek mathematics generally works with numbers in terms of geometric figures, rather than "purely" as number. Square numbers, for example, were described by the Greeks as the areas of squares with certain side lengths, and square roots as the side lengths of squares with a particular area. Both Plato and Descartes wrote about a geometry of idealized mental Forms, but nonetheless, even their geometry still retains some tenuous connection with the physical world of shapes and objects via visualizations and schematic drawings of shapes and objects. The 20th century saw a more extreme form of rejection of the physical, including even the traces of physicality inherent in geometry, with the Bourbaki movement.

Bourbaki as a Culmination of Rejection of the Physical in Mathematics

Again using one school of thought and group of scholars as a marker for larger trends in philosophy and society, it is instructive to look at the work of the Bourbaki group of mathematicians in mid-20th century France as an extreme point in the rejection of embodied, physical ways of doing mathematics.

"Nicolas Bourbaki" was a pseudonym used by a group of European mathematicians who aimed to formalize mathematical systems and create a groundwork of absolute certainty via abstract theorems for mathematics. The efforts of this group came in part as a reaction to earlier philosophers' discovery that it would be very difficult (Frege, 1980; Whitehead & Russell, 2011), or in fact impossible (Gödel, 1992) to set mathematics on such firm and certain grounds.

Where Plato and Descartes did much of their mathematical work via various forms of geometry, the Bourbaki group went further in their antiembodied stance and set themselves against geometric figures of any kind—hence their famous dictum, "Down with Euclid! Death to all triangles!" reported to have been shouted out by leading Bourbaki mathematician Jean Dieudonné at a 1959conference on mathematics education in Réalmont, France (Yaglom, 1981). Mathematics was abstracted to the point where it became a complicated but ultimately meaningless game of moving symbols on paper according to algorithmic rules—meaningless in that this intellectual game was not meant to have signification in terms of the physical world or the situations of everyday life. It was enough for Bourbaki that the system of mathematics was consistent and well-grounded in itself, in an abstract, rule-governed realm of symbolic theorems and proofs. Any recourse to physical existence, including even a minimalist reference sketch of a triangle, was considered excessively embodied.

WHY EMBODIMENT NOW? A POSTMODERN THEORETICAL APPROACH

Where the Enlightenment/Modernist philosophical project promoted a worldview that separated mind and body (and elevated the mental to a much higher status than the physical and sensory), contemporary Postmodern theory throws us back into a fully embodied world where mental and physical ways of being are inseparable. Dating from the mid-20th century, but particularly active since the rise of personal computing and the Internet from the 1980s onward, Postmodernism is an approach to understanding the world as it is being reconfigured in our times.

Postmodern theories in a variety of areas frequently turn to the concept of the embodied mind, and to the variety of ways that sentient beings experience embodiment. In a counter-move to Modernism's search for universal precepts and generalized, abstracted knowledge, Postmodernism situates knowledge in the particularities of bodies, cultures, places, genders, classes, "races", ethnicities, ages, abilities, and so on. Much of Postmodern writing focuses on the relationships between particular ways of knowing based in embodied experiences and the ways these knowledges play out in power structures like colonialism and political struggles.

In mathematics education, Postmodern theories challenge pedagogies that make Modernist assumptions about the purely mental, abstract nature of mathematics learning, and bring us back to body-mind connections in a number of ways.

Understanding "Why Embodiment Now?": A Contemporary Interpretation of McLuhan

Questions about why particular intellectual trends, schools of thought, or new ideas arise at a particular time and place are seldom resolved to everyone's satisfaction. Even in retrospect, it is difficult to be able to sort out which convergences (political, economic, academic, technological, social, religious, etc.) form patterns that might account for particular new preoccupations and new ways of thinking and living. The task is even more difficult, and more urgent, when trying to make sense of one's own contemporary society.

Many theorists in our time have taken up the intellectual task of reintegrating body and embodied learning into many disciplinary areas, and the intensity of this work has increased since about 1980. Others have written wondering or accounting for why there is an increased preoccupation with embodiment at this time (see for example Slingerland, 2008; Wilde, 1999).

I will jump into the fray here with an approach to the question of "Why embodiment now?" based on Marshall McLuhan's influential Postmodern work on theories of technology and culture. McLuhan (1911–1980), the famous Canadian media theorist, drew from the work of his intellectual mentor, economic historian Harold Innis (2008), and contributed to the work of later cultural theorists like Jean Baudrillard (1994) and many others.

First, I would like to offer an explanation of my use of the term *Postmodern* throughout this chapter, a usage that is based in McLuhan's theoretical work (McLuhan & McLuhan, 1988; McLuhan, 2010; McLuhan & Zingrone, 1995). Thinking about cultural and intellectual ways of being and thinking as responses to and outcomes of technological and media change, Modernism (and the so-called Enlightenment) arose from widespread alphabetic literacy starting in the Western world with the invention of the Gutenberg press and the replacement of scant manuscript books with abundant printed ones in the mid-1400s (McLuhan, 1962). McLuhan associates alphabetic literacy and the Enlightenment/Modernist project with the separation of mind and body, radical individualism (and its attendant loneliness and alienation), the valuing of linear, logical ways of thinking, universalist theories, the rise of science, Protestantism, and many other familiar tendencies and tropes of Modernism (see, for example, Toulmin, 1992). The period famously named as Postmodern by Lyotard (1984) and others is one where, as McLuhan asserts, alphabetic literacy and the printing press are in the process of being supplanted by electric and electronic media as the predominant "default" technology of our societies worldwide. This process has been a gradual one over the course of the past century or more, not a sudden rupture that was started and completed in a particular year. The process has greatly accelerated since approximately 1980 with the widespread introduction of personal computing devices and the rapid development of the Internet. Earlier, however, the introduction of telegraphy, telephones, cinema, and electric lights in the second half of the 19th century, and radio and television in the 20th century, already began the transition from the Modern to the Postmodern. McLuhan characterizes the Postmodern era of instant global electronic communications as one of integrative thinking, the change from individualism to "tribal" or communitarian consciousness, the importance of the local, of intuition and faith, of the ear rather than the eye as a dominant sensory modality, and of nonlinear geometries of thought and knowing replacing linearity. It is this era that I refer to as the Postmodern. In our lives in the 20th and 21st centuries, we have been experiencing the rapid (though uneven) transition from the dominance of Modernist ways of thinking and being to those of the Postmodern, and it is very often possible to witness the uneasy coexistence of these modes of being in our times.

To account for "Why embodiment now?" in these Postmodern times, I draw on another aspect of McLuhan's theory that I have found to have great explanatory power: his theory of obsolescence.

McLuhan posited that the media/technologies work us over completely, and that people are usually no more able to have awareness of the "default" media of our culture than fish are able to be aware of the water in which they swim. We shape our tools and technologies, and they immediately shape us in return, in ways we often cannot consciously see or know. However, as soon as the dominant technology of a culture is completely encircled, surrounded or overtaken by a newly dominant technology, the old technology suddenly pops into relief and becomes knowable, visible, obsolete (in that it is no longer the "default" medium, although it may certainly continue to be used), and it instantly becomes an art form (McLuhan, 1974; McLuhan &McLuhan, 1988).

Some examples to clarify this rather startling notion.

- **Horse carts as art form.** With the advent of the motor car, horses and carriages moved from being the default means of transportation and became a novelty and an art form, so that now people will pay large sums of money to ride in a horse-drawn carriage (say, around Central Park).

- **Earth as art form.** McLuhan writes:

> Perhaps the largest conceivable revolution in information occurred on October 17, 1957, when Sputnik created a new environment for the planet. For the first time the natural world was completely enclosed in a man-made container. At the moment that the earth went inside this new artifact, Nature ended and Ecology was born. "Ecological" thinking became inevitable as soon as the planet moved up into the status of a work of art
>
> (McLuhan, 1974, p. 49).

This effect—of seeing Earth, not as "the world" or as our default medium, but as the contents of another technology—was amplified with the moon landing in 1969 and the famous photographs of Earth from space. Suddenly people began to talk about Spaceship Earth and to see Earth as a "fragile blue marble" in space, and the environmental movement immediately took on huge new energy and significance. At these moments, humans generally became aware of Earth as a work of art, and no longer as "the world" or as "just everything"—in other words, Earth ceased to be treated culturally as our unseen default surround medium, and became an art object.

- **Old technologies turning to art forms in our era.** In our current situation of very rapid technological change we have seen many technologies that were formerly "the default" suddenly encircled by new media, obsolesced, and turned into new art forms. Typewriters, rotary telephones, film and Polaroid cameras, handwriting, vinyl records, cassette and VHS tapes, and many other technologies have not completely disappeared, but have gained new value as art forms since becoming "obsolete" in McLuhan's terminology. As McLuhan said, "Obsolescence never meant the end of anything, it's just the beginning" (McLuhan, 1967).

In the present age, with the advent of networked electric/electronic technologies (starting from the telegraph and telephone in the late 19th century), our culturally mediated relationships with our actual bodies have changed. McLuhan points out that any new technology extends some aspect of the body and simultaneously numbs that part of our actual body; for example, cars greatly extend the capabilities of our legs and feet (i.e. moving across the surface of the planet), but at the same time, they numb our legs and feet as we sit immobilized in cars for hours at a time. Networked electric/electronic media of communications extend (and at the same time numb) our entire nervous system.

These networked media also allow us to be present in many places around the world at any given moment, even though our physical bodies are still at home. This effect was present from the earliest days of telegraphy and the telephone, where one's words or voice could be made present around the globe at the speed of electricity. The process was accelerated with radio and television, and greatly accelerated and broadened with the introduction of personal computing and the Internet starting in the 1980s. We can now "be" in multiple places at once through our voices and video images, but also through the virtual embodiment of 3D on-screen avatars, through robotic control of distant objects and tools, and through haptic interfaces. We are just beginning to sort out the multiple ways people can interact between actual and virtual worlds, in mixed reality and augmented reality applications (see, for example, Lindgren & Johnson-Glenberg, 2013). These human-computer interfaces can involve something as minimal as a glance or touch of a fingertip, or as extensive as whole-body movement, locomotion, and voice.

McLuhan saw as early as the 1960s that we were in the process of externalizing our collective neurological system and (just about literally) wrapping it around the globe, through the use of satellites and other wired, wireless, and broadcast technologies (McLuhan, 1964/1994).

Since the 1980s, this process has been sped up and amplified, and its side effects have accelerated too. Living *inside* our own externalized collective nervous system has surrounded our physical bodies with a new default medium (early on, telegraph, telephone, radio and television networks, and now, powerfully, the Internet), and suddenly the "body" has gone from being the unquestioned default medium (the only way to be) to an option, an art form, something to be cultivated, modified, decorated, treasured. We are now, en masse, more able to be living in disembodied ways than ever before in human history, and it is because of this, I argue, that we have suddenly become aware of embodiment as a choice, rather than a necessity. I would posit that this is evidenced by ways that many people began to treat their bodies as art objects or objects of technological manipulation starting in the 1980s, with the much-increased use of ornamentation through interventions like piercings and tattoos, and medicalized manipulation via cosmetic surgery and prostheses, steroids, implants, and cyber-enhancements (see Haraway, 1987).

If the body has now become optional, obsolete (in McLuhan's terms) and an art form, then another, different technology or medium has supplanted the body as our unnoticed default, the waters in which we swim. Has the huge acceleration of technological change made it possible for us to see what this new medium is, and what its effects are, or will that only happen once this also becomes fully surrounded by a yet-newer medium and becomes obsolete? McLuhan's answer might be that we should be paying attention to the leading-edge artists to find out, since artists have the role of "antennae" for the culture, remaining sensitized to changes and perturbations of the field that others may have become numbed to. Avant garde artists, and perhaps academics as well, are responsible as a kind of Distant Early Warning system for the culture, sensing change, exploring and expressing it to everyone else.

Other explanations (at macro and micro levels) for our present preoccupation with body and embodiment can certainly be offered from other points of view, including the political, historical, sociological, and economic. I expect that these alternate explanations will have a number of important elements in common as the effects of the Internet are felt throughout all aspects of our lives. I put forth this McLuhan-esque account based on the relationship between culture and technology as one that deals directly with a methodology for analyzing technological change (McLuhan &McLuhan, 1988) and has the potential for great resonance and explanatory power.

CURRENT APPROACHES TO RESEARCH ON EMBODIMENT IN MATHEMATICS EDUCATION

In this section, I will outline seven approaches to embodiment in contemporary mathematics education research, through:

1) metaphor and language,
2) cognitive science,
3) semiotics,
4) cultural studies,
5) the New Materialism,
6) gesture studies, and
7) arts and performance theory.

Readers should note that this list is not exhaustive—further approaches are certainly possible, and may be developing now. What is more, the seven categories offered here are all interdisciplinary in themselves and may be used in conjunction with one another by particular researchers. Any parsing out of particular approaches and influences will necessarily be considered unsatisfactory by some, as the boundaries among these approaches are porous and changing.

However, provisional as it is, this characterization of seven research approaches does offer an account of some quite distinct starting points that have their own particular and recognizable character. I will include samples from the literature of each research approach, to exemplify the ways each of these approaches plays out (for example, in the choice of material to be considered and the modes of analysis used).

Approaches to Embodiment Through Metaphor and Language

Postmodern approaches to embodiment come from many different disciplinary and interdisciplinary standpoints, several of which will be discussed here. One of the most influential explores the nature of embodied knowledge (generally and in mathematics particularly) via evidence from metaphor and language, led by George Lakoff, Mark Johnson, and Rafael Núñez.

The work of Lakoff, Johnson, and Núñez in the new field of cognitive linguistics, starting in the early 1980s, began by questioning many Modernist assumptions about linguistics and cognitive psychology, and went on to challenge taken-as-given assumptions about mathematics. Although their work in cognitive linguistics does not directly address mathematics *education*, it has certainly had an affect as the groundwork for new ways of conceptualizing mathematics teaching and learning, and Núñez has gone on to collaborate with mathematics educators in his further work.

Johnson (1990, 2008), Lakoff (1990), Lakoff and Johnson (1999, 2003), and Lakoff and Núñez (2000) make the connection between mind and body via embodied image schemata. Stated briefly, an image schema is a structure that brings together our human bodily experiences of the world, ways of languaging that experience, and conceptual metaphors emerging from these complexes of experiences within our particular cultures. The metaphors are embodied because they are initially experienced through movement, locomotion, reaching, grasping, eating, sleeping, moving objects around, noticing differences in temperature, and all the other physical movements and sensations we experience with/as embodied human beings, particularly in early childhood. As we grow up, we also experience the emotions, values, stories, and cultural categories that have emerged around these experiences and become part of language and cultural practices. Starting from these physical experiences and linguistic/cultural meanings accruing to them, we acquire and create the "metaphors we live by," metaphors that give meaning to mathematical concepts as well as other areas of human cultural development.

Lakoff, Johnson, and Núñez begin by exploring and elaborating some of the key image schemata and embodied metaphor systems in contemporary English-speaking societies, and then find the extensions and working-through of these primary embodied metaphors in the abstract concepts within this culture. Embodied metaphor systems and image schemata are shown to underlie conceptualizations in areas as wide-ranging as aesthetics, ethics, and mathematics, and these theorists show the presence of bodily experience as a "live" and productive presence in even the most abstract concepts.

In connecting mental concepts to embodied experiences, Lakoff, Johnson, and Núñez rehabilitate areas of human experience that were rejected by earlier philosophers of language, mathematics, ethics, etc. For example, bodily movement and sensation are no longer viewed here as coarse, base, and deceptive (as they were by Descartes and his followers), but as the very foundations of any kind of conceptual thought and language. Language in use, and so-called paralinguistic functions like gesture, which were rejected by Noam Chomsky in his foundational work in establishing a minimalist modern linguistics (Chomsky, 1993), are brought into the center of linguistics by this work on embodied metaphor. Emotion, banned from Enlightenment/Modernist thought and from mathematics as a deceptive, irrational distraction to logic and reason, is also rehabilitated to a central role in human reasoning. Through their meticulous study of image schemata and embodied metaphor, Lakoff, Johnson, and Núñez build a philosophical case for the inclusion of many "messy" aspects of human life that were excluded by Enlightenment/Modernist philosophers in their quest for purity: that is, the body, the senses, movement, emotion, and the prelinguistic experiences of childhood.

They find that such experiences are the basis not only for competence in terms of physical skills, but for all of human conceptualizations—including the most abstract realms of mathematical thought. (In Lakoff & Núñez, 2000, the culmination of the argument is to show that even Euler's Identity, $e^{(pi)(i)} = -1$, a seemingly highly abstract formulation, is rooted in embodied metaphors based in human sensory, emotional, and cultural experiences.) These findings challenge mathematics educators to make the turn to bodily and sensory experiences, emotions, language, metaphor, and narrative as modalities that are absolutely foundational and essential for any kind of mathematical sense making. Where a Modernist/Enlightenment model of mathematics pedagogy focused on the "delivery" of mathematical concepts via lectures comprising mostly abstract language and notation, the work of Lakoff, Johnson, and Núñez points to the importance of attentiveness to and a renewed pedagogy of body integrated with mind.

As an interesting aside, one reviewer has pointed out to me that some recent notable scientists have taken an "embodied imagination" approach to scientific research via linguistic and narrative strategies. This potentially generative approach goes against formal scientific traditions that decry anthropomorphism and the personalization of imagery in science, nevertheless, it appears to be part of the practice of a number of researchers. Jonas Salk, the researcher who developed the first polio vaccine, writes about imagining himself embodying the entities he studied:

> When I observed phenomena in the laboratory that I did not understand, I would also ask questions as if interrogating myself: "Why would I do that if I were a virus or a cancer cell, or the immune system?" Before long, this internal dialogue became second nature to me; I found that my mind worked this way all the time.
>
> (Salk, 1983, p. 7)

In a similar way, 1983 Nobel laureate cytogeneticist Barbara McClintock talks about studying maize by "being" the maize through a process of imaginative embodiment (as reported in Keller, 1983). Thought experiments (like Einstein's, in which he imagined chasing or riding upon a beam of light) similarly bring the scientist's imagined bodily presence into a research scenario. Interestingly, these examples from the sciences resonate with students talking about 'being the graph' in the Graphs & Gestures Project reported later.

AN EXAMPLE OF AN APPROACH TO EMBODIMENT IN MATHEMATICS VIA METAPHOR AND LANGUAGE

In Núñez, Edwards, & Matos (1999), the authors compare two definitions of continuous mathematical functions: the "natural" and the Cauchy-Weierstrasse definitions. Where the informal, intuitive, "natural" definition describes the graph of a mathematical function using metaphors of motion and travel (source-path-goal schemata), the Cauchy-Weierstrasse definition uses static metaphors of discrete, atomistic points and of things contained within other things (part-whole and container schemata).

The authors suggest that the more "natural" definition of continuity is the older one, coming from the work of Newton, Leibniz, and Euler. This definition seems to arise from the experience of gesturing a graph, and Euler is cited as describing a continuous function as "a curve described by freely leading the hand."

This definition of continuity involves "cognitive contents such as motion, flows, processes, change in time, and wholeness" (p. 54), is thus seen to be more intuitive and more easily accessible than a static metaphor would be, as it arises from everyday experiences and from the very common metaphor of fictive motion. Fictive motion refers to metaphors of movement applied to nonmoving things—for example, when we say things like "the road *travels past* Springfield" or "the bridge *goes over* the river," we imply that the road and bridge are moving, when they are actually static. Similarly, we often talk about mathematical functions using metaphors of fictive motion—for example, when we say "the graph *approaches* an asymptote," "the function *reaches* a limit," or "the curve *oscillates.*"

In contrast, the Cauchy-Weierstrasse definition of continuity, arising from 19th century developments in analysis, treats mathematical functions as static entities comprised of discrete points. Foundational to this definition, points are not conceived of as *locations* on a line, but as the entities *constituting* the line.

These differences are explored in the context of potential student difficulties in reconciling the two definitions in learning calculus. Once students have made sense of the gestural, more natural definition based on a metaphor of fictive motion, they may find it hard to incorporate the later static, atomistic definition into their developing conceptualization of continuity of mathematical functions.

Approaches to Embodiment Through Cognitive Science

The field of cognitive science has grown rapidly since the 1980s, with the accelerated development of computing, computer networks, and robotics and new methods of imaging the brain and brain functions. Cognitive science brings together a number of disciplines including computer science, artificial intelligence studies (AI), philosophy of mind, anthropology, psychology, neuroscience, and linguistics. Research in this area addresses, among other things, philosophical questions about the nature of consciousness, attention, perception, and memory and the possibilities of sentient cognition that is not necessarily human—for example, sentient cognition in other-than-human animals, machines, etc. With a focus on neuroscience and brain imaging, cognitive science also deals with questions of the brain and nervous system as physical entities, and neurological functions as part of body functioning (and so a way of treating embodied learning and knowing at the level of neurons, hormones, brain lesions, and other physical manifestations of the neurological system).

Cognitive science approaches to embodied ways of knowing in mathematics have been influenced by studies like Dehaene's experimental work on human infants' and other-than-human animals' development of concepts of number (Dehaene, 1999) and Devlin's extrapolation from such studies (Devlin, 2006). Dehaene and Devlin use behavioral studies in animal cognition and in infant cognitive development to reflect on the degree of innateness in processes like subitization, estimation, and other elements of number sense. The results of these studies have influenced conceptions of human mathematical ability across life stages, cultures, and languages, and extrapolations from this work continue to influence research in the didactics of mathematics.

Coming from a different aspect of cognitive science, researchers in design and cognitive systems have brought together ideas from the design of human-computer interactions (HCI) and computer modeling with psychological and educational theories of learning to develop "cognitively ergonomic" systems, in which computer interfaces and human mind-bodies respond to and mutually shape one another in a learning setting (see, for example, Abrahamson, 2009, 2010; Holbert & Wilensky, 2012; Antle & Wang, 2013; Lindgren & Johnson-Glenberg, 2013). Attention to the design of interactions, and research on the ways these interact with cultural and bodily norms, plays an important role in the design of hardware, software, interfaces, curriculum, and pedagogy in educational technology for mathematics learning (as well as other areas of the social use of technology). Theoretical work by cognitive scientists like Barsalou (2008, 2009) has grounded much of this work. Also worth noting in this area is work on mirror neurons and embodied learning (for example, Decety & Grèzes, 2006).

Other important studies in embodied learning and the design of human-computer interactions include work exemplified by Hoyles & Noss (2009), Kaput (1994), Fernandes and Healy (2010), Healy and Kynigos (2010), Jackiw and Sinclair (2009), Hegedus and Moreno-Armella (2011), Borba and Villarreal (2005) and others. Much of this work is based in the pioneering studies of Papert (1993) and Turkle (1984). There is a huge literature in the use of technology in mathematics education, and it is beyond the scope of this chapter to fully represent developments in this area, but issues of embodied learning have come to the fore in current thinking about educational technology in our field. Some of the important questions addressed include: relationships between actual and virtual embodiment through an on-screen agent; affordances for learning offered by computer-based static and dynamic imagery; engagement of the imagination through embodied images; the development of mathematical concepts through visual and multisensory (haptic, sonic) engagements with learning technologies; and much more.

Work in embodiment in educational technologies and mathematics learning is not restricted to students' engagement with electronic devices and computers, but often integrates the use of actual physical objects and manipulatives, whole-body activities, paper-and-pencil or chalk-and-blackboard diagrams and symbolic notation, narrative, group discussion, problem solving, and other kinds of multimodal mathematical work. Papert's work with LOGO microworlds and "turtle geometry" in the 1980s offered inspiration for the integration of actual/virtual experiences (see Abelson & diSessa, 1986), along with seminal work on embodied cognition and the use of manipulatives/concrete materials in mathematics education by leading educational theorists like Dienes (1963) and Gattegno (1987) and theorist-practitioners like Castelnuovo (Castelnuovo & Gori-Giorgi, 1976). These researchers took an integrative approach that rejected the drawing of boundary lines between physical and mental aspects of learning, but rather brought multimodal learning experiences together in a conceptualization of embodied cognition. The introduction of electronic, online, and virtual spaces has added new ways of experiencing mathematics through the body, without rejecting nonelectronic approaches. Contemporary researchers working with both virtual and actual mathematical experiences include Nemirovsky (Nemirovsky & Borba, 2003), Noble (Noble, Nemirovsky, Wright, & Tierney, 2001), and Ferrara (Nemirovsky & Ferrara, 2009).

AN EXAMPLE OF AN APPROACH TO EMBODIED MATHEMATICS EDUCATION THROUGH COGNITIVE SCIENCE

Nemirovsky & Ferrara (2009) explore aspects of mathematical imagination and embodied learning through a microanalysis of a student's discourse, gesture, and gaze in a 17-second-long videotaped episode in a secondary school classroom. (Note that very close microanalysis of short episodes of discourse, gesture, and other features of interaction are often undertaken as part of cognitive science-based studies, semiotic studies, and gesture studies, while other approaches to embodiment may take up examples of longer duration, or work with conceptual entities rather than analyzed examples.)

This microanalysis looks closely at a student working with an apparatus that decomposed x- and y-coordinates of the graph of a function, in interaction with the teacher, classmates, and apparatus. The authors identify two cognitive phenomena of interest: "juxtaposing displacements" and "articulating necessary cases," which they see revealed in the student's discourse, gestures, interactions, and use of physical materials. The focus in this article is on the relationship between embodied expression and the development of mathematical imagination.

The authors describe "juxtaposing displacements" as a cognitive move where different aspects of an imagined situation are placed in relation to one another. The effect is compared to the composition of a cubist painting, in which different perspectives and visual planes are juxtaposed as if they were contiguous. This move is hypothesized to exist beyond mathematics learning and perhaps to be a feature of human imaginative cognition more generally.

"Articulating necessary cases" is a described as a cognitive move in contrast to "juxtaposing displacements," as it involves splitting rather than pasting concepts or images together in a kind of collage. In articulating necessary cases, particular cases are split off, sequenced, and explained through rules or principles linked through logical necessity.

Evidence of these two phenomena is found in the student's gestures, gaze, and discourse as she offers mathematical explanations in class. Her cognition vis-à-vis the graph of the mathematical function under discussion is interpreted in terms of the student's mathematical imagination in relationship to her perceptuo-motor activity, using the two cognitive phenomena described. Certain student and teacher interactions in this 17-second classroom incident are seen to be joint utterances, using Gallese's neurocognitive research on "mirror systems" and mirror neurons (see Gallese & Lakoff, 2005). Mathematics learning, using appropriate materials and apparatus, is viewed as a primarily a process of enriching learners' mathematical imagination through embodied experience, and evidenced through embodied, multimodal expression.

Approaches to Embodiment Through Semiotics

Semiotics arose in the 20th century as a field of study used to analyze cultural phenomena via a consideration of signs and their signification. Semiotics is closely connected with structuralism (and its contemporary successor, poststructuralism), and has roots in linguistics (through its founder, Ferdinand de Saussure), mathematics and philosophy (through the work of Charles Peirce), anthropology (through Claude Levis-Strauss), literary criticism and cultural studies (through Roland Barthes), and extends to other areas of culture including film studies, architecture, and education.

A number of prominent contemporary mathematics education theorists ground their embodied mathematics education research in semiotics and related areas of philosophy and linguistics. Semiotics offers theory and analytic methods for making sense of a wide range of mathematical representations and artifacts, including spoken and written language, gesture, mathematical symbolism, diagrams, drawings, and physical and virtual models. Through semiotic concepts like chains of signification, paradigmatic and syntagmatic relationships, denotation and connotation, polysemy, intertextuality, and others, mathematics education researchers have been able to work with (more and less) embodied signs, symbols, and representations to gain new insights into teaching and learning.

Some of the notable scholars working in semiotics as an approach to embodied mathematics learning include Radford (Radford, 2002, 2009, 2010; Radford, Edwards, & Arzarello, 2009; Radford & Puig, 2007), Roth (Givry & Roth, 2006; Roth, 2001, 2010; Roth & Bowen 1998; Roth & McGinn, 1998) Presmeg (Presmeg, 1997, 2003, 2005, 2006, 2008), Arzarello (Arzarello, Paola, Robutti, & Sabena, 2009), Robutti (2006), Ferrara (2006) and Sabena (Sabena, Radford & Bardini, 2005).

AN EXAMPLE OF AN APPROACH TO EMBODIED MATHEMATICS LEARNING THROUGH SEMIOTICS

Arzarello, Paola, Robutti, & Sabena (2009) undertake a microanalysis of multimodal aspects of student and teacher interactions in a high school calculus class, developing the concepts of "semiotic bundles" and "semiotic games" to frame and model observed embodied phenomena involving gesture.

The basic unit of classical semiotic analysis is the sign, as defined by Peirce and other theoretical semioticians. However, such signs are not necessarily multimodal, and have traditionally been viewed in an isolated moment of time in relation to an individual.

Semiotic bundles as described here are collections of activities (including but not limited to gestures, speech, glances, and drawings) that co-occur in typical classroom interactions. Semiotic bundles may include signs made by various students and/or teachers. Semiotic bundles as a concept allows for interactions among people in the class, and for the dynamic development of multimodal semiosis over time. This is a broader, more flexible idea about semiotics than the classical concept of the sign accommodates, and it offers mathematics educators a helpful unit of semiotic analysis for classroom interactions. It also allows for analysis of bodily movement, physical objects, and dynamic interaction among people that brings physicality and intersubjectivity to semiotic classroom analysis. Semiotic bundles can be analyzed synchronically (at a particular moment) and/or diachronically (over a span of time).

Semiotic games here refers mainly to the pedagogic choices made by the teacher in relation to semiotic resources and semiotic bundles developed through teacher-guided classroom interactions. The teacher is viewed as mediating the semiotic resources of the classroom. A teacher's ability to make sense of the embodied, multimodal semiotic bundles developing in the class is seen as a valuable tool in making pedagogic decisions that use such resources to their fullest. Such an analysis can also help the teacher monitor individual students' gestures, drawings, language, and other multimodal, embodied expressions to understand each student's developing mathematical conceptions, and to intervene as needed.

More generally, this study aims to show that the multimodal, embodied, interpersonal, and temporal elements of the semiosis involved in mathematics classrooms form a rich and complex system of meaning-making that goes beyond the linguistic signs of a particular individual.

Approaches to Embodiment Through Cultural Studies

Cultural studies is a contemporary interdisciplinary field of scholarship that investigates power relationships and identities in the context of cultural objects, processes, institutions, and forms. The term *cultural studies* was first used in the mid-1960s, but the field has had "an unprecedented international boom" since the 1980s (Grossberg, Nelson, & Treichler, 1992).

This field of study is grounded in a multiplicity of disciplinary approaches and theories, including those from anthropology, sociology, political science, film and media studies, literature, history, science and technology studies, psychoanalysis, feminist and gender studies, disability studies, and curriculum studies. Through these multiple approaches, cultural studies aims to theorize contemporary life and bring awareness to relationships of oppression and hegemony, liberation and social justice inherent in societies and cultures. As circumstances of life change in the contemporary Postmodern era, cultural studies as a field acknowledges new modalities and ways of living, and the changes in consciousness and power relations that emerge from these changed circumstances.

Cultural studies scholars in feminist, gender, race, and disability studies have been particularly active in raising issues of embodiment as an aspect of Postmodern power relationships. In all these fields, it is acknowledged that persons have experienced subjugation as a direct consequence of being "differently bodied" compared those in positions of power in mainstream, colonialist/patriarchal/heteronormative/racist/ablist societal hierarchies. A focus on embodiment(s) in terms of difference and differential power has led to radical reconceptualization of binaries including feminine-masculine, Black-White, ablebodied-disabled, human-animal, human-machine, and others. Scholars in this field who work from economics, political science, anthropology, and sociology may use theories of embodiment as an approach to challenging norms around binaries like producer-consumer, first world–third world, colonizing-colonized, powerful-powerless, and so on.

In relation to these and other disputed oppositions, cultural theorists challenge watertight categories and exclusionary boundary lines. New theory in this field takes innovative standpoints (often from the point of view of the oppressed and politically disenfranchised) in considering contextualized and embodied experiences of diversity, desire, commodification, community, media influences, identities, cultural tropes, and literacies. Bodily practices and experiences that were considered hidden, private, or taboo have been brought into public and academic discourse, and form the basis for new theory. These radical conceptual challenges are not limited to academic publications, but are put into practice in the arts and in policy making as a basis for fundamental social change and work towards more socially just laws and practices. Cultural studies as a field takes a playful stance in challenging binaries of high culture–low culture, so that diverse phenomena and genres from popular culture (like movies and TV shows, comic books, video games, and popular songs) are given consideration equal to those of so-called high culture.

Through the work of many key cultural theorists—including Grosz (1994), Haraway (1999), Bordo (2003), Hall (1993), Butler (1993), Sheets-Johnstone (1999), Tyler (2000), Csordas (1994), Zizek (1997), Kroker and Kroker (1987), based on earlier philosophical groundwork by Heidegger (1962), Merleau-Ponty (1962/1945), Foucault (1977), Levi-Strauss (1969), Mauss (1954), Lacan (1966), Kristeva (2002), and others—new discourses around body, embodiment, bodily experiences, motion, senses, hybridities, and diversity have entered public, political, artistic, and academic realms. These discussions have brought about struggle and change in societies at large. They have certainly influenced work in mathematics education as well, particularly a number of mathematics education theorists working in areas of equity, culture, and social justice, including Walkerdine (1998), Mendick (2004), Appelbaum (2010), Swanson (2007), De Freitas (2008), Walshaw (2004), and Zevenbergen (2000).

AN EXAMPLE OF AN APPROACH TO EMBODIED MATHEMATICS LEARNING THROUGH CULTURAL STUDIES

Mendick (2004, pp. 43–47) uses a cultural studies analysis of embodied cultural stereotypes of mathematicians in a number of popular feature films to interrogate gender-stereotyping that may affect learners' relationships to mathematics.

Mendick begins with an analysis of her own hybrid identity—as a mathematician, teacher of mathematics, sociologist, and a person deeply connected with popular culture.

As a female mathematician who goes to the movies and pays attention to popular culture, Mendick notices that mathematicians are often stereotyped as "boring, obsessed with the irrelevant, socially incompetent, male, and unsuccessfully heterosexual." The nerdy mathematician is often portrayed as "soft" (soft-bodied, through lack of exercise and healthy food, and through a dichotomization of mind and body), although the mathematics they work on is "hard."

At the same time, there is a paradoxical contrast between the popular culture vision of mathematicians as nerds and, simultaneously, as geniuses and adventurers. The mathematicians in pop culture are often shown as on a quest for rationality, through detective work, espionage, and academic research. These quests are often stereotyped as ending in madness—as if mathematical work itself makes the mathematicians mad.

Mendick looks at four recent films about mathematics (*A Beautiful Mind, Enigma, Good Will Hunting*, and *Pi*) and examines their portrayals of mathematicians in terms of gender and sexuality, madness, rationality, and connection (or more often, disconnection) with a fully embodied, emotionally engaged, connected way of living. Her detailed analysis of the four films shows that mathematicians are stereotyped as male; heteronormative (even in biopics of actual mathematicians who were openly gay or bisexual); on a quest; disconnected from their bodies, emotions, and communities; and tending towards mental illness. In at least one of the films, *Good Will Hunting*, a series of gendered binaries are presented: "mind/body, separation/connection, theory/experience, reading books/living life. Mathematics is attached to the first terms in these oppositions and Will's relationship with his girlfriend Skyla is associated with the second terms" (p. 47). The mathematician in this film eventually abandons mathematics in order to be able to live in a fully embodied, connected, experiential way.

Mendick questions the effects of these kinds of stereotyped media images on students, regardless of gender, who might be considering taking up mathematics. She also wonders why being a mathematician is treated in popular culture as an inborn talent possessed by very few people, while literacy is "seen as an essential part of being fully human" (p. 47).

Approaches to Embodiment Through the New Materialism

It is worth noting a new theoretical approach to embodiment within cultural studies currently being taken up by a number of scholars in mathematics education. The New Materialism is radically material, feminist, and anti-Cartesian. It is a turn against "the linguistic turn" that characterized much of early Postmodern philosophy. The New Materialism frames everything as material, including language, discourse, thought, and concepts. It is a theory of monism, in opposition to Platonic/Cartesian dualism, in which everything that might have earlier been considered abstract is now taken as embodied and physical, although what is meant by the materiality of thought or language remains to be worked out in detail.

Key writers in basic New Materialism theory include Barad (2003), Maclure (2013), Massumi (2002), and Stewart (2007), with work based on theorists that include Butler (1993, 2010), Latour (2007, 2009), Deleuze (1987), Bergson (2004), and Tarde (2010). New Materialism is closely associated with work in the posthuman (see, for example, Weaver, 2010; Lewis & Kahn, 2010). Mathematics educators beginning to work with New Materialism theory and embodied mathematics include De Freitas, Sinclair, Ferrara, and Radford (De Freitas & Sinclair, 2014; Radford 2013; Sinclair, De Freitas, & Ferrara 2013).

AN EXAMPLE OF AN APPROACH TO EMBODIED MATHEMATICS LEARNING THROUGH THE NEW MATERIALISM

De Freitas & Sinclair (2013, pp. 456–468) use the work of Barad and Châtelet to recast the inextricable entanglement of humans, material objects, and mathematical concepts in terms of the "body of mathematics." This recasting of embodiment rejects Platonic/Cartesian boundaries and static or inert characterizations of materials and concepts, taking up instead a feminist practice of studying identity as performative, sociocultural, and situated. Mathematical concepts, manipulative objects, and people doing mathematics are treated as material, embodied and coextensive, mobile and mutually shaping in an unending process of becoming.

In this article, the body is conceived of as a "social entanglement" (p. 456) so that a focus on the individual learner creates a kind of artificial analytical cut between person and sociocultural context. However, the New Materialism goes further than previous sociocultural analyses in mathematics education in seeing human bodies, environments, and materials in a classroom as continually in a state of flux and movement, mutually constituting one another and never fully formed or static. Learners' and teachers' bodies, the classroom itself, manipulatives, and other presences are all both actors and acted upon; none is ever fully formed, finished, or inert.

This radical reframing of the body and interaction goes further in considering mathematical concepts as embodied and material, in the emergent process of becoming in the relational ontology of the "assemblage" that is the classroom.

Coming from a philosophy of the posthuman, and drawing on the work of Haraway and others, this analysis of a "new concept of the self (and of the body) eschews the notion of an isolated human agent acting upon the inert and inanimate world" (p. 457). The body is seen, not as a biologically bounded 'container' nor as an individual cognizing entity, but rather as an ongoing interaction among materials, forces and beings—"a self that constantly projects and extends itself beyond the skin actively engaging and incorporating its material surroundings via the interface of the body" (p. 458).

The authors take on the challenging task of rethinking mathematics in this context, and find Châtelet's concept of the virtual as a key to accounting for the materiality of mathematical ideas and concepts. In this account, "the mathematical concept is always fluid and, in some important sense, unfinished," and is brought into being in material ways through gestures, diagrams, manipulatives, language, digital networks, etc. The authors find hope in opening up the mathematics curriculum through New Materialist perspectives. They conclude that "focusing on acts of embodiment whereby assemblages of concept and learner come in and out of being, and recasting concepts as acts of actualizing the virtual, shifts our attention to a future alive with mathematical potential."

Approaches to Embodiment Through Gesture

With a renewed interest in body and embodied ways of being and knowing, there has been great attention given to gesture, since gesture is a way that aspects of body and physical movement enter into communication and other human activities. Mathematics education has been one of the key disciplines involved from the start in the emerging field of gesture studies, and it is interesting to speculate why this is so.

Gesture studies is a new interdisciplinary field, developed since the 1980s, with a public presence since 2002 through the International Society for Gesture Studies (ISGS, accessible via its active website at http://gesturestudies.com), the journal *Gesture*, and related book publishing (mostly through John Benjamins Publishers in its Gesture Studies book series). Much of the foundational work in gesture studies was developed initially by two University of Chicago psycholinguists, David McNeill (1992, 2000, 2008) and Susan Goldin-Meadow (2003; 2005) and their collaborators, and by other influential gesture theorists including Adam Kendon (2004), Sotaro Kita (2000), Cornelia Müller (Cienki & Müller, 2008), Jürgen Streeck (2009), Gale Stam (McCafferty & Stam, 2008) and others. A brief history of the ISGS and gesture studies as a field can be found in Müller (2002).

Gesture studies had its interdisciplinary origins in psychology, anthropology, and linguistics, but by the third congress of the ISGS (in Chicago, 2007), many other academic disciplines presented research into the nature and uses of gesture. Scholars from computer science, art history, sociology, and music participated in the congress, but so, notably, did many researchers in mathematics education. In fact, mathematics educators made up 10% of conference presenters that year. Work in mathematics education and gesture dates back a few years earlier, to about 2002, and research fora in embodied mathematics and gesture have been part of the influential IGPME (International Group for the Psychology of Mathematics Education) and ICME (International Congress on Mathematical Education) conferences since that time.

Much of the groundwork for the analysis of gesture has come from McNeill's work cited earlier. Mathematics educators (and others) doing this work have benefited from McNeill's foundational work, which includes a taxonomy of gesture phases and types; research into the relationships between gesture and speech, and gesture and thought; the uses and purposes of gesture; gesture phraseology; methodology, methods, and protocols for annotating gesture; gesture and neurological disabilities; cross-cultural studies of gesture; and much more.

A limitation of the use of McNeill's work in education research is that McNeill has chosen to study unconsciously produced speech-accompanying gesture, while educators may sometimes be interested in consciously produced gesture (perhaps on the part of teachers), and consciously taught or elicited gestures (in teachers' pedagogic interactions with students). McNeill's work may still be useful in considering these sorts of gestures, but there may be differences that merit attention in education research contexts.

Much of current mathematics education research involving gesture studies can be characterized as touching on one or several of the following areas.

(i) *Connections with linguistic analysis of classroom interactions:* Microanalysis of very short bursts of speech and accompanying gesture by mathematics learners and teachers, often in the context of group problem solving and instruction, with the aim of accessing aspects of learners' and teachers' unconscious thinking evidenced in gesture.

(ii) *Connections with cognitive and computer design:* analysis of learners' gestures as a resource for the design of "cognitively ergonomic" manipulatives and teaching sequences (both actual and virtual).

(iii) *Connections with philosophical theories of mind, consciousness, language, semiotics and culture:* observation and analysis of gestures around mathematical activity as evidence of qualities and relationships in mind-body-language-culture theory.

(iv) *Connections with theories of curriculum and pedagogy:* observation and teaching/elicitation of gesture as part of design experiments in curriculum and pedagogy aimed at learners' multimodal engagement in mathematical relationships and ideas.

(v) *Connections with cultural studies and studies of diversity:* observations of gesture produced in mathematics learning with reference to gender, social class, ethnicity, culture, (dis)ability, language use, and the many other dimensions of diversity of students physical and sociocultural ways of being.

Gesture studies in mathematics education have not been limited to a particular age group or school grade level, but have spanned all ages, including early childhood, elementary, secondary and tertiary schooling, and out-of-school learning experiences for children and adults in their communities.

Since about 2002, scores of academic articles and chapters have been published on gesture and mathematics education, and this continues to be a very productive area of research in our field. Some of the most influential researchers and papers in this area include Núñez (2004a; 2004b; 2008), Goldin-Meadow (Goldin-Meadow 2014; Goldin-Meadow, Nusbaum, Kelly, & Wagner, 2001), Abrahamson (2004; 2007), Edwards (2003; 2009; Edwards & Moore-Russo 2012), De Freitas and Sinclair (2012; Sinclair et al., 2013), Arzarello (Arzarello & Edwards, 2005; Arzarello, Robutti, & Bazzini, 2005), Radford (2009; Radford et al., 2009), Ferrara and Nemirovsky (2005; Ferrara, 2013; Nemirovsky, Kelton, & Rhodehamel, 2012), Gerofsky (2008; 2010; 2011a), Alibali and Nathan (2012; Alibali et al., 2013; Alibali et al., 2014), Morgan (Morgan & Alshwaikh, 2008), Rotman (2005), Francaviglia (Francaviglia & Servidio, 2011), Frant (Frant, Acevedo, & Font, 2005), Robutti (Robutti, Edwards, & Ferrara, 2012), Healy and Fernandes (2011; Healy, Fernandes, & do Rosário, 2008).

AN EXAMPLE OF AN APPROACH TO EMBODIED MATHEMATICS LEARNING THROUGH GESTURE THEORY

Alibali & Nathan (2012, pp. 248–277) use a close analysis of several examples of teacher and student gestures in classroom interactions to argue that mathematical knowledge is necessarily embodied. Two classes of gesture from McNeill's gesture typology are shown to be commonly used to represent mathematical concepts through action and to ground those concepts in the objects and settings of the teaching/learning environment.

The authors focus on the gestures that teachers and learners produce when explaining mathematical ideas (rather than when negotiating interactions with others in the classroom, etc.) In the process of such explanations, they pay particular notice to David McNeill's categories of *representational gestures* (and its subcategory of *metaphoric gestures*), and *pointing* or *deictic gestures*.

Representational gestures are theorized to "manifest the motoric and perceptual simulations that underlie language and imagery" (p. 254) and reveal conceptual metaphors grounded in bodily experiences. Such gestures are also shown to have the power to enable cognition of objects and situations that are not actually present, recalling Nemirovsky and Ferrara's work on mathematical imagination described earlier on page 71.

Pointing gestures provide evidence that learners' mathematical thinking is grounded in the physical environment of the learning space, and "support the claims that cognition is situated in the environment and that the environment is an integral part of the cognitive system," (p. 255) recalling De Freitas' and Sinclair's work in New Materialist theory described on page 76, although perhaps to a less radical degree.

Alibali and Nathan undertake this analysis with two related aims: first, to advance understanding of the embodied nature of mathematical thinking, learning, and instruction; and second, to help develop an empirical analytic basis for improved mathematical experiences and mathematics pedagogy.

Approaches to Embodiment Through the Arts and Performance Theory

There is a materiality and physicality to all of the fine, performing, and practical arts, and some of these arts undeniably involve the human body. Dance, theater, music, and other forms of performance art involve the artists' physical presence and skills with movement, voice, and instruments; in addition, arts that use recorded performances (live-action film, recorded and sampled music) require artists' physical presence at stages of the work. The making of art is intimately entangled with materials, place, and presence. Sculptors, painters, potters, and weavers all need to become very familiar with their media and develop their physical and design skills in shaping them. Even arts that might seem more ethereal or less physical (say, video animation or poetry) involve materials that must become familiar in the hands, bodies, and voices of the artists, notwithstanding that these materials might include computer applications or language.

The arts and performance also have the power to communicate and to move people in ways that go beyond the limits of propositional language. Effective/affective art works on many levels simultaneously and can help people understand complex relationships in a holistic way. Artworks have the potential to engage the intellect, emotions, kinetic, and sensory experiences and an openness of response all at once.

For mathematicians and mathematics educators, these embodied, affective, intellectual, and intuitive qualities of the arts offer new ways to reach others and communicate the beauty of mathematical patterning. Many people do not have the educational background or interest to access mathematical patterns through the specialized propositional language of proofs, explanations, and equations, but most can appreciate the aesthetic qualities of mathematics when they are expressed via music, dance, painting, photography, sculpture, film, theater, etc. There is the possibility that this aesthetic appreciation may be a starting point for greater experiential and/or propositional understanding of mathematical relations. What is more, learners may be better able to express their own intuitions and questions about mathematical patterns by using color, shape, movement, voice, poetic language, and other artistic modes of expression, rather than being required to work with nothing but formal mathematical symbolism.

A number of mathematicians and mathematics educators have taken up embodied expression through the arts as part of their own mathematical and educational practices. The uptake is based in a number of different premises and on the researchers' academic and artistic positionings:

- A large group of research mathematicians and computer scientists have taken up art forms like sculpture, painting, and digital graphic arts to express or apply their theoretical work in their field. Many of the participants in the annual Bridges Math and Art conference fall into this category; the conference proceedings and gallery (both available on the website, http://bridgesmathart.org) display many beautiful and interesting works. Some of the best-known mathematician artists doing this kind of work include George Hart, Carlo Sequin, Craig Kaplan, Mike Naylor, and Robert Bosch.
- Some artists are interested in creating artwork based on mathematical themes and relationships because these patterns inform their artistic inquiry. Again, many Bridges participants as well as others are doing notable work that falls into this category—for example, Karl Schaeffer and his Dr. Schaffer & Mr. Stern Dance Ensemble, sculptor Nick Sayers, and others like dancer and choreographer Sarah Chase and playwright/mathematician John Mighton.
- Some mathematicians interested in didactics at the university level have developed arts-based resources and pedagogies for teaching undergraduate math classes. A number of these are women mathematicians who aim to make mathematics more accessible to all, and especially to women students, by using traditionally women's arts like needlework to represent mathematical spaces and relationships (see, for example, Taimina, 2009; belcastro & Yackel, 2008, 2011).
- Some mathematics educators working with elementary and secondary schools engage in the arts and mathematical performance with the aim of helping learners learn and understand mathematics better. For most of these educators, student participation as artists is central to the project, and is seen to offer learners a sense of agency, and a way of expressing and exploring mathematical relationships. For example, George Gadanidis, Marcelo Borba, myself and my collaborators have worked on mathematical performances with K-12 students and

teachers and established the Math + Science Performance Festival (http://mathfest.ca), an international online math performance festival/contest, bringing together "live" and digital mathematical performances (Gadanidis & Borba 2008; Gadanidis, Hughes & Borba 2008). Others treat mathematical performances as a spectator activity, notably the MITACS math show/Math Out Loud performances, founded by mathematician Jean-Marie De Koninck and aimed at high school student audiences.

Mathematics educators are exploring both pedagogical and theoretical facets of an arts-based or arts-infused mathematics curriculum, including studies of the aesthetics of mathematics and mathematics education (Sinclair, Pimm, & Higginson, 2006; Sinclair, 2001, 2009; De Freitas, 2010; Gerofsky, Sinclair, & Davis 2003; Gerofsky, 2007, 2009, 2011b). Theoretical groundings for these studies range from more general studies of aesthetics from philosophy and cultural studies (for example, Dissanayake, 1995; Rancière, 2004) to works on performance ethnography (Denzin, 2003, 2006a, 2006b), to the field of performance studies, with roots in both theater and anthropology (Turner, 1986; Conquergood, 2002; Schechner, 2003, 2011).

Some research mathematician–artists have put some of their effort into work that addresses mathematics teaching and learning, even though they would not identify themselves as mathematics educators. These include, most famously, George Hart and Vi Hart, both of whom are continuing to produce very popular, publicly accessible video series on mathematical topics through music, juggling, bell-ringing, origami, poetry, drawing, and sculpture. These and other math/art videos and resources that explore school mathematics topics through embodied arts have become staples of many secondary math classrooms.

AN EXAMPLE OF AN APPROACH TO EMBODIED MATHEMATICS LEARNING THROUGH THE ARTS AND PERFORMANCE THEORY

Gadanidis and Borba (2008) explore the idea of mathematics education as (digital) performance through an analysis of a collaboratively produced set of online videos, *Flatland*, a speculation on the nature of parallel lines. These authors ground their analysis in a number of performance theories, primarily Boorstin's (1990) categories of the experience of performance as voyeuristic, vicarious and/or visceral.

The authors place themselves within the world of performance through their work in songwriting and video production (Gadanidis) and in political theater in Brazil and elsewhere (Borba). The politically activist forum theater work of Augusto Boal informs their sense of engagement of the audience as "spect(actors)," and the idea that performative engagement can bring about positive disruptions to traditional assumptions (in mathematics education as well as political systems).

Their work in digital mathematics performance aims to counter assumptions about mathematics as a cold, inhumane experience; as a series of procedures for generating correct answers; as something best taught in small, easy increments; and as something that involves only known facts. Instead, they want to use performative mathematics as a means to encourage students and teachers to develop a sense of mathematics as warm and human, insightful and imaginative, welcoming curiosity, narrative, and sustained hard work.

In their analysis of embodied, arts-based performances that may be enacted live and/or online, the authors conceive of art and the Internet as other-than-human actors that have the potential to change mathematics as much as mathematics changes them.

Through the arts, Gadanidis and Borba wish to create poetic, storied experiences that partake of the rare and wondrous (as a memorable poem might), and that offer learners chances to ask profound questions and tell tales of the mathematics they have learned (as they might talk about their learning in history, literature, or science class). All too often, these authors point out, mathematics has been treated as routine, procedural, disembodied, and impossible to question or story. An engagement with performance mathematics challenges the underlying assumptions that have made traditional mathematics alienating and may open up new worlds for learners and teachers. The authors suggest that "calling ourselves performance mathematicians creates a shift of identity that impacts on mathematics education, by helping us view mathematics not as confined to classroom activity or to the work of professional mathematicians, but as something that is shared with the wider world" (p. 50).

Summary of Current Approaches to Research on Embodiment in Mathematics Education Presented Here

In the previous section I offered a brief catalogue of seven of the most active and productive of the current approaches to embodiment in mathematics education. For each of these, I have given a characterization of its theoretical roots, its current focus points, some of the terminology used, and some key authors and readings. Here is a condensed recap of these seven approaches.

Embodiment through language and metaphor: Using Lakoff, Johnson and Núñez's work on embodied metaphor, mathematics educators have focused on the relationship among physical bodily experiences (including emotions), the languaging of that experience within cultures, and their relationship to the learning of mathematical conceptual material. The focus on embodied metaphor gives a new, non-Cartesian meaning to mathematical conceptualization.

Embodiment through cognitive sciences: The new field of cognitive science, which includes AI, cognitive neuroscience, computer science, philosophy of mind, and cognitive linguistics (see p. 70), has brought mathematics education researchers to consider embodied learning at the neurological/autonomic systems level, to work on cognitively ergonomic design, to consider virtual as well as actual bodies in learning (for example, to researching mathematics learning in online and hybrid spaces), and to include the more-than-human world in conceiving of mathematical learning and intelligence.

Embodiment through semiotics: Semiotics is an important structuralist philosophical approach based in the Modern era, but heralding (and a foundation of) the Postmodern. Mathematics educators have taken up analytical structures and methods of semiotics to make sense of relationships between different modalities of representation, including speech, writing, diagrams, graphs, films, etc., and interpret these relationships in terms of mathematics teaching and learning.

Embodiment through cultural studies: Mathematics educators concerned with social justice and questions of power, oppression, and liberation may take up theoretical approaches from the Postmodern field of cultural studies to do work about gendered, racialized, class-marked bodies, voices, and presences in mathematics classrooms and to challenge unjust practices.

Embodiment through the New Materialism: As a new and significant subtopic of cultural studies, the New Materialism takes a radically monistic stance to challenge the Cartesian dualism of mind-body. New Materialism asserts that everything—even language and thought—is material. Mathematics education researchers working in this area are beginning to develop field-specific theory about conceptualization, thinking, and material being as part of the learning of mathematics.

Embodiment through gesture: The new interdisciplinary field of gesture studies, based in linguistics, psychology, and computer science, has been taken up with enthusiasm by many mathematics education researchers to use gestural evidence as data in mathematics teaching and learning. Gesture has been shown to offer access to some unconscious process, both cognitive and social, and this has yielded insights into some the unconscious processes of interest in mathematics education.

Embodiment through the arts and performance theory: All of the arts (and especially the performing arts) are embodied in their use of materials and movement and their affect on the senses, emotions, and the physical world. An embodied mathematics through the fine, performing, and practical arts has been a productive new area of research for a number of distinct groups: research mathematicians expressing their findings in artistic ways, artists who have an interest in mathematical themes for their art, postsecondary mathematics educators who want to make learning more accessible to students (particularly women students), educators interested in offering greater access and engagement to elementary and high school math students, and mathematician/artists who are beginning to address educational audiences, through online videos and other projects.

THE GRAPHS & GESTURES PROJECT: MAPPING THE TRAJECTORY OF A RESEARCH PROGRAM IN EMBODIED MATHEMATICS TEACHING AND LEARNING

The seven approaches outlined earlier are recognizable and distinct, but not mutually exclusive, in the practices of mathematics education research. Most researchers interested in embodied mathematics education engage a number of these approaches in the course of a particular piece of research or their research program.

In the final section of this chapter, I will trace the trajectory of my own multiyear Graphs & Gestures Project in embodied mathematics teaching and learning as a exemplar of the ways that such a program might develop, and outline ways that this program was inspired and grounded in multiple approaches taken from those outlined in the previous section. I have chosen to take a macro-level view of a whole research program rather than engage in micro analysis of a few minutes of classroom video, as is often the tradition in articles of this kind. There is potential value in analysis at all levels (micro, meso, and macro). With this example, I intend to add to the literature that examines research programs rather than focuses on research moments.

Introduction to the Graphs & Gestures Project

The Graphs & Gestures Project is an ongoing research program exploring the teaching and learning of the graphs of mathematical functions through gesture, movement, voice, and materials. The project began in 2006, and has focused mainly on secondary and senior elementary school learners in Vancouver, Canada, and Torino, Italy.

This project arose from a small observation and a general interest and attentiveness to the ways that our bodily, sensory, and kinesthetic experiences of the world inform our mathematical understanding. From a hunch—and a feeling that there was something important at play with embodied images of graphs—the project has grown and changed over time. It now includes work with different groups of learners labeled as gifted, "typical," reluctant, dyslexic, and blind and visually impaired. The aims of the project range from the development of basic principles to theory development to interdisciplinary pedagogic design experiments. By mapping the trajectory of Graphs & Gestures over the past eight years, I would like to offer those new to embodied mathematics education a snapshot of a particular "way in" to this area of research. I hope that this will encourage others to find their own way in to this new and promising area.

When an academic researcher, whether new or experienced, embarks on work in a new area, there is some expectation that it will be possible right from the start to delineate a plan for the program of research. This might sometimes be the case, but when working in an area that is still actively developing (as is the case with embodied mathematics learning), there is a sense that the trajectory of the research is a "path made by walking." The researcher may be developing the research program from year to year, and will help develop the theoretical basis for future work through present results, conjectures, and findings.

A methodological article by Bavelas (1987) has been a guide to me in this process, although I was introduced to it after I had begun work in this way for myself. Bavelas, a social psychologist and gesture theorist, advocates for the "care and feeding of hunches" in the initial stages of scientific research and the importance of not foreclosing on one's own new and unfamiliar ideas too early in the research process. She explains that there are many later stages of research where rigor, critique, and the discarding of untenable ideas are essential, but at the early stages, an openness and willingness to entertain wild ideas are necessary to engage creativity in scientific work. It is important for researchers not to foreclose on their own "wild ideas" too early—but once those ideas have had time to develop, it is also important to scrutinize them seriously and critically. A process like Bavelas's schema for permitting creativity in the sciences is playing out in the multiyear Graphs & Gestures Project, and it may serve as an example for others taking on new aspects of mathematics education research.

Years Zero to Eight of the Research

Year Zero: Starting from Teaching Experience and a Hunch

This project began in the year before I began work as a university researcher, while I was still teaching mathematics in secondary school after completing my doctorate. The research questions arose in Year Zero from observations, introspection, and a hunch.

As a high school teacher, I noticed that my colleagues and I used lots of gesture, movement, and vocal sound as we talked about mathematical patterns with our students. Since the main stream of secondary mathematics is focused on mathematical functions, including their graphs, many of these gestures indicated things about the graphs of functions on the Cartesian plane.

One particular incident was the germ of the idea for this project: I was teaching a Math 10 lesson on the maximum region of a quadratic function, which hinged on a graph of a parabola intersected by the line $y = 4$. As a quick check, I asked all the students to show me, simultaneously and through gesture, what the function $y = 4$ looked like. My pedagogic aim was to take a quick poll of the students' knowledge and to see whether they knew that this function would be a horizontal line four units above the origin (and in fact, most students did show me that they knew this).

What struck me at the time, though, was the variety of ways my students gestured this horizontal line. Some made a small gesture pointing with one finger near their nose. Others used two hands in a larger symmetrical gesture at chest level, starting from the middle and extending outwards in both directions. Still others used one or both hands at chest level or below, in a large movement from one side to the other, extending beyond their center of gravity, and sometimes accompanying their gesture with a sound like "whoosh."

I began to wonder about the varied qualities of these student gestures, and especially about the height of the lines they used to represent the function $y = 4$. I realized that I could tell whether a student was showing a horizontal line, but I could not tell how many units above the origin it was supposed to be unless I knew where the origin was situated. This raised two important research questions for me:

(1) Where do people place the x-axis against their body when gesturing the shape of a Cartesian graph?
(2) Is there anything telling about the *qualities* of people's elicited gestures of these graphs (for example, symmetrical or not, one-fingered or two-handed, fast or slow, large or small, accompanied by vocalization or not, etc.)?

Introspection into my own gesturing of Cartesian graphs revealed that, as a default, I tended to place the x-axis at my waist and the origin at my navel (unless the graph lay mostly below the horizontal axis, which would make such a placement difficult to reach in a gesture, in which case I would raise the axis a bit higher). In my role as math teacher, standing rather than sitting at a desk, my movements were large and often accompanied by vocalizations as a way of highlighting particular features of the graph that I wanted students to attend to. I had noticed similar large gestures and vocalizations when observing my colleagues teaching aspects of graphing in their math classes as well. But observation showed me that many students gestured the shapes of graphs differently, and I was curious to explore how these gestures varied, and whether these variations had anything to tell us in terms of mathematics teaching and learning.

My assumption in posing these nascent research questions was that, in embodying a graph through gesture, the person's body, movement, and their conception of the graph must be inextricably co-implicated. The x- and y-axes, and the origin, local maximum and minimum points, roots, slopes, intersection points, and so on are expressed by bodies moving in space as students and teachers gesture, and must necessarily be made in relationship to locations on the gesturer's own body. This assumption aligns most closely with the theoretical constructs of Gesture Theory (elaborated in 3.5), although I was not familiar with this emergent field at that time. There are also potential connections with the sections on "Embodiment through the Arts" and "Embodiment through the New Materialism."

In Year Zero of the project, however, I was not yet aware of these theoretical connections. The research question was in the process of formation as a hunch, and in Year Zero, the work was simply to care for and nourish this hunch.

Years One and Two: Pilot Projects

In my first year as a university professor and researcher, I designed an informal pilot project that began to follow up on my preliminary research questions. The subjects of the pilot project were mostly adults chosen through an opportunistic sampling process—that is, anyone I knew who would agree to participate. That included a score of academic colleagues, graduate students, university staff, friends, and family members.

I selected seventeen graphs of mathematical functions from a calculus course, which I enlarged and mounted on pieces of card. Each participant was videotaped separately facing a camera on a tripod. Participants were instructed to gesture the shape of each graph for the camera, with the optional addition of accompanying their gestures with verbal metaphors and/ or vocalizations.

The resulting videos were analyzed in terms of

- placement of the x- and y-axes against the body,
- symmetrical or asymmetrical gesturing of graphs with bilateral or rotational symmetry,
- for symmetrical gestures, the choice of whether to start at the top and move downwards or vice versa (or to start at the center and move outwards or vice versa),
- acceleration (or lack of acceleration) in the gestures,
- degree of full-body engagement in the gestures, and
- the nature and quality of verbal metaphors and vocalizations, if used.

My analysis of the informal pilot project videos showed that most participants placed the y-axis on the center vertical line of the body (paralleling the spine), although one participant offset the y-axis to either the left or right of his body for each of the graphs. There was great variation in the placement of the x-axis, ranging from waist to nose level, but I observed that a higher placement of the x-axis seemed to co-occur with more limited body movements, little or no acceleration of gestural movements, and few metaphors or vocalizations, while a lower placement of the *x*-axis seemed to co-occur with larger bodily movements, extremes of accelerated/decelerated pace of gesturing, and more use of verbal metaphors and vocalizations.

A number of participants used symmetrical gestures involving both hands moving simultaneously, and these were generally those that also placed the *x*-axis lower. These participants showed an increased verbal attentiveness to the symmetrical nature of the graphs that had symmetries, but so did some of the participants who simply gestured the graphs from left to right or right to left.

Results from Year One led to a more formal pilot project in Year Two, involving 22 students in grades 8 and 11 and their four teachers from three secondary schools representing differing socioeconomic areas of Vancouver, Canada (Gerofsky, 2010). I selected these two age groups (age 13 and 16) because the younger students had done little or no work with the graphs of mathematical functions, and the older students would just have completed a year of intensive work on this topic. I wanted to see whether novice students would gesture the graphs differently than those with a great deal of recent experience in this area. I was also interested in seeing whether teachers gestured the graphs differently from their students or not—or in the other direction, whether students mimicked their teachers' gestures.

Teachers were asked to select a varied group of students from among those who volunteered to participate in the study—varied in terms of gender, cultural background, socio-economic status, and in terms of their interest and/or success in their math courses at school.

For this second pilot study, I limited the printed materials to five of the 17 graphs that had produced the most interesting results in the Year Zero informal study. As in Year Zero, I asked participants to gesture the shapes of the graphs to a camera on a tripod. However, this time I asked for each graph to be gestured three times, with the third time silent. (In the first two gestures, participants were asked to verbalize using metaphors or vocal sounds if they wished, but not to use technical descriptions of the graph's mathematical function, which I had observed tended to inhibit any kind of gesturing.)

In the Year Two pilot project, I visited the schools twice. In the first visit, I videotaped students and teachers gesturing the graphs; during the second, a week later, I interviewed participants about their own sense of their gestures while playing back each participant's video from the previous session. I was interested in knowing whether participants would be aware of the qualities of their own gestures before and while viewing them, and whether their own introspections would help clarify why people gestured the graphs differently from one another.

The research questions for Year Two included the following:

(1) Where do people place the *x*-axis against their body when gesturing the shape of a Cartesian graph? Are people consciously aware of their placement of the *x*-axis as they remember their gestures? How do participants account for this placement upon introspection?

(2) Is there anything telling about the *qualities* of people's elicited gestures of these graphs (for example, symmetrical or not, one-fingered or two-handed, fast or slow, large or small, accompanied by vocalization or not, etc.)? Are there co-occurring qualities in these gestures, and if so, how could these be accounted for?

(3) Do novice learners, experienced learners, and teachers gesture the graphs in distinctive ways? Is there mimicking or transfer between the ways learners and their teachers gesture graphs?

Results from the Year Two pilot project deepened insights that were intuited in the Year One informal pilot study, contributing to the "care and feeding of hunches" by articulating, formalizing, developing, and theorizing early hunches in ways that permitted them to be presented, tested, and scrutinized critically within scholarly communities in mathematics education and gesture theory.

Observations of students and teachers showed a similar bifurcation to that observed in Year One between those who placed the *x*-axis high and low, and similar co-occurring qualities of the gestures associated with each of these extremes of placement of the axis.

Teachers, as might be expected, were more consciously aware of many of the qualities of their gestures, which they deployed thoughtfully as part of their repertoire of presentation skills. In contrast, none of the students was able to recollect where they had placed the *x*-axis against their body until they viewed their gestures on videotape in the second session, and many of them were surprised to notice that they had placed the axis high or low.

Interestingly, though, once they had noticed where they had place the *x*-axis, student participants could readily explain why they had placed the axis at that particular spot. Those who placed the axis high, at nose or throat level, said they wanted to be able to see the graph; those who placed it lower, at heart, waist or hip level, said they wanted to be able to reach it. Those who placed the *x*-axis lower also talked about "riding on the graph," as if the graph were a wave on the ocean, a ski hill or a roller coaster.

When asked where the origin was placed against their body, and why, several students answered very quickly and with assurance, "That's the center of me!" This occurred for an origin placed near the heart, the navel, or the throat. It was interesting to me that the mathematical origin was often identified with the origin or center of the person, and that there was frequently an identification with this potently named point on the Cartesian coordinates and a sense of oneself and one's center.

Later video analysis, following a suggestion by Ferdinando Arzarello, revealed that those who placed the axis high also eye-tracked their own gestures and tended to gesture with one finger (as if it were a pencil), using smaller, very controlled, even gestures at arm's length. Those who placed the axis low did not eye-track their own movements. They tended to gesture with much larger movements, often using both hands together. Following a suggestion by Kathryn Ricketts, I noticed that these participants engaged their spine and the core of their body, and moved off their center of balance, moving both vertically, from low to high, and horizontally, from left to right. The students who placed the *x*-axis high, in contrast, did not engage the spine or core of the body in their gestures, but held quite still, moving mostly one hand and arm and their eyes.

These observations were integrated into the following phrases that capture the bifurcation of gesture and movement types connected with high and low placement of the *x*-axis against the body:

- having the graph "within sight" vs. "within reach,"
- "seeing the graph" vs. "being the graph."

One of the four teachers involved in the Year Two pilot project asked me after the first day with the students whether I could identify which of her students were her "top" math learners, both precise and creative, fully grasping the new math concepts introduced; which were her "average" math students, who worked hard but relied too much on rote memorization rather than a deeper understanding; and which were her students at risk of failing mathematics altogether, and who did not understand nor like math. After having spent only five minutes with each student videotaping them gesturing five graphs, I was able to correctly identify all of her students in these terms. As an exercise, I endeavored to do the same with the other three teachers' students, and there was only one case where my assessment differed from the teacher's (a case where a student consistently gestured only half of every graph that had bilateral symmetry).

My assessments were based on the following observations, only partially articulated at the time: Those students who were "being the graph" were engaging with the shape of the graph more fully and viscerally, while those who "held the graph at arm's length" and gestured only with a carefully controlled fingertip were holding mathematics itself at arm's length, as far away from themselves as possible, and engaging with it in as minimal a way as possible. In terms of developing mathematical understanding, there is a distinction in terms of *mathematical noticing* that emerged in the Year Two pilot project and in later research on the project. Briefly stated, those who engaged with the graph in a visceral way that involved their spine and the core of their body could not help but notice important features of the graph (extrema, slope, discontinuities, etc.) Those who engaged minimally with the graph had a less intense, more minimal experience of noticing such features, and could in fact miss noticing them. Since this kind of mathematical noticing is a basis for an awareness of patterns and relationships, any engagement that enhances "noticing" may also enhance an awareness of mathematical relationships (and may thus have further implications for pedagogical practices).

The students who were "being the graph" were also those who readily produced the most varied verbal metaphors and vocalizations to describe the shape of the graphs. These students seemed to be engaging in rich metaphorical and imaginative analogies to begin to make sense of the graphs. In contrast, the students who talked about "seeing the graph" mostly verbalized the numerical coordinates of points on the graphs—and they seemed to be seeking solely technical descriptions, without a great deal of imaginative or analogical engagement. Based on these observations, I correctly guessed that the students who were "being the graph" were the top mathematics learners, while those who were "seeing the graph" were the average learners who had more difficulty grasping mathematical meanings, relationships, and concepts.

There were a few students who were very hesitant to gesture the shapes of the graphs at all, and who kept returning to scan the printed cards with the graph shapes, starting and restarting their gestures many times without completing them. These students seemed unsure of what to focus on, even at a visual level, and did not seem to know what might be mathematically salient in the graphs. These students typically looked for a singular familiar analogy to the shape of the graph to hang onto as they made their gestures. Unlike the students who were "being the graph," these learners did not generate a profusion of possible metaphors, but clung to a single, inaccurate metaphor as the basis for their description of the graph. For example, when faced with the asymmetrical, rounded graph of a quartic function, one student hesitated for a long time, then could be heard whispering "a W," and then quickly gestured the shape of a symmetrical, sharply angular W three times in succession. These students, who did not discern what was mathematically salient in the graphs, I correctly guessed to be the students at risk of failing their mathematics courses.

Decisions About Research Directions for Year Three

At this stage in the Graphs & Gestures Project, I found myself needing to make a decision about whether to explore and formally test the emergent hypothesis, "Learners whose gestures show them *being the graph* are 'better' mathematics students in some way than those whose gestures show them only *seeing the graph*." Such a study may well be worthwhile as a way of applying a rigorous methodology to following up on an opportunistic, informal observation, and I may engage in this work in upcoming years of the project. There are clear benefits possible to this line of research, including the establishment of an evidential base for new forms of pedagogy, and ways of understanding student engagement and approaches to mathematical topics like graphing.

Along with potential new knowledge, such a study has many potential pitfalls inherent in its design as well. For example, are students consistent in their ways of gesturing a graph—do they always gesture in the same way? What is meant by "better" mathematics students? If the hypothesis were confirmed, would it be applied (inappropriately) to standardized testing of students? (I have already had several private school teachers approach me with the idea of creating a mathematics entrance examination based on assessing applicants' gestured graphs. . .!)

Rather than taking up this topic immediately, I opted for a different (though related) research decision: to work with whole mathematics classes at the senior elementary and secondary levels, using pedagogical design experiments to learn which elements of pedagogy might help all learners to engage in more fully embodied ways with graphs as they learned about aspects of mathematical functions. The decision to focus on pedagogic experimentation at this stage of the research was based on my own commitment to developing more accessible and inclusive approaches to the teaching and learning of mathematics. My own earlier work as a secondary school and adult education teacher has affected my research agenda: I take very seriously the responsibility of offering thoughtful, well-designed pedagogical alternatives to mathematics teachers who are working with groups of students in school and community settings. Pedagogical design experiments give the opportunity to design and test pedagogic innovations based in theoretical and experimental principles, and this is the course the project has taken in Years 3 to 8.

Design Experiments in Schools, Years Three to Eight

In this stage of the project, I began to work with an academic colleague, Kathryn Ricketts, who is both a literacy educator and an acclaimed modern dancer and choreographer. The collaboration brought together my background in mathematics education and Kathryn's knowledge and experience of pedagogy in body and movement work. We also brought several graduate students from mathematics education and interactive arts and technology onto the research team.

Our hypothesis in this work was based on Gattegno's maxim, "only awareness is educable" (Gattegno, 1987, p. 158). We hypothesized that, through greater attention to mathematical properties of graphs via embodied, visceral gesture, movement, and voice, as well as through vivid imagery, narrative, and metaphor, all students could improve their awareness and understanding of the graphs of mathematical functions. Rather than focusing on differentiating between learners who had already acquired this kind of awareness and those who had not, we aimed to raise the awareness of whole groups of students to the level of those "best" mathematics students, and to see whether this would help everyone learn mathematics in a deeper way.

In each year, we worked with different groups of students in both public and private schools in greater Vancouver, Canada and Torino, Italy, and focused on several mathematical topics related to the graphs of functions:

> Year Three, School H (Vancouver public secondary school): Grade 8 math class composed of 2/3 designated "gifted" students and 1/3 "regular" students. **Topic:** Polynomial functions, their roots, and extrema.
>
> Year Four, School H (Vancouver public secondary school): Grade 9 math class of students designated "reluctant math learners", many of whom were dealing with addictions and family dysfunctions, and many of whom missed school frequently. **Topic:** Polynomial functions, their roots, and extrema.
>
> Year Five, School G (Vancouver private elementary school): Grades 6, 7, and 8 classes in a school for students designated "dyslexic." **Topic:** The absolute value of functions.
>
> Years Six & Seven, School K (Vancouver public secondary school): Two students (Grades 10/11 and 11/12) and one vision teacher who were all blind from birth, along with sighted vision teachers and Braille translator. **Topic:** Transformations of functions.
>
> Year Eight, School L (Torino public secondary school of commerce): Grade 12 mathematics day class and Grade 12 mathematics adult education evening class at a high school of commerce. Each of the classes included one blind student whose had gradually lost his or her vision. **Topic:** Maximum regions in quadratic functions.

In all cases, we worked first to create a comfortable context for students and teachers to work with large physical movements, gestures, and voice, something rather rare in mathematics classes. Creating this comfortable context included using spaces where walls and furniture would not get in the way of movement (for example, school drama rooms, the school gym, hallways, outdoor spaces in the schoolyard, or even the regular mathematics classroom with furniture moved to the edges of the room). We chose props and materials that were appealing in their visual, auditory, and tactile qualities: rolls of colorful sewing elastic, heavy brass plumb bobs, oversized "wiki sticks" (wax-saturated string), and buttons, ping pong balls, slides of colorful geometric paintings, and films of roller coasters.

More particularly, we worked initially to acclimatize students to movement and voice through collaboratively designed warm-ups that brought together aspects of movement (core engagement, working with balance, spiraling, crossing the center line of the body, increasing heart rate and breathing), voice (pitch, volume, rhythm, vocal timbre) and aspects of the mathematics we would be addressing (slope, intersections of lines, reflections, translations, maximum/minimum points, asymptotes). Warm-ups used familiar movement metaphors from sports ("throwing a ball") and everyday life (a quick spiral turn with the words "who's there?"; a horizontal "smoothing the tablecloth" gesture with the word "safe"). Through these non-threatening, familiar gestures, whole classes of students gained ease and fluency with movements that engaged spine, core, and viscera, moved them slightly off balance, got them vocalizing, and established correspondences between particular gestural movements, vocal sounds, and mathematical elements. In the context of our guest teaching/research classes (typically, five or six one-hour classes with groups averaging 25 students over the course of five months in each of eight years), only a handful of students expressed any discomfort or asked to be excused from using movement and voice in mathematics class.

After the warm-up, we engaged in design experiments aimed at raising learners' awareness of particular mathematically salient features of graphs related to the mathematical topic at hand. Activities involved the use of multisensory materials (visual, tactile, and auditory), metaphors, images, and narratives, along with engagement in various kinds of movement, gesture, and vocalizations, individually and in groups. The activities and materials were carefully chosen to draw students' attention to particular features of the graphs.

For example, in School H, working on polynomial functions, students took turns placing bright orange dots on the roots of functions on projected slides of graphs. Then, using a stretched length of fuchsia elastic to represent the x-axis, the whole group gestured the shape of the graph in unison, with the whole group using student-chosen vocal sounds to represent the slope and roots of the function. The orange dots and the special sound for the roots ("pah"), along with tangible contact with the elastic x-axis and a slight pause in movement at the roots served to highlight the significance of these points on the curve of the polynomial graphs. The activity of placing the orange dots in consultation with the whole group, and of gesturing and vocalizing the shapes of the graphs together, helped students sort out the difference between the salience of the roots (x-intercepts) for the work we were currently doing, and the nonsalience of the y-intercepts for this work.

In another exercise with the School H classes in Years Three and Four, we worked on having all students engaging with the graphs as if they were landscapes they could "be" in or travel across (an approach I had noticed in the metaphors of the students who were "being the graph" in the Year Two pilot project). In this activity, we projected images of landscape paintings that used shapes very similar to those of polynomial and other mathematical functions. Students started by thinking and then writing about an imagined experience of entering into the landscape of the painting, and picturing what it would feel like, smell like, sound like, and how it would feel to move over that terrain. Then the slide of the painting was replaced by a slide of the graph of the similarly shaped function, which was introduced as a kind of map of the terrain in the previous painting. Once again, students were asked to imagine and write about how it would be to walk or ride over that terrain. Were there sudden drops and precipitous canyons, or was the landscape gently rolling, or a steep climb? Their responses were similar in quality to the metaphorical descriptions that I recorded university calculus lecturers using when they described the graphs of functions in their lectures (Gerofsky, 1996). The secondary school students' vivid descriptions of the graphs as landscape served to highlight mathematically salient features of our discussion (slope, extrema, continuity/discontinuity) through metaphorical and imaginative engagement "as if" the graphs were maps of an appealing or mysterious place.

Work with identified dyslexic, reluctant, and blind or low-vision students developed as we became interested in the potential for movement-enhanced mathematics learning to offer richer, more multisensory contact with mathematical concepts than is typically on offer in school mathematics classes. Key findings included the observation that many identified educational problems and disabilities (dyslexia, hyperactivity, reluctance to learn) seem to disappear once students are released from the confines of rows of desks and the requirement to sit still and quiet for hours. Through multiple potential bodily engagements with mathematical topics through whole-body movement, voice, and metaphor/narrative, most students were willing to try out mathematical experimentation and inquiry. Using posttesting of mathematical topics, we found that even as much as a year later, students were able to reconstruct their learning with a high degree of accuracy, employing gestures, sounds, and metaphors introduced in our design experiment sessions as cognitive resources to remember and make sense of the mathematics.

We chose to work with blind and low-vision learners in researching multimodality and multisensorality in the pedagogy of graphing. Since these students were not able to access the visual representations that are so typically part of mathematics instruction, our research team needed to work with the other senses—sound and touch, including proprioception, movement, balance, and haptics (Paterson, 2007)—in our experimental pedagogy. By learning about the (sometimes scanty and inadequate) existing resources for visually impaired mathematics learners, and developing new resources and approaches based on our earlier work, we were able to start a process of creating better mathematics pedagogies for blind learners. Beyond this laudable but limited result, we were also able to work with the visually impaired students' sighted classmates and teachers in nonvisual, multimodal, and multisensory ways that have the potential of enriching cognitive resources for understanding graphing, not only for blind students, but for most or all students.

Future Directions for the Graphs & Gestures Project

In Years 3 to 8 of this research project in embodied mathematics learning theory and practice, certain lines of inquiry were followed more intensively, while others were set aside. The lines of inquiry that were followed, and which might be further advanced, include:

- developing and testing new, more fully embodied and multisensory pedagogies of graphing;
- through these pedagogies, increasing democratic access to mathematics through embodied ways of knowing for learners who do not learn well in "typical" visually biased, sedentary, less participatory mathematics instruction. These learners might include students identified as dyslexic, hyperactive, attention-deficit, reluctant, and low-vision learners among others, and experimentation could be extended to include other groups often excluded in some way from access to mathematics.

Some lines of inquiry that were introduced in the pilot projects of Years One and Two but not yet followed up on include:

- consideration of the potential importance of other movement aspects of gestured graphs—for example, symmetrical movement, movement that crosses the center line of the body, movement from high-to-low or low-to-high;
- consideration of the potential importance of students producing a variety of different metaphors or narratives for a graph, rather than a singular one;
- more rigorous testing of the informally tested hypothesis that gestural movements for graphs that engage the spine, body core, and viscera, that cross the center line of the body

and that put the body off balance draw attention more powerfully to salient mathematical features than do arms'-length gestures limited to fingers and hands.

Other possible directions include the following:

> Up till now, a number of topics related to graphs of mathematical functions have been the focus of the research team's experimentation. Other mathematical topics, from elementary, secondary and/or post-secondary levels, could also be taken on as part of a more complete research program in developing a pedagogy for embodied mathematics.
>
> Our team has experimented with developing computer-assisted technologies using haptic interfaces and movement-sensor gaming technologies (the Kinect) and the programming of exercise bicycles' onboard computers as ways of bringing together embodied mathematics and computer interfaces (Gerofsky, Savage, & Maclean 2009). Further work could be carried out in this area.

I have worked on developing theoretical approaches that integrate the insights of the Graphs & Gestures Project with broader topics in mathematics, culture, the arts, and education (for example, Gerofsky, 2009, 2011c, 2013; Nicol & Gerofsky, 2009). There is certainly more work needed in this area, and the development of theory may open up new approaches to the practice of mathematics teaching and learning.

Conclusion

This chapter has outlined a number of philosophical issues underlying questions of embodiment/disembodiment in mathematics and mathematics education. I have speculated on the reasons for the spectacular rise in academic and societal interest in issues of embodiment at this particular time in history, based largely on my extension of McLuhan's theories of culture and technology.

The intellectual "landscape" of recent work in embodied mathematics education, from theoretical bases in a number of different disciplines, has contributed to a rather wild proliferation of disparate works in this area, and these differing approaches have been outlined and exemplified.

Finally, I have given the example of my own multiyear Graphs & Gestures Project as a particular exemplification of the trajectory one might take as a researcher interested in developing a research program in democratic access to mathematics learning through embodied ways of knowing.

I hope that this account will help new researchers in this area make sense of the burgeoning research in embodied mathematics learning, and give courage to those who are interested in further pursuing this line of inquiry.

REFERENCES

Abelson, H. & diSessa, A. (1986). *Turtle Geometry: The computer as a medium for exploring mathematics.* Cambridge, MA: MIT Press.

Abrahamson, D. (2004). Embodied spatial articulation: A gesture perspective on student negotiation between kinesthetic schemas and epistemic forms in learning mathematics. In *Proceedings of the Twenty Sixth Annual Meeting of the North American Chapter of the International Group for the Psychology of Mathematics Education* (Vol. 2, pp. 791–797). Windsor, Ontario: Preney.

Abrahamson, D. (2007, June). From gesture to design: Building cognitively ergonomic learning tools. In *Proceedings of the annual meeting of the International Society for Gesture Studies* (pp. 18–21). Evanston, IL: Northwestern University.

Abrahamson, D. (2009). Embodied design: Constructing means for constructing meaning. *Educational Studies in Mathematics, 70*(1), 27–47.

Abrahamson, D. (2010). A tempest in a teapot is but a drop in the ocean: Action-objects in analogical mathematical reasoning. In K. Gomez, L. Lyons, & J. Radinsky (Eds.), *Learning in the disciplines: Proceedings of the 9th International Conference of the Learning Sciences* (Vol. 1, pp. 492–499). Chicago: University of Illinois, ISLS.

Alibali, M.W., & Nathan, M.J. (2012). Embodiment in mathematics teaching and learning: Evidence from learners' and teachers' gestures. *Journal of the Learning Sciences, 21*(2), 247–286.

Alibali, M.W., Nathan, M.J., Wolfgram, M.S., Church, R.B., Jacobs, S.A., Johnson Martinez, C., & Knuth, E.J. (2014). How teachers link ideas in mathematics instruction using speech and gesture: A corpus analysis. *Cognition and Instruction, 32*(1), 65–100.

Alibali, M.W., Young, A.G., Crooks, N.M., Yeo, A., Wolfgram, M.S., Ledesma, I.M., Nathan, M.J., Church, R.B. & Knuth, E.J. (2013). Students learn more when their teacher has learned to gesture effectively. *Gesture, 13*(2), 210–233.

Antle, A. N., & Wang, S. (2013, February). Comparing motor-cognitive strategies for spatial problem solving with tangible and multi-touch interfaces. In *Proceedings of Tangible, Embodied and Embedded Interaction* (pp. 65–72), Barcelona, Spain: ACM Press.

Appelbaum, P. (2010). Sense and representation in elementary mathematics. *Supporting Independent Thinking Through Mathematical Education,* (pp. 10–17).

Arzarello, F., & Edwards, L. (2005). Gesture and the construction of mathematical meaning. In H.L. Chick & J.L. Vincent (Eds.), *Proceedings of the 29th Conference of the International Group for the Psychology of Mathematics Education* (Vol. 1, pp. 123–154). Melbourne: PME.

Arzarello, F., Paola, D., Robutti, O., & Sabena, C. (2009). Gestures as semiotic resources in the mathematics classroom. *Educational Studies in Mathematics, 70*(2), 97–109.

Arzarello, F., Robutti, O., & Bazzini, L. (2005). Acting is learning: focus on the construction of mathematical concepts. *Cambridge Journal of Education, 35*(1), 55–67.

Barad, K. (2003). Posthumanist performativity: Toward an understanding of how matter comes to matter. *Signs, 28*(3), 801–831.

Barsalou, L.W. (2008). Grounded cognition. *Annual Review of Psychology, 59,* 617–645.

Barsalou, L.W. (2009). Simulation, situated conceptualization, and prediction. *Philosophical Transactions of the Royal Society B, 364*(1521), 1281–1289.

Baudrillard, J. (1994). *Simulacra and simulation.* Ann Arbor: University of Michigan Press.

Bavelas, J.B. (1987). Permitting creativity in science. In D.N. Jackson & J. P. Rushton (Eds.), *Scientific excellence: Origins and assessment* (pp. 307–327). Newbury Park, CA: Sage Publications.

belcastro, s.-m. & Yackel, C. (Eds.) (2008). *Making mathematics with needlework.* Wellesley, MA: A. K. Peters.

belcastro, s.-m. & Yackel, C. (Eds.) (2011). *Crafting by concepts.* Wellesley, MA: A. K. Peters.

Bergson, H. (2004). *Matter and memory.* Mineola, NY: Courier Dover Publications.

Boorstin, J. (1990). *The Hollywood eye: What makes movies work.* New York: Harper Collins.

Borba, M., & Villarreal, M.E. (2005). *Humans-with-media and the reorganization of mathematical thinking.* New York: Springer.

Bordo, S. (2003). *Unbearable weight: Feminism, Western culture, and the body.* Berkeley: University of California Press.

Butler, J. (1993). *Bodies that matter: On the discursive limits of "sex."* New York: Routledge.

Butler, J. (2010). Performative agency. *Journal of Cultural Economy, 3*(2), 147–161.

Castelnuovo, E., & Gori-Giorgio, C. (1976). La géometrie projective à l'école. *Educational Studies in Mathematics 7,* 443–463.

Chomsky, N. (1993). A minimalist program for linguistic theory. In K.L. Hale & S.J. Keyser, (Eds.) *The view from Building 20: Essays in linguistics in honor of Sylvain Bromberger* (pp. 1–52). Cambridge, MA: MIT Press.

Cienki, A. & Müller, C. (Eds.). (2008). *Metaphor and gesture.* Amsterdam: John Benjamins.

Conquergood, D. (2002). Performance studies: Interventions and radical research. *TDR/The Drama Review, 46*(2), 145–146.

Csordas, T.J. (Ed.). (1994). *Embodiment and experience: The existential ground of culture and self.* Cambridge, UK: Cambridge University Press.

Decety, J., & Grèzes, J. (2006). The power of simulation: Imagining one's own and other's behavior. *Brain Research, 1079,* 4–14.

De Freitas, E. (2008). Mathematics and its other: (Dis)locating the feminine. *Gender and Education 20*(3), 281–290.

De Freitas, E. (2010). Making mathematics public: Aesthetics as the distribution of the sensible. *Educational Insights, 13*(1).

De Freitas, E., & Sinclair, N. (2012). Diagram, gesture, agency: Theorizing embodiment in the mathematics classroom. *Educational Studies in Mathematics, 80*(1–2), 133–152.

De Freitas, E., & Sinclair, N. (2013). New materialist ontologies in mathematics education: The body in/ of mathematics. *Educational Studies in Mathematics, 83*(3), 453–470.

De Freitas, E. & Sinclair, N. (2014). *Mathematics and the body: Material entanglements in the classroom.* Cambridge, UK: Cambridge University Press.

Dehaene, S. (1999). *The number sense: How the mind creates mathematics.* Oxford: Oxford University Press.

Deleuze, G. (1987). *A thousand plateaus: Capitalism and schizophrenia.* Minneapolis: University of Minnesota Press.

Denzin, N. K. (2003). *Performance ethnography: Critical pedagogy and the politics of culture.* Thousand Oaks, CA: Sage Publications.

Denzin, N. K. (2006a). The politics and ethics of performance pedagogy: Toward a pedagogy of hope. In D. S. Madison & J. Hamera, (Eds.) *The Sage Handbook of Performance Studies* (pp. 325–338). Thousand Oaks, CA: Sage Publications.

Denzin, N. K. (2006b). Pedagogy, performance, and autoethnography. *Text and Performance Quarterly, 26*(4), 333–338.

Descartes, R. (1641). *Meditations on first philosophy.* (J. Cottingham, Trans./Ed.) Cambridge: Cambridge University Press, 1996.

Devlin, K. (2006). *The math instinct.* New York: Basic Books.

Dienes, Z. P. (1963). On the learning of mathematics. *The Arithmetic Teacher 10*(3), 115–126.

Dissanayake, E. (1995). *Homo aestheticus: Where art comes from and why.* Seattle: University of Washington Press.

Edwards, L. D. (2003, April). A natural history of mathematical gesture. In *Proceedings of the American Educational Research Association Annual Conference*, Chicago.

Edwards, L. D. (2009). Gestures and conceptual integration in mathematical talk. *Educational Studies in Mathematics, 70*(2), 127–141.

Edwards, L., & Moore-Russo, D. (2012, July). Embodiment, gesture and multimodality in mathematics. In *Proceedings of the 36th Conference of the International Group for the Psychology of Mathematics Education* (p. 161).

Euclid. (1956). *The thirteen books of the Elements* (Vol. 1, T.L. Heath, Trans.). Mineola, NY: Dover.

Fernandes, S.H.A.A, & Healy, L. (2010). Embodied mathematics: Relationships between doing and imagining in the activities of a blind learner. In M.M.F Pinto & T.F. Kawasaki (Eds.), *Proceedings of the 34th Conference of the International Group for the Psychology of Mathematics Education* (Vol. 2, pp. 345–352). Belo Horizonte, Brazil: PME.

Ferrara, F. (2006, July). Remembering and imagining: Moving back and forth between motion and its representation. In *Proceedings of the 30th Conference of the International Group for the Psychology of Mathematics Education* (Vol. 3, pp. 65–72).

Ferrara, F. (2013). How multimodality works in mathematical activity: Young children graphing motion. *International Journal of Science and Mathematics Education, 12*, 917–939.

Ferrara, F., & Nemirovsky, R.(2005). Connecting talk, gesture, and eye motion for the microanalysis of mathematics learning. *29th Conference of the International Group for the Psychology of Mathematics Education* (Vol. 1, pp. 137–142). Melbourne, Australia.

Foucault, M. (1977). *Discipline and punish.* Toronto: Random House.

Francaviglia, M., & Servidio, R. (2011). Gesture as a cognitive support to solve mathematical problems. *Psychology, 2*, 91.

Frant, J.B., Acevedo, J.I., & Font, V. (2005). Metaphors in mathematics classrooms: Analysing the dynamic process of teaching and learning graph functions. In *Proceedings of the Fourth Congress of the European Society for Research in Mathematics Education* (pp. 82–91).

Frege, G. (1980). *The foundations of arithmetic.* (J. L. Austin, Trans.). Chicago: Northwestern University Press.

Frye, N. (1980). *Creation and recreation.* Toronto: University of Toronto Press.

Gadanidis, G., & Borba, M. (2008). Our lives as performance mathematicians. *For the Learning of Mathematics 28*(1), 44–51.

Gadanidis, G., Hughes, J., & Borba, M.C. (2008). Students as performance mathematicians. *Mathematics Teaching in the Middle School, 14*(3), 168–175.

Gallese, V., & Lakoff, G. (2005). The brain's concepts: The role of the sensory-motor system in conceptual knowledge. *Cognitive Neuropsychology, 22*, 455–479.

Gattegno, C. (1987). *The science of education.* New York: Educational Solutions.

Gerofsky, S. (1996). Selling mathematics: The language of persuasion in an introductory calculus course. In *Proceedings of the 1996 Meeting: Psychology of Mathematics Education* (pp. 409–417). Valencia, Spain.

Gerofsky, S. (2007). Performance space & time. In Gadanidis, G. & Hoogland, C. (Eds.), *Digital Mathematical Performance*. Proceedings of a Fields Institute Symposium, Faculty of Education, University of Western Ontario.

Gerofsky, S. (2008). Gesture as diagnosis & intervention in the pedagogy of graphing: Pilot studies & next steps. In *International Group for the Psychology of Mathematics Education: Proceedings of the Joint Meeting of PME 32 and PME-NA XXX* (pp. 17–21).

Gerofsky, S. (2009). Performance mathematics and democracy. *Educational Insights, 13*(1). Special issue, "Performing the Sign." Retrieved from www.ccfi.educ.ubc.ca/publication/insights/v13n01/toc.html (January 2015).

Gerofsky, S. (2010). Mathematical learning and gesture: Character viewpoint and observer viewpoint in students' gestured graphs of functions. *Gesture, 10 (2–3)*, 322–344.

Gerofsky, S. (2011a). Seeing the graph vs. being the graph. *Integrating Gestures: The Interdisciplinary Nature of Gesture, 4*, 245–256.

Gerofsky, S. (2011b). "Without emotion, there is nothing left but burden": Teaching mathematics through Heathcote's improvisational drama. In R. Sarhangi & C. Sequin (Eds.), *Proceedings of Bridges 2011 Coimbra: Mathematics, Music, Art, Architecture, Culture* (pp. 329–337). University of Coimbra, Portugal.

Gerofsky, S. (2011c). Ancestral genres of mathematical graphs. *For the Learning of Mathematics, 31*(1), 14–19.

Gerofsky, S. (2013). Learning mathematics through dance. In G.W. Hart & R. Sarhangi (Eds.), *Proceedings of Bridges 2013 Eschede, NL: Mathematics, Music, Art, Architecture, Culture* (pp. 337–344). Enschede, NL: Saxon University.

Gerofsky, S., Savage, M. & Maclean, K. (2009). 'Being the graph': Using haptic and kinesthetic interfaces to engage students learning about functions. In Bardini, C. & Fortin, P. (Eds.) *Proceedings of ICTMT 9: The Ninth International Conference on Technology in Mathematics Teaching*, Université de Metz, Metz, France.

Gerofsky, S., Sinclair, N. & Davis, B. (2003). Mathematics and the arts. In B. Davis and E. Simmt (Eds.) *Proceedings of the 2002 Meeting of the Canadian Mathematics Education Study Group.*

Givry, D., & Roth, W.M. (2006). Toward a new conception of conceptions: Interplay of talk, gestures, and structures in the setting. *Journal of Research in Science Teaching, 43*(10), 1086–1109.

Gödel, K. (1992). *On formally undecidable propositions of Principia Mathematica and related systems.* Mineola, NY: Dover.

Goldin-Meadow, S. (2003). *Resilience of language: How gesture creation in deaf students can tell us how all children learn language.* New York: Taylor & Francis.

Goldin-Meadow, S. (2005). *Hearing gesture: How our hands help us think.* Cambridge, MA: Harvard University Press.

Goldin-Meadow, S. (2014). How gesture works to change our minds. *Trends in Neuroscience and Education, 3*(1), 4–6.

Goldin-Meadow, S., Nusbaum, H., Kelly, S.D., & Wagner, S. (2001). Explaining math: Gesturing lightens the load. *Psychological Science, 12*(6), 516–522.

Grossberg, L., Nelson, C. & Treichler, P.A. (Eds.) (1992). *Cultural studies.* New York: Routledge.

Grosz, E. (1994). *Volatile bodies: Toward a corporeal feminism.* Sydney: Allen & Unwin.

Hall, S. (1993). What is this "black" in black popular culture? *Social Justice, 20*(1–2), 104–114.

Haraway, D. (1987). A manifesto for cyborgs: Science, technology, and socialist feminism in the 1980s. *Australian Feminist Studies, 2*(4), 1–42.

Haraway, D. (1999). The biopolitics of postmodern bodies: Determinations of self in immune system discourse. *Feminist theory and the body: A reader, 1*(1), 203.

Havelock, E. (1982). *Preface to Plato.* Cambridge, MA: Harvard University Press.

Healy, L. & Fernandes, S.H.A.A. (2011). The role of gestures in the mathematical practices of those who do not see with their eyes. *Educational Studies in Mathematics, 77*, 157–174.

Healy, L., Fernandes, S.H.A.A., & do Rosário, C.N.S. (2008). The role of gestures in the mathematical practices of blind learners. In *Proceedings of the 32nd conference of the international group for the psychology of mathematics education* (Vol. 3, pp. 137–144). Morelia, Mexico.

Healy, L. & Kynigos, C. (2010). Charting the microworld territory over time: Design and construction in mathematics education. *ZDM—The International Journal on Mathematics Education, 42*, 63–76.

Hegedus, S.J. & Moreno-Armella, L. (2011). The emergence of mathematical structures. *Educational Studies in Mathematics 77*(2–3), 369–388.

Heidegger, M. (1962). *Being and time.* (J. Macquarrie and E. Robinson, Trans.). Oxford: Blackwell.

Holbert, N.R., & Wilensky, U. (2012). Designing video games that encourage players to integrate formal representations with informal play. In *Proceedings of the10th International Conference of the Learning Sciences: The Future of Learning, ICLS 2012.* Vol. 1, pp. 119–126. Sydney, Australia.

Hoyles, C., & Noss, R. (2009.) The technological mediation of mathematics and its learning. *Human Development, 52*(2), 129–147.

Innis, H.A. (2008). *The bias of communication.* Toronto: University of Toronto Press.

Jackiw, N., & Sinclair, N. (2009). Sounds and pictures: Dynamism and dualism in dynamic geometry. *ZDM—The International Journal on Mathematics Education, 41*, 413–426.

Johnson, M. (1990). *The body in the mind.* Chicago: University of Chicago Press.

Johnson, M. (2008). *The meaning of the body: Aesthetics of human understanding.* Chicago: University of Chicago Press.

Kaput, J. J. (1994). The representational roles of technology in connecting mathematics with authentic experience. In R. Biehler (Ed.), *Didactics of mathematics as a scientific discipline* (pp. 379–397). Berlin: Springer.

Keller, E. F. (1983). *A feeling for the organism.* New York: W. H. Freeman & Company.

Kendon, A. (2004). *Gesture: Visible action as utterance.* Cambridge: Cambridge University Press.

Kita, S. (2000). How representational gestures help speaking. In D. McNeill (Ed.), *Language and gesture* (pp. 162–185). Cambridge: Cambridge University Press.

Kristeva, J. (2002). *The portable Kristeva.* New York: Columbia University Press.

Kroker, A., & Kroker, M. L. (1987). *Body invaders.* Victoria, BC: New World Perspectives.

Lacan, J. (1966). *Écrits.* Paris: Le Seuil.

Lakoff, G. (1990). *Women, fire and dangerous things.* Chicago: University of Chicago Press.

Lakoff, G. & Johnson, M. (1999). *Philosophy in the flesh: The embodied mind and its challenge to Western thought.* New York: Basic Books.

Lakoff, G. & Johnson, M. (2003). *Metaphors we live by.* Chicago: University of Chicago Press.

Lakoff, G. & Núñez, R. (2000). *Where mathematics comes from.* New York: Basic Books.

Latour, B. (2007). Can we get our materialism back, please? *Isis, 98*(1), 138–142.

Latour, B. (2009). A collective of humans and non-humans following Daedalus's labyrinth. In *Pandora's hope: Essays on the reality of science studies* (pp. 174–215). Cambridge, MA: Harvard University Press.

Levi-Strauss, C. (1969). *The raw and the cooked.* (J. Weightman & D. Weightman, Trans.) London: Jonathan Cape.

Lewis, T. E., & Kahn, R. (2010). *Education out of bounds: Reimagining cultural studies for a posthuman age.* New York: Palgrave Macmillan.

Lindgren, R., & Johnson-Glenberg, M. (2013). Emboldened by embodiment: Six precepts for research on embodied learning and mixed reality. *Educational Researcher 42*(8), 445–452.

Lyotard, J. F. (1984). *The postmodern condition: A report on knowledge.* (G. Bennington & B. Massumi, Trans.) Minneapolis: University of Minnesota Press.

MacLure, M. (2013). Researching without representation? Language and materiality in post-qualitative methodology. *International Journal of Qualitative Studies in Education, 26*(6), 658–667.

Massumi, B. (2002). *Parables for the virtual: Movement, affect, sensation.* Durham, NC: Duke University Press.

Mauss, M. (1954). *The gift.* (I. G. Cunnison, Trans.). London: Cohen & West.

McCafferty, S. G., & Stam, G. A. (Eds.). (2008). *Gesture: Second language acquisition and classroom research.* Abingdon, UK: Taylor & Francis.

McLuhan, E., & Zingrone, F. (Eds.). (1995). *Essential McLuhan.* Toronto: House of Anansi.

McLuhan, M. (1962). *The Gutenberg galaxy: The making of typographic man.* Toronto: University of Toronto Press.

McLuhan, M. (1964). *Understanding media: The extensions of man.* Cambridge MA: MIT Press, 1994.

McLuhan, M. (1967). *1967 McLuhan television interview.* Retrieved from www.youtube.com/watch?v=OMEC_HqWlBY (December 2013).

McLuhan, M. (1974). At the moment of Sputnik the planet became a global theater in which there are no spectators but only actors. *Journal of Communication, 24*(1), 48–58.

McLuhan, M. (2010). *Understanding me: Lectures and interviews.* (S. McLuhan & D. Staines, Eds.) New York: Random House.

McLuhan, M., & McLuhan, E. (1988). *Laws of media: The new science.* Toronto: University of Toronto Press.

McNeill, D. (1992). *Hand and mind: What gestures reveal about thought.* Chicago: University of Chicago Press.

McNeill, D. (Ed.) (2000). *Language and gesture.* Cambridge: Cambridge University Press.

McNeill, D. (2008). *Gesture and thought.* Chicago: University of Chicago Press.

Mendick, H. (2004). A mathematician goes to the movies. *Research Into Learning Mathematics,* pp. 43–48.

Merleau-Ponty, M. (1945). *Phenomenology of perception.* London: Routledge & Kegan Paul, 1962.

Morgan, C., & Alshwaikh, J. (2008). Imag(in)ing three-dimensional movement with gesture: 'Playing turtle' or pointing? In *Proceedings of the British Society for Research into Learning Mathematics, 28*(3), 136–141.

Müller, C. (2002). *A brief history of the origins of the ISGS.* Retrieved from www.gesturestudies.com/history.php (December 2013).

Nemirovsky, R. & Borba, M. (2003) Perceptual-motor activity and imagination in mathematics learning. In Pateman, N., Dougherty, B., & Zilliox, J. (Eds.). *Proceedings of the 27th Conference of the International Group for the Psychology of Mathematics Education held jointly with the 25th Conference of PME-NA.* Honolulu: University of Hawaii.

Nemirovsky, R., & Ferrara, F. (2009). Mathematical imagination and embodied cognition. *Educational Studies in Mathematics, 70*(2), 159–174.

Nemirovsky, R., Kelton, M. L., & Rhodehamel, B. (2012). Gesture and imagination: On the constitution and uses of phantasms. *Gesture, 12*(2), 130–165.

Nicol, C. & Gerofsky, S. (2009). Mapping multiple worlds: Imagining school mathematics beyond the grid. In Liljedahl, P., Oesterle, S. & Abu-Bakare, V. (Eds.), *Proceedings of CMESG 2009: Canadian Mathematics Education Study Group annual meeting* (pp. 111–116). Toronto: York University.

Noble, T., Nemirovsky, R., Wright, T., & Tierney, C. (2001). Experiencing change: The mathematics of change in multiple environments. *Journal for Research in Mathematics Education*, 85–108.

Núñez, R. (2004a). Do real numbers really move? Language, thought, and gesture: The embodied cognitive foundations of mathematics. *Embodied artificial intelligence* (pp. 54–73). Berlin & Heidelberg: Springer.

Núñez, R. (2004b). Embodied cognition and the nature of mathematics: Language, gesture, and abstraction. In K. Forbus, D. Gentner, & T. Regier (Eds.), *Proceedings of the 26th Annual Conference of the Cognitive Science Society* (pp. 36–37). Mahwah, NJ: Erlbaum.

Núñez, R. E. (2008). A fresh look at the foundations of mathematics: Gesture and the psychological reality of conceptual metaphor. In A. Cienki & C. Müller (Eds.), *Metaphor and gesture* (pp. 93–114). Amsterdam: John Benjamins.

Núñez, R. E., Edwards, L. D., & Matos, J. F. (1999). Embodied cognition as grounding for situatedness and context in mathematics education. *Educational Studies in Mathematics 39*, 45–65.

Papert, S. (1993). *Mindstorms*. New York: Basic Books.

Paterson, M. (2007). *The senses of touch: Haptics, affects and technologies*. New York: Berg.

Plato. (1976). *The meno*. (G.M.A. Grube, Trans.). Indianapolis, IN: Hackett Publishing.

Plato. (2004). *The republic*. (C.D.C. Reeve, Trans.). Indianapolis, IN: Hackett Publishing.

Presmeg, N. C. (1997). A semiotic framework for linking cultural practice and classroom mathematics. In J. A. Dossey, J. O. Swafford, M. Parmantie, & A. E. Dossey (Eds.), *Proceedings of the 19th Annual Meeting of the North American Chapter of the International Group for the Psychology of Mathematics Education* (Vol. 1, pp. 151–156).

Presmeg, N. (2003). Beliefs about the nature of mathematics in the bridging of everyday and school mathematical practices. In *Beliefs: A Hidden Variable in Mathematics Education?* (pp. 293–312). Amsterdam: Springer.

Presmeg, N. (2005). Metaphor and metonymy in processes of semiosis in mathematics education. In *Activity and sign* (pp. 105–115). New York: Springer US.

Presmeg, N. C. (2006). Research on visualization in learning and teaching mathematics. *Handbook of research on the psychology of mathematics education*, 205–235.

Presmeg, N. (2008). Spatial abilities research as a foundation for visualization in teaching and learning mathematics. In *Critical Issues in Mathematics Education* (pp. 83–95). New York: Springer US.

Radford, L. (2002). The seen, the spoken and the written: A semiotic approach to the problem of objectification of mathematical knowledge. *For the Learning of Mathematics, 22*(2), 14–23.

Radford, L. (2009). Why do gestures matter? Sensuous cognition and the palpability of mathematical meanings. *Educational Studies in Mathematics, 70*(2), 11–126.

Radford, L. (2010). The eye as theoretician: Seeing structures in generalizing activities. *For the Learning of Mathematics, 30*(2), 2–7.

Radford, L. (2013). Sensuous cognition. In D. Martinovic, V. Freiman, & Z. Karadag (Eds.), *Visual mathematics and cyberlearning* (pp. 141–162). Dordrecht: Springer.

Radford, L., Edwards, L., & Arzarello, F. (2009). Introduction: beyond words. *Educational Studies in Mathematics, 70*(2), 91–95.

Radford, L., & Puig, L. (2007). Syntax and meaning as sensuous, visual, historical forms of algebraic thinking. *Educational Studies in Mathematics, 66*(2), 145–164.

Rancière, J. (2004). *The politics of aesthetics: The distribution of the sensible*. (G. Rockhill, Trans.). New York: Continuum.

Robutti, O. (2006). Motion, technology, gestures in interpreting graphs. *International Journal for Technology in Mathematics Education, 13*(3), 117–125.

Robutti, O., Edwards, L., & Ferrara, F. (2012, July). Enrica's explanation: Multimodality and gesture. In *Proceedings of 36th Conference of the International Group for the Psychology of Mathematics Education* (p. 27). Taipei, Taiwan.

Roth, W. M. (2001). Gestures: Their role in teaching and learning. *Review of Educational Research, 71*(3), 365–392.

Roth. W. M. (2010). Incarnation: Radicalizing the embodiment of mathematics. *For the Learning of Mathematics, 30*(2), 8–17.

Roth, W. M., & Bowen, G. M. (1998). Decalages in talk and gesture: Visual and verbal semiotics of ecology lectures. *Linguistics and Education, 10*(3), 335–358.

Roth, W.M., & McGinn, M.K. (1998). Inscriptions: Toward a theory of representing as social practice. *Review of Educational Research, 68*(1), 35–59.

Rotman, B. (2005). Gesture in the head: mathematics and mobility. In *Proceedings of the Mathematics and Narrative Conference*. Mykonos, Greece.

Sabena, C., Radford, L., & Bardini, C. (2005). Synchronizing gestures, words and actions in pattern generalizations. In *Proceedings of the 29 PME Conference* (Vol. 4, pp. 129–136). Melbourne, Australia: University of Melbourne.

Salk, J. (1983). *Anatomy of reality: merging of intuition and reason* (Convergence series). New York: Columbia University Press.

Schechner, R. (2003). *Performance theory*. London: Routledge.

Schechner, R. (2011). *Between theater and anthropology*. Philadelphia: University of Pennsylvania Press.

Sheets-Johnstone, M. (1999). *The primacy of movement*. Amsterdam: John Benjamins.

Sinclair, N. (2001). The aesthetic is relevant. *For the Learning of Mathematics, 21*(1), 25–32.

Sinclair, N. (2009). Aesthetics as a liberating force in mathematics education? *ZDM—The International Journal on Mathematics Education, 41*(1–2), 45–60.

Sinclair, N., De Freitas, E., & Ferrara, F. (2013). Virtual encounters: The murky and furtive world of mathematical inventiveness. *ZDM—The International Journal on Mathematics Education, 45*(2), 239–252.

Sinclair, N., Pimm, D., & Higginson, W. (2006). *Mathematics and the aesthetic: New approaches to an ancient affinity*. New York: Springer.

Slingerland, E.E.G. (2008). *What science offers the humanities*. New York: Cambridge University Press.

Stewart, K. (2007). *Ordinary affects*. Durham, NC: Duke University Press.

Streeck, J. (2009). *Gesturecraft: The manu-facture of meaning*. Amsterdam: John Benjamins.

Swanson, D.M. (2007). Cultural beads and mathematical AIDS: A critical narrative of disadvantage, social context and school mathematics in post-apartheid South Africa, with reflections and implications for 'glocal' contexts. *Philosophy of Education Journal, 21*(2), 1–78.

Taimina, D. (2009). *Crocheting adventures with hyperbolic planes*. Wellesley, MA: A. K. Peters.

Tarde, G. (2010). *Gabriel Tarde on communication and social influence: Selected papers*. University of Chicago Press.

Toulmin, S. (1992). *Cosmopolis: The hidden agenda of modernity*. Chicago: University of Chicago Press.

Turkle, S. (1984). *The second self: Computers and the human spirit*. Cambridge, MA: MIT Press.

Turner, V. (1986). *From ritual to theater: The human seriousness of play*. New York: PAJ Publications.

Tyler, I. (2000). Reframing pregnant embodiment. In S. Ahmed, J. Kilby, C. Lury, M. McNeil & B. Skeggs (Eds.), *Transformations: Thinking through feminism* (pp. 288–301). New York: Routledge.

Walkerdine, V. (1998). *Counting girls out: Girls and mathematics*. Abingdon, UK: Psychology Press.

Walshaw, M. (Ed.) (2004). *Mathematics education within the postmodern*. Charlotte, NC: Information Age Publishing.

Weaver, J.A. (2010). *Educating the posthuman: Biosciences, fiction, and curriculum studies*. Rotterdam: Sense Publishers.

Whitehead, A. N., & Russell, B. (2011). *Principia mathematica*. Seaside, OR: Rough Draft Printing.

Wilde, M.H. (1999). Why embodiment now? *Advances in Nursing Science, 22*(2), 25–38.

Yaglom, I.M. (1981). Elementary geometry, then and now. In C. Davis, B. Grünbaum, & F. A. Sherk (Eds.), *The geometric vein* (pp. 253–269). New York: Springer.

Zevenbergen, R. (2000). Cracking the "code" of mathematics classrooms: School success as a function of linguistic, social and cultural background. In J. Boaler (Ed.), *Multiple Perspectives on Mathematics Teaching and Learning* (pp. 201–223). Westport, CT: Ablex.

Zizek, S. (1997). *The plague of fantasies*. London: Verso.

4 Configuring Learning Theory to Support Teaching[1]

David Kirshner

Louisiana State University

> Paradigms, wholly new ways of going about things, come along not by the century, but by the decade; sometimes, it almost seems, by the month. It takes either a preternaturally focused, dogmatical individual, who can shut out any ideas but his or her own, or a mercurial, hopelessly inquisitive one, who can keep dozens of them in play at once, to remain upright amidst this tumble of programs, promises, and proclamations.
>
> (Geertz, 2000, p. 188)

INTRODUCTION

This chapter addresses the multiparadigmatic character of social sciences that Geertz (2000) laments, particularly the presence of multiple, independently conceived notions of learning that educators somehow must negotiate to establish a sound and coherent basis in psychology for theorization of teaching. For education, learning constitutes the essential goal of professional practice. Thus, its diverse theorization in distinct branches of psychology poses a considerable challenge not faced by *paradigmatic professions* like medicine and engineering, those informed by what Kuhn (1970) called *paradigmatic sciences* (e.g., physics, chemistry, biology, genetics, anatomy, etc.) that have achieved a consensus about theory and method. As Kennedy (1999) observed, "The relationship between teaching and learning is the most central issue in teaching, and it is also the most perplexing and least understood" (p. 528).

For the most part, educators' strategy for dealing with psychology's multiple paradigms has consisted simply in identifying with one or another extant branch in an effort to derive guidance for educational practice. Through the past century educators, variously, have found inspiration in behavioral psychology, Gestalt psychology, Dewey's functional psychology, Piagetian developmental psychology, Vygotskian sociocultural theory, ecological psychology, information processing psychology (Gardner, 1987), conceptual change theory, situated cognition theory, and various constructivist and constructionist theories (Spivey, 1997), among others.

The central consequence for education of selecting a single branch from among psychology's offerings might be labeled the *Babel Effect*. Given a diverse menu of psychological approaches, educators in a given era vary in their choice of preferred paradigm. As a consequence, theorists are speaking many different languages as they attempt to articulate foundations for pedagogy, and they are robbed of the opportunity to build a professional discourse of teaching together.

The Babel Effect manifests itself within our pedagogical discourse primarily as complementary tendencies toward conflict and confusion. Conflict arises when educators guided by alternative visions of learning formulate models of teaching practice that are seen as antithetical to one another. Historically, the key example is the conflict between Progressive Educators rallying under the banner of John Dewey's functional psychology and Traditionalists guided by the more reductive sense of stimulus-response learning advanced by Edward Thorndike and his colleagues (Lagemann, 1989). Contemporary conflicts include the "Reading Wars" and the "Math Wars" (Loveless, 2001; these conflicts are analyzed later in the chapter).

Less salient for our community, but more debilitating in its consequence, is the sense of confusion and eventually dissipation that ensues from multiple sources for pedagogical precepts. Within each pedagogical enclave things may not seem terribly amiss. Whether we are behaviorists or constructivists or situativists or critical theorists (to name a few prominent schools) we have coherent and convergent conversations about learning and teaching, and perhaps a sense that we are making progress. But in aggregate, this Balkanization of educational thought is dysfunctional. Unless teachers locate themselves squarely within a single tradition of pedagogical theory—and most don't—they are faced with a discordant array of pedagogical advice:

Learning requires continual practice.	Repetitive practice is the antithesis of learning.
Learning is facilitated by group work.	Individualized study allows each student to progress optimally and at their own rate.
Lecture is the most efficient method to transfer knowledge to students.	Knowledge doesn't transfer but has to be constructed by each individual student.

From this chaotic assembly, only the most general and platitudinous of invocations—"Care about the children. Prepare well for class. Be 'with-it.'" (Pressman, 2007)—escape censure and emerge as uncontested advice for teachers. Our general pedagogical discourse is a poor and pale reflection of the intense intellection within the various enclaves of theory.

To be clear, what is at stake here is not just the rhetoric of pedagogy, but the very character and quality of pedagogical thought and practice. Consider the chain of reasoning underlying development of a chemotherapeutic treatment for cancer. To begin, cell biologists provide insight into cell pathology relevant to this ailment. Then a strategy, say, for interfering with cancer cell reproduction is theorized, and experiments are initiated with lab animals to determine if the strategy has merit. Finally, clinical trials are established to verify efficacy with humans, and to empirically address matters such as dosage levels that theory is insufficiently refined to determine (Arthur & Hancock, 2007).

At the foundation of this collective enterprise is broad agreement across the medical field as to the underlying mechanisms of disease and health. It is this consensus that ensures practitioners are educated in the relevant theories and prepared to expertly perform their assigned role in the treatment process. Surely inductive generalization—noting unexpected successes—and even blind luck have a role to play, but "medicine is a rational enterprise built on a scientific tradition that operates with logical arguments, the laws of causality and the epistemic strategies of observation and experimentation" (Kottow, 1992, p. 19).

In the case of education, the entire infrastructure for rational organization of practice is undermined by the presence of unreconciled theorizations of learning, as emblematized by the typical educational psychology textbook in which the diverse offerings of learning theorists are presented as separate chapters together with recommendations for practice (e.g., Eggen & Kauchak, 2013; Ormrod, 2009). Such an approach abdicates collective responsibility for rationally organized educational practice, leaving individual teachers to find their own way through the thicket of diverse and competing claims (Wojcikiewicz & Wenzel, 2012).

Nothing drives home the ineffectiveness of the current utilization of psychology more strongly than the fact that researchers looking into practices of good teaching ignore learning theory. For instance, in an OECD-funded multinational project in the early 1990s, teachers noted for their excellence were carefully studied to determine effective teaching practices.

A synthesis of findings from each country carried out by Hopkins and Stern (1996) identified the six most important characteristics of excellent teachers, as summarized in Nuthall (2004):

1. a passionate commitment to doing the very best for their students
2. a love of children enacted in warm, caring relationships
3. pedagogical content knowledge, e.g., knowing how to identify, present, and explain key concepts
4. use of a variety of models of teaching and learning
5. a collaborative working style with other teachers to plan, observe, and discuss each other's work
6. a constant questioning of, reflecting on, and modifying of their own practice. (p. 282)

Such an approach to identifying effective teaching practices is the educational equivalent of seeking a cure for cancer by observing the practices of successful physicians. What it yields, as we see, is little more than a catalog of education's bedside manner.

With the exception of educational practices nurtured under the auspices of teams of theorists (e.g., as in design research; see Design-Based Research Collaborative, 2003), to be discussed later, this kind of focus on the surface structure of educational practice is endemic to educational practice: For the most part, "teachers are not explicitly concerned with student learning as they manage student participation in classroom activities . . . [based on the belief that] 'student interest and involvement constitutes both a necessary and sufficient condition for worthwhile learning' (Prawat, 1992, p. 389)" (Nuthall, 2004, p. 276). As Windschitl (2002) noted in an incisive review, even reform pedagogy designed to perturb conventional ideas about teaching and learning is enacted as a kind of mimicry of prescribed methods: "activities, as opposed to ideas, are the starting points and basic units of planning" (p. 138). Except in rare cases, the rich insights into learning that psychologists have generated within psychology's many branches simply are being lost to the profession of teaching.

These travails of educational practice stemming from the multiplicity of learning theories are broadly misunderstood, both by educators and by policy makers. For policy makers (and others in the academy) teaching and the scholarship of teaching is "low-status work" (Lagemann, 2000, p. xii); educators are simply too dull witted (or else too ideologically driven) to figure out what seems a relatively straightforward matter of determining and implementing effective practices. The current policy solution in the U.S. context directs research dollars to the final empirical phase of scientific research—fine-tuning and validating of proposed practices—completely ignoring the need for sound theoretical foundations (Schoenfeld, 2007). Educationists, on the other hand, chalk up the challenges of educational theorizing to the "irreducible complexity" of our domain, seeing theoretical heterogeneity as an index of this complexity, rather than as a fundamental problem in its own right: "What we know about teaching is always contingent on a vast array of intervening variables that mediate between a teacher's action and a student's response" (Labaree, 2000, p. 231; see also Otterness, 2009; Regehr, 2010).[2]

The purpose of this chapter is to articulate a new strategy for exploiting the rich insights into learning that psychology, in its diverse paradigms, has uncovered, without generating the competing prescriptions that divide and weaken the educational enterprise. Given the long-standing and intractable problematic of education's uptake of learning theory, the strategy proposed here is surprisingly straightforward: accept, rather than resist, the multiparadigmatic character of learning theory.

When we educators adopt a single theorization of learning as a basis for pedagogical practice, we are failing to acknowledge that psychology itself has not resolved the multiplicity of learning theory. We are pinning our educational fortunes on the learning theory we hope and believe eventually will prevail, ignoring that psychology, in its multiple paradigms, has produced several distinct theorizations of learning that motivate us as a community.

The alternative proposed here is to work across education to identify the distinct notions of learning that motivate educational practice. Honoring each of these as legitimate, the strategy is to articulate pedagogical practice in genres, each addressing a single notion of learning, and each informed by a theorization specific to that particular notion of learning. This simple move of aligning learning goal → learning theory → pedagogical genre puts educational practice on the same footing as paradigmatic professions like medicine and engineering, in which a single theoretical framework informs prescribed professional practices. The professional educator, therefore, can be schooled in the relevant theorizations for each separate genre and can practice teaching based on a rational plan that explicates how recommended practices are intended to lead to the desired learning outcome. The genres approach yields diversity, but without conflict or confusion endemic to our current discourse.

Before proceeding, it is best to anticipate an objection that may be forming for some readers: how can we take seriously a proposal to construct learning as separate, independent processes in the face of its well-established standing as a complex whole (Regehr, 2010)—multifaceted, to be sure, but composed of mutually interdependent elements (Bransford, Stevens, Schwartz, et al., 2006; Greeno, 2011). Yet the history of psychology does not bear out the current wisdom of learning as a complex whole. Behavioral psychology did not establish itself as a *complement* to mentalistic approaches, but as an *alternative* (Watson, 1913). Likewise sociocultural psychology, cognitive psychology, developmental psychology, and other foundational theories have worked mightily to establish independent claims to account for learning/development. In the current era of dialectical, integrative, and holistic theorizing learning tends to come to us as a complex whole; in a previous era, learning more often came to us as a unitary mechanism (rooted in conditioning, or in developmental schemas, or in serial information processing). My point here is not to settle the matter in advance, but to forestall a priori judgment. A case for the utility of independent theorizations of learning is demonstrated in the current chapter, and it can be assessed directly, on its merits.

The foregoing provides a general rationale for the genres approach, but two clarifications are needed to see the contours of the proposed strategy: the first addresses the role of values decisions in a discursive space that legitimizes separate interpretations of learning; and the second addresses the special character of multiparadigmatic science and its implications for uptake of psychology's learning theories.

Values Decisions

To be sure, the one-to-one alignment of goals to theories to practices advocated does not suddenly transform psychology into a paradigmatic science, nor education into a paradigmatic profession. Indeed, organizing pedagogical practice into independent genres crystallizes a new problematic for education not paralleled within the paradigmatic professions: the need for values decisions pertaining to selection of the teaching genre(s) appropriate for a given student, classroom, subject area, school, or educational jurisdiction.

Values issues concerning learning goals already are implicated in our current educational discourse, as evidenced by conflicts like the Reading Wars and Math Wars (Loveless, 2001). However, in our current discourse in which each sect of theorists recognizes only one's own paradigm as legitimate, one's opponents are cast not only as wrong-headed in their choice of learning goals, but also as misguided in their teaching methods (e.g., Draper, 2002; Klein, 2005). Reifying several distinct theorizations of learning as legitimate, and establishing recognized standards for pedagogical practice associated with each, means that differences about goals no longer bleed over into criticisms of the competence and efficacy of professionals making different values decisions. Teaching assumes a more professional demeanor.

Legitimating various notions of learning and associated genres of teaching also should have the effect of removing the theorist from the fray of values decisions. The learning theorist provides technical knowledge relevant to the shaping of pedagogical practices. However, the genres of teaching are not alternative paths to the same end—this is not about different *learning styles* (North, 2015; Pashler, McDaniel, Rohrer, & Bjork, 2009)—they lead to different ends, and it is properly the province of the world of practice to make the decisions as to what form(s) of learning are to be valued in a given circumstance.

This devolution of values decisions to the world of practice creates a new political dimension of educational policy that may have far-reaching consequence for the organization of schooling: Do teachers decide within their own classrooms? Are these school- or district-level decisions? Do we develop a decentralized model of schooling to allow for more parent choice? Such questions are beyond the scope of the current chapter, but it is worth keeping this consequence of the genres approach in mind.

Theorization in Multiparadigmatic Science

The final issue to be addressed in this introduction concerns the nature of theory development in multiparadigmatic sciences like psychology. Our assumption as educators has been that theorizing in psychology follows the same basic strictures and adheres to the same basic standards as theorizing in any other science. In the next section, I subject this assumption to critical scrutiny from a sociology of science perspective, finding instead that learning theorists are prone to overextension and exaggeration of results, and to systematically minimizing and eliding differences between theoretical approaches.

The consequence for the genres strategy is that after identifying the notions of learning motivating educational practice we cannot simply adopt a ready-made learning theory for each from which to derive guidance for pedagogical practice. Rather, we must compose these theorizations of learning ourselves, drawing selectively from the corpus of results psychologists have obtained relevant to that notion of learning. This usurpation of psychology's traditional role as interpreter of learning theory for educators is bound to create tension between the two fields. However, as we shall see in the sociology of science section, our practice over the past century of selecting one learning paradigm to inform pedagogy, rather than coordinating several paradigms, always has been in the service of psychology's interest in achieving a unified paradigm. Adopting the genres approach in the interests of regularizing our own discourse requires that we step out from behind the shadow of that great science.

Outline of this chapter: Following this introduction, "A Sociological Glimpse at Theorization of Learning" approaches the nature of theory construction in psychology from a sociology of science perspective based on Kuhn's (1970, 2000) analysis of the competitive process through which multiparadigmatic sciences achieve the initial consensus that marks the transition to the status of a mature science. The next section, "Education's Uptake of Learning Theory," reviews the history of education's uptake of learning theory, noting a succession of four phases of thinking about this problem. The following section, "The Genres Approach," identifies the valued notions of learning that motivate educational practice and lays out the constraints on utilizing psychological theory. The next section, "The Crossdisciplinary Framework" (the heart of the chapter), articulates the theorizations of learning and associated genres of teaching. The penultimate section, "Crossdisciplinary Analysis of Pedagogical Practice," applies this coordinated framework of theories and pedagogies to analyzing—and providing new insights into—a wide variety of issues and problems of educational practice. This is intended to make plausible the claim that the genres approach, rather than elaborating a new regime of thought for educational practice, serves to untangle the strands of ideation knotted together within our current integrative discourse about learning and teaching. A concluding section, "Problems and Prospects," reviews the intentions of the chapter and argues for taking the considerable risks associated with this genres approach.

A SOCIOLOGICAL GLIMPSE AT THEORIZATION OF LEARNING

The overall theme of this chapter is that psychology has amassed brilliant and powerful insights into learning that are being underutilized as resources for educational practice owing to the multiparadigmatic character of that science. This is not a problem we can solve by looking to the paradigmatic professions or to the paradigmatic sciences for guidance. We need to carefully and independently analyze the processes of knowledge creation in multiparadigmatic psychology as a first step to outlining a strategy for utilization of its knowledge products. In this section, I take a Sociology of Scientific Knowledge (SSK) perspective to understand the sociological constraints that guide the development of learning theories (Barnes, 1985; Collins & Pinch, 1993).

Sociology of science, and SSK in particular, seeks to identify not only how institutions of science are shaped within the broader cultures in which they are embedded, but how the very knowledge products of those sciences bear the marks of the societal context (Shapin, 1995). The idea that sociological factors constrain scientific theorizing is not one that scientists generally welcome. As Danziger (1990) remarked, psychologists often are uncomfortable with the suggestion that "personal, cultural, and historical factors play important roles in the elaboration and acceptance of psychological theory, . . . this state of affairs is hardly compatible with the claims by the discipline for the objectivity of its insights into human behavior" (p. 5). Indeed, sociology of science perspectives can be "profoundly destabilizing" for scientists whose field of study comes in for critique (Pinch, 2007, p. 266). This is sensitive terrain we traverse.

My analysis of the development of psychological theory is rooted in Thomas Kuhn's (1962, 1970, 2000) well-known theory of scientific paradigms. Taking issue with the long-standing image of scientific progress as an ongoing accumulation of knowledge and technique, Kuhn (1970) distinguished between two kinds of scientific progress. During periods of *normal science*, there is broad agreement among scientists as to the nature of their subject matter and appropriate methods for advancing the science. Indeed, during these periods of paradigmatic consensus progress *is* cumulative—a kind of extended puzzle-solving activity (p. 35). However, as Kuhn (1970) pointed out, normal science is powerful precisely because it is very focused and limited in its scope. As a consequence, it has no way to assimilate "new and unsuspected phenomena [that] are . . . repeatedly uncovered by scientific research" (p. 52). Eventually, someone may take up one or more of these anomalies as sites of investigation outside of the strictures of the existing paradigm. In some cases, these investigations lead to a new theoretical and methodological frame for the science, setting the ground for a period of paradigm conflict and possible *scientific revolution*, after which a new period of normal science ensues (Kuhn, 1970).

In addition to detailing how mature sciences cycle through periods of normal science and revolution, Kuhn (1970) described the process whereby proto-sciences—what he called *pre-paradigm* (p. 17) sciences—mature into paradigmatic sciences. Preparadigmatic sciences are characterized by a multiplicity of scientific schools, each with its own perspective on the new science. The transition from preparadigmatic to paradigmatic coincides with achievement of the science's initial paradigmatic consensus, and hence the first period of normal science. The process is very similar to scientific revolution, except instead of two conflicting paradigms—the established one and the challenger—there are several contenders, all challengers, none already established. It is this process of paradigm competition that will concern us in this section.

There has been considerable discussion as to whether social sciences in general, and psychology in particular, fit Kuhn's definition of preparadigmatic. Driver-Linn (2003) notes that "Kuhn used psychology as an example of a pre-paradigmatic science (to be compared with paradigmatic sciences such as physics)" (p. 272; see Rosenberg, 2005, p. 272, and Staats, 1981, for concurring viewpoints).[3] Nevertheless, opinions have varied.

One point of view that seems to me to be popular with psychologists was voiced by Weimer and Palermo (1973), who observed that psychology achieved an initial consensus around behaviorism and has since had a revolution (cognitive psychology) so it therefore must be paradigmatic. To update the record, we can note that cognitive psychology itself has subsequently clashed with newer upstarts like situated cognition theory (Anderson, Reder, & Simon, 1996, 1997; Greeno, 1997).

The contrary point of view is that whereas behaviorism has fallen from dominance in psychology, it still continues as an active paradigm as evidenced by the continuing presence of journals, conferences, and organizations of its advocates (see Leahey, 1992). Certainly, from our point of view as educators, we *experience* psychology as preparadigmatic, in that contemporary efforts to inform pedagogical practice reference theories of learning in many different branches of psychology (e.g., Eggen & Kauchak, 2013). I proceed with this sociological analysis of learning theory, mindful that psychologists may object to the very idea that psychology is preparadigmatic. Ironically, as we shall see, the act of construing one's field as paradigmatic may itself be a strategy of preparadigmatic competition!

Incommensurability

What is most striking about Kuhn's (1970) theory is his portrayal of the conflicting paradigms as "incommensurable" (p. 4): theorists engaged in different paradigms "see different things, and they see them in different relations to one another" (p. 150). Because the very problems that scientists choose to address are tied to their paradigmatic perspectives, differences of viewpoint can never be resolved through rational debate or adjudicated through empirical evidence. The scientific revolution succeeds if and when the new school is able to offer a sufficiently compelling account of the subject matter to attract established researchers from other schools—and especially new researchers just entering the field—to the new paradigmatic perspective. For the defeated paradigms, "their disappearance is caused by their members' conversion to the new paradigm. But there are always some men who cling to one or another of the older views, and they are simply read out of the profession" (Kuhn, 1970, pp. 18–19). Paradigm shift is ultimately a sociological event as the prior viewpoint is abandoned, not overturned.

Kuhn's notion of incommensurability has been subject to intense critique. Davidson's (1974) much-cited essay argued that the idea of incommensurable theories is incoherent, thereby raising fundamental challenges to Kuhn's thesis. Davidson (1974) objected to Kuhn's (1962) statements that suggested incommensurability implies incomprehensibility across paradigm lines, for example, Kuhn's suggestion that "after discovering oxygen Lavoisier worked in a different world" (1962, p. 118). However, as Oberheim and Hoyningen-Huene (2013) noted, "Kuhn developed and refined his initial idea over the following decades, repeatedly emphasizing that incommensurability [does not] impl[y] incomparability" (p. 3).

My own interpretation is informed by the perceptual dynamics revealed through bi-stable ambiguous figures like the famous vase-faces graphic developed by Danish psychologist Edgar Rubin, see Figure 4.1; one can experience it as a vase or as faces, but not simultaneously. By analogy, the fact that incommensurable theories cannot be brought into the same intellectual frame does not imply an inability for scientists oriented by different paradigms to understand one another, but it does imply that the differences in point of view cannot be resolved within a shared scientific perspective. Thus the process of resolution inevitably has to play out in a

Figure 4.1 Bi-stable ambiguous figure, vase-faces graphic.

broader sociological arena (Kuhn, 1970). This viewpoint is consistent with Kuhn's belief that "revolutionary change in science requires a gestalt switch" (Driver-Linn, 2003, p. 272).[4]

Paradigm Competition

A preparadigmatic science advances to paradigmatic status if and only if one of its paradigms is able to establish itself so completely as to lead to the demise of its competitors. Thus the competition among paradigms is existential, and winning out (or at least fending off attackers) forms the central imperative of each paradigmatic school.[5] As we shall see, this competition among incommensurable paradigms sets up dynamics with respect to both the presentation of psychological theory and the trajectory of such theories that define the very character of preparadigmatic science.

What incommensurability does is create separate intra- and inter-paradigm dynamics of scientific research. Within the paradigm, one is working with colleagues who share one's paradigmatic perspectives to advance knowledge in the field. This work adopts conservative standards of incremental progress and methodological rigor that are hallmarks of normal science and a principal source of its credibility and success (Kuhn, 1970, Chapter 8). But externally, as noted earlier, the battle for supremacy plays out in the sociological realm and depends primarily on one's ability to attract new researchers just entering the field to one's own paradigm. Because the superiority of one position over another cannot be established through rational argument (a consequence of incommensurability), the tendency for theorists is to exaggerate the accomplishments of their school and minimize the uncertainties. This exuberant and optimistic posture marks preparadigmatic science as a distinct kind of scientific enterprise.[6]

We see this discursive dynamic mostly easily in the case of the dominant paradigm in a given era, the one best positioned to establish hegemony over the field. As illustrated with behaviorism and cognitive science, the trajectory for these paradigms moves from initiation to (conservative) extension to (incautious) projection:

Paradigm Initiation: To begin, a paradigm is established around a powerful and distinctive accomplishment that illuminates some aspect of psychological functioning. For behaviorism it was Pavlov's (1897/1910, 1927) discovery of the "conditional reflex" (Murray, 1988) and Thorndike's (1898) discovery of the Law of Effect that formed the eventual basis for classical and operant conditioning, respectively (Hunt, 1993). Based on their studies of animal behavior, these authors established the comparative psychology principle of parsimony first introduced by Morgan (1894/1903) that higher mental processes should not be invoked if the behavior can be explained by lower mental processes. This established a strong break with the mentalism then prevailing in psychological research (Benjamin, 2007, p. 137).

For cognitive science, developments in a variety of fields (neuroscience, logic, anthropology, psycholinguistics, and computer science) coalesced into a new interdisciplinary field challenging the antimentalism enshrined in behavioral psychology (Hunt, 1993). Particularly, the serial digital computer provided an inspectable model of how symbolic elements could be encoded and manipulated computationally to simulate human problem solving (Newell & Simon, 1972). The Information Processing (IP) model became the "guiding metaphor" for cognitive psychology (Hunt, 1993, p. 516).

Paradigm Extension: Next ensues a period of conservative and careful research and theory construction in which the initial insight is extended over the domain of phenomena to which it most directly and obviously applies. For behaviorism, we have refinement and elaboration of classical and operant conditioning extended through experimental research into an antimentalist psychology of human behavior (Murray, 1988). For cognitive science, IP simulation was successfully applied to various domains of logical problem solving and decision making, as well as to subcognitive processes like visual processing (e.g., Marr, 1982), even as cognitive psychologists developed and fine-tuned the basic cognitive structures underlying a wide range of functions: pattern recognition, attention, categorization, and semantic and procedural memory (Gardner, 1987; Smith, 2001).

Paradigm Projection: Eventually, however, to establish hegemony, the paradigm must project itself to phenomena of interest in the broader field remote from its initial sphere of insight. This effort at a big leap in theory distinguishes preparadigmatic science from the incremental progress of normal science, wherein the scientist "concentrate[s] his attention upon problems that he has good reason to believe he will be able to solve" (Kuhn, 1970, p. 164). At this point, preparadigmatic theory tends to move from relative clarity toward opacity, and claims for the accomplishments of the paradigm are most likely to be exaggerated, with hoped-for advances touted as faits accomplis. Reliably, this hegemonic effort is met with push-back from other paradigms, and/or establishment of new paradigms that hope to address these phenomena more successfully.

For behaviorism, this played out in Skinner's (1958a) attempt to extend operant theory from unmediated response conditioning to verbal behavior. This effort was rewarded with a withering critique in which Chomsky (1959) identified such severe weaknesses in Skinner's theory construction as to constitute "play-acting at science" (p. 559). Indeed, this episode is cited as ushering in the ascendancy of cognitivism over behaviorism (Gardner, 1987).

For cognitive psychology, the attempt to project the successes of decontextualized puzzle solving to contextual reasoning critiqued by Lave (1988) generated defections from traditional cognitive science to situated cognition theory (e.g., Brown, Collins, & Duguid, 1989; Greeno, 1993; Hirst & Manier, 1995), a conflict in points of view that remains unresolved (Anderson, Reder, & Simon, 1996, 1997; Anderson, Greeno, Reder, & Simon, 2000; Greeno 1997).

As noted earlier, this pattern of attempting big leaps in theory is uncharacteristic of normal science but is consistent with the sociological process of preparadigmatic competition (Kuhn, 1970). What we can draw from this analysis is that educators should be critical and discerning consumers of psychology's knowledge products: not all claims by psychologists are equally well grounded or credible. But, as we shall see, Education has its own history with respect to Psychology, which conditions obedience and subservience, rather than critical scrutiny.

Psychology and Education

Historically, since the founding of scientific psychology in the late 1800s, education and psychology have been closely intertwined. One of the first preoccupations of the new science was to investigate the educational belief in "transfer of training" (e.g., Thorndike & Woodworth, 1901). Prior to that time, educators had relied on Aristotle's doctrine of Faculty Psychology (reworked over the millennia) as guidance for pedagogy. According to this belief system, the mind could be thought of as consisting of relatively independent "mental faculties" each of which could be strengthened, like a muscle, through exercise. Crucially, "a mind so sharpened and so stored with knowledge was believed ready for any calling; indeed, it was considered 'trained' and equipped for life. Thus . . . transfer of training resulted from sharpening the 'faculties' or powers of the mind, instead of from the specific benefits derived from a particular subject or method of study" (Rippa, 1971, p. 208).

What Thorndike and his colleagues established is that educators had greatly overestimated transfer of training effects (Hall, 2003). These findings discredited education's claims to prepare students for daily life, in the process effectively stripping education of its intellectual authority. Over a short span of years educational psychology emerged as a "guiding science of the school" (Cubberly, 1920, p. 206). Nor was this interest without practical benefit to psychology: "The promise of providing useful answers to practical educational questions may have been the impetus for the establishment of psychology departments in colleges and universities around the turn of the [20th] century" (White, 1991, quoted in Beatty, 1996, p. 102).

It is in this historical context that we need to understand the role that education plays in the psychologists' life-world. Rather than a disinterested senior partner, psychology has maintained a keen interest in how education incorporates psychological theory. As Thorndike (1910) put it, "school-room life itself is a vast laboratory in which are made thousands of experiments of the utmost interest to 'pure' psychology" (p. 12), and many psychologists have actively partici-pated in applying their theories to education.

But it is a mistake for us to interpret the psychologists' contributions to education outside of the general sociological imperatives of their field. Asserting influence over education is an important advertisement of the fitness of one's paradigm. If fear of push-back from other para-digms may serve to moderate rhetorical embellishment of one's scientific accomplishments, no such restraint is evident in pronouncements regarding educational applications. For instance in their landmark Academy of Sciences publication, Bransford, Brown, and Cocking (2000) declare foundations for educational practice that rest on "a new theory of learning [that] is coming into focus" (p. 3). Clearly no responsible paradigmatic science formulates applications to another field based on emergent theorizing. Such pronouncements can only be sensibly interpreted in the context of preparadigmatic competition in which "capturing" education serves to enhance the cachet and credibility of one's paradigm (Beatty, 1996).

I need to stress that what I'm suggesting here is *not* the outlines of a conscious strategy of subterfuge or exaggeration on the part of psychologists but rather the dynamics of how preparadigmatic competition shapes the discursive practice of psychological theorizing. Psy-chologists, confronted with intra- and inter-paradigmatic imperatives of their science, simply have accommodated their world view to enable these two imperatives to be met, the ten-sions between them being borne internally as part of the cultural practice of preparadigmatic science. As a departure from the conservative norms of paradigmatic science, psychologists make bold—even reckless—claims for their paradigm because in their practice of science they have come to sit on the proverbial "edge of their seats" respecting the emergent potential and promise of their paradigm: "Researchers become emotionally involved in their paradigm; it becomes part of their lives" (Hergenhahn, 2009, p. 11). Psychologists' pronouncements reflect the truth they experience.

EDUCATION'S UPTAKE OF LEARNING THEORY

Having presented a picture of how psychology functions as a preparadigmatic science, and of how education is positioned with respect to psychology, I conclude this sociological overview with an analysis of four strategies educators have used to deal with the multiple theorizations of learning that psychology has offered. These strategies are sequential, in the sense that they have been introduced at distinct historical moments in response to problems encountered with previous strategies; however, none has replaced its predecessors and all continue to be utilized today.

Foundational Theory: The initial strategy is to accept guidance for educational practice from advocates of what might be called *foundational* paradigms spawned by major branches of psychology—for example, behavioral, functional (Dewey), Gestalt, developmental, cogni-tive, sociocultural. Foundational paradigms articulate a focused and coherent, but specialized, vision of the learning process. As Alexander (2007) noted, adherents of such theories tend to deny the legitimacy of other theories and other visions as they stake a claim for the sufficiency of their paradigm. As noted earlier, the principal challenge of such theories is one of scope, as theorists seek to convince the field that their seemingly limited paradigmatic perspective actu-ally encompasses remote concerns of the field addressed in other paradigms.

Integrative Theory: Partly as a response to the inability of any foundational paradigm to prevail against its competitors, psychologists have developed what might be termed *integra-tive* theories like social constructivism and situated cognition that attempt to weave together perspectives from the foundational theories (Alexander, 2007, makes essentially the same dis-tinction between foundational and integrative theories, though using a different terminology). Such theories offer education relief from the exclusionary politics of the foundational theories, laying the groundwork for a richer and more encompassing vision of learning, and hence of teaching. That new theories can be created from the combination of existing theories was noted by Kuhn (1970) in his discussion of the preparadigm period before the science of optics coalesced around Newton's *Opticks*. At that time there were "a number of competing schools and sub-schools, most of them espousing one variant or another of Epicurean, Aristotelian, or Platonic theory . . . *and other combinations and modifications besides*" (p. 12, emphasis added). However, the challenges of theorizing linkages across paradigms are not to be underestimated. As Lave (1988) noted, for a true synthesis "units of analysis, though traditionally elaborated separately, must be defined together and consistently" (p. 146).

Holistic Theory: Alternative to the notable efforts of integrative theorists to create a true synthesis, there is a tendency in the literature to provide pedagogical frameworks encompassing a multiplicity of learning paradigms, without resolving their contradictory aspects and implications. This *holistic* tendency is most notably evident in canonical texts of the learning sciences community, *How People Learn* (Bransford, et al., 2000), and *How Students Learn* (Donovan & Bransford, 2005), wherein the authors embrace behaviorism, cognitive psychology, cultural psychology, developmental psychology, Gestalt psychology, information processing theory, neuropsychology, situated cognition, and sociocultural psychology. As noted earlier, all of these are coalescing into "a new theory of learning [that] is coming into focus" (Bransford, et al., 2000, p. 3), a state of affairs that apparently obviates the need to resolve theoretical divergences.

Dialectical Relations and Postpositive Fragmentation: As noted earlier, bona fide integrative theorizing across paradigmatic divides is a challenging undertaking. However, in many current cases, the theories to be integrated are not only understood as incommensurable with one another, but also as dialectically related. For instance, a central assumption of situated cognition theory is that "practice is constituted in a dialectical relation between persons acting and the settings of their activity" (Lave, 1988, p. 145). Likewise, Ernest (1998) finds that "at the center of social constructivism lies an elaborated theory of both individual or subjective knowledge and social or objective knowledge—equally weighted . . . and the dialectical relation between them" (p. 241). Dialectic relations imply "reflexivity" as described by Cobb (2007): "This is an extremely strong relationship that does not merely mean that the two perspectives are interdependent. Instead, it implies that neither exists without the other in that each perspective constitutes the background against which mathematical activity is interpreted from the other perspective" (p. 29).

What dialectical relations do is lock the theories together into a fixed mutual interdependence, but without ever resolving the discrepant viewpoints. This, I would argue, makes a true integrative theory impossible. For example, as Kuhn (1970) noted with respect to the wave/particle dialectic of light, "the period during which light was 'sometimes a wave and sometimes a particle' was a period of crisis—a period when something was wrong—and it ended only with the development of wave mechanics and the realization that light was a self-consistent entity different from both waves and particles" (p. 114). Similarly, a true synthesis of social and cognitive notions of learning must get beyond their dialectical opposition to one another.

Mindful of the severe challenges of integration across paradigms, some of our most sophisticated theorists are coming to question whether establishing epistemic foundations for learning and teaching is even possible. As Sfard (1998) lamented in her essay on incommensurable learning metaphors, we'd best "give up the hope that the little patches of coherence will eventually combine into a consistent global theory. It seems that the sooner we accept the thought that our work is bound to produce a patchwork of metaphors rather than a unified, homogeneous theory of learning, the better for us and for those whose lives are likely to be affected by our work" (p. 12).

Similarly, in framing mathematics education as a *design science*, Cobb (2007) explicitly rejects the possibility of epistemic knowledge as the product of theory/research. For Cobb (2007), the theorist is recast as "*bricoleur* . . . a handy man who invents pragmatic solutions in practical situations. . . . Similarly, I suggest that rather than adhering to one particular theoretical perspective, we act as bricoleurs by adapting ideas from a range of theoretical sources" (p. 29). Indeed, Cobb (2007) "question[s] the assumption that theory consists of decontextualized propositions, statements, or assertions that are elevated above and stand apart from the activities of practitioners" (p. 5), and consequently, he "sh[ies] away from the approach of first surveying currently fashionable philosophical [and psychological] positions and then deriving implications for mathematics education research and practice from them" (pp. 6–7).[7]

In my view, abandoning the pretension that psychological theory has provided epistemic foundations for educational practice is an intellectually responsible answer to our inability to coherently marshal the divergent epistemic knowledge of learning that psychology has generated in its varied paradigms. Still, the postpositive turn away from epistemic knowledge is a drastic step.[8] For in reifying knowledge of learning and teaching as ineluctably local we abandon the possibility that the knowledge base for teaching ever can be systematized, that teacher expertise can be scaled-up beyond the local regime of theory within which it is nurtured, and consequently that teaching ever can attain to the stature and authority of professions whose knowledge base is informed by epistemic science. This is a verdict we shall try to avoid.

THE GENRES APPROACH

The foregoing review of education's uptake of psychological theory highlighted four strategies:

- *Foundational theory:* adopt a single foundational paradigm that provides a clear, but limited, vision of learning.
- *Integrative theory:* adopt an integrative theory struggling to bridge across inconsistent units of analysis.
- *Holistic approach:* ignoring incommensurability, in eclectic fashion, create pedagogical ensembles that draw from a broad range of learning theories.
- *Postpositive approach:* abandoning the possibility of epistemic theorization of learning, reconstitute theory as local to the particular situational interests in a given educational setting.

The genres approach constitutes a new strategy designed to better exploit the significant insights into learning forged within the foundational paradigms. The strategy involves identifying the distinct notions of learning that inspire educational practice, determining the psychological theorization that best explicates each of these, and then using the theorizations to inform the articulation of *genres of teaching*—distinct pedagogical methods, each specific to one of the identified notions of learning. Of course, a theory of learning does not *determine* a teaching method, any more than a theory of cell pathology determines a cure for cancer. Nevertheless, in both cases having a clear understanding of underlying mechanisms is a major asset in formulating sound professional methods. The strategy of aligning learning goals with learning theories with pedagogical practices is intended as an alternative to the current strategies that have led to conflict, confusion, banality, and abandonment, respectively.

Culturally Shared Metaphors for Learning

The first challenge of the genres approach is to identify the notions of learning explored by psychologists that capture our fundamental interests as educators. My personal exploration of the learning theory landscape has evolved over the past 18 years, finally settling into three metaphors for learning: Learning as *habituation*, informed primarily by behavioral psychology; learning as *construction*, informed by developmental psychology (Piaget); and learning as *enculturation*, informed by sociocultural psychology. Remarkably, essentially these same metaphors have been identified by other researchers (Bredo, 1994; Case, 1992; Greeno, Collins, & Resnick, 1996; Richey, Klein, & Tracey, 2011; Shulman, 1987, p. 7; Wojcikiewicz, 2010). Furthermore, these metaphors for learning dovetail with the canonical goals of learning—skills, knowledge (concepts), and dispositions (cultural practices), respectively—that have been identified by the U.S. National Council for Accreditation of Teacher Education (NCATE, 2002; see also AERA, 2005).

Rather than write off this happy convergence to coincidence, I am mindful of the observation of many commentators that psychology often draws from our culture's basic metaphors for its foundational images and intuitions (Fletcher, 1995; Leary, 1994; Olson & Bruner, 1996; Sternberg, 1997). As Fletcher (1995) put it, our culture's "folk psychology is built into scientific psychological theories in a more thoroughgoing fashion than is commonly realized" (p. 97).

Following these observations, the genres approach takes as its working premise that the learning goals motivating educational practice reflect notions of learning that psychologists also have pursued. Thus my intention in articulating genres of teaching is not so much to provide new foundations for pedagogical practice as to disentangle the existing intuitions about teaching and learning knotted together within an integrative theories discourse (Kirshner, 2002). If fully successful, the system of genres that I outline presents a refined and organized version of the varied streams of ideation that already constitute pedagogical thought and practice across the broad spectrum of education.

Utilizing Learning Theory

The second challenge of the genres approach is to identify and utilize the learning theories that best illuminate the metaphors for learning that motivate educators. Given the shared wellspring of metaphors for learning that nourish both education and psychology (Fletcher, 1995; Leary, 1994; Olson & Bruner, 1996; Sternberg, 1997), the obvious strategy would be to adopt extant theories of learning from the menu of available paradigms.

There are two problems with that approach: (A) Although psychology's major learning paradigms do seem to be driven by the metaphors for learning adopted for the genres approach, the match-up is not quite neat. Sometimes more than one branch of psychology is informed by a given metaphor, in which case our theorization of learning may draw from more than one paradigm. Other times, a theory of learning, though inspired primarily by the learning metaphor at hand, adopts a more complex unit of analysis. Such cases may necessitate forays beyond psychology into neighboring disciplines.

(B) As discussed earlier under "Paradigm Projection" (p. 106), the trajectory of learning theory projects beyond the natural, intuitive paradigmatic boundaries in an attempt to encompass notions of learning pursued in other paradigms. Such projection is a necessary part of the competitive process whereby psychology may hope one day to become paradigmatic, but it runs counter to our interest in articulating coherent and distinct theorizations of learning.

These concerns are not just hypothetical; they directly impact the theorizations of all three learning metaphors addressed in the genres approach:

- *Habituation*: (A) The habituation metaphor for learning of skills is informed not only by behaviorism, but also by implicit learning theory of cognitive psychology. (B) Furthermore, despite the nonmentalist rhetoric of behaviorism, applications to education have implicated the learning of "facts" (Skinner, 1958b), which constitutes encroachment of behaviorism onto the terrain of concept learning.
- *Construction*: (B) For the construction metaphor for learning of concepts, both Piaget's developmental psychology (Piaget, 1965/1995) and its interpretation in radical constructivism (von Glasersfeld, 1995) resist the natural solipsistic limitations of the theorizations as they seek to embrace some sense of intersubjectivity.
- *Enculturation*: (A) Despite the clear sociogenetic orientation of sociocultural theory as a basis for theorizing learning of cultural practices, Vygotsky's (1978) vision ultimately is dialectical, thereby necessitating a reliance on sociological theory to explicate the enculturation metaphor.

All of these issues are explored, in depth, in the next section. Their relevance here is to explain the necessity of moving beyond the simple and straightforward strategy of adopting an intact theory of learning from psychology for each of the three learning metaphors. Instead, the genres strategy is to identify the learning theories relevant to each metaphor and, drawing selectively from their results, to assemble a theorization of learning particular to the learning metaphor at hand. A priority in this constructive process is to establish clear boundaries between the learning metaphors. In our current discourse, we typically talk of "understanding the skill," "inculcating thinking skills," and "practicing the concept," each of which intermixes the learning metaphors. A system of genres works only if the learning goals for the genres are distinct from one another, and the selective activity of assembling theorizations works toward that goal.

The result of this selective process, presented in the next section, is a set of theoretical framings of learning that are assembled from psychological theory, but do not directly match the authorized versions of extant theories. Their purpose is to present for educators as clear and focused an analysis as possible of each learning metaphor, as informed by psychological theory. Yet, these sketches of learning are not comfortably part of educational psychology, which as a bona fide branch of psychology "is much determined by the larger field of psychology" (Pressley & Roehrig, 2003, p. 340), and seeks first and foremost to promote the authorized knowledge products of that science. Rather, these sketches of learning come from the education side of the relationship with psychology, a new assertion of autonomy for educators to interpret learning for our own purposes.

Of course this interpretive effort could benefit from positive participation of psychologists, but given the tribal character of science (McRae, 2011) this is improbable. Rather, psychologists are likely to view these unauthorized framings of learning as "weak" psychological theorizing, or perhaps, more generously, simply as "wrong" psychological theorizing.

Educational theorists, too, are likely to be hesitant in embracing the genres approach. As noted earlier, education, has hitherto gained much of its intellectual authority through co-participation with psychology in pursuit of its goals (Lagemann, 2000). As well, as we have evolved into the current era of integrative and dialectical theorizing, philosophical and theoretical breadth and depth have become our markers of academic fitness (see Lester, 2010, p. 82, for a long list of theories invoked by mathematics educators). The reduction of theory to a small set of psychological approaches proposed here goes against this grain. Of course, it is precisely this reduction and organization of theory that enables educational research to attain to what Nuthall (2004) called "pragmatic validity . . . research that actually answers the question of how teaching is related to learning in a way that is comprehensible and practically useful for teachers" (p. 273). Still, this new approach disrupts our hierarchies of status and accomplishment.

In the next section I present the framework of learning theorizations and associated pedagogical methods. I then use the framework as a refractive lens to analyze the learning theory foundations of a wide range of educational practices and problems—from Skinner's programmed instruction to the Reading Wars and the Math Wars to critical pedagogies to metacognitive interests to identity development to ethical issues—in each case bringing a sense of clarity to what otherwise are experienced as deeply complex and sharply contested problematics. In this way, I press the case that the genres approach, though disruptive to our internal and external relations, captures a level of simplicity from which our work as educators can progress.

THE CROSSDISCIPLINARY FRAMEWORK

As noted earlier, the genres approach seeks to assemble theorizations of learning as habituation, construction, and enculturation, each clearly demarcated from the others. In this respect, the three theorizations can be said to constitute a framework of learning theories relevant to

Table 4.1 Crossdisciplinary framework.

LEARNING METAPHOR	Habituation	Construction	Enculturation
WHAT IS ACQUIRED	Skills	Concepts	Dispositions
THEORETICAL RESOURCES	Behaviorism; Implicit Learning Theory	Developmental Psychology; Radical Constructivism	Sociocultural Theory; Sociological Theory
KEY THEORISTS	Thorndike; Skinner; Reber	Piaget; von Glasersfeld	Vygotsky; Parsons
LEARNING PROCESS	Subcognitive connections among input/output elements	Discrepant experience → conceptual restructuring	Osmosis and/or emulation of forms of engagement
PEDAGOGICAL OBJECTIVE	Proficiency With Routine Exercises	More Viable Concept	Culturally Normative Participation
STUDENT-CENTERED PEDAGOGY	Extrinsically Motivated Repetitive Practice	Hypothetical Learning Trajectory	Nurture Classroom Microculture
TEACHER-CENTERED PEDAGOGY	Repetitive Practice	Lecture	Modeling/Coaching (Acculturation)
NECESSARY STUDENT CHARACTERISTIC	Independently Motivated Learners	Metacognitively Sophisticated Learners	Culturally Identified Learners

the practices of teaching. I use the modifier *cross*disciplinary (as opposed to *inter*disciplinary) to emphasize that the branches of psychology (behavioral, developmental, sociocultural) are being coordinated (as opposed to integrated) together, at the same time highlighting their independence from one another as separate sub-*disciplines* of psychology. Table 4.1 provides an overview of the crossdisciplinary framework, which includes three metaphors for learning, associated theoretical resources and theorists, learning goals and processes, and teaching genres.

Student-Centered and Teacher-Centered Pedagogies

As can be seen in Table 4.1, each learning metaphor yields two teaching approaches, depending on whether or not the students possess a key characteristic that facilitates achievement of the given learning goal. The idea is that a student endowed with this characteristic is positioned to utilize instructional resources independently. In this case, a teacher-centered pedagogy is appropriate in which the teacher need only focus on providing the learning resources. However, if students lack the key characteristic, a student-centered pedagogy expands the teacher role to include facilitating student uptake of instructional resources. The relevant student characteristic is indexed to the specific learning metaphor; there is a separate teacher-centered and student-centered pedagogy for each metaphor. This usage differs from standard usage in which *student centered* (or *learner centered*) and *teacher centered* are code for reform-oriented instruction and traditional instruction within a polarized discursive frame (McCombs, 2003).

LEARNING AS HABITUATION

In keeping with Thorndike's connectionism, habituated learning is understood as the association between sense impressions constituting a stimulus and impulses to action constituting a response. Associations are strengthened with use (Law of Exercise), particularly when the behavioral response is closely followed by a satisfying result (Law of Effect; Thorndike, 1911). With repetition, responses to stimuli can become established patterns. This creates the possibility of shaping behavior through administration of rewards and punishments, a matter extensively and productively researched in behavioral psychology (e.g., Ormrod, 2000).

Having first been discovered and studied in the context of (non-human) animal research, a critical aspect of learning from a behaviorist perspective is its operation below the level of conscious thought or intention. As Watson (1913) laid it out in his inaugural vision for the new approach, "I believe we can write a psychology, define it as [the science of behavior], and never go back upon our definition: never use the term consciousness, mental states, mind, content, introspectively verifiable, imagery, and the like" (p. 166).

As the dominant paradigm of psychology through much of the early/middle part of the 20th century, behaviorism exerted a strong influence over education, its antimentalist premise conflicting with educational traditions rooted in notions of mind and consciousness that trace back to Plato (Egan, 1997); indeed, many commentators have lamented the effect that behaviorism had in reducing curriculum to mindless behavior (e.g., von Glasersfeld, 1987; Schoenfeld, 1992). In fact, however, behaviorists rarely have been rigorous in their antimentalist educational projects, most often seeking to attribute acquisition of (low level) information to behavioral learning: "Research that has studied teaching and learning in didactic environments has confirmed the assumptions of behaviorist theory regarding conditions that favor learning of *components of information* and routine skills" (Greeno, Collins, & Resnick, 1996, p. 28, italics added). Indeed, even Skinner (1958b, p. 974) promoted learning of "facts."

Certainly, rote memorization of a string of words (e.g., a telephone number) can be learned as a behavior, and sometimes educators insist on verbatim memorization of say, definitions, in science. "Facts," in this sense, are behaviors. But even in the heyday of behaviorism, behaviorist educators rarely intended or enforced verbatim memorization. For example, in their textbook on behavioral objectives, Sund and Picard (1972) offered as an exemplar: "The child is able to identify the stages of mitosis and to describe in his own words the changes which occur in the cell at each stage" (p. 2). As Chomsky (1959) argued, behaviorists' tolerance for stimuli and responses that are not objectively defined simply imports conceptual content through the back door.

Implicit Learning Theory: For purposes of the crossdisciplinary framework, we need to adhere rigorously to learning of skills as a subcognitive accomplishment. To gain a better sense of habituated learning at the subcognitive level we supplement behavioral theory with the implicit learning domain of cognitive psychology. This area of research demonstrates the scope and power of the cognitive processor to establish complex correlations among stimuli and responses through repetitive engagement in a task domain (Kirsner, Speelman, Maybery, et al., 2013; Reber, 1967). As Reber (1993) noted:

> There are remarkably close ties between the typical experiment on implicit learning and the standard study of conditioning. The commonality lies in the detection of covariation between events, which, I will argue, is the deep principle in processes as seemingly disparate as classical conditioning and implicit learning. Moreover, this conceptual parallel can be shown to hold, even though on the surface the implicit learning experiment appears to be one of abstract induction and the conditioning experiment one of simple association.
>
> (p. 7)

In this tradition of research, complex correlations among stimuli and responses are established through repetitive exposure. In a typical study, subjects are provided some pretext for attending to a stimulus set, without reference to underlying structures that are the actual learning target. For instance, subjects may be directed to memorize a list of letter strings without being told the strings have been generated by a finite state grammar according to fixed rules (Reber, 1967). With sufficient exposure, subjects show evidence of having acquired competencies related to the grammar, for instance, they can identify grammatical strings they've not encountered more frequently than nongrammatical strings consisting of the same letters. Interestingly, subjects in such studies typically have no conscious awareness that they have learned a pattern, or even that there is a pattern to be learned—at least, when conscious knowledge is ascertained through self-reports (Fu, Fu, & Dienes, 2008, p. 186).[9]

Skills Versus Concepts

This idea that habituated learning plays out unconsciously, as patterns of co-occurrence and covariation become operationally linked in the cognitive system, is emphasized in Reber (1993):

> When a cognitive scientist constructs a stimulus environment, he or she may do so on the basis of some set of principles that have the effect of creating an environment that reflects particular patterns of co-occurrence and covariation among its elements. But [for subjects] there are no *rules* here, just patterns of co-occurrence and covariation. The cognitive scientist may *think* that there are rules that characterize these covariations, and in fact, she or he is certainly entertaining a particular clutch of these—namely, the ones begun with.
>
> (p. 116)

Complicating the distinction between skills and concepts is the fact that conscious processes and explicit instruction can play a facilitative role in habituated learning. What explicit instruction about underlying relations does is to focus the perceptual apparatus on relevant aspects of the stimulus display thereby facilitating the implicit process of feature correlation, and consequently increasing the rate of learning. Yet this facilitative effect is independent of actually understanding the underlying relations:

> The most plausible interpretation [of our study] here, and the one that has interesting applications for theories of instruction, is that the function of providing explicit instructions at the outset is to direct and focus the subjects' attention. It alerts them to the kinds of structural relations that characterize the stimuli that follow and permits appropriate coding schemes to be implemented. Yet, these instructions do not teach the grammar in any full or explicit fashion; instead they oriented the subjects toward the relevant invariances in the display that followed.
>
> (Reber, 1993, p. 51)

The fact that instructors may use a set of rules to generate a stimulus set, for example a set of math problems, and that students benefit from explicit presentation of those rules, has led to considerable confusion about the nature of the learning that ensues from repetitive practice. Educators often conclude that students demonstrating intended skills have understood the rules conceptually, and that this understanding is the basis for successful performance (see Kirshner & Awtry, 2004, for an extended discussion). Neither of these conclusions is warranted given the interpretation of habituated learning presented here. Habituated learning is necessarily and exclusively a subcognitive process.

Skills Versus Dispositions

To demarcate skills from dispositions, we return to the issue of objectivity that Chomsky (1959) raised respecting Skinner's (1958a) efforts to extend the analysis of behavior to include verbal behavior. The issue is primarily methodological. Experimentally, or instructionally, one can set out to shape behavior instrumentally only to the extent one can objectively characterize stimulus and response events for organizing regimes of practice and feedback (Ormrod, 2000). For instance, one can shape the habituated response of raising one's hand in class and being recognized by the teacher before speaking because the discrete elements that comprise this event can be objectively characterized. Similarly, one can interpret, say, solving of mixture problems or factoring of polynomials as skills in that each involves discernible, codified problem types and routine solution steps.

However, such methods break down when stimuli and/or responses cannot be objectively demarcated. For instance, nonroutine mathematics problems resist rigid codification, in that expertise in solving requires flexible use of heuristics (Polya, 1957). Use of such *rules-of-thumb* is best conceived of as a cultural disposition rather than a skill, and effective instruction needs be framed in terms of cultural participation rather than repetitive practice. As Stanic and Kilpatrick (1988) noted, 1980s curricula that "reduc[ed] the rule-of-thumb heuristics to procedural skills" (p. 17) failed to nurture in students the art of problem solving. Similarly, one can teach individual behaviors of classroom participation as habituated learning, but classroom citizenship conceived beyond discrete rules of behavior requires an enculturational frame (Millei, Griffiths, & Parkes, 2010).

Habituationist Pedagogies

Teacher Centered: Because habituation learning is based on gradual establishment of feature correlation over repetitive exposure to a stimulus set, the basic requirement of habituationist instruction is to organize systematic repetitive practice across the range of stimulus conditions. Additionally, as noted earlier, demonstration of procedures can serve to activate certain features of the stimulus set that are thereby increasing the rate of habituated learning. Finally, corrective feedback can be crucial for learning, assuring that correct performances are being practiced and learned (Thorndike & Gates, 1929).

   Student Centered: The student's motivation to persist with repetitive practice is a crucial determinant of instructional method. If the student is independently motivated, the teacher-centered instructor's work is simply to provide appropriately structured opportunities to practice. If not, the student-centered habituationist instructor uses a variety of devices to extrinsically motivate students. Behavioral psychology provides significant guidance for provision of rewards and perhaps punishments to sustain engagement, including judicious use of praise and encouragement, game formats and competition, benefits and payment, and the like (Ormrod, 2000).

LEARNING AS CONSTRUCTION

The metaphor of learning as construction is elaborated through Piaget's theorization of conceptual development. Piaget is best known for his macrogenetic studies of how individuals pass through stages of intellectual development. However, it is his microgenetic studies of development in particular conceptual domains (e.g., space, time, number, etc.) that became drivers of pedagogy and research for mathematics and science educators.[10]

   What we pick up on in Piaget's system of ideas is his basic approach to *genetic epistemology*, his viewpoint on the genesis and evolution of our ability to gain knowledge of the world through experience. Rather than an empiricist view in which the structure of the world is directly perceived, Piaget understands knowledge as constructed through our actions on the world:

> In order to know objects, the subject must act upon them, and therefore transform them: he must displace, connect, combine, take apart, and reassemble them. From the most elementary sensorimotor actions (such as pulling and pushing) to the most sophisticated intellectual operations, which are interiorized actions, carried out mentally (e.g., joining together, putting in order, putting into one-to-one correspondence), knowledge is constantly linked with actions or operations.
> (Piaget, 1970/1983, p. 104, quoted in Paz & Leron, 2009, p. 20)

For Piaget, conceptual structures have their basis in the experienced regularities of our actions as they form "action schemas, . . . whatever there is in common between various repetitions or superpositions of the same action" (Piaget, 1971, p. 7). Such schemas form the base of hierarchically organized structures that enable knowledge construction up and down the abstraction ladder:

> If logic and mathematics are so-called "abstract" sciences, the psychologist must ask, Abstracted from what? . . . The origin of these logicomathematical structures should be sought in the activities of the subject, that is, in the most general forms of coordination of his actions, and, finally, in his organic structures themselves [basic infant action reflexes like sucking and grasping].
>
> (Piaget, 1970/1983, p. 106)

From his initial training as a zoologist, Piaget approached conceptual development as adaptation, which he understood as complementary processes of *assimilating* elements of the environment to our existing conceptual structures, and *accommodating* our cognitive structures to better fit with elements of the environment (Piaget, 1977a). The process is dynamically driven by disequilibrium with the environment, which Piaget theorized in terms of cognitive conflicts, contradictions, or discrepancies within cognitive structures, or between expectations and actual events (Sigel, 1979). It is the attempt to achieve a higher equilibrium, or equilibration, that produces learning: "what Piaget calls 'equilibration' is a form of learning . . . that is motivated by conflict and reinforced by conflict reduction" (Berlyne, 1970, p. 968, quoted in Cantor, 1983, p. 44).

Crucially, conflicts must be experienced (in some sense, at some level) in order for them to become productive of conceptual restructuring (Inhelder, Sinclair, & Bovet, 1974). Piaget developed a highly refined set of constructs to understand how experience is recorded in conscious and nonconscious ways within the cognitive system (von Glasersfeld, 1991). Non-conscious *empirical abstraction* involves the isolating of one's experience of sensory properties of an object or situation that can be used to recognize it at a later time. However, for learning to happen—for schemas to be coordinated together into higher level constructs—one needs to reproduce the experience independently of its physical instantiation. This *reflective abstraction* involves a "limited form of awareness" (von Glasersfeld, 1991). This is still different from *reflected abstraction*, a "process of retroactive thematization" (Piaget, 1977b) that we normally associate with conscious reflection. From this we glean that cognitive conflict, as intended by Piaget, is not necessarily what we associate with conscious struggle with an idea or conundrum.

Radical Constructivism: As noted earlier, Piaget's motivating interest was in elaborating the macrogenesis of stages of intellectual development, and his microgenetic studies of conceptual development in particular domains subserved that objective. In this respect, the redirecting of Piaget's genetic epistemology toward microgenesis dramatically extended the scope of the framework from just the core structures of development to include conceptual development in any and all domains (Steffe & Kieren, 1994). Radical constructivism is the epistemological position (or postepistemological position, Noddings, 1990) that takes that broadened mandate of genetic epistemology to heart.

That all concept development is rooted in structures derived from our actions upon the world implies the impossibility of any direct knowledge of the world. For intelligence that serves the organism's adaptation to the world, the question is never "Do my constructed understandings match what is really out there?" but rather, "Do they fit the world in such a way as to enhance my viability?" Constructions that produce dissonance with the world cause perturbations to the cognitive system that may lead to conceptual restructuring and more viable knowledge structures (von Glasersfeld, 1987, 1995).

The idea that all knowledge, including knowledge of other people, is constructed by the individual has led to vociferous criticism of radical constructivism as solipsistic, and consequently as unable to account for intersubjective knowledge (e.g., Gergen, 2002; Howe & Berv,

2000; Lewin, 1995; McCarty & Schwandt, 2000; Phillips, 1995). Piaget, too, faced criticisms that his theory failed to account for the social aspects of human knowledge (e.g., Vygotsky, 1934/1986, pp. 154–155).

Perhaps it was in anticipation of and/or response to such criticisms that both Piaget and von Glasersfeld argued that their theories do account for intersubjective knowledge: "Piaget placed great emphasis on the idea of *decentering*, or attempting to adopt a viewpoint that differs from your own. He used the term *intersubjective operations* to describe thoughts that are directed at another" (Thompson, 2013, pp. 62–63). Likewise, von Glasersfeld (1995), in fending off charges of solipsism, talked of an "intersubjective level" that "reaches beyond the field of our individual experience into that of others" (p. 120).

The complication of one's basic ontology, in an effort to account for intersubjective knowledge, may be necessary for psychological or philosophical theories framed in competitive relation with other theories. However, in this crossdisciplinary project, which seeks after local coherence, the solipsistic limitation of radical constructivism is a crucial asset in framing a constructivist pedagogy that highlights the teacher's isolation from the student—the tentative, conjectural nature of her or his model of students' conceptual structures, and the impossibility of transferring one's own ideas to them.

Student-Centered Constructivist Pedagogy[11]

Once we learn to think within the severe epistemological and theoretical constraints imposed by Piagetian psychology and radical constructivism, the basic approach of student-centered constructivist pedagogy is fairly straightforward to understand (even if dauntingly difficult to enact).

Shorn of intersubjective possibility, the student is seen to learn only from goal-directed encounters with the world, particularly those encounters in which they come to experience dissonances within their conceptual structures. Such a vision of learning would seem to leave little, if any, role for a teacher. Indeed, "for Piaget, the key ingredient of construction episodes was the active self-discovery of discrepancies between current concepts and actual outcomes. He argued that this is absolutely essential for children to stumble across such discrepancies *on their own* if cognitive development is to occur" (Brainerd, 2003, p. 271).

Nevertheless, constructivist researchers, working within his basic framework, have adapted Piaget's clinical interview methods to occasion transitions in children's conceptual structures (i.e., learning) (Cobb & Steffe, 1983; Steffe & Thompson, 2000). This constructivist *teaching experiment* methodology provides grounding for student-centered constructivist methods in this crossdisciplinary framework.

The key point is that the teacher-researcher acts only indirectly to produce learning by shaping a task environment in which the student encounters experiences that may be productive of conceptual restructuring. Learning ensues from the student's actions and reflective dynamics within the task environment: "Learning is not spontaneous in the sense that the provocations that occasion it might be intentional on the part of the teacher-researcher. In the child's frame of reference, though, the processes involved in learning are essentially outside of his or her awareness" (Steffe & Thompson, 2000, p. 290). This is the solipsistic principle in action.

As accounted by Steffe and Thompson (2000), the first requirement for shaping such a task environment is for the teacher to come to have a model of the student's current conceptual structures, including the limitations of those structures relative to a mature understanding of the content to be taught (as construed by the teacher). Whereas this model has on occasion been formulated using Piaget's own theoretical constructs (e.g., Steffe, 1994; Thompson, 1994), much of the detail of Piaget's theory has proven "too vague to provide satisfying explanations" (diSessa, 2006, p. 535; see also Goodson-Espy, 1998). Historically, a variety of framings have served as guides for this modeling including cognitive science (e.g., Sloboda & Rogers, 1987); "conceptual metaphor" (Lakoff & Núñez, 2000); "embodied objects"

(Gray & Tall, 2001); and in science education, fixed misconceptions (based on Kuhn), and malleable preconceptions (diSessa, 2006).

Even though Piaget's theoretical apparatus is rarely used, his basic framework of ideas has been deeply informative as to (A) the nature of a useful model, (B) the characteristics of effective task environments, and (C) the teacher's supporting role in the constructive process.

(A) In concert with Piaget's emphasis on the subject's *actions* as the foundation of conceptual schemas, to the extent possible a model should trace the student's intuitions and preconceptions to physical and perceptual operations. As Lakoff and Núñez (2000) put it, "for the most part, human beings conceptualize abstract concepts in concrete terms, using ideas and modes of reasoning grounded in the sensory-motor system" (p. 5). Probative models of students' understanding should trace back to these perceptual and sensory-motor underpinnings.

(B) In concordance with this first principle, task environments designed to produce conceptual learning should establish activity systems that evoke this perceptual and sensory-motor level of grounding. For, as noted earlier, it is such activity systems that can lead to "reflective abstraction" through which schemas are realigned. This rules out " 'conflict' models of instruction" (diSessa, 2006) that merely provide empirical evidence to contradict the student's explanations or predictions (Confrey, 1990; Simon & Tzur, 2004). Such empirical approaches rely instead on conscious "reflected abstraction," which for Piaget is derivative (von Glasersfeld, 1995). Rather, what is needed are full-blooded activity systems that penetrate to the perceptual and sensory-motor level of conceptual structure, as it is this engagement that provides the positive resources the student draws upon in the reconstructive process. Empirical contradiction is not sufficient.

(C) Finally, for a teacher to effectively support the constructive process she/he must be equipped with more than a model of the initial state of the student's understanding, the end goal of a mature understanding, and perhaps intermediate states the student should pass through en route. The teacher also should be able to anticipate how the student's understanding will be transformed by the tasks that are developed to help move the student forward. This total package sometimes is referred to as a *Hypothetical Learning Trajectory* that "consists of the goal for the students' learning, the mathematical task that will be used to promote student learning, and hypotheses about the processes of student learning" (Simon & Tzur, 2004, p. 91). This interest in the process of conceptual change is motivating revision in the conception of the constructivist teaching experiment:

> In some teaching experiments (e.g., Steffe, 2003), the aim of the retrospective analysis is the characterization of the understandings of the student at different points in the learning process. . . . In our adaptation of the teaching experiment . . . the aim of our analyses is to characterize the flow of the students' (changing) thinking, as opposed to only characterizing the resulting understandings.
>
> (Simon, Saldanha, McClintock, et al., 2010, pp. 91–92)

Pulling all of this together, the teacher/researcher in a constructivist teaching experiment needs a significant knowledge base to develop a working model of the student's conception of the content domain, devise a task environment for the student to restructure that understanding, and perceive, through the student's eyes, how the task domain might facilitate conceptual development.

As well, there are interactive competencies that need to play out as the teacher/researcher facilitates student engagement with the task: first, monitoring uptake of the task, making minor adjustments and redirection to try to ensure the student encounters the task as intended; second, assessing whether engagement with the task is progressing along the lines envisioned (one always needs to be ready to rethink and revise both the model of the student's understanding, and the efficacy of the task environment); third (but very tentatively, without disrupting engagement), helping to juxtapose discrepant elements in the student's workspace so as to enhance the transformative potential of the task; and fourth, encouraging the student through the frustrations that arise when conceptual obstacles are encountered (Steffe, 1991). Finally, excluded from this list is the requirement that the teacher provide a neat and tidy summation of the completed activity. In many cases, the experience should be left raw, so that it can continue to work its magic on the restructuring of schemas. "Retroactive thematization" (Piaget, 1977b, Vol. 1, p. 6) should be allowed to happen spontaneously, or prompted only after a delay; premature closure can curtail the mulling-over process that extends reflective abstraction.

Classroom Implementation

The pedagogical model just described is rooted in a clinical research methodology in which a teacher-researcher attends minutely to the conceptual structures of one or two students engaging with tasks devised specifically for them (Steffe & Thompson, 2000). Given an ontology that understands each person's conceptual structures as the unique product of his/her individual experience, how could this pedagogy possibly have application in a classroom context? The solution to the conundrum is that although constructivism theorizes learning as rooted in individual construction, there turns out to often be great commonality in adaptive structures across individuals; Piaget attributed this to constraints on construction imposed by biological and physical reality (Brainerd, 2003; Glick, 1983).[12]

In practice, though, the classroom is a complicated place to attend to student conceptual construction. Having students work on tasks at their own desks may enable individual students to engage with the task, but it limits the possibilities for verbal expression and teacher mediation. Small-group formats provide opportunity for students to express their understandings, but the group's response to a student's ideas generally will not be tailored toward productive reflection by that student. Whole-class instruction enables a teacher to mediate the conversation, but limits the degree of student expression.

To further complicate matters, the conceptual landscape is comprised not of discrete conceptual structures, but of vertically and horizontally interconnected structures (Hiebert & Carpenter, 1992), including vertical linkages created through reification of processes at one level into conceptual objects at another level (Goodson-Espy, 1998; Sfard & Linchevski, 1994). Thus, in addition to designing lessons that target specific concepts, the student-centered constructivist teacher is constantly alert to opportunities that arise in teaching to support emergence of understanding through connections across contents; one's conceptual agenda often is established interactively. The teacher competencies outlined with respect to the constructivist teaching experiment are crucial; however, their deployment often is highly adaptive to the circumstances at hand.

Despite these limitations and complexities, it seems that student-centered constructivist classroom teaching is fairly robust. Given the wide variety of possible implementation modes, many researchers interested in classroom applications of a psychological constructivist ontology have avoided specifying pedagogical methods at all. For example, in their work with teachers, Cognitively Guided Instruction (CGI) researchers simply educated teachers with respect to children's mathematical constructions and then observed the effects on pedagogy, documenting impressive learning gains for these teachers' students (Carpenter, Fennema, Peterson, & Carey, 1988; Moscardini, 2014). Similarly, in science education, "the very general constructivist heuristic of paying attention to naïve ideas seems powerful. . . . Interventions that merely teach teachers about naïve ideas have been surprisingly successful" (diSessa, 2006, p. 276).

Teacher-Centered Constructivist Pedagogy

The pedagogy of student-centered construction just described is highly demanding, requiring intensive problem solving, a significant knowledge base, and real-time responsiveness on the part of the teacher to orchestrate cognitive dissonances and help make them salient for the learner. This high-intensity effort is needed because of the chancy character of conceptual construction:

> Although the effectiveness of cognitive conflict in leading to subjects' conceptual change is corroborated both in the literature on science education and reading education . . . its effect is not automatic. The effectiveness of cognitive conflict depends on the way comprehension is monitored. It depends, first, on the individual noticing the inconsistency and, second, on the way it is resolved.
>
> (Otero, 1998, p. 149)

Otero's (1998) observation points to the facilitative effect that metacognitive sophistication can bestow upon the learner, as being sensitive to subtle incongruities is the key to stimulating the process of reflective abstraction that can lead to conceptual learning (Simon, Tzur, Heinz, & Kinzel, 2004). In this case, a much simpler teacher-centered constructivist pedagogy can be employed, utilizing the most obvious technique for teaching concepts: lecture, in the form of direct explanation of the mature form of a concept. (Note, this is a very particular version of lecture. Lecture also can include interactive elements, can be delivered with sensitivity to students' likely preconceptions, and can provide other supports for student understanding that push much more toward student-centered constructivist instruction, Brown, Manogue, & Sadownik, 2001.)

For the metacognitively sophisticated student, lecture can succeed because the student, sensitive to tensions between elements of the teacher's explanation and their own intuitions, orchestrates their own cognitive conflicts by generating hypothetical situations that create dissonances with their current conceptual structures. In this case, the teacher's role is limited to organizing and delivering the mature form of the concept. She/he need not have a model of the student's understanding, nor design and mediate tasks relative to that model. Indeed, the teacher need not even adopt a constructivist perspective on learning and teaching, but may happily believe him or herself to be transmitting their understanding directly to the student.

It should be noted that the level of metacognitive capability needed is indexed to the conceptual complexity of the content being taught. Lecture is fully appropriate as a pedagogical method whenever the student's metacognitive sophistication is sufficient to accommodate the gap between current and mature forms of the concept. Students who are relatively sophisticated metacognitively may be unable to productively integrate lecture material concerning very difficult concepts. And even students who are relatively unsophisticated metacognitively can benefit from lecture for simple conceptual content.

LEARNING AS ENCULTURATION

I take *enculturation* to be the process of acquiring dispositions through enmeshment in a cultural community. I interpret *dispositions* broadly as culturally particular ways of engaging with people, problems, artifacts, or oneself. Alternatively, one might say that enculturation is the acquisition of cultural practices, except that as analytic objects, practices are located in the culture, and distributed across actors (Hutchins, 1995; Nardi, 1996), whereas dispositions are properties of an individual. For the purposes of crossdisciplinary theorizing, it seems advantageous to identify learning as attained at the level of the individual (even if the process of learning is social).

The likelihood of acquiring a disposition may be influenced by genetic predispositions. For instance, one might say of someone they have a predisposition toward logical thinking, or they're naturally inclined to be shy. However, predispositions to engage only find expression as dispositions within a cultural context. This interpretation is consistent with the personality theory of German psychologist William Stern, who believed that "all characteristics of personality are properly regarded not as fixed determinants, whether partial or complete, of behavior or states of psychological being . . . but rather as *potentialities*. . . . It is only through extended interaction with the world that the range of such potentialities can gradually become constricted, so that what is initially but a mild tendency in one direction allowing for many other possibilities can become a relative inclination"(Lamiell, 2013, pp. 108–109).

This sense of disposition differs from the more typical cognitive science rendering in which cognitive practices (e.g., critical thinking, metacognition, general problem solving strategies) are naturalized as capabilities of the cognitive apparatus, rather than understood as manifestations of culture at the level of the individual (Scribner & Cole, 1977). Dispositions, thus, are reduced to inclinations or tendencies to employ those capabilities. For instance, Perkins and Ritchhart (2004) present a framework for good thinking based on "viewing dispositions as initiators and motivators of abilities rather than [thinking] abilities themselves" (p. 179).

Internalization of culture is vigorously theorized in the work of Soviet-era psychologist Lev Vygotsky, his many students and collaborators, and in the sociocultural and activity theory schools that ensued. The sociogenetic orientation of Vygotsky's work is clearly expressed in his Genetic Law: "Any function in the child's cultural development appears on stage twice, on two planes. First it appears on the social plane, then on the psychological, first among people as an interpsychical category and then within the child as an intrapsychical category" (Vygotsky, 1978, p. 57).

However, the sociogenetic orientation of Vygotsky's work is complicated by his desire to provide a comprehensive theory of human development and learning that accounts for both shaping and being shaped by culture. Thus he rejected "a static notion of social determination" (Penuel & Wertsch, 1995, p. 84). As Cole (1996) put it, for Vygotsky,

> The dual process of shaping and being shaped through culture implies that humans inhabit "intentional" (constituted) worlds within which the traditional dichotomies of subject and object, person and environment, and so on cannot be analytically separated and temporally ordered into independent and dependent variables.
>
> (p. 103)

What is more, Vygotsky (1978) understood development (i.e., internalization of higher mental cultural practices) and learning (skills and concepts) as mutually interdependent: "Our hypothesis establishes the unity but not the identity of learning processes and internal developmental processes. It presupposes that the one is converted into the other" (pp. 90–91).

Sociological Theory

Although Vygotsky comes closest in psychology to a pure sociogenetic position, his dialectical stance and the integrative complexity of his theories limit the utility of this body of theory as a framework for the enculturation metaphor for learning (though I do draw on specific aspects of sociocultural psychology, and also find great resonance with Vygotsky's own pedagogical insights). Indeed, Western social science has such a strong individualist slant that even in sociology, "most sociologists, both individualists and collectivists, . . . [accept the] position . . . known as *ontological individualism*: the ontological position that only individuals exist" (Sawyer, 2002a, p. 555). Still, within sociology, ideas of *irreducible emergence* stemming from the work of Emile Durkheim are consistent with a social causation position I take to be the essence of the enculturation metaphor: "Durkheim's ([1895] 1964) emergentist account of the autonomy of sociology was foundationally based on emergent (or 'sui generis') social properties having causal force on the individual" (Sawyer, 2002a, p. 558; see Sawyer, 2002b, for a fuller discussion of Durkheim's legacy).

The social psychology of personal space, or proxemics (Hall, 1966; Li, 2001), provides a paradigm example of social causation. Proxemics is the tendency for members of a national culture to draw specific perimeters around their physical bodies for various social purposes. For example, natives of France tend to prefer closer physical proximity for conversation than do Americans (Remland, Jones, & Brinkman, 1991). Clearly, proxemic dispositions are acquired by natives of a culture without volition or conscious awareness, through enmeshment in the cultural milieu. Indeed, according to sociologist Talcott Parsons (1951), for social norms to be "normative" they have to be outside the realm of conscious reflection, or they become merely additional instrumental resources for action:

> There is a range of possible modes of orientation in the motivational sense to a value standard. Perhaps the most important distinction is between that attitude of expediency at one pole, where conformity or non-conformity is a function of the instrumental interests of the actor, and at the other pole the 'introjection' or internalization of the standard so that to act in conformity with it becomes a need disposition in the actor's own personality structure, relatively independently of any instrumentally significant consequences of conformity. The latter is to be regarded as the basic type of integration of motivation with a normative pattern-structure of values. (p. 37)

I take unconscious *introjection* in Parsons' sense as the essential mechanism of enculturation. However, this pure form of enculturation is possible only in a unitary culture in which a single dispositional variation is salient for the subject. One also can come to be enculturated into a subculture with practices that are distinctive among a range of alternative subcultures (e.g., being a jock, being a scientist, being a gang member). In such instances, inductees may actively *acculturate* themselves to a subculture by emulating its distinctive cultural practices. Although acculturation is the more salient process, and historically was identified much earlier (Powell, 1883), it needs to be understood as supplementary to the basic unconscious processes of enculturation going on around it all the time. A culture is comprised of innumerable cultural practices, of which only a limited number can be addressed through conscious strategies of emulation (Kirshner & Meng, 2011).

Student-centered Enculturation Pedagogy

The enculturation/acculturation distinction defines the two pedagogical genres associated with the enculturation metaphor, a student-centered *enculturation pedagogy* appropriate for all students, and a teacher-centered *acculturation pedagogy* appropriate for students who are identified with the reference culture and seek to become part of it. In the enculturation pedagogy, the teacher begins by identifying a reference culture and target disposition(s) within that culture. The instructional focus is on the classroom microculture, which the enculturationist teacher works to shape so that it comes to more closely resemble the reference culture with respect to the target dispositions. Students, thus, come to acquire approximations of the target dispositions through their enmeshment in the surrogate culture of the classroom through the same unconscious processes by which proxemic dispositions are acquired in a national culture. Vygotsky (1926/1997) clearly articulated the foundations of enculturation pedagogy:

> From the psychological point of view, the teacher is the director of the social environment in the classroom, the governor and guide of the interaction between the educational process and the student. . . . Though the teacher is powerless to produce immediate effects in the student, he is all-powerful when it comes to producing direct effects in him through the social environment. The social environment is the true lever of the educational process, and the teacher's overall role reduces to adjusting this lever. . . . Thus, it is that the teacher educates the student by varying the environment.
>
> (p. 49)

Yackel and Cobb (1996) provide valuable perspectives on how such a pedagogy is structured. In their discussion of *sociomathematical norms* as targeted dispositions of mathematical culture (e.g., the appreciation of mathematically elegant solutions) that come to be "interactively constituted by each classroom community" (p. 475), they note what amounts to a "chicken and egg" problem: students can acquire the target dispositions only to the extent these practices already are constituted within the classroom microculture. Yackel and Cobb (1996) borrow the construct of "reflexivity" from ethnomethodology (Leiter, 1980; Mehan & Wood, 1975) to elucidate the problem:

> With regard to sociomathematical norms, what becomes mathematically normative in a classroom is constrained by the current goals, beliefs, suppositions, and assumptions of the classroom participants. At the same time these goals and largely implicit understandings are themselves influenced by what is legitimized as acceptable mathematical activity. It is in this sense that we say sociomathematical norms and goals and beliefs about mathematical activity and learning are reflexively related.
>
> (p. 460)

The solution to this problem constitutes the critical expertise of the enculturationist teacher. As Yackel and Cobb (1996) illustrate, through subtleties of attention and encouragement the teacher, over time, exerts considerable influence on the modes of engagement manifest within the classroom microculture (Vygotsky, 1926/1997). For significant enculturational goals, this must be a progressive agenda in which modes of engagement initially encouraged by the teacher reach a level of general currency in the classroom microculture, eventually to be replaced by yet more sophisticated forms of engagement.

Supposing, for instance, one wishes to teach the characteristic mode of argumentation known as mathematical proof (Pedamonte, 2007; Stylianides & Stylianides, 2009) to young students who typically support their arguments with reference to the authority of textbook and teacher—Harel and Sowder (2007) refer to these as "external conviction proof schemes" (p. 809). By betraying signs of interest whenever internal conviction arguments are offered (regardless how unsophisticated), the teacher may gradually shift the norms of classroom argumentation toward "empirical proof schemes," even though what ultimately is sought are "deductive proof schemes" (p. 809). As in this case, learning of significant cultural practices may require a coordinated effort over months and years.

In keeping with the characterization of enculturation, the critical characteristic of enculturation pedagogy is that the teacher's agenda for participation remain implicit. This does not mean the enculturationist teacher is limited to the (relatively passive) tools of encouragement. As a member of the classroom community, the teacher can introduce modes of engagement through her or his own participation. However, in either case the teacher's agenda for participation must remain implicit (Parsons, 1951). As soon as it becomes explicit, we enter into a politics of cultural identity that demarcates a shift to acculturation pedagogy.

Teacher-Centered Enculturation Pedagogy (Acculturation Pedagogy)

In keeping with the characterization of acculturation, the critical student characteristic that authorizes acculturation pedagogy is self-identification with the reference culture. In this case, the teacher's primary pedagogical role is to model the characteristic practices of the culture. This instructional process provides students who are identified with the reference culture and seek to become part of it an opportunity to appropriate these cultural resources and incorporate them into their evolving repertoire of participatory practices. The instructional process can be informally structured interactively as cultural participation of the teacher with the student (for example, when a mathematician leading investigations with a math club exhibits modes of thinking, values, and problem solving practices that are particular to mathematics culture). In this case, the agenda for appropriation of cultural practices can remain tacit. Alternatively, the teacher can coach the inductee with respect to performance of target cultural practices, in which case the curriculum of cultural practices becomes explicit.

The prerequisite for the acculturationist teacher is that she/he be sufficiently well embedded within the reference culture to model cultural practices effectively—in Ma's (1999) words, "only teachers who are acculturated to mathematics can foster their students' ability to conduct mathematical inquiry" (p. 106). Beyond that, she/he must *signify* for the student as a bona fide member of the reference culture, so that cultural practices modeled by the teacher are experienced as worthy of emulation. Note, this is a different requirement than that specified for the enculturationist teacher whose knowledge of the characteristic practices of the culture must be explicit, and must also include developmental perspectives on those practices.

In school settings, acculturationist pedagogy has obvious application to after-school clubs or to magnet programs into which students have self-selected based on their identity aspirations; however, it may be of limited utility in general K-12 education—and even in much undergraduate level university education! A few years ago, I had the opportunity to coteach a senior-level undergraduate mathematics course with two mathematics colleagues. The purpose of the course was to help students understand, appreciate, and participate more fully in mathematical culture. My colleagues, both senior members of a highly ranked mathematics department, had considerable experience in successfully mentoring doctoral students. The approach they took in our course involved assigning the students problems, discussing the problems with them, and in the process modeling their own unprescribed solution approaches, following fascinating tangents arising from the original problem, communicating their broad perspectives on mathematics, and sharing their excitement and passion for the field. I presume these are methods they would typically employ, with good effect, with doctoral students—students already self-identified as mathematicians. However, the senior undergraduate mathematics majors in the course—many in a teacher education program—generally were not self-identified as mathematicians, and hence were unable to appreciate or make use of the rich cultural resources that these instructors offered.

Identity Politics

As discussed earlier, acculturation pedagogy can be practiced through an informal relationship of students with a teacher-as-cultural-representative, or it can be a formal mentorship in which the curriculum of cultural practices to be mastered is explicit. In the latter case, it is possible to configure instruction so that adoption of cultural practices is mandatory.

In the case of an explicit and mandatory acculturationist curriculum, there is a risk if one applies the pedagogy to students who are not self-identified with the reference culture that the cultural demands of the instruction may produce "intrapersonal conflict" for the student (Brown, 2004, p. 810; see also, Bishop, 2012; Clark, Badertscher, & Napp, 2013; Gutiérrez, 2002; Kincheloe & Steinberg, 2007; Nasir & Saxe, 2003; Rubin, 2007; Vågan, 2011). As Aikenhead and Jegede (1999) noted with respect to science education,

> When the culture of science is generally at odds with a student's life-world, science instruction will tend to disrupt the student's worldview by trying to force that student to abandon or marginalize his or her life-world concepts and reconstruct in their place new (scientific) ways of conceptualizing. This process is *assimilation*. Assimilation can alienate students from their indigenous life-world culture, thereby causing various social disruptions (Baker & Taylor, 1995; Maddock, 1981); or alternatively, attempts at assimilation can alienate students from science.
>
> (p. 274)

Ethical Principle: I don't want to minimize the complexity of ethical questions that flow from the use of acculturationist pedagogy with students who are not already identified with the reference culture—for example, to suggest science should not be a universally required school subject. These questions have a long and important history (Apple & Au, 2014) that is beyond the scope of this chapter. However, the enculturation/acculturation distinction is newly introduced in the crossdisciplinary framework (Kirshner, 2004; Kirshner & Meng, 2011), giving us an opportunity to propose an important principle related to the two enculturation pedagogies: *Ethical concerns regarding intrapersonal cultural conflict that may arise for acculturationist pedagogy do not arise for enculturationist pedagogy.*

The crux of my argument is that in a pluralistic society, cultures are always in transition under the influence of contact with other cultures. Society is teeming with cultural influences that individuals are exposed to in the course of normal social intercourse. In the process, identity structures develop and morph. Yet, as Kim (1988) noted, there are inbuilt "stress-adaptation-growth dynamics of cross-cultural experiences, which bring about cultural strangers' gradual transformation toward increased functional fitness in the host milieu" (p. 200), dynamics that are adaptive to new cultural influences, yet also responsive to the subject's experienced need for cultural continuity. Thus students involved in enculturation pedagogy in which the curriculum of target dispositions is tacit, adapt to the evolving culture of the classroom—or not!—at their own pace, and in their own way.

CROSSDISCIPLINARY ANALYSIS OF PEDAGOGICAL PRACTICE

The Method of Crossdisciplinary Analysis

The metaphors for learning as theorized in the preceding section are taken to reflect our culture's basic understandings of learning (Fletcher, 1995), and thus to drive our varied pedagogical enterprises across the broad spectrum of education. In this respect, the crossdisciplinary framework is intended not so much to provide a new constellation of pedagogical practices, as to organize and refine the varied streams of ideation that currently are tangled together within our integrative discourse (Kirshner, 2002).

To support this claim, I introduce a method of *crossdisciplinary analysis* of pedagogy. This method involves examining the details of implementation to assess whether skills are promoted, whether concepts are promoted, and whether dispositions are promoted. If it seems the answer to any of these is yes, it is incumbent upon the analyst to identify the particular skills, concepts, or dispositions being addressed, to examine the pedagogy to determine whether a student-centered or teacher-centered approach is being used, and to evaluate the efficacy of the pedagogy according to the pedagogical principles laid out in the preceding section. In case multiple pedagogical methods are invoked in the instructional approach, the analyst determines which learning goal predominates and evaluates whether the coordination of pedagogical methods is organized in a coherent and consistent fashion.

In this section, I apply this method to a broad array of key pedagogical practices with the goal of demonstrating that crossdisciplinarity spans the familiar terrain of pedagogical interests—many of which are framed through the integrative and holistic perspectives on learning that currently dominate educational thought. The method of crossdisciplinary analysis serves as a refractive lens, pulling apart the component strands of ideation, often revealing weaknesses and inconsistencies that have been obscured in the prior viewpoint. As well, our current integrative frameworks lead to a kind of homogeneity of thought. The spectrum of reform pedagogies, for instance, involve a balance in which "knowledge is personally constructed and socially mediated" (Windschitl, 2002, p. 137), the variation residing in the degree of emphasis given to each. The crossdisciplinary approach has a different ethos in which, yes, diverse agendas for learning can be coordinated together—but there is no holistic or dialectical imperative to do so. Thus the palette of pedagogical possibility can include wild singletons oriented by a single learning metaphor that we've not previously been able to recognize or appreciate; the final subsection of this section, analyzes one such pedagogical method.

Caveat emptor: Although the individual analyses presented here may be compelling for readers, the broader intention for this section is to support the proposal that a small set of theoretical tools spans (and expands) the totality of our pedagogical interests in promoting student learning. Initially, the analyses presented here may be experienced as independent critiques of educational practices. But over time, and with the experience of performing one's own analyses (these examples are merely illustrative) the critiques coalesce as part of a coherent educational viewpoint. The refractive lens of crossdisciplinarity establishes itself, reflexively, as one's only window to the problems and possibilities of pedagogy.

B. F. Skinner's Programmed Instruction

To illustrate the method of crossdisciplinary analysis, I begin with an instructional method of historical importance. Skinner (1958b) introduced individually paced programmed instruction as an application of behavioral principles, one that he regarded as central to his legacy to education (Morris, 2003). In this instructional format, students are presented with a succession of text fragments (one or two sentences) each with a blank in place of a key word. The students' role is to read the text and supply the missing datum. The frames are sequenced in such a way as to promote incremental progress from simple initial prompts to complex terminal performance. In this way it is anticipated students easily can maintain the 95% success criterion for progress to the next programmed lesson. Feedback is immediate and ongoing so as to reinforce participation (Morris, 2003).

To illustrate programmed instruction, Skinner (1958b, p. 973) presented a science lesson dealing with electric currents and flashlight circuitry (see also Morris, 2003, pp. 242–243). The first few statements from the sequence of 35 statements are given in Table 4.2. We examine this instruction through the three lenses of the crossdisciplinary framework to determine the nature and quality of the learning opportunities provided to students.

Habituation: Given the authorship of these programmed instruction materials, we might expect to find that verbal response skills with respect to science vocabulary are promoted in this curriculum in keeping with the "traditional . . . belief that learning physics means memorizing facts, definitions, and formulas" (White, 1993, p. 5). Indeed, Skinner's (1958b) description of his strategy does touch on repetition of terms:

> Technical terms are introduced slowly. For example, the familiar term "fine wire" in frame 2 is followed by a definition of the technical term "filament" in frame 4; "filament" is then asked for in the presence of the non-scientific synonym in frame 5 and without the synonym in frame 9.
>
> (p. 974)

However, whereas word familiarity may be developed through this lesson, and perhaps some weak association to proximal terms, there is no rehearsal required or memorization being

Table 4.2 Part of a programmed instruction unit used by Skinner (1958b) to illustrate teaching machines.

Sentence to be Completed	Word to be Supplied
1. The important parts of a flashlight are the battery and the bulb. When we "turn on" a flashlight, we close a switch which connects . . . the battery with the _____.	bulb
2. When we turn on a flashlight, an electric current flows through the fine wire in the _____ and causes it to grow hot.	bulb
3. When the hot wire glows brightly, we say . . . it gives off or sends out heat and _____.	light
4. The fine wire in the bulb is called a filament. The bulb "lights up" when the filament is heated by the passage of a(n) _____ current.	electric
5. When a weak battery produces little current, the fine wire, or _____, does not get very hot.	filament
6. A filament which is *less* hot sends out or gives off _____ light.	less
7. "Emit" means "send out." The amount of light sent out, or "emitted", by a filament depends on how _____ the filament is.	hot

tested (in contrast to other examples given in Skinner, 1958b, such as word spellings, p. 972). Indeed, the learning outcomes Skinner (1958b) touts relate to goals of understanding more so than response conditioning:

> The net effect of such material is more than the acquisition of facts and terms. Beginning with a largely unverbalized acquaintance with flashlights, candles, and so on, the student is induced to talk about familiar events, together with a few new facts, with a fairly technical vocabulary. . . . The emission of light from an incandescent source takes shape as a topic or field of inquiry. An understanding of the subject emerges which is often quite surprising in view of the fragmentation required in item building.
>
> (p. 974)

Construction: Examining the pedagogical method with respect to the construction metaphor, we observe that the programmed text forms a kind of lecture on electric current that the student is expected to read and understand, the participatory activity of supplying the missing word serving to ensure the student is attending to and processing each sentence. The primary pedagogical method, therefore, is teacher-centered construction aimed at gaining an understanding of the physics of the light production in a flashlight.

We might ask if a teacher-centered approach is appropriate given the conceptual complexity of electrical current flow. Indeed, Wandersee, Mintzes, and Novak (1994) noted that current flow is regularly misunderstood by students who construct a variety of incorrect conceptual models that science education needs to address:

> Five distinct models of a simple circuit were employed by these students. The "single-wire" notion suggests that current leaves the battery and travels through one wire to a bulb, which serves as a kind of electricity "sink." In the "clashing currents" model, electricity leaves the battery from both terminals and travels toward the bulb, where it is "used up." In addition to these ideas, three kinds of "unidirectional models" were identified. . . . "Unidirectional with conservation" . . . is the scientifically acceptable view.
>
> (p. 182)

Thus Skinner's (1958b) science lesson aims toward a rather cursory understanding of electrical circuits. In this respect, his instructional method, teacher-centered construction, is well matched to the content. For, as noted earlier, lecturing on complex conceptual content would be successful only for students who are metacognitively sophisticated; otherwise, student-centered construction methods would be required.

Enculturation: In addition to teaching the conceptual content, programmed instruction was believed to "teach students to study, for instance, to attend selectively to texts and to reject irrelevant material" (Morris, 2003, p. 244). In the crossdisciplinary framing, these learning goals would count as dispositions—culturally specific forms of engagement.

A full crossdisciplinary analysis would involve identifying the reference culture (perhaps academic culture) in which the intended dispositions are normative, and examining the culture of participation of students in working through this instruction. Students in my graduate course on theories of learning, going through the full sequence of 35 text fragments, report a tendency to word hunt to fill in the blanks, with minimal linguistic and semantic processing. So it is not obvious the extent to which enculturational goals intended by the curriculum are met.

Skinner (1958b) intended his exposition on teaching machines as an illustration of the application of behavioral principles. This is consistent with his effort to interpret language production in behaviorist terms (Skinner, 1958a), which Chomsky (1959) argued did not properly meet behaviorism's own criteria for objective analysis. From our current vantage point, and with the assistance of crossdisciplinary analysis, it seems obvious that the programmed materials presented an explanation of the physics of electrical flow in a flashlight that students were expected to understand. There is no apparent habituated learning agenda being enacted. Thus, to a considerable extent, Skinner was creating conceptually oriented instructional materials without clear principles of learning to guide his efforts.

In the case of these programmed materials, we were lucky: his instructional materials did provide a coherent approach for students to learn concepts, albeit at a rather unambitious level. However, flying without adequate maps is a risky business. As we point the lens of crossdisciplinarity at contemporary education we often find normative curricular methods to be deeply incoherent in their agendas for learning.

The "Reading Wars"

We turn to the Reading Wars, which serves also as an introduction to the next section on the Math Wars. In our current discourse these two controversies are regarded as siblings, rehearsing basic disputes about learning and teaching that trace back over a century of conflict: "The 'education sects' that Dewey described so long ago still exist [today]—in reading, in the proponents of 'whole language' and in 'phonics,' and in math, in the advocates and opponents of 'NCTM math reform'" (Loveless, 2001, p. 2). Through crossdisciplinary lenses, we come to see stark differences in the structure of learning intentions underlying these controversies, and in the quality of the pedagogical practices that ensue.

The Reading Wars pit advocates of "phonics" (Burns, Griffin, & Snow, 1999; Fox, 2000; Stanovich, 1986) against "whole-language" advocates (e.g., Dechant, 1993; Goodman, 1986; Serpell, 2001). The phonics method provides repetitive practice in a systematic and sequential fashion starting with basic linguistic elements (graphemes, phonemes), building up to words, sentences, and more extended texts that incorporate the constituent elements already practiced:

> Phonics advocates see reading primarily as a challenging cognitive, psycholinguistic accomplishment—knowing letters and sounds and being able to perform in a certain way when asked to map one onto the other.
>
> (Snow, 2001, p. 232)

Whole-language methods focus on dispositions of literate society, including inclination to read and strategies of effective reading. Whole-language advocates insist that students' involvement with text always be meaningful in the twin senses that texts are comprehensible[13] and that activities of reading are motivated by personal interest and involvement. The pedagogical method is to create a social community in which children engage with reading and writing in pursuit of their interests and communicative needs:

> Whole-language advocates see reading as a social, cultural activity—participating in communities of practice within which reading and writing are normal activities and thus are acquired as needed by all members.
>
> (Snow, 2001, p. 232)

From a crossdisciplinary reading, both of these pedagogical methods are soundly constituted. Phonics approaches the skills of reading in a systematic and effective fashion through sequenced repetitive practice. Whole language provides a coherent blending of acculturationist support for students' evolving self-identity as readers with the enculturationist strategy of providing a social microculture within which practices of literacy are normative. Indeed, it is telling that antagonists in the Reading Wars rarely criticize their opponents with respect to the learning outcomes actually supported by instruction. Rather phonics advocates worry that whole language leaves students without needed skills (e.g., Dahl, Scharer, Lawson, & Grogan, 1999), while whole language advocates find that phonics methods neglect valued dispositions (e.g., Krashen, 2003).

At a pragmatic level, this might suggest the reasonableness of coordinating these two pedagogies, a suggestion sometimes labeled "a balanced approach" (Honig, 1996). However, our educational discourse, which countenances only one "true" account of learning (and hence of good teaching), makes pragmatic accommodations difficult to realize. The incendiary bitterness of the Reading Wars is well known, having spilled over from the academy into the legislative arena (Boyd & Mitchell, 2001; Goodman, 1998), thereby materially constraining the autonomy of educators to exercise professional judgment.

The "Math Wars"

The Math Wars pits traditionalists combining demonstration/lecture and worksheet drills against reformers who prefer inquiry teaching approaches (Draper, 2002; Klein, 2007; Schoen, Fey, Hirsch, & Coxford, 1999; Wilson, 2003). Traditional textbooks organize mathematics instruction topically, with explanation of the current topic being followed by homogeneously grouped problems related to the content. In this way, concepts and skills are intended to reinforce one another. Reformers generally provide collaborative work on open-ended tasks designed to foster valued mathematical dispositions such as autonomy, creativity, and problem-solving heuristics. As well, the tasks are centered around critical conceptual content, affording development of deep understanding of the content. Thus, in contrast with the Reading Wars, the Math Wars features competing blended pedagogies—skills and concepts versus concepts and dispositions.

Traditional Instruction

Characterizing the instructional position of the traditionalists in the Math Wars is hampered by the fact that "the term 'traditional' was never clearly defined in the debates" (Klein, 2007). Indeed, the Math Wars arose as a reaction to the NCTM's (1989) *Standards*, so much of the traditionalist cause has simply been to retain the traditional methods of U.S. mathematics instruction, which have been characterized as follows: "Teachers present definitions of terms and demonstrate procedures for solving specific problems. Students are then asked to memorize the definitions and practice the procedures" (Stigler & Hiebert, 1999, p. 27). What is not clear is the extent to which demonstration (Clark, Nguyen, & Sweller, 2006) and memorization are intended by traditionalists to be supplemented by explanation of underlying principles (lecture). However, since the ranks of the traditionalists included many prominent university mathematicians (Klein, Askey, Milgram, Wu, et al., 1999), perhaps explanation and demonstration are intended to go hand-in-hand.

   Construction: As explained earlier, from a crossdisciplinary view demonstration of procedures serves habituationist, rather than conceptual goals. Demonstration focuses the perceptual apparatus on relevant aspects of the stimulus display, thereby facilitating subcognitive correlations that are the basis of skilled performance (Reber, 1993). Thus the conceptual agenda is supported only insofar as the instructor interweaves conceptual explanation of why the procedure works along with demonstration of how it works. In cases in which explanation of principles supplements demonstration of procedures, the instructional method is teacher-centered conceptual pedagogy, effective only for those students who are sufficiently sophisticated, metacognitively, to notice incongruities between their own understanding and the explanations offered by the teacher (Otero, 1998). Thus the conceptual intentions of traditional instruction are inconsistently supported, and even then only for a small minority of students.

   Habituation: The habituationist agenda also is compromised in this pedagogical approach. In order to focus on conceptual content, textbooks are organized topically, with homogeneously grouped problem sets meant to reinforce concepts presented in the current chapter. The homogenous grouping of exercises means that, with the exception of review practice tests, there is no opportunity for students to learn to discriminate problem types. Students learn *how* to apply routine solution methods, but not *when* to apply them, making robust skill mastery problematic (Greeno, 1978; VanderStoep & Seifert, 1993).

To understand this limitation of traditional mathematics textbooks it is instructive to consider the method of "gentle repetition" developed in the early 1980s by John Saxon. Saxon's textbooks dispense with the trappings of conceptual explanation, providing only a brief introduction of new content, moving quickly to engaging students in heterogeneous problem sets. In this way, brags Saxon, "as the problems become familiar students can look at a new problem and recognize it by type. This recognition evokes conditioned responses that lead to solutions" (Saxon Publishers, 1992, inside front cover). From a crossdisciplinary perspective, the Saxon approach is effectively structured for habituation learning, and its superiority to traditional approaches to skill development has been empirically documented (e.g., Resendez & Azin, 2007). (As an interesting historical footnote, so distraught was the mathematics education establishment at Saxon's dropping of the trappings of a conceptual agenda that it was a request for advice concerning Saxon texts that prompted the NCTM's initial steps toward its 1989 standards, McLeod, Stake, Schappelle, & Mellissinos, 1995.)

To summarize, traditionalists in the Math Wars support an instructional format that simply juxtaposes problem sets (toward skill development) and lecture (toward concept development), based on the pervasive belief that "conceptual understanding . . . and operational procedures . . . are mutually reinforcing" (National Mathematics Advisory Panel [NMAP], 2008, p. xix). As discussed earlier, this is an illusory belief encouraged by the facilitative effect that explicit presentation of rules plays in the rate of skill acquisition (Kirshner & Awtry, 2004; Reber, 1993). It has kept us from seeing how deficient is the support of both skill development and concept attainment, and, indeed, how these elements of traditional instruction subvert one another.

Reform Instruction

Mathematics education reform participates in a broader pedagogical reform movement generally oriented by the learning metaphors of construction and enculturation as framed in a spectrum of constructivist, social constructivist, situated cognition, and sociocultural theorizations (Donovan & Bransford, 2005). Infrequently, a purely (psychological) constructivist agenda is advanced (Simon, Saldanha, McClintock, et al., 2010; Thompson, 2013), or else one finds goals and methods that are entirely enculturational (Mark, Cuoco, Goldenberg, & Sword, 2010). But these distinctions are not easily marked owing to our current integrative discourse that regards learning as a complex, multifaceted whole, with reform pedagogy "a useful synthesis . . . [wherein] knowledge is personally constructed and socially mediated" (Windschitl, 2002, p. 137).

Typically the reform classroom is structured around *inquiry groups, communities of learners, knowledge-building communities* or other such collaborative fora intended to promote deep understanding of mathematical content in tandem with valued cultural practices, including mathematics-specific practices like mathematical argumentation (proof), problem solving heuristics, and aesthetic values, as well as more general practices of intellectual autonomy, critical thinking, and creativity (e.g., Brown & Campione, 1994; Hutchison, 2012; Mark et al., 2010; NRC, 2000, 2005; Scardamalia & Bereiter, 2003). Instruction typically involves open-ended questions, nonroutine problems, or projects that students work on and discuss. The tasks are chosen for their rich conceptual affordances, so that collaborative discussion and exploration can lead to in-depth understanding of concepts as well as evolution of valued dispositions (Brooks & Brooks, 1999).

From a crossdisciplinary perspective coordination of teaching genres is viable as an instructional strategy, so long as the teacher understands that the constituent teaching approaches are inherently inconsistent with one another and hence inevitably lead to choice points in which one agenda advances only at the expense of the other. As discussed earlier, student-centered construction is very much a teacher-modulated pedagogy. The teacher creates a task environment for the student based on a Hypothetical Learning Trajectory along which student engagement is anticipated to progress. To support the unfolding of this trajectory, the teacher may need to mediate students' initial uptake of tasks and otherwise intensify students' engagement with the task. In contrast, enculturational goals of student autonomy and creativity require the teacher to foster a classroom culture in which students are empowered to pursue evolving interests as they arise in the course of problem solving. Thus the effective reform teacher is in a state of consternation, supporting the cultural dynamics of group interaction while constantly monitoring the conversations, worrying that discussions may not be productive conceptually, and making judicious moment-by-moment decisions about whether (and how) to intervene as a mediator of conceptual construction while doing minimal damage to the agenda of student autonomy and exploration. As Lampert (1985) put it, "the juxtaposition of responsibilities that make up the teacher's job leads to conceptual paradoxes" for which there is no single right choice. The teacher "brings many contradictory aims to each instance of her work, and the resolution of their dissonance cannot be neat or simple" (Lampert, 1985, p. 181, quoted in Ball, 1993, p. 377).

Metacognition

To understand how seriously this hybrid agenda of balancing and juggling is compromised within a rhetoric of reform teaching rooted in integrative or holistic visions of learning/teaching, it is instructive to examine the central and crucial role that metacognition has come to play in contemporary pedagogical theorizing. Indeed, in Bransford, Brown, and Cocking's (2000) canonical text, *How People Learn*, metacognition is emphasized as one of three fundamental aspect of instruction:

> Integration of metacognitive instruction with discipline-based learning can enhance student achievement and develop in students the ability to learn independently. It should be consciously incorporated into curricula across disciplines and age levels.
>
> (p. 21)

Current theoretical interests in metacognition trace back to foundational work of both Vygotsky and Piaget (Fox & Riconscente, 2008). As we have discussed, for Vygotsky, metacognitive capabilities (and other higher mental functions) arise from internalization of social/cultural practices. Olson (2003) applies this perspective to explain how metacognitive capabilities can develop in collaborative groups in that justification of one's ideas to others comes to be internalized as a kind of self-scrutiny: "The normative practice of reason giving and metacognition run together. Explanation, the giving of explicit or public reasons, is . . . the route to metacognition, that is, cognition about cognition" (p. 241).

For Piaget (1975), metacognition figured centrally in his genetic epistemology, deeply implicated in the notion of reflective abstraction, the primary mechanism for conceptual restructuring:

> Reflective abstraction always involves two inseparable features: a "reflechissement" in the sense of the projection of something borrowed from a preceding level onto a higher one, and a "reflexion" in the sense of a (more or less conscious) cognitive reconstruction or reorganization of what has been transferred.
>
> (p.41, quoted in von Glasersfeld, 1991)

Pulling these two strands together, we can begin to see the contradictory implications of Bransford, Brown, and Cocking's (2000) utilization of metacognition in their framing of pedagogical practice, as quoted earlier. On the one hand, "develop[ing] in students the ability to learn independently" (p. 21) is an enculturationist goal of instruction that involves developing students' metacognitive capabilities. As we have discussed, such enculturational agendas unfold over months and years. On the other hand, the idea that "metacognitive instruction with discipline-based learning can enhance student achievement" (p. 21) points to the facilitative role that metacognition plays in concept development. Thus metacognition is revealed as the soft underbelly of reform pedagogy. Like a cat trying to catch its tail, always just out of reach, metacognition is both a goal of instruction and a requirement for its effective realization.

Pointing out the contradictory invocation of metacognition in reform pedagogy is not meant to discredit the agenda of teaching concepts and dispositions in tandem with one another, but rather to highlight the problematic character of such instruction, and the concomitant necessity that teachers be primed to recognize the contradictory imperatives of these teaching genres. But, this need to juggle, to retreat and advance simultaneously, is precisely what is elided in a discourse grounded in holistic thinking based on assumed "synergies" (Bransford et al., 2006), or on integrative sociocultural and situated cognition theorizations in which "the *learning* of a subject's cognitive content is considered a process embedded within the more comprehensive process of enculturation" (Perrenet & Taconis, 2009, p. 182).

There will always be some individual teachers like Lampert and Ball who come to sense and engage with the problematic of multiple learning agendas (see Green, 2014, for an analysis of their influence). But for most teachers, reform is simply enactment of a format of classroom activity, the hope of educational value sustained by "an inordinate amount of faith in the ability of students to structure their own learning" (Windschitl, 2002, p. 138).

In summary, the Math Wars pits traditionalists valuing skills and concepts against reformers intent on fostering concepts and dispositions. In both cases, the good intentions of educators are stymied at the point of intersection of these learning agendas for the simple reason that the assumed concordance of skills and concepts or of concepts and dispositions has not been subjected to critical theoretical scrutiny. In the case of the Reading Wars our students have been lucky; the unnecessary antagonisms are between independently coherent pedagogical visions. In the case of mathematics, in the United States a student's chances of receiving coherently conceived instruction—traditional or reform—are vanishingly small.

Pedagogies of Societal Transformation

This subsection and the next are devoted to the enculturation metaphor as theorized in terms of the enculturation/acculturation distinction. This distinction, separating out unconscious adaptation from conscious emulation, is newly introduced in the crossdisciplinary framework (Kirshner, 2004; Kirshner & Meng, 2011). For instance, Yackel and Cobb (1996) presented a clear theorization of enculturation pedagogy in which the teacher's selective receptivity to student responses fosters the diffusion of desired cultural practices. But they also underscore "the critical and central role of the teacher as a representative of the mathematical community" (p. 475), a hallmark of acculturationist pedagogy, in which the teacher as cultural representative models desired practices for students to emulate. As discussed earlier under "Identity Politics," this distinction is an important one for educators to focus on, as acculturationist instruction can result in "intrapersonal conflict" (Brown, 2004, p. 810).

In the current subsection, the enculturation/acculturation distinction is applied to pedagogies oriented toward improvement of the moral and ethical fabric of the broader society. Collectively, I refer to these as *pedagogies of societal transformation*, including democratic education, liberatory pedagogy, values education, critical literacy, progressive education, character education, and multicultural pedagogy, among others. In our current educational discourse, these pedagogies tend to be marginalized as peripheral to the true academic mission. For instance, in her introduction to a paper on such pedagogies, Cochran-Smith (2004) "takes up the issue of the 'outcomes question' . . . arguing the case for a strong focus on social justice as the necessary *complement* to an ongoing concern with academic excellence and rigor" (p. 193).

In explaining the marginalization of equity discourses, "Secada [1995] noted that mathematics education has traditionally appropriated theoretical constructs from psychology. His basic claim was that research that is not cast in what he termed the 'dominant psychological discourse' is viewed as marginal to the concerns of the field" (Nasir & Cobb, 2002, p. 94). But surely no pedagogical method can aspire to improve the world directly; each must depend on students *learning* (in some sense). Thus pedagogies of societal transformation ought to be accounted for within the same learning framework as any other pedagogies that promote student learning.

Peering through crossdisciplinary lenses, two basic strategies are evident across the broad range of societal transformation pedagogies: *utopian pedagogies* and *critical pedagogies*. Utopian pedagogies (my term)—including democratic education, progressive education, some versions of multicultural pedagogy, and perhaps values education—adopt enculturation teaching methods, creating within the classroom microculture a microcosm of a more ideal society. Students enculturated into the norms of this classroom society then carry their dispositions outward to political and social engagement in the broader society. John Dewey's educational vision included such a utopian strategy:

> When the school introduces and trains each child of society into membership with such a little community, saturating him with the spirit of service, and providing him with the instruments of effective self-direction, we shall have the deepest and best guarantee of a larger society which is worthy, lovely, and harmonious.
>
> (Dewey, 1900, p. 44, quoted in Hall, 2003, p. 16)

In contrast to utopian pedagogies that seek to transform society from within, *critical pedagogies* such as liberatory pedagogy and critical literacy seek to disrupt societal arrangements by having students come to "formulate and agree upon a common understanding about 'structures of oppression' and 'relations of domination'" (Burbules & Berk, 1999, p. 53). The pedagogical method here is acculturationist, the goal being to enlist students as "'transformative intellectuals' (Giroux, 1988), 'cultural workers' (Freire, 1998) capable of identifying and redressing the injustices, inequalities, and myths of an often oppressive world" (Gruenewald, 2003, p. 4). Thus students are being guided toward an identity structure as social change agents, with the teacher serving as an authentic representative of a culture of resistance.

From a crossdisciplinary perspective, the marginalization of equity concerns needs to be understood as part of a broader diminution of the enculturation metaphor within traditional psychological frameworks. We already have noted the absence of any psychological paradigm focused squarely on this metaphor, necessitating a turn to sociological theory as grounding for enculturational learning. Similarly, one finds enculturational interests diminished in integrative pedagogical framings in which enculturational goals always are couple with other learning goals. For instance, Greeno, Collins, and Resnick's (1996) *situative* view is an umbrella for "understand[ing] school learning environments in two ways: their effects on the subject matter knowledge and ability that students acquire, and their effects on the kinds of learners that students become" (p. 31). The crossdisciplinary approach redresses this neglect by ensuring that each learning metaphor informs a dedicated genre of teaching independent of other genres and other theorizations.

The effect of this crossdisciplinary approach is to draw pedagogies of societal transformation into the same pool as other pedagogies that seek to foster students' dispositions. This includes high-status cognitive dispositions like critical thinking, metacognitive sophistication, and logical reasoning that often have been naturalized as part of the cognitive architecture (Perkins & Ritchhart, 2004) rather than recognized as products of cultural enmeshment (Burbules & Berk, 1999; Scribner & Cole, 1977). Furthermore, the method of crossdisciplinary analysis insists that the reference culture for targeted dispositions be identified. Thus, critical pedagogues have an opportunity to point out that even such seemingly innocuous goals as critical thinking reflect class, gender, and race-based priorities (Burbules & Berk, 1999). Of course, the obligation to be explicit about cultural interests applies equally to critical and utopian pedagogies, which may draw unwelcome scrutiny; but overall, the eliding of cultural interests is widely recognized to have contributed to establishing and maintaining societal positions of dominance (Delpit, 2006; Giroux, 1997; Gutstein, 2006; Lerman, 2009; Ostrove & Cole, 2003). Thus, making cultural agendas explicit in the crossdisciplinary approach tends to level the playing field for pedagogies of societal transformation, which hitherto have been more exposed as targets of cultural critique (e.g., see Wasley, 2006, for a discussion of NCATE's dropping of its social justice requirements).

The Remarkable Pedagogy of Christopher Healy

I conclude this section with a crossdisciplinary analysis of Christopher Healy's "Build-A-Book Geometry" course, an unusual offering in which students wrote the textbook collectively, deciding democratically what topics would count as geometric content, and what results are soundly reasoned. Healy began the first of several iterations of his year-long course in 1987 at the working-class California high school where he taught. His instructional format had students working together in small groups to produce ideas related to geometry. Each night, he pored over the reports that the groups produced, selecting some student contributions to be taken up by the class the next day. This did give him some influence on the content addressed by students, but in the periodic meetings in which group members presented ideas to the whole class, he ceded any direct role in adjudicating conclusions reached or the reasoning processes employed:

> After each presentation . . . there is a vote on whether the material presented is true and worthy of entry into the book. This process produces some of the most difficult moments for me, because students have presented and voted down things that I feel are significant parts of geometry. Still, I believe it imperative that I not interfere.
>
> (Healy, 1993a, p. 87)

Healy (1993a, 1993b) used a unique method of constructed journal entries to report on the effects of his course. As intuited by Healy, these journal entries express the thoughts and feelings of his students as they engaged in the course and reflected on various aspects of their lives outside of school. Although individual elements of these constructed journal entries might be questioned on methodological grounds, his overall characterization of the course experience is consistent with actual student statements, as contained in an appendix. Whatever the methodological faults and virtues, these constructed journal entries provide us with a very clear window into what Healy attended to and valued in his interaction with his students—just what we need to perform a crossdisciplinary analysis.

Healy's (1993a, 1993b) reports focus on how his students grappled with the broad autonomy offered to the class, and also how they dealt with personal relations and life plans outside of school. For many students, the course was personally transformative, as illustrated with Chris. As we meet Chris, she is a dependent personality, in need of outside approval through her relationship with her boyfriend, David, and lacking confidence in her mathematical ability: "I do better when I have someone who will tutor me. . . . someone who knows the right answer" (Healy, 1993b, p. 10); and with no plans for further education: "I've got this counselor who thinks I'm going to college (the poor guy just doesn't understand). I don't want to disappoint him, but two more years of this education stuff and I'm done forever" (p. 10). As Healy commented, "At first in my No Book geometry class Chris was a noninvolved student. She just sat there and looked like she was going to let this experience pass her by—until she finally felt strongly enough about something that she got involved" (p. 85).

The key episode for Chris occurred when she became inspired by the proposal that distance need not be defined relative to two points; it could be defined relative to two or more points. She was ready to argue for this, and went up to the board to illustrate her ideas, convincing the class that they needed to reconsider this issue. As Healy noted, "It was not a big deal to the class, but to Chris it was a turning point that affected the way she approached the entire experience. It gave her involvement, confidence, a positive interaction, and a feeling of belonging" (p. 85).

As the course progresses, we see evidence that Chris is reflecting on contrasts between relations of authority in class and at home: "There's no rules in the class, no right or wrong, no ultimates. . . . It's kind of the opposite of my house. In class what we say is important and we talk everything over before we decide on anything. I think people should talk things over—one person shouldn't be dictator" (Healy, 1993b, p. 47). Later, schooling takes a higher priority for her: "It's funny, for some reason going to school and graduating are so important to me now" (Healy, 1993b, p. 80), and eventually: "I'm going to college" (Healy, 1993a, p. 100). As she reflects later, her changes stem from a sense of her own agency and revaluation of her station in life: "The real miracle for me this year was learning that the positive response that really counts doesn't come from outside, it comes from within, If I'm ever going to be someone (and I am), it won't be to please anyone else. I'll do it for me" (Healy, 1993b, p. 163).

Analysis

This pedagogy presents a considerable challenge for crossdisciplinary analysis (and the intrepid reader can pause to self-test their understanding of the framework, by anticipating the cross-disciplinary analysis that follows). Although students in the Build-A-Book course tended to do as well on achievement tests as their peers, clearly the pedagogy itself offered no direct support for skills or for student construction of particular conceptual content. (At best, these might be considered what I call *advertent learning* outcomes that the teacher hopes and expects will occur, but does not directly support.) What is more, the typically emphasized mathematical practices—logical argumentation, problem solving heuristics, aesthetic sensibilities—also are not supported; Healy does not mediate the intellectual environment by expressing interest in or approval of particular mathematical practices. Rather, it seems that something is going on in his classes relative to students' identities. But what is it, and how does Healy's pedagogy produce it?

Having examined what Healy is *not* doing, it's time to turn to what he *is* doing: constituting his classroom as a mathematical community. In this community, students are provided the opportunity to experience themselves as authors of mathematical knowledge and collectively as the adjudicators of mathematical truth. Somehow, from this invitation, personal identities and life aspirations are transformed.

In the crossdisciplinary framework, student self-identification with the reference culture is the prerequisite for an acculturationist pedagogy in which the teacher, as a representative of the culture, models cultural practices. Clearly this is not the pedagogy being enacted in Healy's classroom. First, the students entering the class are not self-identified as mathematicians. Second, Healy does not present himself as a mathematician—he's just perceived as a goofy teacher—nor does he model mathematical dispositions.

Rather, we have to look toward enculturational teaching methods, in which dispositions are grown within the context of the classroom microculture. In this case, the disposition being actively supported in the classroom is mathematical self-identity itself. Indeed, self-identification as a mathematician is a consistent disposition of mathematicians (Burton, 2004), and therefore can, itself, be a goal of enculturation pedagogy. But now we are faced with a further conundrum: According to Healy's (1993b) account, there was only one student in his years of teaching Build-A-Book Geometry who came to perceive himself as a mathematician and to consider a career in that field. Are we, then, to consider Healy's pedagogy as a failure?

Recall that the enculturationist teacher must be equipped not only with an understanding of the target disposition, but also of the intermediate practices students may have to traverse en route to achieving that target. For the working-class students that comprised Healy's classes, these steps would pertain to social class. Mathematicians are part of a high-status professional class. They do not punch time clocks, but work on problems of their own choosing over extended time scales. Collectively, they provide the analytical relations that form the language of science. In these respects, the identity of the mathematician is remote from lower-class expectations of a work life spent in the service of plans, schemes, and enterprises of others (Kenny & Bledsoe, 2005; Burton, 2004).

From this perspective, we can interpret the transitions in self-image and ambition of students like Chris as indicative of a changing sense of class identity. The disposition that Healy cultivated in his students was self-belief in their intellectual efficacy; his methodology, the intense and consistent respect for the ideas they produced as he pored over their work products each evening, until that spirit of importance invaded every nook and cranny of his classroom. As a result, students began to experience themselves not as mathematicians, per se, but as efficacious thinkers and responsible members of a knowledge community, aspects of self-identity that typically demarcate professional-class social identities (Costello, 2005). That's why Healy did not intervene when students got the geometry wrong—not because he didn't care, but because his teaching agenda placed students' own role as adjudicators of mathematical truth ahead of his desire for their understanding of specific content. His pedagogy did not get students all the way to mathematical self-identification, but influencing students' class identity is in itself a major accomplishment[14].

To appreciate the magnitude of Healy's accomplishment, it is useful to compare his methods and results with standard efforts to socialize students to more productive identities as scholars, for instance, by having teachers "serve as models and motivators for students . . . employ[ing] the use of [the teacher's] personal story and history in an effort to provide their students with windows into their experience as mathematics learners" (Clark et al., 2013, pp. 1, 26). As noted earlier, such acculturationist methods have the potential for creating intrapersonal conflict when used with students who are not yet identified with the reference culture. Indeed, educators who employ "upward mobility discourses construct classist hierarchies in schools and classroom practice . . . [that] may unwittingly alienate the very students they hope to inspire" (Jones & Vagle, 2013, p. 129). Healy's Build-A-Book pedagogy is remarkable for its unique enculturationist pedagogy to foster social-class identity, and for the profound effects he achieved with his students.

In sharing Healy's (1993a) account of his pedagogy with graduate students in my Education and Cognition course, the students (most of them experienced teachers) tend to be uncomfortable with Healy's total neglect of skills and concepts in his Build-A-Book geometry course. In the modern history of education, educators sometimes have been guided by behaviorist learning theory (focused on habituationist learning) or by psychological constructivist theory (focused on concept development); as noted in the previous subsection, enculturation learning goals always have been considered auxiliary to the academic mission of schooling. In the crossdisciplinary approach, each of the three learning metaphors is independently theorized, and each forms the basis for dedicated genres of teaching. This enables us to broaden the palette of pedagogical possibility and to appreciate the remarkable accomplishments of teachers like Healy, who step out of the well-worn ruts of received pedagogical wisdom.

PROBLEMS AND PROSPECTS

The past two decades have witnessed a remarkable rise of the concept of "learning" with a subsequent decline of the concept of "education." . . . Despite the omnipresence of the concept of learning in current educational discourse, it is important to see that the new language of learning is not the outcome of one particular process or the expression of a single underlying agenda. It rather is the result of a combination of different, partly even contradictory trends and developments.

(Biesta, 2009, pp. 37, 38)

That the intensification of interest in learning over the past 20 years has not lead to significant improvement in the lives of students and teachers—perhaps even a decline—is troubling. As Biesta's statement suggests, and I have argued, the cause of this malaise owes to a mismatch between psychology's multiple theorizations of learning and education's assumption that good teaching must be characterized as some mutually coherent set of practices. We may disagree about the contents of this set; we may despair at the complexity of ever being able to adequately characterize it; but never once, in a hundred years, has it crossed our minds that multiple, independent theories of learning demand multiple, independent theorizations of teaching.

Why this blind spot? I have argued that we have not chosen to see learning as separate, independently coherent processes, because psychology has not wanted us to. Psychology's historical imperative is to become united around one paradigm, for only thus does an adolescent science reach full paradigmatic maturity (Kuhn, 1970). Education is useful to that quest only insofar as we join the partisan battle by siding with one or another of the protagonists. Reify learning in its separate paradigms, and we subvert the pretensions of sufficiency that paradigms must project out to win converts across paradigmatic boundaries.

At what cost, this acquiescence to psychology's grand design? Instead of letting learning theory, in its diverse paradigms, light the way to our varied aspirations, clinging to the hope or the illusion of unity has brought conflict, confusion, and banality to education. Our now ascendant *design science* mode of pedagogical research (Cobb, 2007; Lesh & Sriraman, 2005; Wittmann, 1995) mires us in theoretical particularism, it being sufficiently challenging just to assemble the theoretical tools to help guide one classroom or one lesson idea. As English (2008) noted, citing Niss (2004), "researchers are not addressing issues that focus on shaping practice, rather their issues focus on practice as an object of research" (p. 10). The prospect of any systematic prescriptive possibility for theory is fading.

Nor does the world of practice look upon the science of learning as a privileged resource for teaching as educators seek foundations for pedagogy oriented by philosophical premises, or political analyses, or neurophysiological data, or moral ideals, or spiritual aspiration, or psychoanalytic method—so that eventually, the marketplace of educational ideas comes more to resemble a bazaar than the organized knowledge base of an established profession.[15] Lending to the carnival atmosphere, astute educational entrepreneurs borrow the patina of scientific respectability—teach the brain!—to bolster the litany of standard-issue pedagogical truisms they are dispensing, reminiscent of the snake-oil salesmen of yore, before medical practice had fully established its scientific basis (see Kirshner, 2012, for a list of websites).

Nor are policy makers—in the United States at least—turning to us for guidance as professional judgment about teaching is replaced by value-added outcome measures of student learning, reduced to a single number, as the determinant of whether a teacher has met her or his professional obligations (Briggs & Domingue, 2011; Scherer, 2011). (This is a narrative we could counter, if only we would organize around the diversity of learning, rather than skirmish among ourselves about its unity.) So irrelevant has our expertise become that the U.S. federal No Child Left Behind Act of 2001 redefined "Highly Qualified Teacher" for middle or secondary grades, removing any reference to pedagogical expertise or training: "the teacher holds at least a bachelor's degree and has demonstrated a high level of competency in each of the academic subjects in which the teacher teaches" (NICHCY, 2009).

In proposing a genres approach, I have argued that multiple theorizations of learning should replace the vain hope that a single theorization can prevail as a source of guidance for pedagogy. In support of that proposal, I have identified diverse metaphors for learning that motivate both psychology and education, formulated theorizations for each, and demonstrated the clarity—across a broad span of educational issues—that can come from looking at educational practice through these multiple lenses, rather than trying to force a unified viewpoint.

Yet, what likely will prove most challenging for educational theorists about the genres proposal is not its multiple instantiations of learning, but its insular character. We are braced by the open-ended nature of our discourse, which invites the challenges and the rewards of theoretical erudition. As partners in psychology's quest for the definitive learning theory, we are engaging with the enduring problems of science. We are part of the intellectual life of our era.

Or do we acknowledge that psychology is an adolescent science, and we share in its hoped-for future glory at the expense of securing a stable knowledge base for teaching, today.

NOTES

1. I am grateful to Steve Wojcikiewicz, whose collaboration in framing the arguments of this chapter has been indispensable.
2. This sense of the complexity of the educational project actually is inherited from psychology itself, where the difficulties in achieving a unified science are attributed to an unruly subject matter: "It is the dilemma of psychology to deal as a natural science with an object that creates history" (Boesch, 1971, p. 9); "Psychology wants to be a natural science about non-natural phenomena" (Vygotsky, 1927/1987, p. 190)–thanks to Mike Cole for these sources.
3. Indeed, Kuhn (1962) acknowledged that "spending the year in a community composed predominantly of social scientists confronted me with unanticipated problems about the differences between such communities and those of the natural scientists among whom I had been trained. . . . Attempting to discover the source of that difference led me to recognize the role in scientific research of what I have since called 'paradigms'" (pp. ix-x, note a).
4. Kuhn (1970) also referenced bi-stable ambiguous figures, but instead focused on a sense of dissolution of the images that can ensue from efforts to switch perspectives: "Aware that nothing in his environment has changed, he directs his attention increasingly not to the figure . . . but to the lines on the paper he is looking at" (p. 114). In this way, Kuhn used the idea of ambiguous figures to reach the conclusion of mutual incomprehensibility across paradigms.
5. Although the competitive function is central to preparadigmatic science, it is rarely an active concern of most psychologists. That's because paradigmatic change, as a sociological process, is enacted over relatively long time periods, and because the competitive ethos conflicts with the norms of paradigmatic science wherein scientists are engaged in a shared quest for truth (excepting local competition over claims to discovery) (Merton, 1942/1973; Sarkar, 2007). Although preparadigmatic science is underpinned by competitive goals, it shares in the espoused ideals of cooperation, a factor that may mitigate against psychologists recognizing the competitive imperative that animates their science. In what follows, I present compelling evidence of preparadigmatic competition, but mindful that many psychological theorists do not perceive their science in this light.
6. I have not found this analysis of distinct intra- and inter-paradigm dynamics of research in the sociology of psychology literature; however, the historical evidence of exaggerated, even reckless, claims reviewed in this chapter seems difficult to explain otherwise.
7. Cobb (2007) bases his objection to the idea of generalized psychological principles in part on his reading of Kuhn's (1962) "analysis of both the processes by which scientists develop theory within an established research tradition and those by which they choose between competing research traditions" (p. 5). For intra-paradigm reasoning, Cobb (2007) takes note of Kuhn's observation that "development and use of theory necessarily involves tacit suppositions and assumptions that scientists learn in the course of their induction into their chosen specialties" (p. 5). He then goes on to inter-paradigm reasoning with the observation that "Kuhn (1962) extended this argument about the tacit aspects of scientific reasoning when he considered how scientists choose between competing research traditions by arguing that 'there is no neutral algorithm of theory-choice, no systematic decision procedure which, properly applied, must lead each individual in the group to the same decision' (p. 200)" (p. 6). Pulling these together, he concludes, quoting Bernstein (1983, p. 47), that scientific reasoning really "is closer to those features of rationality that have been characteristic of the tradition of practical philosophy than to many modern images of what is supposed to be the character of genuine *episteme*" (Cobb, 2007, p. 6).

    In my view, this is a misreading of Kuhn's position. That intra-paradigm scientific reasoning is a cultural practice guided by partly implicit norms does not make it equivalent to the value-laden, socially mediated practices of selecting between competing paradigms. Indeed, Kuhn's (1970) whole point was not to "extend" from normal science to revolution, but rather to distinguish between the practices of logic-based puzzle solving that are characteristic of normal science and "the competition between paradigms [which] is not the sort of battle that can be settled by proofs" (p. 148). Kuhn's (1962/1970) re-characterization of epistemic knowledge as bounded by the paradigmatic world view within which it is created (rather than as objectively true) is not intended to erase the distinction between episteme and techne, nor to diminish the structuring function epistemic knowledge offers for fields of application.

8. Indeed, Sfard's (2008) *commognitive* framework offering a synthesis of communication and cognition signals her return to epistemic theoretical aspirations.
9. Various objective criteria also have been proposed that yield mixed results; or sometimes one's ability to consciously control deployment of one's knowledge is taken to indicate conscious knowledge (Fu et al., 2008).
10. Piaget's microgenetic studies generally served to elaborate and strengthen his macrogenetic theories. However, stage theory encountered problems of décalage or unevenness of expression that challenged the essential idea of stages (Bruner, 1983; Fischer, 1980). This opened up a space for researchers to refocus developmental theory on school contents: "That we finally came to understand that we needed to make our own models to serve our educational purposes rather than to use Piaget's seemed to be a major breakthrough, and it was quite liberating. In fact, the long-lasting effects of this observation can be seen in contemporary constructivist research in which the researchers seek to observe and describe mechanisms that . . . build up mathematical knowledge in a particular learning space" (Steffe & Kieren, 1994, p. 716).
11. The landscape of constructivist learning perspectives is thick and rich (Spivey, 1997). Many have spawned associated *constructivist pedagogies*, none of which is identical with the version offered here.
12. This has been a point of criticism of the Piagetian approach: "By and large, American educational psychologists were not satisfied by this qualification, the reason being that the limitations that are imposed by physical laws and biological structure are vague and general" (Brainerd, 2003, p. 273). Nevertheless, 30 years of teaching experiments reveal that "theoretical constructs that account for the learning of the participating students . . . prove useful when accounting for the learning of other students" (Cobb, Jackson, & Dunlap, p. 483, in this volume).
13. To help clarify the distinction between the enculturation and construction metaphors, it is worth inserting that the goal in reading instruction of having students draw meaning from texts (in general) is an enculturation goal; a culturally specific form of engagement with texts is sought. This is different than the conceptual construction goal of having students understand a particular text in a particular way, for example the relation of madness and femininity in Lady Macbeth's character (Thomas, 2004), which would require a different pedagogy.
14. That identity could be treated as a disposition, and addressed through the same pedagogical methods as any other disposition, was a breakthrough in this analysis and a confirmation of the robust capability of the crossdisciplinary framework. I am grateful to my former graduate student Marie Lord for the extensive discussions coproducing this insight into Healy's pedagogy.
15. Of course, these are valid and valuable sources for pedagogical inspiration, but that inspiration should be mediated by learning theory, insofar as the pedagogical goal is student learning.

REFERENCES

AERA (2005). Annual meeting program. Retrieved from www.aera.net/Portals/38/docs/Annual_Meeting/AM_2005_000_Full%20Program.pdf

Aikenhead, G.S., & Jegede, O.J. (1999). Cross-cultural science education: A cognitive explanation of a cultural phenomenon. *Journal for Research in Science Teaching, 36*(3), 269–287.

Alexander, P.A. (2007). Bridging cognition and socioculturalism within conceptual change research: Unnecessary foray or unachievable feat? *Educational Psychologist, 42*(1), 67–73. Retrieved from www.tandfonline.com/doi/pdf/10.1080/00461520709336919.

Anderson, J.R., Greeno, J.G., Reder, L.M., & Simon, H.A. (2000). Perspectives on learning, thinking, and activity. *Educational Researcher, 29*(4), 11–13.

Anderson, J.R., Reder, L.M., & Simon, H.A. (1996). Situated learning and education. *Educational Researcher, 25*(4), 5–11.

Anderson, J.R., Reder, L.M., & Simon, H.A. (1997). Situative versus cognitive perspectives: Form versus substance. *Educational Researcher, 26*(1), 18–21.

Apple, M.W., & Au, W. (Eds.) (2014). *Critical education* (Vol. 2). New York: Routledge.

Arthur, A., & Hancock B. (2007). *Introduction to the research process*. The National Institute for Health Research, Research Design Services for the East Midlands/Yorkshire & the Humber.

Baker, D., & Taylor, P.C.S. (1995). The effect of culture on the learning of science in non-Western countries: The results of an integrated research review. *International Journal of Science Education, 17*, 695–704.

Ball, D.L. (1993). With an eye on the mathematical horizon: Dilemmas of teaching elementary school mathematics. *The Elementary School Journal, 93*(4), 373–397.

Barnes, B. (1985). *About science*. Oxford: Blackwell.

Beatty, B. (1996). Rethinking the historical role of psychology in educational reform. In D. Olson &. N. Torrance (Eds.), *Handbook of education and human development: New models of learning, teaching and schooling* (pp. 100–116). Cambridge, MA: Basil Blackwell.

Benjamin, L. T., Jr. (2007). *A brief history of modern psychology*. Oxford: Blackwell.

Bernstein, R. J. (1983). *Beyond objectivism and relativism: Science, hermeneutics, and praxis*. Philadelphia: University of Pennsylvania Press.

Biesta, G. (2009). Good education in an age of measurement: On the need to reconnect with the question of purpose in education. *Educational Assessment, Evaluation and Accountability, 21*, 33-46.

Bishop, J. P. (2012). "She's always been the smart one. I've always been the dumb one": Identities in the mathematics classroom. *Journal for Research in Mathematics Education, 43*(1), 34–74.

Boesch, E. E. (1971). Zwischen zwei wirklichkeiten. *Prolegomena zu einer ökologischen psychologie*. Bern: Huber.

Boyd, W. L., & Mitchell, D. E. (2001). The politics of the reading wars. In T. Loveless. (Ed.), *The great curriculum debate: How should we teach reading and math?* (pp. 299–341). Washington, DC: Brookings Institution Press.

Brainerd, C. J. (2003). Jean Piaget: Learning, research, and American Education. In B. J. Zimmerman & D. Schunk (Eds.), *Educational psychology: A century of contributions* (pp. 251–287). Mahwah, NJ: Lawrence Erlbaum Associates.

Bransford, J. D., Brown, A. L., & Cocking, R. R. (Eds.) (2000). *How people learn: Brain, mind, experience, and school* (Expanded Ed.). Washington, DC: Committee on Developments in the Science of Learning, National Research Council.

Bransford, J. D., Stevens, R., Schwartz, D. L., Meltzoff, P. K., Pea, R. D., Roschelle, J., Vye, N., Kuhl, P., Bell, P., Barron, B., Reeves, B., & Sabelli, N. (2006). Learning theories and education: Toward a decade of synergy. In P. A. Alexander & P. H. Winne (Eds.) *Handbook of educational psychology* (2nd ed., pp. 209–244). Mahwah, NJ: Lawrence Erlbaum Associates.

Bredo, E. (1994). Reconstructing educational psychology: Situated cognition and Deweyan pragmatism. *Educational Psychologist, 29*(1), 23–35.

Briggs, D., & Domingue, B. (2011). *Due diligence and the evaluation of teachers*. Boulder, CO: National Education Policy Center.

Brooks, J. G., & Brooks, M. G. (1999). *In search of understanding: The case for constructivist classrooms*. Upper Saddle River, NJ: Prentice Hall.

Brown, A. L., & Campione, J. C. (1994). Guided discovery in a community of learners. In K. McGilly (Ed.), *Classroom lessons: Integrating cognitive theory and classroom practice* (pp. 229–270). Cambridge, MA: The MIT Press.

Brown, B. A. (2004). Discursive identity: Assimilation into the culture of science and its implications for minority students. *Journal of Research in Science Teaching, 41*(8), 810–834.

Brown, G., Manogue, M., & Sadownik, L. (2001). Refreshing lecturing: A guide for lectures. *Medical Teacher, 23*(3), 231–244.

Brown, J. S., Collins, A., & Duguid, P. (1989). Situated cognition and the culture of learning. *Educational Researcher, 18*(1), 32–42.

Bruner, J. (1983). State of the child. *New York Review, 30*(16), 83–89.

Burbules, N., & Berk, R. (1999). Critical thinking and critical pedagogy: Relations, differences, and limits. In T. Popkewitz & L. Fendler (Eds.), *Critical theories in education*. New York: Routledge.

Burns, M. S., Griffin, P., & Snow, C. E. (1999). *Starting out right: A guide to promoting children's reading success*. Washington, DC: National Academy Press.

Burton, L. (2004). *Mathematicians as enquirers: Learning about learning mathematics*. Dordrecht, The Netherlands: Kluwer Academic Publishers.

Cantor, G. N. (1983). Conflict, learning, and Piaget: Comments on Zimmerman and Blom's "Toward an empirical test of the role of cognitive conflict in learning." *Developmental Review, 3*(1), 39–53.

Carpenter, T. P., Fennema, E., Peterson, P. L., & Carey, D. A. (1988). Teachers' pedagogical content knowledge of students' problem solving in elementary arithmetic. *Journal for Research in Mathematics Education, 19*, 385–401.

Case, R. (1992). Neo-Piagetian theories of child development. In R. J. Sternberg & C. A. Berg (Eds.), *Intellectual development* (pp. 161–196). Cambridge, UK: Cambridge University Press.

Chomsky, N. (1959). A review of B. F. Skinner's *Verbal Behavior*. *Language, 35*(1), 26–58.

Clark, L. M., Badertscher, E. M., & Napp, C. (2013). African American mathematics teachers as agents in their African American students' mathematics identity formation. *Teachers College Record, 115*(2). Retrieved from www.tcrecord.org; ID number: 16835; date accessed: 7/26/2013 5:46:27 p.m.

Clark, R. C., Nguyen, F., & Sweller, J. (2006). *Efficiency in learning: Evidence-based guidelines to manage cognitive load*. San Francisco: Pfeiffer.

Cobb, P. (2007). Putting philosophy to work: Coping with multiple theoretical perspectives. In Frank K. Lester, Jr. (Ed.), *Second handbook of research on mathematics teaching and learning* (pp. 3–38). Greenwich, CT: Information Age Publishing.

Cobb, P., & Steffe, L.P. (1983). The constructivist researcher as teacher and model builder. *Journal for Research in Mathematics Education, 14*, 83–94.

Cochran-Smith, M. (2004). Defining the outcomes of teacher education: What's social justice got to do with it? *Asia-Pacific Journal of Teacher Education, 32*(3), 193–212.

Cole, M. (1996). *Cultural psychology.* Cambridge, MA: The Belknap Press.

Collins, H.M., & Pinch, T.J. (1993). *The golem: What everyone should know about science.* Cambridge, UK: Cambridge University Press.

Confrey, J. (1990). A review of the research on student conceptions in mathematics, science, and programming. In C.B. Cazden (Ed.), *Review of research in education* (pp. 3–56). Washington, DC: American Educational Research Association.

Costello, C.Y. (2005). *Professional identity crisis: Race, class, gender, and success at professional schools.* Nashville, TN: Vanderbilt University Press.

Cubberly, E.P. (1920). *The history of education.* Boston: Houghton Mifflin.

Dahl, K., Scharer, P., Lawson, L., & Grogan, P. (1999). Phonics instruction and student achievement in whole language first-grade classrooms. *Reading Research Quarterly, 34*(3), 312–341. doi:10.1598/RRQ.34.3.4.

Danziger, K. (1990). *Constructing the subject.* New York: Cambridge University Press.

Davidson, D. (1974). On the very idea of a conceptual scheme. *Proceedings and Addresses of the American Philosophical Association, 47*, 5–20.

Dechant, E. (1993). *Whole-language reading: A comprehensive teaching guide.* Lancaster, PA: Technomic.

Delpit, L. (2006). *Other people's children: Cultural conflict in the classroom.* New York: New Press.

Design-Based Research Collaborative (2003). Design-based research: An emerging paradigm for educational inquiry. *Educational Researcher, 32*(1), 5–8.

Dewey, J. (1900). *School and society.* Chicago: University of Chicago Press.

diSessa, A.A. (2006). A history of conceptual change research: Threads and fault lines. In R.K. Sawyer, (Ed.), *The Cambridge handbook of the learning sciences* (pp. 265–281). New York: Cambridge University Press.

Donovan, M.S., & Bransford, J.D. (Eds.) (2005). How students learn: *History, mathematics, and science in the classroom.* Washington, DC: National Academies Press.

Draper, R.J. (2002). School mathematics reform, constructivism, and literacy: A case for literacy instruction in the reform-oriented math classroom. *Journal of Adolescent & Adult Literacy, 45*(6), 20–529. Retrieved from http://jwilson.coe.uga.edu/EMAT7050/Students/Ramsey/DraperMathLiteracy.pdg.pdf.

Driver-Linn, E. (2003). Where is psychology going? Structural fault lines revealed by psychologists' use of Kuhn. *American Psychologist, 58*, 269–278. Retrieved from www.radford.edu/~tpierce/622%20files/Driver-Linn%20(2003)%20Kuhn.pdf.

Durkheim, E. (1895/1964). *The rules of sociological method.* New York: The Free Press. (Originally published as *Les règles de la méthode sociologique.* Paris: Alcan, 1895.)

Egan, K. (1997). *The educated mind: How cognitive tools shape our understanding.* Chicago: University of Chicago Press.

Eggen, P., & Kauchak, D. (2013). Educational Psychology: Windows on Classrooms. Boston: Pearson.

English, L.D. (Ed.) (2008). *Handbook of international research in mathematics education* (2nd ed.). New York: Routledge.

Ernest, P. (1998). *Social constructivism as a philosophy of mathematics.* Albany, NY: State University of New York Press.

Fischer, K.W. (1980). A theory of cognitive development: The control and construction of hierarchies of skills. *Psychological Review, 87*, 477–531.

Fletcher, G. (1995). *The scientific credibility of folk psychology.* Mahwah, NJ: Lawrence Erlbaum Associates.

Fox, B.J. (2000). *Word identification strategies: Phonics from a new perspective.* Upper Saddle River, NJ: Merrill.

Fox, E., & Riconscente, M. (2008). Metacognition and self-regulation in James, Piaget, and Vygotsky. *Educational Psychology Review, 20*(4), 373–389.

Freire, P. (1998). *Teachers as cultural workers.* Boulder, CO: Westview Press.

Fu, Q., Fu, X., & Dienes, Z. (2008). Implicit sequence learning and conscious awareness. *Consciousness and Cognition 17*, 185–202.

Gardner, M. (1987). *Riddles of the sphinx and other mathematical puzzle tales.* Washington, DC: Mathematical Association of America.

Geertz, C. (2000). *Available light: Anthropological reflections on philosophical topics.* Princeton, NJ: Princeton University Press.

Gergen, K.J. (2002). Social construction and pedagogical practice. In K.J. Gergen, *Social construction in context* (pp. 115–136). London & Thousand Oaks, CA: Sage Publications.

Giroux, H. (1988). *Teachers as intellectuals: Toward a critical pedagogy of learning*. South Hadley, MA: Bergin Garvey.

Giroux, H. (1997). *Pedagogy and the politics of hope: Theory, culture, and schooling*. Boulder, CO: West view.

von Glasersfeld, E. (1987). Learning as a constructive activity. In C. Janvier (Ed.), *Problems of representation in the teaching and learning of mathematics*. Hillsdale, NJ: Lawrence Erlbaum Publishers, 3–17.

von Glasersfeld, E. (1991). Abstraction, re-presentation, and reflection: An interpretation of experience and Piaget's approach. In L.P. Steffe (Ed.), *Epistemological foundations of mathematical knowledge* (pp. 45–67). New York: Springer-Verlag.

von Glasersfeld, E. (1995). *Radical constructivism: A way of knowing and learning*. New York: Falmer Press.

Glick, J.A. (1983). Piaget, Vygotsky, and Werner. In S. Wapner & B. Kaplan (Eds.), *Toward a holistic developmental psychology* (pp. 35–52). Hillsdale, NJ: Lawrence Erlbaum Associates.

Goodman, K.S. (1986). *What's whole in whole language?* Portsmouth, NH: Heinemann.

Goodman, K.S. (Ed.) (1998). *In defense of good teaching: What teachers need to know about the "Reading Wars."* York, ME: Stenhouse.

Goodson-Espy, T. (1998). The roles of reification and reflective abstraction in the development of abstract thought: Transitions from arithmetic to algebra. *Educational Studies in Mathematics, 36*, 219–245.

Gray. E., & Tall, D. (2001). Relationships between embodied objects and symbolic procepts: An explanatory theory of success and failure in mathematics. *Proceedings of PME 25*, Ütrecht, Holland: University of Ütrecht.

Green, E. (2014). *Building a better teacher: How teaching works (and how to teach it to everyone)*. New York: W.W. Norton & Company Inc.

Greeno, J.G. (1978). Understanding and procedural knowledge in mathematics instruction. *Educational Psychologist, 12*(3), 94–143.

Greeno, J.G. (1993). For research to reform education and cognitive science. In L.A. Penner, G.M. Batsche, H.M. Knoff, & D.L. Nelson (Eds.), *The challenges in mathematics and science education: Psychology's response* (pp. 153–192). Washington, DC: American Psychological Association.

Greeno, J.G. (1997). On claims that answer the wrong question. *Educational Researcher, 26*(1), 5–17.

Greeno, J.G. (2011). A situative perspective on cognition and learning in interaction. In T. Koschmann (Ed.), *Theorizing learning and practice* (pp. 41–72). New York: Springer.

Greeno, J.G., Collins, A.M., & Resnick, L.B. (1996). Cognition and learning. In D.C. Berliner & R.C. Calfee (Eds.), *Handbook of educational psychology* (pp. 15–46). New York: Macmillan.

Gruenewald, D.A. (2003). The best of both worlds: A critical pedagogy of place. *Educational Researcher, 32*(4), 3–12.

Gutiérrez, R. (2002). Enabling the practice of mathematics teachers in context: Toward a new research agenda. *Mathematical Thinking and Learning, 4*, 145–189.

Gutstein, E. (2006). *Reading and writing the world with mathematics: Toward a pedagogy for social justice*. New York, NY: Routledge.

Hall, E.T. (1966) *The hidden dimension*. New York: Doubleday.

Hall, V.C. (2003). Educational psychology from 1820 to 1920. In B.J. Zimmerman & D. Schunk (Eds.), *Educational psychology: A century of contributions* (pp. 3–40). Mahwah, NJ: Lawrence Erlbaum Associates.

Harel, G., & Sowder, L. (2007). Toward comprehensive perspectives on the learning and teaching of proof. In F.K. Lester (Ed.), *Second handbook of research on mathematics education* (pp. 805–842). Charlotte, NC: Information Age Publishers.

Healy, C.C. (1993a). Discovery courses are great in theory, but . . . . In J.L. Schwartz, M. Yerushalmy, & B. Wilson (Eds.), *The Geometric Supposer: What is it a case of?* (pp. 85–104). Hillsdale, NJ: Lawrence Erlbaum Publishers.

Healy, C.C. (1993b). *Build-A-Book Geometry: A story of student discovery*. Berkeley, CA: Key Curriculum Press.

Hergenhahn, B.R. (2009). *An introduction to the history of psychology* (6th ed.). Belmont, CA: Wadsworth, Cengage Learning.

Hiebert, J., & Carpenter, T.P. (1992). Learning and teaching with understanding. In D.A. Grouws (Ed.), *Handbook of research on mathematics teaching and learning* (pp. 65–97). New York: Macmillan Co.

Hirst, W., & Manier, D. (1995). Opening vistas for cognitive psychology. In L.M.W. Martin, K. Nelson, & E. Tobach (Eds.), *Sociocultural psychology: Theory and practice of doing and knowing* (pp. 89–124). New York: Cambridge University Press.

Honig, B. (1996). *How should we teach our children to read?: The role of skills in a comprehensive reading program–A balanced approach*. San Francisco: Far West Laboratory for Educational Research and Development.

Hopkins, D., & Stern, D. (1996). Quality teachers, quality schools: International perspectives and policy implications. *Teaching and Teacher Education, 12,* 501–517.

Howe, K.R., & Berv, J. (2000). Constructing constructivism, epistemological and pedagogical. In D.C. Phillips (Ed.), *Constructivism in education: Opinions and second opinions on controversial issues.* Ninety-ninth Yearbook of the National Society of the Study of Education, Part I (pp. 19–40). Chicago: University of Chicago Press.

Hunt, M. (1993). *The story of psychology.* New York: Doubleday.

Hutchins, E. (1995). How a cockpit remembers its speed. *Cognitive Science, 19,* 265–288.

Hutchison, A. (2012). Mind the gap: Education reform policy and pedagogical practice. *The International Journal of Educational Organization and Leadership, 19,* 1–12.

Inhelder, B., Sinclair, H., & Bovet, M. (1974). *Learning and the development of cognition.* Cambridge, MA: Harvard University Press.

Jones, S., & Vagle, M.D. (2013). Living contradictions and working for change toward a theory of social class–sensitive pedagogy. *Educational Researcher, 42,* 129–141.

Kennedy, M.M. (1999). A test of some common contentions about educational research. *American Educational Research Journal, 36,* 511–541.

Kenny, M.E., & Bledsoe, M. (2005). Contributions of the relational context to career adaptability among urban adolescents. *Journal of Vocational Behaviour, 66*(2), 257–272.

Kim, Y.Y. (1988). *Communication and cross-cultural adaptation: An integrative theory.* Intercommunication Series, 2. Clevedon, England: Multilingual Matters, http://psycnet.apa.org/psycinfo/1988-97819-000.

Kincheloe, J., & Steinberg, S. (2007). *Cutting class: Socio-economic status and education.* Boulder, CO: Rowman & Littlefield.

Kirshner, D. (2002). Untangling teachers' diverse aspirations for student learning: A crossdisciplinary strategy for relating psychological theory to pedagogical practice. *Journal for Research in Mathematics Education, 33*(1), 46–58.

Kirshner, D. (2004). Enculturation: The neglected learning metaphor in mathematics education. In D. McDougall & J.A. Ross (Eds.), *Proceedings of the twenty-sixth annual meeting of the International Group for the Psychology of Mathematics Education, North American Chapter* (vol. 2, pp. 765–772), Toronto: OISE/UT.

Kirshner, D. (2012). *The decline of learning theory as an influence on pedagogy: A crossdisciplinary analysis.* Paper presented at AERA Annual Meeting, Vancouver, Canada, April.

Kirshner, D., & Awtry, T. (2004). Visual salience of algebraic transformations. *Journal for Research in Mathematics Education, 35*(4), 224–257.

Kirshner, D., & Meng, L. (2011). Enculturation and acculturation. In N.M. Seel (Ed.), *Encyclopedia of the sciences of learning* (pp. 1148–1151). Berlin: Springer Publishing.

Kirsner, K. Speelman, C. Maybery, M., O'Brien-Malone, A., Anderson, M., & McCleod, C. (Eds.) (2013). *Implicit and explicit mental processes.* East Sussex, UK: Psychology Press.

Klein, D. (2005). *The state of state MATH standards.* Washington, DC: Fordham Foundation. Retrieved from www.math.jhu.edu/~wsw/ED/mathstandards05FINAL.pdf.

Klein, D. (2007). A quarter century of US 'math wars' and political partisanship. *BSHM Bulletin: Journal of the British Society for the History of Mathematics, 22*(1), 22–33, doi: 10.1080/17498430601148762.

Klein, D., Askey, R., Milgram, R.J., Wu, H., Scharlemann, M., Tsang, B., et al. (1999, November 18). An open letter to United States Secretary of Education, Richard Riley. *The Washington Post.*

Kottow, M.H. (1992). Classical medicine v alternative medical practices. *Journal of Medical Ethics, 18,* 18–22. Retrieved from http://jme.bmj.com/content/18/1/18.full.pdf.

Krashen, S.D. (2003). False claims about phonemic awareness, phonics, skills vs. whole language, and recreational reading. *NoChildLeft.com, 1*(5). Retrieved from www.nochildleft.com/2003/may03 reading.html.

Kuhn, T.S. (1962). *The structure of scientific revolutions.* Chicago: University of Chicago Press.

Kuhn, T.S. (1970). *The structure of scientific revolutions* (enlarged ed.). Chicago: University of Chicago Press.

Kuhn, T.S. (2000). *The road since* Structure*: Philosophical Essays, 1970–1993,* with an autobiographical interview edited by Conant & J. Haugland. Chicago: University of Chicago Press.

Labaree, D.F. (2000). On the nature of teaching and teacher education: Difficult practices that look easy. *Journal of Teacher Education, 51,* 228–233.

Lakoff, G., & Núñez, R.E. (2000). *Where mathematics comes from: How the embodied mind brings mathematics into being.* New York: Basic Books.

Lagemann, E.C. (1989). The plural worlds of educational research. *History of Education Quarterly, 29*(2), 185–214. doi:10.2307/368309. Retrieved from www.jstor.org/stable/368309.

Lagemann, E.C. (2000). *An elusive science: The troubling history of education research.* Chicago: University of Chicago.

Lamiell, J.T. (2013). Critical personalism: On its tenets, its historical obscurity, and its future prospects. In J. Martin & M.H. Bickhard (Eds.), *The psychology of personhood: Philosophical, historical, social-developmental, and narrative perspectives* (pp. 101–123). Cambridge, UK: Cambridge University Press.

Lampert, M. (1985). How do teachers manage to teach? Perspectives on problems in practice. *Harvard Educational Review, 55,* 178–194.

Lave, J. (1988). *Cognition in practice.* Cambridge, UK: Cambridge University Press.

Leahey, T.H. (1992). The mythical revolutions of American psychology. *American Psychologist, 47,* 308–318. Retrieved from www.radford.edu/~tpierce/622%20files/Leahey%20%281992%29%20the%20mythical%20revolutions%20of%20american%20psychology.pdf.

Leary, D.E. (1994). Psyche's muse: The role of metaphor in the history of psychology. In D.E. Leary (Ed.), *Metaphors in the history of psychology* (pp. 1–78). Cambridge, UK: Cambridge University Press.

Leiter, K. (1980). *A primer on ethnomethodology.* New York: Oxford University Press.

Lerman, S. (2009). Pedagogy, discourse and identity. In L. Black, H. Mendick, & Y. Solomon (Eds.), *Mathematical relationships: Identities and participation* (pp. 147–159). New York: Routledge.

Lesh, R., & Sriraman, B. (2005). Mathematics education as a design science. *Zentralblatt für Didaktik der Mathematik, 37*(6), 490–505.

Lester, F.K. (2010). On the theoretical, conceptual, and philosophical foundations for research in mathematics education. In B. Sriraman & L. English (Eds.) (2010). *Theories of mathematics education: Seeking new frontiers* (Advances in Mathematics Education) (pp. 67–85). Berlin/Heidelberg: Springer Science. Reprinted from International Reviews on Mathematical Education, 37(6), 457–467, 2005.

Lewin, P. (1995). The social already inhabits the epistemic: A discussion of Driver; Wood, Cobb, & Yackel; and von Glasersfeld. In L.P. Steffe & G. Gale (Eds.), *Constructivism in education* (pp. 423–432). Hillsdale, NJ: Lawrence Erlbaum Associates.

Li, S. (2001). How close is too close? A comparison of proxemic reactions of Singaporean Chinese to male intruders of four ethnicities. *Perceptual and Motor Skills, 93,* 124–126.

Loveless, T. (2001). Introduction. In T. Loveless (Ed.), *The great curriculum debate: How should we teach reading and math?* (pp. 1–12). Washington, DC: Brookings Institution Press.

Ma, L. (1999). *Knowing and teaching elementary mathematics: Teacher's understanding of fundamental mathematics in China and the United States.* Mahwah, NJ: Lawrence Erlbaum Associates.

Maddock, M.N. (1981). Science education: An anthropological viewpoint. *Studies in Science Education, 8,* 1–26.

Mark, J., Cuoco, A., Goldenberg, E.P., & Sword, S. (2010). Developing mathematical habits of mind. *Mathematics Teaching in the Middle School, 15*(9), 505–509.

Marr, D. (1982). *Vision: A computational investigation into the human representation and processing of visual information.* New York: Freeman.

McCarty, L.P., & Schwandt, T.A. (2000). Seductive illusions: Von Glasersfeld and Gergen on epistemology and education. In D.C. Phillips (Ed.), *Constructivism in education: Opinions and second opinions on controversial issues.* Ninety-ninth yearbook of the National Society of the Study of Education, Part I (pp. 41–85). Chicago: University of Chicago Press.

McCombs, B.L. (2003). A framework for the redesign of K-12 education in the context of current educational reform. Theory Into Practice, 42(2), 93–101.

McLeod, D.B., Stake, R.E., Schappelle, B., & Mellissinos, M. (1995). International influences on the NCTM Standards: A case study of educational change. In D.T. Owens, M.K. Reed, & G.M. Millsaps (Eds.), *Proceedings of the seventeenth annual meeting of the North American Chapter of the International Group for the Psychology of Mathematics Education* (pp. 240–246). Columbus, OH: ERIC Clearinghouse for Science, Mathematics, and Environmental Education.

McRae, M. (2011). *Tribal science: Brains, beliefs, and bad ideas.* St. Lucia, Australia: University of Queensland Press.

Mehan, H., & Wood, H. (1975). *The reality of ethnomethodology.* New York: Wiley.

Merton, R.K. (1942/1973). The normative structure of science. In R.K. Merton, *The sociology of science: Theoretical and empirical investigations* (pp. 267–278). Chicago: University of Chicago Press.

Millei, Z, Griffiths, T.G., & Parkes, R.J. (2010). Re-theorizing discipline in education: Problems, politics, & possibilities. New York: Peter Lang.

Morgan, C.L. (1894/1903). *An introduction to comparative psychology* (2nd ed.). London: Walter Scott Publishing.

Morris, E.K. (2003). B.F. Skinner: A behavior analyst in educational psychology. In B.J. Zimmerman & D. Schunk (Eds.), *Educational psychology: A century of contributions* (pp. 229–250). Mahwah, NJ: Lawrence Erlbaum Associates.

Moscardini, L. (2014). Developing equitable elementary mathematics classrooms through teachers learning about children's mathematical thinking: Cognitively Guided Instruction as an inclusive pedagogy. *Teaching and Teacher Education, 43,* 69–79.

Murray, D. J. (1988). *A history of Western psychology* (2nd ed). Englewood Cliffs, NJ: Prentice Hall.

Nardi, B. A. (1996). Studying context: A comparison of activity theory, situated action models, and distributed cognition. In Nardi, B. A. (Ed.), *Context and consciousness: Activity theory and human-computer interaction* (pp. 69–102). Cambridge, MA: MIT Press.

Nasir, N. S., & Cobb, P. (Eds.). (2002). Editors' introduction to *Diversity, equity, and mathematical learning.* Special issue of *Mathematical Thinking and Problem Solving, 4*(2&3), 91–102.

Nasir, N. S., & Saxe, G. B. (2003). Ethnic and academic identities: A cultural practice perspective on emerging tensions and their management in the lives of minority students. *Educational Researcher, 32*(5), 14–18.

National Council for Accreditation of Teacher Education. (2002). *Professional standards for the accreditation of schools, colleges, and departments of education.* Washington, DC: Author.

National Council of Teachers of Mathematics. (1989). *Curriculum and evaluation standards for school mathematics.* Reston, VA: Author.

National Dissemination Center for Children with Disabilities (NICHCY) (2009). *How NCLB defines "Highly Qualified."* Retrieved from http://nichcy.org/schools-administrators/hqt/nclb.

National Mathematics Advisory Panel. (2008). *Foundations for success: The final report of the National Mathematics Advisory Panel.* Washington, DC: U.S. Department of Education.

National Research Council. (2000). How people learn: Brain, mind, experience, and school. Washington, DC: National Academy Press.

National Research Council. (2005). How students learn: History, mathematics, and science in the classroom. M. S. Donovan & J. D. Bransford (Eds.). Committee on How People Learn: A Targeted Report for Teachers. Division of Behavioral and Social Sciences and Education. Washington, DC: National Academy Press.

Newell, A., & Simon, H. A. (1972). *Human problem solving.* Englewood Cliffs, NJ: Prentice-Hall.

Niss, M. (2004). Key issues and trends in research on mathematical educational. In H. Fujita, Y. Hashimoto, B. Hodgson, P. Yee Lee, S. Lerman, & T. Sawada (Eds.), *Proceedings of the ninth international congress on mathematical education* (pp. 37–57). Dordrecht, Netherlands: Kluwer Academic Publishers. http://link.springer.com/book/10.1007/1-4020-7910-9/page/1.

Noddings, N. (1990). Constructivism in mathematics education. In R. B. Davis, C. A. Maher, & N. Noddings (Eds.), *Constructivist views on the teaching and learning of mathematics. Journal for Research in Mathematics Education*, Monograph Number 4 (pp. 7–18). Reston, VA: National Council of Teachers of Mathematics.

North, A. (2015). Are 'learning styles' a symptom of education's ills? *New York Times, Op Talk,* 2/25/15. Retrieved from http://op-talk.blogs.nytimes.com/2015/02/25/are-learning-styles-a-symptom-of-educations-ills/?smid=fb-share&_r=1.

Nuthall, G., (2004). Relating classroom teaching to student learning: A critical analysis of why research has failed to bridge the theory-practice gap. *Harvard Educational Review, 74*(3), 273–306. Retrieved from http://her.hepg.org/content/e08k1276713824u5/fulltext.pdf.

Oberheim, E., & Hoyningen-Huene, P. (2013). The incommensurability of scientific theories. In E. N. Zalta (Ed.), *The Stanford encyclopedia of philosophy* (Spring Edition). http://plato.stanford.edu/archives/spr2013/entries/incommensurability/.

Olson, D. R. (2003). *Psychological theory and educational reform: How school remakes mind and society.* Cambridge, MA: Cambridge University Press.

Olson, D. R., & Bruner, J. S. (1996). Folk psychology and folk pedagogy. In D. R. Olson & N. Torrance (Eds.), *The handbook of education and human development* (pp. 9–27). Cambridge, MA: Blackwell Publishers.

Ormrod, J. E. (2000). Behaviorist views of learning. In J. E. Ormord, *Educational psychology: Developing learners* (3rd ed.) (pp. 394–432). Upper Saddle River, NJ: Prentice-Hall.

Ormrod, J. E. (2009). *Essentials of educational psychology.* Upper Saddle River, NJ: Merrill.

Ostrove J. M., & Cole E. R. (2003). Privileging class: Toward a critical psychology of social class in the context of education. *Journal of Social Issues, 59,* 677–692. doi:10.1046/j.0022-4537.2003.00084.x.

Otero, J. (1998). Influence of knowledge activation and context on comprehension monitoring of science texts. In D. J. Hacker, J. Dunlosky, & A. C. Graesser (Eds.). *Metacognition in educational theory and practice* (pp. 145–164). Hillsdale, NJ: Lawrence Erlbaum Associates.

Otterness, J. (2009). Teaching and learning—It's not rocket science! *Phi Delta Kappan, 91*(2), 86–88.

Parsons, T. (1951). *The social system.* London: Routledge & Kegan Paul.

Pashler, H., McDaniel, M., Rohrer, D., & Bjork, R. (2009). Learning styles: Concepts and evidence. *Psychological Science in the Public Interest, 9*(3), 105–119.

Pavlov, I. P. (1897/1910). *The work of the digestive glands.* (W. H. Thompson, Trans.) London: Charles Griffin & Co.

Pavlov, I. P. (1927). *Conditioned reflexes: An investigation of the physiological activity of the cerebral cortex.* (G. V. Anrep, Trans./Ed.) London: Oxford University Press.

Paz, T., & Leron, U. (2009). The slippery road from actions on objects to functions and variables. *Journal for Research in Mathematics Education, 40*(1), 18–39.

Pedamonte, B. (2007). How can the relationship between argumentation and proof be analysed? *Educational Studies in Mathematics, 66*(1), 23–41. Retrieved from http://link.springer.com/article/10.1007%2Fs10649-006-9057-x.

Penuel, W.R., & Wertsch, J.V. (1995). Vygotsky and identity formation: A sociocultural approach. *Educational Psychologist, 30*, 83–92.

Perkins, D., & Ritchhart, R. (2004). When is good thinking? In D.Y. Dai & R.J. Sternberg (Eds.), *Motivation, emotion, and cognition: Integrative perspectives on intellectual functioning and development* (pp. 175–194). Mahwah, NJ: Lawrence Erlbaum Associates.

Perrenet, J., & Taconis, R. (2009). Mathematical enculturation: Shifts in problem solving beliefs and behavior during the bachelor programme. *Educational Studies in Mathematics, 71*, 181–198. doi:10.1007/s10649-008-9166-9.

Phillips, D. C. (1995). The good, the bad, and the ugly: The many faces of constructivism. *Educational Researcher, 24*(7), 5–12.

Piaget, J. (1965/1995). *Sociological studies* (T. Brown, R. Campbell, N. Emler, M. Ferrari, M. Gribetz, R. Kitchener, W. Mays, A. Notari, C. Sherrard, and L. Smith, Trans.). New York: Routledge.

Piaget, J. (1970/1983). Piaget's theory. In P.H. Mussen (Ed.), *Handbook of child psychology* (4th ed., Vol. 1, pp. 103–128). New York: John Wiley & Sons.

Piaget, J. (1971). *Biology and Knowledge*. Edinburgh University Press, Edinburgh.

Piaget, J. (1975). *L'equilibration des structures cognitives*. Paris: Presses Universitaires de France.

Piaget, J. (1977a). Problems of equilibration. In M.H. Appel, & L.S. Goldberg, (Eds.), *Topics in cognitive development* (Vol. 1, pp. 3–14). New York: Plenum.

Piaget, J. (1977b). *Recherches sur l'abstraction reflechissante*, Vols. 1 & 2. Paris: Presses Universitaires de France.

Pinch, T. (2007). The sociology of science and technology. In C.D. Bryant & D.L. Peck (Eds.), *21st century sociology: A reference handbook* (vol. 2) (pp. 266–276). Thousand Oaks, CA: Sage Publications.

Polya, G. (1957). *How to solve it: A new aspect of mathematical method* (2nd ed.). Princeton, NJ: Princeton University Press.

Powell, J.W. (1883). Human evolution: Annual address of the President, J.W. Powell, Delivered November 6, 1883. *Transactions of the Anthropological Society of Washington, 2*, 176–208.

Prawat, R.S. (1992). Teachers' beliefs about teaching and learning: A constructivist perspective. *American Journal of Education, 100*, 354–395.

Pressley, M., & Roehrig, A. D. (2003). Educational psychology in the modern era: 1960 to the present. In B.J. Zimmerman & D. Schunk (Eds.), *Educational psychology: A century of contributions* (pp. 333–366). Mahwah, NJ: Lawrence Erlbaum Associates.

Pressman, B. (2007). *Substitute teaching from A to Z*. New York: McGraw-Hill.

Reber, A.S. (1967). Implicit learning of artificial grammars. *Journal of Verbal Learning and Verbal Behavior, 6*, 855–863.

Reber, A.S. (1993). *Implicit learning and tacit knowledge: An essay on the cognitive unconscious* (Oxford Psychology Series No. 19). Oxford, UK: Oxford University Press; New York: Clarendon Press.

Regehr, G. (2010). It's NOT rocket science: Rethinking our metaphors for research in health professions education. *Medical Education, 44*(1), 31–39. Retrieved from www.ncbi.nlm.nih.gov/pubmed/20078754.

Remland, M.S., Jones, T.S., & Brinkman, H. (1991). Proxemic and haptic behavior in three European countries. *Journal of Nonverbal Behavior, 15*(4), 215–232.

Resendez, M. & Azin, M. (2007). *The relationship between using Saxon elementary and middle school math and student performance on California statewide assessments*. Austin, TX: Harcourt.

Richey, R.C., Klein, J.D., & Tracey, M.W. (2011). *The instructional design knowledge base: Theory, research, and practice*. New York: Routledge.

Rippa, S.A. (1971). *Education in a free society* (2nd. ed.). New York: David McKay Company.

Rosenberg, A. (2005). *Philosophy of science: A contemporary approach* (2nd ed.). New York: Routledge.

Rubin, B.C. (2007). Learner identity amid figured worlds: Constructing (in)competence at an urban high school. *The Urban Review, 39*, 217–249.

Sarkar, H. (2007). *Group rationality in scientific research*. New York: Cambridge University Press.

Sawyer, R.K. (2002a). Emergence in sociology: Contemporary philosophy of mind and some implications for sociological theory. *American Journal of Sociology, 107*(3), 551–585. Retrieved from www.jstor.org/stable/10.1086/338780.

Sawyer, R.K. (2002b). Durkheim's dilemma: Toward a sociology of emergence. *Sociological Theory, 20*(2), 227–247. doi:10.1111/1467-9558.00160.

Saxon Publishers (1992). *Saxon Publishers* (a promotional catalogue). Norman, OK: Author.

Scardamalia, M., & Bereiter, C. (2003). Knowledge building. In J.W. Guthrie (Ed.), *Encyclopedia of Education* (2nd ed., pp. 1370–1373). New York: Macmillan Reference, USA.

Scherer, J. (2011). Measuring teaching using value-added modeling: The imperfect panacea. *NASSP Bulletin, 95*(2), 122–140. doi:10.1177/0192636511410052.

Schoen, H. L., Fey, J. T., Hirsch, C. R., & Coxford, A. F. (1999). Issues and options in the Math Wars. *Phi Delta Kappan, 80*(6), 444–453.

Schoenfeld, A. H. (1992). Learning to think mathematically: Problem solving, metacognition, and sense making in mathematics. In D. A. Grouws (Ed.), *Handbook of research on mathematics teaching and learning* (pp. 334–370). New York: Macmillan.

Schoenfeld, A. H. (2007). Method. In Frank K. Lester, Jr. (Ed.), *Second handbook of research on mathematics teaching and learning* (pp. 69–107). Greenwich, CT: Information Age Publishing.

Scribner, S., & Cole, M. (1977). Cross-cultural studies of memory and cognition. In R. V. Kvail, Jr., & J. W. Hagen (Eds.), *Perspectives on the development of memory and cognition* (pp. 239–272). Hillsdale, NJ: Lawrence Erlbaum Associates.

Secada, W. (1995). Social and critical dimensions for equity in mathematics education. In W. Secada, E. Fennema, & L. B. Adajian (Eds.). *New directions for equity in mathematics education* (pp. 146–164). New York: Cambridge University Press.

Serpell, R. (2001). Cultural dimensions of literacy promotion and schooling. In L. Verhoven & C. E. Snow (Eds.), *Literacy and motivation: Reading engagement in individuals and groups* (pp. 243–273). Mahwah, NJ: Lawrence Erlbaum Associates.

Sfard, A. (1998). On two metaphors for learning and the dangers of choosing just one. *Educational Researcher, 27*(2), 4–13.

Sfard, A. (2008). *Thinking as communicating: Human development, the growth of discourses, and mathematizing.* Cambridge, UK: Cambridge University Press.

Sfard, A., & Linchevski, L. (1994). The gains and the pitfalls of reification: The case of algebra. *Educational Studies in Mathematics, 26*, 191–228.

Shapin, S. (1995). Here and everywhere—sociology of scientific knowledge. *Annual Review of Sociology, 21*, 289–321.

Shulman, L. S. (1987). Knowledge and teaching: Foundations of the new reform. *Harvard Educational Review, 57*(1), 1–21.

Sigel, I. E. (1979). On becoming a thinker: A psychoeducational model. *Educational Psychologist, 14*, 70–78.

Simon, M. A., Saldanha, L., McClintock, E., Karagoz Akar, G., Watanabe, T., & Ozgur Zembat, I. (2010). A developing approach to studying students' learning through their mathematical activity. *Cognition and Instruction, 28*, 70–112.

Simon, M. A., & Tzur, R. (2004). Explicating the role of mathematical tasks in conceptual learning: An elaboration of the hypothetical learning trajectory. *Mathematical Thinking and Learning, 6*(2), 91–104.

Simon, M. A., Tzur, R., Heinz, K., & Kinzel, M. (2004). Explicating a mechanism for conceptual learning: Elaborating the construct of reflective abstraction. *Journal for Research in Mathematics Education, 35*(5), 305–329.

Skinner, B. F. (1958a). *Verbal behavior.* New York: Macmillan.

Skinner, B. F. (1958b). Teaching machines. *Science, 128*, 969–977.

Sloboda, J. A., & Rogers, D. (Eds.) (1987). *Cognitive processes in mathematics.* Oxford: Oxford University Press.

Smith, E. E. (2001). Cognitive psychology: History. *International encyclopedia of the social and behavioral sciences.* New York: Elsevier, pp. 2140–2147. Retrieved from http://mechanism.ucsd.edu/teaching/w07/philpsych/smith.cogpsychhistory.pdf.

Snow, C. E. (2001). Preventing reading difficulties in young children: Precursors and fallout. In T. Loveless. (Ed.), *The great curriculum debate: How should we teach reading and math?* (pp. 229–246). Washington, DC: Brookings Institution Press.

Spivey, N. N. (1997). *The constructivist metaphor: Reading, writing, and the making of meaning.* San Diego: Academic Press.

Staats, A. W. (1981). Paradigmatic behaviorism, unified theory, unified theory construction methods, and the Zeitgeist of separatism. *American Psychologist, 36*(3), 239–256. doi: 10.1037/0003-066X.36.3.239.

Stanic, G. M. A., & Kilpatrick, J. (1988). Historical perspectives on problem solving in the mathematics curriculum. In R. I. Charles & E. A. Silver (Eds.), *The teaching and assessing of mathematical problem solving* (pp. 1–22). Hillsdale, NJ: Lawrence Erlbaum Associates; Reston, VA: National Council of Teachers of Mathematics.

Stanovich, K. E. (1986). Matthew effects in reading: Some consequences of individual differences in the acquisition of literacy. *Reading Research Quarterly, 21*, 360–406.

Steffe, L. P. (1991). The constructivist teaching experiment: Illustrations and implications. In E. von Glasersfeld (Ed.), *Radical constructivism in mathematics education* (pp. 177–194). Dordrecht, Holland: Kluwer Academic Publishers.

Steffe, L. (1994). Children's multiplying schemes. In G. Harel & J. Confrey (Eds.), *The development of multiplicative reasoning in the learning of mathematics* (pp. 3–40). Albany: State University of New York Press.

Steffe, L. P. (2003). Fractional commensurate, composition, and adding schemes: Learning trajectories of Jason and Laura: Grade 5. *Journal of Mathematical Behavior, 22,* 237–295.

Steffe, L. P., & Kieren, T. (1994). Radical constructivism and mathematics education. *Journal for Research in Mathematics Education, 25*(6), 711–733.

Steffe, L. P., & Thompson, P. W. (2000). Teaching experiment methodology: Underlying principles and essential elements. In A. Kelly & R. Lesh (Eds.), *Handbook of research design in mathematics and science education* (pp. 267–306). Mahwah, NJ: Lawrence Erlbaum Associates.

Sternberg, R. J. (1997). *Metaphors of mind: Conceptions of the nature of intelligence.* Cambridge, UK: Cambridge University Press.

Stigler, J. W., & Hiebert, J. (1999). *The teaching gap: Best ideas from the world's teachers for improving education in the classroom.* New York: The Free Press.

Stylianides, G. J., & Stylianides, A. J. (2009). Facilitating the transition from empirical arguments to proof. *Journal for Research in Mathematics Education, 40*(3), 314–352.

Sund, R. B., & Picard, A. J. (1972). *Behavioral objectives and evaluation measures: Science and mathematics.* Columbus, OH: Charles Merrill Publishing.

Thomas, C. (2004). Distracted subject: Madness and gender in Shakespeare and early modern culture. Ithaca, NY: Cornell University Press.

Thompson, P. W. (1994). The development of the concept of speed and its relationship to concepts of rate. In G. Harel & J. Confrey (Eds.), *The development of multiplicative reasoning in the learning of Mathematics* (pp. 181–236). Albany: State University of New York Press.

Thompson, P. W. (2013). In the absence of meaning. . . . In Leatham, K. (Ed.), *Vital directions for research in mathematics education* (pp. 57–93). New York: Springer.

Thorndike, E. L. (1898). *Animal intelligence: An experimental study of the associative processes in animals.* New York: Macmillan.

Thorndike, E. L. (1910). The contribution of psychology to education. *Journal of Educational Psychology, 1,* 5–12.

Thorndike, E. L. (1911). *Animal intelligence: Experimental studies.* New York: Macmillan. Retrieved from https://archive.org/stream/animalintelligen00thor#page/n5/mode/2up.

Thorndike, E. L., & Gates, A. I. (1929). The main characteristics of learning. In *Elementary principles of education* (pp. 84–106). New York: The Macmillan Company.

Thorndike, E. L., & Woodworth, R. L. (1901). The influence of improvement in one mental function upon the efficiency of other functions. *Psychological Review, 8,* 247–261.

Vågan, A. (2011). Towards a sociocultural perspective on identity formation in education. *Mind, Culture, and Activity, 18,* 43–57.

VanderStoep, S. W., & Seifert, C. M. (1993). Learning "how" versus learning "when": Improving transfer of problem-solving principles. *The Journal of the Learning Sciences, 3*(1), 93–111.

Vygotsky, L. S. (1926/1997). *Educational psychology* (R. Silverman, Trans.) Boca Raton, FL: St. Lucie Press.

Vygotsky, L. S. (1927/1987). *The historical meaning of the crisis in psychology: A methodological investigation.* New York: Plenum Press.

Vygotsky, L. S. (1934/1986). *Thought and language* (Chapter 6, "The development of scientific concepts in childhood"). Cambridge, MA: MIT Press.

Vygotsky, L. S. (1978). *Mind in society.* Cambridge, MA: Harvard University Press.

Wandersee, J. H., Mintzes, J. J., & Novak, J. D. (1994). Research on alternative conceptions in science. In D. L. Gabel (Ed.), *Handbook of research on science teaching and learning* (pp. 177–210). New York: Macmillan Publishing Company.

Wasley, P. (2006, June 6). Accreditor of education schools drops controversial 'social justice' standard for teacher candidates. *The Chronicle of Higher Education.* Retrieved from http://chronicle.com/article/Accreditor-of-Education/14458/.

Watson, J. B. (1913). Psychology as the behaviorist views it. *Psychological Review, 20,* 158–177.

Weimer, W. B., & Palermo, D. S. (1973). Paradigms and normal science in psychology. *Science Studies, 3,* 211–244.

White, B. Y. (1993). ThinkerTools: Causal models, conceptual change, and science education. *Cognition and Instruction, 10*(1), 1–100. Retrieved from www.jstor.org/stable/3233779?origin=JSTOR-pdf&seq=1#page_scan_tab_contents.

White, S. H. (1991). Three visions of a psychology of education. In L. T. Landsmann (Ed.), *Culture, schooling, and psychological development* (pp. 1–38). Norwood, NJ: Ablex.

Wilson, S.M. (2003). *California dreaming: Reforming mathematics education.* New Haven, CT: Yale University Press.

Windschitl, M. (2002). Framing constructivism in practice as the negotiation of dilemmas: An analysis of the conceptual, pedagogical, cultural, and political challenges facing teachers. *Review of Educational Research, 72*(2), 131–175. Retrieved from http://rer.sagepub.com/content/72/2/131.full.pdf+html.

Wittmann, E. (1995). Mathematics education as a 'design science.' *Educational Studies in Mathematics, 29*, 355–374.

Wojcikiewicz, S.K. (2010). Dewey, Peirce, and the categories of learning. *Education and Culture, 26*(2), 65–82.

Wojcikiewicz, S.K., & Wenzel, A. (2012, April). *Theories of learning as aspects of experience: A philosophical system for reconceptualizing, and teaching, behaviorist, cognitive, and situative perspectives.* Paper presented at AERA Annual Meeting, Vancouver, Canada.

Yackel, E., & Cobb, P. (1996). Sociomathematical norms, argumentation, and autonomy in mathematics. *Journal for Research in Mathematics Education, 27*(4), 458–477.

Section II

Democratic Access to Mathematics Learning

5 Young Children's Access to Powerful Mathematics Ideas

A Review of Current Challenges and New Developments in the Early Years

Joan Moss

OISE of the University of Toronto

Catherine D. Bruce

Trent University

Janette Bobis

The University of Sydney

A CALL TO ACTION

The importance of a sound introduction to mathematics in the early years is buttressed by recent research results that demonstrate the predictive power of early mathematics for later academic and career success (Claessens, Duncan, & Engel, 2009; Duncan et al., 2007; Geary, Hoard, Nugent, & Bailey, 2013; Ritchie & Bates, 2013). In 2007, Duncan et al. identified mathematics skills at kindergarten entry as the best predictor of school achievement, and that this finding was consistent for both boys and girls from high and low socioeconomic backgrounds. More recently, in a tracking study of 1,364 children from 54 months to the age of 15, Watts, Duncan, Siegler and Davis-Kean (2014) found that there were "statistically significant associations between preschool mathematical ability and adolescent mathematics achievement;" moreover, "gains in mathematical knowledge from preschool through first grade are even more predictive of age 15 mathematics achievement than preschool knowledge" (p. 352). Reading and working memory, by comparison, were found to be less predictive of later achievement. Together, these studies strongly indicate that high-quality mathematics learning opportunities, prior to formal schooling and in the first years of school, are crucial.

Fortunately, there is a strong and exciting research base evolving that demonstrates best practices for engaging children in significant mathematics activity. National associations and professional societies, such as the National Council of Teachers of Mathematics (NCTM, 2000) and the National Association for the Education of Young Children (NAEYC/NCTM, 2002), strongly recommend adoption of enriched and expanded mathematics programs in the early years.

Nevertheless, progress in implementing these best practices has been hampered by many factors: for example, the privileging of literacy over math in early years; the discomfort that many early years educators have with mathematics; and, most especially, by common misunderstandings and underestimations of young children's developmental capabilities in the areas of mathematical thinking. These and other factors limit the scope of ambition that teachers and policy makers hold for their young mathematics students. As a result, early years mathematics in many jurisdictions remains narrowly focused on basic counting, sorting, and naming of shapes, or else is relegated to unstructured play, devoid of systematic inquiry (Ginsburg, Lee, & Boyd, 2008).

Although these limitations of the scope and ambition of early childhood mathematics education underserve all children, the imperative of reform takes on added urgency when we consider the differential effects of weak mathematics programming and instruction on children of different social classes. In many countries with tiered education systems, educational expertise is inequitably distributed across income groups, with students of higher socioeconomic status (SES) more likely to obtain instruction conducted in accordance with recommended standards (Arnold & Doctoroff, 2003). A second factor is differences in the socialization experiences that young children of different social classes encounter prior to commencing preschool programs. These differences may privilege more-affluent students' readiness for school mathematics (Clements & Sarama, 2009). In this respect, students from low-resourced communities are more likely to fall behind their peers in early childhood education and elementary school. Fortunately, there is a growing body of research-based programs that have been shown to be promising for all young learners.

In this chapter we consider how to expand both pedagogy and the curriculum for young children to support equitable access to mathematics thinking and ideas. We discuss new research findings on the centrality of early mathematics for long-term overall academic success, and present promising developments in the areas of play and spatial reasoning.

In the first section of this chapter, "Current Issues, Approaches, and Programs for Early Years Mathematics," we summarize key recommendations of leading organizations with a focus on high quality early years mathematics. We review the literature on the gap in preparedness between children from low- and high-resourced communities and review recent research that links early math performance and later academic success. We also offer a description of some representative early year mathematics programs that have been shown to be successful in supporting young learners, particularly those at risk.

In the second section, "Documented Challenges to Mathematically Rich Instruction," we provide an analysis of some of the known impediments to widespread implementation of the recommendations by many professional organizations on early mathematics education. This section also includes a discussion on the attitudes and beliefs about mathematics content and pedagogy for early years classrooms.

The third section, "New Developments in the Field," examines recent developments in the mathematics education research community. The first is an articulation of the various perspectives and findings on the affordances of a playful and guided pedagogy. The second is an expanded conceptualization of early years mathematics curricula to include recent developments in geometry and spatial reasoning. Next, we offer vignettes that bring together guided pedagogy within the context of spatial reasoning to illustrate the sophisticated mathematics thinking that young children can demonstrate.

The next section, "Professional Development for Teachers of Young Children," describes several new models and promising approaches to early years teacher professional learning in mathematics. The chapter finishes with a succinct summary and series of recommendations. Whereas the early childhood years generally are identified as 0–8 years of age, the focus in this chapter is on mathematics teaching and learning in the 4–7 age range, roughly capturing the pre-kindergarten through to first grade span.

CURRENT ISSUES, APPROACHES, AND PROGRAMS FOR EARLY YEARS MATHEMATICS

In the past decade there has been an unprecedented political as well as academic focus on the high importance of mathematics in early years classrooms (Clarke, Clarke & Roche, 2011; Ginsburg et al., 2008; Hachey, 2013; MacDonald, Davies, Dockett, & Perry, 2012; Tirosh, Tsamir & Levenson, 2011; Purpura, Baroody, & Lonigan, 2013). Accumulating evidence confirms that children's mathematics learning in the first six years of life has profound, long-lasting outcomes for students in their later years—not only in relation to their future mathematics achievement but also in terms of overall academic success (e.g., Jordan & Levine, 2009; Duncan et al., 2007). The National Association for the Education of Young Children and the National Council of Teacher of Mathematics (NAEYC & NCTM, 2002) jointly identified mathematics as a crucial area of learning for young children and called for the provision of "high-quality, challenging, and accessible mathematics education for all 3- to 6-year-old children" (NAEYC & NCTM, 2002, p. 1).

Everyday Mathematics and Equity

It is now well known that young children have an intuitive and strong grasp of "everyday mathematics" (Ginsburg et al., 2008, p. 3), as well as having "sophisticated mathematical minds and a natural eagerness to engage in a range of mathematical activities" (English & Mulligan, 2013, p. 1; see also Anthony & Walshaw, 2007; Baroody, Lai, & Mix, 2006; Hunting et al., 2013; Perry & Dockett, 2008; Sarama & Clements, 2009). Even before children enter preschool they develop an *everyday mathematics* that is "surprisingly broad, complex, and sometimes sophisticated" (Ginsburg et al., 2008, p. 3). This everyday mathematics may be innate or drawn from daily experiences, and has been shown to provide the foundation for learning more complex and abstract mathematics throughout school (Jordan & Levine, 2009). Indeed, given the breadth of young children's everyday mathematics, cognitive scientists (West, Denton, & Germino-Hausken, 2000; Baroody & Wilkins, 1999; Hunting, 2003), and math education scholars call for a raising of the curriculum ceiling, because "children often know more than curriculum developers or teachers give them credit" (Sarama & Clements, 2008, p. 68; see also Bruce & Hawes, 2014; Bruce, Moss, & Flynn, 2013).

Unfortunately, not all young children possess—nor have they been exposed to—the same quality of everyday mathematics. Despite many strong universal starting points, there are striking differences in children's mathematics readiness by the time they enter school—differences often attributed to factors related to SES (Baroody, 2006; Case, Griffin & Kelly, 1999; Jordan, Kaplan, Oláh, & Locuniak, 2006; Klibanoff, Levine, Huttenlocher, Vasilyeva, & Hedges, 2006; Lee & Burkam, 2002; Saxe, Guberman, & Gearhart, 1987; Starkey, Klein, & Wakeley, 2004). There is ample research illustrating that kindergarten students from low-resource families lag behind in mathematics knowledge and readiness compared to peers from more affluent families (Alexander & Entwisle, 1988; Claessens et al., 2009; Duncan et al., 2007; Jordan & Levine, 2009). As Clements and Sarama (2011a) note, "some 6-year-olds have not acquired mathematical knowledge that other children acquire at 3 years of age" (p. 5). Although both groups of children may have informal experiences with quantitative situations, those from low-resource communities tend to have fewer opportunities to mathematize this tacit knowledge—that is, to reflect on, and represent, the situations. Research has found that children from low-income families are less able to explain mathematical ideas and processes than their more-privileged peers.

Furthermore, this gap between low-income and middle-income students widens over time in the absence of intervention (Cannon, Jackowitz, & Painter, 2006; Crosnoe & Cooper, 2010). These SES differences pose a major problem in early education contexts with respect to mathematics, where, as we elaborate in this chapter, early competencies have been found to be strong predictors of later academic success, including social studies and reading (Duncan et al., 2007; Verdine et al., 2013).

Mathematics in Kindergarten as the Best Predictor of Later Academic Success

In a landmark set of studies, Claessens, Duncan, and colleagues (e.g., Claessens et al., 2009; Claessens & Engel, 2011; Duncan et al., 2007), found that mathematics skills measured at kindergarten entry were the *best* predictor of later school achievement, and that this finding was consistent for both boys and girls from high and low socioeconomic backgrounds. These studies, involving up to 36,000 students and combining six international data sets, found that children's school-entry mathematics abilities measured at kindergarten were strongly predictive of later academic success, above and beyond the variance accounted for by reading, attention, and socio-emotional skills. Furthermore, the researchers found that "early mathematics skills predicted reading, math, and science achievement as well as grade retention from kindergarten through eighth grade" and that the "importance of these math skills for subsequent achievement increases or is maintained over time." (Claessens & Engel, 2011, p. 2). Further, the findings held true across demographic groups:

> The fact that these early skills are equally important for all children reinforces the need to continue to work to reduce the achievement gap and to ensure that all children 1) begin school with the skills necessary to succeed and 2) are supported adequately in their efforts to continue to learn.
>
> (p. 22)

These and other findings point to the profound importance of early mathematics learning to prepare children for school and life success (Baroody et al., 2006). Jordan and Levine (2009) warn that, without adequate support in the first years of schooling, learners who experience difficulties in mathematics in the early years can experience "a cascade of mathematics failure" (Jordan & Levine, 2009, p. 6) that threatens their ability to catch up (see also Aunola, Leskinen, Lerkkanen, & Nurmi, 2004).

In the interest of establishing equitable starting points for students of all backgrounds, the US National Research Council (NRC) urges policy makers to provide young children with "extensive, high-quality early mathematics instruction that can serve as a sound foundation for later learning in mathematics and contribute to addressing long-term systemic inequities in educational outcomes" (Cross, Woods, & Schweingruber, 2009, p. 2). Baroody et al. (2006) further assert that, "most individual differences are probably due to the lack of opportunity" (p. 200). Therefore establishing the foundations of mathematics knowledge early in formal schooling "seems to be an essential first step for achieving equity (Baroody et al., 2006, p. 202). In the most basic sense, early mathematics education is one of the most important social justice issues.

Policy Directions and Visions of School Mathematics

To elaborate on what is meant by "extensive, high level early mathematics instruction," we look to NAEYC/NCTM and NRC. NAEYC/NCTM (2002) state that mathematics in early years classrooms should address the big ideas in all of the strands of mathematics through the processes of problem solving, analysis, and communication. Further, NRC (2009) declares that early years teaching must be *intentional*. Intentional teaching involves teachers "adapting teaching to the content, type of learning experience, and individual child with a clear learning target as a goal" (NRC, 2009, p. 226).

The intuitive foundational mathematics skills that young children naturally develop are not enough; it is through intentional teaching that children can advance beyond their intuitive mathematics to meaningfully interpret foundational mathematical principles (Ginsburg, 2009; Hachey, 2013).

Early Years Mathematics Programs

Given the moral and practical imperative to improve mathematics programming for young children, some mathematics education researchers and psychologists have been developing comprehensive intervention programs to support closing achievement gaps of children prior to entering formal schooling and in the first years of school.

Since the late 1990s, a number of high quality, research-based, early years mathematics programs have been developed to support young students, particularly children from low-resource communities, to engage in rigorous mathematics learning. Descriptions of the wide range of early years programs is beyond the scope of this chapter. Instead we present four of these programs—Building Blocks, Number Worlds (Rightstart), Pattern and Structure Mathematical Awareness Program, and Big Math for Little Kids—because they span, at a minimum, the pre-kindergarten to first grade (the target age group for this chapter) and, importantly, because the central features of these programs are representative of most of the successful early year mathematics curricula. We have also selected these programs because they specifically address the needs of children at risk and have been empirically tested and shown to be effective in supporting young students to succeed at mathematics beyond their expected levels of competence.

As we note in the descriptions of the four programs there are a number of differences amongst them in terms of scope of topics, level of technology use (for an example of high technology use, see Maschietto & Soury-Lavergne's EducMath program, originating in France), and the overall organization of material. Along with these differences however, the four programs share fundamental principles and features. These commonalities include: (1) the use of the children's mathematical knowledge and interests as a starting point for learning; (2) the understanding that play alone is not enough to ensure deep understanding of foundational mathematics ideas and therefore, mathematics should be introduced and enriched in a planned way; (3) the understanding that activities should be designed and organized based on developmental theory; and (4) the assumption that sensitive adult guidance is required. Each of these programs also involves substantial professional development. Finally, the general hypothesis underlying each program is, to quote (Greenes, Ginsburg, & Balfanz, 2004), "extensive engagement in activities offered. . . may lead to higher levels of competence than ordinarily observed in young children" (p. 164).

Building Blocks—Foundations for Mathematics Thinking Program (Clements & Sarama, 2002)

We begin our discussion of the four selected math programs with Clements' and Sarama's Building Blocks curriculum, which, to date, has undergone several phases of rigorous evaluation and has been shown to be highly successful. (See Clements and Sarama, 2008 and Clements, Sarama, Spitler, Lange, & Wolfe, 2011 for details of randomized controlled studies showing strong effect sizes of the program.) Designed for students from pre-kindergarten through second grade, the Building Blocks program has been created to support young students to gain competence in the domains of: (1) number concepts (in particular, in subitizing, counting and arithmetic operations); and (2) spatial and geometric concepts, and processes. Clements and Sarama state that they selected these topics because they are "mathematically foundational, generative for, and interesting to young children" (p. 6). Within these two areas, three mathematical themes are integrated: patterns, data and sorting, and sequencing (Sarama, 2004). The activities included in Building Blocks are aimed at "finding the mathematics in, and developing mathematics from children's everyday activity" (Sarama & Clements, 2002, p. 93).

While this program involves a wide range of classroom activities, a particular feature of Building Blocks is the prominent use of computer software designed as part of the curriculum (Sarama, 2004; Clements & Sarama, 2002). The software component supports students' modeling and mathematizing and, importantly, allows for individualized learning experiences.

A second important feature of this program, and one that is a foundational contribution, is the incorporation of rigorously researched learning trajectories that underlie each topic and subtopic. Learning trajectories, first introduced and used in the Netherlands within the Realistic mathematics program (Gravemeijer, 1994), and also developed and used by Dutch researchers (Van den Heuvel-Panhuizen, 2008; Van den Heuvel-Panhuizen & Buys, 2008; Van den Heuvel-Panhuizen, Kühne, & Lombard, 2012), constitute the core around which all educational activities are structured in the Building Blocks program. These trajectories involve descriptions of successive levels of mathematical reasoning towards a goal of a specific topic and are embedded in the instructional activities that enable students to progress from one level to another. For example, in the geometry strand in the area of composing and decomposing, students move from the level of "Pre-Composer," a level in which the child manipulates shapes as individual pieces and is yet unable to combine them to compose large shape; to "Picture Maker," in which the student chooses shapes using gestalt configuration and a pick-discard strategy; to "Shape Composer," in which the child is able to combine shapes to make new shapes with anticipation.

The Number Worlds Program (Griffin, 2004)

The design of the Number Worlds program (originally called Rightstart; see Griffin, Case, & Siegler, 1994) also is heavily grounded in a developmental trajectory approach. However, in this program, the focus is exclusively on number development and is underpinned by the central conceptual structure theory for whole number development (e.g., Case & Okamoto, 1996). Briefly, a central conceptual structure is defined as a powerful organizing knowledge network that plays a central role in enabling individuals to master the problems that a domain presents. The proposal is that the central conceptual structure for number is built on the integration of two separate competencies/schemas, that young children (3 years old) possess: one is an initial counting schema, and the other, a global quantity comparison scheme that is intuitive and involves a nonnumerical sense of quantity. As documented in extensive cognitive developmental research (summarized in Griffin & Case, 1996), it is the merging of these two separate schemas at the age 5 or 6 that supports the formation of a single, superordinate conceptual structure for number.

Griffin, Case and Siegler (1994) propose that this structure is an internal counting line, a continuum increasing in one-unit steps, to which the child has access when solving mathematical tasks and learning new ideas. Once the child has developed the central conceptual structure, they are able to use the counting numbers without needing the presence of physical objects to make a variety of quantity judgments, such as determining how many objects they would have altogether if they had four of something and received three more. One of the motivating factors for the creation of the Number Worlds program was research revealing that a substantial number of children living in low-income communities in Canada and the United States start school at age 6 without this conceptual structure in place and are at risk for significant mathematics difficulties (Griffin et al., 1994).

Based on this developmental central conceptual structure theory, activities in the Number Worlds program follow a specific order. It begins by presenting students with activities to help them build each separate competence/schema and then to integrate them. Thus, the Number Worlds program provides activities that involve quantities, counting, and formal symbols, and is organized to provide multiple opportunities for constructing relationships among the three aspects. Importantly, the program provides a carefully graded sequence of activities that enable students to use their current understandings to construct new understandings at the next level up.

Activities in the pre-kindergarten program enable 4-year-old students to use their conceptual structures to acquire the foundational knowledge that they will need later. Activities in the kindergarten program allow students to construct and consolidate their central conceptual structure. Within each grade level, activities have also been classified at three levels of developmental complexity. A seamless sequence of activities permits individual students to start at an appropriate individual level and to move through the normal developmental progression at a suitable pace.

Finally, in the Number Worlds program games are used to expose young students to five different forms of number representation that are common in our culture: groups of objects in

Object Land, dot-set patterns and numerals in Picture Land, position on a path or line in Line Land, position on a vertical scale in Sky Land, and position on a dial in Circle Land.

Expanded programs for four grade levels (pre-K–2) enable students to forge connections among these "lands" at increasing levels of complexity.

Pattern and Structure Mathematical Awareness Program (Mulligan & Mitchelmore, 2009, 2013)

The Australian early years mathematics program, Pattern and Structure Mathematical Awareness Program (PASMAP), consists of a series of learning experiences developed for children in kindergarten through Grade 2, and is based on the assumptions that awareness of pattern and structure is a fundamental requirement for understanding mathematics; and that pattern and structure can be learned through appropriate learning experiences and explicit teaching (Mulligan & Mitchelmore; see also English, 2012, 2013). The authors of this program assert that the early development of patterning and structural thinking in mathematics is critical to the abstraction and generalization of mathematical ideas and relationships. In the authors' view, mathematical development depends to a large extent on the structure of students' thinking and how well this reflects the structure of mathematical concepts and relationships. For example, children need to recognize mathematical structure and how it is generalized in order to understand how the number system is organized by grouping in tens, and how equal groups form the basis of multiplication and division concepts (Mulligan, Prescott, Papic, & Mitchelmore, 2006). Research conducted by Mulligan and team reveals that children with a strong sense of structure can more easily recognize similarities and differences in new mathematical patterns, whereas children with low structure tend to focus on more superficial features of patterns and relationship. The result for students who do not have a strong sense of structure is that they are less likely to transfer their understanding (Mulligan & Mitchelmore, 2013; Mulligan et al., 2006).

Theoretically, PASMAP is grounded in the proposed existence of an Awareness of Mathematical Pattern and Structure (AMPS) construct. The degree to which children recognize and apply pattern and structure is referred to as their AMPS. According to this theory, the AMPS construct generalizes across many early mathematical concepts and is correlated with children's mathematical understanding. The AMPS construct, which Mulligan and Mitchelmore (2013, p. 35) classify in five developmental levels, from "Prestructural" to "Advanced Structural," involves both cognitive and metacognitive abilities: cognitive involves knowledge of structure, and metacognitive involves a tendency to seek and analyze patterns.

PASMAP consists of guidelines for a large number of learning sequences designed to support young students' pattern awareness in the first three years of formal schooling. Amongst the learning sequences included in PASMAP are patterning, structured counting, place value, partitioning and sharing, measurement, grid structure, geometry, and symmetry and transformation. Each separate learning sequence follows an identical developmental pattern of learning experiences for the students and is comprised of four separate stepwise components. (1) The initial activities in the learning sequence involves various types of "modeling" where students either copy, model, or describe a pattern or structure within the topic. The teacher's role in this first set of activities is to support students in understanding the essential features of the pattern or relation. (2) The second set of activities involves "representing." Here the children are required to physically draw the pattern or a model of the pattern while it is still visible. This experience reinforces child understanding and representational skill. (3) Next in the learning sequence are activities involving "visualization." To this end the tasks students engage with involve drawing or symbolizing without being able to see the original structure. (4) Finally, children work towards making "generalizations": at this stage of the process teachers explicitly support students in understanding the structure of the pattern and work with students to find similar patterns in other contexts. PASMAP can be implemented as a complete mathematics program that aligns with the Australian mathematics curriculum (Australian Curriculum, Assessment, and Reporting Authority, 2014). Alternatively, learning sequences from PASMAP can be integrated with existing mathematics programs to support particular aspects of the curriculum such as patterns and algebra.

Big Math for Little Kids (Greenes et al., 2004)

The Big Math for Little Kids program is a mathematics curriculum designed to facilitate mathematics learning for pre-kindergarten to first grade students (Greenes et al. 2004). The program is the most comprehensive of the four described in this section and includes six units (number, shape, measurement, constructing and partitioning numbers, patterns and logic, and navigation and spatial concepts). The program is designed to be used in whole-class and small-group settings, as well as with individual students. It contains a sequence of enjoyable activities designed to promote both mathematical understanding and language (Greenes et al., 2004). This program is firmly grounded in the intensive research and observational studies of young children's spontaneous mathematics in preschool settings. Unlike the other programs presented here, which follow highly specified trajectories, the Big Math for Little Kids program focuses on a variety of types of activities, games, tasks, stories, and verbal expression in an integrated framework. In fact, storybooks were developed for each of the strands in the program.

Central among the goals of Big Math for Little Kids is to support all students, including those at risk, to verbalize their mathematics and to learn to mathematize. The Big Math for Little Kids program should encourage "thinking like a mathematician," promote language development, and foster student reflection (Greenes et al., 2004). The intensive language focus of the Big Math for Little Kids program emanates from research by Greenes and colleagues. In particular, the focus on language and metacognition in the Big Math for Little Kids program stems from research on the well-known lag in performance between high- and low-SES students in verbal number sense, addition, and subtraction. The research revealed, for example, that while both high- and low-SES students employed similar strategies when presented with addition and subtraction problems (such as counting on from the larger number, or "derived facts"), what differed was the way that these two groups of children articulated these strategies and understandings, with the lower SES group experiencing much more difficulty (Ginsburg & Pappas, 2004). Big Math for Little Kids has a promising record of success (e.g., Presser, Clements, Ginsburg & Ertle, 2012) and in particular, demonstrates a gap-closing intervention in the form of a mathematically rich program that benefits all students.

Some Concluding Thoughts on Early years Mathematics Programs

The four math programs described share some common underpinning beliefs: First, programs and related instruction are impactful when they are research-based and developmentally sound. Second, the learning builds on a child's current mathematical knowledge. Third, children benefit from a planned program that is carefully guided by adults who draw children's attention to the mathematics at hand. And fourth, children come to be able to engage in significant mathematics when the tasks are well constructed with appropriate materials and ideas. We suggest that there are several other foundations to quality mathematics programming for young children, including (1) the importance of daily/regular mathematics learning opportunities; (2) the importance of teacher-student interaction over peer interactions when developing and solidifying mathematics ideas; and (3) the value of multiple teaching contexts and less reliance on student rotation through centers (e.g., Bruce et al., 2013; Ginsburg et al., 2008).

While it is helpful to know that well-constructed programs are available, it is also important to underline that despite the existence of these exemplars, there is limited rich mathematics programming occurring in many classrooms. There are a host of reasons why this may be the case. For example, teachers of young children may not be comfortable teaching mathematics, or may hold beliefs about mathematics learning that run counter to the most fundamental principles of the programs mentioned in this chapter. Of particular concern is the pervasive underestimation of student interests and abilities in mathematics, leading to strongly restricted mathematics programs of counting and naming shapes (Ginsburg et al., 2008). These, and other existing challenges, are discussed next.

DOCUMENTED CHALLENGES TO MATHEMATICALLY RICH INSTRUCTION

While the arguments, and visions, for high-quality early years mathematics programs are well researched and well articulated, the kinds of systemic changes needed to realize these visions for early years mathematics are not easily achieved. Here we outline some of the main challenges to mathematically rich instruction in the early years.

Negative Attitudes, Beliefs, and Lack of Interest in Mathematics Content and Pedagogy

Mathematics educational research has identified a host of challenges in the domain of attitudes and beliefs toward mathematics itself and in turn, how it should be taught. Teachers of young children often report anxieties, discomfort, and difficulties teaching mathematics (Copley, 2004; Lee & Ginsburg, 2007). Compared to other elementary educators, kindergarten to grade 4 teachers (working with children of ages 4 through 10), have reported the most strongly negative attitudes toward mathematics (Kolstad & Hughes, 1994). Many teachers of young children also admit to not seeing themselves as teachers of mathematics—what Ginsburg and Ertel (2008) call an "identity issue." Further, many teachers of young children report selecting a career in educating young children (rather than older students) *because* they do not like mathematics or they do not want to teach mathematics (Ginsburg & Ertel, 2008). In a survey of primarily female preservice elementary teachers ($n = 384$), Perry (2011) found that those preservice teachers who chose careers in elementary education reported notably low confidence levels in learning mathematics—lower on average than those women who chose careers in other fields.

These challenges facing teachers of early years mathematics must not be interpreted as a criticism of educators, but of systemic, cultural and historical factors. As Stipek (2013) cogently writes, "we cannot blame the teachers. Until recently we have not expected instruction in mathematics in early childhood education programs. And in addition to not being trained, many are not comfortable with their own mathematical skill" (in Ginsburg et al., 2008, p. 13).

The overall challenge arises from the scarcity of examples and models of effective early years mathematics teaching. In fact, early years mathematics teaching, learning, and related educational research receives relatively little focus internationally from the mathematics education community. In our recent search of peer-reviewed mathematics education journals, the term "early childhood mathematics education" found only 83 scholarly articles between 2005 and 2013 (approximately 10 articles per year) over all mathematics education journals (ProQuest search, May 2014).

This overall low interest may explain a related devaluing of mathematics teaching in early years classrooms. Ginsburg, Lee, and Boyd (2008) found that "in general, early childhood teachers do not place a high value on teaching mathematics" (p. 10). Rather, helping children develop socially and emotionally (Kowalski, Pretti-Frontczak, & Johnson, 2001; Lee, 2006; Lin, Lawrence, & Gorrell, 2003) and protecting them from tedium and stress have been reported as top priorities for educators of young children (Lee, 2006; Lee & Ginsburg, 2007). Further, many educators believe that their students will eventually catch up to their peers mathematically, regardless of what happens during their early childhood years (Lee & Ginsburg, 2007, 2009).

As Lee and Ginsburg's studies point out, teachers believe that young children are not ready for, nor are they interested in mathematics, that young children are not capable of high level or abstract reasoning, and that simple numbers and shapes are the most appropriate mathematics content in early years of schooling. A final complication is a widely held belief that mathematics should not be a stand-alone subject, but should rather be integrated into other learning where students "don't even know they are doing math." Indeed, a play approach to mathematics has wide currency: many teachers of early years strongly hold to the belief that all mathematics activity should emerge from child-directed play. While there is widespread agreement that young children learn through actively constructing their mathematics knowledge, there are still many questions about the kinds of pedagogy that are appropriate for early years mathematics learning.

The Belief That All Mathematics Learning Should Emerge From Children's Unguided Play

In this section, we elaborate on the predominant play pedagogy and the potential limitations of unguided play for deep learning in mathematics. There is no dispute that play is central to early years education and is acknowledged as an important mode of engaging students in mathematics learning in early years (e.g., Bergen, 2009; Caldera et al., 1999; Perry & Dockett, 2002). Amongst the many other affordances of play for learning, play has been reported to support the development of dispositions and habits of mind valued in mathematics education, such as curiosity, creativity, and acceptance of multiple routes or multiple possible answers to the same problem (Ginsburg, 2006; NAEYC/NCTM, 2002; Dockett & Perry, 2007). However, while play offers extensive possibilities, it "does not guarantee mathematical development" (NAEYC/NCTM, 2002, p. 6; cited in de Vries, Thomas, & Warren, 2010, p. 717). "Children do learn from play, but it appears that they can learn much more with artful guidance and challenging activities provided by their teachers" (Seo & Ginsburg, 2004, p. 103). Furthermore, Sarama and Clements (2009) argue that when children play with mathematics-related objects by themselves, it is unlikely that their play will facilitate the learning of the intended concepts.

Among the many challenges cited of a play-only approach is that the learning program can become "a grab bag of any mathematics-related experiences that seem to relate to a theme or project" (NAEYC/NCTM, 2002, p. 8). Further, drawing out the mathematics through teachable moments, when they are recognized, is "extraordinarily difficult" (Ginsburg & Ertle, 2008, p. 47). In a play-based mathematics program there is also little opportunity for teachers to support the critical process of mathematization: redescribing, abstracting, generalizing, and giving language to that which is first understood at an intuitive and informal level (Clements and Sarama, 2009, p. 244). Both exploiting the teachable moment and supporting mathematization is a sophisticated process that demands a nuanced mathematics knowledge and heightened attention to what mathematics children are actually doing and thinking about in their play (Clements & Sarama, 2009; Ginsburg et al., 2008; Perry & Dockett, 2008). As Ginsburg and Ertel (2008) assert, play alone likely does not address the gap in abilities for students from low-resource communities who may suffer from lack of opportunity to engage with mathematics (see also Bowman, Donovan, & Burns, 2001; Starkey & Klein, 2008).

Narrow Conceptions of What Mathematics Should Be Taught

The limitations of unstructured and nonmathematized play, coupled with a general lack of interest in mathematics for young children, is concerning. As a result, there are wide reports of a limited content palette of early years mathematics programs (Balfanz, 1999) that focus on counting to 20, repeating patterns, and naming shapes (Copley, 2004; Frede, Jung, Barnett, Lamy, & Figueras, 2007; Graham, Nash, & Paul, 1997), leaving young children undernourished in their mathematical development (Ginsburg et al., 2008).

Fortunately, there are some very promising new developments in the field that may offer a way forward in response to the current call to action.

NEW DEVELOPMENTS IN THE FIELD

We turn now to some new developments in the field of mathematics for young children with the potential of offering children improved access to a deeper and broader range of mathematics learning opportunities. In the first of these developments, we present the benefits of a *playful pedagogy*. Next, we discuss the potential benefits of a mathematics curriculum that includes a much stronger emphasis on spatial reasoning. Then we combine these two developments in the form of three vignettes to illustrate the sophisticated and genuine reasoning of young children as they participate in classroom lessons that focus on geometry and spatial reasoning.

New Research Findings on the Effectiveness of a Playful Pedagogy

There is accumulating evidence over the last decade that a middle ground between unguided play and direct instruction may be most effective in supporting young students in learning mathematics. Variously called *guided discovery* (Baroody et al., 2006), *guided play* (Singer, Golnikoff, & Hirsh-Pasek, 2006), or *structured play* (Bruce & Flynn, 2012), this middle ground approach integrates the child-centered engagement of play with curricular goals and enabling children to maintain a large degree of control over their learning.

In a particularly detailed study, Baroody et al. (2006) articulated a helpful continuum of pedagogies for early years mathematics based on their classroom observations. The continuum is described at four points, from (1) *traditional direct-instruction*, to (2) *guided discovery learning via an adult-initiated task*, to (3) *flexible guided discovery learning via a child-initiated task*, and finally to (4) *unguided discovery learning via a child-initiated task*. The continuum of types were distinguished by identifying who was initiating the task or learning (the child or the teacher) and the degree of teacher "guidance" (from none to fully) that occurred during the task. Baroody and colleagues' observations of children in classrooms found that guided discovery and flexible guided discovery (the two categories in the center of the continuum) were the most promising approaches for learning mathematics, but that each one of these approaches held an important place in early years classrooms.

More recently, Fisher, Hirsh-Pasek, Newcombe, and Golinkoff (2013) tested the efficacy of a pedagogical approach that they referred to as *guided play*. In this study, the researchers asked: What would a pedagogy look like that combined early years' teachers' attention to the whole child and the inclusion of play and choice, with elementary-grade practices of robust content and attention to learning trajectories? The authors reported on results of a teaching experiment with kindergarten-aged children in which they compared the efficacy of children's learning about properties of geometric shapes in three conditions: direct instruction, guided play, and free play. Although the scope of this chapter does not allow for a full description of their methods and results (please see Fisher et al., 2013 for the full report) we take time here to provide some details of the experimental intervention to illuminate the way the researchers operationalized this construct of guided play.

In this study, 70 4- to 5-year-old children were introduced to the properties of four geometric shapes (triangles, rectangles, pentagons, and hexagons) and were randomly assigned to one of three learning/teaching modes: guided play, free play, or direct instruction. Researchers chose 4–5 year olds because they typically display some knowledge of shapes and often rely heavily on visual representations in their mathematics meaning making. The goal of the experimental intervention was that the students would recognize shapes not only in their canonical form (regular), which is typical of students in the age range (Van Hiele, 1999), but that they would also be able to identify irregular shapes (irregular in orientation or lengths of sides) as *real* shapes. In addition, the study assessed whether these young students would reject distractor shapes that closely resembled one of the four target shapes but had incorrect features. In mathematics education terms, the goal of the teaching experiment was to move students from a simply visual recognition of the shapes to a more analytical one.

Interestingly, the conditions of the guided play and direct instruction approaches were similar in more ways than they were different. In both of these conditions the teacher-researcher introduced the child to a play-like scenario about the secrets of shapes. In both the guided and direct-instruction conditions the researcher began with the following text: "Did you know that all shapes have secrets?" In the direct-instruction condition, the experimenter continued by saying: "Today I am going to *tell* you the secret of the shapes." By contrast in the guided play condition the researcher said: "Today I need your *help in discovering the secret* of the shapes." The researchers explained the difference as one of telling (direct) versus one that involved the students in inferring (guided).

As the lesson progressed, the teacher in the direct-instruction condition defined the properties (secrets) of each shape. In the guided-play condition, the instructor encouraged the students to focus on and identify what they saw as similar in each shape category. Essentially in both conditions the students were asked to focus on the similarities amongst the individual shapes: however, in the direct instruction condition, the experimenter was teaching by *telling* versus in the guided play condition the researcher was teaching by *implying* (Fisher et al., 2013).

Results revealed that children in the guided-play and direct-instruction conditions both made progress. However, the students in the guided-play condition made significantly more progress and showed deeper conceptual processing of shape features, and they were better able to extrapolate, compared to students who were taught through direct instruction. The children in the free play condition did not improve at all. This group showed no change in understanding.

The results of this study point to the greater efficacy of the guided but playful approach to mathematics learning. The study is also useful in helping to define and operationalize through a detailed example, a model for a middle ground approach to mathematics teaching of young children that clearly sits in the middle between play and direct instruction: a playful and intentional pedagogy.

It is important to note that on the other side of the early years pedagogy debate are proponents for direct instruction. The assertion is that direct instruction is more efficient and facilitates children's learning more effectively than other approaches (Stockard & Engelmann, 2008). However, while this approach is gaining in popularity in countries such as the United States, the United Kingdom and Australia, in reality there has been little conclusive research to support the efficacy of direct instruction in early years settings (Diamond, Barnett, Thomas, & Munro, 2007), particularly in the area of mathematics learning (Fisher, Hirsh-Pasek, Newcombe, & Golinkoff, 2013). Indeed there are some reports that state direct instruction interventions in early years are seen by some as undermining later development and learning (Hirsh-Pasek, Hyson, & Rescorla, 1990; Marcon, 2002). The conflicting findings to date point to the need for additional and precise comparative studies with children ages 4 through 7.

A Growing Knowledge and Interest in the Affordances of a Spatial Approach to Young Children's Mathematics

Another recent development in the growing field of mathematics education research with young children is examining the potential benefits of a mathematics curriculum that builds on and expands children's geometric and spatial reasoning abilities. This very recent development is not yet fully realized and has emerged since the previous edition of this *Handbook*.

The inclusion of geometry in early years classrooms has, for the most part, been dominated by recognizing and naming shapes (Copley, 2004). Freudenthal (1981) asserted that geometry is the most neglected subject of mathematics teaching, referring to geometry as the "forgotten" strand in pre-kindergarten through senior school mathematics curricula. Although Clements and Sarama (2011b) have led the way in championing the importance of geometry in early years, it has received much less research emphasis in the mathematics education literature than has number (NRC, 2009). Indeed the concern about the minimal role of geometry in early years curriculum and up through the grades has been recognized for decades. A search of the mathematics education research literature in early years reveals that, with the exception of a handful of programs (Casey et al., 2008; Clements & Sarama, 2007; Levenson, Tirosh, & Tsamir, 2011; Van den Heuvel-Panhuizen & Buijs, 2005), there has been a notable absence of program focus on young children's learning in the area of geometry.

Van den Heuvel-Panhuizen and Buijs (2005) urge us to provide "more space for geometry in primary school" (p.145). This call for increased attention on geometric thinking is important because of its foundational role in overall mathematics, "where students learn to reason and to see the axiomatic structure of mathematics" (NCTM, 2000, p. 41). In its *Principles and Standards for School Mathematics* document, the NCTM parses geometry in the early years (K–2) mathematics programs into four categories of activity: (1) analyzing properties of two- and three-dimensional geometric figures; (2) locating objects in space and describing spatial relationships; (3) applying transformations and using symmetry; (4) using visualization and spatial reasoning. Although now over 10 years old, this set of descriptions moves well beyond typical classroom learning for 4–8 year olds at present, and helps set an agenda for renewed mathematics education research energies. Within each of these four NCTM categories of geometry activity, spatial reasoning is prominent. Spatial reasoning of young children, including the ability to visualize, engage in perspective taking, situate oneself and other objects in space, and to mentally rotate figures, is proving to be a key predictor of overall mathematics abilities (Mix & Cheng, 2012; Verdine et al., 2013).

To date, the study of spatial reasoning has been largely conducted within the domains of cognitive sciences and psychology (Gathercole & Pickering, 2000; Levine, Huttenlocher, Taylor, & Langrock, 1999; Cheng & Mix, 2012; Newcombe, 2010, 2013; Newcombe & Frick, 2010). One particularly promising finding reported in an award-winning meta-analysis is that spatial reasoning is malleable: it can be improved with practice and training for people of all ages (Uttal et al., 2013). Recent findings connecting spatial reasoning abilities to the science, technology, engineering, and mathematics (STEM) disciplines, have begun to attract the attention of some mathematics and science educators, as well as mathematics education researchers who are now exploring how spatial reasoning can be embedded in mathematics programs that are grounded in classroom-based research initiatives (Battista, 2007; Clements & Sarama, 2011a; Sinclair & Bruce, 2014; Van den Heuvel-Panhuizen & Buys, 2008; Whiteley, 2002). Currently, as with geometry in general, there are minimal high-quality, field-tested resources for teachers that focus on building spatial reasoning (Clements & Sarama, 2011a; Ehrlich, Levine, & Goldin-Meadow, 2006) although some classroom field-tested resources that intentionally zero in on spatial reasoning (Stipek, 2013), are now being developed to accompany these recent findings on its importance. (See, for example, Clements & Sarama, 2002; Moss et al., 2012; Bruce, Flynn, McPherson, & Bennett, 2012.)

Reports from the United Kingdom (Jones, 2000), Australia (MacDonald et al., 2012) and in the United States (Clements and Sarama, 2011b) further corroborate these findings and suggest that the lack of focus on early geometry learning is of international concern. For example, a recent U.S. study tested 81 kindergarten teachers, more than half whom had MA degrees or higher, on their mathematical content knowledge of number sense, patterning, ordering, shapes, spatial sense, and comparison problems. The teachers scored lowest in their knowledge of spatial sense, obtaining a mean score of 44.23 compared to a mean score of 89.12 on the test of number sense (Lee, 2010).

The lack of attention paid to, and understanding of, geometry and spatial thinking is troubling given its fundamental importance to the development of mathematics. As Clements and Sarama (2011) point out, geometry is a special kind of language through which we communicate ideas that are essentially spatial, "from number lines to arrays, even quantitative, numerical, and arithmetical ideas rest on a geometric base" (p. 134). In addition, they note that geometry spans mathematics and science and is central to other disciplines such as physics, chemistry, biology, geology, geography, art, and architecture (Wai, Lubinski & Benbow, 2009). Furthermore, the work of developmental psychologists solidifies the importance of spatial thinking in mathematics in general. Over a century of psychological research supports the close relationship between spatial and mathematical processes, so much so, that Mix and Cheng (2012) claim that "the relation between spatial ability and mathematics is so well established that it no longer makes sense to ask whether they are connected" (p. 206). A recent meta-analysis has shown that spatial reasoning is malleable and can be improved with practice and training in people of all ages (Uttal et al., 2013). Furthermore, Newcombe, Uttal, and Sauter (2013) suggest that by providing instructional support to enhance young children's spatial reasoning, we are opening up possibilities for their long-term interest and engagement with STEM-related activities. More specifically, Verdine et al. (2014), suggest that incorporating spatial reasoning into early years math will have a "two-for-one" effect that yields benefits both for spatial reasoning as well as mathematical development (p. 6). Moreover, teaching spatial ability enhances children's mathematical attitude (Casey et al., 2008; Van den Heuvel-Panhuizen & Buys, 2008).

Illustrative Vignettes That Reveal Sophisticated Spatial Reasoning of Young Children in the Context of a Playful Pedagogy

In the sections that follow we present three examples of young children's (ages 4 to 6) mathematical reasoning as they engage with a range of carefully designed mathematics activities that have a particular emphasis on spatial reasoning. These vignettes are drawn from our research classrooms (predominately in underprivileged communities) and represent the kinds of sophisticated mathematical reasoning that can emerge when children are invited into stimulating and structured learning opportunities focused on powerful mathematics.

Exploring Congruence in a Kindergarten Classroom: A Two-Dimensional Pentomino Challenge

The task featured in this first vignette challenged students to generate 12 pentomino figures representing the full set of noncongruent two-dimensional figures that can be comprised of five squares (in which the squares are edge-aligned, see Figure 5.1).

To begin, the children were introduced to a narrative where they were asked to help Princess Kate assemble 12 magic keys (pentomino figures) to rescue her Prince William from the tower of the evil witch. Next the teacher established rules for assembling pentomino figures from five squares and then invited a student to come up to the interactive whiteboard to find/assemble and to move five squares together to form the first of the 12 pentomino configurations. See Figure 5.2.

The teacher then proceeded to assemble a second figure on the whiteboard, congruent to the first but oriented in a rotation of 180 degrees of the first (Figure 5.3).

The teacher then addressed the students.

Teacher: There, now I have a *new* magic key.
Students: (*excited calling out*) No, it's the same! It's the same!
Teacher: (*feigning ignorance*) What do you mean, it's the same?
Sam: You can rotate it and it will be the same (*moving his arms*).

Figure 5.1 The complete set of 12 pentomino configurations.

Teacher: (*Next, the teacher picked a plastic model of the same pentomino figure, which she displayed, to the children in still another orientation.*) What about this one? Do you think this one is the same as well?

Students: No, it's the same too!

Students: (*multiple voices*) You just have to make it go the same way and you will see.

Once the children had demonstrated their understanding that these first three pentominoes were congruent and only therefore represented a single one of the 12 possibilities, they were asked to sit in small groups to find as many unique combinations of five squares as possible. See Figures 5.4a and 5.4b.

In the final step in the lesson, the students were asked to share and compare their assembled figures to collectively identify the 12 distinct pentomino figures. Surprisingly, in the course of presenting and describing their pentomino figures, one student, Mante, made an observation that the pentomino she had built might look like an open box if it were folded.

Figure 5.2 Student drags squares on the interactive whiteboard to construct one of the 12 pentomino figures while following the restrictions of the configurations. Once her figure was complete, the teacher acknowledged that the student's shape was indeed a "magic key."

Figure 5.3 The teacher constructs a congruent figure in different orientation.

Figure 5.4a Students assembling configurations of five squares.

Figure 5.4b Students assembling configurations of five squares.

The discussion that took place is captured in the transcript below:

Teacher: Who would like to describe the shape of one of their magic keys?

Mante: (*Holding up a pentomino in the shape of a cross:*) It's a plus.

Teacher: Yes, Mante, it does look like a cross. Is there a different way you might describe
              that shape? Mante? Lana?

Mante: It's like an X for a pirate's treasure, or, it could like turn into a box!
Teacher: How could you turn it into a box?
Student: But it's a box without a top. You lift these sides up, but you need one more . . . one more on top to get a cube.

The teacher encouraged the students to investigate further (see Figure 5.5).

As shown in this particular vignette, the 4–6 year old students not only assembled and distinguished each of the 12 pentomino figures, but they also initiated—with the help of a peer—the dynamic connection between two- and three-dimensional figures through first mentally and then physically folding the nets to make "boxes without tops." Furthermore, in this task students engaged in the forms of geometric reasoning specified by NCTM, such as recognizing and applying translations, rotations, and reflections to discriminate between congruent and noncongruent figures.

Location, Orientation, and Positional Language: A Grade 1 Barrier Game

In this second vignette, we highlight the discussion of a pair of 7-year-old students as they played shape-based barrier games designed to focus on location and orientation and positional language of shapes with the aid of cookie sheets and magnetic shapes.

The lesson from which the vignette is taken had a number of steps. As a starting point, students were given cookie sheets sectioned into six equal parts and six different magnetized shapes. Then, working in pairs with a barrier in place between the pairs of students, the person in the role of challenger covered full grid by placing each of their shapes in one of the grid sections and then described to his/her partner where each shape was located in the grid and how it was oriented.

In the next stage of the barrier game, which added an increased level of challenge, the grid was removed and this time the designer children composite composed figures using Tangram pieces to assemble designs that resembled horses, houses, arrows, rockets, etc. Again, the children kept a barrier between them so that one partner created a composite figure design (using

Figure 5.5 Students use paper folding to determine which pentomino configurations make an open box.

Figure 5.6 Two children in grade 1 playing a barrier game with a red folder acting as the barrier, and each child having their own set of green magnetic Tangram figures and cookie sheet.

a variety of smaller shapes), and described it to the other partner, who could not see the design (see Figure 5.6).

In the following transcript, the composer/challenger (Ben) is describing his figure and trying to provide as much detail as possible to his partner. Ben's partner (Shay) is asking additional directional questions as needed:

Ben: So the right corner of the triangle is touching the side of the tray.
Shay: A certain way?
Ben: It is. It is kind of like a boat. Now put a stretched out triangle on the short side.
Shay: On the left or the right?
Ben: The left. And now put a triangle, so it fits on the other small side.
Shay: The right.
Ben: Yup. (*pause*)
Ben: And the whole thing is like a triangle stretched out upways and sideways, on both sides.

Upon completion of the game, the partners compared their designs to determine whether they were exact matches or whether there were some differences (Figure 5.7).

Ben: You didn't do something right, but they are very very close. Look at this (*points to his own design*) and now look at yours (*points to same area of the design his partner made*). Look, look. Is there a space there? (*points to design his partner made*). But is there a space here? (*points to his design*).
Shay: OK (*Shay shifts the base of her design over approximately 1 cm to the left*).

The designs now match exactly.

In this transcript, Ben is referring to several important geometric and mathematical ideas: the overall location and orientation of shapes within the rectangular frame of the cookie sheet;

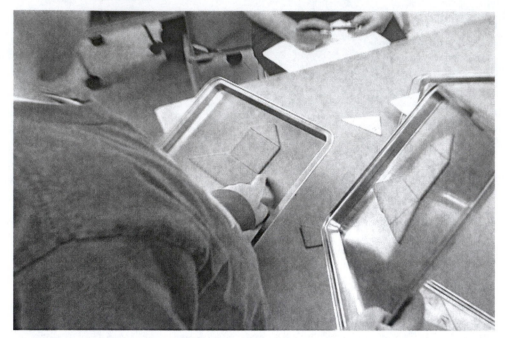

Figure 5.7 Two children compare their designs after completing the Barrier Game.

the relative location of figures to one another; and the composition of the overall composite shape (a large triangular looking figure "stretched out upways and sideways"). Finally, the composer, Ben demands precision by pointing out the minor variation between his design and his partner's design. In asking his partner questions, and pointing to the area that is not an exact match (and without touching Shay's design), he encourages his partner to adjust his design to complete the exchanges and the game, Shay slides the figure over slightly to create an exact match with Ben's. The level of geometric and spatial reasoning, persistence and precision involved in this task (difficult for many adults) is remarkable to observe in these two 7 year olds.

The Three-, Four- and Five-Cube Challenge: A Lesson in Discovering Equivalence of Three-Dimensional Figures

The third vignette focuses on geometry and transformations with an emphasis on children's reasoning about three-dimensional figures. The examples of students' thinking that we present in the vignette come from a grade 1 lesson designed by a Math for Young Children lesson study teacher team. The overarching goal of the lesson was to support students to engage with the challenging concept of congruence/equivalence of three-dimensional figures: or, as the teachers described the goal, "to help students to realize that certain three-dimensional shapes are the same despite differences in their orientations."

This lesson was designed in a number of steps of increasing difficulty. Specifically, the students were asked first to find all of the possible configurations using three interlocking cubes, then to find as many unique configurations as possible using four cubes, and then five cubes. The initial three-cube challenge (which results in only two unique figures) was introduced as a means to help the students to discover the principles of equivalence despite position or orientation. The four- and five-cube challenges were significantly more difficult, requiring the students to imagine and build the multiple combinations in which the interlocking cubes could be combined to create new figures—a total of eight possible figures with four cubes and 29 with five cubes.

The lesson participation structures were designed so that students could recognize equivalence in two ways: one through visual inspection and mental rotation and the other through building, comparing, and manipulating the actual figures. The first brief set of exchanges we present occurred between students midway through the lesson and exemplifies students' abilities to reason about equivalence through visualization and mental rotation.

Student 1: (*Holding up a figure she had assembled with 5 cubes:*) Does anyone have this shape? It is a "W."

Student 2: I was about to make that "W" but then I realize I have already made it except it looks like an "M."

Similarly:

Student 3: I have a shape that's like a throne. Did anyone else make one?

Student 4: I have one in my collection too, except mine is rotated and it looks like a table.

The way these students reasoned showed that they were using visualization and thinking/ seeing their figures holistically.

While the young students in our research classrooms were able to recognize congruence amongst shapes, as exemplified in the previous transcript, the majority of students had trouble with three-dimensional figures that were mirror images of each other. The confusion arose because students had learned, when working with two-dimensional figures, that shapes that are mirror images of each other are congruent. Thus it was perplexing for the students when they worked with three-dimensional figures, to come to understand that mirror figures were *not* equivalent.

To illustrate what we mean by mirror-image figures, Figure 5.8 presents a photo of the complete set of four-cube figures in which the last two figures at the far right are mirror images of one another and are unique in structure.

Indeed, as the final transcript illustrates, the mirror image problem not only challenged students but also proved to be challenging for adults—the teachers and researchers.

The last transcript comes from the final part of the lesson, when the students were challenged to find all of the possible unique figures that could be created with five cubes. After the students had been given 10 minutes to work in pairs to build as many five-cube figures as they could, the teacher then asked pairs of students to join together in groups of four and to pool their combined figures, assess the new combined collection of shapes, and eliminate those configurations that were the same.

Ryan and his small group looked at the collection of shapes that they had combined. Ryan stared for a long time at two shapes on the mat and then picked them up and rotated them repeatedly. He then approached the teacher, who was working with another group of children, and held out his two figures.

Ryan: I think these are different but I am not sure.

Teacher: Hmm. . . What do you think? (*Pause*) Ryan, let me have them. They look the same to me.
(*The teacher takes the two figures and sets them down next to each other and rotates one to consider this problem.*) I am sorry, Ryan, but I am not sure.

Figure 5.8 Unique configurations that can be built using sets of four interlocking cubes.

Ryan takes the two shapes, confers with his group and then comes back to the teacher.

Ryan: They are different. No matter what you do to this one (*Ryan physically rotates one of the figures*), you can not make it look the same as this one. They're different. I know because you would have to take this cube (*points to one cube in the configuration*) and move it. You can't make this one fit into that one.

Some Concluding Thoughts on New Approaches in the Field

The types of dynamic student activities presented in the three vignettes are uncommon in early years geometry lessons and activities. In terms of cognitive demand, the mental rotation required of the students is challenging. Some research suggests that mental rotations are more a strength for males than females (e.g. Jansen, Schmelter, Quaiser-Pohl, Neuburger, & Heil, 2013; Levine et al., 1999; Tzuriel & Egozi, 2010), but both boys and girls enjoyed these activities and persisted in constructing the cube configurations. In working with one group of 7 year olds, the class found 26 of the 29 configurations for five cubes. These results are consistent with other children at different sites in the same Math for Young Children project. These examples of sophisticated mathematical ideas also illustrate how a playful pedagogy combined with clear mathematics goals enable children to clearly exceed typical curriculum expectations and typical trajectories. These specific examples have come from our own research projects but are also representative of the kinds of mathematical reasoning that is becoming more frequently reported in the mathematics education literature. See, for example, Sinclair's work with young children in dynamic geometry environments (Sinclair & Crespo, 2006; Sinclair & Jackiw,

Figure 5.9 Students considering equivalence of mirror shapes.

Figure 5.10 Student discusses mirror shapes with the teacher.

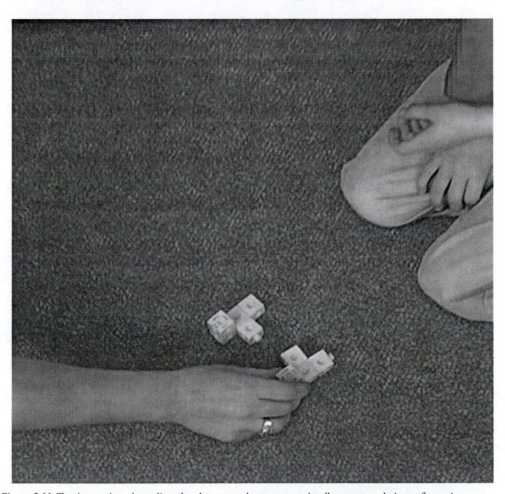

Figure 5.11 Teacher and student align the shapes on the carpet to visually compare their configuration.

2011; Sinclair & Moss, 2012); English's work on data management and metarepresentations (e.g., English 2004); and the extensive literature that looks at the development of patterning and algebraic reasoning (Blanton & Kaput 2003; Brizuela, Martinez, & Cayton-Hodges, 2013; Carraher, Martinez, & Schlieman, 2008; Moss & London-McNab, 2011; Papic, Mulligan, & Mitchelmore, 2011; Radford, 2008; Warren & Cooper, 2008).

The final new development that we highlight is inextricably connected to the other developments identified in previous sections of this chapter—namely, teacher professional development. In this next section, we examine promising approaches to teacher professional development as a critical feature of shifting mathematics curriculum, its implementation, and classroom practice.

PROFESSIONAL DEVELOPMENT FOR TEACHERS OF YOUNG CHILDREN

Central to the process of enhancing young children's opportunities to learn mathematics are teacher knowledge of, confidence in, and attitudes toward mathematics teaching (MacDonald et al., 2012). Unfortunately, as indicated in earlier sections of the chapter, studies report that many early years educators do not identify themselves as teachers of mathematics (Ginsburg & Ertel, 2008), are ambivalent towards mathematics (Hunting et al., 2013), or even report a dislike for mathematics (Kolstad & Hughes, 1994). These challenges should not be taken as criticism of teachers but as a reflection of systemic, cultural, and historical factors (Stipek, 2013). Historically, we have underestimated the knowledge required for engaging young children in mathematics activity. As Stipek (2014) observed, not only do teachers need specific knowledge of the mathematics content they are teaching, but they also need to be able to assess their students and support them to progress through more advanced levels.

Given the critical role teachers play in developing a solid, mathematics foundation for their students (e.g., Simpson & Linder, 2014; Shulman 1986; Ball, Thames, & Phelps, 2008), professional development programs that support teachers of young children are of extreme importance. Research-based professional development programs undertaken across many parts of the world show that the mathematical knowledge and understanding of young children can be enhanced as a result of their teachers' involvement in high-quality and sustained programs of professional development (Anderson, Bobis & Way, 2008; Bobis et al., 2005; Bruce et al., 2013; Clements & Sarama, 2013; Fennema et al., 1996; Guskey, 2003; Moss, Hawes, Naqvi & Caswell, 2015).

Promising Mathematics Programs That Incorporate Professional Development

In the last decade, there have been high-caliber examples of successful professional development programs designed to support the implementation of specific research-based mathematics curricula for young students, such as *Mathematical Awareness Program, Count Me In Too*, and the *Numeracy Development Project* (Bobis et al., 2005), National Literacy and Numeracy Strategies (Aubrey, 2004; Aubrey, Dahl, & Godfrey, 2006), Patterns and Early Algebra Professional Development Program (Papic, 2013) and Curious Minds (van Nes & de Lange, 2007). Earlier we described four such programs: Big Math for Little Kids (Greenes et al., 2004), Building Blocks (Clements & Sarama, 2007), Number Worlds (Griffin, 2007) and PASMAP (Mulligan & Mitchelmore, 2009). Each of these programs is accompanied by substantial professional development programs that have resulted in significant gains in children's mathematics learning. Despite obvious differences in their mathematics content areas, the professional development components of these programs have four common structures: (1) Each provides workshops for the educator participants near the start of the school year as well as regular workshops throughout the school year. (2) Each provides individualized supports for teachers in the form of classroom-based coaching. (3) Each is designed around a coherent curriculum grounded in research and in standards for early math learning and teaching. (4) In addition, each program is comprehensive and of sufficient duration for educator participants to explore and develop a deep understanding of its content. When examined together, these programs also include some key characteristics of exemplary professional development for early years mathematics educators.

Characteristics of Effective Professional Development for Early Years Teachers

The robust literature on mathematics professional development focuses predominantly on teachers of older students. However, in 2010, Zaslow, Tout, Halle, Whittaker, and Lavelle conducted a thorough evaluation of 18 early childhood professional development programs in mathematics and literacy. The evaluation identified common features across the professional development programs that were effective in supporting child learning.

Classroom-Embedded and Practice-Focused Professional Learning Programs

A common feature of successful professional development is that it is embedded in practice. A practice-focused approach prioritizes working in classrooms and with children—what Webster-Wright (2009) calls "active engagement in practice" (p. 723) in her review of over 200 studies on professional development. This approach stands in contrast to a more traditional knowledge-based approach to professional development, where the underlying assumption is that teachers will simply and successfully translate the context-void knowledge into their classroom practice (Bruce, Esmonde, Ross, Gookie, & Beatty, 2010). Increasingly, research reveals that introducing teachers to general concepts about children's mathematical development works better when the concepts are illustrated through directly and collaboratively working with children (Moss et al., 2015) in a tight alignment of practice and knowledge. We conjecture that a practice-focused approach to professional development is particularly successful in supporting early years teachers who are initially hesitant, and even possibly resistant, to teaching mathematics.

Although there are many variations and features of the practice-focused approach to professional development, Zaslow et al. (2010) highlight "coaching" wherein an experienced educator/researcher, part of the professional development research team, supports individual teachers by modeling teaching, coteaching, and providing feedback through shared reflection. According to the Zaslow report, this kind of coaching can happen on-site or through technology. The use of technology can work in two ways: a video library can provide documented examples of exemplary practice; and teachers can record their own teaching, send it to their coaches, and receive feedback.

Clearly Articulated and Specific Objectives for Professional Development

Important findings emerging from the Zaslow et al. (2010) report also dealt with both the breadth of the goals of the professional development program, and how these goals were to be communicated. Amongst their findings was that the effects of the professional development were stronger when the goals were specific rather than open-ended (Fukkink & Lont, 2007, cited in Zaslow, 2010) and were clearly articulated and communicated to the participants of the professional development program. Amongst the communication methods cited was the availability of a manual for each participant that laid out the full program. The meta-analysis also stressed the importance of familiarizing the participants with the measures used in the program as another way to deepen their understanding of the goals of the program (Hamre, Pianta, Burchinal, & Downer, 2010).

Although specifying and communicating goals is understood to be important for successful professional development for all educators, Zaslow emphasizes that—for the teaching and learning of mathematics in early years—the communication of goals is particularly important to the process. Citing Clements et al., (2011) she proposes that a clear articulation of the specific concepts and skills targeted in the program, along with an explanation and how a focus on these concepts and skills is part of the learning sequence, builds upon previous learning and prepares a foundation for later learning (Zaslow, 2010).

Implementation and Use of Information From Child Assessments

An important finding across multiple studies is that effective professional development programs often incorporate training for teachers and other educators, to both conduct child assessments and to use this information to inform instruction and monitor children's progress (Mast & Ginsburg, 2010; Moss et al., 2015; Tirosh, Tsamir, Levenson, & Tabach, 2011; Zaslow et al., 2010). As Ginsburg (2009) observed, while the use of assessments to inform instruction may serve different professional development purposes, this practice of observing students during task-based assessments can be particularly important to early years mathematics educators, allowing them to become acquainted with foundational sequences of mathematical learning. In the Math for Young Children project, teachers were invited to, and supported in, developing their own student interview tasks to understand more about their students' thinking in precise mathematics content areas (Bruce et al., 2013; Moss et al., 2015).

Sustained Professional Development of Sufficient Duration

In an analysis of the extant empirical research on the effects of professional development on teacher knowledge and change in practice, Desimone (2011) identified the importance of sufficient time for the professional development experience to have an effect in changing practice for teachers. Based on her analysis, Desimone recommended a 20-hour minimum of contact hours, over at least four to five months. This sustained professional development model is a central feature of the Building Blocks professional development program, for example, which includes nine days of training as well as 16 hours of on-site coaching.

Other important characteristics related to sustained professional development programs include involving educators (1) in actively working on mathematics challenges on a regular basis; and (2) in cycles of collaborative co-planning of tasks, classroom implementation, and purposeful reflection (Bobis, Higgins, Cavanagh, & Roche, 2012; Bruce et al., 2013; Clements et al., 2011; Goldsmith, Doerr, & Lewis, 2014; Papic, 2013; Timperley, Wilson, Barrar, & Fung, 2007; Warren & Quine, 2013). This purposeful reflection has been highly successful when working with the educators of children from disadvantaged backgrounds in the first two years of school: Warren and Quine (2013) implemented a professional development program that incorporated ongoing discussions with experts in the field and cycles of reflection as the teachers tested out new teaching approaches and resources in their classrooms. The researchers found that building early childhood educators' confidence in mathematics over time was critical to the success of the professional development program.

Lesson Study as a Form of Professional Development for Mathematics Teachers of Young Children

In Japan, lesson study has been a dominant and powerful form of professional development for the past century (Murata, 2013; Takahashi & Yoshida, 2004). In the late 1990s, lesson study was introduced in the United States (see Chokshi & Fernandez, 2004; Lewis, Perry, & Murata, 2006) and has since spread through North America and pockets of Europe (with the World Association of Lesson Studies international conference hosted in Sweden in 2013) and Eurasia (see Doig, Groves, & Fujii, 2011). Takahashi and Yoshida (2004) identified three characteristics of lesson study that have appeal to teachers on this global stage: First, lesson study is embedded in the authentic environment of classrooms. Second, students and student learning are a strong point of focus. Third, lesson study supports teachers as the actors of instructional change. In the lesson study cycle, participants engage in iterative cycles beginning with defining a problem, setting goals, designing a lesson or series of lessons, teaching the lesson, reflecting on lesson success, and finally making further revisions (e.g., Lewis et al., 2006). Recently, a set of customized adaptations to the lesson study process have been introduced in professional development projects for early years mathematics teachers (see Moss et al., 2015). The Math for Young Children project—a professional development initiative on geometry and spatial reasoning in the early years—has, since 2011, adapted lesson study with teams of early childhood educators (ECEs), kindergarten to second grade teachers, mathematics instructional leads, school administrators, and university mathematics educators who have collaborated on new approaches to the teaching and learning of geometry and spatial reasoning. Perhaps more than other types of professional development for teachers of young children, lesson study provides teachers with a vivid picture of their own students' interests, assets, and challenges. As noted by Copley and Padrón (1999), collaborative teacher professional development experiences enable participants to be sensitive to and focus on the diversity of children in their communities including those with special needs, children who are culturally and linguistically marginalized, and children who come from disadvantaged socioeconomic backgrounds.

CONCLUSIONS AND RECOMMENDATIONS

In this chapter we aimed to capture some of the most recent developments in mathematics education research that focus on children ages 4–7. We have discussed the ambitious recommendations of NCTM, NAEYC, and other organizations for the provision of rigorous mathematics learning for all; identified the potential inequities that can arise based on differences in backgrounds and mathematics readiness in the first years of schooling; described a representative sampling of early years curricula to support young learners in performing above-typical expectations; and signaled a renewed international interest in young children's mathematics learning.

In summary, we highlight five important and productive areas of recent mathematics education research:

1. The development by educational researchers of a robust cluster of longitudinal studies showing the importance of early mathematics as a best predictor of overall school success (e.g., Claessens & Engel, 2013);
2. Mathematics education studies that are pushing the upper boundaries of what was previously held knowledge of the capabilities of young learners (e.g., English & Mulligan, 2013);
3. Exciting research findings on the characteristics of professional development for early years teachers that broaden our repertoire of ways to contextualize and customize professional learning in practice-oriented models;
4. Newfound evidence of the potential of spatial reasoning as a foundation and possible gateway to early years mathematics learning (e.g., Van den Heuvel-Panhuizen, Elia & Robitzsch, in press);
5. Research-based insights into early years mathematics pedagogy demonstrating the positive impact of intentional teaching and structured, yet playful, mathematics learning opportunities (e.g., Fisher et al., 2013).

With the evidence and developments in mind, we suggest that collective efforts need to be further directed to supporting educators of young children in implementing high-quality classroom practices that further the mathematics learning of all children. The three vignettes offered in this chapter from our Math for Young Children research classrooms encapsulate and substantiate the value of these efforts, particularly in underresourced communities. The vignettes addressed all five areas noted: They explicitly focused on children aged 4–7, with the knowledge that this is a crucial time in children's mathematics development that has long-term implications (Area 1). The three vignettes provided examples of innovative lesson ideas and tasks that address important mathematics content that is usually reserved for older students (Area 4). The types of sophisticated spatial reasoning that the young children exhibited in the vignettes, such as reasoning about reflections, rotations, translations and visualizations provide a strong example of what it means to reexamine the boundaries of our knowledge of young children's capabilities (Area 2). The vignettes also served to illustrate a playful guided pedagogy approach (Area 5) that combines open-ended and play-filled but planned activities with strong curricular goals. Finally, to address new visions of professional development (Area 3), the Math for Young Children program employed a highly collaborative and classroom-embedded structure, in order to develop, test, and refine lessons and interventions. There is a range of programs across the globe with similar interests and developments—and while we are encouraged by the burgeoning and international interest in research on young children's mathematics learning, we also acknowledge that there is more work to be done, particularly in terms of scalability and equity issues. To further the call to action in this chapter, we offer several considerations for an immediate and future research agenda.

Study the Processes Involved in Teaching Mathematics to Young Children

The research base on young children's mathematical development and mathematics programs is increasing, yet there is limited aligned research that investigates mathematics teaching processes when working with young children. In a clear and compelling manner, Ginsburg, Lewis, and Clements (2008) argue that:

> A crucial set of questions revolves around teaching. Many of the studies attempt to ensure the fidelity of instruction, in the sense of determining whether teachers teach the material more or less as intended. But the studies pay very little, if any, attention to the ways in which teachers implement the activities, incorporate them into their own teaching styles, find some topics easier to teach than others, interpret the materials, adjust teaching to meet student needs, and understand (or misunderstand) the competence of their students. Teachers are at the heart of any program and curriculum, yet the present studies tell us little about their roles in the enterprise.
>
> (p. 9)

Mathematics has received less attention at the early childhood level. We are only at the beginning stages of developing a substantive knowledge base on how to teach it and how young children learn it. Most of the cognitive developmental research that has provided a revolution in the way we conceptualize young children's mathematical abilities does not focus on teaching or the processes of teaching. Thus exploratory and formalized research that focuses on teaching, teacher moves, and on children's learning from teaching in classroom contexts is needed. It is anticipated that findings from this kind of research would ultimately be of high practical value to teachers of young children.

Increase the Focus on Mathematics in Educator Preparation Programs

Many preparation programs for early years educators do not include much explicit mathematics content. Even preservice programs that train teachers of elementary school age may not be up-to-date in terms of current research, programming, policy, or mandates for math in the early years (see Schoenfeld & Stipek, 2011). One strategy for beginning to address this challenge could involve an increase in the stringency of preservice courses to require classroom place-ments in early years settings. Greater attention to the deep mathematics content knowledge that educators of preschool, and the first years of schooling, require is also essential. Given the rapid growth of in-service professional development programs for mathematics, there may be the potential to bring some of these models and practices to preservice education programs. Ginsburg's focus on practice (Ginsburg, Hyson, & Wood, 2014) is still under development but makes a coherent attempt to bridge these worlds of mathematics content learning, preservice programming, and in-service professional development.

Expand and Refine the Range of Tools for Measuring Professional Development Outcomes

As outlined in the professional development section of this chapter, current research points to some key features of professional learning programs for mathematics teachers of young chil-dren, with an emphasis on measuring student achievement as the metric of success. Although student achievement is of critical importance, what seems to be lacking are research questions and related metrics for assessing teacher shifts in attitudes (Anderson et al., 2008), beliefs (Bruce et al., 2010), and practices (Tout, Zaslow, & Berry, 2006) as a result of the professional development opportunities for these teachers of young children. This gap in the research is partly due to the resource intensity and financial demands of carefully studying shifts in class-room practice and teacher attitudes, but is also due to the complexity of teasing apart the causal factors: Is it coaching, technology uses, face-to-face interactions, small group collaborations, in-classroom experiences, video use/analysis, or a host of other factors that are having the greatest impact on teaching practice and beliefs? (See Zaslow et al., 2010.) What are the criti-cal combinations of professional development features in the particular context of mathematics learning environments for young children? These questions are considerably challenging given the complexities of the classroom setting and the range of children learning in those settings.

Push the Upper Boundaries of Mathematics Curriculum for Young Children

"Mounting evidence illustrates that young children have the interest and capacity to learn meaningful mathematics at early ages" (Newton & Alexander, 2013, p. 23). Researchers are continuing to expand the knowledge base of what young children know and can do, and the refinement of assessment tools is central to this expansion. For example, for decades children were tested on mental rotations using images (drawings) of two-dimensional and three-dimensional figures only, rather than using real figures. With the introduction and refine-ment of the three-dimensional mental rotation blocks task (Bruce & Hawes, 2014; Hawes, Lefevre, Xui, & Bruce, 2014)—a new tool for assessing mental rotations—researchers have learned that children at age 5 have the ability to mentally rotate three-dimensional figures, a skill deemed too complex for 5 year olds in previous research trials. This one example, and many other recent studies, call into question long-held beliefs that young children are inca-pable of considering abstract or sophisticated mathematics ideas (English & Mulligan, 2013; Ginsburg, 2009). When combined, the mounting evidence of what young children know and can do has the potential to push up against or even remove current curriculum ceilings in order to expose young children to more sophisticated mathematics ideas. This upward move-ment includes keen attention to the development of high-quality mathematics tasks for young children that are engaging; involve important mathematics content; require problem solving, effort, and persistence; encourage children to work collaboratively; embed ongoing feedback to inform children's actions; and provide opportunities for children to develop a sense of ownership, self-direction, and accomplishment (Schoenfeld & Stypek, 2011) As Perry and Dockett (2013) remind us, "Children are unlikely to demonstrate their full potential unless they are provided with the challenging and supportive contexts that allow them to do so

(Bobis et al., 2012; Hunting, Mousley, & Perry, 2012)" (p. 156). We suggest, along with Stylianides and Stylianides (2013), that there is still more work to be done involving systematic classroom-based studies that demonstrate what children can learn in classroom contexts, and that compare pedagogical approaches in their effects on the development of children's mathematics understanding, ultimately moving toward a "no-ceiling" approach to curriculum development and implementation (Bruce et al., 2013).

Advance the Equity Agenda

This chapter has highlighted some of the inequities and risks that children from underserved communities may face in terms of their mathematical development. This is not new, as Ginsburg and Russell (1981) called for mathematics research on disadvantaged children over 30 years ago. Yet studies of young children's mathematics in some underresourced contexts, such as many aboriginal populations, are just now beginning to be reported. One of the main challenges to this work is identifying particular strengths and "points of leverage" that help young children develop to their potential and close learning gaps, because the "research on these children yields results that are far more complex than usually assumed" (Schoenfeld & Stipek, 2011, p. 4). Extending the existing research on the implementation of mathematics programming and interventions that support the needs of children from low-resourced backgrounds, including robust studies on the role of mathematics language, the role of spatial reasoning, the effects of structured yet playful mathematics tasks, and the impact of providing opportunities to learn, is urgent.

Final Thoughts

Researchers of young children and educators alike are reaching a state of constructive urgency in relation to the study and implementation of pedagogies that foster deep mathematics understanding, particularly given the recent and profound socio-economic learning gaps revealed in the literature. The raising of voices in early years mathematics education and related research is just beginning to garner interest and legitimacy in the wider research and policy arenas to precipitate the necessary prioritizing of early years mathematics and the shifting of funding priorities. Vigorous research programs, knowledge mobilization, and implementation of researched-effective pedagogy and curricula are indeed at the heart of our work over the next two decades in mathematics education research with young children.

REFERENCES

Alexander, K. L., & Entwisle, D. R., (1988). Achievement in the first 2 years of school: Patterns and processes. *Monographs of the Society for Research in Child Development, 53*(2, Serial No 218).

Anderson, J., Bobis, J., & Way, J. (2008). Teachers as learners: Building knowledge in and through the practice of teaching mathematics. In H. Forgaz, A. Barkatasas, A. Bishop, B. Clarke, S. Keast, W. T. Seah, P. Sullivan, & S. Willis (Eds.), *Research in mathematics education in Australasia 2004–2007* (pp. 313–335). Rotterdam, The Netherlands: Sense Publishers.

Anthony, G., & Walshaw, M. (2007). *Effective pedagogy in mathematics/pāngarau*. Wellington, New Zealand: Ministry of Education.

Arnold, D. H., & Doctoroff, G. L. (2003). The early education of socioeconomically disadvantaged children. *Annual Review of Psychology, 54*, 517–545.

Aubrey, C. (2004). Implementing the foundation stage in reception classes. *British Educational Research Journal, 30*(5), 633–656.

Aubrey, C., Dahl, S., & Godfrey, R. (2006). Early mathematics development and later achievement: Further evidence. *Mathematics Education Research Journal, 18*(1), 27–46.

Aunola, K., Leskinen, E., Lerkkanen, M.-K., & Nurmi, J.-E. (2004). Developmental dynamics of math performance from preschool to grade 2. *Journal of Educational Psychology, 96*(4), 699–713.

Australian Curriculum, Assessment, and Reporting Authority (2014). *The Australian Curriculum.* Retrieved from www.australiancurriculum.edu.au/Curriculum/Overview

Balfanz, R. (1999). Why do we teach children so little mathematics? Some historical considerations. In J.V. Copley (Ed.), *Mathematics in the early years* (pp. 3–10). Reston, VA: National Council of Teachers of Mathematics.

Ball, D. L., Thames, M. H., & Phelps, G. (2008). Content knowledge for teaching: What makes it special? *Journal of Teacher Education, 59*(5), 389–407.

Baroody, A.J. (2006). Why children have difficulties mastering the basic number combinations and how to help them. *Teaching Children Mathematics, 13*(1), 22–31.

Baroody, A.J., Lai, M., & Mix, K.S. (2006). The development of young children's early number and operation sense and its implications for early childhood education. In B. Spodek & O. Saracho (Eds.), *Handbook of research on the education of young children* (Vol. 2, pp. 187–221). Mahwah, NJ: Erlbaum.

Baroody, A.J., & Wilkins, J.L.M. (1999). The development of informal counting, number, and arithmetic skills and concepts. In J. Copeley (Ed.), *Mathematics in the early years, birth to five.* Reston, VA: National Council of Teachers of Mathematics.

Battista, M.T. (2007). The development of geometric and spatial thinking. In F. Lester (Ed.), *Second handbook of research on mathematics teaching and learning* (pp. 843–908). Reston, VA: National Council of Teachers of Mathematics.

Bergen, D. (2009). Play as the learning medium for future scientists, mathematicians, and engineers. *American Journal of Play, 1*(4), 413–428.

Blanton, M., & Kaput, J. (2003). Developing elementary teachers' algebra eyes and ears. *Teaching Children Mathematics, 10*(2), 70–77.

Bobis, J., Clarke, B., Clarke, D., Thomas, G., Wright, R., Young-Loveridge, J., & Gould, P. (2005). Supporting teachers in the development of young children's mathematical thinking: Three large scale cases. *Mathematics Education Research Journal, 16*(3), 27–57.

Bobis, J., Higgins, J., Cavanagh, M., & Roche, A. (2012). Professional knowledge of practising teachers of mathematics. In J. Greenlees, T. Logan, T. Lowrie, A. MacDonald, & B. Perry (Eds.), *Review of Australasian mathematics education research: 2008–2011* (pp. 313–341), Rotterdam, The Netherlands: Sense Publishers.

Bowman, B., Donovan, M. S., & Burns, M.S. (Eds.). (2001). *Eager to learn: Educating our preschoolers.* Washington, DC: National Academy Press.

Brizuela, B. M., Martinez, M. V., & Cayton-Hodges, G. A. (2013). The impact of early algebra: Results from a longitudinal intervention. *Journal of Research in Mathematics Education / Revista de Investigación en Didáctica de las Matemáticas, 2*(2), 209–241.

Bruce, C., Esmonde, I., Ross, J., Gookie, L., & Beatty, R. (2010). The effects of sustained classroom-embedded teacher professional learning on teacher efficacy and related student achievement. *Teaching and Teacher Education, 26*(8), 1598–1608.

Bruce, C. & Flynn, T. (2012). Integrating instruction and play in a Kindergarten to Grade 2 lesson study project. In L. R. Van Zoest, J. J. Lo, & J. L. Kratky, (Eds.), *Proceedings of the 34th annual meeting of the North American Chapter of the International Group for the Psychology of Mathematics Education* (pp. 853–856). Kalamazoo, MI: Western Michigan University.

Bruce, C., Flynn, T., McPherson, R., Bennett, S. (2012). *Mathematics for Young Children.* Retrieved from http://tmerc.ca/m4yc/.

Bruce, C. D., & Hawes, Z. (2014). The role of 2D and 3D mental rotation in mathematics for young children? What is it? Why is it important? And what can we do about it? *ZDM: The International Journal on Mathematics Education, 47*(3), 1–14. doi: 10.1007/s11858-014-0637

Bruce, C., & Moss, J. & Flynn, T. (2013). A "no-ceiling" approach to young children's mathematics: Preliminary results of an innovative professional learning program. In M. Martinez, & A. Castro Superfine (Eds.), *Proceedings of the 35th annual meeting of the North American Chapter of the International Group for the Psychology of Mathematics Education* (p. 911). Chicago, IL: University of Chicago.

Bruce, C.D., Moss, J., Sinclair, N., Whiteley, W., Okamoto, Y., McGarvey, L., . . . Davis, B. (2013, April). *Early years spatial reasoning: Learning, teaching, and research implications.* Paper presented at the NCTM research presession: Linking research and practice, Denver, CO.

Caldera, Y., McDonald Culp, A., O'Brien, M. Truglio, R., Alvarez, M., & Huston, A. (1999). Children's play preferences, construction play with blocks, and visual-spatial skills: are they related? *International Journal of Behavioural Development, 23* (4), 855–872. doi:10.1080/016502599383577

Cannon, J.S., Jacknowitz, A., & Painter, G. (2006). Is full better than half? Examining the longitudinal effects of full-day kindergarten attendance. *Journal of Policy Analysis & Management, 25*(2), 299–321. doi:10.1002/pam.20174

Carraher, D., Martinez, M., & Schlieman, A. (2008). Early algebra and mathematical generalization. *ZDM: The International Journal on Mathematics Education, 40*, 3–22.

Case, R., Griffin, S., & Kelly, W. (1999). Socioeconomic gradients in mathematical ability and their responsiveness to intervention during early childhood. In D. Keating & C. Hertzman (Eds.), *Developmental health and the wealth of nations: Social, biological, and educational dynamics* (pp. 125–152). New York: Guilford Press.

Case, R., & Okamoto, Y. (1996). The role of central conceptual structures in the development of children's thought. *Monographs of the Society for Research in Child Development, 61*(1–2, Serial No. 246).

Casey, B.M., Andrews, N., Schindler, H., Kersh, J.E., Samper, A., & Copley, J. (2008). The development of spatial skills through interventions involving block building activities. *Cognition and Instruction, 26,* 269–309.

Cheng, Y.L., & Mix, K.S. (2012). Spatial training improves children's mathematics ability. *Journal of Cognition and Development.* Advanced online publication. doi: 10.1080/15248372.2012.725186

Chokshi, S., & Fernandez, C. (2004). Challenges to importing Japanese lesson study: Concerns, misconceptions, and nuances. *Phi Delta Kappan* (March), 520–525.

Claessens, A., Duncan, G., & Engel, M. (2009). Kindergarten skills and fifth-grade achievement: Evidence from the ECLS-K. *Economics of Education Review, 28,* 415–427.

Claessens, A. & Engel, M. (2011, April). *How important is where you start? Early mathematical knowledge and later school success.* Paper presented at the 2011 Annual Meeting of the American Educational Research Association (AERA), New Orleans, LA.

Claessens, A. & Engel, M. (2013). How Important is where you start? Early mathematics knowledge and later school success. *Teachers College Record, 115,* 1–29.

Clarke, D., Clarke, B., & Roche, A. (2011). Building teachers' expertise in understanding, assessing and developing children's mathematical thinking: the power of task-based, one-to-one assessment interviews. *ZDM: The International Journal on Mathematics Education, 43*(6–7), 901–913.

Clements, D.H., & Sarama, J. (2002). *Effects of a preschool mathematics curriculum: Summary research on the Building Blocks project.* University of Buffalo, State University of New York. Retrieved from gse.buffalo.edu/org/buildingblocks/index_2.htm

Clements, D.H., & Sarama, J. (2007). Effects of a preschool mathematics curriculum: Summative research on the Building Blocks project. *Journal for Research in Mathematics Education, 38*(2), 136–163.

Clements, D.H., & Sarama, J. (2008). Experimental evaluation of the effects of a research-based preschool mathematics curriculum. *American Educational Research Journal, 45,* 443–494.

Clements, D.H., & Sarama, J. (2009). *Learning and teaching early math: The learning trajectories approach.* New York: Routledge.

Clements, D., & Sarama, J. (2011a). Early childhood mathematics intervention. *Science, 333,* 968–970.

Clements, D.H., & Sarama, J. (2011b). Early childhood teacher education: The case of geometry. *Journal of Mathematics Teacher Education, 14*(2), 133–148.

Clements, D.H.,, & Sarama, J. (2013). Rethinking early mathematics: What Is research-based curriculum for young children? In L. English & J. Mulligan (Eds.), *Reconceptualizing early mathematics learning* (pp. 121–148). New York: Springer.

Clements, D.H., Sarama, J., Spitler, M. E., Lange, A. A., & Wolfe, C. B. (2011) Mathematics learned by young children in an intervention based on learning trajectories: A large-scale cluster randomized trial. *Journal for Research in Mathematics Education, 42*(2), 127–166.

Copley, J.V. (2004). The early childhood collaborative: A professional development model to communicate and implement the standards. In D.H. Clements & J. Sarama (Eds.), *Engaging young children in mathematics: Standards for early childhood mathematics education* (pp. 401–414). Mahwah, NJ: Lawrence Erlbaum Associates.

Copley, J. V., & Padron, Y. (1999). Preparing teachers of young learners: Professional development of early childhood teachers in mathematics and science. *Dialogue on early childhood: Science, mathematics, and technology education.* Washington, DC: American Association for the Advancement of Science (AAAS).

Crosnoe, R., & Cooper, C.E. (2010). Economically disadvantaged children's transition into elementary school: Linking family process, school contexts, and educational policy. *American Educational Research Journal, 47*(2), 258–291.

Cross, C.T., Woods, T.A., & Schweingruber, H. (Eds.) (2009). *Mathematics learning in early childhood.* Washington, DC: National Academies Press.

de Vries, E., Thomas, L., & Warren, E. (2010). Teaching mathematics and play-based learning in an indigenous early childhood setting: Early childhood teachers' perspectives. In L. Sparrow, B. Kissane, & C. Hurst (Eds.), *Shaping the future of mathematics education: Proceedings of the 33rd annual conference of the Mathematics Education Research Group of Australasia* (pp. 719–722). Fremantle: MERGA.

Desimone, L. (2011) A primer on effective professional development. *Phi Delta Kappan, 92*(6), 68–71.

Diamond, A., Barnett, W.S., Thomas, J., & Munro, S. (2007). Preschool program improves cognitive control. *Science, 318,* 1387–1388. doi:10.1126/science.1151148

Dockett, S. & Perry, B. (2007). *Starting school: Perceptions, experiences and expectations.* Sidney: University of New South Wales Press.

Doig, B., Groves, S. & Fujii, T. (2011). The critical role of task development in lesson study. In L.C. Hart et al., (eds.), *Lesson study research and practice in mathematics education,* Springer: New York.

Duncan, G.J., Dowsett, C.J., Claessens, A., Magnuson, K., Huston, A.C., Klebanov, P., . . . & Japel, C. (2007). School readiness and later achievement. *Developmental Psychology, 43,* 1428–1446.

Ehrlich, S., Levine, S.C., & Goldin-Meadow, S. (2006). The importance of gesture in children's spatial reasoning. *Developmental Psychology, 42*(6), 1259–1268.

English, L.D. (2004). Promoting the development of young children's mathematical and analogical reasoning. In L. D. English (Ed.), *Mathematical and analogical reasoning of young learners.* Mahwah, NJ: Lawrence Erlbaum Associates.

English, L.D. (2012). Data modelling with first-grade students. *Educational Studies in Mathematics Education, 81*(1), 15–30.

English, L. D. (2013). Reconceptualizing statistics learning in the early years. In L. D. English & J. Mulligan (Eds.). *Reconceptualizing early mathematics learning,* (pp. 67–82). New York: Springer.

English, L. D. & Mulligan, J. (2013). Perspectives on reconceptualizing early mathematics learning. In L. D. English & J. Mulligan (Eds.), *Reconceptualizing early mathematics learning* (pp. 121–148). New York: Springer.

Fennema, E., Carpenter, T.P., Franke, M.L., Levi, L., Jacobs, V.R., & Empson, S.B. (1996). A longitudinal study of learning to use children's thinking in mathematics instruction. *Journal for Research in Mathematics Education, 27*(4), 403–434.

Fisher, K.R., Hirsh-Pasek, K., Newcombe, N., & Golinkoff, R.M. (2013). Taking shape: Supporting preschoolers' acquisition of geometric knowledge through guided play. *Child development, 84*(6), 1872–1878.

Frede, E., Jung, K., Barnett, W.S., Lamy, C.E., & Figueras, A. (2007). *The Abbott preschool program longitudinal effects study (APPLES).* Rutgers, NJ: National Institute for Early Education Research.

Freudenthal, H. (1981). Major problems of mathematics education. *Educational Studies in Mathematics, 12,* 133–150.

Fukkink, R., & Lont, A. (2007). Does training matter? A meta-analysis and review of caregiver training studies. *Early Childhood Research Quarterly, 22*(3), 294–311.

Gathercole, S.E., & Pickering, S.J. (2000). Assessment of working memory in six- and seven-year old children. *Journal of Educational Psychology, 92,* 377–390.

Geary, D. C., Hoard, M. K., Nugent, L., & Bailey, D. H. (2013). Adolescents' functional numeracy is predicted by their school entry number system knowledge. *PLoS ONE, 8,* e54651. doi:10.1371/journal.pone.0054651

Ginsburg, H.P. (2006). Mathematical play and playful mathematics: A guide for early education. In D. Singer, R.M. Golinkoff, & K. Hirsh-Pasek (Eds.), *Play = Learning: How play motivates and enhances children's cognitive and social-emotional growth* (pp. 145–165). New York: Oxford University Press.

Ginsburg, H. P. (2009). The challenge of formative assessment in mathematics education: Children's minds, teachers' minds. *Human Development, 52,* 109–128. doi: 10.1159/000202729

Ginsburg, H.P., & Ertel B. (2008). Knowing the mathematics in early childhood mathematics. In O. Saracho & B. Spodek (Eds.), *Contemporary perspectives on mathematics in early childhood education* (pp. 45–66). Charlotte, NC: Information Age Publishing.

Ginsburg, H. P., Hyson, M., & Woods, T. A. (Eds.). (2014). *Preparing early childhood educators to teach math: Professional development that works.* Baltimore, MD: Paul H. Brookes Publishing.

Ginsburg, H.P., Lee, J.S., & Boyd, J.S. (2008). Mathematics education for young children: What it is and how to promote it. *Social Policy Report of the Society for Research in Child Development, 22,* 3–23.

Ginsburg, H. P., Lewis, A., & Clements, M. (2008). *School readiness and early childhood education: What we can learn from federal investments in research on mathematics programs?* A working paper prepared for a working meeting on recent school readiness research: Guiding the synthesis of early childhood research. Washington, DC: October 21–22. Retrieved from http://aspe.hhs.gov/hsp/10/School Readiness/apb3.pdf.

Ginsburg, H.P., & Pappas, S. (2004). SES, ethnic, and gender differences in young children's informal addition and subtraction: A clinical interview investigation. *Journal of Applied Developmental Psychology, 25,* 171–192.

Ginsburg, H. P., & Russell, R. L. (1981). Social class and racial influences on early mathematical thinking. *Monographs of the Society for Research in Child Development, 46* (6, Serial No. 193).

Goldsmith, L. T., Doerr, H.M., & Lewis, C.C. (2014). Mathematics teachers' learning: a conceptual framework and synthesis of research, *Journal of Mathematics Teacher Education, 17*(1), 5–36.

Graham, T.A., Nash, C., & Paul, K. (1997). Young children's exposure to mathematics: The child care context. *Early Childhood Education Journal, 25*(1), 31–38.

Gravemeijer, K. (1994). *Developing realistic mathematics education*. Utrecht: Freudenthal Institute.

Greenes, C., Ginsburg, H., & Balfanz, R. (2004). Big math for little kids, *Early Childhood Research Quarterly, 19*, 159–166.

Griffin, S. (2004). Number Worlds: A research-based mathematics program for young children. In D. H. Clements, J. Sarama, & A.-M. DiBiase (Eds.), *Engaging young children in mathematics: Standards for early childhood mathematics education* (pp. 325–342). Mahwah, NJ: Lawrence Erlbaum Associates.

Griffin, S. (2007). Early intervention for children at risk of developing mathematical learning difficulties. In D. B. Berch & M. M. Mazzocco (Eds.), Why is math so hard for some children? The nature and origins of mathematical learning difficulties and disabilities (pp. 373–396). Baltimore, MD: Brookes Publishing.

Griffin, S., & Case, R. (1996). *Number worlds: Kindergarten level*. Durham, NH: Number Worlds Alliance.

Griffin, S., Case, R., & Siegler, R. (1994). Rightstart: Providing the central conceptual prerequisites for first formal learning of arithmetic to students at risk for school failure. In K. McGilly (Ed.), *Classroom lessons: Integrating cognitive theory and classroom practice* (pp. 24–49). Cambridge, MA: MIT Press.

Guskey, T. R. (2003). What makes professional development effective? *Phi Delta Kappan, 84*(10), 748–750.

Hachey, A. (2013). The early childhood mathematics education revolution. *Early Education and Development, 24*, 419–430.

Hamre, B. K., Pianta, R. C., Burchinal, M., & Downer, J. T. (2010, March). *A course on supporting early language and literacy development through teacher-child interaction: Effects on teacher beliefs, knowledge and practice*. Presentation at the Meetings of the Society for Research in Educational Effectiveness, Washington, DC.

Hawes, Z., Lefevre, J., Xui, C., & Bruce, C. (2014). Development of a new reliable 3D mental rotation blocks task (3D MRBT) for clinical interviews, *Mind, Brain and Education, 8*(3).

Hirsh-Pasek, K., Hyson, M., & Rescorla, L. (1990). Academic environments in preschool: Do they pressure or challenge young children? *Early Education and Development, 1* (6), 401–423.

Hunting, R. (2003). Part–whole number knowledge in preschool children. *Journal of Mathematical Behavior, 22*, 217–235.

Hunting, R., Bobis, J., Doig, B., English, L., Mousley, J., Mulligan, J., . . . Young-Loveridge, J. (2013). *Mathematical thinking in preschool children in rural and regional Australia: Research and practice*. Camberwell: ACER Press.

Hunting, R. P., Mousley, J. A., & Perry, B. (2012). A study of rural preschool practitioners' views on young children's mathematical thinking. *Mathematics Education Research Journal*. doi:10.1007/ s13394–011–0030–3

Jansen, P., Schmelter, A., Quaiser-Pohl, C., Neuburger, S., & Heil, M. (2013). Mental rotation performance in primary school age children: Are there gender differences in chronometric tests?. *Cognitive Development, 28*(1), 51–62.

Jones, K. (2000). Teacher knowledge and professional development in geometry. In Rowland, T. (Ed.), *Proceedings of the British Society for Research into Learning Mathematics 20*(3).

Jordan, N., Kaplan, D., Olah, L. N., & Locuniak, M. (2006). Number sense growth in kindergarten: A longitudinal investigation of children at risk for mathematics difficulties. *Child Development, 77*, 153–175.

Jordan, N., & Levine, S. (2009). Socioeconomic variation, number competence, and mathematics learning difficulties in young children. *Developmental Disabilities Research Reviews, 15*, 60–68.

Klibanoff, R., Levine, S. C., Huttenlocher, J., Vasilyeva, M., & Hedges, L. (2006). Preschool children's mathematical knowledge: The effect of teacher "math talk." *Developmental Psychology, 42*(1), 59–69.

Kolstad, R. K., & Hughes, S. (1994). Teacher attitudes towards mathematics. *Journal of Instructional Psychology, 21*, 44–48.

Kowalski, K., Pretti-Frontczak, K., & Johnson, L. (2001). Preschool teachers' beliefs concerning the importance of various developmental skills and abilities. *Journal of Research in Childhood Education, 16*, 5–14.

Lee, J. S. (2006). Preschool teachers' shared beliefs about appropriate pedagogy for 4-year-olds. *Early Childhood Education Journal, 33*(6), 433–441.

Lee, J. S. (2010). Exploring kindergarten teachers' pedagogical content knowledge of mathematics, *International Journal of Early Childhood, 42*, 27–41. doi:10.1007/s13158-010-0003-9

Lee, J. S., & Ginsburg, H. P. (2007). Preschool teachers' beliefs about appropriate early literacy and mathematics education for low- and middle-socioeconomic children. *Early Education and Development, 18*(1), 111–143.

Lee, J. S., & Ginsburg, H. P. (2009). Early childhood teachers' misconceptions about mathematics education for young children in the United States. *Australasian Journal of Early Childhood, 34*(4), 37–45.

Lee, V. E, & Burkam, D. T. (2002). *Inequality at the starting gate: Social background differences in achievement as children begin school*. Washington, DC: Economic Policy Institute.

Levenson, E., Tirosh, D., & Tsamir, P. (2011). *Preschool geometry theory, research, and practical perspectives.* Rotterdam, The Netherlands: Sense Publishers.

Levine, S. C., Huttenlocher, J., Taylor, A., & Langrock, A. (1999). Early sex differences in spatial skill. *Developmental Psychology, 35*(4), 940–949.

Lewis, C., Perry, R., & Murata, A. (2006). How should research contribute to instructional improvement: The case of lesson study. *Educational Researcher, 35*(3), 3–14.

Lin, H-L., Lawrence, F. R., & Gorrell, J. (2003). Kindergarten teachers' views of children's readiness for school. *Early Childhood Research Quarterly, 18*(2), 225–237.

MacDonald, A., Davies, N., Dockett, S., & Perry, B. (2012). Early childhood mathematics education. In B. Perry, T. Lowrie, T. Logan, A. MacDonald & J. Greenlees (Eds.). Research in Mathematics Education in Australasia 2008–2011 (pp. 169–192). Rotterdam, The Netherlands: Sense Publishers.

Marcon, R. (2002). Moving up the grades: Relationship between preschool model and later school success. *Early Childhood Research and Practice, 4*(1), 1–23.

Mast, J. & Ginsburg, H. (2010). Child study/lesson study: Developing minds to understand and teach children. In N. Lyons (Ed.), *Handbook of reflection and reflective inquiry: Mapping a way of knowing for professional reflective inquiry* (pp. 257–271). New York: Springer.

Mix, K. S., & Cheng, Y-L. (2012). The relation between space and math: Developmental and educational implications. *Advances in Child Development and Behavior*, 197–242.

Moss, J., Caswell, B., Chang, D., Hawes, Z., Naqvi, S., & Tepylo, D. (2012). *Math for Young Children.* Retrieved from www.oise.utoronto.ca/robertson/Inquiry-based_Mathematics/Math_For_Young_Children/index.html.

Moss, J., Hawes, Z., Naqvi, S., & Caswell, B. (2015). Adapting Japanese Lesson Study to enhance the teaching and learning of geometry and spatial reasoning in early years classrooms: A case study. *ZDM: The international journal on mathematics education, 15*(3).

Moss, J. & London-McNab, S. (2011) An approach to geometric and numeric patterning that fosters second grade students' reasoning and generalizing about functions and co-variation. In J. Cai & E. Knuth (Eds.), *Early algebraization: A global dialogue from multiple perspectives (Advances in Mathematics Education).* New York: Springer.

Mulligan, J. T., & Mitchelmore, M. (2009). Awareness of pattern and structure in early mathematical development. Mathematics Education Research Journal, 21(2), 33–49.

Mulligan, J. T., & Mitchelmore, M. C. (2013). Early awareness of mathematical pattern and structure. In L. D. English & J. Mulligan (Eds.). *Reconceptualizing early mathematics learning* (pp. 29–45). New York: Springer.

Mulligan, J. T., Prescott, A., Papic, M., & Mitchelmore, M. C. (2006). Improving early numeracy through a Pattern and Structure Mathematics Awareness Program (PASMAP). In P. Grootenboer, R. Zevenbergen & M. Chinnappan (Eds.), Identities, cultures and learning spaces: Proceedings of the 29th annual conference of the Mathematics Education Research Group of Australasia, (pp. 376–383). Canberra: MERGA.

Murata, A. (2013). Diversity and high academic expectations without tracking: Inclusively responsive instruction. *The Journal of Learning Sciences, 21*(2), 312–335.

National Association for the Education of Young Children and the National Council of Teachers of Mathematics. (2002). *Position statement: Early childhood mathematics: Promoting good beginnings.* Retrieved from www.naeyc.org/about/position/psmath.asp.

National Council of Teachers of Mathematics (2000). Principles and standards for school mathematics. Reston, VA: Author.

National Mathematics Advisory Panel. (2008). *Foundations for success: The final report of the National Mathematics Advisory Panel.* Washington, DC: U.S. Department of Education.

National Research Council. (2009). *Mathematics learning in early childhood: Paths toward excellence and equity.* Committee on Early Childhood Mathematics, C. T. Cross, T. A. Woods, & H. Schweingruber (Eds.), Center for Education, Division of Behavioral and Social Sciences and Education. Washington, DC: The National Academies Press.

Newcombe, N. (2010). Picture this: Increasing math and science learning by improving spatial thinking. *American Educator, 34*(2), 29–35.

Newcombe, N. S. (2013). Seeing relationships: Using spatial thinking to teach science, mathematics, and social studies. *American Educator, 37*(1), 26–31.

Newcombe, N., & Frick, A. (2010). Early education for spatial. intelligence: Why, what, and how. *Mind, Brain and Education, 4*(3), 102–111.

Newton, K., & Alexander, P. (2013). Early mathematics learning in perspective: Eras and forces of change. In L. English & J. Mulligan (Eds.). *Reconceptualizing early mathematics learning,* (pp. 5–28). New York: Springer.

Papic, M. (2013). Improving numeracy outcomes for young Australian Indigenous children through the Patterns and Early Algebra Preschool (PEAP) Professional Development (PD) Program. In L.

D. English & J. Mulligan (Eds.). *Reconceptualizing early mathematics learning* (pp. 253–281). New York: Springer.

Papic, M., Mulligan, J.T., & Mitchelmore, M.C. (2011). Assessing the development of preschoolers' mathematical patterning. *Journal for Research in Mathematics Education, 42*(3), 237–268.

Perry, C. (2011). Motivation and attitude of preservice elementary teachers toward mathematics. *School Science and Mathematics, 111*(1), 2–10.

Perry, B., & Dockett, S. (2002). Young children's access to powerful mathematical ideas. In L. D. English (Ed.). *Handbook of international research in mathematics education: Directions for the 21st century* (pp. 81–111). Mahwah, NJ: Lawrence Erlbaum.

Perry, B. & Dockett, S. (2008). Young children's access to powerful mathematical ideas. In L. D. English (Ed.), *Handbook of international research in mathematics education* (2nd ed., pp. 75–108). New York, Routledge.

Perry, B., & Dockett, S. (2013). Reflecting on young children's mathematics learning. In L. D. English & J. T. Mulligan (Eds.), *Reconceptualizing Early Mathematics Learning*, Springer Series: Advances in Mathematics Education, 149–162.

Presser, A. L., Clements, M., Ginsburg, H., & Ertle, B. (2012). *Effects of a preschool and kindergarten mathematics curriculum: Big Math for Little Kids* (pp. 1–55). Retrieved from cct.edc.org/sites/cct.edc.org/files/publications/BigMathPaper_Final.pdf

Purpura, D. J., Baroody, A. J., & Lonigan, C. J. (2013). The transition from informal to formal mathematical knowledge: Mediation by numeral knowledge. *Journal of Educational Psychology, 105*, 453–464.

Radford, L. (2008). Iconicity and contraction: A semiotic investigation of forms of algebraic generalizations of patterns in different contexts. *ZDM: The International Journal on Mathematics Education, 40*, 83–96.

Ritchie, S. J., & Bates, T. C. (2013). Enduring links from childhood mathematics and reading achievement to adult socioeconomic status. *Psychological Science, 24*(7), 1301–1308. doi: 10.1177/0956797612466268

Sarama, J. (2004). Technology in early childhood mathematics: Building Blocks™ as an innovative technology-based curriculum. In D.H. Clements, J. Sarama & A.-M. DiBiase (Eds.), *Engaging young children in mathematics: Standards for early childhood mathematics education* (pp. 361–375). Mahwah, NJ: Lawrence Erlbaum Associates.

Sarama, J., & Clements, D.H. (2002). Building Blocks for young children's mathematical development. *Journal of Educational Computing Research, 27*(1&2), 93–109.

Sarama, J., & Clements, D. H. (2008). Linking research and software development. In G. W. Blume & M. K. Heid (Eds.), *Research on technology and the teaching and learning of mathematics: Vol. 2. Cases and perspectives* (pp. 113–130). New York: Information Age Publishing.

Sarama, J., & Clements, D.H. (2009). *Early childhood mathematics education research: Learning trajectories for young children*. London: Routledge.

Saxe, G. B., Guberman, S. R., & Gearhart, M. (1987). Goals and contexts: A reply to the commentaries. Reply to commentaries of *Social Processes in Early Number Development* (1987), *Monographs for the Society for Research in Child Development, 52*(2), 160–163.

Seo, K., & Ginsburg, H. (2004). What is developmentally appropriate in early childhood mathematics education? Lessons from new research. In D. Clements, J. Sarama, & A. Dibiase (Eds.), *Engaging young children in mathematics: Standards for early childhood mathematics education* (pp. 91–104). Hillsdale: Erlbaum.

Schoenfeld, A., & Stipek, D. (2011). *Mathematics matters: Children's mathematical journey starts early*. Report of a conference held November 7–8. Berkeley CA. University of California Berkeley.

Shulman, L. (1986). Those who understand: Knowledge growth in teaching. *Educational Researcher, 15*(2), 4–14.

Simpson, A., & Linder, S. (2014). An examination of mathematics professional development opportunities in early childhood settings. *Educational Journal, 42*(5), 335–342.

Sinclair, N., & Bruce, C. (2014). Spatial reasoning for young learners (research forum). In Liljedahl, P., Nicol, C., Oesterle, S., & Allan, D. (Eds.). *Proceedings of the Joint Meeting of PME 38 and PME-NA 36* (Vol. 1). Vancouver, Canada: PME.

Sinclair, N., & Crespo, S. (2006). Learning mathematics with dynamic computer environments. *Teaching Children Mathematics 12*(9), 436–444.

Sinclair, N., & Jackiw, N. (2011). *TouchCounts* [computer software]. Tangible Mathematics Project, Simon Fraser University.

Sinclair, N., & Moss, J. (2012). The more it changes, the more it becomes the same: The development of the routine of shape identification in dynamic geometry environments. *International Journal of Education Research, 51&52*, 28–44.

Singer, D., Golinkoff, R. M., & Hirsh-Pasek, K. (Eds.). (2006). *Play = Learning: How play motivates and enhances children's cognitive and social-emotional growth.* New York: Oxford University Press.

Starkey, P., & Klein, A. (2008). Sociocultural influences on young children's mathematical knowledge. In O. Saracho & B. Spodek (Eds.), *Contemporary perspectives on mathematics in early childhood education* (pp. 253–276). Charlotte, NC: Information Age Publishing.

Starkey, P., Klein, A., & Wakeley, A. (2004). Enhancing young children's mathematical knowledge through a pre-kindergarten mathematics intervention. *Early Childhood Research Quarterly, 19,* 99–120.

Stipek, D. (2013). Mathematics in early childhood education: revolution or evolution? *Early Education and Development, 24*: 431–435. doi: 10.1080/10409289.2013.777285

Stipek, D. (2014). Play and mathematics: An equation that works. *Preschool Matters . . . Today! A blog of the National Institute for Early Education Research.* Retrieved from http://preschoolmatters. org/2014/03/14/play-and-mathematics-an-equation-that-works/

Stockard, J., & Engelmann, K. (2008). *Academic kindergarten and later academic success: The impact of direct instruction* (Technical Report 2008-7). Eugene, OR: National Institute for Direct Instruction.

Stylianides, A. J., & Stylianides, G. J. (2013). Seeking research-grounded solutions to problems of practice: Classroom-based interventions in mathematics education. *ZDM: The International Journal on Mathematics Education, 45*(3), 333–340.

Takahashi, A., & Yoshida, M. (2004). Ideas for establishing Lesson-Study communities. *Teaching Children Mathematics* (May), 436–443.

Timperley, H., Wilson, A., Barrar, H., & Fung, I. (2007). *Teacher professional learning and development: Best evidence synthesis iteration [BES].* Wellington, New Zealand: Ministry of Education.

Tirosh, D., Tsamir, P., & Levenson, E. (2011). Using theories to build kindergarten teachers' mathematical knowledge for teaching. In K. Ruthven & T. Rowland (Eds.), *Mathematical Knowledge in Teaching* (pp. 231–250). Dordrecht: Springer.

Tirosh, D., Tsamir, P., Levenson, E., & Tabach, M. (2011). From preschool teachers' professional development to children's knowledge: Comparing sets. *Journal of Math Teacher Educators, 14,* 113–131.

Tout, K., Zaslow, M. & Berry, D. (2006). Quality and qualifications: Links between professional development and quality in early care and education settings. In M. Zaslow & I. Martinez-Beck (Eds.). *Critical issues in early childhood professional development.* Baltimore, MD: Brookes Publishing.

Tzuriel, D., & Egozi, G. (2010). Gender differences in spatial ability of young children: The effects of training and processing strategies. *Child development, 81*(5), 1417–1430.

Uttal, D. H., Meadow, N. G., Tipton, E., Hand, L. L., Alden, A. R., Warren, C., & Newcombe, N. S. (2013). The malleability of spatial skills: A meta-analysis of training studies. *Psychological bulletin, 139*(2), 352.

Van den Heuvel-Panhuizen, M. (Ed.) (2008). *Children learn mathematics. A learning-teaching trajectory with intermediate attainment targets for calculation with whole numbers in primary school.* Rotterdam /Tapei: Sense Publishers.

Van den Heuvel-Panhuizen, M., & Buijs, K. (2005). *Young children learn measurement and geometry. A learning-teaching trajectory with intermediate attainment targets for the lower grades in primary school.* Utrecht, The Netherlands: Freudenthal Institute.

Van den Heuvel-Panhuizen, M., & Buys, K. (Eds.). (2008). *Young children learn measurement and geometry.* Rotterdam, The Netherlands: Sense Publishers.

Van den Heuvel-Panhuizen, M., Elia, I. & Robitzsch, A. (in press). Kindergartners' performance in two types of imaginary perspective taking. *ZDM: The International Journal on Mathematics Education (3).*

Van den Heuvel-Panhuizen, M., Kühne, C., & Lombard, A. P. (2012). *Learning pathway for number in the early primary grades.* Illovo, South Africa: Macmillan.

Van Hiele, P. (1999). Developing geometric thinking through activities that begin with play. *Teaching Children Mathematics* (February), pp. 310–316.

van Nes, F., & de Lange, J. (2007). Mathematics education and neurosciences: Relating spatial structures to the development of spatial sense and number sense. *The Montana Mathematics Enthusiast, 4*(2), 210–229.

Verdine, B. N., Golinkoff, R., Hirsh-Pasek, K., Newcombe, N., Filipowocz, A. T., & Chang, A. (2013). Deconstructiong builidng blocks: Preschoolers' spatial assembly preformance relates to early mathematics skills. *Child Development.* doi: 10.1111/cdev.12165

Wai, J., Lubinski, D., & Benbow, C. P. (2009). Spatial ability for STEM domains: Aligning over fifty years of cumulative psychological knowledge solidifies its importance. *Journal of Educational Psychology, 101,* 817–835.

Warren, E., & Cooper, T. J. (2008). Generalising the pattern rule for visual growth patterns: Actions that support 8 year olds thinking. *Educational Studies in Mathematics, 67,* 171–185.

Warren, E., & Quine, J. (2013). Enhancing teacher professional development for early years mathematics teachers working in disadvantaged contexts. In L. D. English & J. Mulligan (Eds.). *Reconceptualizing early mathematics learning (pp. 283–308).* New York: Springer.

Watts, T., Duncan, G., Siegler, R., & Davis-Kean, P. (2014). What's past is prologue: Relations between early mathematics knowledge and high school achievement. *Educational Researcher, 43* (7), 352–360.

Webster-Wright, A. (2009). Reframing professional development through understanding authentic professional learning. *Review of Educational Research, 79*(2), 702–739.

West, J., Denton, K., & Germino-Hausken, E. (2000). *America's kindergarteners. Statistical analysis report*, NCES2000–070. Washington, DC: U.S. Department of Education, Office of Educational Research and Improvement, National Center for Education Statistics.

Whiteley, W. (2002). Teaching to see like a mathematician. *Presentation at the Visual Representation and Interpretation conference*, Liverpool, UK. Retrieved from www.math.yorku.ca/~whiteley/Teaching_to_see.pdf.

Zaslow, M. (2010) Quality Measurement in Early Childhood Settings. In M. Zaslow, I. Martinez-Beck, K Tout , T Halle H P. Ginsburg & M. Hyson (Eds.), *Towards the identification of features of effective professional development for early childhood educators.* Prepared for Policy and Program Studies Service, Office of Planning, Evaluation and Policy Development, U.S. Department of Education. Retrieved from www.ed.gov/about/offices/list

Zaslow, M., Tout, K., Halle, T., Whittaker, J. V., & Lavelle, B. (2010). *Towards the identification of features of effective professional development for early childhood educators.* Prepared for Policy and Program Studies Service, Office of Planning, Evaluation and Policy Development, U.S. Department of Education. Retrieved from www.ed.gov/about/offices/list.

6   Powerful Ideas in Elementary School Mathematics

David W. Carraher

TERC

Analúcia D. Schliemann

Tufts University

INTRODUCTION[1]

We develop here the idea that functions, and more generally, relations, have a critical role to play throughout elementary school mathematics education. This claim is based on the notions that functions and relations are already implicit throughout the content of present-day elementary mathematics curricula, that they merit greater prominence in elementary education, and that they are accessible to young students. We argue that fostering students' early understanding of functions and relations can deepen and integrate their knowledge about topics in the current curriculum, increase their ability to make mathematical generalizations, and better prepare them for a later, more formal introduction to algebra and functions.

By the early introduction of functions and relations, we have in mind approaches that differ notably from formal axiomatic approaches. To be sure, formal rules of syntax gradually take on importance, but young students' reasoning about functions gains considerable support from representing and reflecting on the structure of situations described through word problems.

The first half of the chapter looks at how functions and relations bear on common topics and representations in elementary mathematics. We begin by presenting four recurring powerful ideas, beginning with the idea that the operations of arithmetic are themselves functions. From the standpoint of mathematics, the four ideas are fairly straightforward and uncontroversial, as are the definitions of function and relation. Even so, they merit careful scrutiny because they are not widely acknowledged in elementary mathematics education. As we shall see, this stems in part from differences in how functions and relations may be represented in the elementary classroom and their conventional forms in mathematics.

The remainder of the chapter focuses on research and theory about elementary school students learning under circumstances in which functions and other relations are assigned a more prominent role in the curriculum. In many places we draw on our own longitudinal classroom investigations from Grades 2 through 8 (Carraher, Schliemann, & Brizuela, 2000, 2005; Carraher, Schliemann, & Schwartz, 2008; Carraher, Schliemann, Brizuela, & Earnest, 2006, 2014; Schliemann, Carraher, & Brizuela, 2007, 2012; Schliemann, Carraher, & Caddle, 2013; Schliemann, Carraher, Goodrow, Caddle, & Porter, 2013).

Three main bodies of work contribute to the present analysis: (1) *early algebra* research (e.g., Blanton, 2008; Blanton & Kaput, 2000; Brizuela & Earnest, 2008; Brizuela & Schliemann, 2004; Cai & Knuth, 2011; Carpenter & Franke; 2001; Carpenter, Franke, & Levi, 2003; Carraher, Schliemann, & Brizuela, 2000, 2005; Carraher, Schliemann, & Schwartz et al., 2008; Carraher, Schliemann, Brizuela, & Earnest et al., 2006, in press; Davydov, 1991; Dougherty, 2008; Carraher & Schliemann, 2007; Kaput, 1998; Moss & Beatty, 2006; Schliemann et al., 2007, 2012), (2) studies of *additive* and *multiplicative structures* (e.g. Carpenter, Moser, &

Romberg, 1982; Harel & Confrey, 1994; Lesh & Landau, 1983; Vergnaud, 1982, 1983, 1994), and (3) work on *functions* (e.g., Romberg, Fennema, & Carpenter, 1993; Sfard, 1991; Dubinsky & Harel, 1992; Schwartz, 1996; Schwartz & Yerushalmy, 1992).

POWERFUL IDEAS

Elementary school mathematics introduces students to the operations and properties of integers, to rational numbers via fractions and decimals, and to basic ideas about geometry and measurement. It places considerable emphasis on the mastery of key representational systems associated with place-value notation, written expressions and equations (without variables), tables, number lines, simple graphs, and mathematical statements in natural language, such as word problems. The history of mathematics education is replete with attempts to implement powerful ideas in elementary school mathematics. For example, in the early 20th century, learning theorists from a behaviorist school of thought (e.g. Thorndike) advocated teaching methods aimed at reinforcing desired behaviors of students, typically, the solving of routine arithmetical computations and word problems. In the second half of the 20th century proponents of the "New Mathematics Movement" attempted to make elementary school mathematics more powerful using ideas from set theory that, in the 19th century, had helped provide coherent and rigorous foundations for arithmetic. Although the mathematical rationale of the movement was generally acknowledged as sound, the outcomes fell far short of their aspirations.[2] An historian of mathematics might stress time-honored mathematical ideas and notational advances, such as the invention of the place value system that, once adopted, allowed people to solve a wider range of problems with less effort than ever before and paved the way for further advances, such as algebraic notation. More recently, mathematics educators have highlighted the importance of what students already know, how they reason, and how their reasoning plays a role in learning the content of mathematics (e.g. Langrall, Mooney, Nishet, & Jones, 2008).

For the purposes of this chapter, "powerful ideas" include those that facilitate in-depth learning, understanding, and teaching of key mathematical content areas and promote key long-term developments. We will build the present analysis around four powerful ideas, listed in Table 6.1, that foreshadow what is to come. Their meaning and implications will become clearer as the analysis unfolds.

The first powerful idea is that the operations of arithmetic are literally defined as functions. Indeed, they are the first examples of functions that students encounter in mathematics. However, the domain and codomain of functions, which are the source of variables, tend to be tacit at best. In addition, the overwhelming majority of problems posed in elementary school concern bound, rather than free, variables.

The second powerful idea highlights why functions and relations deserve a more prominent role. These concepts are critical for the expansion of elementary students' concept of number beyond the natural numbers and for the introduction of variables as placeholders for elements of sets.

Table 6.1 Four powerful ideas.

(1) The four basic operations of arithmetic—addition, subtraction, multiplication, and division—are functions.

(2) Mathematical generalizations can be fostered by making the domain and codomain of functions prominent and leaving otherwise bound variables free to vary.

(3) Functions and relations help integrate arithmetic, algebra, and geometry.

(4) Equations and inequalities can naturally be interpreted as the comparison of two functions.

The third powerful idea concerns the role of functions in uniting arithmetic, algebra, and geometry. It is precisely the abstract nature of functions that permits and, from a pedagogical standpoint, requires them to be represented in such diverse forms, most notably as data tables, as points on the line and graphs in the Cartesian plane, as arithmetic and algebraic expressions, as diagrams, and as statements in spoken and written language.

The fourth powerful idea builds on the fact that equations and inequalities can be regarded as the comparison of two functions across their domains. Equations may be regarded as statements expressing the conditions under which two functions provide the same output for a given input. Likewise, inequalities can be interpreted as statements representing the conditions under which one of the functions yields a greater output than the other function. Equations and inequalities conventionally take the form of algebraic notation. However, they can be expressed through any of the various forms for representing functions.

From an educational standpoint, the ideas we propose confer power to the extent that they contribute to student learning. So, equally important are pedagogical insights about how to successfully plan, stage, and implement programs of instruction, drawing upon tools for representing, deriving, and communicating mathematical ideas. Their impact also depends on the degree to which curricula and classroom activities make use of research regarding how students reason and learn about selected topics. This is one reason we include detailed descriptions of studies on students learning in classrooms.

What ideas qualify as powerful also depends to a degree on the abilities and concepts one hopes to foster. In the present chapter we will be focusing in particular on students' ability to model situations described in word problems. By modeling situations we mean providing coherent and useful descriptions of how various quantities of interest are interrelated. Note that, throughout this paper, we take *quantity* to represent a "property of a phenomenon, body, or substance, where the property has a magnitude that can be expressed as a number and a reference" (JCGM, 2012, p. 2); this convention is consistent with certain usages in mathematics (e.g. Whitney, 1968a) and mathematics education Fridman (1991). In principle, descriptions of how quantities are interrelated may enable the student to make inferences about one quantity from information about others. They should serve to handle particular cases as well as a range of cases with varying values.

Accordingly, we will be paying attention to the students' growing use of variables in their models of situations. As is to be expected, this requires examining students' uses of notation for stating relationships among numbers and quantities, fixed and variable. It also demands special attention to how students use natural language to express models. And as numbers and numeric operations increasingly take on geometric form as positions, distances, and ultimately transformations on the real line and in the plane, it becomes necessary to pay close attention to how students use number line diagrams and graphs to express relationships.

Viewing basic topics of elementary school mathematics through the lens of functions and relations can serve to unite—for teachers as well as students—key ideas and techniques that might otherwise seem unrelated. It can facilitate problem solving by making more readily accessible the tools through which relations and functions are routinely represented: number lines, bar diagrams, graphs, arithmetic and algebraic notation, tables, and specialized language structures. It also better prepares students for mathematics in middle and high school, minimizing difficulties that are exacerbated by excessively computational approaches to arithmetic (Booth, 1988; Kaput, 1998; Lacampagne, 1995; Schliemann et al., 2007; Schoenfeld, 1995). A major challenge for educators consists in finding opportunities for switching the focus from computations on specific values to relationships among sets of values.

Additive, Multiplicative, and Linear Structures

In past decades mathematics education researchers increasingly examined knowledge about arithmetical operations beyond knowing how to compute sums and differences, products, and quotients (Carpenter et al., 1982; Lesh & Landau, 1983; Schwartz, 1996; Vergnaud, 1982, 1983, 1994). One often employs the terms "additive and multiplicative structures" to encompass this broader sort of arithmetical knowledge.

In the present context, the term *structure* alludes to the logical relations among the quantities in a problem. *Additive structures* are associated with statements of the form $A + B = C$ and variants such as $C - B = A$ and $C - A = B$, where the letters, A, B, C, etc., may stand for numbers or for quantity values of multitudes or magnitudes; they also correspond to inequalities such as $A + B < C$. *Multiplicative structures* entail problems that might be represented by $A \times B = C$ and variants such as $C \div B = A$. *Linear structures* are those associated with an equation such as $A \times B + C = D$. Such relational structures are attributed to word problems regardless of whether the problems contain algebraic notation and whether they expressly include variables.

Problems having the same relational structure may nonetheless be conceptualized as having different structures in another sense. As much research has shown (e.g., Vergnaud, 1982), young students may treat problems of part-whole compositions (C consists of two parts, A and B), transformations (A undergoes the additive change, B, resulting in C), comparisons (A is greater than C by B), and net changes (the composition of change A with change B constitutes a net change, $A + B$) as having different "conceptual structures," even though they have the same underlying relational structure, $A + B = C$ (Vergnaud, 1982). Unfortunately, to refer to part-whole compositions, transformations, and so on, as *structures* is potentially misleading because one hopes that students will ultimately realize that conceptual structures may obscure a common underlying relational structure. Teachers need to be cognizant of both kinds of structure and realize that the relational structure is the more elusive of the two.

The rich features of situations also may obscure underlying relational structures. Furthermore, the relational structure is less salient in problems that assign values to all or all but one of the variables. In effect, when all but one variable are bound, students are prone to regard the unbound variable as a secret or missing number rather than as a placeholder for all elements of a domain. There are ways to address this issue. Indeed, we will examine examples in which problems are formulated in such a way as to leave variables "free to vary."

Nonmathematicians commonly conflate the operations of arithmetic with the specific procedures or rules used for computing sums, differences, products, and quotients. This view is problematic, for it implies that alternative procedures necessarily constitute different operations. The ancient Egyptians "doubling and halving" procedure, though certainly different from modern column multiplication, is nonetheless a valid form of multiplication. Likewise, a Brazilian street vendor's mental calculation of the difference, 200–35, entails the operation of subtraction even if it does not make use of the minus sign, place value notation, and column-wise computation (Carraher, Carraher, & Schliemann, 1985).

The symbolic forms of problems are a critical component of mathematical knowledge and problem solving that we must keep in mind in the upcoming analysis. They need to be distinguished from the underlying relational structure of problems.

Algebraic Structures

We are trying to weigh the relative merits of treating the operations of arithmetic as functions. In this venture, another sort of structure can be of help in providing a deeper understanding of the properties of the arithmetical operations. In mathematics, *algebraic structures* correspond to the sets or classes of numbers under consideration and, in a looser sense, to the properties of operations defined over those sets. For elementary school mathematics, the initial algebraic structure will be the natural or counting numbers, 1, 2, 3. . . Throughout elementary school the students expand their understanding of numbers to include integers, rational numbers, in the form of fractions and decimal numbers, and eventually the real numbers. As new, more inclusive, classes of numbers enter the scene, the arithmetic properties of the operations will change. For real numbers, these properties include the additive and multiplicative properties of closure, commutativity, associativity, distributivity, identity, inverse, and order properties such as transitivity and additive and multiplicative compatibility (Rosen, 2012). Not all of these properties hold for the other, "earlier," less-inclusive classes of numbers. As we proceed to reconceptualize the operations of arithmetic as functions, we need to keep in mind that the domains of the functions and relations, the very numbers the student will presumably be working with, will be changing. The operation of division over natural or counting numbers is not closed. That is one of the reasons that integer division, or more precisely, division of natural numbers with a remainder, is the first form of division that students encounter. Rational numbers open the door to long division, a different function from integer division. Multiplication of counting numbers never results in a product less than the multiplicand. This property no longer holds for integers and rational numbers. As we shall see, functions and relations, which bring domains into the light of day, can help teachers and curriculum developers take into account the student's evolving sense of what numbers are.

Syntactical Structure

Consider an algebraic expression in conventional form such as $2x + 3$. The syntactical structure of the expression may be clearly represented through tree notation:

> Tree notation expresses the hierarchy of operations in an expression through the vertical arrangement of nodes. As well, in tree notation letters are used to represent operations that may be indicated only tacitly by positioning of symbols in ordinary notation.
> (Kirshner & Awtry, 2004, pp. 232–233)

Syntactical structure may also be expressed by a string of characters that depicts the level and order of operations through bracketing. For instance, in Wolfram Language, aka Mathematica, the expression $2x + 3$ in full form is represented as "Plus [3,Times[2,x]]." A treeform diagram of the expression is generated by the code, TreeForm [$2x + 3$]. In addition, tree structure can be described and clarified through "precise declarative accounts of algebraic structures and processes" (Kirshner & Awtry, 2004, p. 249) embodied in spoken or written language.

Although syntactical structures are important for students' mastery of arithmetic and algebra, we will not focus on such structures in the present analysis.

Relations and Functional Relations (Functions)

To appreciate the mathematical meaning of a relation, consider tables, that is, tabular representations of data or information. For most purposes, any table of information can be regarded as a relation. Each tuple—that is, ordered pair, triple, quadruple, etc., that makes up a row of information—is a member of the relation.[3]

For convenience, consider the set numbers that a single dice can return: $\{1, 2, 3, 4, 5, 6\}$. The possible outcomes for a pair of dice, along with their sum, are the triples $(1, 1, 2)$, $(2, 1, 3)$, $(1, 2, 3)$, $(2, 2, 4)$, . . ., $(6, 6, 12)$. In mathematics one often takes the set of tuples as the relation itself. This notion of a relation as a list of cases applies as well to infinite sets, such as the integers, rationals, or real numbers. Of course, we cannot make a table of infinite length. But we can imagine such a table—and we can work, together with students, on a subset of such a table even though it does not comprise the entire relation.

If we exclude empirical data (rainfall data, position time pairs on an actual trip), most relations of interest to elementary school mathematics may also be described through words and algebraic notation. For example, "given the integers n, m that are elements in the set $\{1, 2, 3, 4, 5, 6\}$ and s that is an element of $\{2, 3, 4, . . .12\}$, the relation can be described as $\{n, m, n + m\}$" Note that we may describe the relation equally well as the triples $\{n=s-m,\ m,s\},\{n,s-n,s\}$, or even $\{n=s-m, m=s-n, s=n+m\}$. It does not matter that, in real life, one first throws the dice and then sums the outcomes to get the total. A relation need not convey a sense of input and output.

The reader will note that some representations of the described relation highlight subtraction while others highlight addition. From a relational point of view, every addition problem is a subtraction problem—actually, two subtraction problems. Every division problem can be regarded as a multiplication problem, provided the divisor is not zero. Two symbolic representations of a relation are interchangeable if they correspond to the same tuples.

One of the principal virtues of a relational approach to addition and subtraction is the degree to which it facilitates the reformulation of an indirect problem as a direct problem. Consider the following simple problem:

> Some birds are sitting in a tree. Two more birds fly to the tree, and then there are five. How many birds were there in the tree at first?
>
> (Mikulina, 1991, p. 186)

The problem is indirect because a valid solution is not produced by carrying out addition as alluded to in the story through the phrase "Two more birds fly to the tree." One can represent the relational structure of the problem as $x+2=5$ but one more straightforwardly solves this missing addend problem by recognizing that the structure may also be represented by $x=5-2$. We might justify this rewriting of the relation through rules of syntax. But the young student may initially find it more natural to work through the relation in story form, coming to the realization that the current covey of birds in the tree consists of those that were there from the beginning together with those that arrived later. Eliminating the "joiners" from the current set of birds leaves the original birds; subtracting the number of joiners from the current number of birds yields the number of the original birds.

A relational approach aims at describing how diverse numbers or quantities in a problem fit together. This supports the discovery of alternative, yet equivalent, symbolic formulations that can then be more easily simplified. Eventually rules of syntax can guide the rewriting; but in the beginning, the student's understanding of the semantics of the problem may be the principal driver for finding equivalent expressions.

A (binary) *function* is a relation in which each and every "piece of information" (element) from one set (the domain) is associated with a single piece of information from the second set, the codomain or target. We exemplify this for the case of multiplication. The "times seven" table represents the relation $\{(1,7),(2,14),(3,21),(4,28),\ldots,(12,84)\}$. There is an implied asymmetry, a direction, reflected in the functional notation, $x \mapsto 7x$ (to be read as "x maps to $7x$"), where x stands in for the elements in the domain and $7x$ for elements in the codomain. This asymmetry—"you can always produce f(x) from x"—is consistent with the view that a function is a unidirectional procedure or a process. However, there are many occasions in which one needs to view a function as an object that can be acted upon and compared with other functions (see Sfard, 1991, for the distinction of function as a process versus function as an object). As we shall see, in treating equations and inequalities as comparisons of functions, it is useful to think of functions both as processes and as objects.

When one conceives of multiplication as a binary function, each element in the first set is itself an ordered pair, (x, y). For example, we may represent multiplication as the function $(x, y) \mapsto x \times y$. The relation can also be represented as $\{(x,y), x \times y\}$.

A functional approach to arithmetic provides students with opportunities to analyze physical quantities and situations and to build and understand mathematics concepts. It can empower teachers and students to learn the standard topics in a deeper, more interconnected way. From the decimal system, to arithmetic operations, to fractions, ratio, and proportion, a functional approach can pave the way for a smooth transition to the middle and high school curriculum and to the future learning of algebra (Schoenfeld, 1995; Schliemann et al., 2012) and even calculus (Oehrtman, Carlson, & Thompson, 2008).

First, by recognizing arithmetic operations as functions, teachers will more easily pay attention to domain and codomain of arithmetic operations (Powerful Idea #2). This is important given that young students typically enter school with a limited understanding of natural numbers and, yet, by the end of elementary school, will be expected to have become familiar with operations (hence functions) over integers and rational numbers, each class of which introduces additional properties, new notational and representational advances (unary operators, fractional and decimal forms, additional uses of the number line, etc.), and new kinds of situations to be modeled.

Second, treating the operations of arithmetic as functions offers many opportunities for using variables (Powerful Idea #2). Computable functions, namely, those for which outputs can be uniquely determined from inputs by using an algorithm (a clearly specified list of steps or formula), consist of variables, constants, and operators that, when configured in certain ways, enable focusing on sets of values rather than individual values. This shift in focus from particular numbers to variables encourages the production of mathematical generalizations.

Third, by treating the operations of arithmetic as functions, mathematical structures and relations become more evident. Mathematical structures reveal themselves through features shared by different actions, such as computations. (For example, the sequence of computations $1 \times 3 + 7, 2 \times 3 + 7, 3 \times 3 + 7, 4 \times 3 + 7$ highlights the invariant syntactical structure, $\square \times 3 + 7$). Over time, relatively deep structures, will become increasingly accessible.

Fourth, when viewing the basic operations of arithmetic as functions, algebra, algebraic thinking, and geometry are seen as inherent to arithmetic and arithmetical reasoning (Powerful Ideas #3 and 4). This can mitigate the clash between arithmetic and algebra that many students currently experience when, after years of dealing with a computational view of arithmetic, they are formally introduced to algebra.

As we will attempt to show, a functional approach to elementary school mathematics can be closely allied with other powerful ideas such as generalizing, modeling, and using multiple representations. It leads to viewing isolated examples and topics as instances of more abstract ideas and concepts. We believe that such ideas can make a difference in teaching and learning at the elementary school level.

LEARNING ABOUT ADDITIVE RELATIONS

What opportunities are there for young students to learn about additive relations in the broad sense in which we are using the term? To make relations explicit, one needs to introduce variables. This leads us to ask, "How can young children understand variables, if at all, and use them in discussing relations?"

A variable is a short name or placeholder for a set of elements. Although this may seem far removed from everyday experience, we regularly use words and expressions to stand for indeterminate and variable quantities. For example, a service charge might be set as 15% of the cost of dinner, *whatever that cost may be.*

Relations, including functions, are fundamentally about associations between sets (of elements) that we denote through variables. When the elements in question are *numbers*, the variable can be thought of as a generalized number. Sometimes the elements in question are understood to be values associated with quantities such as number of items, length, time, or mass, or of derived quantities such as speed, density, or person-hours. In such cases the variables may be referred to as *variable magnitudes* (Aleksandrov, 1999) or *variable quantities*. It is a matter of considerable debate how to meaningfully bridge the realms of numbers and quantities. Some would hold that students learn about numbers and then apply this knowledge to situations involving quantities. Others suggest that students acquire mathematical knowledge primarily through extra-mathematical situations.

Relations and Additive Structures

In the 1960s a group of Soviet researchers (see Davydov, 1991), initiated a long-term program to introduce students to algebra from their very first days in school. Despite the well-documented success of the program and the care with which the ideas were developed and published, the approach has enjoyed relatively little influence on early mathematics curricula outside of the former Soviet republics. Studies by Dougherty (2008) and Schmittau and Morris (2004) are notable exceptions.

Schmittau and Morris (2004) provide a useful description of the initial activities of the Davydov approach in first grade, which highlights additive relations among physical quantities:

> The grade 1 curriculum begins with an exploration of quantitative properties of real objects. Length, width, volume, area, and weight, are examples of "quantities." Children learn to isolate and identify a single quantitative property of an object (e.g., the surface area of a glass) and to abstract it from the object's spatial orientation. They learn to compare objects and to determine whether they are equal with respect to some quantitative property, and to use a line segment model to represent the results of their comparison of quantities. Initially they draw two equal line segments, "||," to indicate that two objects are equal with respect to some property and two unequal line segments to show that they are not equal. Children then learn to use an uppercase letter to represent a quantitative property of an object, and to represent equality and inequality relationships with the signs =, ≠, >, and <. For example, they compare the lengths of two boards, name the lengths A and B, and represent the relationship between them as $A = B, A \neq B, A > B, A < B$. There is no reference to numbers during this work: "A" represents the unmeasured length of the board.
>
> (Schmittau and Morris, 2004, p. 60)

The authors further note that an inequality (e.g. $K > D$, where K and D are, for example, the unmeasured lengths of two objects) leads naturally to an equation involving three objects: "If $K > D$ (by A) then $K - A = D$ and $K = D + A$" (Schmittau & Morris, 2004, p. 64).

The Davydov approach takes welcome steps in the direction of giving algebraic expression to relations. It introduces variable notation while stopping short of explicitly introducing variables as placeholders for all elements in a set.

Addition and Subtraction as Functions

From here on, we describe in detail examples of classroom discussions that took place in our longitudinal intervention studies designed to investigate a particular approach to functions and other relations in elementary school. We will argue that the data provide evidence that participating students understand a relation as a correspondence between two variables, not simply between two numbers or quantity values. This would suggest that relations and functions, in the particular sense adopted here, are within reach of even young elementary students.

The first example comes from a three-year intervention, from third through fifth grade, in which students were introduced to variables and functions (Carraher, Schliemann, & Schwartz, 2008). In four third grade classrooms of 8 and 9 year olds, the instructor told the students he was going to discuss the number of candies that two students, John and Mary, had. In his left hand he held a box of candies that he identified as John's candies. In his right hand he held a similar-looking box, Mary's box, along with three loose candies taped onto the top. He stated that there was exactly the same number of candies inside each box, although Mary had three additional candies atop her box.

Unlike standard addition problems given to third-grade students, this problem does not have a unique solution in that many ordered pairs representing John's and Mary's amounts satisfy the constraints of the problem. Given that an actual box contains a fixed amount at a given time, the lesson introduces a tension between the empirical reality (How many candies are actually in the boxes?) and the logical possibilities (What are all the possible pairs of amounts that satisfy the conditions of the problem?).

At the beginning of the lesson, the students treated the problem as being about specific amounts, an interpretation the instructor did not immediately attempt to dispel. The boxes were circulated among the students who, perhaps not surprisingly, hefted and shook them to help estimate the amounts. Because packing paper prevented the candies from rattling, the instructor had to reassure students not only that the boxes contained candies but also that they contained precisely the same number of candies. After this, the students were asked to individually draw or describe on paper what they knew or could say about the number of candies John and Mary had. Approximately two-thirds of the students attributed a specific value to John's and Mary's amounts. In the majority of cases the number ascribed to Mary was three greater than the number ascribed to John. Some students refrained from attributing specific values and described instead the relation between the amounts, namely, that Mary had three more than John, or that Mary had more than John. In isolated cases, a student used a symbol (a question mark or an empty square or box) to indicate unknown amounts; in such cases, however, the same type of placeholder was used for John's and Mary's amounts.

After collectively reviewing the students' work, the teacher asked each student to state the number of candies they thought John and Mary might have had. The teacher registered students' estimates on a whiteboard in a three-column data table, with a student's name and her estimates for John and Mary's amounts in each row. Afterwards, and without opening the boxes, the teacher initiated a discussion about the validity of the various guesses, that is, about which answers were in accordance with how the problem was stated. The teacher's intent was to shift the conversation from the actual number of candies to all ordered pairs of numbers consistent with the narrative. Here is where the table's role as a tool for displaying relations was put to use.

Occasionally, a student gave an answer that violated the constraint that Mary had three more candies than John, for example, by proposing that John had seven candies while Mary had 13. Other students quickly noticed such inconsistencies and claimed that the ordered pair could not be correct. From our perspective they were claiming that the pair was not in the relation. They pointed out that, even though there could be any amount in the boxes, the amount in each box had to be the same and Mary had to have exactly three more candies than John. Students eventually agreed that once an amount is attributed to one of the students, the other student's amount must take on a particular value. They also reached the consensus that any and all answers consistent with the information given in the problem were legitimate. As one student expressed it, once the invalid pairs were removed from the table: "Everybody had the right answer because everybody. . . has three more [for Mary], always."

In one classroom, a student had offered to represent the amounts in the box by a question mark and, with the instructors' guidance, the student proposed to represent Mary's amount as "? + 3." In another classroom, the instructor proposed using the letter N to represent the indeterminate or variable amount. Students first speculated that N could be 19, 90, or 14 (N is the14th letter in the alphabet). The instructor recommended that they adopt the convention that N stands for any number and asked: "How many should we say that Mary has if John has N candies, and N can stand for anything?" Several students suggested that Mary's amount also be called N. The instructor then asked, "Well, if we write N here [on the blackboard, next to the N assigned to John] doesn't that suggest that they [John and Mary] have the same amount? Students at first rejected this proposal, claiming that N "could mean anything." The instructor agreed, but raised the issue that "some people would look at it [the adoption of N to represent both John's and Mary's amounts] and say it's the same anything if you're calling them both N." A student then proposed to represent Mary's amount as $N + 3$ and explained: "I thought, 'cuz she could have three more than John. Write N plus three 'cuz she could have any amount plus three." Another student agreed, explaining " 'cuz if it's any number, like if it's ninety, you could just, like add three and it'd be ninety-three."

In the four classrooms students eventually adopted the convention that if N represents the amount of candy in a box, Mary's amount might be called "N plus three." (In one classroom, a student submitted, with a gleam in his eye, that if there were 1 billion candies in each box, Mary would have 1 billion and three candies!) The student clearly realized that 1 billion candies could not possibly fit in the box; his point appears to have been that the wording of the problem did not exclude this possibility. In a sense, the student was attempting to test the limits of the domain the teacher would consider legitimate. He was playfully overlooking the physical constraints and focusing solely on the constraints imposed by the wording of the problem.

Some may regard the inherent ambiguity of the problem as a possible source of confusion. Yet it is the story's ambiguity that allows the teacher and students to hold a meaningful discussion about the sort of truth they were to pursue: empirical truth, consistent with the "facts on the ground" or logical proof consistent with the wording of the problem. Through such conversations students can begin to appreciate the tension between realistic considerations (there is only one answer for the number of candies John and Mary have) and logical possibilities (valid answers are those consistent with the information given, regardless of whether they correspond to a particular case at hand).

The results from the Candy Boxes task suggest that young students can learn to shift their focus from individual instances to sets of numbers and their interrelations (Powerful Idea #2). In this view the mathematical object is no longer a relation between two constants but rather the relation between two variables. More recent work by Brizuela, Blanton, Gardiner, Newman-Owens, & Sawrey, (in press) found that even first and second graders can discuss problems and come to use variables to represent relations among quantities. But we must be careful not to overinterpret promising first steps: the Candy Boxes lesson represented the beginning of a long conversation about variables that extended over months and years and across a wide variety of contexts.

Representing Additive Functions on a Number Line

The Candy Boxes activity introduced third graders to functions through a table of values, simple algebraic notation, and number lines. One of the long-term goals was to exploit key geometrical representations for expressing relations on the number line and in the Cartesian plane. Here we briefly describe how additive relations are introduced as displacements on the number line, preparing students for dealing later with transformations of the real line. We also show how variables enter the discussion through what we called the "N-number line" or the "variable number line."

In the classroom research the number line was first introduced by means of a length of twine stretched across the classroom with numerals to represent successive integers attached at approximately one-foot intervals. Students at first tended to consider only the numerals shown on the twine but, after discussing where the number line would finish, they quickly came to regard the number line as an imaginary construct that can "go through walls" and continues indefinitely in opposing directions. In subsequent lessons, number lines were represented on paper or projected onto a large screen. To emphasize intervals, as opposed to points on the number line, arrows linking points on the same line represented changes in values, and longer arrows connecting shorter ones were used to lead students to consider shortcuts that went from the tail of the first arrow to the head of the last arrow. For example, the operation "$+ 7 - 9$" could be composed and represented as subtracting 2, something occasionally referred to as a "shortcut."

Whereas we might think of a number line as the embodiment of the continuous and dense real line (a mathematical object), young students are likely to interpret number lines as holding nothing but integers separated by voids. Students are sometimes inclined to consider the difference between numbers on the number line as the number of tick marks between one number and the other rather than distances as measured by some unit of distance or metric. Getting students to think of numbers and number operations as entailing distances, slopes and rates of change, and geometric transformations (translations, dilations, reflections, etc.) is a long-term process of unifying arithmetic and geometry that culminates in analytic geometry. We may informally refer to this process as helping students move "onto the real line" and later "onto the coordinate plane."

Students also used number lines to model additive relations in word problems by displacing themselves along a number line drawn on the classroom floor or by showing displacements on paper. In preparation for the work with positive and negative integers, in one of the lessons we proposed a situation involving money and debts (see Carraher et al., 2006 and Peled and Carraher, 2008, for details on the challenges and progress made by third graders on adopting the conventions for representing problems on the number line).

We later introduced the "*N number* line"—a variation (Figure 6.1) where positions were identified as $N - 2$, $N - 1$, N, $N + 1$, $N + 2$, etc. Such a representation allowed students to represent additive relations as functions of one variable.

Students were asked to solve addition and subtraction problems with indeterminate values and to focus on variables and notation for variables.

Solving Multistep Additive Problems Using the *N Number* Line

The following description of a lesson in a third-grade classroom of 16 students shows how the variable number line helped students reflect upon and represent the following statements of a multistep problem involving addition and subtraction and, at the end, solve the problem (see Figure 6.1):

> Mary and John each have a piggy bank.
> On *Sunday* they both had the same amount in their piggy banks.
> On *Monday*, their grandmother comes to visit them and gives $3 to each of them.
> On *Tuesday*, they go together to the bookstore. Mary spends $3 on Harry Potter's new book. John spends $5 on a 2001 calendar with dog pictures on it.
> On *Wednesday*, John washes his neighbor's car and makes $4. Mary also made $4 babysitting. They run to put their money in their piggy banks.

Only after the whole story had been discussed and represented through Wednesday were the students shown the additional statement:

> On *Thursday* Mary opens her piggy bank and finds that she has $9.

They were then asked to determine how much money was initially in each piggy bank, how much money John and Mary each ended up with, and the difference between their final amounts.

Representing Unknown Amounts

After a class discussion about each step of the problem, students worked alone or in pairs to provide their own written accounts about the information given. Members of the research

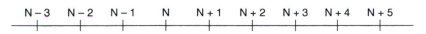

Figure 6.1 The *N* number line. This was used to represent successive additive operations upon an indeterminate number or amount, *N*.

team asked individual students to explain what they were doing and raised questions that encouraged them to develop more adequate representations. We will highlight main points related to students' insights and representations. For a detailed description of the lesson implementation (see Carraher et al., 2006 and Carraher et al., in press).

Sunday: After a student read the *Sunday* part for the whole class, the instructor asked whether anyone knew how much money each of the characters in the story had. The students agreed that they did not, and did not appear to be bothered by that. A few uttered: "*N*" and one of them stated, "*N*, it's for anything." Others called out "any number" and "anything." A student proposed, "You could make [sic] some money in them, but it has to be the same amount" and, when the instructor reminded him that the amount was unknown, the student suggested that he could write *N* to represent the unknown amount. They all started writing in their handouts, which contained a copy of the *N number* line. The instructor reminded them that they could use the *N number* line and drew a copy of the *N number* line on the board.

After approximately three minutes, four students had attributed specific values for Mary and John on Sunday, five represented the amount as *N*, two placed a question mark inside or next to each piggy bank, and five drew piggy banks with no indication of what each would contain (Figure 6.2).

One of the students (first example in Figure 6.2) explained that she used *N* because "You don't know how much amount they have" and "*N* means any number." When further asked, "Is it that they have, like, ten dollars each?" she answered: "No. . . . Because we don't know how much they have."

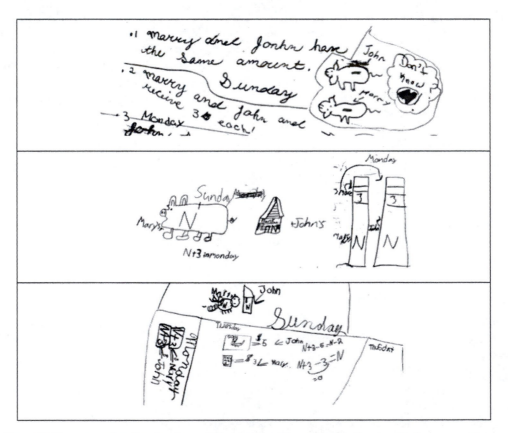

Figure 6.2 Three examples of students' use of *N* to represent the amounts in the piggy bank.

Representing Changes in Unknown Amounts

Monday: When the students read that each child received $3 on Monday, they inferred that Mary and John would continue to have the same amount of money as each other and that they both would have $3 more than the day before. A student proposed that, on Monday, they would each have N plus 3 "Because we don't know how much money they had on Sunday, and they got plus, . . . and they got three more dollars on Monday." The second and third examples in Figure 6.2 show spontaneous depictions of $N + 3$. As one student explained, "when the grandmother came to visit them they had like, N. And then she gave Mary and John three dollars. That's why I say [pointing to $N + 3$ on paper] N plus three."

By the end of the lesson, students' written work showed that 11 of the 16 students had adopted $N + 3$ for the amounts on Monday, one student used specific amounts in his work sheet, and four produced drawings that could not be interpreted, or written work that included N but inconsistently, as in $N + 3 = N$.

Operating on Unknowns With Multiple Representations

Tuesday: Some students wondered whether there would be enough money in the piggy banks on Tuesday for the purchases. A student suggested that the children in the story probably had $10; others assumed that there must be at least $5 in each piggy bank by the end of Monday, otherwise John could not have bought a $5 calendar. The students also concluded that, at the end of Tuesday, John and Mary would have different amounts of money and that Mary would have more money than John, but the same amount that she had on Sunday.

The instructor encouraged the class to use the N *number* line to represent what has happened from Sunday to Tuesday. With input from the students, she drew arrows going from N to $N + 3$ and back to N again to show the changes in Mary's amounts. In parallel, she used algebraic notation, narrating the changes from Sunday to Tuesday, step by step, and getting students' input while she wrote $N + 3 - 3$. She then wrote a bracket under +3–3, with a 0 below it, and extended the notation to $N + 3 - 3 = N + 0 = N$. A student explained how the $3 spent cancels out the $3 given by the grandmother: "Because you added three, right, and then she took, she spent those three and she has the number she started with." With the students' input, the instructor eventually wrote $N + 3 - 5$ to express John's amount at the end of Tuesday. Some students suggested that this amount was equal to "N minus 2," an inference that she registered as $N + 3 - 5 = N - 2$.

The bottom example in Figure 6.2 shows that, for Tuesday, the student first drew iconic representations of the calendar and the book next to the values $5 and $3, respectively. While discussing with an in-class interviewer, he wrote the two equations ($N + 3 - 5 = N - 2$ and $N + 3 - 3 = N$), using the N *number* line as support for his decisions (Powerful Idea #3). Later, when he learned that N was equal to 5 (from the information about the amount on Thursday) he wrote 8 next to $N + 3$ on the Monday section of his worksheet.

Wednesday: Students concluded that on Wednesday Mary and John would end up with different amounts, then explained that Mary would have $N + 4$ and John $N + 2$. A student volunteered to show why $N + 3 - 3 + 4$ equals $N + 4$ by crossing out the subexpression $+ 3 - 3$ saying, "We don't need that anymore." Another student stated that this is the same as 0.

The students then took turns helping the instructor write out an equation conveying what happened to John's amounts throughout the week. Going through each step in the story, they built the equation $N + 3 - 5 + 4 = N + 2$. Before they agreed upon the expression for the right-hand side of the equation, the instructor had to help them visualize the operations leading to $N + 2$ on the N *number* line, starting with +3 – 5 and then –2 + 4 leading to 2. As one of the students explained: "N is anything, plus 3, minus 5, is minus 2; N minus 2 plus 4, equals (while counting on his fingers) N plus 2." This student also grouped the numbers differently, first adding 3 and 4 and then taking away 5, giving the instructor the opportunity to stress that the order of operations did not matter.

Solving the Problem Once the Solution Set Is Constrained to a Single Value.

Thursday: When a student learned that Mary ended with $9, several children suggested aloud that N had to be 5. Some of them claimed that John (whose amount was represented by $N + 2$) had "two *more*," apparently meaning "two more than N." Others answered 7, by adding $5 + 2$ or by subtracting 2 from Mary's final amount of 9. One student expressed that $N + 2$ (John's amount) is two less than $N + 4$ (Mary's amount).

The instructor concluded the lesson by working with the students in filling out a 2-by-4 table displaying the amounts that Mary and John had across the four days. Some students suggested expressions with unknown values; others suggested using the actual values, as inferred after the information about Thursday's events.

This early work on number lines not only helped students better solve arithmetic problems, but also prepared them to later work in the Cartesian space. This transition was achieved by first representing in parallel number lines and then rotating one of them to become perpendicular to the other, thereby creating a coordinate space.

The N Number Line in a New Context: Differences Between Heights

It is possible to mix unbound measures with known measures. Figure 6.3, for instance, exemplifies a problem that provides specific differences in heights among children while leaving the heights of the three protagonists unbound, that is, free to vary (Carraher et al., 2006). Representing the relationships among heights—whether through a drawing, through alternative verbal descriptions, or through equations—may initially be challenging for third graders. But in the course of a single lesson or two, students become comfortable with such problems.

The following week, in the eighth lesson in third grade, we asked the same group of students to work on the problem in Figure 6.3 (see Carraher et al., 2000, 2007, for a previous analysis of the same problem with another group of students). The problem states the differences in heights among three characters without revealing their actual heights. The heights could be thought to vary insofar as they could take on a set of possible values. The point of researching the issue was to see what sense the students made of such a problem.

After discussing each statement in the problem, the instructor encouraged the students to focus on the differences between the protagonists' heights (see Carraher, Brizuela, & Earnest, 2001, for details on this first part of the class) and to represent the problem on individual

Tom is 4 inches taller than Maria.

Maria is 6 inches shorter than Leslie.

Draw Tom's height, Maria's height, and Leslie's height.

    Show what the numbers 4 and 6

refer to.

Maria   Maria's Height

Figure 6.3 The Heights Problem.

worksheets. Most of the students used vertical bars or lines to show the three heights (see example in Figure 6.4).

To our surprise, one of the students chose to represent the heights on a variable number line, much like the one they had been working with during previous meetings (see Figure 6.5). The instructor adopted her number line as a basis for a class discussion of the relations among the heights and about her assumption that Maria is located at N on the variable number line (middle number line in Figure 6.6). In the discussion, most students easily accepted that if Maria's height was located at N on the line, Tom's height should be at $N + 4$ and Leslie's at $N + 6$.

It is impressive that the student realized that the N *number* line would help to clarify the problem at hand, and that the remaining students easily accepted her idea and represented

Figure 6.4 A student's drawing and notation for the Heights Problem.

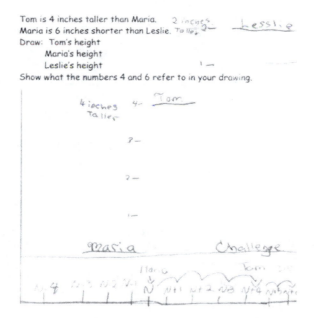

Figure 6.5 A student's drawing (notches) showing differences but no origin. She also uses a variable number line that becomes the basis of subsequent discussion.

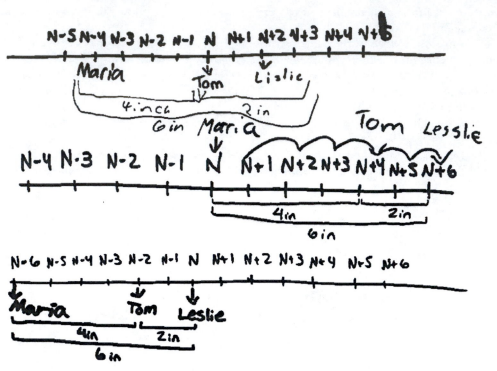

Figure 6.6 Three "variable number line" representations drawn by students and their teacher to discuss the cases where Maria is attributed the height of *N* (middle number line); Leslie is assigned the height of *N* (the bottom number line); and the Tom is assigned a height of *N* (the upper number line).

Tom and Leslie's heights ($N + 2$, $N + 4$, respectively), from Maria's (N). The instructor then pushed the students even further, asking them to assume, instead, that Leslie's height was N. They noted that Tom's height would be $N - 2$ and Maria's would be $N - 6$ (the bottom number line in Figure 6.6). They determined this by making the appropriate displacements on the variable number line. When the instructor proposed them to place Tom at N, again, after some adjustment to the work of a student who counted points instead of intervals, Leslie was correctly placed at $N + 2$ and Maria at $N - 4$ (top number line in Figure 6.6).

By the end of the lesson, the students were relating the given numerical differences to algebraic notation, line segment diagrams, number lines (including variable number lines), subtraction, counting, and natural language descriptions. The fluidity with which they moved from one representational form to another suggests a flexible understanding of *additive structures*. Their willingness to use N to represent the height of any of the three characters in the story (as long as the relations among the three heights are kept invariant) shows an encouraging degree of robustness in their thinking.

Further Challenges in Learning About Additive Relations and Structures

In the preceding examples, we focused on the progress young students can make in identifying additive structures and reasoning about variables. We should be careful not to underestimate the time and effort such progress demands. Students may quickly accept the idea that there are negative integers on the number line and yet remain puzzled when negative numbers arise in extra-mathematical contexts. Many students, for example, think of monetary amounts as physical commodities that they can hold in their hand. By this standard, the least amount that they can have is no money at all. The idea that they might spend more money than they have, and express the result of this action as a negative value, demands that they view debits as negative amounts and, ultimately, a net balance as a sum of credits and debits. The interested reader will find useful discussions of such issues by Peled and Carraher (2008).

LEARNING ABOUT MULTIPLICATIVE AND LINEAR RELATIONS AMONG QUANTITIES

Multiplication and division are generally modeled by, or serve as models of, situations involving unlike quantities or a combination of numbers and quantities. Students face situations in which, of the two inputs, multiplier and multiplicand (a) one refers to a quantity while the other will refer to a number (six seconds times five) or (b) the two entities refer to different kinds of quantities (e.g. a distance multiplied by a speed resulting in a time or a length times a length yielding an area). Thus, multiplication and division of quantities exhibit an asymmetry that does not occur in the realm of number, where two numbers are input, resulting in a third number.

As Vergnaud (1983) notes, understanding multiplication as part of the conceptual field of multiplicative structures rests on understanding proportionality. We would add that a deep understanding of multiplication is grounded on an understanding of linear functions.

This situation has led some to propose that quantities be explicitly integrated into the mathematical models used to solve applied problems (Whitney1968a, 1968b). For the present discussion, to the extent that quantities play a role in how students conceptualize mathematical problems, we will need to take them into account as we examine issues regarding multiplicative structures.

Viewing Multiplicative Structures as Relations

Let's now examine the prospects of introducing multiplicative problems and linear functions wherein relations among variables are given a prominent role. We will examine two successive lessons about the seating capacity around configurations of dinner tables (see detailed analysis by Carraher, Martinez, & Schliemann, 2008), implemented during the latter half of third grade. The 15 students in the classroom were part of another three-year longitudinal classroom intervention and attended a Boston school in a minority and immigrant community. The previous 33 lessons aimed at helping students to note and articulate the general relations they see among variables. During the lessons, students attempted to represent and determine, using data tables and mathematical notation, the relation between the number of tables and the number of people who can be served.

In the first lesson the tables were separated and four people could be seated at each one. In the second, tables were set end to end in a line that grew with each additional table. The two tasks corresponded, respectively, to the functions $f(n) = 4n$ and $g(n) = 2n + 2$, where n refers to the number of tables and $f(n)$, $g(n)$ refer to the number of people that can be seated at n tables. The tasks were introduced to the third grade students as a word problem.

The Separated Dinner Tables Problem

The constraint of filling each dinner table was clarified during a 10-minute discussion about the terms *maximum* and *minimum*: For a separated table, "zero seats" was the minimum and four was the maximum number of people at each table. The students' task was to determine the maximum number of people that could be seated at varying numbers of separated dinner tables.

The students then completed a handout for one, two, three, and nine dinner tables and the instructor registered the agreed-upon results in tabular form on the whiteboard. The gap between the rows for three and for nine tables was intended to interrupt a column-wise, building-up strategy (see Schliemann, Carraher, & Brizuela, 2001 and Vergnaud, 1983) and to encourage students to consider within-row, input-output, an approach considered more congenial to closed form expressions of the function. The students filled in the data table in the handouts by multiplying the number of dinner tables by four, by adding four plus four, plus four repeatedly (once for each dinner table), and by adding four to the number of people in the prior row. One student noted that, when the rows of the data table were not arranged in a regularly increasing fashion, it was difficult to make use of the values in one row to obtain to values in the next.

In the discussion of the meaning of the written computations within the dinner table context, children at first described what we might term "number of people per table" as "number of people." The instructor systematically rephrased children's statements or helped them to do so, differentiating between total number of people and number of people per table. A student, building on previous work on notation for variables, proposed to use t for the number of tables and stated that "four times t" expresses the total number of people.

The problem was also used to give rise to discussions regarding the inverse function, $t = p/4$: To answer the question "What if we have 20 people total?" a student said that four times five is 20 and that you can think of 20 divided by five and the answer is four. Another proposed that one can also think of 20 divided by four, and a third one viewed the question as, "Four times what number equals 20?"

The Joined Dinner Tables Task

In the lesson on joined dinner tables, we examined the various ways in which students attempt to determine the relation between the number of tables and the number of people who can be served, with particular regard to what the elements in an equation refer to.

The instructor first reviewed the previous lesson and students recalled what they had done then. Five minutes into the lesson the instructor asked them to determine how many people could sit at two tables that are joined together. Students concluded that the answer was six people. The instructor counted along the outside edges of two tables drawn on the board and asked: "Now, how come that when we had two tables there were eight and, now we have two tables and we have six?" A student, pointing in the drawing at the two inside edges where the tables meet and where guests cannot sit explained: "Because of these two sides, right here." After agreeing that seats would be lost between adjacent tables, other students discussed how many people would sit at two and at three joined tables. A student attempted to generalize how seating capacity increased according to the number of tables by saying: "You keep adding two."

The instructor then built a data table on the board, with headers for the number of dinner tables (t) and the maximum number of people (p) that could sit at separate tables (the Tuesday column), and at joined tables (Thursday), as shown in Figure 6.7. Working together with the children, she filled in the results for two and three separate dinner tables, and then when they are joined. As each row of data was completed she contrasted the results for the two situations. Again, some students expressed, for the joined dinner tables, that "You are adding two each time."

Fifteen minutes into the lesson, to motivate students to seek a general rule for relating the number of tables to the number of seats, instead of simply extending the number of people by two each time a table was added, the instructor asked: "How many people could be seated at 100 tables?" One student answered 200 people, and another said 101, apparently just trying to guess. As the instructor reminds them of the previous lesson, several students mention that they had to multiply by four. After some discussion, with input from the students, she writes the equation $t \times 4 = p$ for the case of separate tables and asks them to state what each of its elements stands for. She rephrases students' suggestions and expresses that t stands for number of tables, 4 for number of people per table, and p for total number of people. Before going back to the question on the number of people that can sit at 100 joined tables, she asks the students to propose a formula for the case of joined tables.

Figure 6.7 Table relating the number of dinner tables to number of people that could sit if the tables were separated (Tuesday) or joined (Thursday).

One of the students, pointing to each row in the data table on the board shown in Figure 6.7, examines how the seating capacity of joined tables differs from the seating capacity of separate tables and mentions that, as the number of tables increases, joined tables hold ever-fewer guests than separate tables. The instructor agrees with the student but stresses that she is looking for a general statement that does not rely upon the number of people for separate dinner tables. She then asks, once more, how many people can sit at 100 tables. A student predicts that 202 people can be seated at 100 tables. She agrees with him and proposes that the students move to working in small groups on their handouts (Figure 6.8).

Most children chose to draw tables and count the number of external table edges to determine the number of people who could sit at the joined tables. This may appear unnecessary, given that they had already discussed the same case as the data table on the board was filled in. However, the drawings constituted a path to the multiple types of generalizations the children came to develop as they attempted to represent a general rule corresponding to the closed form expression of the function and as they attempted to answer the question: "If I tell you the number of dinner tables lined up, how can you figure out the maximum number of people that can sit down?"

While working in small groups, a student proposed a general rule and described it as: "t times two plus two equals p." In another group, a student generated drawings for each case and successively added two for the next total. When a researcher in the classroom asked him to find the number of people for 100 tables, he stated that 202 people could sit at the tables and generated a general rule for the function. He later explained to the whole class, drawing a long rectangle on the board: "'cuz if you have one table, on that side is 100, 100 over there [along the other long side] and then two over here [at the heads of the table]. . . 200 plus 2 equals 202." When asked to propose a formula for "whatever number of tables," she proposed "t times two plus two" and wrote on the board $t \times 2 + 2$. Another student suggests surrounding $t \times 2$ by parentheses. The instructor writes the equation $(t \times 2) + 2 = p$ on the board and asks the students to state what each element in the equation represented.

The equation $(t \times 2) + 2 = p$ constitutes a closed form representation of the relation between the number of joined dinner tables and the maximum number of people that could be seated. In the class handouts, eight of the 15 children attending the lesson answered the question "If I tell you the number of dinner tables lined up, how can you figure out the maximum number of people that can sit down?" The other seven relied on drawings and counting or didn't answer the question. A review of the videos of the lesson and of their written work showed that, in their development towards the closed form representation favored by the instructor,

In your restaurant, square <u>dinner tables</u> have are always arranged together in a single line. Below, figure out the <u>maximum number of people</u> you can seat.

Dinner tables		Number of people
1 		4
2 		
3		
4		
5		
6		
7		

Figure 6.8 Handout for the Dinner Tables Problem.

the students produced several equivalent expressions that fall into one of two broad categories: a recursive formula versus a closed form expression. They were alternative correct representations for the relation (see details in the original paper by Carraher, Martinez, & Schliemann, 2008). The classroom discussions and the students' written work stress the conceptual shift that some students need to go through to abandon their own models and construct something that is closer to the mathematical relationships and representations we want them to learn. It shows how students can come to gradually appropriate the general representational tools of mathematics.

EQUATIONS AND INEQUALITIES AS THE COMPARISON OF FUNCTIONS

Equations and inequalities can be interpreted as a comparison of functions (Powerful Idea #4). Let us exemplify and explain.

Some authors (e.g. Filloy and Rojano, 1989) have noted that many students who are just beginning to study algebra will find an equation such as $w + 8 = 3 \times w$ to be challenging because the variable, w, appears on both sides of the equal sign. The difficulty presumably lies in operating on (or with) the so-called unknown.

Subtracting w from each side of the equation yields the equation $8 = 2w$. This equation may be solved by dividing each side by 2 and obtaining a solved equation in the canonical form, x = 4. But by interpreting the equation, $w + 8 = 3 \times w$, as a comparison of the function $w + 8$ with the function $3 \times w$, novel ways for approaching the solution to equations emerge.

We noted that functions may be expressed through a variety of forms, including graphs and verbal formulations. For example, the graph of the function $w + 8$ can be plotted as a line, with slope of 1 that intersects the point (0,8). Likewise, the function $3 \times w$ can be plotted as a line of slope 3 that passes through the origin.

We have designed lessons for students as young as 9 years that exploit the interpretation of an equation as the comparison of functions. One implementation employed the functions $w + 8$ and $3 \times w$ we have been discussing; the lesson and results are described in detail elsewhere (Carraher, Schliemann, & Schwartz, 2008). Here we will summarize the points of interest to the present chapter.

We posed the following problem to students in the latter part of fourth grade (about 10 years old):

> Mike has $8 in his hand and the rest of his money is in his wallet;
>> Robin has exactly three times as much money as Mike has in his wallet.
> What can you say about the amounts of money Mike and Robin have?

The first statement was intended to embody the function, $w + 8$. The second statement was to embody the function $3 \times w$.

It took approximately 10 minutes of class discussion, led by the instructor, to reach an agreement about the asserted relation that Robin had three times as much money as Mike had in his wallet. Until then, many interpreted the statement as meaning that Robin's amount was three times Mike's total amount. Then the students were asked to individually represent the situation in writing. Over 60% of the students used algebraic notation to capture the functional relationships among the variables (Figure 6.9).

However, as the discussion progressed, most students believed that one of the boys had more money than the other. They were then encouraged to examine the amounts in the wallet as well as Mike's total and Robin's total under scenarios that varied according to the amount

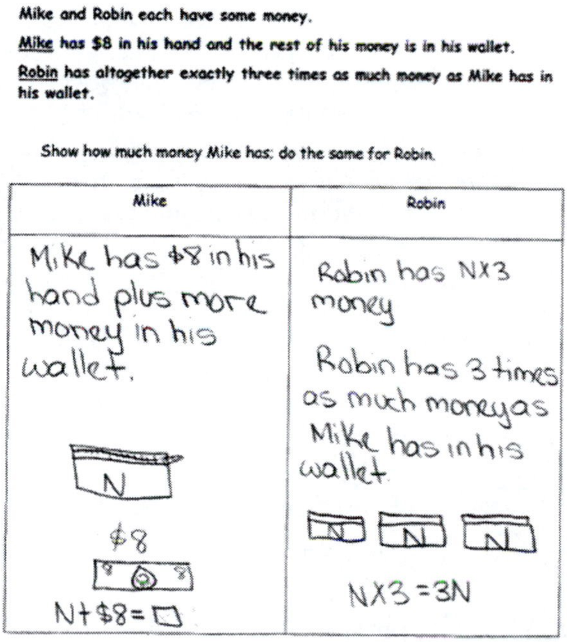

Figure 6.9 An 11-year-old student's representation of the wallet problem.

of money in the wallet. The instructor showed how to fill in the three-column table (w, $w +$ 8, and $3w$) for the cases where the wallet had $0, $1, and $2. They then produced data tables and graphs relating possible amounts in the wallet to the amounts Mike and Robin each would have. By examining the data table and the graphs they found that when there was $4 in the wallet they would have the same amount of money; for amounts smaller than $4 Mike would have more money; and for those larger than $4 Robin would have more.

Over the course of two lessons, the students came to realize, and to express comfortably in their own words, which if either of the boys had more money. The students realized that the answer to this question depended on how much money was in the wallet: when there was less than $4 in the wallet, Mike had more money, when there was exactly $4 in the wallet, the boys had the same amounts, and when there was more than $4 in the wallet, Robin had more.

They spoke of the wallet as "filling up" as they scanned over increasing values in the wallet. They noted that Mike's total was increasing more slowly (by $1 for each additional dollar the wallet held) than Robin's total, which increased by $3 for each additional dollar in the wallet.

It was clear from the discussions and the student work that the students were treating the amount of money in the wallet, as well as the students' amounts, as variables and the amounts of Mike and Robin as functions.

For them, w (the amount of money in the wallet) was not an "unknown" but instead a variable. The functions were equal only for the case when there was $4 in the wallet. For all other conditions, one of the boys had more money than the other.

We interpret such results as showing that fairly young students can work with and understand variables as placeholders for sets (rather than simply a single missing value) and algebraic expressions as denoting functions that can be compared.

We have also found that fourth grade students can learn to act directly on the algebraic representations of equations. This required additional instruction regarding subtleties of notation usage that we will not describe here. We believe that facility with syntactic rules can and should build upon the intuitions that students build and extend when algebra is employed to model quantitative situations. At some point, we would hope and expect that students will eventually be able to treat algebraic expressions as providing sufficient information for deriving new expressions. We happen to believe, however, that this is better viewed as a long-term goal rather than a starting point for learning about functions. And, even so, there will always be occasions for using algebra to model extra-mathematical situations.

In our classroom intervention studies, fourth and fifth graders proceeded to learn about the Cartesian space, and to solve equations by comparing two functions by drawing the graph of each function and by using the syntactic rules of algebra, topics that typically only appear in middle and high school. It suffices to say that, as they were attempting to solve problems related to the situations we brought to the classroom, they were applying number facts and dealing with arithmetic operations. Most importantly, they were beginning to master relations among sets of quantities and numbers.

Written assessments at the end of each year of the intervention showed that the treatment students outperformed their peers in all grades. At the end of the project (fifth grade), the treatment students fared better than controls on algebra problems. The power of our approach was also measured two and three years later. Then, participating students were more successful than their peers in learning to solve more advanced algebra problems and better profited from algebra instruction in seventh and eighth grade (see detailed report by Schliemann et al., 2012).

DISCUSSION AND CONCLUSIONS

Many curriculum developers and mathematics educators have failed to note that addition, subtraction, multiplication, and division operations are defined as functions and that this idea can provide important insights for elementary school mathematics. In introducing arithmetic operations as functions, it is crucial to consider situations and quantities that may lead to discussion of the covariation between two sets of values, the mathematical representations that may help highlighting the covariation of the two sets, and students' own ways of first approaching the proposed situations. Within a relational approach to arithmetic, topics in the curriculum are viewed as instances of more abstract ideas and concepts. This not only enriches children's understanding of arithmetic, but can also build the foundations for the meaningful learning of elementary algebra.

However, elementary school students do not need to be acquainted with terminology surrounding functions (function, domain and codomain, ordered pairs, Cartesian product). Nonetheless, a certain degree of formalization is desirable even at the elementary level. It is important and feasible that elementary school students learn to use and master other key representations, including number lines, graphs of functions, and algebraic notation. This, of course, requires careful planning and design of situations that, over the long run, strike a balance between theorems-in-action and theorems (Vergnaud, 1996), between intuition and logic (Poincaré, 1969), and between using and reflecting upon mathematical tools and ideas.

In traditional elementary school curricula, young students are introduced to mathematical relations indirectly through number facts or simple problems such as $6 + 4 = \square$. However, two of the variables have been bound, a consequence of which is that the equation will be true if and only if the third variable equals 10. And the fact that the third variable is already isolated on one side of the equation eliminates the need to state the relation in another, equivalent form, using the operation of subtraction. Addition and subtraction entail different calculation procedures. But the very same relations can be represented through addition and subtraction when the relations are described through equations or inequalities. Equivalent forms are understood as conveying the same information. Likewise, by introducing the equals sign together with other relational operators ($>, <, \geq, \leq$), a major opportunity is gained for emphasizing variables, not simply "unknowns."

One need not wonder that young students are inclined to believe that "=" stands for "makes" or "yields" (Kieran, 1981); that is precisely how it is introduced and explained to them. But the equals sign means much more than this. The relational operators, $\langle, \leq, =, \geq, \rangle$ are comparison operators. The algebraic expression of a relation, regardless of which operator is used, can always be regarded as a comparison of an amount (magnitude or multitude) on one side of the operator with the amount on the other. This same approach can be extended to equations with one or more unbound variables.

In the Candy Boxes problem, we saw that young students could quickly grasp the idea of the function $x + 3$, or the relation between x and $x + 3$, without assigning a value to x and while fully realizing that x could stand for any number of candies that could conceivably fit in the box. In the problem of comparing two students' amounts of money over several days, students were able to operate on variable amounts, only later solving the problem for particular value of x after they were told that, on Thursday, the amounts, the students had become equal.

However, even when students are willing to treat quantities as variable, there may be additional issues to explore. Imagine a fourth grade student who is facing the relation $x < 6$. She might place her finger at 6 on a number line and claim that numbers to the left of that position satisfy the relation, $x < 6$, and that numbers to the right of 6 make the relation false ("they are greater than 6"). So far, so good. But more is required for us to conclude that the relation the student is referring to is the relation we may have in mind. Does she believe that the relation holds for all values in the domain, for example, real numbers? What about –7, –8, and so on? Does the student believe negative integers are less than 6? What about fractions? Does the student believe 2/3 and –3/17 to be among the numbers to the left of 6? Does she realize that there are infinitely many fractions to the right of 6 and also infinitely many between 5.5 and 6? We cannot conclude that a student has the same understanding of a particular relation that we do merely because we are in agreement for a few selected cases.

We do not wish to imply that teachers should attempt to introduce real numbers explicitly early on. It will take years just to gain an initial grasp of rational numbers through fractions and decimals; real numbers will take even longer to master. Nor do we wish to argue that algebraic notation be the sole means for examining relations, especially with young students. Relations can also be expressed in natural language, for instance, in statements in word problems. They can be described with tables of data. Relations can also be represented through diagrams, displacements on a number line, or graphs in the coordinate plane. Students learn about and express their understanding of relations, including functions, while using multiple representations in concert.

Functions can initially be taught to and understood by children as a dependency of one amount on another—and they need to be first introduced to view, rather than the more abstract, modern view of functions as ordered pairs.

Elementary teachers and textbooks tacitly work with functions well before they introduce the term *function*. Exposing the functional character of arithmetic explicitly helps elementary school children shift their focus from individual numbers to sets of numbers and quantities (i.e., variables) and their interrelations. This shift naturally leads students to consider relationships between variables. Isolated examples can always be treated as instances of more general cases. "Plus three" can be viewed as an operation on an indeterminate number, a variable. Eventually students can begin to appreciate numeric operations as movements on (transformations of) the number line (i.e. the real line).

CLOSING THOUGHTS

We focused here on four powerful ideas. There are several other powerful ideas that played roles in the present analysis and may be of interest to mathematics educators at the elementary school level:

- Every arithmetic expression is a particular instance of one or more algebraic expressions.
- Every mathematical idea of importance is embodied in multiple representations; some hinge on connections among multiple representations.
- Variables are symbols representing sets of numbers or quantities. Although the elements of the sets may refer to properties of real-world objects, events, or phenomena, students need to understand when the elements of a domain are established solely through the affordances and constraints of statements in the form of language or mathematical statements.
- Expanding number from the naturals to include positive rationals, integers, rationals, and reals requires assimilating many new ideas about what numbers are for and how they can be expressed. The operations of arithmetic over these classes of numbers also have different sets of properties.
- Amounts, whether numbers or values of quantities, can be composed and decomposed in many ways.
- Numbers and quantities can be represented in space both as locations and movements (first on the number line) and, from middle school onwards, in the plane and beyond.

The sort of deep mathematical understanding we would like students to develop will not be achieved through an occasional inclusion of the term *function* in the early mathematics curriculum any more than will embracing slogans such as "Pay attention to students' reasoning," "Algebra for all," or "Promote discussions and interaction among students." The devil is in the details. Specific topics and examples raise a host of issues for curriculum developers, teachers, and, ultimately, students to contend with. For example, in discussing the order of decimal numbers, issues regarding place value notation and the location of points on the real line must be considered. Teachers need to realize that students need to reconcile how the ordering of decimal numbers builds on, yet differs from, the ordering of integers. It will be even more challenging to establish conventions for displaying operations on the line and in the plane. Ultimately, success in learning potentially powerful ideas will heavily depend on the staging and sequencing of learning activities as well as the continued engagement of students, each of which can benefit from the growing expertise of their teachers.

We focused, in this chapter, on a handful of potentially powerful ideas. Since they can be succinctly stated, it may be tempting to believe that they lend themselves to straightforward implementations in the classroom. This is only partly true. The sort of tasks discussed here, such as the candy boxes problem, the heights problem and the wallet problem, seem to be ordinary arithmetic word problems. But, in the hands of a skilled teacher, students soon find that the problems raise issues that they and their peers may not immediately agree upon and settle. This occurs especially when a problem leaves one or more quantities free to vary. Students commonly propose answers or best guesses using their intuitions and prior knowledge about related situations. They work, so to speak, with a 'logic of meanings' (Piaget and Garcia, 1991; Schliemann, 1998) tied closely to the situation at hand. Pedagogically, this may be a useful starting point but it is unsatisfactory as an end point. A supportive mathematics teacher will want to encourage formalizations of the problem,[4] formalizations that will rely on conventional representational tools of mathematics including tables, number line diagrams, graphs in the plane, and a variety of notations. As syntactical and relational structures become more prominent, students' understanding relies less and less on references to particular, extra-mathematical features.

NOTES

1. We thank the National Science Foundation for funding the classroom studies described in this chapter through Grants #9722732, #9909591, and #0310171. We are also grateful to our many collaborators over the years. Among those, we specially thank Bárbara M. Brizuela, a permanent contributor to all studies, and Montserrat Teixidor-i-Bigas for our many discussions on mathematics content as we jointly work in the Poincaré Institute for Mathematics Education (NSF Grant #0962863). The views presented here represent the work of the authors and not necessarily the funding agency.
2. Functions played a prominent role in "New Mathematics." but they were introduced in very different ways from those to be discussed here.
3. We are defining a relation for our present purposes. How relations are conceptualized by teachers and students is an important but very different issue.
4. Here a "formalization" refers loosely to any representation that serves to highlight the underlying structure of a problem, thereby portraying the problem as one instance of a class of problems having a similar structure.

REFERENCES

Aleksandrov, A. D. (1999). A general view of mathematics. In Aleksandrov, A. D., & Kolmogorov, A. N. (Eds.). (1999). *Mathematics: its content, methods and meaning.* N. Chelmsford, MA: Courier Dover Publications.

Blanton, M. (2008). *Algebra and the elementary classroom: Transforming thinking, transforming practice.* New York: Pearson Education.

Blanton, M., & Kaput, J. (2000). Generalizing and progressively formalizing in a third grade mathematics classroom: Conversations about even and odd numbers. In M. Fernández (Ed.), *Proceedings of the 20th Annual Meeting of the for the Psychology of Mathematics Education, North American Chapter* (p. 115). Columbus, OH, ERIC Clearinghouse (ED446945).

Booth, L.R. (1988). Children's difficulties in beginning algebra. In A.F. Coxford & A.P. Shulte (Eds.), *The ideas of algebra, K-12: 1988 Yearbook* (pp. 20–32). Reston, VA: National Council of Teachers of Mathematics.

Brizuela, B.M., Blanton, M., Gardiner, A., Newman-Owens, A., & Sawrey, K. (in press). A first grade student's exploration of variable and variable notation. *Estudios de Psicología.* Abingdon, UK: Taylor & Francis.

Brizuela, B.M., & Earnest, D. (2008). Multiple notational systems and algebraic understandings: The case of the "best deal" problem. In J. Kaput, D. Carraher, & M. Blanton (Eds.), *Algebra in the Early Grades* (pp. 273–301). Mahwah, NJ: Lawrence Erlbaum Associates.

Brizuela, B.M., & Schliemann, A. D. (2004). Fourth graders solving linear equations. *For the Learning of Mathematics, 24*(2), 33–40.

Cai, J. & Knuth, E. (Eds.). (2011). Early algebraization: A global dialogue from multiple perspectives. New York, NY: Springer.

Carpenter, T. P., & Franke, M. (2001). Developing algebraic reasoning in the elementary school: Generalization and proof. In H. Chick, K. Stacey, J. Vincent, & J. Vincent (Eds.), *The future of the teaching and learning of algebra. Proceedings of the 12th ICMI Study Conference* (Vol. 1, pp. 155–162). Melbourne, Australia: The University of Melbourne.

Carpenter, T.P., Franke, M.L., & Levi, L. (2003). *Thinking mathematically: Integrating arithmetic and algebra in elementary school.* Portsmouth, NH: Heinemann.

Carpenter, T.P., Moser, J.M., & Romberg, T.A. (1982) (Eds.), *Addition and subtraction: A cognitive view.* Hillsdale, NJ: Lawrence Erlbaum Associates.

Carraher, D. W., Brizuela, B. M., & Earnest, D. (2001). The reification of additive differences in early algebra. In H. Chick, K. Stacey, J. Vincent, & J. Vincent (Eds.), *Proceedings of the Twelfth ICMI Study Conference: The future of the teaching and learning of algebra* (Vol. 1, pp. 163–170). Melbourne, Australia: University of Melbourne Press.

Carraher, D.W., Martinez, M., & Schliemann, A. D. (2008). Early algebra and mathematical generalization. *ZDM – The International Journal on Mathematics Education, 40*(1), 3-22.

Carraher, D. W. & Schliemann, A. D. (2007) Early algebra and algebraic reasoning. In F. Lester (ed.) *Second handbook of research on mathematics teaching and learning: A project of the National Council of Teachers of Mathematics* (Vol 2, pp. 669–705). Charlotte, NC: Information Age Publishing.

Carraher, D.W., Schliemann, A. D., & Brizuela, B. (2000, October*). Early algebra, early arithmetic: Treating operations as functions.* Plenary address at the 22nd Meeting of the Psychology of Mathematics Education, North American Chapter, Tucson, AZ (available in CD-ROM).

Carraher, D.W., Schliemann, A. D., & Brizuela, B. (2005). Treating operations as functions. In D. Carraher & R. Nemirovsky (Eds.), *Monographs of the Journal for Research in Mathematics Education, 8,* CD-ROM only.

Carraher, D.W., Schliemann, A. D., Brizuela, B.M., & Earnest, D. (2006). Arithmetic and algebra in early mathematics education. *Journal for Research in Mathematics Education, 37*(2), 87–115.

Carraher, D. W., Schliemann, A. D., Brizuela, B., & Earnest, D. (2014). Arithmetic and Algebra in early Mathematics Education. In E.A. Silver & P.A. Kenney (Editors). *Lessons Learned from Research: Volume 2. Useful Research on Teaching Important Mathematics to All Students.* Reston, VA: National Council of Teachers of Mathematics.

Carraher, D.W., Schliemann, A. D., & Schwartz, J.L. (2008). Early algebra is not the same as algebra early. In J. Kaput, D. Carraher & M. Blanton (Eds.), *Algebra in the early grades.* Mahwah, NJ: Lawrence Erlbaum Associates.

Carraher, T.N., Carraher, D.W., & Schliemann, A. D. (1985). Mathematics in the streets and in schools. *British Journal of Developmental Psychology, 3*(1), 21–29.

Davydov, V.V. (1991). *Psychological abilities of primary school children in learning mathematics* (Vol. 6). Reston, VA: National Council of Teachers of Mathematics.

Dougherty, B. (2008). Measure up: A quantitative view of early algebra. In J. Kaput, D. Carraher, & M. Blanton (Eds.), *Algebra in the early grades.* Mahwah, NJ: Lawrence Erlbaum Associates.

Dubinsky, E., & Harel, G. (Eds.) (1992). *The concept of function: Aspects of epistemology and pedagogy.* Washington, DC: Mathematical Association of America.

Filoy, E., & Rojano, T. (1989). Solving equations: The transition from arithmetic to algebra. *For the Learning of Mathematics, 2,* 19–25.

Fridman, L.M. (1991). Features of introducing the concept of concrete numbers in the primary grades. In V.V. Davydov (Ed.), *Psychological abilities of primary school children in learning mathematics. Vol 6: Soviet studies in mathematics education* (pp. 148–180). Reston, VA: National Council of Teachers of Mathematics.

Harel, G. & Confrey, J. (1994) (Eds.), *The development of multiplicative reasoning in the learning of mathematics.* Albany: State University of New York Press.

JCGM (2012) International vocabulary of metrology: Basic and general concepts and associated terms (VIM, 3rd ed.). Sèvres, France: Bureau Internacional de Poids et Measures (BIPM), Joint Committee for Guides in Metrology, JCGM 200:2012 (JCGM 200:2008 with minor corrections). Retrieved from www.bipm.org/en/publications/guides/, May 5, 2015.

Kieran, C. (1981). Concepts associated with the equality symbol. *Educational Studies in Mathematics, 12,* 317–326.

Kaput, J. (1998). Transforming algebra from an engine of inequity to an engine of mathematical power by "algebrafying" the K–12 curriculum. In National Council of Teachers of Mathematics and Mathematical Sciences Education Board Center for Science, Mathematics and Engineering Education, National Research Council (Sponsors). *The Nature and Role of Algebra in the K-14 Curriculum* (pp. 25–26). Washington, DC: National Academies Press.

Kirshner, D., & Awtry, T. (2004). Visual salience of algebraic transformations. *Journal for Research in Mathematics Education, 35*(4), 224–257.

Lacampagne, C.B. (1995). *The Algebra Initiative Colloquium.* Washington, DC: U.S. Department of Education, OERI.

Langrall, C., Mooney, E. S., Nishet, S. & Jones, G. S. (2008). Elementary school students' access to powerful mathematical ideas. In L. D. English & D. Kirshner (Eds.) *Handbook of international research in mathematics education* (2nd ed., pp. 109–135). New York, Routledge.

Lesh, R. A & Landau, M. (Eds.) (1983). *Acquisition of mathematics concepts and processes.* New York: Academic Press.

Mikulina, G. G. (1991). The psychological features of solving problems with letter data. In V. Davydov (Ed.), *Soviet studies in mathematics education* (vol. 6, pp. 181–232). Reston, VA: National Council of Teachers of Mathematics.

Moss, J. & Beatty, R. (2006). Knowledge building in mathematics: Supporting collaborative learning in pattern problems. *Computer-Supported Collaborative Learning, 1,* pp. 441–465.

Oehrtman, M.C., Carlson, M.P., & Thompson, P.W. (2008). Foundational reasoning abilities that promote coherence in students' understandings of function. In M.P. Carlson & C. Rasmussen (Eds.), *Making the connection: Research and practice in undergraduate mathematics* (pp. 27–42). Washington, DC: Mathematical Association of America.

Peled, I., & Carraher, D.W. (2008). Signed numbers and algebraic thinking. In J. Kaput, D.W. Carraher, & M. Blanton (Eds.), *Algebra in the early grades.* Mahwah, NJ: Lawrence Erlbaum Associates.

Piaget, J., & Garcia, R. (1991). Vers une logique des significations. Geneva: Murionde Editeur.

Poincaré, H. (1969). Intuition and logic in mathematics. *The Mathematics Teacher, 62*(2), pp. 205–212.

Romberg, T., Fennema, E., & Carpenter, T. (1993) (Eds.) *Integrating research on the graphical representation of functions* (pp. 41–68). Hillsdale, NJ: Lawrence Erlbaum Associates.

Rosen, K. (2012). Axioms for the real numbers and positive integers. In *Discrete Mathematics and its applications* (pp. A1–A6). New York: McGraw-Hill.

Schliemann, A. D. (1998). Logic of meanings and situated cognition. *Learning and Instruction, 8*(6), pp. 549–560.

Schliemann, A. D., Carraher, D. W. & Brizuela, B. M. (2001). When tables become function tables. In M. v. d. Heuvel-Panhuizen (Ed.), *Proceedings of the 25th Conference of the International Group for the Psychology of Mathematics Education* (Vol. 4, pp. 145–152). Utrecht, The Netherlands: Freudenthal Institute.

Schliemann, A. D., Carraher, D.W., & Brizuela, B.M. (2007). *Bringing out the algebraic character of arithmetic: From children's ideas to classroom practice.* Hillsdale, NJ: Lawrence Erlbaum Associates.

Schliemann A. D., Carraher D. W., & Brizuela B. M. (2012). Algebra in elementary school. In L. Coulange & J.-P. Drouhard (Eds.) *Enseignement de l'algèbre élémentaire: Bilan et perspectives* (pp. 109–124). Special Issue of *Recherches en Didactique des Mathématiques.*

Schliemann, A. D., Carraher, D. W., & Caddle, M. (2013). From seeing points to seeing intervals in number lines and graphs. In B. Brizuela & B. Gravel (Eds.) *Show me what you know: Exploring representations across STEM disciplines.* New York: Teachers College Press.

Schliemann, A. D., Carraher, D. W., Goodrow, A., Caddle, M., & Porter, M. (2013). Equations in elementary school. In A.M. Lindmeier & A. Heinze (Eds.). *Proceedings of the 37th Conference of the International Group for the Psychology of Mathematics Education* (Vol. 4, pp. 161–168). Kiel, Germany: PME.

Schmittau, J. & Morris, A. (2004) The development of algebra in the elementary mathematics curriculum of V. V. Davydov. *The Mathematics Educator, 8*(1), 60–87

Schoenfeld, A. (1995). Report of Working Group 1. In C.B. Lacampagne (Ed.), *The Algebra Initiative Colloquium: Vol. 2. Working Group Papers* (pp. 11–18). Washington, DC: U.S. Department of Education, OERI.

Schwartz, J.L. (1996). *Semantic aspects of quantity.* Unpublished manuscript, MIT and Harvard Graduate School of Education, Cambridge, MA.

Schwartz, J. & Yerushalmy, M. (1992). Getting students to function on and with algebra. In E. Dubinsky & G. Harel (Eds.), *The concept of function: Aspects of epistemology and pedagogy* (pp. 261–289). Washington, DC: Mathematical Association of America.

Sfard, A. (1991). On the dual nature of mathematical conceptions: Reflections on processes and objects as different sides of the same coin. *Educational Studies in Mathematics 22,* 1–36.

Vergnaud, G. (1982). A classification of cognitive tasks and operations of thought involved in addition and subtraction problems. In T.P. Carpenter, J.M., Moser, & T.A. Romberg (Eds.), *Addition and subtraction: A cognitive view* (pp. 39–59). Hillsdale, NJ: Lawrence Erlbaum Associates.

Vergnaud, G. (1983). Multiplicative structures. In R.A. Lesh & M. Landau (Eds.), *Acquisition of mathematics concepts and processes* (pp. 127–174). New York: Academic Press.

Vergnaud, G. (1994). Multiplicative conceptual field: What and why? In G. Harel & J. Confrey (Eds.), *The development of multiplicative reasoning in the learning of mathematics* (pp. 41–59). Albany: State University of New York Press.

Vergnaud, G. (1996). The theory of conceptual fields. In L. Steffe & P. Nesher (Eds.), *Theories of mathematical learning* (pp. 219–239). Mahwah, NJ: Lawrence Erlbaum Associates.

Whitney, H. (1968a). The mathematics of physical quantities: Part I: mathematical models for measurement. *American Mathematical Monthly, 75*(2), 115–138.

Whitney, H. (1968b). The mathematics of physical quantities, Part 2: Quantity structures and dimensional analysis. *American Mathematical Monthly, 75*(3), 227–256.

7 Students' Access to Mathematics Learning in the Middle and Junior Secondary Schools

Teresa Rojano

Center for Research and Advanced Studies of the National Polytechnic Institute (Cinvestav)

INTRODUCTION

This chapter focuses on analyzing the role of sense development and meaning assignment as processes that give access to middle and junior secondary school students (MJSS) to lifelong mathematics learning. Much has been written about the concept that achieving lifelong mathematics learning for all depends to a good extent on individuals having contact with sources of meaning that are aligned with their daily lives, age group, school level, and prior mathematics experience.

From the works of the 90s by Arcavi (1994) on symbol sense, up to the recent studies by Hoch and Dreyfus (2006) on structure sense in high school algebra, all provide theoretical and empirical inputs that make it possible to raise the research questions concerning the learning of mathematical contents, in such a way that the essence of lifelong learning underlies the very notion of sense production. Added to the foregoing studies is research in mathematics education that adopts a semiotic approach, such as the works of Filloy, Rojano, and Puig (2008), Otte (2005), Puig (2003), Presmeg (2005), and Radford (2000), for instance.

Some of those new ways of raising the theme of lifelong mathematics learning are sketched here, attempting to illustrate the new focus via concrete examples. Also dealt with is the thesis that assignment of meaning is the result of developing sense through actions of reading/ transforming *texts*[1] that are presented to students during the process of teaching them mathematics. It is also argued that delving deeper into those processes of meaning production (semiosis) and of their relationship with the mathematics and linguistic experience of MJSS students will make it possible to conceive teaching models that are appropriate for this student population. In order to accomplish that deepening, a proposal is made in the subsection entitled "Sense Production in Mathematics Learning: The Case of Algebraic Read-Writing." The proposal is grounded in the theoretical elements (inspired by notions of semiotics) developed by Filloy and coauthors, and extensively presented in recent publications (for example in Filloy et al., 2008; Filloy, Rojano, & Solares, 2010; Rojano, Filloy, & Puig, 2014). It is noteworthy to mention that when these authors speak of sense and meaning production processes, they are not referring to those processes solely associated with mathematical signs or expressions. They associate them with *texts* composed of signs of a heterogeneous nature, which in addition to the signs of mathematics proper, can also include signs from natural language, figures, diagrams, representations of situations from daily life or the physical world, scenes on a computer screen, etc. The previously mentioned subsection also includes introduction of a broad notion of mathematical sign system that allows for inclusion of the *texts* described here.

As well, this version of the chapter revisits the theme of the influence of digital technologies in the teaching and learning of mathematics. In more particular terms, the chapter analyzes aspects and modes of technology use that offer MJSS students the possibility of having democratic access to mathematics knowledge. The term *democratic access* is understood in a broad sense, so that, inter alia, it can include early introduction (in MJSS) to advanced mathematics topics, as well as a practical approach to the complex notions of the mathematics of variation and modeling. For example, research topics derived from the following are addressed: 1) the possibility of incorporating, by way of using Dynamic Geometry programs, three-dimensional geometry topics into the middle school curriculum; 2) the possibility of using computer algebra systems (CAS) either to reduce the emphasis on the manipulative aspects of algebra and focus student work on conceptual tasks (Kieran, 2007) or to promote both the conceptual and technical aspects of mathematics (Lagrange, 2003); and 4) the possibility of using recent versions of spreadsheets that offer a friendly environment to different groups of students for mathematical modeling activities.

Some of the most renowned didactical potentials of digital technologies include deploying multiple representations of mathematics concepts and objects, and of the dynamic interconnections between them. The latter gives learning technology environments a sources-of-meaning nature that differs from that of the sources of meaning that pertain to static representations. In turn, the foregoing gives cause for raising the hypothesis that in such environments, meaning production processes also have a different nature, amongst other reasons, due to the type of interaction between the user and the dynamic representations of the objects of knowledge. Using the terms introduced at the beginning of this section, one can hence hypothesize that the read/transformation processes of the *texts* in a teaching model that incorporates digital technologies are different because of their dynamic and interactive nature. That possible relationship between the nature of representations (or *texts*) and processes of semiosis is not discussed in this chapter. The hypothesis will be left as material for future research instead.

On another line of thought, albeit along the same line as digital technologies, the evolution of these tools is also discussed, as will their role in the projection of future research. In the recent versions for mobile devices (digital tablets, for example) of technology learning environments or *microworlds* developed and used in the 90s, users can practically touch and physically manipulate multiple representations of mathematical objects. This probably will have an impact on the epistemological and cognitive levels of mathematics learning. Whereas with incorporation of intelligent systems into the microworlds, means of feedback that are already known can be optimized and new ones imagined. Later on in this chapter, there is also a discussion concerning how the foregoing innovations and the connectivity via the Internet might change the way in which digital technologies can be integrated into the mathematics curriculum. This is anticipated to occur both in terms of the educational material and contents accessible on the cloud, and because students and teachers can work collaboratively within virtual communities. These new scenarios can in turn become the subject of research for mathematics education, specifically in MJSS.

In short, the two themes discussed in this chapter are research into lifelong mathematics learning, based on development of sense and assignment of meaning; and democratic access to mathematics knowledge in MJSS, by way of using the more recent versions and modes of digital technologies. It has already been made clear that the link between the foregoing two lines of research will not be analyzed here. It is rather being proposed that it be dealt with in future works.

The two following sections deal with the themes of life-long mathematics learning and democratic access to mathematics knowledge in MJSS. The first one begins with a review of what some official education documents consider lifelong learning n mathematics and in the second describes a variety of conceptions about sense in mathematics in the research literature. At the end of this portion of the chapter, it is intended to connect mathematics sense development processes with lifelong learning.

ACCESS TO LIFELONG MATHEMATICS LEARNING IN THE MJSS

The goal of enabling students to use mathematics knowledge learned at school in varying contexts and beyond their school lives has become universal. That is to say that it is present in different forms in the curricular mathematics documents of many countries and in the documents of world organizations. Some of such documents include the specific goal of taking students toward a mathematics learning that will not only allow them to move fluently through their different school levels, but rather also that will make it possible for them to approach problems in their post-school lives in a scientific and flexible manner. For instance, in *Principles and Standards for School Mathematics* (NCTM, 2000), that goal is formulated in terms of a conception of learning mathematics with understanding, as opposed to a mechanical and memory-based learning process (NCTM, 2000, pp. 20–21). In that document, while referring to the research of Bransford, Brown, and Cocking (2000) it is pointed out that conceptual comprehension is one of the important components of proficiency, which, together with factual knowledge and procedural facility, enable students to flexibly use their knowledge, appropriately applying what they have learned in one setting in another. That same document also refers to the work of Schoenfeld (1988), who asserts that when students connect, in a meaningful way, the new knowledge with already existing knowledge, they then are able to make sense of mathematics and their applications. In the National Curriculum of Mathematics of the UK (Stage 3), the following objective is stressed: "The study of mathematics should enable pupils to apply their knowledge, skills and understanding to relevant real-world situations" Qualifications and Curriculum Authority (2007). The official documents of the Ministry of Education in Mexico point out that one of the main objectives of the 2006 Reform of the Secondary School curriculum is that "students not only study and learn more but that they learn meaningfully and use what they learn not only to solve particular problems, but are able to pose new questions and study by themselves continuously" (SEP, 2006, p. 9).

With respect to this generalized interest of having students make flexible and sensible use of learned mathematics (during and after school), within the sphere of the research, the currents of *realistic mathematics* (Gravemeijer, 1994, 2004; Streefland, 1991; Van Den Heuvel-Panhuizen, 2003) and *mathematics in context* (Sierpinska, 1995) have contributed essential elements. The underpinning thesis in both currents is the idea that if the teaching of mathematics uses problem situations (realistic or contextual in general) as the starting point, the students will have the extra-mathematical referents and meanings associated with the knowledge built. This will then make it possible for them to apply that knowledge in situations and to problems of varying contexts, and that entire cycle will help the students to make sense of school mathematics.

It should however be noted that in addition to the relevance of the connection with situations of daily life or with context problems, research has indicated that the sense of mathematics is also found in mathematics itself. And there, from a broad point of view, this chapter emphasizes the need to undertake research into the processes by which sense is produced and by which meanings are assigned on the basis of contexts, be they of a mathematical or extra-mathematical nature. The chapter also emphasizes the importance of focusing that research on production of meaning by MJSS students, but not just around symbols and concepts, rather also on mathematics methods. In order to provide a broad spectrum of related research, the next section refers to a series of authors who have broached the topic of the sense of mathematics from different perspectives and with respect to different aspects of school mathematics. Even though one of the examples discussed pertains to the university level, the case is indeed relevant to any school level in view of the fact that it clearly illustrates the determining role that appropriate use of notation can play in the resolution of mathematics problems.

SENSE AND ASSIGNING MEANING IN MATHEMATICS

During several decades of intensive research on the difficulties faced by students in learning mathematics, emphasis was placed on the study of conceptualization processes in particular mathematical contents (for instance, concepts of fraction, variable, proportionality), as well as on the analysis of frequent and persistent errors that were reported at the beginning of the 80s. In this respect, the analysis carried out by Kieran (1981) on the interpretations of the sign "="

and the English Concepts in Secondary School Mathematics and Science (CSMS)[2] project that deals with literal equations and expressions in algebra stand out. As of that analysis of errors, there arose the research line of reading-interpretation of mathematics symbols by learners. This line of research has continued to be cultivated from varying perspectives, some of which area of interest has extended into the study of the processes by which meaning and sense are assigned to mathematical symbolism.

Examples are presented in this section that are taken from both the works of the line of interpretation of mathematics expressions and symbols (Arcavi, 1994; Hoch, 2007; Hoch & Dreyfus, 2006), and the works interested in more general signification processes (semiosis) in mathematics (Presmeg, 2005). Important and practical contributions are identified in both cases for the teaching and learning of mathematics in MJSS.

Later, in the same section, the findings of several studies are presented, also with a semiotic approach, albeit focused specifically on algebraic concepts and methods of MJSS (Filloy et al., 2008) and on generalization processes (Radford, 2000).

In the next subsections, arguments are presented concerning the reasons that signification processes that foster strategic thinking among students can evolve into lifelong mathematics learning.

Symbol and Structure Sense in the Learning of Mathematics

In a 1994 essay, Arcavi speaks of "symbol sense" as a series of skills that, inter alia, include "the intuitive feel for when to call on symbols in the process of solving a problem, and conversely, when to abandon a symbolic treatment for better tools" (Arcavi, 1994, p. 25). The foregoing author also refers to symbol sense as certain types of instantiations, such as "interrupting a mechanical symbolic procedure to inspect or to reconnect oneself to the underlying meanings" (Arcavi, 1994, p. 27). To illustrate the latter skill, Arcavi resorts to the example of a secondary school student who, in an equation simplification process to obtain the solution, arrives at the equation $3x + 5 = 4x$. Instead of mechanically carrying out the corresponding algebraic manipulation (subtracting the $3x$ term from both sides of the equation), she stopped and changed to a different approach (*symbol reading*), and saw that in order to obtain the $4x$ term on the right, based on the $3x$ term on the left, it was enough to just add an x on the left side and as a result, 5 should be the value of x. With respect to this case, Arcavi asserts that although the standard algebraic method and the student's method are mathematically indistinguishable, there is an important difference at the psychological level and that the example is a "small but healthy instance of symbol sense" (Arcavi, 1994, p. 27).

In more recent work, Hoch and Dreyfus (2006) and Hoch (2007) speak of "structure sense" for high school algebra, as the capability that students have to: 1) recognize a familiar structure in its simplest form; 2) deal with a compound term as a single entity and, through an appropriate substitution, recognize a familiar structure in a more complex form; and 3) choose appropriate manipulations to make best use of a structure. Based on the foregoing definition, the authors formulated a structure sense teaching approach for grade 11 students by using tasks such as the following sequence of exercises, 1–5, taken from Hoch & Dreyfus, 2010, p. 530). The purpose of these tasks was to have students familiarize themselves with equations that could be perceived with a quadratic or linear structure, if the variable is considered as a product (for instance, xy).

1. Find xy : $8xy + 15 = 0$
2. Find xy : $8x^2y^2 + 6xy - 9 = 0$
3. Find $3xy$: $17xy - 25 = 13 + xy$ 90
4. Find $2xy$: $34xy - 4x^2y^2 = 10xy - 13$
5. Find x : $17x^2 - 45 = 0$

Faced with this list of exercises during an interview with instruction the students were asked about the structure of the equations, so that afterward they could formulate other similarly structured equations and, in some cases, so that they could indicate efficient ways of resolving them. In Exercise 5, the students were asked if the equation would have to have a different structure if the instruction was to "find the value of x^2."

In both of the previous cases, the authors resort to a catalogue of skills to communicate the meaning of symbol sense and structure sense. Moreover, even if in their studies one can note an absence of theorization, those works are still very useful both to verify whether the students possess the skills described or not, and to propose and test teaching approaches that help them to develop those skills (such as the example of linear or quadratic structure of the equations in the exercise from Hoch & Dreyfus, 2010).

The researches undertaken by Arcavi (1994), and Hoch and Dreyfus (2006), together with the studies by Linchevski and Liveneh (1999), and Griffin (2004) on number sense are located in the sphere of strategic thinking in mathematics. Given that characteristic, these works open the door to extending the possibility of teaching strategic thinking to a variety of algebraic topics and problem solving of the MJSS curriculum. For instance, on the one hand it would be important to identify manifestations of number and symbol sense among students at that school level, when they are asked to apply the Cartesian method (method of "putting into an equation") in the resolution of word problems or the algebraic methods in resolution of both linear and quadratic equations and linear equation systems with two unknown quantities. Such findings would be very useful for delving deeper into the analysis of the interaction between the strategic thought of students with their use of methods established at school. On the other hand, formulating and testing teaching sequences relative to structure sense in the algebra of MJSS represents an interesting didactic challenge, as well as the possibility of changing the focus in the didactics of symbolic algebra at this school level.

Moreover, in the light of the fundamentally symbolic and structural nature of mathematics, development of strategic thinking related to symbol and structure sense are an essential component for mathematics learning at higher educational levels and throughout life.

Comprehension of Mathematics as Semiosis Processes

On a par with the works of Arcavi (1994) and of Hoch and Dreyfus (2006), some authors express their concern to develop theory that attempts to explain the processes by which meaning is assigned in mathematics, and in their research they resort to semiotics or the science of signs. Generally, in semiotic approaches to the problems raised in mathematics education, comprehension of mathematics concepts and symbols is remitted to semiosis processes. That is to say that they are remitted to processes of producing and operating with signs in order to produce meaning.

The processes of semiosis and their components are conceived in different ways, according to the varying authors and currents of semiotics. In this section, reference is made to elements of the theory of Peirce (1931–1958), given that further along in this chapter there is a discussion concerning mathematics education studies that are based on such theory. One of the characteristics of that theory is that the processes, rather than the signs themselves, are emphasized (Hoopes, 1991)—and that emphasis is present even in the very idea of sign. In Peirce's multiple definitions, he points out that signs are not characterized by a signifier/signified dyadic relationship (as is proposed in the theory of Saussure), but they are rather triadic between the sign (S), its object (O), and a mind (the interpretant I) for which the sign is related to its object in such a way that, for certain purposes, it can be treated as if it were that other[3]. Hence, in the triad (S, O, I) S and I are signs, and I is a new sign S', which in the mind creates another sign as interpretant, I', of object O, that is to say a new cognition I', such that the object O is the link between the two triads (S, O, I) and (S', O, I'). This has to do with the open nature of the sign of a semiosis process that has no end, as explained by Peirce in one of his definitions:

Sign [Lat. *signum*, a mark, a token]: Ger. *zeichen*; Fr. *signe*; It. *Segno*. (1) Anything which determines something else (its *interpretant*) to refer to an object to which itself refers (its *object*) in the same way, the interpretant becoming in turn a sign, and so on *ad infinitum*.

(Peirce, 1931–1958, Vol. 2, p. 169), ()

Just as Peirce (1868) proposes several definitions, he also proposes several typologies of signs, one of which consists of three categories: icons, indices and symbols. This typology defines the way in which the sign refers to its object: the icon by a quality of its own, the index by real connection to its object, and the symbol by a habit or rule for its interpretant.[4]

In the field of mathematics education, the more or less recent publication of collections of works on semiotics and mathematics and on semiotics and mathematics learning reveal the noted interest in that field for this type of approach (see, for instance, Hoffmann, Lenhard, & Seeger, 2005; Radford, Schubring, & Seeger, 2008). Among the authors who share this interest and incorporate elements of Peirce's theory in their studies is Otte (2005). This author proposes to study fundamental problems of mathematics comprehension from the standpoint of semiotics. Such problems include mathematical objects and the proof paradox (Otte, 2005, p. 9). Otte analyzes the role of the categories of signs that were formulated by Peirce (icons, indices, and symbols) in mathematics signification. Whereas Presmeg (2005), inspired by Otte's ideas, studies the definition of those categories of representation in terms of metaphors and metonymies, and formulates a nested model of signs that is based on Peirce's triadic formulation (for a description on the model, see Presmeg, 2005, pp. 106–107). Using an anecdote about a session of class with university students, Presmeg illustrates how, through a change of notation, relations among the lengths of segments of a geometric figure become clear to her and to her students. In her anecdote, the measurements had to be used to demonstrate the existence of the Nagel point of a triangle, which is the point of intersection of the line segments from the vertices of the triangle to the points of tangency of the opposite escribed circles (in Figure 7.1, N is the Nagel point of the triangle ABC).

The change of notation consisted of expressing the AB segment as $c1 + c2$; the BC segment as $a1 + a2$; and the AC segment as $b1 + b2$. With this, during the analysis of figure, it became clear that $c1+c2+a1$ and $b2+b1+a2$ were semi-perimeters of the ABC triangle; this fact that enabled them to carry out the required proof that had remained "hidden" while the notation using capital letters for the AB, BD, AC and CD segments were used. In Presmeg's own words:

> In semiotic terms the representamen on one day $AB + BD = AC + CD$ was not a sufficiently iconic likeness of the semi-perimeter of the triangle to make it clear, firstly, that the object *was* a semi-perimeter, and secondly, that each of the six given expressions represented a semi-perimeter, and that they were therefore all equal to one another. Somehow the representamen $c1 + c2 + a1 = b2 + b1 + a2$ together with the similar equations, had helped to make the relationships apparent. Both of these representations were symbolic: both were conventional ways of expressing relationships among the lengths of line segments. In both cases, the interpretants were all-important in determining the outcomes of the actions taken, successful or otherwise. The difference between the two symbols appears to reside in their metaphoric and metonymic features, that is, how they behaved as icons and indices in representing the abstract structure of the configuration of circles and lines [. . .]. As a metaphor, the icon of a lower-case representamen was more efficient in suggesting an interpretant that would unpack the relationships.

(Presmeg, 2005, pp. 113–114)

Presmeg's anecdote, analyzed with respect to the metaphorical and metonymic traits of the symbols, is an example of the relevance of the notations used in mathematics teaching and in professional mathematics work, itself. This particular case demonstrates that the signs or representamen play (for themselves and acting in their capacity of icons) a determining role in signification processes vis-à-vis certain parts of a geometric configuration, processes through

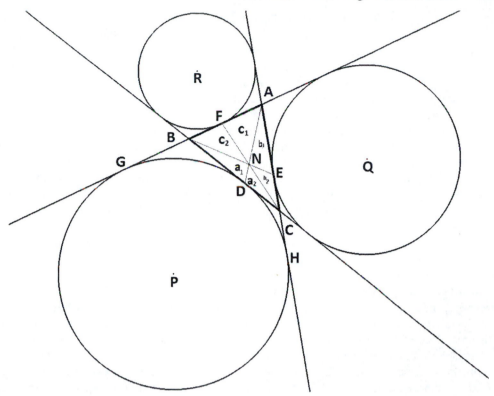

Figure 7.1 Nagel point N of a triangle ABC (Presmeg, 2005, p. 112).

which relations among the elements of the configuration, which are the basis of the required demonstration, become evident. It is noteworthy to mention that even if this example corresponds to topics of university geometry (Nagel point; Ceva theorem), the theoretical explanations of the signification processes can well be applied to topics and cases of MJSS mathematics, such as shape, space and measurement, statistics, and representation (not necessarily algebraic) of situations and word problems.

Sense Production in Mathematics Learning: The Case of Algebraic Read-Writing

As mentioned previously, in the line of research that deals with the reading (interpretation) of algebraic symbols, researchers have studied the manners in which 11–16 year old students tend to read algebraic symbols by attempting to unravel the nature of those readings (Booth, 1984; Filloy & Rojano, 1989; Freudenthal, 1983; Kieran, 1981; Küchemann, 1981). Some authors approached the problem from the standpoint that considers algebra to be a language. In this sense, one should clarify that research that resorts to semiotics differ from research that uses linguistics: the latter studies mathematics as a language and analyzes its syntactic and semantic aspects (see Drouhard, 1992; Kirshner, 1987, 1989); whereas the former studies mathematics as a system of signs. The latter gives rise to the inclusion of not just mathematics signs, but also of the signs of vernacular language and of other types of signs as well. This is very advantageous in the field of mathematics education because in that field the mathematics *texts* involved in teaching and learning are made up of signs that come from different systems (Puig, 2003).

With the broad notion of Mathematical Sign System (MSS) originally formulated by Filloy (1993), which includes the productions of students when they resolve a mathematics task, Filloy et al. (2008) adapt elements of Peirce's theory on processes of semiosis to describe the *text* reading/transformation processes of one MSS in mathematics learning and teaching situations (in this case, the *texts* can be tasks or problems that are proposed to the students and/or their productions as they broach and resolve the tasks or problems). As mentioned earlier, according to Peirce's theory, the condition of the sign's openness in an unending process of semiosis is derived from the link that is established between the two triads (S, O, I) and (S', O, I'), through O (Peirce, 1931–58, p. 135). In the work of Filloy et al. this process of semiosis is conceived with respect to texts and not to isolated signs, and this makes it possible to speak of chains of reading/transformation of texts in which a text T is read and transformed into a new text T', which is opened to a new reading (for a mind) to be transformed into another text T''. From that perspective, differentiation among T, T' and T'' is actually a distinction between positions of a text in an ad infinitum process of reading/transformation (Filloy, et al., 2008, p. 125). In Peirce's theory, processes of semiosis lead to production of sense with respect to signs; while in Filloy et al., production of sense in the learning and teaching of mathematics arises in processes of reading/transformation of mathematical texts (under the broad notion of mathematical texts referred to earlier).

Now, in the field of learning and teaching MJSS algebra, the interest lies in studying production of sense both with respect to concepts (for instance, the concept of unknown, variable, function) as well as to methods (for example, algebraic methods for resolution of equations and word problems). Previous research has shown that at the school level in question, learning algebraic concepts and methods implies crucial transitions in student thought. Such transitions include: expanding conceptions such as that of equality or of variable; overcoming the difficulty of operating with unknown quantities; moving from arithmetic or intuitive methods in the resolution of word problems to the method of "putting into equation" the statement of a problem (Cartesian method). Some of those transitions have recently been researched from the standpoint of the above-cited processes of reading/transformation of texts. For example, Filloy, Rojano and Solares (2010) carried out a study with secondary school students in which they conducted clinical interviews that included sections with instruction. The study deals with learning algebraic resolution of problems with two unknown quantities, in which the progress of the students is analyzed in terms of their ability to operate the unknown when this unknown is represented by an expression that involves a second unknown. In curricular terms, the study was undertaken when the students had already mastered algebraic resolution of a linear equation, but they still had to learn classic algebraic methods for resolving systems of two linear equations with two unknown quantities, of the type specified here:

$$Ax + By = C$$
$$Dx + Ey = F$$

With x and y as unknowns, and A, B, C, D, E and F as known quantities, and for the resolution of which it is eventually necessary to operate the unknown at a second level of representation. That is to say, expressed as:

$$y = \frac{C - Ax}{B}, \ B \neq 0$$

At the beginning of the interview, the students were asked to take on a word problem with two unknown quantities. Over the course of their resolutions (which, before the instruction, began with intuitive strategies), it became clear that in order to progress in line with the algebraic syntax toward working with two unknown quantities, it was not sufficient for them to have overcome the difficulties involved in operating one unknown in linear equations, nor was it enough to name the two unknowns with letters. It is rather necessary to imbue operating with a single unknown, expressed in terms of the other unknown, with sense, and this in turn implies endowing the equalization and algebraic substitution with new sense (Filloy et al., 2010, p. 76). In order to illustrate such processes of semiosis, which lead to sense production with respect to operating unknowns and to algebraic substitution, an interview episode with L (a student who participated in the study) is reproduced here. In this episode L was presented with the "Age Problem," which involves two unknown quantities (Filloy et al., 2010, p. 4).

As was mentioned before, at the moment of the interview, L mastered the algebra syntactic rules to solve linear equations with one unknown, but had not been taught the algebraic methods to solve systems of two linear equations with two unknowns. At this stage of the interview, L had already solved simpler problems with two unknown quantities and was taught (during the interview) how to translate this sort of problems into a system of equations.

The Age Problem: The age difference between Juan and Carlos is 12 years. Within four years, Juan, who's the older of the two, will be twice Carlos's age. How old are they both now?

L used the letters J and C to represent the unknown quantities (Juan's and Carlos's ages) and translated the word problem into the following system of equations:

$$J - C = 12$$
$$J + 4 = 2(C + 4)$$

This translation into the algebraic code is an important act of reading/transformation of the text corresponding to the word problem.

L could find Juan's age when Carlos's age had a specific value, but was unable to find the algebraic expression that enables one to calculate Juan's age in terms of Carlos's age ($J = C + 12$). She could not operate on the unknowns J and C, because she did not know their numerical values. In other words, to read/transform the *text* corresponding to the equation system she needed to assign a numerical value to one of the unknowns (C).

In order to help L obtain the appropriate expression, the interviewer (I) suggested she thinks again of unknown C as a known number:

I: Here you have that Juan's age minus Carlos's age equals 12. If we had a number here, for example 10, could you find Juan's age value?
I points to the equation $J - C = 12$, and writes 10 below C in that equation.
L: Yes! Adding these two.
L points to 10 and 12.
I: OK. So, if we knew Carlos's age, could we calculate Juan's age?
L: Yes!
I: How?
L: By adding Carlos' age to 12.
I: Then, if I represent Carlos's age with C, how much is the value of Juan's age?
I points to C and J in the equation: $J - C = 12$.
L: I don't know it yet.

Although L was competent in solving linear equations with one unknown, she was unable to undertake a suitable reading/transformation act of the text $J - C = 12$ in order to produce the expression $J = C + 12$. Then I intervened:

I: What would J's value be? It is a number, a number you don't know, but it is a number. Suppose that I already knew what number it is, but I do not want to tell you. I'll call it C. I tell you: it is C. Then, how much is the value of Juan's age?
I points to J in $J - C = 12$.
L: C plus 12.
L writes $J = C + 12$, and after a while, she also writes $(C + 12) + 4 = 2(C + 4)$,
and then she simplifies to $(C + 12) + 4 = 2C + 8$.
I: What did you do? Why did you put that here?
I points to $C + 12$ in the equation $(C + 12) + 4 = 2C + 8$.

L: So that . . . Do you remember when *P* . . . when here . . . we replaced it with five *a* ?
Well, here I substituted *J* by *C* plus 12, so that there are only *C*s.

L points to the perimeter problem (a problem that she had just solved during the interview). Then she indicates the *J* in the equation $J + 4 = 2C + 8$, and $C + 12$ in the equation $(C + 12) + 4 = 2C + 8$.

L explains her reasoning as follows: "I substituted *J* by *C* plus 12 so there are only *C*s." Here she refers to the equation she obtained in terms of the unknown *C*: $(C + 12) + 4 = 2C + 8$.

At this point, L solves this equation without any trouble, obtaining $C = 8$. Then she obtained $J = 20$ by substituting the value of *C* in $J = 12 + C$.

The interviewer's intervention, suggesting that L think of *C* as a known quantity, together with L's reference to a previous simpler problem solved by her, was determinant in the sense production with respect to read/transform the equation $J - C = 12$ in $J = C + 12$ and substitute the letter *J* by $C + 12$ in the equation $J + 4 = 2(C + 4)$. This moment of sense production was crucial for L to recover her syntactic competence of solving linear equations with one unknown and consequently to be able to solve the system of two linear equations with two unknowns.

In operational terms, in equation systems such as those above, substitution of $y = \dfrac{C - Ax}{B}$ in the second equation, together with a reference to what *y* represents in the context of the problem, leads the majority of students to make sense both of the equalization of expressions that result from the substitution, as well as of the substitution method itself for resolution of systems of two equations with two unknown quantities (Filloy et al., 2010, pp. 70–75).

Studies such as that described here are examples of the fact that transition processes that move toward competent use of the MSS of algebra are ongoing throughout MJSS. They furthermore go through critical points that demand sense production vis-à-vis algebraic actions, such as substitution and equalization, and this goes beyond achieving an "adequate" reading—interpretation of algebraic signs. Under this perspective, which conceives the learning and teaching of mathematics as processes of semiosis (of production of sense) by way of actions of reading/transformation of mathematics texts, it is possible to revisit old research problems, such as progress in the mathematics thought of MJSS students, from particular to general, from numerical to algebraic, from concrete to abstract. It should be noted that achieving this type of progress among MJSS students prepares them for long-term mathematics learning because things of a general nature, of a symbolic nature (algebraic), and of an abstract nature are endemic to mathematical thinking.

Signs and Meanings in Mathematics Generalization

In Radford's (2000) study on signs and meanings in the emerging algebraic thought of students, he uses a socio-cultural theoretical framework that also includes a semiotic perspective. On the one hand, this framework is based on the Vygostkian idea that our cognitive functioning is affected by the use of signs, while on the other, it is based on the idea that the signs with which an individual acts and thinks belong to symbolic cultural systems that transcend the individual level. In this way, the signs that an individual thinks with are framed by meanings and rules of social usage, and they provide that individual with social means of semiotic objectification (Radford, 2000).

According to that perspective, Radford (2000) conceives learning algebra "as the appropriation of a new and specific mathematical way of acting and thinking which is dialectically interwoven with a novel use and production of signs whose meanings are acquired by the students as a result of their social immersion into mathematical activities" (p. 241). Radford uses this theoretical approach to analyze data from a study with eighth grade students, whose main purposes are: "1) To investigate the way in which students use signs and endow them with meaning during their very first tasks related to the algebraic generalization of patterns. And 2) to provide accounts about the students' emergent algebraic thinking" (Radford, 2000, p. 238). In relation to both purposes, this author presents the analysis of protocols from a small group of students that engaged in a generalization activity that consisted of finding a formula to calculate the number of elements in figure *n* in a figurative sequence. Figure 7.2 shows the task presented to the students.

From a semiotic analysis of an episode in which students worked on Figure 12 of the sequence, in their way to produce a general formula, Radford reports that

> objectification of generality was discursively elaborated as *potential act* articulated in two key linguistic elements: the use of deictic terms and adverbs of generative action out of which a concrete example (here the Figure [7.2] of the sequence) functioned as a metaphor. The metaphoric Figure [7.2], crafted with terms like 'rank', 'vertical' and 'horizontal' allowed the students to accomplish an apprehension and a discursive representation of the general and provided them with a way for expressing the general through the particular. In addition, the objectification of the general in natural language proved to be fundamental to the rise of the symbolic formula in that the symbolic formula appeared as contracted or abbreviated speech. An important result was to have identified that the letter-signs resulting from this process of semiotic objectification correspond to the category of *indexes*.
>
> (Radford, 2000, pp. 260–261).

Using the bingo chips provided, reproduce the following sequence:

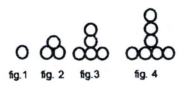

fig. 1   fig. 2   fig. 3   fig. 4

Continue the sequence up to and including figure 6.

a) How many circles would figure number 10 have in total?

b) How many circles would figure number 100 have in total?

c) You are now going to write a message to another Grade 8 student from another class clearly explaining what s/he must do in order to find out how many circles there are in any given figure of the sequence.

Message:

d) Find a formula to calculate the number of circles in figure number "n".

Figure 7.2 Problem presented to the students during the small group activity (Radford, 2000, p. 254).

In another part of the article, Radford concludes that "the passage from a non-symbolic to a symbolic algebraic expression of generality means two ruptures: one with the sensual geometry of the patterns and the other with the numerical feature of them." (Radford, 2000, p. 261). These quotations from Radford's article illustrate the semiotic and socio-cultural nature of the theoretical approach he uses in the analysis of students' productions when they interact with a variety of MSS. Furthermore, the case reported demonstrates that using such a semiotic standpoint, new findings concerning generalization processes in secondary school students (a theme widely researched during the last three decades) arise. Among these findings are: 1) the metaphoric nature of the processes that allowed students to verbalize the general, in a way, that they could express the general through the particular; and 2) the findings concerning the students' breaking away from certain traits of the particular along the way from nonsymbolic expression to symbolic expression of generalities.

A New Way of Viewing Mathematics Learning

Reference has been made in this section to a variety of research focused on studying the processes by way of which meaning and sense are assigned to mathematical signs and texts (please consider the previously described broad notion of *texts*). Empirical findings and theorizations from this research have given rise to a new way of viewing mathematics comprehension and learning. It has been argued that this new view enables delving into the analysis of the transitions of the mathematical thought of MJSS students, and that these transitions involve essential changes in the relationship of learners with mathematical sign systems. It is conjectured that based on a deepening of those transitions, teaching approaches that favor them can be designed and, in this manner, help students to advance toward learning the mathematics of higher levels of education.

DIGITAL TECHNOLOGIES AND MJSS MATHEMATICS

In the second edition of this *Handbook*, this author (Rojano, 2008) presented an analysis of the role that digital technologies can play in the teaching and learning of generalization and mathematics of variation in MJSS. Such analysis made it clear that, based on research done in the 90s, it was feasible to introduce MJSS students to complex mathematical ideas at an early age. This was because the research in question showed the potential of those technologies to help students with regularity symbolization processes for figurative and numerical sequences, as well as in the analysis of variation phenomena in multiple representations, without the students having to deal with the analytical expressions of functions (Rojano, 2008). The edition in question also mentioned the possibility of incorporating topics of three-dimensional geometry into the curriculum of that school level, by using new versions of Dynamic Geometry programs with which it is possible to manipulate three-dimensional figures and study and visually discover their geometric properties (Rojano, 2008, pp. 146–148). In this section, the theme of "digital technologies—mathematics of MJSS" is taken up again, with emphasis placed on the possible impact of technological evolution on the curriculum and classroom practices.

Technological Innovation and Curricula of MJSS

Despite certain skepticism that still exists among the community of mathematics teachers and school authorities concerning the potential impact of digital technologies on mathematics curricula, the findings of empirical studies undertaken over the last decade, in which a large variety of specialized software and applications were used, have indeed wielded influence on curricular changes at different levels (Sutherland & Rojano, 2012), and particularly at the MJSS level. This influence can be seen in terms of how digital technologies have helped to: 1) Connect different curricular areas (for instance, mathematics and natural sciences, exploiting the possibility of working with multiple representations of concepts or situations that are dynamically linked to one another). 2) Give students early access to powerful mathematical ideas, such as for instance, the possibility of introducing the study of mathematics of variation as of the elementary level. 3) Enable students to analyze large sets of authentic data in themes of statistics, and information presentation and management. 4) Incorporate new topics into the curriculum. 5) Eliminate classic curricular themes (Royal Society & JMC, 1997). Such is the case of the UK where a good deal of manipulative algebra was taken out of the curriculum in the 90s. In that curricular proposal, resolution of equations and problems is done by trial and refinement with the help of a calculator. It is worth mentioning that some time later and due to findings reported with respect to research on the didactics of algebra, educational authorities retracted the decision and today one can see a notable presence of topics related to paper-and-pencil algebra in the UK's curriculum (Sutherland, 2007).

In terms of particular topics of the MJSS curriculum, some of the more recent developments have become potential factors of change. For example, recent developments in three-dimensional Dynamic Geometry (DG) enable students to obtain visual information regarding three-dimensional figures. Hence, themes of spatial geometry that had traditionally been reserved for university curriculum and that required analysis of analytical expressions of the figures or mastery of advanced mathematics properties and theorems, can now be broached by junior secondary school students (Figure 7.3).

On the basis of research carried out in CAS environments, researchers have found that it is possible to reduce the emphasis on manipulative aspects of algebra and to focus the work of students on conceptual tasks (Kieran, 2007) or to promote both conceptual and technical aspects of mathematics (Artigue, 2002; Lagrange, 2003).

The open-source Dynamic Geometry software program Geogebra favors the connection between Euclidean geometry, Cartesian geometry, and analytical geometry. While in reference to software that was not specifically designed for educational purposes, recent versions of spreadsheets offer a friendly environment for mathematical modeling activities that involve multiple mathematics representations and simulators of physical world phenomena (Horton & Leonard, 2005).

In spite of the fact that such innovations may influence changes in official curricula, there is a need to study their influence on the enacted curriculum of MJSS, for which there are robust

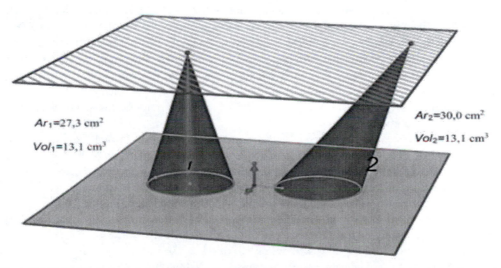

$Ar_1 = 27,3 \text{ cm}^2$

$Vol_1 = 13,1 \text{ cm}^3$

$Ar_2 = 30,0 \text{ cm}^2$

$Vol_2 = 13,1 \text{ cm}^3$

Figure 7.3 Cabri-3D Geometric Figure. Through dragging the vertices of the cones, it can be shown that cones with equal bases and with the same height can have different areas but the same volume.

theories in existence today on processes of instrumentation, of orchestration (Trouche, 2004), and of semiotic mediation (Bartolini & Mariotti, 2008) in the mathematics classroom. This opens promising areas for future research.

Technological Innovation and Classroom Practices

The introduction of digital technology to schools has lead to a myriad of modes of using that technology, amongst which are those that have attempted to keep pace with technological innovation. Such is the case of use of calculators and personal computers in the classroom, which are supplemented by use of the electronic whiteboard. In the latter mode, individual or team work can be combined with displays on the large screen of student productions, hence creating the right conditions for group discussions, comparison of solutions, and institution-alization of knowledge (Trouche, 2004) amongst other practices for social construction of knowledge.

Over the course of the last 10 years, government projects with those characteristics were implemented in several regions of the world. In Mexico, interactive materials in line with the free primary school textbook program were developed for display and manipulation on interactive whiteboards (Trigueros et al., 2006). While in the UK, mass use of whiteboards was introduced in compulsory teaching classrooms (Kenewell, 2009). Despite the fact that neither of the foregoing two experiences reported very optimistic results with respect to use of the interactive whiteboards, one can say that with the modes of use that stemmed from the technology, the very notable dichotomy of the 80s came to an end. This dichotomy concerned technologies designed for personal and private use (such as graphic calculators) on the one hand, and the technologies with which personal work was made public (such as personal com-puters), on the other (Rojano, 2014).

On a very different line of thought, albeit also related to the transformation of practices, technological innovations have been developed more recently that are changing the conditions for learning mathematics. For instance, access on mobile devices (through the network) to new applications (apps for tablets) and to interactive materials developed in previous decades (for example, GD, spreadsheets, CAS) can encourage more flexible multimodal use of digital technology, both in terms of teaching and learning (Hegedus & Tall, Chapter 23 in this vol-ume). In particular, the possibility of doing individual work on those devices, with applications designed for self-study, places the learner at the center. Moreover, in this case the digital tech-nology functions as a means for autonomous learning and lifelong learning. In those develop-ments the emphasis on teaching is reduced, as is the case of Apple iPad apps such as iFactor and iFactor Pro, which were designed for factorization of quadratic expressions and for resolution of second-degree equations, respectively. Such applications can be used to verify the results of tasks done previously by students with paper and pencil algebra, and hence supporting those students in developing their manipulative algebra skills. Those types of applications have the trait of presenting, in an automated fashion, families of algebraic problems or exercises that include variants in the structure of the expressions and in the numerical domain of equation coefficients and solutions.

Apps have also been developed for tablets in which users practically "touch" and manipulate the geometric objects, without mediation of a mouse or keyboard. With such direct interaction with the object of knowledge, one would imagine that working with those materials would have repercussions at the cognitive and epistemological levels; that is to say, it will have an effect on the manner in which students build mathematics knowledge (Figure 7.4).

Other innovations include an intelligent support system that provides feedback to users when they work in a digital learning environment. This includes the software eXpresser, which was developed in the London Knowledge Lab (www.lkl.ac.uk) and with which students work in a microworld to learn generalization on the basis of building and analyzing patterns in figurative sequences (Figure 7.5). While a task is being worked on, the system poses the user

Figure 7.4 Direct manipulation of a geometric figure on the touch screen of a digital tablet. Sources: Hegedus (2012); James Kaput Center, University of Massachusetts (www.kaputcenter.umassd.edu).

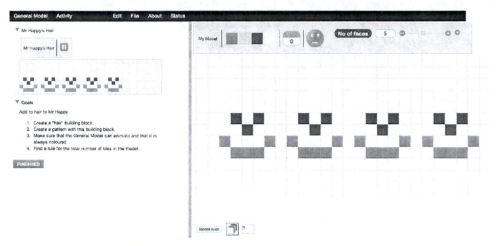

Figure 7.5 eXpresser screen. On the left there is a window of the general world, and on the right a "my world" window. Intelligent support feedback appears in the top right hand of the screen.

questions or prompts him/her at specific points deemed by the activity designers to be "learning opportunities" (Noss et al., 2009).

In the *Intelligent Dialogue* interactive units, developed in collaboration by the Laboratorio de Innovación Tecnológica y Educativa (LITE) (Laboratory for Technological and Educational Innovation) and the Instituto de Matemáticas (Mathematics Institute) of the National University of Mexico (UNAM), there is a simultaneous display on the screen of a microworld window and a chat window that are dynamically linked to each other (see *Diálogos con Prometeo*, http://arquimedes.matem.unam.mx/Dialogos/). The system enters into a dialogue with users while they are working in the microworld. In this case, interaction is with the two systems. One action by the student in the microworld can lead to a question or a suggestion by the system in the chat window. In turn, the answers given by the user in that window can lead to feedback in both windows. Like in eXpresser, the design of interactive Intelligent Dialogues includes previously identified critical feedback points. In specific cases, when unit

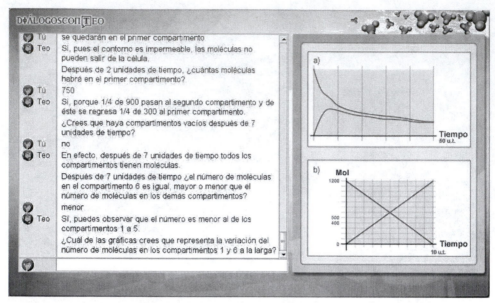

Figure 7.6 Screen for the molecular diffusion model in Intelligent Dialogues. On the right, the microworld window opens (graphics with parameters that can be varied) and, on the left, the dialogue window appears.

content includes science-modeling activities, those points correspond to behavior prediction points of a phenomenon, confirming a conjecture or validating the model (Figure 7.6).

It is important to point out that in the two preceding examples, interactions between the user and the digital environment are of a complex nature. They differ significantly from the type of applications that used to be developed in the 80s with artificial intelligence systems and that lead to the so-called tutorials, the design of which was based on models of programmed learning (Rojano & Abreu, 2012). In fact, that complex interaction is related to the intentionality of the didactic design, given that in both cases the intelligent support is conceived as a timely, specific, and personalized support, as a supplement to feedback from the teacher or classmates. That is to say, that the design of those tools includes the intention of helping to transform classroom practices in terms of the possibilities offered by focused feedback (Noss et al., 2009; Rojano & García-Campos, 2014). The emergence of novel modes of usage, derived from digital innovations, leads to the need for the corresponding research that can be used to verify the didactic and digital design hypothesis, for devices apps and specialized software. In other words, the future of digital technology usage for teaching and learning mathematics ought not only to depend on technological evolution, rather it ought also to depend on the findings of research that make the potential and limitations of those innovations transparent for teachers and curriculum designers (Rojano, 2014).

LIFELONG LEARNING, DIGITAL TECHNOLOGIES AND SIGNIFICATION IN MATHEMATICS: FINAL REMARKS

This chapter is located in the *Handbook* section entitled "Democratic Access to Mathematics Learning" and in the light of that title, in the initial sections this author has raised the need to deepen our knowledge of the processes by way of which meanings are assigned and sense is produced among MJSS students with respect to mathematics objects, symbols, texts, and methods. The fact that part of the contents of the chapter was devoted to this theme is due to the implicit hypothesis that access to lifelong learning in mathematics depends first and foremost on those signification processes. In the brief overview undertaken of the research that has focused on the study of meaning (and of sense) in mathematics, special reference has been made to studies that adopt a semiotic approach; that is to say, to those that conceive of learning in mathematics as processes of semiosis. The decision to discuss this type of approach, instead of the *realistic mathematics* and *mathematics in context* currents, is not due to a lack of appreciation for the important contribution that the foregoing currents have made to research into the mathematics—real-world relationship as a source of meanings in teaching of mathematics (Gravemeijer, 2004; Sierpinska, 1995; Streefland, 1991; and Van Den Heuvel-Panhuizen, 2003)—but rather because semiotic approaches make it possible to hone the analysis of learners' relationships with the mathematical sign systems involved in learning. The interest in bringing semiotic approaches to the table, specifically in this chapter devoted to MJSS mathematics, also has to do with the fact that the transitions needed in the thought processes of adolescent students in order for them to gain access to the mathematics thought of that level assume deep changes in their manner of reading/interpreting/transforming mathematical signs, notations, and texts. The processes of reading mathematical texts have been illustrated by way of examples of different levels of domains of knowledge, such as that of geometry (Presmeg's anecdote) and that of algebra (second level of representation of the unknown in resolution of systems of linear equations with two unknown quantities; resolution of word problems using the Cartesian method; algebraic expression of generality). Although in some cases the examples presented are from tertiary (structure sense and symbol sense) and university (the metonymical and metaphorical nature of signs) levels, this author has pointed out the advisability of taking up once again the themes and foci proposed in those examples and extending them to problems pertaining to MJSS.

The section "Sense and Assigning Meaning in Mathematics" is in its entirety an invitation (exhortation) for theoretical reflection on the manners in which MJSS students comprehend and handle the sign systems involved in teaching and learning mathematics. The foregoing is offered as an answer to the enormous cumulous of data collected by empirical studies on the read-writing of mathematics symbols that have been undertaken over the past decades and that, inter alia, have confirmed the difficulties reported by research of the 80s and 90s. It is worth mentioning that some of these studies have as well advanced our theoretical knowledge concerning the origin and nature of such difficulties.

Also in view of the theme of the *Handbook* section entitled "Democratic Access to Mathematics Learning," and with more of a practical than theoretical vision in mind, in this chapter efforts were made to refresh thought on the role played by digital technologies, precisely in that democratic access to mathematics knowledge. This author opted to reflect on the possible influence, in this sense, of technological innovations on both the official mathematics curriculum and MJSS classroom practices. The reason for this was that the role of technology learning environments as a gateway to powerful mathematical ideas had already been broached in the second edition of this *Handbook*. In this version, the author has pointed out the importance of incorporating into teaching new developments (such as three-dimensional versions of Dynamic Geometry or intelligent support that accompany the microworlds) with associated research that make it possible to understand the magnitude of the didactic potential of such developments and the feasibility of generalizing their usage. The objective of this is to reduce the discrepancy that presently exists between the findings of intensive research that for decades has pointed to the didactic virtues of digital learning environments in mathematics and their minimal influence over the curriculum, and the use of such environments in mathematics classes (Artigue, 2007).

A forecast was also made, namely that the availability of interactive materials (new and old) on the Cloud and on mobile devices will wield a significant influence over the social aspects of building mathematics knowledge, both due to the new possibilities of interaction and collaboration among communities of students and teachers, and to the facilities that such availabilities will proffer for self-study. It is noteworthy to mention that the foregoing forecast has to do with the role that digital technologies (in their most modern versions) may have in lifelong mathematics learning.

Though the study of particular problems related to the two aspects dealt with (technological innovation-mathematics curriculum and technological innovation-mathematics practices) has not been raised here, emphasis has indeed been placed on the need to orient a portion of research efforts toward aspects that aim to close the gap between research and practice.

NOTES

1. The mathematical *texts* considered here are made up of a set of heterogeneous signs. The signs that are usually considered as specific to mathematics are only part of the signs used in these *texts*, together with the signs of natural language, figures, and diagrams, as well as signs from technology environments (See Filloy, Rojano, & Puig, 2008, Chapter 8).
2. This British project was funded by the Social Science Research Council and undertaken by a research team at the Chelsea College (University of London). It was fully reported in Hart (1981). One of the main features of the CSMS mathematics outcomes was "an unexpectedly high incidence of certain wrong answers which suggested the presence of misconceptions leading to inappropriate strategies." (Booth, 1984, Preface).
3. Peirce (1931–1958) introduces the *interpretant* term as follows: "A sign [. . .] addresses somebody, that is, creates in the mind of that person an equivalent sign, or perhaps a more developed sign. That sign which it creates I call the interpretant of the first sign. The sign stands for something, its object." (Peirce, 1931–1958, Vol. 2.228, p. 135).
4. An *icon* (also called *likeness* and *semblance*) is a sign that denotes its object by virtue of a quality which is shared by them but which the icon has irrespectively of the object. The icon (for instance, a portrait or a diagram) *resembles or imitates* its object. An *index* is a sign that denotes its object by virtue of an *actual connection* involving them, one that Peirce also calls a *real relation* in virtue of its being irrespective of interpretation. A *symbol* is a sign that denotes its object solely by virtue of the fact that it will be interpreted to do so. The symbol consists in a natural or conventional or logical rule, norm, or habit, a habit that lacks (or has shed) dependence on the symbolic sign's having a resemblance or real connection to the denoted object. Thus, a symbol denotes by virtue of its interpretant. Its sign-action (semiosis) is ruled by a habit, a more or less systematic set of associations that ensures its interpretation (Peirce, 1868).

REFERENCES

Arcavi, A. (1994). Symbol sense: Informal sense-making in formal mathematics. *For the Learning of Mathematics, 14*(3), 24–35. Retrieved from http://flm-journal.org/index.php?do=show&lang=en&show Menu=14%2C3.

Artigue, M. (2002). Learning mathematics in a CAS environment. The genesis of a reflection about instrumentation and the dialectics between technical and conceptual work. *International Journal of Computers for Mathematical Learning, 7*, 245–274. doi:10.1023/A:1022103903080

Artigue, M. (2007). *L'impact curricular des technologies sur l'éducation mathématique [The curricular impact of technology on mathematics education]*. Paper presented at the XII CIAEM Conference, Querétaro, Mexico. Retrieved from www.centroedumatematica.com/ciaem/?q=es/node/237.

Bartolini, M., & Mariotti, A. (2008). Semiotic mediation in the mathematics classroom: Artifacts and signs after a Vygotskian perspective. In L. English (Ed.), *Handbook of international research in mathematics education* (2nd ed., pp.746–783). New York: Routledge.

Booth, L. (1984). *Algebra: Children's strategies and errors*. Windsor, Berkshire: NFER-NELSON.

Bransford, J., Brown, A., & Cocking, R. (Eds.) (2000). *How people learn: Brain, mind, experience, and school*. Washington, D.C.: National Academy Press.

Drouhard, J. P. (1992). *Les écritures symboliques de l'algèbre élémentaire [The symbolic writings of elementary algebra]*. Doctoral dissertation, Université Paris 7. Retrieved from http://tel.archives-ouvertes. fr/tel-00925358.

Filloy, E. (1993). Tendencias cognitivas y procesos de abstracción en el aprendizaje del algebra y de la geometría [Cognitive tendencies and processes of abstraction in the learning of algebra and geometry]. *Enseñanza de las Ciencias 11*(2), 160–166. Retrieved from http://ddd.uab.cat/record/18?ln= carecord/14?ln=ca.

Filloy, E. & Rojano, T. (1989). Solving equations: The transition from arithmetic to algebra. *For the Learning of Mathematics, 9*(2), 19–25. Retrieved from http://flm-journal.org/index.php?do=show &lang=en&showMenu=9%2C2.

Filloy, E., Rojano, T., & Puig, L. (2008). *Educational algebra. A theoretical and empirical approach*. New York: Springer.

Filloy, E., Rojano, T., & Solares, A. (2010). Problems dealing with unknown quantities and two different levels of representing unknowns. *Journal for Research in Mathematics Education*, 41 (1), 52–80. Retrieved from www.nctm.org/publications/article.aspx?id=26190.

Freudenthal, H. (1983). The algebraic language. In H. Freudenthal, *Didactical phenomenology of mathematical structures* (pp. 461–490). Dordrecht: Reidel. doi:10.1007/0–306–47235-X_16

Gravemeijer, K. (1994). *Developing realistic mathematics education*. Utrecht, The Netherlands: Freudenthal Institute.

Gravemeijer, K. (2004). Local instruction theories as means of support for teachers in reform mathematics education. *Mathematical Thinking and Learning*, 6 (2), 105–128. doi:10.1207/s15327833mtl0602_3

Griffin, S. (2004). Building number sense with Number Worlds: A mathematics program for young children. *Early Childhood Research Quarterly*, 19 (1), 173–180. Retrieved from www.sciencedirect.com/science/article/pii/S0885200604000146.

Hart, K. (1981). Children's understanding of mathematics: 11–16. London: John Murray

Hoch, M. (2007). *Structure sense in high school algebra*. Unpublished doctoral dissertation, Tel Aviv University, Israel.

Hoch, M., & Dreyfus, T. (2006). Structure sense versus manipulation skills: An unexpected result. In J. Novotná, H. Moraová, M. Krátká, & N. Stehlíková (Eds.), *Proceedings of the 30th Conference of the International Group for the Psychology of Mathematics* Education, *3*, 305–312. Prague, Czech Republic: PME.

Hoch, M., & Dreyfus, T. (2010). Developing Katy's algebraic structure sense. *Proceedings of CERME 6*, January 28–February 1, 2009, Lyon France © INRP 2010. Retrieved from www.inrp.fr/editions/cerme6.

Hoffmann, M.H.G, Lenhard, J., & Seeger, F. (Eds.) (2005). *Activity and sign. Grounding mathematics education*. New York: Springer.

Hoopes, J. (Ed.) (1991). *Peirce on signs. Writings on semiotics by Charles Sanders Peirce*. Chapel Hill: University of North Carolina Press.

Horton, R.M., & Leonard, W. H. (2005). Mathematical modeling in science: Using spreadsheets to create mathematical models and address scientific inquiry. *The Science Teacher*, 72(5), 40–45.

Kennewell, S. (2009). *Reflections on the interactive whiteboard phenomenon: A synthesis of research from the UK*. Portugal: Observatório dos Recursos Educativos. Retrieved from www.ore.org.pt/filesobservatorio/pdf/KENNEWELL.pdf.

Kieran, C. (1981). Concepts associated with the equality symbol. *Educational Studies in Mathematics*, 12, 317–26. doi:10.1007/BF00311062

Kieran, C. (2007). Research on the learning and teaching of school algebra at the middle, secondary, and college level: Building meaning for symbols and their manipulation. In F. Lester (Ed.) *Second handbook of research on mathematics teaching and learning* (pp. 707–762). Charlotte, NC: Information Age Publishing.

Kirshner, D. (1987). *Linguistic analysis of symbolic elementary algebra*. Unpublished doctoral dissertation, University of British Columbia.

Kirshner, D. (1989). The visual syntax of algebra. *Journal for Research in Mathematics Education*, 20, 274–287. Retrieved from www.nctm.org/publications/article.aspx?id=38660.

Küchemann, D. (1981). Algebra. In K. Hart (Ed.) *Children's understanding of mathematics 11–16* (pp. 102–119). London: Murray.

Lagrange, J-B (2003). Learning techniques and concepts using CAS: A practical and theoretical reflection. In J. T. Fey (Ed.) *Computer algebra systems in secondary school mathematics education* (pp. 269–283). Reston, VA: National Council of Teachers of Mathematics.

Linchevski, L. & Liveneh, D (1999). Structure sense: The relationship between algebraic and numerical contexts. *Educational Studies in Mathematics*, 40 (2), 173–196. Retrieved from www.jstor.org/stable/3483083.

National Council of Teachers of Mathematics. (2000). *Principles and standards for school mathematics*. Reston, VA: National Council of Teachers of Mathematics.

Noss, R., Hoyles, C., Mavrikis, M., Geraniou, E., Gutierrez-Santos, S., & Pearce, D. (2009). Broadening the sense of "dynamic": A microworld to support students' mathematical generalization. In Special Issue of *ZDM: The International Journal on Mathematics Education, Transforming mathematics education through the use of dynamic mathematics technologies, 41*(4), 493–503. doi:10.1007/s11858–009–0182–8

Otte, M. (2005). Mathematics, sign and activity. In M.H.G. Hoffmann, J. Lenhard, & F. Seeger (Eds.), *Activity and sign. Grounding mathematics education* (pp. 9–22). New York: Springer.

Peirce, C. S. (1868). On a new list of categories. *Proceedings of the American Academy of Arts and Sciences 7*, 287–298.

Peirce, C. S. (1931–1958). *Collected papers of Charles Sanders Peirce.* C. Hartshorne & P. Weiss, Eds. (Vols. 1–6) and A. Burks, Ed. (Vols. 7–8). Cambridge, MA: The Belknap Press of Harvard University Press.

Presmeg, N. (2005). Metaphor and metonym in processes of semiosis in mathematics education. In M.H.G. Hoffmann, J. Lenhard, & F. Seeger (Eds.) (2005). *Activity and sign. Grounding mathematics education* (pp. 105–115). New York: Springer.

Puig, L. (2003). Signos, textos y sistemas matemáticos de signos [Signs, texts and mathematical sign systems]. In E. Filloy (Ed.) *Matemática Educativa: Aspectos de la investigación actual* (pp. 174–186). México: Fondo de Cultura Económica/Cinvestav.

Qualifications and Curriculum Authority (2007). *Mathematics. Programme for key state 3 and attainment targets* (p. 145). Retrieved from http://webarchive.nationalarchives.gov.uk/20130123124929/http://media.education.gov.uk/assets/files/pdf/q/mathematics%202007%20programme%20of%20study%20for%20key%20stage%203.pdf.

Radford, L. (2000). Signs and meanings in students' emerging algebraic thinking: A semiotic analysis. *Educational Studies in Mathematics, 42,* 237–268. doi:10.1023/A:1017530828058

Radford, L., Schubring, G., & Seeger, F. (Eds.) (2008). *Semiotics in mathematics education.* Rotterdam/Taipei: Sense Publishers.

Rojano, T. (2008). Mathematics learning in the middle school/junior secondary school: Student access to powerful mathematical ideas. In L. English (Ed.) *Handbook of International Research in Mathematics Education* (2nd ed., pp. 136–153). New York: Routledge.

Rojano, T. (2014). El futuro de las tecnologías digitales en la educación matemática: Prospectiva a treinta años de investigación intensiva en el campo. [The future of digital technologies in mathematics education: A prospective after 30 years of intensive research in the field]. *Educación Matemática,* número especial: 25 años [special issue: 25 years], 11–30. Retrieved from www.revista-educacion-matematica.com/volumen-25/numero-e/11-30.

Rojano, T., & Abreu, J-L (2012). Dialogues with Prometheus: Intelligent support for teaching mathematics. In C. Kynigos, J-E Clayson, & N. Yiannoutso (Eds.) *Proceedings of the Constructionism 2012 Conference* (pp. 544–548). Athens, Greece.

Rojano, T., Filloy, E., & Puig, L (2014). Intertextuality and sense production in the learning of algebraic methods. *Educational Studies in Mathematics, 87*(3), 389–407. Retrieved from http://link.springer.com/article/10.1007/s10649-014-9561-3.

Rojano, T., & García-Campos, M (2014). Intelligent dialogues with tertiary education pupils. Working with parameterized modeling activities. In P. Liljedahl & C. Nicol (Eds.), *Proceedings of the 38th Conference of the International Group for the Psychology of Mathematics Education, 6,* 210. July 15–20, Vancouver: Simon Fraser University/British Columbia University.

Royal Society/JMC (1997). Teaching and learning algebra pre-19. *Report of a Royal Society/Joint Mathematical Council Working Group* (pp. 3–4). London: Royal Society.

Schoenfeld, A. (1988). When good teaching leads to bad results: The disasters of well taught mathematics classes. *Educational Psychologist, 23,* 145–166. doi:10.1207/s15326985ep2302_5

Secretaría de Educación Pública (SEP). (2006). *Reforma de la educación secundaria. Fundamentación curricular. Matemáticas* [Reform of secondary school education. Curricular foundations. Mathematics].

Sierpinska, A. (1995). Mathematics: "In context," "pure," or "with applications"? *For the Learning of Mathematics, 15*(1), 2–15. Retrieved from http://flm-journal.org/index.php?do=show&lang=en&showMenu=15%2C1.

Streefland, L. (Ed.) (1991). *Fractions in realistic mathematics education. A paradigm of developmental research.* Dordrecht: Kluwer Academic Publishers.

Sutherland, R. (2007). *Teaching for learning mathematics.* Maidenhead: Open University Press.

Sutherland, R., & Rojano, T. (2012). Technology and curricula in mathematics education. In S. Lerman (Ed.) *Encyclopedia of mathematics education.* New York: Springer.

Trigueros, M., Lozano, M., Sandoval, I., Lage, A., Jinich, E., García, H., & Tovilla, E. (2006). Developing resources for teaching and learning mathematics with digital technologies in *Enciclomedia,* a national project. In C. Hoyles, J. B. Lagrange, L. H. Son, & N. Sinclair (Eds.) *Proceedings of the 17th Study Conference of the International Commission on Mathematical Instruction* (pp. 556–563). Hanoi Institute of Technology and Didirem Université Paris 7.

Trouche, L. (2004). Managing the complexity of human/machine interactions in computerized learning environments: Guiding students' process through instrumental orchestrations. *International Journal of Computers for Mathematical Learning, 9,* 281–307. doi:10.1007/s10758-004-3468-5

Van den Heuvel-Panhuizen, M. (2003). The didactical use of models in realistic mathematics education: An example from a longitudinal trajectory on percentage. *Educational Studies in Mathematics, 54*(1), pp. 9–35. doi:10.1023/B:EDUC.0000005212.03219.dc

8 Mathematical Structure, Proof, and Definition in Advanced Mathematical Thinking

Joanna Mamona-Downs and Martin L. N. Downs

University of Patras, Greece

INTRODUCTION

As mathematical thought matures, it is often convenient to map the advance by referring to transitional stages. These can be quite minor and local, for instance when hierarchical levels of understanding for a concept are identified in a relatively stable mathematical context, or can be more far-reaching when the concepts themselves are in flux and different definitions are crafted accordingly to the state reached in a mathematical theory. Transitional stages can be gradual or abrupt. An institutional change tends to accelerate the sophistication in how mathematics is treated, and this is especially pressing when one considers the difference between the character of mathematics taught at high school and that taught at the tertiary level. (In the United States, this institutional change might be best reflected when a student enters the program of senior study at university.) Many students find this transition difficult, finding the style of the presentation of mathematics at university very different to what they were accustomed before (see for example De Guzmán, Hodgson, Robert, & Villani, 1998). It is natural to question whether the institutional change by itself is responsible in creating these difficulties. Students are abruptly faced with the apparent detached character of formalization and new standards set for argumentation that are largely foreign to the school experience. Is there a way to direct students' learning of mathematical ideas in a "continuous" manner avoiding such "ruptures"? Some educators claim that, indeed, there is a way. For example, Rasmussen, Zandieh, King, & Teppo (2005) advocate the construction of "advancing mathematical activity . . . to think about the transition from informal to more formal mathematical reasoning" (p. 71). From another study, Marrongelle & Rasmussen (2008), it is clear that this approach is regarded to be more or less universal in application, suggesting it has the potential to instruct mathematics as a "continuum." From this stance, there cannot be a tight characterization for the term *Advanced Mathematical Thinking*, a topic espoused by many mathematics educators considering the special needs to cope with tertiary level mathematics.

Even though guided reinvention or rediscovery (we shall not make a distinction here) is a legitimate tactic in teaching mathematics on occasion, it is questionable whether this tactic is feasible, or even desirable, to apply on a grand scale. At the university level, many defined mathematical objects gain conceptual weight only after determining a coherent set of properties that those objects possess in common. Concerns in progressing mathematical theory are dominant, affecting the way in which presentation is styled. From this perspective, mathematics develops by recognizing structural affordances, and the institutional change can be regarded as being useful in stressing that a new mindset is now in place. The educator's role then is to study how students cope with the resultant new codes of practice and to suggest means of support for students to fulfill them.

Mathematical theories partially covered at high school then re-treated at the tertiary level are of particular interest when studying transitional issues. The most evident example is Calculus as presented at school and a first course on Real Analysis as taught at university. Many students are flabbergasted by the contrast between the two; bringing out an axiomatic system for the real numbers allows proofs of properties that before were largely taken for granted. Also, in some countries, certain basic notions of linear algebra are introduced in higher streams of secondary school; the topics typically covered are vector spaces, independence or dependence of a set of vectors, and solving systems of linear equations. A comparison study in Selinski (2012) contrasts school and university students' performance on such topics. What is reported is a difference in students' disposition, "particularly towards new mathematical experiences" (p. 403). To be more specific, the undergraduates were able to give examples of linear spaces beyond real vector spaces whereas the school students could not. In one way this is not surprising from experiential grounds, but still fitting a theory on objects of differing type strongly suggests that an axiomatic system has been appropriated. If a characterization of "advanced mathematics" is desired, working according to a set of axioms is one of the most convincing candidates. In David Tall's characterization of "Three Worlds of Mathematics," the third world deals with the nature of mathematics based on axiomatic systems; in Tall (2004), it is stated: "This I have called the 'formal-axiomatic world' or 'formal world', for short. It turns previous experiences on their heads, working not with familiar objects of experience, but with axioms that are carefully formulated to define mathematical structures in terms of specified properties. Other properties are then deduced by formal proof to build a sequence of theorems" (pp. 30–31). From this perspective, then, it becomes crucial to scrutinize the character and role of "mathematical structure," and this will form a major topic of this chapter.

In discussing mathematical structure, it is evident that differing agendas can be pursued. Our particular approach will be rather coarse: we aim to seek out facets of structure that underlie the formal-axiomatic world. But we will be interested also in aspects of structure supporting mathematical thought from a more naturalistic or instrumental platforms, representing at large the usual practices found at school. Hence we envisage that by discerning two broad "types" of structure teachers will be more equipped in explaining to their students what is at issue in the transition to university study.

In suggesting a "world" representing "advanced mathematics" there should be an appreciation of what types of activities would be promoted. In this respect, there is a significant shift in how questions are posed. Instead of tasks with the command "find" (or the like), most now have the command "show" or "prove." Instead of an answer, the output is an appropriate argument respecting the laws of logic and the standards and conventions set in the working technical language. In practical terms, though, the real crux lies in the processes of drawing out the structure linking the premises and the proposed inference. Also, in an environment driven by axiomatic systems, the motivation behind forming definitions tends to be traceable in their potential in furthering mathematical theory. Because of the prominent role played by equivalent statements in advanced mathematics, there are many cases where the status of proof and definition can be interchanged. This means that an exhaustive discussion on proof cannot be made without an accompanying discussion on definition.

This chapter then considers three related themes—namely mathematical structure, proof and definitions—all taken from an educational viewpoint. As the literature on the character and role of structure is rather diverse, we devote two sections to the subject. The first represents our own outlook according to our particular purposes; the second attempts to give a broader account of the different ways that other researchers have approached the issue of structure, but by necessity the discourse is selective. Next is a section concerning proof, succeeded by one on definitions. For these two sections we have a dual aim: to give a sample of the lines that recent educational literature has taken on proof and definition, and then to discuss the extent the studies referred to reveal thinking in terms of structure. As many of the studies mentioned do not have an explicit agenda on the topic of structure, the second aim is achieved at a rather attributive level only. In the concluding section, a little is said on mathematical theory building vis-à-vis structure and on the practical educational benefits in taking a structural perspective.

ON STRUCTURE IN MATHEMATICS

From philosophical, psychological, and educational sources it is seen that there are many slants taken on the character of structure in mathematics. Given this, it is in place to explain the role of structure vis-à-vis this particular chapter. Indeed, as the chapter deals with topics concerning proof and definitions, the pertinence to structure might not be so immediate and needs some explanation.

In this, we start with a simple example. In Rickart (1996) there is an anecdote about an occasion when the author asked his young son this succession of questions: How many prongs are there on his fork? What is the number of spaces between the prongs? On imaging a fork with any number of prongs how many spaces are there? The child immediately answered each question correctly. The author later relates this incident to structure, or structure sense, and indeed as a basic exemplar. The fact that the child was able to answer a question on a property of some imaginary object was taken as evidence of this. The author did not pursue the encounter further at the time, though. Let us propose a hypothetical follow-up. First we might ask the child *why* the number of spaces is one less than the number of the prongs. Possibly the child would answer in a way indicating that the answer simply comes from an assumption from the experienced case of four prongs, or else give reasoning embracing all the cases. The latter would suggest structural apprehension more than the former. The child may explain that each space "goes" with the prong to its immediate left, so the prong to the extreme right is not associated to a space. The idea of a one-to-one correspondence then underlies the explanation. Now we stray beyond what one could expect from the child in raising the question: If you forget about the spaces and prongs, can you still retain the argument used outside its original context? Via some mathematical terminology you can. The prong and space case is an instance of the following: Suppose that for the finite set A and the set B with b an element of B there is a bijection between A and $B - \{b\}$, then $|A| = |B| - 1$.

The motive in going through the example was to illustrate that structure takes two forms: there is structure that is identified in the environment that which one is working on, and there is structure that is specified by a property without being explicit to the circumstances for which the property holds. The first form is accessible by young students, but the second depends on appreciation of given abstract definitions leaning to the axiomatic character of mathematics typically met at the tertiary level. However, there can be a meeting between the two forms; in particular, taking specific instantiations of a structure that has a formal character can help to explain why the structure is discerned. For example, the plane isometries that preserve a plane figure are often called the *symmetries of the figure* and hold the group conditions. The abstract structure of the definition of a group then can be used to define symmetry in other situations (via group actions).

In talking about these two forms of structure we acknowledge that we are being coarse. Indeed when the child imagines the situation of a fork having any number of prongs it could be said that an intermediate shift in the comprehension of the structure occurs. Then we have three stages that bear some similarities to a hierarchy on thinking in terms of structure due to Van Hiele (1986); here descriptive, relational and theoretical levels are distinguished. But from the vantage of advanced mathematics the main interest is what lies at the theoretical level, and for this a detailed discussion of structure at other levels is not a priority.

Even though the mathematics education literature is aware of these two major forms of structure—one based on perception and observation, the other on imposing certain conditions and what follows in consequence—from our reading there is little that attempts to build a model incorporating both. This is rather surprising. Both highlight thinking that deals with organizational aspects in instigating argumentation. Observations often come in the form of identifying correspondences, and conditions often allude to restrictions put on (formal) functions. In this respect, organizing argument around aspects of invariance often comes to the fore.

Let us illustrate. We consider the geometric mean and the arithmetic mean of a finite set of real numbers. Let n be the number of elements in the set. The two means have structure imposed on them by their definitions, but allow also some informal interpretation. For instance, the arithmetic mean equals the constant value were you to imagine that all the elements had the same contribution to the total. Also, note that the two averages have completely the same structure but applied to two different operations; this is evident as if the word *arithmetic* is replaced by *geometric* in the informal interpretation nothing else is changed (apart from the value of the total). A standard theorem states if there are at least two different numbers contained in the set then the arithmetic mean is greater to the geometric mean. One approach in proving the inequality is as following: note that there must be an element x_1 with value greater than the arithmetic mean and another x_2 with value less. Consider their distances from the arithmetic mean, and take the least; denote it by d. Now we take a "new" set; elements x_1 and x_2 are replaced by $x_1 - d$ and $x_2 + d$, the others are unchanged. By design, the arithmetic mean is preserved, and it is guaranteed that an element in the new set, but not in the old, takes the value of the arithmetic mean. The effect on the geometric mean has to be determined; the geometric mean increases or decreases depending on the sign of $(x_1 - d)(x_2 + d) - x_1 x_2$. This expression reduces to $d[(x_1 - x_2) - d]$, and as $(x_1 - x_2) - d$ is positive by construction, the geometric mean always increases. Now recur the action until the resulting set consists of just one element, the arithmetic mean "repeated" n times. In this case, the arithmetic mean equals the geometric mean; we have shown that the geometric mean of the original set is less than that for the final set, so the result has been proved. To summarize, for any set the strategy is to form a (finite) sequence of sets (starting with that set) such that the arithmetic mean is preserved, and the sequence is made in such a way to successively increase the number of elements having the value of the arithmetic mean until all elements have it; we have deliberately driven things towards what we know and can handle. In this, the crafting of conditions to avail a construction (i.e. the sequence of sets), the identification and using of relationships, and the organizing of argumentation around aspects of invariance are very much in evidence. Here we note that the usage of the required symbolism is relatively light; a sense of structure brings efficiency in the employment of notation.

The perspective of structure that we take admits intuitive ideas modeled into available channels of mathematical expression as well as imposed definitional constructions. For both cases, we do not think of structure as an inflexible base for thought, but rather structure supports the making of constructions that have significance in raising mathematical issues and then how to deal with these issues. Many of the issues would concern establishing proposed properties, so lean towards the proof tradition. The emphasis on constructions involves definition making at various levels. Also we deem factors of presentation important, as these depend on a good grasp of the workable technical language for which its efficacy in turn depends on structural appreciation.

We contend that a structural outlook can be profitable in analyzing students' behavior in proof making/reading, and in designing/handling definitions. But a major concern of this chapter is to give a résumé account of the current educational literature on the teaching and learning of topics that concern proof and definition at high school and university levels. In the relevant sections, what has been said about structure often takes a background role, but we believe that the reader would recognize factors that are consistent to the structural viewpoint as described above. In this, the reader may care to consider the extant that the implied structure leans towards the formal-axiomatic world.

STRUCTURE AS IT IS DISCUSSED IN THE LITERATURE

We discuss how the mathematics education community treats the notion of structure in general. Of course the word *structure* is often taken casually, but there is continued interest to feature "structure" prominently in frameworks or as the main topic of study. We start by stating chosen descriptors of structure from the literature.

The following characterization is due to Mason, Stephens, & Watson (2009):

> We take mathematical structure to mean the identification of general properties which are instantiated in particular situations as relationships between elements. . . . a relationship is some connection or association between elements or subsets which have been themselves been discerned.
>
> (p. 10)

This is very much in line with the first form of structural appreciation mentioned in the previous section; for example, the appearance of the word *properties* (rather than "conditions" or "consequences") suggests that a relationship is intuited. Not surprisingly, here mathematical structure is regarded relevant to all age bands.

As a global description of structure can seem elusive, some expositions of structure deliberately select topics deemed particularly pertinent to aspects of structure. For example, in Niss (2006) the themes selected are: "The formation, nature, and role of mathematical concepts; the need for and role of mathematical proof; and symbolism and formalism in mathematics" (p. 51). This choice has similarities to our position stated in the previous section. Concepts and definitions are intimately related, with an interest in which is posited first. What qualifies an argument as proof has prompted long debate between mathematicians, philosophers, and educators, and it is perhaps best conducted in terms of the role of structure in mathematics. Finally, the respective roles of symbolism and formalism are discussed, leading up to the following claim:

> Mastery of symbolism and formalism requires students to develop a kind of "controlled schizophrenia" between intuition (and sense-making) and formalism that allows them to switch between the two so as to distinguish between interpretation and meaning, on the one hand, and notation and rules, on the other hand.
>
> (Niss, 2006, p. 61)

This is in accordance with our presentation of the proof concerning arithmetic and geometric means given earlier.

We move on to another definition. It is taken from Novotná & Hoch (2008):

> The term *algebraic structure* is usually used in abstract algebra and may be understood to consist of a set closed under one or more operations, satisfying some axioms.
>
> (p. 94)

This involves a specialized form of structure, but is consistent to many mathematicians' first interpretation of the word. In this context, structure prompts working from given conditions that leans more towards the syntactic rather than the semantic; also the focus predominately stays at the fundamentals. However, "Axioms result from necessity, not from some arbitrary decree, and this reason is often misunderstood" (Artmann, 1988, p. 23). Conception still has its role if it is agreed that it embraces the building up of insight (cf. Tall & Vinner, 1981). In this respect, mathematicians are interested to convey aspects of structure especially in drawing out issues or programs, even though they might not explicitly use the word. Below is an extract from an introductory chapter from a textbook on Group Theory:

> effect a division of the original classification problem into two parts: (i) find finite simple groups of all possible types (the 'building blocks' of finite group theory), (ii) solve the extension problem (that is, find how the building blocks fit together).
>
> (Rose, 1978, p. 9)

This extract is interesting as it has a component of analogical expression lying outside the technical language. From a formal viewpoint this component is superfluous and without meaning.

Nonetheless, the informal statements seem to stress a structural understanding and voice a long-term aim in terms of insight. This exemplifies informal language acting as a kind of meta-commentary on what is done on the formal level. This is an important factor in breaking the negative image many students harbor that university-level mathematics is just a meaningless manipulation of symbolism.

Novotná and Hoch (2008) introduce the terms *structure sense* and *algebraic structure*. Structure sense seems to represent a source of evaluation of what structural bases yield cognitively over what is merely referential to the particular mathematical field considered, here abstract algebra. Thus there is a distinction made between working from the axioms and sense making in the formal environment. From our perspective, this distinction is not made; the term *structure sense* is regarded as redundant because the word *structure* encompasses sense making anyway.

The definition of structure in Novotná and Hoch (2008) was specific to a particular mathematical domain. This suggests that it might be useful to draw up lists of arenas in mathematics and its learning and teaching that are particularly relevant to structure. The following list is due to Zalman Usiskin.

> The first mathematical structures that I think of are the obvious ones: the structures of algebra, namely groups, rings, vector spaces, fields, etc. Then there are categories, which might be thought of as structures of structures. But even the objects within these structures might be viewed as structures. For instance, a matrix is a structure of data; a network is another type of structure of data; a relation is a third type of structure.
>
> Then there are the logical structures. What follows from what? What can you prove given such and such?
>
> But there are also historical structures. This development led to that development which led to a third development, etc. These structures are not as rigorous as the structures of algebra or of logical structures, but there is a sense to them that can make them quite important for extracting meaning from a concept.
>
> There are also algorithmic structures. Algorithms are embedded in other algorithms, lead to more algorithms.
>
> There are interest structures—something reminds you of something else; that reminds you of more.
>
> There are also pedagogical structures, namely sequences and networks of activities that we put together for the purpose of a student's learning a particular bit of mathematics.
>
> So we might say that there are formal structures and informal structures. We study relationships among formal structures by looking for morphisms and other functions that might relate them. We study informal structures by looking for commonalities.
>
> (personal communication, January 2014)

This list casts a picture of remarkable variety in the role of structure and suggests various different perspectives: for example, structure as a part of mathematics, structure as a part of understanding mathematics, structure as triggering connections within mathematics, structure as playing a role in teaching. The last item arguably is closest in representing the "mean" viewpoint of educators interested in incorporating aspects of structure in their studies, without necessarily invoking the notion of a morphism.

In characterizing a notion that seems rather intangible, one legitimate approach is to summon up situations where the notion is deemed relevant and then draw out similarities in the various situations that can help in forming a characterization. Hence it is important to have lists like one drawn out by Usiskin. But in the end the sheer diversity found makes it difficult to extract commonalities. Because of this, educators are mainly interested in forming more direct general frameworks. A natural consideration here is that structural awareness promotes thinking in terms of "mathematical objects" and in how they interact. Cognitively, models of "objectification" such as Action Process Object Schema (APOS) (e.g. Cottrill, et al., 1996) can be useful for studying students' understanding of foundational concepts. Also the position taken that the status of a mathematical object is cemented when it is acted on highlights structural affordances. However, these models may be not so efficient for the appropriation of objects that rise whilst considering mathematical activities such as problem solving and designing constructions. In talking about objects, it should not be forgotten that mathematicians also use the word *entity*. Some educators take the two words as synonymous (e.g. Font, Godino & Gallardo, 2013), but elsewhere *entity* has a broader meaning. For example, in Prasada, Ferenz, and Haskell (2002) we find: "Object construals require thinking of the structure as being non-arbitrary, whereas substance construals require thinking of the structure as being arbitrary" (p. 141). This suggests that there are different levels of concreteness in structure. An entity is unspecified whereas an object is at least partially determined. So, an existential proof deals with an entity rather an object. This point is important to make as basing mathematics from an axiomatic approach can involve instances of inconsistency, i.e., cases where an axiomatic system cannot be fulfilled by any object, but before an inconsistency is established it is sensible to talk about potential entities.

Thinking in terms of objects invites analysis of "inner" structure and, by operations applied to an object, invites consideration of larger structures that contain the object. Hence an object can be thought of as being "placed" within a mathematical system, where the system can be thought of as the arena constraining the structure (Rickart, 1996). A system typically contains various types of objects, and for each type subobjects and superobjects can be specified in relation to any particular object. The structure is explored by revealing correspondences between the various families of objects concerned (e.g., Mamona-Downs & Downs, 2004).

However this picture is not really quite complete. There is always a drive to create new objects related to the old to enhance the scope of the structure. An example is the notion of equivalence and equivalent relations. Equivalence plays a crucial part of structural thinking because it determines which objects are thought to lie naturally in the same body or class. This determination is made on abstract structural grounds. In Hamdan (2006), students are asked to make meaningful connections between some notions that are pertinent to the idea of equivalent relation; partition, equivalence classes, and the fiber structure of a function.

Also it is limiting to think that structure is delineated by a mathematical system. One role of structure is to extract method or technique from a particular argument or mathematical situation in readiness for instantiation elsewhere. This issue is sometimes referred to as the *transfer problem* (e.g., Lobato & Siebert, 2002). Related to this, the same problem posed in various mathematical topics can bring out common structural understanding between them (Kondratieva, 2011). Also there are functional devices that mathematically determine whether two objects share common structure, like isomorphisms, homomorphisms, and other "morphisms." An account of the history of mathematics structure vis-à-vis isomorphism can be found in Timmermans (2012). Informal forms of isomorphism are sometimes discussed in the mathematics education literature (e.g., Greer & Harel, 1998), and there are several studies extant on student's understanding of formal isomorphism, for example Weber and Alcock (2004) for group isomorphism and Ebert, Ebert, and Klin (2004) for graph isomorphism.

Our current focus is on mathematical objects; in the previous section we talked about constructions. It could be argued that the notion of a mathematical construction is inherently dependent on realizing objects. For example, in the argument we gave showing that the arithmetic mean is greater or equal to the geometric mean, a process is made which when finished represents a finite sequence of sets; the recognition of the sequence means that an object has been realized. The process underlying the object is deliberately designed to determine the inequality, so the process/object acts as a construction. Stressing the object component helps in forming the original strategy.

As we have seen, the play and relativity concerning mathematical objects is highly intricate; not much of this is caught at the school level. The role of structure is to yield an overall coherent view of the system considered; as put by Dreyfus and Eisenberg (1996):

> there is a central core of concepts and relationships that, once grasped and integrated, allow one to organize the entire topic and conceive its unity. It can be observed that once a student gets to this stage, the amount of knowledge involved seems to collapse; examples that were completely disjoint now turn out to be essentially identical.
>
> (p. 267)

ON PROOF

There is much latitude in interpreting the character of proof. One factor in this is whether mathematics primarily concerns the attainment of results, or proposes potential consequences from the givens and then asks for verification. The latter fits better to the proof "culture." Further, from a perspective in building up and presenting mathematical theory, it is convenient to simply state a likely consequence as if it were no longer provisional. Hence typically the command "prove" occurs far more often than "prove or disprove" in exercises found in mathematics textbooks. In this respect, it is convenient to employ two different words to serve a distinction; these words are *proposition* and *statement*. Here the word *statement* is not taken as in its usual usage in logic, but a shortening for *authoritative statement*, i.e., a "true" statement for which its truth was established in the past. A proposition can be refuted, but a statement is *assumed* to be true. For a proposition, an argument is made to decide its status (i.e., true or false). For a statement, the argument does not deal with determining a final state, but acts as a channel for verification and articulation. For many students this can be difficult to swallow; it is bad enough to impose a proposition that they did not have any part in forming, but then further to suggest a priori that the proposition is true, as in the case of a statement, might well seem excessive. A format is made: state the premises, state an inference, and only after demonstrate the inference. Unsurprisingly, some educators advocate a characterization of proof avoiding such formatting. Such a characterization often involves the making of a conjecture and then giving an argument to resolve its status. For example, Pedemonte (2007) focuses on the "cognitive unity" between the reasoning in building up a conjecture and in the construction of an allied "proof"; in many cases a "proof" can seem more natural if the content matter of the relevant theorem was indeed first raised in the form of a conjecture. However, the format is too pervasive for educators to try to sidestep completely as it constitutes a major part of how mathematics is documented at the research level.

From now on mostly we will discuss proof in the context of demonstrating statements. As the statement is assumed to be true, the onus is on finding a suitable and efficient argument. The center of attention is on the argument itself. This situation can make students uneasy and uncertain about what argumentation qualifies as proof. There are educational studies dealing with this issue; one tactic employed is to distribute a list of given arguments where the items differ in the degree of validity and completeness, and ask students for their opinion to the status of each item vis-à-vis proof. For example, Weber (2010) found that senior undergraduates do not regard empirical work as proof, but most accepted diagrammatic argumentation, and are readily swayed by familiar form than content. Also they tended not to check seemingly deductive argumentation carefully, and even if an error is recognized sometimes its ramifications on the basic structure are not appreciated or considered.

The part that proof takes in modeling physical or "real-like" situations can be confusing for students. In Martinez & Brizuela (2009) there is a summary of a framework due to Chevallard (1989). According to this the main stages of modeling are (1) Identification of Variables and Parameters, (2) Establishing Relations between Variables and Parameters, and (3) Working the Model to Establish New Relationships. Also there is a distinction made between the intra-mathematical context and the extra-mathematical context. Extra-mathematical modeling concerns determining a mathematical system to accommodate the structure implicit in the context. For example, the classic problem of tiling the chessboard by 2 × 1 tiles with two opposite corner squares removed is readily reasoned through as having no solution by imagining that for each tile one of its squares is marked, the other not. But the argument has perceptual aspects, so it cannot strictly be considered as a proof; the argument, though, can be modeled into the environment of a Cartesian product and *only in that environment* a proof is available (Mamona-Downs & Downs, 2011). In general, modeling from the phenomenal world can *involve* mathematical proof but the processes in casting the model itself lie beyond what mathematical expression can allow, so modeling and proof are two separate types of accomplishment.

Since a statement given to students typically is assumed established, they can ask about their need to prove it. As the mathematics becomes more abstract, though, the givens and an ensuing statement can easily become detached from each other cognitively. To state, for instance, that "a compact set in a metric space is equivalent to a set satisfying the condition that any open cover of the set has a refinement to a finite cover" can be disorienting and seem arbitrary. (Even if it's true, so what?) The proof has an explanatory role *why* such strange looking connections occur and what significance they have beyond verification. There is a well-circulated anecdote about Pierre Deligne who on the completion of an involved proof on the blackboard made a plea to his audience: "I would be grateful if anyone who has understood this demonstration would explain it to me." A proof often can seem utilitarian rather than carrying any real sense of purpose. Recently there has been an interest in the literature about the "purposes" of proof; one that figures prominently is to make the premise, consequence, and proof appear as a single cognitive unit (cf., Barnard, 1998). Another rests on the simple observation that some proofs can be parsed for general techniques that can be extracted from the argumentation supporting the proof. This topic of course is hardly new to mathematic education; an influential study by de Villiers with the title: "The role and function of proof in mathematics" was published in 1990. But a paper by a mathematician, Rav (1999), talking about the possible role that proof has in raising insight, connections, and generalization as well as technique extraction gave the area new momentum (e.g., Hanna & Barbeau, 2008). The message is that the total knowledge of mathematics accrues from proof itself as much as it does from the statements that are validated. A "good" proof is not simply judged from its explanatory power but also from the tools that it provides; hence there are influences towards meaning in abstraction and increased functionality at the same time. Creating tools involves reorganization of the existing specific structure in a form that can be applied elsewhere. Students are rarely informed about such purposes in the course of instruction; however, this omission could be regarded as a secondary concern in the face of the difficulties they display with proof in the first instance.

There is yet a further reason why students do not feel comfortable with proof. The whole mathematical glossary can seem to be prearranged in order to facilitate proof (Downs & Mamona-Downs, 2005). An impression can be left that a vacuous intellectual game is being played. To defuse this, a sense of building mathematical theory must be distilled (cf., Balacheff, 2010), and in particular how definitions are decided on in order to base the rest of the work. The role of definitions will be discussed in the next section. Keeping a sense of theoretical development can help students, provided they are capable of thinking in the formal language. Often they do not have this facility (Thurston, 1995), and this lack can be debilitating especially at the fundamental stages (cf., Moore, 1994).

We continue by discussing difficulties in the *actual practice* in forming and reading proof. First, students have to fathom what a task is asking for. Typically, there are two separate parts, one setting out the conditions and the other a consequence. Both have to be understood, and because of the formal language used it can be challenging just to comprehend what is being proposed. A part of the challenge lies in "unraveling" the logical form of statements (Selden, McKee & Selden, 2010). From a study of mathematicians' practice concerning proof (Wilkerson-Jerde & Wilensky, 2011), mathematicians tend to "deconstruct" the ideas implicit in a statement to identify its subcomponents. If students do not do this, they are impeded in conceiving a meaningful mathematical issue that would motivate their future thinking. A second difficulty is due to many students harboring an image of proof as a sequence of deductive steps getting from "A" to "B"; this leaves them to have the impression that logic automatically drives the direction of a proof. This is not helpful, especially in initializing a proof: logical considerations are at play when constructing a proof but logic on its own cannot support points of strategy. There is an important problem-solving element in undertaking proof (Mamona-Downs & Downs, 2013). However, the current way that problem solving is taught tends to avoid settings that are overtly theoretical. It is not surprising, then, that there are reports that courses in problem solving do not transfer well to other courses (Yusof & Tall, 1999).

From our perspective of proof, rules of predicate logic must be explicitly respected. But students can find logical aspects in the construction of a proof difficult, and can accept argumentation that is glaringly faulty. The problem is mainly due to the lack of a sense of meaning in the working language and of structural awareness. It is difficult for a student to understand what counts as an implication, as often what is involved in passing from one line to the next in an argument is far more than what can be justified from a single deductive step. Also an implication can take different logical forms; see Durand-Guerrier (2003). The appreciation and handling of multiple quantifiers are especially troublesome; see for example Pinto (1996). Indirect proof often confounds student understanding. Proof by contradiction is particularly taxing on the cognition; you have to argue "positively" on a proposition expected to be false. Leron (1985) suggests that some cases of proof by contradiction can be replaced by a constructive procedure; he states that this has an extra advantage in terms of proof purposes as mentioned above. However, proof by contradiction is a tactic too pervasive in "advanced" mathematics to bypass. In Antonini and Mariotti (2006), a closer analysis of the logic that supports proof by contradiction is made together with the resultant demands on students' comprehension.

Often in tackling a task it is essential to identify a "means of entry" stimulating a line in argumentation, and this is equally true for tasks in a proof format as it is for those that are not. Such means of entry emerge through observations of relationships, perhaps realized after some exploratory work. Students have to be persistent in trying out various ideas, something that demands commitment. After the initial breakthrough, provisional further stages in the process of proving likely would be forthcoming. For example, according to Raman, Sandefur, Birky, Campbell, & Somers (2009) a student starts with identifying key ideas that initialize thinking about the emerging proof, then develops technical handles to allow coherent writing and finally reformulates this to achieve a perceived standard form. Alcock (2010) discusses the modes of thinking that students need to be successful provers from a mathematician's point of view; these are termed *instantiation, structural thinking, creative thinking*, and *critical thinking*. For teaching purposes, the opinion was that instructors should place more stress on the structural component, but all four should be present and coordinated.

Even if a student attains a good relational and instrumental understanding of a proof, she/he still might have problems in writing down the proof in what is regarded as an acceptable form. Two main difficulties are first, "translating" ideas into an established mathematical glossary, and, second, deciding what parts of a proof can be safely missed out (e.g., when the term "it is clear that" is sanctioned). Such presentational concerns can influence how students think about proof in general. Putting emphasis on presentation suggests that the role of a proof is not just about verifying the statement, but also about verifying its own grounds of argumentation. Also a presentation can seem to resemble a documentary artifact. But producing such an artifact presumably would involve an act of mediated restructuring. There are some papers extant on how lecturers present proof in their courses, but little about the processes in refining argument to a presentational style. For example, Mills (2011) reports on lecturers' expectations in how students should react whilst a proof is being presented; sometimes students are required to provide factual information, sometimes to contribute to the forming of key ideas.

Weber (2012) interviewed mathematicians about how they presented proofs at class; one result was that the interviewees used superficial methods to assess students' understanding of a proof, perhaps taking the final form of the presentation too much as a model.

We end this section by saying a little about proof reading. The reading of a proof can be done at various levels, from parsing the proof to a thorough reading. For parsing, we agree with a statement made by Polya (1954): "The advanced reader who skips parts that appear to him too elementary may miss more than the less advanced reader who skips parts that appear to him too complex" (p. xi). However, from now we restrict our attention to comprehensive readings. Evidently it is difficult to study directly students' thinking processing whilst reading proof, as there is not a concrete "output," but there are indirect methods to measure the level of comprehension. Weinberg and Wiesner (2011) report that students' reading is constrained by the "closed structure" found in textbooks and the sense of authority that they cast. In Weber and Mejia-Ramos (2011) mathematicians are interviewed about their habits and practice in reading proofs, including some points of didactical significance; line-by-line reading is distinguished from a reading identifying and relating the overarching methods in a proof. The latter is conjectured to involve the formation of "structural-intuitive evidence" where a mental appraisal is available to check the plausibility of the formal argument. Mejia-Ramos, Fuller, Weber, Rhoads, & Samkoff, (2012) give a model of the components in proof reading, but it is rather vague in its implementation. Any structural consideration involved in the original forming of the proof should be recoverable but not necessarily on reading merely at the literal level. The research area of proof reading really is still at its infancy, especially in how reading impacts students' ability in processing the production of proof.

ON CONCEPTUALIZATION AND DEFINITIONS

In an influential paper, Tall and Vinner (1981) introduce the notions of *concept image* and *concept definition*. Here the concept image consists of "the total cognitive structure that is associated with the concept, which includes all the mental pictures and associated properties and processes ideally," whereas the concept definition is taken as "a form of words used to specify that concept" (p. 152). The concept definition once interiorized by learners is held as a specific part of the concept image. In contrast, in Davis and Vinner (1986), the term *concept image* is distinguished from the formal definition, and the term *concept definition* is not mentioned. The first of these two papers refers to insight drawn from the definition itself as well as initial intuitions that precede its formation. The second is more concerned with how the initial intuitions arise in the first place, and how instruction has a role in garnering them; from this perspective, "seemingly unavoidable misconceptual stages" appear. For both there seems to be an assumption that the definition has already been decided on by some form of authority. More recently there is a tendency to portray simultaneous development on "definition construction processes" and "concept formation processes" (Ouvrier-Buffet, 2006). Hence we have a situation where design directed towards instrumental understanding and design directed towards relational understanding meet; a growing appreciation of underlying structure is important in this wedding.

There are numerous educational studies reporting that some students can recapture by themselves a form of the formal definition through guided reinvention. Some deal with fundamental definitions, some deal with adapting known definitions in new domains, others with cementing past knowledge previously held only at an intuitive level. The last can bring in surprises to students; for example, several papers take the position that $(-8)^{1/3}$ should be regarded as undefined in the context of the school curriculum (e.g., Woo & Yim, 2008).

Typical influences in such student-centered recovery of established definitions are Realistic Mathematics Education (Gravemeijer, 1999); the use of metaphor (Lakoff & Nunez, 2000); the production, retrieval, and analysis of examples; and adapting conditions to cope with unexpected contingencies and change in the conceptual focus, rather in the spirit of Lakatos (1976). A good exemplar of this recent trend is given in Zandieh and Rasmussen (2010), where students are requested to give definitions of planar triangles and then to adapt these for the sphere. From the data collected, the authors propose a framework with four strands: situational, referential, general, and formal activity. The situational and referential activities tend to deal with existing aspects of the concept image; the general and formal tend to expand it to more unfamiliar territory.

Currently there is a surge in the amount of research devoted to students' ability to exemplify effectively, or what students can make out of examples that they already have at hand. We recognize that exemplification is important in many situations especially in the context of conjectures, but here we are only interested in its significance vis-à-vis definition. Traditionally, central formal definitions are presented without much commentary at the lecture hall, but can be followed by giving examples in order to orient the student. Dahlberg and Housman (1997) conducted a study where an unfamiliar definition is given, and it was shown that the students who were generating *their own examples* were the better in garnering primal conceptual input. This suggests that students' generation of examples is important in initializing the concept image after the definition is stated. For reform-oriented instruction, examples precede the definition. Students are challenged to extract the essential structure common in the examples to construct the (desired) definition. The richness and reliability of the sources of the examples (student-generated or otherwise) depends on the strength of the existing concept image. Some educators talk about the importance for a student to build up an (individual or collective) "example space" for a particular mathematical topic where the form of the definitions made is influenced by theoretical considerations; an influential work in this area is Watson and Mason (2005). Curley and Meehan (2010) designed a frame that gave opportunities for students to form a wide net of examples for various topics in Real Analysis; it was not clear whether the activity encouraged accurate portrayals of the relevant concept definitions, but the exercise helped students to appreciate some aspects of the mathematical field better. Other authors report that example use is more conducive to some mathematical fields than others (e.g., Zaslavsky & Shir, 2005). This is not surprising; for example, when the theory is flowing smoothly in dealing with a succession of linked mathematical issues (as in a first course in complex analysis) the definitions formed are made in order to serve the theoretical drive, and examples tend to be demoted to the status of illustration and application.

Edwards and Ward (2004) state that students have difficulties in understanding the very nature of mathematical definitions, and "should have experiences that focus on the use of mathematical definitions and experiences in the process of defining" (p. 422). The same authors caution, though, that activities designed for generating definitions can reduce to "games that are won if the student can guess what the teacher is thinking" (Edward & Ward, 2008, p. 230). The question "Are students truly motivated when asked to participate in defining activities?" is an authentic concern. Related to this, the processes in forming definitions can be described in terms of phenomenology; here, a major component is "intention" where the intention is expounded from intuitive sources, and the definition is either organized to meet the intention or is scrutinized in terms of how well it represents the intention or explains why and how the original intention must be compromised (e.g., Asghari, 2004).

At school, definitions can be descriptive, admit perceptual factors, and allow hidden assumptions. Students enter university and face a completely different climate. We illustrate this. The most natural definition for a quadrilateral includes "crossed quadrilaterals," but most students do not want to regard a crossed quadrilateral as a quadrilateral. In fieldwork conducted by De Villiers (1998), some students tried to sum up the interior angles of the four vertices of a crossed quadrilateral, but from their working through they were getting the same total as gotten from "ordinary quadrilaterals"; so it seemed that their attempt in distinguishing the two was failing. The usual image of what is an interior angle is disturbed when you apply it to a precise definition for a crossed quadrilateral. The point here is that the students knew that they needed a further condition in distinguishing crossed quadrilaterals, but they failed to readjust a definition aspect, which ensured that the condition was applied consistently to both ordinary and crossed quadrilaterals. In introducing the condition, the students were working maturely, but not so when they took interior angles perceptually against the usual convention (i.e., taking angles consistently anti-clockwise).

Sometimes the role of a definition is weak cognitively; the definition is just there for mathematical endorsement. For example, a (real) sequence is defined as a function of the natural numbers into the reals; what is really conveyed is an (infinite but "countable") ordered list of real numbers. This informal reading even invites a special symbolism; instead of the standard formatting of function, i.e., f: $N \rightarrow R$ and f(n) for the value of f at $n \in N$, we typically write down (a_n) for the sequence and a_n to denote the value of the nth term. The adapted form accentuates the idea of "position" in the ordering of the terms (Vollrath, 1994). Form in general is an important theme vis-à-vis definition; to illustrate, there is no real difference between sequences and series, but the theory from the "series" perspective proves to be very distinct with far-going ramifications. (Students can have difficulty in accepting partial sums, so the identification of a series as a sequence would not be realized, see Martínez-Planell, Gonzalez, DiCristina, & Acevedo, 2012.) Also, although the presentation of a formal definition tends to be stated in its most utilitarian form, the definition can be reformulated to stress other purposes. For example, let us consider limits of a function in the Reals. An alternative version to the usual statement of the definition is as follows: f has limit l at x iff for every interval centered at l there is an interval centered at x for which, except possibly at x itself, f maps into that interval. Such a reading might be more conducive in extending the definition to other systems (Mamona-Downs, 2014).

Another way the relativity of definitions crops up is in the context of (logically) equivalent definitions. Here a definitional statement implies another statement, and conversely this second statement implies the first. Then you can regard any one of the two to be the definition and the other as a consequence; any result gotten from either is validated for both. This allows switching of perspectives that is completely mathematically controlled. Equivalent definitions can be effected by adapting the existing conditions in the same system, or can be more radical in equating the roles of two sets of properties taken from two different systems. (The many forms of the completeness property of the reals illustrate both cases; see Bergé, 2008). In Parameswaran (2010), some mathematicians expressed that "equivalent reformulations of definitions enrich understanding." Preferences from a set of equivalent definitions on epistemic, cognitive, and instructional grounds are examined in Wilhelmi, Godino, and Lacasta (2007). The paper refers to problem-solving techniques afforded by the various choices of definition available and discusses evoked meanings from operative and discursive viewpoints as well as whether they are partial or holistic in character. Of course, students may create more than one definition based on contrasting aspects of their concept image, especially when working in groups. A natural question to ask them is whether the definitions are different cognitively, and if they are equivalent; the study in Leikin and Winicki-Landman (2000) follows this direction.

In our discussion it is clear that definitions carry differing role and status. In Ouvrier-Buffet (2011) a typology of definitions due to Lakatos is described. Three types are distinguished: naïve definitions, zero-definitions, and proof-generated definitions. Naïve definitions are to specify and name, and they do not evolve; a zero-definition is one that is designed to respect original conceptual bases, a proof-generated definition either rises from "monster barring" activities or when the conceptual base is compromised by a need to prove a desired theorem. In other words, we "tinker" the definition in order for the theorem to be provable, an approach suggesting that one is responding to structural considerations.

In general, the topic of definitions and definition making is central to structural thinking; we lay down the "laws" that our working must adhere to in an arena that has to be specified. Also, defining has a design aspect in making such laws workable and in harmony with the original intent; this can lead to very interesting aspects in modeling. There are many types of definitions, depending on their envisaged purpose, giving much scope for educational research on the student response. Students' understanding of equivalent definitions is particularly important to study, as it exposes different bases of structure with differing working potential; see e.g., Mamona-Downs and Megalou (2013).

EPILOGUE

This chapter has a narrower scope than the corresponding chapters in the two previous editions of the *Handbook*, and takes a rather different form. All three versions, though, highlight the role of structure in Advanced Mathematical Thinking. The present work, though, is more directed to themes explicitly concerning proof and definition, and in consequence topics such as affect, a wider vision of explaining and reasoning, and the current state of established educational theories are not emphasized as before. We contend that the most vibrant areas in Advanced Mathematical Thinking research today concern guided reinvention of proof and conceptually based definitions, the need for students to read given proofs in a proactive manner, and the need for students to experience the interplay (or even interchange) between definitions and what is proved. In this light, it is heartening that many educators now are communicating with working mathematicians, throwing light on mathematicians' beliefs and practice in their teaching.

Even in the proof/definition perspective that we adopt there are omissions. For example, we do not discuss the difference between the material that the instructor presents and the activities that students are asked to perform in their assignments. Some tasks put to students would indeed involve forming a proof of a statement beyond those presented in class, but others would be to test basic understanding, to give exercise in procedures and algorithms, and to *apply* established statements/theorems (for which a proof may be required, or may not). Some educators claim that the activities given to students in the typical traditional tertiary-level class lean too much on procedural work and on memory of bookwork. Of course, one would like students to be active in creating mathematics that is new to them, but a lot of practice and cultivating a retentive memory are also beneficial in such an accumulative discipline as mathematics. This leads to another theme not directly tackled in this chapter: even though there is some reference to positioning within a mathematical theory, the forming of theories in mathematics is not dealt with as a separate topic. Theory making could be regarded as being complementary to proof and definition in completing a whole vista of the role of structure in mathematics. For example, a metric space naturally leads to the notion of an open set; working with open sets one soon obtains a reformation (concerning proof) that is independent of the original conditions of a metric space. This is accommodated in a more general definition of open sets that motivates the notion of topological spaces where the original conceptual base of "distance" is now redundant. It can be a challenge for an educator to undertake a study on students' apprehension of mathematical theory as it unfolds; for successful students the current knowledge must be malleable, with its content filtered for local usage as well as for deciding what to retain on the long term. It can be difficult to deliver an introduction of what a course is about because much of the language needed has to be developed *over* the course. There are manifold ways to nuance the presentation of the theory, but perhaps it is unrealistic to treat a whole theory through student activities as espoused by advocates of reinvention. However, when the instructor dictates the direction of the material, there is a danger that the student finishes a course without appreciating the whole "tissue" of what has been achieved. There are very few expositions of mathematical theory building in the literature; one that has been well circulated is due to Chevallard (1998), in which "theory" is one component out of four in a "mathematical organization." The notion of a mathematical organization stresses the different choices in the material that covers a course. In contrast, in tertiary-level mathematics the sense of developing a single theory is often strong enough to carry it through the entire course. But are students conscious of it? The topic of students' appreciation of mathematical theory should have more attention than it presently has.

We continue with some reflections more geared to actual teaching practices. It is one thing to ponder the importance of structure in mathematics in a rather detached fashion; it is another to translate this into practical suggestions of pedagogical value. In this regard, we revisit the contention that the present problem solving agenda is inadequate to cope with many theoretical settings in mathematics; such claims have contributed to recent expressions of doubt about the viability of regarding problem solving as an autonomous topic (e.g., Sweller, Clark & Kirschner, 2010). We consider that what is currently understood by the term *problem solving* needs enrichment from a structural standpoint. In this one central factor would be an investigation of how constructions are conceived of and employed; this done, one could consider the resultant adaptations needed on the established mainstays in the theory of problem solving such as heuristics and control. Constructions are interesting in that they can merge definitional concerns with those in developing tools for the furtherance of argumentation. Another factor to keep in mind is that the presentation of a proof tends to repress the processes in designing those constructions on which the proof depends. This has prompted some researchers to advocate a proof presentation that lays out its content in a top-to-bottom fashion (e.g., Leron, 1983). The field remains under-researched, however. It is important to study how well undergraduates are equipped to make their own constructions, and how to support them in this type of activity.

We end up by returning to the theme of guided reinvention. This is a possible strategy to ease the transition from the mathematics learned at high school to that at university. The two types of structure (observational and formal) that we mention at the start of the chapter would blend to a degree. But we have also pointed to its infeasibility as a general instructional practice. When learning tertiary-level mathematics, the rate that new ideas are introduced and the changes in how mathematical knowledge is documented necessitate a new mode of processing from given material; from this point of view it is a luxury to prompt students to produce ideas new to them but established in theory, and in the long run it can go against the general enculturation in how ideas evolve and intertwine. We think that guided reinvention is yielding some interesting results, but in the end it has to be tailored within some larger model of scaffolding (i.e., first give support, then fade it out).

REFERENCES

Alcock, L. (2010). Mathematicians' perspectives on teaching and learning of proof. *Research in Collegiate Mathematics Education, CBMS Issues in Mathematics Education, 16,* 63–91.

Antonini, S., & Mariotti, M. A. (2006). Abduction and the explanation of anomalies: The case of proof by contradiction. *Proceedings of the CERME, 6,* 322–331. Lyon, France.

Artmann, B. (1988). *The concept of number: From quartenions to monads and topological fields.* New York/ Chichester: John Wiley & Sons.

Asghari, H.A. (2004). Organizing with a focus on defining. A phenomenographic approach. In A.B. Fuglestad, (Ed.) *Proceedings of the 28th PME Conference, 2,* 63–70. Bergen, Norway.

Balacheff, N. (2010). Bridging knowing and proving in mathematics: A didactical perspective. In G. Hanna, H.N. Jahnke, & H. Pulte (Eds.) *Explanation and proof in mathematics. Philosophical and educational Perspectives* (pp. 115–137). New York: Springer.

Barnard, T. (1998). Compressed units of mathematical thought. *Journal of Mathematical Behavior, 17*(4), 401–404.

Bergé, A. (2008). The completeness property of the set of real numbers in the transition from calculus to analysis. *Educational Studies in Mathematics, 67*(3), 217–235.

Chevallard, Y. (1989). Le passage de l'arithmétique á l'algébrique dans l' enseignement des mathématiques au college. *Petit X, 19,* 43–72.

Chevallard, Y. (1998). Analyses des practiques enseignantes et didactique des mathematics : l'approche anthropologique. *Actes de l' École d'été de la Rochelle, 19*(2), 91–118.

Cottrill, J., Dubinsky, E., Nichols, D., Schwingendorf, K., Thomas, K., & Vidakovic, D. (1996). Understanding the limit concept: Beginning with a coordinated process scheme. *Journal of Mathematical Behavior, 15*(2), 167–192.

Curley, N., & Meehan, M. (2010). Example generation exercises in an introductory analysis course. *MSOR Connections, 10*(1), 49–51.

Dahlberg, R.P., & Housman, D.L. (1997). Facilitating learning events through example generation. *Educational Studies in Mathematics, 33*(3), 283–299.

Davis, R.B., & Vinner, S. (1986). The notion of limit: Some seemingly unavoidable misconception stages. *Journal of Mathematical Behavior, 5*(3), 281–303.

De Guzmán, M., Hodgson, B.R., Robert, A., & Villani, V. (1998). Difficulties in the passage from secondary to tertiary education. In G. Fischer and U. Rehmann (Eds.), *Proceedings of the International Congress of Mathematicians*, (Vol 3., pp. 747–762). Berlin: Documenta Mathematica.

De Villiers, M. (1998). An alternative approach to proof in Dynamic Geometry. In R. Lehrer & D. Chazan (Eds.), *Designing learning environments for developing understanding of geometry and space* (pp. 369–393). Mahwah, NJ: Lawrence Erlbaum Associates.

Downs, M., & Mamona-Downs, J. (2005). The proof language as a regulator of rigor in proof, and its effect on student behavior. *Proceedings of CERME, 4*, 1748–1757. Sant Feliu de Guixols, Spain.

Dreyfus, T., & Eisenberg, T. (1996). On different facets of mathematical thinking. In R.J. Sternberg & T. Ben-Zeev (Eds.). *The nature of mathematical thinking* (pp. 253–284). Mahwah, NJ: Lawrence Erlbaum Associates.

Durand-Guerrier, V. (2003). Which notion of implication is the right one? From logical considerations to a didactic perspective. *Educational Studies in Mathematics, 53*(1), 5–34.

Ebert, C., Ebert, G., & Klin, M. (2004). From the principle of bijection to the isomorphism of structures: an analysis of some teaching paradigms in discrete mathematics. *ZDM: The International Journal on Mathematics Education, 36*(5), 172–183.

Edwards, B.S., & Ward, M.B. (2004). Surprises from mathematics education research: Student (mis)use of mathematical definitions. *The American Mathematical Monthly, 111*(5), 411–424.

Edwards, B.S., & Ward, M.B. (2008). The role of mathematical definitions in mathematics and in undergraduate mathematics courses. In M.P. Carlson & C. Rasmussen (Eds.), *Making the connection; Research and Teaching in Undergraduate Mathematics Education* (pp. 223–232). Washington, DC: Mathematical Association of America.

Font, V., Godino, J.D., & Gallardo, J. (2013). The emergence of objects from mathematical practices. *Educational Studies in Mathematics, 82*(1), 97–124.

Gravemeijer, K. (1999). How emergent models may foster the constitution of formal mathematics. *Mathematical Thinking and Learning, 1*(2), 155–177.

Greer, B., & Harel, G. (1998). The role of isomorphisms in mathematical cognition. *The Journal of Mathematical Behavior, 17*(1), 5–24.

Hamdan, M. (2006). Equivalent structures on sets: Equivalence classes, partitions and fiber structures of functions. *Educational Studies in Mathematics, 62*(2), 127–147.

Hanna, G., & Barbeau E. (2008). Proofs as bearers of Mathematical Knowledge. *ZDM: The International Journal on Mathematics Education, 40*(3), 345–353.

Kondratieva, M. (2011). The promise of interconnecting problems for enriching students' experiences in mathematics. *The Montana Mathematics Enthusiast, 8*(1&2), 355–382.

Lakatos, I. (1976). *Proofs and refutations: The logic of mathematical discovery*. Cambridge: Cambridge University Press.

Lakoff, G., & Nunez, R.E. (2000). *Where mathematics comes from*. New York: Basic Books.

Leikin, R., & Winicki-Landman, G. (2000). On equivalent and non-equivalent definitions II. *For the Learning of Mathematics, 20*(2), 24–29.

Leron, U. (1983). Structuring mathematical proofs. *The American Mathematical Monthly, 90*(3), 174–184.

Leron, U. (1985). A direct approach to indirect proofs. *Educational Studies in Mathematics, 16*(3), 321–325.

Lobato, J., & Siebert, D. (2002). Quantitative reasoning in a reconceived view of transfer. *Journal of Mathematical Behavior, 21*(1), 87–116.

Mamona-Downs, J. (2014). *Reconciling two non-equivalent definitions for the limit of two-variable real functions*. Talk presented at the MAA Joint Mathematics Meeting, Baltimore, MD.

Mamona-Downs, J., & Downs, M. (2004). Realization of techniques in problem solving: The construction of bijections for enumeration Tasks. *Educational Studies in Mathematics, 56* (2&3), 235–253.

Mamona-Downs, J., & Downs, M. (2011). Proof: A game for pedants? *Proceedings of CERME, 7*, 213–223, Rzeszów, Poland.

Mamona-Downs, J., & Downs, M. (2013). Problem solving and its elements in forming proof. *The Mathematics Enthusiast, 10*(1), 137–162.

Mamona-Downs, J., & Megalou, F. (2013) Students' understanding of limiting behavior at a point for functions from R² to R. *Journal of Mathematical Behavior, 32*(1) 53–68.

Marrongelle, K., & Rasmussen, C. (2008). Meeting new teaching challenges: Teaching strategies that mediate between all lecture and all student discovery. In M. Carlson, & C. Rasmussen (Eds.), *Making the connection: Research and teaching in undergraduate mathematics education* (pp. 167–178). Washington, DC: The Mathematical Association of America.

Martinez, M.V., & Brizuela, B.M. (2009). Modelling and proof in high school. In M. Tzekaki, M. Kaldrimidou, & H. Sakonidis (Eds.) *Proceedings of the 33rd PME Conference, 4,* 113–120. Thessaloniki, Greece.

Martínez-Planell, R., Gonzalez, A.C., DiCristina, G., & Acevedo, V. (2012). Students' conceptions of infinite series. *Educational Studies in Mathematics, 81*(2), 235–249.

Mason, J., Stephens, M., & Watson, A. (2009). Appreciating mathematical structure for all. *Mathematics Education Research Journal, 21*(2), 10–32.

Mejia-Ramos, J.P., Fuller, E., Weber, K., Rhoads, K., & Samkoff, A. (2012). An assessment model for proof comprehension in undergraduate mathematics. *Educational Studies in Mathematics, 79*(1), 3–18.

Mills, M. (2011). Mathematicians' pedagogical thoughts and practices in proof presentation. In S. Brown, S. Larsen, K. Marrongelle, & M. Oehrtman (Eds.) *Proceedings of the 14th Conference for Research in Undergraduate Mathematics Education, 4,* 167–172. Portland, Oregon.

Moore, R.C. (1994). Making the transition to formal proof. *Educational Studies in Mathematics, 27*(3), 249–266.

Niss, M. (2006). The structure of mathematics and its influence on the learning process. In J. Maasz & W. Schloeglmann (Eds.), *New Mathematics Education Research and Practice* (pp. 51–62). Rotterdam: Sense Publishers.

Novotná, J., & Hoch, M. (2008). How structure sense for algebraic expressions or equations is related to structure sense for abstract algebra. *Mathematics Education Research Journal, 20*(2), 93–104.

Ouvrier-Buffet, C. (2006). Exploring mathematical definition construction processes. *Educational Studies in Mathematics, 63*(3), 259–282.

Ouvrier-Buffet, C. (2011). A mathematical experience involving defining processes: In-action definitions and zero-definitions. *Educational Studies in Mathematics, 76*(2), 165–182.

Parameswaran, R. (2010). Expert mathematicians' approach to understanding definitions. *The Mathematics Educator, 20*(1), 43–51.

Pedemonte, B. (2007). How can the relationship between argumentation and proof be analysed? *Educational Studies in Mathematics, 66*(1), 23–41.

Pinto, M.M.F. (1996). *Students use of quantifiers.* Paper presented to the Advanced Mathematical Thinking Working Group at the Twentieth Conference of the International Group for the Psychology of Mathematics Education, Valencia, Spain.

Polya, G. (1954). *Mathematics and plausible reasoning.* Princeton, NJ: Princeton University Press.

Prasada, S., Ferenz, K., & Haskell, T. (2002). Conceiving of entities as objects and as stuff. *Cognition, 83*(2), 141–165.

Raman, M., Sandefur, J., Birky, G., Campbell, C., & Somers, K. (2009). "Is that a proof?": Using video to teach and learn how to prove at university level. In F.-L. Lin, F.-J. Hsieh, G. Hanna & M. de Villiers (Eds.), *Proceedings of the ICMI Study 19 Conference: Proof and Proving in Mathematics Education, 2,* 154–159. Taipei, Taiwan.

Rasmussen, C., Zandieh, M., King, K., & Teppo, A. (2005). Advancing mathematical activity: A practice-oriented view of Advanced Mathematical Thinking. *Mathematical Thinking and Learning, 7*(1), 51–73.

Rav, Y. (1999). Why do we prove theorems? *Philosophia Mathematica, 7*(1), 5–41.

Rickart, C. (1996). Structuralism and mathematical thinking. In R.J. Sternberg & T. Ben-Zeev (Eds.), *The nature of mathematical thinking* (pp. 285–300). Mahwah, NJ: Lawrence Erlbaum Associates.

Rose, J.S. (1978). *a course on group theory.* Cambridge: Cambridge University Press.

Selden, A., McKee, K., & Selden, J. (2010). Affect, behavioural schemas and the proving process. *International Journal of Mathematical Education in Science and Technology, 41*(2), 199–215.

Selinski, N.E. (2012). Examining students' mathematical transition between secondary school and university: working with vectors and linear independence. In S. Brown, S. Larsen, K. Marrongelle & M. Oehrtman (Eds.), *Proceedings of the 15th Conference on Research in Undergraduate Mathematics Education, 1,* 403–416. Portland, Oregon.

Sweller, J., Clark, R., & Kirschner, P. (2010). Teaching general problem-solving skills is not a substitute for, or a viable addition to, teaching mathematics. *Notices of the AMS, 57*(10), 1303–1304.

Tall, D. (2004). Introducing three worlds of mathematics. *For the Learning of Mathematics, 23*(3), 29–33.

Tall, D., & Vinner, S. (1981). Concept image and concept definition in mathematics with particular reference to limits and continuity. *Educational Studies in Mathematics, 12*(2), 151–169.

Thurston, W. P. (1995). On proof and progress in mathematics. *For the Learning of Mathematics, 15*(1), 29–37.

Timmermans, B. (2012). Prehistory of the concept of mathematical structure: Isomorphism between group theory, crystallography and philosophy. *The Mathematical Intelligencer, 34*(3), 41–54.

Van Hiele, P. (1986). *Structure and insight. A theory of mathematics education.* Orlando, FL: Academic University Press.

Vollrath, H. J. (1994). Reflection on mathematical concepts as starting points for didactical thinking. In R. Biehler, W. Scholz, R. Strasser, & B. Winkelmann (Eds.), *Didactics of mathematics as a scientific discipline* (pp. 61–72). Dordrecht: Kluwer Academic Publishers.

Watson, A., & Mason, J. (2005). *Mathematics as a constructive activity: learners generating examples.* Mahwah, NJ: Lawrence Erlbaum Associates.

Weber, K. (2010). Mathematics majors' perceptions of conviction, validity, and proof. *Mathematical Thinking and Learning, 12*(4), 306–336.

Weber, K. (2012). Mathematicians' perspectives on their pedagogical practice with respect to proof. *International Journal of Mathematical Education in Science and Technology, 43*(4), 463–482.

Weber, K., & Alcock, L. (2004). Semantic and syntactic proof productions. *Educational Studies in Mathematics, 56*(2–3), 209–234.

Weber, K., & Mejia-Ramos, J. P. (2011). Why and how mathematicians read proofs: An exploratory study. *Educational Studies in Mathematics, 76*(3), 329–344.

Weinberg, A., & Wiesner, E. (2011). Understanding mathematics textbooks through reader-oriented theory. *Educational Studies in Mathematics, 76*(1), 49–63.

Wilhelmi, M. R., Godino, J. D., & Lacasta, E. (2007). Didactic effectiveness of mathematical definitions. The case of the absolute value. *International Electronic Journal of Mathematics Education, 27*(2), 3–9.

Wilkerson-Jerde, M. H., & Wilensky, U. (2011). How do mathematicians learn math?: Resources and acts for constructing and understanding mathematics. *Educational Studies in Mathematics, 78*(1), 21–43.

Woo, J., & Yim, J. (2008). Revisiting 0.999. . . and $(-8)^{1/3}$ in school mathematics from the perspective of the algebraic permanence principle. *For the Learning of Mathematics, 28*(2), 11–16.

Yusof, Y. M., & Tall, D. (1999). Changing attitudes to university mathematics through problem solving. *Educational Studies in Mathematics, 37*(1), 67–82.

Zandieh, M., & Rasmussen, C. (2010). Defining as a mathematical activity: A framework for characterizing progress from informal to more formal ways of reasoning. *The Journal of Mathematical Behavior, 29*(2), 57–75.

Zaslavsky, O., & Shir, K. (2005). Students' conceptions of a mathematical definition. *Journal for Research in Mathematics Education, 36*(4), 317–346.

9 Reform as an Issue for Mathematics Education Research
Thinking About Change, Communication, and Cooperation

Michael N. Fried and Miriam Amit

Ben Gurion University of the Negev

Mathematics education research is a theoretical and practical enterprise. But even in its most theoretical form, it aims ultimately to bring about changes for the better in what we teach, how we teach, and what we hope learners will learn. In this way, mathematics education research, whether theoretical or practical, is never far from the effort to *reform* mathematics teaching and learning. How fruitful actual reforms will be depends not only on the quality of the particular proposals we make but also on how well we understand the nature and processes of reform. While some of these processes are completely general, others are connected specifically with mathematics education and are distinct enough to warrant giving the investigation of reform in mathematics education a permanent place in the overall program of mathematics education research.

But how should such an investigation proceed? What kind of thing is its object? The wide range of efforts referred to as reform movements makes even the basic question of what reform is not easy to answer, and it may be that only an intimation of a definition is possible at all. Whatever else it may be, however, a reform movement is a phenomenon that necessarily takes in the whole complex of students, teachers, researchers, parents, and politicians; it is motivated by societal, scientific, and technological needs, as well as by research in mathematics and general education—and it is inescapably a phenomenon connected with values. The phenomenon of reform, since it is so close, as we said, to the core of mathematics education, must, for this reason, be at least as complex as mathematics education itself. The general thesis behind this chapter, then, is that research into reform must reflect this complexity. It must take into account the social and historical nature of reform, its local and global aspects, its response to changing technologies and changing interests in mathematics and science—and it must avoid reducing reform to any one of these. Such an inquiry, naturally, must be of a different kind than other more usual forms of educational research—more reflective, more retrospective, more holistic.

Our discussion begins with one of the main undercurrents of the chapter, namely that research is intertwined with reform as one of its motives, components and results. From there, we continue with the question of "reform researchers" and their methodologies. The two sections are intimately connected since the methodology of research on reform is conditioned by the necessity of research being itself part of the reform process: models for such self-referential research exist in mathematics education, but it may be that these have their clearest application in reform movement research. Moreover, since, as we have said, reform research must be reflective, the sometimes uneasy relationship between research and practice must itself be a matter the researcher on reform must both confront and study.

Following this discussion, we set out two central directions for reform research. The first, which we place under the general heading "communication," concerns the complexity of reform in its most literal sense, namely, its embracing of different populations representing different interests, areas of expertise, and needs—a diversity providing fertile ground for cooperation and mutual enrichment, but also for misunderstanding and tension. The second direction concerns the problem at the heart of reform phenomena, the problem of change. Reform has everything to do with change: researchers on reform must consider how reform effects change and especially the response to change. The latter is particularly important since recent reforms have been conceived with an eye to the rapid changes in society, knowledge, and technology. At another level, the response to change includes also a lack of response or resistance to change; one aspect of this that we will highlight is change that is not change, the mere appearance of change that we call *pseudo-change*.

As some final words, we will reiterate a point lying beneath the surface throughout our chapter, namely that reform research must be ever cognizant of the place of values in processes of reform. This is so for the simple reason that the researcher, in wishing to bring about a change and needing to explain and justify a change, must give firm attention to the definition of ends. But defining ends means defining *desirable* ends; it is for this reason, at bottom, that reform researchers must be completely cognizant of the question of values. Questions of content, in this regard, can never be completely value-neutral, keeping in mind that even "usefulness" is a value! So, defining ends must take place in a wide forum involving the views not only of other mathematics education researchers but also of mathematicians, scientists, philosophers, and historians. This, together with the general complexity of reform, suggests that reform research may in fact involve a cooperative effort among these different intellectual disciplines rather than a narrow subspecialty of mathematics education research. The chapter ends, therefore, with a call for such cooperation.

Before beginning, we ought to say a word about what is *not* included in this chapter—for properly treating the subject of reform and how it should figure in mathematics education research requires a monograph (at least!), and so in a chapter as short as this one we have to remain silent about material that otherwise would be criminal to leave out. First, we give only limited detail about specific reform movements in the past. This is particularly lamentable since the study of reform must be to a greater extent than other forms of mathematics education research a historical enterprise; indeed, one is likely to gain more by the long perspective of time than the critical examination (not always disinterested) of modern developments. That said, we can refer the reader to a longer version of this chapter that contains much of the missing historical detail, namely, Amit and Fried (2008), as well as older works such as Howson, Keitel, and Kilpatrick (1981) and Griffiths and Howson (1979), which contain broad overviews of past reforms. Finally—and this we say truly with a heavy heart—little attention is given to the many questions connected to social justice, including immigrant and low-income populations. We justify this move on the grounds that these many questions are very close to those asked by the extensive research being done specifically on social justice in mathematics education. The large collection of papers in Atweh, Graven, Secada, and Valero (2011) is a source we can recommend.

RESEARCH AS A COMPONENT AND RESULT OF REFORM

As we stated at the outset, even when it is being most theoretical, the ultimate end of mathematics education research must be the improvement of mathematics education, so that almost all mathematics education research in this sense could be connected with the reform of mathematics education. Certainly this is true of efforts directed towards curriculum design and development, learning materials, and learning environments. Moreover, the role constructivist theories occupy in the *National Council of Teachers of Mathematics Standards* (NCTM, 1989, 2000), for example, show how basic research can be a component of a reform in mathematics education. Basic research cannot determine the values towards which a reform strives (see

Amit & Fried, 2008), but it is plain that reform would be empty without research. In the more recent reforms, at least, the influence of research has been weighty indeed. The curious fact is that the influence has tended to be *mutual*, that is, not only has research shaped reform, but reform has also shaped research! This is clear when one considers that the period in which a genuine community of researchers in mathematics education began to crystallize was precisely the period of major reform in the 1950s and 1960s (see Kilpatrick, 1992, pp. 23–29). And this was true not only of the research community in the United States, but also in Europe. One need only look at the development of the Commission Internationale pour l'Etude et Amélioration de l'Enseignment des Mathématiques (CIEAEM), which, beginning in 1950, simultaneously became a nucleus of reform, as its name promised, and, under the leadership of Gattengo, an active forum for research aiming to bring together "epistemologists, logicians, psychologists, mathematicians, pedagogues" (Félix, 1998, p. 18).

A telling example of how reform affects research was the National Longitudinal Study of Mathematical Abilities (NLSMA) set up in 1961 to assess the efforts of the School Mathematics Study Group (SMSG). The NLSMA, for all its faults and despite its questionable value as an instrument of assessment for the "new math," was truly a *consequence* of the "new math" reform and did have a tremendous influence on the course of educational research. About this, Kilpatrick (1992 says:

> [The NLSMA] brought together psychologists and mathematicians to develop instruments for assessing reasoning ability, the ability to apply mathematics in nonroutine contexts, and attitudes toward various facets of mathematics—instruments that were used in both subsidiary and ensuing research studies. It developed and refined new techniques for analyzing the multiple effects of complex treatments on nonrandomly chosen groups. And it trained quite a few researchers in mathematics education.
>
> (p. 29)

In this connection, it is worth noting that some of the basic themes developed later by the NLSMA were already beginning to take form in 1959, only a year after the SMSG itself was founded. On a recommendation from the Advisory Committee, Begle set up an ad hoc committee consisting of three distinguished psychologists who "outline a plan for some needed research [regarding psychological problems relevant to the teaching of mathematics]. SMSG was particularly interested in evaluating the effectiveness of its new mathematics programs in relation to children's attitudes, motives, anxieties, and skills" (Wooton, 1965, p. 56–57, 95–96). The example of the NLSMA is important since it shows that the growth and development of a research community during the reform years of the 1950s and 60s was not by chance, but actively encouraged as a natural part of the reform process.

Such encouragement, of course, is equally characteristic of the Standards period in the 1990s and early 2000s, as can be seen in this statement by Romberg and Collins (2000):

> Propelled by the need to educate all of America's students to levels of achievement in mathematics and science not thought possible over a decade ago, the challenge of the reform movement is to create classrooms where all students have the opportunity to understand mathematical and scientific ideas. This assertion is based on the belief that there is a direct and powerful relationship between student understanding and student achievement. In fact, the way to achieve the high expectations that we have for all students rests on their understanding of important mathematical and scientific ideas taught in school classrooms by professional teachers. This challenge needs to be addressed directly by researchers so that real change in the teaching and learning of mathematics and science occurs in the next decade. A sustained research program, conducted collaboratively with school personnel in school classrooms, needs to be carried out.
>
> (pp. 82–82)

The statement shows clearly how reform sets an agenda for action, informed by research as well as the social importance of mathematics education, and in doing so it simultaneously sets an agenda for research itself, thus illustrating and reinforcing the idea that the reform movement and the research community mutually influence and shape one another. How this mutual dependence between research and reform may also bring in political and social considerations is an area necessary to investigate in itself. But we need now to move on to consider "reform research," its characteristics and its place in the general community of researchers and educators. For, to date, there is no *explicit* subfield of research in mathematics education called "reform research," and it is the main purpose of this chapter to give a sketch of some aspects of what such research ought to be.

"REFORM RESEARCHERS" AND THEIR METHODOLOGIES

Even in the brief description just given, one can see how a community of researchers can crystallize in times of reform. It is one of the laudable aspects of the research community in general that it is, truly, a *community*; it is not so specialized that researchers in the different branches of mathematics education research cannot find common ground and a common language. Reform researchers must be members of this same community, however, their relationship to it is unique because of the nature of the inquiry to which they are dedicated. This is for the simple reason that reform movements, whether by design or necessity, take in almost all aspects of mathematics education. They take in content, and thus, curriculum development; they take in means, and thus, teaching methods, learning environments, and technology; they take in societal needs, and thus, national priorities and economic development, as well as social justice and empowerment. Connected with all of these, moreover, is an unavoidable concern with values, for as one writer put it, all education is "value saturated" (Egan, 2005, p. 39). But what distinguishes a reform from other attempts at improving education is the necessity of seeing all these aspects as an integrated whole. One can say then that the reform process aims at a systemic improvement of education; that is, it takes as its object not curriculum or teaching style or learning environments individually, but an entire matrix combining content, means, social needs, and values with the populations of students, teachers, researchers, parents, and politicians.

To make a biological analogy, the reform process is directed towards the ecology of education (see Goodlad, 1987). The ecological viewpoint of the living world takes into account physiology, genetics, chemistry, and so on insofar as these contribute to making the living world a single complex system; the reform process is similarly directed towards a single complex system. The research community, as we have seen, is an essential part of that system, defining it and being defined by it. Thus, just as the human beings who study ecological systems are simultaneously part of such systems, researchers of reform are, in the same way, part of the object they study. This can be said, to some degree, also about other branches of research in mathematics education, but there is a difference. In most kinds of educational research, the effect of researchers must be taken into account only because the *ideal* situation in which researchers have no effect on their subject, in which they are unseen, unheard, and unfelt observers, can never be fully realized. In reform research, by contrast, the researcher is *essential* part of the object of research. Moreover, because researchers are no less part of the general research community than any other kinds of researchers, they are as much defining and being defined by reform, the very thing they are studying. These considerations have immediate implications for the question of methodology.

Traditional research methodology, based on the methodological ideal in the natural sciences, aims to keep researchers apart from the phenomena being studied, both with respect to the researchers' physical presence and to their values and particular worldview; the methodology of reform research, by contrast, must conceive of the researcher as taking part in the process of reform and possessing definite values and goals. In some sense, the way reform researchers are themselves entangled in their subject is parallel to the position of the sociologist or historian, and, indeed, the study of reform is in some degree the study of an historical process. Interestingly enough, historiography too, like educational research, at one time aimed to be "simply a science, no less and no more" (Bury, 1956, p. 223), and, like educational research, eventually came to accept, for the most part, a view such as this of the historian E. H. Carr (1967):

> Human beings are not only the most complex and variable of natural entities, but they have to be studied by other human beings, not be independent observers of another species . . . The sociologist, the economist, or the historian needs to penetrate into forms of human behaviour in which the will is active, to ascertain why the human beings who are the object of his study will to act as they did. This sets up a relation, which is peculiar to history and the social sciences, between the observer and what is observed. The point of view of the historian enters irrevocable into every observation which he makes; history is shot through and through with relativity.
>
> (p. 70)

The lesson of this is that reform research must give an account of a process from an insider's point of view; therefore, it must, like the historian's account, be reflective and even introspective. The methodology that flows from this alone is something similar to what Howson et al. (1981, p. 195) call an "official biography" or the "rigorous journal." The most well-known examples, although they were not necessarily intended to be rigorous assessments of a reform (as Wooton (1965, p. vii) makes a point of saying), were certainly Wooton's 1965 account of the School Mathematics Study Group (SMSG) (Wooton, 1965), and Thwaites' 1972 account of the British response to the challenge of Sputnik, the School Mathematics Project (SMP). In principle, however, there is no reason why such "official biographies" could not be rigorous examinations in the way biographies' historical figures can also be a work of rigorous scholarship. It may well be, in fact, that a written quasi-historical account is the best way to take stock of the reform movement's accomplishments and reflect on the rightness of the goals it set for itself and the values it assumed. An account such as this can be factual and, at the same time, be reflective in a way tomes of statistics can never be. In this connection, it is telling that in a recent volume edited by Senk and Thompson (2003) on the progress of the Standards-Based Reform movement the first and last parts are decidedly historical in character.

But reform researchers are not only insiders, they are *active* insiders; an account is not enough, rather, it must bring researchers and the other players in the reform process into the circle of defining and being defined by the reform. The methodology of reform research must, therefore, answer both the need to be reflective and the need to be active.

There are some existing models for this kind of research. One that comes quickly to mind is *action research* or *participatory research*. Carr and Kemmis (1986) describe action research as follows:

> Action research is simply a form of self-reflective enquiry undertaken by participants in social situations in order to improve the rationality and justice of their own practices, their understanding of these practices, and the situations in which the practices are carried out.
>
> (p. 162)

Even from this short description, it is plain that action research contains many of the elements that we have described as desiderata for reform research: it is reflexive, that is, there is no clear division between the researcher and the researched; it considers ends and values; and it is directed towards action (e.g. Dick, 1999; Elliott, 1978). Moreover, action research also employs such means as journal writing, which are themselves consistent with the methodological modes for reform research that we have already mentioned. As Elliott (1978) describes, "In explaining 'what is going on' action research tells a 'story' about the event by relating it to a context of mutually interdependent contingencies, i.e. events which 'hang together' because they depend on each other for their occurrence" (p. 356).

An important aspect of action research is its *cyclical* or *iterative* character. It alternates between action and reflection. Moreover, cycles are contained in cycles: "Larger cycles span whole phases of a research program" (Dick, 1999, p. 3). These wider cycles continually broaden and deepen the teachers' and all other participants' understanding, and can also broaden the range of participation, including "professional" researchers whose own field of action goes beyond the individual classroom. This is important, for it answers two apparent weaknesses of action research as a model for reform research methodology, namely, 1) that the participants may not possess the appropriate theoretical background to reflect deeply enough on their practice; 2) that action research seems to be *local* in nature (a single class-room, a single school) whereas reform is very broad in scope and must see the classroom in a very broad context. The fact that there is cycling at all means that the theoretical background which the "professional" researcher supposedly possesses is not a fixed body of knowledge, but knowledge continually being reviewed and revised in the cycling process, and that the "professional" researcher and teacher-researcher alike, therefore, must view themselves as learners and partners in learning. Moreover, this partnership in learning, which ideally should be ever expanding (see Dick, 1999, p. 4), affords the researcher the broad view appropriate to the phenomenon of reform.

The cyclical character of action research and its focus on practice is shared also by the Japa-nese Lesson Study, popularized in the West by Stigler and Hiebert's well-known book, *The Teaching Gap* (Stigler & Hiebert, 1999). With some variations, the Lesson Study consists of four stages: 1) an investigation (involving examination of content and specific teaching goals); 2) the lesson planning; 3) the "research lesson" in which the lesson is carried out and data on its relative success or failure are collected; 4) reflection and improvement (Lewis, Perry, & Hurd, 2009; see also Shimizo, 1999). What is significant is that this cycle of practice and reflec-tion is done collaboratively–and this can occur not only at the local level of a school but also at higher levels. For this reason, the Lesson Study has great ability to create a working community of teachers and researchers, as stressed by Gunnarsdóttir and Pálsdóttir (2011) in their work on the Lesson Study in Iceland. It also has the ability to engage researchers and practition-ers directly in the attempt to implement and, most important for us, to understand a reform (Perry & Lewis, 2009, give particular attention to this aspect of the Lesson Study approach): it is, like all participatory approaches, a means of reform as well as a means of examining reform in a continuous, iterative fashion.

Needless to say, the approaches for reform research methodology given here are consist-ent with general contemporary trends in mathematics education. For example, in describing "Some Shifts in Emphasis in Educational Research in Mathematics and Science" Kelly and Lesh, (2000, p. 37, Table 2.1) note, among other shifts: less emphasis on "researcher remoteness or stances of 'objectivity'" and more emphasis on "researcher engagement, participant-observer roles"; less emphasis on "researcher as expert: the judge of the effectiveness of knowledge transmission using prescripted measures" and more emphasis on "researcher as coconstruc-tor of knowledge: a learner-listener who values the perspective of the researcher subject, who practices self-reflexivity"; less emphasis on "simple cause-and-effect or correlational models" and more emphasis on "complexity theory; systems thinking; organic and evolutionary models of learning and system change." Underlying these trends is the general understanding that research must be characterized by a *diversity* of methodologies. It is evident, thus, that if gen-eral educational research is marked by a diversity of methodologies, the same must be true, a fortiori for reform research whose complex object demands many views to arrive at some sense of the whole. Thus, different methodologies such as those contained in the historiographical and action research models, presented earlier, must be brought together as complementary parts of a whole reform research effort.

But now we must turn to two main areas that reform research must keep within its sight. These are, as we said, communication, and the problem of change, the response to change, and "pseudo-change."

COMMUNICATION

In the attempt to describe the situation of reform researcher, we adopted the metaphor of ecology. That metaphor served to emphasize the fundamental fact that reform occurs at the level of an entire community of interested parties and agents of change, "policy makers" and "policy agents" (Niss, 2014), and researchers of all types. Thus, in the student-teacher-researcher-parent-politician complex, reform researchers have a central role in building an intellectual foundation for the reform and in communicating the principles of the reform to all those affected by it, as well as investigating breakdowns of communication. The *lack* of communication between researchers and the public and between researchers and mathematics teachers (and here, as we will see, researchers include mathematicians as well as mathematics educators) can truly threaten the success of reform. How far that can happen was made clear in an eloquent way by Usiskin (1999–2000) and again by Battista (1999). Battista, in particular, implied that this lack of communication is more than the absence of communication, but almost active noncommunication (mostly on the part of the public towards the research community): "Too often the educational programs and methods used in schools are formulated—by practitioners, administrators, laypeople, politicians, and professors of education—*with a total disregard* for scientific research" (Battista, 1999, p. 431, emphasis added). One must ask, however, whether the research community itself has done enough to *foster* an atmosphere of communication.

Whatever the case, it is clear that the problem of communication is critical and requires understanding to solve. For reform researchers, therefore, this problem of communication must be a central concern, especially in one of its special forms: *the problem of theory and practice.* Indeed, the degree to which theory is put into practice is a reflection of the *mutual* comprehension of researchers and teachers. Obviously, it is in the language of practice that the public, as well as teachers and students, will come to know reform.

There are four main channels through which research communicates to teachers and to the public: 1) journals; 2) teacher-training courses; 3) textbooks and other learning materials; 4) popular media. Teacher training is by far the most direct and in some ways the ideal channel for communication. In the context of general educational reform, Kennedy (2005) tells us that teachers indicated professional training to be the most significant source of their own educational change (p. 217). Even here, though, communication should not be taken for granted. As Kennedy (2005) goes on to point out:

> sources of knowledge outside the classroom, such as professional development programs and institutional policies, *can* have very strong and powerful influences on practice, even though they often don't. Their influences are uneven, either because they are transient or because they are inconsistently and unevenly communicated to teachers.
>
> (p. 224)

But if professional training is potentially the most powerful channel by which research can reach teachers, the channel via textbooks and other learning material is the most common. Moreover, textbooks are probably the most immediate determinants of practice. The process by which textbooks are produced and adopted also provides a good example of the difficulties of communication, and, hence, ought to be among the foci of reform research.

Ginsburg, Klein, and Starkey (1998) have examined the process of textbook production and dissemination in the United States, highlighting the complicated dynamics existing among researchers, government and professional groups, publishers, and teachers. It is difficult to find the first thread in this complex web of relationships, but the role of government is as good a place as any to start. Ginsburg et al. (1998) explain that many states "require publishers to receive official approval before their textbooks may be offered for sale" (p. 432). The approval criteria used at the time by many state governments relies heavily on the NCTM Standards (NCTM, 1989) and are informed by the research community. The extent to which ideas from research have influenced such approval can be seen in the 1992 version of the *California Framework* (California Department of Education, 1992) discussed in some detail by Ginsburg, et al. (1998) :

> Drawing on its interpretation of constructivism, the California Framework requires what some in the state have seen as a radical approach to the creation of textbooks. The Frame-work decrees that, to be adopted by schools in California, curriculum materials must stress meaningful learning, the construction of knowledge, independent thinking, and extended investigations and explorations; and the Framework requires publishers to downplay rote learning, memorization, and the passive absorption of knowledge.
>
> (p. 433)

Editorial staffs of publishers accommodate the state criteria by studying the Standards, by reading NCTM journals such as *Teaching Children Mathematics*, and by attending professional conferences. Moreover, "The editorial staff are often former teachers and other individuals with a sincere interest in helping children learn" (Ginsburg et al. (1998), p. 434). In this connection, it is important to point out that the role of the editorial staff in producing a textbook goes beyond being a mere forum where books are accepted or rejected; the editorial staff and, for that matter, the marketing staff have great influence not only on the final form of a textbook but also on its content.

With government approbation and encouragement of reform efforts on the one hand, and an earnest willingness of publishers to produce acceptable material on the other, the circumstances seem perfect for a smooth working relationship between researchers, teachers, and the public and a real opportunity for constructive communication. Unfortunately, governments must consider voters and publishers, sales. This would remain only a hypothetical issue if there were complete unanimity in support for the general direction and specific details of the reform, but this is never the case. There are those who object to change in principle, that what is traditional is best a priori. There are those who simply do not understand the reform at hand, and there those who do understand it but reject the values it promotes. Some of these objections are rational and some are not, but they all can contribute to a heated atmosphere that the popular press is ever willing to report and that politician and publisher alike cannot ignore. The brunt of these pressures and counterpressures is largely borne by the publisher, and "The result," writes Ginsburg et al. (1998, p. 437) "is a complex series of compromises. Given the goal of maximizing sales (and profits), publishers naturally wish to have their textbook cake and eat it too. To some extent, publishers try to satisfy all sides in the controversy." So, instead of producing textbooks with a clear strategy and clear outlook, publishers tend to produce textbooks rife with mixed messages.

The help such textbooks can provide in informing teachers' classroom practice is moot, and the damage they may cause in the hands of teachers who have qualms about the merits of reform can be great. One must never forget that textbooks must be used, and the way they are used depends on the readiness and understanding of the user. Again as Ginsburg et al. (1998) puts it:

> But consider the extent to which the research-oriented textbook pages make demands on teachers. These pages do not offer a cookbook for teaching; they are not "teacher-proof." Just the opposite is true: the constructivist approach depends on the intelligence of the teacher, who must construct an understanding of the child's learning in order to foster it. To use these pages, teachers must think in a flexible manner, responding to the needs and

unique constructions of individual children. Textbook pages are merely a resource; they can set direction but cannot guarantee what teachers will do.

(pp. 440–441)

So, communication between researchers and teachers through the channel of textbooks can break down first at the stage where the textbook is produced and then—partly because of the way the textbook is finally produced—at the stage where the textbook is actually used in the classroom. The problem is compounded by the ability of textbooks to *appear* to satisfy reform recommendations and of teachers to *appear* to use them with understanding and in the right spirit—an ability that mirrors that uncanny ability of people to appear as if they are engaged in genuine dialogue though no one is genuinely listening or genuinely trying to communicate ideas.

The failure to communicate through the channel of textbooks may be inherent in the nature of textbooks themselves. We have spoken about the obstacles to producing a textbook that reflects clearly and consistently what research has found out about learning and teaching mathematics. However, the mere fact that teachers and students are meant to be a *final* destination for textbooks and that, ideally, a textbook aims to be inclusive and authoritative, means that as a channel of communication textbooks are essentially *one-way*: researchers, writers, and editorial staffs stand on one end, disseminating reform ideas to teachers and students who stand on the other. But for theory and practice to meet, communication must be *two-way and continuous*. As Lesh and Lovitts, 2000, say, "In mathematics and science education, the flow of information between researchers, and practitioners is not the kind of one-way process that is suggested by such terms as *information dissemination*. Instead, to be effective, the flow of information usually must be cyclic, iterative, and interactive" (p. 54). However, at present it is difficult to see what kind of published learning material *could* bring about this sort of two-way and continuous communication. Yet, it is imperative to try and find such material. The theoretical and practical problems with textbooks, thus, suggest that reform researchers must redefine their own role in communicating ideas about teaching and learning and, at the same time, explore new means of communication—and, both these ends, of course, require a deep look at the problem of communication itself.

A different kind of failure of communication from that between researchers and teachers is a communication gap within the research community itself, namely, between academic mathematicians and academic mathematics educators. Since the 1990s, the relationship between these two communities has been a rocky one (see Amit & Fried, 2008, for a description of the earlier prominence of mathematicians in mathematics education and mathematics education reform). Gerald Goldin (2002) used terms such as "chasm," "gulf," and "divide" to describe the strained relations between the two communities and identified fundamental differences in their outlooks going beyond mere predilection (see also Cuoco, 2003). This tension between university mathematics education researchers and university mathematicians means, then, that when one speaks about the "academic research community" one must be wary about treating the academic community as one unified group: one must ask not only whether the university dominates but also which part.

The potential for this tension to have a detrimental effect on reform efforts can be seen in the atmosphere surrounding the validation committee of the Common Core State Standards. Many of the figures on the validation committee were educational or mathematics educational researchers as well as teachers and educational administrators. Although it is true there were few mathematicians on the committee, it must be said that one of the lead writers of the Mathematics Standards (Common Core State Standards Initiative, 2012), William McCallum, was a prominent university mathematician. Nevertheless, another mathematician, James Milgram, who sat on the original validation committee, gave testimony for Indiana Senate Education Panel opposing the Common Core, saying that, "[The Common Core and Indiana] standards were authored with the help of the professional mathematics community as distinguished from the mathematical education community. But—as someone who was at the middle of overseeing the writing process—my main duty on the CCSSO [Council for Chief State School Officers] Validation Committee—it became clear that the professional math community input to CCSSI was often ignored" (Milgram, 2013).

But difference does not have to lead to tension. That the university does not speak with a single voice—if it remains within the bounds of cultured academic debate—may in fact provide an opportunity to deepen our understanding for what is needed for change. *This* potential can be seen in the series of discussions between mathematicians (including, interestingly enough, James Milgram) and mathematics educators that led the document, "Reaching for Common Ground in K–12 Mathematics Education" (Ball et al. (2005)); that document outlined "fundamental premises" shared by both groups and specific "areas of agreement" on the improvement of mathematics education. Jeremy Kilpatrick, who was also a participant in these discussions—and who also sat on the Common Core State Standards validation committee—makes it clear, however, that cooperation does not always come with fireworks:

> My experience with the Common Ground Committee, whose work was funded by the National Science Foundation and Texas Instruments., was similar to an experience I had had some three decades earlier with Morris Kline, one of the most outspoken critics of the new math in U.S. schools. When you have a conversation with people who have expressed strong views about a topic like school mathematics, and you get them away from microphones and reporters—or in today's world, away from tweets and blogs—they moderate their language substantially. You discover that there are many areas of mutual agreement that might not have surfaced previously. Consequently, I strongly believe that mathematicians and mathematics educators already occupy considerable common ground.
>
> (Kilpatrick, 2014, p. 342)

How to provide the conditions allowing the potential for cooperation to overcome the potential for tension between the disciplines of mathematics and mathematics education is hardly self-evident and needs to be studied (Fried & Dreyfus, 2014). Mathematical training or mathematics educational training alone cannot be sufficient, but both are necessary; knowledge of the values and aims of both together, perhaps, with a modicum of conflict management, are essential ingredients to progress on this front.

CHANGE, THE RESPONSE TO CHANGE, AND PSEUDO-CHANGE

The most obvious set of questions with which reform research must be concerned is that set of questions related to change: for reform is all about change; a reform movement is both an agent of change and a response to change. As an agent of change, it must be ever cognizant of students, teachers, researchers, parents, and politicians as a single complex. As a response to change, it must take into account not only the state of mathematical knowledge and of research in mathematics education but also of society and its needs. Thus, these two aspects of change organize that matrix of factors which, as we said earlier, characterize the object of reform.

The basic questions one would think to ask about reform as an agent of change are questions such as: How can change be effected? Is change truly *being* effected? When and how can one judge the results of change? Given the complex picture of reform that we have been developing until now—in which the distinction between researcher and practitioner, between mover and moved, is blurred, and in which there is much interaction and mutual influence among all those involved in reform—these questions, simple and obvious though they may seem, must be put somewhat differently. The basic question in this light ought to be: How do teachers and researchers learn and change while *at the very same time* be facilitators of change?

The question can be asked equally, and more tellingly, in a negative form: What happens when the cycle of learning and doing *is broken*? This would be a trivial question if the breaking of that cycle meant the unambiguous cessation of the reform effort, but that is rarely the case. Most often the resulting failure of reform is, rather, a kind of pseudo-change or "pseudo-reform": materials are produced that *seem* to conform to reform recommendations but, in truth, embody the very practices the reform aims to amend (see Ginsburg, et al. (1998), pp. 434, 438). Teachers use reform material in class, perhaps even attend in-service courses and programs on reform principles, yet often persist teaching in a way completely against the spirit of the reform (as Robert B. Davis used to say "They've got the words, but not the music")— often because of achievement-oriented administrators who also *appear* to accept reform ideas! Pseudo-reform is the expression of the failure to change and also a barrier to further change; it is, thus, exactly the negation of the process of changing and being changed that signifies healthy reform. Making pseudo-reform an object for reflection within the cycle of learning and doing, accordingly, can at once invigorate and safeguard that cycle.

We might remark in passing that the phenomenon of pseudo-reform is probably also behind the curious fact that writers on one reform or another often refer to the problem of drills and memorization *as if these were advocated* by the previous generation of reformers. Of course, the truth is that hardly anyone who has thought at all deeply about education ever completely advocated drills and memorization. This applies not only to modern thinkers, but also thinkers as far back as Milton and Montaigne—and even Plato, who, for example, teases his companion Phaedrus for merely memorizing without truly understanding a tract on love. Even the Jesuits, who used to say *Repetitio mater studiorum est* [!], did not think that memorization was the *only* mother of studies. The problem seems to be that it is all too easy (and sometimes all too convenient!) to mistake the non-reform practices—drilling and memorizing—hidden under the guise of reform *for the reform itself*! Understanding pseudo-reform and learning to recognize it is thus essential not only for the success of a present reform, but also for the fair evaluation of past reforms.

The next question (What is the proper *pace* of reform?) bridges the two aspects of change and reform. Clearly, it can be taken as a question about implementation, and therefore a question about reform as an *agent* of change. For example, one of the important characteristics of curriculum development projects, which are usually connected with reform movements, is that they set for themselves a definite period of time to accomplish their goals (Griffiths & Howson, 1979, pp. 145–146). Prescribing the amount of time for a project seems to go against the view of reform in which methods and strategies are continually being redefined (that is, always being *emergent*); it appears problematic in the way that setting a definite time for an open and free dialogue is. Yet, whether it is for a dialogue or a reform project, a specified time period is certainly a practical necessity. So the reform researcher must surely ask how to balance this practical need of defining a schedule for reform with the flexibility needed for methods and strategies to be truly emergent.

The question of pace also brings us directly to questions related to reform *as a response* to change. This is particularly true with regards to recent reform movements such as Standards-based reform. These movements have been conditioned by the assumption that the world is rapidly changing and that mathematics education must change with it. Though this may be a slight oversimplification, we can say that there are three, not utterly distinct, ways relevant to mathematics education in which the world is understood to be changing: 1) in the state of mathematical knowledge and knowledge in mathematics education; 2) in the demands of society and economy; 3) in the means available for communication, production, and scientific inquiry. These require a corresponding educational response as to content, ends, and means.

The changing state of mathematical and scientific knowledge was obviously behind the "modernization" motive of the "new-math" reform. The changes that this implied for mathematics education had to do largely with the selection of mathematical topics and the mode in which the selected topics should be presented. In any time of reform, however, the way the reform responds to the change in mathematical knowledge is deeply connected with the way mathematical knowledge grows.

Now, the growth of mathematical knowledge is a rather complex process involving both a cumulative *body of knowledge*—specific mathematical theorems, objects, concepts, and procedures—and shifting views as to what is important in mathematics, what should be considered rigorous, and even what is a proper mathematical *object* (what Elkana has called *images of knowledge*; see, for example, Corry, 1989; Davis & Hersh, 1981, Elkana, 1981). Leo Corry (1989) describes the distinction as follows:

> The body of knowledge includes theories, "facts," methods, and open problems. The images of knowledge serve as guiding principles, or selectors; they pose and resolve questions that arise from the body of knowledge, but are not part of and cannot be settled within the body of knowledge itself. For example, the images of knowledge help to resolve such questions as the following: Which of the open problems of the discipline most urgently demands attention?
>
> (p. 411)

While it is often difficult to separate the *body* from the *images* of mathematical knowledge, the way reform responds to change here must, in general, take both these aspects of mathematical change into account. How images of knowledge may play a part can be seen, for example, in diminished importance of classical geometry during the "new math" reform. That reordering of mathematical priorities was partly the result of *a view of mathematics* in which logico-algebraic structure was taken to be the true heart of the subject. With that, Dieudonné could say, "the whole course [of plane Euclidean geometry] might, I think be tackled in two or three hours—one of them being occupied by the descriptions of the axiom system, one by its useful consequences and possibly a third one by a few mildly interesting exercises" (in Howson et al., 1981, p. 102). A different image of mathematical knowledge played a part in determining the mathematical content of the standards-based reform. About that, Kilpatrick (1997) pointed out, "A large part of the standards-based reform is built of the view that mathematics itself has become more computational and less formal" (p. 957). For the reform researcher, then, it is important to maintain a firm awareness that during a period of reform teachers and students may have to accustom themselves not only to new topics but also to new ways of thinking about the general character of mathematics. That said, because the *body* of mathematical knowledge is *cumulative* and that new knowledge rarely *contradicts* the old, the school mathematics program tends to have a relatively stable core. Researchers, teachers and students have some base from which they can build the new ways of thinking entailed by reform.

The nonlinear changes in the images of knowledge share the character of and are partly dependent on equally nonlinear changes in the conditions and demands of society and the economy. This has always been true to some extent, but today the rate of these societal and economic changes is, perhaps, unprecedented. The implications for education are clear. As Hass (1964) noted already 50 years ago, "change is so rapid in our innovating, industrial society, that *today's education is unsuited for tomorrow's world and is as outmoded as the Model-T for the world of 20 years from tomorrow*—the world whose leaders are now in the classrooms of America" (p. 143, emphasis added). Changing demands of the economy, in particular, were among the central preoccupations of the NCTM Standards (NCTM, 1989, 2000) and justified setting the goal of encouraging of "mathematically literate workers":

> The economic status quo in which factory employees work the same jobs to produce the same goods in the same manner for decades is a throwback to our industrial-age past. Today, economic survival and growth are dependent on new factories established to produce complex products and services with very short market cycles. It is a literal reality that before the first products are sold, new replacements are being designed for an ever-changing market. . . . Traditional notions of basic mathematical competence have been outstripped by ever-higher expectations of the skills and knowledge of workers; new

methods of production demand a technologically competent work force. The *U.S. Congressional Office of Technology Assessment* (1988) claims that employees must be prepared to understand the complexities and technologies of communication, to ask questions, to assimilate unfamiliar information, and to work cooperatively in teams. Businesses no longer seek workers with strong backs, clever hands, and "shopkeeper" arithmetic skills.

(NCTM, 1989, p. 3)

That the same economic concern is still at work today can be seen, for example, in Dan Ben-David's response to Israel's poor performance on the PISA examinations:

A country in perpetual danger since its birth cannot allow itself to whither economically or technologically and it will continue to be required to develop abilities that do not exist in other countries. A small economy that needs to withstand existential pressures in such a hostile neighborhood must understand that its economic future depends on technological, scientific and medical innovation. In this kind of a reality it is not too difficult to understand the future implications of providing its top pupils with an educational toolbox of poorer quality than that provided by 24 or the 25 Western countries with whom Israel must compete in the global marketplace.

(Ben-David, 2011, p. 334)

Unlike the changes in mathematical knowledge, it is unclear that in these rapid-nonlinear changes there is any stable core of content on which a reform curriculum can be built. Obviously, for reform to respond by continually changing the curriculum is neither feasible nor desirable. But what is the right response to such changes? What kind of strategy should curriculum designers adopt to answer these constantly changing economic demands? The overall direction of the recent reforms has been to stress a curriculum that makes the student flexible and adaptable rather than "learned." Accordingly, the curriculum does not aim to provide specific content but the *conditions* for learning and doing mathematics. Thus, in the original Standards the NCTM set as one of the social goals of education "lifelong learning" whereby "Problem solving—which includes the ways in which problems are represented, the meanings of the language of mathematics, and the ways in which one conjectures and reasons—must be central to schooling so that students can explore, create, accommodate to changed conditions, and actively create new knowledge over the course of their lives" (NCTM, 1989, p. 4). In other words, the very general notions stressed by the Standards—problem solving, mathematical reasoning, communication—embody the ideal of a mathematically educated person as one *capable* of learning mathematics, that is, one who has a well-based *potential* for acquiring and using specific mathematical content. This is why the 1989 Standards summarized the NCTM's outlook with the expression "mathematical power." It is worth pointing out in this connection that *power* and *potential* share the same Latin root: *posse*, "to be able" or "capable."

This emphasis on *potential* to learn mathematical content is seen also in reform ideas that are keenly interested in maintaining a connection with concrete mathematical content. For example, one has the Danish competencies approach, KOM, (Niss & Højgaard, 2011). Niss describes its core as follows:

Possessing *mathematical competence*—i.e. mastering mathematics—is an individual's capability and readiness to act appropriately, and in a knowledge-based manner, in situations and contexts in which mathematics actually plays or potentially could play a role.

A mathematical *competency* is a distinct major constituent in mathematical competence. The KOM Project identifies eight such mathematical competencies: Mathematical thinking; Mathematical problem handling; Mathematical modelling; Mathematical reasoning; Representing mathematically; Handling mathematical symbolism and formalism;

Communicating mathematically; Dealing with (physical) aids and tools for mathematical activity.

(Niss, 2014, p. 270)

To some extent this can also be seen in the notion of Habits of Mind developed by June Mark, Al Cuoco, and Paul Goldenberg (see Goldenberg, 2014), which has been adopted by the Common Core State Standards. Indeed, the connection between competencies and "habits of mind" is made explicitly in this statement from the California Orange County department of education site:

> The introductions to both the English language arts and mathematics CCSS [Common Core State Standards] include descriptions of 21st Century Competencies. These cognitive and psychological aptitudes are described in the English language arts standards as "Capacities" and in the mathematics standards as "Practices.". These are referred to as "Habits of Mind" which operate in tandem with the academic content in the standards.
>
> (OCDE, 2011)

Making modes of thinking, rather than specific objects of thought, the focus of the mathematics program may well be the answer to the problem of providing relatively stable curricula able to respond to the unstable ever-changing demands of society and the economy. It is certainly an answer very much in line with a rationalist tradition that, since Descartes at least, gives method precedence over substance—a tradition in which general education in modern democracies is deeply entrenched (see Brann, 1979, pp. 129–149). But that same tradition is fraught with difficulties. Thus, while we may tentatively accept the general approach of reform programs leaning in this direction, what the right educational response to our rapidly changing society must remain a question and subject of inquiry for reform research.

The problem of changing means available for communication, production, and scientific inquiry, is, of course, the problem of technology. In some respects, the difficulties for reform arising from the pace of technological change are the same as those just discussed, as are the approaches open to reform to solve those difficulties. However, a few more words are in order.

Although there are those who think that the use of graphing calculators and computers can dull mathematical thinking (e.g., Neal Koblitz, 1996), it is fair to say that most see technology as an unavoidable and welcome aspect of the modern world (see Wong, 2003 for an overview of the issues connected with curriculum). Roitman (1997) lists four questions that she reasonably takes to be the relevant questions concerning any use of technology in the classroom:

- What mathematics is reflected in the use of technology?
- What efforts are made to ensure that the mathematics is significant and correct?
- How does the use of technology engage students in realistic and worthwhile mathematical activities?
- How does the use of technology elicit the use or enable deeper understanding of mathematics that it is important to know and be able to do? (p. 7)

Roitman's four questions are no less pertinent today and are still addressed in one form or another in the vast and ever-growing literature on technology in mathematics education: Jim Kaput, who was a leading figure and pioneer among this group of researchers, addressed many of these questions directly or in connection with his development of SimCalc. But here reform research risks stepping out of its bailiwick, for the proper consideration of Roitman's questions really demands precisely the kind of independent research effort that Kaput and others like him have pursued. It is clear, though, that the degree to which expectations of a technology-oriented reform are fulfilled is proportional to the seriousness with which these questions are asked—and *for this* reform research does have a role in providing and developing models whereby these crucial questions are continually asked and continually at work inform-ing the cycling process of practice and reflection. Just providing computers or graphing calcu-lators in the schools is obviously not enough, as has been recently pointed out trenchantly in a general context by Larry Cuban (2006). In fact, because computers are physical objects one can point at—and often very attractive ones—merely supplying such technology without teach-ers and researchers reflecting on their wise use can easily become a variety of pseudo-reform: the technology becomes visible but ineffectual.

CONCLUDING THOUGHTS: CONTENT, VALUES, AND COOPERATION

What we have just said about reform research and technology seems to suggest that reform research is concerned only that questions of content are asked, how they are asked, and when they are asked, rather than with the questions themselves. This is consistent with some of the other things we have said about reform research, for example, its overriding concern with the existence, manner, and extent of communication. But is reform research really only concerned with the "mechanics" of reform—only that there be communication, but not what is being communicated, only that there be questions, but not with the substance of the questions? Such a view would be a distortion and definitely *not* consistent with one other point that we emphasized about reform research, namely, that it be *active*.

We argued that the active involvement of reform research in reform followed from the very nature of reform in that its object is a complex-interacting system of which researchers are themselves an integral part. The reform researcher is not only studying and monitoring the flow of information within that system *ab extra*, as it were, but is exchanging ideas with teachers, stu-dents, parents, and other researchers, influencing them and being influenced by them, watch-ing change occur and being changed. The reform researcher will, therefore, of necessity be continuously engaged in a dialogue concerned with the content and the values of the reform.

A metaphor that helps clarify the peculiar position reform researchers occupy in this dia-logue is that of moderators for discussions among experts. In such discussions, moderators are not expected to have all the expertise of the participants, but they are expected to be able to listen well and ask guiding questions, and this, in turn, demands an intelligent grasp of the content of the discussion. More than this, however, moderators must have an acute awareness of the general picture arising out of the discussion, since it is the responsibility of the modera-tor, not so much that the discussion reach this or that specific conclusion, but that discussion keeps its general subject and general goals in sight. In short, the moderator must continually coordinate the substance and ends of the discussion.

Where the discussion corresponds to the reform movement, the necessity of such a coor-dination effort is completely evident. For—as should be clear from our considerations of the motives for reform—reform needs to be viewed not as a mere corrective, but as a concrete expression of a total vision of mathematics education. Moreover, this total vision is one arising out of the efforts and thoughts of *all* those involved in the reform effort, and of others too. By the latter, we have in mind (besides those involved in fields of study and action concerned specifically with mathematics education) also philosophers, anthropologists, sociologists, and historians, to name a few.

This is all the more true in light of what was said earlier about images of knowledge: our very understanding of mathematics and of the ends of mathematics education is as much deter-mined by culture and society as by logic and objective mental activity. Thus, the point of view of the historian or the anthropologist should be of immense help in defining the values behind the seemingly detached mathematics of the classroom. Mathematics education, in this regard, must never be provincial. Reform research, in particular, must see itself fostering a sense of openness and of cooperation among those concerned with a wide range of human activity.

In what we have said, we have really set out only the most basic requirements of reform research and only a very general picture of the reform researcher. For the latter especially we have had to rely on numerous metaphors: the researcher as ecologist, as complex-system analyst, as discussion moderator. The need of such metaphors is a sign that in speaking about reform research we are speaking about something genuinely new, something still lacking definition, still lacking precision. We should like to see this new field reach the same level of clarity attained by other areas of educational research. The only way this can be achieved is if researchers—guided by these general metaphors and released from all other paradigms of educational research—will go out into the field, allow themselves to become immersed in actual reform efforts, and, yet, maintain enough self-possession to soberly document what they find. We believe this represents a worthy challenge: it may, in fact, become emblematic for other future challenges for educational research.

REFERENCES

Amit, M., & Fried, M.N. (2008). The complexities of change: aspects of reform and reform research in mathematics education. In L. English (Ed.), *Handbook of International Research in Mathematics Education* (2nd Ed., pp. 385–414). New York: Routledge.

Atweh, B., Graven, M., Secada, W., & Valero, P. (Eds.) (2011). *Mapping equity and quality in mathematics education*. Dordrecht: Springer

Ball, D.L., Ferrini-Mundy, J., Kilpatrick, J., Milgram, J.R., Schmid, W., & Schaar, R. (2005). Reaching for common ground in K–12 mathematics education. *Notices of the American Mathematical Society, 52*(9), 1055–1058.

Battista, M.T. (1999). The mathematical miseducation of America's youth. *The Phi Delta Kappan, 80*(6), 424–433.

Ben-David, D. (2011). Israel's educational achievements: Updated international comparisons. In D. Ben-David (Ed.), *State of the nation report: Society, economy and policy in Israel 2010*. Jerusalem: Taub Center of Social Policy Studies in Israel.

Brann, E.T.H. (1979). *Paradoxes of education in a republic*. Chicago: University of Chicago Press.

Bury, J.B. (1956). History as a science. In F. Stern (Ed.), *The varieties of history* (pp. 209–223). New York: Meridian Books.

California Department of Education (1992). *Mathematics framework for California public schools: Kindergarten through grade twelve*. Sacramento, CA: California Department of Education.

Carr, E.H. (1967). *What is history?* Harmondsworth, UK: Penguin Books.

Carr, W., & Kemmis, S. (1986). *Becoming critical. Education, knowledge and action research*. Lewes, UK: Falmer.

Common Core State Standards Initiative. (2012). *Mathematics standards*. Retrieved from www.core-standards.org/Math (accessed August 20, 2013).

Corry, L. (1989). Linearity and reflexivity in the growth of mathematical knowledge. *Science in Context, 3*, 409–440.

Cuban, L. (2006). The laptop revolution has no clothes. *Education Week 26*(8), 29. Retrieved from www.edweek.org/ (accessed August 20, 2013).

Cuoco, A. (2003). Teaching mathematics in the United States. *Notices of the American Mathematics Society, 50*(7), 777–787.

Davis, p. J., & Hersh, R. (1981). *The Mathematical Experience*. Boston: Birkhäuser.

Dick, B. (1999). Sources of Rigour in Action Research: Addressing the Issues of Trustworthiness and Credibility. A paper presented at the *Association for Qualitative Research Conference "Issues of rigour in qualitative research"* at the Duxton Hotel, Melbourne, Victoria, 6–10 July 1999.

Egan, K. (2005). Students' development in theory and practice: The doubtful role of research. *Harvard Education Review, 75*(1), 25–41.

Elliott, J. (1978). What is action-research in schools? *Journal of Curriculum Studies, 10*, 355–357.

Elkana, Y. (1981). A programmatic attempt at an anthropology of knowledge. In E. Mendelson & Y. Elkana (Eds.), *Sociology of the Sciences: Vol. 5. Sciences and Cultures* (pp. 1–76). Dordrecht: Reidel.

Félix, L. (1998). Essai sur l'histoire de la CIEAEM. In T. Bernet & F. Jaquet (Eds.), *La CIEAEM au travers de ses 50 premières rencontres: Matériaux pur l'histoire de la Commission*. Neuchâtel, Switzerland.

Fried, M.N., & Dreyfus, T. (Eds.) (2014). *Mathematics and mathematics education: Searching for common ground*. New York: Springer.

Ginsburg, H.P., Klein, A., & Starkey, P. (1998). The development of children's mathematical thinking: Connecting research with practice. In I. Sigel & A. Renninger (Eds.), *Handbook of Child Psychology, 5th Ed.: Vol. 4. Child Psychology and Practice* (pp. 401–476). New York: John Wiley & Sons.

Goldenberg, P. (2014). "Mathematical Literacy": An Inadequate Metaphor. In M.N. Fried & T. Dreyfus, (Eds.), *Mathematics and Mathematics Education: Searching for Common Ground* (pp. 139–156). New York: Springer.

Goldin, G.A. (2002). Connecting understandings from mathematics and mathematics education research. In A.D. Cockburn & E. Nardi (Eds.), *PME26: Proceedings of the 26th Annual Conference 1* (pp. 161–166). Norwich, UK: University of East Anglia.

Goodlad, J.I. (1987). Towards a healthy ecosystem. In *The Ecology of School Renewal: 86th Yearbook of the National Society for the Study of Education, Part I* (pp. 210–221). Chicago: University of Chicago Press.

Griffiths, H.B., & Howson, A.G. (1979). *Mathematics, society and curricula*. London: Cambridge University Press.

Gunnarsdóttir, G.H., & Pálsdóttir, G. (2011). Lesson Study in teacher education: A tool to establish a learning community. In M. Pytlak, E. Swoboda, & T. Rowland (Eds.), *CERME7 Proceedings of the Seventh Congress of the European Society for Research in Mathematics Education*. Rzeszow, Poland. Retrieved from www.cerme7.univ.rzeszow.pl (accessed August 20, 2013).

Hass, C.G. (1964). Who should plan the curriculum? In A. Crow & L.D. Crow (Eds.), *Vital Issues in American Education* (pp. 143–148). New York/Toronto/London: Bantam Books.

Howson, G., Keitel, K., & Kilpatrick, J. (1981). *Curriculum development in mathematics*. Cambridge: Cambridge University Press.

Kelly, A.E., & Lesh, R. (2000). Trends and shifts in research methods. In A. Kelly, & R. Lesh (Eds.) *Handbook of Research Design in Mathematics & Science Education* (pp. 35–44). Mahwah, NJ: Lawrence Erlbaum Associates.

Kennedy, M. (2005). *Inside teaching: How classroom life undermines reform*. Cambridge, MA: Harvard University Press.

Kilpatrick, J. (1992). History of research in mathematics education. In D.A. Grouws (Ed.), *Handbook of Research on Mathematics Teaching and Learning* (pp. 3–37). New York: Macmillan Publishing Company.

Kilpatrick, J. (1997). Confronting reform. *American Mathematical Monthly, 104*, 955–962.

Kilpatrick, J. (2014). We must cultivate our common ground. In M.N. Fried & T. Dreyfus, (Eds.), *Mathematics and Mathematics Education: Searching for Common Ground* (pp. 337–343). New York: Springer.

Koblitz, N. (1996). The case against computers in K–13 math education (kindergarten through calculus). *The Mathematical Intelligencer, 18*, 9–16.

Lesh, R., & Lovitts, B. (2000). Research agendas: Identifying priority problems and developing useful theoretical perspectives. In A. Kelly & R. Lesh (Eds.), *Handbook of Research Design in Mathematics & Science Education* (pp. 45–72). Mahwah, NJ: Lawrence Erlbaum Associates.

Lewis, C.C., Perry, R.R., & Hurd, J. (2009). Improving mathematics instruction through lesson study: A theoretical model and North American case. *Journal of Mathematics Teacher Education, 12*, 285–304.

Milgram, J. (2013). Testimony to the Indiana Senate Education Committee. Retrieved from http://hoosiersagainstcommoncore.com/james-milgram-testimony-to-the-indiana-senate-committee/ (accessed August, 28, 2013).

NCTM (National Council of Teachers of Mathematics). (1989). *Curriculum and evaluation standards for school mathematics*. Reston, VA: Author.

NCTM (National Council of Teachers of Mathematics). (2000). *Principles and standards for school mathematics*. Reston, VA: Author. Retrieved from http://standards.nctm.org (accessed August 20, 2013).

Niss, M. (2014). Mathematics and mathematics education policy. In M.N. Fried & T. Dreyfus (Eds.), *Mathematics and Mathematics Education: Searching for Common Ground* (pp. 261–275). New York: Springer.

Niss, M., & Højgaard, T. (Eds.) (2011). *Competencies and mathematical learning. Ideas and inspiration for the development of mathematics teaching and learning in Denmark*. IMFUFA-text number 485. Roskilde, Denmark: Roskilde University.

OCDE (Orange County Department of Education). (2011). Common Core State Standards for California. Retrieved from www.ocde.us/CommonCoreCA/Pages/default.aspx (accessed May 22, 2014).

Perry, R.R. & Lewis, C.C. (2009). What is successful adaptation of Lesson Study in the U.S.? *Journal of Educational Change, 10*(4), 365–391.

Roitman, J. (1997). A mathematician looks at the standards. Retrieved from www.stolaf.edu/other/extend/Expectations/nise.html (accessed August 20, 2013).

Romberg, T.A. & Collins, A. (2000). The impact of standards-based reform on methods of research in schools. In A. Kelly & R. Lesh (Eds.) *Handbook of Research Design in Mathematics & Science Education* (pp. 73–86). Mahwah, NJ: Lawrence Erlbaum Associates.

Senk, S.L. & Thompson, D.R. (Eds.) (2003). *Standards-based school mathematics curricula: What are they? What do students learn?* Mahwah, NJ: Lawrence Erlbaum Associates.

Shimizu, Y. (1999). Aspects of mathematics teacher education in Japan: Focusing on teachers' roles. *Journal of Mathematics Teacher Education, 2*(1), 107–116.

Stigler, J.W. & Hiebert, J. (1999). *The teaching gap.* New York: The Free Press.

Thwaites, B. (1972). *SMP: The first ten years.* Cambridge: Cambridge University Press.

Usiskin, Z. (1999–2000). Educating the public about school mathematics. *UCSMP Newsletter* (26, Winter), 4–12.

Wong, N.Y. (2003). The influence of technology on the mathematics curriculum. In A.J. Bishop, M.A. Clements, C. Keitel, J. Kilpatrick & F.K.S. Leung (Eds.), *Second international handbook of mathematics education* (pp. 271–321). Dordrecht: Kluwer Academic Publishers.

Wooton, W. (1965). *SMSG: The making of a curriculum.* New Haven/London: Yale University Press.

10 Prospective Mathematics Teachers' Learning and Knowledge for Teaching

João Pedro da Ponte

Universidade de Lisboa

Olive Chapman

University of Calgary

INTRODUCTION

What is the nature of current research on the education of prospective elementary and secondary school teachers of mathematics? In Ponte and Chapman (2008) we addressed this question based on a review of studies published in 1998 to 2005. In this chapter we build on this work by extending the review from 2006 to 2013. We begin with a brief sketch of the landscape of teacher education that provides an organizing image for the relations among the main topics and the related issues addressed in the chapter. We then present and discuss studies that provide insights into these various topics, which include: the nature of prospective teachers' mathematics knowledge; knowledge of mathematics teaching; professional identity; learning approaches to support development of, or growth in, this knowledge; and teacher education program elements. We end with a reflection on the nature of this domain of research, and on the opportunities and constraints it offers for moving the field of mathematics teacher education forward.

Landscape of Prospective Teacher Education

Prospective mathematics teacher education is a complex process with many interacting elements. Figure 10.1 represents this complexity as a landscape of key elements, with the development of the prospective teachers' knowledge of mathematics and mathematics teaching located in the center of it. While these two elements are often considered independently, they are represented as inherently interconnected. They are perhaps the key focus in mathematics teacher education. They are also shown to be situated in the development of prospective teachers' identity, which includes factors such as values, beliefs, habits, norms, dispositions, and in general, ways of being a teacher. Identity ultimately develops in reference to the group identity of the teachers' professional community, which includes the preceding three elements, thus establishing its importance. Finally, Figure 10.1 shows several factors interacting with this group of inner elements in the landscape that impact the nature of prospective teacher education programs. These include:

- Prospective teachers' characteristics, for example, their beliefs, attitudes, knowledge, conceptions, and skills prior to entering the program.
- Program instructors' and other participants' characteristics, for example, their beliefs, attitudes, knowledge, conceptions, and personal features. (Other participants include cooperating teachers and students involved in the prospective teachers' field experiences.)
- Program elements such as teaching approaches, purposes, and objectives; curriculum and materials: assessment instruments and procedures; and the overall organization and

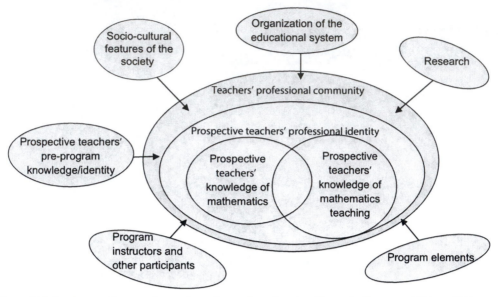

Figure 10.1 Landscape of prospective mathematics teacher education (Ponte & Chapman, 2008, p. 226).

pedagogical features of the program (e.g., ways of working/learning emphasized, personal relationships between prospective teachers and other participants, access to resources, and use of Information and Communication Technology).

• Sociocultural features of the society, including the roles and values promoted by ministries of education, school administrators, parents, media, and the general public.

• Organization of the educational system, including ways of accessing teacher education and entering the profession, certification, contracts, career features, and curriculum organization.

• Research, for example, its emphases, values, priorities, ways of disseminating results and relationships with the field of practice (Ponte & Chapman 2008, p. 226).

While this landscape highlights the complex structure of prospective teacher education, underlying it are issues that still further add to this complexity. For example, there are many contradictions and conflicts bearing on the mission of prospective teacher education to transform the identity of prospective teachers from that of student to that of teacher and preparing them to assume their professional roles. There are many ways of being a teacher, and the teacher's identity is a multifaceted notion. There are also conflicting visions of the mathematics curriculum and between what is considered important for prospective teachers to learn and what they actually learn. In addition, there are conflicting visions between university and school contexts, and among the perspectives of the direct participants in the teacher education process and other interested stakeholders. Research also adds a layer of complexity to understanding teacher education: studies place different emphases on many aspects of the mathematics curriculum and often derive conflicting recommendations regarding prospective teachers' learning and appropriate learning opportunities.

Focus of Chapter

The comprehensive view of prospective teacher education presented in Figure 10.1 offers many possibilities for framing a paper about this field. However, given that this chapter is an update of the review in Ponte and Chapman (2008), we decided to focus on the same three central elements of the landscape: knowledge of mathematics, knowledge of mathematics teaching, and teachers' professional identity (Figure 10.1). We also address teacher education program elements that are connected to other elements of Figure 10.1 and recently have gained more prominence in research.

Our intent is to highlight examples of studies on prospective mathematics teachers' knowledge, learning, and identity and program features over the period 2006–2013 as a way of understanding current trends in research to establish meaningful and effective prospective teacher education. We offer brief descriptions only of the aims and findings of these studies, which enables us to include a broader range of examples. We organize our discussion of these studies in five sections following this introduction: "Prospective Teachers' Knowledge of Mathematics," "Prospective Teachers' Knowledge of Mathematics Teaching," and "Prospective Teacher's Identity." Each of these sections focuses on the ways the knowledge is conceptualized and developed. The following section, "Teacher Education Settings, Activities, and Tools," highlights innovative features that have become significant in teacher education in the last few years. Finally, in "Concluding Reflections" we offer a reflective summary of prospective mathematics teachers' learning and discusses general issues concerning the state of research on their knowledge and development.

PROSPECTIVE TEACHERS' KNOWLEDGE OF MATHEMATICS

There is general consensus that teachers need to hold sound content knowledge as this affects both what they teach and how they teach it. It is, therefore, no surprise that teachers' knowledge of mathematics continues to be a central theme in research on prospective mathematics teacher education. While some studies have begun to investigate ways to measure mathematical knowledge for teaching, the prominent focus is still the nature of prospective teachers' knowledge from a qualitative research perspective. This section addresses these studies of prospective teachers' learning with attention to the perspectives of mathematical knowledge considered, issues identified with this knowledge, and how its development has been facilitated in mathematics education courses.

Perspectives of Knowledge of Mathematics

Teachers who do not have a strong knowledge of mathematics are likely to be limited in their professional competence, but having such knowledge does not guarantee that one will be an effective mathematics teacher. Whereas quality teaching is directly related to subject matter knowledge, the nature of this knowledge is a critical factor in this relationship. Ma (1999) argued that, to be effective, teachers need a profound understanding of fundamental mathematics. This understanding must be deep, broad, and thorough, and it must go beyond being able to compute correctly. This perspective underlies the scope of mathematics recommended for teaching. For example, the National Council of Teachers of Mathematics (NCTM) described it as: "The content and discourse of mathematics, including mathematical concepts and procedures and the connections among them; multiple representations of mathematical concepts and procedures; ways to reason mathematically, solve problems, and communicate mathematics effectively at different levels of formality" (NCTM, 1991, p. 132). Similarly, Kilpatrick, Swafford, and Findell (2001) described it as:

> Knowledge of mathematical facts, concepts, procedures, and the relationships among them; knowledge of the ways that mathematical ideas can be represented; and the knowledge of mathematics as a discipline—in particular, how mathematical knowledge is produced, the nature of discourse in mathematics, and the norms and standards of evidence that guide argument and proof.
>
> (p. 371)

Table 10.1 Examples of perspectives of teachers' mathematics knowledge studied.

Topic	Dimension	Studies
Whole numbers	Reasoning	Lo, Grant, & Flowers, 2008
Whole/rational numbers	Reasoning	Seaman & Szydlik, 2007
Rational numbers	Reasoning	Son & Crespo, 2009
Ratio and proportion	Concepts/procedures	Bartell, Webel, Bowen, & Dyson, 2013
Equations	Concepts/procedures/representations	Lo & Luo, 2012
Functions	Language/communication	Tobias, 2013
	Concepts/problem solving	Pitta-Pantazi & Christou, 2011
	Concepts/reasoning	Prediger, 2010
	Representations/reasoning	Caglayan, 2013
	Representations	Davis, 2009
	Representations/definitions	Steele, Hillen, & Smith, 2013

In addition to the issue of describing this knowledge, studies have begun to deal with the issue of measuring it for practicing teachers. For example, Hill, Blunk, et al. (2008) compared results of a testing instrument to assess the "mathematical knowledge for teaching" with those of a quantitative observational instrument to measure the "mathematical quality of instruction" and found a strong positive association. Krauss et al. (2008) constructed tests to measure the "pedagogical content knowledge" and the "content knowledge" of secondary mathematics teachers to investigate whether these categories of knowledge can be distinguished empirically, and whether the mean level of knowledge and the degree of connectedness between them depend on mathematical expertise. Findings showed that the secondary mathematics teachers with in-depth mathematical training outscored other teachers on both knowledge categories and exhibited a higher degree of cognitive connectedness between the two knowledge categories. More recently, Beswick, Callingham, and Watson (2012) used an instrument designed to measure multiple facets of middle school mathematics teacher knowledge. They found that teacher knowledge can be conceived of as a unidimensional construct with four increasing hierarchical levels: *Personal Numeracy, Pedagogical Awareness, Pedagogical Content Knowledge Emergence,* and *Pedagogical Content Knowledge Consolidation.*

Table 10.1 presents studies that cover some of the dimensions of the perspectives of mathematics knowledge for teaching that we have discussed. In particular, they suggest a trend of viewing prospective teachers' mathematics knowledge in terms of particular concepts, procedures, representations, and reasoning processes associated with the school curriculum. They touch on a wide variety of curriculum topics. In the next section we elaborate on the sample of studies in Table 10.1.

Issues With Prospective Teachers' Knowledge of Mathematics

A common theme of studies on prospective teachers' mathematics knowledge is that it has serious issues that teacher education programs ought to address. Llinares and Krainer (2006) and Ponte and Chapman (2006) referenced studies over a 30-year period that identified several issues with teachers' knowledge in relation to what is considered to be adequate to teach mathematics. These issues include misconceptions for different topics of school mathematics, such as numbers and number theory; geometry; measurement; ratio and proportion; algebra, functions, and calculus; probability and statistics; set theory; logic and proof; problem posing; and problem solving. Our previous findings (Ponte & Chapman, 2008) and the current review of studies continue to reflect this trend of identifying limitations with, or raising concerns about, prospective teachers' mathematics knowledge. Table 10.2 provides examples of these issues based on our previous findings.

One area of mathematics that received significant attention by researchers in the last eight years is rational numbers. Studies continue to address prospective teachers' knowledge of

Table 10.2 Examples of issues with prospective teachers' knowledge of mathematics.

- Procedural attachments that inhibit development of a deeper understanding of concepts related to the multiplicative structure of whole numbers
- Influence of primitive, behavioral models for multiplication and division
- Adequate procedural knowledge but inadequate conceptual knowledge of division and sparse connections between the two
- Inability to establish connections among different representations of a concept (rational numbers, functions)
- Difficulties in the language of fractions, functions and equations
- Distorted definitions and images of rational numbers
- Lack of ability to connect real-world situations and symbolic computations
- Lack of sensitivity to the different meanings of variables
- Difficulty in processing geometrical information and lack of basic geometrical knowledge, skills and analytical thinking ability
- Inadequate logical reasoning
- Difficulty in making reasoned conjectures and in using definitions and properties to justify assertions

rational numbers in different ways. For example, Tobias (2013) examined how prospective elementary teachers developed an understanding of language use for defining the whole and found that even when important mathematical ideas were appropriated (such as fractions depending on a whole or group, defining an "of what," and knowing what the denominator represents) some participants still had difficulty in distinguishing among the terms "of a," "of one," "of the," and "of each." Son and Crespo (2009) studied prospective teachers' reasoning and response to a student's nontraditional strategy in fraction division and found that some participants solved tasks using numerical fractions as "indicated division" as well as the commutative property whereas other used fractions in "a general form" and used algebraic methods. They also found that participants with a deeper understanding of the mathematical basis regarding fractions of this student's strategy tended to think that students learn by explaining and justifying their ideas to each other. In a different cultural context, Lo and Luo (2012) studied the knowledge of fraction division of Taiwanese prospective elementary teachers and found that most participants had developed a secure knowledge of this operation but tasks of representing fraction division through word problems and diagrams proved to be challenging even for proficient prospective teachers.

Some studies also indicate the importance of algebraic thinking and proof as a research focus. For example, Stephens (2006) examined the awareness of equivalence and relational thinking depicted by prospective elementary teachers, finding that most participants demonstrated an awareness of relational thinking in noticing opportunities offered by the tasks to engage students and also in tracing such thinking in students' productions. However, many were not aware of elementary students' misconceptions about the meaning of the equal sign. In relation to proof, Stylianides, Stylianides, and Philippou (2007) examined prospective elementary and secondary mathematics teachers' knowledge of proof by mathematical induction and found that participants had difficulties concerning the essence of the base step of induction, the meaning associated with the inductive step, and the domain of discourse.

A trend in current studies is to draw on the distinction made by Ball, Thames, and Phelps (2005; 2008) between *common content knowledge* (i.e., knowledge associated with recognizing wrong answers, spotting inaccurate definitions in textbooks, and using notation correctly) and *specialized content knowledge* (i.e., knowledge associated with analyzing errors and evaluating alternative ideas, giving mathematical explanations, using mathematical representations, and being explicit about mathematical language and practice). This distinction stands on the notion that "studying what teachers know is insufficient to solving the problem of understanding the knowledge that is needed for teaching. What is missing with all the focus on teachers is a view of mathematical knowledge in the context of teaching" (Ball, Lubienski, & Mewborn, 2001, p. 450). This means that there is an important distinction between knowing how to do mathematics problems and knowing mathematics in ways that enable its use in teaching. From this perspective, the sample of studies described suggests that prospective teachers' common content knowledge and specialized content knowledge is likely to be problematic and require ongoing attention in teacher education.

Development of Prospective Teachers' Knowledge of Mathematics for Teaching

Given the concerns about prospective teachers' mathematics knowledge, it also is not surprising that the literature has been addressing ways to enhance it in teacher education. For example, Watson and Mason (2007) indicated that courses should include features that prompt participants to:

- engage in mathematical thinking through working on suitable mathematics tasks;
- reflect on the experience of doing mathematics tasks individually or with others;
- analyze task structure, including the purpose and affordances, and experiment with extending and varying task structure and task presentation;
- challenge approaches dominated by procedures that depend on rote memorization and mechanical use of algorithms and routines; and
- observe and listen to learners, by observing classes or videos and interacting with learners.

The underlying premise of such suggestions is not simply to provide prospective teachers with more mathematics, but, more importantly, to allow them to understand and reconstruct what they know with more depth and meaning. In particular, they should engage in learning or relearning the mathematics they will teach consistent with current curriculum recommendations for mathematics education. The following studies provide evidence of the nature and the effectiveness of such suggestions in teacher education courses.

Steele et al. (2013) described teacher learning in a teaching experiment consisting of a content-focused methods course involving mathematical knowledge for teaching function. The goal was the development of mathematical knowledge that built on individual teachers' prior knowledge as well as the development of a stronger collective understanding of function. Course design began with the identification of function-related mathematical tasks, cases, and student work that represented a variety of types of functions and non-functions. The course was anchored by linear and quadratic relationships most common in secondary mathematics. Participants, including prospective teachers in the course, showed growth in their ability to define function, to provide examples of functions and link them to the definition, to make connections between function representations, and to consider the role of definitions in mathematics and the K–12 classroom.

In Lo et al. (2008), prospective teachers participated in a one-semester course in which a typical lesson began with a brief introduction of a task, followed by individual problem solving, small group discourse, and then whole-class discussion where different strategies and justifications were presented, clarified, and compared. This cycle may repeat two to three times during a lesson. Focusing solely on the whole number multiplication portion of the course (which consist of four lessons) after students previously worked on developing and justifying reasoning strategies for addition and subtraction, the authors found growth in the participants' knowledge of this concept. In another study, Crespo and Sinclair (2008) explored the problem-posing behavior of prospective elementary teachers in a mathematics methods course framed in a "pedagogy of inquiry" rather than a "pedagogy of presentation" to give them opportunities to read, explore, and investigate forms of mathematics teaching that value and promote students' sense making and reasoning. The course included engaging the participants in doing mathematics. Two interventions designed for the study were integrated within the course's goals and tasks: exploration of a mathematical situation as a precursor to mathematical problem posing and development of aesthetic criteria to judge the mathematical quality of the problems posed. Results showed that both interventions led to improved problem posing and mathematically richer understandings of what makes a problem "good."

Finally, Prediger (2010) examined students' perspectives of equations, equalities, and meanings of the equal sign using an example of concrete sequence of learning as part of a teacher education course on school algebra and its teaching and learning for prospective middle-school teachers. The first activity in the sequence was the writing of a spontaneous, individual analysis of a teaching episode. It was followed by a discussion of different suggestions and evaluation of the answers of colleagues. In the second activity, the learning situation was enriched by another teaching episode, video recorded in a grade 11 calculus course. The approach allowed the participants to construct didactically sensitive mathematical knowledge for teaching and developed subjective needs for a deeper analysis.

These studies illustrate how the features indicated by Watson and Mason (2007) may be put into practice. They suggest that a variety of approaches may lead to positive learning outcomes for prospective teachers. The studies also suggest a current trend of having prospective teachers probe more deeply fundamental mathematical ideas from the school curriculum linked to the learner's activity and related mathematical understanding. Teachers are asked to revisit familiar content and to examine it in ways unfamiliar to them in order to get to the underlying meanings of the mathematics concepts and procedures and how they may develop in the classroom context. A central goal of such studies, then, is considering approaches for helping prospective teachers to understand deeply the mathematics they teach.

PROSPECTIVE TEACHERS' KNOWLEDGE OF MATHEMATICS TEACHING

In addition to content knowledge, teachers need sound pedagogical knowledge for mathematics. Thus, the nature and development of knowledge for teaching mathematics continue to receive attention in research on prospective mathematics teachers. In this section, we discuss a sample of studies we reviewed to highlight what they focused on in terms of the perspectives and issues of the knowledge and approaches used to facilitate its development.

Perspectives of Knowledge of Mathematics Teaching

As with content knowledge, a unique body of knowledge of mathematics teaching that teachers should hold is not clearly defined. However, developments in research on mathematics education since the 1970s indicate the need for teachers to take into account students' thinking and learning processes. These factors are reflected in current theories of the nature of this knowledge. For example, building on Shulman's (1986) notion of pedagogical content knowledge (PCK), Ball and colleagues (Ball et al., 2008; Hill, Ball, & Schilling, 2008) described mathematics knowledge for teaching in terms of three types of knowledge:

- *Knowledge of content and students*, that is, "content knowledge intertwined with knowledge of how students think about, know, or learn this particular content" (Hill, Ball et al., 2008, p. 375). This includes knowledge associated with teachers having to anticipate student errors and common misconceptions, interpret students' incomplete thinking, and predict what students are likely to do with specific tasks and what they will find interesting or challenging.
- *Knowledge of content and teaching*, that is, knowledge about how to *build* on students' thinking and how to address student errors effectively. This includes knowledge associated

with teachers having to sequence content for instruction, recognize instructional pros and cons of difficult representations, and size up mathematical issues in responding to students' novel approaches.

* *Knowledge of curriculum*, that is, the familiarity with the full range of programs, instructional materials, and tools available for teaching particular concepts at different levels.

Our review of recent studies of prospective mathematics teachers suggests that there is consistency between these proposed dimensions of knowledge of mathematics teaching and those that researchers have explored in their studies. Table 10.3 provides specific examples of this knowledge as used in such studies. As discussed in the next section, there are issues with this knowledge for prospective teachers.

Issues With Prospective Teachers' Knowledge of Mathematics Teaching

Our previous findings (Ponte & Chapman, 2008) and current review of studies continue to reflect a trend of issues with prospective teachers' knowledge of mathematics teaching. Some of the issues raised in studies in our previous review included holding naive beliefs about teaching and learning, having difficulty in explaining students' errors, having little knowledge of the difficulties children experienced with word problems and possible sources of these difficulties, focusing only on the correctness of their students' answers, being inclined to asking questions that focused on getting students to an answer, and a having limited capacity to carry out active sense making with their students. Current studies we reviewed add to this list as in the following examples.

Using a framework designed to discriminate among tasks according to their cognitive complexity, Osana et al. (2007) examined the nature of prospective teachers' evaluations of elementary mathematics problems. Findings demonstrated that, overall, the prospective teachers had more difficulty accurately classifying problems considered to represent high levels of cognitive complexity compared to simpler problems. Those with strong mathematics knowledge were able to sort the problems more accurately than those with weaker content knowledge. Morris, Hiebert, and Spitzer (2009) studied the successes and challenges **that** prospective teachers were likely to experience as they unpacked lesson-level mathematical learning goals (i.e., identify subconcepts and subskills that feed into target learning goals). Findings indicated that they could identify mathematical subconcepts of learning goals in supportive contexts but could not spontaneously apply a strategy of unpacking learning goals to plan for, or evaluate, teaching and learning. Finally, Karp (2010) analyzed the experiences of secondary school prospective teachers during a teaching methods course offered prior to their student teaching, but involving actual teaching and reflexive analysis of it. Findings indicated that participants possessed insufficient knowledge of content and students, as seen, for example, by their difficulties with

Table 10.3 Examples of prospective teachers' knowledge of mathematics teaching studied.

(Mis)conceptions—fraction multiplication	Isiksal & Cakiroglu, 2011
Teaching ratio and proportion	Ben-Chaim, Keret, & Ilany, 2007
Teaching geometry	Nason, Chalmers, & Yeh, 2012; Barrantes & Blanco, 2006
Providing explanations	Charalambous, Hill, & Ball, 2011
Evidence of conceptual understanding	Bartell et al., 2013
Multiple representations/meanings	Ryken, 2009
Appraising elementary tasks	Osana, Lacroix, Tucker, & Desrosiers, 2007
Using curriculum material/textbooks	Lloyd, 2008; Nicol & Crespo, 2006; Davis, 2009
Planning and evaluating instruction	Morris, Hiebert, & Spitzer, 2009
Problem-solving instruction	Karp, 2010
Evaluating students' achievement	Spitzer, Phelps, Beyers, Johnson, & Sieminski, 2011
Analyzing mathematics teaching	Alsawaie & Alghazo, 2010

understanding students' thinking. While the number of mathematics courses they completed was high, in general, their ability to listen to their students and to react to what they said was largely limited by their own mathematical knowledge and conceptions of mathematics.

While, as the preceding studies suggest, there are ongoing concerns about prospective mathematics teachers' knowledge, other studies also suggest a shift to addressing what they know or are able to do, thus moving away from the deficiency perspective to one of understanding their sense making. For example, Isiksal and Cakiroglu (2011) studied prospective teachers' knowledge of common conceptions and misconceptions that grade 6–7 students have about multiplication of fractions, the sources of these misconceptions, and the pedagogical strategies they knew to overcome these misconceptions. Findings indicated five types of prospective teachers' perceptions of children's mistakes: based on algorithms, on inappropriate intuitions, on formal knowledge of fraction operations, on misunderstanding fraction symbolism, and on misunderstanding the problem. The participants also suggested three categories of strategies (based on teaching methods, formal knowledge of fractions, and psychological constructs) that could be used to overcome these difficulties. In another study, Barrantes and Blanco (2006) examined prospective primary school teachers' conceptions of teaching and learning school-level geometry and found that the participants could be distributed in three groups: those fully convinced by traditional forms of teaching; those holding traditional inclination with innovative features (the majority); and those similar to the second group but openly showing a rejection of the traditional tendencies. The researchers' overall conception is that geometry should be taught in the same way as other parts of mathematics, except for geometrical figures and models that should be handled and manipulated by students.

Finally, two other studies focused on teaching resources. Nicol and Crespo (2006) considered how four prospective teachers interpreted and used textbooks while learning to teach mathematics and found that they had varied approaches, ranging from adherence, to elaboration, to creation. Lloyd (2008) focused on one prospective teacher's interactions with mathematics curriculum materials from two distinct programs used during her internship in a kindergarten classroom and found that although she used each curriculum in distinct ways, her curriculum use was adaptive in both cases.

This sample of studies on prospective teachers' knowledge of mathematics teaching indicates both limitations and sense making in the three areas of student, teaching, and curriculum associated with Ball et al.'s (2008) view of pedagogical content knowledge. These studies suggest that teacher education needs to continue to find meaningful ways to address ongoing concerns and to build on the sense making of prospective teachers. The next section considers some of these ways that have been researched in the period of our review.

Development of Prospective Teachers' Knowledge of Mathematics Teaching

Our previous findings (Ponte & Chapman, 2008) indicated two themes that were central to the approaches used in studies on development of prospective mathematics teachers' knowledge of teaching: reflection and integrating content and pedagogy. Reflection is considered important for prospective teachers to address their preeducation-program sense of what teaching methods are good or bad, which they use to frame their learning. As Jaworski and Gellert (2003) explained, when prospective teachers enter initial mathematics teacher education they already have extensive knowledge about mathematics teaching, but this knowledge is limited because it is based mainly on their experience as students. The implication, then, is that it is important for programs to engage prospective teachers in learning opportunities that enable them to reconstruct their initial knowledge and understanding of mathematics teaching. This requires awareness and scrutiny of this prior knowledge. Reflection is a key process for achieving this. However, while this perspective of reflection on self was a focus in studies in our previous review (Ponte & Chapman, 2008), it is less so in current studies. Instead, there seems to be a shift away from reflecting on initial personal theories and conceptions but an ongoing focus on PCK that includes integrating content and pedagogy, the second theme in our previous findings. This latter theme deals with ways to develop new understandings of mathematics teaching, which is evident in many of the studies in our current review. Table 10.4 summarizes examples of key items in the interventions studied to promote development of such knowledge of mathematics teaching.

The following summaries of some of these studies highlight these interventions and the impact on the prospective teachers' learning. For example, Spitzer et al. (2011) studied an intervention to support beginning prospective elementary teachers in improving their ability to recognize and evaluate evidence of student achievement in a mathematical lesson. The intervention included a lesson engaging participants in making claims about student achievement, considering information that suggested their initial claims were incorrect, and examining the source of their errors, and a second lesson using a card-sorting task to further develop their understanding of the need for alignment between evidence of student understanding and the learning goal under consideration. Participants were given seven cards, each listing a different learning goal related to decimal concepts, and 12 cards, each providing a sample student response. The learning goal cards included both conceptual and procedural goals, and the student response cards included both revealing and nonrevealing evidence. Participants were asked to match each learning goal card with the student response cards that constituted evidence of achievement of that particular learning goal. Findings indicated that the participants' ability to evaluate evidence improved: for example, they were more likely to rely on student thinking as evidence and were better able to recognize when evidence was not relevant to a learning goal. However, less improvement occurred in their ability to identify evidence that is not revealing of students' understanding (e.g., detailed procedural steps).

Focusing on mathematical tasks, Charalambous et al. (2011) studied whether prospective teachers could learn to provide explanations during their teacher preparation. If so, what did this learning entail and what contributed to it? The intervention was a content course, built around rich problems and aimed at helping participants develop flexible understanding of important ideas and processes within the realm of number theory and operations. It also offered them opportunities to practice using representations, providing explanations, and analyzing others' thinking. Findings, based on four prospective teachers, indicated that they all made progress in learning to provide instructional explanations to varying degrees.

Some studies explicitly addressed PCK. For example, Nason et al. (2012) studied changes that occurred to prospective teachers' knowledge about the teaching and learning of primary school geometry and factors that influenced those changes. Intervention involved a lesson-plan study of geometry within a computer-supported collaborative learning environment. Findings indicated that the intervention facilitated considerable growth in the participants' PCK in terms of organization, representation, and presentation of content in the lesson plans and the quality and sequencing of questions. İmre and Akkoç (2012) studied the development of elementary prospective teachers' PCK of number patterns in terms of knowledge of students' understanding and difficulties, and knowledge of pattern-specific strategies and multiple representations to apply these strategies. The intervention consisted of field work during a practicum in elementary schools (grades 1–8) and weekly on-campus classes to reflect on their

Table 10.4 Examples of key items of approaches for knowledge of mathematics teaching studied.

Structured tasks	Spitzer et al., 2011
Investigative tasks	Ben-Chaim et al., 2007
Video-lesson analysis	Alsawaie & Alghazo, 2010
Weekly field work and micro-teaching	İmre & Akkoç, 2012
Lesson plan study	Nason et al., 2012
Rich mathematical problems	Charalambous et al., 2011
Classroom artifacts	Ryken, 2009
Textbooks	Davis, 2009

experiences in schools and conduct micro-teaching activities. Findings indicated improvement of the three participants' knowledge, including the way they took students' understanding of and difficulties with patterns into account and used pattern-specific strategies during the abduction phase in their teaching. Also, Davis (2009) studied the influence of reading and planning from two differently organized mathematics textbooks on high-school prospective teachers' PCK and content knowledge of exponential functions. On the posttest, their PCK grew based on their use of the textbook that focused more on the places where students might experience difficulties.

Finally, classroom artifacts played a role in some studies as in Ryken (2009) that studied how the act of representing helped prospective elementary teachers determine differences in the quality of students' representations, the problem-solving challenges encountered, and whether analyzing visual representations enhance pedagogical reasoning. The participants engaged in two tasks: a mathematics lesson in which they represented a children's story mathematically and a master's project in which they used artifacts collected during student teaching to reexamine their teaching practices. Findings revealed that analyzing representations helped the prospective teachers rethink their teaching practices.

These studies suggest that a variety of approaches with positive learning outcomes could be used to facilitate the development of prospective teachers' knowledge of mathematics teaching. The focus is on situations that are directly related to school mathematics. These approaches are related to two categories that Ball et al. (2008) identified as PCK: addressing knowledge of mathematics and learners, and of mathematics and teaching. Thus a central goal for such studies is considering approaches that will help teachers to understand their students and how to engage them deeply in the mathematics they teach. Ball et al. (2008) suggest a trend similar to the focus on "content and pedagogy" we identified in Ponte and Chapman (2008). However, the apparent decrease in focus on reflection on preprogram knowledge could be a result of an increase on the focus on student thinking as well as some overlap between studies we have categorized as dealing with identity discussed next.

PROSPECTIVE TEACHERS' IDENTITY

While the notion of identity has different meanings based on different theoretical perspectives, in Ponte and Chapman (2008) we made a case for prospective teachers' professional identity being about the professional self they construct and reconstruct in becoming and being teachers. It includes their appropriation of the values and norms of the profession, their core beliefs about teaching and about themselves as teachers, a vision of what it means to be an "excellent teacher" and of the kind of teacher they want to be, a sense of self as a learner, and a capacity to reflect on experience. This perspective provides our basis for identifying studies in relation to identity.

In Ponte and Chapman (2008) we indicated that identity was an underrepresented area of research on prospective mathematics teachers. Our current review suggests that there were few studies dealing explicitly with identity as a main focus. However, many studies continue to partly or implicitly address related features of identity based on the preceding definition of it. In this section, we discuss a sample of such studies to highlight examples of these features of identity and the development of them. Table 10.5 summarizes these features and studies we consider.

Features of Prospective Teachers' Identity

The following summaries of some studies in Table 10.5 highlight these features of identity in terms of how they are interpreted and related to prospective mathematics teachers. In Llewellyn (2009), identity is regarded in terms of gender, control, choice, and confidence

Table 10.5 Examples of features of prospective teachers' professional identity studied.

Gender, control, choice, and confidence	Llewellyn, 2009
Professional goals, values	Goos & Benninon, 2008
Oppressive and liberative teaching practices	Yow, 2012
Efficacy beliefs	Swars, Smith, Smith, & Hart, 2009
Views of a "good teacher"	Charalambous, Philippou, & Kyriakides, 2008
Mathematical motivation	Lavy & Shriki, 2008
Mathematical sophistication	Newton, 2009
Reasoning attitude	Jansen, 2009
Reflection on own teaching	Seaman & Szydlik, 2007
Reflective stance	Peretz, 2006
	Jansen & Spitzer 2009
	Stockero, 2008

within mathematical discourses. These discourses are often gendered, can overlap, and can be both productive and restrictive while they work to normalize (or not) the identity of the prospective teacher. Findings for the two prospective primary school teachers showed that, despite their similar actual mathematical attainment, there was a striking difference between Alex's (male) self-positioning as a "mathematics person" and Sam's (female) placing outside of the discourse of "mathematics person" through some unstable conception of confidence. Both sought to be in control of mathematics.

In Newton (2009), identity is implied in terms of motivation, defined as value, self-concept of ability, and anxiety. The study examined prospective elementary school teachers' motivations for working with fractions before and after taking a course designed to deepen their understanding of elementary school mathematics. At posttest, participants' value (importance and usefulness of fractions) and self-concept of ability increased while anxiety decreased, but these changes differed by instructor. In Jansen (2009), identity is regarded also in terms of motivation, defined to be a motive (e.g., a wish, intention, or drive) to engage in a specific activity. It can be achieved through interactions of multiple values, beliefs, and goals. The study addressed what motivates prospective elementary teachers to participate in whole-class discussions during mathematics content courses for teachers. Results indicated that they were motivated by positive utility values for participating, to demonstrate competence, or to help others. Negative utility values for participating were expressed by those who preferred to learn through actively listening and were likely to report having a shy personality.

Some studies included beliefs, as in Seaman and Szydlik (2007) where identity is implied in terms of mathematical sophistication, which is related to beliefs about the nature of mathematical behavior. The study examined prospective teachers' understandings of basic mathematical tasks to determine their use or non-use of various indicators of mathematical sophistication. Participants displayed a set of values and avenues for learning mathematics that was so impoverished and different from that of the mathematical community, that their attempts to create fundamental mathematical understandings were often unsuccessful. In Yow (2012), identity is regarded in terms of one being an "oppressive" or "liberative" teacher, and a practice is oppressive or liberative depending on the belief, motive, or intention behind the action. The study considered how prospective secondary teachers viewed themselves as oppressive or liberative mathematics teachers. Findings indicated that they were more likely to write liberative scenarios about their practice than oppressive ones.

One study that mentioned reflection is Jansen and Spitzer (2009), where identity is implied in terms of reflective thinking skills, in particular prospective teachers' ability to describe and interpret their own teaching. The study examined prospective middle school mathematics teachers' reflective thinking skills to understand how they learned from their own teaching practice when engaging in a modified lesson-study experience. Findings indicated that, when describing their students' thinking, participants focused on identifying students' specific mathematical understandings and differentiating between individual students' thinking. Most of them were moving toward reflective thinking.

Collectively, these studies provide important ways of thinking about and understanding different aspects of prospective mathematics teachers' identity. They also raise issues with these features of identity: for example, issues with confidence, anxiety, motivation, values, and mathematical sophistication. This suggests that teacher education needs to continue to find meaningful ways to facilitate the development of prospective teachers' professional identity. The next section considers some of these ways that have been researched in the period of our review.

Development of Prospective Teachers' Identity

The development of a teacher's identity is a continuing and dynamic process affected by multiple influences beginning before entry into an education program and with formal teacher education being only one stage of it. However, based on the studies we reviewed, our focus is on interventions to facilitate development carried out in the context of teacher education programs. As we discussed in Ponte and Chapman (2008), development of identity tends to be a byproduct of teacher education rather than a targeted outcome. These programs could include development of features such as the images, values, and norms of prospective teachers concerning their professional roles (about students, other teachers, and the community) and themselves as teachers. They also could include development of activities related to field experiences, such as observing the practice of experienced teachers or reflecting on one's own practice as student teacher. These possibilities provide a basis for identifying studies that deal with identity development.

Our previous findings (Ponte & Chapman, 2008) indicated two themes that were explicit or implicit in the interventions used in studies on development of prospective mathematics teachers' identity: (i) inquiry/reflection of/on practice and (ii) reflection on self before, during, and after the practicum and other field experiences. In both cases, the development of reflective skills is as important as the development of new knowledge and views. Our findings of current studies suggest an ongoing trend of explicit and implicit focus on reflection: for example, reflection is implied through group communication, during mathematical activities, and interaction with others during practicum, and it is explicit in working with a video case. However, there is less explicit focus of reflection on self or practicum teaching. We illustrate this in the following sample of studies in which we identify the features of identity implied and highlight the nature and impact of the intervention on them.

Goos and Benninon (2008) stands out in our examples as it explicitly mentions identity in framing the work. The intervention involved a website established to encourage professional discussion among prospective teachers outside class times and during the practicum periods, and also to provide continuing support when they became beginning teachers. The researchers imposed minimal structure on communication, allowing the participants to use the site in ways that met their needs. The study investigated how this online community, focused on becoming a teacher of secondary school mathematics, emerged and was sustained. Findings indicated that the emergent design of the community contributed to its sustainability in allowing the prospective teachers to define their own professional goals and values.

Another exception involves explicit focus on reflection. In Stockero (2008), identity is implied in terms of a reflective stance. The intervention involved a middle-school mathematics methods course with a goal to help prospective teachers realize that not all students think about mathematics in the same way and that understanding their thinking is central to the meaningful development of mathematical ideas. The course used a video-case curriculum as a major instructional tool to develop the prospective teachers' reflective stance. The prospective teachers showed changes in their level of reflection, their tendency to ground their analyses in evidence, and their focus on student thinking.

Some studies included a focus on changing beliefs/image as in these examples. In Swars et al. (2009), identity is regarded in terms of pedagogical beliefs, efficacy beliefs, and anxiety. The intervention involved a two-course mathematics methods sequence and field placements. The first course on grades PreK–2 presented a paradigm shift in what it means to know and do mathematics, how children learn mathematics with understanding, and how teachers can support children's problem solving and construction of understanding. The second course, on grades 3–5, allowed more time for continued development toward a constructivist perspective. Across both courses, there were extensive field experiences. The results indicated that anxiety and efficacy beliefs were impacted positively. In Charalambous et al. (2008), identity is also implied in terms of beliefs—that is, efficacy beliefs, defined as one's beliefs about one's ability to organize and execute tasks to achieve specific goals. The intervention was a field-experience course. The prospective teachers' interaction with their mentors, university tutors, peers, and pupils impacted their efficacy beliefs in diverse ways: for example, mentors informed their efficacy beliefs by modeling teaching and providing feedback and by the latent messages that their behavior conveyed to them. In addition, in Lavy and Shriki (2008), identity is regarded in terms of image of the "good teacher," which is associated with the teacher's personality. The intervention involved computerized project-based learning in a course that focused on teaching middle school and engaged prospective teachers in worthwhile mathematical tasks, discussions of pedagogical and mathematical issues, and examination of their beliefs about teaching and learning mathematics. Before the study, their image of the "good teacher" was a "motherly" character whose main concern was to reduce the fear of mathematics and encourage students especially when they fail. After the study, their image shifted to a figure that encourages the students to see the beauty of mathematics.

Finally, in Peretz (2006), identity is implied in terms of reasoning attitude, that is, improving reasoning includes changing attitudes. The intervention was a constructivist Teaching–Learning–Space used to get prospective elementary school teachers to unpack and reconstruct a deeper and more flexible understanding of basic mathematical concepts, which for the most part they already "know." The main goals were to encourage prospective teachers to understand their mathematical "doings" and to promote a reasoning attitude within them, rather than just teaching them the basic arithmetical concepts. Findings showed that the approach can help prospective elementary school teachers to change their attitudes towards reasoning in mathematics.

In Ponte and Chapman (2008) we concluded that the studies we reviewed at that point suggested that inquiry of one's own practice could be a powerful way of constructing knowledge, an intensive activity that may lead teachers to reflect on themselves, to learn about themselves, and to direct their own development. The current studies contribute less to this and more to our understanding of different features of identity and how different activities are successful in promoting identity development. They do imply the importance of reflection and inquiry in these activities, but we still have much to learn about the conditions at the personal, collective, and program levels that may foster such activities. We need more studies that focus more explicitly on mathematical identity to understand meaningful intervention to facilitate its development.

Teacher Education Settings, Activities, and Tools

The organization of teacher education and its relation to the social and educational context are important aspects of prospective teacher education. In this section we identify a new trend that has gained attention in recent studies. In particular, we discuss institutional elements that shape specific aspects of teacher education and program elements that frame learning activities and contexts with a focus on practicum, lesson study, video/multimedia cases, and online settings. Whenever possible we strive to relate these elements to the program study plans, the nature of the participants' activity, the relation between mathematics content and mathematics teaching didactics (PCK), and the relation of program activities to actual classroom practice and school culture.

General Aspects

Based on data from a survey of 21 countries/regions, Tatto, Lerman and Novotna (2010) indicated that in most cases prospective mathematics teacher education is carried out at universities. However, economic constraints seem to have generated a trend to move prospective mathematics teacher education towards primary and secondary schools. Everywhere, prospective teacher education is strongly regulated at the national or local level. There are two main forms of organization for these programs: "concurrent preparation," prevalent for primary teachers, in which general education and professional education are provided jointly in a single program; and "consecutive preparation," prevalent for secondary teachers, that establishes two separate periods for both kinds of preparation. Teacher educators tend to be mathematicians for the mathematics courses, general educators for the pedagogy courses, and mathematics educators for the didactic courses. In some cases, mathematics educators assume the responsibility for courses in didactics, mathematics, and pedagogy. The emphasis on mathematics content knowledge varies widely, but tends to be high for secondary teachers and low for primary teachers. In contrast, the emphasis on didactics and pedagogy tends to be high in most countries/regions in the survey, although this is more noticeable at secondary level. In most cases the entry level into teacher education is at the end of secondary education; however, in three countries (England, Germany, and Italy) it is after an initial undergraduate degree. In some countries a master degree is necessary to become a teacher.

The varieties of prospective teacher education routes, including some in which academic teacher education is minimal or nonexistent, and the different emphasis on different strands (content, pedagogy, didactics, teaching practice), show that teacher education is still not completely established as a professional field. This suggests that researchers, besides being concerned with specific features of prospective teacher education, also need to attend to such global issues in order to promote more coherence and quality in the process of preparation of new teachers and its acceptance by decision makers and the society in general.

Practicum and Lesson Study

The practicum, internship, field experience, or student teaching periods in schools has a long history of being recognized as a key element of teacher preparation. Tatto et al. (2010) indicated that periods of practice in schools vary from 45 days to two years in most countries/regions in their survey. This variation in time and organizational features show that the purpose and role of this element of teacher education is still not well established at an international level. In some cases it seems that the major aim is to provide a smooth transition from the status of prospective teacher towards that of in-service teacher—helping the development of most-needed survival skills—whereas in other cases, it seems to be regarded as a key stage of the development of an integrated set of competencies necessary for effective mathematics teaching. However, regardless of the aim, school-based experiences can allow prospective teachers to develop their professional competence and identity, integrating and developing new knowledge and attitudes, based on what they learned in university courses or other formal and informal situations. The way this enhances the quality of a teacher's preparation depends on the nature of the experience provided, especially if it is based on well-structured activities (Wilson, Floden, & Ferrini-Mundy, 2001). Such activities depend on the characteristics of the cooperating school, the cooperating teacher, and the articulation between school activities and university supervision, as evidenced in some studies.

For example, Peterson and Williams (2008) studied the learning opportunities provided by the interactions between a prospective teacher and cooperating teacher, analyzing the core themes that emerged from their conversations. Whereas one prospective/cooperating teacher pair focused on controlling student behavior and rarely talked about mathematics for teaching, another pair focused on students' active participation and their understanding of mathematics in the lesson. The authors suggested such different experiences in the practicum can have a deep effect on prospective teachers' understanding of mathematics and mathematics teaching. Another study by Leatham and Peterson (2010) focused on cooperating teachers' perceptions of the purpose of student teaching. From a survey of 45 secondary mathematics cooperating teachers, they concluded that the most common purposes were interacting with experienced teachers, having real classroom experiences, and learning about classroom management while the most common roles for cooperating teachers were providing opportunities for experience, modeling, reflection, and sharing knowledge. The cooperating teachers saw themselves as experienced teachers but not as teacher educators.

A general concern is the mismatch between the curriculum advocated in teacher education programs and what prospective teachers often find in schools, which can lead to what is learned at the university being contradicted and dismissed during the practicum experiences. This concern is implied by Rhoads, Radu, and Weber (2011) who analyzed the experiences of nine prospective high-school mathematics teachers in their practicum. The results indicated that most of the participants supported reform-oriented teaching and conceptual understanding in mathematics, but all were paired with cooperating teachers who valued traditional instruction and procedural understanding. However, some of these prospective teachers had positive experiences with their cooperating teachers, valuing constructive critical feedback associated with concrete recommendations for improvement, freedom to use their own teaching methods, and a friendly and supportive relationship. In another study, Philipp et al. (2007) examined the effects of early field experiences carried out in schools and in a laboratory environment, on the mathematics content knowledge and beliefs of 159 prospective primary-school teachers enrolled in the first of four mathematics content courses of the program. They concluded that the prospective teachers who studied children's mathematical thinking while learning mathematics improved their mathematical content knowledge and developed new refined beliefs about mathematics, teaching, and learning more than those of the other groups.

Another organizational setting that recently has been used in several studies in the preparation of prospective teachers is lesson study, which involves a cyclic process of planning and testing teaching. For example, Fernandez and Zilliox (2011) designed instructional experiences for prospective primary and secondary teachers based on features of lesson study. The 36 secondary participants carried out repeated cycles of planning, implementing, and revising lessons in a micro-teaching setting with videotaped lessons while the 48 prospective primary teachers carried out similar activities in actual schools. Findings indicated that they were able to expose their beliefs and practices to peers and other participants, trialing and revising their beliefs and practices, led by the dynamic of the lesson study cycles. The experiences helped them to understand and implement reform-oriented teaching practices. Murata and Pothen (2011) had prospective teachers read about lesson study, watch videos, read research-related readings, and do assignments such as looking at data from teacher interviews and student assessment data, and writing a reflection paper. They concluded that the participants developed an understanding of the importance of student learning, enhanced their understanding of the mathematics content, developed skills for designing and evaluating lessons and for interacting with the children, and learnt how to collaborate with other teachers. In addition, Ricks (2011), working with four prospective secondary teachers also in a lesson study, suggested that their reflection may be conceptualized in two main categories, one related to specific episodes unconnected to future activity, and another connecting reflective episodes into a cyclic progression in which experimental action supported the refinement of ideas.

Considering several studies conducted in the frame of lesson study, Potari (2011) concluded that two factors were most important: (i) the role of teacher educators as facilitators of prospective teachers' learning through different degrees of guidance and support, and (ii) the role of group collaboration providing the opportunity to share ideas, see teaching and learning in new perspectives, develop a sense of belonging, and develop a sense for mathematics teaching toward reform-oriented practices. These can support the integration of planning, study of curriculum documents and relevant research findings, observation, and reflection. The drawbacks are time and organizational effort required.

Video and Multimedia Cases and Online Settings

In the last few years many studies have addressed the potential of multimedia cases and video clips in prospective teacher education. For example, Santagata, Zannoni, and Stigler (2007) used unedited videos of entire lessons to support lesson analysis for prospective secondary mathematics teachers. The focus was on parts of the lesson and learning goals, students' thinking and learning, and possible alternative teaching strategies. Participants commented on events they found interesting regarding teachers' actions and decisions, students' behavior and learning, and mathematics content. Findings indicated that they improved significantly, moving from simple descriptions of what they saw on the video to analyses focused on the observable effects of teacher actions on student learning. In another study, Alsawaie and Alghazo (2010) explored the effect of using a methodology of video lesson analysis on the ability of prospective middle- and high-school mathematics teachers to analyze mathematics teaching. The experimental group analyzed 10 video lessons on their own time throughout the semester, interacting via discussion forums using the Blackboard online platform. Both the experimental and the control group wrote a pre- and a postintervention analysis of a video lesson. Findings indicated that the intervention improved the experimental group's ability to analyze mathematics teaching while little improvement occurred for the control group.

Regarding multimedia cases, McGraw, Lynch, Koc, Budak, and Brown (2007) studied their potential as tools in teacher education. They examined online and face-to-face discussions that took place within heterogeneous groups composed of prospective middle and secondary mathematics teachers as well as in-service mathematics teachers, mathematicians, and mathematics teacher educators. After a first activity based on the notion of task cognitive demand, the participants viewed and discussed a multimedia case designed by the researchers that included video clips and transcripts of classroom activities, and provided many possibilities for examining teaching and learning. Findings indicated that most discussions within small groups tended to focus on issues of task implementation in the classroom.

As the preceding sample of studies suggest, multimedia cases and video clips can be useful resources in prospective mathematics teacher education, enabling easy access to rich representations of practice. In these studies, whereas some researchers chose to use video clips that represented classroom work with very little editing structure, others designed sophisticated multimedia materials combining video, single images, and text, with many interactive features. In general, many kinds of explorations are possible in both cases. However, a critical issue is how these materials and explorations are integrated in the main goals and other activities in teacher education programs.

The use of online settings in prospective teacher education has also developed recently as evidenced in Alsawaie and Alghazo (2010). In another study, Llinares and Valls (2007, 2010) examined how participation and reification of ideas about mathematics teaching emerged in the discussions about mathematics teaching based on the analysis of video cases. Prospective primary teachers, as part of a mathematics methods course, participated in two virtual learning environments that integrated the analysis of video clips, online discussions, and essay writing about key aspects of mathematics teaching. Findings indicated that the structure of the learning environments supported their inquiry and knowledge-building through activities like identifying, interpreting, and designing. Llinares and Valls (2010) also indicated that relevant aspects to explain the prospective teachers' learning included the specific questions posed in online discussions, the way in which the theoretical information was used to frame and to interpret the events from mathematics teaching, and the characteristics of engagement with others participating in the online discussions. In addition, Fernández, Llinares, and Valls (2012) sought to characterize prospective mathematics teachers' development of professional noticing of students' mathematical thinking in online contexts. They concluded that the online discussions supported this development because of the role of writing, that is, the final written text supported the collaborative activity.

Online environments extend the range of possible forms of work in prospective teacher education. Most often they are integrated with face-to-face activities. The research carried out so far shows that, by integrating individual reflections and collective online discussions, suitable learning experiences may be provided to promote the development of prospective teachers' professional knowledge and competencies.

CONCLUDING REFLECTIONS

The education of prospective teachers who teach mathematics, either as specialists in the discipline or along with other curriculum subjects, constitutes one of the main fields of activity of mathematics educators. In this chapter, we presented examples of recent international research in this field with special attention to studies carried out in the last eight years in the domains of the nature and development of prospective mathematics teachers' knowledge of mathematics and teaching mathematics and their identity and the learning contexts involved. In this final section we reflect on the trend in research process and findings, and some ongoing issues.

Trends in Research Process

In the last eight years there were important efforts to carry out large-scale research projects dealing with prospective teacher education, teacher knowledge, and teacher quality of instruction, drawing on sophisticated measuring instruments and large samples of participants. However, similar to our findings in Ponte and Chapman (2008), most of the studies we discussed in this chapter are qualitative case studies or small-scale studies using instruments and processes of data collection such as interviews, observations, classroom productions, and journal writing of the prospective teachers, researchers' field notes, audio, and video recording, questionnaires, and tests. This suggests that studies of prospective teacher education continue to privilege small-scale designs and qualitative techniques. This is understandable given the resources necessary to carry out large-scale quantitative studies and the potential of qualitative designs to address issues intimately related to personal meaning, institutional practices, and traditions. However, specific aspects of these methods of some of these studies prompt us to raise several issues.

The fact that many qualitative studies draw on an insider's perspective (i.e., the research-instructor in an intervention) may be regarded as a positive feature of practitioners (e.g., teacher educators) researching their own practice. To provide a balanced perspective and to add new perspectives and questioning power to this field, these studies need to be combined with studies involving an external perspective and meta-studies. Many qualitative studies have remarkable designs and methodological quality. However, others are mostly one-off activities or involve design problems. For example, there are situations where studies are not designed as case studies of individuals but findings are presented as such. For example, many studies involving an intervention to support prospective teachers' learning are based on courses usually taught by the researcher. In some instances, findings are not reported for all participants in the course, but only for one to four of them and, in some cases, report varying degrees of progress in these participants' learning. There are also issues of variables that are not accounted for in these intervention studies, for example, the dependence of the intervention on the instructor. As one study (Newton, 2009) reported, changes for participants differed by instructors who used the same intervention. These situations involving sample size and confounding variables make it difficult to understand the overall effectiveness of the interventions involved and to evaluate and compare strategies. The design of quantitative studies needs also further refinements, especially regarding consistency of sampling procedures, construct validity, and accuracy of measurements.

Trends in Findings

In spite of possible limitations noted, the studies discussed in this chapter offer some key insights about teacher learning. For example, studies continue to show that there are deficiencies in prospective teachers' knowledge of mathematics and mathematics teaching that require special attention in teacher education. They also suggest that a variety of instructional approaches can make a difference to the quality of this knowledge, such as building on prospective teachers' sense making of mathematics and mathematics learning by involving them in activities that bear on fundamental mathematical ideas at the school level and focusing on the learner's thinking. Inquiring in one's practice has proven to be a powerful way of constructing knowledge about mathematics, about students, about teaching, and about oneself. Several studies show cases of success in which prospective teachers are beginning to develop an identity and assume practices aligned with current mathematics curriculum perspectives. The number of studies addressing features of identity suggests recognition of their importance in promoting and understanding teacher learning. In addition, several studies show the important possibilities provided by new technological media, especially video and online settings, whereas reminding us of the critical role of teacher educators and the construction of collaborative settings as a basis for the development of the teacher education process.

Ongoing Issues

In spite of the success of these studies in facilitating prospective teachers' learning, as we discussed in Ponte and Chapman (2008), what is asked of teacher education can be viewed as an impossible task. In a short time, it must prepare a young (perhaps immature) person to assume a highly complex professional function that involves conducting mathematical activity with large groups of students (20 to 40 or more), who often have little interest in mathematics, have serious affective and social needs, and come from increasingly mixed cultural settings. Further, we ask new teachers to engage in practices that are compatible with innovative curriculum orientations but generally are not the established school approach.

Given such features of teaching, the teacher education agenda is not to find a universal solution to prospective teacher education. It is likely more productive to seek local progress. In this respect, research shows that we may provide prospective teachers with opportunities that will allow them to understand, appreciate, and embrace the complexity of their practice as a basis for ongoing inquiry. Such inquiry may facilitate developing more holistic, grounded notions of teaching and learning mathematics. While research studies suggest strategies that provide some direction for meeting this challenge, true progress will require a relationship among the teacher education institution, the schools, and the educational authorities that provides not only a strong synergy between the work at the university and the participating schools, but also supports novice teachers in the initial phase of their career in education. There are also important issues concerning the interface of mathematics education with educational policy, school administration, and program evaluation that need more attention by mathematics education researchers.

Although prospective mathematics teacher education has gained better understanding of processes by which one learns how to teach mathematics and be a professional teacher and is exploring new technological environments and tools, many questions still remain in this field. As we learn more, many of these questions may remain difficult to answer because local conditions vary widely. Prospective teacher education is not a closed system, but a subsystem that depends on other larger social systems that also evolve in relation to the larger social changes. Such inherent incompleteness is a major challenge and source of interest.

REFERENCES

Alsawaie, O.N., & Alghazo, I.M. (2010). The effect of video-based approach on prospective teachers' ability to analyze mathematics teaching. *Journal of Mathematics Teacher Education, 13*(3), 223–241.

Ball, D. L., Lubienski, S. T., & Mewborn, D. S. (2001). Research on teaching mathematics: The unsolved problems of teachers' mathematical knowledge. In V. Richardson (Ed), *Handbook of research on teaching* (4th ed., pp. 433–456). Washington, DC: AERA.

Ball, D. L, Thames, M.H., & Phelps, G. (2005). *Articulating domains of mathematical knowledge of teaching*. Paper presented at the American Education Research Association Conference, Montreal, Canada.

Ball, D.L., Thames, M.H., & Phelps, G. (2008). Content knowledge for teaching: What makes it special? *Journal of Teacher Education, 59*(5), 389–407.

Barrantes, M., & Blanco, L.J. (2006). A study of prospective primary teachers conceptions of teaching and learning school geometry. *Journal of Mathematics Teacher Education, 9*(5), 411–436.

Bartell, T.G., Webel, C., Bowen, B., & Dyson, N. (2013). Prospective teacher learning: recognizing evidence of conceptual understanding. *Journal of Mathematics Teacher Education, 16*(1), 57–79.

Ben-Chaim, D., Keret, Y., & Ilany, B.-S. (2007). Designing and implementing authentic investigative proportional reasoning tasks: The impact on pre-service mathematics teachers' content and pedagogical knowledge and attitudes. *Journal of Mathematics Teacher Education, 10*(4–6), 333–340.

Beswick, K., Callingham, R., & Watson, J. (2012). The nature and development of middle school mathematics teachers' knowledge. *Journal of Mathematics Teacher Education, 15*(2), 131–157.

Caglayan, G. (2013). Prospective mathematics teachers' sense making of polynomial multiplication and factorization modeled with algebra tiles. *Journal of Mathematics Teacher Education, 16*, 349–378.

Charalambous, C.Y., Hill, H. C., & Ball, D. L. (2011). Prospective teachers' learning to provide instructional explanations: how does it look and what might it take? *Journal of Mathematics Teacher Education, 14*(6), 441–463.

Charalambous, C.Y., Philippou, G. N., & Kyriakides, L. (2008). Tracing the development of preservice teachers' efficacy beliefs in teaching mathematics during fieldwork. *Educational Studies in Mathematics, 67*, 125–142.

Crespo, S., & Sinclair, N. (2008). What makes a problem mathematically interesting? Inviting prospective teachers to pose better problems. *Journal of Mathematics Teacher Education, 11*(5), 395–415.

Davis, J.D. (2009). Understanding the influence of two mathematics textbooks on prospective secondary teachers' knowledge. *Journal of Mathematics Teacher Education, 12*, 365–389.

Fernández, C., Llinares, S., & Valls, J. (2012). Learning to notice students' mathematical thinking through on-line discussions. *ZDM: The International Journal on Mathematics Education, 44*, 477–459.

Fernandez, M. L., & Zilliox, J. (2011). Investigating approaches to lesson study in prospective mathematics teacher education. In L. C. Hart, A. Alston & A. Murata (Eds.), *Lesson study, research and practice in mathematics education* (pp. 85–102). Dordrecht: Springer.

Goos, M., & Benninon, A. (2008). Developing a communal identity as beginning teachers of mathematics: Emergence of an online community of practice. *Journal of Mathematics Teacher Education, 11*, 41–60.

Hill, H., Ball, D.L., & Schilling, S.G. (2008). Unpacking pedagogical content knowledge: Conceptualizing and measuring teachers' topic-specific knowledge of students. *Journal for Research in Mathematics Education, 39*(4), 372–400.

Hill, H.C., Blunk, M.L., Charalambous, C.Y., Lewis, J.M., Phelps, G.C., Sleep, D.L. (2008). Mathematical knowledge for teaching and the mathematical quality of instruction: An exploratory study. *Cognition and Instruction, 26*, 430–511.

İmre, S.Y., & Akkoç, H. (2012). Investigating the development of prospective mathematics teachers' pedagogical content knowledge of generalising number patterns through school practicum. *Journal of Mathematics Teacher Education, 15*(3), 207–226.

Isiksal, M., & Cakiroglu, E. (2011). The nature of prospective mathematics teachers' pedagogical content knowledge: The case of multiplication of fractions. *Journal of Mathematics Teacher Education, 14*, 3, 213–230.

Jansen, A. (2009) Prospective elementary teachers' motivation to participate in whole-class discussions during mathematics content courses for teachers. *Educational Studies in Mathematics*, (2009) 71:145–160.

Jansen, A., & Spitzer, S.M. (2009). Prospective middle school mathematics teachers' reflective thinking skills: Descriptions of their students' thinking and interpretations of their teaching. *Journal of Mathematics Teacher Education, 12*(2), 133–151.

Jaworski, B., & Gellert, U. (2003). Educating new mathematics teachers: Integrating theory and practice, and the roles of practicing teachers. In A. J. Bishop, M. A. Clements, C. Keitel, J. Kilpatrick & F.K.S. Leung (Eds.), *Second international handbook of mathematics education* (pp. 829–875). Dordrecht: Kluwer.

Karp, A. (2010). Analyzing and attempting to overcome prospective teachers' difficulties during problem-solving instruction. *Journal of Mathematics Teacher Education, 13*(2), 121–139.

Kilpatrick, J., Swafford, J., & Findell, B. (Eds.). (2001). *Adding it up: Helping children learn mathematics.* Washington, DC: National Academy Press.

Krauss, S., Brunner, M., Kunter, M., Baumert, J., Neubrand, M., Blum, W., & Jordan, A. (2008). Pedagogical content knowledge and content knowledge of secondary mathematics teachers. *Journal of Educational Psychology, 100*(716–715).

Lavy, I., & Shriki, A. (2008). Investigating changes in prospective teachers' views of a "good teacher" while engaging in computerized project-based learning. *Journal of Mathematics Teacher Education, 11*(4), 259–284.

Leatham, K.R., & Peterson, B.E. (2010). Secondary mathematics cooperating teachers' perceptions of the purpose of student teaching. *Journal of Mathematics Teacher Education, 13*(2), 99–119.

Llewellyn, A. (2009). "Gender games": A post-structural exploration of the prospective teacher, mathematics and identity. *Journal of Mathematics Teacher Education, 12*(6), 411–426.

Llinares, S., & Krainer, K. (2006). Mathematics (student) teachers and teacher educators as learners. In A. Gutierrez & P. Boero (Eds.), *Handbook of research on the psychology of mathematics education: Past, present and future* (pp. 429–460). Rotterdam: Sense Publishers.

Llinares, S., & Valls, J. (2007). The building of pre-service primary teachers' knowledge of mathematics teaching: interaction and online video studies. *Instructional Science, 37*(3), 247–271.

Llinares, S., & Valls, J. (2010). Prospective primary mathematics teachers' learning from online discussions in a virtual video-based environment. *Journal of Mathematics Teacher Education, 13*(2), 177–196.

Lloyd, G.M. (2008). Curriculum use while learning to teach: One student teacher's appropriation of mathematics curriculum materials. *Journal for Research in Mathematics Education, 39*(1), 63–94.

Lo, J.-J., Grant, T.J., & Flowers, J. (2008). Challenges in deepening prospective teachers' understanding of multiplication through justification. *Journal of Mathematics Teacher Education, 11*, 5–22.

Lo, J.-J., & Luo, F. (2012). Prospective elementary teachers' knowledge of fraction division. *Journal of Mathematics Teacher Education, 15*(6), 481–500.

Ma, L. (1999). *Knowing and teaching elementary mathematics.* Mahwah, NJ: Lawrence Erlbaum Associates.

McGraw, R., Lynch, K., Koc, Y., Budak, A., & Brown, C.A. (2007). The multimedia case as a tool for professional development: An analysis of online and face-to-face interaction among mathematics pre-service teachers, mathematicians, and mathematics teacher educators. *Journal of Mathematics Teacher Education, 10*(2), 95–121.

Morris, A.K., Hiebert, J., & Spitzer, S.M. (2009). Mathematical knowledge for teaching in planning and evaluating instruction: What can preservice teachers learn? *Journal for Research in Mathematics Education, 40*(5), 491–529.

Murata, A., & Pothen, B.E. (2011). Lesson study in preservice primary mathematics methods courses: Connecting emerging practice and understanding. In L.C. Hart, A. Alston, & A. Murata (Eds.), *Lesson study, research and practice in mathematics education* (pp. 103–116). Dordrecht: Springer.

Nason, R., Chalmers, C., & Yeh, A. (2012). Facilitating growth in prospective teachers' knowledge: teaching geometry in primary schools. *Journal of Mathematics Teacher Education, 15*(3), 227–249.

National Council of Teachers of Mathematics. (1991). *Professional standards for teaching mathematics.* Reston, VA: Author.

Newton, J.N. (2009). Instructional practices related to prospective elementary school teachers' motivation for fractions. *Journal of Mathematics Teacher Education, 12*, 89–109.

Nicol, C., & Crespo, S. (2006). Learning to teach with mathematics textbooks: How preservice teachers interpret and use curriculum materials. *Educational Studies in Mathematics, 62*, 331–355.

Osana, H., Lacroix, G., Tucker, B.J., & Desrosiers, C. (2007). The role of content knowledge and problem features on preservice teachers' appraisal of elementary tasks. *Journal of Mathematics Teacher Education, 9*(4), 347–380.

Peretz, D. (2006). Enhancing reasoning attitudes of prospective elementary school mathematics teachers. *Journal of Mathematics Teacher Education, 9*(4), 381–400.

Peterson, B.E., & Williams, S.R. (2008). Learning mathematics for teaching in the student teaching experience: Two contrasting cases. *Journal of Mathematics Teacher Education, 11*(6), 459–478.

Philipp, R.A., Ambrose, R., Lamb, L.L.C., Sowder, J.T., Schappele, B.P., Sowder, L., et al. (2007). Effects of early field experiences on the mathematics content knowledge of prospective and beliefs of primary school teachers: An experimental study. *Journal for Research in Mathematics Education,* *38*(5), 438–476.

Pitta-Pantazi, D., & Christou, C. (2011). The structure of prospective kindergarten teachers' proportional reasoning. *Journal of Mathematics Teacher Education, 14*(2), 149–169.

Ponte, J. P., & Chapman, O. (2006). Mathematics teachers' knowledge and practices. In A. Gutierrez & P. Boero (Eds.), *Handbook of research on the psychology of mathematics education: Past, present and future* (pp. 461–494). Rotterdam: Sense Publishers.

Ponte, J. P., & Chapman, O. (2008). Preservice mathematics teachers' knowledge and development. In L. D. English (Ed.) Handbook of international research in mathematics education: Directions for the 21st century (2nd Ed., pp. 225–263). New York: Routledge.

Potari, D. (2011). Response to part II: Emerging issues from lesson study approaches in prospective mathematics teacher education. In L. C. Hart, A. Alston, & A. Murata (Eds.), *Lesson study, research and practice in mathematics education* (pp. 127–132). Dordrecht: Springer.

Prediger, S. (2010). How to develop mathematics-for-teaching and for understanding: The case of meanings of the equal sign. *Journal of Mathematics Teacher Education, 13*(1), 73–93.

Rhoads, K., Radu, I., & Weber, K. (2011). Teacher internship experiences of prospective high school mathematics teachers. *International Journal of Science and Mathematics Education, 9*(4), 975–998.

Ricks, T. E. (2011). Process reflection during Japanese lesson study experiences by prospective secondary mathematics teachers. *Journal of Mathematics Teacher Education, 14*(4), 251–267.

Ryken, A. (2009). Multiple representations as sites for teacher reflection about mathematics learning. *Journal of Mathematics Teacher Education, 12,* 347–364

Santagata, R., Zannoni, C., & Stigler, J. W. (2007). The role of lesson analysis in preservice teacher education: An empirical investigation of teacher learning from a virtual video-based field experience. *Journal of Mathematics Teacher Education, 10*(2), 123–140.

Seaman, C. E., & Szydlik, J. E. (2007). Mathematical sophistication among preservice elementary teachers. *Journal of Mathematics Teacher Education, 10*(3), 167–182.

Shulman, L. S. (1986). Those who understand: Knowledge growth in teaching. *Educational Researcher, 15*(2), 4–14.

Son, J.-W., & Crespo, S. (2009). Prospective teachers' reasoning and response to a student's non-traditional strategy when dividing fractions. *Journal of Mathematics Teacher Education, 12,* 235–261.

Spitzer, S. M., Phelps, C. M., Beyers, J.E.R., Johnson, D.Y., & Sieminski, E. M. (2011). Developing prospective elementary teachers' abilities to identify evidence of student mathematical achievement. *Journal of Mathematics Teacher Education, 14,* 67–87.

Steele, M. D., Hillen, A. F., Smith, M. S. (2013). Developing mathematical knowledge for teaching in a methods course: The case of function. *Journal of Mathematics Teacher Education, 16,* 451–482.

Stephens, A. C. (2006). Equivalence and relational thinking: Preservice elementary teachers' awareness of opportunities and misconceptions. *Journal of Mathematics Teacher Education, 9*(3), 221–248.

Stockero, S. L. (2008). Using a video-based curriculum to develop a reflective stance in prospective mathematics teachers. *Journal of Mathematics Teacher Education, 11*(5), 373–394.

Stylianides, G. J., Stylianides, A. J., & Philippou, G. N. (2007). Preservice teachers' knowledge of proof by mathematical induction. *Journal of Mathematics Teacher Education, 10*(3), 145166.

Swars, S. L., Smith, S. Z., Smith, M. E., & Hart, L. C. (2009). A longitudinal study of effects of a developmental teacher preparation program on elementary prospective teachers' mathematics beliefs. *Journal of Mathematics Teacher Education, 12*(1), 47–66.

Tatto, M. T., Lerman, S., & Novotna, J. (2010). The organization of the mathematics preparation and development of teachers: A report from the ICMI Study 15. *Journal of Mathematics Teacher Education, 13*(4), 313–324.

Tobias, J. M. (2013). Prospective elementary teachers' development of fraction language for defining the whole. *Journal of Mathematics Teacher Education, 16*(2), 85–103.

Watson, A., & Mason, J. (2007). Taken-as-shared: A review of common assumptions about mathematical tasks in teacher education. *Journal of Mathematics Teacher Education, 10*(4), 205–215.

Wilson, S. M., Floden, R. E., & Ferrini-Mundy, J. (2001). *Teacher preparation research: Current knowledge, gaps, and recommendations.* Washington, DC: University of Washington Center for the Study of Teaching and Policy.

Yow, J. A. (2012). Prospective teacher beliefs about liberative and oppressive mathematics teaching practices: A first step toward equitable instruction. *Journal of Mathematics Teacher Education, 15*(1), 83–96.

11 Educating Future Mathematics Education Professors[1]

Jeremy Kilpatrick and Denise A. Spangler
University of Georgia

In the first decades of the 20th century, anyone looking at the pioneering doctoral programs in mathematics education being established by David Eugene Smith at Teachers College, Columbia University, and Felix Klein at the University of Göttingen could not have envisioned the variegated landscape of such programs a century later. Similarly, no one today can with any confidence predict how mathematics education professors will be educated during the next generation, let alone the next century. In this chapter, we examine those features of programs for educating the professorate in mathematics education that ought to persist even as programs come and go; technology advances; instructional media and delivery systems get reconfigured; faculty hiring and working conditions change; and both mathematics and mathematics education curricula are revised in various directions. We explore what it might mean to prepare doctoral students for their future roles as professors of mathematics education.

A NEW GENERATION

Today's doctoral programs in mathematics education are numerous and extremely varied (see Andžāns, Bonka, & Grevholm, 2008, for examples from around the world). Some are located in departments of mathematics or mathematical sciences, where mathematics education might be viewed as a (multidisciplinary) mathematical science. The term *didactics of mathematics* is sometimes used to label such programs. The location is likely to be an artifact of history. The university in which the program is situated might have originated as a normal school or other pedagogical institution whose mathematics department came to encompass, and offer doctoral degrees in, both mathematics and mathematics education. When doctoral programs in mathematics education are located in a department of mathematics or mathematical sciences, a new faculty member in mathematics education might be expected to be especially well prepared in mathematics.

An alternative is for the program in mathematics education to have been placed in a department, school, or college of education that originated outside the university and then was incorporated into it as education gained status as a scholarly field. In a few cases, the program might be located in a separate department of mathematics education or mathematics didactics, but it is much more likely to reside in a department of pedagogy, subject-matter didactics, curriculum and instruction, or general education. Much depends on the size of the program and on its history within the university of which it is a part. The location of the program within the university, however, is generally not the main source of variance in programs.

Some universities have multiple doctoral programs in mathematics education, whereas others share a doctoral program in mathematics education with one or more other universities. An example of an institution with multiple programs is Teachers College, Columbia University, where there are programs in mathematics education leading to the Doctor of Education

(Ed.D.), the Doctor of Education in the College Teaching of an Academic Subject (Ed.D.C.T.), and the Doctor of Philosophy (Ph.D.). According to Reys, Glasgow, Teuscher, and Nevels (2007), approximately 15% of 70 U.S. institutions with doctoral programs in mathematics education grant both the Ed.D. and the Ph.D. Worldwide, a distinction is often made between the two degrees, with the Ph.D., the "research doctorate," seen as more scientific, contributing to knowledge, and the Ed.D., the "professional doctorate," as more applied, contributing to policy or professional practice (Bernstein et al., 2014, p. 25; de Ibarrola & Anderson, 2014, p. xi). Across institutions and countries, however, there is considerable variation in how the two kinds of programs differ, and there are likely as many differences within Ph.D. programs and within Ed.D. programs as there are between the two types of programs.

Increasingly in recent years there have been instances, particularly in Europe, in which institutions have collaborated to support doctoral studies in mathematics education. The European Union's ERASMUS (*Eu*Ropean Community *A*ction *S*cheme for the *M*obility of *U*niversity *S*tudents) Program has given grants to support internships and student exchanges across doctoral programs, and the European University Association has established the so-called European doctorate (*Doctor Europæus*), which requires that the doctoral research, thesis approval, languages of the thesis defense, and thesis examination board span several European countries. In a fine example of cross-national cooperation, the Nordic Graduate School in Mathematics Education (Grevholm, 2008), which existed from 2004 to 2009, held workshops, seminars, and summer schools for students from about 40 institutions in the Nordic and Baltic countries. During its six-year duration, students in the school successfully defended over 50 doctoral dissertations in mathematics education (Grevholm, 2009). Although that project has ended, similar examples of such cooperation can be expected to emerge around the world as more countries discover the value of regional programs.

Cross-institutional programs can also provide a means for developing countries to harness the resources needed if they are to provide doctoral education in the absence of a critical mass of either faculty or students at a single institution. From 1997 to 2004, for example, the National Research Foundation of South Africa and the U.S. National Science Foundation jointly sponsored an annual Research School in South Africa where doctoral students in mathematics and science education from around the country and region had opportunities to work for a week with scholars from several countries, including the United States, the United Kingdom, and South Africa (Mewborn, 2008; for more details on research in mathematics education in South Africa, see Vithal, Adler, & Keitel, 2005). Since 2003, the Southern African Association for Research in Mathematics, Science, and Technology Education (SAARMSTE; see www. saarmste.org/) has been hosting the Research School. The school, now a three- to four-day residential workshop, provides some 40 to 50 participants, mainly from southern Africa, with an opportunity to learn about various aspects of the research process. It is attended for doctoral students, postdoctoral fellows, and supervisors in mathematics, science, and technology education. At the school, experienced researchers from universities around the world conduct plenary sessions and workshops on issues of research design, data collection, data analysis, and writing for publication. The participants can get feedback on their research activities and their writing from experienced researchers as well as become acquainted with other new scholars from the region. The Research School is only one of many activities of the SAARMSTE that are intended to build capacity in education research in southern Africa.

Some doctoral programs in mathematics education, especially in North America, consist primarily of several years of coursework followed by qualifying examinations and a dissertation. Students take graduate courses in mathematics, mathematics education, psychology, research methods, and other areas of interest to the student or emphasized by the institution. There is often a requirement that the student spend a certain number of terms in residence at the institution. In contrast, other doctoral programs assume that, by admitting students who already possess a master's degree, additional coursework can be deemphasized or eliminated.

In such programs, many of which are in the European Higher Education Area (Curaj, Scott, Vlasceanu, & Wilson, 2012), students enter the program with a master's degree and begin by engaging in independent research guided by a professor, with perhaps some coursework or intense independent study as needed.

In the United Kingdom, for example, the main (and in many cases only) component of the research doctorate is a thesis or portfolio of original research that is then examined by an expert panel appointed by the university. In Australia and New Zealand, coursework has not ordinarily been part of doctoral programs, but it has become much more common during the past decade. In a recent online survey of doctoral students in five Australian universities (Kiley, Bell, & Feng, 2013), 39% of the more than 700 respondents had undertaken or were undertaking coursework, and 57% agreed that it should be part of the doctoral program. The meaning of the term *coursework*, however, is not always clear, as Margaret Kiley of the Australian National University, who has been studying the phenomenon, revealed in an interview (Van, 2012):

> When you actually spoke to those involved with the introduction of coursework and asked what that was, there was an amazing variety of understandings of what "coursework" might be. For example, you've got people who think coursework is about research methods, those who would call coursework "research processes"—all the things to do with how to do research. For others coursework is actually disciplinary knowledge: advanced disciplinary knowledge. And those two of course are quite different.
>
> (p. 119)

As the availability of online courses, and perhaps even entire doctoral programs, becomes more pervasive, one might expect residence requirements to be abandoned and coursework requirements to change, becoming more tailored to the interests and qualifications of the student. Individual programs are likely to change their shape and nature during the coming generation, but the great variety to be found among programs internationally seems unlikely to diminish.

NEEDED PROFICIENCY

Although there is great variety in the location and configuration of doctoral programs, it is reasonable to expect that there will continue to be some commonalities in the proficiencies of doctoral students seeking to become professors of mathematics education. Certainly proficiencies will vary based on individual aspirations and interests and the emphases in specific programs, but there are categories of proficiency one would expect to see in all future mathematics education professors; namely, proficiency with mathematics and with teaching. Given that professors of mathematics education need preparation in both mathematics and education, there is almost no possibility that their doctoral program can supply them with all the preparation they will need in both fields, so whatever education they receive ought to equip them to acquire additional proficiency once they are on the job.

Mathematical Knowledge, Skills, and Abilities

Anyone being educated to become a professor of mathematics education obviously needs a strong education in mathematics. How extensive should that be? In some doctoral programs in mathematics education, the assumption is made that students finishing the program ought to have studied graduate-level mathematics to at least the equivalent of a master's degree in mathematics. Other programs ask for more mathematics than that, particularly if the student is seeking a position to prepare undergraduate mathematics instructors. Some programs ask for less mathematics, however, particularly if the student is seeking a position to prepare primary school mathematics teachers. Dossey and Lappan (2001) offer guidelines for mathematics course offerings for the different specializations available in U.S. doctoral programs that may apply to programs in other countries as well.

The question of what mathematics a mathematics educator needs to know was addressed more than a century ago by Felix Klein. In 1908, he published the first volume of his groundbreaking *Elementarmathematik vom höheren Standpunkte aus* (Elementary Mathematics from a Higher Standpoint), which was his attempt to raise the level of secondary mathematics instruction by equipping prospective teachers with a more comprehensive view of the content they would be teaching. He had expressed his views of mathematics education in his inaugural address (*Antrittsrede*) of 1872 when he became professor at Erlangen at the age of 23. The problem of the secondary school curriculum was, for Klein, neither insufficient time nor inadequate content: it was the absence of a revitalized, more spirited treatment of the content that would reflect a better understanding of the mutual connections between problems in the various domains of mathematics:

> We, as university teachers, require not only that our students, on completion of their studies, know what must be taught in the schools. We want the future teacher to stand *above* his subject, that he have a conception of the present state of knowledge in his field, and that he generally be capable of following its further development.
>
> (Klein, in Rowe, 1985, p. 139)

Discussing the mathematics a teacher needs to know, Klein (1924/1932) wrote: "The teacher's knowledge should be far greater than that which he presents to his pupils. He must be familiar with the cliffs and the whirlpools in order to guide his pupils safely past them" (p. 162). The metaphor here is that of guide, someone who knows the mathematical terrain well and can conduct his or her students through it without them getting lost or injured. Klein went on to discuss how the novice teacher needs to be equipped to counteract common misperceptions of mathematical ideas:

> If you lack orientation, if you are not well informed concerning the intuitive elements of mathematics as well as the vital relations with neighboring fields, if, above all, you do not know the historical development, your footing will be very insecure. You will then either withdraw to the ground of the most modern pure mathematics, and fail to be understood in the school, or you will succumb to the assault, give up what you learned at the university and even in your teaching allow yourself to be buried in the traditional routine.
>
> (Klein, 1924/1932, p. 236)

Consequently, Klein's approach to mathematics for prospective teachers put considerable emphasis on applications, geometric illustrations, space perception, the concept of function, and the historical development of the field. As two examples of the greater knowledge teachers should have, he thought they should understand the function-theoretic nature of the logarithm and also know something of non-Euclidean geometry even though neither topic, in his view, should be part of regular school instruction.

Klein's efforts anticipated later attempts to characterize the particular sort of mathematical proficiency needed by teachers—not simply a firm knowledge of the content to be taught in school but also an understanding of where that knowledge fits into the rest of mathematics, how it might come to be grasped by the novice, and what learning difficulties it might present: part of what has come to be called *mathematical knowledge for teaching* (Ball, Thames, & Phelps, 2008; Bass, 2005; Bromme, 1994; Carrillo, Climent, Contreras, & Muñoz-Catalán, 2013; Rowland, Turner, Thwaites, & Huckstep, 2009; Silverman & Thompson, 2008).

Our argument here is that the potential mathematics education professor needs that sort of proficiency, too.

Claiming that all mathematical knowledge for teaching (MKT) is specialized, Carrillo et al. (2013) modified the MKT idea, proposing instead what they call *mathematics teachers' specialized knowledge* (MTSK). The mathematical knowledge aspect of MTSK has three elements: *knowledge of topics* (KOT), *knowledge of the structure of mathematics* (KSM), and *knowledge about mathematics* (KAM). In our view, all three elements should be included in the mathematical knowledge, skills, and abilities expected of future mathematics education professors, appropriate to the level at which they plan to work.

KOT is the knowledge of the concepts and procedures relevant to a topic in school mathematics together with an understanding of the theoretical basis for those concepts and procedures. Any teacher should have knowledge that is more formal and at a higher level than that of his or her students. For example, although one's students might know only that the order in which two numbers are added does not matter, as a teacher, one needs the more technical knowledge that addition (as well as multiplication but not subtraction or division) is commutative. Similarly, the mathematics education professor should possess KOT that is more formal and at a higher level than that of the undergraduate and graduate students he or she is teaching. For instance, a mathematics education professor teaching prospective lower secondary school teachers should have a robust understanding of proportional reasoning, including the technical differences between fractions and ratios, when those differences matter, and when they do not.

KSM is the knowledge of the structure of the discipline of mathematics: its fundamental concepts, operations, and their properties and how they are organized into various systems. For example, a teacher of mathematics needs to know the properties of each of the number systems to be found in the school curriculum, including the natural numbers, integers, rational numbers, real numbers, and complex numbers. Similarly, the mathematics education professor should possess knowledge not only of the interrelationships among topics in a branch of mathematics but also of how the various branches of mathematics are related. If the teacher of mathematics needs a view of mathematics from 6,000 meters, the mathematics education professor needs a view from 12,000 meters.

KAM is knowledge about how mathematics is created and established. It includes knowing ways of producing syntactic knowledge in mathematics; knowing aspects of mathematical communication, reasoning, and evaluating; knowing how to define and use definitions; being able to establish relations, correspondences, and equivalences; and being able to select representations, argue, generalize, and explore. For example, any teacher of mathematics should know what his or her students think an explanation is. "What do they think it means to 'know' or to 'do' mathematics?" (Ball, 1990, p. 259). The mathematics education professor should also understand how new knowledge is created and verified in the field and how the discipline regulates knowledge development.

We find that the Carrillo et al. (2013) formulation of the mathematical knowledge aspect of MTSK constitutes a useful framework for thinking about the specialized types of mathematical knowledge that a mathematics education professor, as well as a teacher of school mathematics, needs. That knowledge is quite different from the mathematical knowledge needed and used by the ordinary citizen, the professional in another field, or even the research mathematician. It involves the application of mathematics to the field of teaching. As Bass (2005) observed: "*Mathematics education is not mathematics.* It is a domain of professional work that makes fundamental use of highly specialized kinds of mathematical knowledge, and in that sense it can, I suggest, be usefully viewed as a kind of applied mathematics" (p. 418).

Pedagogical knowledge, skills, and abilities. Along with the mathematical knowledge aspect of MTSK, Carrillo et al. (2013) analyzed its pedagogical knowledge aspect.[2] That aspect also has three elements: *knowledge of features of learning mathematics* (KFLM), *knowledge of mathematics teaching* (KMT), and *knowledge of mathematics learning standards* (KMLS). All three elements should be included in the pedagogical content knowledge, skills, and abilities expected of future mathematics education professors.

KFLM is concerned with understanding how mathematics is learned. What are the features of the mathematics learning process, and how are students thinking when they are engaged in mathematical learning activities? By knowing both the specific mathematical topic and the specific group of students and by being familiar with a model or theory of learning, a teacher can anticipate the difficulties the students might have in learning it (Grossman & Schoenfeld, 2005). For example, the teacher might understand that given a problem requiring proportional reasoning, some of his or her students might try adding rather than multiplying to find the missing quantity. As an extension of these ideas, the mathematics education professor should know a variety of learning theories, and understand when each one is most appropriately applied to a particular piece of content or a particular group of learners. The professor should have a broad understanding of typical student errors, misconceptions, and strategies for solving problems in the content areas most appropriate to his or her work (e.g., primary, secondary, or tertiary). In contrast to the teacher noted earlier who applies this knowledge to a particular group of learners, a professor of mathematics education should be able to apply his or her knowledge more generally. In addition, the professor needs to know what the available research says about the unique learning needs and propensities of adult learners as well as those of children.

KMT involves pedagogical knowledge related to specific mathematical content. The teacher knows resources appropriate to a mathematical topic, including textbooks and other instructional materials. That knowledge allows the teacher to choose or produce a particular representation or a structured sequence of examples to illustrate the topic. KMT is not simply a general knowledge of mathematics and of teaching it; KMT is pedagogical knowledge integrated with specific mathematical content knowledge that constrains the resulting teaching. For example, the teacher might know that one sequence of quadratic equations is more helpful than another when students are learning to solve such equations and might therefore choose to use the former sequence. Again, the mathematics education professor also needs more generalized KMT and should, for example, be able to independently generate a variety of sequences of quadratic equations and articulate the advantages and disadvantages of each. Through a careful selection of numbers and contexts, the professor should be able to construct mathematical tasks for prospective teachers that would demand a solution method beyond simple cross-multiplication. In addition, the professor needs knowledge of appropriate representations and instructional materials for both children and adult learners, and he or she should be able to evaluate a variety of such things.

KMLS is pedagogical knowledge of the school mathematics curriculum across the grades, including knowledge of appropriate instructional materials, evaluation instruments, and standards. KMLS is designed to extend beyond the teacher's immediate context to objectives and performance measures developed by outside agencies, such as examination boards and professional associations. For example, the teacher who knows that the ministry of education has revised the syllabus for the school-leaving certificate in mathematics so that geometry proofs using transformations are no longer accepted will be able to adjust his or her instruction to better prepare students for the corresponding certificate examination. The mathematics education professor certainly needs extensive KMLS, whether the national system is centralized or not but especially if prospective teachers of mathematics in the program will be headed for schools with a variety of curriculum and assessment formats.

Future mathematics education professors will need to acquire the requisite pedagogical knowledge discussed both as part of their doctoral program and outside it, both before they take their first faculty positions and throughout their careers. University courses and seminars can provide helpful theoretical frameworks for understanding mathematics teaching and learning, but only extensive experience in mathematics and mathematics education classrooms can make those frameworks come alive and help the future professor organize and build up his or her pedagogical knowledge.

NEEDED EXPERIENCE

Field Experience Teaching Mathematics

Anyone seeking a position as a faculty member in mathematics education ought to be familiar with what it means to teach mathematics in school or college. If the prospective mathematics educator has not been inside a school or college classroom as a regular teacher of mathematics, he or she will not be able to speak authoritatively to prospective mathematics teachers about what they will encounter when they take teaching positions. Those doctoral students who intend to work in teacher preparation should gain some experience in primary, secondary, or tertiary classrooms during their doctoral study. Doctoral students who pursue their degrees in other than their home country and intend to seek employment in the new country need classroom experiences, even if they have taught in their home countries. This experience need not take the form of student teaching but should include opportunities to observe and engage in mathematics instruction.

Given the complexities of schools and difficulties of finding sufficient high-quality placements for teacher education students, placing doctoral students in schools or colleges can be difficult. Thus it is worth considering alternative models of field experience. In his discussion of the professional development of teachers, John Dewey (1904/1964) argued that teaching demands preparation in both theoretical and practical work. Teachers need to be prepared to address questions of the relationship between subject-matter knowledge and educational theory while simultaneously managing the daily routines of classroom practice. Dewey termed a focus on the theoretical aspects of teaching the *laboratory* approach and a focus on the practical aspects, the *apprenticeship* approach (Philipp et al., 2007). The laboratory approach allows the prospective teacher to attend to how students learn, understand, and do mathematics before having to teach a lesson. It is "forward-looking" (p. 443), whereas the apprenticeship approach "helps practicing teachers learn how to do that which is currently being done" (p. 443). Effective teacher preparation demands both approaches, but it tends to be dominated by apprenticeship activities such as student teaching and other field experiences in schools and colleges (McIntyre, Byrd, & Foxx, 1996).

The research of Philipp et al. (2007) demonstrated the relative effectiveness of a laboratory approach in which two treatments to acquaint prospective elementary school teachers with children's mathematical thinking (either by watching videos or by watching videos and working with children) were compared with two apprenticeship treatments that involved visiting elementary school mathematics classes (either typical classes or classes selected because their teachers had participated in reform-based professional development efforts). Philipp et al. found that the laboratory approach was only modestly better than the apprenticeship approach in improving prospective teachers' mathematical knowledge, but it improved their beliefs about children's learning and thinking much more strikingly than the apprenticeship approach. The work of Philipp et al. suggests that, for future mathematics education professors, deliberately structured experiences outside the classroom can take the place of direct classroom experiences teaching school or college mathematics, at least for some purposes.

Field Experience Teaching Mathematics Education

As future university faculty members, doctoral students can expect to be called upon to teach a range of mathematics education courses, including content and methods courses for prospective and practicing teachers, and theory courses on a range of topics (such as assessment, learning, teaching, curriculum) for master's and doctoral students. Doctoral programs generally do not provide explicit preparation for teaching such courses. Some doctoral students get the opportunity to serve as teaching assistants or instructors of record for undergraduate courses as part of their assistantship duties, but many doctoral students have other assistantship duties (such as research) or no assistantship at all. Given that teaching will almost certainly be expected of all future university or college faculty members, doctoral programs should deliberately and systematically prepare students for that role through internships or field experiences. Such an internship or field experience would involve the doctoral student in all aspects of instruction, including global planning for the course; daily planning, selection and implementation of in-class and out-of-class tasks; construction of assessment rubrics; consultation with individual students outside of class; and assigning grades—all under the guidance of a seasoned faculty member. The intern and faculty member would engage in discussions about the rationale behind various decisions to help the intern gain a sense of all that goes into designing and teaching undergraduate courses. The point is not that there is one correct way to teach such courses that doctoral students should learn, but rather that doctoral students should have the opportunity to see the range of decisions that go into designing and implementing a course so that they are prepared to think through those decisions themselves.

Emphasizing the need to attend more to the laboratory approach and less to the apprenticeship approach in teacher preparation, Feiman-Nemser (2012) points out:

> According to Dewey, the supreme mark of a teacher is the ability to interpret and activate students' motivational and intellectual processes. This means seeing what is going on in students' minds and figuring out how to engage them in worthwhile learning.
>
> (p. 12)

Moving to the preparation of teacher educators, she makes a similar argument, asserting that

> the preparation of teacher educators must include experience with professional practice. Put slightly differently, in order to learn how to teach teachers effectively, aspiring teacher educators must have experiences with the tasks and ways of thinking fundamental to learning teaching.
>
> (Feiman-Nemser, 2013, p. 190)

To learn from experience, according to Feiman-Nemser (2013), teacher educators need to overcome obstacles posed by their familiarity with classroom teaching, the transitory quality of experience, and the isolated character of teaching. She recounts what she has learned about the role of experience over decades of teaching doctoral students, pointing out that those students need to analyze their prior teaching experience from new perspectives, engage in and analyze the firsthand experience they are gaining as course instructors and what she calls "field instructors," and work together to observe and investigate various forms of recorded experience. For "the teaching experiences of novice teacher educators [to become] an educative resource . . . requires the design of professional learning opportunities that allow teacher educators to learn in and from their practice and the practice of others" (p. 206). Such learning opportunities are rarely included in doctoral programs, but future mathematics education professors are not likely to encounter them otherwise.

Although most doctoral students in mathematics education will have taken graduate level theory courses, they likely will not have had any reason to see the "behind the scenes" work that goes into crafting such courses. Generally, the first time they will have an opportunity to think deeply about the construction and implementation of such courses will be when they are faced with teaching them. Expectations vary from institution to institution regarding how much freedom an instructor has to modify, adapt, or create a syllabus, but even when standard syllabi exist, they often do not convey the full range of decisions that an instructor must make. New professors often then find themselves constructing syllabi based on their experiences as students but without the benefit of the rationales that went into developing those experiences. Perhaps this task is part of the learning curve that is best accomplished on the job, as not all doctoral students will be expected to teach these sorts of courses.

Research Experience

The field of mathematics education has not simply grown over the past century or so; it has also changed dramatically. Early researchers in mathematics education, for example, attempted to follow the model of the natural sciences by setting up experiments, controlling variables, and measuring effects using quantitative methods (Kilpatrick, 1992). Abandoning that model in the mid-20th century, researchers began using so-called qualitative research methods to interpret the teaching and learning of mathematics by observing mathematics classes as well as interviewing teachers and learners. Today's researchers often use combinations of qualitative and quantitative methods. The popularity of mixed-method research has meant that future professors of mathematics education need to be educated in understanding and employing both kinds of methods, which has added to the preparation they need. Further, there is now a substantial research literature—as shown by the chapters in the present *Handbook*—with which those prospective professors need to be acquainted.

The independent research project for the dissertation or thesis is the gold standard for the doctoral degree, yet many doctoral graduates of mathematics education programs will take faculty positions in which conducting original research is not part of their job responsibilities. Traditional doctoral programs have culminated in a thesis, dissertation, or portfolio that reports on some research work they have done. The purpose of the written document has been to certify that the candidate is capable of making an original, independent, and significant contribution to the field. The university typically convenes a group of experts to judge the contribution. They may be faculty members at the university, or outside experts may be brought in to assist in the process. In the Scandinavian countries, candidates may face one or more "opponents" brought in from outside to contest the arguments the candidate has made in the dissertation.

One alternative in practice by some scholars today is to require that the student conduct research within the sphere of inquiry in which the major professor is working. The benefits of this arrangement are that the student works with a well-established literature base, theoretical frameworks, and data collection and analysis techniques, and that the research that comes out of the dissertation contributes to an ongoing line of inquiry. Further, the major professor is better equipped than otherwise to offer support and suggest directions for further work. In this scenario, the doctoral student might still collect original data (most certainly would analyze the data, whether newly collected or existing) and would engage in writing up the problem statement, literature review, methods, and results. Thus, the student would be prepared for many aspects of research but would not necessarily get much experience conceptualizing and designing a study from scratch.

Another alternative to the individual research project is what has been termed the *Mode 2* educational model for doctoral education (Nerad & Trzyna, 2008, pp. 305–306) in which an often-interdisciplinary group of students and senior researchers work together on a marketable project. Complaints about large numbers of new doctoral degree holders unable to secure faculty positions have led funders of some programs in the social sciences and education to support Mode 2 in an effort to duplicate the apparently more successful practices of doctoral programs in the natural sciences and engineering. "Mode 2 doctoral education offers the possibility of organizing world-class doctoral study through networks of cooperation with scholars and universities across the globe as well as with scholars in many different academic disciplines" (Nerad & Trzyna, 2008, p. 306). It remains to be seen, however, whether or how far doctoral programs in mathematics education move toward adopting a Mode 2 approach.

Certainly conceptualizing and designing studies are experiences that doctoral students need if they intend to go on to careers in which they will be doing independent research in the future, but do students with other career aspirations need those experiences? Might these students be better served by learning how to apply literature, theoretical frameworks, and methods in the context of their major professor's line of inquiry? Of course, that raises the question of who would decide which students should do original research and when that decision would be made.

Although not all future mathematics education professors will be employed in positions that require them to create new knowledge by conducting research, all will be consumers of research and need to be prepared for that role. As consumers, professors are expected to use research to inform their instruction, read research reports to keep abreast of changes in the field, and engage with policy makers and the general public about research results. Professors of mathematics education need to have a solid understanding of what education research can and cannot tell us, an understanding of research design sufficient to allow them to critique published research articles and find flaws in arguments presented in the media, a familiarity with the most commonly used research methods, and a capacity to learn new methods as they emerge.

Currently, quantitative, qualitative, and mixed methods designs are commonly used in research in mathematics education, so it behooves professors to be familiar with all three and have a depth of understanding in at least one. Given that many policy decisions are based on particular interpretations of small slices of research, future professors need to be knowledgeable about and able to dissect bodies of work and even translate them for lay people, such as policy makers. Further, a great deal of research about issues in education is being conducted by those outside of the field, such as economists and sociologists. It is critically important that the professor of mathematics education possess the knowledge and vocabulary to talk with such researchers about their work. The profession depends on the use of peer reviewers for journal articles, book chapters, and grant proposals, providing another reason for professors to have substantial knowledge of research methods. Although it is increasingly common for research teams to include methodologists who specialize in determining the methods to be used in conducting a study, the mathematics educators on the team still need to be conversant with the research methods in order to draw sensible conclusions, even if they do not have the skills to analyze the data using sophisticated techniques and software. As with most aspects of the knowledge base for being a professor, research methods are constantly changing, so in addition to learning about current methods of research, future professors of mathematics education need to have the confidence and propensity to learn about emerging methods at a level sufficient for interpreting research results.

PROFESSIONAL IDENTITY

Like the professions of medicine and law, the profession of education requires that professors in the field be equipped to engage in both research and professional practice. Unlike medicine and law, however, schools of education in most countries have relatively little control over who becomes certified to enter the profession. Teacher preparation, especially for prospective primary and middle grades teachers, is often available through a variety of alternatives to college and university programs. Professors of mathematics education may therefore need to be more than simply researchers and practitioners. They may need to represent the field not only to their fellow practitioners but also to policy makers, parents, and the general public. They need to be promoters of their subject, building a research environment if one does not already exist; establishing projects that help to make mathematics education a more visible, credible field; and engaging with issues connected to mathematics in the broader society. In other words, they need to develop a professional identity (Grevholm, 2010).

The work of a university professor who is also a professional mathematics educator always spans more than just teaching and research. At the institutional level, faculty members serve on departmental, college, and university governance committees (such as a curriculum committee or student academic appeals committee), advise students, serve as major professors for doctoral students, direct independent studies for students, and write and read comprehensive exams for graduate students, among other tasks. The future mathematics education professor is likely to be expected to conduct a variety of activities to establish an academic reputation, including identifying and formulating research problems, seeking funding to conduct research, carrying out and writing up research studies, reporting on scholarly work at conferences and in academic publications, reviewing funding proposals and journal manuscripts, and a host of other academic activities. Most of these activities are unlikely to have received extensive attention in the prospective professor's doctoral program—although some might have been treated in depth—so he or she will need to acquire experience with them on the job. Years ago, Walbesser and Eisenberg (1971) addressed the question of the research competencies needed by mathematics educators and detailed a sequence of seminars at the University of Maryland that were designed to provide such competencies, but unless an institution has a fairly sizable doctoral program in mathematics education, it is unlikely to be able to offer such seminars.

Professors of mathematics education also engage in a host of activities at the institution and in the profession that are much less obvious to doctoral students. Often, such professors are expected to influence educational policy. They may be among the few people in academe who can speak with authority about the teaching and learning of mathematics and how those activities are being conducted and being debated in their country and internationally. Part of their professional identity, for at least some future professors of mathematics education, will require them to use their knowledge and skills to defend the discipline and the students and teachers who are being affected by changes in educational policy.

Many an assistant professor has been heard to lament, "But they didn't teach me how to do that!" Those of us conducting doctoral programs may assume that immersion in the academic and professional milieu will translate into knowing how to do these things, or perhaps we believe that students can (and should) figure these things out on their own when they become faculty members. Some individual faculty members and some programs do explicitly include some of these items in doctoral education, most commonly engaging doctoral students in joint reviews of conference proposals and journal articles. Certainly, doctoral programs in mathematics education cannot prepare students for every situation they will encounter in their professional lives, but what would it mean to provide students with internships that would deliberately expose them to a broader range of activities included in the life of a professor?

It might be a useful exercise to consider how Feiman-Nemser's (2001) continuum of tasks of teaching might be applied to doctoral programs in mathematics education. She subdivides the tasks of teaching into those that are best learned during the preservice years, in the induction years, and through professional development later in one's career. Her continuum is based on the most crucial items for teachers to learn at each point in their careers and the capacity of institutions (teacher education institutions, schools, and professional development experiences) to foster particular kinds of learning. Faculty members at doctoral-granting institutions might engage in an analysis of the various aspects of being a professor and identify those that are best learned while a doctoral student versus those that are best learned on the job or through targeted support later in one's career.

MANY PATHS

The report of the first U.S. national conference on doctoral programs in mathematics education in 1999 was entitled *One Field, Many Paths* (Reys & Kilpatrick, 2001). The term *many paths* was chosen because the conference had revealed that those programs were enormously diverse in goals, content, structure, requirements, operation, and virtually every other respect. That diversity is even greater when one looks outside the United States at doctoral programs around the world. Although most graduates of such programs are likely to be involved in some sort of teacher preparation or professional development, other options are increasingly available in tertiary education or outside. The situation worldwide is even more complicated than that portrayed in *One Field, Many Paths*, as doctoral students come from a variety of backgrounds (classroom teacher, student of graduate level mathematics), go through the variety of doctoral programs noted earlier, and go on to a host of career options (including mathematics education professor teaching primarily content courses, mathematics education professor teaching primarily methods courses, or mathematics education professor teaching both content and methods courses). One of the oldest clichés in the business is that a professor's education is a lifelong process. Trite or not, we see that assertion as an enduring truth for the years to come. Two decades or so of formal education along with several years of experience teaching mathematics and mathematics education can provide only the rudiments of the education one needs to fill adequately the position of professor of mathematics education. The biggest challenge to the education of future professors of mathematics education is how to arrange that process to provide a sensible balance between one's formal studies, organized experience, and on-the-job learning.

NOTES

1. We are grateful to Barbro Grevholm, University of Agder, and Robert E. Reys, University of Missouri, for their comments on an early draft.
2. In some countries, *subject-matter didactical knowledge* would be used in preference to *pedagogical knowledge* in this context.

REFERENCES

Andžāns, A., Bonka, D., & Grevholm, B. (Eds.). (2008). *Selected papers of the ICME 11 Discussion Group 12: Rethinking doctoral programs in mathematics education*. Rīga: University of Latvia, Mācību grāmata. Retrieved from http://math.unipa.it/~grim/icme11_dg12_proceedings_final.pdf.

Ball, D.L. (1990). The mathematical understandings that prospective teachers bring to teacher education. *Elementary School Journal, 90*, 449–466.

Ball, D.L., Thames, M.H., & Phelps, G. (2008). Content knowledge for teaching: What makes it special? *Journal of Teacher Education, 59*, 389–407.

Bass, H. (2005). Mathematics, mathematicians, and mathematics education. *Bulletin of the American Mathematical Society, 42*, 417–430.

Bernstein, B.L., Evans, B., Fyffe, J., Halai, N., Hall, F.L., Jensen, H.S., Marsh, H., & Ortega, S. (2014). The continuing evolution of the research doctorate. In M. Nerad & B. Evans (Eds.), *Globalization and its impacts on the quality of PhD education: Forces and forms in doctoral education worldwide* (pp. 5–30). Rotterdam, the Netherlands: Sense Publishers.

Bromme, R. (1994). Beyond subject matter: A psychological topology of teachers' professional knowledge. In R. Biehler, R.W. Scholz, R. Sträßer, & B. Winkelmann (Eds.), *Didactics of mathematics as a scientific discipline* (pp. 73–88). Dordrecht, the Netherlands: Kluwer.

Carrillo, J., Climent, N., Contreras, L.C., & Muñoz-Catalán, M.C. (2013, February). *Determining specialized knowledge for mathematics teaching*. Paper presented in Working Group 17 at the Eighth Congress of European Research in Mathematics Education (CERME 8), Manavgat-Side, Antalya, Turkey.

Curaj, A., Scott, P., Vlasceanu, L., & Wilson, L. (Eds.). (2012). *European higher education at the crossroads: Between the Bologna Process and national reforms*. Dordrecht, the Netherlands: Springer.

de Ibarrola, M., & Anderson, L.W. (Eds.). (2014). *The nurturing of new educational researchers: Dialogues and debates*. Rotterdam, the Netherlands: Sense Publishers.

Dewey, J. (1964). The relation of theory to practice in education. New York: Random House. (Original work published 1904.)

Dossey, J.A., & Lappan G. (2001). The mathematics education of mathematics educators in doctoral programs in mathematics education. In R.E. Reys & J. Kilpatrick (Eds.), *CBMS Issues in Mathematics Education: Vol. 9. One field, many paths: U.S. doctoral programs in mathematics education* (pp. 67–72). Providence, RI: American Mathematical Society.

Feiman-Nemser, S. (2001). From preparation to practice: Designing a continuum to strengthen and sustain teaching. *Teachers College Record, 103*, 1113–1055.

Feiman-Nemser, S. (2012). *Teachers as learners*. Cambridge, MA: Harvard Education Press.

Feiman-Nemser, S. (2013). The role of experience in the education of teacher educators. In M. Ben-Peretz (with S. Kleeman, R. Reichenberg, & S. Shimoni) (Ed.), *Teacher educators as members of an evolving profession* (pp. 189–210). New York: Rowan & Littlefield.

Grevholm, B. (2008). A Norwegian doctoral programme in didactics of mathematics—Doctoral programmes in the Nordic research communities. In A. Andžāns, D. Bonka, & B. Grevholm (Eds.), *Selected papers of the ICME 11 Discussion Group 12: Rethinking doctoral programs in mathematics education* (pp. 26–43). Rīga: University of Latvia, Mācību grāmata. Retrieved from http://math.unipa.it/~grim/icme11_dg12_proceedings_final.pdf.

Grevholm, B. (2009). Nordic collaboration in mathematics education research. *Nordic Studies in Mathematics Education, 14*(4), 89–100.

Grevholm, B. (2010). Mathematics teacher education: A Scandinavian perspective. In G. Anthony & B. Grevholm (Eds.), *SMDF Papers: No. 8. Teachers of mathematics: Recruitment, retention, professional development and identity* (pp. 93–100). Kristiansand, Sweden: Svensk förening för MatematikDidaktisk Forskning.

Grossman, P.L., & Schoenfeld, A. (with Lee, C.D.). (2005). Teaching subject matter. In L. Darling-Hammond, J. Bransford, P. LePage, K. Hammerness, & H. Duffy (Eds.), *Preparing teachers for a changing world: What teachers should learn and be able to do* (pp. 201–231). San Francisco, CA: Jossey Bass.

Kilpatrick, J. (1992). A history of research in mathematics education. In D.A. Grouws (Ed.), *Handbook of research on mathematics research and teaching* (pp. 3–39). New York: Macmillan.

Kiley, M., Bell, K., & Feng, L. (2013, November). *Report of the online surveys related to OLT-funded project: Coursework in Australian Doctoral Education: What's happening, why, and future directions?* (Report to the Council of Deans and Directors of Graduate Studies in Australia [DDOGS]). Canberra: Australian National University, Centre for Higher Education, Learning & Teaching. Retrieved from http://chelt.anu.edu.au/doctoral-coursework/presentations.

Klein, F. (1932). *Elementary mathematics from an advanced standpoint: Arithmetic, algebra, analysis* (3rd Ed., Vol. 1). (E.R. Hedrick & C.A. Noble, Trans.) New York: Macmillan. (Original work published 1924.)

McIntyre, D.J., Byrd, D.M., & Foxx, S.M. (1996). Field and laboratory experiences. In J. Sikula (Ed.), *Handbook of research on teacher education* (2nd ed., pp. 171–193). New York: Simon & Schuster Macmillan.

Mewborn, D.S. (2008). Program delivery issues, opportunities, and challenges. In R.E. Reys & J.A. Dossey (Eds.), *CBMS Issues in Mathematics Education: Vol. 15. U.S. doctorates in mathematics education: Developing stewards of the discipline* (pp. 129–136). Providence, RI: American Mathematical Society.

Nerad, M., & Trzyna, T. (2008). Globalization and doctoral education—toward a research agenda. In M. Nerad & M. Heggelund (Eds.), *Toward a global PhD? Forces and forms in doctoral education worldwide* (pp. 300–312). Seattle: University of Washington Press.

Philipp, R.A., Ambrose, R., Lamb, L.L., Sowder, J.T., Schappelle, B.T., Sowder, L., Thanheiser, E., & Chauvot, J. (2007). Effects of early field experiences on the mathematical content knowledge and beliefs of prospective elementary school teachers: An experimental study. *Journal for Research in Mathematics Education, 38*, 438–476.

Reys, R.E., & Kilpatrick, J. (Eds.). (2001). *CBMS Issues in Mathematics Education: Vol. 9. One field, many paths: U.S. doctoral programs in mathematics education.* Providence, RI: American Mathematical Society.

Reys, R., Glasgow, R., Teuscher, D., & Nevels, N. (2007). Doctoral programs in mathematics education in the United States: 2007 Status Report. *Notices of the American Mathematical Society, 54*(11), 1283–1293.

Rowe, D.E. (1985). Felix Klein's "Erlanger Antrittsrede": A transcription with English translation and commentary. *Historia Mathematica, 12*, 123–141.

Rowland, T., Turner, F., Thwaites, A., & Huckstep, P. (2009). *Developing primary mathematics teaching: Reflecting on practice with the knowledge quartet.* London: Sage.

Silverman, J., & Thompson, P.W. (2008). Toward a framework for the development of mathematical knowledge for teaching. *Journal of Mathematics Teacher Education, 11*, 499–511. Retrieved from http://pat-thompson.net/PDFversions/2008SilvermanThompsonMKT.pdf.

Van, L.K. (2012). First course: Formal coursework and the new Australian PhD: An interview with Margaret Kiley. *Digital Culture & Education, 5*(2), 119–126. Retrieved from www.digitalcultureandeducation.com/cms/wp-content/uploads/2013/11/van.pdf.

Vithal, R., Adler, J., & Keitel, C. (Eds.). (2005). *Researching mathematics education in South Africa: Perspectives, practices and possibilities.* Pretoria, South Africa: Human Sciences Research Council.

Walbesser, H.H., & Eisenberg, T. (1971). What research competencies for the mathematics educator? *American Mathematical Monthly, 78*, 667–673.

Section III

Transformations in Learning Contexts

12 Problem Solving in a 21st-Century Mathematics Curriculum

Lyn D. English

Queensland University of Technology

Julie Gainsburg

California State University, Northridge

Problem solving makes a wonderful banner under which to march as long as no one looks too closely at what others mean by the term.

(Kilpatrick, 1981, p. 2)

INTRODUCTION

Research on problem solving in the mathematics curriculum has spanned many decades, yielding pendulum-like swings in recommendations on various issues. Ongoing debates concern the effectiveness of teaching general strategies and heuristics, the role of mathematical content (as the means versus the learning goal of problem solving), the role of context, and the proper emphasis on the social and affective dimensions of problem solving (e.g., Lesh & Zawojewski, 2007; Lester, 2013; Lester & Kehle, 2003; Schoenfeld, 1985, 2008; Silver, 1985). Various scholarly perspectives—including cognitive and behavioral science, neuroscience, the discipline of mathematics, educational philosophy, and sociocultural stances—have informed these debates, often generating divergent resolutions. Perhaps due to this uncertainty, educators' efforts over the years to improve students' mathematical problem-solving skills have had disappointing results. Qualitative and quantitative studies consistently reveal mathematics students' struggles to solve problems more significant than routine exercises (OECD, 2014; Boaler, 2009).

Another perspective on problem solving considers the demands of modern life and work. We acknowledge that preparation for adult work and life is not the only goal of mathematics education. We contend, however, that for the vast majority of students (who will not become academic mathematicians), enhancing their opportunities and performance in work and life should indeed be the main purpose for mathematics education. Worldwide, linking mathematics education and workplace preparedness has become a central policy theme (Grubb & Lazerson, 2004; Mehta, 2013; Miller, n.d.), while linking with life enhancement is less so. Nevertheless, insufficient effort has been made to move beyond this policy rhetoric—to critically examine the mathematical demands of 21st-century work and life, and to consider how these demands should reshape mathematics education. This chapter aims to contribute to this effort. We examine how employers, workers, economists, and other scholars portray the problem-solving demands of modern work and life, and the contributions of schooling. We then consider how certain historical problem-solving debates could be resolved if the overriding purpose of mathematics instruction were to prepare students to meet the demands of work and life today.

One difficulty immediately arises when investigating problem solving in mathematics education: Numerous interpretations of *problems* and *problem solving* have been offered over the years with no universally accepted definitions (English & Sriraman, 2010; Lesh & Zawojewski, 2007; Lester, 2013; Schoenfeld, 2013; Toerner, Schoenfeld, & Reiss, 2008; Zawojewski, 2010). The domain of problem solving is broad, resulting in the myriad approaches to defining it. In 1981, Kilpatrick complained that the "imprecise and indiscriminate use" of the terms *problem* and *problem solving* "allows numerous sins to be committed in their name" (p. 2), and the situation seems hardly improved today.

Traditionally, problems have been defined as tasks in which the solver does not know how to arrive at an answer. Lester (2013) reviews numerous examples of this sort of definition, such as Duncker's: "A problem arises when a living creature has a goal but does not know how this goal is to be reached" (1945, p. 1). Newell and Simon (1972) echoed this notion of blockage but included a motivational aspect: "A person is confronted with a problem when he wants something and does not know immediately what series of actions he can perform to get it" (p. 72). Some more recent definitions of mathematical problem solving still refer to the uncertainty of solution, such as Mamona-Downs and Downs's (2013) notion of "engagement on any mathematical task that is not judged procedural or the student does not have an initial overall idea how to proceed in solving the task" (p. 139). Other scholars recognize the breadth of the notion, as can be seen in English and Sriraman's (2010) simple statement regarding their use of the term *problem solving*: "in a broad sense to cover a range of activities that challenge and extend one's thinking" (p. 263). Also offering a broad, albeit more comprehensive, view is Hegedus's definition:

> We take a very broad view of what is mathematical problem-solving viewing it as an enterprise of collaborative investigation where multiple approaches are valid. It is not just about solving a specific problem, which has a specific answer or application into the real world, but rather it is an investigation that might have multiple approaches and where students can make multiple observations.
>
> (2013, p. 89)

These newer interpretations of problems and problem solving reflect dissatisfaction with the traditional notions and their unhelpfulness for the teaching of problem solving (Lester, 2013).

Taking the perspective of preparation for adult work and life, another ambiguity emerges: Should *problems* in mathematics education refer to *mathematical* problems (posed, solved, and concluded in the domain of mathematics) or to real-world problems and problems in other domains (such as science or business) that can be solved by applying mathematics? In our research for this chapter, we tried to stay open with regard to the meaning of *problem solving in mathematics education*, to avoid arbitrarily constraining our interpretations of what 21st-century demands might require of mathematics education.

We structure the remainder of our chapter as follows. First, we review briefly some key debates in mathematical problem-solving research of past decades. We then review the literature about the demands of modern work and life. Here, we examine drivers of change in the workplace and everyday life, the nature of quantitative problems that need to be solved in these changing contexts, and the competencies required in doing so. Finally, we return to the key debates to discuss possible resolutions suggested by the research about problem solving in the 21st century.

DEBATES (AND DISAPPOINTMENTS) OF MATHEMATICAL PROBLEM-SOLVING RESEARCH

Promoting mathematical problem solving has been a long-standing, often contentious endeavor. The importance of problem solving in the mathematics curriculum has been universally recognized, and scholars have advanced numerous strategies for building students' competencies in solving multiple problem types. The 1980s was to be the "decade of problem solving," with the National Council of Teachers of Mathematics' (NCTM) *An Agenda for Action* recommending the mathematics curriculum be organized around problem solving (1980, p. 2). Recent years have seen a resurgence of interest in problem solving among mathematics-education researchers, as evidenced by the many publications devoted to numerous issues pertaining to problem-solving theory and practice, both in school and beyond. For example, the 2013 special issue of *The Mathematics Enthusiast* (Vol. 10, nos. 1–2) aimed to address "the current trends in problem solving research and . . . the main results that influence teachers' practices and curricula design" (Moreno Armella & Santos-Trigo, 2013, p. 4). In another journal special issue (*ZDM*, Vol. 39, nos. 5–6), Toerner, Schoenfeld, and Reiss (2008) edited a review of problem-solving developments around the world. And a recent special issue of *Educational Studies in Mathematics* (Vol. 83, no. 2013) and an edited book, *Problem Posing: From Research to Effective Practice* (Singer, Ellerton, & Cai, 2013) were devoted entirely to the topic of problem *posing*.

Unfortunately, this decades-long focus on mathematical problem solving, while yielding important insights into the phenomenon, has not produced clear guidance for educational practice. Questions about how to promote problem-solving competency remain; indeed, we contend that they have become more perplexing in light of proliferating interpretations of problems and problem solving, the recent emphasis in many countries on equitable education for a greater range of students, and the changing demands of work and society. In particular, certain unresolved debates appear to impede our forward movement. We review some of those debates here.

Teaching Problem Solving versus Teaching Mathematics *through* Problem Solving

Should the overarching goal of using problems in the mathematics classroom be to teach problem solving per se, or to teach mathematical content, using problem solving as a vehicle? Some scholars (e.g., Anderson, 2014) blame disappointing student gains on the traditional treatment of classroom problem solving, where it is independent of, and isolated from, the development of core mathematical ideas, understandings, and processes. In school, problem solving often takes the form of application ("story") problems at the end of the textbook chapter, positioning it as an add-on task, presumably to promote the ability to apply already-learned content. Such problems rarely serve either the purpose of teaching problem solving or building or deepening the knowledge of that content (Anderson, 2014). But the limited research attention to how concept development might be accomplished *through* problem solving indicates that problem solving has not been seen as playing a central role in the curriculum but rather has been pushed to the periphery (Rigelman, 2013). Also needed are studies that explore whether both goals can be accomplished at once, examining the impact of problem-driven conceptual development on the development of problem-solving competencies (Lester & Charles, 2003; Schoen & Charles, 2003). In sum, while more recent scholarship favors problem solving as a means for developing mathematics-content understanding as opposed to an end in itself, the debate is far from settled.

The Effectiveness of Heuristics and General Skills

Closely related to the debate about the purpose of problem solving in the classroom is a second debate about how to teach students to solve problems. Earlier scholarship rested on the notion of problem solving as a general ability (or ability set) that could be developed across content areas or even in a decontextualized manner. Perhaps the most contentious facet of this debate has been the efficacy of teaching general strategies and heuristics—the tools of an "expert" problem solver—instigated largely by Polya's seminal book, *How to Solve it* (1945). This book has long been regarded as a valuable resource for improving students' abilities to solve unfamiliar problems by offering a list of steps and solution strategies to take when "stuck." Despite some evidence that such tools can contribute to successful problem solving, they nevertheless appear not to have delivered the improvements in problem solving that educators envisioned many years ago (e.g., Lesh & Zawojewski, 2007; Lester & Kehle, 2003; Schoenfeld, 2013; Silver, 1985).

Other general competencies have also been associated with problem solving. Metacognition (the reflection of the solver on his or her thinking and solving processes) is presumed to influence problem solving, with more sophisticated levels of self-awareness and explicitness about strategies being associated with greater success in solving problems (Kapa, 2001; Schneider & Artelt, 2010). Over the years, numerous instructional interventions have been developed and implemented to enhance metacognition as an indirect means of improving problem-solving competence (e.g., Goos, Galbraith, & Renshaw, 2002; Kramarski, Weisse, & Kololshi-Minsker, 2010). Social skills such as collaboration and communication have also been linked to problem-solving competence and, again, targeted directly with instructional interventions (Goos & Galbraith, 1996; McKenna & Agogino, 2004).

Overall, there appears little evidence to suggest that improving these general skills or heuristics leads to greater success in solving problems (mathematical or otherwise) (Lester, 2013), though other positive outcomes surely result. One explanation for this limited success is that these general skills are often presented as a collection of separate entities to be learned and applied, without students fully knowing and understanding why, when, and how to do so (e.g., English & Sriraman, 2010; Lesh & Zawojewski, 2007; Lester, 2013). Another explanation is that problem-solving skills and heuristics, initially conceived to be used interactively with students engaged in authentic problem solving, are often incorporated into textbooks didactically and thus reduced to procedural algorithms (Stanic & Kilpatrick, 1989).

The Role of Context and Authenticity

Mathematics educators frequently debate the role of realistic contexts in teaching. Students' difficulties in applying mathematical concepts and abilities (that they presumably have learned in school) outside of school, or in other classes, such as those in the sciences, have been amply documented (de Abreu, 2002; Greiffenhagen & Sharrock, 2008; Nunes, Schliemann, & Carraher, 1993). A prevailing explanation for these difficulties is the context-specific nature of learning and problem solving. That is, problem-solving competencies that are learned in one situation take on features of that situation; transferring them to a new problem in a new context poses challenges (Lobato, 2003; Hohensee, 2014). This view of problem solving would also explain why acquiring general (heuristic, metacognitive, and social) skills might do little to improve problem-solving competence; indeed, it challenges the existence of "problem-solving competence" as a unitary phenomenon. One resolution is to situate mathematics learning in real-world problem-solving contexts, although the problem remains that mathematics learned in one context does not easily transfer to other contexts. Additional concerns have been raised regarding the equitability of contextualizing mathematics instruction. Lubienski (2000) found children from low-income households less able to access the mathematics in a contextualized curriculum, while Cooper and Dunne (1998) showed low-income students scoring more poorly on contextualized assessment questions. Both studies concluded that the context presented a distraction that higher income students knew to ignore. Finally, importing real-world problems and contexts into the classroom necessarily reduces their authenticity, for pedagogical and logistical reasons. As Bakker, Kent, Derry, Noss, and Hoyles (2008) warned, we cannot simply reproduce workplace experiences within the classroom in the hope of increasing students' chances of success beyond school. More research is needed to settle questions about whether teaching mathematics through real-world problem contexts improves students' abilities to solve a range of problems in adulthood and, if so, how authentic those contexts must be.

What Mathematical Content to Teach

A more general debate that overlaps with the issue of problem solving concerns what mathematical content is most important to teach. This question, too, can be answered from many perspectives, including the perpetuation of the discipline, the preparation of future mathematicians, readiness for future mathematics or other classes, and personal intellectual development or enjoyment. Again, the perspective we take here is preparation to meet the demands of modern work and life, with full recognition that this is only one of many valid goals.

In the next section, we examine how employers, workers, economists, and other scholars portray the problem-solving demands of modern work and life and the contributions of schooling, as a means of shedding new light on these classic debates.

THE DEMANDS OF 21ST-CENTURY WORK AND LIFE

Drivers of Change

The very phrase "21st-century demands" implies a view that life and work today significantly differ from life and work even a few decades ago, in ways that alter cognitive requirements and obligate new educational priorities. Before examining those new requirements and priorities, we first ask what has driven change in life and work and what is the basis for claims that their requirements are different.

Those who believe 21st-century life and work has changed significantly point to several sources. Technological advances and ubiquity are perhaps the most commonly cited drivers of change (Brynjolfsson & McAfee, 2011; Goldin & Katz, 2008; Handel, in press). In the workplace, computers and robots now accomplish routine or manual tasks that once required human actors (Autor, Levy, & Murnane, 2003; Partnership for 21st-Century Skills [P21], 2008). This development, in turn, purportedly requires workers to have higher-level problem-solving skills (Kaput, Noss, & Hoyles, 2008; Hoyles, Noss, Kent, & Bakker, 2010; P21, 2008). Multiple explanations have been offered for the mechanism by which technology elevates cognitive demands on the workforce as a whole. Automation by computers or robots may be *replacing* low-cognitive-level jobs, leaving only higher-level jobs remaining. Alternately, technology may be *transforming* what were once low-level jobs, because working *with* technology, or coping with technological change requires higher levels of cognition (Schultz, 1975; Welch, 1970 [both cited in Pellegrino & Hilton, 2012]). Or the mechanism may be less direct: some research finds that company-level technology investments yield productivity gains only when accompanied by organizational changes such as new strategies, processes, practices, and structures (P21, 2008). Thus, technology may be altering the cognitive demands on workers by changing their organizational roles, engaging them, for example, in self-managed teams, information sharing, and/or decentralized decision making.

Which, if any, of these mechanisms accurately ties technological advances to increased cognitive demands at work is uncertain. As Brynjolfsson and McAfee write, "Digital technologies are one of the most important driving forces in the economy today. They're transforming the world of work and are key drivers of productivity and growth. Yet their impact on employment is not well understood, and definitely not fully appreciated" (2011, p. 9). Handel's (in press) study of U.S. workers challenges both the job-replacement and job-transformation explanations. Furthermore, changes in organizational structures and practices that elevate cognitive demands on workers, such as flatter hierarchies and greater use of teams (Tucker, 2013), may have other causes than technology. Globalization and intensifying international competition are offered as other major drivers of elevated cognitive demands in the workplace (Hoyles et al., 2010). Most employers surveyed by the Partnership for 21st-Century Skills felt global competitiveness had shifted the importance of certain skills and competencies in their companies. Other change drivers—some of which are interdependent with technology, globalization, and each other—include the transformation from a manufacturing to a service or information economy (P21, 2008; Reich, 1991[cited in Pellegrino & Hilton, 2012]), the rapid pace of change in business (P21, 2008), mass customization of products, and elevated standards for communication with customers (Hoyles et al. 2010).

Despite these economic changes, there is some debate about whether the cognitive demands of the workplace, overall, are actually rising. Levy and Murnane (2004 [cited in Pellegrino & Hilton, 2012]) argue that the modern workplace increasingly requires the ability to solve non-routine problems, as well as complex communication competencies and verbal and quantitative literacy. Yet a meta-analysis by Bowles, Gintis, and Osborne (2001), as well as other studies reviewed by Pellegrino and Hilton (2012), show small to no correlations between scores on basic cognitive tests and earnings since the 1970s, suggesting that the labor-market demand for cognitive competencies has been static. Also debated is whether changes in workforce needs, if they do exist, constitute a crisis, as many proclaim. In the U.S., for example, STEM fields may be enjoying high job growth (Langdon, McKittrick, Beede, Khan, & Doms, 2011) but experts (e.g., Atkinson & Mayo, 2010; Salzman, Kuehn, & Lowell, 2013) differ in their assessments of employers' ability to fill those new positions. Other experts (Barton, 2000; Pellegrino & Hilton, 2012) also note an elevated premium on college degrees but question the reason. Rather than requiring college-level skills and knowledge, employers may seek a college degree only as a means of screening for basic skills, persistence, or work ethic (Murnane & Levy, 1996; Vedder, Denhart, & Robe, 2013).

Perhaps the new environmental condition that matters most to education is ideational. Mehta (2013) describes how the 1983 report *A Nation at Risk* linked—to a degree not seen before—schooling to individual and national economic success, thus engendering a new paradigm. This paradigm presumed that schools (not social forces) should be held responsible for academic achievement, were substantially underperforming in this role, and could be compelled to improve through monitoring by standardized cognitive tests—presumptions that have opened the door for and legitimized a dramatic shift from local to federal control of U.S. public schools. The implication of this new paradigm for our discussion is that notions of elevated cognitive demands on today's workers may not reflect actual economic or technological developments as much as a new perspective on the purpose of schooling (and policies that embody this perspective) that directly ties education to the quality of the workforce.

Overall, despite general agreement that broad economic and technological change has occurred in the past few decades, its impact on employment and its cognitive demands are not well established. Handel (in press) sums up the situation: "Researchers have only a cloudy sense of the levels and kinds of job skill requirements, rates of change, the dimensions along which job skills are changing, and the interrelationships between skills, technology, and employment involvement" (p. 3).

Unsurprisingly, given a current policy environment that prioritizes economic gain among the purposes of education, less research has targeted the changed demands of 21st-century life outside of work. A major source of such scholarship is Decision Research (www.decision-research.org), a nonprofit organization that investigates human judgment, decision making, and risk. Multiple studies from this group document recent movement in the areas of health care and personal finance towards greater consumer decision making, at the same time that available information about these areas is burgeoning. In health care, "Coverage choices are becoming more complicated and varied, health delivery systems more complex, and evidence of provider quality and treatment efficacy more transparent. Consumers therefore require more knowledge and greater skill to take full advantage of new sources of information and to make appropriate choices" (Hibbard, Peters, Dixon, & Tusler, 2007, p. 380). In one study, 50% of people seeking information about cancer first consulted the Internet; only 25% first consulted a doctor (Nelson, Fagerlin, & Peters, 2008). Much of this health-care and financial information is represented by statistics (e.g., regarding risks and benefits) and graphs (e.g., survival and mortality curves), as well as in complex documents and forms (e.g., from insurers). One's ability to understand this information has obvious consequences for one's health and well-being (Nelson et al., 2008).

In 1988, Davis observed that virtually all aspects of modern life had become mathematized, including driving, warfare, and even aesthetic judgment. He argued that citizens now needed not technical mathematical skills as much as an understanding of the ways mathematics shaped their lives, so that they could participate knowledgeably in social decisions rather than ceding control to a mathematically expert elite. In 2015, Davis's observation has only become truer. (Indeed, this sort of socio-mathematical savvy might allow people to more critically analyze policy rhetoric about the economic imperatives for increased schooling or cognitive skill!)

Problems Faced in 21st-Century Life and Work

Whether or not the demands of 21st-century work and life have changed considerably, and regardless of the reason, it is still meaningful to ask about the nature of the problems that need to be solved there. Most investigations into the cognitive requirements of the modern workplace are general: asking large groups of employers what they desire from workers; or trying to correlate levels of schooling with employment, earnings, or national productivity. Smaller-grained studies of the kinds of intellectual problems that arise in work (or everyday life) are few and, by necessity, highly context specific. Such studies are usually ethnographic and thus, while providing a thorough characterization of problems in particular workplaces or everyday settings, are difficult to generalize across adult activity.

Much of the ethnographic research about the kinds of problems modern workers need to solve has been conducted by the Techno-Mathematical Literacies in the Workplace Project. Between 2003 and 2007, Hoyles, Noss, Kent, Bakker, and colleagues followed midlevel workers in IT-intensive settings: five manufacturing companies and two finance companies. While the problems these workers solved on a regular basis varied considerably, commonalities were observed within and across companies. All of the work centered on highly mathematized processes, for example, statistical process control (SPC) in manufacturing and the calculation of interest rates in finance. Graphs, charts, spreadsheets, and computer simulations displayed the input variables and output data for these processes. Everyday problems involved the impact of changes in input variables on output data, requiring workers to interpret these technological displays. The research team coined the term *techno-mathematical literacies* (TmL) to capture the ways that mathematical processes were understood with and through technological representations. Hoyles et al. (2010) observed that in these workplaces, "Calculation and basic arithmetic are of subsidiary importance compared to a conceptual grasp of how, for example, process improvement works, how graphs and spreadsheets may highlight relationships, and how systematic data may be used with powerful, predictive tools to control and improve processes" (p. 168). Unfortunately, many workers lacked sufficient TmL to solve their everyday problems effectively. The team concluded that the workers' "major skills gap" could be closed not with more mathematical training (e.g., to understand the algebra in which the processes were formally described) but with a deeper understanding of the mathematical models underlying the processes. Bakker et al. (2008) further investigated the nature of problem solving engaged in by workers using SPC, in contrast to the statistical reasoning required in school tasks. They found that both forms of problem solving aim for generalization, use data as evidence, employ probabilistic language, and compare data against models. But SPC involves generalizing about a *process* (rather than a population, as in school tasks) and its goal is (a decision about) action, to reduce output discrepancies. Thus, SPC requires *abductive* inference (explaining data anomalies as results of process events or conditions) rather than *inductive* (simply predicting data patterns). Also, unlike school tasks, which often entail suppressing context, interpreting SPC data relies on context (e.g., cost, knowledge of process).

Gainsburg's (2006, 2007a, 2007b) findings from her ethnographic study of structural engineers echo the findings of the TmL team. The phenomena at the center of the engineers' problem solving were not processes per se but structures and their behavior. However, the need to understand underlying models that were represented mathematically (and technologically) was just as crucial. Indeed, in Gainsburg's assessment, "The heart of the intellectual work of structural engineers is the application of mathematical representations and procedures to solve design problems, which usually requires the selection, adaptation, or creation of a model" (2007b, p. 38). In structural engineering, mathematical models are unavoidable because the structures do not yet exist. A main source of problems is the complexity and uniqueness of each building, which preclude the simple application of established procedures. Structural engineers need a deep understanding of structural behavior, combined with conceptual fluency with usually basic mathematics, to create models that accurately represent the proposed building or elements. As with midlevel manufacturing and financial work, the problems that structural engineers must solve are, at root, about prediction, and the tools that support that prediction are mathematical models and processes.

It is important to note that not only do these ethnographic findings not necessarily generalize across workplaces, they do not even represent the work of all employees within these fields. For example, a study by Kent and Noss (2002) of a much larger structural-engineering firm than the ones studied by Gainsburg painted a different picture: Here, the creation of mathematical models was assigned to mathematical specialists and not generally handled by engineers (also Dudley, 2010). Similarly, in the manufacturing firms in the TmL project, higher-level employees interacted with the processes in ways that required more formal mathematical understanding and manipulation, while lower-level workers presumably never solved problems involving mathematically described processes.

Handel (in press) conducted a rare example of a broader investigation about the nature of problems encountered across a spectrum of work settings. In his survey of 2,000 workers across a range of U.S. workplaces, only 22% of the respondents reported having to solve "hard" problems "often" in their jobs; about 33% said they rarely or never had to do so. While the frequency of hard problems did not vary greatly by broad occupational type, it was somewhat correlated with the level of formal education a job required. The contrast between Handel's findings and those of the TmL team and Gainsburg is striking. One explanation might be that the latter focused on unusually challenging jobs. A different explanation might be methodological: people are known to be poor describers of their own activity. In particular, when reporting on their mathematical problem solving, people default to school-type characterizations of mathematics (formal and algorithmic), which are rarely evident in their work (Hoyles, Noss, & Pozzi, 2001). Ethnographers generally take a broader view of mathematics and "see" the same people using mathematics to solve everyday problems. It must also be noted that the TmL team detected problems that could have been (better) solved with more significant understanding and quantitative reasoning than they actually were. Thus, the TmL team described problems in the workplaces they studied that were only hypothetically challenging. Had Handel surveyed these same workers, they might also have reported that they rarely solved hard problems.

Outside the workplace, the Decision Research group portrays the kind of problems that people encounter in making everyday decisions about personal health care. These portrayals appear to be based on the researchers' experience or literature reviews and not systematic research. Reyna, Nelson, Han, and Dieckmann (2009) and Hibbard et al. (2007) describe typical problems related to personal health care: having to perform basic arithmetic operations on information embedded in a document, interpreting the information on medication prescription or nutritional labels, choosing among hospitals based on comparative data, and estimating risk magnitudes. While these problems sound less challenging than those facing engineers and midlevel manufacturing and finance workers, they may be more problematic for most people because they arise infrequently and thus never become routine, as do many workplace problems. Indeed, as will be discussed later, most people struggle to solve these health care–related problems.

In sum, we lack a comprehensive view of the kinds of problems people must solve in 21st-century work and life, but generalizations are probably impossible anyway. Some workers solve complex problems that require mathematical interpretation and reasoning, some do not, and some who don't would probably accomplish their jobs better if they did. The advent of sophisticated, mathematized processes and computerized representations of their output may have elevated the need for people to "make sense of mechanism" (Kaput, Noss, & Hoyles, 2008), as is the case for structural engineers and midlevel manufacturing and finance workers, but more research is needed to determine the ways and extent to which this is true and for what segments of the population.

Competencies Required by 21st-Century Work and Life

Researchers have taken many routes to try to determine the competencies required by modern work and life. At the most macroscopic end are studies that examine the impact of schooling in general on national and individual economic outcomes. These studies are valuable in that they measure real outcomes, but they offer only blunt proxies for cognitive competencies and problem-solving success. They are relevant to our discussion only if we presume that "going to school" yields competencies needed in the workplace and that economic gains indicate worker effectiveness in solving workplace problems—presumptions we problematize later.

Very generally speaking, time spent in school correlates with both individual and national economic gains (Barton, 2000; Bowles, Gintis, & Osborne, 2001; Cawley, Heckman, & Vytlacil, 2001; Goldin & Katz, 2008; Heckman, Stixrud, & Urzua, 2006; Tienken, 2008). Unclear, however, is *why* schooling produces economic gains—what schooling imparts that matters (Pellegrino & Hilton, 2012). An obvious explanation—that schooling impacts the economy by increasing cognitive ability—has been tested repeatedly, with conflicting or inconclusive results (Bowles et al., 2001; Cawley et al., 2001, Hanushek & Woessman, 2008, 2011; Murnane, Willett, & Levy, 1995; OECD, 2010). Furthermore, the impact of schooling on national economic outcomes may vary by educational level. The effect is unquestionably strong in developing countries. Elevating a national average from elementary to middle-school education, or elevating low cognitive abilities to moderate ones, yields greater economic gains than adding years of more advanced schooling or high-level cognitive skills (Bowles et al., 2001; Hanushek & Woessmann, 2008; Tienken, 2008). (In fact, Tienken argues that causality runs in the opposite direction in highly educated countries: thriving economies beget high education levels.) The value of college, however, has recently come under scrutiny. College degrees certainly advantage individuals in employment seeking (Greenstone & Looney, 2011; Zaback, Carlson, & Crellin, 2012), but experts differ on how much countries stand to gain by increasing their college-going populations (e.g., Goldin & Katz, 2008; Handel, in press; Lim & Kim, 2013; Vedder, Denhart & Robe, 2013; Wolf, 2009).

Technology appears to mediate the relationship between schooling or cognitive ability and economic outcomes, although, again, there is little agreement about how. Goldin and Katz (2008) contend that rising U.S. income inequality is the combined result of technological advances and a drop in college-degree completion—a low-supply, high-demand situation that elevates the individual economic return on a college degree. Closer inspection, however, reveals a "hollowing out" effect: midlevel white-collar work is disappearing, due, as some argue, to automation, rendering the greatest job growth at the "ends," in areas of low and high cognitive demand (manual labor and cutting-edge innovation) (Barton, 2000; Brynjolfsson & McAfee, 2011; Krugman, 2011). This bodes poorly for increased college education as an overall workforce-development strategy. Globally, technology exerts varied demands on different nations' needs for cognitive ability. To make economic progress, developing countries need only imitate other countries' technologies (an endeavor with lesser cognitive requirements) while developed countries must advance through innovation, which requires greater cognitive skill (Hanushek & Woessmann, 2008, 2011).

Many studies have attempted to trace the economic effects of schooling to specific courses, particularly mathematics, again with conflicting findings. Altonji (1995) found each additional 10th–12th-grade mathematics course predicted a very small earnings benefit for individuals, compared to the benefit of a year of school in general, and no benefit to wage *growth* over the first few years of work. Levine and Zimmerman (1995) documented a somewhat larger wage benefit for high-school mathematics courses, but only for female college graduates. These weak effects for mathematics courses may be a function of averaging a range of high-school courses, possibly diluting stronger earnings returns to more advanced courses with the weaker returns to more basic courses. Interestingly, Bishop and Mane (2004) found that, among high-school courses, career-and-technical-education courses had the biggest earnings impact, an effect that was amplified for students who attended college.

The difficulty of attributing the economic outcomes of schooling to specific courses raises the question: What skills, knowledge, or behaviors are learned in school that matter in the workplace? Various surveys of employers reveal their desire for workers who possess "soft skills" related to collaboration and communication, personal attributes like industriousness and perseverance, and general, higher-order, cognitive skills used in problem solving and critical thinking. Three-hundred Fortune 500 executives surveyed by MetLife (2010) felt the most important areas for college and career readiness were problem-solving skills, critical-thinking skills, clear and persuasive writing, and the ability to work both independently and on teams; they considered higher-level mathematics and science skills far less important. Similarly, 100 U.S. business leaders surveyed by the Business Council (2013) rated the most important skills/capabilities for workers, in order, as work ethic, teamwork, decision making, critical thinking, basic reading and math, and computer literacy. The Partnership for 21st-Century Skills identified four broad areas of employer-desired skills: *core subjects and 21st-century themes; learning and innovation skills; information, media, and technology skills;* and *life and career skills* (P21, 2009). Learning and innovation skills subdivided into three categories: *creativity and innovation, critical thinking and problem solving,* and *communication and collaboration*. Relevant to our chapter is their articulation of *critical thinking and problem solving*:

- Reason Effectively
  - Use various types of reasoning (inductive, deductive, etc.) as appropriate to the situation.
- Use Systems Thinking
  - Analyze how parts of a whole interact with each other to produce overall outcomes in complex systems.
- Make Judgments and Decisions
  - Effectively analyze and evaluate evidence, arguments, claims and beliefs.
  - Analyze and evaluate major alternative points of view.
  - Synthesize and make connections between information and arguments.
  - Interpret information and draw conclusions based on the best analysis.
  - Reflect critically on learning experiences and processes.
- Solve Problems
  - Solve different kinds of nonfamiliar problems in both conventional and innovative ways.
  - Identify and ask significant questions that clarify various points of view and lead to better solutions.

Overall, such employer surveys are useful for their "close-to-the-ground" perspective on the requirements of the 21st-century workplace, but they do not empirically link these competencies to actual outcomes such as productivity, employment, or wages. (A 2013 Gallup study of recent graduates, ages 18–35, however, links school experience with these skills to self-reported success in the workplace.) Such surveys may, however, help explain the mechanisms by which schooling contributes to such outcomes. Studies comparing high-school graduates to earners of high-school equivalency-exam certificates suggest that valuable "noncognitive traits" are acquired through attendance in school and rewarded with increased earnings, especially for women and for men in low-skill markets (Heckman et al., 2006). Relatedly, Cawley et al. (2001) found that specific behavioral and social skills impacted earnings independently of cognitive skills, although they seemed to operate by increasing school attendance and performance. Unfortunately, these and other reports (Business Council, 2013; Fischer, 2013; P21, 2006) make clear that many U.S. workers, even those with college degrees, lack the interpersonal and problem-solving skills, and the work ethic, that employers desire.

What of the *mathematical* requirements of modern work and life? In contrast with current policy rhetoric, researchers have observed that most work over the past few decades has involved only basic mathematics. In the 1995 National Job Task Analysis (Packer, 1997), 3,000 U.S. workers across levels reported on the skill requirements of their jobs. Only one of the 25 competencies that they rated most important (Number 14) was mathematical: "perform arithmetic." Further analysis showed that the content of the most basic high-school algebra and geometry courses more than covered the mathematical skill requirements of the vast majority of workers. Apparently little has changed since the 1990s. Handel (in press) interviewed 2,000 workers across levels and found that, whereas most workers used arithmetic on the job and about 66% used fractions, decimals, and percentages, only about 25% used more advanced mathematics, usually simple algebra. (In an interesting exception, 15% to 30% of "skilled blue-collar workers" used geometry, trigonometry, inferential statistics, and complex algebra—similar to the rates of use among managers and professionals—while all other groups rarely did.) The U.S. Bureau of Labor Statistics confirms these worker self-reports of low mathematics requirements in its 2001–2012 projections for job openings (Barton, 2006). So, too, do the findings of a National Center on Education and the Economy (NCEE) (2013) study of U.S. community colleges. (Because community colleges provide the bulk of U.S. vocational education, their course requirements arguably represent a baseline for career readiness.) For the initial credit-bearing courses in the eight most popular community-college programs, middle-school-level mathematics—especially arithmetic, ratio, proportion, expressions, and simple equations—was most important. Only one program required Algebra 2. Yet many programs required mathematical skills not emphasized in high school: schematics, geometric visualization, complex applications of measurement, mathematical modeling, statistics, and probability. As with soft, social, and general problem-solving skills, many workers and community college students lack even these basic mathematical skills (Murnane & Levy, 1996; NCEE, 2013; Packer, 1997). We have previously noted the shortcoming of such studies: They are constrained by their respondents' mathematical skills. They cannot reveal whether improved mathematical skill, understanding, or application ability among workers would increase the number of topics and level of mathematics they used and whether that would, in turn, enhance their productivity or work quality.

More or better mathematics learning might also enhance life outcomes. Studies conducted by the Decision Research group showed more numerate people making better health and financial decisions and enjoying better health and financial outcomes. Echoing workplace studies, these authors report that many people lack the requisite numeracy for such decisions, even though the mathematics involved is basic, suggesting that improved mathematical skill would enhance many lives (Peters, Hibbard, Slovic, & Dieckmann, 2007). Their methodology is, in itself, illuminating: *Numeracy* is treated as a somewhat hybrid construct, measured by a test of quantitative reasoning in context. As such, it is theoretically decoupled from schooling, education level, and intelligence (Nelson et al., 2008; Peters & Levine, 2008). That is, the independent variable (numeracy) captures the ability to apply particular mathematical concepts, overlapping somewhat with the dependent variable (making real-world decisions involving quantity). This might shed some light on why years of high-school mathematics—a purer measure of mathematical competence—poorly predicts workplace performance (i.e., earnings):

The mathematics in high-school courses is probably more topically advanced than necessary for real-world decisions, but such courses do not enable students to apply mathematics in real-world problem solving. As Pellegrino and Hilton (2012) note, "Over a century of research on transfer has yielded little evidence that teaching can develop general cognitive competencies that are transferable to any new discipline, problem, or context, in or out of school" (p. 8).

How and Where Might 21st-Century Competencies Be Developed?

Despite their pessimism about teaching for transfer, Pellegrino and Hilton (2012) conclude their review of 21st-century competencies with a call for exactly that. Indeed, for them, what makes something a 21st-century competence is that a person can apply it in situations different from the one in which it was learned. Drawing on a large body of education research, they propose that schooling should aim for "deep learning"—an understanding of the general principles or structures that underlie concepts and problems—because deep learning promotes transfer.

Pellegrino and Hilton concede uncertainty about what schooling imparts that promotes positive outcomes in 21st-century work and life, and even about whether the current labor market truly demands increased cognitive competence. Regardless of this uncertainty, or maybe due to it, they put their faith in school-based improvements to promote adult success. Specifically, they recommend transforming teaching to focus on:

* underlying principles
* the process of learning
* high-level skills, even if low-level skills have not yet been mastered
* learning skills and concepts in a specific domain
* the conditions for application
* using multiple representations, especially graphic or tactile
* integrating noncognitive skills
* giving the learning process ample time.

These recommendations are presumed to increase the likelihood of transfer and produce more effective problem solvers in an unpredictable and fast-changing workplace or society because the knowledge and skills learned can be employed flexibly and across a range of problem situations. Still, Pellegrino and Hilton acknowledge the power of context, recommending teaching the use of skills and knowledge in specific domains, making explicit the conditions in which the knowledge might be applied, and assessing its application. As such, Pellegrino and Hilton's recommendations (albeit not aimed at mathematics specifically) depart from a view that prevailed for decades: that mathematics education provides general mental training/discipline that can transfer across fields (Stanic & Kilpatrick, 1989).

Responding to the low level of mathematical topics required in profession-oriented community-college courses and students' inability to apply even this low-level mathematics, the NCEE's (2013) recommendations for mathematics education generally echo Pellegrino and Hilton's. The NCEE urges K–12 schools to spend far more instructional time on proportional relationships, percents, graphical representations, functions, expressions, and equations, emphasizing conceptual understandings of these topics and their application to practical problems. Contradicting current policy statements, but reflecting Pellegrino and Hilton's appeal for ample time to the learning process, the NCEE argues against requiring Algebra 2 in high school and advises delaying Algebra 1 for some students. Further, the NCEE advocates for multiple mathematical paths, not just the traditional one leading to calculus. Options in statistics, data analysis, and applied geometry, for example, would better reflect the mathematics used across occupations and retain more students in the STEM pipeline.

Other scholars (e.g., Bishop, 1993; Fischer, 2013; Harvard Graduate School of Education [GSE], 2011) argue for contextualized or job-specific learning, either in school or in workplace settings. Noting differences among the qualities that constitute "readiness" for the workplace, college, and healthy personal development, respectively, the *Pathways to Prosperity* report (Harvard GSE, 2011) concludes that "a more holistic approach to education—one that aims to equip young adults with a broader range of skills—is more likely to produce youth who will succeed in the 21st century" (p. 4). This more holistic education includes vocational education, career counseling from the early grades, and structured workplace experiences in high school. The report lauds work-related K–12 educational experiences such as the engineering curriculum, "Project Lead the Way", California's "Linked Learning" initiative, robotics competitions, and various career-and-technical and career-academy programs. And while over 90% of the U.S. CEOs surveyed by the Business Council (2013) rated secondary and four-year college education "very/most important" for a top-quality workforce, 82% felt the same way about "on-the-job training." The TmL researchers aimed their interventions at experienced workers but proposed that gaps in adult TmL might be lessened by school instruction that acknowledged the importance of context, real-world constraints, action, and responsibility (Bakker et al., 2008). Empirical support for this idea comes from the Gallup (2013) study showing that school experience with real-world problem solving, more than with any other 21st-century skill, predicted self-reported success at work.

The potential contributions of work-based or work-related learning to 21st-century problem solving are twofold: First, it provides realistic contexts for learning that could help overcome the failure of abstract, general knowledge to transfer and thus promote the use of academic knowledge for solving real problems. (Less clear, however, is whether context-specific learning enables knowledge to be used in solving problems beyond the context in which it was learned [Cognition & Technology Group at Vanderbilt, 1990].) Second, work-related learning is likelier to engender the soft skills and attitudes desired by employers, especially if it involves work on projects with real purposes and clients. But blending work (or real-world) situations and classroom learning is not a straightforward matter. The TmL researchers warn that, "Formulating potential implications of workplace research for school education is a tricky business. . . . One should not make the mistake to try and copy workplace situations in school education" (Bakker et al., 2008, p. 142). Indeed, a current topic of contention is whether 21st-century competence is better learned in school or in workplace or other out-of-school settings (Fischer, 2013). Fifty-nine percent of the young employees in the Gallup (2013) study reported learning most of the skills needed in their current job outside of school, but this percent dropped significantly for college graduates. The implications of these findings are unclear: they may suggest room for improvement in the way high schools prepare students for the workplace, or they may indicate that the kinds of jobs filled by high-school graduates rely less on intellectual, school-taught skills than do jobs requiring a college degree.

ADVANCING PROBLEM SOLVING IN THE MATHEMATICS CURRICULUM

Recent research about 21st-century work and life, summarized in the prior section, yields conflicting perspectives about how technology has impacted workplace problem solving and whether cognitive demand is rising in general. Nevertheless, some principles emerge from this research with direct relevance to mathematics education:

- Problem solving in work and life requires a more solid and flexible grasp of basic mathematics than much of the population currently possesses. Advanced mathematics courses do not appear to be the solution.
- Certain noncognitive and general skills (that are typically underpromoted in education) are critical for workplace problem solving. Many of these are cognitively high level.
- Many jobs, particularly in IT-intensive fields, require an understanding of conceptual models that underlie processes or systems ("making sense of mechanism"), which in turn requires

interpretations of complex representations within the work context and a deep understanding of the work domain.

- In some contrast, everyday life decisions increasingly require interpreting quantitative data in various complex forms, in multiple, unfamiliar domains.
- The ability to apply one's training and knowledge to novel, unfamiliar problems (transfer) is highly privileged by employers, and is presumed most effectively fostered when learning occurs in work-based contexts on the job or replicated in schools.

In light of these principles, we revisit the debates presented earlier and consider how we might approach mathematical problem solving within the school curriculum for the purpose of preparing students for success in 21st-century work and life.

Problem Solving: Process and Content

Earlier, we described a decades-long debate on teaching problem solving versus teaching mathematics *through* problem solving. Mathematical-content knowledge per se is almost never an explicit goal of employers, but their clear desire for workers who are effective problem solvers implicitly argues for schools to teach problem solving as an end in itself. Thus, despite the mathematics-education community's recent bent towards problem solving as a vehicle for learning mathematical content, we recommend honoring both goals. We advocate restructuring this debate to ask, instead, how we might design problems that are sufficiently cognitively demanding to foster both significant mathematical content and effective problem-solving capabilities. As a start, we might consider redefining problem solving as an experience where the solver or a collaborating group "needs to develop a more productive mathematical way of thinking about the given situation" (Lesh & Zawojewski, 2007, p. 782). The focus then becomes one of learning or idea generation, rather than the application of problem-solving processes or strategies. Hence, one key feature of problem solving that promotes both process and content is the opportunity for student generation of mathematical ideas, indeed, even before such content is formally introduced.

This feature of idea generation reflects calls for more cognitively challenging tasks that encourage high-level thinking and reasoning, have multiple points of entry, and enable the use of varied solution approaches. Unfortunately, as Silver, Mesa, Morris, Star, and Benken (2009) report, emphasis in the 1990s on the importance of cognitively demanding tasks (e.g., Stein, Grover, & Henningsen, 1996) appears to have gone largely unheeded. This is a pity because Stein et al.'s criteria provide a pertinent basis for designing mathematics-curriculum problems that target 21st-century demands related to communication and other general problem-solving skills. For example, problems with high cognitive demand require students to explain, describe, and justify; make decisions, choices, and plans; formulate questions; apply existing knowledge and create new ideas; and represent their understanding in multiple formats. Students are likely to face such demands when encountering problems outside of school, where uncertainty and a broadening of mathematical content call for problem solvers who have the disposition and ability to generate mathematical knowledge on an "as-needed basis." Although debates continue about whether the cognitive challenges of the workplace are truly increasing, we do know that more skillful decision making and problem solving are needed in all avenues of life, where solving information-laden problems has become increasingly vital to one's overall health, well-being, and achievements.

General Skills and Heuristics

Collectively, the general skills for successful problem solving advocated by employer groups and mathematics educators share some features, although recommendations for fostering these skills remain challenging and, at times, contradictory. From the extensive literature on general skills, the four broad areas of employer-desired skills that have been identified by the Partnership for 21st-Century Skills (P21, 2010) appear particularly pertinent. These areas, which we have delineated in a prior section, include effective reasoning, using systems thinking, making judgements and decisions, and solving problems. These skill areas are reflected in recent writings of Schoenfeld (2011, 2013) and Lester (2013), who raise the importance of recognizing and constructing patterns of inference and making careful judgments during the problem-solving process. Schoenfeld's (2013) inclusion of solvers' beliefs and dispositions about themselves and the discipline being engaged, together with their "decision-making mechanism" (p. 17), is an interesting extension of his earlier work, in which "dispositions, beliefs, values, tastes, and preferences" (Schoenfeld, 2010, p. 29) were identified as core features of successful problem solving. More recently, Swanson (2013) also highlighted the importance of students' beliefs and orientations when faced with challenging mathematics problems. She aptly titled her article "Overcoming the Run Response," invoking the fear such problems can instill in students. In revealing students' emotional reactions to these problems, Swanson stressed the importance of self-awareness and regulation, in other words, metacognition. Metacognition, in broad terms, is increasingly recognized as playing a critical role in successful problem solving, both within and beyond the curriculum (e.g., Lester, 2013; Pellegrino & Hilton, 2012). Lester's (2013) inclusion of "intuition" as one of the key components of successful problem solving further supports the recognition of general cognitive components, provided students become conscious of their intuitions and can evaluate their implications for the problem at hand. Yet, as he and others (e.g., Schneider & Artelt, 2010) have lamented, we still know little about how to develop students' metacognitive abilities. Indeed, current approaches may be inherently self-contradictory (see Kirshner, Chapter 4 in this volume).

The extent to which these competencies and dispositions exist as general abilities that individuals can possess and apply across domains, much less be taught, remains unclear. The strong consensus on their importance in the workplace could mean employers have actually seen workers—their most valuable ones—repeatedly solve nonroutine problems, implying that such general competencies exist. Even so, *nonroutine* should not be confused with *contextually unfamiliar*, a broader condition. Exemplary workers have the ability to solve novel problems within their domain (e.g., auto mechanics) but there is no reason to expect this ability to extend to problems in other domains (e.g., cooking). This distinction might inform the issue of problem-solving heuristics: within-domain heuristics (e.g., for mathematical problem solving, as Polya's were originally intended) might hold promise, but not cross-domain heuristics. Still, even the observation of able solvers of nonroutine problems within a domain does not guarantee that within-domain heuristics explain their success or even exist. Clearly, more research is needed on within-domain problem-solving expertise and how it is learned.

Contexts and Authenticity

It is apparent that domain knowledge is key to workplace problem solving. Beyond specific job training, however, it is hard to see how to address this in schools. Further, while it may be possible to succeed at work with expertise in only a single domain, everyday life decisions occur in multiple domains encountered too infrequently to become familiar (e.g., medical and financial decisions). Still, with little research support for the transfer of mathematical skills learned in the abstract to contextual problems, it seems advisable to engage students in learning to solve contextualized problems with mathematical tools and in making sense of models (real-world systems and processes that mathematically relate quantities). As more classrooms employ context-based mathematical learning and modeling, more research can be conducted on the effect of such education on students' problem-solving ability in future courses, work, and life—specifically, how well learning to use mathematics to solve problems in certain contexts (in school) prepares students for doing so in other contexts outside of school.

Even if such transfer remains hard to prove, there are other reasons to teach mathematics in the context of solving realistic problems. It offers a more realistic view of real-world problem solving, which is usually interdisciplinary and dependent on contextual specifics (unlike traditional school math problems); this view should better prepare students for such problem solving. It could also reveal the nature of various workplaces, thus building career awareness and a general understanding of what adult work requires. Realistic problem solving could also invoke and build noncognitive skills desired by employers, such as collaboration and communication. It might also build positive dispositions towards the use of mathematics in solving real-world problems, convincing students that mathematical tools can be useful in problem solving, developing self-efficacy in the use of those tools, and showing that persistence is often required.

Mathematical Content

Here, the message from the research is clear: For solving the vast majority of problems arising in work and life, only basic mathematics is needed, but people need to be far more fluent with its use and application than they are today. The current press to expose more students to more advanced mathematics topics before college appears to head in the wrong direction, especially when these topics are covered rapidly and cursorily. More advisable would be spending more time with each topic, enriching students' understanding by using the topic to solve a variety of mathematical and real problems. For most students, a goal of mastery of basic algebra and geometry by the end of high school seems most justified, with the addition of the less-traditional topics of statistics, data analysis, and solid geometry.

Despite the shortcomings of transfer research, the finding by the TmL researchers of the importance of understanding the conceptual models underlying real-world processes supports the idea that deep understanding of somewhat generalizable concepts is more efficacious in promoting problem-solving ability, at least within a domain, than shallower, situation-specific, procedural knowledge. This suggests that whatever the mathematical content (and whatever the context), the primary goal for teaching should be deep understanding of the underlying principles and concepts. This should work in both directions: problem solving in real contexts can contribute to a deep understanding of mathematical concepts and principles, and applying mathematical tools to real problems can contribute to a deep understanding of the concepts and principles underlying the real-world systems or phenomena. The sentiments of employers and the observations by workplace ethnographers underscore the importance of learning and metacognition on the job: successful engineers, scientists, and technology workers use mathematics or quantitative reasoning to better understand the systems at the heart of their work, at the same time honing their mathematical or quantitative "tools" for future problem solving. Schools should make explicit to students that this learning cycle is part of what the best STEM workers do.

MATHEMATICAL MODELING—ONE WAY TO PREPARE FOR 21ST-CENTURY DEMANDS

Mathematical modeling is becoming increasingly important in the workplace and in many other avenues in life. The terms *models* and *modeling* have been interpreted variously in the literature (e.g., English, 2013; Gainsburg, 2006; Lesh & Doerr, 2003; Lesh & Zawojewski, 2007; Stillman & Galbraith, 2011), with debate over whether these are components of the broad problem-solving spectrum or entities in their own right. Without taking a stance on this debate, we consider modeling a powerful vehicle for bringing features of 21st-century problems into the mathematics classroom.

Modeling has an extensive history within the mathematics community, as can be seen in the 1983 establishment of International Conferences on the Teaching of Mathematical Modeling and Applications (ICTMA; Kaiser, 2010). Various interpretations and forms of models and modeling exist, even within the ICTMA community, but we refer to Lesh and Fennewald's (2010) basic "first-iteration definition of a model," namely, "A model is a system for describing (or explaining, or designing) another system(s) for some clearly specified purpose" (p. 7). This interpretation is especially germane to fields beyond mathematics education, including engineering and other mature science domains. Some of the experiences that engage students in modeling from this perspective have been described as model-eliciting activities (MEAs; English, 2007; Hamilton, Lesh, Lester, & Brilleslyper, 2008; Lesh & Doerr, 2003), where the focus is on the processes of interpretation and reinterpretation of problematic information, and on the iterative development of mathematical ideas as models are formed, tested, and refined in response to certain specifications. MEAs give students the opportunity to create, apply, and adapt mathematical and scientific concepts in interpreting, explaining, and predicting the behavior of real-world based problems such as those that occur in engineering (e.g., Gainsburg, 2006).

Exposure to statistical information in these MEAs provides a valuable basis for developing the skills that consumers need in working effectively with data. Interpreting and understanding the implications of insurance documents, financial agreements, and political agendas, to name a few, requires an ability to deal with complex information. Modeling problems present students with such data, which must be interpreted, differentiated, prioritized, and coordinated to produce a solution model. Furthermore, students' modeling work often elicits nontraditional mathematics topics for their grade level, because different types of quantities and operations are needed to deal with realistic situations. For example, MEAs often involve accumulations, probabilities, frequencies, and ranks, with the associated operations of sorting, organizing, selecting, quantifying, weighting, and transforming large data sets (Doerr & English, 2003; Lesh, Zawojewski, & Carmona, 2003). Integral to the mathematizing process are the myriad representational media required in expressing and documenting the models, including computer-based graphics, tables, lists, paper-based diagrams and graphs, and oral and written communication (Lesh & Harel, 2003). Because these representations embody the factors, relationships, and operations that students considered important in creating their models, MEAs offer an additional benefit to teachers and researchers: powerful insight into the growth of students' mathematical thinking.

As we noted in our discussion on 21st-century demands, the importance of understanding the underlying models that are represented mathematically and technologically is crucial in many fields, including engineering, finance, manufacturing, and agriculture. Virtually all aspects of modern life have been mathematized using the modeling components we have highlighted; our future citizens need to be aware of, and understand how, this mathematization shapes their lives in so many ways. In preparing our students to become mathematically aware, consideration needs to be given to how we might select contexts that approximate authenticity and foster an appreciation of learning through classroom problem solving. Modeling problems also foster the types of general skills that employers demand in the workplace and that citizens need for maximum societal participation. Such skills include critical and innovative thinking, complex reasoning, metacognitive actions, and collaboration and communication within and across disciplines. In sum, modeling activities represent an excellent example of an instructional strategy that should promote the kind of learning valued in 21st-century work and life.

CONCLUDING POINTS

We commenced this chapter by reviewing some of the key debates on mathematical problem solving over past decades. Given that these debates remain largely unresolved, we turned to research on the demands of modern work and life and examined drivers of change in these settings. We considered the nature of the problems that need to be solved in these changing contexts and the competencies required for dealing effectively with the challenges that arise. In light of this research, we revisited mathematics education and suggested how we might better prepare students for successful problem solving in the 21st century.

Where do we stand then, with regard to suggestions for how we might advance students' problem solving in today's world? Clearly, there are many courses of action that might be adopted and, with the diverse range of learning contexts we face, no one set of recommendations would suit all school systems. Nevertheless, we have focused on ways in which we might teach problem-solving processes in conjunction with developing mathematical content, how we might address context and authenticity, and how general skills might be developed to enhance problem-solving success in the modern workplace and life. Many challenges remain, however, in implementing our recommendations and issues for further investigation abound. We address just a couple of such issues in closing.

We have given MEAs as an example of a rich source for developing both problem-solving processes and mathematical content as well as providing authentic contexts and fostering general skills. Other cognitively demanding problem types that offer similar learning opportunities should also be incorporated within the mathematics curriculum. Interdisciplinary problems that require synthesizing knowledge from across STEM domains—for example, problems in an engineering context—can be appealing and authentic, but they remain rare in the mathematics curriculum (English, Hudson, & Dawes, 2012; Suh, Seshaiyer, Moore, Green, Jewell, & Rice, 2013).

Modifying "traditional" mathematical problems to foster idea generation rather than mere procedural application is another area in need of attention. Such modification can be both teacher and student initiated. Teachers can restructure existing problems to be interdisciplinary (perhaps in collaboration with teachers of other subjects), so that obvious solution paths become less apparent, not all of the required mathematics is presented, and a more open approach to solution is encouraged. And the renewed interest in problem posing offers valuable suggestions for engaging students in adapting, creating, and solving their own problems, beginning with such experiences in the earliest years of schooling. For example, English and Watson (2014) have shown how problem posing can be integrated within the regular mathematics curriculum in the areas of statistics and probability, where students direct their own investigations.

Thinking more broadly, we advocate an increased awareness of mathematical problem solving beyond the classroom and greater insights into how the demands of the 21st century are impacting our lives. While we cannot simply transport the mathematical problems of the outside world into the classroom, there are many ways in which we can more realistically contextualize "school problems." Such recontextualization should incorporate a transition to more cognitively challenging problems—ones which stimulate curiosity, foster critical thinking, promote creative solutions, and feature multiple entry and exit points for increased access by a range of students.

REFERENCES

Altonji, J. G. (1995). The effects of high school curriculum on education and labor market outcomes. *The Journal of Human Resources, 30*(3), 409–438.

Anderson, J. (2014). Forging new opportunities for problem solving in Australian mathematics classrooms through the first national mathematics curriculum. In Y. Li & G. Lappan (Eds.), *Mathematics curriculum in school education* (pp. 209–230). Dordrecht: Springer.

Atkinson, R. D., & Mayo, M. (2010). *Refueling the U.S. innovation economy: Fresh approaches to science, technology, engineering, and mathematics (STEM) education*. The Information Technology & Innovation Foundation. Retrieved from www.itif.org/files/2010-refueling-innovation-economy.pdf.

Autor, D., Levy, F., & Murnane, R. (2003). The skill content of recent technological change: An empirical exploration. *Quarterly Journal of Economics, 118*(4), 1279–1333.

Bakker, A., Kent, P., Derry, J., Noss, R., & Hoyles, C. (2008). Statistical inference at work: Statistical Process Control as an example. *Statistics Education Research Journal, 7*(2), 130–145.

Barton, P.E. (2000). *What jobs require: Literacy, education, and training, 1940–2006*. Educational Testing Service Policy Information Report.

Barton, P.E. (2006). *High school reform and work: Facing labor market realities*. Educational Testing Service Policy Information Report.

Bishop, J. (1993). Improving job matches in the U.S. labor market. Brookings Papers on Economic Activity. *Microeconomics, 1993*(1), 335–400.

Bishop, J.H., & Mane, F. (2004). The impacts of career-technical education on high school labor market success. *Economics of Education Review, 23*, 381–402

Boaler, J. (2009). *The elephant in the classroom: Helping children learn and love maths*. London: Souvenir Press.

Bowles, Ginits, & Osborne (2001). The determinants of earnings: A behavioral approach. *Journal of Economic Literature, 39*(4), 1137–1176.

Brynjolfsson, E. & McAfee, A. (2011). *Race against the machine: How the digital revolution is accelerating innovation, driving productivity, and irreversibly transforming employment and the economy*. Lexington, MA: Digital Frontier Press.

Business Council. (2013, May). *CEO survey results: The Business Council survey of CEOs in collaboration with the Conference Board*. Retrieved from www.thebusinesscouncil.org/assets/TCB_BCS_MAY_2013.pdf.

Cawley, J., Heckman, J.J., & Vytlacil, E.J. (2001). Three observations on wages and measured cognitive ability. *Labour Economics, 8*(4), 419–442.

Cognition & Technology Group at Vanderbilt. (1990). Anchored instruction and its relationship to situated cognition. *Educational Researcher, 19*(6), 2–10.

Cooper, B. & Dunne, M. (1998). Anyone for tennis? Social class differences in children's responses to national curriculum mathematics testing. *The Sociological Review, 46*(1), 115–148.

Davis, P.J. (1988). Applied mathematics as social contract. *Mathematics Magazine, 61*(3), 139–147.

de Abreu, G. (2002). Mathematics learning in out-of-school contexts: A cultural psychology perspective. In L.D. English (Ed.). *Handbook of International research in mathematics Education* (pp. 323–353). Mahwah, NJ: Lawrence Erlbaum Associates.

Doerr, H.M., & English, L.D. (2003). A Modeling perspective on students' mathematical reasoning about data. *Journal for Research in Mathematics Education, 34*(2), 110–136.

Dudley, U. (2010). What is mathematics for? *Notices of the AMS, 57*(5), 608–613.

Duncker, K. (1945). On problem solving. *Psychological Monographs, 58*(5).

English, L.D. (2007). Interdisciplinary modelling in the primary mathematics curriculum. In J. Watson & K. Beswick (Eds.), *Mathematics: Essential research, essential practice. Proceedings of the 30th annual conference of the Mathematics Education Research Group of Australasia* (Vol. 2, pp. 275–284). Adelaide: MERGA.

English, L.D. (2013). Complex modelling in the primary and middle school years: An interdisciplinary approach. In G. Stillman, G. Kaiser, W. Blum, & J. Brown (Eds.), *Mathematical modelling: Connecting to practice—Teaching practice and the practice of applied mathematicians* (pp. 491–505). New York: Springer.

English, L.D., Hudson, P.B., & Dawes, L. (2012). Engineering design processes in seventh-grade classrooms: Bridging the engineering education gap. *European Journal of Engineering Education, 37*(5), 436–447.

English, L.D., & Sriraman, B. (2010). Problem solving for the 21st century. In B. Sriraman & L.D. English (Eds.), *Advances in Mathematics Education. Theories of mathematics education: Seeking new frontiers* (pp. 263–285). New York: Springer.

English, L.D., & Watson, J.M. (2014). Statistical literacy in the elementary school: Opportunities for problem posing. In F. Singer, N. Ellerton, & J. Cai (Eds.), *Problem posing: From research to effective practice*. Dordrecht: Springer.

Fischer, K. (2013). The employment mismatch. *The Chronicle of Higher Education* (March 4). Retrieved from http://chronicle.com/article/The-Employment-Mismatch/137625/#id=overview.

Gainsburg, J. (2006). The mathematical modeling of structural engineers. *Mathematical Thinking and Learning, 8*(1), 3–36.

Gainsburg, J. (2007a). The mathematical disposition of structural engineers. *Journal for Research in Mathematics Education, 38*(5), 477–506.

Gainsburg, J. (2007b). Problem solving and learning in everyday structural engineering work. In R.A. Lesh, E. Hamilton, & J. Kaput (Eds.), *Foundations for the future in mathematics education* (pp. 37–56). Mahwah, NJ: Lawrence Erlbaum Associates.

Gallup (2013, May 28). *21st century skills and the workplace: A 2013 Microsoft Partners in Learning and Pearson Foundation study*. Retrieved from www.gallup.com/services/176699/21st-century-skills-workplace.aspx.

Goldin, C. & Katz, L.F. (2008). *The race between education and technology*. Cambridge, MA: Harvard University Press.

Goos, M., & Galbraith, P. (1996). Do it this way! Metacognitive strategies in collaborative mathematical problem solving. *Educational Studies in Mathematics, 30*, 229–260.

Goos, M., Galbraith, P., & Renshaw, P. (2002). Socially mediated metacognition: creating collaborative zones of proximal development in small group problem solving. *Educational Studies in Mathematics, 49*, 193–223.

Greenstone, M. & Looney, A. (2011). *Where is the best place to invest $102,000—In stocks, bonds, or a college degree?* Report from the Hamilton Project, Brookings. Retrieved from www.brookings.edu/research/papers/2011/06/25-education-greenstone-looney.

Greiffenhagen, C., & Sharrock, W. (2008). School mathematics and its everyday other? Revisiting Lave's 'Cognition in Practice.' *Educational Studies in Mathematics, 69*, 1–21.

Grubb, W.N., & Lazerson, M. (2004). The education gospel: The economic power of schooling. Cambridge, MA: Harvard University Press.

Hamilton, E., Lesh, R., Lester, F., & Brilleslyper, M. (2008). Model-eliciting activities (MEAs) as a bridge between engineering education research and mathematics education research. *Advances in Engineering Education, 1*(2), 1–25.

Handel, M.J. (in press). What do people do at work? A profile of U.S. jobs from the survey of workplace skills, technology, and management practices (STAMP). In F. Green & M. Keese (Eds). Paris: OECD Publishing.

Hanushek, E.A., & Woessmann, L. (2008). The role of cognitive skills in economic development, *Journal of Economic Literature, 46*(3), 607–668.

Hanushek, E.A., & Woessmann. L. (2011). How much do educational outcomes matter for developed countries? *Economic Policy, 26(67)*.

Harvard Graduate School of Education (GSE). (2011, February). *Pathways to prosperity: Meeting the challenge of preparing young Americans for the 21st century*. Report from the Pathways to Prosperity Project.

Heckman, J.J., Stixrud, J., & Urzua, S. (2006). The effects of cognitive and noncognitive abilities on labor market outcomes and social behavior. *Journal of Labor Economics, 4*(3), 411–482.

Hegedus, S. (2013). Young children's investigating advanced mathematical concepts with haptic technologies: Future design perspectives. *The Mathematics Enthusiast, 10*(1–2), 87–108.

Hibbard, J.H., Peters, E., Dixon, A., & Tusler, M. (2007). Consumer competencies and the use of comparative quality information: It isn't just about literacy. *Medical Care Research and Review, 62*(4), 379–394.

Hohensee, C. (2014). Backward transfer: An investigation of the influence of quadratic functions instruction on students' prior ways of reasoning about linear functions. *Mathematical Thinking and Learning, 16*(2), 135–174.

Hoyles, C., Noss, R., Kent, P., & Bakker, A. (2010). *Improving mathematics at work: The need for techno-mathematical literacies*. London: Routledge.

Hoyles, C., Noss, R., & Pozzi, S. (2001). Proportional reasoning in nursing practice. *Journal for Research in Mathematics Education, 32*, 4–27.

Kapa, E. (2001). A metacognitive support during the process of problem solving in a computerized environment. *Educational Studies in Mathematics, 47*, 317–336.

Kaiser, G. (2010). Introduction: ICTMA and the teaching of modelling and applications. In R. Lesh, P. Galbraith, C. R. Haines, & A. Hurford (Eds.), *Modeling students' mathematical modeling competencies* (pp. 1–2). New York: Springer.

Kaput, J., Noss, R., & Hoyles, C. (2008). Developing new notations for a learnable mathematics in the computational era. In L. D. English (Ed.), *Handbook of international research in mathematics education* (2nd ed., pp. 693–715). New York: Routledge.

Kent, P., & Noss, R. (2002, January). *The mathematical components of engineering expertise: The relationship between doing and understanding mathematics*. Paper submitted to the Institution of Electrical Engineers Annual Symposium on Engineering Education, London.

Kilpatrick, J. (1981). One point of view: Stop the bandwagon, I want off. *Arithmetic Teacher, 28*(8), 2.

Kramarski, B., Weisse, I., & Kololshi-Minsker, I. (2010). How can self-regulated learning support the problem solving of third-grade students with mathematics anxiety? *The International Journal on Mathematics Education, 42* (2), 179–193.

Krugman, P. (2011, March 9). Degrees and dollars. *New York Times*. Retrieved from www.nytimes.com/2011/03/07/opinion/07krugman.html.

Langdon, D., McKittrick, G., Beede, D., Khan, B., & Doms, M. (2011). *STEM: Good jobs now and for the future. U.S. Department of Commerce, Economics and Statistics Administration*. Retrieved from www.esa.doc.gov/Reports/stem-good-jobs-now-and-future.

Lesh, R. & Doerr, H.M. (2003). Foundations of a models and modeling perspective on mathematics teaching, learning, and problem solving. In R. Lesh & H.M. Doerr (Eds.), *Beyond constructivism:*

Models and modeling perspectives on mathematics problem solving, learning, and teaching (pp. 3–33). Mahwah, NJ: Lawrence Erlbaum Associates.

Lesh, R., & Fennewald, T. (2010). Introduction to part 1 modeling: What is it? Why do it? In R. Lesh, P. Galbraith, C. R. Haines, & A. Hurford (Eds.), *Modeling students' mathematical modeling competencies* (pp. 5–10). New York: Springer.

Lesh, R., & Harel, G. (2003). Problem solving, modeling, and local conceptual development. *Mathematical Thinking and Learning, 5*(2–3), 157–189.

Lesh, R. & Zawojewski, J.S. (2007). Problem solving and modeling. In F. Lester (Ed.), *Second handbook of research on mathematics teaching and learning* (pp. 763–804). Charlotte, NC: Information Age Publishing.

Lesh, R., Zawojewski, J., & Carmona, G. (2003). What mathematical abilities are needed for success beyond school in a technology-based age of information? In R. Lesh & H. M. Doerr (Eds.), *Beyond constructivism: Models and modeling perspectives on mathematics teaching, learning, and problem solving.* Mahwah, NJ: Lawrence Erlbaum Associates.

Lester, F.K., Jr. (2013). Thoughts about research on mathematical problem-solving instruction. *The Mathematics Enthusiast, 10*(1&2), 245–278.

Lester, F.K., Jr., & Charles, R.I. (Eds.). (2003). *Teaching mathematics through problem solving: Grades pre-K–6.* Reston, VA: National Council of Teachers of Mathematics.

Lester, F.K., Jr., & Kehle, P.E. (2003). From problem solving to modeling: The evolution of thinking about research on complex mathematical activity. In R. Lesh & H. Doerr, (Eds.), *Beyond constructivism: Models and modeling perspectives on mathematics problem solving, learning and teaching* (pp. 501–518), Mahwah, NJ: Lawrence Erlbaum Associates.

Levine, P.B., & Zimmerman, D.J. (1995). The benefit of additional high-school math and science classes for young men and women. *Journal of Business and Economic Statistics, 13*(2), 137–149.

Levy, F., & Murnane, R.J. (2004). *The new division of labor: How computers are creating the next job market.* Princeton, NJ: Princeton University Press.

Lim, G, & Kim, C. (2013). Who has to pay for their education? Evidence from European tertiary education. *Educational Researcher, 42*(4), 250–252.

Lobato, J. (2003). How design experiments can inform a rethinking of transfer and vice versa. *Educational Researcher, 32*(1), 17–20.

Lubienski, S. (2000). Problem solving as a means toward mathematics for all: An exploratory look through a class lens. *Journal for Research in Mathematics Education, 31*(4), 454–482.

Mamona-Downs, J., & Downs, M. (2013). Problem solving and its elements in forming proof. *The Mathematics Enthusiast, 10*(1–2), 137–162.

McKenna, A.F., & Agogino, A.M. (2004, April). Supporting mechanical reasoning with a representationally-rich learning environment. *Journal of Engineering Education,* 97–104.

Mehta, J. (2013). How paradigms create policies: The transformation of American educational policy, 1980–2001. *American Educational Research Journal, 50*(2), 285–324.

MetLife. (2010). *The MetLife survey of the American teacher: Preparing students for college and careers.* Retrieved from www.metlife.com/teachersurvey.

Miller, R. (n.d.). *Education and economic growth: From the 19th to 21st century.* Paper commissioned by Cisco Systems. Retrieved from www.cisco.com/web/strategy/docs/education/eeg_what_research_says.pdf.

Moreno Armella, L., & Santos-Trigos, M. (2013). Introduction to international perspectives on problem solving research in mathematics education. *The Mathematics Enthusiast, 10*(1–2), 3–8.

Murnane, R.J., & Levy, F. (1996). *Teaching the new basic skills: Principles for educating children to thrive in a changing economy.* New York: The Free Press.

Murnane, R.J., Willett, J.B., & Levy, F. (1995). The growing importance of cognitive skills in wage determination. *The Review of Economics and Statistics, 77*(2), 251–266.

National Center on Education and the Economy (NCEE). (2013, May). *What does it really mean to be college and work ready? The mathematics required of first year community college students.* Retrieved from www.ncee.org.

National Council of Teachers of Mathematics. (1980). *An agenda for action.* Reston, VA: Author.

Nelson, W., Fagerlin, A., & Peters, E. (2008). Clinical implications of numeracy: Theory and practice. *The Society of Behavioral Medicine, 35,* 261–274. Retrieved from http://link.springer.com/article/10.1007%2Fs12160-008-9037-8.

Newell, H.A., & Simon, A.H. (1972). Human problem solving. Englewood Cliffs, NJ: Prentice Hall.

Nunes, T., Schliemann, A. D., & Carraher, D.W. (1993). *Street mathematics and school mathematics.* Cambridge: Cambridge University Press.

OECD. (2010). *The high cost of low educational performance: The long-run economic impact of improving PISA outcomes.* Paris: OECD Publishing. Retrieved from www.oecd-ilibrary.org/education/the-high-cost-of-low-educational-performance_9789264077485-en.

OECD (2014). *PISA 2012 results: What students know and can do: Vol. 1. Student performance in mathematics, reading and science—Volume 1*. Paris: OECD Publishing. Retrieved from www.oecd.org/pisa/keyfindings/pisa-2012-results-volume-I.pdf.

Packer, A. (1997). Mathematical competencies that employers expect. In L.A. Steen (Ed.), *Why numbers count: Quantitative literacy for tomorrow's America* (pp. 137–154). New York: College Entrance Examination Board.

Partnership for 21st Century Skills. (2006). *Are they really ready to work? Employers' perspectives on the basic knowledge and applied skills of new entrants to the 21st century U.S. workforce*. Retrieved from www.p21.org.

Partnership for 21st Century Skills. (2008). *21st century skills, education and competitiveness: A resources and policy guide*. Retrieved from www.p21.org.

Partnership for 21st Century Skills. (2009). *P21 framework definitions*. Retrieved from www.p21.org.

Pellegrino, J.W., & Hilton, M.L. (Eds.) (2012). *Education for life and work: Developing transferable knowledge and skills in the 21st century*. Washington, DC: National Academies Press. Retrieved from www.nap.edu/catalog/13398/education-for-life-and-work-developing-transferable-knowledge-and-skills.

Peters, E., Hibbard, J., Slovic, P., & Dieckmann, N. (2007). Numeracy skill and the communication, comprehension, and use of risk-benefit information. *Health Affairs, 26*(3), 741–748.

Peters, E., & Levin, I.P. (2008). Dissecting the risky-choice framing effect: Numeracy as an individual-difference factor in weighting risky and riskless options. *Judgment and Decision Making, 3*(6), 435–448.

Polya, G. (1945). *How to solve it*. Princeton, NJ: Princeton University Press.

Reyna, V. F., Nelson, W. L., Han, P. K., and Dieckmann, N. F. (2009). How numeracy influences risk comprehension and medical decision making. *Psychological Bulletin, 135*(6), 943–973.

Rigelman, N.R. (2013). Become a mathematical problem solver. *Mathematics Teaching in the Middle School, 18*(7), 416–423.

Salzman, H., Kuehn, D., & Lowell, L. (2013, April 24). Guestworkers in the high-skill U.S. labor market: An analysis of supply, employment, and wage trends. *EPI Briefing Paper #359*, Economy Policy Institute. Retrieved from www.epi.org/files/2013/bp359-guestworkers-high-skill-labor-market-analysis.pdf.

Schneider, W., & Artelt, C. (2010). Metacognition and mathematics education. *ZDM: The International Journal on Mathematics Education, 42*, 149–161.

Schoen, H.L., & Charles, R.I. (2003). *Teaching mathematics through problem solving: Grades 6–12*. Reston, VA: National Council of Teachers of Mathematics.

Schoenfeld, A.H. (1985). *Mathematical problem solving*. Orlando, FL: Academic Press.

Schoenfeld, A.H. (2008). Problem solving in the United States, 1970–2008: Research and theory, practice and politics. In G. Törner, A.H. Schoenfeld, & K. Reiss (Eds.), Problem solving around the world—Summing up the state of the art. *ZDM: The International Journal on Mathematics Education*, special issue (1).

Schoenfeld, A.H. (2013). Reflections on problem solving theory and practice. *The Mathematics Enthusiast, 10*(1&2), 9–34.

Schultz, T.W. (1975). The value of the ability to deal with disequilibria. *American Economic Review, 13*(3), 827–846.

Silver, E. (Ed.). (1985). *Teaching and learning mathematical problem solving: Multiple research perspectives*. Hillsdale, NJ: Lawrence Erlbaum Associates.

Silver, E.A., Mesa, V., Morris, K.A., Star, J.R., & Benken, B.M. (2009). Teaching mathematics for understanding: An analysis of lessons submitted by teachers seeking NBPTS certification. *U.S. Educational Research Journal, 46*(2), 501–531.

Singer, F., Ellerton., N., & Cai, J. (Eds.). (2015). *Mathematical problem posing: From research to effective practice*. Dordrecht: Springer.

Stanic, G.M.A., & Kilpatrick, J. (1989). Historical perspectives on problem solving in the mathematics curriculum. In R. I. Charles & E.A. Silver (Eds.), *The teaching and assessing of mathematical problem solving* (Vol. 3, pp. 1–22). Reston, VA: National Council of Teachers of Mathematics.

Stein, M. K., Grover, B. W., & Henningsen, M. (1996). Building student capacity for mathematical thinking and reasoning: An analysis of mathematical tasks used in reform classrooms. *American Education Research Journal, 33*, 455–488.

Stillman, G., & Galbraith, P. (2011). Evolution of applications and modelling in a senior secondary curriculum. In Kaiser, G., Blum, W., Borromeo Ferri, R., & Stillman, G. (Eds.), *Trends in teaching and learning of mathematical modelling: ICTMA14* (pp. 689–699). New York: Springer.

Suh, J.M., Seshaiyer, P., Moore, K., Green, M., Jewell, H., & Rice, I. (2013). Being an environmentally friendly package engineer. *Teaching Children Mathematics, 20*(4), 261–263.

Swanson, R.E. (2013). Overcoming the run response. *Mathematics Teaching in the Middle school, 19*(2), 94–99.

Tienken, C. H. (2008). Rankings of international achievement test performance and economic strength: Correlation or conjecture? *International Journal of Education Policy & Leadership, 3*(4).

Toerner, G., Schoenfeld, A. H., & Reiss, K. (Eds.). (2008). *Problem Solving Around the World—Summing up the State of the Art. ZDM: The International Journal on Mathematics Education,* 39(5–6), plus special issue (1).

Tucker, M. (2013, June 6). A framework for thinking and learning. *Education Week.* Retrieved from http://blogs.edweek.org/edweek/top_performers/2013/06/a_framework_for_thinking_and_learning.html.

Vedder, R., Denhart, C., & Robe, J. (2013). *Why are recent college graduates underemployed? University enrollments and labor-market realities.* Center for College Affordability and Productivity. Retrieved from http://centerforcollegeaffordability.org/uploads/Underemployed%20Report%202.pdf.

Welch, F. (1970). Education in production. *Journal of Political Economy, 78*(1), 35–59.

Wolf, A. (2009, July-August). Misunderstanding education: Why increasing enrollments can't and won't fix the economy. *Change.* Retrieved from www.changemag.org/July-August 2009/full-mis understanding.html.

Zaback, K., Carlson, A., & Crellin, M. (2012). *The economic benefit of postsecondary degrees: A state and national-level analysis.* Report from the State Higher Education Executive Officers. Retrieved from www.sheeo.org/sites/default/files/publications/Econ%20Benefit%20of%20Degrees%20Report%20 with%20Appendices.pdf.

Zawojewski, J. (2010). Problem solving versus modeling. In R. A. Lesh, P. L. Galbraith, C. R. Haines, & A. Hurford (Eds.). *Modeling students' mathematical modeling competencies* (pp. 237–244). Dordrecht: Springer.

13 Critical Issues in Culture and Mathematics Learning

Peter Appelbaum

Arcadia University, Philadelphia, United States

Charoula Stathopoulou

University of Thessally, Volos, Greece

It has become routine to tentatively suggest that people should no longer be willing to think of mathematics and mathematics education as far removed from culture, politics, and controversy. There is a long tradition of such scholarship (Zaslavsky, 1973a, 1973b; Pinxten, van Dooren, & Harvey, 1983; D'Ambrosio, 1985; Mellin-Olsen, 1987; Pinxten, van Dooren, & Soberon, 1987; Bishop, 1988a, 1988b; Ascher, 1991; Gerdes, 1992, 1994, 1996; Lerman, 1994; Skovsmose, 1994, 2004, 2011; Appelbaum, 1995; Baker, Clay, & Fox, 1996; Barton, 1996a; Powell & Frankenstein, 1997; Dowling, 1998; Eglash, 1999; Boaler, 2000; Martin, 2000; Adler, 2001; de Abreu, Bishop, & Presmeg, 2002; Gutstein, 2003; Kumashiro, 2009; Presmeg, 2007). Increasing attention to the effects of globalization, international economic and cultural proliferation, and a surge of migration and immigration leading to ever-diverse communities, has buttressed interest in cultural contexts of education in general, and mathematics education in multicultural communities in particular. Lerman (2000) dubbed this the "social turn" at the turn of the century. Yet, after at least 40 years of scholarship, as indicated by our brief representative sample of references, research and practice in mathematics education rarely moves beyond a surface suggestion that culture might be relevant to explore the nuances and complexities of mathematics and mathematics education as culturally constructed, embedded in cultural contexts, or as a component of socio-political institutions of power and authority.

A brief flirtation with multicultural methods in the 1980s and 1990s led to many suggestions for classroom activities that connect mathematics to: games and practices from non-Western cultures (see, e.g., Zaslavsky, 1993; 1996, & 1998; Whitin & Wilde, 1995, Lipka, Sharp, Adams, & Sharp, 2007); nonstandard calculation procedures and algorithms (Stathopoulou & Kalabasis, 2002; Moreira, 2003; Knijnik, Wanderer, & Oliveira, 2005; Stathopoulou, 2005; Moreira & Pires, 2012; Orey & Rosa, 2008); multiple representations of mathematical concepts (Favilli, 2007; Gerdes, 1988, Barton, 1995; Palhares, 2012), and to a cultural pride linked to mathematics (Matthews, 1989; Appelbaum, 1995; Moses & Cobb, 2001; Gutstein, 2003). There has been a recent effort in this century to develop school mathematics activities and projects that take advantage of the funds of knowledge that students bring to school from home and community cultures (see, e.g., Gerdes, 1988; Civil & Kahn, 2001; Stathopoulou, 2006; Klein & Showalter, 2012). However, there remains a limited focus on using social practices from "other," nonmainstream cultures to lure learners into an understanding of traditional mathematics content (Bazin & Tamez, 2002). Few culturally sensitive curricular practices that work with the culturally specific knowledge that learners bring to school support these learners taking what is enhanced or refined in school back into home cultures. Even the more politically sensitive approaches to mathematics teaching and learning (Civil, 2002; Frankenstein, 1987; Gutstein & Peterson, 2005) assume the mathematics to be politically neutral, however politicized its applications. And few research projects, curriculum development efforts, or cross-cultural collaborations in mathematics education take seriously the notion that potentially confusing and complex multiplicities of cultures and identities are manifest in what might be taken on first glance to be a single, monolithic "culture" in contemporary, postcolonial, creolized "inter-cultural" contexts (Appelbaum, 1995, 2008; Valero & Stentof, 2010; Swanson & Appelbaum, 2013; Chronaki, 2005).

As recently as 2007, Norma Presmeg wrote that mathematics education had "experienced a major revolution in perceptions," so that "mathematics, long considered value- and culture-free, is indeed a cultural product, and hence that the role of culture—with all its complexities and contestations—is an important aspect of mathematics education" (Presmeg, 2007, p. 435). As late as the revised edition of *Against Common Sense*, Kevin Kumashiro could write, "More than any discipline, math is considered by many people to be the least influenced by social factors, and, therefore, to be the most bias-free of all subjects being taught and learned in school. People have told me that race might matter when treating students of color differently in a math classroom, but race has little, if anything, to do with adding and subtracting numbers" (Kumashiro, 2009, p. 111). How has it come about that he needs to write this as late in history as 2009? Virtually the same comments can be found in most of the references already cited in this paragraph, from at least as long ago as the 1970s.

It is time to take stock of mathematics education and culture, in order to understand the range of working definitions that are commonly muddled and confused in professional and public discourse. It is perhaps time also to consider alternatives to "culture" as a central concept in mathematics education. Approaches to mathematics education and culture take different forms depending on how one conceives of mathematics, (mathematics) education, and culture. One can imagine a three-dimensional set of axes with categories along each of these dimensions, so that the combinations of presumptions about each of these terms and the practices they represent come together in any given research project or reflection on mathematics education to create a common-sense "reality" that is made "real" by this work. If we take a look at only two of these at a time (given the limitations of a text-based chapter, this is the easiest way to represent such interactions, but also, it is useful to isolate the interactions taken two dimensions at a time to introduce this idea of complex interactions), we can visualize subsets of the larger taxonomy. (See Table 13.1)

We share Table 13.1 not to establish an exhaustive taxonomy, but to communicate the variety of assumptions that a typical research project, curriculum design, or development effort carries with it as common sense. In order to study and understand issues of culture and mathematics learning/teaching, one needs to consider various lenses from mathematics education, educational anthropology, sociology, sociolinguistics, and critical theory, and so on. In general, the questions in this chapter assume that knowledge is related to experience in inhabited social and cultural worlds, and that knowledge passes through social and cultural systems and institutions through norms, values, conventions, and practices. At the same time, those socializing norms, values, conventions, and practices pass through structures of reality and ideology associated with knowledge. Knowledge and culture cannot be extricated from each other, and neither one should be conceived as a context for the other.

Approaches to mathematics education and culture establish forms of reality and common sense through the application of distinctions, often without any clear attention to these distinctions. In this way, these approaches create implicit—sometimes explicit—assumptions about dichotomies such as in-school and out-of-school learning, formal and informal education, teaching and learning, mathematics and culture, student or teacher identity and mathematics, and so on. For example, if we carry out a project or teach a school mathematics lesson trying to make it more meaningful and relevant to some students in the classroom by noting that they are members of a nonmainstream subculture, we are reducing the uniqueness of each individual to a set of stereotypical assumptions from a generic caricature of this subculture. Each individual may or may not fit this set of assumptions. Indeed, most of the learners in this

Table 13.1 Complex interactions of mathematics, (mathematics) education, and culture.

Culture → Mathematics ↓	Culture is not taken as relevant to mathematics.	Culture is a context in which mathematics occurs.	Culture is a web of webs of meaning and interpretation.	Culture cannot be separated from social instantiations of power and inequity.	Culture is also a tool and form of economic power and authority.
Mathematics is a set of methods for formulating and solving problems	Mathematics is a collection of tools and knowledge essential for everyday life and for economic success in a global marketplace.	Mathematics is a collection of tools and knowledge that are developed in a particular culture dependent on needs specific to that culture.	Mathematics is a collection of practices through which people understand their reality by defining and solving problems.	Mathematics is a collection of tools and knowledge that not only depends on social instantiations but also depends on power relationships.	School mathematics is a pipeline to higher education and careers associated with power and authority.
Mathematics is a universal, global language.	Mathematics is a bridge across nations and subcultures, helping with communication and progress.	Mathematical concepts are common across all cultures.	Mathematics helps people communicate across cultures by sharing a common language.	Mathematics can be used to enact increasingly more or less equitable social systems.	Advanced knowledge of mathematics enables some to wield power over others.
Mathematics constitutes a "culture" in that is a collection of social practices.	People can "learn" mathematics if educators help them make transitions among everyday life cultures and the cultures of school mathematics.	School mathematics is a collection of enculturation practices.	School mathematics is an entry into worlds of aesthetics, logic, and wonder, and a key to the great ideas of humanity.	Mathematics is associated with intelligence, rationality, and privilege.	Those with mathematical skills are valuable to those in power.
Mathematics as social practices differs across and within social and cultural contexts.	Mathematics educators will be more successful if they can make connections between home cultures and the culture of school mathematics.	In different cultures, we find different mathematical needs, and different ways of developing mathematical knowledge.	There are many unique ways of mathematizing one's world.	Valued forms of mathematical skills and concepts are those forms of mathematics associated with dominant cultural groups.	Mathematics curricula that celebrate indigenous and folk traditions of mathematics are explicit political challenges to dominant groups.

Western Mathematics as a collection of social practices is both part of, and enables, dominant cultural interactions among people, perpetuating forms of colonialism and imperialism, and erasing variations from awareness.	School mathematics is implicated in forms of social inequity. For example, mathematics might be a gatekeeper or pipeline to occupations that bring agency and status.	Learners might experience conflicts between home cultures and school cultures of mathematics that would prevent them from excelling at mathematics in school.	School mathematics may or may not resonate with the values and desires of learners whose home cultures have different values and desires.	School mathematics is a tool of unequal outcomes and experiences that reproduce social inequalities in society.	Mathematical models are used to determine policies and programs for international development.
Mathematics education can be a specific genre of critical pedagogy, helping people to name and change their world as their refine and extend mathematical skills and concepts.	Mathematics can be useful as a tool for solving social problems and for individual empowerment.	Mathematics can be used to recognize events of inequality in society, since it is a marker of differences across cultures: while there are commonalities of mathematical activity across cultures, specific practices distinguish one culture from another.	Mathematics is a collection of ways of making meaning and interpreting experience. Changing ones mathematics changes one's understanding of reality; changing one's common-sense assumptions changes one's mathematical practices.	Mathematics education as a genre of critical pedagogy is a tool for people's awareness about culture, connections with social instantiations, and the reproduction of social inequalities.	Mathematics education as a genre of critical pedagogy promotes a culture of deliberation grounded in challenging oppression, exploitation, and exclusion.

situation are members of multiple subcultures at the same time, and are in any given moment having experiences that resonate with cultural habits and dispositions from more than one of these subcultures. We want to use categories based on cultural distinctions to analyze situations, because this seems like the only reasonable, common-sense way for us to make sense of the setting and the people in it. Yet, as soon as we use these distinctions, we are already aware of the variations within any given group that seem more extreme than differences between groups. And as soon as we try to take into account the variations within any given group, we are already aware of the ways in which these variations are inadequate to capture the variations within any one individual within that group. That is, borders between categories are permeable, so that (to keep this simple) say, a Catholic, Latina girl in a Chicago classroom may or may not be having an experience consistent with what her teacher might expect of a learner recently relocated from New Jersey with her Cuban-American, Jewish father, working in a small group with her Chicano best friend and a recent immigrant from Albania. In other words, each learner is determined to some extent by the cultural contexts that are part of their life; yet, as individuals, learners have a repertoire of behaviors and ways of making meaning out of experience that are specific to them.

It is increasingly challenging to exploit all resources available in the interests of mathematics learners, given the myriad of types of resources and locations of these resources; at the same time, conflicts exist in most discussions of education broadly conceived about the role of mathematics in the lives of children and adults—both in the present and in their futures, in terms of both individual and societal needs. These conflicts and associated confusions regarding the role(s) of mathematics are made more complex by the expectations for mathematics and mathematics learning, more or less culturally determined, that meet each other in educational encounters. This chapter addresses these issues through the variety of cultural approaches to mathematics education pedagogy and research that have become significant in the field, including mathematics as a culture; funds of knowledge pedagogies; ethnomathematical critiques and approaches to teaching and learning; popular culture studies; public pedagogies; and critical mathematics education. These are not separate, analytic categories, but mutually informing strands of interwoven discourse. Given space restrictions endemic to a research handbook, and the important interrelations of those newly significant approaches in the field of mathematics education, we do not address here every conceivable aspect of culture, nor do we focus on characteristics or components of culture such as language and organizational climate, which deserve attention elsewhere. We also limit our discussion to mathematics learning, saving culture and mathematics teaching for another comprehensive synthesis.

We have chosen to use "culture" to refer to aspects of cultural contexts, and more specifically, aspects of culture related to learning and knowledge, rather than to speak of culture in general. We do this to avoid the discontinuity that appears at school through dichotomies of formal and informal learning, distinguished by the role of a designer or evaluator of learning experiences not present in the learning context that is necessary for "formal" learning to take place. Culture, more broadly, is both "an historically transmitted pattern of meanings embodied in symbols, a system of inherited conceptions expressed in symbolic forms by means of which men communicate, perpetuate, and develop their knowledge about and their attitudes toward life" (Geertz, 1973a, p. 89), and those "webs of significance" people themselves spin (Geertz, 1973b, p. 5).

CULTURE OF MATHEMATICS

One notion is that mathematical thinking is a particular culture of its own, independent of social categories such as race, class, gender, ethnicity, religion, sexual orientation, and so on. Alan Bishop's (1988a; 1988b) early work in this area offers a broad, universal set of intellectual practices that could be taken as "mathematical," independent of the particular social context:

counting, measuring, locating, designing, playing, and explaining. The apparent universality of mathematics results, according to Bishop, from the universality of the adaptive, human goals that define these six types of activities, rather than the a priori nature of mathematical principals. Bishop assumed the cultural universality of the activities, but emphasized the diversity found in symbolic mathematical technologies produced by the activities within varying cultural contexts. There are at least four implications of this initial foray into mathematics and culture:

(1) If we start from the premise that there are particular and unique ways of being mathematical, then school mathematics experiences are either experiences of enculturation (as in the title of Bishop's book), in which younger members of the culture are enabled to become more sophisticated, grown-up, members of that culture over time; or acculturation, in which there are power relations between those who are more or less sophisticated and experienced, and in which those whose identity is more closely affiliated with the dominant, school mathematical culture have advantages in these power relations; or both. In this sense, the term *learning* in the title of our chapter might be suitably replaced by *enculturation, acculturation*, or both.

(2) Mathematics might involve its own "register" and/or "language" that must be learned and practiced in order for people to become better able to function in a mathematical culture.

(3) Mathematics might be a family of practices that embrace and maintain particular values (Bishop 1988a,b, 2007). For example, Bishop's empirical comparison of mathematics with science distinguished the epistemological commitment to rationalism and objectivism, the pursuit of control and progress, and the strong adherence to openness and mystery that characterizes mathematics as a field of practices with the subtly contrasting commitments of science to a rationalism and objectivism more distinguished by analogical thinking and the identification of problems, control associated with paradigms and circumstances rather than security, progress focused more on plausible alternatives, openness more aligned with human construction than with verification. Mystery for mathematics is, according to Bishop, more associated with abstraction, wonder, dehumanized knowledge, and intuition, while for science mystery is characterized by guesses, daydreams, curiosity, and fascination (Bishop, 2007, pp. 127–28). Values also enter into discussion of mathematics education when one considers cultural contexts. For example, Seah (2004) describes the socialization experiences of immigrant teachers in Australia in terms of interactions between cultural values. Home cultures were regarded as shaping personal values, and consequently, worldviews pertaining to education, mathematics, and mathematics teaching and learning; at the same time, students of school mathematics were found to acquire an internally consistent set of mathematical values that affirms Bishops' categories, seemingly immune to cultural differences. Most importantly, according to Seah (2004), a shift from examining teachers' negotiation of perceived value differences to exploring the nature of those differences pointed to the co-construction of social values independent of a teacher's agency and more associated with a broader context of socialization. Values, in this sense, are inculcated through experience (Andersson & Seah, 2013). It is interesting, however, as noted by Grootenboer, Lomas and Ingram (2008), that research in this area has not yet adequately addressed this experience through direct, classroom-based studies of that experience, but rather through self-reporting by mostly secondary students in surveys and interviews.

(4) It becomes confusing to tease out how mathematics in this broadly universal conception is and is not imbricated in a colonialist enterprise. The expectation of a universality at some level carries with it some elements of the Western, ideological framework of mathematics as neutral and distant from culture, so that an analysis on this macro level creates a continuity with that perspective, rendering local variations across cultures and subcultures less significant or seemingly irrelevant. Every mathematical knowledge not

historically and culturally embedded in Western mathematics is measured and defined by Western mathematics. Indeed, it has become central to the study of mathematics and mathematics education to view mathematics as a cultural construct, and to recognize the potential for research based on such a view to contribute to the development of both mathematics and mathematics education (Barton, 1996b, p. 9; Appelbaum, 1995; Davis & Hersh, 1986). (Even this notion of mathematics and mathematics education as a cultural construct carries with it the colonialist legacy of anthropological study, which itself is a "Western" epistemological project that needs self-interrogation. This might explain, for example, the dominance of Western researchers in the citations included in this chapter; cultural perspectives are historically located in European and Western academic traditions, reflected in the literature that has grown out of these traditions.)

When speaking of early years of schooling, enculturation is not really apprenticeship within the child's own culture since a school curriculum has already decided before the arrival of the child what and how he or she will learn. In this sense, no school experiences are ever enculturation. We inherit the term *enculturation* from the title of Alan Bishop's (1988b) book; yet he himself later used the more appropriate concept *acculturation*, given that every learner grapples with cultural conflicts (Bishop, 2002). A psychological approach that contrasts with the socio-cultural orientation discussed here would make an analogous distinction: enculturation can be understood as acquiring the characteristics of a subculture, in this case, mathematics, through being enmeshed within that culture; while acculturation would refer to "fitting in" to a cultural milieu by emulating the characteristics of those who are already members of that milieu (Kirshner, 2004). Here milieu refers to broader social interactions beyond the focus on "register." The cultural perspective emphasizes how intercultural experiences are always bound up in unequal power relations that serve important roles in the experiences of those involved. We might say that school mathematics serves through acculturation important functions in social and cultural reproduction, contributing to the development of "reasonable" people who reason in particular ways, and who are also able to be governed by systems of power and established authorities (Cline-Cohen, 1982; Walkerdine, 1987; Appelbaum, 1995). At the same time, an awareness of the special vocabulary of school mathematics, and the idiosyncratic ways of working as a student of mathematics that help learners succeed in such a context, offers useful ideas for supporting learners of mathematics who are not yet demonstrating mastery of the material. This cultural approach distinguishes between the subject knowledge of a course in mathematics and the norms and expectations that teachers of mathematics might have for learners in the course.

Sometimes described as "academic literacy," the norms and expectations for how one works and demonstrates learning in a school context have been shown to be teachable and assimilable when made explicit to the students, and when practiced as explicit ways of working (Appelbaum, 2008; Polya, 1945; Mason, Burton, & Stacey, 1985; Brown & Walter, 2005; Cotton, 2010). To use Geertz's image of *webs of signification*, the culture of a mathematics classroom is the tangled interweaving of webs of meaning and interpretation brought to the classroom by teachers, learners, broader characteristics of the social milieu of the school and society, etc. The academic literacy expectations structure the potential interactions that occur in educational encounters, constraining and enabling activity, interpretations, expectations, fears and desires.

Nasir, Hand, and Taylor (2008) distinguish between "cultural" knowledge and "domain" knowledge: "that is, knowledge derived from settings outside of school, typically in students' homes and communities, . . . and . . . knowledge valued in the practices prescribed by mathematicians and math educators" (p. 187). They note the importance of discerning how the features of different social contexts mediate what is learned in interaction with the proclivities and dispositions of the learners. When mathematics and culture are constructed in this way, it becomes possible to ask what might be done to help learners who are not demonstrating knowledge to do so more successfully, as in closing a racial or ethnic achievement gap, or in minimizing gaps between current levels of performance and predetermined, "levels of excellence." It becomes possible, as well, to describe ways that learners apparently demonstrate mathematical skills in everyday contexts that they do not demonstrate in school contexts. Yet, this seeming "progress" in understanding things also constructs what is possible to say about mathematics education and culture: distinguishing between cultural and domain "knowledge" presumes knowledge as something that can be taken or transferred out of one social context and put into another. While it appears to be a major shift in thinking about the nature and role of culture in learning, it merely reproduces common-sense distinctions between knowledge and culture that do not address the ways that knowledge and culture are mutually determined, and inseparable. When we separate mathematics as a domain of knowledge from mathematics education as a cultural system, we run the risk of reifying mathematics as a universal body of knowledge, even if we want to de-center this universal domain, placing it alongside everyday, out-of-school, informal, and home mathematical practices. What is more relevant about different contexts of mathematics learning is how communication of mathematical ideas and practices create a negotiation of what constitutes "learning," "knowing," "mathematics," and so on.

It may seem powerful to distinguish between mathematics in and out of school, because it allows us to indicate the importance of accounting for alignment and power in analyzing language in a mathematics classroom (Nasir et al., 2008; Lerman, 2001). In this way, research can delineate features of mathematics classrooms that clash or resonate with home and neighborhood cultures, and thus establish initially unobservable, now visible, systematic forms of power that lead to inequity. Some features of pedagogical practices support and constrain different forms of knowing and being for students in a general sense; at the same time, we might unravel how different forms of knowing and being mathematical may or may not be available or possible for specific individuals or particular groups of students (Presmeg, 2002; Atweh, Graven, & Secada, 2011). Nevertheless, it is important to note that such assumptions about mathematics education and culture prevent mathematics education researchers and educators from undertaking their work independent of the history of their field. For example, the history of school mathematics as a form of cultural practice replicates the idea that one can separate some knowledge from others, and then wonder who has the right or authority to decide what knowledge is of most worth; this could go unnoticed unless one sees the interconnections between culture and education. Some scholars have suggested that the dichotomy between "everyday" and "school" mathematics is false (Mellin-Olsen, 1987; Appelbaum, 1995; Moschkovich, 2007). Others (e.g., Gutiérrez, 2002a; 2002b; Gutstein, 2003; 2006) maintain that knowledge of mathematics must include as part of knowing mathematics an ability to critique the role of mathematics in society and to use mathematics as a tool for social justice. Already in the phrasing of such utopian goals we miss the mark of rethinking mathematics and mathematics education itself.

FUNDS OF KNOWLEDGE AND CRITICAL MATHEMATICS EDUCATION

Culture sometimes enters into discussions of mathematics education policy and practice as a response to increased diversity among the teachers and learners of the mathematics. For example, increased immigration in Europe and elsewhere has created a relatively new "problem" of integrating immigrants into mainstream society while also helping new members of the community to learn mathematics. In North and South America, immigration combined with the legacy of slavery and long-standing border crossings of citizens has led to multiply complex, multilingual and multiethnic communities. Members of nondominant groups are often constructed as culturally different, despite generations of cohabitation. The dominant society appears innocent when social and economic differences are interpreted as cultural. It is difficult to disconnect cultural differences from political choices. For example, in recent years, Roma children in Greece were prevented by parents of non-Roma students from attending local schools. It is not a cultural choice not to be at school in this situation, but the result of long-standing efforts on the part of members of dominant groups in society to prevent Roma children access to the public schools[1].

Marta Civil (2008) quotes Peter Gates (2006, p. 391):

> In many parts of the world, teachers—mathematics teachers—are facing the challenges of teaching in multiethnic and multilingual classrooms containing, immigrant, indigenous, migrant, and refugee children, and if research is to be useful it has to address and help us understand such challenges.

Given a history of schooling that sees immigration and other forms of diversity as creating new problems for schools, a particularly political act on the part of educators is to turn the tables on the ordering of culture and knowledge, breaking down the appearance of these as categories. Instead of looking for successful ways to support learning by culturally diverse students, the question becomes how to take advantage of the knowledge that learners bring with them to school from their home and community environments (Civil, 1996; 2008; Lipka & Mohatt, 1998; Gorgorió & Planas, 2001; Lipka, 2005; D'Ambrosio, 2006; Klein & Showalter, 2012). Civil (1996) asked,

> Can we develop learning experiences that tap on students' areas of expertise and at the same time help them advance in their learning of mathematics? And, What are the implications of critical pedagogy for the mathematics education of "minority" and poor students?
> (Civil, 1996, quoted in Civil, 2008, p. 3)

Her responses have been grounded, as have the responses of other mathematics educators, in theories of funds of knowledge (González, Moll, & Amanti, 2005), which refer to the knowledge and experiences that exist in any household, and that could be refined, extended, and built upon in schools and other educational settings. On one level, advocates of funds of knowledge research and pedagogical practices simply emphasize the need for teachers to better understand their students and their families. On another level, this work requires that teachers, curriculum developers, and researchers engage in collaborative action research in multicultural contexts if they are to adequately know about and eventually work with the funds of knowledge that learners bring to educational encounters (Dominguez, 2012; Radosavljevic, 2012; Willey, Lopez Leiva, & Vomvoridi-Ivanovic, 2012; Gerardo, Gutiérrez & Irving, 2012; Diéz-Palomar, 2012). This perspective has led to serious efforts to include families and community members in school learning activities, to systematic use of experiences with families and in out-side-of-school social contexts as field work for preservice teachers, and to a rise in after-school and weekend curricula that focus on community involvement.

For some educators, a lack of facility with indigenous and folk traditions is further understood to undermine potentially successful mathematics education experiences (D'Ambrosio, 2006; Fasheh, 2012). Others emphasize the need not only to build on funds of knowledge brought into school from outside experience, but to also take school mathematical experiences back out into everyday life in ways that support and nurture culturally specific values and goals (Mukhopadhyay & Roth, 2012; Klein & Showalter, 2012). On yet a more important level, funds of knowledge research and practice undermine a common-sense separation between home and school, recognizing that learning occurs not just in both, but that learning experiences in one or another of these places—along with learning on the street, while playing video games at a shopping mall, listening to music, and so on—is never only in that one place, but pulls together experiences across any and all such places, with resonances, dissonances, and combined reverberations.

Assumptions about the location and nature of mathematics learning are similarly challenged by *critical mathematics education*, another subfield concerned with the social and political aspects of mathematics learning. Critical mathematics education focuses on providing access to mathematical ideas for all, independent of race, gender, class, and other categories of social distinction. It addresses the use and function of mathematics-in-practice, whether as an advanced, technological application, or as everyday experience. Within classrooms, critical mathematics education supports democratic forms of pedagogy, in which ideas are presented and negotiated together toward the cultivation of democratic citizenship. Critical mathematics education demands a critical perspective on both mathematics and the teaching/learning of mathematics. In doing so, it takes one step further in questioning our assumptions about what mathematics education could mean and what democratic participation should mean.

Ole Skovsmose (1994) describes a classroom in which critical mathematics education is taking place as one in which the students (and teachers) are attributed a "critical competence." Decisive and prescribing roles are abandoned in favor of all participants having control of the educational process. Instead of merely forming a classroom community for discussion, Skovsmose (1994) suggests that the students and teachers together must establish a "critical distance." What he means is that seemingly objective and value-free principles for the structure of the curriculum are put into a new perspective, and that such principles are revealed for the teachers and learners as value-loaded, necessitating critical consideration of contents and other subject-matter aspects as part of the educational process itself.

Keitel, Klotzman, and Skovsmose (1993) describe mathematics as a technology with the potential to work for democratic goals, and make distinctions between different types of knowledge based on the object of the knowledge. The first level of mathematical work, they write, presumes a true-false ideology and corresponds to much of what we witness in current school curricula. The second level directs students and teachers to ask about right method: Are there other algorithms? Which are valued for our need? The third level emphasizes the appropriateness and reliability of the mathematics for its context. This level raises the particularly technological aspect of mathematics by investigating specifically the relationship between means and ends. The fourth level requires participants to interrogate the appropriateness of formalizing the problem for solution: a mathematical/technological approach is not always wise and participants would consider this issue as a form of reflective mathematics. At the fifth level, a critical mathematics education studies the implications of pursuing special formal means; it asks how particular algorithms affect our perceptions of (a part of) reality, and how we conceive mathematical tools when we use them universally. Thus the role of mathematics in society becomes a component of reflective mathematical knowledge. Finally, the sixth level examines reflective thinking itself as an evaluative process, comparing Levels 1 and 2 as essential mathematical tools, Levels 3 and 4 as the relationship between means and ends, and Level 5 as the global impact of using formal techniques. On Level 6, reflective evaluation as a process is noted as a tool itself and as such becomes an object of reflection. When teachers and students plan their classroom experiences by making sure that all of these levels are represented in the group's activities, it is more likely that students and teachers can be attributed the critical competence envisioned as the more general goal of mathematics education, building upon and refining the funds of knowledge that teachers and students bring to the experiences.

One important direction for critical mathematics education is in the examination of mathematics as a culture to be crafted in educational experiences, and in particular, to critically consider the authority to phrase the questions for discussion. Who sets the agenda in a critical thinking classroom? Stephen Brown and Marion Walter (2005) laid out a variety of powerful ways to rethink mathematics investigations through *The Art of Problem Posing*, and in doing so present a number of ideas for enabling students both to "talk back" to mathematics and to use their problem solving and problem posing experiences to learn about themselves as problem solvers and posers. In the process, they help frame yet another dilemma for future research in mathematics education: Is it always more democratic if students pose the problem? The kinds of questions that are possible, and the ways that we expect to phrase them, are to be examined by a critical thinker. Susan Gerofsky (2001, 2010) noted that the questions themselves reveal more about our fantasies and desires than about the mathematics involved.

Finally, it becomes crucial to examine the discourses of mathematics and mathematics education in and out of school and popular culture (Appelbaum, 1995). Critical mathematics education asks how and why the split between popular culture and school mathematics is evident in mathematical discourse, and why such a strange dichotomy must be resolved between mathematics as a "commodity" and as a "cultural resource." Mathematics is a commodity in our consumer culture because it has been turned into "stuff" that people collect (knowledge) in order to spend later (on the job market, to get into university, etc.). But it is also a cultural resource in that it is a world of metaphors and ways of making meaning through which people can interpret their world and describe it in new ways. Critical mathematics educators recognize the role of mathematics as a commodity in our society, but they search for ways to effectively emphasize the meaning-making aspects of mathematics as part of the variety of cultures. In doing so, they make it possible for mathematics to be a resource for political action. In formulating a democratic, critical mathematics education, it is also essential that teachers grapple with the serious multicultural indictments of mathematics as a tool of postcolonial and imperial authority. What we once accepted as pure, wholesome truth is now understood as culturally specific and tied to particular interests. Philip Davis and Reuben Hersh (1986) and David Berlinski (2000), for instance, have described some aspects of mathematics as a tool in accomplishing a fantasy of control over human experience. They use the examples of math-military connections, math-business connections, among others (See also, Schoenfeld, 1991; Gutstein, 2012).

Mathematics can serve the good as well as the evil: the power of mathematics is at least double edged. On one hand great achievements in arts, science, and technology are mathematically based. On the other, mathematics is implicated in technologically caused catastrophes (Atweh, 2007; D'Ambrosio, 2006). Yet this does not mean that mathematics itself is some neutral tool that might be used one way or the other, nor does it mean that the way we teach mathematics leads to "good" applications or "bad": mathematics, mathematics education, and culture, as mutually determined and evolving, together create what we call *mathematics*, what we identify as *mathematics education*, and what we label *culture*, after the fact.

Skovsmose (2004) argues that the socio-political roles of mathematics, its meaning, its uses, and its application, are not essentially determined within mathematics itself. There is no intrinsic connection between mathematical knowledge and how to use it once it is situated in a cultural context. In the same way, mathematics education also has no fixed, agreed-upon method of working with mathematical knowledge. How to represent mathematics and how to handle it is always a compendium of choices, circling back upon culture in this mutually evolving fashion. Even a mainstream curriculum that is teaching traditional mathematical knowledge implies a perspective on how mathematics is handed down from one generation to another (François, 2007). Mathematics education is therefore critical in the sense that it is situated in uncertainty. This uncertainty is grounded in the nature of mathematics, a human practice determined by contingency at the moment of its construction. A second aspect—and perhaps the more important aspect—of this uncertainty is the fact that the result of that human practice, namely the mathematical knowledge, will be applied by human beings with their diverse and sometimes conflicting needs, beliefs, and interests. This is what makes mathematics uncertain and why mathematics education is critical per se. The fact that educators and researchers now acknowledge these uncertainties makes mathematics education a "critical mathematics education:" there is no fixed curriculum, nor are there predetermined content and methods; mathematics education as a profession has become the act of reflecting on the nature and the function of mathematics, time and again.

ETHNOMATHEMATICS, MULTICULTURALISM, AND DIVERSITY EDUCATION

Mathematics educators ask why students—and people, in general—do not generally see mathematics as helping them to interpret events in their lives or to gain control over human experience. They search for ways to help students appreciate the marvelous qualities of mathematics without glorifying its historic roots in militarism and other fantasies of control. Funds of knowledge approaches embrace the skills and concepts that students bring with them from everyday life into school, often culturally different from, if mathematically equivalent to, the practices that are demanded of learners. Ethnomathematics, the anthropological study of mathematical practices not necessarily rooted in Western European history, makes it clear that mathematics and mathematical reasoning are cultural constructions (Bishop, 1988b; Barton, 1996a; D'Ambrosio, 1987, 1988; Favilli, 2007; Gutstein et al., 1997.) See Barton, 1996b, for a thorough review of definitions of ethnomathematics, and Barton, 1996c, for a discussion of ethnomathematics as a research program that examines how cultural groups understand, articulate, and use the concepts and practices that we describe as mathematical, "whether or not the cultural group has a concept of mathematics" (Barton, 1996c, p. 214). This raises the challenge to embrace the global variety of cultures of mathematical activity, and to confront the politics that would be unleashed by such attention in a typical Amero-European school.

Multicultural education has taken a variety of forms in the past century, ranging from an awareness that some learners need special attention addressing cultural needs, to a more politicized sensitivity to the ways that school practices might undermine altruistic goals of educational systems, to explicitly constructing school experiences that promote and advocate social change (Appelbaum, 2002; Sleeter & Soriano, 2012; Sleeter & Grant, 2007). Multicultural *mathematics* education has taken shape in analogous ways. Early efforts used non-Western activities as examples through which learners could "see" mathematical concepts and skills in action; some educators tried to connect personally with students' home cultures by using games and activities associated with what the educators knew about the home culture. Later uses of non-Western examples made an effort to integrate culture and mathematics in more nuanced ways—for example, by studying the diversity of *mancala* versions across African cultures as both mathematical and cultural, rather than as an excuse to practice counting or grouping; in such classrooms, it became possible to ask how the different versions lead to different strategies and to different mathematical decisions.

What multicultural and ethnomathematics approaches share is an insistence on attention to cultural differences and a special concern for students who come from socially vulnerable groups. Initially, most educators find such an insistence to be an important contribution to equity and social democratic understanding. However, members of groups other than the dominant group tend within a multicultural framework to be constructed as different in a sense that is "other" to the mainstream, dominant culture. An excellent example of how this plays out in an epistemological way is the questioning of codified curricula as being "watered down" by the inclusion of non-Western problems, algorithms, and aesthetic applications of mathematics (Atweh, Forgasz, & Nebres, 2001; Olin, 2003; Orey and Rosa, 2008; Sykes, 1995). While one might see certain activities as mathematical when interpreted through a lens of "modern mathematics," some mathematicians sometimes claim that the activities are not inherently mathematical, and that they are not even mathematical when practiced in their original, social context; at other times, we find complaints that the time taken to place the mathematics into the non-Western context is not justified given the tangential connections that are attempted.

Ron Eglash (1999) proposed a continuum of mathematized activities, ranging from a non-mathematical practice that is possible to interpret mathematically if so desired, toward an explicit use of abstraction, theorization, and exploration, to a meta-abstraction of alternative theories. Yet, such a continuum perpetuates a Western comprehension of mathematical action premised on a centrality of abstraction, theory, and meta-analysis that may or may not be valid across cultures, in an ethnomathematical sense; it also further normalizes Western mathematics to which "other" cultures of mathematics would be compared, further extending the problematic nature of multicultural efforts grounded in the concept of culture itself. In contemporary societies, various cultural groups are not "other," but instead are part of the mosaic of cultures that make up the community in which the school is found and the mathematics is learned. Multiculturalism can also run the risk of promoting ethnocentrism and marginalization of immigrant groups (Govaris & Antwniadou, 2000; Radtke 1994). A rich, diverse mathematics education would position itself as alternative to multiculturalism, recognizing that intercultural relationships are (almost always) asymmetrical, and that intercultural education should aim to repair the damages caused by attention to what once might have been called "egregious cultural differences."

For these reasons, many educators have come to define their work, not in terms of multiculturalism, but instead in terms of "diversity education" (Appelbaum, 2002; Nolan, 2009; Swanson, 2010; Walshaw, 2010; Martin & Gohlson, 2012). Diversity education takes as a given the state of formal educational systems as posing for students of every conceivable subgroup differences that must be confronted. One example of this is the ways that performance is commonly evaluated in relation to formal education's measures, independent of where and how students begin, and independent of how the confrontation with differences is experienced. In the case of Roma students, who typically are very effective in complex, mental calculations, yet who are perceived as challenged by formal, school mathematics, teachers in Greek schools following an official curriculum are not interested in such skills. Meanwhile, grade 4 Latina/o youth in Philadelphia are observed composing their own investigations of the common characteristics of trapezoids, parallelograms, rhombi, and kites on the playground at recess, yet are described by their teachers as unprepared for grade-level geometry based on a district diagnostic test of shape names and area models of fractions. Learners are subjected to decisions made by authorities that address a view of the larger society without regard for the nuances of differences and the ways that power unfolds through forms of mathematics education. This is further illustrated by the emphasis on "problem solving," collaboration, and "communities of learning," which have been shown to sanctify mathematics and mathematicians as possessing authoritative knowledge over increasing realms of human phenomena, narrowing in the process the boundaries of possible action and critical thought, and extending the ways that pedagogical attention to "equity" with "no child left behind" increasingly divide, demarcate, and exclude particular children from participation in school mathematics (Popkewitz, 2004). At the same time, an emphasis on educational reform built upon "culture" independent of critical cultural studies clouds the supposedly transparent mathematics in a cacophony of confusion, where students are seduced into the ambiguity of problems while teachers are bewildered by the plethora of "different" cultures bringing a myriad of assumptions to the classroom (Zolkower, 1995). Some mathematics educators worry about the ways that culture in the mathematics classroom makes possible actions only visible in places where things are "not supposed to make sense" (Zolkower, 1995, p. 154), a departure from tradition that it seems many teachers are not ready to make.

Instead of removing the differences, or criticizing current practices as harmful to social justice, diversity educators work *with* the recognition of difference and promote direct attention to how the use of cultural difference by a language of multiculturalism might be coopted *for* social justice. Unlike Zolkower's fear of culture leading to a slippage away from a dominant construction of mathematical knowledge, diversity educators trouble notions of difference as perpetuating inequality, questioning any assignation of resistance to learning as a sign of cultural difference. Diversity educators search for those times and places where the function of something designated as "cultural difference" serves to support a new version of racism or marginalization—as, for example, in the expression, "culturally incompatible"—in order to respond together with their students (Balibar & Swenson, 2003; Govaris & Antwniadou, 2000; Skovsmose & Penteado, 2011; Mishra, 2012). Indicative of the slippery slope from cultural awareness into political oppression is the analysis of cultural difference frameworks in apartheid South Africa by Vithal and Skovsmose (1997) in their article, "The End of Innocence." Within the subfield of ethnomathematics, such concerns have been voiced in terms of restoring cultural dignity and offering the intellectual tools for the exercise of citizenship (D'Ambrosio 1999).

SOCIOPOLITICAL TURN

Rochelle Gutiérrez (2010) uses the phrase "sociopolitical turn" to describe a growing body of researchers and practitioners who foreground the political and engage in the tensions that surround that work. In a synthetic introduction to a 2010 special issue of *the Journal of Research in Mathematics Education* devoted to equity, she summarized three types of theoretical perspectives that begin with knowledge, power, and identity as interwoven and arising from (and constituted within) social discourses. Adopting such a stance means for these perspectives the uncovering of taken-for-granted rules and ways of operating that privilege some individuals and exclude others. Gutiérrez characterized work grounded in these theories as pursuing not only a better understanding of mathematics education in all of its social and cultural forms, but also working in such a way that contributes directly to the transformation of mathematics education to privilege more socially just practices. The first of her examples is critical mathematics education, discussed earlier in this chapter. The second, growing out of the North American context where social justice studies often obscure a direct reference to racial inequality, is the combination of "critical race theory" and "Latcrit theory," which privilege the voices of scholars of color and the experiences of students and teachers, and which work against popular discourses that suggest such experiences are subjective, illegitimate, or biased.

Critical race theory and Latcrit theory use counternarratives and storytelling to make experiences of marginalized subcultures clear; the stories capture uniqueness as overcoming racial inequality instead of as cultural difference (Leonard & Martin, 2013; Martin, 2000, 2009; Téllez, Moschkovich, & Civil, 2011). There have not been many publications using critical race theory or Latcrit theories in mathematics education, yet those that do draw on these frameworks offer convincing claims about the value of deconstructing race and racism in particular as a means to highlight whiteness as property and its relation to "normality," to value the strategies and strengths of people of color, to highlight community wealth, and to challenge commonly held beliefs about a racial hierarchy or a neutral society (Gutiérrez, 2010; Tate, 1997; Tate & D'Ambrosio, 1997).

Gutiérrez brings together researchers and theorists who attend to discourses as an entry into many of these issues under the collective term, "poststructural," her third example of the sociopolitical turn. In such approaches to mathematics education, learners, teachers, and researchers are both results of and producers of discourses. Because discourses are inherently social, political, historical, and connected with the construction of meaning, these approaches share much with those ways of thinking about mathematics education that are connected to a concern with culture. In this subfield, however, meaning, reasoning, knowledge, action, learning, and so on, are products of discourses, not characteristics of culture, and are also constantly renegotiated in social and cultural contexts, finding their meaning in the outcomes of actions and interactions moment by moment (see, e.g., Appelbaum, 1995, 2008; Walshaw, 2007). In other words, meanings that people make of themselves and their world are forever being created in and through interactions with others, in larger social and political contexts, with discourses that are themselves renewed and modified through these experiences and events. Discourses are sometimes confused with paradigms, since they connote taken-for-granted ways of interacting and operating, and because they are part of what comes to be expected and experienced as "normal."

An example described by Gutiérrez (2010) is the achievement gap in the United States. Discourses of difference create this state of things that people take as normal and comprehensible, and refer to as a "gap." Although the supposed "gap" might be better understood as one of excellence in pedagogy and resources provided (Tate, 1997; Tate, Anderson, & King, 2011), it is what people take as the normal state of things because it has been repeated and reported upon in so many ways. That this gap presumes a dominant, White majority as a norm is never explicitly considered; that there are many brilliant, Black children routinely demonstrating excellence in multiple ways (Leonard & Martin, 2013) is not part of this discourse. Alternative stories do not enter common-sense decision making.

The importance of understanding discourses in this way is that they produce common sense "truths": rather than reflecting some clear sense of reality, they structure reality for people. Similar examples can be unraveled for what discourses construct as "achievement," "equity," and "mathematics" itself. Gutiérrez writes,

> Unless learners and practitioners have the means to challenge these discourses or re-inscribe them with other meanings, they can come to believe they are successful or unsuccessful based on the discourses that operate in schooling practices. As such, they may evaluate themselves (often unconsciously), perhaps even reign in particular behaviors so as to be in line with what we think of as habits of successful learners or practitioners (a form of internal surveillance).
>
> (p. 43)

As an example of how attention to discourse can address what might otherwise be considered a "cultural" issue, we can consider Gutiérrez's example of specified algorithms being required in a school curriculum. When learners are asked to "show their work," this practice can lead to immigrant students discounting the knowledge of their parents who have learned mathematics in other countries (or, more generally, in other communities or other cultural contexts even if those "foreign" algorithms are correct. Of course, we might go even further with our analysis: Such practices define some algorithms and forms of knowledge not only as correct, but as foreign, despite the fact that their very presence in the community belies their exoticism and demonstrates their presence in the multicultural society. In this latter sense, culture has become a tool of ignorance, whether it is perpetuating a lack of personal awareness or disguising knowledge.

PUBLIC PEDAGOGY

Reading some of our discussion of critical mathematics education and diversity education, one might wonder if the concept of "culture" has run its course for mathematics education. There is a trajectory of awareness and perspective that begins with seeing culture as relevant to teaching and learning mathematics, moving on to questioning common pedagogical practices because of a cultural understanding, then to seeing limitations of culture as possibly too crude to comprehend an individual's ever-evolving collection of cultural identities, and later to recognizing culture as a tool of ignorance. It is tempting to propose replacing culture with more useful tools, such as race, immigration status, power, and so on.

Yet it might be that culture is not so much a conceptual tool to be brought into use within education, but rather that education can be a tool of conceptual use within culture. When we stop to think about it, there is no experience that is not educational. A person is always learning. Walking down the street, we learn where and when we can and cannot be (sometimes with help from uniformed representatives of a state), how trees and animals can and should share public spaces with us, and what it means to live in a community. In community gardens and graffiti tagging we learn how to reclaim public spaces to be used in new ways. We listen to music, dance with others, cull something to eat from found plants despite a drought, and learn what is possible, new ways to feel and solve problems, how to decide when someone has an expertise we can share. In a profoundly deep way, "culture" is not a context in which we live, but the result of what we are always learning and what we are always learning from. Instead of asking what culture can do for mathematics teaching and learning, and how we might better understand mathematics education with culture, we might benefit more from understanding what mathematics teaching and learning can do for culture and the understanding of culture. Just as culture is a web of meanings and interpretations, not a context, education is also a web of evolving meanings and interpretations-in-action.

This switch to the mathematics education of culture leads educators and researchers to consider mathematics teaching and learning that takes place on television, in public protest, in social media, and other aspects of everyday life. "Education is an enveloping concept, a dimension of culture that maintains dominant practices while also offering spaces for their critique and reimagination." (Sandlin, Schultz, & Burdick, 2009, p. 1). Often, the forms of mathematics education that are studied in this way—as important features of culture and popular media—take place outside of traditional classroom walls. For example, one can study or facilitate the mathematics of music videos and video games, street theater, or mathematics cafés that meet in church basements or neighborhood nail salons (Appelbaum, 1995; 2012). This study would not be in the service of clever ways to "trick" students into focusing on school mathematics (See, e.g., Burks, 2010; Chappell & Thompson, 2009; Popmatics, 2010), but rather to understand how people are learning and refining mathematical skills and concepts by their participation in these social, cultural activities. These forms of teaching and learning do not concern themselves with the limitations of schools and school structures, and because of this they offer opportunities to expand our comprehension of the universe of mathematics education that is taking place in the lives of all people every day, and at the same time, they offer a seemingly unlimited well of new possibilities for mathematics curriculum and mathematics pedagogies. They are "public pedagogies" (Sandlin et al., 2009; Trifonas, 2012), that is, spaces, sites, and languages of learning and education that are growing and proliferating outside of the traditional institutions of schooling—yet they are pedagogies that are just as crucial to our understanding of the development of individuals, intellectual work, and social change, if not more so, than what takes place in classrooms.

The study of public pedagogies might help those working in schools to bring ways of working and creating that are successful outside of school back into classrooms, as "playbooks" to guide new forms of school learning (Goble, 2013); there is the further potential that educators can reframe school mathematics experiences as only one of many forms of acculturation into/with mathematics that characterize contemporary mathematics learning. However, public pedagogies are also a possible alternative future for mathematics education unrestricted by the traditions and politics of state-sponsored or otherwise designed and organized educational institutions.

LEARNING MATHEMATICS

There was a time not long ago when "culture" was adopted as a tool by mathematics educators for improving the efficiency and efficacy of school mathematics pedagogy. "On the other hand," write Rosa and Orey (2011), "the learning of mathematics has always been associated with the schooling process, that is, it was thought that mathematical concepts and skills were acquired only if individuals went to school" (p. 7). This is an example of how school mathematics and culture mutually buttress common sense about mathematics and mathematics learning. What does it mean to "learn" mathematics? The answer to this question circles back to what people have "learned," which, in many cultures, is related to school experiences only, despite tangled webs of mathematical experiences and personal transformations in multiple sites of formal and informal education, everyday life, and public pedagogical encounters. School mathematics continues in many instances to be a process of appropriating techniques and skills. When this circles back upon what might be identified culturally as "mathematical," many experiences that could be otherwise defined as mathematical learning are overlooked, dismissed, or ridiculed.

When "culture" is added to the collection of analytic tools for comprehending mathematics learning, we have emphasized in this chapter that learners cannot be defined in terms of "a" culture, but rather that we are always referring to multiple, overlapping, and potentially conflicting subcultures. At the same time, "learning" cannot be isolated from culture, since learning both defines and is defined by the multiplicity of cultures to which we refer in the plural. Although many researchers have been interested in connecting culture and mathematics learning (as is evident in the persistence of such dichotomies as formal-informal learning, school-extracurricular learning, academic-nonacademic learning, and so on) these distinctions have not been sufficient to address the facilitation of learning, especially learning by members of minority and marginalized groups. We suggest that it is useful to avoid the dichotomies when referring to knowledge and learning. Knowledge is everywhere created and transformed in every moment; there is a complex web of meanings and interpretations among people and within learners, which, ironically, in turn, is itself part of a complex web of meanings and interpretations. "Culture" does not give answers to problems of mathematics education; issues of power, authority, and policy need to be included in any attempt to understand culture and mathematics learning. Unless these and other issues of postcolonial intercultures are centered in our analyses, we run the risk of limiting ourselves to naïve yet symbolically violent versions of assimilation and acculturation to the dominant culture, such as in those found contemporary efforts to integrate culturally different children into a mainstream school culture.

A culture of questioning (Giroux, 2011) might be culled from those aspects of critical multiculturalism, diversity education, ethnomathematics, critical race theory, Latcrit theories, and the emerging interest in public pedagogies. In these efforts, mathematics educators collaborate to be part of the creation of new institutions and public pedagogies that promote a culture of deliberation grounded in challenging oppression, exploitation, and exclusion. In this sense, we flip the direction of mutual influence, and focus on those ways that mathematics learning becomes part of efforts to construct a culture that creates ideological and structural conditions necessary for the development of an informed public, and new discourses for thinking through the processes of oppression, exploitation, and exclusion.

NOTES

1. The European Court of Human Rights condemned Greece for violation of the right to education and the provisions of the Convention prohibiting discrimination. Twenty-three Roma parents had complained about the exclusion of children from primary schools in Sofades Karditsa, and the subsequent, compulsory education in separate schools for Roma children. (See TVXS, http://tvxs.gr/news/ελλάδα/πρόστιμο-για-αποκλεισμό-παιδιών-ρομά-από-σχολεία.)

REFERENCES

de Abreu, G., Bishop, A. J., & Presmeg, N. C. (Eds.). (2002). *Transitions between contexts of mathematical practices.* Dordrecht, The Netherlands: Kluwer Academic Press.

Adler, J. (2001). *Teaching mathematics in multilingual classrooms.* Dordrecht, The Netherlands: Kluwer.

Andersson, A. & Seah, W. T. (2013). Facilitating mathematics learning in different contexts: The values perspective. *Proceedings of the seventh international mathematics education and society conference (MES7), 1*(2), 193–202. International Mathematics Education and Society Conference (MES7), South Africa.

Appelbaum, P. (1995). *Popular culture, educational discourse, and* mathematics. Albany, NY: State University of New York Press.

Appelbaum, P. (2002). *Multicultural and diversity education: A reference handbook.* Santa Barbara, CA: ABC-CLIO.

Appelbaum, P. (2008). *Embracing mathematics: On becoming a teacher and changing with mathematics.* New York: Routledge.

Appelbaum, P. (2012). *Democracy & mathematics circles/Le démocratie et les cercles mathématiques.* Prezi for a workshop held at the International Commission for the Study and Improvement of Mathematics Teaching, Rhodes, Greece. Retrieved from http://prezi.com/s_3pvca2bb8j/democracy-mathematics-circles-le-democratie-et-les-cercles-mathematiques/.

Ascher, M. (1991). *Ethnomathematics: A multicultural view of mathematical ideas.* Pacific Grove, CA: Brooks/Cole.

Atweh, B., Forgasz, H., & Nebres, B. (Eds.). (2001). *Sociocultural research on mathematics education: An international perspective.* Mahwah, NJ: Lawrence Erlbaum Associates.

Atweh, B. (2007, November). Pedagogy for socially response-able mathematics education. In *Proceedings of the annual conference of the Australian Association of Research in Education.* Fremantle, West Australia. Retrieved from www.aare.edu.au/07pap/atw07600.pdf.

Atweh, B., Graven, M., & Secada, W. (Eds.) (2011). *Mapping equity and quality in mathematics education.* Dordrecht, The Netherlands: Springer.

Baker, D., Clay, J., & Fox, C. (1996). *Challenging ways of knowing in English, maths and science.* Bristol, PA: Falmer Press.

Balibar, E. & Swenson, J. (2003). *We, the people of Europe? Reflections on transnational citizenship.* Princeton, NJ: Princeton University Press.

Barton, B. (1995). Making sense of ethnomathematics: Ethnomathematics is making sense. *Educational Studies in Mathematics, 31*(1–2), pp. 201–233.

Barton, B. (1996a). Anthropology perspectives on mathematics and mathematics education. In A. Bishop, M. A. Clements, C. Keitel-Kreidt, J. Kilpatrick, & F. K-S. Leung (Eds.), *International handbook of mathematics education* (pp. 1035–1053). New York: Springer Publishing.

Barton, B. (1996b). *Ethnomathematics: Exploring cultural diversity in mathematics.* Unpublished doctoral dissertation, the University of Auckland.

Barton, B. (1996c). Making sense of ethnomathematics: Ethnomathematics is making sense. *Educational Studies in Mathematics, 31*(1–2), 201–233.

Bazin, M., & Tamez, M. (2002). *Math and science across cultures: Activities and investigations from the Exploratorium.* New York: The New Press.

Berlinski, D. (2000). *The advent of the algorithm: The idea that rules the world.* New York: Harcourt Brace.

Bishop, A. (Ed.). (1988a). *Mathematics education and culture.* Dordrecht, The Netherlands: Kluwer Academic Publishers.

Bishop, A. (1988b). *Mathematical enculturation: A cultural perspective on mathematics education.* Boston, MA: Kluwer Academic Publishers.

Bishop, A. (2002). Mathematical acculturation, cultural conflicts, and transition. In G. de Abreu, A. Bishop, & N. Presmeg, (Eds.), *Transitions between contexts of mathematical practices* (pp. 193–212). Dordrecht, The Netherlands: Kluwer Academic Publishers.

Bishop, A. (2007). Values in mathematics and science education: An empirical investigation. In U. Gellert & E. Jablonka (Eds.), *Mathematisation and demathematisation: Social, philosophical, and educational ramifications* (pp. 123–139). Rotterdam, The Netherlands: Sense Publishers.

Boaler, J. (Ed.) (2000). *Multiple perspectives on mathematics teaching and learning.* Westport, CT: Ablex.

Brown, S., & Walter, M. (2005). *The art of problem posing.* Mahwah, NJ: Lawrence Erlbaum Associates.

Burks, R. (2010). "Survivor" math: Using popular culture to enhance learning mathematics. *PRIMUS: Problems, Resources, and Issues in Mathematics Undergraduate Studies, 21*(1), 62–72.

Chappell, M. & Thompson, D. (2009). *Math, culture, and popular media: Activities to engage middle school students through film, literature, and the Internet.* Portsmouth, NH: Heinemann.

Chronaki, A. (2005). Learning about 'learning identities' in the school arithmetic practice: The experience of two young minority Gypsy girls in the Greek context of education. *European Journal of Psychology of Education, 20*(1), pp. 61–74.

Civil, M., & Kahn, L. (2001). Mathematics instruction developed from a garden theme. *Teaching Children Mathematics, 7*(7), 400–405.

Civil, M. (1996). *Teaching mathematics to minority students: Dilemmas I face.* Paper presented at working group 22 (Mathematics, Education, Society and Culture) at the 8th International Congress on Mathematical Education (ICME). Sevilla, Spain.

Civil, M. (2002). Everyday mathematics, mathematicians' mathematics, and school mathematics: Can we bring them together? In B. Brenner & J. Moschkovich (Eds.), *Everyday and academic mathematics in the classroom* (pp. 40–62). Reston, VA: National Council of Teachers of Mathematics.

Civil, M. (2008). *Mathematics teaching and learning of immigrant students. A look at the key themes from recent research.* Prepared for ICME Survey Team 5: Mathematics Education in Multicultural and Multilingual Environments, Monterrey, Mexico. Retrieved from http://math.arizona.edu/~cemela/english/content/ICME_PME/MCivil-SurveyTeam5-ICME11.pdf.

Cline-Cohen, P. (1982). *A calculating people: The spread of numeracy in early America.* Berkeley: University of California Press.

Cotton, T. (2010). *Understanding and teaching primary mathematics*. Edinburgh Gate: Pearson Education.

D'Ambrosio, U. (1985). Ethnomathematics and its place in the history and pedagogy of mathematics. *For the Learning of Mathematics, 5,* 44–48.

D'Ambrosio, U. (1987). Reflections on ethnomathematics. *International Study Group on Ethnomathematics Newsletter, 3*(1), 3–5.

D'Ambrosio, U. (1988). Ethnomathematics: A research program in the history of ideas and in cognition. *International Study Group on Ethnomathematics Newsletter, 4*(1), 5–8.

D'Ambrosio, U. (1999). Ethnomathematics and its first international congress. *ZDM: The International Journal on Mathematics Education, 31*(2), 50–53.

D'Ambrosio, U. (2006). *Ethnomathematics*. Rotterdam, The Netherlands: Sense Publishers.

Davis, P., & Hersh, R. (1986). *Descartes' dream: The world according to mathematics*. San Diego, CA: Harcourt, Brace, Jovanovich.

Diéz-Palomar, J. (2012). *Family mathematics education: Improvement performance beyond the classroom walls*. Paper presented at the American Educational Research Association, Vancouver, Canada.

Dominguez, D. (2012). *When home came to school: Mexican mothers and their children finding (and solving) mathematical problems in their life experiences*. Paper presented at the American Educational Research Association, Vancouver, Canada.

Dowling, P. (1998). *The sociology of mathematics education: Mathematical myths/pedagogic texts*. Bristol, PA: Falmer Press.

Eglash, R. (1999). *African fractals: Modern computing and indigenous design*. New Brunswick, NJ: Rutgers University Press.

Fasheh, M. J. (2012). The role of mathematics in the destruction of communities, and what we can do to reverse this process, including using mathematics. In Skovsmose, O. & Greer, B. (Eds.), *Opening the cage: Critique and politics of mathematics education* (pp. 93–106). Rotterdam, The Netherlands: Sense Publishers.

Favilli, F. (Ed.) (2007). Ethnomathematics and mathematics education. *Proceedings of the 10th international congress of mathematics education, discussion group 15: Ethnomathematics*. Pisa: Tipografia Editrice Pisana.

François, K. (2007). The untouchable and frightening status of mathematics. In K. Francois & J.-P. van Bendegem (Eds.), *Mathematics education library: Vol. 42. Philosophical dimensions in mathematics education* (pp. 13–39). New York: Springer.

Frankenstein, M. (1987). Critical mathematics education: An application of Paulo Freire's epistemology. In I. Shor (Ed.), *Freire for the classroom: A sourcebook for liberatory teaching* (pp. 180–210). Portsmouth, NH: Boyton/Cook.

Gates, P. (2006). The place of equity and social justice in the history of PME. In A. Gutiérrez & P. Boero (Eds.), *Handbook of research on the psychology of mathematics education: Past, present and future* (pp. 367–402). Rotterdam, The Netherlands: Sense Publishers.

Geertz, C. (1973a). Religion as a cultural system. In *The interpretation of cultures* (pp. 87–125). New York: Basic Books.

Geertz, C. (1973b). Thick description: Toward an interpretive theory of culture. In *The interpretation of cultures* (pp. 3–30). New York: Basic Books.

Gerardo, J. M., Guitiérrez, R., & Irving, S. (2012). *Playing games to "change the game": Preservice teachers learning to support Latina/o adolescents through an after-school mathematics club*. Paper presented at the American Educational Research Association, Vancouver, Canada.

Gerdes, P. (1988). On possible uses of traditional Angolan sand drawings in the mathematics classroom, *Educational Studies in Mathematics, 19*(1), 3–22.

Gerdes, P. (1992). On the history of mathematics in Africa south of the Sahara. *AMUCHMA Newsletter, 9,* 3–32. Maputo: Higher Pedagogical Institute.

Gerdes, P. (1994). Reflections on ethnomathematics. *For the Learning of Mathematics, 14*(2), 19–21.

Gerdes, P. (1996). Ethnomathematics and mathematics education. In A. Bishop, M. A. Clements, C. Keitel-Kreidt, J. Kilpatrick, & F. K-S. Leung (Eds.), *International handbook of mathematics education* (pp. 909–943). New York: Springer-Verlag.

Gerofsky, S. (2001). Genre analysis as a way of understanding pedagogy in mathematics education. In J. Weaver, M. Morris, & Peter Appelbaum (Eds.), *(Post) modern science (education): propositions and alternative paths* (pp. 147–176). New York: Peter Lang.

Gerofsky, S. (2010). The impossibility of "real-life" word problems (according to Bakhtin, Lacan, Zizek and Baudrillard). *Discourse, 31*(1), 61–74.

Giroux, H. A. (2011). *On critical pedagogy. Bloomsbury Publishing Inc.1385 Broadway, 5th Floor New York, NY 10018*

Goble, R. (2013). *Making curriculum pop: A resource sharing community for educators interested in better practices and teaching with pop culture*. Retrieved from http://mcpopmb.ning.com/.

González, N., Moll, L., & Amanti, C. (Eds.) (2005). *Funds of knowledge: Theorizing practice in households, communities, and classrooms.* Mahwah, NJ: Lawrence Erlbaum Associates.

Gorgorió, N., & Planas, N. (2001). Teaching mathematics in multilingual classrooms. *Educational Studies in Mathematics, 47,* 7–33.

Govaris, C., & Antwniadou, A. (2000). Children of immigrants in a Greek kindergarten. *International Journal of the Humanities, 3*(1), 113–118.

Grootenboer, P., Lomas, G., & Ingram, N. (2008). The affective domain and mathematics education. In B. Perry, T. Lowrie, T. Logan, A. MacDonald, & J. Greenlees, (Eds.), *Research in mathematics education in Australasia 2008–2011* (pp. 23–37). Rotterdam, The Netherlands: Sense Publishers.

Gutiérrez, R. (2002a). Beyond essentialism: The complexity of language in teaching mathematics to Latina/o students. *American Educational Research Journal, 39*(4), 1047–1088.

Gutiérrez, R. (2002b). Enabling the practice of mathematics teachers in context: Toward a new equity research agenda. *Mathematical Thinking and Learning, 4*(2–3), 145–187.

Gutiérrez, R. (2010). The sociopolitical turn in mathematics education. *Journal for Research in Mathematics Education, 44*(1), 37–68.

Gutstein, E. (2003). Teaching and learning mathematics for social justice in an urban, Latino school. *Journal for Research in Mathematics Education, 34,* 37–73.

Gutstein, E. (2006). *Reading and writing the world with mathematics: Toward a pedagogy for social justice.* London: Taylor & Francis.

Gutstein, E. (2012). Mathematics as a weapon in the struggle. In B. Greer & O. Skovsmose (Eds.), *Opening the cage: Critique and politics of mathematics education* (pp. 23–48). Rotterdam, The Netherlands: Sense Publishers.

Gutstein, E., Lipman, P., Hernández, P., & de los Reyes, R. (1997). Culturally relevant mathematics teaching in a Mexican American context. *Journal for Research in Mathematics Education, 28*(6), 709–737.

Gutstein, E., & Peterson, B. (Eds.) (2005). *Rethinking mathematics: Teaching social justice by the numbers.* Milwaukee, WI: Rethinking Schools.

Keitel, C., Klotzmann, E., & Skovsmose, O. (1993). Beyond the tunnel vision: Analyzing the relationship between mathematics, society and technology. In C. Keitel & K. Ruthven (Eds.), *Learning from computers: mathematics education and technology* (pp. 243–279). New York: Springer-Verlag.

Kirshner, D. (2004). Enculturation: The neglected learning metaphor in mathematics education. In D. McDougall & J.A. Ross (Eds.), *Proceedings of the twenty-sixth annual meeting of the International Group for the Psychology of Mathematics Education, North American Chapter* (Vol. 2, pp. 765–772). Toronto: OISE/UT.

Klein, R. & Showalter, D. (2012). Where's the math? In J. Díez-Palomar & C. Kanes (Eds.), *Family and community in and out of the classroom: Ways to improve mathematics achievement* (pp. 115–122). Barcelona: Univ. Autònoma de Barcelona.

Knijnik, G., Wanderer, F., & Oliveira, C.J. (2005). Cultural differences, oral mathematics and calculators in a teacher training course of the Brazilian Landless Movement. *ZDM: The International Journal on Mathematics Education, 37*(2), 101–108.

Kumashiro, K. K. (2009). *Against common sense: Teaching and learning toward social justice.* London: Taylor & Francis.

Leonard, J., & Martin, D. B. (Eds.) (2013). *The brilliance of Black children in mathematics: Beyond the numbers and toward new discourse.* Charlotte, NC: Information Age Publishers.

Lerman, S. (Ed.). (1994). *Cultural perspectives on the mathematics classroom.* Dordrecht, The Netherlands: Kluwer Academic Press.

Lerman, S. (2000). The social turn in mathematics education research. In J. Boaler (Ed.), *Multiple perspectives on mathematics teaching and learning* (pp. 19–44). Westport, CT: Ablex.

Lerman, S. (2001). Cultural, discursive, psychology: A sociocultural approach to studying the teaching and learning of mathematics. *Educational Studies in Mathematics, 46*(1–2), 133–150.

Lipka, J. (2005). Math in a cultural context: Two case studies of a successful culturally based math project. *Anthropology and Education Quarterly, 36*(4), 367–385.

Lipka, J., & Mohatt, G.V. (1998). *Transforming the culture of schools: Yup'ik Eskimo examples. Sociocultural, political, and historical studies in education.* Mahwah, NJ: Lawrence Erlbaum Associates.

Lipka, J. Sharp, N., Adams, B., & Sharp, F. (2007). Creating a third space for authentic biculturalism: Examples from math in a cultural context. *Journal of American Indian Education, 46* (3), 94–115.

Martin, D.B. (2000). *Mathematics success and failure among African-American youth: The roles of socio-historical context, community forces, school influence, and individual agency.* Mahwah, NJ: Lawrence Erlbaum Associates.

Martin, D. B. (Ed.) (2009). *Mathematics teaching, learning, and liberation in the lives of Black children.* London: Routledge.

Martin, D. B. & Gohlson, M. (2012). On becoming and being a critical Black scholar in mathematics education: The politics of race and identity. In *Opening the cage: Critique and politics of mathematics education* (pp. 203–222). Rotterdam, The Netherlands: Sense Publishers.

Mason, J., Burton, L., & Stacey, K. (1985). *Thinking mathematically*. Reading, MA: Addison-Wesley.

Matthews, J. (1989). *Escalante: The best teacher in America*. New York: Henry Holt & Co.

Mellin-Olsen, S. (1987). *The politics of mathematics education*. Dordrecht, The Netherlands: D. Reidel.

Mishra, V. (2012). *What was multiculturalism?* Melbourne: Melbourne University Publishing.

Moreira, D. (2003). A Matemática na educação familiar: Memórias escolares, ideias sobre a Matemática e relação educativa em grupos domésticos de baixa escolaridade. *Quadrante. Revista de Investigação em Educação Matemática, 12*(2), 3–23.

Moreira, D., & Pires G. (2012). O processo educativo das crianças ciganas e a aprendizagem da matemática. A. I. Afonso (Ed.), *Etnografias com ciganos. Diferenciação e resistência cultural* (pp. 71–87). Lisboa: Edições Colibri.

Moschkovich, J. N. (2007). Examining mathematical discourse practices. *For the Learning of Mathematics, 27*(1), 24–30.

Moses, R., & C. Cobb. (2001). *Radical equations: Civil rights from Mississippi to the algebra project*. Boston, MA: Beacon Press.

Mukhopadhyay, S., & Roth, W. M. (2012). *Alternative forms of knowing (in) mathematics: Celebrating diversity of mathematical practices*. Rotterdam, The Netherlands: Sense Publishers.

Nasir, N. S., Hand, V., & Taylor, E. V. (2008). Culture and mathematics in school: Boundaries between "cultural" and "domain" knowledge in the mathematics classroom and beyond. *Review of Educational Research, 32*, 187–240.

Nolan, K. (2009). Mathematics in and through social justice: Another misunderstood marriage? *Journal of Mathematics Teacher Education, 12*(3), 205–216.

Olin, D. (2003). Crash course: Ethnomathematics. *New York Times* (February 23). Retrieved from www.nytimes.com/2003/02/23/magazine/23CRASH.html.

Orey, D. C., & Rosa, M. (2008). Ethnomathematics and cultural representations: Teaching in highly diverse contexts. *Acta Scientiae, 10*(1), 27–46.

Palhares, P. (2012).. Mathematics education and ethnomathematics. A connection in need of reinforcement. *REDIMAT-Journal of Research in Mathematics Education, 1*(1), 79–92.

Pinxten, R., van Dooren, I., & Harvey, F. (1983). *Anthropology of space*. Philadelphia, PA: University of Pennsylvania Press.

Pinxten, R., van Dooren, I., & Soberon, E. (1987). *Towards a Navajo geometry*. Ghent, Belgium: KKI Press.

Polya, G. (1945). *How to solve it: A new aspect of mathematical method*. Princeton, NJ: Princeton University Press.

Popkewtiz, T. (2004). The alchemy of the mathematics curriculum: Inscriptions and the fabrication of the child. *American Educational Research Journal, 41*(1), 3–34.

Popmatics. (2010). *The intersection of pop culture and mathematics: Creating a generation of mathematicians*. Retrieved from http://popmatics.wordpress.com/.

Powell, A., & Frankenstein, M. (1997). *Ethnomathematics: Challenging Eurocentrism in mathematics education*. Albany, NY: State University of New York Press.

Presmeg, N. (2002). Beliefs about the nature of mathematics in the bridging of everyday and school mathematical practices. In G. Leder, E. Pehkonen, & G. Torner (Eds.), *Beliefs: A hidden variable in mathematics education?* (pp. 293–312). Dordrecht, The Netherlands: Kluwer Academic Publishers.

Presmeg, N. (2007). The role of culture in teaching and learning mathematics. In F. Lester (Ed.), *Second handbook of research on mathematics teaching and learning* (pp. 435–460). Reston, VA: National Council of Teachers of Mathematics.

Radosavljevic, A. (2012). *Mathematics socialization through games: Bilingual third graders after school*. Paper presented at the American Educational Research Association, Vancouver, Canada.

Radtke, F. (1994). The formation of ethnic minorities and the transformation of social into ethnic conflicts in a so-called multicultural society—the case of Germany. In J. Rex & B. Drury (Eds.), *Ethnic mobilisation in a multi-cultural Europe* (pp. 30–37). Aldershot: Avebury.

Rosa, M., & Orey, D. C. (2011). Ethnomathematics: The cultural aspects of mathematics. *Revista Latinoamericana de Etnomatemática, 4*(2), 32–54.

Sandlin, J., Schultz, B., & Burdick, S. (2009). *Handbook of public pedagogy: Education and learning beyond schooling*. New York: Routledge.

Schoenfeld, A. (1991). On mathematics as sense-making: An informal attack on the unfortunate divorce of formal and informal mathematics. In J.F. Voss, D. N. Perkins, & J. W. Segal (Eds.), *Informal reasoning and education* (pp. 311–343). Cambridge, MA: Harvard University Press.

Seah, W. T. (2004). Shifting the lens of inquiry into the socialization of mathematics teachers. Nature of value differences. In I. Putt, R. Faragher, & M. McLean (Eds.), *Proceedings of the 27th annual conference of the mathematics education research group of Australasia* (Vol. 2, pp. 501–508). Townsville: James Cook University.

Skovsmose, O. (1994). *Toward a philosophy of critical mathematics education.* Dordrecht, The Netherlands: D. Reidel.

Skovsmose, O. (2004). Critical mathematics education for the future. In Niss, M. & Emborg, E. (Eds.), *Proceedings of the 10th international congress on mathematics education (ICME).* Retrieved from www.educ.fc.ul.pt/docentes/jfmatos/areas_tematicas/politica/CME_for_the_Future.pdf.

Skovsmose, O. (2011). *An invitation to critical mathematics education.* Rotterdam, The Netherlands: Sense Publishers.

Skovsmose, O., & Penteado, M. G. (2011). In B. Atweh, M. Graven, & W. Secada (Eds.), *Mapping equity and quality in mathematics education* (pp. 77–90). Dordrecht, The Netherlands; Springer.

Sleeter, C. E., & Grant, C. (2007). *Making choices for multicultural education: Five approaches to race, class and gender.* New York: Wiley.

Sleeter, C. E., & Soriano, E., (Eds.). (2012). *Creating solidarity across diverse communities: International perspectives.* New York: Teachers College Press.

Stathopoulou, Ch. (2005). *Ethnomathematics: Exploring the cultural dimension of mathematics and of mathematics education.* Athens: Atrapos.

Stathopoulou, Ch. (2006). Exploring informal mathematics of craftsmen in the designing tradition of 'Xysta' at Pyrgi of Chios. *For the Learning of Mathematics, 26*(3), 9–14.

Stathopoulou, Ch., & Kalabasis F. (2002). Teaching mathematics to first grade Romany children, through familiar every day money dealings. In P. Volero & O. Skovsmose (Eds.), *Proceedings of the Mathematics Education and Society Conference* (pp. 507–514). Helsingør, Denmark: Danmarks Paedagogiske Universitet.

Swanson, D. (2010). Paradox and politics of disadvantage: narratizing critical moments of discourse and mathematics pedagogy within the "glocal." In M. Walshaw (Ed.), *Unpacking pedagogy: New perspectives for mathematics* (pp. 245–263). Greenwich, CT: Information Age Publishing.

Swanson, D. & Appelbaum, P. (2013). Refusal as a democratic catalyst for mathematics education development. *Pythagoras, 33*(2). Retrieved from www.pythagoras.org.za/index.php/pythagoras/article/view/189.

Sykes, C. (1995). *Dumbing down our kids: Why American children feel good about themselves but can't read, write, or add.* New York: St. Martin's Griffin.

Tate, W. (1997). Critical race theory and education: History, theory, and implications. *Review of Research in Education, 22,* 195–247.

Tate, W. F., Anderson, C. R., & King, K. (Eds.) (2011). Disrupting tradition: Pathways for research and practice in mathematics education. Reston, VA: National Council of Teachers of Mathematics.

Tate, W. F., & D'Ambrosio, B. S. (Eds.) (1997, January). Equity, reform, and research in mathematics education, Journal for Research in Mathematics Education, 28(6), 650–782.

Téllez, K., Moschkovich, J. & Civil, M. (2011). *Latinos/as and mathematics education: Research on learning and teaching in classrooms and communities.* Charlotte, NC: Information Age Publishing.

Trifonas, P. (2012). *Learning the virtual life: Public pedagogy in a digital world.* New York: Routledge.

Valero, P. & Stentof, D. (2010). The "post" move of critical mathematics education. In H. Alrø, O. Ravn, & P. Valero (Eds.), *Critical mathematics education: Past, present and future: Festschrift for Ole Skovsmose* (pp. 183–196). Rotterdam, The Netherlands: Sense Publishers.

Vithal, R., & Skovsmose, O. (1997). The end of innocence: A critique of "ethnomathematics." *Educational Studies in Mathematics, 34*(2), 131–157.

Walkerdine, V. (1987). *The mastery of reason: Cognitive development and the production of meaning.* New York: Routledge.

Walshaw, M. (2007). *Working with Foucault in education.* Rotterdam, The Netherlands: Sense Publishers.

Walshaw, M. (2010). The performance of self in the art of research. *Educational Insights, 13*(1). Retrieved from www.ccfi.educ.ubc.ca/publication/insights/v13n01/articles/walshaw/index.html.

Whitin, D., & Sandra Wilde. (1995). *It's the story that counts: More children's books for mathematical Learning, K–6.* Portsmouth, NH: Heinemann.

Willey, C., Lopez Leiva, C. A., & Vomvoridi-Ivanovic, E. (2012). *Reconnecting with powerful, personal resources to teach and learn mathematics: Experiences of three Latina/o preservice teachers.* Paper presented at the American Educational Research Association, Vancouver, Canada.

Zaslavsky, C. (1973a). *Africa counts: Number and pattern in African culture.* Boston, MA: Prindle, Weber & Schmid.

Zaslavsky, C. (1973b). Mathematics in the study of African culture . *Arithmetic Teacher, 20,* 532–535.

Zaslavsky, C. (1993). *Multicultural mathematics: Interdisciplinary cooperative-learning activities.* Portland, ME: J. Weston Walch.

Zaslavsky, C. (1996). *The multicultural math classroom: bringing in the world.* Portsmouth, NH: Heinemann.

Zaslavsky, C. (1998). *Math games and activities from around the world.* Chicago: Chicago Review Press, 1998.

Zolkower, B. (1995). Math fictions: What really solves the problem? *Social Text, 43*(3), 133–162.

14 Mathematics Education and Democracy
An Open Landscape of Tensions, Uncertainties, and Challenges

Ole Skovsmose

Aalborg University

Miriam Godoy Penteado

Universidade Estadual Paulista

In their classic study assuming the perspective of analytical philosophy, Benn and Peters (1959) relate democracy to notions such as justice, equality, freedom, and responsibility. A further investigation of justice is provided by Rawls (1971/1999), who begins his inquiry in analytic philosophy but expands his investigations beyond this tradition. Ideas about deliberative democracy, as for instance presented by Bohman and Rehg (1997), relate the notion of democracy to participation, negotiation, and dialogue. Democracy can also be related to citizenship, autonomy, human rights, and inclusion. Together all such notions belong to an extended family of open concepts.

Democracy is derived from the Greek: *demos* means "people," and *cratos* means "rule"; so, literally speaking, "democracy" means "ruled by people." What can be referred to as classic democracy was realized in ancient Greece, but also criticized by prominent philosophers including Plato and Aristotle. Democratic ideals were advocated by Locke in *Two Treatises of Government* (1689/1988). Here he elaborated many topics that formed the liberal tradition in democracy, for instance concerning representation and private property. He also addressed slavery, which he found possible to justify. We find democratic ideals suggested by Rousseau in *The Social Contract*, first published in 1762. Rousseau poses the question: Who is the sovereign? In a monarchy the answer is simple: the king. According to Rousseau, the answer is just as simple when we consider a democracy: the people are the sovereign. This brings Rousseau to claim that in a democracy it should be possible for people actually to participate in the governing. In this way he shares ideas with the classic model of democracy. In *Capitalism, Socialism and Democracy* (1943), Schumpeter suggests an interpretation of democracy that is very remote from Rousseau's. According to Schumpeter, the role of the people in a democracy is to produce a government and only this. Thus democracy has nothing to do with participation and public decision making, except for the election of the person to be put in power. According to Schumpeter, democracy works perfectly well in huge societies. The democratic method simply takes the form of a "competitive struggle," and people's democratic activity consists solely in casting their votes.

Drawing on these comments, we want to stress that the apparently straightforward notion of democracy takes us a long way round among many other notions and ideals. Democracy can be clarified only through concepts just as complex as itself. As our departure for discussing mathematics education and democracy, we want to recognize the openness of democracy as well as of the extended family of related concepts.

THE DEWEY HARMONY

Dewey's conception of democracy is far removed from any technocratic interpretation as suggested by Schumpeter; it is closer to Rousseau's interpretation. Dewey (1966) sees democracy as a "way of life," and in *Democracy and Education* (1916), as well as in subsequent writings, he presents visions of a profound harmony between a democratic way of life and educational processes.

The basis for claiming this harmony is found in Dewey's philosophic pragmatism and in the way he sees sciences. According to him, science must refrain from any form of dogmatism. Every issue must be investigated without preconceptions, and inquiry processes are crucial for any such activity: one experiences something, one questions something, one recognizes something as a problem, one addresses the problem, one makes experiments, one provides tentative conclusions, and one questions any such conclusions. This way one enters an open process. One is researching.

According to Dewey (1938/1963, 1974), research processes are similar to learning processes, in particular when learning takes place in settings inspired by investigative approaches. Furthermore, Dewey finds that democratic processes can be characterized as inquiry processes. In other words, democracy and education share the procedures characteristic of the scientific method. As a consequence, an education organized in terms of inquiry processes becomes an education for democracy. This is the principal idea of what we refer to as the *Dewey harmony*.

With respect to mathematics education one finds many expressions of this harmony. Let us just refer to one such example, which is clearly expressed in the title of a paper written by Hannaford (1998): "Mathematics Teaching Is Democratic Education." In this straightforward way, Hannaford claims the existence of an intrinsic connection between mathematics education and democracy. This is due to the very nature of, on the one hand, a democratic way of life, and, on the other hand, the mathematical way of thinking. In both cases, rational arguments function as the principal tools.

AN APORETIC CONDITION

The Dewey harmony forms part of a more general Modern Outlook, which claims the existence of a profound harmony between scientific thinking and discoveries, mathematical rationality, technological enterprises, educational processes, democratic ways of life, welfare, and socio-political progress in general. In particular, science and technology has been conceptualized as the engine of progress.[1] This Modern Outlook has also been referred to as the "grand narrative" of Modernity (Lyotard, 1979/1984).

Modernity is a broad label; it refers to the scientific revolution, the period of Enlightenment, and it includes the scientific and technological optimism that prospered during the 19th century. Only in the later part of the 20th century was this outlook broadly questioned. A basic element of this questioning is the claim that the Modern Outlook includes a false self-understanding: the grand narratives of Modernity represent only myths.

We cannot ignore that the most brutal forms of colonization accompanied by racism formed part of Modernity. Racism did not operate as a popular preconception only: during the 19th century it was assumed to have a scientific underpinning. Through, for instance, meticulous phrenological studies one tried to distinguish between developed and less developed human races. Such studies were accompanied by linguistic studies trying to trace the linguistic expression of such stipulated differences.[2] One could interpret the Holocaust as a pathological event in Modern history, as not forming part of the history of "progress." Contrary to this "explaining away" of the Holocaust, Bauman (1989) emphasizes that it was precisely modern technology, modern bureaucracy, and modern management that made the Holocaust function with all its devastating efficiency. In fact, Modernity includes a range of examples that reveal the grand narratives of Modernity as a false self-portrayal.

Throughout Modernity, the democracy-is-not-for-them argument has been applied again and again. As an example, Said (1979, p. 31 ff.) points out that in 1910 in the English Parliament it was explicitly stated by Arthur James Balfour (Prime Minister 1902–1905 and Foreign Secretary 1916–1919) in a debate addressing Egypt that democracy was not for the "Orientals." This democracy-is-not-for-them argument was basic to the apartheid regime in South Africa: Blacks had to be excluded. For long periods the same argument barred woman from participating in democracy, thus women only got the right to vote in United Kingdom in 1928, in France 1944, in Switzerland in 1971, while in Saudi Arabia they are promised to be allowed to vote in 2015. The democracy-is-not-for-them argument has operated as an integral part of different Modern interpretations of democracy.

The grand narrative of Modernity represents myths more that reality, and the very notion of Modernity might be obsolete. Beck (1986/1992, 1999) explores the notion of the risk society, which includes the idea that science and technology not only contribute to the solutions of problems, but also formulate a part of the very production of those problems. Michael Gibbons et al. (1994) address what they call the Mode-2 society, characterized by the fact that science and knowledge production in general has come to operate under market conditions. Castells (1996, 1997, 1998), addresses the complexity of the information age and demonstrates how modern technology has impacts on all spheres of life, including the processes of globalization. All such studies point towards the closing of the so-called Modern period.

Leaving aside the Modern self-understanding, we come to face a new framing of the discussion of education and democracy. Thus, we cannot assume the existence of any intrinsic harmony between education and democracy in general, nor between mathematics education and democracy in particular. We cannot assume the existence of any profound harmony between scientific thinking, mathematical rationality, technological enterprises, educational processes, democracy, and progress in general. We cannot rely on any uniform interpretation of notions belonging to the extended family of open concepts related to democracy as, for instance, justice, equality, and freedom. Like democracy itself, such notions do not have any essence. Instead we have to do with contested concepts.[3] These can be interpreted in different ways; they can include conflicting perspectives and assume particular interests. There is no general perspective that helps to provide some universal interpretations of such concepts. Together with such contested concepts we are operating in socio-political contexts filled with tensions and contradictions. As a consequence, we come to face profound uncertainty, which we refer to as an *aporetic condition*.[4]

That mathematics is also subjected to the aporetic condition is emphasized by D'Ambrosio in the following observations:

> In the last 100 years, we have seen enormous advances in our knowledge of nature and in the development of new technologies. [. . .] And yet, this same century has shown us a despicable human behavior. Unprecedented means of mass destruction, of insecurity, new terrible diseases, unjustified famine [. . .] are matched only by an irreversible destruction of the environment. Much of this paradox has to do with an absence of reflections and considerations of values in academics, particularly in the scientific disciplines, both in research and in education. Most of the means to achieve these wonders and also these horrors of science and technology have to do with advances in mathematics.
>
> (D'Ambrosio, 1994, p. 443)

Mathematics can be associated with processes that are out of democratic control, processes that can provide wonders as well as horrors. D'Ambrosio also refers here to mathematics education, and we recognize "mathematics education and democracy" as an open landscape of tensions, uncertainties, and challenges.[5] As a consequence, we recognize the complexity of the politics of mathematics education.[6]

In the next section, "Mathematics in School Practices" we explore mathematics education for democracy in terms of different formulations of mathematics education for social justice.

We also consider what kind of disciplining might be exercised through the school mathematics tradition. Finally, we consider the possibility that dealing with these traditions may ensure profound forms of social inclusion. Acknowledging the aporetic condition, however, we cannot expect that relating mathematics education and democracy would lead us towards any particular educational program or towards some curriculum guidelines. The aporetic condition is accompanied by profound uncertainties.

However, through the notion of *pedagogical imagination* we reach the constructive part of operating within an aporetic condition. In the section "Pedagogical Imagination," we provide a general presentation of the notion. We also discuss two particular issues concerning the direction of imagination: (1) mathematics in society and technology and (2) mathematics in students' life-worlds. In the final section, "An Open Landscape," we acknowledge "mathematics education and democracy" as a fertile ground for such imagination.

MATHEMATICS IN SCHOOL PRACTICES

The discussion of mathematics education and democracy cannot concentrate on school education alone. Learning mathematics can take place in many other contexts, and in all of these contexts one can consider what it could mean to try to pursue democratic ideals. However, in this chapter we do concentrate on school practices.

If one assumes a Modern Outlook, the Dewey harmony also applies to mathematics education. When properly organized, mathematics education forms part of a democratic endeavor. Our point, however, is that one cannot set out with any such assumption. We find instead that mathematics education can be performed with reference to any form of political interest. We do not find that mathematics education contains any particular democratic essence.[7] It could come to operate as a democratic force, but also as a disciplining device—to use a term explored by Foucault (1991). In schools, mathematics education operates within the aporetic condition. It represents tensions, challenges, and uncertainties that we are able to address only through contested concepts.

Narratives About Mathematics Education for Social Justice

Mathematics education for social justice has been explored in several books and articles (D'Ambrosio, 2012; Frankenstein, 2012; Gates, 2006; Gutstein, 2012a; Sriraman, 2008; and Wager & Stinson, 2012). Apparently, social justice represents a crucial feature of democracy, as does responsiveness. Thus responsive mathematics education tries to make students able to respond to forms of domination as critical citizens. This approach has been elaborated in depth in *Culturally responsive mathematics education* (Greer, Mukhopadhyay, Powell, & Nelson-Barber, 2009). The principal idea is to establish a mathematics education that makes students able to "respond to authority," which is crucial idea of deliberative democracy.

Similar perspectives have been presented by Gutstein (2006) in *Reading and writing the world with mathematics*. Here he draws on ideas formulated by Freire, who talks about "reading the world" as a metaphor for interpreting the world, including all its forms of domination and suppression, and about "writing the world" as an expression of changing the world. Gutstein illustrates how such reading-writing can be developed with reference to mathematics. One can read the world through numbers and figures, and on this basis one might become able to write the world.

Mathematics education for social inclusion has many ramifications. There are studies addressing students in vulnerable social conditions (see, for instance, Vithal, 2009) and others including students with special educational needs, such as blind or deaf students (Healy & Fernandes, 2011; Marcone & Penteado, 2013). The point is not to see inclusion as a one-way process of bringing groups back to "normality," but as a mutual process of interaction. Many studies have evolved around the notion of equity (see, for instance Forgasz & Rivera, 2012), and many ethnomathematical studies address issues like social justice and inclusion (see, for instance, D'Ambrosio, 2006).

These studies aim at creating the possibility that all people could participate in mathematical practices. However, we do not want to rush towards the conclusion that such proposals ensure a mathematics education for democracy. Any suggestion for a mathematics education for social justice operates within the aporetic condition. This means that we cannot provide any straightforward identification of what socio-political functions such an education might serve, even when applying the notion of "social justice." All approaches include contradictions, and the basic notions through which we may address these approaches are all contested. We are really dealing with an open landscape.

The School Mathematics Tradition

Let us consider what might be called *mainstream* mathematics education. One could claim that education on a grand scale is a principal democratic concern. The overall importance of education was recognized by the Enlightenment movement, and since then general education has been associated with the development of democracy. Education was taken as a defining characteristic for the development of citizenship. Literacy was considered a democratic concern, and so was mathemacy in its different interpretations (see, for instance, Chronaki, 2010). Following on from this perspective, one can see the school mathematics tradition as a most important foundation for ensuring democratic citizenship.

Let us, however, consider the school mathematics tradition from a different perspective by paying attention to some of its particular features:

(1) The activities in the classroom are first of all defined through the chosen textbook. The teacher provides an exposition on a particular topic, which defines the tasks for the students. This way, the "acted out" curriculum becomes defined through the textbook.

(2) The mathematical exercises play a dominant role, as solving preformulated exercises is widely considered essential for the learning of mathematics. These exercises demonstrate three particular characteristics: all the information given is exact, and should not be questioned; all the information given is necessary for solving the exercises, and also sufficient as no other information is needed; the exercises have one and only one correct answer.

(3) One important feature of classroom practice is to eliminate errors. There are many possibilities for making errors: an algorithm can be conducted wrongly; a wrong algorithm can be applied; an exercise can be copied incorrectly from the textbook; the wrong exercise can be performed, etc. All forms of errors have to be eliminated, as "doing things correctly" is considered equivalent to "learning mathematics."

(4) The students' performance has to be evaluated. This can be done through the teacher's questioning approach; through the teacher's control of the students' solutions of exercises; and through different forms of tests. It can also be achieved through the exams at the end of the school year.

Considering the content of the many exercises, that define the school mathematics tradition, one can hardly claim that working with such exercises provides any deeper understanding of mathematics. However, one can pay attention not to the content, but to the form of these exercises. They operate as a long sequence of commands: "Construct a triangle. . .!" "Solve the equation. . .!," "Calculate the distance between . . . !," etc. Taking a command as given is a defining element of a logic of commands.

In this sense, the school mathematics tradition might be seen as providing a form of social control through a disciplining of thought, which in turn might serve its main functions within the given socio-economic order of society. These observations can be related to Foucault's discussion of governability. In order to be able to properly govern, the state needs to make the population governable; mathematics education can be seen as contributing to such disciplining, for instance by exercising a logic of command. Such observations, then, bring us to question the existence of any intrinsic connection between the school mathematics tradition and democratic ideals.

Tradition or Alternative?

Let us now consider the Algebra Project in the United States as organized by Robert Moses. The project was expanded radically in 1982 from teaching mathematics in one school to, by the end of the 1990s, incorporating more than 200 schools. Moses participated in the Black civil rights movement, and the Algebra Project became part of the overall struggle for human rights. The Algebra Project tried to improve the quality of mathematics education in poor communities. The explicit goal of the project was to provide better access for Black students to further education, and Moses saw algebra as playing a crucial role in gatekeeping. The aim of the project was to take students who had low scores in the mathematics tests and prepare them for college entrance by the end of high school.

The Algebra Project included many educational initiatives relating the content of mathematics to the students' own contexts. However, a main aim was to ensure Black students gained access to the established educational system. Thus the aim was not to provide a new curriculum more suited to the students' needs as citizens, but exactly to engage the students more successfully in the existing traditional curriculum. This curriculum operated in a powerful way by assuming the logic of the gatekeeper. The project was not intended to eliminate the gatekeeper, but to beat the gatekeeper at its own game. The Algebra Project was not trying to change the logic of the system; the aim was instead to make Black students able to cope with this logic.

As suggested in the books *Culturally responsive mathematics education* (Greer et al., 2009) and *Reading and writing the world with mathematics* (Gutstein, 2006), mathematics education for social justice can be approached by exploring numbers and figures with respect to, say, salary, house prices, and health security, potentially also providing students with an insight into the way injustice operates. However, one can also think of the Algebra Project as education for social justice precisely because it acknowledges the importance of the school mathematics tradition in providing (or denying) access to further education. In order to counteract the exclusion of marginalized groups, it becomes important to master the very tradition that is at the root of their marginalization. In all circumstances, the Algebra Project illustrates the contested nature of ways of pursuing social justice through mathematics education.

PEDAGOGICAL IMAGINATION

We must address mathematics education and democracy within an aporetic condition. As mentioned earlier, due to the contested nature of the concepts we are using, we cannot expect to identify any specific program that defines a mathematics education for democracy, and certainly not in terms of any curriculum proposal. However, contested concepts might have other functions than providing analytical clarity and proper justifications for particular educational approaches.

Educational research can take as a point of departure observations of educational practices. One can observe what is taking place; one can provide accurate and valid descriptions; and on this basis try to provide a theory. Theorizing, however, can also address what has not taken place, but what could come to take place. Thus educational research could address, not only what is, but also what is not (yet). It could address educational possibilities, and of course all of this also applies to research in mathematics education (Skovsmose, 2009a).

In order to explore educational possibilities, pedagogical imagination has an important role to play. One can relate this notion to *sociological imagination,* as coined by Wright-Mills (1959). By sociological imagination he understood a conception of alternatives to what in fact is taking place. Such imagination helps to reveal that some "sociological facts" are not necessary facts, but contingent facts: they could be different. A sociological imagination is crucial for showing that socio-political alternatives are possible. A pedagogical imagination has a similar role to play: it helps to reveal that alternative educational practices might be possible. What could be taken for granted, say in terms of educational traditions, are not educational necessities, but contingencies.

A pedagogical imagination needs fuel, and such imaginations need to be conceptualized. Contested concepts belonging to the extended family of democracy might help us in expressing such imaginations. Thus we see the open landscape of mathematics education and democracy as fertile ground for pedagogical imagination. However, it is important to keep in mind that pedagogical imaginations themselves will be contested.

With respect to the practices of mathematics in school, we can think of the different alternative narratives of mathematics education for social justice as expressions of pedagogical imagination. Thus the notion of democracy brings us to consider different interpretations of citizenships. Citizenship concerns participation and autonomy, and one can think of citizenship as including a capacity of "responding to authority." One can also interpret citizenship with references to "reading and writing the world." Certainly citizenship also means inclusion. Other very different contested concepts can as well be related to democracy. Thus Valero, García, Camelo, Mancera, and Romero (2012) explore the notion of dignity, and Swanson and Appelbaum (2012) consider refusal as a democratic catalyst. All such notions are contested, but as such they can shape pedagogical imaginations.

In the following we will explore other more particular directions of pedagogical imagination by considering (1) mathematics in society and technology, and (2) mathematics in the students' life-worlds.

Mathematics in Society and Technology

As part of the Modern Outlook, mathematics was celebrated as a form of sublime human rationality, and this celebration formed some of the "grand narratives": that mathematics provides a unique insight in nature, which means that mathematics can be considered the language of science; that mathematics, through its broad range of applications, represents the rationality of technology-based progress; and that mathematics stands out as a pure science due to its objectivity and neutrality.

Such grand narratives, however, need to be substituted by a group of very different and even contradictory "small narratives" about mathematics, which cannot be added up to a general celebration of mathematics. Contradictory small narratives can be associated with the many different forms of mathematics in action. Thus mathematics becomes an integral part of technology, which we interpret in the broadest possible way. Thus, we do not only refer to technological artifacts: washing machines, TV sets, robots, electronic networks, etc. We also refer to forms of automatization, procedures for financial transactions, and forms of surveillance and control, etc. All forms of daily practices—our *life-worlds*—become continuously defined and redefined through mathematics in action.[8] Mathematics operates as an ongoing democratic challenge. Let us refer to a few more particular forms of mathematics in action.

One can consider a computer as a mathematical algorithm, materialized in an electronic format. In this sense a computer is a conglomerate of mathematical constructs. We find such constructs in all forms of modern information and communication technology. For instance, mathematics is crucial for the functioning of the Google Page Rank System. This system is brought in action every time one uses Google to search for something on the Internet. What appears on screen is not a direct result of one's search, but of page rankings provided by a predesigned mathematical algorithm. This is a specific illustration of the fact that our knowledge is now more than ever before structured by technology.

The new possibilities for processing and circulating information, together with new forms of communication (as illustrated by social media), bring about new challenges for democracy. Are we dealing with a technology that supports individual participation and autonomy? Does the very same technology at the very same time open new possibilities for controlling and suppressing?

Processes of production take new forms due to automatization and robotting. Any production process—of cars, airplanes, washing machines—is established through a certain balance between automatic processes, technical management, and manual labor. However, this balance is always changing as new technology makes new forms of automatization possible. Processes of robotting are formed through mathematics: both the construction of proper robots as well as in the combination of mechanical and manual elements in the production process. The whole scientific structuring of production processes is a feature of a society, where science itself has gone on the market. In this structuring mathematics in action forms a defining element.

Processes of surveillance are formed through computing and mathematics. It is possible to generate huge amounts of data, and the automatic processing of data constitutes a part of any form of modern schemes of surveillance having to do the financial transactions, security matters, marketing strategies, etc. The so-called whistle blowers have drawn our attention to the fact that a worldwide web of surveillance is not only possible but is already exercised. A mathematics-based Big-Brother negation of democratic principles has become a central feature of our time.

The hectic mathematics-based development of technology includes many contradictions. We are referring to powerful actions that represent horrors as well as wonders. They represent all sorts of human values: mathematics-based actions can be risky, expensive, benevolent, brutal, cynical, efficient, etc. This spectrum cannot be captured by some grand narrative about mathematics. Mathematics in action includes tensions and contradictions. One finds all kind of narratives about horrors and wonders.

Let us consider mathematics education as taking place at universities—not only the education of future mathematicians, but as well the education of engineers, computer scientists, economists, etc. Expertise is needed with reference to all forms of mathematics in action. Such expertise could be an unreflective and obedient application of techniques and procedures. We refer to this as *one-dimensional expertise*. All forms of expertise could turn one-dimensional if they concentrate on specific technical questions such as "How do we do it?" and ignore questions like "Why do it? and "Why is it done that way?" If we, however, explore expertise through notions like citizenship, autonomy, and responsibility, the challenge becomes: "How do we provide an education that is not only developing a technical expertise within a certain domain, but at the same time is providing a panorama of reflections about the application of this domain?" Possible answers would bring us to conceptualize a two-dimensional expertise, a reflective expertise, as an important educational task.[9] Thus we might identify a fruitful route for pedagogical imagination along a sequence of concepts: democracy, citizenship, participation, autonomy, responsibility, and refection on mathematics in action.

Reflections on mathematics, however, do not concern the formation of expertise only. Such reflection concerns all forms of mathematics education. We live in a mathematized society, where an apparent demathematization also plays its part (see, Gellert & Jablonka, 2009; Jablonka, 2010; and Jablonka & Gellert, 2007). Demathematization refers to the processes of mathematics operating in an invisible format. Thus the mathematics of the Google Page Rank System do not appear in any search processes. Notions like democratic control, democratic access to decision making, critique of decision procedures, and deliberation all bring fuel to pedagogical imagination concerning how to address the mathematization and demathematization of society. Also in this case, notions like responsiveness and reading and writing the world can turn out to be constructive for identifying educational possibilities.[10]

Mathematics in Students' Life-Worlds

Discussions of mathematics education and democracy also concern the students' perspectives and their possibilities in life. (They also concern the life of the teachers; however, due to the limitations of space, we are not going to address this latter issue here.) We will consider what directions pedagogical imaginations might take when we consider these perspectives and possibilities.

In order to explore the students' perspectives we draw on the notion of life-world. Husserl (1936/1970) presented this notion as an unstructured phenomenon, representing a pure foundation for any form of structuring. The notion of life-world, however, can be given a radically different interpretation as an experienced world structured by social, political, economic, cultural, and discursive forces. We see life-worlds this way, and we will address two features of the students' life-worlds: their foregrounds and their experiences of meaning.

The foreground of a person refers to opportunities and obstructions that the social, political, economic and cultural situation provides for her or him (Skovsmose, 2014). A foreground can be seen as a province of a life-world, but simultaneously it reaches beyond this world by including possibilities and hopes as well as obstructions and desolation. A foreground represents the horizon of a life-world. Naturally, the foreground is not composed of any well-defined space of possibilities. Instead one can see the foreground as a flux of possibilities and obstructions, of hopes and despair. Horizons are ever changing. A foreground is not just there spread out in front of a person. It is an evolving phenomenon.

One can think of foregrounds in individual terms, but it might be more useful to think of them in collective terms since interpretations of possibilities are elaborated through patterns of interaction and communication. People from the same community can be submitted to the same basic life conditions and in this sense have similar foregrounds. Foregrounds are collective, but still include individual features. When only desolate possibilities are experienced by a student, we talk about a ruined foreground. A foreground can be ruined due to social, economic, political, and cultural violence. During the apartheid regime in South Africa, the destruction for Black people's possibilities was an integral part of the system. There is, however, a broad range of examples of foregrounds being configured through processes of social exclusion (Baber, 2007).

We see mathematics education as playing an important role in the formation of students' foregrounds. Let us illustrate with the following statement by Volmink (1994):

> Mathematics is not only an impenetrable mystery to many, but has also, more than any other subject, been cast in the role as an 'objective' judge, in order to decide who in the society 'can' and who 'cannot'. It therefore serves as the gate keeper to participation in the decision making processes of society. To deny some access to participation in mathematics is then also to determine, a priori, who will move ahead and who will stay behind.
>
> (pp. 51–52)

This is a strong statement about the role that mathematics education exercises in shaping the students' foregrounds in a way that might be characterized as violent. It is such forms of violence that the Algebra Project was trying to cope with, in the most direct way, by adding more possibilities to the students' foregrounds.

A radically different formation of possibilities is expressed by Lupes, one of Gutstein's students:

> With every single thing about math that I learned came something else. Sometimes I learned more of other things instead of math. I learned to think of fairness, injustices and so forth everywhere I see numbers distorted in the world. Now my mind is opened to so many new things. I'm more independent and aware. I have learned to be strong in every way you can think of it.
>
> (Lupes, quoted from Gutstein, 2003, p. 37)

Through his mathematic education, Lupes came to see the world differently. He learned about fairness and injustice. His life-world changed; his foreground as well. We see meaning as a network of relationships within life-worlds, but simultaneously as relationships reaching beyond. Thus we find the meaning that students might associate with learning activities in the classroom is related to experienced relationships between their foregrounds and these activities. We can read Lupes's comment as an illustration of this idea.

Notions like life-world, foreground, meaning, and possibility also belong to the extended family of open concepts related to democracy. Let us now see how they might help directing pedagogical imagination. We illustrate with two examples.

As part of a project taking place in a poorer neighborhood in Rio Claro, a city in the interior of the São Paulo state, we were teaching a group of students considered by teachers to be the most difficult in the classroom. They were always causing problems by being noisy, fighting, and obstructing the lessons. They had shown no interest whatsoever in mathematics. We met with these 12 students in the computer room. It turned out that it was not that difficult to engage them in working with computers. For many, school was the only place where they had the opportunity to touch a keyboard. So what kind of activities might make sense to them? Many! For instance, working with dynamic geometry. They were fascinated by the movement on the screen, dragging a corner of a triangle here and there. They experienced many things for the first time, like the magic that in any triangle the sum of internal angles results always in 180 degrees. This kind of activity seemed to make sense to them. But why? Again, one need not think of meaning as having to do with familiarity. Meaning also has to do with engaging students' foregrounds. It has to do with reaching out towards the horizons of the students' life-worlds. Working with computers might bring about new imaginations of possibilities: "This could also be for me."[11]

In a public school also located in Rio Claro, the teacher whom we were working with wanted to introduce project work in mathematics. She asked her students what topics they were interested in. Several proposals were put forward, but one captured the interest of all the students: they wanted to work with surfing and surfboards. The teacher, however, was dubious. She did not consider this topic would provide any relevant possibilities. The school after all was located in a poor neighborhood, and Rio Claro is far from the sea. Most likely the students would never have been to the beach and never have seen the ocean. How could working with surfing make any sense to them? If one relates meaning first of all to the students already-established experiences and to their backgrounds, surfing seems to make no sense—it is without "real" meaning. However, meaningfulness might also be related to the students' foregrounds, to their hopes and aspirations. Considering their possible horizons, elaborating a project about surfing could become extremely meaningful.

Exploring the properties of a triangle and considering the mathematics of surfing may indeed be meaningful to many children, as the experience of meaning has much to do with features of the horizon of students' life-worlds, their foregrounds. Contested notions like foreground and meaning might encourage pedagogical imagination to consider the construction of possibilities for students and together with students.[12] Such constructions concern the students' horizons. They have to do with possibilities that intentions for learning could be directed towards, and in this way provide meaning for the students' activities. Thus one might identify a fruitful route for pedagogical imagination along the sequence of concepts: democracy, possibility, horizons of life-worlds, foregrounds, and meaning.

AN OPEN LANDSCAPE

The Modern Outlook provided one framing of the discussion of mathematics education and democracy. Within the grand narratives of Modernity, democracy included a range of intrinsic good qualities due to the assumed "essence" of democracy. This framing stipulated a harmony between educational processes and democratic ideals. More generally, it outlined the exist-ence of an overall harmony between scientific thinking, mathematical rationality, technological development, educational processes, and social progress in general.

If we, however, acknowledge an aporetic condition, we cannot assume any such harmony. We cannot assume that notions such as social justice, equality, and freedom maintain certain universal qualities. We cannot assume that democracy is a transparent notion; instead it could be filled with ambiguities. In general, we recognize democracy as well as its extended family of related notions as being contested: they can be related to very many different, and also contra-dictory, interests and priorities.

This does not mean, however, that we should try to leave aside such notions. They have important roles to play. Although they cannot provide universal justifications of educational projects such as "mathematics education for social justice," "inclusive mathematics educa-tion," or "mathematics education for democracy," they can provide resources for pedagogical imagination. Contested concepts might help formulate new educational possibilities. As a con-sequence, we consider "mathematics education for democracy" to be an open landscape filled with tensions, uncertainties, and challenges.

ACKNOWLEDGMENTS

To some extent this text draws on Skovsmose and Penteado (2012), and we thank the edi-tors for permission to do so. We also want to thank Peter Gates, Denival Biotto Filho, Renato Marcone, Lessandra Marcelly Silva, and Guilherme Gomes da Silva for their many helpful comments and suggestions.

NOTES

1. For a discussion of the notion of progress, see Bury (1932/1955) and Nisbet (1980).
2. A fascinated study of the intimate relationship between linguistic studies and a racist outlook is found in Bernal (1987).
3. The notion of "essentially contested concept" has been discussed in Gallie, (1956), while the also related notion of "explosive concepts" has been discussed in Skovsmose (2005).
4. In Ancient Greek, *aporia* could refer to "a question for discussion," "a difficulty" or "a puzzle." The origin of the word is *a-poria*, which means "without *poria*," which means. "without direction." The dialogues of the younger Plato are often characterized as aporetic. Here conflicting interpretations of a philosophic issue are presented, but the very conflict remains unsolved. For a discussion of aporia, see Part 3 in Skovsmose (2005).
5. In Aguilar and Zavaleta (2012) one finds a comprehensive review of literature concerning mathemat-ics education and democracy. See also Brijlall, Bansilal, and Moore-Russo (2012), Daher (2012), Khuzwayo and Bansilal (2012), Orrill (2001), Skovsmose (1990, 1998), Skovsmose and Valero (2001, 2002), Skovsmose and Penteado (2012), Vithal (2010, 2012), Vithal and Skovsmose (2012), Tate (1996), and Woodrow (1997).
6. An important presentation of this area is found in Mellin-Olsen (1987). Profound explorations of politics of mathematics education are found in Powell and Frankenstein (Eds.) (1997), Gutstein (2012b), Valero (2002), and Vithal (2003). See also Skovsmose and Greer (eds.), (2012), which has the subtitle "Critique and Politics of Mathematics Education." Further studies are found in, for instance, Alrø, Ravn, and Valero (2010), Appelbaum (1995), Johnston and Yasukawa (2001), Martin (2009), Pais (2012), and Vithal (1999).
7. See, for instance Mehrtens (1993) for a study of mathematics education during the Nazi period in Germany.
8. See, for instance, Skovsmose (2012).
9. See Skovsmose, Valero, and Ravn Christensen (2009) for discussions of university education and Skovsmose (2009b) for a discussion of "critical expertise."
10. In these comments about mathematics in society and technology we have not referred to ethnomath-ematics interpreted as the mathematics of marginalized groups. It is, however, important to reflect on all forms of mathematics. One needs to consider all forms of ethnomathematics in action and the

possible qualities of such actions: Could they be risky, expensive, benevolent, brutal, cynical, efficient, etc.? Could they include "horrors" and well as "wonders"? Our point is that also any form of ethno-mathematics is subjected to aporetic conditions.

11. See also Penteado and Skovsmose (2009), Skovsmose and Penteado (2011, 2012).

12. The importance of addressing the students' perspective has, also been emphasized by Martin (2009), Mhlolo and Schäfer (2012).

REFERENCES

Alrø, H., Ravn, O., & Valero, P. (Eds.) (2010). *Critical mathematics education: Past, present, and future*. Rotterdam: Sense Publishers.

Aguilar, M.S., & Zavaleta, J.G.M. (2012). On the links between mathematics education and democracy: A literature review. *Pythagoras*, *33*(2). Retrieved from www.pythagoras.org.za/index.php/pythagoras/issue/view/21

Appelbaum, P.M. (1995). *Popular culture, educational discourse, and mathematics*. Albany, NY: State University of New York Press.

Baber, S.A. (2007). *Interplay of citizenship, education and mathematics: Formation of foregrounds of Pakistani immigrants in Denmark*. Unpublished doctoral dissertation. Aalborg: Aalborg University.

Bauman, Z. (1989). *Modernity and the holocaust*. Cambridge, UK: Polity Press & Blackwell Publishing.

Beck, U. (1992). *Risk society*. London: Sage Publications. (First German edition 1986.)

Beck, U. (1999). *World risk society*. Cambridge, UK: Polity Press.

Benn, S.I., & Peters, R.S. (1959). *Social principles of the democratic state*. London: Allen & Unwin.

Bernal, M. (1987). *Black Athena: Afroasiatic roots of classical civilization: Vol. 1. The fabrication of Ancient Greece, 1785–1985*. New Brunswick, NJ: Rutgers University Press.

Bohman, J., & Rehg, W. (Eds.). (1997). *Deliberative democracy: Essays on reason and politics*. Cambridge, MA: The MIT Press.

Brijlall, D., Bansilal, S., & Moore-Russo, D. (2012). Exploring teachers' conceptions of representations in mathematics through the lens of positive deliberative interaction. *Pythagoras*, 33(2). Retrieved from www.pythagoras.org.za/index.php/pythagoras/issue/view/21

Bury, J.B. (1955). *The idea of progress: An inquiry into its origin and growth*. With an introduction by Charles A. Bead. New York: Dover Publications. (First published 1932.)

Castells, M. (1996). *The information age: Economy, society and culture: Vol. 1. The Rise of the Network Society*. Oxford: Blackwell Publishers.

Castells, M. (1997). *The information age: Economy, society and culture: Vol. 2. The Power of Identity)*. Oxford: Blackwell Publishers.

Castells, M. (1998). *The information age: Economy, society and culture: Vol. 3. End of Millennium)*. Oxford: Blackwell Publishers.

Chronaki, A. (2010). Revisiting mathemacy: A process-reading of critical mathematics education. In H. Alrø, O. Ravn, & P. Valero (Eds.), *Critical mathematics education: Past, present and future* (pp. 31–49). Rotterdam: Sense Publishers.

Daher, W. (2012). Student teachers' perceptions of democracy in the mathematics classroom: Freedom, equality and dialogue. *Pythagoras*, *33*(2). Retrieved from www.pythagoras.org.za/index.php/pythagoras/issue/view/21

D'Ambrosio, U. (1994). Cultural framing of mathematics teaching and learning. In R. Biehler, R. W. Scholz, R. Strasser, & B. Winkelmann (Eds.), *Didactics of mathematics as a scientific discipline* (pp. 443–455). Dordrecht: Kluwer.

D'Ambrosio, U. (2006). *Ethnomathematics: Link between transitions and modernity*. Rotterdam: Sense Publishers.

D'Ambrosio, U. (2012). A broad concept of social justice. In A.A. Wager & D.W. Stinson (Eds.), *Teaching mathematics for social justice: Conversations with mathematics educators* (pp. 201–213). Reston, VA: National Council of Mathematics Teachers.

Dewey, J. (1963). *Experience and education*. New York: Macmillan Publishing Company (First edition 1938.)

Dewey, J. (1966). *Democracy and education*. New York: The Free Press (First edition 1916).

Dewey, J. (1974). *On education*. (R. D. Archambault, Ed.) Chicago: The University of Chicago Press.

Forgasz, H., & Rivera, F. (Eds.) (2012). *Towards equity in mathematics education: Gender, culture, and diversity*. New York: Springer.

Foucault, M. (1991). *Discipline and punish: The birth of the prison*. London: Penguin Books. (First French edition 1975.)

Frankenstein, M. (2012). Beyond math content and process: Proposals for underlying aspects of social justice education. In A.A. Wager & D.W. Stinson (Eds.), *Teaching mathematics for social justice:*

Conversations with mathematics educators (pp. 49–62). Reston, VA: National Council of Mathematics Teachers.

Gallie, W. B. (1956). Essentially contested concepts. *Proceedings of the Aristotelian Society, 56,* 167–198.

Gates, P. (2006). The place of equity and social justice in the history of PME. In A. Gutérrez & P. Boero (Eds.), *Handbook of research on the psychology of mathematics education: Past, present and future* (pp. 367–402). Rotterdam: Sense Publishers.

Gellert, U., & Jablonka, E. (2009). The demathematising effect of technology: Calling for critical competence. In P. Ernest, B. Greer, & B. Sriraman (Eds.), *Critical issues in mathematics education* (pp. 19–24). Charlotte, NC: Information Age Publishing.

Gibbons, M., Limoges, C., Nowotny, H., Schwartzman, S., Scott, P., & Trow, M. (1994). *The new production of knowledge: The dynamics of science and research in contemporary societies.* London: Sage Publications.

Greer, B. Mukhopadhyay, S., Powell, A.B., & Nelson-Barber, S. (Eds.) (2009). *Culturally responsive mathematics education.* New York: Routledge.

Gutstein, E. (2003). Teaching and learning mathematics for social justice in an urban, Latino school. *Journal for Research in Mathematics Education, 34,* 37–73.

Gutstein, E. (2006). *Reading and writing the world with mathematics: Toward a pedagogy for social justice.* New York & London: Routledge.

Gutstein, E. (2012a). Reflections on teaching and learning mathematics for social justice in urban schools. In A.A. Wager & D.W. Stinson (Eds.), *Teaching mathematics for social justice: Conversations with mathematics educators* (pp. 63–78). Reston, VA: National Council of Mathematics Teachers.

Gutstein, E. (2012b). Mathematics as a weapon in a struggle. In O. Skovsmose & B. Greer (Eds.), *Opening the cage: Critique and politics of mathematics education* (pp. 23–48). Rotterdam: Sense Publishers.

Hannaford, C. (1998). Mathematics teaching is democratic education. *ZDM: The International Journal on Mathematics Education, 98*(6), 181–187.

Healy, L., & Fernandes, S.H.A.A. (2011). The role of gestures in the mathematical practices of those who do not see with their eyes. *Educational Studies in Mathematics, 77,* 157–174.

Husserl, E. (1970). *The crisis of European sciences and transcendental phenomenology.* (D. Car, Trans.) Evanston, IL: Northwestern University Press. (First German version 1936.)

Jablonka, E. (2010). Reflections on mathematical modelling. In H. Alrø, O. Ravn, & P. Valero (Eds.), *Critical mathematics education: Past, present and future* (pp. 89–100). Rotterdam: Sense Publisher.

Jablonka, E., & Gellert, U. (2007). Mathematisation—demathematisation. In U. Gellert & E. Jablonka (Eds.), *Mathematization and de-mathematization: Social, philosophical and educational ramifications* (pp. 1–18). Rotterdam: Sense Publishers.

Johnston, B., & Yasukawa, K. (2001). *Numeracy: Negotiating the world through mathematics.* In B. Atweh, H. Forgasz, & B. Nebres (Eds.), *Sociocultural research on mathematics education* (pp. 279–294). Mahwah, NJ: Lawrence Erlbaum Associates.

Khuzwayo, H.B., & Bansilal, S. (2012). Granting learners an authentic voice in the mathematics classroom for the benefit of both the teacher and the learner. *Pythagoras, 33*(2). Retrieved from www.pythagoras.org.za/index.php/pythagoras/issue/view/21

Locke, J. (1988). *Two treatises of government.* (P. Laslett, Ed.). Cambridge, UK: Cambridge University Press. (First published 1689.)

Lyotard, J. F. (1984). *The postmodern condition: A report on knowledge.* (G. Bennington & B. Massuni, Trans.) Manchester: Manchester University Press. (Original French edition 1979.)

Marcone, R., & Penteado, M.G. (2013).Teaching mathematics for blind students: A challenge at university. *International Journal for Research in Mathematics Education, 3,* 23–35.

Martin, D.B. (2009). *Mathematics teaching, learning, and liberation in the lives of black children.* New York: Routledge.

Mehrtens, H. (1993). The social system of mathematics and National Socialism: A survey. In S. Restivo, J.P. van Bendegem, & R. Fisher, R. (Eds.), *Math worlds: Philosophical and social studies of mathematics and mathematics education* (pp. 219–246). Albany, NY: State University of New York Press.

Mellin-Olsen, S. (1987). *The politics of mathematics education.* Dordrecht, The Netherlands: Reidel Publishing Company.

Mhlolo, M.K., & Schäfer, M. (2012). Towards empowering learners in a democratic mathematics classroom: To what extent are teachers' listening orientations conducive to and respectful of learners' thinking? *Pythagoras, 33*(2). Retrieved from www.pythagoras.org.za/index.php/pythagoras/issue/view/21

Nisbet, R.A. (1980). History of the idea of progress. New York: Basic Books.

Orrill, R. (2001). Mathematics, numeracy, and democracy. In L. A. Steen (Ed.), *Mathematics and democracy. The case for quantitative literacy* (pp. 8–20). Princeton, NJ: The National Council on Education and the Disciplines & The Woodrow Wilson National Fellowship Foundation.

Pais, A. (2012). A critical approach to equity. In O. Skovsmose & B. Greer (Eds.), *Opening the cage: Critique and politics of mathematics education* (pp. 49–92). Rotterdam: Sense Publishers.

Penteado, M.G., & Skovsmose, O. (2009). How to draw with a worn-out mouse? Searching for social justice through collaboration. *Journal for Mathematics Teacher Education, 12*(3), 217–230.

Powell, A.B., & Frankenstein, M. (Eds.). (1997). *Ethnomathematics: Challenging Eurocentrism in mathematics education*. Albany, NY: State University of New York Press.

Rawls, J. (1999). *A theory of justice*. Oxford: Oxford University Press. (First published 1971.)

Rousseau, J. J. (1968). *The social contract*. London: Penguin Books (First French edition 1762.)

Said, E.W. (1979). *Orientalism*. New York: Vintage Books.

Skovsmose, O. (1990). Mathematical education and democracy. *Educational Studies in Mathematics, 21*, 109–128.

Skovsmose, O. (1998). Linking mathematics education and democracy: Citizenship, mathematics archaeology, mathemacy and deliberative interaction. *ZDM: The International Journal on Mathematics Education, 98*(6), 195–203.

Skovsmose, O. (2005). *Travelling through education: Uncertainty, mathematics, responsibility*. Rotterdam: Sense Publishers.

Skovsmose, O. (2009a). Researching possibilities. In M. Setati, R. Vithal, C. Malcolm, & R. Dhunpath (Eds.), *Researching possibilities in mathematics, science and technology education* (pp. 105–119). New York: Nova Science Publishers.

Skovsmose, O. (2009b). Towards a critical professionalism in university science and mathematics education. In O. Skovsmose, P. Valero, & O. Ravn Christensen (Eds.), *University sciences and mathematics education in transition* (pp. 325–346). New York: Springer.

Skovsmose, O. (2012). Symbolic power, robotting, and surveilling. *Educational Studies in Mathematics, 80*(1), 119–132.

Skovsmose, O. (2014). *Foregrounds*. Rotterdam: Sense Publishers.

Skovsmose, O., & Greer, B. (Eds.) (2012). *Opening the cage: Critique and politics of mathematics education*. Rotterdam: Sense Publishers.

Skovsmose, O., & Penteado, M.G. (2011). Ghettoes in the classroom and the construction of possibilities. In B. Atweh, M. Graven, W. Secada, & P. Valero. (eds.), *Mapping equity and quality in mathematics education* (pp. 77–90). New York: Springer.

Skovsmose, O., & Penteado, M.G. (2012). Mathematics education and democracy: An on-going challenge. In S. Kafoussi, C. Skoumpourdi & F. Kalavasis (Eds.), *International Journal for Mathematics in Education, 4*, 15–29.

Skovsmose, O., & Valero, P. (2001). Breaking political neutrality: The critical engagement of mathematics education with democracy. In B. Atweh, H. Forgasz, & B. Nebres (Eds.), *Sociocultural research on mathematics education* (pp. 37–55). Mahwah, NJ, & London: Lawrence Erlbaum Associates.

Skovsmose, O., & Valero, P. (2002). Democratic access to powerful mathematical ideas. In L. English (Ed.), *Handbook of international research in mathematics education* (pp. 383–407). Mahwah, NJ: Lawrence Erlbaum Associates.

Skovsmose, O., Valero, P., & Ravn Christensen, O. (Eds.) (2009). *University sciences and mathematics education in transition*. New York: Springer.

Sriraman, B. (Ed.) (2008). *The Montana Mathematics Enthusiast: Monograph 1. International perspectives on social justice in mathematics education*. Charlotte, NC: Information Age Publishing, Inc.

Swanson, D., & Appelbaum, P. (2012). Refusal as a democratic catalyst for mathematics education development, *Pythagoras, 33*(2). Retrieved from www.pythagoras.org.za/index.php/pythagoras/issue/view/21

Tate, W.F. (1996). Mathematizing and the democracy: The need for an education that is multicultural and social reconstructionist. In C.A. Grant & M.L. Gómez (Eds.), *Making schooling multicultural: Campus and classroom* (pp. 185–201). Englewood Cliffs, NJ: Prentice Hall.

Valero, P. (2002). *Reform, democracy, and mathematics education: Towards a socio-political frame for understanding change in the organization of secondary school mathematics*. Unpublished doctoral dissertation. Department of Curriculum Research, The Danish University of Education, Copenhagen.

Valero, P., García, G., Camelo, F., Mancera, G., & Romero, J. (2012). Mathematics education and the dignity of being. *Pythagoras, 33*(2). Retrieved from www.pythagoras.org.za/index.php/pythagoras/issue/view/21

Vithal, R. (1999). Democracy and authority: A complementarity in Mathematics Education? *ZDM: The International Journal on Mathematics Education, 99*(1), 27–36.

Vithal, R. (2003). *In search of a pedagogy of conflict and dialogue for mathematics education*. Dordrecht: Kluwer Academic Publishers.

Vithal, R. (2009). Researching, and learning mathematics at the margin: From "shelter" to school. In P. Ernest, B. Greer, & B. Sriraman (Eds.), *Critical issues in mathematics education* (pp. 475–484). Charlotte, NC: Information Age Publishing.

Vithal R. (2010). Democratising mathematics education doctoral research teaching and learning: Undoing the North-South divide. In H. Alrø, O. Ravn, & P. Valero, P. (Eds.), *Critical mathematics education: Past, present and future* (pp. 197–207). Rotterdam: Sense Publisher.

Vithal, R. (2012). Mathematics education, democracy and development: Exploring connections. *Pythagoras, 33*(2). Retrieved from www.pythagoras.org.za/index.php/pythagoras/issue/view/21.

Vithal, R. & Skovsmose, O. (Eds.) (2012). Mathematics education, democracy and development. *Pythagoras, 33*(2). Retrieved from www.pythagoras.org.za/index.php/pythagoras/issue/view/21.

Volmink, J. (1994). Mathematics by all. In S. Lerman (Ed.), *Cultural perspectives on the mathematics classroom* (pp. 51–68). Dordrecht, The Netherlands: Kluwer Academic Publishers.

Wager, A.A., & Stinson, D.W. (Eds.) (2012). *Teaching mathematics for social justice: Conversations with mathematics educators*. Reston, VA: National Council of Mathematics Teachers.

Woodrow, D. (1997). Democratic education: Does it exist—especially for mathematics education? *For the Learning of Mathematics, 17*(3), 11–16.

Wright-Mills, C. (1959). *The sociological imagination*. Oxford: Oxford University Press.

15 Toward a Sociology of Mathematics Education

Examining Democratic Access in U.S. Schools

Celia Rousseau Anderson

University of Memphis

William F. Tate

Washington University in St. Louis

> Historically, research in mathematics education has been more closely aligned with the scientific research movement. . . . The traditional paradigmatic boundaries of mathematics education are drawn from two fields of study—mathematics and psychology. . . . Most discussions related to "democratic access" are limited to a focus on classrooms, and more specifically, individual student cognition.
>
> (Tate & Rousseau, 2002, p. 273)

In a previous edition of this *Handbook*, we observed that the focus of research on equity or democratic access had, to that point, been on classrooms and individual students within those classrooms (Tate & Rousseau, 2002). We also pointed to the paradigmatic foundations of much of mathematics education research—mathematics and psychology. Since that time, research on equity and democratic access has begun to expand beyond the walls of the classroom and beyond the psychological focus of earlier scholarship. In this edition of the *Handbook*, we take a new look at the existing research and recent trends related to democratic access and propose future directions that would expand further the paradigmatic boundaries of mathematics education.

As we have in previous editions of this *Handbook*, we focused our review and analysis in this chapter on social science studies conducted to better understand mathematics education in the United States (Rousseau-Anderson & Tate, 2008; Tate & Rousseau, 2002). While there are certainly similarities in the schooling conditions of various countries, we make no claim that our review is global in nature. In fact, one of the fundamental arguments that we make in this chapter is the necessity to examine issues of democratic access with an eye on the context. For this reason, we have chosen to focus on democratic access in U.S. schools.

To illustrate the importance of context, we offer a specific case within a U.S. school. The case was part of a larger study conducted by one of the authors. We use this vignette to set the stage for the discussion of the recent research and to explore a framework for equity scholarship in mathematics education. We will revisit the vignette at various points throughout the chapter.

It is important to note at the outset that this vignette is situated in a specific context that we describe as "urban." Moreover, we also make repeated reference throughout the chapter to research related to the conditions of urban schools. Because scholars use the descriptor "urban" in many different ways, we seek here to clarify our use of the term. In the *Handbook of Urban Education* (Milner & Lomotey, 2014), the editors outline three of the primary ways used by contributors to frame "urban" education: the size of the city, the students in the schools, and the resources available to schools. While these three aspects of urban education are related, we use "urban" in this chapter in a manner consistent with the first approach—as a descriptor of a city environment, reflecting a dense, large, metropolitan area. Like Milner (2012), we acknowledge that even within this framing of "urban," there are different realities for schools that are related to the size, history, and resources of the city. It is, in fact, the contextual significance of the school's location that is the focus of this chapter. We concur with Small's (2014) argument that "differences among cities matter . . . To ignore heterogeneity for the sake of simplification is to favor convenience over common sense, to risk having a search for a single archetype slip our thinking into stereotype" (para 21 and 22). Whether urban or non-urban, we assert that the issue of "place" is important for understanding opportunity to learn in mathematics education. Using the following vignette, we seek to illustrate how the specific urban setting potentially shapes mathematics teaching at this school.

URBAN MIDDLE SCHOOL: CLASSROOM VIGNETTE

There were 16 students in the classroom: 14 African American students and 2 Latino students. There were nine girls and seven boys. The students were arranged into groups of four and were completing a worksheet. The worksheet included two tables that the students were to fill in with the numbers of vertices, faces, and edges of prisms and pyramids. The students also had a reference sheet with drawings of prisms and pyramids.

As the activity progressed, several students raised their hands to ask questions of the teacher. In most cases, an individual student asked the teacher a question and the teacher responded directly to that individual, while the other students in the same small group continued working on the task. After getting the same question from multiple students, the teacher made an announcement to the entire class, "Remember that I told you not to do questions three and six. Mark those off on your paper." The two questions that the teacher eliminated asked the students to use the cases they had recorded to make a generalization about the relationships between the vertices, faces, and edges of any prism or pyramid.

As students finished the task, several conferred with others sitting next to them to compare answers. Once students were confident that they had completed the task, they took out other assignments, often from a different class (e.g., several students pulled out novels assigned for an English class). Students in the same group did not necessarily finish the task at the same time. A few students were still working when the teacher announced that class was ending. She instructed the students to turn in their worksheets and told them that they would discuss the activity the next day. As the class ended, she said, "One thing I noticed is that many of you are still getting mixed up on the difference between vertices, faces, and edges. And some of you are not clear on the difference between a prism and a pyramid. We will go back over that tomorrow."

An interview with the teacher after the lesson revealed that she decided to omit the generalization questions because she believed that they would be too difficult for her students. She said that the students would either not know how to respond to the questions or would become frustrated and give up. For this reason, she believed that it was better to skip these questions. As she explained, her main goal was for the students to identify vertices, faces, and edges and have an idea of what different prisms and pyramids looked like. She thought that this was an appropriate goal for the students in her class. She also noted that the state standardized test included questions that only asked the students to identity whether a figure was a prism or pyramid and the number of vertices, faces, or edges. As a result, she thought it was more appropriate to focus on the content that was included on the test. The students in her classes had not been successful previously on the state standardized test. During the year prior to the observation, only 19% of students in the school tested at a level considered to be "proficient" or "advanced" on the test. This compared with a statewide rate of 47% proficient or advanced for the same year.

One approach to analyzing this classroom episode is to focus on the characteristics of the classroom instruction and the interactions within this classroom. From this perspective, we note immediately that, although the classroom was organized into small groups, there was very little collaboration apparent among the students. Most worked independently within their groupings. Additionally, although the task involved counting the vertices, faces, and edges of polyhedra, the students had only two-dimensional renderings of the prisms and pyramids for reference. An examination of the task itself revealed that the removal of the two generalization questions significantly altered the nature of the task. By removing these questions, the teacher had effectively changed the level of cognitive demand (Stein, Smith, Henningsen, & Silver, 2009) of the task, making it a procedural task involving counting. Additionally, the teacher's comments at the end of class focused on the students' identification of the parts of the polyhedra, rather than their understanding of relationships among these parts.

This "first look" at the classroom has focused on the interactions among students, the nature of the classroom task, and the teacher's statements to the class. If we were to extend this line of inquiry, we might analyze further the interactions within this class session or extend the analysis to other classroom episodes of this teacher. However, as yet, this analysis has not interrogated directly issues of equity or opportunity to learn. In this chapter, we seek to illustrate an approach to the study of equity in mathematics education. We intend to use this vignette to provide examples of the central questions related to the nature of democratic access in this setting.

TOWARD A SOCIOLOGY OF MATHEMATICS EDUCATION[1]

Several scholars have noted the growing attention to equity in mathematics education (Lubienski, 2007). For example, Gutierrez (2013) noted that "'talk' of equity has become more mainstream in the mathematics education community" (p. 2). Our own review of the mathematics education literature for this chapter confirmed that scholarship related to equity appears to have grown significantly since the previous editions of this Handbook were prepared. Moreover, recent research related to equity has pushed the traditional boundaries of mathematics education. According to the National Council of Teachers of Mathematics Research Committee (2005), this expansion was necessary:

> For researchers to contribute more fully to equity, we may need to break with tradition, expand boundaries, and cross into fields outside mathematics education *and* outside education. . . . The complexity of teaching and learning, and its intersection with equity and social justice issues, demands more than the narrow confines that any one field can provide.
>
> (pp. 96–97)

In fact, several authors writing on equity have pointed to the influences of fields beyond mathematics education. For example, in describing the chapters in their book on equity in mathematics classrooms, Nasir and Cobb (2007) note that the contributors employ concepts from a range of fields outside education.

Similarly, a recent Equity Special Issue of the JRME focused on issues of *power* and *identity*. The editors characterized these foci as reflective of the "sociopolitical turn" in mathematics education research. According to Gutierrez (2013), the sociopolitical turn represents the shift in theoretical perspectives that "see knowledge, power, and identity as interwoven and arising from (and constituted within) social discourses" (p. 4). This shift has required that scholars expand beyond traditional boundaries of mathematics education: "Conducting research that highlights the dynamic nature of identity and the production of power in social interactions requires knowing multiple literatures outside the field of mathematics education and finding appropriate ways to draw upon them" (Gutierrez, 2013, p. 21). Gutierrez goes on to argue that scholarship reflecting the sociopolitical turn has come from researchers with one foot in mathematics education and the other foot in a different discipline.

One of the common places for this "other foot" to be found is in sociology (Martin, 2009b, 2011; Nasir & de Royston, 2013; Stinson, 2006). Sociology is one of the primary fields identified as contributing to scholarship representing the sociopolitical turn (Gutierrez, 2013; Nasir & Cobb, 2007; Stinson, 2006; Stinson & Bullock, 2012). Yet, while the need to expand the boundaries of mathematics education has been argued extensively, there is an inherent tension in doing so. Lubienski (2007) identifies this as one of the challenges of doing work that interrogates equity in the classroom. The need to have a foot in two distinct fields can be difficult, as it requires having a simultaneous grounding, both theoretical and methodological, in mathematics education and sociology. However, it is in this intersection that much of the recent research related to equity can be found. Since much of our own research has spanned these two disciplines, we seek in this chapter to explore the intersection of mathematics education and sociology and the ways that this intersection both reflects and expands upon the more recent scholarship on equity in mathematics education.

We must first acknowledge that there is an existing body of scholarship in sociology of mathematics education that has informed scholarship related to equity (Gutierrez, 2013; Gutierrez & Dixon-Roman, 2011). Specifically, scholars have previously outlined characteristics of a perspective on the sociology of mathematics education that attends to social aspects of and influences on mathematics teaching and learning. For example, Dowling (1998) describes his book *The Sociology of Mathematics Education: Mathematical Myth/Pedagogical Texts* as focusing on "the theoretical space . . . concerned with patterns of relationships between individuals and groups and the production and reproduction of these relationships in cultural practices and in action" (p. 1). He further describes this space as an intersection of "social activity theory" and school mathematics.

In addition, Restivo (2007) has also outlined a perspective on the sociology of mathematics education. Specifically, Restivo describes the sociology of mathematics education as the sociology of the mind in relation to mathematics teaching and learning. According to Restivo and Bauchspies (2006), the sociology of mathematics education is "transforming the sociology of mathematics and the sociology of the mind into pedagogical tools for mathematics educators" (p. 198).

Similarly, Mesquita, Restivo, and D'Ambrosio (2011) draw attention to the role of the sociology of mathematics in understanding mathematics education. In particular, they focus on the social life of mathematics to highlight the role of power and culture in establishing the mathematics that is valued. They connect these social processes to mathematics education.

> The sociology of mathematics has had a strong influence on mathematics education. It has revealed the role of informal and non-formal mathematics in formal mathematical practices; it has helped to explore all mathematics as an outcome of interactions among many social facts, including economics and political and cultural acts.
>
> (p. 53)

Thus, although they do not outline a sociology of mathematics education per se, Mesquita and her colleagues connect the sociology of mathematics to the structure of mathematics education, highlighting the importance of taking a sociological perspective.

While acknowledging the existing scholarship on the sociology of mathematics education, our approach to conceptualizing the integration of sociology and mathematics education differs in some ways from the work described previously. In part, this difference is likely due to the site of origin. We conceive of a sociology of mathematics education that would reflect the application of the sociology of education to mathematics education. In contrast to drawing from sociology of mathematics or sociology in general, this approach would build on the existing research from sociology of education that focuses on equity and access. We believe that grounding a sociology of mathematics education in this manner would allow researchers to more effectively build upon the theoretical perspectives and methodologies that have been utilized within sociology of education and create a more robust framework for examining issues of equity and access in school mathematics.

Sociology of education as a subfield of sociology is dedicated largely to the study of how formal schooling influences individuals and the ways society affects education (both formal and informal). Four major questions that drive research in the sociology of education are as follows:

1.   How does education socialize?
2.   What role does education serve in credentialing?
3.   How do various entities in society influence education?
4.   What role does education play in creating and maintaining social inequality?

In the following sections, we examine each of these questions with regard to research in mathematics education. In this way, we seek to outline what a sociology of mathematics education could look like and how it builds on existing scholarship.

SOCIALIZATION

One direction of recent research related to equity and democratic access can be seen in the 2013 Special Equity Issue of the JRME. In describing the focus of the issue, the members of the editorial panel note that they took a particular approach to equity by seeking work that "highlighted how identity and power play out in mathematics teaching and learning in schools and in broader policies and practices of mathematics education" (D'Ambrosio et al., 2013, p. 5). This focus on identity and power reflects prominent themes of recent scholarship related to equity and democratic access. Moreover, this focus also reflects the socialization processes of mathematics education. In other words, this scholarship addresses the question: How does mathematics education socialize?

The attention to power in recent mathematics education scholarship provides evidence of shifts in the theoretical perspectives and disciplinary orientations of researchers who focus on equity. Moving from the psychological and classroom-focused orientation of earlier work, more recent research has begun to explore the ways that larger social discourses and relations shape the socialization of students and teachers within mathematics. In particular, several scholars have offered a poststructural perspective on power, drawing on the work of Foucault (Stinson, 2013; Valero, 2007; Walshaw, 2013). For example, Valero (2007) describes power as distributed in social relations and happening through "the everyday participation of actors in social practices, in the creation of their meaning, and in the constitution of their associated practices" (p. 226). Similarly, Walshaw (2013) asserts that power is constituted in discourse "structuring collective life and shaping individual identity" (p. 102). These conceptions draw attention to "the microphysics of power in mathematics education practices" (Valero, 2007) and demand consideration of structures operating both in and out of schools (Nasir & Cobb, 2007).

One example of a poststructural perspective on power can be seen in Walshaw's (2013) examination of the experiences of a secondary school student and a preservice teacher. Specifically, her analysis considers the operation of governance and agency (or lack thereof) in their experiences. She argues that this approach sheds light onto the ways through which "power insinuates itself into the discourses and practices of school and classroom life" (p. 116). In other words, this research reflects the ways that power operates to socialize both students and teachers.

In addition, as indicated in the focus of the JRME Special Issue, a significant portion of the recent research related to power in mathematics education has simultaneously focused on the development of identity. According to Martin (2006),

> Mathematics identity refers to the dispositions and deeply held beliefs that individuals develop, within their overall self-concept, about their ability to participate and perform effectively in mathematical contexts and to use mathematics to change the conditions of their lives. A mathematics identity encompasses a person's self-understanding of himself or herself in the context of doing mathematics. It also encompasses how others 'construct' us in relation to mathematics.
>
> (p. 206)

In this way, the study of mathematics identity overlaps with the discussion of power in mathematics education. Researchers with a focus on identity "view the math classroom as both a space where students develop a sense of themselves as doers and learners of math and where broader issues of power and access play out in fundamental ways" (Nasir, Hand, & Taylor, 2008, p. 206). Mathematics instruction is viewed simultaneously as shaping students' understanding of the social and socio-mathematical norms (Yackel & Cobb, 1996) involved in learning mathematics as well as influencing students' understandings of themselves as mathematics learners (Martin, 2006).

For example, Varelas, Martin, and Kane (2012) highlight this simultaneous influence through a framework that focuses on the interplay between content learning and identity instruction. They assert that "integrally connected and intertwined with content learning (CL) is identity construction (IC)—how children see themselves and how others see them vis-à-vis disciplinary knowledge and practices" (p. 323). In describing emerging research on African American students, they note that mathematics identities are "strong correlates" of mathematics success or failure. Moreover, they cite the significance of teachers' classroom practices in shaping students' identities. One example of this influence can be seen in Berry's (2008) study of successful African American males in mathematics. One of the key findings of his research involved the significance of identity. According to Berry, each of the themes that emerged from his research involved "identity-shaping experiences that describe how these boys shape their understandings of and persistence with mathematics" (p. 477). This attention to identity is one example of more recent trends in equity research in mathematics education.

Berry's study is also an example of the intersection between emerging research on identity and a concomitant focus on race. According to Martin (2009a), a small number of scholars "have begun to examine issues pertaining to the co-construction of mathematics identity and racial identity so as to better understand the mathematical experiences, particularly success of African American learners through their own voices" (p. 28). Similarly, in their review of research on culture in mathematics, Nasir et al. (2008) cite a focus on racialized identities in mathematics classes as one of three lenses that researchers have used to understand culture and math learning.

For example, like Berry, Stinson (2013) examined the experiences of successful African American male students. In the study, he considers the ways through which the "discourses" from the larger sociocultural context interacted with the identity formation of the students. He argues, in fact, that the participants' mathematics identities "cannot be fully understood in their complexities decontextualized from how these young men negotiated some of the broader unjust sociocultural discourses that surround African American male adolescents" (p. 87). In this way, the identity formation process has both classroom-based influences (through instruction) as well as larger societal influences related to race and racial discourses.

The importance of understanding identity development as a process that involves experiences and discourses from within schools and the larger culture is also highlighted in Nasir and de Royston's (2013) work. In their analysis of the experiences of African American students, they note the differing value placed on students' cultural capital depending on their context and point to the role of power in this valuation. According to the authors, their analyses "illustrated that race and identity are an important part of understanding the access to cultural practices and the types of capital expressed and taken up within them" (Nasir & de Royston, 2013, p. 283). They further argue that understanding the ways that power operates through the ascription of value to particular cultural practices is an important direction for mathematics education research.

In a similar manner, Nasir and Shah (2011) have examined the ways that "racialized narratives" shape students experiences. In particular, they identify these racial narratives as "cultural artifacts" and describe how these narratives shape students' perceptions of self as well as their positioning of other students'. According to Nasir and Shah, "racialized narratives about students' intellectual and mathematical abilities play a central role in processes of positioning and identification" (p. 27). They assert that understanding these narratives and how they play out in schools and classrooms is critical for making sense of African American students' mathematical identities and engagement.

The more recent focus on the racialized experiences of African American students in mathematics is also reflected in edited volumes dedicated to this topic (e.g. Leonard & Martin, 2013; Martin, 2009a). Several chapters within these volumes focused specifically on mathematics socialization. For example, Jackson's (2009) chapter from the edited volume *Mathematics Teaching, Learning, and Liberation in the Lives of Black Children* describes the instructional practices of a middle-school mathematics teacher and the role of these practices in the socialization of two African American students. Jackson also interrogates the ways that larger discourses about students shape what happens in the classroom. According to Jackson, the teacher's classroom "as all classrooms, was a nexus of discourses about youth, about mathematics, and about pedagogy. The local practices were influenced by discourses about poor children of color and mathematics that circulated outside of [the school]" (p. 195). The study provides insight into the interactions of the local context in shaping teachers' expectations and, subsequently, students' experiences.

Each of these recent areas of focus within equity research in mathematics education (power, identity, and race) represents a piece of the puzzle with regard to addressing the question: How does mathematics education socialize? Yet, as we seek to illustrate in the next sections, the factors associated with the socialization function cannot be separated from the other questions that frame a sociology of mathematics education. For example, studies related to identity (e.g., Jackson, 2009; Stinson, 2013) have pointed to the role of society and larger sociocultural discourses in shaping the socialization process. These results point us back to questions related to the influence of society and the creation of inequality. Thus, the questions that we use to frame the sociology of mathematics education are interconnected and cannot be fully addressed in isolation. However, before exploring the other questions that comprise the framework, we return briefly to the opening vignette.

Vignette Revisited: How Does Mathematics Education Socialize?

To illustrate further the nature of the more recent research and the ways that it expands beyond prior views of mathematics teaching and learning, we return to the vignette described at the beginning of this chapter. Previously, we described one way to approach the analysis of the observed classroom—an analysis that focused on issues of teacher instructional practices, task selection, and student interaction. Certainly, such an analysis is crucial in understanding the nature of mathematics instruction. Research on equity in mathematics education has expanded to consider additional aspects of mathematics teaching and learning. For example, one approach to understanding student learning and equity in the vignette classroom could involve an examination of student identity. Consistent with research by Stinson (2013) and

Berry (2008), we might focus on successful students within this mathematics classroom and seek to understand the ways that their mathematics identity is shaped by factors both within the school and within the larger society, including the ways that race and racial discourses influence identity development. This attention to race might also involve an investigation of the role of race in shaping instruction. For example, like Jackson (2009), we could examine the role of race and racial discourses in shaping the teacher's beliefs and expectations. Why did the teacher view her students as unable or unwilling to complete the "hard" questions on the polyhedra task? What is the role of race and the larger racial discourse in shaping these expectations? And how did the low achievement of the school shape these expectations? Moreover, the achievement level of the school might also interact with issues of power and agency. Given the accountability in this context, what level of surveillance did the teacher experience with regard to the curriculum? How did that surveillance shape her teaching practice or sense of agency with regard to the curriculum? These are but a few of the questions that we might seek to answer about the socialization processes that are operational in this context.

CREDENTIALING

In addition to its socialization function, mathematics education also serves in credentialing. Our chapter in the previous edition of this *Handbook* (Rousseau-Anderson & Tate, 2008) explored the differential credentialing opportunities for both students and teachers in U.S. schools. In the chapter entitled, "Still Separate, Still Unequal: Democratic Access to Mathematics in U.S. Schools," we examined several different "levels" of inequity in mathematics education, including differential access to coursework and teacher quality. Students' access to specific coursework and teachers' levels of preparation reflect the credentialing function of mathematics education. In this chapter, we describe recent research as well as shifts in the landscape with regard to the credentialing function of mathematics education.

College-preparatory courses in mathematics serve a credentialing function for students, indicating which students have the academic preparation for success in postsecondary mathematics. As a result, examining access to such courses (and the credentials they offer) is crucial from an equity perspective. In the previous edition of this *Handbook*, we reviewed several studies that demonstrated that predominantly minority schools are less likely to provide access to college preparatory courses than schools with majority White populations. This differential access applied to courses at several different levels of mathematics: early Algebra I (in eighth grade), advanced mathematics courses beyond Algebra II in high school, and Advanced Placement courses in high school that offer college credit. In general, these studies revealed that schools with higher proportions of students of color and low-income students offered fewer of the courses that serve to credential a student as being on a college-bound trajectory (Rousseau-Anderson & Tate, 2008).

One approach to addressing credentialing differences involves reducing access to lower-level courses and ensuring that more students take higher-level courses. As we outlined in an earlier edition of this *Handbook*, past research has suggested that constraining the curriculum in this manner is part of creating more equitable opportunities (Tate & Rousseau, 2002). Yet, much of this research has utilized large-scale, national data sets or smaller case studies of schools to compare schools that offer different levels of access to credentialing courses. What happens when the goal of a more constrained curriculum is applied as a universal policy?

Allensworth, Nomi, Montgomery, and Lee (2009) examined the implementation of a mandated college preparatory curriculum in Chicago. The policy established ninth grade Algebra I as a requirement, effectively eliminating lower-level remedial mathematics courses. The study by Allensworth and her colleagues explored the effects of this universal mandate in Chicago Public Schools. The results of their study indicate that, at least at one level, the policy was successful in equalizing opportunities for the credential represented in Algebra I. Once implemented, the policy eliminated racial disparities in Algebra I enrollment that existed prior to the curriculum change. Additionally, students in all ability groups were more likely to earn an Algebra I credit by the end of ninth grade, a credential that students in the lower-level ability groups had been denied previously.

However, the results also indicated that simply mandating a constrained curriculum might not be an effective means to achieve the goals of promoting access to advanced mathematics and further credentialing. Despite the improved access to ninth grade Algebra I, students were no more likely to obtain credits in upper-level mathematics or attend a four-year college (Allensworth et al., 2009). According to Allensworth and her colleagues, "most of the benefits of the 'College Prep for All' policy suggested by the extant research were unrealized" (p. 383). The effort to improve the credentialing of students in mathematics through constraining the curriculum met with limited success. While the researchers suggested several potential reasons for the limited impact, one of the issues that they raised involves the preparation of teachers and the quality (as opposed to the content) of instruction. The policy implemented in Chicago addressed initially the content of instruction without intervening on the quality by providing additional professional development for teachers.

Another approach to eliminating the problem of access to higher mathematics education credentials is to raise state-mandated math graduation requirements. Since the release of recommendations found in *A Nation at Risk* (National Commission on Excellence in Education, 1983), there has been a near-universal commitment at the state level to demand more mathematics and science content of all high school students in the United States. To achieve this goal states have increased their course graduation requirements (CGR) for the high school diploma. Raising CGRs is thought to improve the intellectual preparedness of graduates for postsecondary education. Very little attention has been paid to the intended and unintended consequences of this policy strategy on the credentialing function of schools. Plunk, Tate, Bierut, and Grucza (2014) examined the effects of raising mathematics and science CGRs in 44 states on high school students' rates of school dropout, beginning college, and obtaining any college degree. Using logistic regression with Census and American Community Survey data ($n = 2,892,444$), they found that high school dropout rates increased as states mandated more math and science CGRs, reaching 11.41% when students were required to take six math and science requirements, compared to 8.6% for students without a requirement. Results also varied by gender and race, with the dropout rate for some demographic groups increasing by as much as five percentage points. Their research suggests that many schools were ill-prepared to support students for the tougher mandated graduation standards. In addition, for students exposed to higher math and science graduation requirements who do graduate, there was no across-the-board increase in college enrollment or college degree attainment. Differences in subgroups based on sex and race/ethnicity included higher CGRs being associated with a decrease in the likelihood of Black women and Hispanic men and women enrolling in college after graduating from high school. However, higher CGRs were associated with an increase in the likelihood that Hispanics and nonmigrant[2] Black women who enrolled in college would earn a degree.

Plunk et al. (2014) argued that the negative effect of increasing math and science CGRs on high school dropout patterns extends beyond the credentialing function. For example, Lochner and Moretti (2001) estimated that a 1% reduction in the national high school dropout rate would have resulted in 400 fewer murders and 8,000 fewer assaults, and that a 1% reduction for all men ages 20–60 would save the United States as much as $1.4 billion per year in reduced costs from crime incurred by victims and society at large. These cost-benefit estimates highlight the relevance of the math and science CGR effect on high school dropout. In addition, Carnevale, Rose, and Cheah (2011) estimated that over a 40-year career, earning a high school diploma adds 33% more to lifetime earnings, which translates to almost $9,000 per year. There is a significant economic penalty for individuals who do not complete high school. Thus, student credentialing matters because there are individual and societal consequences.

Moreover, the importance of credentialing also extends to teachers. The preparation and credentialing of teachers have been demonstrated as a critical predictor of student achievement and learning. It is also one of the key factors in any examination of equity and democratic access. "In the United States, teachers are the most inequitably distributed school resource" (Darling-Hammond, 2010, p. 40). As we outlined in the previous edition of this *Handbook*, teacher quality in U.S. schools varies greatly by the students served. Students of color and students from low-income backgrounds are more likely to have less-qualified teachers, as measured by certification status, degree, and teaching experience (Rousseau-Anderson & Tate, 2008). Moreover, these differences in teacher quality are related to differences in achievement. According to Darling-Hammond (2010), "studies have found that, at the school, district, and even state levels, the proportion of teachers who are inexperienced, underprepared, or uncertified has a significant negative effect on student achievement after controlling for student characteristics like poverty and language background" (p. 49). Thus, the issue of teacher credentialing is crucial for any understanding of the nature of inequity in U.S. schools. In order to better understand issues related to teacher credentialing, we examine research related to teacher shortages, teacher turnover, and alternative pathways to teaching.

According to Ingersoll and Perda (2009), "contemporary educational thought holds that one of the pivotal causes of inadequate school performance is the inability of schools to adequately staff classrooms with qualified teachers, especially in fields such as mathematics and science" (p. 1). They note that primary causes commonly associated with this shortage are teacher retirement and inadequate production of new teachers. However, in a study of national data on teacher staffing, they found that, while the perception of a shortage was accurate, the reasons behind the shortage were inconsistent with the conventional wisdom. Of the school subjects included in the study, mathematics experienced the most serious hiring and recruitment problems (Ingersoll & Perda, 2009). The results indicated that 54% of secondary schools had job openings for mathematics teachers and about 41% of these indicated serious difficulties filling these openings. In other words, 22% of all secondary schools in the national sample had difficulties filling mathematics positions with qualified teachers. The researchers also found that, contrary to popular belief, the reasons for this shortage were not an inadequate production of new teachers to keep pace with retirements. Even in mathematics, the number of new teachers produced from teacher preparation programs exceeded retirements. Rather, the shortage appeared to occur when preretirement turnover was taken into account. Specifically, new teacher production does not keep pace with the number of teachers leaving before retirement. "Turnover is a major factor behind the problems that many schools have staffing their classrooms with qualified mathematics, science, and other teachers" (Ingersoll & Merrill, 2013 p. 23).

Moreover, the turnover is not equitably distributed across states, districts, or schools within districts. According to Ingersoll and Merrill (2013), 45% of teacher turnover of all public schools in 2004–2005 took place in just 25% of schools. High-poverty, high-minority, urban, and rural schools had the highest rates of turnover. Similar results on the distribution of teacher turnover have been found in other studies. For example, in a study by Frankenberg (2006) of over 1,000 teachers, 61% of teachers in schools with the lowest shares of Black and Latino students reported that they are not at all likely to leave teaching in the next few years, while less than half (40%) of teachers in high-minority schools expressed similar confidence that they will be teaching in three years. Similarly, in a study of Georgia public schools, Freeman, Scafidi, and Sjoquist (2005) found that teacher turnover (specifically, White teacher turnover) was much greater in schools with higher percentages of Black students.

Why are higher rates of teacher turnover in high-minority and high-poverty schools an equity concern? In part, the unequal distribution of teacher turnover is a concern due to its relationship to teacher experience. Given the association between teacher experience and achievement (Fetler, 1999), the higher levels of teacher turnover and lower levels of teacher experience point to different opportunities in high-minority and low-income schools. However, additional research suggests that the impact of teacher turnover on achievement may go beyond teacher experience and may also vary by context. A study by Ronfeldt, Loeb, and Wyckoff (2013) of students in New York City confirms the negative impact of teacher turnover on student achievement. The results indicate that, while some of the negative impact of teacher turnover is explained by changes in the distribution of teacher experience, a substantial amount remained unexplained by longevity. Even in cases in which teachers of comparable levels of experience replaced the teachers leaving the system, student achievement was lower. In addition, Ronfeldt and colleagues noted that even the achievement of the students whose teachers did not leave was worse in years of higher turnover, and this effect was found mostly in lower-performing schools. "Results suggest that teacher turnover has a significant and negative impact on student achievement in both math and ELA. Moreover, teacher turnover is particularly harmful to the achievement of students in schools with larger populations of low-performing and Black students" (Ronfeldt et al., 2013, p. 30). Thus, one of the equity considerations with regard to teacher credentialing involves the inequitable distribution of teacher turnover.

One strategy for addressing turnover and the subsequent teacher shortfall in hard-to-staff schools and districts has been to provide alternative pathways to teaching. These pathways reduce the requirements for initial entry to teaching, allowing teachers to begin teaching before completing all of the requirements for licensure (Clark et al., 2013; Darling-Hammond, Holtzman, Gatlin, & Heilig, 2005; Heilig & Jez, 2010). One of the primary examples of these alternative pathways is Teach for America (TFA). Founded in 1990, Teach for America is a national organization that recruits, selects, trains, and supports new teachers (Clark et al., 2013). According to its Web site (www.teachforamerica.org), the organization serves 48 sites, including several of the nation's urban school districts. The organization typically recruits individuals directly from undergraduate programs. The Teach for America "corps members" need not have completed any previous teacher preparation training. They participate in a five-week training program over the summer before beginning full-time teaching. They commit to teach for two years and participate in additional training toward licensure during those two years. While the overall number of Teach for America corps members is small, relative to the larger population of U.S. teachers, the expedited pathway to teaching represented by TFA and the concentration of the program in high-minority, low-income school districts makes TFA a noteworthy entity in any discussion of teacher credentialing and democratic access in mathematics education in U.S. schools.

Some research suggests that TFA corps members may be making a positive impact on mathematics teaching and learning in the high-needs schools that they serve. A recent report prepared for the Institute of Education Sciences of the U.S. Department of Education (Clark et al., 2013) compared TFA corps members to teachers who either entered teaching through a traditional teacher preparation program or through another alternative certification program. The results of this study indicated that, in mathematics, TFA teachers were more effective than teachers with whom they were compared. Students of TFA corps members outperformed students of traditionally licensed teachers on end-of-year mathematics assessments at a statistically significant level. They also scored higher than teachers from other alternative licensure programs.

Similarly, Kane, Rockoff, and Staiger (2008) compared TFA corps members with uncertified teachers and traditionally licensed teachers in New York City schools. They also found that students in the classrooms of TFA corps members scored higher relative to traditionally certified teachers, controlling for years of experience and students' prior achievement. However, the TFA corps members exhibited significantly lower retention rates than teachers entering through other routes. The five-year retention rate for traditionally certified teachers in the population was approximately 50%, compared to only 18% for TFA corps members.

Despite the positive results in some studies, the picture with respect to the effectiveness of TFA corps members and other alternatively licensed teachers is not completely straightforward. For example, in a longitudinal study of the Houston, Texas, school district, Darling-Hammond et al. (2005) found that the effectiveness of TFA corps members varied. TFA corps members who had completed the requirements to achieve a standard certification performed at a level equivalent to other certified teachers, after controlling for several factors, including experience. However, over the period covered by the study, researchers found that TFA corps members were less and less likely to have achieved certification and their overall effectiveness changed. "When compared to less well qualified teachers, TFA teachers appeared to have a neutral or positive effect. When compared to a pool of teachers who were on average better qualified, TFA teachers appeared to have a negative effect" (p. 22). Similarly, Darling-Hammond and her colleagues note that other large, well-controlled, longitudinal studies have shown similar results. "Teachers who entered teaching without full preparation . . . were significantly less effective when they started than fully prepared beginning teachers working with similar students" (p. 47). Yet, the gap in effectiveness closed once alternatively licensed teachers, including TFA corps members, had completed the certification process.

Thus, the picture with regard to the effectiveness of TFA is not entirely clear. It is beyond the scope of this chapter to provide a more comprehensive review of the research literature related to TFA or to attempt to reconcile the differences in results. Our purpose in highlighting a portion of the research on TFA is to suggest that the landscape of teacher credentialing is complex and context dependent. Based on the body of existing research, we would argue that the optimal scenario regarding teacher credentialing would be a fully certified teacher with a degree in mathematics and longevity in the classroom (Darling-Hammond, 2010; Rousseau-Anderson & Tate, 2008). That optimal scenario, however, does not reflect the teacher pool in many urban districts and low-income schools. Darling-Hammond et al. (2005) note that TFA operates in districts that hire many uncertified teachers. "Our analyses suggest that in contexts where many teachers have little preparation and where there is high turnover, TFA may make a positive contribution" (Darling-Hammond et al., 2005, p. 21). As Darling-Hammond and her colleagues suggest, because TFA corps members make a two-year commitment, they can actually provide more stability than the existing teacher pool in some urban districts. Similarly, Kane et al. (2008) acknowledged the much higher turnover rate of TFA corps members over five years, but argued that the relative effectiveness of TFA teachers potentially offsets this turnover. In both cases, these conclusions point to the importance of understanding teacher credentialing in context. Although TFA is only one example of the alternative pathway programs operating in U.S. schools, it is instructive as a case insofar as it highlights the various factors involved in teacher staffing and credentialing. The interplay of teacher shortages, teacher turnover, and the strategies that are employed to address those shortages, particularly in the schools serving low-income students and students of color, contribute to a complex picture with regard to teacher quality, credentialing, and equity in mathematics.

Vignette Revisited: Mathematics Education and Credentials

The issue of the credentialing process (particularly, teacher credentialing) is also relevant to understanding the classroom described in the vignette. The teacher in the classroom vignette was in her third year of teaching at the time of the observation. She held an alternative certification, which reflected the fact that she had not completed a teacher education program prior to beginning a full-time teaching position. At the time of the observation, she was in the process of completing the requirements for regular licensure. However, she did not hold a degree in mathematics and was in the process of completing a generalist middle-grades teacher preparation program (not specific to mathematics).

Moreover, her level of credentialing was not unique within the school. Of the nine mathematics teachers in the school, only two had more than three years of experience. Only two of the nine teachers had completed a teacher education program prior to their first year of full-time teaching—and only three of the nine held a regular teaching license. The remaining six were teaching through an alternative certification process (i.e., teaching full-time prior to completing a teacher preparation program). Moreover, four of the six were TFA corps members. We assert that understanding our observations in the vignette classroom requires attention to these factors of teacher quality and credentials. Yet, as noted in the previous section, the picture with respect to teacher credentialing in this context is complex. It would be tempting to view the credentials of the teachers as a primary contributor to the low achievement of the school, due to lack of prior training and limited experience. Moreover, other research points to the importance of sustained opportunities to participate in professional development and build professional community in order to transform instruction and improve student learning (Gamoran et al., 2003; Horn & Little, 2009). The teachers at the vignette school had not experienced the benefits of this type of long-term participation in a professional community. However, as Darling-Hammond et al. (2005) suggest, the TFA corps members and teachers from other alternative certification programs might actually be more effective and have greater longevity than the general teacher pool in an urban district, like that of the vignette school, in which many uncertified teachers are hired.

Similarly, the picture with respect to student credentialing is equally complicated. Approximately 40% of eighth graders at the school complete Algebra I, with the remainder completing Algebra I in the ninth grade. Yet, as in the study of Allensworth et al. (2009) of reform in Chicago, this early algebra credential has not translated into significant numbers of students obtaining higher-level credentials in mathematics. Fewer than 5% of the 12th graders at the vignette school enroll in Advanced Placement Calculus. Thus, while the school curriculum includes no remedial mathematics courses, students are not completing the most advanced courses in significant numbers. As is the case with teacher credentialing, the process of student credentialing is not entirely straightforward. We see part of the picture, but are nevertheless missing some crucial pieces that are likely related to the other questions that comprise our framework. For example, how might the socialization process relate to the failure of the school to "pump" students to the highest levels of mathematics? And how does this lack of student credentialing contribute to ongoing inequity?

MAINTAINING INEQUITY AND THE ROLE OF SOCIETY: A GEOSPATIAL PERSPECTIVE

While the research reviewed in the preceding sections sheds light on processes related to democratic access, we assert that our understanding of mathematics education in classrooms and schools is incomplete without attending to the role of society and the perpetuation of inequity through the system of mathematics education. In recent years, several scholars in mathematics education have grappled with these questions with regard to U.S. schools. For example, Tate (2008) has explored the intergenerational impact of poor teacher quality in mathematics, highlighting the ways that the system perpetuates inequity in mathematics education. Similarly, multiple contributions to the recent Special Equity Issue of JRME raised questions with regard to the role of mathematics education in the maintenance of inequity (Gutierrez, 2013; JRME Equity Special Issue Editorial Panel, 2013; Martin, 2013).

However, we take a slightly different approach to the examination of these questions regarding the role of mathematics education and the impact of society. As indicated in the previous sections and the discussion of the vignette, the operation of these systems (e.g., with regard to teacher credentials) often involves dynamics that are shaped at a local level (e.g., teacher shortages in particular schools and districts). As a result, we argue the need for an approach that takes various levels of context into account. A geospatial perspective on the study of equity and opportunity to learn offers a lens to examine layered context.

> Geospatial perspective calls for the addition of a geographic lens that focuses on place and space as important contextual variables. A geospatial view increases our understanding of

education, health, and other social variables by framing research in the context of neighborhoods, communities, and regions.

(Tate, Jones, Thorne-Wallington, & Hogrebe, 2012, p. 426)

Such a perspective interrogates the influence of context on issues of access and opportunity. In particular, a geospatial perspective can help us to better understand why space and location are predictors of mathematics understanding and attainment. This perspective bridges the macro and the micro by considering the larger factors that shape opportunity at a local level. In contrast to large-scale analyses that use national, regional, or statewide data sets, a geospatial perspective acknowledges the differences among locations and spaces within the same state or region.

This approach has been used to interrogate the factors that shape mathematics learning in urban spaces. For example, Hogrebe and Tate (2012) examined relationships between Algebra I performance and a variety of district-level variables with the goal to understand whether these relationships differed by location. Their results indicate that, in fact, the relationships between Algebra I scores and several variables (free-and-reduced lunch percent; minority percent; discipline incident rate; master's degree percent; and local revenue percent) tended to be stronger around the larger urban metropolitan areas of the state. These relationships were obscured in larger statewide analyses. According to the authors, the findings "suggest that research on the equity movement in mathematics education . . . must take local context into account. . . . While some variables may not appear to be strongly related to Algebra I performance when examined globally across a state, significant relationships existed regionally" (p. 22). They conclude that "place matters" in the study of equity in mathematics education.

Although not taking an explicitly geospatial perspective, other studies related to mathematics education have gone beyond the reporting of global differences to consider the underlying geography of opportunity that might contribute to those differences. For example, Hill and Lubienski (2007) studied a large sample of teachers in California. Using a measure of mathematics knowledge for teaching, they found a relationship between the teachers' mathematics knowledge for teaching and the school population. "Schools enrolling larger number of low-income and minority students employed teachers who had, on average, slightly less mathematical knowledge for teaching than their counterparts in more affluent schools" (p. 764). Hill and Lubienski then push beyond this more global result to highlight previous findings that teachers often teach in schools near those that they attended as a student (Loeb & Reininger, 2004). They note the cycle that this creates: "Schools that fail to adequately prepare teachers, in terms of mathematical knowledge, may suffer the consequences when these students return to teach in later years" (p. 765). At this point, the global finding of inequitable opportunity in the form of teacher quality is translated into a local cycle of intergenerational reproduction of poor content knowledge. Hill and Lubienski then note that universities in these areas have a role in breaking this cycle. "By strengthening the amount and quality of [content and methods] course work for teachers, *particularly in institutions whose graduates migrate largely to high-minority, high-poverty schools*, teacher educators might substantially reduce educational inequities by lessening disparities in the distribution of knowledgeable teachers" (p. 766, emphasis added). In this way, the focus on the contextual factors that shape patterns of unequal opportunity leads to tangible strategies that can be proposed at a local level.

Vignette Revisited: Three Rivers and a Geospatial Perspective

To illustrate how "place matters" in the understanding of equity in mathematics education, we return again to our opening vignette. The school described in the vignette serves a community that we will call "Three Rivers." Three Rivers is an incorporated area of approximately 40,000 residents within a larger U.S. city. The community is served by three high schools. The graduation rates of these schools for the 2012–2013 school year were 58%, 41.6%, and 84.1%. Only one of the three schools approached the statewide graduation rate of 87.2%. These relatively low graduation rates are also reflected in postsecondary attainment. According to the U.S. Census Bureau, in the zip code that encompasses most of Three Rivers, only 45% of the population of residents 25 years or older hold a high school diploma, and only 7.1% of residents hold a Bachelor's degree or graduate/professional degree. On the other end of the educational spectrum, less than one-third of eligible preschool-age children attend school prior to kindergarten.

Moreover, the struggles of the Three Rivers schools are not reflected only in the relatively low graduation rates. Under the current accountability system within the state, schools with achievement levels that put them in the bottom 5% statewide are subject to takeover. During the 2012–2013 school year, 83 schools in the state were identified in the bottom 5%. Of the 83 schools, 12 were located in the Three Rivers community. Thus, although Three Rivers represents only about 0.6% of the state population, its schools made up over 14% of those in the lowest-performing bracket. In fact, 12 out of the 18 schools located in Three Rivers were in the bottom 5% of schools statewide.

Yet, in addition to the educational outcomes, a geospatial perspective would also consider other neighborhood and community factors that are not typically considered in mathematics education research. For example, over a period of several years, the Three Rivers area has suffered from the loss of large plants that provided blue-collar jobs for many in the community. Currently, the unemployment rate in the community is 17%; and six out of 10 children in the community of over 40,000 live within the federal definition of poverty (Waters, 2012). Additionally, the area has led the state in subprime mortgages and foreclosures for the past decade. The high rate of foreclosures has led to a substantial number of vacant homes and has contributed to significant drops in property values (Moore, 2013). Aggregate home values in the area dropped from $667 million in 2005 to $332 million in 2010 (Waters, 2012).

In addition to the economic factors, there are several health-related indicators that are relevant for understanding the community and its schools. According to the U.S. Department of Agriculture (www.ers.usda.gov), several areas of the community are considered "food deserts"—a designation that reflects lack of access to grocery stores or supermarkets. The community also has the highest rate of teen pregnancies, low-birth-weight babies, and infant mortality in the county (Warren, 2011; Waters, 2012). These non–school-based factors have important implications for cognitive and academic performance (Tate et al., 2012).

We wish to be clear on one point: The purpose of constructing this picture of the context is not to suggest that these factors operate in a deterministic manner (i.e., that the task of achieving equity is impossible due to the conditions in the community). Rather, the goal in describing this case and the geospatial context is to suggest that our understanding of mathematics teaching and learning is severely limited when we focus only on the classroom (or even the school) as the locus of interest. This focus potentially restricts our understanding of the factors that shape teaching and learning in the setting (e.g., issues of teacher quality and experience, achievement levels in surrounding schools from which many students are transferring, curricular pressure related to the accountability status of the school, etc.). Yet, in addition to limiting our understanding of the factors that influence teaching and learning, an analysis that is not situated spatially limits the quality of our intervention decisions.

As we have argued elsewhere, we must, at some point, move beyond analysis to the design of more equitable opportunities for traditionally underserved students (Tate & Rousseau, 2007). Arguably, it is in this design stage that the geospatial perspective takes on its most important role. We are not suggesting that the analyses described earlier with regard to this school are not potentially important for understanding equity and access. Understanding the nature of classroom interactions provides insight into opportunity to learn at this site. Investigating the socialization process and examining the credentialing function are crucial. But a viable design for improving teaching and learning in this setting requires attention to location.

For example, given the relatively low preschool attendance rate, an approach to improving equity in this context would focus potentially on early childhood education (Tate et al., 2012).

Given the high levels of teacher attrition and the proportion of TFA corps members, strategies focused on teacher retention become relevant with attention to the context. Another target might focus on efforts to mitigate the effects of summer learning loss that is likely to impact students in this low-income community. Health-related issues, such as ensuring access to nutritious high-quality foods at school, are potential components of an intervention that considers the context. Parental education programs to help parents and guardians better support their children academically also become a priority in a context in which high school graduation rates and postsecondary completion rates are low. Similarly, the low levels of postsecondary attainment in the community are reflected in the small number of teachers who reside in the community. This suggests the need to connect the school to the surrounding neighborhoods and to increase opportunities for teacher preparation for persons from the community. In addition to more traditional interventions, a design approach that is situated in a geospatial perspective would take into account the community context—not simply to note this as background to the study but as an integral consideration in the intervention design. Such a perspective takes into consideration not only the ways that society influences mathematics education but also the ways that mathematics education contributes to inequity. This approach has the potential to interrupt the intergenerational cycle of low mathematics achievement and educational attainment.

CONCLUSION

As noted at the beginning of the chapter, the vignette was based on ongoing observations of a school in an urban school district. Since the time of the observation represented in the vignette, two of the nine mathematics teachers in the school (including the teacher described in the vignette) have resigned. Both teachers left their positions in the middle of the school year. The school replaced one teacher with a licensed teacher with three years of experience. The other teacher was replaced by a first-year Teach for America corps member. Before the replacements arrived, the students in the two classrooms had uncertified substitute teachers for almost one month.

We share this epilogue to the vignette because we view it as illustrative of the complex and dynamic challenges of U.S. mathematics education, particularly in urban schools. It also reflects the complexity that we, as researchers, must be able to address in any effort to make sense of mathematics teaching and learning in schools such as the one described in the vignette. In our earlier scholarship related to equity we have described several variables associated with greater opportunity to learn in mathematics education: professional development, instructional time, curriculum, quality of curricular materials, etc. (Rousseau-Anderson, 2007; Tate & Rousseau, 2007). An examination of the vignette school considering these factors reveals the complexity of the picture with regard to access and opportunity to learn. On one hand, the school provides substantially greater instructional time in mathematics than other schools in the community. The curricular materials used by the school are (what we consider to be) high quality and were selected to align with national standards. The mathematics teachers receive approximately 60 hours of professional development during the school year, specifically on mathematics content and pedagogy. A substantial number of eighth graders take and pass Algebra I—and the school-level achievement in mathematics is higher than nearby schools in the community. On the other hand, the teacher turnover rate (particularly in mathematics) is high. Overall, the mathematics teachers are relatively inexperienced, with few credentials. Few students matriculate through the most advanced mathematics courses—and the school-level achievement in mathematics is well below the state average. Moreover, the vignette classroom reflected several patterns observed in the classrooms of other mathematics teachers at the school (e.g., limited cognitive demand of tasks, procedural focus of instruction, limited student discourse, ineffective or limited use of cooperative learning, etc.). So, what sense can we make of mathematics teaching and learning in this setting? How does democratic access in this setting relate to larger research findings in mathematics education? These are, in part, the challenges that bring us to the framework we have outlined in this chapter.

If we are to understand and to address effectively the issues represented in the vignette example, we must expand even further beyond the paradigmatic boundaries of mathematics education. In particular, we argue for a sociology of mathematics education that draws from sociology of education. In fact, the growth and development of sociology of education as a sub-discipline of sociology has a potential parallel to the need for a sociology of mathematics education. In describing the growth of sociology of education as a field within sociology, Hallinan (2000) noted that there emerged a need to develop theoretical frameworks that went beyond those available in sociology. General sociological theories failed to account for the unique environment and population of schools and did not account for "causes and consequences of interinstitutional and intrainstitutional variation in schooling processes" (p. 3). Sociologists of education were in need of theories that would explain the social processes that occur in schools and distinguish schools from other social institutions (Hallinan, 2000). According to Hallinan, sociology of education turned to other areas for theoretical ideas about schools. In much the same way, it is clear from our review of more recent literature that mathematics educators, particularly those focused on issues of democratic access, have seen the need to make a similar turn in order to understand the social and institutional influences on mathematics education.

Another parallel between the development of sociology of education and sociology of mathematics education can be found in the need to engage simultaneously analyses at multiple levels. In addition to theories that took into account the operation of educational institutions as distinct from other social institutions, sociologists of education have noted a need for micro-level and macro-level analyses. For example, Cohen (2000) argued that research on equality of educational opportunity engages two sets of inequalities simultaneously at both the societal and institutional level and the classroom level. She argued that:

> Research on equality of educational opportunity at the societal or regional level alone will neglect the experiences of students within classrooms and schools. These experiences are the most proximate causes of educational success or failure. . . . Similarly, work with the concept of equal opportunities only at the level of the classroom will neglect the big picture of the social location of that classroom in relationship to inequalities in the larger society and in the organization of the school. Moreover, inequalities at the societal level interpenetrate inequalities at the classroom level in complex ways.
>
> (p. 265)

In many ways, this need for integration of individual and contextual analyses is the same challenge facing researchers in mathematics education. In the previous edition of this chapter, we examined research that had, at that time, been conducted at the classroom level (Rousseau-Anderson & Tate, 2008). We noted two primary themes in the classroom-based research: (1) students can be unintentionally marginalized in the classroom as a result of unstated norms and power structures; and (2) the factors that shape participation are not limited to conditions inside the classroom. Other influences are operational (e.g., socioeconomic status, culture, language, grouping practices, and so on). These findings suggested to us that investigations of access cannot be limited to the mathematics classroom, but must take into consideration broader factors. In the same chapter, we also examined research at a structural level that involved patterns of differential opportunities across schools, districts, etc. We noted, at that time, the need for scholarship that engaged multiple levels of analysis and sought to understand better the ways that the macro-level forces shape what happens at a micro-level in classrooms.

What we have seen develop in the mathematics education literature in recent years is a shift toward research that considers this interplay. This is illustrated in the "sociopolitical turn" in mathematics education (Gutierrez, 2013). It can also be seen in some of the more recent scholarship that traces the impact of larger discourses and structures in the development of student identity (Berry, 2008; Nasir & de Royston, 2013; Stinson, 2013) and instructional practices within the classroom (Jackson, 2009).

Yet, despite this apparent shift, we assert that we are still in need of a sociology of mathematics education that could serve much the same role as sociology of education does as a subdiscipline of sociology. Specifically, a sociology of mathematics education would expand on the existing sociopolitical turn by developing and adapting theoretical models that take into account the specific conditions that shape equity in mathematics education. These models would engage research from sociology of education, while simultaneously considering how equity concerns in mathematics education might operate differently than other disciplines. Further, the attention to macro- and micro-level factors directs us to take a geospatial perspective on equity in mathematics education. We assert that this geospatial perspective offers one way to understand more fully the interplay of the macro- and micro-levels in the education of traditionally underserved students. This focus on the importance of context is a theme that recurred in our review of recent research. A truly geospatial perspective would take into account multiple factors at the local level that might be related to educational achievement and attainment. These factors would include, but not be limited to, employment and other economic indicators, preschool education, prenatal care, access to health care, postsecondary opportunities and attainment, etc. These factors are well beyond the scope of traditional mathematics education scholarship—yet attention to these factors is necessary to understand the nature of democratic access at a local level and to design interventions that are likely to be successful.

One example of the significance of a geospatial perspective can be seen in the research of Mesquita, Restivo, and D'Ambrosio (2011) in Brazil. According to the authors, the study sought to "make sociological sense of lived mathematics experiences" of "asphalt children" in São Paulo. Their approach took into account the geographical, historical, social, cultural, and policy dynamics of the urban setting of São Paulo and the specific conditions of the children involved in the study. In so doing, they create a picture of the "multiple, systemic, and complex interdependencies" related to mathematics experiences of this population.

Thus, this study is an example of the use of a sociological lens that considers the multiple factors shaping mathematics and mathematics education in a specific geospatial location. As such, it provides insight into the type of research that we submit is important for mathematics education. We should note, however, that the research by Mesquita et al. (2011) focused on the mathematics knowledge and experiences of children in nonschool settings. In particular, they attended to the "lack of links between the school knowledge-making and the knowledge-making in use" (p. 118) and concluded that the academic environment engaged in chronic omission of the mathematics "knowledges" of asphalt children. The type of research that we call for would engage in a similar analysis of the role of location, history, economics, policy, and culture in shaping opportunities for children. However, we assert the need for a parallel line of research situated within and around schools in order to better understand how to create more equitable opportunity to learn through schooling.

Research on equity and democratic access in mathematics education has made a "turn" in recent years away from a strict focus on mathematics and psychology. We submit that this move to go beyond the traditional paradigmatic boundaries is a positive step toward understanding the nature of inequity and access in mathematics education in the United States. However, in places such as Three Rivers, the next (urgent) steps require design—and this design involves a geospatial perspective that considers all the factors that shape equity and access in a neighborhood and engages all of the entities that can intervene in that community. We will know that we have achieved some measure of success with respect to equity and democratic access when the zip codes of places like Three Rivers no longer have predictive value with regard to mathematics education and achievement.

NOTES

1. We use the indefinite article *a* in describing our view of sociology of mathematics education to acknowledge that there are other existing approaches that integrate sociology and mathematics education and that these approaches differ substantively from the framework we are using.
2. "Nonmigrant" refers to students who were born in the state in which they attended high school.

REFERENCES

Allensworth, E., Nomi, T., Montgomery, N., & Lee, V. (2009). College preparatory curriculum for all: Academic consequences of requiring Algebra and English I for ninth graders in Chicago. *Educational Evaluation and Policy Analysis, 31*, 367–391.

Berry, R. (2008). Access to upper level mathematics: The students of successful African American middle school boys. *Journal for Research in Mathematics Education, 39*, 464–488.

Carnevale, A. P., Rose, S. J., & Cheah, B. (2011). *The college payoff: Education, occupations, lifetime earnings.* Washington, DC: Georgetown University Center on Education and the Workforce.

Clark, M., Chiang, H., Silva, T., McConnell, S., Sonnenfeld, K., Erbe, A., & Puma, M. (2013). *The effectiveness of secondary math teachers from Teach for America and the Teaching Fellows programs* (NCEE 2013–4015). Washington, DC: National Center for Education Evaluation and Regional Assistance, Institute of Education Sciences, U.S. Department of Education.

Cohen, E. (2000). Equitable classrooms in a changing society. In M. Hallinan (Ed.), *Handbook of the Sociology of Education* (pp. 265–283). New York: Kluwer.

D'Ambrosio, B., Frankenstein, M., Gutierrez, R., Kastberg, S., Martin, D., Moschkovich, J., Taylor, E., & Barnes, D. (2013). Introduction to the JRME Equity Special Issue. *Journal for Research in Mathematics Education, 44*(1), 5–10.

Darling-Hammond, L. (2010). *The flat world and education: How our commitment to equity will determine our future.* New York: Teachers College Press.

Darling-Hammond, L., Holtzman, D., Gatlin, S. J., & Heilig, J. V. (2005). Does teacher preparation matter? Evidence about teacher certification, Teach for America, and teacher effectiveness. *Education Policy Analysis Archives, 13*(42), 1–51.

Dowling, P. (1998). *The sociology of mathematics education: Mathematical myths/pedagogical texts* London: Routledge.

Fetler, M. (1999). High school staffing characteristics and mathematics test results. *Education Policy Analysis Archives, 79*(9), 1–22.

Frankenberg, E. (2006). The segregation of American teachers. Cambridge, MA: The Civil Rights Project at Harvard University.

Freeman, C., Scafidi, B., & Sjoquist, D. (2005). Racial segregation in Georgia public schools, 1994–2001: Trends, causes, and impact on teacher quality. In J. Boger & G. Orfield (Eds.), *School resegregation: Must the South turn back?* (pp. 143–163). Chapel Hill, NC: University of North Carolina Press.

Gamoran, A., Anderson, C., Quiroz, P., Secada, W., Williams, T., & Ashmann, S. (2003). *Transforming teaching in math and science: How schools and districts can support change.* New York: Teachers College Press.

Gutierrez, R. (2013). The sociopolitical turn in mathematics education. *Journal for Research in Mathematics Education, 44*(1), 37–68.

Gutierrez, R., & Dixon-Roman, E. (2011). Beyond gap gazing: How can thinking about education comprehensively help us (re)envision mathematics education? In B. Atweh, M. Graven, W. Secada, & P. Valero (Eds.), *Mapping equity and quality in mathematics education* (pp. 21–34). London: Springer.

Hallinan, M. (2000). Introduction: Sociology of education at the threshold of the twenty-first century. In M. Hallinan (Ed.), *Handbook of the sociology of education* (pp. 1–12). New York: Kluwer.

Heilig, J.V., & Jez, S. J. (2010). *Teach for America: A review of the evidence.* Boulder, CA & Tempe, AZ: Education and the Public Interest Center & Education Policy Research Unit.

Hill, H., & Lubienski, S. (2007). Teachers' mathematics knowledge for teaching and school context: A study of California teachers. *Educational Policy, 21*(5), 747–768.

Hogrebe, M., & Tate, W. (2012). Place, poverty, and algebra: A statewide comparative spatial analysis of variable relationships. *Journal of Mathematics Education at Teachers College, 3*, 12–24.

Horn, I., & Little, J. (2009). Attending to problems of practice: Routines and resources for professional learning in teachers' workplace interactions. *American Educational Research Journal, 47*, 181–217.

Ingersoll, R., & Merrill, L. (2013). *Seven trends: The transformation of the teaching force.* Philadelphia, PA: Consortium for Policy Research in Education.

Ingersoll, R., & Perda, D. (2009). *The mathematics and science teacher shortage: Fact and myth.* Philadelphia, PA: Consortium for Policy Research in Education.

Jackson, K. (2009). The social construction of youth and mathematics: The case of a fifth-grade classroom. In D. Martin (Ed.), *Mathematics teaching, learning, and liberation in the lives of Black children* (pp. 175–198). New York: Routledge.

JRME Equity Special Issue Editorial Panel. (2013). Addressing racism. *Journal for Research in Mathematics Education, 44,* 23–36.

Kane, T., Rockoff, J., & Staiger, D. (2008). What does certification tell us about teacher effectiveness? Evidence from New York City. *Economics of Education Review, 27,* 615–631.

Leonard, J., & Martin, D. (Eds.). (2013). *The brilliance of Black children in mathematics: Beyond the numbers and toward new discourse.* Charlotte, NC: Information Age.

Lochner, L., & Moretti, E. (2001). *The effect of education on crime: Evidence from prison inmates, arrests, and self-reports* (No. w8605). Cambridge, MA: National Bureau of Economic Research.

Loeb, S., & Reininger, M. (2004). *Public policy and teacher labor markets: What we know and why it matters.* East Lansing: Education Policy Center at Michigan State University.

Lubienski, S. (2007). Research, reform, and equity in U.S. mathematics education In N. Nasir & P. Cobb (Eds.), *Improving access to mathematics: Diversity and equity in the classroom* (pp. 10–23). New York: Teachers College Press.

Martin, D. (2006). Mathematics learning and participation as racialized forms of experience: African American parents speak on the struggle for mathematics literacy. *Mathematical Thinking and Learning, 8*(3), 197–229.

Martin, D. (2009a). Liberating the production of knowledge about African American children and mathematics. In D. Martin (Ed.), *Mathematics teaching, learning, and liberation in the lives of Black children* (pp. 3–35). New York: Routledge.

Martin, D. (2009b). Researching race in mathematics education. *Teachers College Record, 111*(2), 295–338.

Martin, D. (2011). What does quality mean in the context of White institutional space? In B. Atweh, M. Graven, W. Secada, & P. Valero (Eds.), *Mapping equity and quality in mathematics education* (pp. 437–450). London: Springer.

Martin, D. (2013). Race, racial projects, and mathematics education. *Journal for Research in Mathematics Education, 44*(1), 316–333.

Mesquita, M., Restivo, S., & D'Ambrosio, U. (2011). *Asphalt children and city streets: A life, a city, and a case study of history, culture, and ethnomathematics in São Paulo.* Boston, MA: Sense Publishers.

Milner, H. (2012). But what is urban education? *Urban Education, 47,* 556–561.

Milner, H., & Lomotey, K. (Eds.)(2014). *Handbook of urban education.* New York: Routledge.

Moore, L. (2013, April 6). [Three Rivers] homeowners suffer greatest property value losses in reappraisal. *The Commercial Appeal.*

Nasir, N., & Cobb, P. (Eds.). (2007). *Improving access to mathematics: Diversity and equity in the classroom.* New York: Teachers College Press.

Nasir, N., & de Royston, M. (2013). Power, identity, and mathematical practices outside and inside school. *Journal for Research in Mathematics Education, 44*(1), 264–287.

Nasir, N., Hand, V., & Taylor, E. (2008). Culture and mathematics in school: Boundaries between "cultural" and "domain" knowledge in the mathematics classroom and beyond. *Review of Research in Education, 32,* 187–240.

Nasir, N., & Shah, N. (2011). On defense: African American males making sense of racialized narratives in mathematics education. *Journal of African American Males in Education, 2*(1), 24–45.

National Commission on Excellence in Education. (1983). *A nation at risk: The imperative for educational reform.* Washington, DC: United States Department of Education.

National Council of Teachers of Mathematics Research Committee. (2005). Equity in school mathematics education: How can research contribute? *Journal for Research in Mathematics Education, 36*(2), 92–100.

Plunk, A., Tate, W., Bierut, L., & Grucza, R. (2014). Intended and unintended effects of state-mandated high school science and mathematics course graduation requirements on educational attainment. *Educational Researcher, 43*(5), 230–241.

Restivo, S. (2007). Theory of mind, social science, and mathematical practice. In B. van Kerkhove & J. P. van Bendegem (Eds.), *Perspectives on mathematical practices: Bringing together philosophy of mathematics, sociology of mathematics, and mathematics education* (pp. 83–106). Dordrecht: Springer.

Restivo, S., & Bauchspies, W. (2006). The will to mathematics: Minds, morals, and numbers. *Foundations of Science, 11,* 197–215.

Ronfeldt, M., Loeb, S., & Wyckoff, J. (2013). How teacher turnover harms student achievement. *American Educational Research Journal, 50*(1), 4–36.

Rousseau-Anderson, C. (2007). Examining school mathematics through the lenses of learning and equity. In G. Martin & M. Strutchens (Eds.), *The learning of mathematics: 2007 yearbook* (pp. 97–113). Reston, VA: National Council of Teachers of Mathematics.

Rousseau-Anderson, C., & Tate, W. (2008). Still separate, still unequal: Democratic access to mathematics in U.S. schools. In L. English (Ed.), *Handbook of international research in mathematics education* (2nd ed., pp. 299–318). New York: Routledge.

Small, M. L. (2014, March 17). No two ghettos are alike. *The Chronicle Review*. Retrieved from http://m.chronicle.com/article/No-Two-Ghettos-Are-Alike/145301 (August 1, 2014).

Stein, M. K., Smith, M., Henningsen, M., & Silver, E. (2009). *Implementing standards-based mathematics instruction: A casebook for professional development* (2nd ed.). New York: Teachers College Press.

Stinson, D. (2006). African American male adolescents, schooling (and mathematics): Deficiency, refection, and achievement. *Review of Educational Research, 76*(4), 477–506.

Stinson, D. (2013). Negotiating the "white male myth": African American male students and success in school mathematics. *Journal for Research in Mathematics Education, 44*(1), 69–99.

Stinson, D., & Bullock, E. (2012). Critical postmodern theory in mathematics education research: A praxis of uncertainty. *Educational Studies in Mathematics, 80*, 41–55.

Tate, W. (2008). The political economy of teacher quality in school mathematics: African American males, opportunity structures, politics and method. *American Behavioral Scientist, 51*(7), 953–971.

Tate, W., Jones, B., Thorne-Wallington, E., & Hogrebe, M. (2012). Science and the city: Thinking geospatially about opportunity to learn. *Urban Education, 47*, 399–433.

Tate, W., & Rousseau, C. (2002). Access and opportunity: The political and social context of mathematics education. In L. English (Ed.), *Handbook of international research in mathematics education* (pp. 271–299). Mahwah, NJ: Lawrence Erlbaum Associates.

Tate, W., & Rousseau, C. (2007). Engineering change in mathematics education: Research, policy, and practice. In F. Lester (Ed.), *Second handbook of research on mathematics teaching and learning* (Vol. 2, pp. 1209–1246). Greenwich, CT: Information Age Publishing.

Valero, P. (2007). A socio-political look at equity in the school organization of mathematics education *ZDM: The International Journal on Mathematics Education, 39*, 225–233.

Varelas, M., Martin, D., & Kane, J. (2012). Content knowledge and identity construction: A framework to strengthen African American students' mathematics and science learning in urban elementary schools. *Human Development, 55*, 319–339.

Walshaw, M. (2013). Post-structuralism and ethical practical action: Issues of power and identity. *Journal for Research in Mathematics Education, 44*(1), 100–118.

Warren, B. (2011, September 2). County's infant mortality rate stirs plea. *The Commercial Appeal*.

Waters, D. (2012, December 2). [Three Rivers] community becomes lab for do or die experiment. *The Commercial Appeal*.

Yackel, E., & Cobb, P. (1996). Sociomathematical norms, argumentation, and autonomy in mathematics. *Journal for Research in Mathematics Education, 27*(4), 458–477.

16 Mathematics Learning In and Out of School

Towards Continuity or Discontinuity?

Guida de Abreu

Oxford Brookes University, Oxford, UK

Sarah Crafter

Institute of Education, London, UK

INTRODUCTION

Globalization and unprecedented levels of migration were partly responsible for the expansion of research on mathematical learning in and out of school, including a focus on multicultural settings within Western societies. This new focus often falls under the umbrella of research on home-school mathematics (e.g. Andrews & Yee, 2006; Civil & Andrade, 2002; Civil & Menéndez, 2011; Hughes & Pollard, 2006). In many Western countries, immigration is substantially changing the ethnic and cultural composition of the school population. This diversity within schools poses major challenges to systems of education developed to serve the needs of homogeneous monocultural groups (Abreu & Elbers, 2005; Cole, 1998). Questions around the experiences and achievements of students from different cultural, ethnic, social, economic, and linguistic groups in-school mathematics became salient and in need of discussion (Abreu, 2014; Civil, 2008; Gorgorió, Abreu, Cesar, & Valero, 2005).

This chapter revisits research on the relationship between mathematical practices in and out of school. It traces the evolution of research from an examination of the cultural nature of school and out-of-school mathematical practices, to current research that attempts to understand the experiences of the person as a participant in these practices. A focus on practice (i.e. the activity, how it is organized, how it is understood, and its specific purposes) initially contributed to mapping the differences between in- and out-of-school mathematics, and subsequently offered insight into the diversity of school mathematical practices in different settings. For example, school mathematics in a school setting is a different practice from school mathematics in the home setting. Or, for immigrant students, school mathematics in the host country is a different practice from their home country. A focus on the person—such as a student, a teacher, a parent—as a participant gives insight into the way they experience and negotiate differences between mathematical practices. Our major interest resides in examining the implications of these processes to the understanding of school mathematical learning. What makes mathematical practices experienced as continuous or discontinuous between in-school and out-of-school settings?

This review begins with an historical background on how developments in (cross-) cultural psychology contributed to our understanding of the cultural nature of mathematical cognition, learning, and practices. This is followed by a review of research that explores mathematical learning as a socio-culturally mediated process, considering processes of cultural mediation (the role of cultural tools, both mental and physical) and social mediation (the role of institutions, social interactions and other types of social processes). The final section focuses on the person as a participant in multiple social and cultural practices, and covers recent studies on multicultural settings (the role of the individual in the reconstruction of the cultural and the social at the psychological level).

The structure of the chapter reflects the movement in the cultural psychology of mathematics education: from an understanding of the mathematics of particular cultural and social groups to the understanding of the person as a participant in sociocultural practices. This movement also reflects different perspectives on the examination of the role of culture on psychological development (Abreu, 2014). The initial work in this area examined mathematics in everyday life (Carraher, Schliemann, & Carraher, 1988; Rogoff & Lave, 1984) and focused on the shared cultural practices of groups and communities. This body of research illustrated fundamental differences between in- and out-of-school mathematics, such as different systems of mathematical knowledge (e.g. measurement systems used in and out of school), strategies used to solve problems, and social norms regulating mathematical practices. "Cultural discontinuity" emerged as an explanatory concept to explain differences and mismatches between learning and uses of mathematics in and out of school.

More recent work recognizes the "discontinuities" of mathematical practices both at cultural and social levels. However, discontinuity is not the center of the analysis, but the "point of departure" (de Haan & Elbers, 2008) or point of rupture in the way a person experiences transitions between practices (Abreu, Crafter, Gorgorió, & Prat, 2013). This perspective examines dynamic aspects of culture, i.e., the way a person experiences participation and transitions in multiple mathematical practices, such as his or her experiences of home-school mathematics and how this impacts on the construction of knowledge, meaning, and identities (Abreu, 2014; Anderson & Gold, 2006; Cobb & Hodge, 2002; Chronaki, 2005; Gorgorió & Abreu, 2009; Nasir & Cobb, 2002). This provides a complementary analysis exploring what contributes to experiencing continuities and discontinuities across different mathematical practices, such as home and school mathematics.

PERSPECTIVES ON THE CULTURAL NATURE OF MATHEMATICS LEARNING IN OUT-OF-SCHOOL PRACTICES

Insights into the nature of mathematics learning in out-of-school practices were initially data driven, grounded in ethnographic-type descriptions, and linked to different disciplines. For example, two disciplines that have approached the problem from a sociocultural stance are ethnomathematics education (D'Ambrosio, 1985) and developmental psychology (Nunes, Schliemann, & Carraher, 1993). As illustrated in Table 16.1, studies along these lines provided complementary perspectives in the analysis of mathematics learning outside school.

Table 16.1 Two perspectives on outside school mathematics.

	Ethnomathematics education *(D'Ambrosio, 1985)*	*Developmental psychology* *(Nunes et al., 1993)*
Level of analysis	Sociogenetic level: Historical and anthropological analysis of the mathematics of different sociocultural groups.	Ontogenetic level: Analysis of the individual's psychological processes involved in learning and using mathematics in specific sociocultural contexts.
Focus of analysis	Relationship between social-political order and individual learning: How the value social groups attribute to certain forms of mathematics mediates its transmission and appropriation.	Relationships between culture and cognition: How specific cultural tools mediate mathematics cognition.

These previously distinct foci of enquiry are now overlapping to some extent, as researchers seek to find ways to look at the intersection of micro and macro contexts of mathematical practice. Thus, a psychological analysis at the ontogenetic level, as for example, how a learner develops understanding of basic arithmetic sums (e.g. adding and subtracting), also requires the understanding of the sociogenetic level, i.e., for example, what type of strategies and resources are socially valorized and promoted in educational settings (e.g. using number lines to solve sums).

Cultural Psychology and Mathematical Cognition

Efforts to understand the relationship between mathematical thinking and culture can be traced to the interest of Western science in testing the universality of cognitive development and to the expansion of Western style of schooling in other societies (Cole, Gay, & Glick, 1968). The latter included mathematics as one of the key subjects in the elementary curriculum. Cole (1977, 1995) recounted his first task in cross-cultural research as being "to figure out why Liberian children seemed to experience so much difficulty learning mathematics" (Cole, 1995, p. 23). He also noted that his "graduate training was in the tradition of American mathematical learning theory, which at that time entailed the use of algebra and probability theory to provide a foundation for discovery of presumably universal laws of learning." This happened about 40 years ago, and as he confessed, he "knew almost nothing about the teaching of mathematics, and even less about Liberia" (Cole, 1995, p. 24). Cole and his collaborators soon grew skeptical about their own knowledge and methods. In the course of a classification study, which required participants to sort objects, it was observed that the Liberians tended to use different groupings depending on the way the task was presented to them.

Cole's observations at first glance exposed the inadequacy of research procedures that were drawn from his training as a psychologist in the United States and subsequently applied to other cultural contexts. However, as cautioned by Rogoff and Lave (1984), this does not allow us to jump to the conclusion that variation between cultural groups could be explained solely in terms of inadequacies of research procedures, either in tests and tasks or in the difficulties of communication between researchers and participants. These explanations would reduce the differences in performance to differences in "display" (Shweder, 1990) and presuppose that in ideal testing circumstances the differences should disappear. Cole and his colleagues observed that differences could be linked to the tools used as mediators to practice. To their surprise, the differences were not only linked to a tool being available, but also to a more complex organization of the tool itself. Hand spans and foot lengths were tools used both in the United States and by the Kpelle of Liberia. When Cole and his colleagues tested both Americans and Kpelle in tasks that required estimating length with hand spans and foot lengths, the Americans performed better despite the familiarity of both groups with the tools. Further analysis revealed that although both groups were familiar with these length measures, the Kpelle did not relate different measures in a system, thus making the task more difficult to accomplish. In contrast, the Americans were familiar with well-articulated systems, such as inches, feet, and yards that enabled them to translate between the measures. Observations of this kind revealed the need for a shift from studying products to studying processes. This shift is at the heart of the movement from cross-cultural to cultural psychology (Cole, 1995).

A basic claim shared by the principal proponents of cultural psychology (see Stiegler, Shweder, & Herdt, 1990) is that the adoption of such a perspective offers the possibility of accounting for diversity in human psychological functioning. Of course, understanding variations between groups and individuals has been at the core of psychology, but the mainstream approach searches for its sources in the universality of the mind and the presence or absence of capacities, properties, traits, and so forth. Cultural psychology searches for the sources of diversity in socioculturally specific experiences. Proponents of cultural psychology approaches share the view that understanding diversity requires attention to the interplay between the individual, society and culture.

These insights marked the starting of a new era in psychological approaches to mathematics learning outside school. The revised theoretical and methodological foundations led to the emergence of new research programs, such as the series of "street mathematics" studies carried out by Nunes and her colleagues in Brazil in the 1980s (Carraher et al., 1988; Nunes et al., 1993). Research in "everyday cognition," "situated cognition," and "mathematics learning in and out of school" flourished in the 1980s with seminal research works being published (see, for instance, Lave, 1988; Rogoff & Lave, 1984; Saxe, 1991). A major influence on psychologists working in this area has been Vygotsky's (1978) notion of cultural mediation. This notion was applied to understanding the role of tools or artifacts in mediating mathematical action and thinking in specific social practices (Resnick, Pontecorvo, & Säljö, 1997).

There were two distinct phases in the investigation of cultural influences on mathematics learning in out-of-school contexts. In the first phase, scholars traveled to other countries to investigate the mathematical thinking and learning of foreign people. Although not always made explicit, this traveling was often politically motivated. The second phase involved the researchers' return to their home countries. This also had a politically motivated dimension, coming from the researchers themselves, who realized that the lessons learned abroad could throw light on the learning of diverse groups in their own country.

Studies of Out-of-School Mathematics in Non-Western Cultures

Some of the pioneering studies of mathematics in out-of-school contexts were carried out in non-Western cultures (Brenner, 1983; Gay & Cole, 1967; Lave, 1977; Pettito & Ginsburg, 1982; Saxe, 1982; Saxe & Posner, 1983). These studies can now be considered landmarks in view of the realization of psychologists that cultural differences are not necessarily associated with deep cognitive differences. They also persuaded psychologists to rethink their research methodology. Instead of taking school knowledge as the reference and formulating tasks from this perspective to see whether individuals transfer to other settings, the researchers engaged in ethnographic observations in outside-school contexts. In these studies one can see—along with some traditional cross-cultural concepts—the emergence of new constructs such as apprenticeship, distinct arithmetic systems, and strategies that mark a new era of research in out-of-school mathematics. One also can see how unexpected findings have challenged views about key constructs that have been used to explain mathematical thinking and learning in and out of school. Among the key constructs challenged were the notion of transfer and the concrete versus abstract dichotomy (ideas linked to a universalistic, culture-free, view of mathematical cognition and learning) (Nunes, 1992b).

Out-of-school practices in non-Western cultures provided an environment suitable for empirical testing of the power of transfer of school-related skills. In these settings, researchers could easily find people with different degrees of exposure to schooling, from none to advanced levels. This situation also meant that the learning of mathematical skills required for specific crafts and professions were often embedded in the apprenticeship. Within the same group it was possible to find people who varied both in terms of levels of skill in the profession and in terms of their levels of schooling. Various researchers took advantage of these naturally occurring situations to disentangle the effects of schooling on cognitive development (Greenfield & Lave, 1982).

A classic example is the work of Jean Lave among the tailors of Monrovia, Liberia. As an anthropologist, she spent several months observing the work of master and apprentice tailors. This enabled her to gain access to the arithmetic tailors used, such as estimating size, in inches, of the waistbands of pairs of trousers. Lave then used this knowledge to develop a strategy to study the impact of schooling and tailoring on mathematical skills. Her strategy consisted of devising arithmetical tasks that varied according to their degree of familiarity with tailoring or schooling practices. She then applied the tasks to tailors who also varied in two dimensions: (1) none to 10 years of schooling; and (2) a few months to 25 years of tailoring experience. Lave observed specific effects. Schooling contributed more to performance in school-oriented tasks and tailoring to the tailoring-oriented tasks. On the basis of these findings, Lave concluded that "It appears that neither schooling nor tailoring skills generalize very far beyond the circumstances in which they are ordinarily applied" (Greenfield & Lave, 1982, p. 199). This study was only a starting point for a challenge of the view that schooling has general cognitive effects that would transfer and generalize across practices (Lave, 1988).

Research that followed an ethnographic approach challenged the notion of cognitive transfer and demonstrated that inclusion of cultural practices in analyzing mathematical cognition is complex. Saxe (1982, 1991) illustrated the impact of cultural practices on cognition by studying the Oksapmin, an indigenous community in Papua New Guinea, who used a 27-body-part counting system. Saxe's analysis showed that the introduction of Western-style practices such as schooling and currency impacted on mathematical cognition. For example, he found that people with little participation in commercial activities continued to use traditional counting systems based on body parts, whereas the others who actively participated in economic exchanges had adopted a hybrid counting system combining body parts and numerical representation. His return to the Oksapmin community 20 years later (Saxe & Esmonde, 2005) further supports the initial results showing that changes in cultural practices, i.e. economic exchange, are associated with new forms of mathematical cognition. The shift in the meaning of the concept *fu* is an example, as the word changed from being used as an intensive quantifier meaning "a complete group of plenty" to being used as "double a numerical value." Saxe's work is unique in demonstrating the interrelationship between participation in organized cultural practices and development of mathematical cognition. One can hypothesize that, to some degree, Saxe's observations may be replicated when learners are exposed to school practices that are different from their everyday outside school practices. However, it is very likely that the most common methodological approaches based on standardized measurements make "invisible cognitive adaptations that individuals create to local conditions" (Saxe, 2012, p. 235)

Everyday Mathematics in the Context of Western Societies

The insights gained into non-Western cultures have encouraged outside school research in the researchers' own cultures (Andrews & Yee, 2006; Baker, Street, & Tomlin, 2006; Carraher, Carraher, & Schliemann, 1982; Lave, 1988; Masinglia, 1994; Murtaugh, 1985; Scribner, 1984; Winter, Salway, Yee, & Hughes, 2004). Lave's seminal piece of work on the Adult Maths Project, conducted in the United States, showed distinct contrasts between, for example, performance on a school-like test (average 59% correct answers) and arithmetical performance in the supermarket (98%). According to Lave (1988), the key issue is the interpretation of "everyday." She distinguished between a functionalist view in which "the label 'everyday' is heavy with negative connotations emanating from its definition in contrast to scientific thought" (p. 14) and a practice theory view, in which "the everyday world is just that: what people do in daily, weekly, monthly cycles of activity" (p.15). In Lave's perspective "school" is one type of everyday setting, and as in any other setting, success and failure in mathematical tasks might best be understood in terms of relations between persons, their activities, and contexts rather than solely in terms of cognitive strategies.

Arcavi's (2002) examination of the concept of "everyday" asked the question "Everyday for whom?" (p. 13). He suggested that "everyday" depends on the context and practice within which the mathematics takes place. Sometimes, because of the context, the activity may not be recognized as one that is mathematical. He also suggests that we can bridge contexts of "everydayness" by also seeing the "everyday" in academic mathematics settings and "realistic" mathematization (such as problem solving).

CULTURAL MEDIATION OF MATHEMATICAL THINKING AND LEARNING

Different Tools in Different Practices

Having established that performance in a mathematical task was linked to the context of the practice, such as in-school versus out-of-school context, research moved on to explore the cognitive and social processes associated with different performances. For example, Terezinha Nunes and her colleagues (Carraher et al., 1982, Nunes, 1992a; 1992b; Nunes & Bryant, 1996), while investigating the mathematics of street children in Brazil, reflected on the processes that explained: "How is it that the same children offered two different performances in problems apparently similar, depending on their use of oral or written strategies?" Their careful examination of "oral" and "written" arithmetic revealed key differences between the two forms. Thus, oral arithmetic: (i) Preserves the relative value of number; (ii) proceeds in the order we speak, from large to small numbers; (iii) allows different types of manipulation, such as dealing with different values and then adjusting; and (iv) preserves the meaning of the situation. Written arithmetic: (i) sets the relative value of number aside; (ii) usually follows the opposite order in which we speak; (iii) given numbers are strictly adhered to in problem solving; and (iv) sets the meaning of the situation aside. Nunes's analysis highlighted the fact that common errors in both written and oral calculations were linked not only to the functioning of the mind, but were also inherently linked to specific organizations of systems of representations—to the tool that mediated the person's mathematical action. Cultural practices provide tools that both expand and impose limits on the mathematical operations the person can carry out (Nunes, 1992b; Nunes & Bryant, 1996).

Bose and Subramaniam's (2011) ongoing studies in India show that this approach is still very important in understanding the different performances of the same people in different practices. In their studies they explore and characterize the nature and extent of everyday mathematics knowledge and involvement in economic activities amongst middle-grade students from schools located in a large low-income area in Mumbai. Their findings show that the students developed sound knowledge of currency handling in "everyday mathematics," including doing arithmetic operations on the currency involving multidigit numbers (Bose & Subramaniam, 2011). However, similarly to the studies carried out in Brazil (e.g. Nunes et al., 1993), the students' ability to handle oral strategies was better than their attempts at written approaches. These findings are supported by a study in Lebanon with street vendors who, even when faced with formal school-like tests, attempted to inject everyday meaning into the figures to try and make sense of them (Jurdak & Sharhin, 1999).

Another finding from Subramaniam and Bose (2012) is that in everyday household-based activities, the use of a diverse modes and units of measurement is evident. In contrast, they report that in "modern Indian school mathematics textbooks this diversity is not found and only standard units are taught using standard measuring instruments like a ruler or weighing balance" (p. 1982). They suggest that the concept of "demathematization" can explain why mathematics used in informal practices in out-of-school contexts are not part of the school curriculum. In both examples (i.e. currency and measurement), it is apparent that the everyday context exposes the students to different cultural tools. The authors acknowledge that in their studies the implications for the way the students experience the transition between their everyday and their school mathematics remains to be explored. However, in their view, the restricted view of measurement in current school textbooks may make it difficult for the students to see the connection between what they learn in school and their rich experiences of measurement outside school.

This type of evidence allows for a connection between the analysis of empirical data and Vygotsky's notion of cultural mediation of psychological functioning. Within this perspective a central focus of the studies has been on understanding what are the tools or artifacts used in specific social practices and their role in mediating mathematical action and thinking. Systems of representations, such as mental tools, can be seen as sharing some properties with tools used to operate in the physical environment. For instance, using a bike as a means of transport compared with using a car shapes the action in different ways. Similarly, using oral arithmetic as means to solve a mathematical problem shapes the action differently from using written arithmetic.

Unique Appropriation of Cultural Tools

Most of the theoretical advances mentioned earlier have resulted from studies conducted within traditional out-of-school practices, such as street vending, farming, and carpentry. There was also a tendency in these studies to describe patterns that applied to the whole community. This means that there is still a need to explain how individual diversity can emerge. Abreu explored this issue, reflecting on her study with sugarcane farmers. Between 1995 and 1998, she carried out an investigation into the use and understanding of mathematics by sugarcane farmers in the northeast of Brazil (Abreu, 1998b, 1999). Her motive to engage in this particular project was to gain an understanding of why the farmers had difficulties in appropriating modern technology. Both theoretically and methodologically, Abreu's study was informed by the so-called everyday cognition approach (Rogoff & Lave, 1984), and by a Vygotskian view of mathematics learning as the internalization of sociocultural tools.

The ethnographic approach led Abreu (1998b, 1999) to describe the particular mathematics used by the farmers, which differed from school mathematics. For instance, they had specific length and area measures, formulas to calculate areas, and a variety of oral strategies to solve sums that involved both additive and multiplicative structures. In addition, the findings from the interviews about the strategies used by the farmers revealed the way their experiences with the use of specific tools mediated their cognition. By concentrating on the similarities of tool use among farmers, evidence that showed unique appropriation of the tools was overlooked and the mechanisms behind this were not explored. The analysis did not address development at the level of the individual. Nevertheless, this latter type of analysis may well clarify the origins of diversity among individuals in similar cultural practices.

Looking retrospectively at the data, one can see two distinct patterns of the farmers' reconstruction of cultural knowledge. For instance, reexamining their procedures for calculating the areas of quadrilateral and triangular plots of land, one can see more than one pattern. In the most prevalent pattern, farmers followed a convention. For example, the area of a triangular plot of land was found by multiplying the average of the two opposite sides by one half of the length of the remaining side $\{Area = [(a + b) / 2] \times (c / 2)\}$. For those following this pattern, it is as if personal knowledge mirrored the conventional cultural knowledge, a truly Vygotskian account of a reconstruction of the social at a psychological level. A less-common pattern seems to indicate a more complex process. For instance, instead of following the conventional procedure, one of the farmers multiplied one of the sides by half the length of the smaller side of the triangle $\{Area = [b \times (a / 2)]\}$. When asked why he had not averaged the "opposite sides," he said that could not be done and went on to explain that the largest side was discounted because it can be seen as equivalent to the diagonal of a quadrilateral. Thus, using it in the formulae would result in overestimating the area of the triangle (Abreu, 1998b). In this pattern, there was an indication of uniqueness: personal knowledge was grounded in cultural knowledge, but it was not a copy of it. The reference to the diagonal of a triangle also suggests that the unique solution could be a hybrid form that combines pieces of knowledge from farming practices with pieces from school practices. This pattern is in agreement with Saxe's observations of the impact of being exposed to new practices on cognition.

The Use of Tools in Transitions between Practices

Evidence that what one person learns in one practice does not always translate to other practices makes it possible to question traditional explanations of transfer in terms of an automatic cognitive process. It is also the case, however, that people move between practices and that some overlapping between uses of knowledge has been observed. Some researchers have argued that it is important to explain these movements by using a developmental dimension in the investigations (Abreu, 1998a; Saxe, 1991; Van Oers, 1998). Saxe (1991) addressed developmental issues in his investigations among Brazilian candy sellers (boys aged between 6 and 15 years). His study involved ethnographic observations in which the specific mathematics of candy selling was described and demonstrated through structured interviews. One example examined how children decided the price of candies for retail sale. Saxe observed that younger children were more likely to rely on other people (wholesale store clerks, parents, or colleagues) while the older ones did the calculations themselves. Among the children who did the calculations, he observed that they predominantly made use of practice-linked strategies. He also observed, however, that some children used school-linked strategies, which in fact involved the appropriation of both practice and school-based mathematics. Saxe's developmental approach provided two new insights into the way transitions between out-of-school and in-school mathematical practices may be conceptualized. The first is to regard these transitions as a constructive developmental process taking shape over time through a progressive appropriation and specialization of forms of knowledge. The second is to regard these transitions as a socially supported process.

Saxe's insights can be applied to understanding learners in transition between different school mathematical practices, as is the case of many immigrant school students. The socio-developmental nature of transition processes were observed in our case study analysis of Felipe, an immigrant student in a secondary school in Catalonia (Abreu et al., 2013). In Chile, Felipe used to like mathematics and was considered a good student doing well in the subject. This was the self-image he continued having of himself in Catalonia until the moment he failed his school mathematics assessments. At this stage he was surprised to find, like many other immigrant students, that mathematical operations and strategies were not the same as he had experienced in Chile. Trying to make sense of what happened to him when interviewed, he talked about the importance of time (developmental process) and significant others (socially supported process). Looking back, Felipe stressed the importance of time in two ways: first, the time it took him to become aware of what was happening and how it affected his school career. His grades in mathematics make it seem impossible for him to pursue his choice of university degree. Second, he talked about the way parents and teachers could have played a role in helping him become aware of the differences and addressing issues at an earlier stage.

The focus on the use of cultural tools for people who experience transitions between mathematical practices shows that (i) participation in different mathematical practices has implications for mathematical cognition, as the participant may, for example develop new hybrid strategies; (ii) that these practices are socially organized and that significant others play a role in the way a person appropriates mathematical knowledge; (iii) that shifts in mathematical cognition occur as constructive developmental processes; and (iv) that school mathematics is better conceptualized as a variety of specific "school mathematical" practices that are distinctive depending on their contexts. This last point allow us to draw on the insights of research on out-of-school mathematics to understand mathematical learning in current globalized and multicultural societies, where it is common that learners experience transitions between different school mathematical practices—for example, transitions between school mathematics at school and school mathematics at home, and transitions between school mathematics of the home country and school mathematics of a host country.

SOCIAL MEDIATION OF MATHEMATICAL LEARNING

As described earlier, studies on out-of-school mathematics arose from cross-cultural psychology and this seems to have shaped the way the impact of the social was initially explored. First, the studies carried out on a variety of out-of-school practices in different cultures pointed to links between the uses of mathematical tools and sociocultural and institutional contexts. Second, the notion that the tools with one uses to think are cultural generated interest in a particular type of asymmetric social interaction: between someone who is more knowledgeable and someone who is less knowledgeable, such as parent-child, teacher-pupil, or master-apprentice. We first review some key studies under these two foci and then explore the impact of changes on the macro-social level.

The Mediating Role of Social Institutions

In the sequence of out-of-school studies that suggested the use of tools was linked to the context of the practices, researchers explored the applicability of these ideas to formal institutional contexts. Research on cultural aspects has addressed context-specific cognition related to activities (e.g., tailoring, schooling, selling), while research on social aspects has addressed issues related to the social institutions where these activities take place. Examples of such studies are Säljö and Wyndhamn (1993) and Schubauer-Leoni (1990). Both investigated the applicability of the ideas to different contexts within school by comparing performance inside and outside the mathematics classrooms. Säljö and Wyndhamn found that Swedish students, when asked to solve postage problems, called on different strategies according to the context in which the task was presented. In the context of a mathematics lesson, 57% of the students attempted some type of calculation. In a social studies lesson, however, only 29% used calculations. In this context most of the students found the solution by reading the postage table. Schubauer-Leoni and collaborators (Schubauer-Leoni, 1990; Schubauer-Leoni and Perret-Clermont, 1997) found that 8- and 9-year-old Swiss children used different solutions to addition problems according to the context in which they were tested. Only three out of 34 pupils used conventional arithmetical notation when tested outside the classroom, compared with 17 out of 39 pupils when tested in the classroom. Because the cultural artifacts available were similar, one can hypothesize that differences in the solution were related to "multitude of genres" (Minick, Stone, & Forman, 1993). Mathematics, like language, provided different uses that emerged as a function of the ways tasks are interpreted. The institutional place where the activities were presented to the children provided different frames for the interpretation of the task and allowed them a choice of tools. These findings add another dimension to the understanding of continuities and discontinuities in the use of mathematical knowledge across practices. They suggest that institutional discursive practices (Walkerdine, 1988) regulate uses of mathematical knowledge, and consequently, patterns of development.

The Mediating Role of Social Interactions

Although the influence of social interactions in learning is one of the main lines of investigation in sociocultural theory, most of the empirical research in mathematics learning has been conducted either in controlled experimental situations or in classrooms (Cobb, 1995; Forman, Larreamendy-Joerns, Stein, & Brown, 1998; Schubauer-Leoni & Perret-Clermont, 1997). Thus analyses of social interactions specific to the transmission and appropriation of mathematical knowledge in out-of-school practices are scarce (Hyde, Else-Quest, Alibali, Knuth, & Romberg, 2006; Saxe, 1996; Vandermaas-Peeler, Nelson, Bumpass, & Sassine, 2009).

Saxe, Guberman, and Gearhart (1987) introduced detailed analysis of social interactions in out-of-school mathematics by researching number practices in White families living in Brooklyn, New York. They sampled families from both working- and middle-class groups with young children aged 2.5 to 4 years. Previous research had revealed that children of this age developed some basic mathematical knowledge, but the enculturating processes through which these children acquired this knowledge had not been addressed. By conducting in-depth interviews with the mothers, Saxe et al.'s research revealed the social structuring of early number practices at home. These practices had been organized taking into account age and class differences. For instance, the younger children tended to be engaged in less-complex activities, while the older children engaged in more-complex activities. Furthermore, analyses of mother-child video-taped interactions revealed the dialectical nature of the process: "mothers were adjusting their goal-related directives to their children's understandings and task-related accomplishments and children were adjusting their goal-directed activities to their mothers' efforts to organize the task" (Saxe, 1996, p. 292).

Further support that families play a part in the structuring of practices that contribute to the child's development of mathematical cognition outside school was obtained in Guberman's (1996) study with Brazilian families. Children from working-class families in Brazil often engage in commercial transactions. Taking this into consideration, Guberman observed and interviewed parents of Brazilian children aged 4 to 14 years. He explored how parents structured their children's learning of mathematics by varying the degree of responsibility assigned to the child in purchasing tasks. His findings revealed four levels of engagement in purchase tasks that were related to increasing arithmetical complexity. For instance, at Level 1, the child is given the exact amount of money needed for the purchase. At Level 2, the child is not given an exact amount and is told to wait for the change. At Level 3, the child is required to check the change. At Level 4, the child is expected to calculate the cost of the purchase. Identification of currency and the requirement to make calculations varied in complexity from Levels 1 to 4. Guberman concluded that "even in activities distal from direct verbal interaction with parents, children learning often is regulated by parents" (p. 1621).

The types of mathematical competencies studied by Saxe and Guberman have often been referred to as *informal mathematics*. Furthermore, some authors assert that "much of this informal mathematics can develop in the absence of adult instruction; indeed, many adults are quite surprised to learn how much their young children or students know in this area" (Ginsburg, Choi, Lopez, Netley, & Chao-Yuan, 1997, p. 165). Saxe and Guberman's findings do, however, suggest that the absence of formal instruction cannot be confused with lack of socially organized activities that support a child's development of mathematical concepts. In fact, in the same way that adults would not often define their uses of mathematics in outside school activities as mathematical, they would likewise not define their children's practices as mathematical (see also O'Toole & Abreu, 2005). The mediating role of adults and more expert peers in structuring and supporting the new generations in their local practices, however, is revealed when explored in systematic research.

The need for basic research exploring parent-child interactions associated with mathematics learning in the home is noted in the literature. Hyde et al. (2006), for example, argue that "Parents are a largely untapped resource for improving the mathematics performance of American children" (p. 136). The importance of home mathematical practices and of a socio-cultural approach in their study was applied to predominantly White mothers, which the authors acknowledge as a limitation of their study, as ethnic minority parents may differ. However, their main findings actually reflect those from studies with other cultural groups; i.e., the way mothers interact with their children is impacted by their mathematical knowledge and by their self-confidence. In our studies we have opted for referring to self-confidence as part of mathematical identities, a concept that better reflects a socio-cultural approach to mathematics learning (see for example, Abreu, 1995; Crafter & Abreu, 2010). Indeed, a recent study by Newton and Abreu (2014) exemplifies how the concept of identity can offer new insights on the way parents interact with their children. Using a dialogical self approach, Newton's analysis suggested that the parent's mathematical identity, in the form of positioning the "self" (the parent) and "other" (the child) was seen to influence mathematical activities during parent-child interaction. In his study, how the parent perceived the mathematical identity of their child was more important in determining mathematical activity than the parent's own mathematical identity. This was seen in the way parental practice reflected: children's feelings and emotions regarding mathematics, children's perceived competencies at mathematics, and children's attitude towards mathematical activity.

The Impact of Macro-Social Change

In current societies, with increasing levels of cultural change, new communication technologies, and the unprecedented levels of traveling and migration, it is likely that both adults and children frequently experience exposure to change and coexisting practices. Sociocultural approaches to mathematics learning, in particular those based on initial interpretations of Vygotsky and apprenticeship models, are recognized as providing a limited account of the impact of the societal changes on learning (Forman, Minick, & Stone, 1993; Goodnow, 1990). Studies of interactions following a Vygotskian approach were criticized for providing "descriptions of perfectly orchestrated dyads" (Litowitz, 1993, p. 187) and for a lack of consideration of the influences of the wider social structure (Stone, 1993). We revisit Abreu's research with the sugarcane farmers (Abreu, 1998b) to illustrate how a change on the macro-cultural impacts on an individual participant. At the time of Abreu's field work in the farming community, the farmers were in the midst of coping with one of these external demands. Changes in the Brazilian economy at a macro level led the government to impose new criteria for the payment of sugarcane.

The first impact of the change was that it required a type of mathematical knowledge most of farmers did not have. Traditional mathematics (Abreu, 1999) enabled the farmers to grasp some understanding of the new system, such as when comparing whether they were making or losing money, but it was limited when they had to read and interpret tables combining different variables and when they were required to understand concepts such as percentages, decimals, and positive and negative numbers. The second type of impact was on the farmers' identities. The changes made them experience loss of control, it brought uncertainty, and it threatened their standing. They were not sure where they stood, whether they could contract services, whether they could borrow money from the bank, and perhaps more importantly, whether they could survive in business. The third impact was that exposure to technological innovation and modern institutions (e.g., schools, banks) over time raised the farmers' awareness that some forms of knowledge are more powerful than others, and also that some are more accepted than others. For the person, changes in macro-social structures can have different types of impact, which can be linked both to mathematical knowledge itself, and to the way knowledge influences identities.

The insights gained from the farmers can be applied to explore the impact of changes in school mathematical curriculum on parents. Our studies in England have shown the crucial impact that the introduction of a National Numeracy Strategy had on the relationship between home and school mathematics. The mathematics that children are learning in today's primary schools is different from the parents own school mathematics. Several studies with the parents revealed that these changes had an impact on the way they try to make sense of new mathematical knowledge (e.g. understanding new strategies, understanding a number line), on their identities (in terms of how parents feel able to support their children), and in their relationship with their children (who often resist the parents' knowledge as different from the school). Despite schools' attempts to help the parents to catch up with curriculum changes, such as running workshops for parents, it was apparent many parents still struggled (see for example, Crafter, 2012; McMullen & Abreu, 2011; Newton & Abreu, 2012). This is an area that needs further research as there are gaps in the understanding of the impact of parental involvement in their children's school mathematics.

Another key example of the impact of societal changes is the examination of practices, such as peer collaboration, that may have worked in monocultural classrooms but do not necessarily work in multicultural classrooms. This is exemplified by Elbers and de Haan

(2005). They examined the construction of word meaning by students in a multicultural mathematics classroom at a Dutch primary school. The school where they worked had 80% of the students from a minority background, mainly Moroccan and Turkish, and the teachers followed a pedagogy that promoted peer collaboration. Elbers and de Haan recorded and examined the way students deal with language problems in mathematical tasks that originate from minority students' unfamiliarity with specific Dutch words and expressions. The initial expectation was that clarifying cultural meanings of Dutch words was crucial for the students to overcome their language problems—but their analysis pointed out something different. Their study showed that minority students: (1) do not ask for clarification of word meaning during teacher-fronted classroom instruction; (2) do raise problems with word meanings when working in groups, but their conversations about word meaning are restricted to their collaborative group activities. The clarification of meaning was made part of the mathematical discourse, even in groups with Dutch children who potentially did have access to the wider cultural discourse. When providing explanations the Dutch students did not elucidate the meaning of the unfamiliar words in broad cultural terms but gave minimal information, which was sufficient for minority students to solve the task. These findings suggest that the institutional practices take for granted the students' access to cultural meanings. Peer collaboration in the classroom investigated by Elbers and de Haan required the Dutch students to take on the role of helping classmates from a diversity of cultural and linguistic backgrounds. This is a completely new challenge that required them to engage in forms of interaction unfamiliar to them. Future research has to address the development and promotion of new forms of interaction and classroom communication that better support access to the mathematical curriculum cultural meanings (Abreu & Elbers, 2005; Elbers & de Haan, 2005).

FROM CULTURAL AND SOCIAL MEDIATION TO THE PERSON AS PARTICIPANT IN MULTIPLE MATHEMATICAL PRACTICES

The insights from the research outlined earlier contributed to the development of socio-cultural approaches to mathematical learning that apply to all learners. These insights offered a new lens to explore the learning of children from home cultures different from their school culture. The evidence that children and young people (such as the Brazilian street children) developed competence in out-of-school mathematics begged for an explanation as to why they were failing in their school mathematics. Along the same lines researchers working with immigrant and minority communities started exploring relationships between home–school mathematics (e.g. the work of Marta Civil in the United States, see Civil, 2008). Initially, the notion of home mathematics underlying these studies was based on engagement with informal working activities (e.g., street vending, farming, dressmaking).

Over time the notion of home mathematics evolved to include a wider range of "everyday" practices including both implicit (spontaneous) numeracy practices such as playing games, cooking, and baking, and more explicit numeracy practices such as counting, using money, and school mathematics at home. The need to distinguish between these different types of numeracy at home has been recognized as crucial to the understanding of the impact of outside-school mathematics on school mathematics learning (Crafter & Abreu, 2011; LeFevre et al., 2009; Vandermaas-Peeler et al., 2009). This is a sign that the notion of home numeracy practices is starting to be recognized as mainstream and relevant to the understanding of the mathematical learning of all children. We would argue, however, that an understanding of home–school mathematics needs more than a description of the numeracy practices; it needs a clear account of the ways the key actors (child, parent, and teacher) participate in and experience these practices.

Children's Participation in Home Mathematics

Observations from Abreu's studies with schoolchildren in Brazil and Portugal (Abreu, 1995; Abreu, Bishop, & Pompeu, 1997) revealed a new angle on how they participated in outside-school mathematical practices. Instead of a common pattern of enculturation into home practices, evidence of heterogeneity emerged. Shopping activities related to the everyday life of the family—for example, fetching bread, fruit, or vegetables—were common practices among the children in Abreu's studies. Interviews with children engaged in similar practices revealed differences in what the child was in charge of: (i) some of the children just did the shopping, and adults took responsibility for economic exchanges (that is, they fully accepted the vendor's sums and change or their parents took responsibility for that); (ii) some of the children shared the responsibility with their parents or with other adults; and (iii) some of the children described themselves as being in charge of the economic decisions involved. The manner in which the children experienced this situation seemed to influence the extent to which they used mathematics in the home practices. At a first glance, these forms of engagement can be seen as developmental. Indeed, it is not difficult to see some resemblance with Guberman's (1996) levels of engagement. However, in-depth comparative case study analysis suggested that the diversity could be linked to the way parents supported their children's engagement in out-of-school practices, including other factors than the children's developmental level. For instance, children's accounts suggested that not all the families engaged their children in the use of traditional home mathematics.

It seems common understanding that diversity in participation results in different degrees of mastery of knowledge. However, the way people gain an understanding of the social world around them involves other social processes. Children and young people develop an understanding of the valorization of coexisting mathematical practices and associated social identities, which make them active agents in the way they participate in the practices (Abreu & Cline, 2003) Drawing on Tajfel (1978), participating in mathematical practices results in two key processes: First it results in the process of social categorization, i.e., "the ordering of the social environment in terms of groupings of persons in a manner which makes sense to individuals" (Tajfel, 1978, p. 61). Second, social comparison emerges from a human tendency to evaluate the ordering within the system of values of a society. These processes contribute to an individual's development of social identities: i.e., how a membership in particular community of practice contributes to an understanding of who they are and where they stand.

The findings from Abreu and her colleagues' studies indicated that children had developed ways of categorizing some practices of their community as involving uses of mathematics and others as not involving them. For instance, in the farming community in Brazil (Abreu, 1995), it was more likely that children would categorize working in an office as a practice in which people use mathematics than working on a sugarcane farm. In England (Abreu & Cline, 2003), few children categorized driving a taxi as a practice that requires the use of mathematics, but they could see shopping as one that does. They also associated performances in school mathematics with given social identities. For instance, for tasks in which they had to choose adults who might have been good or bad at school, the children chose more adults in white-collar professions (office workers) as possibly having been the best in school mathematics; conversely children chose those in blue-collar professions and other low social status practices as possibly the worst.

We argue that these social-psychological processes are key to explain processes of mathematical learning as intersecting with processes of identity development. Studies in cultures where home mathematics is distinct from school mathematics (Abreu, 1995), and studies with immigrant and minority students, illustrated that children and young people become aware of the differences between their home and their school practices (see Abreu, Bishop, & Presmeg, 2002a; Abreu & Elbers, 2005). In addition, some of these studies have shown that students talked about these differences in relation to how they perceived their home cultural identities as intersecting with their school mathematical learning. Gorgorió, Planas, and Vilella (2002) clearly illustrated this intersection when they reported the case of Saima, a 15-year-old Indian girl, who expressed the feeling of being displaced in the Catalonian mathematical classroom. As she said, "Miss, I'm wrong in your class . . . I do the same mathematics as boys, but I will not do the same work . . . I do not want to be a mechanic. Please, can I do mathematics for girls?" (p. 44). Saima's positioning was constructed at the intersection of her gender identity, her cultural identity, and her identity as a mathematical learner.

Crafter and Abreu (2010) also found evidence of a similar developmental process in her study with learners in multiethnic mathematical classrooms in England. They examined the case of Monifa, a 10-year-old daughter of a Nigerian family, who developed awareness that the differences between the mathematical practices of her father and her teacher were linked to their cultural identities. As Monifa explained: "Sometimes they just explain it differently. . . . Because my dad would have done it differently and it's where we come from because my dad was taught in Nigeria, and he taught in Nigeria. And Miss Durham has been here. So, they do it in different ways." When recounting an event where the teacher tried to convince her that her father's solution was not appropriate, she said: "I wasn't too keen but I understand my dad's more so I went with my dad. But she is my teacher in school, so. . . . ." Monifa's view was that the best way of coping for her would be to stick to each mathematical practice according to the context. But, as she explained, the practices of the school and home often made requests on her that made her feel as if she were "two people": "It's like I'm two people at the same time and it's just hard." Case studies such as Saima's and Monifa's illustrate that some students develop awareness of the significance of their cultural identity in their school mathematical learning, experienced in this case, as a discontinuity. They also suggest that to cope with discontinuity these students have engaged with complex identity work, which requires them to articulate the impact of differences between home and school mathematical practices in relation to identities.

Parents Participation in Their Children's School Mathematics

Observations such as those outlined earlier motivated our inclusion of parents in research investigating how children experience the relationship between their home and school mathematics. It seemed likely that parents were playing a key role in the diversity among children in their reconstruction of the cultural systems of knowledge of the home practices. It also seemed likely that they were playing a part (sometimes unintentional) in the way the children were developing their identities as mathematical learners. But the dynamics through which their influences operated were unclear. Were their own valorizations of the coexisting mathematical practices the crucial factor? Or was their influence shaped in interactions (and perhaps negotiations) with the children themselves (i.e., a joint construction)? To explore these issues, the research strategy adopted with the Brazilian schoolchildren (Abreu, 1995) was expanded to include a parental perspective. The new studies were conducted in multiethnic primary schools in England (Abreu & Cline, 1998; Abreu, Cline, & Shamsi, 2002b; Abreu & Cline, 2005; O'Toole & Abreu, 2005).

For the initial studies, schools with representative numbers of children from Bangladeshi (Abreu & Cline, 1998) and Pakistani families living in England were selected (Abreu et al., 2002b; Abreu & Cline, 2005). The patterns of achievement of children in these multiethnic schools had some similarities to the schools in Brazil. Children of Bangladeshi and Pakistani origin, on average, underachieved in English schools (OFSTED, 1999). Nonetheless, as in Brazil, within any single-year group, there was variation in performance among the children from the same home group, which included both high and low achievers. It was also likely that there were differences between children's home and school mathematics because their parents experienced a different culture and a different school system through having gone to school in their country of origin. Therefore, it was possible to follow the original question: "Do the children who succeed [in school mathematics] establish a different relationship with their home knowledge than the ones who fail?" (Abreu, 1995, p. 124), by incorporating a parental perspective. That is, if children establish a different relationship do parents play a role and, if so, what does that role involves?

Parents' more vivid accounts of their engagement in helping the children with mathematics at home were related to school mathematics. It was also in these accounts that both children and parents made explicit the differences between the way mathematics was tackled in the child's school and at home (Abreu & Cline, 2005; Abreu et al., 2002b). Accounts from the parents showed that differences between home and school mathematics could be experienced in terms of:

- The content of school mathematics and in the strategies used for calculations (examples included differences in algorithms for subtraction and division);
- The methods of teaching and the tools used in teaching (for example, methods for learning times tables, use of calculators);
- The language in which they learned and felt confident doing mathematics.

Apart from the differences related to language, the first two differences applied to both groups studied, i.e., White-British and Asian-British parents. They seem to be linked to the parents' experience of a different school system (immigrant parents) and or to changes in the curriculum over time in England. This meant that in both ethnic groups, if parents (relatives) were to support the child at school properly, they had to figure out the necessary process of transition between their own mathematical practices and the ones the child was experiencing (Abreu et al., 2002b).

Differences within the same ethnic group emerged when we focused the analysis on (i) the influences of the parents' positions in the way they tackled the differences, and (ii) a comparison between information obtained from the parent and their child regarding representations, experiences, and negotiations of differences between home and school mathematics (Abreu & Cline, 2005). There was some evidence that the way parents structured their support to their children was likely to be colored by their own positions about which form of knowledge they valued more. For instance, they took positions regarding the language by which mathematics was communicated, or regarding the importance of knowing the times tables by heart.

Abreu and her colleagues' (2002b) examination of the patterns of interaction between the child and the parent's experiences offered further insight into the emergence of within group diversity. Comparative case study analysis highlighted some possible links between patterns of interaction and children's performances. Comparison of two Pakistani children, both in Year 2, and in the same mathematics class, showed that for the low-achieving child, there was a discontinuity between the child's preferences and the way the parents were trying to support him in learning school mathematics. His parents were not aware that the transition exposed the child to differences between the way they taught mathematics to him at home and the way he was learning at school. The child's accounts revealed that he believed the teacher knew better than his mother did and that he preferred the English language. At home, however, his parents were teaching him in Urdu, and did not show any awareness that the change in language at school could cause him difficulties. This seemed a case in which the parents' representations of primary school mathematics were still associated with their own schooling. Difficulties in communication with the school might have reinforced their representation. By contrast, in the case of the high achiever, there was continuity in the way differences in methods, language, and identities were negotiated. In this case, the parents—in particular the mother—had developed representations of home and school learning that included a theory of how her child might experience the transition. For this child, the differences between the mother and his teacher's mathematics did not mean that home practices had "inferior status." Like the low achiever, he also preferred the English language, but in this case the mother was prepared to help the child bridge the gap between the two languages.

A basic distinction between the low achiever and the high achiever was seen in the parents' awareness of the existence of differences in their own ways of doing mathematics and those that their child was being taught at school. The parent of the high achiever also showed more awareness of the child's preferences. The success was then achieved through sensitive interactions, in which the mother learned from the child and then adjusted her strategies to fit with his needs and preferences. A case study with a White-British parent, however, showed that being aware of the difference was not enough to support a child. In this case, the mother had developed an acute sense of the differences between her methods and those of the child, but was experiencing it as a burden. Therefore, interactions conducive to success seemed to require awareness of differences, flexible adjustment, and specialized mathematical knowledge. In sum, including the perspective of parents revealed the intersection of the social, cultural, and individual. It showed that parents did not just recreate their own mathematical background for their children. They deliberately selected some forms of knowledge from those available in their culture as appropriate to transmit to their children and rejected or hid other forms. Finally, the actions of some parents seemed to take into account the active role of the child.

This area was further investigated using the concept of cultural models and resources to give insight into how parents make sense of their child's mathematics learning (Crafter, 2012). Cultural models are patterns and meanings that help us make sense of our experiences. When faced with new experiences parents would need to draw on existing cultural models to make sense of those. In which case, what resources do parents draw on during the process of this sense making? Interviews with 28 parents revealed that the type of resources used to make sense of home-school mathematics depended on what parents were focusing on. For example, when trying to understand the child's achievement, parents would look towards the teacher, exam results, and their own models of child development to incorporate new information into existing cultural models (Crafter, 2012). The use of resources to expand one's understanding of home-school mathematics was precarious. Parents often misunderstood the messages teachers gave them about their child's achievement, the way exam results were reported were hard for parents to understand, and parents' understandings of child development (and therefore the expectations for what a child can perform at a particular age) did not always match the school's. Using the child as a resource for completing mathematics homework could be more problematic for parents whose children did not understand the mathematics or who were generally resistant to completing it.

The question of what counts as mathematics in culturally diverse homes also warrants some attention. For example, some parents were skilled at explicitly undertaking activities that the child may, or may not, be aware involves learning mathematics. Or, parents know that an activity like cooking explicitly uses mathematics but they do not know how to make this activity into one involving calculation. Equally, mathematics may be implicit in home activities without parents being aware that they are doing mathematics (Crafter & Abreu, 2013). Vandermaas-Peeler et al. (2009) also argue that distinguishing different types of parents' home numeracies is important to understand children's mathematical development. In their study they distinguish "*socio-cultural numeracy exchanges*, explaining the use and value of money or numbers in routine activities such as shopping or cooking, and *mathematical exchanges*, including counting, quantity or size comparisons" (p.67, our emphasis).

To sum up, the need to distinguish between different types of parental numeracy practices is now gaining wider acceptance and is being advocated as a potential avenue to understand the impact of parents on their child's school mathematical learning (see for example, LeFevre, et al., 2009). Socio-cultural studies suggest complex ways of exploring these practices taking into account the intricate relationships between knowledge construction and identities.

CONCLUDING THOUGHTS

In conclusion, we would like to reflect on the extent that accounts of how learners 'experience relationships between mathematical learning in and out of school are emphasizing continuity or discontinuity between these practices. There is not a simple explanation for this relationship. We discerned distinct phases on the research to elaborate our thinking.

Research since the 1970s on out-of-school mathematics has followed the same direction as that of Vygotsky's theory on the impact of culture in the mind. According to Minick et al. (1993), Vygotskian research of the late 1970s and early 1980s tested the plausibility of the theoretical framework. It was one-dimensional and focused on a discussion around the relationship between cognition and cognitive tools. This is reflected in the initial studies on out-of-school mathematics that explored the cultural nature of mathematical tools, such as counting systems, and how these were appropriated and used as cognitive tools. The emphasis on this initial work was on the differences between out-of-school and in-school mathematics. It was apparent that there was discontinuity between the practices, as competence in one practice did not predict performance in the other practice. This applied in both directions. One could be competent in out-of-school mathematics and also having difficulties at school. In the same vein, one could be competent in school mathematics and not perform well in out-of-school mathematics (e.g. see Nunes et al., 1993).

Following this period, during the late 1980s and 90s the framework was broadened to pay attention to processes of social mediation. The attention to social institutions and social interactions became apparent when research in out-of-school mathematics shifted from cross-cultural comparisons to social practices within the Western societies. Contrasting out-of-school and in-school mathematics took another turn here. It became clear that both institutions and participants in social interactions played a part in the continuity and discontinuity between the practices. Social representations of what counts as school mathematical knowledge and about the learning process can be seen as influencing the continuity and discontinuity. Thus, for example, the representation that certain forms of out-of-school mathematics are poorly valued at school may contribute to discontinuity. This also applies to the representation of school mathematical practices over time, as for example, in the context of societal changes, parents' school mathematics can be represented as "old fashioned." From a social perspective, participation in mathematical practices becomes a process of understanding and construction of social and cultural identities (Abreu, 1995; Abreu & Cline, 2003; Crafter & Abreu, 2010). The issues of continuity and discontinuity become both issues of connecting mathematical concepts, tools, understandings, and issues of identity. Connecting out of-school and in-school mathematics also involves dialogue and negotiation between identity positions of the self and significant others. These insights contributed to a third turn in this field of research that focuses on the person as a participant in multiple mathematical practices. From this perspective, discontinuity is a starting point. Research explores trajectories of participation, attempting to make sense of the processes that result in a person experiencing discontinuity in practices over time and across practices, and the processes that enable change and facilitate continuity.

As far as educational policy is concerned, there has been very little change in the last decade. Research in out-of-school contexts as well as in mathematical learning in multicultural schools suggests that in situations where home backgrounds differ markedly from school backgrounds, children might benefit from an approach that helps them bridge gaps and cross boundaries (Abreu et al., 2002a). This is still far from being the way curricular reforms are implemented in England. The numeracy framework in England emphasizes the need for parents and communities to be involved in their children's mathematics education to ensure achievement (Abreu & Cline, 2005; Brown, Askew, Baker, Denvir, & Millet, 1998). The parents' involvement, however, is not seen in terms of helping the children to integrate home and school numeracies (Abreu & Cline, 2005). It is instead portrayed in unidirectional terms, in which the parents are expected to support school numeracies, but no attention is given to home numeracy practices.

Although these policies are in line with representations of teachers and parents, who view the school mathematics as the relevant one for the child's success in today's society, they might fail to take into account the actual experiences of the developing child (Abreu & Cline, 2005).

Research on the development of immigrant children does suggest that successful pathways are associated with transcultural identities that promote a creative acquisition of competencies from the culture(s) of origin and the host culture (Suárez-Orozco & Suárez-Orozco, 2001). The case studies reported in the previous section suggest that mathematics education is far from understanding how to design classroom practices that enable children to see distinct mathematical practices as part of their transcultural identities. The social and cultural basis of representations from teachers, parents, and curriculum planners need to be understood along with an examination of their impact on the way learners experience transitions between their school and out-of-school mathematical practices.

REFERENCES

Abreu, G. de (1995). Understanding how children experience the relationship between home and school mathematics. *Mind, Culture and Activity: An International Journal, 2*(2), 119–142.

Abreu, G. de (1998a). The mathematics learning in sociocultural contexts: The mediating role of social valorisation. *Learning and Instruction, 8*(6), 567–572.

Abreu, G. de (1998b). Reflecting on mathematics in and out of school from a cultural psychology perspective. In A.O.A.K. Newstead (Ed.), *PME—The International group for the psychology of mathematics education* (Vol. 1, pp. 115–130). Stellenbosh, South Africa: PME.

Abreu, G. de (1999). Learning mathematics in and outside school: Two views on situated learning. In J. Bliss, R. Saljo, & P. Light (Eds.), *Learning sites: Social and technological resources for learning* (pp. 17–31). Oxford: Elsevier Science.

Abreu, G. de (2014). Cultural diversity in mathematics education. In *Encyclopedia of mathematics education* (pp. 125–129). Dordrecht, The Netherlands: Springer.

Abreu, G. de, Bishop, A., & Pompeu, G. (1997). What children and teachers count as mathematics. In T. Nunes & P. Bryant (Eds.), *Learning and teaching mathematics: An international perspective* (pp. 233–264). Hove, UK: Psychology Press.

Abreu, G. de, Bishop, A., & Presmeg, N. (2002a). *Transitions between contexts of mathematical practices.* Dordrecht, The Netherlands: Kluwer.

Abreu, G. de, & Cline, T. (1998). Studying social representations of mathematics learning in multiethnic primary schools: Work in progress. *Papers on Social Representations, 7*(1–2), 1–20.

Abreu, G. de, & Cline, T. (2003). Schooled mathematics and cultural knowledge. *Pedagogy, Culture and Society, 11*(1), 11–30.

Abreu, G. de, & Cline, T. (2005). Parents' representations of their children's mathematics learning in multiethnic primary schools. *British Educational Research Journal, 31*(6), 697–722.

Abreu, G. de, Cline, T., & Shamsi, T. (2002b). Exploring ways parents participate in their children's school mathematical learning: Case studies in a multi-ethnic primary school. In G. de Abreu, A. Bishop, & N. Presmeg (Eds.), *Transitions between contexts of mathematical practices* (pp. 123–147). Dordrecht, The Netherlands: Kluwer.

Abreu, G. de, Crafter, S., Gorgorió, N., & Prat, M. (2013, February). Understanding immigrant students' transitions as mathematical learners from a dialogical self perspective. CERME 8. Antalya, Turkey. Retrieved from http://cerme8.metu.edu.tr/wgpapers/WG10/WG10_de_Abreu.pdf

Abreu, G. de, & Elbers, E. (2005). Introduction: The social mediation of learning in multiethnic schools. *European Journal of Psychology of Education, 20*(1), 3–11.

Anderson, D.D., & Gold, E. (2006). Home to school: Numeracy practices and mathematical identities. *Mathematical Thinking and Learning, 8*(3), 261–286.

Andrews, J., & Yee, W.C. (2006). Children's 'funds of knowledge' and their real life activities: Two minority ethnic children learning in out of school contexts in the UK. *Educational Review, 58(4),* 435–449.

Arcavi, A. (2002). The everyday and the academic in mathematics. *Journal for Research in Mathematics Education, 11,* 12–29.

Baker, D.A., Street, B.V., & Tomlin, A. (2006). Navigating schooled numeracies: Explanations for low achievement in mathematics of UK children from low SES background. *Mathematical Thinking and Learning, 8(3),* 287–307.

Bose, A., & Subramaniam, K. (2011). Exploring school children's out of school mathematics. In *Proceedings of the 35th Conference of the International Group for the Psychology of Mathematics Education* (Vol. 2, pp. 177–184).

Brenner, M. (1983). *The practice of arithmetic in Liberian schools*. Paper presented at the American Anthropological Association, Chicago.

Brown, M., Askew, M., Baker, D., Denvir, H., & Millet, A. (1998). Is the national numeracy strategy research-based? *British Journal of Educational Studies, 46*(4), 362–385.

Carraher, T., Carraher, D., & Schliemann, A. (1982). Na vida, dez; na escola, zero. Os contextos culturais da aprendizagem da matematica. *Cadernos de Pesquisa, 42,* 76–86.

Carraher, T. N., Schliemann, A. D., & Carraher, D. W. (1988). Mathematical concepts in everyday life. In G. Saxe & R. M. Gearhart (Eds.), *Children's mathematics: New directions in child development* (pp. 71–88). San Francisco: Jossey Bass.

Chronaki, A. (2005). Learning about "learning identities" in the school arithmetic practice: The experience of two minority gypsy girls in the Greek context of education. *European Journal of Psychology of Education, 20*(1), 61–74.

Civil, M. (2008, July). *Mathematics teaching and learning of immigrant students: A survey of recent research*. Manuscript prepared for the 11th International Congress of Mathematics Education (ICME) Survey Team 5: Mathematics Education in Multicultural and Multilingual Environments, Monterrey, Mexico.

Civil, M., & Andrade, R. (2002). Transitions between home and school mathematics: rays of hope amidst the passing clouds. In G. de Abreu, A. Bishop, & N. Presmeg (Eds.), *Transitions between contexts of mathematical practice* (pp. 149–169). Dordrecht, The Netherlands: Kluwer.

Civil, M., & Menéndez, J. M. (2011). Impressions of Mexican immigrant families on their early experiences with school mathematics in Arizona. In R. Kitchen & M. Civil (Eds.), *Transnational and borderland studies in mathematics education* (pp. 47–68). New York: Routledge.

Cobb, P. (1995). Mathematical learning and small group interaction: four case studies. In P. Cobb & H. Bauersfeld (Eds.), *The emergence of mathematical meaning* (pp. 25–129). Hillsdale, NJ: Lawrence Erlbaum Associates.

Cobb, P., & Hodge, L. L. (2002). A relational perspective on issues of cultural diversity and equity as they play out in the mathematics classroom. *Mathematical Thinking and Learning* (Special Issue, "Diversity, Equity and Mathematical Learning"), *4*(2–3), 249–284.

Cole, M. (1977). An ethnographic psychology of cognition. In P. N. Johnson-Laird & P. C. Wason (Eds.), *Thinking* (pp. 468–482). Cambridge: Cambridge University Press.

Cole, M. (1995). Culture and cognitive development: From cross-cultural research to creating systems of cultural mediation. *Culture & Psychology, 1,* 25–54.

Cole, M. (1998). Can cultural psychology help us to think about diversity? *Mind, Culture and Activity, 5*(4), 291–304.

Cole, M., Gay, J., & Glick, J. (1968). Some experimental studies of Kpelle quantitative behaviour. *Psychonomic Monograph, 2*(10).

Crafter, S. (2012). Making sense of homework: Parental resources for understanding mathematical learning in multicultural settings. In E. Hjörne, G. van der Aalsvoort, & G. de Abreu (Eds.), *Learning, social interaction and diversity—Exploring identities in school practices* (pp. 53–68). Sense Publications.

Crafter, S., & Abreu, G. de (2010). Constructing identities in multicultural learning contexts. *Mind, Culture and Activity, 7*(2):102–118.

Crafter, S., & Abreu, G. de (2011). *Teachers' discussions about parental use of implicit and explicit mathematics in the home*. Seventh Conference of the European Society for Research in Mathematics Education (9–11 February, Rzeszow, Poland). Working Group 10.

Crafter, S., & Abreu, G. de (2013). Exploring parents' cultural models of mathematical knowledge in multiethnic primary schools. In G. Marsico, K. Komatsu, & A. Iannaccone (Eds.), *Crossing boundaries: Intercontextual dynamics between family and school* (pp. 209–228). Charlotte, NC: Information Age Publication.

D'Ambrosio, U. (1985). *Socio-cultural basis for mathematics education*. Campinas, Brasil: Unicamp.

de Haan, M., & Elbers, E. (2008). Diversity in the construction of modes of collaboration in multiethnic classrooms. In B. van Oers, W. Wardekker, E. Elbers, & R. van der Veer (Eds.) *The transformation of learning: advances in cultural-historical activity* (pp. 219–241). Cambridge: Cambridge University Press.

Elbers, E., & de Haan, M. (2005). The construction of word meaning in a multicultural classroom. Mediational tools in peer collaboration during mathematics lessons. *European Journal of Psychology of Education, 20*(1), 45–59.

Forman, E., Larreamendy-Joerns, J., Stein, M. K., & A. Brown. (1998). "You're going to want to find out which and prove it": Collective argumentation in a mathematics classroom. *Learning and Instruction, 8*(6), 527–548.

Forman, E.A., Minick, N., & Stone, C.A. (Eds.). (1993). *Contexts for learning*. Oxford: Oxford University Press.

Gay, J., & Cole, M. (1967). *The new mathematics and an old culture: a study of learning among the Kpelle of Liberia*. New York: Holt, Rinehart, & Winston.

Ginsburg, H.P., Choi, Y.E., Lopez, L.S., Netley, R., & Chao-Yuan, C. (1997). Happy birthday to you: Early mathematical thinking of Asian, South American, and U.S. children. In T. Nunes & P. Bryant (Eds.), *Learning and teaching mathematics* (pp. 163–207). Hove, UK: Psychology Press.

Goodnow, J.J. (1990). The socialization of cognition: What's involved? In J.W. Stiegler, R.A. Shweder, & G. Herdt (Eds.), *Cultural psychology* (pp. 259–286). Cambridge: Cambridge University Press.

Gorgorió, N., & Abreu, G. de (2009). Social representations as mediators of practice in mathematics classrooms with immigrant students. *Educational Studies in Mathematics, 72*(1), 61–76.

Gorgorió, N., Abreu, G. de, César, M., & Valero, P. (2005). *Issues and challenges of researching mathematics education in multicultural settings*. Paper presented at the CERME 4 — The Fourth Conference of the European Society for Research in Mathematics Education, Sant Feliu de Guixols, Spain.

Gorgorió, N., Planas, N., & Vilella, X. (2002). Immigrant children learning mathematics in mainstream schools. In G. de Abreu, A. Bishop, & N. Presmeg (Eds.), *Transitions between contexts of mathematical practice* (pp. 23–52). Dordrecht, The Netherlands: Kluwer.

Greenfield, P., & Lave, J. (1982). Cognitive aspects of informal education. In D.A. Wagner & H.W. Stevenson (Eds.), *Cultural perspectives on child development*. San Francisco: Freeman.

Guberman, S.R. (1996). The development of everyday mathematics in Brazilian children with limited formal education. *Child Development, 67*, 1609–1623.

Hughes, M., & Pollard, A. (2006). Home-school knowledge exchange in context. *Educational Review, 58*(4), 385–395.

Hyde, J.S., Else-Quest, N.M., Alibali, M.W., Knuth, E., & Romberg, T. (2006). Mathematics in the home: Homework practices and mother—child interactions doing mathematics. *Journal of Mathematical Behavior, 25*(2), 136–152.

Jurkak, M., & Sharhin, I. (1999). An ethnographic study of the computational strategies of a group of young street vendors in Beirut. *Educational Studies in Mathematics, 40*, 155–172.

Lave, J. (1977). Cognitive consequences of traditional apprenticeship training in West Africa. *Anthropology and Education Quarterly, 8*(3), 177–180.

Lave, J. (1988). *Cognition in practice*. Cambridge: Cambridge University Press.

LeFevre, J.A., Skwarchuk, S.L., Smith-Chant, B.L., Fast, L., Kamawar, D., & Bisanz, J. (2009). Home numeracy experiences and children's math performance in the early school years. *Canadian Journal of Behavioural Science, 41*(2), 55–66.

Litowitz, B.E. (1993). Deconstruction in the Zone of Proximal Development. In E. Froman, N. Minick, & C.A. Stone (Eds.), *Contexts for learning* (pp. 184–185). Oxford: Oxford University Press.

Masinglia, J.O. (1994). Mathematics practice in carpet laying. *Anthropology & Education Quarterly, 25*, 430–461.

McMullen, R., & Abreu, G. de (2011). Mothers' experiences of their children's school mathematics at home: The impact of being a mother-teacher. *Research in Mathematics Education,13*(1), 59–74.

Minick, N., Stone, C.A., & Forman, E.A. (1993). Integration of individual, social, and institutional processes in accounts of children's learning and development. In E.A. Forman, N. Minick, & C.A. Stone (Eds.), *Contexts for learning* (pp. 3–16). Oxford: Oxford University Press.

Murtaugh, M. (1985). The practice of arithmetic by American grocery shoppers. *Anthropology and Education Quarterly, 16*(3), 186–192.

Nasir, N.S., & Cobb, P. (2002). Diversity, equity, and mathematical learning. *Mathematical Thinking and Learning, 4*(2 & 3), 91–102.

Newton, R., & Abreu, G. de (2012). Parents as mathematical facilitators: analyzing goals in parent-child mathematical activity. In F.J. Diez-Palomar and C. Kanes (Eds.), *Family and the community in and out of the classroom: Ways to improve mathematics achievement*. Barcelona: Universitat Autonoma de Barcelona, Servei de Publicacions.

Nunes, T. (1992a). Cognitive invariants and cultural variation in mathematical concepts. *International Journal of Behavioral Development, 15*(4), 433–453.

Nunes, T. (1992b). Ethnomathematics and everyday cognition. In D.A. Grouws (Ed.), *Handbook of research on mathematics teaching and learning* (pp. 557–574). New York: Macmillan.

Nunes, T., & Bryant, P. (1996). *Children doing mathematics*. Oxford: Blackwell.

Nunes, T., Schliemann, A., & Carraher, D. (1993). *Street mathematics and school mathematics*. Cambridge: Cambridge University Press.

OFSTED. (1999). *Raising the attainment of minority ethnic pupils*. School and LEA responses: Office of Her Majesty's Chief Inspector of Schools.

O'Toole, S., & Abreu, G. de (2005). Parents' past experiences as a mediational tool for understanding their child's current mathematical learning. *European Journal of Psychology of Education, 20*(1), 75–89.

Pettito, A. L., & Ginsburg, H. P. (1982). Mental arithmetic in Africa and America: Strategies, principles, and explanations. *International Journal of Psychology, 17*, 81–102.

Resnick, L. B., Pontecorvo, C., & Säljö, R. (1997). Discourse, tools and reasoning. In L. B. Resnick, C. Pontecorvo, R. Säljö, & B. Burge (Eds.), *Discourse, tools and reasoning: Essays on situated cognition* (pp. 1–20). New York: Springer and NATO Scientific Affairs Division.

Rogoff, B., & Lave, J. (Eds.). (1984). *Everyday cognition: Its development in social context.* Cambridge, MA: Harvard University Press.

Säljö, R., & Wyndhamn, J. (1993). Solving everyday problems in the formal setting. An empirical study of the school as context for thought. In S. Chaiklin & J. Lave (Eds.), *Understanding practice: Perspectives on activity and context* (pp. 327–342). Cambridge: Cambridge University Press.

Saxe, G. B. (1982). Culture and the development of numerical cognition: Studies among the Oksapmin of Papua New Guinea. In C. G. Brainerd (Ed.), *Children's logical and mathematical cognition* (pp. 157–176). New York: Springer Verlag.

Saxe, G. B. (1991). *Culture and cognitive development: studies in mathematical understanding.* Hillsdale, NJ: Lawrence Erlbaum Associates.

Saxe, G. B. (1996). Studying cognitive development in sociocultural context: The development of a practice based approach. In R. Jessor, A. Colby, & R. Shweder (Eds.), *Ethnography and human development* (pp. 275–303). Chicago: The University of Chicago Press.

Saxe, G. B. (2012). Approaches to reduction in treatments of culture-cognition relations: Affordances and limitations. Commentary on Gauvain and Munroe. *Human Development, 55,* 233–242.

Saxe, G. B., & Esmonde, I. (2005). Studying cognition in flux: A historical treatment of Fu in the shifting structure of Oksapmin Mathematics. *Mind, Culture & Activity, 12*(3–4), 171–225.

Saxe, G. B., Guberman, S. R., & Gearhart, M. (1987). Social processes in early number development. *Monographs of the Society for Research in Child Development, 52*(2), 1–137.

Saxe, G. B., & Posner, J. (1983). The development of numerical cognition: Cross-cultural perspectives. In H. P. Ginsburg (Ed.), *The development of mathematical thinking* (pp. 291–317). London: Academic Press.

Schubauer-Leoni, M. L. (1990). Ecritures additives en classe ou en dehors de la classe: Une affaire de contexte. *Resonances, 6,* 16–18.

Schubauer-Leoni, M.-L., & Perret-Clermont, A.-N. (1997). Social interactions and mathematics learning. In T. Nunes & P. Bryant (Eds.), *Learning and teaching mathematics: An international perspective* (pp. 265–283). Hove, UK: Psychology Press.

Scribner, S. (1984). Cognitive studies of work. *The Quarterly Newsletter of the Laboratory of Human Cognition, 6* (Special Issue), 1–50. San Diego: University of California.

Shweder, R. A. (1990). Cultural psychology—What is it? In J. W. Stiegler, R. A. Shweder, & G. Herdt (Eds.), *Cultural psychology* (pp. 1–43). Cambridge: Cambridge University Press.

Stiegler, J. W., Shweder, R. A., & Herdt, G. (Eds.) (1990). *Cultural psychology.* Cambridge: Cambridge University Press.

Stone, C. A. (1993). What is missing in the metaphor of scaffolding? In E. A. Forman, N. Minick, & C. A. Stone (Eds.), *Contexts for learning: Sociocultural dynamics in children's development* (pp. 169–183). Oxford: Oxford University Press.

Suárez-Orozco, C., & Suárez-Orozco, M. M. (2001). *Children of immigration.* Cambridge, MA: Harvard University Press.

Subramaniam, K., & Bose, A. (2012). Measurement units and modes: The Indian context. *Proceedings of the 12th International Congress on Mathematical Education (ICME-12)* (Vol. 1983).

Tajfel, H. (1978). Social categorisation, social identity and social comparison. In H. Tajfel (Ed.), *Differentiation between social groups: Studies in social psychology of intergroup relations* (pp. 61–76). London: Academic Press.

Vandermaas-Peeler, M., Nelson, J., Bumpass, C., & Sassine, B. (2009). Numeracy-related exchanges in joint storybook reading and play. *International Journal of Early Years Education, 17*(1), 67–84.

Van Oers, B. (1998). From context to contextualising. *Learning and Instruction, 8*(6), 473–488.

Vygotsky, L. (1978). *Mind in society: The development of higher psychological processes.* Cambridge, MA: Harvard University Press.

Walkerdine, V. (1988). *The mastery of reason.* London: Routledge.

Winter, J., Salway, L., Yee, W. C., & Hughes, M. (2004). Linking home and school mathematics: The home school knowledge exchange project. *Research in Mathematics Education, 6*(1), 59–75.

17 Perspectives on Complex Systems in Mathematics Learning

Brent Davis

University of Calgary, Canada

Elaine Simmt

University of Alberta, Canada

Over the past two decades, interest in complex systems has emerged in the mathematics education community among both researchers and practitioners, appearing as calls to move from hierarchy-based to network thinking (Burton, 1999), to be attentive to nested and intertwining complex learning systems (Davis & Simmt, 2003), and as a source for new topics of study. In this paper we provide an overview of complexity and point to its presence and impact in the field.

WHAT IS COMPLEX?

Perhaps the most frequently encountered statement in reviews of complex systems research is there is no unified definition of such key terms as *complex* and *complexity* among researchers. Rather than opening with a one-size-fits-all description, then, accounts of complexity research tend to begin by invoking some manner of Aristotle's observation that "the whole can be greater than the sum of the parts." Complexity researchers, that is, are interested in those phenomena that do not reveal themselves—and that, in fact, might disintegrate—under the reductive scrutiny of analytic science.

This is not to say that complex systems researchers are uninterested in constituent parts or governing laws. The point, rather, is that some phenomena manifest traits and capacities that cannot be predicted or explained in terms of components and rules, in part because those complex phenomena change over time. Invoking principles that are more reliant on Darwin than Newton, complex systems researchers investigate both how interacting parts enable systems' global behaviors and how those systems relate to and interact with other phenomena in their environments. Such emphases are clearly not "new." Indeed, the first major development in the emergence of complexity research was the recognition that there is a class of phenomena that cannot be understood in terms of simple cause–effect dynamics. In the Western world, that recognition was formally announced in the 1800s through the work of Darwin and his contemporaries, but it took more than a century for the sensibility to percolate to and through other branches of academic inquiry.

With that slow percolation, complexity research only cohered as a discernible movement in the physical and information sciences in the middle of that 20th century, with the social sciences and humanities joining in its development in more recent decades. To a much lesser (but noticeably accelerating) extent, complex systems research has been embraced by educationists whose interests extend across such levels of phenomena as genomics, neurological processes, subjective understanding, interpersonal dynamics, cultural evolution, and global ecology.

Our thesis is that complex systems research is itself an example of what it studies: an emergent phenomenon in which similar but nonetheless diverse elements coalesce into a

416

coherent, discernible unity that cannot be appreciated as a sum of its constituents. A sense of its internal diversity might be gleaned from some of the varied terms for complex systems that have arisen in different fields, including *complex adaptive systems* (physics), *nonlinear dynamical systems* (mathematics), *dissipative structures* (chemistry), *autopoietic systems* (biology), *healthy organisms* (health care), *organized complex systems* (information science), *social systems* (sociology), and simply *systems* (cybernetics) (Mitchell, 2009). This range of titles and interests is both boon and bane. On the positive side, it offers a sense of the breadth of phenomena and diversity of interest that are addressed within discussions of complexity. On the negative, it points to the reason why there is no readily comprehensible, unified description of complexity: researchers tend to structure definitions around their particular research interests.

Instead of lamenting this tendency toward diverse definitions, we use it to structure this chapter. Embracing the fact that there is no simple consensus, this writing is organized around varied responses to the question, "What is complexity?" In the process, we describe and illustrate some of the ways complexity discourses have been (and, in some cases, might be) taken up in mathematics education research, how particular interpretations of complexity tend to be tethered to specific researcher interests, and why engaging with emergent topics and interpretations might matter for projects within mathematics education. Specifically, the chapter is developed around the following four perspectives on complexity:

- Complexity as an historical discourse—i.e., complexity is an instance of what it describes, a self-organizing, emergent, evolving coherence.
- Complexity as a disciplinary discourse—i.e., complexity is a digitally enabled, modeling-based branch of mathematics.
- Complexity as a theoretical discourse—i.e., complexity is the study of learning systems.
- Complexity as a pragmatic discourse—i.e., complexity is a means to nurture emergent possibility.

We use this organizational strategy not merely as a means to categorize foci of discussion and research contributions. It is also used to acknowledge the noncompressibility of complexity discourses. As with most academic domains, debates have opened up among proponents, as some argue for the necessity of rigorous evidence and mathematical model-ability, while others contend that standards derived from complexity research in other domains (in particular, physics) cannot be imposed on phenomena that are specific to education.

COMPLEXITY AS AN HISTORICAL DISCOURSE

It is useful to be aware of some of the varied attitudes toward complex systems research that are present among mathematics education researchers. To that end, we offer some brief historical notes on the evolution of different sensibilities among complexivists, starting with the domain-defining realization that there exist many self-organizing, self-maintaining phenomena, and complexity is itself one of them.

When we speak of complexity research as an historical discourse we are suggesting that as a phenomenon it is an embodiment of its own history. That is, complexity research is a phenomenon that has arisen and continues to co-dependently arise with/in its grander ecosystems of the academic, social, and more-than-human worlds. It has emerged from the interaction of theorists and theories in time, space, and discourse domains. It is a system that defines and is defined by its own history but is coupled with its environment that enables and constrains possibilities for its evolution (Maturana & Varela, 1992). More concisely, it is an example of what it describes, a self-organizing, emergent coherence that is self-modifying in relation the medium in which it exists.

This point might be illustrated through an abridged account of the emergence and evolution of the domain. As historians note, any such undertaking entails a series of arbitrary selections—and, among complexivists, one of the most common of these is the practice of starting such histories in the middle of the 20th century (see, e.g., Waldrop, 1992; Mitchell, 2009). This decision is well justified in the fact that it was at that point that interdisciplinary discussions began to gain some momentum. At the same time, it can obscure the fact that many of the movement's orienting insights and interpretive tools had already been developed in different disciplines. For example, as already mentioned, evolutionary theory is key to complexity discourses. Of comparable importance were developments in mathematics such as Poincaré's research into the infinite complication that can arise in "simple" nonlinear systems. Developed more than a century ago, his "qualitative dynamics" has been central in the mathematical theory of dynamical systems.

Many other contributing moments could be identified prior to the mid-20th-century moment of shared realization among researchers across several disciplines that they were interested in a similar sort of unruly phenomenon. Dubbed *complexity theory* by proponents, studies associated with the nascent movement were focused mainly on description. The major accomplishment of complexity research of the time—or Complexity 1.0, one might say—was a cross-disciplinary recognition of a class of nonreducible, emergent phenomena that would not surrender their secrets to the tools of classical, analytic science. Infusing this movement was a new set of images and metaphors to describe these diverse phenomena. Images based in Euclidean geometry and dynamics framed by classical physics were gradually replaced by images drawn from fractal geometry (e.g., scale independence, unexpected detail) and the structural dynamics of biology (e.g., ecosystemic organizations, dynamic interdependencies). A principal visual metaphor at the time was that of nested systems (see Figure 17.1a.), reflecting the important insights that systems were both irreducible (i.e., they must be studied at the levels of their emergence) and comprised similarly complex systems.

As more and more phenomena were recognized as complexly emergent and more and more fields of inquiry came to be involved in the project of complexity research, the focus of study was elaborated beyond description of complex dynamics into analyses of the similar roots, structures, and consequences of these dynamics. This "Complexity 2.0" phase roughly spanned 1980 through 2000, and was marked in the field with a shift in self-reference from "complexity theory" to "complexity science." It was characterized by increasing use of such notions of recursive processes within cycles of development and growth (see Figure 17.2b for one of the principal visual metaphors of the time), with the notion of "living systems" prevailing in comparisons of complex and not-complex entities. It was a time of explosive growth in complexity research, spurred by developments in mathematical modeling that afforded a

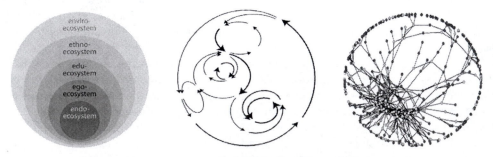

Figure 17.1 Three important visual metaphors within complexity research corresponding to the major emphases within three phases of the movement—(a) nested systems, (b) entangled dynamics, and (c) decentralized networks.

means to test hypotheses without impacting sensitive ecologies. Indeed, as evidenced by the recipients of Nobel Prizes in physics, medicine, chemistry, and economics, it was the coming of age of complexity. The winners in 1980 might be retroactively interpreted in terms of complexity theory, but few were explicitly aligned with the movement. By 2000, all of the winners were clearly and explicitly complexivist.

Since the turn of the century, complexity research has become decidedly more pragmatic in its emphases. Elaborating its ongoing interests in description and analysis, a strongly articulated component of the current work is on occasioning the emergence of complex phenomena—that is, not just identifying them, not just better understanding what makes them go, but more deliberate efforts to trigger them into being, to support their development, and to sustain their existence. As might be expected, the foci of discussions have shifted to reflect this concern with pragmatics, and are now largely organized around matters of scale-free connective networks (see Figure 17.1c) and the way that these networks enable learning systems. Much of this hands-on work is highly speculative, and a more tentative emphasis is reflected in a tendency to refer to the field as *complexity research* (or simply *complexity*) rather than *complexity theory* or *complexity science*.

With this shift toward pragmatics and the combined notions of nested, co-entangled, and networked learning systems, complexity/systems research has reached a place where it can be of great use to mathematics educators. As a review of the contents of the current issue of any leading journal in the field will reveal, the field of mathematics education has grown to encompass a broad range of interests, greatly elaborated from the psychological and epistemic foci that dominated only a few decades ago. Researchers are currently concerned with multiple levels of organization (e.g., individual learners, classrooms, schools, school districts, disciplinary knowledge, society), co-specifying dynamics (e.g., between teachers and learners, between knowledge and action) and complex associations (e.g., among people, among ideas). Across the diversity of these interests, mathematics education research remains an explicitly pragmatic enterprise. It is charged with the tasks of supporting the wellness and possibility of individuals while supporting the maintenance and evolution of society. "Complexity 3.0" enables this work.

Of course, and reemphasizing the central point of this section, a complex system is one that embodies its own history. Emergent mindsets within the moment, then, do not replace prior emphases. They are elaborations. While different mindsets occasionally exist in tension, all three foci—on description, analysis, and pragmatics—are well represented in current complexity research. This point should become clearer over the next three sections of this chapter.

COMPLEXITY AS A DISCIPLINARY DISCOURSE

While complexity research spans many domains, for the purposes of understanding its relevance to mathematics education, it can be useful to focus on that part of the movement that is properly a strand of mathematical study. Indeed, the nested, emergent, and networked—that is, complex—character of mathematics itself is brought in sharp relief when the discipline is seen as both nesting and nested in complexity research. We endeavor to develop this point in this section, as we explore complexity as a disciplinary discourse in mathematics education, a domain concerned with the ways that social conditions, cultural tools, and mathematics content interact in the evolution of the curriculum and teaching approaches (see Ernest, 2011).

Two illustrations of the emergence of complexity in mathematics are useful: the first is one that traces the mathematical study of complex dynamic systems from the time of Newton to the present; the second is one that illustrates the emergence of a new branch of mathematics and a defining element of complexity—namely, network theory. Together these two instances illustrate the evolution of complexity in mathematics and provide critical insights into complex systems.

Prior to the advent of rapid and inexpensive computational power, the modeling of systems was largely focused on those dynamics that could be studied through differential linear equations. Poincaré was notable among those who examined nonlinear dynamical systems, doing so from a theoretical perspective. However, while it is now clear that he understood a number of features of chaotic and dynamical systems, at the time his insights were regarded as qualitative, speculative, and largely unproven (Bell, 1937). The computational power of digital technologies in the second half of the 20th century opened up the possibility of working on the problems of systems numerically, at which time the investigation of dynamical systems began to flourish. Computing power brought about possibility of doing "experimental mathematics"[1] (Borwein & Devlin, 2008) and numerical analysis, triggering a rebirth of the modeling of nonlinear dynamical systems.

Importantly, digital computing provided not only a means of computing extremely large data sets and iterating functions through hundreds of thousands of repetitions, it also provided means for converting numerical data to visual representations, enabling the generation of new insights and, consequently, new forms of mathematics. This work is evident in applied mathematics and central to computing science and machine learning (Mitchell, 2009). The mid-20th century brought about many insights into features of nonlinear dynamical systems that had not previously been observed or constructed, including notions of fractal dimension, chaos, phase space, attractors, and sensitivity to initial conditions. More recently, graph theory as introduced by Euler in the 18th century has been taken up and elaborated in the study of networked systems. In particular, the realization that a decentralized network structure is the fingerprint of a complexity system garnered intense interest from various disciplines in the natural sciences and the human sciences. The temporal gap between graph theory and network theory was in large part due to the difference in possibilities in analytical approaches to graphs and the affordances that computers created for modeling systems. A similar story involves the modeling of iterative and nonlinear dynamical systems.

It is important to emphasize that what is most critical here was not the rapid increase in mathematical knowledge that accompanied the rise of the digital era; it was the clear and sudden elaboration in how mathematics was conducted. Such analyses of the history of mathematics underscore the realization that the discipline of mathematics evolves over time (Bell, 1937; Fauvel & Grey, 1987), influencing and influenced by social and cultural interaction (Ernest, 1994; Cohen and Stewart, 1995). Contemporary mathematics is steeped in its history and emerges out of it—and at the same time is in a constant state of change. As Foote (2007) illuminates, even those mathematical systems that are based on simple axiomatic foundations lead to entirely unexpected "macroscopic" outcomes, including implications and applications that reach well beyond their historical beginnings. That is, mathematics is a complex system. In a similar sense, school mathematics can be argued to be a complex system, with practices, purposes, entailments, and consequences that extend well beyond its initial foci and intentions.

On this matter, a frequent criticism of school mathematics is its curricula are a poor fit for contemporary circumstances. For the most part, the contents of school mathematics have changed little over recent centuries and continue to reflect the needs and obsessions of 16th and 17th-century Europe, when publicly funded and mandatory education spread across the continent to address the emergent knowledge requirements of an industrialized society. At that time, only a small proportion of pupils moved on to the equivalent of today's high school. That curriculum was set to meet the needs of the elite student who would challenge examinations to get into the prestigious civil service (particularly the engineering corps). Archibald (2007), a historian of mathematics, points out that the curriculum developed in the 19th century lives on today in high school mathematics, in spite of the fact that contemporary high schools serve a much wider population than the mathematically elite of 19th-century Europe. Circumstances and sensibilities have changed, along with the needs of a mathematically literate citizen. But so too have the affordances of the world in which we live: availability of data, speed at which information is shared, and the means of handling information. As Lesh (2010) noted, complexity has emerged as "an important topic to be included in any mathematics curriculum that claims to be preparing students for full participation in a technology-based *age of information*" (p. 563).

An important qualification must be made here, as the suggestion is *not* that study of complex systems is new, but that this mathematics for school represents a significant shift from traditional emphases. In fact, Descartes, Newton, and many of their contemporaries were well aware of complex phenomena at the time of the emergence of modern schooling. However, because of the intractability of many nonlinear differential equations, when they came up in research, they were routinely replaced by linear approximations (Stewart, 1989). Lecturers and texts followed suit in omitting nonlinear accounts; hence generations of students were exposed to oversimplified, linearized versions of natural phenomena. In other words, non-complex mathematics prevailed in public schools not because it was ideal but because it lent itself to calculations that could be done by hand. Ultimately that emphasis is complicit with a resilient worldview of a clockwork reality. Kaput (1992) argued, the advent of powerful computing technologies over the past half century can help to restore an appreciation of the relentless nonlinearity of the universe. That is, due to their power, digital technologies have not just opened up new vistas of calculation, they have triggered epistemic shifts as they contribute to redefinitions of what counts as possible and what is expressible. This insight has been engaged by many mathematics education researchers (e.g., English, 2011; Moreno-Armella, Hegedus, & Kaput, 2008; Hoyles & Noss, 2008).

As a branch of mathematics with possibilities for schooling, then, research on complex systems has deep historical roots and a wealth of applications. Complexity thus represents an important strand of mathematical inquiry, with subtopics that include dynamic modeling, systems thinking, network analysis, and fractal geometry—among others—and concepts such as sensitivity to initial conditions, attractor basins, scaling factors, network stability, and cascading failures. Themes that have been developed within the field of mathematics education as possible curriculum topics include mathematical modeling, data modeling, and a range of systems-based approaches for applications in engineering and other STEM domains. Three examples are offered: powerful programming languages appropriate to young learners but with utility for all levels; data management and associated modeling strategies; and mathematical modeling.

Notable in this regard is the seminal work of Seymour Papert (e.g., 1980), particularly his development of the Logo programming language in the late 1970s. The language was designed to be usable by young novices and advanced experts alike. It enabled users to solve problems using a mobile robot, the "Logo turtle," and eventually a simulated turtle on the computer screen. While not intended explicitly for the study of complexity, Logo lent itself to recursive programming (an instance of C 2.0) and was thus easily used to generate fractal-like images and to explore applications dynamically—opening the door to more complexity-specific topics.

To that end, different developers have since offered Logo-based platforms that are explicitly intended to explore complex systems (and other) applications. Notable in this regard are StarLogo (lead designer, Mitchell Resnick; http://education.mit.edu/starlogo/) and NetLogo (lead designer, Uri Wilensky; http://ccl.northwestern.edu/netlogo/). Both platforms were developed in the 1990s and extended Papert's original Logo program by presenting the possibility of multiple, interacting agents (turtles). This feature renders the applications useful for simulating ranges of complex phenomena. Both StarLogo and NetLogo include extensive online libraries of already-programmed simulations of familiar phenomena (e.g., flocking birds, traffic jams, disease spread, and population dynamics) and less-familiar applications in a variety of domains such as economics, biology, physics, chemistry, neurology, and psychology. At the same time, the platforms preserve the simplicity of programming that distinguished the original Logo (e.g., utilizing switches, sliders, choosers, inputs, and other interface elements), making them accessible for even young learners. Other visual programming languages have been developed that are particularly appropriate to students (e.g., Scratch, http://scratch.mit. edu, and ToonTalk, www.toontalk.com).

Over the past few decades, hundreds of speculative essays and research reports (see, e.g., the NetLogo reference page, http://ccl.northwestern.edu/netlogo/references.shtml) have been published on these and other multi-turtle programs. Regarding matters of potential innovations for school mathematics, in addition to well-developed resources, there have been extensive discussions. There exists a substantial empirical basis for moving forward on the selection and development of curriculum content that is fitted to themes of complexity. Not surprisingly, then, with the ready access to computational and imaging technologies in most school class-rooms, some (e.g., Jacobson & Wilensky 2006) have advocated for the inclusion of such topics as computer-based modeling and simulation languages, including networked collaborative sim-ulations (see Kaput Center for Research and Innovation in STEM Education, www.kaputcenter. umassd.edu). In this vein, complexity is understood as a digitally enabled, modeling-based branch of mathematics that opens spaces (particularly in secondary and tertiary education) for new themes such as recursive functions, fractal geometry, and modeling of complex phenomena with mathematical tools such as iteration, cobwebbing, and phase diagrams.

The shift in sensibility from linearity to complexity is seen as more important than the development of the computational competencies necessary for sophisticated modeling—a matter that serves as a growing focus among mathematics educators with an interest in modeling, including The International Community of Teachers of Mathematics Modeling Applications (ICTMA; see Lesh, Galbraith, Haines, & Hurford, 2010). To this end, data management and associated modeling strategies have emerged as particularly prominent (and relevant) topics, likely spurred by the density of data made available by current information technologies. English (2006, 2008), for example, has examined data modeling in the early years and engineering education in the middle school years with a view toward developing children's mathematics thinking in manners that have significant utility in the evolving world. Lesh and Doerr (2003) and Lesh et al. (2010) covered similar ground in their development of a modeling-centric approach to mathematical problem solving, noting that an emphasis on complexity entails shifts in thinking not just about the nature of problem solving situations, but also about the nature of the "things" that are being interpreted mathematically and the nature of the mathematical thinking that is needed. Indeed, the very role of mathematics in one's life has been argued to be transformed through this shift in curriculum emphasis. As Lesh (2010) pointedly described, "whereas the entire traditional K–14 mathematics curricu-lum can be characterized as a step-by-step line of march toward the study of single, solvable, differentiable functions, the world beyond schools contains scarcely a few situations of single actor–single outcome variety" (p. 564). Extending this thought, Lesh highlighted that ques-tions and topics in complexity and data management are not only made more accessible in K–14 settings through digital technologies, but also current tools have made it possible to render some key principles comprehensible to young learners in manners that complement traditional curriculum emphases.

Despite the growing research base and the compelling arguments, however, few contempo-rary programs of study in school mathematics have heeded such admonitions for change. It is perhaps for this reason that many mathematics education researchers have focused on familiar topic areas (such as the data management examples just mentioned) as means to incorporate studies of complexity into school mathematics. Discussions of and research into possible sites of integration have spanned all grade levels and several content areas, and proponents have tended to advocate for complexity-content, but in a less calculation-dependent format.

Alongside discussions of the possible content of school mathematics are discussions of complexity-informed and technology-enabled means of engaging with learners, all framed by a growing realization that the what, the how, the who, the where, and the when of mathematics learning cannot be pried apart. Such emergent, complexity-informed pedagogical issues are addressed in subsequent sections.

COMPLEXITY AS A THEORETICAL DISCOURSE

As noted in the introductory section of this chapter, *complexity* tends to be defined in terms of the particular interests of researchers. For example, biologists tend to talk about complexity in terms of living systems, physicists in terms of nonlinear dynamical systems, and information scientists in terms of evolving networks. It should not be surprising, then, that among educational researchers, one definition has a particular resonance: a complex system is one that learns. Indeed, perhaps the best-developed aspect of complex systems research within the field of mathematics education is around researchers' understandings of and contributions to theories of learning.

On this count, still-heard descriptors such as "new paradigm" and "emerging worldview" are perhaps not appropriate when it comes to manifestations of complexity thinking in the field, where core principles of complexity (if not the explicit movement) have a deep history. In particular, several theories of learning that have been prevalent for many decades are readily aligned with complexivist sensibilities. For example, one would be hard pressed to find recent research on mathematics learning that is not deeply committed to such notions as co-participation, inextricable entanglements, decentralized structures, co-adaptive dynamics, self-determination, and nonlinear unfoldings. But perhaps the clearest evidence of the prevalence of sensibilities that are sympathetic to complexity is the frequent usage of the notion of *emergence*, in descriptions of individual learning (e.g., Lesh & Doerr, 2003; van Oers, 2010; Proulx, 2013, Bowers & Nickerson, 2001), the products of mathematical understanding (Cobb, 1999; Font, Godino, & Gallardo, 2013), the structures of personal knowing (e.g., ACT-R theory: Anderson & Labiere, 1998; Implicit Learning Theory: Reber, 1993); tools of learning (Hershkowitz & Schwarz, 1999), collective knowledge production (Cobb & Bauersfeld, 1995; Burton, 1999; Davis & Simmt, 2006; Martin & Towers, 2011), teachers' dynamic knowledge of mathematics (Davis, 2011; Davis & Renert, 2014), and the open-ended character of mathematics knowledge itself (Foote, 2007; Hegedus & Moreno-Armella, 2011).

Notably, the discourse of emergence is not necessarily rooted in complexity research. Its variety of sources includes psychology, sociology, and philosophy (Sawyer 2002a, 2002b), and usages of *emergence* are frequently left undefined. Relatively few researchers have explicitly likened complex systems to learners (e.g., Wilensky & Resnick, 1999; Stroup & Wilensky, 2000; Davis & Simmt, 2003; Lesh & Doerr, 2003, Kilgore, 1999). However, the frequent use of *emergence* signals an important and broad appreciation of the adaptive, irreducible, unprescribable, yet-coherent natures of knowledge, knowledge production, and knowledge-producing systems.

Before engaging in a complexity-based reading of a few of the more prominent theories of learning in the field, it is useful to be explicit about some of the key aspects of a complex (learning) form/phenomenon/entity—hereafter referred to simply as a *learner*. In brief, a learner is a perceptible coherence that

- co-dependently arises with the world in the co-implicated interactions of multiple agents/systems (e.g., neurons, instantiations, schemata, persons, social clusters, subcultures, species),
- is typically conceived/perceived and characterized as a body and/or in embodied terms (e.g., a person, a body of knowledge, a social corpus, the body politic),
- manifests features and capacities that are not observed in constituting agents/systems,
- maintains itself over some period of time, and
- evolves in response to both internal and external dynamics in manners that are better described in terms of adequacy/sufficiency (i.e., fitness among subagents and between agent and environment) than optimality/efficiency (i.e., match between internal and external).

To be clear, the claim here is *not* that prominent theories of learning in the field of mathematics education draw on complex systems thinking. In fact, it is more the reverse: complex systems research, as a domain, has cohered around studies of sorts of phenomena and dynamics that have been the focus of mathematics education research for many decades. As such, complexity research should be construed more in terms of a domain to which researchers of learning might contribute and less a domain from which they might draw. This detail might be underscored by noting that the bulleted points, noted above, were proposed in one way or another by multiple learning theorists long before the field of complexity studies arose. For example, in the 1700s Kant described a concept as a structured cluster of representations that can be used to collect objects, scenarios, or sequences of events or relations—a notion that directly informed Piaget's (1953) account of a *schema* as a mental framework that is created as a child interacts with/in physical and social environments, and integrates sensorimotor, symbolic, and operational instantiations.

What complexity discourses offer, then, is not a new description, but interpretive devices that derive from the study of a great diversity of complex, emergent forms. That is, complex systems research presents a frame that brings diverse theories of learning into productive conversation, as it simultaneously highlights common ground (e.g., the bulleted points earlier) and important divergences (Davis, Sumara, & Luce-Kapler, 2008). Significantly, in complexity terms, those divergences arise because learning theorists are studying learning at many different levels—and a core tenet of complex systems research is that behaviors and laws that are appropriate at one level of activity may not apply at another (see Laborde, Perrin-Glorian & Sierpinska, 2005). Phrased differently, phenomena must be studied at the levels of their emergence (Cohen & Stewart, 1995).

Before addressing some of the details of the divergences among theories of learning, it is worth noting a further contribution of complex systems thinking to studies of learning and learners. Concerned as they are with such a range of adaptive phenomena, complexity researchers have developed several empirical tools that can be used to distinguish whether or not a particular phenomenon is indeed complex. For example, in terms of internal structure, the agents that comprise a complex unity organize themselves in a decentralized network (see Watts, 2003). As well, one can expect ubiquitous power law distributions when complex activity is present (e.g., in social systems, there tend to be a great many people of lower status and many fewer of higher status; in active classrooms, there tend to be very many brief articulations and very few extended ones; in languages, a few words are encountered with very high frequency while most are rarely used; see Buchanan, 2002). A further feature of a complex system is the presence of multiple feedback loops that work in concert to modulate its internal coherence and maintain its external fit with its context (Pirie & Kieren, 1994).

These qualities might be illustrated with the broad example of human knowledge, as efforts to map out domains and their interconnections reveal both decentralized network structures and power law distributions.[2] The same appears to be true of mathematics—supporting, increasingly, characterizations of the domain as "a living, breathing, changing organism" (Burger & Starbird, 2005, p. xi) that "emerges as an autopoietic [i.e., self-creating and self-maintaining] system" (Sfard, 2008, p. 129). More pointedly, Foote (2007) has argued that mathematics is an adaptive, complex system that is approaching the limits of human verifiability. Such characterizations are a far cry from the rather static, certain, and linearized portrayals of mathematics in artifacts intended for schools.

Similarly, theories of learning that might be aligned with complexivist sensibilities are a far cry from cause–effect accounts (e.g., behaviorism, cognitivism) that dominated educational research for much of the 20th century. Today there are dozens—perhaps hundreds—of theories of learning at play in the mathematics education literature. Some researchers see this proliferation of perspectives as a fracturing of the field. Indeed, much of the educational literature over the past decade has been focused on specifying the fine-grained distinctions among different frames—between, for example, radical constructivism and social constructivism, between actor-network theory and activity theory, between embodied cognition and enactivism, and so on. In contrast, from a complexity perspective, it is more useful to focus not on where theories fracture but on how they might complement and elaborate one another. To this end,

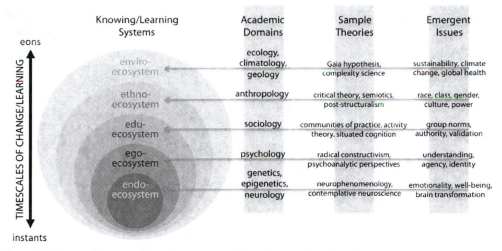

Figure 17.2 Some of the nested complex systems of interest to mathematics educators.

one useful strategy is to compare their units of analysis. Phrased differently, it is useful to ask, "Who/what is posited as the learner within each theory?"

Figure 17.2 is intended to gesture toward the conclusion that, when learners and learning phenomena of interest to mathematics educators are understood as co-implicated systems, a range of theories become necessary to grapple with the many issues the field must address (cf. Lemke, 2000). No single perspective will do. Each of the entries in the "Sample Theories" column (among others, of course) is well represented in the current mathematics education literature, each is principally concerned with one particular knowing/learning system, each is tethered to specific methodological traditions ("Academic Domains"), and each tends to gravitate toward particular concerns ("Emergent Issues"). In more concise terms, each is a theory of a complex system—and their common ground (i.e., the sorts of details mentioned in the bulleted points earlier) is as vital as their separate emphases.

These level-specific complexities—and the collected, inter-theory complexity that emerges when they are considered simultaneously—are vital for the project of mathematics education. Sophisticated and effective mathematics pedagogies demand sophisticated insights into the complex dynamics of knowing and learning in all their manifestations.

To recap, then, among educationists interested in complexity, there is frequent resonance with the notions that a complex system is one that knows (i.e., perceives, acts, engages, develops, etc.) and learns (adapts, evolves, maintains self-coherence, etc.). This interpretation reaches across many systems that are of interest among educators, including physiological, personal, social, institutional, epistemological, cultural, and ecological systems. Unfolding from and enfolding in one another, it is impossible to study one of these phenomena without studying all of the others. Once again, this sensibility has been well represented in the mathematics education research literature for decades in the form of varied theories of learning. Among others, radical constructivism, socio-cultural theories of learning, embodied, and critical theories can all be read as instances of complexity theories. That is, they all invoke bodily metaphors, systemic concerns, evolutionary dynamics, emergent possibility, and self-maintaining properties.

COMPLEXITY AS A PRAGMATIC DISCOURSE

There is an ongoing debate within the field of complex systems research that is often characterized in terms of a tension between "hard" and "soft" complexity. The hard deals with well-defined, readily modeled phenomena, the soft with hazily bounded phenomena that defy quantification and that can be approximated only through modeling— the break often coincides with the separation of the physical and social sciences.

Perhaps unsurprisingly, given the way it straddles the discipline of mathematics and the field of education, this same tension is well represented within mathematics education research (cf. Hurford, 2010). Nevertheless, there is a vibrant and productive community within the field that is taking on such "softer" questions around the pragmatic implications for the decidedly complex space of the mathematics classroom. These efforts are largely oriented by the realization that beliefs on the nature of mathematics have been infused into the teaching of mathematics throughout the history of formal education. From a master and apprentices working with straight edge and compass to demonstrate earth measures, to a professor lecturing to a group of pupils on the integration of a function, to a teacher facilitating student inquiry into simulations, pedagogical settings are influenced by beliefs on the nature of the mathematics being taught and learned.

In other words, mathematics pedagogy itself is a complex phenomenon that emerges from the interaction of teachers, mathematics, and students, all of which in themselves are complex learning systems. With complexity having emerged in the last century as a prominent discourse in mathematics and science, there are new metaphoric lenses to interpret and enable productive, "intelligent" classrooms. Central to this sort of transition is a shift from learning theories that focus principally on individuals' inner understandings to theories that are designed to foster collective understanding (Towers, Martin, & Heater, 2013). As Kilgore (1999) noted, the dominant shared meaning and identity of the collective is most closely related to collective social action: "People collectively develop solutions to societal problems, a process that Milbrath (1989) calls 'learning our way out'" (Kilgore, p. 196). In other words, for schooling in general and mathematics education in particular, it has become important to create experiences for learners that encourage collective action and that draw on collective possibility.

Traditionally, in school mathematics, even when it is granted that the group is critical to sense making and knowledge generation, individual learning has most often served as the principal focus (e.g., Cobb & Bauersfeld, 1995; Lerman, 2000; Sfard, 2008). This tendency is not surprising in a society in which the individual is viewed as the primary agent having autonomy and responsibility. Complexivist researchers do not contest this focus. However, they often problematize the bifurcation of the independently constituted individual and varied collective foci of the formal education, thus advocating a sensibility that is attentive to mutual influence across levels. As Kilgore (1999) argued, "understanding learning in social movements requires not only a concept of the group as a learner and constructor of knowledge, but also an understanding of the centrality of the group's vision of social justice that drives it to act—mostly in conflict with other groups—in the larger social, economic, and political field of meaning making" (p. 191). Phrased differently, people coming together around an issue demonstrate collective behavior/learning through a focus that is neither the individual nor the group but the emergent product of their actions and interactions.

So, what might teaching and learning look like at a time when the mathematics is framed as a complex, dynamic phenomena rather than a fixed collection of facts? Or when individuals are seen not as the locus of learning, but as complex learners that are nested in grander learning systems? Or when we note that mathematics itself is a decentralized network and many of the hubs of activity use experimental methods and are completely dependent on technology to run data sets and create visualizations of potential relationships? In other words, what kind of pedagogies, curricula, and classrooms might be occasioned by a contemporary mathematics of complexity?

Efforts to address such questions are well under way. For example, as already noted in the section on complexity as a disciplinary discourse, there are innovative classes and research projects that invoke modeling (Lesh & Doer, 2003), collaborative and collective data collection and analysis (Jacobson & Wilensky, 2006), and the study of complex phenomena (English, 2008). These might all be construed as instances in which the focus is shifted away from controlling the mathematics that students must replicate, and toward creating space for and nurturing common experiences and other redundancies in which mathematical thinking might flourish. Refocusing traditional curricula can make space for the collective learner to emerge. Interactive classrooms are ripe with the possibility of the emergence of a collective learning system. But, as Davis and Simmt (2003) developed, they need to be allowed to function as a collective—presenting issues of control (e.g., mathematical authority can no longer be vested exclusively in the teacher and/or textbook); diversity (e.g., variation among students becomes an asset that can be used by the collective for specialized tasks and thinking); redundancy (e.g., the teacher must provide experiences to serve as common places for the students so they might be able to interact with each other); and interconnectivity (e.g., ideas must have a means of interacting, through group sharing).

There are many examples of classrooms functioning well as collective mathematics learners, but most research reports do no explicitly present them as such. Exceptions include Davis and Simmt (2003) and Martin and Towers (2011), who ask us to consider not the individual meaning maker but instead the knowledge that emerges from the collective activity of co-acting learners. In an inquiry class where learning is more about being mathematical and less about learning some particular thing, the collective learner emerges and with it new mathematics. Teaching is therefore "a complex act of participation in unfolding understandings" (Martin & Towers, 2011, p. 425). To the extent the collective learner emerges in mathematics classes, there is individual knowledge made public, there are a bumping up of ideas, there emerges a shared project, and there is collective action on a task that produces the emergent learner, and products attributed to the group.

Networks, for example, have been explored as a new pedagogy, as demonstrated in some of the work at the Kaput Center. In 2003 Roschelle, Vahey, Tatar, Kaput, and Hegedus explored the use of hand-held computer technologies to create within-classroom networks. They described five key considerations of networked mathematics classes: network extent and generality (e.g., extending network outside of class, constraining it to the inside only, including members, including non-members etc.); network topology (e.g., hub and spokes, multiple hubs, cascades); anonymity and group display (i.e., features where students may be anonymous or tracked); types of network functions (e.g., distributing information, differentiating information, contributing information, collecting information and aggregating information); and representational integration (e.g. when and how functions are communicated and represented).

The omnipresence of information and communication technologies—mobile, highly connected, fast, and flexible—is a good place to start thinking about the potential shape of mathematics education in a complex infused environment. Two current and popular manifestations of mathematics "lessons" have emerged in this context: the video lesson and massive online courses.

With regard to the former, the Internet is a repository for a great number of instructional videos. Although many of the clips are concerned with do-it-yourself projects, ranging from tying a Windsor knot to fixing a bathroom toilet, a good number are explicitly related to school topics and content. Indeed, YouTube has an education channel in which much of the content is school related. One of the advantages of current information and communications technologies is that, with access to the Internet, it is possible to find an explanation-based tutorial for almost any topic covered in school mathematics, and students use these (as demonstrated by the millions of hits on the Khan Academy, for example). Not without irony, however, in spite of the tremendous power for supporting connectivity and collaboration, the Internet's main influence on mathematics pedagogy so far appears to be more to further entrench centuries-old sensibilities than to introduce new possibilities. Mathematics tends to be presented in a procedural, "how to" format; practice tends to be focused more on automaticity than meaning; and an individual may interact with and learn from other individuals (in the case of blogs), but there is nothing specific in the design of a posted video that occasions collectivity or a collective learner. The sole significant innovation of on-demand video appears to be the "flipped classroom"—which is claimed to afford a more human experience by enabling every student to work on his or her own time (Khan, 2011, March), amplifying rather than challenging the individual-centric emphasis of modern schooling.

This situation might be contrasted with affordances of massive open online courses (MOOCs), another instructional strategy afforded by current Information and Communications Technologies. As an educational "space," a MOOC has the potential to occasion many sorts of collectivity. They may be an infrastructure from which a collective learning system can emerge. Although MOOCs are one-to-many (one teacher–many students) they are made up of an emergent and unbounded landscape (topology) of neighboring interactions: there is within them incredible diversity of individual and subgroup learners (*massive* ensures this), yet there is also adequate sameness (redundancy) through language groups, background experience, etc. In the MOOC we see the emergence of subsystems by language groups, topic interest, forms of inquiry, and manners of working (Nixon et al., 2013), and it is out of these subsystems that the MOOC is maintained and evolves.

Drawing on complexity principles to interpret the MOOC phenomenon, some critical ingredients for collective emergence come into sharp relief. For example, in the one-to-many format, while there is a localized source of energy-rich matter from which individual agents draw, control of the phenomenon is actually decentralized. The only aspect that the teacher controls is the initial distribution of information. No individual learner is compelled to take up any or all of the aspect of the course in the way that he or she is compelled to do so in traditional schools. The control is distributed through infrastructure that enables individuals and groups of individuals to interact and co-act.

However, it is perhaps overly optimistic to suggest that MOOCs are fecund sites for the emergence of complex co-activity, particularly in light of the fact that most MOOCs are rooted in assumptions and the visions of learning that are readily aligned with traditional schooling. As McLuhan (1964/2013) noted, new media use the old as content. The new technology is always first used in ways of the previous generation. The MOOC might thus at first seem like just a hyper-efficient means to manage a classic approach—namely, the lecture. However, because of the learning platforms and their affordances, a MOOC has potential to be more than another video or another textbook. It presents the possibility of a landscape for learners to cluster into collectives to explore ideas, techniques, and practices. It is around this possibility that a MOOC differs from Web-based instructional videos. Such topic-specific video clips may give the teacher an opportunity to flip her or his classroom, but the result is likely to be an amplification of established sensibilities rather than an opening of new possibilities—unless opportunities are made for the learners to work collectively on mathematics. The key difference afforded by the MOOC lecture, then, in not the small change in delivery, but in the possibilities that arise with such a large number of interacting participants.

Recently, another massive online approach is being offered as a possibility for education. With the great interest in massive multiplayer online gaming, the Education Arcade at MIT has created a game specifically to promote mathematics and science learning.[3] This game is currently in the pilot phase, but it has the potential to be an environment for collective learning. The architecture of the game, the multiple players, and the collective action toward various goals all provide possibilities for complex emergence.

To be clear, the suggestion here is not at all that mathematics educators should consider MOOC-like structures. Rather, the point is that when complexity is taken up as a pragmatic discourse, it does more than offer suggestions on more productive engagements within traditional classroom structures. It challenges many of the foundational principles of those structures.

CLOSING REMARKS

In his influential *Finite and Infinite Games*, James Carse (1987) distinguished between two sorts of rule-governed engagements: For finite games, the rules are fixed *boundaries* that constrain the play and delimit possibilities. For infinite games, the rules are more akin to shifting *horizons*—in the language of complexity, emergent possibilities—that move with the play. Among Carse's examples of finite games are athletic engagements (e.g., most sports), academic engagements (e.g., debates), and intercultural engagements (e.g., wars). Not surprisingly, he also includes schooling. For infinite games he offers only one example: life. We would offer others—including, for example, mathematics.

Among other contrasts, finite games have definite beginnings and ends—and the goal is to win—whereas it is not always clear when an infinite game began and when it might be over. Further, the goal of the infinite game is not to win, but to stay in the game. To that end, if it seems that an infinite game is approaching an end, the players are obligated to change the rules in order to continue the play. (This is the reason we include mathematics as an infinite game. As its history shows, the rules of engagement have changed as the domain has evolved.)

Both types of games can serve as instances of complex emergence. The difference is that, for one, the rules are immutable, and for the other, the rules and the systems are both emergent. With regard to a distinction among complexity researchers, finite games are akin to the sorts of phenomena that are of interest among those who study "hard complexity" through computer modeling, controlled experimentation, and so on. Infinite games are more the fodder of those who are interested in phenomena that might be modeled, but for which the models never really suffice. For instance, it is one thing to watch a simulation of the emergence and spread of an idea in a population, and it is quite another to be a teacher in a classroom where knowledge is actually being generated. The model is a useful device for enabling perception, but it is a poor substitute for the actual phenomenon.

Complexivists Cohen and Stewart (1995) made a similar point in a somewhat different manner, by crossing the words *simplicity* and *complexity* to generate the terms *simplexity* and *complicity*. For them, simplexity refers "to the process whereby a system of rules can engender simple features. Simplexity is the emergence of large-scale simplicities as direct consequences of rules" (p. 411). Among the illustrative examples they offer are Newton's laws and formal mathematics, whose "properties are the direct and inescapable consequences of the rules" (p. 412). Other instances that might be mentioned are those that Carse identified as finite games.

A core issue among complexivists, Cohen and Stewart noted, is that simplexities (finite games) have not only been taken as models, but they have also been mistaken as the way things really are. In an effort to interrupt this deeply entrenched habit, Cohen and Stewart proposed the notion of complicities as a category of phenomena in which "totally different rules converge to produce similar features, and so exhibit the same large-scale structural patterns" (p. 414). That is, complicities can are structurally similar to simplexities—hence the fidelity of the latter in modeling the former.

There is a crucial difference, however. In an echo of the ancient caution against mistaking the map for the territory, Cohen and Stewart summarized, "Simplexity merely explores a fixed space of the possible. . . . Complicity enlarges it" (p. 417). It is a sensibility that is echoed in among a growing number of voices in the field of mathematics education. Consider an imperative from Laborde, Perrin-Glorian, and Sierpinska (2005), for example:

> To see beyond the banality, it is necessary to abandon the psychological-cognitive perspective and look at the classroom situation as an integral but dynamic system evolving in time. . . . For a mathematical debate to take place in the classroom, then, students should not consider the work of verbalization of their mathematical work as an isolated, individual school task to be evaluated by the teacher and then quickly forgotten, but as a mere phase in a collective project of common knowledge construction. The class must work as a system, to produce a system of knowledge and this implies the necessity of "record keeping" or memory.
>
> (p. vi)

This manner of thinking is amplified even more as one considers the potential of technology to connect and amplify possibilities. As mathematics educators whose work is informed by complexity research, we cannot help but read such statements as invitations to think in terms of our complicity in infinite games, rather than the maintenance of simplexities in a finite game.

More pointedly, we close with the question of whether it is adequate or appropriate for mathematics education researchers to take up complexity as a means to make sense of long-standing practices. Complexity may be taken up as one theory among many others. However, it is potentially a game-changing discourse.

NOTES

1. See Borwein & Devlin (2008). See also http://mathworld.wolfram.com/ExperimentalMathematics.html.
2. Many examples are provided at the Visual Complexity Web site, www.visualcomplexity.com. A particularly cogent mapping of knowledge domains has been generated by the International Institute for General Systems Studies, and is available at www.iigss.net/files/gPICT.pdf.
3. See The Radix Endeavor, http://education.mit.edu/projects/radix-endeavor.

REFERENCES

Anderson, J. R., & Lebiere, C. (1998). Learning. In J. R. Anderson & C. Lebiere (Eds.), *The atomic components of thought* (pp. 101–142). Mahwah, NJ: Lawrence Erlbaum Associates.

Archibald, T. (2007, April). *History of changing the culture: From the French revolution to the 21st century.* Paper presented at Changing the Culture, Simon Fraser University, Vancouver, Canada. Abstract retrieved from www.pims.math.ca/educational/changing-culture/2007

Bell, E. T. (1937). *Men of mathematics: The lives and achievements of the great mathematicians from Zeno to Poincaré.* New York: Simon & Schuster.

Borwein, J., & Devlin, K. (2008). *The computer as crucible: an introduction to experimental mathematics.* Natick, MA: A. K. Peters.

Bowers, J. & Nickerson, S. (2001). Identifying cyclic patterns of interaction to study individual and collective learning. *Mathematical Thinking and Learning, 3*(1), 1–28, doi:10.1207/S15327833MTL0301_01

Buchanan, M. (2002). *Ubiquity: Why catastrophes happen.* New York: Broadway Books.

Burger, E. B., & Starbird, M. (2005). *The heart of mathematics: An invitation to effective thinking* (2nd ed.). Emeryville, CA: Key College Publishing.

Burton, L. (Ed.). (1999). *Learning mathematics: From hierarchies to networks.* London: Falmer.

Carse, J. (1987). *Finite and infinite games.* New York: Simon & Schuster.

Cobb, P. (1999). Individual and collective mathematical development: the case of statistical data analysis. *Mathematics Thinking and Learning, 1*(1), 5–43.

Cobb, P., & Bauersfeld, H. (Eds.). (1995). *Emergence of mathematics meaning: Interaction in classroom cultures.* Hillsdale, NJ: Lawrence Erlbaum Associates.

Cohen, J. S., & Stewart, I. (1995). *Collapse of chaos: Discovering simplicity in a complex world.* London: Penguin.

Davis, B. (2011). Mathematics teachers' subtle, complex disciplinary knowledge. *Science, 332,* 1506–1507.

Davis, B. & Renert, M. (2014). *The math teachers know: Profound understanding of emergent mathematics.* New York: Routledge.

Davis, B., & Simmt, E. (2003). Understanding learning systems: Mathematics education and complexity science. *Journal for Research in Mathematics Education, 34*(2) 137–167.

Davis, B., & Simmt, E. (2006). Mathematics-for-teaching: An ongoing investigation of the mathematics that teachers (need to) know. *Educational Studies in Mathematics, 61*(3) 293–319.

Davis, B., Sumara, D., & Luce-Kapler, R. (2008). *Engaging minds: Changing teaching in complex times.* New York: Routledge.

English, L. D. (2006). Mathematical modeling in the primary school: Children's construction of a consumer guide. *Educational Studies in Mathematics, 62*(3). 303–329.

English, L. D., (2008). Introducing complex systems into the mathematics curriculum. *Teaching Children Mathematics, 15*(1), 38–47.

English, L. D. (2011). Complex learning through cognitively demanding tasks. *Mathematics Enthusiast, 8*(3). 483–506.

Ernest, P. (1994). *Social constructivism and the psychology of mathematics education*. London: Falmer.

Ernest, P. (2011). *The unit of analysis in mathematics education: Bridging the political-technical divide*. Paper presented at the Mathematics Education and Contemporary Theory. Manchester Metropolitan University, July 17–19, 2011.

Fauvel, J. & Grey, J. (1987). *The history of mathematics: S reader*. London: Macmillan Education with The Open University.

Font, V., Godino, J. D., & Gallardo, J. (2013). The emergence of objects from mathematical practices. *Educational Studies in Mathematics, 82*(1), 97–124.

Foote, R. (2007). Mathematics and complex systems. <A3+7>*Science*</A3+7>, <A3+7>*318*</A3+7>, 410–412.

Hegedus, S. J., & Moreno-Armella, L. (2011). The emergence of mathematical structures. *Educational Studies in Mathematics, 77*(2–3), 369–388.

Hershkowitz, R., & Schwarz, B. (1999). The emergent perspective in rich learning environments: some roles of tools and activities in the construction of sociomathematical norms. *Educational Studies in Mathematics, 39*(1–3), 149–166.

Hoyles, C., & Noss, R. (2008). Next steps in implementing Kaput's research programme. *Educational Studies in Mathematics, 68*(2), 85–94.

Hurford, A. (2010). Complexity theories and theories of learning: literature reviews and syntheses. In B. Sriraman & L. D. English (Eds.), *Theories of mathematics education: Seeking new frontiers* (pp. 567–590). New York: Springer.

Jacobson, M., & Wilensky, U. (2006). Complex systems in education: Scientific and educational importance and research challenges for the learning sciences. *Journal of the Learning Sciences, 15*(1), 11–34.

Kaput, J. J. (1992). Technology and mathematics education. In D. A. Grouws (Ed.), *Handbooks on mathematics teaching and learning* (pp. 515–556). New York: Macmillan.

Khan, S. (2011, March). *Let's use video to reinvent education*. TED2011. Retrieved from www.ted.com/talks/salman_khan_let_s_use_video_to_reinvent_education

Kilgore, D. (1999). Understanding learning in social movements: A theory of collective learning. *International Journal of Lifelong Education, 18*(3), 191–202. doi: 10.1080/026013799293784

Laborde, C., Perrin-Glorian, M., & Sierpinska, A. (Eds.) (2005). *Beyond the apparent banality of the mathematics classroom*. New York: Springer.

Lemke, J.L. (2000). Across the scales of time: Artifacts, activities, and meanings in ecosocial systems. *Mind, Culture, and Activity, 7*(4), 273–290.

Lerman, S. (2000). The social turn in mathematics education. In J. Boaler (Ed.), *Multiple perspectives on mathematics education* (pp. 19–44). Westport, CT: Ablex.

Lesh, R. (2010). The importance of complex systems in K–12 mathematics education. In Sriraman, B. & English, L. D. (Eds.), *Theories of mathematics education: seeking new frontiers* (pp. 563–566). Berlin: Springer.

Lesh, R., & Doerr, H. (Eds.) (2003). *Beyond constructivism: Models and modeling perspectives on mathematics problem solving learning and teaching*. Mahwah, NJ: Lawrence Erlbaum Associates.

Lesh, R., Galbraith, P. L., Haines, C. R., & Hurford, A. (Eds.). (2010). *Modeling students' mathematical modeling competencies*. New York: Springer.

Martin, L.C., & Towers, J. (2011). Improvisational understanding in the mathematics classroom. In R. K. Sawyer (Ed.), *Structure and improvisation in creative teaching* (pp. 252–278). New York: Cambridge University Press.

Maturana, H., & Varela, F. (1992). *The tree of knowledge: The biological roots of human understanding*. Boston: Shambhala Publications.

McLuhan, M. (1964/2013). Understanding media: The extensions of man. Berkeley, CA: Gingko Press.

Milbrath, L. W. (1989). *Envisioning a sustainable society: Learning our way out*. Albany, NY: State University of New York Press.

Mitchell, M. (2009). *Complexity: A guided tour*. Oxford, UK: Oxford University Press.

Moreno-Armella, L., Hegedus, S. J., & Kaput, J. J. (2008). From static to dynamic mathematics: Historical and representational perspectives. *Educational Studies in Mathematics, 68*(2), 99–111.

Nixon, L., Kendle, M., Bowdoin, D., Bailey, A., Wressell, L., Alshammari, M., Agra, E., & Donaldon, J., (2013). *Massively open: How massive open online courses changed the world*. CreateSpace Independent Publishing Platform.

Papert, S. (1980). *Mindstorms: children, computers, and powerful ideas*. New York: Basic Books.

Piaget, J. (1953). *The origin of intelligence in the child*. London: Routledge and Kegan Paul.

Pirie, S., & Kieren, T. (1994). Growth in mathematical understanding: How can we characterise it and how can we represent it? *Educational Studies in Mathematics, 26*(2), 165–190.

Proulx, J. (2013). Mental mathematics, emergence of strategies, and the enactivist theory of cognition. *Educational Studies in Mathematics*. doi:10.1007/s10649-013-9480-8

Reber, A. S. (1993). *Oxford Psychology Series: No. 19. Implicit learning and tacit knowledge: An essay on the cognitive unconscious.* Oxford, UK: Oxford University Press; New York: Clarendon Press.

Roschelle, J., Vahey, P., Tatar, D., Kaput, J., & Hegedus, S. J. (2003). Five key considerations for networking in a handheld-based mathematics classroom. In N. A. Pateman, B. J. Dougherty, & J. T. Zilliox (Eds.), *Proceedings of the 2003 Joint Meeting of PME and PMENA* (Vol. 4, pp. 71–78). Honolulu: University of Hawaii.

Sawyer, R. K. (2002a). Emergence in psychology: Lessons from the history of non-reductionist science. *Human Development, 45,* 2–28.

Sawyer, R. K. (2002b). Emergence in sociology: Contemporary philosophy of mind and some implications for sociological theory. *American Journal of Sociology, 107*(3), 551–585.

Sfard, A. (2008). *Thinking as communicating: Human development, the growth of discourses, and mathematizing.* New York: Cambridge University Press.

Stewart, I. (1989). *Does God play dice?* Cambridge, MA: Blackwell.

Stroup, W. M., & Wilensky, U. (2000). Assessing learning as emergent phenomena: moving constructivist statistics beyond the bell curve. In A. E. Kelly & R. A. Lesh (Eds.), *Handbook of Research in Mathematics and Science Education* (pp. 877–911). Mahwah, NJ: Lawrence Erlbaum Associates.

Towers, J., Martin, L., & Heater, B. (2013). Teaching and learning mathematics in the collective. *Journal of Mathematical Behavior, 32,* 424–433.

van Oers, B. (2010). Emergent mathematical thinking in the context of play. *Educational Studies in Mathematics, 74*(1–3), 23–37.

Waldrop, M. M. (1992). *Complexity: The emerging science on the edge of order and chaos.* New York: Simon & Schuster.

Watts, Duncan (2003). *Six degrees: The science of a connected age.* New York: W.W. Norton & Company.

Wilensky, U., & Resnick, M. (1999). Thinking in levels: A dynamic systems approach to making sense of the world. *Journal of Science Education and Technology, 8*(1), 3–19.

Section IV
Advances in Research Methodologies

18 Researching Mathematical Meanings for Teaching[1,2]

Patrick W. Thompson

Arizona State University

Research on mathematical knowledge for teaching (MKT) has the goal of trying to find relationships among the mathematics that teachers know, their instruction, and students' learning. The underlying assumption seems to be that if we find these relationships, and if we then help teachers obtain the appropriate knowledge, they will be positioned to teach better and support better student learning. This conceptualization of research on MKT seems quite plausible—until we ask, "What do we mean that a teacher *knows* something? How can a teacher knowing something help a student know it, too?" Answers to these questions will reveal the importance of being clear about what we presume we are assessing when we assess teachers' MKT and about why we even care to assess it.

WHAT IS *KNOWLEDGE* AND WHY DO WE CARE?

Mason and Spence (1999) analyzed historical uses of "knowledge" and quickly determined that *knowing* is much more useful for thinking about teaching and learning than is *knowledge*. *Knowing* connotes activities of a knower, while *knowledge* connotes facts—justified true beliefs. They argued that thinking about teachers' *knowledge* leads us to separate knowers from what they know, which has the consequence of separating, in our thinking, what teachers know from their thinking, deciding, and acting. Mason and Spence urged us to think instead about teachers' *acts of knowing*, which brings us closer to describing sources of teachers' actions and decisions. Within their acts of knowing Mason and Spence distinguished two broad kinds: *knowing about* (knowing-that, knowing-how, knowing-why) and *knowing-to*, "active knowledge which is present in the moment when it is required" (Mason & Spence, 1999, p. 135).

Mason's and Spence's stance on knowledge versus knowing is in line with Glasersfeld's explanations that to interpret Piaget's concept of knowledge we need to think quite differently about knowledge than as justified true belief. He explained that we need to understand Piaget's use of knowledge as connoting the dynamic, adaptive, and organized functioning of an organism's neural system—and as having reference only within the organism's experience (Glasersfeld, 1978, 1981, 1985). Put another way, "knowledge" and "knowing" are the same concept in Piaget's genetic epistemology. As I will explain in later sections, *knowing-to*, as described by Mason and Spence, can be characterized more expansively by appealing to Piaget's notion that a scheme is a meaning—an organization of actions, images, and other meanings. Thus, one *knows-to* act in a particular way in a particular context because the actions implied by one's understanding of a context are in the scheme to which you assimilated the context. In this regard, I hasten to add that Piaget had an expansive meaning of action, as "all movement, all thought, all emotion that responds to a need" (Piaget, 1968, p. 6). Thus, when Piaget spoke of schemes, he had in mind organizations of mental and affective activity whose contents could be highly nuanced and could contain several layers of structure.

Hill and Ball's Learning Mathematics for Teaching (LMT) project demonstrated that there is a correlational link between K–8 mathematics teachers' mathematical knowledge for teaching as measured by their LMT instrument and the mathematical quality of teachers' instruction (MQI) as measured by their MQI instrument (Charalambous & Hill, 2012; Hill, 2011; Hill, Blunk, Charalambous, Lewis, Phelps, Sleep, & Ball, 2008; Hill & Charalambous, 2012). At the same time, Schilling, Blunk, and Hill (2007) point out that they tacitly assumed in developing the LMT assessment that knowledge held by teachers, specifically their knowledge of content and students (KCS), was declarative.

> When we began developing items in this domain [KCS], we hypothesized that teachers' knowledge of students existed separately from their mathematical knowledge and reasoning ability. We thought of such knowledge as "declarative," or factual knowledge teachers have of student learning. Results from these validation studies, however, suggest that this "knowledge" may actually contain both elements of mathematical reasoning and knowledge of students and their mathematical trajectories.
>
> (Schilling, et al., 2007, p. 121)

The approach to investigating teachers' MKT that I describe in this chapter builds from Schilling et al.'s observation that our understanding of MKT can be broadened profitably by shifting our focus from teachers' (declarative) mathematical knowledge, to focus instead on teachers' mathematical meanings. This shift is essentially from a philosophically mainstream view of knowledge as justified, true belief about things external to the knower, to a Piagetian perspective in which meaning and knowledge are largely synonymous, and both are grounded in the knower's schemes.

This shift allows us to move, for example, from asking what teachers *know* about equations to what teachers *mean* by an equation. Compare Teacher 1's and Teacher 2's meanings of algebraic equations.

Teacher 1 thinks that any mathematical statement that contains an equal sign is an equation. Upon seeing an algebraic equation Teacher 1 thinks "do the same thing to both sides to keep the equation balanced," thinks that a solution is the number in the final step that produces a statement like "$x = $ (number)," and has the goal of reaching the final step. Teacher 1 also feels confused about differences among equations and identities, and between equations and functions. Teacher 1 thinks they should all be called equations because they all contain an equal sign.

Teacher 2 thinks that an algebraic equation is a statement of equality together with the question, "For what values of the variable(s) will this statement be true?" Teacher 2 has the goal of answering that question, and thinks to put the equation into an equivalent form that can be solve by inspection. Teacher 2 thinks of a "step" as applying an equivalence-preserving transformation to one or both sides of the equation so that it is closer to being solvable by inspection.[3] Teacher 2 has no difficulty distinguishing between equations and functions and between equations and identities. To Teacher 2, a function is a statement about a relationship between two quantities' values. An identity is an equation that is true for all values in the equation's domain. Teacher 2 realizes that all statements with an equal sign *could* be called "equations." However, she realizes also that to do so, the general meaning of an equation would have to be that an equation represents its solution set and that she would therefore need to define functions as sets of ordered pairs—ideas that she feels are too general for her students.

Both teachers could exhibit similar performances in answering questions about equations and procedures for solving them. Their different meanings, however, would provide different potentialities regarding what they say to students *about* equations and equation solving.

The mathematical knowledge that matters most for teachers resides in the mathematical meanings they hold. Teachers' mathematical meanings constitute their images of the mathematics they teach and intend that students have. Teachers' mathematical meanings guide their instructional decisions and actions (Thompson, 2013). Dewey (1910) said as much when he elaborated the connection between thinking and meaning: "That thinking both employs and expands notions, conceptions, is then simply saying that in inference and judgment we use meanings, and that this use also corrects and widens them" (Dewey, 1910, p. 125). Dewey also alerted us to the dangers of being vague about our central constructs:

> Vagueness disguises the unconscious mixing together of different meanings, and facilitates the substitution of one meaning for another, and covers up the failure to have any precise meaning at all.
>
> (Dewey, 1910, p. 130)

Vagueness in our meaning of knowledge becomes especially problematic when we set out to assess it. We place ourselves in the uncomfortable position of defining knowledge, or types of it, in the same way that many psychologists use the idea of operational definition to define intelligence—intelligence is defined to be what intelligence tests assess. Bridgman, who originated the method of operational definition, roundly criticized using a measure of a construct to define that construct: "Without doubt it is possible to apply the procedure suggested here, but I believe that the situation seldom arises which one would be content to treat finally by any such method as this" (Bridgman, 1955, Chapter 1, Kindle Locations 507–508). Without explication, the word *knowledge* becomes a primitive term in research on mathematical knowledge for teaching, open to any interpretation that a person can pack into it.

I will not try to explicate what others might mean by knowledge in discussing what teachers know and how what they know is related to what they do. To do so would take us into a morass of philosophical disputes, such as knowledge versus belief (Thompson, 1992) and constructivism versus realism (Glasersfeld, 1992; Howe & Berv, 2000; Phillips, 2000; Suchting, 1992)—disputes that turn out to be immaterial for the purpose of improving mathematics teaching. Instead, I will argue here, as I have argued elsewhere (Thompson, 2013), that a focus on teachers' mathematical meanings, as opposed to their mathematical knowledge, offers a fruitful approach to uncovering important sources of teachers' instructional decisions and actions, and provides useful guidance for designing teachers' professional development.

In this chapter I make two proposals. The first is that a focus on teachers' mathematical meanings, in line with Mason and Spence's focus on *knowing-to*, is more productive for understanding and improving teachers' instruction than is a focus on mathematical knowledge. With meaning defined appropriately, a focus on meanings positions us to help teachers focus on creating instruction that helps students develop productive meanings. The second proposal is a means to gain insight into mathematical meanings teachers have. To do this requires a theory of meaning as well as a set of techniques that can be used at scale for creating useful models of teachers' mathematical meanings—models that provide guidance in designing mathematics teachers' professional development that helps them to help their students create coherent mathematical meanings.

Finally, an example might give further clarity to the distinction between knowledge and meaning. Suppose a child lays three meter sticks end to end, and then is given a fourth meter stick to lay down. Upon putting it down, we ask, "How much did you add to the total length?" ("A meter.") The child *knows* that he added a meter. But what did it *mean* to him? Did he mean that he added one more stick called "a meter"? Or did he mean that he added a meter in length that is constituted by centimeters, which in turn are constituted by millimeters, which in turn are constituted by (and so on). Understanding what people mean gives more insight into their thinking than does understanding what they believe to be true.

EXAMPLES OF INVESTIGATING TEACHERS' MEANINGS

Two examples will set the stage for discussing the idea of meaning, and mathematical meanings for teaching, and how one might assess them. They are drawn from *Mathematical Meanings for Teaching Secondary Mathematics* (MMTsm), a 43-item diagnostic instrument designed for use in mathematics professional development.[4,5]

Example 1: Meanings of "Over"

We noticed that English speakers often speak of average speed as "Distance over time" and represent it with a symbolic expression like d/t. However, what "over" means to persons saying this was unclear to us. Are they speaking of a spatial arrangement of symbols? Or are they thinking that two things happened concurrently—something moved and some amount of time elapsed?

We designed an item (Figure 18.1) to see the extent to which teachers distinguish or confound "over" as meaning spatial arrangement of symbols versus "over" as meaning that two events happened or are happening concurrently. The difference in these meanings can reflect an importance difference regarding what teachers intend that students understand from their instruction of average rate of change. If teachers intend to convey only a spatial arrangement of symbols, then their utterances are about marks as written and are not about what students should understand about variables varying or about the meaning of quotient within a context.

The purpose of Part A in Figure 18.1 was to have teachers commit to a meaning of "over" in a context where, when interpreted normatively, it means "during." The purpose of Part B was to give teachers an opportunity to show how they interpreted the context in which "over" occurred while expressing it symbolically. Since the statement is about a change in mass, the symbolic representation of it should reflect a change in mass that happened as time passed from one moment in time to another. Since the function f gives the culture's mass at moments in time, and since the change in time is represented by "Δx," one representation of the change in mass would be $f(x + \Delta x) - f(x) = 4$ or $f(x_0 + \Delta x) - f(x_0) = 4$, where x_0 refers to a specific moment in time.

Figure 18.2 contains one teacher's response to Parts A and B. In Part A, the teacher said that "over" means "during," but went on to say that you also can think of "over" as meaning a ratio. This teacher's Part B response shows more than that, "over" brings to mind a spatial arrangement of symbols. It reveals two additional issues: (1) the teacher defined "$f(x)$" in terms of an expression in which "x" does not appear, and (2) used "$f(x)$" to represent a rate of change even though the text stated that "the function f gives the culture's mass at moments in time."[6]

A college science textbook contains this statement about a function f that gives a bacterial culture's mass at moments in time.

The change in the culture's mass over the time period Δx is 4 grams.

Part A.   What does the word "over" mean in this statement?

Part B.   Express the textbook's statement symbolically.

Figure 18.1 An item to investigate teachers' meanings of "over." © 2014 Arizona Board of Regents. Used with permission.

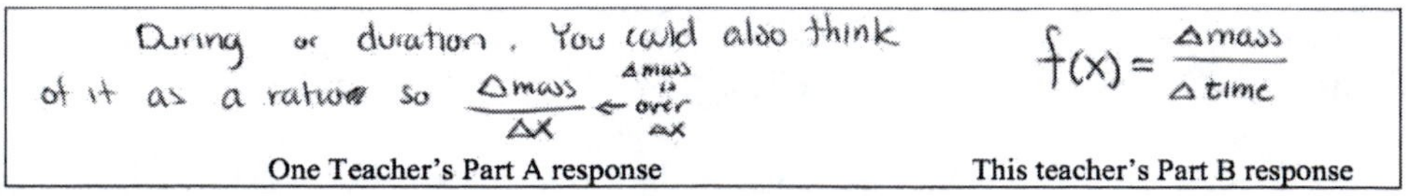

One Teacher's Part A response   This teacher's Part B response

Figure 18.2 A teacher's responses to questions in Figure 18.1.

We designed a scoring rubric to capture the range of meanings we discerned from responses given in summer 2013 by 96 high school mathematics teachers in the Midwest and Southwest United States. Table 18.1 and Table 18.2 show gradations among levels of responses to Parts A and B, respectively. We put any response equivalent to "during" at the highest level for Part A of Figure 18.1, and any response like "$f(x + \Delta x) - f(x) = 4$" or "$m_{t_2} - m_{t_1} = 4$" where $t_2 - t_1 = \Delta x$" at the highest level for Part B. While a method for creating rubrics that focus on meanings is discussed in a later section, for now it is worth pointing out that though this item's design emerged from being attentive to teachers' and students' meanings in prior research and in our daily work with teachers, the rubrics for scoring responses to Figure 18.1 emerged from analyzing teachers' responses to the item itself. When distinguishing between levels of responses, we continually asked, "How might a student interpret what the teacher produced? How productive would it be for students' development of coherent meanings were a teacher to express what he or she did?"

In subsequent tables I share results of our scoring for Figure 18.1 to illustrate how a focus on teachers' meanings can provide useful information about their thinking. Table 18.3 summarizes teachers' responses to Part A: 61% of responses were assigned Levels A3 or A2 (teachers spoke of "over" in a way that suggested something happening during a passage of time) while 32% were assigned Level A1 (they specifically mentioned that "over" meant division or ratio in the statement about a change of mass over a time interval). Table 18.3 also breaks down responses by teachers' undergraduate major. "Math" points to teachers who received a B.Sc. in

Table 18.1 Rubric for scoring Figure 1, Part A. © 2014 Arizona Board of Regents. Used with permission.

A3:	Teacher said "during," or otherwise referred to the culture's mass in relation to a passage of time.
A2:	Any of the following: • The teacher conveyed "during" but represented the time interval using a symbol other than Δx. • The teacher described "over" as meaning an amount of time.
A1:	The teacher conveyed that "over" means division, regardless of saying anything else.
A0:	Any of the following: • The teacher wrote "I don't know." • The scorer cannot interpret what the teacher meant by "over." • The teacher's response is not described by any of levels A1 to A3.

Table 18.2 Rubric for scoring Figure 1, Part B. © 2014 Arizona Board of Regents. Used with permission.

B4:	The teacher represented a difference in the mass of a culture at different moments in time, with the resulting difference being 4. If the teacher used a variable other than "m" or "y" to stand for mass instead of using $f(x)$, or a variable other than x to represent elapsed time, the letter must be defined.
B3:	Any of the following: • The teacher wrote a statement like $\Delta m = 4$ or $\Delta y = 4$. • The teacher represented a difference of masses that equals 4 using a letter other than m or y to represent mass, **and** said that their variable represents mass. In addition, the teacher did not represent a time interval.
B2:	• Teacher's response contains a combination of $\Delta m = 4$ and $\Delta m / \Delta x = 4$.
B1:	The teacher wrote a quotient showing the *change* in mass divided by the *change* in time is equal to 4 (with or without a unit), or some algebraically equivalent statement.
B0b:	The teacher's response conveys division but the response is not described by level B1.
B0a	Any of the following: • The teacher wrote "I don't know" • The scorer cannot interpret the teacher's response. • The teacher's response is not described by any of Levels B0b to B3.

Table 18.3 High school mathematics teachers' responses to Figure 1, Part A ($n = 96$).

A-Level	Math	MathEd	Other	Total
A3	11	15	16	42
A2	5	4	8	17
A1	9	14	8	31
A0	1	3	1	5
No Ans	1	0	0	1
Total	27	36	33	96

Table 18.4 High school mathematics teachers' responses to Figure 1, Part B ($n = 96$).

B-Level	Math	MathEd	Other	Total
B4	0	2	1	3
B3	1	2	2	5
B2	2	0	0	2
B1	10	13	11	34
B0b	7	11	6	24
B0a	5	8	12	25
No Ans	2	0	1	3
Total	27	36	33	96

mathematics; "Math Ed" points to teachers who received a B.Sc. or B.A. in secondary mathematics education; "Other" is any other undergraduate degree. As shown in Table 18.3, 59% of Math majors, 53% of Math Ed majors, and 73% of Other majors answered at Levels A3 or A2.

Table 18.4 shows the classification of teachers' symbolic representations of the entire statement: 3% of responses were at Level B4; 5% of responses were at Level B3, 60% of responses were at Level B1 or Level B0b, and 26% were placed at Level B0a. Responses at levels B1 and B0b contained a quotient or the equivalent of a quotient (e.g., $\Delta m = 4\Delta x$). Figure 18.3 shows four examples of Level B0a responses. The first two responses in Figure 18.3 are by teachers holding a degree in mathematics; the second two are by teachers holding a degree in mathematics education.

Table 18.3 shows the majority of teachers responding at a high level regarding a meaning of "over" while Table 18.4 shows the majority of teachers responding at a low level regarding a representation of the entire statement—representing it with a quotient or with a wholly inappropriate response. Table 18.5 examines the relationship between teachers' responses to Parts A and B: 100% of teachers who responded at a low level (A0 or A1) for Part A scored at a low level (B0a, B0b, B1, or B2) for Part B. Moreover, 51 of 59 teachers (86%) who scored at a high level for Part A (A2 or A3) scored at a low level for Part B (B0a, B0b, B1, or B2). This suggests strongly that the phrase "change in mass over change in time" triggered a variety of meanings among teachers, most of which were unlike the meaning that the culture's mass changed by some amount while elapsed time changed by some amount.

It is worthwhile to unpack two implications of what we learned from this item. The first regards mathematical modeling—teachers understanding situations described verbally and describing their understandings symbolically. The second regards what teachers might convey to students unthinkingly about fractions.[7]

Modeling. In this item, the textbook's statement is read normatively as being about a change in mass that happened during a change in time. That such a large percentage of teachers

$$f(t) = m$$
$$f(m) = 4$$

B.Sc. Math

$$M(\Delta x) = M + 4$$

B.Sc. Math

$$f(x) = 4$$

B.Sc. Math Ed

$$f(x) = bx \cdot 4$$

B.A. Math Ed

Figure 18.3 Examples of Level B0a responses.

Table 18.5 Relationship between teachers' responses to Part A and to Part B of Figure 1 ($n = 96$).

	B4	B3	B2	B1	B0b	B0a	No Ans	Total
A3	2	4	2	12	4	17	1	42
A2	1	1	0	4	3	7	1	17
A1	0	0	0	17	14	0	0	31
A0	0	0	0	1	3	1	0	5
No Ans	0	0	0	0	0	0	1	1
Total	3	5	2	34	24	25	3	96

associated the statement fundamentally with a ratio suggests that they did not interpret the statement in terms of the quantities involved (a difference of masses and a difference of times) and a relationship between them (concurrence). This raises the possibility that teachers' meanings for the quantities and relationships that any rate of change entails are muddled when they teach the idea of rate of change or model situations that involve a rate of change. Put another way, "over" meaning a spatial arrangement of symbols is in line with "*more* means addition, *less* means subtraction, *of* means multiplication"—meanings that muddle young children's thinking when solving arithmetic word problems.

What teachers convey to students about fractions. Teachers should be alert to how students interpret "*a/b*". We would hope they attend to whether their students assimilate "*a/b*" just as two numbers separated by a slash mark or that they also assimilate it to a scheme that relates the value of *a*, the value of *b*, and their relative size. This second meaning can be expressed as "*a/b* is a number *m* that tells you that *a* is *m* times as large as *b*."[8] The second meaning of "*a/b*" is the meaning of quotient, and is related tightly to past research on ratio-as-measure (Lobato & Thanheiser, 2000; Simon & Blume, 1994). Teachers who read "*a/b*" as "*a* over *b*" and for whom "over" implies a spatial arrangement seem unlikely to worry about whether students are developing the quotient meaning of "*a/b*." Cameron Byerley is investigating the viability of this claim.

Example 2: An Item to Investigate Teachers' Meanings for Slope

We often see teachers teach the idea of slope simply as a computation, expressed as "rise over run" or "the change in *y* divided by the change in *x*." We also often see it taught as a property of a triangle drawn against a graph. These are unproductive meanings for students to have. They only work to answer the question, "What is the slope?" It is important for students to understand that the idea of slope is tightly bound to the idea of relative size of changes in two quantities, which then ties the idea of slope to the idea of constant rate of change. It is also important for students to understand that a graph's slope is independent of axes' scales and independent of the coordinate system in which the graph is made.[9]

With this in mind, we designed the item in Figure 18.4 to probe teachers' meanings of slope in regard to relative size of changes and to issues of axes' scales. Part A requests a *numerical* value for *m* even though the coordinate system's axes are sans numbers. If you see the line

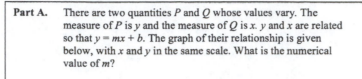
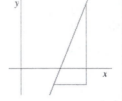

| **Part A.** | There are two quantities P and Q whose values vary. The measure of P is y and the measure of Q is x. y and x are related so that $y = mx + b$. The graph of their relationship is given below, with x and y in the same scale. What is the numerical value of m? |
| **Part B.** | What would be the numerical value of m if the y-axis were changed so that the distance between 0 and 1 is 2 times as large as the original? |

Figure 18.4 An item to investigate teachers' meanings of slope. © 2014 Arizona Board of Regents. Used with permission.

Table 18.6 Teachers' responses to Part A and Part B of Figure 4 ($n = 96$).

| | | \multicolumn{6}{c}{**Part B Response**} |
		Same	*Double*	*Half*	*Other*	*No Ans*	*Total*
Part A *Response*	*Close Num*	2	30	15	3	0	50
	Far Num	1	4	2	1	0	8
	Diff Quot	4	10	6	1	1	22
	Other	6	3	0	1	3	13
	No Ans	0	0	0	0	3	3
	Total	13	47	23	6	7	96

segments as representing amounts of change in x and y, and if you understand the quotient $\Delta y / \Delta x$ as the measure of Δy in units of Δx, then you can decide to estimate the numerical value of m simply by physically measuring Δy using Δx as a unit. The change in y is 2.5 times as large as the change in x, so $m = 2.5$.[10]

We included Part B to see whether teachers thought of the line's slope as being a property of the triangle *itself* instead of as a relative size of changes that the horizontal and vertical segments *represent*. When the y-axis is enlarged by a factor of 2, and remembering that the graph represents the relationship between values of x and values of y, the value of m remains the same because the change in y that the vertical segment represents does not change. Interviews with students and teachers convinced us that if someone's meaning for slope is a property of a triangle, then he or she will say either that the slope will be twice as large (if imagining that the triangle stretches) or half as large (if imagining that the y-axis is rescaled but the triangle remains the same).

Table 18.6 shows responses from the group of 96 high school mathematics teachers mentioned in the prior example. Rows describe responses to Part A. *Close Num* means a numerical estimate from 2 to 3. *Far Num* means a numerical estimate less than 2 or greater than 3. *Diff Quot* means a response like "$\Delta y / \Delta x$" or "$(y_1) / (x_1)$." *Other* responses included "y/x," "P/Q," and "$m = (y - b) / x$." Columns describe responses to Part B.

Table 18.6 shows that 52% of the teachers gave a numerical approximation that was close to 2.5. Many of them showed work that suggested measuring Δy in units of Δx. However, 90% (45/50) of these teachers who gave a close approximation for Part A answered either "double" or "half" to Part B. This suggests that though they understood slope to be about relative size, they compared side-lengths of a triangle and not what those lengths represented. Teachers answering Part A with a number outside the "close" range seemed to give numerical values as an index of the line's perceptual "slantiness." These responses did not contain work to suggest that the teacher measured the length of one segment in terms of the length of the other. Teachers who gave a symbolic response (*Difference Quotient* or *Other*) to Part A had the highest percentage of "same" on Part B. We suspect that this was because they focused on symbolic formulas, which they could think of as remaining the same regardless of how, or whether, they interpreted the graph. The results in Table 18.6 suggest that a large percentage of these 96 teachers thought that "slope" meant a property of a triangle drawn against a graph that either reflects the relative size of its legs or that is associated with a computational formula.

TEACHERS' MATHEMATICAL MEANINGS

The items in the previous section share a trait: they were designed to elicit teachers' interpretations of a statement or setting about an idea that recurs in mathematics teaching, and then to elicit implications in teachers' thinking that their interpretations held. This design strategy is rooted in a theory of meaning that is based on Piaget's notion of *assimilation to a scheme*. In this section I will unpack the idea of assimilation and explain its connection to assessing teachers' mathematical meanings for teaching mathematics.

A sense of absorption is commonly associated with *assimilate*. Object A is assimilated to Object B when A is transformed to become part of B. As Piaget famously stated in elaborating his meaning of assimilation, "A rabbit that eats a cabbage doesn't become cabbage; it's the cabbage that becomes rabbit—that's assimilation. It's the same thing at the psychological level. Whatever a stimulus is, it is integrated with internal structures" (Bringuier, 1980, p. 42). By this Piaget meant that a person experiences the structures that are activated through assimilation, not the stimulus that an observer views as separate from the experiencer. To illustrate this distinction, suppose that a person, deep in thought, rounds a corner on the streets of Chicago and looks up at what we call the Willis Tower and sees the Empire State Building, recalling the dinner he had in it. This person *assimilated the Empire State Building*—despite it being 1286 kilometers away. His experience was that he saw the Empire State Building, even if he eventually corrected himself by realizing that he was in Chicago, not New York.[11]

Another way to understand assimilation in Piaget's theory is to think of meanings that come to a person's mind upon encountering a situation. What looks like absorption (taking in the situation) actually is the person's imbuement of meaning to the situation.

> Assimilating an object to a scheme involves giving one or several meanings to this object, and it is this conferring of meanings that implies a more or less complete system of inferences, even when it is simply a question of verifying a fact. In short, we could say that an assimilation is an association accompanied by inference. (Johnckheere, Mandelbrot, & Piaget, 1958, p. 59) as quoted in (Montangero & Maurice-Naville, 1997, p. 72).

Johnckheere et al.'s reference to "a more or less compete system of inferences" was their way to talk about the implicative nature of meanings. A person's meaning in a situation is what comes to mind immediately together with what is ready to come to mind *next*. The implicative nature of meanings is at the heart of Piaget's notion of scheme (Piaget & Garcia, 1991). Thompson, Carlson, Byerley, and Hatfield (2014), building from Harel's (2008, 2013) notions of ways of understanding and ways of thinking, captured the implicative nature of meaning in their system for differentiating among various forms of understanding (Table 18.7).

Understanding in the moment addresses what a person understands of something said, written, or done in the moment of understanding it. All understandings are understandings-in-the-moment. Some understandings might be a state that the person has struggled to attain at that moment through functional accommodations of existing schemes (Steffe, 1991). This is an understanding that can be easily lost once the person's attention moves on; it is typical of when a person makes sense of an idea for the first time. The *meaning of an understanding* is the space of implications that the current understanding mobilizes—actions, operations, or

Table 18.7 Thompson and Harel's definitions of understanding, meaning, and way of thinking. (Thompson et al., 2014)

Construct	Definition
Understanding (in the moment)	Cognitive state resulting from an assimilation
Meaning (in the moment)	The space of implications existing at the moment of understanding
Understanding (stable)	Cognitive state resulting from an assimilation to a scheme
Meaning (stable)	The space of implications that results from having assimilated to a scheme. The scheme is the meaning, what Harel previously called a *way of understanding*.
Way of Thinking	Habitual anticipation of specific meanings or ways of thinking in reasoning

schemes that the person's current understanding suggests.[12] An understanding is *stable* if it is the result of an assimilation to a scheme. A scheme, being stable, then constitutes the space of implications resulting from the person's assimilation of anything to it.[13] The scheme is the meaning of the understanding that the person constructs in the moment. As an aside, schemes provide the "way" in Harel's "way of understanding" (Harel, 2013). Finally, Thompson et al. (2014) characterize "way of thinking" as a person having developed a pattern for utilizing specific meanings or ways of thinking in reasoning about particular ideas.

The previous section's examples were designed to gain insight into aspects of teachers' meanings. The first example examined their meanings of "over" as revealed in their linguistic and mathematical descriptions of two events' concurrence. The second example examined their meanings of slope. In neither example can we say that we determined teachers' meanings. The best we can say is that we gained insight into their meanings. Since meanings are schemes ("implications of an understanding"), their boundaries and connections with other meanings are often subtle and sensitive to context. Thus, diagnoses of teachers' meanings to support the design of professional development require a battery of items that reveal broader schemes, or clear indicators of limited meanings, among a body of related mathematical ideas. I address this issue in the next section.

ASSESSING TEACHERS' MATHEMATICAL MEANINGS FOR TEACHING

To assess teachers' mathematical meanings for teaching requires that the assessment designers have a theory of the meanings they intend to assess. Assessment designers must say what they will take to constitute productive and less productive meanings for students' learning regarding a mathematical idea—and an explanation of why one is more productive than another. Productive meanings are *propaedeutic* (preparing the student for future learning) and they lend coherence to the meanings students already have.

A theory of meanings-to-be-assessed should also draw from research on meanings that prove to be problematic when students have them. For example, research on students' understandings of fractions shows that "*a* out of *b*" as a meaning for *a/b* is highly detrimental for students' later mathematical learning (Carpenter, Coburn, Reys, & Wilson, 1976; Norton & Wilkins, 2009; Thompson & Saldanha, 2003; Torbeyns, Schneider, Xin, & Siegler, 2014; Vinner, Hershkowitz, & Bruckheimer, 1981). Teachers who have unproductive meanings can easily convey them to students unthinkingly (Izsák, 2012; Thompson, 2013), so it is essential to create assessment items that give teachers the opportunity to display unproductive meanings as well as productive ones. The next section illustrates the process for designing such items in the context of the concepts of variation and covariation.

Continuous Variation and Covariation

It is well established that students profit by thinking that values of variables vary continuously on a connected subset of the real numbers (Castillo-Garsow, 2010; Confrey, 1994; Confrey & Smith, 1995; Thompson, 1994a). The idea that variables' values vary continuously is the basis for thinking covariationally, which is an essential component of understanding functions, graphs, and relationships (Carlson, Jacobs, Coe, Larsen, & Hsu, 2002; Thompson, 1994b).

To assess teachers' meanings for continuous variation and covariation, we must first say precisely what we mean by "understanding continuous variation" and "understanding continuous covariation" and how teachers' thinking might be at different levels regarding them. Table 18.8 and Table 18.9 are a culmination of prior research on students' understandings of

Table 18.8 Meanings of continuous variation behind the MMTsm.

Meanings of Continuous Variation	
Level	*Description*
Smooth Continuous Variation	The individual thinks of variation of a variable's value as the variable's magnitude increasing in bits while anticipating simultaneously that within each bit the variable's value varies smoothly.
Chunky Continuous Variation	The individual thinks of variation of a variable's magnitude as increasing by intervals of a fixed size. The individual imagines, for example, the variable's value varying from 0 to 1, from 1 to 2, from 2 to 3 to (and so on). Values between 0 and 1, between 1 and 2, between 2 and 3 "come along" by virtue of each being part of a chunk, but the quantity does not have them as a value in the same way it has 0, 1, 2, etc. as values. Chunky continuous variation is *not* just thinking that increases happen in whole number amounts. Thinking of a variable's value going from 0 to 0.25, 0.25 to 0.5, 0.5 to 0.75, and so on (while thinking that entailed intervals "come along") is just as much thinking with chunky continuous variation as is thinking of increases from 0 to 1, 1 to 2, and so on.
Discrete Variation	The individual thinks of a variable as taking specific values. The individual sees the variable's value changing from a to b by taking values $a_1, a_2, \rightleftharpoons, a_n$, but does not envision the variable taking any value between a_i and a_{i+1}.
No Variation (NV)	The individual envisions a variable as having a fixed value. It could have a different fixed value, but that would be simply to envision another scenario.
Variable as Letter (VL)	A variable is a letter. It has nothing to do with variation.

Table 18.9 Meanings of continuous covariation behind the MMTsm.

Meanings of Continuous Covariation	
Level	*Description*
Smooth Continuous Covariation (SCC)	The individual envisions changes in one variable's value in relation to changes in another variable's value where variables vary smoothly and continuously.
Chunky Continuous Covariation (CCC)	The individual envisions chunky continuous variation in one variable's value in relation to chunky continuous variation in another variable's value.
Coordination of Values (CV)	The individual coordinates the values of one variable with values of another variable with the anticipation of creating a discrete collection of pairs $(x, f(x))$.
Precoordination of Values (PCV)	The individual envisions two variables' values varying together but asynchronously (one variable changes, then the second variable changes, then the first, etc.). The individual does not anticipate creating pairs of values.
Variation but No Coordination (VNC)	The individual has no image of variables varying together. The individual focuses on one or another variable's variation with no coordination of values.

variables, functions, and rate of change (Carlson, et al., 2002; Castillo-Garsow, 2010; Confrey, 1992; Confrey & Smith, 1995; Saldanha & Thompson, 1998; Thompson & Thompson, 1996; Thompson, 1994a, 2011; Thompson & Thompson, 1994).

Table 18.8 describes different levels at which someone could think of a variable's value varying. The two highest levels of thinking are about a meaning of variation that creates continuous intervals. The distinction between the two levels is that a person thinking at the highest level has a recursive anticipation that any variation can be refined (Thompson, 2011, p. 47). A person at the second level ("chunky") envisions variation over an interval in fixed increments without the accompanying image that variation happens within each increment, as if laying rulers end-to-end. The lower three levels capture thinking about variation as an act of replacement—the individual thinks of a variable's value as something that is substituted for the letter.

Table 18.9 imports the meanings of continous variation (Table 18.8) into meanings of covariation. Table 18.9 could be expanded to account for the possibility that an individual conceives of two variables having different kinds of variation, but in practice this has not been workable.

Figure 18.5 shows the fourth version of one of several items that we designed to assess teachers' meanings of covariation. The highest level of reasoning we anticipated is this: If you imagine the ball bobbing, and if you coordinate small changes in displacement in a direction with small changes in total distance, you will realize that the two changes are always the same magnitude but possibly in different directions. Thus, the graph's slope will be ±1 over *any* interval in which the ball's displacement changes without changing direction.

We designed the item in Figure 18.5 purposely to exclude considerations of the ball's speed and its elapsed time. Our intention was to create a situation that forced teachers to conceptualize both quantities in the covariation. Our reason for this was that teacher interviews in the early stages of the item's development convinced us, in line with prior research, that teachers could envision an event happening in time without actually conceptualizing time as a quantity.

Table 18.10 summarizes responses from 111 high school mathematics teachers in the Midwest United States who took the Summer 2012 version of the MMTsm. It is split into two groups: responses that involved some description of variation (*n* = 17) and responses that contained no description of variation (*n* = 94). Only 10 responses (9%) spoke of displacement and total distance covarying.

The item in Figure 18.5 was extremely difficult to score, for two reasons: First, teachers often used poor grammar and vague language. Second, surprising to us, most teachers explained the graph in ways having nothing to do with the quantities involved and their variation. Instead,

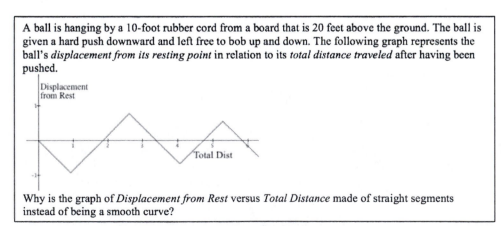

A ball is hanging by a 10-foot rubber cord from a board that is 20 feet above the ground. The ball is given a hard push downward and left free to bob up and down. The following graph represents the ball's *displacement from its resting point* in relation to its *total distance traveled* after having been pushed.

Why is the graph of *Displacement from Rest* versus *Total Distance* made of straight segments instead of being a smooth curve?

Figure 18.5 Version 4 of an item to assess covariational reasoning. © 2014 Arizona Board of Regents. Used with permission.

Table 18.10 Responses by high school mathematics teachers in Summer 2012 to the item in Figure 5 (*n* = 111).

Response	Freq
1. Covaried distance and displacement	10
2. Coordinated distance and displacement	3
3. Varied total distance, mentioned displacement, but no covariation	3
4. Varied displacement, mentioned total distance, but no covariation	1
5. Used physical situation wrongly to explain the graph	22
6. Used graph to describe the ball's behavior	29
7. Measuring distance implies a linear graph	16
8. Other	27

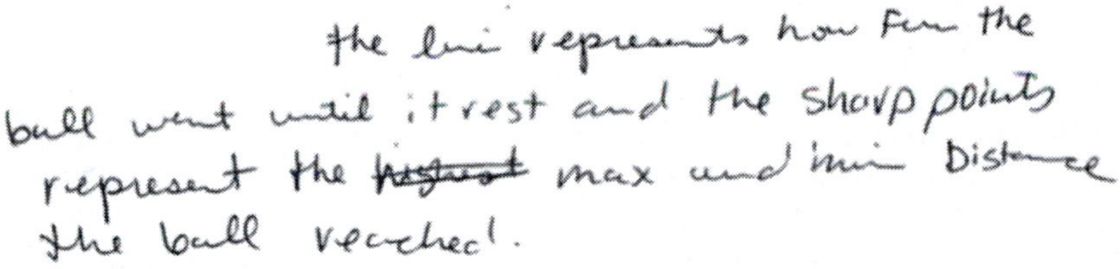

the line represents how far the ball went until it rest and the sharp points represent the ~~highest~~ max and min distance the ball reached.

Figure 18.6 Example of a response that explains the ball's movement based on properties of the graph in Figure 18.5.

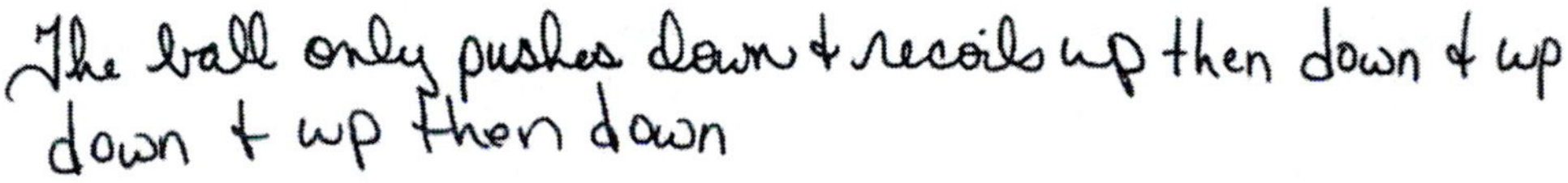

The ball only pushes down & recoils up then down & up down + up then down

Figure 18.7 Example of response that uses physical situation to explain the graph in Figure 18.5.

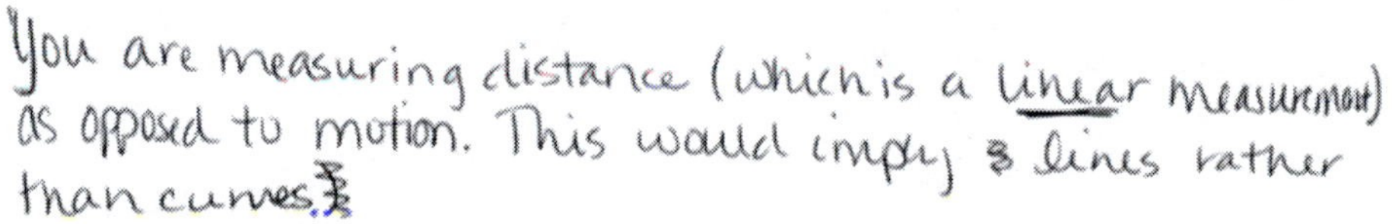

You are measuring distance (which is a linear measurement) as opposed to motion. This would imply 3 lines rather than curves.

Figure 18.8 Example of response that explains the graph in Figure 18.5 in terms of the theme that distance is a linear measurement.

many teachers took the graph as given and tried to use its properties to explain the situation (Figure 18.6). Other teachers tried to explain the graph in terms of what happens when a ball bobs up and down (Figure 18.7). Yet other teachers tried to explain the graph in terms of an overarching theme (Figure 18.8). Finally, many teachers mentioned time in their responses to Figure 18.5.

These non-covariational responses led us to add categories of "thematic thinking" (categories 5 and 7 in Table 18.10), "shape thinking" (category 6 in Table 18.10), and "nonresponsive" to our theoretical framework. We added these categories in order to capture ways of thinking that teachers exhibited in response to an item that is ostensibly about covariation, but which elicits responses having nothing to do with covariation. We also modified the item to alert teachers explicitly that they should not incorporate time into their explanations.

Our difficulty in developing a scoring rubric for Version 4 of this item (Figure 18.5) led us to create a multiple-choice version (Figure 18.9), where the options were worded to reflect the kinds of thinking we detected in teachers responses to Figure 18.5. We anticipated that we would see an increase in responses aligned with smooth continuous covariation (option *d*) simply because teachers might see that it is the most reasonable explanation even though it might not occur to them spontaneously. Indeed, we thought it entirely possible that most teachers would recognize option *d* as the response they should select.

Option *a* reflects thematic thinking (TT). Option *b* reflects chunky covariational thinking (CCC). Option *c* reflects coordination of variations (CV). Option *e* reflects shape thinking (ST)—using properties of the graph to describe properties of the situation. We were unable to include an option that would reflect precoordination ways of thinking, largely because our descriptions were too long. We included Part B as a second opportunity for teachers to express shape thinking, or to recognize the inappropriateness of the student's shape thinking, but we do not yet have data on Part B.

Table 18.11 shows responses from 96 high school mathematics teachers who took the Summer 2013 version of the MMTsm (which did not include Part B). It shows that we were correct to anticipate a higher rate of responses aligned with smooth and chunky continuous covariation—but since 67% of responses were other than *d*, our concern was unfounded that making the item multiple-choice would "give away" what we considered the most appropriate response. Also, Table 18.11 shows that no teacher selected option *e* (shape thinking). This was our motive for including Part B. We are collecting data on Part B with 200 high school mathematics teachers in Summer 2014. Interviews with teachers, and trials with senior mathematics majors, suggest to us that Part B will elicit shape thinking among teachers who are prone to think this way.

I mentioned earlier that a teacher's response to a single item is not sufficient to gain insight into the boundaries and connections within his or her meanings—that to do this requires multiple items that involve aspects of a meaning in different settings. My final example is of

---

A ball is hanging by a 10-foot rubber cord from a board that is 20 feet above the ground. The ball is given a sharp push downward and is left free to bob up and down.

The graph on the left represents the ball's *displacement from its resting point* in relation to its *time elapsed* since being pushed. The graph on the right is the ball's *displacement from its resting point* in relation to its *total distance traveled* since being pushed.

Part A. Why is the graph of *Displacement from Rest* versus *Total Distance* made of straight segments?

> *Select the best answer.*
>   a.   Distance, which is a linear measurement, must be represented with a straight segment.
>   b.   A change of one in displacement corresponds to a change of one in total distance.
>   c.   The ball's displacement in either direction is correlated with changes in total distance.
>   d.   Any small change in displacement in a direction is the same magnitude as the change in total distance.
>   e.   The graph represents the motion of the ball. The graph is made of line segments, demonstrating that the ball travels in a linear fashion.

Part B. A student said, "The graph on the right shows that the ball's speed is constant between about 1 and 2.5 seconds." Is the student's statement true? Explain.

Figure 18.9 Version 10 of item in Figure 5. © 2014 Arizona Board of Regents. Used with permission.

Table 18.11 Responses to Figure 9 (Version 10 of the item in Figure 5) by 96 high school mathematics teachers in Summer 2013.

Response	Math	MathEd	Other	Total
d (SCC)	7	12	11	30
b (CCC)	9	12	8	29
c (CV)	5	7	4	16
a (TT)	4	4	8	16
I Don't Know	0	1	0	1
No Ans	1	0	2	3
No Time	1	0	0	1
Total	27	36	33	96

In a lesson on linear equations, Darren, a student in Mrs. Bryant's class, asked, "Mrs. Bryant, why do they call x a variable in $3x + 7 = 12$ when x can be only one number? Didn't you say that a letter that stands for just one number is a constant?"

How would you respond?

Figure 18.10 Item to investigate teachers' conceptions of variation in equations. © 2014 Arizona Board of Regents. Used with permission.

a variation item (Figure 18.10) given in a context where the question is not about variation or covariation directly. Rather, it addresses the seeming contradiction described by Chazan (1993) that many students worldwide experience while studying algebra: Why do we call "x" a variable in equations like $3x + 7 = 12$ when it stands for just one number?

The conundrum that this item raises is an artifact of the way many teachers and textbooks speak of equations. They convey to students that equations have a particular form (formula on one side, number on the other) and that they are triggers for a special collection of activities that should end when you get a letter on one side of an equal sign and a number on the other. Thus, students learn that the letter in the equation you start with stands for the number(s) your equation-solving activities end with. The meaning that a variable in an equation stands only for a solution is highly debilitating for students' making meaning of related ideas. For example, in $y = mx + b$ students must distinguish between x and y as variables (in the sense that we envision their values varying) and m and b as constants (meaning, they can have different values, but we envision any value of m and b being fixed while values of x and y vary). Also, the meaning that a variable in an equation stands just for a solution is incoherent with solving equations graphically. If a solution is the only possible value of x in $3x + 7 = 12$, then any graph we draw would have only the point $(5/3, 12)$ on it. Later in their study of mathematics, students must think of both m and x as variables in $y = mx + b$ and that the two together create a surface whose cross-sections are lines. Thus, our intention for the item in Figure 18.10 was to see the extent to which teachers hold meanings that would support students' thinking "in an equation, x stands for the equation's solutions."

Table 18.12 displays the rubric we developed for scoring responses to Darren's question. Level 4 responses conveyed the message that you can think of the value of x varying in magnitude just as in non-equation settings. Level 3 responses conveyed the message that x can have different values, but the values are substituted for x.[14] Level 2 responses separated the meaning of variables into two categories—a meaning for variables used in functions and a meaning for

Table 18.12 Rubric for scoring teachers' responses to Darren's question in Figure 10. © 2014 Arizona Board of Regents. Used with permission.

Level 4	The teacher conveyed that the value of x varies in the sense of varying values or of a magnitude growing larger, and conveyed that a solution to the equation is a value of x that makes the statement $3x + 7 = 12$ true.
Level 3	The teacher conveyed a sense that we substitute values for x (including "x can be any number" or "x can be many numbers"), and that we are looking for the number or numbers that make the statement $3x + 7 = 12$ true.
Level 2	The teacher conveyed that x could be used in more than one way. For instance, when x is in equations, it stands just for a solution, but when it is in something like $y = 3x + 7$, x can vary (or, it can stand for any number).
Level 1	A Level 1 response conveys that x represents a single value (possibly not until we solve for it). Responses at this level support the idea that x does not vary, or at most that the value of x changes depending on the value on the right hand side of the equal sign.
Level 0	Any of the following: • Scorer cannot interpret the teacher's response. • The teacher wrote "I don't know" or equivalent. • The teacher addressed the question with incoherent reasoning. • The teacher stated that a variable is just a letter, and makes no further statements that fit in a higher level. • The teacher's response does not fit into Levels 1 to 4.

Table 18.13 High school mathematics teachers' responses to Figure 10 in Summer 2013 ($n = 96$).

	Math	MathEd	Other	Total
Level 4	1	1	2	4
Level 3	2	3	3	8
Level 2	4	9	8	21
Level 1	18	20	17	55
Level 0	1	3	3	7
No Ans	1	0	0	1
Total	27	36	33	96

variables used in equations. Level 1 responses agreed with Darren's interpretation—that in equations, a letter in an equation stands only for its solutions.

Table 18.13 displays our scoring of 96 high school mathematics teachers in Summer 2013 using the rubric in Table 18.12. I include teachers' initial major to show that responses' levels were largely independent of major. It shows that only 13% of these teachers resolved the conundrum at the highest two levels, that 22% said that the meaning of x depends on whether it occurs in an equation or in a function, while 57% essentially agreed with Darren that x is a constant in the equation $3x + 7 = 12$. Level 1 included responses like, "Yes, x stands for only one number in $3x + 7 = 12$. But it would stand for a different number in $3x + 7 = 14$."

Table 18.14 examines the relationship between teachers' responses to the Bouncing Ball item and to Darren's question. Responses to neither item are predictive of responses to the other. We see this as an artifact of two things: (1) We created an overestimate of teachers' covariational thinking by making the Figure 18.9 item multiple choice, and (2) the Figure 18.10 item, for many teachers, triggered an "equation" scheme in which the idea of variable is isolated from the idea of variation. In either case, our recommendation to these teachers' professional development leaders was that they work with teachers to build meanings of variation and covariation so that they are coherent across the topics of functions and equations.

Table 18.14 Relationship between responses to items in Figure 9 and Figure 10 (*n* = 96).

		Bouncing Ball					
		d (SCC)	b (CCV)	c (CV)	a (TT)	Other	Total
x varies	Level 4	1	0	2	0	1	4
	Level 3	5	2	1	0	0	8
	Level 2	9	6	3	3	0	21
	Level 1	11	21	9	11	3	55
	Level 0	3	1	0	2	1	7
	No Ans	0	0	1	0	0	1
	Total	29	28	16	16	5	96

An Item's Focus

Results from assessing teachers' meanings for "over" (Figure 18.1), their covariational reasoning (Figure 18.9), and their meanings for variation (Figure 18.10) highlight an issue that will be faced in designing any assessment of meaning: A meaning can never be isolated in teachers' responses to an item; teachers often activate many meanings when interpreting an item. For example, in the "over" item (Figure 18.1), many teachers incorporated their meanings of function and their meanings for ratio into their responses. In the Bouncing Ball item (Figure 18.9), even though we designed it to focus on covariation, teachers saw two graphs, which certainly activated their schemes for graphs. Also, the item describes a ball bobbing on a rubber cord; teachers certainly envisioned its behavior idiosyncratically. Teachers also thought of a variety of quantities, some of which turned out to be immaterial to the question—such as that the ball bounces in time and with a velocity. In the "*x* varies" item (Figure 18.10), the question is about variables and constants, but in the context of discussing an equation. Teachers certainly activated their meanings for equations as well as their meanings for "constant" and "variable."[15]

Thus, in devising a scoring rubric one must identify the rubric's focus. In the "over" item, we chose to ignore aspects of responses that revealed problematic meanings for function notation and for rate of change—simply because not all teachers thought to use function notation or to mention rate of change in their responses. For most items, we chose to ignore arithmetic errors because the items' foci were on something that was immaterial to correct calculations. The idea of *focus* in designing and scoring an item is tantamount to deciding to which aspects of teachers responses you will attend, which also entails the willingness to ignore other aspects of teacher's thinking that are revealed in their responses, no matter how interesting those revelations are.

METHODOLOGICAL ISSUES IN ASSESSING TEACHERS' MATHEMATICAL MEANINGS FOR TEACHING MATHEMATICS

Our overall method for developing the MMTsm resembles the methods used by Hestenes and colleagues to create the *Force Concept Inventory*, or FCI (Hestenes, Wells, & Swackhamer, 1992; Savinainen & Scott, 2002) and by Carlson and colleagues to create the *Precalculus Concept Assessment*, or PCA (Carlson, Oehrtman, & Engelke, 2010): (1) Create a draft item, interview teachers (in service and preservice) using the draft item. A panel of four mathematicians and six mathematics educators also reviewed draft items at multiple stages of item development. In interviews, we looked for whether teachers interpret the item as being about what we intended. We also looked for whether the item elicits the genre of responses we hoped (e.g., we do not want teachers to think that we simply want them to produce an answer as if to a routine question). (2) Revise the item; interview again if the revision is significant. (3) Administer the collection of items to a large sample of teachers. Analyze teachers' responses in terms of the meanings and ways of thinking they reveal. (4) Retire unusable items. (5) Interview teachers regarding responses that are ambiguous with regard to meaning in cases where it is important to settle the ambiguity.(6) Revise remaining items according to what we learned from teachers' responses, being always alert to opportunities to make multiple-choice options that teachers are likely to find appealing according to the meaning they hold. (7) Administer the set of revised items to a large sample of teachers. (8) Devise scoring rubrics and training materials for scoring open-ended items; revise items only when absolutely necessary.

Though the overall method described resembles the development of the FCI and PCA, our focus on assessing teachers' meanings rather than performance introduced many new issues. In this section I share issues to which we found ourselves attending methodically in our attempts to assess teachers' mathematical meanings for teaching. They can be grouped into three themes: (1) item design, (2) rubrics for scoring, and (3) aggregating data. Though it is these three themes I will expand, a general comment to frame them might be helpful. You will profit by approaching the task of designing items to assess mathematical meanings much like you would a design experiment (Brown, 1992; Cobb, Confrey, diSessa, Lehrer, & Schauble, 2003). The difference between a design experiment and what I outline in this section is that within the cycle of design-evaluate-redesign you will have mini-cycles with the same structure, and you will maintain a more intimate dialectic between design and theory throughout the design and refinement process.

Designing Items

The foremost characteristic of meanings is that they are invoked in an act of interpretation. An item to assess teachers' mathematical meanings must therefore be designed so that teachers reveal something about their interpretation of it. Ideally, it will invite teachers to think that the meanings that come to their minds in understanding the item are the ones that the item writers want them to share. Next, an item must have a focus—a meaning that you deem important enough to merit devoting one or more of a relatively small number of items to it. Finally, the collection of meanings you assess must form a coherent background for the assessment itself. The collection must address the body of ideas that comprise the conceptual skeleton of the elementary, middle, or secondary curriculum for which teachers taking the assessment are responsible. These three considerations undergird the design of individual items.

Start with Meanings That Matter to Students, Both Positively and Negatively

Research on teachers' and students' mathematical understandings and thinking often provides inspiration for items, as do ways of thinking by teachers and by students that you notice in your everyday interactions with them. Research on students' or teachers' performance that emphasizes correct responses is usually not helpful. Research that reveals *sources* of students' productive and unproductive meanings and ways of thinking are more useful. For example, APOS (Action, Process, Object Scheme) theory (Arnon, et al., 2014; Dubinsky & McDonald, 2001) describes students' difficulties with the idea of function as a mapping of the function's domain onto its image. The idea that a function maps a set of values A to a set of values B entails thinking that the function is evaluated at *every* element of A, and that every value of the function is an element of the set B. One might get at teachers' thinking regarding the idea of mapping a set to a set by asking something like the item in Figure 18.11.[16]

Part (a) asks what the expression $f([0.5, 1.5])$ *might* mean, not what it *does* mean. It asks teachers to make a meaning for the expression even if they've never seen this notation. The purpose would be to see whether teachers could think about what it *might* mean to have an interval of numbers instead of a single number as input to a function. Part (b) gives teachers an opportunity to express whatever meaning they expressed in Part (a) more concretely. This

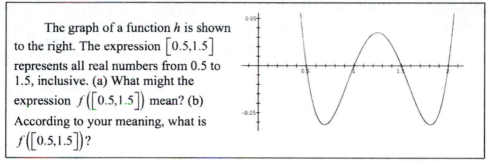

The graph of a function h is shown to the right. The expression $\left[0.5, 1.5\right]$ represents all real numbers from 0.5 to 1.5, inclusive. (a) What might the expression $f\left(\left[0.5, 1.5\right]\right)$ mean? (b) According to your meaning, what is $f\left(\left[0.5, 1.5\right]\right)$?

Figure 18.11 Potential item to probe teachers' meaning for function as mapping.

could reveal that they have an intuitive scheme for mapping a set that they cannot articulate, or it could reveal that their verbal formulation of a meaning for $f[0.5, 1.5)$ is not grounded in a scheme of actions and operations.

Leverage the Implicative Nature of Meanings

To leverage the implicative nature of meanings, one asks for a teacher's response and then follows up with a question to reveal what the teacher's response implies for him or her. Examples of this strategy appear earlier in the chapter.

Raise Issues of Conflicting Meanings That Often Arise, or that a Teacher Should Anticipate, in Students' Thinking

The research literature on students' understandings of important mathematical ideas is a rich source for items that probe teachers' meanings. For example, it is well known that students often interpret graphs that show a function's rate of change as if the graph is of the function itself, such as mistaking a speed-time graph for a distance-time graph (Monk, 1992; Monk & Nemirovsky, 1994; Oehrtman, Carlson, & Thompson, 2008). A common explanation is that students did not pay attention to the axes' labels. We included an item on the MMTsm that showed a graph that represented the rate of change of a bacterial culture's mass relative to elapsed time since the measurements began, with axes clearly labeled "g/hr" and "hr." We asked, "Over what time intervals is the culture's mass increasing?" On the next page we presented the same graph with one point highlighted, and asked teachers to explain what the point represented. Then we asked teachers whether they would like to change their answer to the first part. Some teachers responded to the first part as if the graph showed the culture's mass, not its rate of change, interpreted the point correctly, and then changed their answer to Part A. These teachers had not attended to the axes labels and changed their response when their attention was drawn to them. Other teachers interpreted the graph as if about mass, interpreted the point as if about a rate of change, and left their answer to Part A the same. For these teachers, their original interpretation of the graph was stable. We interpret this as suggesting that, to these teachers, graphs are about amounts. It is also consistent with a form of reasoning about graphs that I mentioned earlier—shape thinking. We cannot be certain of either hypothesis without follow-up interviews, but these teachers' original interpretation was certainly resistant to perturbation.

Request Symbolic Responses Sparingly

Teachers often use symbolism idiomatically—the expression itself has meaning to them, but the meaning of the whole does not derive from meanings of its parts. Request symbolic responses only when it is important to see how teachers express their meanings symbolically and only in cases where you have another window to the meaning they think they are expressing.

Decide Early on an Item's Focus

Since meanings are schemes, an item can invoke multiple meanings in the person responding to it. See the discussion of *focus* on page 451.

Pilot Items Early and Often

It is essential that you conduct interviews on as many items as your resources allow. Of course, we all operate with limited resources, so you must decide strategically on which items you will interview. It is also useful to share items with mathematicians with whom you've established a working relationship. It is imperative that you also share your rationale for the item and what you hope teachers will reveal in their responses.

Scoring Responses and Refining Items

Our method for developing scoring rubrics and for refining items is inspired by the work of Wilson and Draney at the UC Berkeley Evaluation and Research (BEAR) Center (Kennedy & Wilson, 2007; Wilson & Sloane, 2000). That work focuses on creating construct maps and progress variables that form the basis of instruments that use a developmental perspective on students' learning to assess students' progress—to evaluate learning progressions. BEAR assessments are given on multiple occasions to track students' progress over large periods of time in learning a body of interrelated ideas and ways of thinking.

MMTsm items, however, do not come with models for the development of meanings they assess. Teachers are not first-time learners of these ideas. Rather, in many instances they developed unproductive meanings as students, and then spent years learning to cope with mathematics instruction that they were unprepared to understand—developing ways to satisfy demands to perform without having a basis in meaning. Moreover, experienced teachers, over time, often develop curricular meanings that overlay meanings they already possessed. As a result, it is rare that we can place teachers' meanings on a developmental scale regarding progress in learning an idea. Our approach instead became to design rubrics to reflect levels of *productive* meaning—where "productive" is judged by the criterion of how useful a meaning would be for students' future mathematical learning were a teacher to convey it to them. Levels of productive meaning do not form a progression in the sense that we envision teachers going through lower levels to reach higher levels. But the levels do impose order on teachers' responses on a scale that is relevant to teaching the idea being assessed, and we may expect responses by teachers who are involved in professional development to attain higher levels when responding to an item on successive occasions.

It is essential that each free-response item have a scoring rubric. Your assessment will be unusable outside your project without scoring rubrics.

As mentioned earlier, our method for developing scoring rubrics derives from the work of Wilson and Draney. It has five phases that describe the scoring of items that have gone through the development phase of interviews and small-scale piloting, and for which you now have a large number of responses.

Phase 1: Grounded theory. In the first phase you approach responses with the open attitude espoused by Strauss and Corbin (1998), but the "openness" is theoretical. Attend to how well you can make sense of teachers' responses using the theory of meaning behind the item. In this phase we sometimes made major changes to an item and placed the item in the pool awaiting further development without trying to score responses, or we discarded the item altogether. With some items we found that we could make sense of teachers' responses if we modified its theory of meaning. In other cases, we made minor changes to the item to use in later testing, but proceeded to analyze responses to the current item as given to teachers.

Phase 2: Group responses. When an item elicits responses that you feel give insights into teachers' meanings or ways of thinking, you then proceed to group responses by levels of productive meaning. In this case, "meaning" is *the researcher's* attribution of meanings and ways of thinking that would explain why a teacher wrote what he or she wrote. Our team found it useful to conduct these analyses individually with subsets of responses to an item and then report our analyses to the team for discussion. Lengthy discussions of individual responses, over time, will increase the overall coherence of the scoring scheme for all responses. I hasten to add that it will often happen that you cannot describe a group of responses in terms of meanings that teachers might have had. But you may still be able to describe a group of responses in terms of meanings that you envision students might construct were teachers to say in class what they said in their responses to the item.

Phase 3: Codify your criteria for grouping responses. It is in the third phase that you begin to have something that resembles a scoring rubric for an item. Your aim will be that the criteria's descriptions allow a scorer to place any response at a particular level. Sometimes a teacher's response will fit two levels. In this case the scoring rubric must say whether to place the response at the higher or lower level. The response in Figure 18.2 (meaning of "over") is an example of this. The teacher said that "over" means "during" and the teacher said that "over" means a ratio. We decided to state clearly that responses like this should go at the lower level.

Phase 4: Small-scale interscorer trials. The rubric is ready to be "stress tested" after it has reached its first stable state. Select a small random sample of responses (we used samples of size 10) and have several team members score them independently *according to the rubric*. Team discussions of scoring discrepancies often lead to further revisions of the rubric during the discussion. When consensus has been reached on a rubric it is ready for interscorer agreement testing.

Phase 5: Interscorer agreement and scoring all responses. For efficiency we combined the scoring of all responses with scoring for interscorer agreement. We had 112 responses to score on each item of the MMTsm. Two team members each scored 66 responses, 46 that were unique to a scorer and 20 that were common to the two scorers.[17] Scorers scored their respective responses independently, entering scores in a spreadsheet. The team discussed discrepancies between scores on common responses. Some discrepancies were accepted as unavoidable error, which left the rubric intact. Other discrepancies pointed to problems with the rubric that, upon revision, eliminated the discrepancy. If we changed a level's description, each scorer revisited responses unique to his response set whose scores might be affected by the rubric's revisions.

It should be obvious that the method for developing a scoring rubric described here is an exercise in reflecting abstraction (Piaget, 2001). The shifts from Phase 1 to Phase 5 reflect the team members' progressive thematization of their thinking about the responses that an item elicits from teachers. A scoring rubric, in its final form, therefore reflects a scheme that the rubric designers built by continually reflecting on their actions of making sense of teachers' responses.

Aggregating Data

Our goal for the MMTsm, from the outset, was to create an instrument whose results could inform teachers and their professional development leaders about areas in which teachers might work to strengthen their mathematical meanings for teaching and areas in which they have productive meanings. The issue of aggregating data, then, is really the issue of how to report results in a way that helps teachers improve their mathematics teaching and helps professional developers design an evidence-based intervention. Each item is rich in the information it provides about teachers' meanings. But results cannot be reported item-by-item. We also faced the problem that one mix of meanings on a set of related items can have very different implications for teaching and for professional development than another mix of meanings.

We are facing the issue of data aggregation as of this writing, and at this moment I cannot offer a solution. We hope that the data we've collected and scored are amenable to a variant of the BEAR assessment system, a system that was designed for tracking students' progress within a learning progression. But it is not clear to me that it even makes sense to look for structure among levels of productive mathematical meanings in responses to MMTsm items. Lower levels of a scoring rubric tend to be about unproductive meanings teachers might convey to students instead of about meanings they have.

For professional development projects currently using the MMTsm, we will report very simple profiles for individual teachers: scaled-level scores for groups of items within the MMTsm item categories along with brief statements about what scores in different ranges mean regarding mathematical meanings for teaching that concept area. We have no illusions that this will be especially meaningful to teachers except to alert them that there might be something they should work on. However, we expect this information to be very helpful to leaders of the teachers' professional development projects. Project teams attend an 18-hour workshop on the MMTsm, its design, and on using the rubrics so score teachers' responses. The workshop, and the rubrics' supporting materials, also goes into great detail about implications for student learning that we foresee responses at the different levels having. It is this aspect of the MMTsm that we see having the greatest potential impact—alerting professional development leaders about the mathematical meanings they will be attempting to affect in their projects and why affecting them is important.

Two large projects are using the MMTsm as a measure of their yearlong projects' impact on teachers' mathematical meanings for teaching secondary mathematics. Their use of the MMTsm will allow us to inquire into two questions: (1) Can we be confident that gains on the MMTsm actually reflect higher quality and more coherent meanings? (2) Is it possible for teachers' scores to go *down* over the period of a year, and if so, why? Both questions require qualitative methods that we hope will yield results that triangulate with what we think teachers' responses to the MMTsm tell us.

CONNECTING ASSESSMENTS OF MATHEMATICAL MEANINGS TO CLASSROOM INSTRUCTION

I discuss the idea of teaching as a form of conversation in (Thompson, 2013) and explain how successful conversation relies in principle on participants' conscious attention to their and others' meanings. I cannot repeat that discussion here. One point, however, deserves mentioning: Teachers convey meanings to students in the sense that students strive to understand what their teacher wants them to do or to understand, building meanings in the process. This happens regardless of whether teachers are aware of the meanings they possess, and it happens regardless of the coherence of the teacher's meanings. A teacher's aim should be that the meanings students build from instruction are meanings worth having for a lifetime. Teachers' instruction should support students in creating coherent meanings of the mathematics the teacher is teaching, and those meanings should lay a foundation for students' future learning. Attention to teachers' mathematical meanings for teaching mathematics will support this broad goal.

Having high-quality, coherent meanings is an essential aspect of high-quality instruction—but it is only a piece of high quality instruction. Other factors will affect whether teachers convey productive mathematical meanings to their students:

- The teacher has meanings. Is the teacher aware of them? Is the teacher oriented to conveying them to students?

- Does the teacher reflect on activities and problems that might give students an occasion to transform their current meanings into desired meanings?
- Does the teacher care about the meanings students construct from what he or she does and says, and convey that care to students? Is the teacher oriented to notice students' meanings, and adjust instruction accordingly?

CONCLUSION

In this chapter I argued in principle and by example that a focus on teachers' mathematical meanings for teaching mathematics is both important and potentially productive regarding the improvement of teachers' teaching, which I take as necessary for the improvement of students' mathematical learning. I also outlined a method for developing items and instruments that focus on teachers' mathematical meanings for teaching mathematics. In this concluding section, I will speak about how we can link research and assessment more intimately than simply using the results of each in the activities of the other.

Assessment as a Context and Source for Research

While developing the MMTsm, we often found that existing research was inadequate to guide an item's design or to make sense of teachers' responses. For example, in designing items to investigate teachers' meanings for function we discovered that function notation is a far more complex notion for teachers than existing research on function suggests (Musgrave & Thompson, in press; Yoon, Hatfield, & Thompson, in press). This led to function notation becoming one of the identified areas in which we attended to teachers' meanings, which in turn has led to an expansion of our understanding of the conceptual requirements for students and teachers to use functions as models of dynamic situations. We anticipate that these developments will lead to new directions in research on students' and teachers' understandings of function.

More broadly, a focus on creating items that assess teachers' meanings will reveal lacunae in past research related to that those meanings, largely because you will need to address issues of teachers' and students' thinking that past research finessed. When this happens, you can both address the issue within your overall scheme for the assessment's design while simultaneously putting it on your and others' agendas for future research.

Finally, we are now planning proposals to use the MMTsm to draw national and international comparisons—not as a horse race among groups, but to investigate whether differences among teachers' mathematical meanings for teaching might be a partial explanation for differences among nations' mathematics education outcomes.

Research as Source for Assessment

I mentioned that research on students' and teachers' mathematical thinking often provides inspiration for deciding upon the areas that your assessment will cover and for items to include in it. There is, however, another important way in which we can leverage the conduct of research on mathematical thinking, especially qualitative research, to inform future assessments: In doing qualitative research on students' or teachers' mathematical thinking, one is attentive to nuances in individuals' thinking that point to understandings, meanings, or ways of thinking that might prove explanatory with regard to why it is reasonable, from the individuals' perspectives, that they do what they did. If researchers were to think also about the prevalence of any of these as possible explanations of phenomena that have already been witnessed broadly, they would have the beginning of an assessment focus. If in addition they were to fine-tune their tasks so that they could be given outside of interviews, and responses could be scored with that focus, they would have early drafts of assessment items.

Striving for Common Measures

While writing this chapter, the MMTsm team and I struggled with the question of what to include as examples of items that focus on teachers' mathematical meanings for teaching. We were reluctant to include actual MMTsm items, for the simple reason that if we amortize the amount spent by the National Science Foundation across items and scoring rubrics, each item and its rubric cost, on average, over $35,000. These items are not easy to create. I could have used discarded items, and they would have served the purpose of this chapter.

We decided collectively that I should use actual items and include our data on them, for three reasons. The first reason is that most people with whom we shared results are truly surprised by them—they were unaware of teachers' difficulties with mathematical meanings that they thought were largely unproblematic. We decided that it is important that the mathematics education community realize the depth of a problem that has gone largely unnoticed. The second reason that we decided to include actual items and data on them is to encourage others to use them, or the MMTsm in its entirety, in their research. It is only through the use of common measures that research results are comparable, and the use of common measures also supports the development of common conceptions of what is being measured. The third reason for including actual items and their data is that they are better than the discarded items, and we wanted to share the best items we could in hopes that they would inspire others to create even better ones.

NOTES

1. Research reported in this article was supported by National Science Foundation Grant No. MSP-1050595. Any recommendations or conclusions stated here are the author's and do not necessarily reflect official positions of the NSF.
2. I thank John Mason, David Kirshner, Lyn English, Mark Wilson, Karen Draney, and Cameron Byerley for their thoughtful comments and suggestions on earlier drafts.
3. This narrative also assumes that the teacher has a rich meaning of "equivalence-preserving transformation."
4. MMTsm team members are Stacy Musgrave, Ioanna Mamona, Cameron Byerley, Neil Hatfield, Hyunkyoung Yoon, Surani Joshua, Ben Whitmire, Mark Wilson, Karen Draney, Perman Gochyyev, Diah Wihardini, Dong Hoon Lee, and JinHo Kim.
5. The MMTsm assesses teachers' mathematical meanings in the areas of variation and covariation, function (definition, notation, and modeling), frames of reference, magnitude, proportionality, rate of change, and structure.
6. A later section discusses general issues of method. One of the issues is that of "focus." Teachers' responses often tell you far more about their thinking than an item was designed to tap. What you decide to ignore in teachers' responses to a particular item is as important as what you decide to look for.
7. My use of "convey" is not the same as "transmit." A meaning that a teacher conveys to a student is the meaning the student constructs in attempting to understand what the teacher meant.
8. This is precisely the meaning of division stated in the Grade 5 mathematics textbook published by the Japan Ministry of Education (2008).
9. The graph of $y = 3x + 2$ has a constant slope of 3 even when graphed in a polar coordinate system or in a log-log coordinate system—and its graph does not appear to be a line in either one.
10. The graph in the actual item was much larger than it appears here, making physical measurement quite easy.
11. I am indebted to Les Steffe for this example.
12. I use the word *space* instead of *set* because meanings do have structure. Actions imply other actions by creating conditions for further action. The structure of a person's meaning arises from the structure of the interconnections among actions, images, and schemes that constitute it in that person's reality.
13. One of Piaget's definitions of *scheme* was, "[Schemes are] organized totalities [of actions and operations] whose internal elements are mutually implied" (Piaget, 1952, p. 405)
14. One reviewer of this chapter suggested that what we have as Level 3 in Table 12 should be the highest level. I respectfully disagree. Students and teachers who have the meaning of variables in equations as described in Level 4 see greater coherence among ideas of functions, graphs, equations, and solutions

to an equation. In effect, they will see an equation's solution set S as $S = \{x \in D \mid f(x) = c\}$, where D is a function's domain and c is in the function's image. To think of values of x in D that make the statement true, one must envision the possibility of all values of x in D, which is what the meaning of continous variation described here affords.

15. For example, some teachers declared "x" is a variable by virtue of being a letter, and that only specific numbers, represented with numerals, are constants.
16. This is item is not on the MMTsm.
17. The solution to $2x + 20 = 112$ is 46.

REFERENCES

Arnon, I., Cottril, J., Dubinsky, E., Oktac, A., Fuentes, S. R., Trigueros, M., & Weller, K. (2014). *APOS Theory: A framework for research and curriculum development in mathematics education*. New York: Springer.

Bridgman, P. W. (1955). *Reflections of a physicist* (Kindle ed.). Retrieved from Amazon.com.

Bringuier, J. C. (1980). *Conversations with Jean Piaget*. Chicago: University of Chicago Press.

Brown, A. L. (1992). Design experiments: Theoretical and methodological challenges in creating complex interventions in classroom settings. *Journal of the Learning Sciences, 2*, 141–178. Retrieved from www.jstor.org/stable/1466837. doi:10.2307/1466837

Carlson, M. P., Jacobs, S., Coe, E., Larsen, S., & Hsu, E. (2002). Applying covariational reasoning while modeling dynamic events: A framework and a study. *Journal for Research in Mathematics Education, 33*, 352–378.

Carlson, M. P., Oehrtman, M. C., & Engelke, N. (2010). The precalculus concept assessment (PCA) instrument: A tool for assessing students' reasoning patterns and understandings. *Cognition and Instruction, 28*, 113–145.

Carpenter, T. P., Coburn, T. G., Reys, R. E., & Wilson, J. W. (1976). Notes from National Assessment: Addition and multiplication with fractions. *The Arithmetic Teacher, 23*, 137–142. Retrieved from www.jstor.org/stable/41191386. doi:10.2307/41191386

Castillo-Garsow, C. C. (2010). *Teaching the Verhulst model: A teaching experiment in covariational reasoning and exponential growth*. Ph.D. dissertation, Arizona State University, Tempe, AZ. Retrieved from http://pat-thompson.net/PDFversions/Theses/2010CastilloGarsow.pdf.

Charalambous, C. Y., & Hill, H. C. (2012). Teacher knowledge, curriculum materials, and quality of instruction: Unpacking a complex relationship. *Journal of Curriculum Studies, 44*, 443–466.

Chazan, D. (1993). F(x)=G(x)?: An approach to modeling with algebra. *For the Learning of Mathematics, 13*, 22–26.

Cobb, P., Confrey, J., diSessa, A., Lehrer, R., & Schauble, L. (2003). Design experiments in educational research. *Educational Researcher, 32*, 9–13.

Confrey, J. (1992). Using computers to promote students' inventions on the function concept. In S. Malcom, L. Roberts, & K. Sheingold (Eds.), *This year in school science 1991* (pp. 141–174). Washington, DC: AAAS.

Confrey, J. (1994). Splitting, similarity, and rate of change: A new approach to multiplication and exponential functions. In G. Harel & J. Confrey (Eds.), *The development of multiplicative reasoning in the learning of mathematics* (pp. 293–330). Albany: State University of New York Press.

Confrey, J., & Smith, E. (1995). Splitting, covariation and their role in the development of exponential function. *Journal for Research in Mathematics Education, 26*, 66–86.

Dewey, J. (1910). *How we think*. Boston: D. C. Heath.

Dubinsky, E., & McDonald, M. A. (2001). APOS: A constructivist theory of learning in undergrad mathematics education research. *New ICME Studies Series, 7*, 275–282.

Glasersfeld, E. v. (1978). Radical constructivism and Piaget's concept of knowledge. In F. B. Murray (Ed.), *Impact of Piagetian Theory* (pp. 109–122). Baltimore, MD: University Park Press.

Glasersfeld, E. v. (1981). The concepts of adaptation and viability in a radical constructivist theory of knowledge. In I. Sigel & R. M. Golinkoff (Eds.), *Piagetian Theory and Research: New Directions and Research* (pp. 87–95). Hillsdale, NJ: Lawrence Erlbaum Associates.

Glasersfeld, E. v. (1985). Reconstructing the concept of knowledge. *Archives de Psychologie, 53*, 91–101.

Glasersfeld, E. v. (1992). Constructivism reconstructed: A reply to Suchting. *Science & Education, 1*, 379–384.

Harel, G. (2008). What is mathematics? A pedagogical answer to a philosophical question. In R. B. Gold & R. Simons (Eds.), *Current issues in the philosophy of mathematics from the perspective of mathematicians* (pp. 265–290). Washington, DC: Mathematical Association of America.

Harel, G. (2013). Intellectual need. In K. Leatham (Ed.), *Vital directions for research in mathematics education* (pp. 119–151). New York: Springer.

Hestenes, D., Wells, M., & Swackhamer, G. (1992). Force concept inventory. *The Physics Teacher, 30*, 141–158.

Hill, H.C. (2011). Measuring the mathematical quality of instruction. *Journal of Mathematics Teacher Education, 14*, 25–47.

Hill, H.C., Blunk, M.L., Charalambous, C.Y., Lewis, J.M., Phelps, G.C., Sleep, L., et al. (2008). Mathematical knowledge for teaching and the mathematical quality of instruction: An exploratory study. *Cognition and Instruction, 26*, 430–511.

Hill, H.C., & Charalambous, C.Y. (2012). Teacher knowledge, curriculum materials, and quality of instruction: Lessons learned and open issues. *Journal of Curriculum Studies, 44*, 559–576. doi:10.1080/00220272.2012.716978

Howe, K.R., & Berv, J. (2000). Constructing constructivism, epistemological and pedagogical. In D. C. Phillips (Ed.), *Constructivism in education: Opinions and second opinions on controversial issues*, Yearbook of the National Society for the Study of Education (pp. 19–40). Chicago: University of Chicago Press.

Izsák, A. (2012). Measuring mathematical knowledge for teaching fractions with drawn quantities. *Journal for Research in Mathematics Education, 43*, 391–427.

Japan Ministry of Education. (2008). *Japanese Mathematics Curriculum in the Course of Study* (A. Takahashi, T. Watanabe, & Y. Makoto, Trans.). Madison, WI: Global Education Resources.

Johnckheere, A., Mandelbrot, B.B., & Piaget, J. (1958). *La lecture de l'expérience [Observation and decoding of reality]*. Paris: P.U.F.

Kennedy, K.A., & Wilson, M.R. (2007). Using progress variables to map intellectual development. In R.W. Lissitz (Ed.), *Assessing and modeling cognitive development in schools: Intellectual growth and standard setting*. Maple Grove, MN: JAM Press.

Lobato, J., & Thanheiser, E. (2000). Using technology to promote and examine students' construction of ratio-as-measure. In *Proceedings of the 22nd annual meeting of the North American chapter of the International Group for the Psychology of Mathematics Education* (Vol. 2, pp. 371–377). Tucson, AZ: PME-NA.

Mason, J., & Spence, M. (1999). Beyond mere knowledge of mathematics: The importance of knowing-to act in the moment. *Educational Studies in Mathematics, 38*, 135–161. doi:10.1023/A:1003622804002

Monk, G.S. (1992). Students' understanding of a function given by a physical model. In G. Harel & E. Dubinsky (Eds.), *The concept of function: Aspects of epistemology and pedagogy* (pp. 175–194). Washington, DC: Mathematical Association of America.

Monk, S., & Nemirovsky, R. (1994). The case of Dan: Student construction of a functional situation through visual attributes. In E. Dubinsky, A.H. Schoenfeld, & J.J. Kaput (Eds.), *Research in Collegiate Mathematics Education, 1*, Issues in Mathematics Education (pp. 139–168). Providence, RI: American Mathematical Society.

Montangero, J., & Maurice-Naville, D. (1997). *Piaget or the advance of knowledge.* (A. Curnu-Wells, Trans.) Mahwah, NJ: Lawrence Erlbaum Associates.

Musgrave, S., & Thompson, P.W. (in press). Function notation as idiom. In P. Liljedahl & C.C. Nicol (Eds.), *Proceedings of the 38th Meeting of the International Group for the Psychology of Mathematics Education*. Vancouver, BC: PME.

Norton, A.H., & Wilkins, J.L.M. (2009). A quantitative analysis of children's splitting operations and fraction schemes. *Journal of Mathematical Behavior, 28*(2), 150–161.

Oehrtman, M.C., Carlson, M.P., & Thompson, P.W. (2008). Foundational reasoning abilities that promote coherence in students' understandings of function. In M.P. Carlson & C. Rasmussen (Eds.), *MAA Notes. Making the connection: Research and practice in undergraduate mathematics* (pp. 27–42). Washington, DC: Mathematical Association of America.

Phillips, D. C. (2000). An opinionated account of the constructivist landscape. In D. C. Phillips (Ed.), *Yearbook of the National Society for the Study of Education. Constructivism in education: Opinions and second opinions on controversial issues* (pp. 1–16). Chicago: University of Chicago Press.

Piaget, J. (1952). *The origins of intelligence in children.* New York: W.W. Norton.

Piaget, J. (1968). *Six psychological studies.* New York: Vintage Books.

Piaget, J. (2001). *Studies in reflecting abstraction.* (R.L. Campbell, Trans.) New York: Psychology Press.

Piaget, J., & Garcia, R. (1991). *Toward a logic of meanings.* Hillsdale, NJ: Lawrence Erlbaum Associates.

Saldanha, L.A., & Thompson, P.W. (1998). Re-thinking co-variation from a quantitative perspective: Simultaneous continuous variation. In S.B. Berenson & W.N. Coulombe (Eds.), *Proceedings of the Annual Meeting of the Psychology of Mathematics Education—North America*, (Vol. 1, pp. 298–304). Raleigh, NC: North Carolina State University. Retrieved from http://pat-thompson.net/PDFversions/1998SimulConVar.pdf.

Savinainen, A., & Scott, P. (2002). The force concept inventory: a tool for monitoring student learning. *Physics Education, 37*, 45–52. doi:10.1088/0031-9120/37/1/306

Schilling, S.G., Blunk, M., & Hill, H.C. (2007). Test validation and the MKT measures: Generalizations and conclusions. *Measurement, 5*, 118–128. doi:10.1080/15366360701487146

Simon, M.A., & Blume, G.W. (1994). Mathematical modeling as a component of understanding ratio-as-measure: A study of prospective elementary teachers. *Journal of Mathematical Behavior, 13*, 183–197. doi:10.1016/0732-3123(94)90022-1

Steffe, L.P. (1991). The learning paradox. In L.P. Steffe (Ed.), *Epistemological foundations of mathematical experience* (pp. 26–44). New York: Springer-Verlag.

Strauss, A.L., & Corbin, J. (1998). Basics of qualitative research: Techniques and procedures for developing grounded theory (2nd ed.). Thousand Oaks, CA: Sage Publications.

Suchting, W.A. (1992). Constructivism deconstructed. *Science & Education, 1*, 223–254.

Thompson, A.G. (1992). Teachers' beliefs and conceptions: A synthesis of research. In D.A. Grouws (Ed.), *Handbook of research on mathematics teaching and learning* (pp. 127–146). New York: Macmillan.

Thompson, A.G., & Thompson, P.W. (1996). Talking about rates conceptually, Part II: Mathematical knowledge for teaching. *Journal for Research in Mathematics Education, 27*, 2–24.

Thompson, P.W. (1994a). The development of the concept of speed and its relationship to concepts of rate. In G. Harel & J. Confrey (Eds.), *The development of multiplicative reasoning in the learning of mathematics* (pp. 179–234). Albany: State University of New York Press.

Thompson, P.W. (1994b). Students, functions, and the undergraduate mathematics curriculum. In E. Dubinsky, A.H. Schoenfeld, & J.J. Kaput (Eds.), *Research in collegiate mathematics education: Vol. 1. Issues in Mathematics Education* (pp. 21–44). Providence, RI: American Mathematical Society.

Thompson, P.W. (2011). Quantitative reasoning and mathematical modeling. In L.L. Hatfield, S. Chamberlain, & S. Belbase (Eds.), *WISDOMe Monographs. New perspectives and directions for collaborative research in mathematics education* (pp. 33–57). Laramie: University of Wyoming.

Thompson, P.W. (2013). In the absence of meaning. In K. Leatham (Ed.), *Vital directions for research in mathematics education* (pp. 57–93). New York: Springer.

Thompson, P.W., Carlson, M.P., Byerley, C., & Hatfield, N. (2014). Schemes for thinking with magnitudes: A hypothesis about foundational reasoning abilities in algebra. In L.P. Steffe, L.L. Hatfield, & K.C. Moore (Eds.), *WISDOMe Monographs: Vol. 4. Epistemic algebra students: Emerging models of students' algebraic knowing* (pp. 1–24). Laramie: University of Wyoming.

Thompson, P.W., & Saldanha, L.A. (2003). Fractions and multiplicative reasoning. In J. Kilpatrick, G. Martin, & D. Schifter (Eds.), *Research companion to the Principles and Standards for School Mathematics* (pp. 95–114). Reston, VA: National Council of Teachers of Mathematics.

Thompson, P.W., & Thompson, A.G. (1994). Talking about rates conceptually, Part I: A teacher's struggle. *Journal for Research in Mathematics Education, 25*, 279–303.

Torbeyns, J., Schneider, M., Xin, Z., & Siegler, R.S. (2014). Bridging the gap: Fraction understanding is central to mathematics achievement in students from three different continents. *Learning and Instruction, 37*(1), 5–13. doi:10.1016/j.learninstruc.2014.03.002

Vinner, S., Hershkowitz, R., & Bruckheimer, M. (1981). Some cognitive factors as causes of mistakes in the addition of fractions. *Journal for Research in Mathematics Education, 12*, 70–76.

Wilson, M.R., & Sloane, K. (2000). From principles to practice: An embedded assessment system. *Applied Measurement in Education, 13*, 181–208.

Yoon, H., Hatfield, N., & Thompson, P.W. (in press). Teachers' meanings for function notation. In P. Liljedahl & C.C. Nicol (Eds.), *Proceedings of the 38th Meeting of the International Group for the Psychology of Mathematics Education*. Vancouver, BC: PME.

19 Measurement Challenges in Mathematics Education Research

Rosemary Callingham

University of Tasmania

Mathematics education research has developed over the last 50 years from its early grounding in psychology into a rich and diverse field of endeavor. At the same time, there is a growing international concern that we are failing the upcoming generations. In many Western countries, fewer school students are undertaking mathematics at high levels. There are calls for improved curricula, better teaching, and structural changes to education systems that will lead to more people wanting to take up mathematics teaching as a career—and a constant refrain of increased accountability. Schoenfeld (2008, p. 513) suggested that the difficulties faced by mathematics education were twofold. Internal to the field, as it expands and takes on new theories and methodologies, is the necessity to "develop and impose the highest standards for its own conduct." To meet external demands for sound and trustworthy information, the methods used should "gather evidence that provides solid warrants for the claims being made." These demands create significant challenges for mathematics education research in designing studies that are rigorous and methodologically sound, and that provide information to practitioners, including policy makers, curriculum and resources developers, teachers, parents, and their students, that meets their very diverse expectations.

At the heart of these issues is the notion of measurement. Regardless of the methodology chosen, are we truly gathering data about the intended construct—whether that be achievement or performance in mathematics, beliefs, and attitudes towards mathematics, "best practice" in classroom teaching, or curriculum materials, for example—or are we in reality addressing some other underlying characteristic or trait? A related but not trivial question concerns the ways in which the research team's perspectives or beliefs privilege particular approaches—to teaching, to research design, or to analyses. Such matters have the potential to distort research outcomes in fundamental ways that go beyond simply having diverse interpretations of the data collected: they reach into the heart of the research itself, affecting the research questions posed, the research design, and data collection and analysis. These challenges for measuring mathematical constructs exist whether the study is qualitative or quantitative, large or small scale, funded or unfunded, mandated or grassroots.

At this point it is necessary to consider what I mean by "measure." An exploration of several online and hardcopy dictionaries reveals two clear meanings of the word as a verb: to determine the *quantity* of something using an instrument of some form with standard units, and to ascertain the *quality* of something by making an assessment against some defined standard. Measurement thus encompasses both quantitative and qualitative approaches to research. That is not to say that there are no tensions existing between these two paradigms, but it does suggest that in essence they are the same endeavor, using different approaches to achieve the same end, which is to increase the knowledge base about mathematics education.

The qualitative/quantitative divide, however, still exists in the minds of some researchers, and more particularly in the views of consumers of mathematics education research. Researchers of both persuasions may feel at times that their study has not been funded, or their paper

462

has been rejected, on the grounds of not conforming to some perceived "norm" of good research. Pragmatists may adopt a "mixed-methods" approach, arguing that this can cover the best of both worlds. Such views, however, seem to miss the point: the research question, arising from a consideration of a particular situation and a review of prior work, is the determinant of the method. Unless the target construct is clearly defined and the study deeply conceptualized, it matters little what approach is taken. The measures, of quantity or quality, will not be dependable and the study will ultimately be untrustworthy.

It may be useful at this point to consider what is meant by *mathematics education research*. Niss (1999) defined it as "the scientific and scholarly field of research and development which aims at identifying, characterizing, and understanding phenomena and processes actually or potentially involved in the teaching and learning of mathematics at any educational level" (p. 5). Mason (2002) used the term *disciplined noticing*. It relates to mathematics only—it is domain specific (Seldon, 2002)—although connected to the larger field of educational research more generally. It may include studies of individuals, classrooms, systems, or nations. As such it is a broad domain, able to encompass a wide range of theories and perspectives, drawing on psychology and social sciences as required.

This breadth, however, poses significant challenges. Some may consider mathematics education research to be a mile wide but an inch deep, with such a range of interests that nothing is considered in depth. Others may think of it as within an ivory tower, disconnected from the reality of mathematics, its learning and teaching. Such views are exacerbated by internecine disputes, especially those between mathematicians and mathematics educators such as the well documented "math wars" (e.g., Klein, 2007, Schoenfeld, 2004). The term *education* may itself impact perceptions of mathematics education research. The value and nature of educational research more broadly has been in the spotlight for many years. Burkhardt and Schoenfeld (2003), for example, stated "Educational research is not very influential, useful, or well-funded" (p. 3) and went on to argue that educational research required significant realignment to bring research and practice closer together in meaningful ways. Among their suggestions was a call for a "reasonably stable theoretical base" (p. 10) accompanied by a greater consistency and standardization of methods and instruments. Given the current situation in mathematics education, the field may have much ground still to cover.

Schoenfeld (2008, p. 487) suggested several criteria for making judgements about the quality of mathematics education research:

- Descriptive power
- Explanatory power
- Scope
- Predictive power
- Rigor and specificity
- Falsifiability
- Replicability, generality, and trustworthiness
- Multiple sources of evidence (triangulation)

These criteria provide a framework against which a published study may be counted, and may aid in determining the study's quality or worth. These criteria do not favor any particular approach to research: they allow for both qualitative and quantitative approaches, and avoid common value judgements such as "effectiveness" or "best practice."

The structure of this chapter is as follows. Research traditions in mathematics education will be briefly reviewed to provide some context for the discussion. The nature of knowledge forms privileged by different research approaches, and researchers' own perspectives and beliefs, will then be canvased, followed by a consideration of the impact of these issues on what is measured, or is measurable. Finally, Schoenfeld's (2008) criteria will be applied to three studies as case studies of quality mathematics education research.

RESEARCH TRADITIONS IN MATHEMATICS EDUCATION

Early research into the learning and teaching of mathematics—mathematics education—was drawn largely from the field of psychology and used methods and approaches pertinent to that field. The work of Richard Skemp (1971), for example, was pioneering and led to the foundation of the PME (Psychology of Mathematics Education) organization. Studies were small-scale, based on a hypothesis, and used experimental or quasi-experimental designs. Consider the study by Bell described by Skemp (1971, pp, 47–50) relating to networks. The hypothesis was that learning with understanding leads to greater transferability. In brief, a group of 11-year-old students ($n = 12$) who had been taught Euler's rule for traversability of networks including an explanation for why it works considerably outperformed two other similar groups on a novel set of networks. One of these two groups had been taught the rule alone, and the third group had not been taught the rule at all. Of interest was the finding that the first two groups, both of which had been taught the rule, performed identically on a first group of network problems. In the novel situation, with harder networks, the group taught for understanding performed far better. This study is typical of early studies in mathematics education. They were, in effect, laboratory-style studies drawing on the Western psychological tradition.

The work of Swiss psychologist Jean Piaget changed the way that educational researchers thought about children's cognitive development. His notion of stages of development was based on one-to-one clinical interviews in which children completed carefully designed tasks, many of which were based on mathematical concepts (e.g., Piaget, 1941/1952; Piaget & Inhelder, 1947/1956). He considered the quality of a child's response to develop a hierarchical framework that, he claimed, children moved through in an invariant sequence as their understanding developed. Although today some of Piaget's methods are questioned, and the lock-step approach to cognitive development has been largely superseded by more complex theories, his work has been highly influential in educational research.

In a similar fashion, coming from a psychology background but within a different tradition, the work of Krutetskii (1976) "influenced generations of researchers" (Mason & Johnston-Wilder, 2004, p. 119). Like Piaget, he also used clinical interview techniques described by Presmeg (2014) as a "precursor to the qualitative methodologies that followed" (p. 9). Krutetskii described insights and approaches to problem solving that were used by students identified as gifted in mathematics, and initiated the term *a mathematical cast of mind* to describe individuals who not only solved mathematical problems correctly but did so "elegantly." He was interested not only in what mathematically gifted children knew but also in how they used that knowledge to solve problems.

In contrast, studies that have addressed mathematics performance or achievement have often come from the psychometric tradition. Written tests of mathematics have been used since 1830 and public examinations have been the norm since the early 20th century. Underpinning studies of this type are a drive for standardization—the test used is administered under identical conditions to all students—in the belief that this approach is equitable. Often driven by the American Psychological Association or similar organizations, this logical positivist research tradition emphasizes validity and reliability, usually defined statistically (Cherryholmes, 1988). The data generated from these activities have been used by researchers to establish factors, such as socio-economic status, that influence mathematics achievement, and to compare achievement by different groups, such as indigenous status, jurisdiction, or gender. Although such activity as measuring mathematical performance, especially through national or international surveys, may not always be recognized as mathematics education research, the findings are widely used and publicized in many instances, and are often used as a basis for policy development.

In parallel with social science research more broadly, mathematics education research began to draw on other traditions. Interpretive studies are now commonplace, where researchers aim to describe and explain behaviors. Learning mathematics, or any other subject, is seen as part of a social practice codified in educational institutions and schools (Eisenhart, 1988). Bishop (1985) referred to studies focused on classroom transactions, for example, as having a "social construction" frame. Postmodern approaches consider issues of power within social institutions (Goldin, 2003). Many others could be described.

The point is that there is now a broad range of theories, methods, frameworks, and techniques available to researchers in mathematics education. These diverse approaches come from a range of philosophical perspectives (Bredo, 2012) and draw on different epistemological traditions (Kelly, 2012). The educational research community itself is divided and unable to find common ground. It has proven difficult to identify agreed standards against which to test the quality of any particular study. The sometimes competing demands have created a situation in which some researchers—especially those inexperienced in the field—"go fishing" for a theoretical approach after collecting some data, rather than developing a sound rationale for their research method. Mathematics education researchers are not immune from such challenges.

As the field has taken on a broadly more sociological flavor, cultural differences in research traditions have emerged. Sririman and Törner (2008), for example, described the disunity among mathematics education research traditions within Europe. They suggested that this arises because of different approaches to "mathematics didactics." Tsatsaroni, Lerman, and Xu (2003) considered the theories in use in mathematics education in the early 21st century. They found that while most studies used an explicit theory and also had an orientation towards empiricism, the nature of the theories had changed over time. The orientation towards psychological and mathematical studies had dropped, whereas research based on a range of socio-cultural theories had increased. More recently, Ross and Onwuegbuzie (2014), considering methodologies rather than theories, showed that in the period 2006 to 2010, there was an increase in the number of articles published in the *Journal for Research in Mathematics Education* that used mixed research designs, and that the quantitative approaches used in these mixed designs were at a lower end of a complexity scale. These meta-analyses of published articles appear to indicate a trend towards using more qualitative research designs, underpinned by a wide range of theories.

Lerman (2010) suggested that this proliferation of theories, and hence methodologies, is inescapable and warns that "there is cause to have some worries about how these theories are being used" (p. 107). As an example, there is a considerable body of research that indicates that "direct instruction" (the practice of the teacher controlling all dialogue in the classroom using a well-scripted and structured process of instruction) is more effective than what are often termed "reform" approaches, where students are provided with activities that allow them to construct their own understanding in mathematics (e.g., Becker, 1992; Wilson, Andrew, & Below, 2006). Opponents of the direct instruction approach argue that students taught through this approach become procedural users of mathematics only and do not develop deep connected mathematical knowledge (e.g., Boaler, 2002; Brown, Askew, Hodgen, Rhodes, & Wiliam, 2003). These two views are based on fundamentally different philosophies of mathematics learning and teaching (Ewing, 2011). Without understanding or recognizing how these views differ, research findings can be misinterpreted, and the limitations of a research study may go unacknowledged. These considerations give rise to questions about researchers privileging one form of knowledge over another. The next section addresses this notion more explicitly.

PRIVILEGING FORMS OF (MATHEMATICS EDUCATION) KNOWLEDGE

The understanding that researchers bring to their work about mathematics—its learning and teaching—inevitably influences the nature and scope of their research studies. In addition, because little research exists outside a political reality, funding may be tied to specific approaches. These factors may consciously or unconsciously impact on the design and conduct of a specific research project. In this section I consider the effects of such influences and the challenges that ensue for researchers as a result.

It is difficult, probably impossible, to be completely objective about the subject of any research study. The action of deciding to engage in a particular study is itself the result of personal interest, background, and inclination and is influenced by training and the local context. Context plays an important part in any study undertaken within an education setting.

There are two ways in which context may influence a study. The first is the actual social context within which the study is set. The second is the researcher context that informs the conduct of the study. For clarity I will refer to the first as "environmental" context and the second as "instrumental" context.

The environmental context, by its very nature, can inhibit the generalizability of any study. No two educational contexts are identical, even within the same school. Indeed Lietz (2009), reporting on data from the Programme for International Student Assessment, or PISA (www.oecd.org/pisa), indicated that in many Western countries, including Australia, Canada, and the UK, approximately 20% of the differences in student performance was found between schools, and approximately 80% was attributable to differences between students within schools: that is, in-school variance was greater than between school variance. Finland was an exception with only 5% of variance occurring between schools and Germany, in contrast, showed 52% of the variance occurring between schools. These findings suggest that the environmental contexts within which participating schools operated—which may include aspects such as the organization of the educational systems, approaches to teaching, and educational values—appear to impact on students' performances. This point has been the subject of a number of comparative studies across cultures, particularly between East Asian and Western countries, exploring environmental contexts among nations. For example, East Asian students, such as those from Korea, Shanghai, and Hong Kong, tend to perform at a high level on mathematics tests and many factors have been identified as having a likely influence on their performance, including cultural values (Leung, 2005a; Li, 2004), teacher knowledge (Leung, 2005b; Ma, 1999), expectations of schooling (Wardlaw, 2006), and language (Callingham, 2013). There are contextual influences at all levels—international, national and local—and the mathematics education researcher in choosing the unit of analysis needs to be mindful of these potential effects. The multiplicity of factors and broad differences between and within countries, districts, and schools indicate that environmental context is likely to threaten generalizability and replicability. The mathematics education researcher still, however, has a responsibility to ensure that studies are undertaken with rigor. The different environmental contexts must be recognized and acknowledged, and the findings of the study have to be interpreted in the light of the environmental contextual influences. The difficulties provide some limitations to claims of generalizability but do not necessarily negate the validity of any one study.

Consider as an example that body of work that could be characterized as "workplace mathematics" or "everyday mathematics." Carraher, Carraher, and Schliemann (1985) conducted a study into the calculation skills of young people in Brazil that was in many ways seminal in the field. They used a combination of research approaches, including participant observation in which a researcher posed as a customer and purchased items from the youngster, and a formal clinical interview (termed the *formal test*) in which subjects attempted mathematics problems based on the ones that they had solved informally in the street sales situation. They found that the youngsters involved solved problems in context—both informally in the marketplace and when orally presented with word problems—significantly better than they did context-free mathematics problems that were mathematically identical to those embedded in context. Clements (2004, p. 186) pointed out that this study was "the forerunner of numerous subsequent investigations . . . into the often peculiar calculation skills of persons immersed in particular 'cultures'." These types of studies are still happening.

As the field developed, a more critical stance was taken. Mary Harris (1997), for example, pointed out the complexity of mathematics in the largely female field of textiles and suggested that if the mathematical skills of women engaged in textile work were formally recognized, women could potentially gain better employment. Hoyles and her associates (Hoyles, Noss, Kent, & Bakker, 2010) used the notion of *boundary objects* to develop technology-based tools for improving workplace training, emphasizing the collaborative aspects of the study both to make the tools useful and ensure their take-up and use. In these latter two studies predominantly qualitative approaches were used to provide rich descriptions. The studies themselves were specific to their contexts.

Cultural mathematics developed in other ways as well. Bishop (1988) brought together many different studies to argue that although mathematics is a cultural phenomenon, nevertheless there are common threads. There have been many cultural studies of mathematics including counting and number systems (e.g., the work of Lean cited in Owens, 2001). The field of "ethnomathematics" (D'Ambrosio, 1985) is concerned with those ways in which different cultures have developed diverse mathematics, depending on the needs within the particular society. It has a number of different foci, including one of empowerment through mathematics and criticisms of the Eurocentric nature of school mathematics (e.g., Powell & Frankenstein, 1997).

The point here is not that the cultural aspect of mathematics education is a diverse field, rather it is that it is an umbrella encompassing many different studies, none of which is truly replicable or generalizable because of its situated nature (Lave, 1988). Like a dot in a pointillist painting, every mathematics education cultural research study carries limited information, bounded by time and place. Taken together, however, the body of work reveals a rich and subtle picture of the place of mathematics in the world, historically and currently. Mathematics education researchers need to be mindful of where their study fits within the wider field, and how it contributes to that field within its own environmental context.

The previous discussion referred to the environmental contexts in which a study may be located. The influences of the researchers' own environments may themselves exert subtle influences on the decisions that are made about the conduct of the project itself through the personal biases that any research team or individual may bring to a study. Shulman (1987) indicated that educational ends, purposes, and values are part of the knowledge base of all teachers, and hence, also of educational researchers. Researchers cannot isolate themselves from their environment; the best that can be done is to acknowledge the influence of prior experiences, previous research understandings, and personal preferences. Interestingly, researchers who use qualitative approaches may explicitly address such issues. Rarely, however, are such considerations made when a quantitative study is being designed. This kind of influence is what I term *instrumental* context.

It should be emphasized that in discussing the notion of bias, I am not referring to prejudice or unfairness. Rather it is those dispositions towards one theory over another, or in the choice of a particular research approach, that emerge from background, training, culture, and personal experiences. The research questions developed, the instruments used, the sample chosen, the data collected and so on are all subject to the internal, often unexamined, attitudes, beliefs, and dispositions of the individual researcher. Researchers should examine their thinking deeply, and acknowledge that there may be a variety of ways of addressing the same problem or of interpreting the same results, even when the environmental contexts are taken into account.

As an example, consider a number of approaches to examining the nature of pedagogical content knowledge (PCK) in mathematics. Shulman (1987) first defined PCK as

> the blending of content and pedagogy into an understanding of how topics, problems, or issues are organized, represented, and adapted to the diverse interests and abilities of learners, and presented for instruction. Pedagogical content knowledge is the category most likely to distinguish the understanding of the content specialist from that of the pedagogue.
>
> (p. 8)

Since Shulman first described PCK, there has been considerable interest in attempting to identify and measure PCK in the context of mathematics. In the United States, a team led by Ball explored the notion of knowledge for teaching (Ball, Thames, & Phelps, 2008) by considering the ways in which teachers needed to know and understand mathematics that went beyond simply being able to undertake mathematical problems. They developed a model of knowledge for teaching that included both mathematical knowledge (subject matter knowledge) and PCK, with several subdomains within each of these two categories. Using this basis, they developed instruments to measure elementary school teachers' knowledge for teaching mathematics. Analysis of data from initial administration of the instruments suggested three factors: two content knowledge factors addressing knowledge of number and operations, and knowledge of patterns, functions, and algebra; and a student factor, termed *knowledge of students and content* (Hill, Schilling, & Ball, 2004). The choice of mathematical content was confined to areas of importance in the local curriculum. In contrast, in Australia Callingham and Watson (2011) chose to focus on statistics as a newer component of the curriculum and one that was known to be problematic for teachers. Their items asked teachers to anticipate students' likely correct and incorrect responses to statistical questions, and to indicate what they would do to move students' knowledge forward. The content knowledge was present but the emphasis in the measures was on knowing about students' knowledge, based on teachers' own statistical understanding. A third approach to the measurement of PCK was taken by Baumert and his associates in Germany (Baumert et al., 2010) in which they proposed three facets of high school teachers' PCK: tasks in which teachers were asked to recognize a variety of possible solution paths; students, addressing common mistakes and misconceptions; and instruction, addressing the range of representations and approaches to teaching.

These three quantitative studies aimed at identifying and measuring teachers' PCK all took different perspectives based on researchers' understanding, experience, and context. The US study (Ball et al., 2008) placed an emphasis on teachers' mathematical knowledge in the areas of arithmetic operations and patterns and relationships. Their knowledge of students was also linked to content, reflecting a belief about the critical importance of core mathematical concepts. In contrast, the Australian statistics-based study (Callingham & Watson, 2011) focused on teachers' knowledge of likely student difficulties and development of student understanding. Implicit in the decision to make students the focus was a recognition that teachers themselves were unsure of their own statistical knowledge and that to ask them directly to solve statistical problems would have been threatening. The European study (Baumert et al., 2010) considered aspects such as the choice of teaching tasks and multiple solution paths, privileging a particular didactic tradition. It is clear that there are overlaps, but each measure developed appears to have been influenced by the researchers' backgrounds and traditions, leading to different instrumental contexts.

Baumert et al. (2010) conjectured that a teacher's background and experience would influence the development of PCK. Teachers training at different institutions, even within the same country, may experience very different emphases in their education. Chick (2011) described the challenges experienced in deciding what aspects of PCK in mathematics to address, both in teaching and research. She stated

> we demigod-like educators think we have power to direct people on this path to enlightenment. We choose what aspects of PCK to emphasise based, if you like, on our PCK for PCK. We cannot do all we would like (we are not omnipotent) but our expertise is the basis for choices about what to include. We exhibit a self-asserted omniscience that we are doing what is best.
>
> (p. 1)

Clearly, regardless of whether a particular study is qualitative or quantitative, it is not context free. Some aspects of mathematical knowledge, understanding, beliefs, and attitudes, or skill will inevitably be privileged over others. The important point for any researcher is to accept and acknowledge these differences. Unless these aspects are recognized the value of the research in providing descriptive or explanatory power may be distorted. These considerations point towards the postmodern dilemma of pluralism and localization. Walshaw (2004) noted

> As a crucial component of our complex societies, mathematics education is an evolving, self-critical enterprise—constantly on the lookout for creative solutions and new ways of looking, interpreting and explaining.
>
> (p. 2)

Mathematics education researchers, while continuing to embrace new approaches, theories, and techniques, need to take care not to ignore prior work—that is they must recognize and acknowledge the heritage and traditions both within the field and their own circumstances, and frame their work accordingly.

The two previous sections have served to highlight the intricacy of mathematics education research. Not only is there a raft of possible theories that lead to a range of methodological choices, but these theories can also be applied in a variety of environmental contexts by researchers who bring their own perspectives to bear, influencing the instrumental contexts. Given this complexity, it seems unlikely that the field is moving towards a unified theory of mathematics education, or if indeed this goal is sensible (Sririman & English, 2010). The mathematics education researcher of necessity must rely on the professional judgement and knowledge of the research team, being explicit about the theoretical underpinnings of the study and the inherent strengths and limitations of the supporting philosophy. The important message is that having a theory is essential to provide a rationale and platform on which to build the study. Lerman (2010) reported that around 10% of reported mathematics education studies in the period from 1996 to 2001 did not use an explicit theory of any type. As with teaching, having no solid basis for the decisions and choices that arise throughout a research study is like walking on quicksand—at any moment the luckless researcher can sink in the mire of competing interpretations of the data. I sometimes see research students struggling to write a thesis from a poorly conceptualized study, attempting to make sense of a disordered collection of disparate information. Being clear about the theoretical perspective allows the researcher to justify the research design and focuses attention on the relevant data to collect. Considerations of what information is needed to answer the research question inevitably leads to discussion about measures and measurement. This aspect of research is addressed in the next section.

MEASURES AND MEASUREMENT IN MATHEMATICS EDUCATION

Issues around the nature of the measurement—of quality or quantity—appear to be rarely acknowledged or discussed in mathematics education research. These matters are, however, fundamental to meeting the kinds of criteria to which Schoenfeld (2008) referred. Cobb, Confrey, diSessa, Lehrer, and Schauble (2003, p. 12), in the context of design experiments, made the point that "all measurements (even observations) are indexes to constructs of interest, not the constructs themselves." They went on to point out that

> Measures are created, not found, and decisions about the creation of measures are among the most important made. An otherwise impeccable design will produce no useful information about the phenomena of interest if problems of construct validity are not successfully resolved. Measures that are feasible to administer, and that produce precise and reliable scores, may or may not adequately capture the phenomenon of interest.
>
> (p. 12)

There are a number of important points here. The idea that a measure is not simply waiting to be discovered but is purposefully manufactured to capture indicators of the focus of the study is critical. No study exists in a vacuum: however apparently unstructured or naturalistic the data collection purports to be, there must be some underlying construct of interest to the researcher or the study itself becomes questionable. The development of some measure bridges the gap between the theory espoused and the observed phenomenon.

As an example, an exercise I set for my research methods students is to go and observe people at an eating place. No other instructions are given. When the students report back, it is obvious that they all focus on different aspects—the type of food, the conversations happening, the use of space—and that without some frame of reference the observations are fairly useless. Even when a frame of reference is supplied retrospectively, the data are too diffuse to be used to make sensible inferences about the new focus of attention. The point is simply and quickly made that having some framework or theory, usually based on previous research reported in the literature, is essential in order to construct measures of the target behavior.

Because measures are constructed, the validity of the construct is important. The notion of validity has been challenged in relation to qualitative data, but Messick (1991) argued for a holistic view where the idea of a "score" that is used as a measure encompasses

> any coding or summarization of observed consistencies or performance regularities on a test, questionnaire, observation procedure, or other assessment device (such as work samples, portfolios, or realistic problem simulations). This general usage subsumes qualitative as well as quantitative summaries.
>
> (p. 1)

Regardless of the form in which the data are collected, the construct itself must carry useful, interpretable information if it is to contribute to the study. Consideration of the construct needs to go beyond content alone and take account of such matters as values and utility. It should also be recognized that establishing validity is always a matter of argument, and that as new evidence is produced the validity of the construct may change, for better or worse.

As an example of the different ways in which measures may be constructed, I return to the body of work that addresses that complex construct of PCK. In the three studies discussed in the previous section (Ball et al., 2008; Baumert et al., 2010; Callingham & Watson, 2011) attempts were made first to define components of the construct and then to write items that would address these components. The focus in each study, despite the differences, was on the appropriate mathematical understandings of teachers that were needed to develop students' understanding. In contrast, two other studies, Rowland, Huckstep, and Thwaites (2005) and Chick, Baker, Pham, and Cheng (2006), took a qualitative approach to identify the actions that teachers use when teaching. Their focus was the process of teaching. Rowland et al. (2005) used 24 videotaped lessons from elementary preservice teachers towards the end of their teacher education course. Using an inductive approach they identified a "knowledge quartet," based on identifying larger themes from the 18 codes that they created during analysis of their data. These themes—termed *foundation, transformation, connection*, and *contingency*—aimed to capture what teachers were doing in the process of teaching and were used to frame discussions with preservice teachers about their teaching practice. Chick and her colleagues used a combination of interviews, questionnaires, and classroom observations to consider aspects of mathematics teaching, and hence developed a framework for examining PCK in relation to specific aspects of mathematics (Chick, Pham, & Baker, 2006). They described three facets of teachers' knowledge: pedagogical knowledge in a content context, content knowledge in a pedagogical context, and a category that was "clearly PCK" involving a symbiotic relationship between pedagogy and content.

Of interest here is that although the two approaches—quantitative and qualitative—to the consideration of PCK were different, they both provided sound and valid data for the purposes that were intended. The three quantitative studies aimed to identify how much PCK teachers had and ultimately to use the measure of that PCK as one variable in identifying factors that impacted on students' learning. In contrast, the two qualitative studies aimed to consider teaching in action and to use the data as a basis for discussions with preservice and in-service teachers. All the studies focused on the relationship between mathematical knowledge and pedagogy that is at the heart of the PCK construct. Of particular note, however, is that based on the same body of previous research identified in the literature, the aims of the studies and the nature of the research questions drove the methodology used. These five studies exemplify the importance of having a strong theoretical basis on which to frame an investigation and from which to develop measures, quantitative or qualitative, of the target construct.

These PCK studies also bring attention to the utility of the studies and what Messick (1991) referred to as "consequential validity." The different types of PCK study described earlier had different intentions. The three quantitative studies aimed ultimately to explore the links between teachers' knowledge and students' outcomes, whereas the objective of the two qualitative studies was to open conversations with teachers about the nature of teaching mathematics. The nature and use of the data collected was appropriate and provided no adverse consequences. Unfortunately, sometimes research findings are used carelessly, often by influential nonresearchers, with unanticipated consequences. Consider for example the consequences of using data from large-scale national or international testing programs, such as the National Assessment of Educational Progress (NAEP) (e.g., National Center for Educational Statistics, 2014). There is growing evidence (e.g., Berliner, 2011) that as a consequence of the emphasis on high-stakes testing, the curriculum offered in school becomes curtailed, and that this in turn affects outcomes for students later. Rather than improving the quality of education, the intense focus on performance is detrimental to education more broadly. Research programs such as NAEP in the United States, and its equivalents in many other countries, are intended to provide a series of snapshots of a system, rather than data that can provide worthwhile evidence at the school or individual level. The data are being used beyond their design limitations and the consequential validity is weak.

Returning to the comments of Cobb et al. (2003) quoted earlier, constructing measures is a key aspect of any research study. Quality measures, used appropriately, provide rigorous evidence about the focus of study. Rasch measurement (Bond & Fox, 2007) provides one approach to developing rigorous measures within a qualitative inferential framework. Using the interactions between questions (test items, hierarchically coded interviews or observations, Likert scale surveys) and persons (teachers, students) it is possible to produce an interval-level ordered conjoint scale that can be used to explore, describe, or explain relationships between the items and persons. Measures produced by the model are a sound basis for comparing groups, considering interactions, or predicting outcomes. In the editorial to a special issue of the *Mathematics Education Research Journal* addressing uses of Rasch measurement in mathematics education research, the editors wrote:

> First, we believe strongly that all research should have a strong conceptual basis and should be supported by rigorous techniques. Conceptualising a research study requires a deep consideration of the ideas of others, and interpretation of those ideas within the set of values and beliefs each researcher brings to the research process—a qualitative framework. Second, we believe that research approaches should be defensible and rigorous, and that quantitative techniques can provide a sound basis for such an approach. There is an important caveat, however: *Measurement is a means to an end, not an end in itself, and must be used properly.*
>
> (Callingham & Bond, 2006, p. 7).

This caveat is an important one. It relates to Schoenfeld's (2008) calls for mathematics education research to provide sound evidence for the claims made, and goes further to suggest that how that information is used also has an impact, incorporating the notion of consequential validity. It is a legitimate research activity to develop an instrument to measure, for example, attitudes towards mathematics that may take various forms (Aiken 1970)—but that instrument has to produce measures that have descriptive power (e.g., Leder, 1985), explanatory power (e.g., Ma & Kishor, 1997), or predictive power (e.g., Neale, 1969). Ultimately it is the meaning ascribed to the measure that impacts.

The notion of *meaning* is a philosophical one. Mundey (1986) suggested "The hallmark of a meaningless proposition is that its truth-value depends on what scale or coordinate system is employed, whereas meaningful propositions have truth-value independent of the choice of representation, within certain limits" (p. 392). Comments such as this have implications for the development of ways of measuring a construct, whatever that construct might be, in mathematics education. The ideal, perfect-world construct may not exist, but the ideal should be the basis for the development of any survey, test, observation, or interview schedule that might be used to measure a construct. All too often, however, any relationship between the ideal and the components that the instrument purports to measure goes unexamined (Fisher, 2004), apart from a cursory review by a panel of researchers.

Fisher (2004) argued that

> Research methods embodying integrated qualitative-quantitative mathematics have two crucial advantages over currently popular methods in the social sciences. The first is that strict criteria exist for knowing when mathematically transparent representation, and so, quantification, has been provisionally achieved. The second is the foundation this achievement lays for creating and maintaining universal uniform metrics as a common language for the exchange of value.
>
> (p. 441)

These conditions—achievement of quantification and the establishment of a universal measurement scale—are then open to falsifiability, one of Schoenfeld's (2008) criteria for mathematics education research. The research becomes transparent in its meaning and can thus be questioned. It is this questioning that moves the field forward.

There is, however, a subtle distinction between Fisher's (2004) approach and the positivist paradigm. Fisher proposes the ideal and aims to fit the data obtained from the measures employed to that ideal. In contrast, the usual positivist approach is to attempt to fit a model to the data obtained from the measures. The underlying assumption in the latter approach is that the measures are the construct. The clarity and transparency of the research is not clearly established, leaving open the potential for confusion and reducing the capacity for falsifiability. Fisher is arguing for the use of numbers because of the precision of meaning they carry when the instruments used to generate these numbers conform to an ideal model.

Such a requirement taken at face value appears to challenge qualitative methodologies. Often, however, qualitative researchers use frequency counts of some action, comment, or code to build their argument. If, however, the investigation is truly about quality—as qualitative research implies—it should be possible to match the actions or observations to a set of standards. Defining a set of standards implies an ideal to which the construct should matched, which is the same activity as recommended by Fisher. Using techniques such as Rasch measurement, the levels of quality identified can be transformed into a true measurement scale. It is the underlying ideal construct that provides the basis for judgements that then can be coded numerically without compromising the qualitative approach.

The work of Long, Wendt, and Dunne (2011) provides an example of this dual approach. They considered proficiency in multiplicative thinking, one of the important staging posts in developing mathematical understanding in the middle years of schooling (Siemon, 2013; Siemon, Bleckly, & Neal, 2012). Items were selected from the Trends in International Mathematics and Science Study (TIMSS) (International Association for the Evaluation of Educational Achievement, 2007) to address a theorized conceptual domain of multiplicative thinking, including addressing ratio, proportion, and percent, and intentionally covering a wide range of difficulty, based on released TIMSS data. These items were administered to 330 South African students in Grades 7 to 9. In addition, a group of students from high-, middle-, and low-proficiency bands was interviewed, with items for interview chosen in such a way that, for example, a high proficiency student would answer a relatively easy item, and a low proficiency student might receive a more difficult item. In this way the nature of the students' thinking at different proficiency levels was able to be identified.

From the initial Rasch analysis of the test items a hierarchy of items was identified that were first grouped by identifying appropriate cut points on the scale—a qualitative interpretation of quantitative data. These initial item groupings were examined for common themes and cognitive demands. The interviews provided identification of particular types of error associated with levels of competency and the difficulty of the items. Combining all of this information allowed researchers to identify patterns of thinking that were demonstrated as students displayed greater competency. More importantly, some fine-grained identification of the needs of specific individuals was possible that enabled teachers to target their teaching more effectively. The combination of quantitative precision and qualitative interpretation provided insights that neither approach would have done if used in isolation.

Nevertheless, there are many studies that provide sound evidence but do not conform to this approach. Any diagnostic tool, by definition, seeks responses that do not conform to an ideal so that studies aiming to identify students' misconceptions, for example, will not fit the model. Stacey and Steinle (2006), for example, worked to identify misconceptions about decimals. They used a carefully designed diagnostic test based on available literature that required students to compare pairs of decimal numbers. Their aim was to identify patterns of responses and to see how these patterns changed as students moved through schooling. This approach is best characterized as "mapping" learning as students moved between different categories of response, as opposed to measuring learning, where students show an increasing quantity of understanding of the core construct as they learn more. The Rasch model is not appropriate for activities of this type, but it is worth noting that the research design used by Stacey and Steinle conformed to the model described earlier. They developed a strong conceptual framework, based on previous work, designed and delivered an appropriate test, and then analyzed the results using a combination of quantitative (percentages in categories and so on) and qualitative (descriptions of typical errors) analysis to identify patterns in students' thinking.

Instruments developed for diagnosis are legitimate but cannot provide information about students' mathematical achievement, and they should not be used for that purpose. Similarly many cross-cultural studies aim to identify similarities and differences, again a diagnostic activity. Studies such as these map the territory rather than make judgements about a situation. The measures used are categorical and descriptive, but may become the basis for later development of tools to consider increasing quality or quantity.

Sound measurement is the foundation of quality research in mathematics education. Identifying and defining the construct provides specificity and rigor, and identifies the scope of the study. The measures used must meet expectations for descriptive, diagnostic, explanatory, or predictive power. Clarifying the underlying construct provides transparency so that studies can be judged in terms of replicability, generality and trustworthiness. Using sound measurement techniques provides for falsifiability, and from a clear discussion of the target construct it is easier to develop multiple ways of collecting data. Sound measurement allows for all of Schoenfeld's (2008) criteria to be met.

The previous sections have attempted to map the territory of mathematics education research from the particular perspective of considering measures as the basis for quality outcomes. In the next section three case studies are presented, with a focus on the measures used and testing the projects against Schoenfeld's criteria.

CASE STUDIES FROM MATHEMATICS EDUCATION RESEARCH

In this section three case studies are used to exemplify aspects of mathematics education research. The first of these is PISA, run across many countries under the auspices of the Organization for Economic Cooperation and Development (OECD). The second is the Learners' Perspective Study (www.lps.iccr.edu.au/), an international umbrella for considering ways in which students' learn mathematics in different countries. The last study, StatSmart, (Callingham & Watson, 2007) is typical of many small- to mid-scale studies funded by national bodies. In each case only publically available material has been used as a source of information. This material includes reports, Web sites, and published books and papers. The three studies were chosen because of the availability of information, and because they are distinctively different in their aims and methodologies: PISA uses quantitative approaches to conduct large-scale studies; the Learners' Perspective Study uses qualitative approaches that are applied in a range of situations; and the StatSmart project used a mixed-methods approach in a longitudinal study.

Case Study 1: PISA

PISA aims to provide evaluative information to governments about the outcomes from their education systems. Surveys are used on a triennial basis—2003, 2006, 2009, 2012—to consider three aspects of schooling: reading, science, and (of specific interest) mathematics. Unlike other international surveys, such as the Trends in Mathematics and Science Study (http://timssandpirls.bc.edu), PISA does not use the mathematics curriculum as a basis. Instead the tests used assess the extent to which 15-year-old students are equipped to meet the demands of postschool life as full participants in society. Background questionnaires are also used to provide information about the context and aid in the interpretation of the findings. Surveys are conducted every three years with a sample of 15-year-old students, and in each survey one particular topic—reading, science, or mathematics—is the focus, although the other two are also tested to provide intermediate data. The tests are scaled using Rasch measurement so that the outcomes are directly comparable over time, giving governments an opportunity to monitor progress.

PISA has a strong theoretical framework. The focus is mathematical literacy, defined as

> The capacity to identify, to understand, and to engage in mathematics and make well-founded judgements about the role that mathematics plays, as needed for an individual's current and future private life, occupational life, and social life with peers and relatives, and life as a constructive, concerned, and reflective citizen.
>
> (OECD, 2003, p.10)

Underpinning this definition is the concept of *mathematization* (de Lange, 1987), a notion founded in the European tradition of mathematics teaching (Jablonka & Gellert, 2007). Mathematization involves perceiving the mathematics inherent in a situation and using these mathematics to then solve authentic (in the sense of real-world) problems. In PISA, the constraints of the testing format does not permit a full assessment of the capacity to mathematize; a compromise is made by identifying elements of the process and developing items that address these elements (OECD, 2003). Over time the theory behind PISA has developed. In 2012, the most recent assessment, financial literacy and problem solving were also considered, in line with participating countries' interests in these areas. At each iteration of the project, the theoretical framework is reconsidered and items are written to address the specific elements of the framework used for a particular survey.

There have been criticisms of PISA. Most recently Heinz-Dieter Meyer (2014) wrote an open letter to the director of PISA that focused largely on the uses of PISA data. Meyer criticized, among other aspects, the development of international rankings; short-term policy fixes to improve standings; and the focus on narrow, measurable domains rather than such attributes as "physical, moral, civic, and artistic development." Other criticisms have been of a technical nature (e.g., Goldstein, 2004; Kreiner & Christensen, 2014). These technical criticisms focus on the nature of the Rasch model used for scaling including issues such as fit to the model and item bias (DIF). All of these issues, in both social and technical domains, become important when ranking becomes the predominant focus. It is worth noting, however, that ranking was never the intention behind PISA but political, social, and economic environments have driven this agenda.

In terms of Schoenfeld's (2008) criteria, PISA has a clearly defined scope, based on a framework agreed to by participating countries. The study has rigor and specificity in both the methodology and reporting. Breaches of the sampling frame, for example, are considered and reported, and technical reports are provided that detail the analyses conducted. The collection of multiple sources of data, including detailed context questionnaires and surveys about special topics from students as well as teachers, helps to provide both descriptive and explanatory power. The criticism of PISA demonstrates the capacity for falsifiability, but may, to some extent, challenge its trustworthiness even though the methodology provides replicability, and generality. PISA may also fall down on predictive power, although it should be remembered that the purpose is to provide systems and governments with a snapshot of performance, not to predict future development or to provide a ranking system.

Case Study 2: The Learners' Perspective Study

The Learners' Perspective Study (www.lps.iccr.edu.au) aims to examine patterns of participation in "competently taught eighth-grade mathematics classrooms." There are now 16 international teams participating in the study, in countries as diverse as Australia, Japan, Norway, Israel, the UK, and the United States. Using a systematic approach, a series of lessons is videotaped for analysis, to answer six general research questions:

1. Within the classrooms studied in each country, is there evidence of a coherent body of student practice(s), and to what extent are these practices culturally specific?
2. What are the antecedent and consequent conditions and actions (particularly learner actions) associated with teacher practices identified in earlier studies as culturally specific and nationally characteristic?
3. To what extent does an individual teacher employ a variety of pedagogical approaches in the course of teaching a lesson sequence?
4. What degree of similarity or difference (both locally and internationally) can be found in the learner (and teacher) practices occurring in classrooms identified by the local education community as constituting sites of competent teaching practice?
5. To what extent are teacher and learner practices in a mutually supportive relationship?
6. To what extent are particular documented teacher and learner practices associated with student construction of valued social and mathematical meanings?

(Learners' Perspective Study, n.d.)

More specific research questions may also be posed by local teams. The focus is on what actually happens in mathematics classrooms taught by teachers deemed by local standards as competent in teaching mathematics. Results have been widely disseminated in a series of books (Clarke, Keitel, & Shimizu, 2006; Clarke, Emanuelsson, Jablonka, & Mok, 2006; Kaur, Anthony, Ohtani, & Clarke, 2013; Shimizu, Kaur, Huang, & Clarke, 2010). and other publications.

Multiple sources of data are collected about each lesson sequence. These sources include videos of the classroom using three cameras, one focused on the teacher, one on a pair of target students, and one on the whole class; field notes; video-stimulated recall interviews with teachers and students; teacher questionnaires; students' work samples; and teacher resources. These data are analyzed collaboratively, using frameworks developed by the project.

Unlike PISA, the study is not government or system focused, although there are implications for professional learning and teacher education. As such, it attracts less high-stakes attention. The study provides useful, detailed information about classroom discourse in cultural settings in ways that allow comparisons of practice without making judgements about whether one practice is better than another. The local culture may well influence how data of this type are interpreted. Clarke (2013) stated

> Any demands for evidence-based instructional advocacy must acknowledge the cultural specificity of the analytical tools by which such evidence is generated. It follows that the advocacy arising from such research will also be culturally framed and constrained.
>
> (p. 32)

The value of research such as the Learners' Perspective Study is in pointing out the cultural differences in situations where there is a risk that familiar practice is assumed as the best or only way of teaching. It reminds us to examine our own biases as mathematics education researchers.

The Learners' Perspective Study has valuable descriptive power arising from multiple data sources that are collected in the same way, and analyzed collaboratively, across diverse cultures. The scope is broad, encompassing both teacher actions and student discourse, and the complexity of classroom interactions among teachers and students. The trustworthiness arises from the collaborative endeavor—there is no attempt to impose a particular cultural lens, but the data collection and analysis promote replicability. The design of the study is rigorous and has a specific focus, despite the breadth. It does not pretend to provide predictive or explanatory power, although the outcomes may give rise to conjectures that address these aspects of Schoenfeld's (2008) criteria. The falsifiability of the study is low. As a cross-cultural, descriptive study it is difficult to see how the research could be challenged in a general sense, although details can always be questioned. The Learners' Perspective Study provides a good example of qualitative research that meets high standards of research endeavor.

Case Study 3: StatSmart

The third case study is typical of research funded at a local level. StatSmart was a three-year Australian study that aimed to collect longitudinal data about the effects of a professional learning program for teachers on their students' learning outcomes. Statistics was the target understanding, because this is an area of the mathematics curriculum in which teachers were known to lack confidence. The study had a complex design (Callingham & Watson, 2007) in which data were collected from students twice in their first year of the project, before and after they had undertaken a statistics unit. Typically this testing was about six months apart. All students then did a follow-up longitudinal test one year after their posttest. Teachers also undertook a profiling instrument (Watson, 2001) and care was taken to be able to link individual teachers to the students in their classes. Most teachers completed this at least twice and many three times over the three years of the project. In addition data were collected through interviews with teachers, and at the professional learning sessions presented as part of the study. Altogether data were collected from 34 teachers in 15 schools representative of all types of school, in three different states in Australia, together with nearly 1,000 of their students in Grades 5–10. Students and teachers were tracked across time. In addition to reports to the Australian Research Council and project partners who funded the study, findings were disseminated through publications and conference presentations.

The extent of StatSmart was similar to many nationally funded studies around the world. Although the study had limited scope, within the focus on statistics it did address both students' and teachers' understanding. Generalizability was limited because of the nature of the teacher sample. It was not possible to recruit a random sample of teachers, and those that did participate were highly experienced and interested in teaching statistics. The student data, however, together with the background data on their teachers and schools did provide explanatory power, and results on earlier tests did predict outcomes on later ones. There was also evidence that teachers influenced their students, although this outcome was far from clear.

The overall design provided rigor. The study provided limited descriptive power but the quantitative approach taken, underpinned by Rasch measurement, was open to falsifiability. The multiple sources of data collected over three years provided some triangulation, although the outcomes might have been enhanced by additional observational data. For a small-scale study typical of those funded to small research teams, StatSmart was able to meet many of Schoenfeld's (2008) criteria.

All three case studies met some aspects of Schoenfeld's criteria, and it is unlikely that any one would meet all of them. Of particular note is that all these studies had a strongly articulated theoretical framework and clear intentions. The methodology used was chosen to best answer the research questions that arose from the aims of the studies.

Questions could be asked about the utility of these studies. The two more academic studies (the Learners' Perspective Study and StatSmart) have potential to inform policy makers' decisions about professional learning, but may not have been able to realize that potential. PISA, however, does have impact—sometimes in inappropriate ways, which was the issue at the heart of Heinz-Dieter Meyer's open letter. There is little doubt, however, that through judicious use of the data, some countries have been able to improve those mathematics education outcomes measured by PISA. The use of the data by policy makers and others is out of the hands of researchers to a large extent.

If mathematics education research is to have the impact it deserves, researchers have to become more aware of directly marketing their findings outside the world of academia. As illustrated by the case studies, mathematics education research can meet high standards internally, using sound methods that support any claims that are made. Selling this quality to non-researchers in the education field is one of the next big challenges for mathematics education.

REFERENCES

Aiken, L. R., Jr. (1970). Attitudes toward mathematics. *Review of Educational Research, 40*(4), 551–596.

Ball, D. L., Thames, M. H., & Phelps, G. (2008). Content knowledge for teaching: What makes it so special? *Journal of Teacher Education, 59*(5), 389–407.

Baumert, J., Kunter, M., Blum, W., Brunner, M., Voss, T., Jordan, A., Klusmann, U., Krauss, S., Neubrand, M., & Tsai, Y-M. (2010). Teachers' mathematical knowledge, cognitive activation in the classroom, and student progress. *American Educational Research Journal, 47*(1), 133–180.

Becker, W. C. (1992). Direct instruction: A twenty year review. In R. P. West, & L. A. Hamerlynck (Eds.). *Designs for excellence in education: The legacy of B. F. Skinner* (pp. 71–112). Longmont, CO: Sopris West.

Berliner, D. (2011). Rational responses to high stakes testing: the case of curriculum narrowing and the harm that follows. *Cambridge Journal of Education, 41*:3, 287–302. doi:10.1080/03057 64X.2011.607151

Bishop, A. J. (1985). The social construction of meaning—a significant development for mathematics education. *For the Learning of Mathematics, 5*(1), 24–28.

Bishop, A. J. (1988). *Mathematical enculturation: A cultural perspective on mathematics education.* Dordrecht: Kluwer.

Boaler, J. (2002). *Experiencing school mathematics: Traditional and reform approaches to teaching and their impact on student learning.* Mahwah, NJ: Lawrence Erlbaum Associates.

Bond, T. G., & Fox, C. M. (2007). *Applying the Rasch model: Fundamental measurement in the human sciences* (2nd ed.). Mahwah, NJ: Lawrence Erlbaum Associates.

Bredo, E. (2012). Philosophies of educational research. In J. L. Green, G. Camilli, & P. B. Elmore (Eds.) *Handbook of complementary methods in education research.* New York: Routledge.

Brown, M., Askew, M., Hodgen, J., Rhodes, V., & Wiliam, D. (2003). Individual and cohort progression in learning numeracy ages 5–11: Results from the Leverhulme 5-year longitudinal study. *Proceedings of the International Conference on Mathematics and Science Learning* (pp. 81–109). Taiwan, Taipei.

Burkhardt, H., & Schoenfeld, A. H. (2003) Improving educational research: Toward a more useful, more influential, and better-funded enterprise. *Educational Researcher, 32*(9), 3–14.

Callingham, R. (2013). Chinese students and mathematical problem solving. In S. Phillipson, H. Stoeger, & A. Ziegler (Eds.) *Exceptionality in East Asia. Explorations in the actiotope model of giftedness* (pp. 86–99). Abingdon, Oxon: Routledge.

Callingham, R., & Bond, T. G. (2006). Research in mathematics education: Insights from Rasch measurement. *Mathematics Education Research Journal, 18*(2), 1–10.

Callingham, R., & Watson J. M. (2007, December). *Overcoming research design issues using Rasch measurement: The StatSmart project.* Paper presented at the Australian Association for Research in Education International Educational Research Conference 2007, Fremantle, Australia. Retrieved from www.aare.edu.au/07pap/cal07042.pdf.

Callingham, R., & Watson, J. M. (2011). Measuring levels of statistical pedagogical content knowledge. In C. Batanero, G. Burrill, & C. Reading (Eds.) *Teaching statistics in school mathematics—Challenges for teaching and teacher education: A joint ICMI/IASE study* (pp. 283–293). Dordrecht, The Netherlands: Springer.

Carraher, T. N., Carraher, D. W., & Schliemann, A. D. (1985). Mathematics in the streets and schools. *British Journal of Psychology 3,* 21–29.

Cherryholmes, C. H. (1988). Construct validity and discourses of research. *American Journal of Education, 96*(3), 421–457.

Chick, H. L. (2011). God-like educators in a fallen world. In J. Wright (Ed.) *Proceedings of the annual conference of the Australian Association for Research in Education.* Retrieved from www.aare.edu.au/publications-database.php/6143/god-like-educators-in-a-fallen-world.

Chick, H. L., Baker, M., Pham, T., & Cheng, H. (2006). Aspects of teachers' pedagogical content knowledge for decimals. In J. Novotná, H. Moraová, M. Krátká, & N. Stehlikóvá (Eds.) *Proceedings of the 30th Conference of the International Group for the Psychology of Mathematics Education* (Vol. 2, pp. 297–304). Prague: PME.

Chick, H. L., Pham, T., & Baker, M. (2006). Probing teachers' pedagogical content knowledge: Lessons from the case of the subtraction algorithm. In P. Grootenboer, R. Zevenbergen, & M. Chinnappan (eds.), *Identities, cultures and learning spaces. Proceedings of the 29th annual conference of Mathematics Education Research Group of Australasia* (pp. 139–146). Sydney: MERGA.

Clarke, D. J. (2013). Contingent conceptions of accomplished practice: The cultural specificity of discourse in and about the mathematics classroom. *ZDM: The International Journal in Mathematics Education 45*(1), 21–33.

Clarke, D. J., Emanuelsson, J., Jablonka, E., & Mok, I.A.C. (2006). *Making connections: Comparing mathematics classrooms around the world.* Rotterdam, The Netherlands: Sense Publishers.

Clarke, D. J., Keitel, C., & Shimizu, Y. (2006). *Mathematics classrooms in twelve countries: The insider's perspective.* Rotterdam, The Netherlands: Sense Publishers.

Clements, M. A. (Ken) (2004). Perspective on "Mathematics in the streets and schools." In T. P. Carpenter, J. A. Dossy, & J. L. Koehler (eds.) *Classics in mathematics education research.* Reston, VA: National Council of Teachers of Mathematics.

Cobb, P., Confrey, J., diSessa, A., Lehrer, R., & Schauble, L. (2003). Design experiments in educational research. *Educational Researcher, 32*(1), 9–13.

D'Ambrosio, B. (1985). Ethnomathematics and its place in the history and pedagogy of mathematics. *For the Learning of Mathematics, 5,* 44–8.

de Lange, J. (1987). *Mathematics, insight and meaning.* Utrecht, The Netherlands: Utrecht University.

Eisenhart, M. A. (1988). The ethnographic research tradition and mathematics education research. *Journal for Research in Mathematics Education, 19*(2), 99–114.

Ewing, B., (2011). Direct instruction in mathematics: Issues for schools with high indigenous enrolments: A literature review. *Australian Journal of Teacher Education, 36*(5), 63–91.

Fisher, W. P., Jr. (2004). Meaning and method in the social sciences. *Human Studies: A Journal for Philosophy and the Social Sciences, 27*(4), 429–54.

Goldin, G. A. (2003). Developing complex understandings: On the relation of mathematics education research to mathematics. *Educational Studies in Mathematics, 54,* 171–202.

Goldstein, H. (2004). International comparisons of student attainment: Some issues arising from the PISA study. *Assessment in Education, 11,* 319–330.

Harris, M. (1997). *Common threads: Women, mathematics and work.* London, UK: Trentham Books.

Hill, H. C., Schilling, S. G., & Ball, D. L. (2004). Developing measures of teachers' mathematics for teaching. *Elementary School Journal, 105,* 11–30.

Hoyles, C., Noss. R., Kent, P. & Bakker, A. (2010). *Improving mathematics at work: The need for techno-mathematical literacies.* Abingdon, Oxon: Routledge.

International Association for the Evaluation of Educational Achievement. (2007). *TIMSS 2003. Mathematics items.* Chestnut Hill, MA: Boston College.

Jablonka, E. & Gellert, U. (2007). Mathematisation—demathematisation. In E. Jablonka & U. Gellert (Eds.) *Mathematisation and demathematisation. Social, philosophical and educational ramifications.* Rotterdam, The Netherlands: Sense Publishers.

Kaur, B., Anthony, G., Ohtani, M., & Clarke D. J. (2013). *Student voice in mathematics classrooms around the world.* Rotterdam, The Netherlands: Sense Publishers.

Kelly, G.J. (2012). Epistemology and educational research. In J.L. Green, G. Camilli, & P.B. Elmore (Eds.) *Handbook of complementary methods in education research*. New York: Routledge.

Klein, D. (2007). A quarter century of US 'math wars' and political partisanship. *BSHM Bulletin: Journal of the British Society for the History of Mathematics, 22*(1), 22–33.

Kreiner, S., & Christensen, K.B. (2014). Analyses of model fit and robustness. A new look at the PISA scaling model underlying ranking of countries according to reading literacy. *Psychometrika, 79*(2), 210–231.

Krutetskii, V.A. (1976). *The psychology of mathematical abilities in schoolchildren*. Chicago: University of Chicago Press.

Lave, J. (1988). *Cognition in practice: Mind, mathematics and culture in everyday life*. Cambridge, UK: Cambridge University Press.

Learners' Perspective Study (n.d.). *About the study*. Retrieved from www.lps.iccr.edu.au/index.php/about-the-project

Leder, G. (1985). Measurement of attitude to mathematics. *For the Learning of Mathematics, 5*(3), 18–21.

Lerman, S. (2010). Theories of mathematics education: Is plurality a problem? In Sririman, B. & English, L. (Eds.) *Theories of mathematics education. Seeking new frontiers*. Heidelberg: Springer.

Leung, K.S.F. (2005a, August). *In the books there are golden houses: Mathematics assessment in East Asia*. Plenary address to the ICMI 3rd East Asian Regional Conference on Mathematics Education, Shanghai.

Leung, K.S.F. (2005b). Some characteristics of East Asian classrooms based on data from the 1999 TIMSS video study. *Educational Studies in Mathematics, 60*, 199–215.

Li, J. (2004). A Chinese cultural model of learning. In L. Fan, N-Y, Wong, J. Cai, & S. Li (Eds.) *How Chinese learn mathematics: Perspectives from insiders* (pp. 124–156). Singapore: World Scientific Publishing.

Lietz, P. (2009). *Variance in performance between students within schools and between schools*. Melbourne, VIC: Australian Council for Educational Research. Retrieved from www.ican.sa.edu.au/files/links/ACER_DECS_variance_report.pdf.

Long, C., Wendt, H., & Dunne, T. (2011). Applying Rasch measurement in mathematics education research: steps towards a triangulated investigation into proficiency in the multiplicative conceptual field. *Educational Research and Evaluation: An International Journal on Theory and Practice, 17*(5), 387–407.

Ma, L. (1999). *Knowing and teaching elementary mathematics: Teachers' understanding of fundamental mathematics in China and the United States*. Mahwah, NJ: Lawrence Erlbaum Associates.

Ma, X. & Kishor, N. (1997). Assessing the relationship between attitude toward mathematics and achievement in mathematics: A meta-analysis. *Journal for Research in Mathematics Education, 28*(1), 26–47.

Mason, J. (2002). *Researching your own practice: The discipline of noticing*. London: Routledge Falmer.

Mason, J. & Johnston-Wilder, S. (2004). *Fundamental constructs in mathematics education*. London: Routledge.

Messick, S. (1991). Validity of test interpretation and use. In M.C. Alkin, (Ed.), *Encyclopedia of Educational Research* (6th ed.), New York: Macmillan. Retrieved from http://files.eric.ed.gov/fulltext/ED395031.pdf.

Meyer, H-D. (2014) *Open letter to Andreas Schleicher, OECD, Paris*. Retrieved from www.ilsole24ore.com/pdf2010/Editrice/ILSOLE24ORE/ILSOLE24ORE/Online/_Oggetti_Correlati/Documenti/Notizie/2014/05/invalsi-pisa.pdf?uuid=AB212FIB.

Mundey, B. (1986). On the general theory of meaningful representation. *Synthese, 67*, 391–437.

National Center for Education Statistics. (2014). *The condition of education: Mathematics performance*. Washington, DC: National Center for Education Statistics, Institute of Education Sciences, US Department of Education. Retrieved from http://nces.ed.gov/programs/coe/indicator_cnc.asp.

Neale, D. (1969). The role of attitudes in learning mathematics. *The Arithmetic Teacher, 16*(8), 631–641.

Niss, M. (1999). Aspects of the nature and state of research in mathematics education. *Educational Studies in Mathematics, 40*, 1–24.

Organisation for Economic Cooperation and Development (OECD). (2003). *The PISA 2003 assessment framework*. Paris: OECD. Retrieved from www.oecd.org/education/school/programmeforinternationalstudentassessmentpisa/33692793.pdf.

Owens, K. (2001). The work of Glendon Lean on the counting systems of Papua New Guinea and Oceania. *Mathematics Education Research Journal, 13*(1), 47–71.

Piaget, J. (1941/1952). *The child's conception of number*. London: Routledge & Kegan Paul. (Original work published 1941.)

Piaget, J. & Inhelder, B. (1947/1956). *The child's conception of space*. London: Routledge. (Original work published 1947.)

Powell, A., & Frankenstein, M. (1997). *Ethnomathematics: Challenging Eurocentrism in mathematics education*. Albany: State University of New York Press.

Presmeg, N. (2014). A dance of instruction with construction in mathematics education. In U Korten-kamp, B. Brandt, C. Benz, G. Krummheuer, S. Ladel, & R. Vogel. (Eds.) *Early mathematics learning. Selected papers of the POEM conference 2012* (pp. 9–17). New York: Springer. Retrieved from www. springer.com/gp/book/9781461446774.

Ross, A., & Onwuegbuzie, A. J. (2014). Complexity of quantitative analyses used in mixed research articles published in a flagship mathematics education journal. *International Journal of Multiple Research Approaches, 8*(1), 80–90.

Rowland, T., Huckstep, P., & Thwaites, A. (2005). Elementary teachers' mathematics subject knowledge: The knowledge quartet and the case of Naomi. *Journal of Mathematics Teacher Education, 8*, 255–281.

Schoenfeld, A. H. (2004). The math wars. *Educational Policy 18*(1), 253–286.

Schoenfeld, A. H. (2008). Research methods in (mathematics) education. In L. D. English (Ed.), *Handbook of international research in mathematics education* (2nd ed.). New York: Routledge.

Seldon, A. (2002). *Two research traditions separated by a common subject: Mathematics and mathematics education.* Cookeville, TN: Tennessee Technological University. Retrieved from https://www.tntech. edu/files/math/reports/TR_2002_2.pdf.

Shimizu, Y., Kaur, B., Huang, R., & Clarke, D. J. (2010). *Mathematical tasks in classrooms around the world.* Rotterdam, The Netherlands: Sense Publishers.

Shulman, L. S. (1987). Knowledge and teaching: Foundations of the new reform. *Harvard Educational Review, 57*, 1–22.

Siemon, D. (2013). Launching mathematical futures: The key role of multiplicative thinking. In S. Hernert, J. Tillyer & T. Spencer. (Eds.) *Mathematics: Launching Futures*, Proceedings of the 24th Biennial Conference of the Australian Association of Mathematics Teachers (pp. 36–52). Adelaide, Australia: AAMT.

Siemon, D., Bleckly, J. & Neal, D. (2012). Working with the big ideas in number and the Australian Curriculum Mathematics. In W. Atweh, M. Goos, R Jorgensen, & D. Siemon (Eds.) *Engaging the Australian Curriculum Mathematics—Perspectives from the field* (pp. 19–46). Mathematical Education Research Group of Australasia. Retrieved from www.merga.net.au/sites/default/files/editor/books/1/Chapter%202%20Siemon.pdf.

Skemp, R. (1971). *The psychology of learning mathematics.* Harmondsworth, UK: Penguin Books.

Sriraman, B., & English, L. D. (2010). Surveying theories and philosophies of mathematics education. In B. Sriraman, & L. D. English (Eds.), *Theories of mathematics education. Seeking new frontiers.* Heidelberg: Springer.

Sriraman, B., & Törner, G. (2008). Political union/mathematics educational disunion. In L. D. English (Ed.), *Handbook of international research in mathematics education* (2nd ed.). New York: Routledge.

Stacey, K., & Steinle, V. (2006). A case of the inapplicability of the Rasch model: Mapping conceptual learning. *Mathematics Education Research Journal 18*(2), 77–92.

Tsatsaroni, A., Lerman, S., & Xu, G. (2003). *A sociological description of changes in the intellectual field of mathematics education research: Implications for the identities of academics.* Paper presented at the annual meeting of the American Educational Research Association, Chicago. ERIC# ED482512.

Walshaw, M. (2004) Introduction: Postmodernism meets mathematics education. In M. Walshaw (Ed.) *Mathematics education within the postmodern.* Charlotte, NC: Information Age Publishing.

Wardlaw, C. (2006, September). *Mathematics in HK/China. Improving on being first in PISA.* Address to the 50th Anniversary Meeting of the Australian Mathematical Society, Sydney.

Watson, J. M. (2001). Profiling teachers' competence and confidence to teach particular mathematics topics: The case of chance and data. *Journal of Mathematics Teacher Education, 4*, 305–337.

Wilson, L., Andrew, C., & Below, J. (2006). A comparison of teacher/pupil interaction within mathematics lessons in St Petersberg, Russia and North-East of England. *British Educational Research Journal, 32*(3), 411–441.

20 Design Research
An Analysis and Critique

Paul Cobb

Vanderbilt University

Kara Jackson

University of Washington

Charlotte Dunlap

Vanderbilt University

In this chapter, we delineate the prototypical characteristics of the design research methodology and describe what is involved in conducting a design study to investigate either students' learning in a particular mathematical domain or teachers' development of increasingly sophisticated forms of practices. In addition, we discuss some of the common limitations of design studies, thereby identifying areas for attention in future studies of this type.

Design studies entail "engineering" participants' development of particular forms of practice while systematically studying the development of those practices and the context in which they emerge, which includes the designed means of support (Schoenfeld, 2006). Design studies are therefore both pragmatic and theoretical in orientation (Design-Based Research Collaborative, 2003). Pragmatically, they involve investigating and improving a design for supporting learning. Theoretically, they involve developing, testing, and revising conjectures about both learning processes and the means of supporting that learning (Gravemeijer, 1994b). The resulting theory then constitutes the rationale for the design.

Design studies can be conducted in a diverse range of settings that vary in type and scope. At one end of the spectrum, in *one-on-one design studies* a researcher conducts a series of individual teaching sessions with each of a small number of students in order to study the process of learning in a particular mathematical domain (e.g., Cobb & Steffe, 1983; Simon et al., 2010). At the other end of the spectrum, in *organizational design studies* a research team collaborates with teachers, school administrators, and other stakeholders to investigate and support the development of school and school district capacity for instructional improvement in mathematics (e.g., Cobb & Jackson, 2012; Fishman, Marx, Blumenfeld, & Krajcik, 2004). In this chapter, we focus on two common types of design studies:

- *Classroom design studies* in which a research team collaborates with a mathematics teacher (who might be a research team member) to assume responsibility for instruction in order to investigate the process of students' learning in a particular mathematical domain (e.g., Lamberg & Middleton, 2009; Lehrer & Kim, 2009; Simpson, Hoyles, & Noss, 2006; Stephan & Akyuz, 2012).
- *Professional development design studies* in which a research team works with a group of practicing mathematics teachers to support their development of increasingly sophisticated instructional practices (e.g., Cobb, Zhao, & Dean, 2009; Lesh & Kelly, 1997; Zawojewski, Chamberlin, Hjalmarson, & Lewis, 2008).

In general, it is appropriate to conduct these two types of design studies when research problems have the following two characteristics. First, the goal is to understand either how students develop specific forms of mathematical practice or how teachers develop particular forms of instructional practice. However, these developments rarely occur in situ and are therefore difficult if not impossible to study by conducting observational investigations. An interventionist methodology such as design research that aims to bring about the intended developments in order to study them is therefore appropriate. Second, current research on the process of supporting the development of the focal practice is inadequate and cannot inform the formulation of viable instructional or professional development designs. A bootstrapping methodology such as design research in which designs are improved in the course of iterative cycles of design and analysis is therefore appropriate.

Five crosscutting features characterize all types of design studies, including those that investigate students' and teachers' learning. Although some of these features are shared with other methodologies, when taken together they differentiate design research from other approaches. The first crosscutting feature is that, ideally, design studies address the types of problems that arise for practitioners as they attempt to support students' or teachers' learning, and thus contribute directly to improving the quality of educational practice.

The second feature is the highly interventionist nature of the methodology. The intent when conducting a design study is to investigate the possibilities for educational improvement by supporting either students' or teachers' development of relatively novel forms of practice in order to study their development. Consequently, the type of instruction or professional development enacted in the course of a study usually differs significantly from typical instructional or teacher education practice. The process of engineering the forms of learning being studied provides the research team with both considerable control compared with naturalistic investigations, and with the opportunity to identify forms of supports that are necessary for the development of the focal practices.

The third feature is that design studies have a strong theoretical as well as a pragmatic orientation. A primary purpose when conducting a design study is to develop theory that comprises substantiated conjectures about both processes of learning and the means of supporting that learning. These theories are modest in scope and focus on either students' development of particular types of mathematical reasoning in the classroom or teachers' development of particular forms of instructional practice in the context of professional development.

The fourth feature is that design studies involve testing and, if necessary, revising or abandoning conjectures about students' or teachers' learning processes and the means of supporting that learning. This process of testing and revising conjectures and thus of improving the associated design for supporting participants' learning involves iterative cycles of design and analysis. At any point in a design study, the evolving instructional or professional development design reflects then-current conjectures about the process of the participating students' or teachers' learning and the means of supporting it. Ongoing analyses of both the participants' activity and of the enacted supports for their learning provide opportunities to test, refine, and revise the underlying conjectures, and these revisions in turn inform the modification of the design.

The fifth crosscutting feature is that, as a consequence of the concern for theory, design studies aim for generalizability. Although a design study is conducted in a limited number of settings, the intent is not merely to investigate the process of supporting a particular group of students' or teachers' learning. Instead, the research team frames the initial design formulated when preparing for a study and the learning processes it is intended to support as an instance of a broader class of phenomena, thereby making them susceptible to theoretical analysis.

In the following sections, we first give a brief historical overview of the design research methodology to clarify its antecedents in both the learning sciences and mathematics education. We then discuss, in turn, classroom design studies and professional development design studies. For each type of study, we first consider a key research tool, the interpretive framework that the research team uses to make ongoing interpretations of participants' activity, and the enacted supports for their learning. For each, we then discuss the phases of preparing for a study, experimenting to support learning, and conducting retrospective analyses of data generated in the course of the study. Finally, we take a critical perspective by discussing some of the common limitations of each type of design study, thereby indicating areas for improvement in future studies of this type.

HISTORICAL OVERVIEW

The five defining features of design studies foreground the intimate relation between theory and practice. Methodologies in which instructional design serves as a context for the development of theories of learning and instruction have a long history, particularly in the former Soviet Union (Menchinskaya, 1969). However, the term *design research* emerged relatively recently in the learning sciences and is most closely associated with Ann Brown (1992) and Alan Collins (1992). In proposing design studies that investigated learning as it occurred in complex settings such as classrooms, Brown and Collins sought to overcome the perceived limitations of traditional studies of cognition that involve the control of variables in relatively artificial laboratory settings. They developed an analogy with design sciences such as aeronautical engineering to emphasize that the methodology is highly interventionist and has a theoretical as well as a pragmatic intent. As they explained, an aeronautical engineer creates a model that embodies theoretical conjectures, investigates how the model behaves under certain conditions, and generates data in order to test and revise the conjectures inherent in the model. Similarly, researchers conducting a design study create an initial design for supporting envisioned learning processes, investigate how the design plays out in practice, and generate data in order to test and revise theoretical conjectures inherent in the design.

Although design research in the learning sciences and in mathematics education is highly compatible, the histories differ. The emergence of the learning sciences from cognitive science signaled a relatively radical change of priorities (cf. DeCorte, Greer, & Verschaffel, 1996). In contrast, the development of design research in mathematics education has been more evolutionary and builds on two prior lines of research: the constructivist teaching experiment and Realistic Mathematics Education developed at the Freudenthal Institute in The Netherlands.

Steffe and his colleagues drew heavily on earlier Soviet work when they developed the constructivist teaching experiment methodology in the late 1970s and early 1980s (Cobb & Steffe, 1983; Steffe, 1983; Steffe & Kieren, 1994; Steffe & Thompson, 2000). The purpose of the teaching experiment as formulated by Steffe was to enable researchers to investigate the *process* by which individual students reorganize their mathematical ways of knowing. To this end, a researcher typically interacts with students one-on-one and attempts to precipitate their learning by posing theoretically motivated tasks and by asking follow-up questions, often with the intention of encouraging the student to reflect on her or his mathematical activity. The primary products of a constructivist teaching experiment typically consist of conceptual models composed of theoretical constructs that account for the learning of the participating students. Such constructs prove useful when accounting for the learning of other students, and can thus inform teachers' decision making (Thompson & Saldanha, 2000). Although the researcher acts as a teacher in this methodological approach, the primary emphasis is on the interpretation of students' mathematical reasoning rather than on the development of instructional designs.

Subsequent attempts to adapt the constructivist teaching experiment methodology to the classroom setting involved creating sets of instructional activities. However, the primary focus of these classroom experiments was on the development of explanatory constructs rather than the improvement of instructional designs (Cobb, Yackel, & Wood, 1995). For example, the intent of one series of analyses was to develop an interpretive framework that situated students' mathematical learning within the social context of the classroom (Cobb & Yackel, 1998). In retrospect, it is now apparent that a limitation in this work was the lack of specific, empirically grounded design heuristics that could inform the development of instructional activities.

The second line of research on which design research in mathematics education draws, Realistic Mathematics Education (RME), complemented the constructivist teaching experiment by focusing primarily on the design of instructional sequences rather than the development of explanatory theoretical constructs (cf. Gravemeijer, 1994b; Streefland, 1991; Treffers, 1987). RME researchers' work in developing, trying out, and modifying instructional sequences in a wide range of mathematical domains was oriented by Freudenthal's (1973) notion of mathematics as a human activity and informed by his didactical phenomenology of mathematics. The heuristics for instructional design in mathematics education that RME researchers proposed were delineated by reflecting on the process of designing and improving these specific instructional sequences (Gravemeijer, 1994a; Treffers, 1987).

It should be apparent from this brief historical account of design research that the initial focus was on supporting and investigating students' learning and that the methodology was only later extended to investigate teachers' learning. This historical overview also indicates that two types of conceptual tools are essential when conducting a design study to investigate and support either students' or teachers' learning: an interpretive framework for making sense of participants' activity in the complex settings in which design studies are conducted, and a set of design heuristics or principles that can guide the development of specific designs.

CLASSROOM DESIGN STUDIES

Interpretive Framework

In conducting a classroom design study, the research team makes ongoing interpretations of both the students' mathematical activity and the classroom learning environment. These interpretations necessarily involve suppositions and assumptions about mathematical learning processes and about the aspects of the classroom learning environment that are potentially important supports for students' learning. For example, some researchers assume that mathematical learning is a process of individual cognitive reorganization that occurs as students attempt to solve tasks and respond to the teacher's questions in the classroom (Clements & Sarama, 2004; Saldanha & Thompson, 2007). For these researchers, aspects of the classroom learning environment influence the process of students' learning by precipitating students' internal reorganization of their reasoning. Researchers who adopt this perspective on learning tend to foreground mathematical tasks together with physical, symbolic, and computer-based tools, and the teacher's questions, as key supports for students' learning. In contrast, other researchers assume that students' mathematical learning is situated with respect to classroom mathematical practices that are constituted collectively by the teacher and students (Doorman, Drijvers, Gravemeijer, Boon, & Reed, 2013; Kwon, Ju, Kim, Park, & Park, 2013; Lehrer, Kim, & Jones, 2011; Stephan & Akyuz, 2012). For these researchers, aspects of the classroom learning environment influence not merely the process of students' learning but its products, including the forms of mathematical reasoning that they develop. Researchers who take this latter perspective on learning typically focus on the affordances of classroom tasks and tools, and on the nature of classroom norms and the quality of classroom discourse as potential supports for students' learning.

A research team's suppositions and assumptions about mathematical learning are consequential because they influence ongoing design and instructional decisions. For example, Stephan and Akyuz (2012) conducted a classroom design study in which they supported the development of seventh-grade students' understanding of integers and the meaning of the minus sign. These concepts are typically included in elementary and middle-grades curricula but continue to prove problematic for students, in part because they are often reduced to procedures whose meaning can be lost (Byrnes, 1992). Stephan and Akyuz's (2012) design for supporting the participating students' learning involved problem scenarios that focused on monetary transactions and the use of the vertical number line as a tool for solving these problems. The authors drew on the emergent interpretive perspective that treats individual students' mathematical reasoning as acts of participating in collective classroom mathematical practices. Operationalizing this perspective involved strategic collection and analysis of classroom video data in addition to individual student interviews. Documenting shifts in classroom mathematical practice involved analyzing classroom discourse as both an indicator of individual mathematical reasoning and as a signal of what had become taken-as-shared within the class.

As a further example, Kwon et al. (2013) used Toulmin's (1958) scheme of argumentation as an overarching framework when they traced developments in how eighth-grade students justified their reasoning about geometric patterns. Using this framework, the researchers made interpretations of classroom events that informed the design of the various components of the classroom learning environment which were central to the design. Components included tasks that necessitated students' explicit justification of their reasoning, the organization of classroom activities, and the teacher's use of discursive moves that supported students' development of more complex and elaborated forms of argumentation. In addition, Kwon et al. used this framework when they conducted retrospective analyses of data generated during the study to connect the students' increasingly sophisticated mathematical arguments to the designed supports for their learning.

In our view, it is essential that researchers conducting a classroom design study make explicit the theoretical commitments inherent in their interpretive perspective, given the role of these commitments in orienting the design of supports for students' learning. By articulating the key constructs used when interpreting the students' mathematical activity and the classroom learning environment, the research team subjects these constructs to public debate and scrutiny. Classroom design studies conducted from a range of different perspectives can make important contributions. However, we also note that a considerable body of evidence has accumulated in the years since Brown's (1992) and Collins' (1992) pioneering work that indicates the forms of mathematical reasoning children and adults develop are shaped by the settings of their learning and, in particular, by the collective practices in which they participate while learning (Doorman et al., 2013; Hall, 2001; Hoyles, Noss, & Pozzi, 2001; Kwon et al., 2013).

Preparing for a Classroom Design Study

Specifying Goals for Students' Mathematical Learning

As we have indicated, classroom design studies are useful in testing and revising conjectures about students' development of domain-specific forms of reasoning that rarely occur in situ. In specifying the forms of mathematical reasoning that constitute the goals for students' learning, it is therefore critical to question how the mathematical domain under consideration is typically represented in curricula by identifying the central, organizing mathematical ideas. Clearly, any prior studies that have investigated the possibilities for students' mathematical learning in the focal mathematical domain are relevant in this regard. A significant number of classroom design studies have been conducted that focus on elementary domains such as early number, whereas the relevant research base of some secondary and university level domains is extremely thin.

Although the formulation of student learning goals might also be informed by national or state policy documents that detail standards for students' mathematical learning, the goals proposed for a design study typically involve a significant reconceptualization of the relevant standards. For example, the learning goals that Stephan and Akyuz (2012) formulated for their seventh-grade design study in which they investigated students' learning in the domain of integers departed from then-current state standards by emphasizing how students come to reason quantitatively about integers.

In addition to taking account of policy recommendations, the delineation of learning goals might draw on analyses of the disciplinary practice of professionals. For example, Lehrer, Schauble, Strom, and Pligge (2001) discussed a series of design studies conducted in elementary classrooms in which they first supported students' development of mathematical models that involved similarity and ratio so that students could then investigate the volume, weight, and density of different types of materials. They explained that their decision to introduce mathematical modeling and the investigation of physical attributes of materials sequentially rather than simultaneously was in response to "typical forms of integration" (p. 43) of mathematical tools and scientific contexts, which often underestimate the power of students' conceptual reasoning about the former and reduce the latter to an inauthentic context for employing procedures. As a consequence, the design studies they conducted aimed to support students' development of practices that are nearly invisible in school science but are central to the work of practicing scientists: using mathematics as a tool to reason about and model differences in the properties of materials. As a further example, Cheeseman, McDonough, and Ferguson (2012) challenged the contention that the flexible use of formal units for measuring mass is beyond first-grade students. Their design study resulted in an instructional sequence that took students from concrete and comparative heuristic measurement routines to more formalized use of tools and units, and resulted in student learning about mass and measurement typically reserved for students in older grade levels. In both of these examples, the learning goals that oriented the entire instructional design effort took account of disciplinary practice.

Documenting Instructional Starting Points

In addition to specifying explicit learning goals, it is also important to identify the aspects of students' current reasoning on which instruction can build before attempting to formulate conjectures about students' development and the means of supporting it. Prior research, such as interview and observational studies, can be useful in indicating students' initial reasoning. However, it is often necessary to create additional forms of assessments when preparing for a design study, especially if little prior work has been conducted in the relevant domain or if the proposed learning goals differ significantly from those addressed by typical instruction. These assessments usually take the form of one-on-one interviews but might also involve observations of students as they attempt to reason through tasks. In addition, written assessments can be used if the research base is strong enough to guide the development of tasks that are aligned with the overall intent of the study. For example, Stephan and Akyuz (2012) used interviews and written assessments both to identify instructional starting points and to complement classroom observations as a way of tracking developments in the participating students' reasoning during the study.

Delineating an Envisioned Learning Trajectory

The next step in preparing for a classroom design study is to develop an initial design by specifying an envisioned or hypothetical learning trajectory that comprises testable conjectures about both significant developments in students' reasoning and the specific means of supporting these developments (Simon, 1995). In this regard, it is important to clarify the design heuristics or principles that informed the development of the initial design. For example, Stephan and Akyuz's (2012) envisioned trajectory for students' learning was informed by RME and included explicit conjectures about how students' reasoning about integers might develop as they used a series of increasingly sophisticated symbolic tools to solve a sequence of instructional tasks. Similarly, Wawro, Rasmussen, Zandieh, and Larson (2013) drew on RME as they formulated their initial design for supporting college students' learning in linear algebra. For their part, Lehrer et al.'s (2001) initial conjectures included possible benchmarks in students' developing reasoning about volume and similarity together with possible types of tasks and symbolic tools. Their design of instructional tasks was informed by the heuristic that mathematical models of scientific phenomena are analogies that show and hide (or distort) different aspects of a reality (cf. Hesse, 1965). The instructional sequence that they tested and improved exploits this "mismatch, or residual between the model and the world" (Lehrer et al., 2001, p. 52) in order to support students in formulating, critiquing, and revising models of the relations between volume, weight, and density.

It is worth noting that the intent when assessing the potential of particular types of tasks and of physical or symbolic tools is to anticipate the student learning opportunities that might arise if they were to be used in the classroom. In our view, it is therefore essential to envision how the tasks and tools might actually be enacted in the classroom by considering the nature of classroom norms and discourse (Gravemeijer & Cobb, 2006). This attention to the means of support sets an envisioned learning trajectory apart from the notion of a developmental trajectory as typically used in cognitive and developmental psychology by underscoring that the envisioned developments will not occur unless appropriate supports are enacted in the classroom. It is in this sense that the forms of learning being investigated are "engineered" in the course of a design study.

In our experience, prior studies that are useful in informing the delineation of an envisioned learning trajectory focus on learning goals that are at least partially compatible with those of the planned study and include reports of the process of students' learning, the instructional setting, and the supports for that learning. Because the number of such studies is limited in many domains, the initial conjectures about students' learning and the means of supporting it are often provisional and eminently revisable. The process of formulating the envisioned learning trajectory is nonetheless valuable because the research team is then in a position to improve its initial design in a data-driven manner once it begins experimenting in the classroom.

Placing the Study in Theoretical Context

An overriding goal when conducting a classroom design study is to produce "humble theory" (Cobb, Confrey, diSessa, Lehrer, & Schauble, 2003) that can provide others with useful guidance as they attempt to support students' learning in other settings. It is therefore critical when preparing for a design study to place it in a larger theoretical context by framing it as a paradigmatic case of a broader class of phenomena. For example, Stephan and Akyuz (2012) and Lehrer et al. (2001) both sought to develop a *domain-specific instructional theory*. Stephan and Akyuz (2012) framed their study as a case of supporting the development of middle-grades students' reasoning about integers, and Lehrer et al. (2001) framed their study as a case of supporting elementary students' learning in particular mathematical and science domains.

These illustrations do not, of course, exhaust the possibilities. A series of design studies can, for example, serve as the context in which to revise and refine an initial interpretive framework that does useful work in informing the generation, selection, and assessment of design alternatives. Examples of frameworks developed in this way include the theory of meta-representational competence (diSessa, 1992, 2002, 2004), the theory of quantitative reasoning (Smith & Thompson, 2007; Thompson, 1994, 1996), the theory of actor-oriented abstraction (Lobato, 2003, 2012), and the emergent perspective on students' mathematical learning in the social context of the classroom (Cobb, Stephan, McClain, & Gravemeijer, 2001). In each of these cases, the framework was revised in response to issues encountered while using it to make sense of classroom events. As a consequence, the resulting framework does not stand apart from the practice of experimenting to support learning but is instead grounded in it. Such frameworks can function both as a source of guidance for instructional design and as tools for making sense of what is happening in the complex setting of the classroom (diSessa & Cobb, 2004).

Experimenting to Support Learning

The objective when conducting any type of design study is not to demonstrate that the envisioned learning trajectory works. The primary goal is not even to assess whether it works, although the research team will necessarily do so. Instead, the purpose when experimenting to support learning is to improve the envisioned trajectory developed during the preparation phase of the study. Improvement happens through testing and revising conjectures about both students' prospective learning processes and the specific means of supporting it.

Data Collection

Decisions about the types of data that need to be generated in the course of a study depend on the theoretical intent of the design study. The data have to make it possible for the research team to address the broader theoretical issues of which the learning setting under investigation is a paradigm case when subsequently conducting retrospective analyses. At a minimum, the research team has to collect data that allows them to document both the process of students' learning in the classroom sessions and the evolving classroom learning environment, which includes the enacted supports for the students' learning. Thus, as we have noted, Stephan and Akyuz (2001) conducted pre- and post-interviews and also used written assessments to assess shifts in individual students' reasoning about integers. Additionally, they video-recorded all classroom sessions and made copies of all the students' written work so that they could document the classroom mathematical practices that were established in the course of the study. The analysis of these data allowed the research team to investigate how the students' participation in successive practices both supported and constrained the development of the students' reasoning about integers.

Existing instruments are often not adequate because classroom design studies typically aim at novel learning goals. As a consequence, the research team usually has to devise ways of documenting the students' developing reasoning and key aspects of the classroom learning environment. The data collected in the course of a classroom design study are therefore usually qualitative for the most part. For example, one of the goals of Lehrer et al.'s (2001) study was to investigate how students might come to reason about density quantitatively. It would have been relatively straightforward to develop a pencil-and-paper assessment of students' proficiency in executing procedures for finding and comparing the densities of different materials. However, the challenge of documenting how the students' reasoning about density developed in relation to the designed classroom learning environment required that the research team conduct video-recorded one-on-one pre- and post-interviews with the participating students, video-record all classroom sessions, and make copies of all the artifacts that the students produced during the study.

Iterative Cycles of Design and Analysis

The iterative nature of a design study is a key aspect of the methodology. Each cycle involves designing instruction, enacting that design during a classroom session, and then analyzing what transpired in the classroom in order to plan for upcoming sessions. The overall goal in enacting successive design and analysis cycles is to test and improve the envisioned learning trajectory formulated during the preparation phase. As part of this testing and revision process, it is essential to have debriefing meetings after each classroom session in which members of the research team share and debate their interpretations of classroom events. Once the team has reached consensus, it can then prepare for upcoming classroom sessions by designing (or revising existing designs for) instructional tasks and considering other means of support (e.g., the renegotiation of classroom norms).

It is also useful to have longer research team meetings periodically in order to take stock of the ongoing process of testing and revising conjectures. The purpose of these meetings is to outline a revised learning trajectory for the entire study that takes account of the revisions made thus far. In our view, ensuring that there is a reflexive relationship between local judgments (e.g., the specific tasks that will be used in a particular session and the mathematical issues on which the teacher might press students) and the longer term learning goals and overall learning trajectory should be a basic tenet of design research (Simon, 1995).

Conducting Retrospective Analysis

The final phase of a design study involves conducting retrospective analyses by drawing on the entire data set generated while experimenting in the classroom. The ongoing analyses conducted while the study is in process usually relate directly to the immediate pragmatic goal of supporting the participating students' learning. In contrast, retrospective analyses seek to place this learning and the means by which it was supported in a broader theoretical context by framing it as a paradigmatic case of a more encompassing phenomenon. For ease of explication, we assume that one of the primary theoretical goals of a classroom design study is to develop a domain-specific instructional theory.

Kelly (2004) observed that methodologies are underpinned by distinct argumentative grammars that link research questions to data, data to analysis, and analysis to final claims and assertions. He noted that the argumentative grammar of mature methodologies, such as randomized field trials, can be described separately from the details of any particular study, and then went on to observe that there is no agreed-upon argumentative grammar for design research. As a consequence, "design studies lack a basis for warrant for their claims" (p. 119). This is clearly a severe weakness of the methodology. We therefore propose an argumentative grammar for classroom design studies and then discuss issues of trustworthiness specific to classroom design studies in the following paragraphs.

Argumentative Grammar

The first step in the proposed argumentative grammar is to demonstrate that the students would not have developed the documented forms of mathematical reasoning but for their participation in the design study. Assuming that sound procedures have been employed to assess developments in the students' reasoning, this step in the argument is usually straightforward because classroom design studies aim to investigate students' development of novel forms of reasoning that rarely emerge in the context of typical mathematics instruction. The team can therefore draw on prior interview and observational studies to show that the documented forms of reasoning are relatively rare. As Brown (1992) made clear, the suggestion that the students' learning can be attributed to the Hawthorne Effect is not viable because the research team has predicted the forms of reasoning the students would develop when preparing for the study.

The second, more demanding, step in the proposed argumentative grammar is to show that the findings are potentially generalizable by delineating the aspects of the investigated learning process that can be repeated in other settings. This concern for replicability does not imply that a design should be realized in precisely the same way in different classrooms. Instead, the intent is to inform others as they customize the design to the settings in which they are working by differentiating between the necessary and the contingent aspects of the design. A primary concern when conducting a retrospective analysis of the entire data corpus is to document how each successive form of reasoning emerged as a reorganization of prior forms of reasoning, and to identify the aspects of the classroom learning environment that supported the students' development of these successive forms of reasoning. The resulting domain-specific instructional theory explains how the students' learning was engineered by explicating what Brown (1992) characterized as the coupling between successive developments in their reasoning and the relevant aspects of the classroom learning environment, including the designed supports as they were enacted in the classroom. The likelihood that the research team will be able to construct a robust theory of this type is greater if it takes a broad view of possible supports that extends beyond instructional tasks and tools, and if it employs an interpretive framework that treats students' mathematical learning as situated with respect to the classroom learning environment.

It is important to note that in explaining how students' learning was supported in the design study classroom, retrospective analyses of the type that we have outlined differentiate the necessary aspects of the classroom learning environment from those that are contingent and might be varied by researchers working in other settings. For example, the sequence of instructional tasks that Stephan and Akyuz (2012) used took the notion of net worth as a grounding context for reasoning about positive and negative integers. Their retrospective analysis indicated that this task context directly supported and was necessary for the students to come to reason about integers quantitatively. Their analysis also indicated that the students' use of particular symbolic tools (such as the vertical number line), teacher press on particular issues (e.g., "Who is worth more?"), and students' use of certain gestures to indicate differences and changes in quantities were also necessary, whereas the specific number combinations used in tasks were contingent and might be varied by others building on their work.

It should be clear that the generalizability of the findings of a design study is not based on a representative sample and what Maxwell (2004) called a *regularity type of causal description* that captures observed regularities across a number of cases. Instead, it is based on a *process-oriented explanation* of a single case "that sees causality as fundamentally referring to the actual causal mechanisms and processes that are involved in particular events and situations" (Maxwell, 2004, p. 4). In this regard, Maxwell drew on Shadish, Cook, and Campbell (2002) to clarify that process-oriented explanations are concerned with "the mechanisms through which and the conditions under which the causal relationship holds" (p. 4). In the case of a domain-specific instructional theory, the mechanisms are the processes by which specific aspects of the learning environment support particular developments in students' reasoning, and the conditions are the students' reasoning at a particular point in a learning trajectory.

In summary, the argumentative grammar that we have outlined involves:

- Demonstrating that the students would not have developed particular forms of mathematical reasoning but for their participation in the design study.
- Documenting how each successive form of reasoning emerged as a reorganization of prior forms of reasoning.
- Identifying the specific aspects of the classroom learning environment that were necessary rather than contingent in supporting the emergence of these successive forms of reasoning.

In presenting this argumentative grammar, we have spoken as though a robust instructional theory can be developed in the course of a single study. However, this is not always the case, especially if the research base on which the team can build when formulating initial design conjectures is thin. Instead, it is sometimes necessary to conduct a series of studies in which the findings of one study inform the initial design for the next study (Gravemeijer & Cobb, 2006). For example, the domain-specific instructional theories that Stephan and Akyuz (2012) and Lehrer et al. (2001) developed were refined while conducting a series of studies. Even when a single study does appear to be sufficient, we believe it is useful to conduct follow-up trials with a range of participants in a variety of settings. These trials are not necessarily full-scale design studies but focus on customizing the design while working in a new setting.

Trustworthiness

Trustworthiness is concerned with the reasonableness and justifiability of claims and assertions about both successive developments in the participating students' reasoning and the aspects of the classroom learning environment that supported those developments. Clearly, a discussion of the basic tenets of qualitative data analysis is beyond the scope of this chapter. However, we should acknowledge that analyzing the large longitudinal data set generated in the course of a classroom design study can be challenging. It is nonetheless essential to analyze the entire data corpus systematically while simultaneously documenting all phases of the analysis process, including the evidence for particular inferences. Only then can final claims and assertions be justified by backtracking through the various levels of the analysis, if necessary, to the original data sources (e.g., video recordings of classroom sessions and audio-recorded student interviews). It is the documentation of the research team's data analysis process that provides an empirical grounding for the analysis. The documentation of this process enables other researchers to differentiate systematic analyses in which sample episodes are used to illustrate general assertions from untrustworthy analyses in which a few possibly atypical episodes are used to support unsubstantiated claims. Additional criteria that enhance the trustworthiness of a retrospective analysis include both the extent to which it has been critiqued by other researchers who do not have a stake in the success of the study, and the extent to which it derives from a prolonged engagement with students and teachers (Taylor & Bogdan, 1984). This latter criterion is typically satisfied in the case of classroom design studies and constitutes a strength of the methodology.

PROFESSIONAL DEVELOPMENT DESIGN STUDIES

As we have indicated, classroom design studies are frequently conducted to develop domain-specific instructional theories that consist of:

- A substantiated learning process that culminates with students' attainment of significant learning goals in a particular mathematical domain.
- The demonstrated means of supporting that learning process.

Similarly, a primary goal when conducting a professional development design study is to develop what we call a *practice-specific professional development theory* that consists of:

- A substantiated learning process that culminates with mathematics teachers' development of particular forms of instructional practice.
- The demonstrated means of supporting that learning process.

Pragmatically, professional development design studies involve supporting teachers in improving specific aspects of their instructional practice. Following Ball and Cohen (1999), we take it as given that teacher professional development should center on "the critical activities of the profession" and "emphasize question, investigations, analysis, and criticism" (p. 13). Theoretically, professional development design studies involve developing, testing, and revising conjectures about both the process by which teachers develop increasingly sophisticated instructional practices and the means of supporting that development. In this regard, Grossman, Compton, et al. (2009) observed that "practice in complex domains involves the orchestration of skill, relationship, and identity to accomplish particular activities with others in specific environments" (p. 2059). As a consequence, the conjectures about teachers' learning are not restricted to directly observable aspects of teaching (e.g., questioning students) but can include a focus on the development of particular types of knowledge (e.g., knowledge of students' mathematical reasoning in a particular domain) and beliefs (e.g., beliefs about the mathematical capabilities of particular groups of students) that are implicated in the enactment of particular instructional practices (cf. Bannan-Ritland, 2008).

As a point of clarification, we use the term *professional development* (PD) to refer to activities that are intentionally designed to support teachers' learning. PD therefore includes both pull-out sessions for teachers from a number of schools or from a single school that are led by a researcher or by a facilitator who is a member of the research team, and one-on-one support in which a researcher or a coach who is a member of the research team works with individual teachers in their classrooms.

The number of PD design studies that have been conducted is relatively small compared with classroom design studies. However, many of the basic tenets of PD design studies parallel those of classroom design studies. We will therefore focus primarily on the instances in which tenets have to be modified significantly and on additional issues that need to be addressed when conducting a PD design study.

Interpretive Framework

The interpretive framework that a research team uses when conducting a PD design study explicates its suppositions and assumptions about the process of teachers' learning and about aspects of the PD learning environment that are necessary rather than contingent in supporting that learning. This framework should address two issues that do not typically arise when conducting classroom design studies: situating participants' activity with respect to school settings and accounting for the relations between their activity across two settings.

Situating Teachers' Activity with Respect to School Settings

A key difference between classroom design studies and PD design studies concerns the extent to which it is possible (and desirable) to insulate participants from the requirements and expectations of their schools. In classroom design studies, researchers typically isolate the study classroom to the greatest extent possible when negotiating entrée to the site. In contrast, it is usually not possible to renegotiate the school settings in which the participating teachers work when developing sites for a PD design study. We view this as an advantage given that the influence of professional development on what teachers do in their classrooms is mediated by the school settings in which they teach (e.g., Bryk, Sebring, Allensworth, Luppesco, & Easton, 2010; Cobb, McClain, Lamberg, & Dean, 2003; Coburn, 2003; Grossman, O'Keefe, Kantor, & Delgado, 2013). Key aspects of school settings include the instructional materials and associated resources to which teachers have access and that they are expected to use (e.g., pacing guides and curriculum frameworks), the people to whom teachers are accountable and for what they are held accountable (e.g., school principals' expectations for mathematics instruction), and the formal and informal sources of support on which teachers can draw to improve their instructional practices (e.g., school and district PD, colleagues to whom they can turn for advice about instruction).

In light of this difference between classroom and PD design studies, it is important that the interpretive framework a research team uses when conducting a PD study situates the participating teachers' activity with respect to key aspects of the settings in which they work (cf. Zawojewski et al., 2008). For example, the framework that Cobb, McClain, et al. (2003) used in a PD design study that focused on teaching statistical data analysis in the middles grades drew primarily on Wenger's (1998) theoretical analysis of communities of practice. This approach involved documenting the practices of members of distinct communities that had a stake in middle-grades mathematics teaching and learning (e.g., school leaders, district math leaders), and analyzing the connections between communities in terms of boundary encounters, brokers, and boundary objects. This attention to the school settings in which the teachers worked resulted in greater explanatory power when accounting for the teachers' activity in both PD sessions and their classrooms. This in turn enabled the research team to adjust their PD design accordingly.

Situating Teachers' Activity with Respect to the PD Learning Environment

It is also important that the interpretive framework the research team uses situates teachers' activity with respect to the PD learning environment, including the social norms established in the sessions, the PD activities in which they engage, the tools they use, and the terminology and discourse constituted during sessions. The research team's design efforts should focus on these aspects of the PD learning environment, as a considerable body of evidence indicates that they influence the practices and associated forms of reasoning that the participating teachers develop (e.g., Horn, 2005; Kazemi & Franke, 2004; Putnam & Borko, 2000; Sherin & Han, 2004). The research teams' assumptions about teachers' learning and the PD learning environment are therefore consequential because they influence ongoing design decisions.

Accounting for the Relations Between Teachers' Activity Across Settings

In a classroom design study, the research team typically focuses on supporting students' learning within a single setting, the classroom. In contrast, the intent of a PD design study is to engage teachers in activities in one setting, the PD sessions, with the explicit goal of supporting their reorganization of their activity in another setting, the classroom. As a consequence, designs for supporting teachers' learning necessarily involve suppositions and assumptions about the relations between teachers' activity across these two settings (Cobb, Zhao, et al., 2009; Kazemi & Hubbard, 2008). As Kazemi and Hubbard (2008) and Cobb, Zhao, et al. (2009) observe, PD has traditionally reflected an assumption that the relation between a PD session and a teacher's classroom is unidirectional; teachers' activity in PD sessions is assumed to impact what they do in their classrooms. However, a model of practice-based PD challenges this assumption by proposing that teachers' ongoing practice serves as an important resource for teachers' learning (Cobb, Zhao, et al., 2009; Kazemi & Hubbard, 2008).

The assumptions a research team makes about the relations between teachers' activity across the two settings impacts both the design and the interpretation of teachers' activity. It is therefore important for researchers conducting PD design studies to be explicit about how they conceptualize these relations. For example, in the PD design experiment that focused on statistical data analysis, Cobb, Zhao, et al. (2009) found that although the participating teachers readily analyzed student work in PD sessions, they did not view this activity as relevant to their classroom practice. It subsequently became apparent that while the research team assumed the teachers would view student work as a "resource for the prospective planning of future instruction" (p. 188), they used it in the classroom solely for "retrospective assessment." This finding led the research team to modify their interpretive framework to take account of how artifacts were used in each setting, and how each influenced the other. They were then in a position to adjust their design for supporting the teachers' learning to take account of this relation.

Preparing for a PD Design Study

To avoid repetition, we take our discussion of classroom design studies as a point of reference and limit our discussion to issues that are specific to PD design studies.

Specifying Goals for Teachers' Learning

Parallel to classroom design studies, PD design studies are useful in testing and revising conjectures about teachers' development of forms of instructional practice that rarely occur in situ and for which viable designs do not currently exist for supporting the development of the focal practices and associated forms of beliefs and forms of knowledge. The forms of instructional practice that constitute the goals of a PD design study should be specified in as much detail as possible to orient the formulation of an initial design. In our view, it is essential that the targeted forms of practice can be justified in terms of student learning opportunities. This implies that the first step in delineating the goals for teachers' learning is to clarify goals for students' mathematical learning (e.g., develop conceptual understanding as well as procedural fluency, explain and justify solutions, make connections among multiple representations). The second step is to then draw on current research on mathematics teaching to identify instructional practices that have been shown to support students' attainment of these mathematics learning goals. For example, current research suggests that if students are to develop conceptual understanding as well as procedural fluency, it is important that teachers routinely pose and maintain the rigor of cognitively demanding tasks (Henningsen & Stein, 1997), elicit and build on student thinking to advance an instructional agenda (Franke, Kazemi, & Battey, 2007), and orchestrate whole-class discussions in which students are pressed to make sense of each other's solution in relation to important mathematical ideas (Stein, Engle, Smith, & Hughes, 2008). These (and other) findings can inform the specification of goals for teachers' learning.

Documenting Instructional Starting Points

In addition to specifying explicit learning goals, it is important to identify aspects of teachers' current practices and relevant forms of knowledge on which PD can build before attempting to formulate conjectures about teachers' development of the target forms of practice and the means of supporting that development. Determining which instructional starting points to document will depend on the goals of the study. For example, it may be important to document the participating teachers' mathematical knowledge for teaching (Hill, Schilling, & Ball, 2004) or their conceptions of the mathematical capabilities of traditionally underserved groups of students (Jackson & Gibbons, 2014). Documenting starting points usually involves classroom observations, assessments (of mathematical knowledge for teaching, for example), and interviews. In addition, it is important (though atypical) to document the school settings in which the participating teachers work as these settings will mediate the influence of the PD on the participating teachers' classroom practices.

Delineating an Envisioned Learning Trajectory

The next step in preparing for an experiment is to delineate an envisioned learning trajectory by formulating testable conjectures about significant developments in teachers' classroom practices, knowledge, and beliefs, and the means of supporting these developments. In doing so, it is necessary to consider how their learning in the PD sessions might relate to changes in their classroom practices as they are situated in the school settings in which they work. The current literature on teacher learning and on professional development includes only a few analyses that report actual trajectories of mathematics teachers' development of particular forms of practice (see, e.g., Franke, Carpenter, Levi, & Fennema, 2001; Kazemi & Franke, 2004; van Es & Sherin, 2008). However, the literature on teacher learning and on professional development is useful in suggesting potentially productive means of supporting teachers' learning. For example, there is some evidence that in-service teacher PD that impacts classroom instruction shares the following qualities: it is sustained over time, involves the same group of teachers working together, is focused on issues central to instruction, and is organized around the instructional materials that teachers use in their classrooms (Darling-Hammond, Wei, Andree, Richardson, & Orphanos, 2009; Garet, Porter, Desimone, Birman, & Yoon, 2001; Kazemi & Franke, 2004; Little, 2003).

In our view, the findings of recent research on practice-based preservice teacher education (e.g., Ball, Sleep, Boerst, & Bass, 2009; Lampert, Beasley, Ghousseini, Kazemi, & Franke, 2010; Lampert et al., 2013; McDonald, Kazemi, & Kavanagh, 2013) is particularly relevant in informing the design and enactment of supports for in-service teachers' learning and merits further investigation in the context of in-service teacher PD. This body of research, which is grounded theoretically in analyses of how professionals develop complex forms of practice, suggests it is crucial that teachers are provided opportunities to engage in both pedagogies of investigation and enactment (Grossman, Compton, et al., 2009; Grossman, Hammerness, & McDonald, 2009) that are organized around target instructional practices (e.g., eliciting and building on student thinking to accomplish an instructional agenda). Pedagogies of investigation involve analyzing and critiquing representations of practice such as student work and video-cases of teaching (Borko, Jacobs, Eiteljorg, & Pittman, 2009; Kazemi & Franke, 2004; Sherin & Han, 2004). Pedagogies of enactment involve planning for, rehearsing, and enacting aspects of practice in a graduated sequence of increasingly complex settings (e.g., teaching other teachers who play the role of students, working with a small group of students, teaching an entire class). Opportunity for teachers to co-participate in activities that approximate the targeted practices with more accomplished others are crucial to pedagogies of enactment (Bruner, 1996; Forman, 2003; Lave & Wenger, 1991).

In addition to indicating potentially productive types of PD activities, the current literature on teacher learning and professional development can inform the practices of facilitators in leading the enactment of those activities that can be justified in terms of teacher learning opportunities. In our view, the recent developments in preservice teacher education that we have cited are particularly promising for in-service teacher education because they reflect a bidirectional view of the relation between teachers' activity in PD sessions and their classrooms. However, because research on the processes by which teachers develop particular forms of practice is relatively thin, initial design conjectures will almost certainly be provisional and thus eminently revisable.

Placing the Study in Theoretical Context

The intent of a PD design study is to produce knowledge that will be useful in providing guidance to others as they attempt to support teachers' learning in other settings. As is the case with classroom design studies, it is therefore important to frame a PD design study explicitly as a paradigmatic case of a broader class of phenomena, for example, teachers' development of particular practices (e.g., eliciting and responding to student thinking), knowledge (e.g., of students' reasoning in a particular mathematical domain), and/or beliefs (e.g., about the mathematical capabilities of particular groups of students).

Experimenting to Support Learning

The objective when experimenting to support the participating teachers' learning is to improve the envisioned trajectory by testing and revising conjectures about both the prospective learning processes and the specific means of supporting it.

Data Collection

The data collected have to make it possible for the research team to address the broader theoretical issues under investigation when conducting retrospective analyses. At a minimum, researchers will need to collect data to document:

- Relevant aspects of the school context that might mediate the impact of the PD on teachers' resulting practices, knowledge, and/or conceptions.
- Relevant aspects of the PD learning environment, including the enacted supports for the participating teachers' learning.
- The process of the teachers' learning in the PD sessions.
- Developments in the teachers' classroom practices.

The data are likely to be primarily qualitative, given the focus on accounting for the *process* by which teachers learn, and the means by which it is supported. However, it is reasonable to include validated quantitative instruments, such as an assessment of teachers' mathematical knowledge for teaching (Hill, Ball, & Schilling, 2008), if they fit with the theoretical intent of the study and contribute to the research team's understanding of teachers' ongoing learning (cf. Lesh & Kelly, 1997).

Cycles of Design and Analysis

In PD design studies, the cycles comprise a PD session together with the researchers' debriefing meetings held after the meeting to conduct an initial (ongoing) analysis of what transpired and to plan for future sessions. The cycles depend on the frequency of the PD sessions and are therefore usually less frequent than the daily cycles of a classroom design study. In the debriefing meetings, it is important to take account of the school settings in which the teachers work when developing explanations of their activity in PD sessions as well as of their classroom instruction.

Conducting Retrospective Analysis

As is the case for classroom design studies, ongoing analyses conducted while a PD design study is in progress contribute to the immediate pragmatic goal of supporting the participating teachers' learning, whereas retrospective analyses treat the teachers' learning and the means by which it was supported as paradigmatic of a more encompassing phenomenon. In discussing retrospective analyses, we assume that one of the primary goals of the study is to develop a practice-specific PD theory.

Argumentative Grammar

The argumentative grammar that we propose for PD design studies parallels that for classroom design studies. The two major differences concern accounting for changes in the teachers' activity across settings, and the need to take account of the mediating role of the school context. Although trustworthiness is central to the argumentative grammar for PD design studies, we do not discuss it explicitly because the issues addressed when discussing classroom design studies apply equally to PD design studies.

Similar to classroom design studies, the first step in the proposed argumentative grammar is to demonstrate that the teachers would not have developed the documented forms of instructional practice but for their participation in the design study. This is usually straightforward because PD design studies typically investigate teachers' development of forms of instructional practice that rarely occur in situ and for which viable designs do not currently exist.

The second step in the argumentative grammar involves showing that the findings are potentially generalizable. This can be accomplished by delineating the aspects of the investigated learning processes and the means of supporting them that are necessary rather than merely contingent, and by reporting how the school settings in which the teachers worked mediated the influence of the PD on their classroom practices. Similar to classroom design studies, this does not imply that a design should be repeated with absolute fidelity. Instead, the intent is to inform others of the necessary aspects of the PD design and of the school settings so that they can customize the design to the settings in which they are working. This entails conducting an analysis of the entire data corpus to document how the teachers developed increasingly sophisticated forms of instructional practice, to identify aspects of the PD learning environment that supported the teachers' development of these practices, and to clarify the mediating role of the school settings in which the teachers worked.

The resulting practice-based professional development theory explains how the teachers' learning was engineered by specifying relations between successive developments in teachers' practice and the relevant aspects of the PD learning environment and the school settings. The likelihood that the research team will be able to construct a robust theory of this type is greater if they take a broad view of the school settings in which teachers work and if they employ an interpretive framework that treats teachers' learning as situated with respect to the PD learning environment and school settings.

Similar to classroom design studies, the generalizability of the findings of a PD design study is based on a process-oriented explanation, in which the mechanisms through which and the conditions under which teachers developed the documented forms of practice are reported. In the case of a practice-specific professional development theory, the mechanisms are the process by which specific aspects of the PD learning environment support teachers' successive reorganizations of their practices. The conditions are the teachers' practices at a particular point in the substantiated learning trajectory and specific aspects of the school settings.

In summary, the argumentative grammar for a PD design study involves:

- Demonstrating that the participants would not have developed particular forms of practice but for their participation in the design study.
- Identifying the specific aspects of the PD learning environment that were necessary rather than contingent in supporting the emergence of these successive forms of practice.
- Clarifying how specific aspects of the school settings mediated the influence of the teachers' learning in PD sessions on their classroom practice.

Given that the research base on which a team can build when formulating initial design conjectures for a PD design study is thin, it is unlikely that a robust practice-specific PD theory can be developed in the course of a single study. Therefore, as is the case for classroom design studies, it is probably necessary to conduct a series of studies in which the findings of one study inform the initial PD design for the next study.

As an additional observation, much of what we have said about investigating and supporting teachers' learning can be generalized to the investigation of the learning of members of other role groups whose practices are implicated in school and district instructional improvement efforts, including mathematics coaches, school leaders, or professional development facilitators. The goal of such studies would be to develop a practice-specific professional development theory that consists of:

- A substantiated learning process that culminates with the target role group's development of a particular form of (coaching, school leadership, or facilitation) practice.
- The demonstrated means of supporting that learning process.

In our view, it is reasonable to extrapolate from the teacher learning literature because there is little research on supporting coaches', school leaders', and professional development facilitators' learning.

CURRENT LIMITATIONS OF DESIGN STUDIES

To this point, we have focused on the potential contributions of design studies. It is also important to take a critical stance by considering general limitations of such studies. In discussing classroom design studies, we highlighted a major current limitation that applies to the design research methodology more generally: the lack of an explicit, agreed-upon argumentative grammar. As we indicated, this is a severe weakness that must be addressed if design research is to become a mature methodology with explicitly codified standards that can be used to judge the quality of proposals for and reports of particular classroom and professional development design studies.

A second major limitation of both types of design studies concerns the limited attention that is typically given to issues of equity. It is important to acknowledge that the complexity of students' and teachers' learning, and of the designed learning environments, makes it impossible to specify completely everything that transpires in the course of a design study (Cobb, Confrey, et al., 2003). Choices therefore have to be made when framing a design study as a paradigmatic case of a broader class of phenomena. It is nonetheless striking that few classroom and professional development design studies have been conducted that focus explicitly on equity in student learning opportunities. In this regard, a classroom design conducted by Enyedy and Mukhopadhyay (2007) is a rare exception: they attempted to support students in making increasingly sophisticated statistical arguments by drawing on their out-of-school knowledge of city neighborhoods. In reporting their findings, Enyedy and Mukhopadhyay observed that there was an inherent tension between honoring the students' local knowledge while establishing disciplinary norms of argumentation.

The failure to attend explicitly to issues of equity reflects the assumptions that designs that effectively support all students' learning can be developed without attending explicitly to issues of equity, and that designs and forms of instructional practice that are judged to be productive are necessarily equitable. In our view, both these assumptions are suspect. In our view, attending to issues of equity in classroom design studies entails documenting the distribution of students' learning opportunities and, perhaps, the development of their mathematical identities (cf. Cobb, Gresalfi, & Hodge, 2009). In the case of professional development studies, it entails specifying intended instructional practices for participating teachers for which there is evidence that these practices will support the learning of diverse groups of students or, at a minimum, a conceptual analysis that indicates they have this potential.

A third major weakness concerns the frequent failure of researchers conducting classroom and PD design studies to design for scale when preparing for studies, thereby limiting the potential pragmatic payoff and relevance of their work beyond the research community. This weakness is especially evident in many classroom design studies, as researchers conducting such studies often give little consideration to the knowledge and skill that teachers would have to develop to enact the design effectively. In many cases, the learning demands appear to be unrealistic for most teachers given their current instructional practices. This weakness is also evident in many PD design studies, though in a less extreme form because researchers conducting this type of study cannot typically insulate teachers from the school settings in which they work. However, members of the research team often "camp out" in a small number of schools as central providers of support, failing to take account of the atypical expertise they bring to supporting the participating teachers' learning. One of the strengths of the design research methodology is that it enables researchers to explore what is possible in students' or teachers' learning. As a consequence, there is typically a significant discontinuity between typical forms of education and those that are the focus of classroom and PD design studies. However, the possibility that the design developed and refined in the course of a design study might contribute to improvements in classroom teaching and learning on a large scale will be significantly reduced unless researchers consider not merely their own but others' capacity to support students' or teachers' learning when formulating the design.

One approach for circumventing this limitation is to give at least as much weight to the problems of practice that school personnel identify as to researchers' assessments of what counts as theoretically interesting problems about students' or teachers' learning (cf. Bannan-Ritland, 2008). In this approach, researchers might take practitioners' concerns as their starting point and negotiate how those issues are framed so that the study is both pragmatically and theoretically significant. For example, a study that begins with teachers' concern about motivating students might reframe the focal issue in terms of cultivating students' mathematical interests or supporting their development of productive mathematical identities. In this and similar instances, the design research methodology would approach its full potential by exploring what is possible in students' or teachers' learning in a manner that is likely to have implications for educational improvement more generally.

The fourth limitation that we identified is specific to classroom design studies and concerns the lack of attention to the instructional practices of the teacher in the study. Most researchers who conduct classroom design studies would readily acknowledge that the study teacher plays a central role in supporting the participating students' learning. However, these teachers' instructional practices are rarely the focus of explicit analysis. This is unfortunate because these teachers typically enact relatively sophisticated practices. Analysis of their practice could therefore contribute to the delineation of key aspects of inquiry-oriented mathematics instruction. This would in turn help clarify the goals for teachers' learning that should be targeted in teacher professional development in general, and in professional development design studies in particular. Kwon et al.'s (2013) investigation of the development of mathematical argumentation is a rare exception as they framed the study teacher's discursive moves as a key designed support for the participating students' learning. Such attention to the study teacher's practices can inform efforts to support the implementation of instructional sequences developed during a classroom design study in other contexts.

The final limitations are specific to PD design studies. Most of the small number of studies of this type that have been conducted have focused exclusively on teachers' participation in the PD sessions. In our view, it is also essential to document changes in the quality of the participating teachers' instructional practices by, at a minimum, conducting pre- and post-observations of their classroom teaching. In addition, researchers conducting PD design studies have rarely attempted to document the settings in which the participating teachers work. As a consequence, the teacher group is, in effect, located in an institutional vacuum. The generalizability of study findings is thus threatened, making it difficult if not impossible for other researchers to adapt the PD design to the school contexts in which they are working. In reviewing reports of professional development design studies, it also became apparent that clear standards should be established for reporting such studies. A significant proportion of the reports we reviewed failed to provide information about the design principles that underpin the PD design, the conjectures about teachers' learning and the specific means of supporting their learning, the relation between teachers' participation in professional development activities and their classroom practice, and the aspects of school settings that mediate teachers' development of the intended forms of instructional practice. Carefully planned and executed PD design studies that are adequately reported are urgently needed as they can make critical contributions to the development and refinement of practice-specific professional development theories. The failure to include this essential information in published reports makes it difficult for research teams to learn from and build on prior studies. This, in turn, limits the possibility that the field will develop robust theories regarding how teachers can be supported to develop productive forms of practice.

REFERENCES

Ball, D. L., & Cohen, D. K. (1999). Developing practice, developing practitioners: Toward a practice-based theory of professional education. In G. Sykes & L. Darling-Hammond (Eds.), *Teaching as the learning profession: Handbook of policy and practice* (pp. 3–32). San Francisco: Jossey Bass.

Ball, D. L., Sleep, L., Boerst, T., & Bass, H. (2009). Combining the development of practice and the practice of development in teacher education. *Elementary School Journal, 109*(5), 458–474.

Bannan-Ritland, B. (2008). Teacher design research: An emerging paradigm for teachers' professional development. In A. E. Kelly, R. Lesh & J. Y. Baek (Eds.), *Handbook of design research methods in education: Innovations in science, technology, engineering and mathematics learning and teaching* (pp. 246–262). New York: Routledge.

Borko, H., Jacobs, J., Eiteljorg, E., & Pittman, M. E. (2009). Video as a tool for fostering productive discussions in mathematics professional development. *Teaching and Teacher Education, 24,* 417–436.

Brown, A. L. (1992). Design experiments: Theoretical and methodological challenges in creating complex interventions in classroom settings. *Journal of the Learning Sciences, 2,* 141–178.

Bruner, J. (1996). *The culture of education.* Cambridge, MA: Harvard University Press.

Bryk, A. S., Sebring, P. B., Allensworth, E., Luppesco, S., & Easton, J. Q. (2010). *Organizing schools for improvement: Lessons from Chicago.* Chicago: University of Chicago Press.

Byrnes, J. P. (1992). The conceptual basis of procedural learning. *Cognitive Development, 7*(2), 235–257.

Cheeseman, J., McDonough, A., & Ferguson, S. (2012). The effects of creating rich learning environments for children to measure mass. In J. Dindyal, L. P. Cheng & S. F. Ng (Eds.), *Mathematics education: Expanding horizons (Proceedings of the 35th annual conference of the Mathematics Education Research Group of Australasia).* Singapore: MERGA.

Clements, D.H., & Sarama, J. (2004). Learning trajectories in mathematics education. *Mathematical Thinking and Learning, 6*, 81–89.

Cobb, P., Confrey, J., diSessa, A., Lehrer, R., & Schauble, L. (2003). Design experiments in educational research. *Educational Researcher, 32*(1), 9–13.

Cobb, P., Gresalfi, M., & Hodge, L.L. (2009). An interpretive scheme for analyzing the identities that students develop in mathematics classrooms. *Journal for Research in Mathematics Education, 40*, 40–68.

Cobb, P., & Jackson, K. (2012). Analyzing educational policies: A learning design perspective. *The Journal of the Learning Sciences, 21*(4), 487–521.

Cobb, P., McClain, K., Lamberg, T., & Dean, C. (2003). Situating teachers' instructional practices in the institutional setting of the school and district. *Educational Researcher, 32*(6), 13–24.

Cobb, P., & Steffe, L. (1983). The constructivist researcher as teacher and model builder. *Journal for Research in Mathematics Education, 14*, 83–94.

Cobb, P., Stephan, M., McClain, K., & Gravemeijer, K. (2001). Participating in classroom mathematical practices. *The Journal of the Learning Sciences, 10*(1–2), 113–163.

Cobb, P., & Yackel, E. (1998). A constructivist perspective on the culture of the mathematics classroom. In F. Seeger, J. Voigt & U. Waschescio (Eds.), *The culture of the mathematics classroom: Analysis and changes* (pp. 158–190). New York: Cambridge University Press.

Cobb, P., Yackel, E., & Wood, T. (1995). The classroom teaching experiment. In P. Cobb & H. Bauersfeld (Eds.), *Emergence of mathematical meaning: Interaction in classroom cultures* (pp. 17–24). Hillsdale, NJ: Lawrence Erlbaum Associates.

Cobb, P., Zhao, Q., & Dean, C. (2009). Conducting design experiments to support teachers' learning: A reflection from the field. *Journal of the Learning Sciences, 18*, 165–199.

Coburn, C.E. (2003). Rethinking scale: Moving beyond numbers to deep and lasting change. *Educational Researcher, 32*(6), 3–12.

Collins, A. (1992). Toward a design science of education. In T. Scanon & T. O'Shey (Eds.), *New directions in educational technology* (pp. 15–22). New York: Springer.

Darling-Hammond, L., Wei, R.C., Andree, A., Richardson, N., & Orphanos, S. (2009). *Professional learning in the learning profession: A status report on teacher development in the United States and abroad*. Dallas, TX: National Staff Development Council.

DeCorte, E., Greer, B., & Verschaffel, L. (1996). Mathematics learning and teaching. In D. Berliner & R. Calfee (Eds.), *Handbook of educational psychology* (pp. 491–549). New York: Macmillan.

Design-Based Research Collaborative. (2003). Design-based research: An emerging paradigm for educational inquiry. *Educational Researcher, 32*(1), 5–8.

diSessa, A.A. (1992). Images of learning. In E. d. Corte, M.C. Linn, H. Mandl & L. Verschaffel (Eds.), *Computer-based learning environments and problem solving* (pp. 19–40). Berlin: Springer.

diSessa, A.A. (2002). Students' criteria for representational adequacy. In K. Gravemeijer, R. Lehrer, B. v. Oers & L. Verschaffel (Eds.), *Symbolizing, modeling and tool use in mathematics education* (pp. 105–129). Dortrecht: Kluwer.

diSessa, A.A. (2004). Metarepresentation: Native competence and targets for instruction. *Cognition and Instruction, 22*(3), 293–331.

diSessa, A.A., & Cobb, P. (2004). Ontological innovation and the role of theory in design experiments. *Journal of the Learning Sciences, 13*, 77–103.

Doorman, M., Drijvers, P., Gravemeijer, K., Boon, P., & Reed, H. (2013). Design research in mathematics education: The case of an ict-rich learning arrangement for the concept of function. In T. Plomp & N. Nieveen (Eds.), *Educational design research—Part B: Illustrative cases* (pp. 425–446). Enschede, The Netherlands: SLO.

Enyedy, N., & Mukhopadhyay, S. (2007). They don't show nothing I didn't know: Emergent tensions between culturally relevant pedagogy and mathematics pedagogy. *Journal of the Learning Sciences, 16*, 139–174.

Fishman, B., Marx, R.W., Blumenfeld, P., & Krajcik, J.S. (2004). Creating a framework for research on systemic technology innovations. *Journal of the Learning Sciences, 13*, 43–76.

Forman, E.A. (2003). A sociocultural approach to mathematics reform: Speaking, inscribing, and doing mathematics within communities of practice. In J. Kilpatrick, W.G. Martin, & D. Schifter (Eds.), *A research companion to principles and standards for school mathematics* (pp. 333–352). Reston, VA: National Council of Teachers of Mathematics.

Franke, M.L., Carpenter, T.P., Levi, L., & Fennema, E. (2001). Capturing teachers' generative change: A follow-up study of professional development in mathematics. *American Educational Research Journal, 38*(3), 653–689.

Franke, M.L., Kazemi, E., & Battey, D. (2007). Mathematics teaching and classroom practice. In F.K. Lester (Ed.), *Second handbook of research on mathematics teaching and learning* (pp. 225–256). Greenwich, CT: Information Age Publishers.

Freudenthal, H. (1973). *Mathematics as an educational task*. Dordrecht, The Netherlands: Reidel.

Garet, M., S., Porter, A. C., Desimone, L., Birman, B. F., & Yoon, K. S. (2001). What makes professional development effective? Results from a national sample of teachers. *American Educational Research Journal, 38*, 915–945.

Gravemeijer, K. (1994a). *Developing realistic mathematics education.* Utrecht, The Netherlands: CD-ß Press.

Gravemeijer, K. (1994b). Educational development and developmental research. *Journal for Research in Mathematics Education, 25*, 443–471.

Gravemeijer, K., & Cobb, P. (2006). Design research from the learning design perspective. In J. v. d. Akker, K. Gravemeijer, S. McKenney, & N. Nieveen (Eds.), *Educational design research* (pp. 17–51). London: Routledge.

Grossman, P., Compton, C., Igra, D., Ronfeldt, M., Shahan, E., & Williamson, P. W. (2009). Teaching practice: A cross-professional perspective. *Teachers College Record, 111*(9), 2055–2100.

Grossman, P., Hammerness, K., & McDonald, M. (2009). Redefining teaching, re-imagining teacher education. *Teachers and teaching: Theory and practice, 15*(2), 273–289.

Grossman, P., O'Keefe, J., Kantor, T., & Delgado, P. C. (2013, April). *Seeking coherence: Organizational capacity for professional development targeting core practices in English language arts.* Paper presented at the annual meeting of the American Educational Research Association, San Francisco, CA.

Hall, R. (2001). Schedules of practical work for the analysis of case studies of learning and development. *Journal of the Learning Sciences, 10*, 203–222.

Henningsen, M., & Stein, M. K. (1997). Mathematical tasks and student cognition: Classroom-based factors that support and inhibit high-level mathematical thinking and reasoning. *Journal for Research in Mathematics Education, 28*(5), 524–549.

Hesse, M. B. (1965). *Forces and fields: A study of action at a distance in the history of physics.* Totowa, NJ: Littlefield, Adams. & Co.

Hill, H. C., Ball, D. L., & Schilling, S. G. (2008). Unpacking pedagogical content knowledge: Conceptualizing and measuring teachers' topic-specific knowledge of students. *Journal for Research in Mathematics Education, 39*(4), 372–400.

Hill, H. C., Schilling, S. G., & Ball, D. L. (2004). Developing measures of teachers' mathematics knowledge for teaching. *The Elementary School Journal, 105*(1), 11–30.

Horn, I. S. (2005). Learning on the job: A situated account of teacher learning in high school mathematics departments. *Cognition and Instruction, 23*, 207–236.

Hoyles, C., Noss, R., & Pozzi, S. (2001). Proportional reasoning in nursing practice. *Journal for Research in Mathematics Education, 32*(1), 4–27.

Jackson, K., & Gibbons, L. (2014, April). *Accounting for how practitioners frame a common problem of practice—students' struggle in mathematics.* Paper presented at the National Council of Teachers of Mathematics Research Conference, New Orleans, LA.

Kazemi, E., & Franke, M. L. (2004). Teacher learning in mathematics: Using student work to promote collective inquiry. *Journal of Mathematics Teacher Education, 7*, 203–235.

Kazemi, E., & Hubbard, A. (2008). New directions for the design and study of professional development: Attending to the coevolution of teachers' participation across contexts. *Journal of Teacher Education, 59*, 428–441.

Kelly, A. E. (2004). Design research in education: Yes, but is it methodological? *Journal of the Learning Sciences, 13*, 115–128.

Kwon, O. N., Ju, M-K., Kim, R. Y., Park, J. H., & Park, J. S. (2013). Design research as an inquiry into students' argumentation and justification: Focusing on the design of intervention. In T. Plomp & N. Nieveen (Eds.), *Educational design research—Part B: Illustrative cases.* Enschede, The Netherlands: SLO.

Lamberg, T., & Middleton, J. A. (2009). Design research perspectives on transitioning from individual microgenetic interviews to a whole-class teaching experiment. *Educational Researcher, 38*(4), 233–245.

Lampert, M., Beasley, H., Ghousseini, H., Kazemi, E., & Franke, M. L. (2010). Using designed instructional activities to enable novices to manage ambitious mathematics teaching. In M. K. Stein & L. Kucan (Eds.), *Instructional explanations in the disciplines* (pp. 129–141). New York: Springer.

Lampert, M., Franke, M. L., Kazemi, E., Ghousseini, H., Chan Turrou, A., Beasley, H., . . . Crowe, K. (2013). Keeping it complex: Using rehearsals to support novice teacher learning of ambitious teaching. *Journal of Teacher Education, 64*(3), 226–243.

Lave, J., & Wenger, E. (1991). *Situated learning: Legitimate peripheral participation.* London: Cambridge University Press.

Lehrer, R., & Kim, M. J. (2009). Structuring variability by negotiating its measure. *Mathematics Education Research Journal, 21*(2), 116–133.

Lehrer, R., Kim, M. J., & Jones, S. (2011). Developing conceptions of statistics by designing measures of distribution. *ZDM: The International Journal on Mathematics Education, 43*, 723–736.

Lehrer, R., Schauble, L., Strom, D., & Pligge, M. (2001). Similarity of form and substance: Modeling material kind. In S.M. Carver & D. Klahr (Eds.), *Cognition and Instruction: Twenty-five years of progress* (pp. 39–74). Mahwah, NJ: Lawrence Erlbaum Associates.

Lesh, R., & Kelly, A.E. (1997). Teachers' evolving conceptions of one-to-one tutoring: A three-tiered teaching experiment. *Journal for Research in Mathematics Education, 28*(4), 398–430.

Little, J.W. (2003). Inside teacher community: Representations of classroom practice. *Teachers College Record, 105*, 913–945.

Lobato, J. (2003). How design experiments can inform a rethinking of transfer and vice versa. *Educational Researcher, 32*(1), 17–20.

Lobato, J. (2012). The actor-oriented transfer perspective and its contributions to educational research and practice. *Educational Psychologist, 47*(3), 232–247.

Maxwell, J.A. (2004). Causal explanation, qualitative research, and scientific inquiry in education. *Educational Researcher, 33*(2), 3–11.

McDonald, M., Kazemi, E., & Kavanagh, S.S. (2013). Core practices and pedagogies of teacher education: A call for a common language and collective activity. *Journal of Teacher Education, 64*(5), 378–386.

Menchinskaya, N.A. (1969). Fifty years of Soviet instructional psychology. In J. Kilpatrick & I. Wirzup (Eds.), *Soviet studies in the psychology of learning and teaching mathematics* (Vol. 1, pp. 5–27). Stanford, CA: School Mathematics Study Group.

Putnam, R.T., & Borko, H. (2000). What do new views of knowledge and thinking have to say about research on teacher learning? *Educational Researcher, 29*(1), 4–15.

Saldanha, L., & Thompson, P. (2007). Exploring connections between sampling distributions and statistical inference: An analysis of students' engagement and thinking in the context of instruction involving repeated sampling. *International Electronic Journal of Mathematics Education, 2*, 270–297.

Schoenfeld, A.H. (2006). Design experiments. In P.B. Ellmore, G. Camilli, & J. Green (Eds.), *Complementary methods for research in education.* Washington, DC: American Educational Research Association.

Shadish, W.R., Cook, T.D., & Campbell, D.T. (2002). *Experimental and quasi-experimental designs for generalized causal inference.* Boston: Houghton Mifflin.

Sherin, M.G., & Han, S.Y. (2004). Teacher learning in the context of video club. *Teaching and Teacher Education, 20*, 163–183.

Simon, M.A. (1995). Reconstructing mathematics pedagogy from a constructivist perspective. *Journal for Research in Mathematics Education, 26*, 114–145.

Simon, M.A., Saldanha, L., McClintock, E., Karagoz Akar, G., Watanabe, T., & Ozgur Zembat, I. (2010). A developing approach to studying students' learning through their mathematical activity. *Cognition and Instruction, 28*, 70–112.

Simpson, G., Hoyles, C., & Noss, R. (2006). Exploring the mathematics of motion through construction and collaboration. *Journal of Computer Assisted Learning, 22*(2), 114–136.

Smith, J.P., & Thompson, P.W. (2007). Quantitative reasoning and the development of algebraic reasoning. In J.J. Kaput, D.W. Carraher, & M.L. Blanton (Eds.), *Algebra in the early grades* (pp. 95–132). Mahwah, NJ: Lawrence Erlbaum Associates.

Steffe, L. (1983). The teaching experiment methodology in a constructivist research program. In M. Zweng, T. Green, J. Kilpatrick, H. Pollak, & M. Suydam (Eds.), *Proceedings of the Fourth International Congress on Mathematical Education* (pp. 469–471). Boston: Birhauser.

Steffe, L., & Kieren, T.E. (1994). Radical constructivism and mathematics education. *Journal for Research in Mathematics Education, 25*, 711–733.

Steffe, L., & Thompson, P.W. (2000). Teaching experiment methodology: Underlying principles and essential elements. In A.E. Kelly & R. Lesh (Eds.), *Handbook of research design in mathematics and science education* (pp. 267–307). Mahwah, NJ: Lawrence Erlbaum Associates.

Stein, M.K., Engle, R.A., Smith, M.S., & Hughes, E.K. (2008). Orchestrating productive mathematical discussions: Five practices for helping teachers move beyond show and tell. *Mathematical Thinking and Learning, 10*(4), 313–340.

Stephan, M., & Akyuz, D. (2012). A proposed instructional theory for integer addition and subtraction. *Journal for Research in Mathematics Education, 43*, 428–464.

Streefland, L. (1991). *Fractions in realistic mathematics education. A paradigm of developmental research.* Dordrecht, The Netherlands: Kluwer.

Taylor, S.J., & Bogdan, R. (1984). *Introduction to qualitative research methods: The search for meanings* (2nd ed.). New York: John Wiley & Sons.

Thompson, P.W. (1994). Images of rate and operational understanding of the Fundamental Theorem of Calculus. *Educational Studies in Mathematics, 26*, 229–274.

Thompson, P.W. (1996). Imagery and the development of mathematical reasoning. In L.P. Steffe, P. Nesher, P. Cobb, G. Goldin, & B. Greer (Eds.), *Theories of mathematical learning* (pp. 267–283). Hillsdale, NJ: Lawrence Erlbaum Associates.

Thompson, P.W., & Saldanha, L.A. (2000). Epistemological analyses of mathematical ideas: A research methodology. In M. Fernandez (Ed.), *Proceedings of the Twenty-Second Annual Meeting of the North American Chapter of the International Group for the Psychology of Mathematics Education* (Vol. 2, pp. 403–407). Columbus, OH: ERIC Clearinghouse for Science, Mathematics, and Environmental Education.

Toulmin, S.E. (1958). *The uses of argument*. Cambridge: Cambridge University Press.

Treffers, A. (1987). *Three dimensions: A model of goal and theory description in mathematics instruction—The Wiskobas Project*. Dordrecht, The Netherlands: Reidel.

van Es, E.A., & Sherin, M.G. (2008). Mathematics teachers' "learning to notice" in the context of a video club. *Teaching and Teacher Education, 24,* 244–276.

Wawro, M., Rasmussen, C., Zandieh, M., & Larson, C. (2013). Design research within undergraduate mathematics education: An example from introductory linear algebra. In T. Plomp & N. Nieveen (Eds.), *Educational design research—Part B: Illustrative cases* (pp. 905–925). Enschede, The Netherlands: SLO.

Wenger, E. (1998). *Communities of practice: Learning, meaning, and identity*. New York: Cambridge University Press.

Zawojewski, J., Chamberlin, M., Hjalmarson, M.A., & Lewis, C. (2008). Developing design studies in mathematics education professional development: Studying teachers' interpretive systems. In A.E. Kelly, R. Lesh, & J.Y. Baek (Eds.), *Handbook of design research methods in education: Innovations in science, technology, engineering and mathematics learning and teaching* (pp. 219–245). New York: Routledge.

21 The Intertwining of Theory and Practice
Influences on Ways of Teaching and Teachers' Education

Annalisa Cusi

University of Torino

Nicolina A. Malara

University of Modena and Reggio Emilia

INTRODUCTION

In the last decades the role of theory in Mathematics Education (ME) has so increased that Artigue (2011) speaks of "theoretical explosion in ME," and surveys and books about theories of ME have been published with the aim of comparing and reflecting on different studies and trying to constitute a common ground for scholars (Lerman, 2006; Cobb, 2007; Simon, 2009; Sriraman & English, 2010).

Niss (2007) stresses the benefits that theory offers: it provides explanations or predictions of certain phenomena; it helps and guides action and behavior in specific implementations in order to achieve certain goals; but, most importantly, it provides a structured set of lenses through which it is possible to look at phenomena and methods in order to answer research questions. Silver and Herbst (2007) underline that at the beginning research in ME has been done to respond to problems derived from practice but, in time, theory has assumed its own character, becoming central in ME research. They also highlight a widespread prejudice about theory among teachers and practitioners, who often conceive it as irrelevant for practice. This fact has been also stressed by Roesken (2011) and Boaler (2008), who declare that few researchers manage to uncover something that makes a real difference to children and adults in their experience of mathematics. Sowder (2007) observes that the reason why many teachers do "not believe theories about student learning" is that often researchers do not "work with teachers on classroom research that builds on and tests the theories about student learning" (p. 214).

In the research arena, in some cases ME tends to be accepted at the level of pure scientific speculation, with no connection to the most pressing needs of teachers and without taking into account the teachers' reality and the constraints of their environment. Kieran, Krainer, and Shaughnessy (2013) claim that a distinctive gap between research and practice is created because too often in ME research teachers are viewed as "recipients."

Since the 1980s, some important scholars, such as Kilpatrick (1981) and Freudenthal (1983), pinpointed this separation. Wittmann (2001), quoting also other researchers, argues in favor of a reorientation of research towards practice. Other scholars underline that the communication of research results must be increased among teachers (Bishop, 1998; Lester & Wiliam, 2002; Boaler, 2008). In particular Boaler (2008) observes that the impact of research on practice would be stronger if researchers, in the planning of their studies, would consider what are the arguments that may engage teachers and the issues with which they may identify.

Yet, other scholars underline the benefits for teachers arising from their interaction with researchers on theoretical questions related to the classroom activity in the realm of teacher education programs (Jaworski, 2008; Kieran et al., 2013; White, Jaworski, Agudelo-Valderrama, & Gooya, 2013).

In tune with these and other studies (see for instance Mason, 1990), we are convinced that theory could play the role of a fundamental mediator in reducing the gap between research and practice, and that a fruitful interrelation between these two poles could be fostered if suitable research projects and teacher education programs were conceived with the aim of both actively involving teachers in the field of practice and, at the same time, motivating them to approach theory to elicit indications and tools to analyze their own practice.

In a previous work (Malara & Zan, 2008), it has been suggested that a possible way of minimizing the research/practice gap could be to focus, in tune with an idea of teacher as a decision maker, on teacher education programs where teachers and researchers are dialogically involved. In particular, it has been stressed that teachers and researchers play a fundamental role within these programs in mediating between theory and practice, highlighting how, on one side, the contact with theory changes teachers' decision processes, and therefore their practice, and, on the other side, the contact with practice changes researchers' decision processes, and therefore theory.

For these reasons, in this chapter we discuss the relationship between theory and practice, looking at the research on mathematics teacher education that underlines the role of theory in restructuring both the teacher's knowledge for teaching and the teacher education practice.[1] Specifically, we will discuss two main themes: (1) the implications, for both research and teacher education, of the idea of teacher as a decision maker; (2) the use of theory as a lens to reflect on teachers' practice in teacher education programs, with a focus on the results from our experience and on the new research perspectives offered by these results.

THE TEACHER AS A DECISION MAKER: IMPLICATIONS FOR BOTH TEACHER EDUCATION AND RESEARCH ON IT

In a previous work (Malara & Zan, 2008) a vision of teaching as an activity of problem solving and problem posing has been proposed, stressing that the complexity of teaching processes implies that every teacher is required not only to find a solution to the problems arising in the classroom, but first of all to identify them. One of the main implications of this vision is that in teaching mathematics a teacher must do much more than merely convey knowledge through the "right" words or actions. He/she has the responsibility not only of creating an environment that allows pupils to build up mathematical understanding, but also of making hypotheses about pupils' conceptual constructs and the possible didactical strategies to help them modify such constructs. Therefore, in agreement with some U.S. scholars (see for instance Carpenter, 1988), we focus on the role played by the teacher as a decision maker. With this expression we intend a thoughtful professional who brings into the class a socio-constructive and evolutive vision of mathematics, who is aware of his/her role, and who is able to consciously observe and control his/her behavior when facing contingent actions and making sudden decisions. In our educational programs we work with and for teachers with the aim of making them become more sensitive and effective decision makers.

In the last decades, researchers have underlined the need of considering teacher and students variables in the contexts in which they are placed, as Lerman (2000) stresses, speaking of a "social turn in mathematics education research." This new perspective has led, initially to studies on students' learning in social settings through nonroutine tasks and, more recently, to the study of teachers' learning and change, professional growth and identity. In tune with this evolution, we will focus on this second aspect.

Starting with Shulman's work (1986), many researchers have considered the manifold components of the knowledge necessary to the teachers practice (Cochran-Smith & Lytle, 1999; Sowder, 2007; Ball, Thames, & Phelps, 2008). Recently Barwell (2013) has written on the importance of focusing on teachers' knowledge about the dynamics that characterize students' thought processes during class activities. Moreover, Schoenfeld (2013) has stressed the importance of studying the interaction between teachers' knowledge, resources, goals, beliefs, and orientations and their in-the-moment decision making. This position is consistent with the studies (Malara & Zan, 2008; Thames & Van Zoest, 2013; Sowder, 2007; Roesken, 2011) that discuss the crucial role played by an investigation in situ of the interrelationships between teacher knowledge, beliefs, and emotions because it allows the teachers to become aware of the mismatch between their espoused beliefs and the beliefs that emerge from practice.

Two themes can be considered the most relevant trends of the studies on and with teachers: (1) to understand how teachers learn from their experiences; and (2) to change teachers' knowledge, beliefs, and practice (Goos, 2013).

With reference to these themes, we agree with Thames and Van Zoest (2013), who stress the need of developing studies aimed at the analysis of the effects of specific teacher actions on students' learning. We are, in fact, convinced that these kinds of studies may engender what Goos (2013) calls "productive tensions between teachers' thinking, actions, and professional environments" that "can become opportunities for teacher change" (p. 521). We refer to the term *teacher change* in the sense of "teacher's aware professional evolution" that occurs in time and that can imply a shift of his/her paradigms.[2] Chapman and Heater (2010), studying teachers involved in a developmental program, state that the change needed to traditional teachers to become nontraditional inquiry-oriented teachers is not simple to achieve because the level of change that the teachers desire is often different.

The problematic questions linked to an effective teacher change have been discussed also by Simon (2013), who explains teachers' resistance to change, admitting that it is very difficult for any experience to profoundly affect the complex structures that constitute the basis for teachers' practices and strictly influence what teachers do and their way of interpreting everything that happens ("major assimilatory structures of teachers"). He therefore recognizes the importance of the role played by researchers in promoting effective opportunities for teacher change.

We are convinced that in order to foster teacher change it is necessary to study individual teachers in depth and to provide detailed analyses of their teaching processes, sharing with them this analysis and helping them to develop resulting reflections (Malara & Zan, 2008; Cusi & Malara, 2012, 2013). The role played by teachers' reflection and awareness for effective changes will be discussed in the next section.

THE ROLE OF THEORY FOR THE DEVELOPMENT OF TEACHERS' AWARENESS: A FOCUS ON TEACHER EDUCATION PROGRAMS

Since the 1990s, research in mathematics teaching insists on the need for teachers' reflection about their own practice (Mason, 1998, 2002; Jaworski, 1998). Referring to Schön, Jaworski introduces the term *reflective practice* to define the kind of practice that results from this reflection: "The essence of reflective practice in teaching might be seen as the making explicit of teaching approaches and processes so that they can become the objects of critical scrutiny" (1998, p. 7). Through reflective practice teachers become aware of *what* they are doing and *why*: awareness is therefore the product of a process of reflection.

Mason (1990, 1998, 2002) emphasizes the role of awareness in teaching. He distinguishes between (1) *awareness-in-action*, which is defined as "the powers of construal and of acting in the material world"; (2) *awareness-in-discipline*, that is, the awareness of awareness-in-action; and (3) *awareness-in-counsel*, which represents the awareness of the whole educative project.

According to Mason (1998, 2008), fostering students' development of an explicit awareness of their awareness-in-action requires teachers to become aware "not simply of the fact of different ways of intervening, but of the fact of subtle sensitivities that guide or determine choices between types and timings of interventions" (2008, p. 49). Therefore teacher educators should foster in teachers relevant shifts of attention, directing their attention toward constructs, theories, and practices that can inform and guide their future choices.

Jaworski (2004) has stressed the value not only of teachers' critical reflection about their practice, but also of the sharing of these reflections between teachers and between researchers and teachers within a community of inquiry. She stresses that this dialogical model is particularly relevant to teacher professional development because it makes teachers conduct research on their own practice and, consequently, develop a critical intelligence and an increasing awareness of the different aspects to be faced during the teaching processes.

Boaler (2008) states that it is necessary to build a "culture in which teachers see themselves as needing to learn from research on a regular basis" (p. 100) because, in this way, teachers may be encouraged to think that research results would be helpful to their teaching. She therefore stresses the need of a radical shift that involves "changing the teaching profession to be one that conducts its own research" (p. 101). Lerman (2013), too, underlines the need of involving teachers in the analysis of their practice, making them active parts of research projects.

We are in tune with these positions and believe that suitable research projects and teacher education programs should be conceived with the aim of actively involving teachers in the field of practice and, at the same time, motivating them to approach theory to elicit useful tools to analyze their own practice. In the last decade, different teacher education paths have been planned with the aim of fostering a real teachers' involvement and their active collaboration with researchers. In these cases the teacher education process acquires the typical characteristics of a path of introduction to research (Jaworski, 2006; Cusi & Malara, 2011, 2012; Mellone, 2011; Potari, 2013). In most of these projects the teachers play the role of "teacher-researchers." This term has been used with different meanings, but in our view a distinctive character of the teacher-researcher is his/her conquest of an autonomous relationship with theory, as a result of an effective long-term dialogue with researchers.

In a recent work Jaworski (2012) uses the term *teacher-as-inquirer* to indicate the role played by teachers who collaborate in research projects and are motivated to undertake inquiry-based practice, to give time to collaboration with didacticians,[3] and to engage seriously with reflective developmental practice. Also the work done by Goodchild (2008) can be considered in this perspective. Goodchild claims that "developmental research in communities of inquiry is 'good' research in the ethical sense" because "it empowers teachers, students, and didacticians, to begin to take control of their professional practices and empowers them to be, in their school teams, self-sufficient in development" (2008, pp. 214–215).

Potari (2013) has implemented a course for teachers aimed at fostering their construction of bridges between the activity of research and the activity of teaching, where the reference to the theory is fundamental. She states that during the course the teachers undertook actions such as "reading and presenting research papers focusing on the research goals, the tasks used, and the main findings; reflecting on what ways they could use research findings in their teaching; designing mathematical examples and tasks and justifying their choices based on research; analyzing mathematics tasks, classroom dialogues, and students' work by using analytical models offered by research; collaborating with other teachers on designing, implementing, and evaluating a classroom intervention based on research findings with a focus on students' mathematical understanding" (Potari, 2013, p. 512).

As we will explain in the following section, our approach is in tune with the choice of working on theory in order to make the teachers acquire new useful tools that can help them become more sensitive in perceiving and interpreting class processes.

THEORY AS A LENS TO REFLECT ON TEACHERS' PRACTICE: OUR METHODOLOGY OF WORK WITH AND FOR TEACHERS

In our previous studies (Malara, 2003; Malara & Zan, 2008; Cusi & Malara, 2008, 2012; Cusi, Malara, & Navarra, 2011)—realized in the realm of the Aral Project[4]—we have introduced our methodology of work with and for teachers. In tune with what we have presented here, our research is based on the hypothesis that observation and critical-reflective study of socio-constructive classroom processes are necessary conditions to foster teachers' development of awareness about the roles they must play in the class, the dynamics that characterize the mathematical collective construction, and the variables that intervene (Malara, 2003). In the perspective of constituting a community of inquiry, the teachers are organized in groups according to the activities that they experiment with in their classes. Each group is coordinated by a researcher-mentor, who frequently has face-to-face and e-mail exchanges with the teachers. Periodically, work sessions conducted by the project leader, and joint meetings with all the teachers and researchers involved in the research are realized.

Our aim is to make teachers: (a) acquire an increasing capability of interpreting the complexity of class processes and reflecting on the effectiveness of the role they play; (b) develop awareness about the effects of their micro-decisions; (c) become able to better control their behaviors and communicative styles; and (d) observe, during the development of class activities, the influence of this critical-reflective study on students' behaviors and learning.

In order to fulfill these objectives, we involve teachers in a complex activity of critical analysis of the transcripts of audio recordings[5] concerning classroom processes and associated reflections. This activity is aimed at throwing light on the interrelation between students' construction of knowledge and the teacher's behaviors in guiding them perform this construction. The analysis is carried out by developing what we call *Multi-commented Transcripts* (MT).

The development of MT starts when the experimenters-teachers send the transcripts of their lessons, together with their comments and reflections, to mentors-researchers. Subsequently, the mentors-researchers make their own comments and send them back to the authors, to other teachers involved in similar activities, and sometimes to other researchers. Often, the authors make further interventions in this cycle, commenting on comments or inserting new ones.

The main characteristic of this methodology is the "choral" exchange that is at the basis of MT and of the richness of the reflections that emerge from the comments. Since MT outline an overall frame of teacher's didactical action, they could help in highlighting if the didactical praxis is coherent with the references to the involved theory. In this way, MT become useful working tools for teachers and researchers, providing them with new elements that can help enhance their interventions. Moreover, they foster—through a comparison between different teachers and periodic shared reflections—the identification of the distinctive elements of teachers' actions and a reflection on their effectiveness.

The critical analysis we developed with teachers through the MT methodology enabled us to perceive, in spite of the support given by theoretical studies, some teachers' incapability of critically controlling class processes (see for example, in Cusi et al., 2011, our categorization of metacognitive and nonmetacognitive teachers in their action in the classroom and in the a posteriori reflection upon their action). For this reason, our objective in the work with teachers is to provoke shifts of attention for them in the reflection on their actions, moving from a focus on student behaviors to a focus on teachers' attitudes and behaviors, and on their effects on students (Malara & Navarra, 2011).

In order to promote these shifts of attention, we have recently modified our methodology for working with teachers. The hypothesis underlying this methodology is that the development of teachers' awareness-in-discipline could be fostered if the usual activities of reflection on their practice are carried out in reference to specific indicators. These indicators provide teachers with "theoretical lenses" to which they can refer as interpretative keys in the analysis of class processes.

As we will clarify in the following, this approach is in tune with both the learning study's distinguishing features (Marton & Morris, 2002) and with the approach presented by Potari (2013), which shares the same objective of supporting "teachers to develop an inquiry stance of mathematics teaching that could form a solid base for their autonomous development as mathematics teachers" (p. 512).

Our current teacher education processes are characterized by a constant dialectic between theoretical aspects related to classroom actions and didactical implementations. Before describing this new methodology in detail, we present a theoretical construct we have shared with teachers for the analysis of their practices.

A THEORETICAL CONSTRUCT FOR THE ANALYSIS OF TEACHER'S ACTIONS

During our previous studies aimed at fostering a constructive didactic of algebra as a tool for thinking (Cusi & Malara, 2009, 2013), we developed a theoretical construct conceived as a means to study the teacher's actions during class activities. In the analysis performed through this theoretical construct, the specific mathematical content (in our case the construction of proofs through algebraic language) is taken into account.

In our research work, in fact, our constant objective is to combine two poles that seem to be "dangerously" separated in literature (Harel, 2010[6]; Roesken, 2011[7]): content to be taught and teacher's actions.

This construct, which will be referred to as $M\text{-}_{AE}AB$ (acronym for *Model of Aware and Effective Attitudes and Behaviors*), specifies a set of characters and actions that outline a profile of a teacher who is able to effectively guide his/her students in the processes of reasoning's construction through algebraic language (see Cusi & Malara, 2009, 2013; Cusi, 2008).

The $M\text{-}_{AE}AB$ construct has been conceived within a theoretical frame essentially constituted by two triads of components: the first triad is related to the development of the mathematical content in the teaching/learning process and refers to the role played by algebraic language in the construction of thinking; the second triad refers to the social dimension of the teaching/learning processes and to the role played by the teacher during class activities.

The first triad considers three aspects that are connected to students' development of reasoning through algebraic language: (a) the idea of *conceptual frames* introduced by Arzarello, Bazzini, and Chiappini (2001),[8] who have highlighted the importance of activating different conceptual frames and of changing from one frame to another in order to correctly interpret the different algebraic expressions constructed while solving a problem; (b) the concept of *anticipating thought* developed by Boero (2001), who has focused on the role it plays in the construction of reasoning through processes of transformation; (c) the concept of *representation register* analyzed by Duval (2006), who has identified in the coordination of different registers a key aspect for the learning of mathematics.

Our research work (Cusi, 2009) has enabled us to show that an effective use of algebraic language for the construction of proofs requires the application and combination of three main key components: (a) the appropriate activation and coordination between different conceptual frames; (b) the activation of appropriate anticipating thoughts; and (c) the coordination between algebraic and verbal registers.

Since we are convinced that students' development of these competencies is strictly related to both the teacher's way of acting while he/she faces the class activities and the time he/she devotes to meta-aspects and to reflections, the second triad of our theoretical frame refers to methodological aspects and to the socio-constructive dynamics involved in the teaching/learning processes. It therefore considers three main components that have to be conceived on the same level.

The first component of this triad is Vygotskyan. Our source of inspiration was Vygotsky's emphasis (1978) on the central role that the child's imitation of the adult's actions plays in his/

her mental development. Vygotsky stresses the importance of an instruction aimed at stimulating students' activation of internal learning processes through their interaction with the teacher and/or with more expert classmates, because this interaction enables them to reach an higher level of mental development. As regards the activities that involve the construction of reasoning through algebraic language, we are convinced that it is necessary for students to be immersed into contexts (such as those advocated by Schoenfeld (1992) within which mathematical sense-making is practiced and developed in a way that fosters students' conquest of a real awareness of the meaning of class activities. For this reason, the second component of our second triad is Leont'ev's work (1978) on the interrelation between the activities realized in social contexts and the development of a real awareness about the meaning of these activities. Leont'ev stresses, in particular, that the knowledge assimilated by students can really educate them only if they are previously educated to an aware relationship with knowledge.

Vygotsky and Leont'ev ideas on the centrality of interaction in both the learning processes and the processes of construction of meaning about learning represent an important reference for our planning of class activities.

Moreover, Vygotsky's stress on the importance of the role played by the adult in encouraging the child's transition from a potential to an actual mental development led us to define a first idea of the teacher's action. This idea is in tune with the theory of cognitive apprenticeship (Collins, Brown, & Newman, 1989), the third component of the second triad.

Through this theory, Collins et al. (1989) propose a model of instruction that takes inspiration from apprenticeship in practical professions. The authors highlight some key aspects of apprenticeship that could become useful references in the teaching of specific subjects such as problem solving, reading comprehension, or writing. In particular, they focus on the fact that, differently from those students who receive a traditional "transmissive" teaching, apprentices can "see" the processes of work in the same moment in which they are realized. But, while manual labor activities—the object of traditional apprenticeship—are directly observable, the practice of problem solving, reading comprehension, and writing is not directly observable because thinking processes are mainly invisible.

The cognitive apprenticeship theory intends to "make thinking visible." Collins et al. (1989) identified four dimensions (content, method, sequencing, and sociology) to which they associate a set of meaningful characters for constructing and evaluating learning contexts. We focus on two dimensions in particular that constitute the main reference in our analysis of teaching/learning processes: method and sociology.

Method refers to those teaching methods that, according to Collins et al. (1989), should be designed to give students the opportunity to observe, engage in, and invent or discover expert strategies in context. Among them, modeling, coaching, scaffolding, and fading play key roles in fostering students' development of grounded abilities through processes of observation and guided practice. *Modeling* requires an expert to carry out a task externalizing his/her internal processes—that is, the heuristics and the activated control processes—in order to enable students construct a conceptual model of the processes required to perform a task. *Coaching* is the expert's observation of students while they are facing a task, in order to give them stimuli, supports, feedback, and possibly new tasks aimed at making them improve their performance. *Scaffolding* refers both to the support the teacher gives students in carrying out a task and to the gradual removal of this support to enable students to autonomously complete the task. Collins et al. (1989) introduce the term *fading* to objectify this second significant aspect of scaffolding.

The methods referred to as *articulation* and *reflection* characterize the activities aimed at making students both focus on their observation of experts' approaches and learn how to consciously control their own strategies. Articulation involves those methods aimed at getting students to articulate their knowledge, reasoning, or problem-solving processes. Reflection involves those methods that are aimed at making students compare their own problem-solving processes with those of an expert, another student, and even an internal cognitive model of expertise.

The sociology dimension refers to the social aspects of the learning environment: in cognitive apprenticeship, apprentices learn to develop abilities in the context of their application to problems, within a culture focused on and defined by expert practice.

We think that the cognitive apprenticeship paradigm could also be a useful reference for both teachers and researchers in their planning, implementation, and joint analysis of the teaching/learning processes aimed at fostering an effective use of algebraic language as a thinking tool. We believe that the games of interaction and coordination between the syntactical level, the interpretative level, and the level of activation of anticipating thoughts (which can be automatically set up by an expert) should be "made visible" to novices in order to make them acquire and understand their meaning. Therefore the hypothesis on which our research is based is that students should acquire the teacher's attitudes and behaviors during class interaction through a process of cognitive apprenticeship that enables students to progressively construct the competencies and awareness necessary to effectively face proofs through algebraic language. In this way students can internalize the teacher's strategies and develop (thanks to the meta-reflections about the actions that they have performed) a real awareness of the activities realized in the class.

The idea of a teacher who is able to activate in his/her students processes of "imitation," in a Vygotskyan[9] sense, to foster their assimilation of specific suitable strategies for an effective approach to problem-solving activities, led us to focus on one of the possible roles that a teacher could play in his/her classes: the role of model (that becomes particularly meaningful in relation to the activities on which our research is focused). This idea is also in tune with what Lerman (2000) suggests: "The teacher may perform the role of 'master' for some students in relation to some aspects of what we might call the mathematical identities produced" (p. 33).

Mason's (2008) interpretation of the role played by the mathematics teacher during class activities is also consistent with this idea. Mason stresses that, in order to realize real mental development, it is important not to underestimate the problem of the widespread discrepancy between what the teacher thinks he/she is communicating to students and what they really understand. According to Mason, this problem can be solved if the teacher works in his/her class with the constant aim of "educating awareness," initially using particular repeated prompts, and then using less and less direct prompts, or using meta-questions aimed at helping students internalize these prompts so that they can autonomously refer to these stimuli in specific situations, even when the teacher does not explicitly remind students of them.

The characters highlighted by the M-$_{AE}$AB construct are those of a teacher who acts with the main aim of "making thinking visible" and, at the same time, is aware of the incidence of his/her actions for the students' development of awareness. These characters have been identified thanks to the analysis of both small group activities carried out by students aged 15–16 and the collective discussions conducted by their teachers during teaching experiments aimed at introducing activities of proof construction through algebraic language. This analysis enabled us to show the effects of the different approaches of the teachers involved in our experimentations, from the point of view of both students' manifested awareness and their achieved competencies. Through the comparison between teachers' different approaches we were able to make clearly evident that inappropriate teacher choices prevent students from acquiring the necessary competencies and from developing awareness; at the same time it allowed the identification of the teacher's characters that foster the construction of the key competencies for an effective development of algebraic thinking (Cusi, 2008; Cusi & Malara, 2009).

A first group of these characters refer to the roles that a teacher should play in order to pose him/herself not as a "mere expert" who proposes effective approaches, but as a learner who faces problems with the main aim of making visible the hidden thinking, with the aims, the meaning of the strategies, and the interpretation of results. These roles, which could be placed within the categories of modeling and coaching, are that of: (a) *investigating subject*, who stimulates an attitude of research towards the problem being studied, and as a constituent part of the class in the research work being activated; (b) *practical/strategic guide*, who shares (rather than transmits) with his/her students the adopted strategies and the knowledge to be locally activated; (c) *activator of interpretative processes* and *activator of anticipating thoughts*, who simulates and provokes the construction of the key-competencies for the development of thought processes through algebraic language.

The second group of characters refers to the roles that the teacher plays when he/she becomes a point of reference for students to help them clarify salient aspects at different levels and become aware of the meaning of the realized activities and of the learning processes themselves. These roles, which could be placed within the categories of articulation and reflection, are that of: (a) *guide in controlling the meaning* of the constructed algebraic expressions, at both the syntactical and the semantic level, in order to maintain a harmonized balance between these two aspects; (b) *reflective guide*, who makes students reflect on the effective approaches carried out during class activities and helps them identify effective practical/strategic models from which they can draw their inspiration; (c) *activator of reflective attitudes* and *activator of meta-cognitive acts*, with the aim of instilling the control of the global sense of the activated processes (see also Cusi & Malara, 2013, where these two groups of roles are presented showing the links with the underpinning two triads of theoretical components).

A PATH FOR TEACHER EDUCATION AIMED AT MAKING TEACHERS DEVELOP NEW AWARENESS

We can now present in detail the activities—preliminary to those devoted to a shared critical reflection (through the MT methodology)—that we have inserted within our methodology of work with teachers. They are characterized by a moment of study/reflection and a moment of action/reflection.

The *moment of study/reflection* is subdivided into two phases: (1) the *theoretical study* of research papers; and (2) the *analysis of the practice of others*, namely activities of analysis of extracts of class discussions conducted during previous experimentations, aimed at showing how the use of the theoretical constructs previously introduced enables us to highlight problematic or effective aspects related to the teacher's actions.

The *theoretical study* (Phase 1) is at three levels: the sense of the discipline, the study of the processes that intervene, and the modeling of the teacher's actions (in particular, the $M\text{-}_{AE}AB$ construct is introduced).

During the activities of *analysis of the practice of others* (Phase 2), teachers are required to analyze the extracts of collective discussions about the construction of proofs through algebraic language, focusing on the approach of the teacher and on students' interventions, trying to individuate, referring to the identified lenses: (a) the moments in which the teacher plays roles in tune with the $M\text{-}_{AE}AB$ construct; (b) the moments in which the teacher's approach distances itself from the one that could be characterized through the $M\text{-}_{AE}AB$ construct; (c) the positive and/or negative effects of the teacher's work on students, in terms of competencies and awareness shown by students during the collective discussion.

The teachers are involved in two further interrelated phases, constituting the moment of action/reflection: (3) the *phase of planning/action*, namely the design of activities to be proposed to their classes, planning the methodology to be adopted referring to the introduced theoretical constructs (*planning*), and the subsequent implementation of the activities in the classes (*action*); (4) the *phase of analysis of one's own practice*, i.e. the analysis of the activities planned during Phase 3, to be developed through reflections generated by an observation of class processes referring to specific theoretical lenses.

During the *phase of planning/action* (Phase 3), in particular, teachers are asked to work on some proof problems that require students to identify regularities, and to construct conjectures starting from numerical explorations and prove the conjectures.

Before the action in the classes, teachers have also to develop: (a) an a priori analysis of the problems to be proposed, considering in particular the possible conjectures that students can produce and the main difficulties they can face, especially during the proving phase; and (b) the planning of the methodology to be adopted with the objective of acting in tune with the M-$_{AE}$AB construct in facing proof problems. After the action in the classes, during the *phase of analysis of one's own practice* (Phase 4), the teachers have to propose an a posteriori analysis of the transcripts of the activities they have carried out, similar to the one developed during Phase 2.

We think that the work developed during Phases 2 and 4 of our path is in tune with what Sowder (2007) observes (quoting Richert's, 1991, research) about the role played by the study of written cases of classroom events, which "present the dilemmas of teaching, the tradeoffs, the uncertainties. They capture teacher actions as they exist in the uncertain context where those actions occur . . . [they] provide the potential for connecting the act of teaching with the cognitions and feelings that both motivate and explain the act. They offer a vehicle for making the tacit explicit" (Richert, 1991, p. 117).

Thanks to the enhancement of the preliminary moment of study/reflection and action/reflection—according to the above-mentioned modalities—our methodology of work with teachers can be now outlined with this structure (which is schematized in Figure 21.1): (1) theoretical study; (2) analysis of the practice of others; (3) planning/action in the classes; (4) analysis of one's own practice; and (5) critical shared reflection through the MT.

Our approach is consistent with the cyclic path of planning-implementation-reflection that, according to Thames and Van Zoest (2013), "can lead teachers to revisit and substantially expand on, and demand more of, their mathematical understanding in ways that matter for their learning and their teaching" (p. 589). We must however notice that, in our case, the phases of planning-implementation-reflection are part of a wider path, within which the theoretical study and analysis play an essential role. We can therefore again notice the affinity between our work with teachers and the methodology adopted by Potari (2013), which is characterized by phases of reading and analysis of research papers, designing of mathematical tasks on the basis of research results, and analysis of mathematics tasks and classroom activities using analytical models offered by research.

If we consider what Sowder (2007) states (quoting Borko & Putnam, 1995), we can observe that making teachers analyze their own practice through theoretical lenses could enable them

Our Methodology of work with teachers

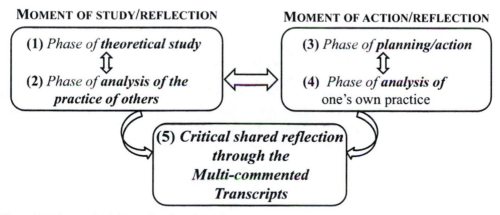

Figure 21.1 Our methodology of work with teachers.

to contextualize research results and therefore their new theoretical knowledge. According to Sowder, in fact, an approach that gives "opportunities to construct knowledge of subject matter and pedagogy in an environment that supports and encourages risk taking and reflection" (Sowder, 2007, p. 11) can foster change, and can make teachers aware that they are both objects and agents of change.

In the next section we will present an example of the work carried out by a teacher during the Phase 4 of our teacher education path. We chose this extract because it testifies: (a) the support given by the theoretical lenses in enabling the teachers to analyze in detail their own actions, (b) the difficulties that teachers could face during this type of activity.

AN EXAMPLE OF "ANALYSIS OF ONE'S OWN PRACTICE" AND SOME META-THEORETICAL CONSIDERATIONS ON OUR NEW METHODOLOGY OF WORK WITH AND FOR TEACHERS

The example we are presenting involves a teacher (T) who appears both to have really understood the roles that should be played in order to act in tune with the typical characters of the $M_{-AE}AB$ construct and to be able to critically analyze her approach during class activities. However, she reveals some blocks in using the construct itself in the analysis she develops.

The following discussion concerns the analysis of the strategies carried out by groups of students of T's class to face this problem: "Consider a natural number. Calculate the sum between this number and its two consecutive numbers. What can you observe? Can you prove what you assert?"[10]

The extract of the discussion is shown in the first column of Table 21.1.[11] The second column contains the comments proposed by T in the a posteriori analysis she developed during Phase 4 of our path, referring to the theoretical lenses provided by the $M_{-AE}AB$ construct. (Each comment is inserted next to the intervention it refers to.) Our comments, developed referring to the same theoretical lenses, are included in the third column. We have proposed them at a later stage in order to recognize harmony or contrast between T's interpretations of her interventions and our interpretations. Our comments were shared with T later in Phase 5 of our path. At the bottom of the table there is a spontaneous reflection, proposed by T when she sent us her analysis.

As our comments in the third column highlight, T's approach testifies that she has really internalized the typical characters highlighted by the $M_{-AE}AB$ construct. Focusing, till the beginning of this discussion's excerpt, on the objective of the formalization and manipulation that the class is carrying out, T poses herself as an activator of anticipating thoughts and interpretative processes. At the same time, she does not lose sight of the meta-dimension of the activity, posing herself as a reflective guide and proposing questions aimed at enabling students make the meaning of the adopted approach explicit.

These observations enable us to understand the level of awareness developed by T—thanks to the previous activities of our teacher education path—about the attitudes and behaviors to be activated when these specific activities are proposed.

Despite the interesting reflections she proposes, T does not use the theoretical terms of the $M_{-AE}AB$ construct to describe and objectify her approach. For example, she makes use of the term "model of reasoning," recalling the idea of $M_{-AE}AB$, instead of specifying that her intervention reveals an attempt of posing herself as an "activator of anticipating thoughts." Similarly, she observes that her intervention has the aim of "activating a reflection," without objectifying her role through the concept of "activator of reflective attitudes." Even if she proposes correct reflections from a practical point of view, she therefore hasn't yet developed the necessary self-confidence to analyze her actions according to these theoretical terms. T, in fact, is able to "describe" her own practice, but she does that without referring to general terms. She is able to recognize the typical characters of the $M_{-AE}AB$ construct, but she does not make them explicit, choosing to refer to them through concrete examples.

Table 21.1 An example of "Analysis of One's Own Practice."

Discussion extract	T's interpretation of her roles referring to the M-$_{AE}$AB construct	Our interpretation of T's roles referring to the M-$_{AE}$AB construct
In a first phase of the discussion, the class agrees upon this conjecture: the sum is always a multiple of 3 (the conjecture has been proposed by the student F). Another student (L) declares that she has also found that it is not a simple multiple of 3, but the product between 3 and the consecutive of the initial number. In the following, the teacher (T) begins the discussion about the possible construction of the proof of this conjecture.		
T 46: Let's start from this sum, which must be a multiple of 3. F, if you propose me this conjecture, what is the starting point and what is your objective? **F8:** I first considered some examples, then I found the conjecture and I started to generalize.	*Attempt to pose myself as a model of reasoning.*	*Focus on the objective:* *T poses herself as an activator of anticipating thoughts.*
T 47: What did you try to reach? **F9:** A rule that is invariant for every example.		*T poses herself as an activator of anticipating thoughts.*
T 48: A rule that is always valid . . . but what do I have to read? Where do I want to go? . . . mixing in order to go . . . where? You want a multiple of three, so what do you want? **F11:** I want . . . I want a *3n*	*Intervention strong conditioning, as the student's replay shows.*	*Focus on the objective, with an attempt to highlight and explain the effective strategies to be carried out (she poses herself as a reflective guide).*
T 50: A *3n* because I want a 3 multiplied by something. And you, L, according to what you have proposed, what do you want to have in the end? . . . What must the mixing give you? **L8:** It must give *nx + 1* . . .	*Intervention that is not meaningful with respect to a situation that should have required an in-depth analysis. The attempt itself of using a certainly not technical term— "mixing"—does not help and creates additional confusion (even though it wasn't the first time I used it).*	*Focus on the objective, with an attempt to highlight and explain the effective strategies to be carried out (she poses herself as a reflective guide).*
After a long discussion the class propose the following initial expression: n + (n + 1) + (n + 1 + 1). T makes students reflect on how this expression can be transformed, with the aim of reaching the predetermined objective, applying suitable properties of numerical operations (associative, commutative, distributive). The students correctly suggest to transform the initial expression into 3n + 3.		
T 93: So, F, we have now 3n + 3. **F29:** I wasn't able to go further than this. Actually it is enough for me to say that the final number is always a multiple of 3. It is enough. **T 94:** Why? **F31:** Because 3n is a multiple of 3 and, if we sum 3 to 3n we obtain the following multiple of 3. **T 95:** But we haven't arrived to what we wanted. We fixed an objective, but we stopped before. Is there a reason to arrive to 3 multiplied by something? . . .	*This intervention is aimed at activating a global reflection, in order also to stimulate a point of the justification that (in the a-priori analysis of the problem) was considered a delicate one. In fact, in contrast with the conclusion expressed in F31—according to which the thesis was proved even if the expected expression wasn't obtained—the intervention T95 aims at provoking a further reflection, posing herself as a model.*	*T poses herself as an activator of interpretative processes.* *T poses herself as an activator of reflective attitudes.*
T's a posteriori reflections: *With respect to the previous laboratory[i], the analysis of my interventions in the class was more difficult and complex. Even though my memory helped me in integrating the too restrictive vision provided by the mere discussion's transcripts, the self-criticism and/or the need of avoiding critiques forced me to not propose an objective analysis. What I said is not meant to be an excuse for what I am going to write. On the contrary, it represents the requirement of an external point of view, an eye, complementary to mine, that could help me more objectively analyze my way of proceeding during the class discussion.*		

[i] T refers to the activities of *analysis of the practice* of others (Phase 2), that she has previously faced.

516 *Cusi & Malara*

We must stress that this problem did not emerge during the phase of "analysis of others' practice" (Phase 2), during which T was able to directly refer to the terms of the M-$_{AE}$AB construct. We think that this missed objectification of the activated processes should be ascribed to difficulties with the passage from an experience of observation of others to an experience of observation of self, as T's a posteriori reflection testifies: "the self-criticism and/or the need of avoiding critics forced me to not propose an objective analysis." With regard to T's way of analyzing her own practice (referring to shared theoretical lenses), she can be described as a "teacher in transition." However, at the same time, T shows that she is aware she is, if we use Vygotskyan terms, in a zone of proximal development.

We can recall some of these considerations to reflect on our teacher education path and on the highlighted problems. T's request for an "external point of view," of an eye complementary to hers that could help her to develop an objective analysis of her "way of proceeding during the class discussion" testifies that overcoming this phase of transition requires the intervention of one or more external observers, who guide the teacher, through a continuous comparison, in the work of making the activated processes explicit. This kind of path requires, therefore, the constitution of a dialogical relationship between teachers and researchers, within which (in tune with the paradigm of developmental research) the analysis of micro-situations is carried out with the aim of developing teachers' real awareness of their own practice. This awareness can be obtained through the objectification realized thanks to the use of theoretical constructs, which can therefore play the role not only of tools of analysis but also of ways to communicate with teachers and to model the processes of reflection.

For this reason we must stress the need and the value of a dialogical comparison between teachers and researchers, which enables researchers to guide teachers in the complex work of theoretical analysis of their own practice, helping them describe and comment on their actions through the theoretical lenses for observation, in a scaffolding process aimed at a *modeling of reflection*. Researchers' interventions have to aim at provoking the necessary shifts of attention for teachers, in order to produce a real awareness-in-discipline about their capability of both acting in the class and reflecting (a-posteriori) on their own practice. Thanks to this work, teachers can progressively become capable of performing an auto-analysis and aware of the character of their actions, learning how to autonomously control them.

As Mason (2008) observes when he describes what happens to a student who internalizes the stimuli received by his/her teacher, this process fosters the teacher's internalization of the researchers' stimuli, so that the activity of reflection moves from a process "in themselves" to a process "for themselves."

FINAL REFLECTIONS

Starting from some reflections on the recognized relevance of addressing theory with reference to the teacher's practice, in this chapter we have focused on the theme of the integration of research and practice in teacher education programs. Potari (2013) stresses some fundamental questions related to this theme. Among them: "Can the findings and methodological as well as theoretical tools that have been developed in the community of researchers be meaningful for the teachers? What kind of conflicts and contradictions seem to emerge from this integration?" (p. 2).

Our vision of the teacher as a decision maker and our experience as both researchers and teacher educators has suggested to us how to address these research questions. In order for theoretically relevant research to have a direct and effective influence on teachers, some fundamental conditions have to be met: (1) teachers must be able to "absorb" this research and become aware of its incidence in their professionalism and "decision making"; (2) the research itself must be conveyed in forms that are accessible also to practitioners; and (3) institutional initiatives have to be promoted, in a perspective of long-life learning, to increase knowledge, exchange, and communication between teachers and researchers so that consolidated research results can become constructs and terms used for practice and in practice. In tune with these ideas, the methodology that characterizes our work with teachers is, therefore, conceived as a way of fostering teachers' development of a "theoretical awareness" (i.e. an awareness of the usefulness of theory in their professionals experience) that could enable him/her become a more effective decision maker.

The approach we have presented is in tune with the evolution of those theoretical studies that have led to an improvement of the teachers' developmental practices in the realm of educational projects realized by means of activities of joint actions and reflections between researchers. Through the support that researchers give to teachers in their approach to the theoretical study, the acquired theoretical references frame and scaffold the teachers' analysis of their own practice, helping the gradual development of self-awareness and the growth of a new identity.

The $M-_{AE}AB$ theoretical construct—a research product initially conceived as a tool for researchers in their analysis of the teaching/learning processes—has now become, thanks to the evolution of our methodology, a tool for teacher education practice. The example we have proposed shows how this construct could be used by teachers (initially in the "analysis of the practice of others" and then also in the "analysis of one's own practice") to identify their attitudes and behaviors in guiding students toward an aware and effective construction of mathematical meanings. This observation enables to focus on a first significance of this example: the evolution of a dialogic comparison between researchers and teachers can reduce the separation between theory and practice.[12] For this reason, our approach could be considered a meaningful prototype of desirable training processes, since it represents an example of the kind of research that, according to Goodchild (2008), can have a positive influence on both research and practice for teachers, students and researchers themselves.

However, our example also testifies the difficulties faced by teachers in overcoming the gap between analyzing the practice of others and analyzing their own practice. Despite the real appreciation of theory that teachers display, their assimilation of the theoretical lenses seems to be slow and difficult, probably because of the emotional distance it requires and because of the difficulties they face in confronting themselves. This difficult assimilation could be explained by referring to Simon's (2013) idea of "major assimilatory structures of teachers." Simon, indeed, highlights that these structures, which determine what teachers perceive and the sense made of these perceptions, are unlikely to be affected directly by a single type of teacher professional development experience. He stresses that "the challenge is to develop comprehensive approaches to teacher education and professional development that are monitored in terms of teachers' ongoing assimilation of these experiences" (Simon, 2013, p. 581).

This consideration enables us to shift our attention to the possible ways in which the kind of research we are performing can really affect practice, overcoming what Simon calls "teachers' resistance to change."

A possible focus of our future studies could be to plan appropriate training activities in preservice education, with the aim of enabling future teachers to develop those sensitivities that could minimize the gap between the analysis of the other practice and the analysis of their own practice.

Another possible answer to the question of developing a research that could really affect practice is developing these educational activities in the long term. However a long-term development requires a socio-educational political plan that involves a sharp dialogue between the research world and the world of educational institutions, at all levels (local, national and international). This would involve also the training of teacher educators in order to allow a real circulation of these methodologies. As regards these aspects, attention has recently been focused on the institutional contexts of reference for teachers and on the influences of the practice they promote in order to foster teacher professional development (Krainer, 2011; Arzarello et al., 2014).

A fundamental—and still open—aspect to be considered is how to test the teacher change and the stability of this change, considering the long time this complex process requires. Although many studies have proposed different ways of describing teacher change (see for instance Sowder, 2007), the problem of how to test teacher change is still open, as Koellner et al. (2007) testify, stating that most of professional development programs "are still in their infancy with respect to research data on their enactment and impact" (p. 300). Moreover, even if sometimes teacher change could be observed, the constitution of a new stable teacher identity is difficult to highlight, because of the lack of both long-term institutional teacher education paths and effective tools to analyze this complex evolution.

Another final reflection could be made in relation to the way that the effects of teacher education on student learning are measured. An analytical study of the interrelationships between the teacher's evolution and the mathematical growth of students, to be developed within communities of inquiry through articulated experimentations, is required. This kind of investigation is complex but desirable.

NOTES

1. The concept of *teacher's practice* to which we will refer is an open and complex one by Simon and Tzur (1999): "By teachers' practice, I mean not only everything teachers do that contributes to their teaching (planning, assessing, interacting with students) but also everything teachers think about, know, and believe about what they do. In addition, teachers' intuitions, skills, values, and feelings about what they do are part of their practice. Thus, we see a teacher's practice as a conglomerate that cannot be understood by looking at parts split off from the whole (i.e., looking only at beliefs or methods of questioning or mathematical knowledge)" (pp. 253–254).

2. Roesken (2011) stresses that terms such as "teacher change," "professional development," "professional growth," "teacher development . . . are used simultaneously but not consistently in the international discussion to describe the field of providing help for practicing teachers" (p. 7). She develops a detailed study on the differences and the interconnections among these notions, to which we refer for an in-depth analysis.

3. In this chapter and also in Goodchild (2008) university researchers are referred to as *didacticians* because teachers are also held to be researchers.

4. The ArAl Project (Malara & Navarra, 2003) is a wide and articulated project devoted to the renewal of arithmetic and algebra teaching, as well as to the professional development of teachers. It promotes, since early grades, a relational view of arithmetic and a linguistic and socio-constructive approach to algebra conceived as a tool for reasoning. It develops through two intertwined educational paths: the first one is devoted to the planning and the implementation of class activities and to the analysis of students learning; the second is aimed at a renovation of teacher professionalism through individual and shared reflective practices on the activated didactical processes.

5. As it has also been stressed in Malara and Zan (2008), we think that the use of videos of classroom processes in teacher education is important because it can help teachers analyse the use and incidence of nonverbal language, as well as the participation of the whole class. However we believe that the videos, because of their dynamicity, do not enable an analytical study of class processes. Moreover, as observed by Coles (2013), during the analysis of videos teachers often divert from the objective of their observation, making judgments instead of trying to interpret the reasons of their actions. Thanks to the transcripts, the interaction process becomes crystallized, enabling both to analyze the different micro-situations and the specific expressions used and to connect and globally control them.

6. Harel (2010) stresses that "attention to mathematical content is peripheral in many current frameworks and studies in mathematics education. . . . Often, upon reading a report on such a study, one is left with the impression that the report would remain intact if each mention of different academic subject such history, biology, or physics. There is a risk that, if this continues, mathematics education research will likely lose its identity"(p. 343).

7. Roesken (2011) states that the issue raised by Ball (2000) should not be neglected, that our tendency to focus either on the cognitive domain (e.g. knowledge) or teachers' action "is yet one more recent form of fragmentation in teachers education, and in particular, in our efforts to help teachers acquire usable content knowledge" (p. 246).

8. Arzarello et al. (2001) define *conceptual frames* as an organized set of notions (mathematical objects, properties, algorithms to be used, reasoning strategies, and so on), which suggests how to reason, manipulate formulas, and anticipate results while coping with a problem.

9. In order to better highlight the meaning of this term, we quote Vygotsky's words: "Children can imitate a variety of actions that go well beyond the limits of their own capabilities. Using imitation, children are capable of doing much more in collective activity or under the guidance of adults" (1978, p. 88).

10. Once the required conjecture has been formulated (that is: the sum is always a multiple of 3 and, in particular, the triple of the consecutive of the initial number), the student has to activate the frame "consecutive number" in order to generate the expression $n + n + 1 + n + 2$. Afterward, if the expression $3n + 3$ is produced by a correct syntactical transformation, the frame "multiple" (and a consequent correct anticipating thought) must be activated in order to become aware of the need of factorizing the expression into the new expression $3(n + 1)$, which can better highlight, through a good coordination between the frame "multiple" and the frame "consecutive number," what has been conjectured.

11. The teacher chose to separately enumerate in sequence her interventions (indicated with T) and her students' interventions (every student is represented with a different letter).

12. This is in tune with what has been discussed in Malara and Zan (2008), where the positive effects, on both theory and practice, of the dialogical interchanges between teachers and researchers are highlighted.

REFERENCES

Artigue, M. (2011). Review of Bharath Sriraman & Lyn English, "Theories of mathematics education—seeking new frontiers." *Research in Mathematics Education, 13*(3), 311–316.

Arzarello, F., Bazzini, L., & Chiappini, G. (2001). A model for analyzing algebraic thinking. In R. Sutherland, T. Rojano, A. Bell, & R. Lins (Eds.), *Perspectives on school algebra* (pp.61–81). Dortrecht: Kluwer Academic Publishers.

Arzarello, F., Robutti, O., Sabena, C., Cusi, A., Garuti, R., Malara, N. A., & Martignone, F. (2014). Meta-didactical transposition: a theoretical model for teacher education programs. In A. Clark-Wilson, O. Robutti, & N. Sinclair (Eds.), *The mathematics teacher in the digital era: Vol. 2. An international perspective on technology focused professional development* (pp. 347–372). Dordrecht: Springer.

Ball, D. (2000). Bridging practices. Intertwining content and pedagogy in teaching and learning to teach. *Journal of Teacher Education, 5*(3), 241–247.

Ball, D. L., Thames, M. H., & Phelps, G. (2008). Content knowledge for teaching: What makes it special? *Journal of Teacher Education, 59*(5), 389–407.

Barwell, R. (2013), Discursive psychology as an alternative perspective on mathematics teacher knowledge. *ZDM: The International Journal of Mathematics Education*, 45, 595–606.

Bishop, A. J. (1998). Research and practioners. In J. Kilpatrick & A. Sierpinska (Eds.), *Mathematics education as a research domain: A search for identity* (pp. 33–45). Dordrecht: Kluwer Academic Publishers.

Boaler, J. (2008). Bridging the gap between research and practice: International examples of success. In M. Menghini, F. Furinghetti, L. Giacardi, & F. Arzarello (Eds.), *The first century of the international commission on mathematical instruction* (1908–2008) (pp. 91–112). Roma: Instituto della Enciclopedia Italiana.

Boero, P. (2001). Transformation and anticipation as key processes in algebraic problem solving. In R. Sutherland, T. Rojano, A. Bell, & R. Lins (Eds.), *Perspectives on school algebra* (pp. 99–119). Dordrecht: Kluwer Academic Publishers.

Borko, H., & Putnam, R. (1995). Expanding a teachers' knowledge base: A cognitive psychological perspective on professional development. In T. Guskey & M. Huberman (Eds.), *Professional development in education: New paradigms and practices* (pp. 35–65). New York: Teachers College Press.

Carpenter, T. (1988). Teaching as problem solving. In R. Charles & E. Silver (Eds.), *The teaching and assessing of mathematical problem solving* (pp. 187–202). Hillsdale, NJ: Lawrence Erlbaum Associates.

Chapman, O., & Heater, B. (2010). Understanding change through a high school mathematics teacher's journey to inquiry-based teaching. *Journal of Mathematics Teacher Education, 13*, 445–458.

Cobb, P. (2007). Putting philosophy to work: Coping with multiple theoretical perspectives. In F. K. Lester, Jr. (Ed.), *Second handbook of research on mathematics teaching and learning: A project of the National Council of Teachers of Mathematics* (pp. 3–38). Charlotte, NC: Information Age.

Cochran-Smith, M., & Lytle, S. (1999). Relationship of knowledge and practice. Teacher learning in communities. In A. Iran-Nejad & P. D. Pearson (Eds.), *Review of Research in Education* (Vol. 24, pp. 249–305). Washington, DC: American Educational Research Association.

Coles, A. (2013). Using video for professional development: the role of the discussion facilitator. *Journal of Mathematics Teacher Education, 16*, 165–184.

Collins, A., Brown, J. S., & Newman, S. E. (1989). Cognitive apprenticeship: Teaching the craft of reading, writing, and mathematics. In L. B. Resnik (Ed.), *Knowing, learning and instruction* (pp. 453–494). Hillsdale, NJ: Lawrence Erlbaum Associates.

Cusi, A. (2008). An approach to proof in elementary number theory focused on representation and interpretation aspects: The teacher's role. In B. Czarnocha (Ed.), *Handbook of mathematics teaching research* (pp. 107–122). Rzeszów: Rzeszów University Press.

Cusi, A. (2009). Interrelation between anticipating thought and interpretative aspects in the use of algebraic language for the construction of proofs. In V. Durand-Guerrier, S. Soury-Lavergne, & F. Arzarello (Eds.), *Proceedings of 6th CERME Conference* (pp. 469–478). Lyon: Service des publications, INRP.

Cusi, A., & Malara, N. A. (2008). Approaching early algebra: Teachers educational process and classroom experiences. *Quadrante, 16*(1), 57–80.

Cusi, A., & Malara, N. A. (2009). The role of the teacher in developing proof activities by means of algebraic language. In M. Tzekaki, M. Kaldrimidou, & H. Sakonidis (Eds.), *Proceedings of the 33rd Conference of the International Group for the Psychology of Mathematics Education* (Vol. 2, pp. 361–368). Thessaloniki, Greece.

Cusi, A., & Malara, N. A. (2011). Analysis of the teacher's role in an approach to algebra as a tool for thinking: problems pointed out during laboratorial activities with perspective teachers. In M. Pytlak, T. Rowland, & E. Swoboda (Eds.), *Proceedings of the 7th Congress of the European Society for Research in Mathematics Education* (pp. 2619–2629). Rzeszow, Poland.

Cusi, A., & Malara, N. A. (2012). Educational processes in early algebra to promote a linguistic approach: behavior and emerging awareness in teachers. In L. Coulange, J.P. Drouhard, J.L. Dorier, & A. Robert (Eds.), *Recherches en didactique des mathématiques, Numéro spécial hors-série, Enseignement de l'algèbre élémentaire: bilan et perspectives* (pp. 299–319). Grenoble: La Pensée Sauvage.

Cusi, A., & Malara, N. A. (2013). A theoretical construct to analyze the teacher's role during introductory activities to algebraic modelling. In B. Ubuz, C. Haser, & M. A. Mariotti (Eds.), *Proceedings of the 8th Congress of the European Society for Research in Mathematics Education* (pp. 3015–3024). Antalya, Turkey.

Cusi, A., Malara, N. A., & Navarra, G. (2011). Early algebra: Theoretical issues and educational strategies for bringing the teachers to promote a linguistic and metacognitive approach to it. In J. Cai & E. Knuth (Eds.), *Early algebraization: Cognitive, curricular, and instructional perspectives* (pp. 483–510). Berlin-Heidelberg: Springer.

Duval, R. (2006). A cognitive analysis of problems of comprehension in a learning of mathematics. *Educational Studies in Mathematics, 61*, 103–131.

Freudenthal, H. (1983). Major problems of mathematics education. In M. Zweng, T. Green, J. Kilpatrick, H. Pollack, & M. Suydam (Eds.), *Proceedings of the Fourth International Congress on Mathematical Education* (pp. 1–7). Boston: Birkhäuser.

Goodchild, S. (2008). A quest for 'good' research: The mathematics teacher educator as practitioner researcher in a community of inquiry. In B. Jaworski & T. Wood (Eds.), *International handbook of mathematics teachers education: Volume 4. Mathematics teacher educator as a developing professional* (pp. 201–220). Rotterdam: Sense Publishers.

Goos, M. (2013). Sociocultural perspectives in research on and with mathematics teachers: a zone theory approach. *ZDM: The International Journal of Mathematics Education, 45*, 521–533.

Harel, G. (2010). Commentary on 'On the theoretical, conceptual, and philosophical foundations for research in mathematics education'. In B. Sriraman & L. English (Eds.), *Theories of mathematics education: Seeking new frontiers* (pp. 87–95). Berlin/Heidelberg: Springer Science.

Jaworski, B. (1998). Mathematics teacher research: Process, practice and the development of teaching. *Journal of Mathematics Teacher Education, 1*, 3–31.

Jaworski, B. (2004). Grappling with complexity: Co-learning in inquiry communities in mathematics teaching development. In M.J. Hoines & A.B. Fuglestad (Eds.), *Proceedings of the 28th Conference of the International Group for the Psychology of Mathematics Education* (Vol. 1n pp. 17–36). Bergen, Norway.

Jaworski, B. (2006). Theory and practice in mathematics teaching development: Critical inquiry as a mode of learning in teaching. *Journal of Mathematics Teacher, 9*, 187–211.

Jaworski, B. (2008), Development of mathematics teachers educators and its relation to teaching development. In B. Jaworski & T. Wood (Eds.), *International handbook of mathematics teachers education: Volume 4. Mathematics teacher educator as a developing professional* (pp. 335–361). Rotterdam: Sense Publishers.

Jaworski, B. (2012). Mathematics teaching development as a human practice: Identifying and drawing the threads. *ZDM. The International Journal on Mathematics Education, 44*, 613–625.

Kieran, C., Krainer, K., & Shaughnessy, J. M. (2013). Linking research to practice: Teachers as key stakeholders in mathematics education research. In M. A. Clements, A. Bishop, C. Keitel-Kreidt, J. Kilpatrick, & F.K.S. Leung (Eds.), *Third international handbook of mathematics education* (pp. 361–392). New York: Springer Science & Business.

Kilpatrick, J. (1981). The reasonable ineffectiveness of research in mathematics education. *For the Learning of Mathematics, 2*(2), 22–29.

Koellner, K., Jacobs, J., Borko, H., Schneider, C., Pittman, M.E., Eiteljorg, E., Bunning, K., & Frykholm, J. (2007). The problem-solving cycle: A model to support the development of teachers' professional knowledge. *Mathematical Thinking and Learning, 9*(3), 273–303.

Krainer, K. (2011). Teachers as stakeholders in mathematics education research. In B. Ubuz (Ed.), *Proceedings of the 35th Conference of the International Group for the Psychology of Mathematics Education* (Vol. 1, pp. 47–62). Ankara, Turkey.

Leont'ev, A. N. (1978). *Activity, consciousness and personality.* Englewood Cliffs, NJ: Prentice Hall.

Lerman, S. (2000). The social turn in mathematics education research. In J. Boaler (Ed.), *Multiple perspectives on mathematics teaching and learning* (pp. 19–44). Westport, CT: Ablex Publishing.

Lerman, S. (2006). Theories of mathematics education: Is plurality a problem? *ZDM: The International Journal of mathematics Education, 38*, 8–13.

Lerman, S. (2013). Theories in practices: Mathematics teaching and mathematics teachers education. *ZDM: The International Journal of Mathematics Education, 45*, 623–631.

Lester, F., & Wiliam, D. (2002). On the purpose of mathematics education research: Making productive contributions to policy and practice. In L. English (Ed.), *Handbook of international research in mathematics education* (pp. 489–506). Mahwah, NJ: Lawrence Erlbaum Associates.

Malara, N. A. (2003). Dialectics between theory and practice: Theoretical issues and aspects of practice from an early algebra project. In N. A. Pateman, B. J. Dougherty, & J. T. Zilliox (Eds.), *Proceedings of the 27th Conference of the International Group for the Psychology of Mathematics Education* (Vol.1, pp. 33–48). Honolulu.

Malara, N.A., & Navarra, G. (2003). *ArAl Project: Arithmetic pathways towards pre-algebraic thinking.* Bologna: Pitagora.

Malara, N. A., & Navarra, G. (2011). Multicommented transcripts methodology as an educational tool for teachers involved in early algebra. In M. Pytlak, E. Swoboda, & T. Rowland (Eds.), *Proceedings of the 7th Congress of the European Society for Research in Mathematics Education* (pp. 2737–2745). Rzeszow (Poland).

Malara, N.A., & Zan, R. (2008). The complex interplay between theory and practice: reflections and examples. In L. English (Ed.), *Handbook of international research in mathematics education* (2nd ed., pp. 539–564). New York: Routledge.

Marton, F., & Morris, P. (2002). *What matters? Discovering critical conditions of classroom learning.* Goteborg: Acta Universitatis Gothoburgensins.

Mason, J. (1990). Reflection on dialogue between theory and practice, reconciled by awareness. In F. Seeger & H. Steinbring (Eds.), *The dialogue between theory and practice in mathematics education: Overcoming the broadcast metaphor. Proceedings of the Fourth Conference on Systematic Cooperation Between Theory and Practice in Mathematics Education.* Materialen und Studien, band 38 (pp. 177–192). Bielefeld: Institut für Didaktik der Mathematik.

Mason, J. (1998). Enabling teachers to be real teachers: Necessary levels of awareness and structure of attention. *Journal of Mathematics Teacher Education, 1*, 243–267.

Mason, J. (2002). *Researching your own practice: The discipline of noticing.* London: Falmer Press.

Mason, J. (2008). Being mathematical with and in front of learners. In B. Jaworski & T. Wood (Eds.), *International handbook of mathematics teachers education: Volume 4. Mathematics teacher educator as a developing professional* (p. 31–55). Rotterdam: Sense Publishers.

Mellone, M. (2011). The influence of theoretical tools on teachers' orientation to notice and classroom practice: A case study. *Journal of Mathematics Teacher Education, 14*, 269–284.

Niss, M. (2007). Reflections on the state and trends in research on mathematics teaching and learning. From here to utopia. In F. K. Lester, Jr. (Ed.), *Second handbook of research on mathematics teaching and learning: A project of the National Council of Teachers of Mathematics* (pp. 1293–1312). Charlotte, NC: Information Age Publishing.

Potari, D. (2013). The relationship of theory and practice in mathematics teacher professional development: An activity theory perspective. *ZDM: The International Journal of Mathematics Education, 45*, 507–519.

Richert, A.E. (1991). Using teacher cases or reflection and enhanced understanding. In A. Lieberman & L. Miller (Eds.), *Staff development for education in the '90s: New demands, new realities, new perspectives* (pp. 113–132). New York: Teachers College Press.

Roesken, B. (2011). *Hidden dimension in the professional development of mathematics teachers.* Rotterdam: Sense Publishers.

Schoenfeld, A.H. (1992). Learning to think mathematically: Problem solving, metacognition, and sense-making in mathematics. In D. Grouws (Ed.), *Handbook for research on mathematics teaching and learning* (pp. 334–370). New York: Macmillan.

Schoenfeld, A. H. (2013). Classroom observations in theory and practice. *ZDM: The International Journal of Mathematics Education, 45*, 607–621.

Shulman, L. S. (1986). Those who understand: Knowledge growth in teaching. *Educational Researcher*, 15, 4–14.

Silver, E. A., & Herbst, P. G. (2007). Theory in Mathematics Education Scholarship. In F. K. Lester, Jr. (Ed.), *Second Handbook of Research on Mathematics Teaching and Learning: A project of the National Council of Teachers of Mathematics* (pp. 39–67). Charlotte, NC: Information Age Publishing.

Simon, M. (2009). Amidst multiple theories of learning in mathematics education. *Journal for Research in Mathematics Education, 40*(5), 477–490.

Simon, M. (2013). Promoting fundamental change in mathematics teaching: A theoretical, methodological, and empirical approach to the problem. *ZDM: The International Journal of Mathematics Education, 45*, 573–582.

Simon, M., & Tzur, R. (1999). Explicating the teacher's perspective from the researchers' perspective: generating accounts of mathematics teachers' practice. *Journal for Research in Mathematics Education, 30*, 252–264.

Sowder, J. T. (2007). The mathematical education and development of teachers. In F. K. Lester, Jr. (Ed.), *Second handbook of research on mathematics teaching and learning: A project of the National Council of Teachers of Mathematics* (pp. 157–223). Charlotte, NC: Information Age Publishing.

Sriraman, B., & English, L. (2010). *Series advances in mathematics education. Theories of mathematics education—Seeking new frontiers.* Berlin/Heidelberg: Springer Science.

Thames, M., & Van Zoest, L. (2013). Building coherence in research on mathematics teacher characteristics by developing practice-based approaches. *ZDM: The International Journal of mathematics Education, 45*, 583–594.

Vygotsky, L. S. (1978). *Mind in society: The development of higher mental processes.* Cambridge MA: Harvard University Press.

White, A. L., Jaworski, B., Agudelo-Valderrama, C., & Gooya, Z. (2013). Teachers learning from teachers. In M. A. Clements, A. Bishop, C. Keitel-Kreidt, J. Kilpatrick, & F.K.S. Leung (Eds.), *Third international handbook of mathematics education* (pp. 393–430). New York: Springer Science & Business.

Wittmann, E. C. (2001). Developing mathematics education in a systematic process. *Educational Studies in mathematics, 48*, 1–20.

22 Knowledge Creation Through Dialogic Interaction Between the Practices of Teaching and Researching

Kenneth Ruthven

University of Cambridge, UK

Simon Goodchild

University of Agder, Norway

INTRODUCTION

This chapter focuses on how the interplay between the practices of researching and teaching can help to foster development of knowledge about and for mathematics teaching. It will treat *researching* and *teaching, researcher* and *teacher*, simply as convenient typifications, recognizing the possibility that institutions and individuals may participate in both practices and take on both roles. Moreover, as the previous sentence illustrates, this chapter will reserve *practice* for use in the sense of social practice; it will employ the more direct terms *teacher* and *teaching* to refer to what some sources speak of as *practitioner* and *practice*. Building on the view widely held amongst mathematics educators that any communal knowledge base for mathematics teaching should draw both on craft knowledge created within the practice of teaching and on scholarly knowledge created within the practice of researching, the particular focus of this chapter will be on synergy between these practices, and on knowledge conversion between them.

KNOWLEDGE CREATION AND CONVERSION WITHIN TEACHING

Knowledge Creation Within Teaching: The Significance of Craft Knowledge

Craft knowledge refers to the professional knowledge that teachers use in their day-to-day classroom teaching, action-oriented knowledge that is not generally made explicit by teachers, which they may indeed find difficult to articulate, or which they may even be unaware of using.

> [C]raft knowledge describes the knowledge that arises from and, in turn, informs what teachers do. As such, this knowledge is to be distinguished from other forms of knowledge that are not linked to practice in this direct way. Craft knowledge is not, therefore, the kind of knowledge that teachers draw on when explaining the thinking underlying their ideal teaching practices. Neither is it knowledge drawn from theoretical sources. Professional craft knowledge can certainly be (and often is) informed by these sources, but it is of a far more practical nature than these knowledge forms. Professional craft knowledge is the knowledge that teachers develop through the processes of reflection and practical problem-solving that they engage in to carry out the demands of their jobs.
>
> (Cooper & McIntyre, 1996, p. 76)

523

There is, then, a process of knowledge creation within teaching. Through experimenting and problem solving in the course of teaching, and through re-presenting teaching and reflecting on it, craft knowledge is developed and shared within the profession. This can also incorporate a process of knowledge conversion; by contextualizing and activating scholarly knowledge within teaching, it can be brought to contribute to the development of craft knowledge.

> From a cognitive point of view, professional knowledge is developed as a product of professional action, and it establishes itself through work and performance in the profession, not merely through accumulation of theoretical knowledge, but through the integration, tuning and restructuring of theoretical knowledge to the demands of practical situations and constraints.
>
> (Bromme & Tillema, 1995, p. 262)

Moreover, knowledge conversion can proceed in the opposite direction, through eliciting craft knowledge and codifying it. Thus articulated through researching, craft knowledge can be brought to contribute to the further development of scholarly knowledge.

The next two sections illustrate knowledge conversion between teachers' craft knowledge and researchers' scholarly knowledge by considering two projects chosen because they are recognized as significant pioneering contributions to the field, conducted in unusual depth. While the projects share a concern with the teaching of mathematics at the elementary-school level, the second can be seen as providing a counterpoint to the first, not just in its pedagogical stance but in the form of knowledge conversion involved. Thus, whereas the first project illustrates an approach to eliciting and codifying craft knowledge as scholarly knowledge, the second, conversely, illustrates an approach to contextualizing and activating scholarly knowledge as craft knowledge.

Eliciting and Codifying Craft Knowledge: The Example of Expert Direct Instruction

A program of research that demonstrated the possibilities of eliciting and codifying the craft knowledge of teachers was conducted by Leinhardt and her associates (1988a; 1989; Leinhardt, Putnam, Stein, & Baxter, 1991), employing concepts and methods drawn from a strand of cognitive science research that focuses on the analysis of expertise. Instruction was analyzed by observing teachers in action in the classroom, and by interviewing them about their thinking. Teachers were identified as "experts" on the basis of their consistency in producing both high gains in student achievement and high levels of final achievement. Compared with novice teachers, the instruction—and underlying cognition—of these expert teachers was characterized in the following terms:

> Expert teachers use many complex cognitive skills, weaving together elegant lessons that are made up of many smaller lesson segments. These segments, in turn, depend on small, socially scripted pieces of behavior called *routines*, which teachers. . . use extensively. Expert teachers also have a rich repertoire of instructional scripts that are updated and revised throughout their personal history of teaching. Teachers are flexible, precise and parsimonious planners. That is, they plan what they need to but not what they already know and do automatically. Experts plan better than novices in the sense of efficiency and in terms of the mental outline from which they operate. . . From that more global plan. . . they select an agenda for a lesson. . . The agenda serves not only to set up and coordinate the lesson segments but also to lay out the strategy for actually explaining the mathematical topic under consideration. The ensuing explanations are developed from a system of goals and actions that the teacher has for ensuring that the students understand the particular piece of mathematics.
>
> (Leinhardt et al., 1991, p. 88)

As analyzed here, then, the expertise of outstanding teachers is many-layered. Most readily articulated are the processes of deliberate analysis involved in the pre-active framing of a lesson agenda, in its interactive accomplishment—and adaptation—within the lesson, and in post-active review. Most easily neglected are those largely reflex aspects of action and interaction, exemplified by the classroom routines through which the stability and predictability of classroom activity is produced. Leinhardt suggests that: "[the] importance [of routines] is often overlooked because spontaneity, flexibility and responsiveness are so highly valued in our culture, especially by educators" (1988a, p. 49). Equally, one could conjecture that routines receive less recognition precisely because they have become so reflex for expert teachers, in contrast to those aspects of teaching that command their deliberate attention and continue to exercise them.

This body of work analyses teachers' pedagogical knowledge and reasoning in terms of constructs of "script," "agenda," and "explanation." A teacher's script for a particular curricular topic is viewed as a loosely ordered repertoire of goals, tasks, and actions, continually developed and refined over time; it incorporates sequences of action and argumentation, relevant representations and explanations, and markers for anticipated student difficulties. The most important feature of a script is the way in which it acts as an organizing structure, coordinating knowledge of subject and pedagogy with reasoning about actions and goals, hence underpinning the efficient and cohesive planning and development of lessons. Such a script provides a matrix of knowledge supporting the setting of a lesson "agenda": a mental plan including lesson goals, actions through which these goals can be achieved, expectations about the sequencing of actions through the lesson, and important decision points within the lesson. The agendas of the expert teachers studied by Leinhardt showed more developed instructional logic and smoother flow, and they took more account of students' actions and reasoning, and sought more evidence of these. A crucial element of any script is its "explanation" of each new idea. Several elements contribute to the effectiveness of the explanations of expert teachers: anticipation of prerequisite ideas and skills; motivation of the new idea; specification of its conditions of use; principled legitimation of the new idea; integration of different elements of the explanation; and completion of the explanation.

An unexpected finding concerned the way in which expert teachers attended to the thinking of students:

> [Teachers] did build models, but in different ways than we had anticipated. Teachers seem to construct flags for themselves that signal material that will cause difficulty as it is being learned, and then they adjust their teaching of the topic in response to those flags or to past successes. They seem to diagnose their teaching and its cycle rather than diagnosing the mental representation of a particular student. A major goal of teaching seems to be to move through a script, making only modest adjustments on line in response to unique student needs.
>
> (Leinhardt, 1988a, pp. 51–52)

Indeed, this was one consideration that led to the value of the teaching practice of which these studies built a model being questioned by some mathematics educators: "[O]n at least two points is this model lacking: the mathematics that students are being asked to learn and the lack of attention to individuals" (Fennema & Franke, 1992, p. 159). These two points were related: "Although teachers may be able to achieve short-term computational goals without attending to students' knowledge, they may need to understand students' thinking to facilitate students' growth in understanding and problem solving" (Carpenter, Fennema, Peterson, Chiang, & Loef, 1989, p. 502).

Leinhardt did acknowledge the need to study other forms of teaching:

> Although our experts have been shown to be responsive and supportive of student efforts to learn key concepts and procedures, the content, method, and direction of their lessons

are situated primarily with the teacher. Cognitively based learning theories, however, suggest that it is pedagogically sound and cognitively necessary for students to have a role in determining the method and direction of their own learning . . . A key feature of [future] studies will be the distinction between the explanations that are essentially designed by teachers in advance, and those which students play an active role in constructing during classroom dialogue.

(Leinhardt et al., 1991, p. 111)

However, conducting such studies is problematic if teachers have not developed pedagogical models compatible with such cognitively based learning theories. A major limitation inherent in simply studying expert teachers within an established pedagogical system is confinement to that system. The development of new forms of pedagogy calls for some form of intervention.

Contextualizing and Activating Scholarly Knowledge: The Example of Cognitively Guided Instruction

A program of research into Cognitively Guided Instruction (CGI) (Carpenter et al., 1989; Peterson Fennema, & Carpenter, 1991; Fennema, Carpenter, Franke, Levi, Jacobs, & Empson, 1996) addressed this issue of how new forms of pedagogy might be developed through contextualizing and activating scholarly knowledge. Its central hypothesis was that:

Research provides detailed knowledge about children's thinking and problem solving that, if available to teachers, might affect their knowledge of their own students and their planning of instruction.

(Carpenter et al., 1989, p. 502)

This quotation signals that it is important to distinguish multiple senses of "knowledge" about "children's thinking" in considering this body of work. First, there is an important distinction between some overarching model of children's thinking, as against information about the thinking of particular children. There is then a further distinction between such models in general, as against the particular one adopted by the researchers. The scholarly knowledge primarily in play in this project was a cognitive model (developed by Carpenter and his colleagues in earlier research) that classified arithmetic word problems and the solution strategies adopted by students, and described progression in students' thinking in terms of their changing use of particular types of solution strategy in response to particular types of problem.

Another study examined what knowledge experienced teachers already had available to analyze such issues (Carpenter, Fennema, Peterson, & Carey, 1988). Teachers were presented with tasks related to teaching, such as creating a word problem corresponding to a given number equation, assessing the relative difficulty of word problems, and—after viewing particular students solving problems—predicting how students would solve others. Most teachers proved relatively successful on such tasks, particularly those involving the types of problem commonly encountered at the grade level at which they taught. Although many teachers found it difficult to articulate the basis on which they made such judgments, they clearly had developed relevant knowledge. Moreover, the form that this craft knowledge took seems to have reflected the circumstances of their teaching. Teachers appear to have been oriented towards helping students to infer the computation expected through identifying cue words within a problem statement or visualizing the action involved.

By contrast, the CGI program was based on the conjecture that organizing classroom activity around less-structured problem solving, and developing pedagogical strategies to focus attention on the solution strategies devised by students themselves, would prove beneficial to student learning. Consequently, the professional development program associated with CGI aimed to familiarize teachers with the particular research-based model developed by Carpenter and colleagues, as a more powerful means of conceptualizing problem and strategy types, and of relating these to problem difficulty and student progression. Carefully chosen videotaped recordings of individual children solving problems were used as the stimulus for discussions aimed at highlighting key distinctions within the model, and at clarifying its use to characterize the mathematical thinking of particular children. Teachers were also encouraged to test out the model by presenting agreed problems to children in their own class and recording their solutions for further discussion in workshops.

In addition, teachers were invited to reflect on how the model could be exploited in teaching. While the program emphasized that it was teachers themselves who were best placed to make informed decisions about how the model should and could be used in their classrooms, the researchers acknowledge their influence on teachers' thinking about such matters:

> We do not believe that we did not influence directly what teachers did in classrooms. The mathematical content we showed and discussed with them was based almost exclusively on word problems. The videotapes were of individual interviewers asking a child to solve word problems, waiting while the child solved the problem, and asking questions such as "How did you get that answer?" or "Could you show me what you did?" Teachers were encouraged to ask children to solve word problems and ascertain how the problems were solved. We did not, however, directly prescribe either pedagogy or curriculum for teachers.
> (Fennema et al., 1996, pp. 408–409)

The double negative in the opening sentence of this quotation, the distinction between "influence" at the start and "prescribe" at the close, signals the complexities and ambiguities of the line that the researchers were treading in their relationships with teachers. What this approach recognized was that the types of questioning shown in the research interviews with single students would need adaptation in order to become functional components of classroom teaching aimed at the longer-term traversal of a curriculum by a whole class of students. Equally, teachers would have to integrate use of the cognitive model into facets of their practice such as lesson planning, classroom organization, and interactive questioning, by adapting established aspects of their craft knowledge and possibly developing them to create new approaches to planning, organization, and questioning.

Indeed, it transpired that this process of knowledge conversion through which teachers appropriated the cognitive model and adapted their craft knowledge accordingly could lead teachers to use the model in ways not anticipated by the researchers. A further study reported on an exceptional teacher who had already established a powerful social environment for learning in her classroom. She had been able to contextualize and activate the cognitive model for her purposes in managing that environment, to strengthen the challenges she set for her students and to sharpen her understanding of their responses. However, the researchers were surprised by some features of her approach:

> Ms J did not use knowledge of children's thinking in the way we had anticipated . . . Because these problems were organized into a hierarchy of difficulty determined by the reasonably well-defined levels that children move through as they learn to solve the problems, we expected that teachers would . . . use the knowledge more or less as a template to assess what . . . students knew and then to systematically select more difficult problems for the children to solve . . . The hierarchy of problem types and solution strategies would be used systematically to make both daily and long-term instructional decisions. Ms J did not do what we had anticipated. Although at times she made use of the specifics of the hierarchy . . . we were unable to identify any systematic way in which she selected problems . . . Instead, she used the knowledge about problem types to dramatically broaden the scope of her curriculum and her expectations of children. She used all problem types from almost

the first week of school, and children in her class had many opportunities to solve all types of problems using whatever solution strategy they chose.

(Fennema et al., 1993, p. 578)

CGI, thus, provides a particularly fully researched example of a program that has enabled teachers to contextualize and activate scholarly knowledge in their professional work, provoking a corresponding adaptation and development of their craft knowledge.

A DIALOGIC CYCLE OF KNOWLEDGE CREATION AND CONVERSION

Establishing a Dialogic Cycle: Coupling the Construction and Conversion of Scholarly and Craft Knowledge

These examples point to a dialogic cycle of knowledge creation (Ruthven, 2002). In one phase of this cycle (exemplified by the CGI program), scholarly knowledge is (re)contextualized and activated within teaching, stimulating (re)construction of craft knowledge. In the complementary phase (exemplified by the Leinhardt program), craft knowledge is elicited and codified through researching, stimulating (re)construction of scholarly knowledge. In both phases, conversion involves the filtering and reformulating of knowledge: only certain derivatives of scholarly knowledge will prove capable of being productively incorporated within craft knowledge; equally, only some derivatives of craft knowledge will prove able to be fruitfully appropriated as scholarly knowledge.

Huberman (1993) has pointed to the benefits of "sustained interaction" between researchers (or researching) and teachers (or teaching), and to how the disruptions of taken-for-granted views that arise in the course of such collaboration stimulate rethinking:

[O]nce they get beyond the initial discomfort of defining common meanings and of working out the social dynamics of their encounters, each party is bound to be surprised or annoyed or even shaken by some of the information and the reasoning put forth by the other party. Both bodies of knowledge are "valid," albeit on different grounds, and

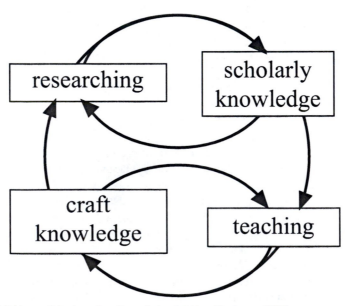

Figure 22.1 Establishing a dialogic cycle of knowledge creation (Ruthven, 2002).

both are contending for salience and prominence. Were the researchers and [teachers] to remain among themselves, there would probably be far fewer instances of cognitive shifts.

(Huberman, 1993, p. 50)

Clearly, then, such sustained interaction can make an important contribution to the professional development of teachers. This has encouraged approaches to professional development in which scholarly knowledge from research is tested by teachers in their own classrooms in terms of the insight it provides into teaching and learning processes, and of the support it offers in improving the quality of these processes. However, because teaching calls for "a highly efficient collection of heuristics . . . for the solution of very specific problems" (Leinhardt, 1988b, p. 146), an essential component of the dialogic knowledge-creation cycle outlined earlier is development of appropriate craft knowledge by teachers participating in the research. Eliciting and codifying this craft knowledge has the potential to improve the effectiveness with which coaching of other teachers can be undertaken, by providing more explicit frameworks for analyzing teaching processes, for articulating mechanisms and functions, and for understanding adaptation to different conditions.

The resources and strategies available to teachers shape not only their approaches to teaching but also their thinking about it. Initiating and sustaining the dialogic cycle of knowledge creation and conversion can be assisted by seeking to develop some kind of didactical apparatus, and the modes of activity and forms of discourse that mediate use of that apparatus. In the earlier illustration of CGI, for example, key artifacts were the map of problem types and solution strategies, and the repertoire of interaction patterns and questioning forms employed to probe students' reasoning. Likewise, in the earlier illustration of expert direct instruction, research analysis provided explicit models of didactical systems and their component parts in terms of prototypical "scripts," "agendas," and "explanations" for particular topics. Structuring apparatus of these types can provide important underpinning for the wider diffusion and adaptation of new knowledge (Ruthven, 2005). First, such apparatus has a symbolic function, signifying the associated didactical system. Second, of course, it has a pragmatic function, providing a means of structuring and regulating activity in accordance with the didactical system. Third, this apparatus and its associated discourse have an epistemic function, crystallizing the key ideas of the didactical system. Finally, inasmuch as such apparatus and its associated discourse incorporate explicit flexibility (and are seen as doing so), they serve a heuristic function, assisting thoughtful interpretation and local reformulation of the didactical system.

Since initial presentation of the dialogic cycle model (Ruthven, 2002), two particular proposals have been made on how to realize and develop it further around particular forms of structuring apparatus. The next two sections of the chapter explore these.

Developing the Dialogic Cycle: Design and Analysis of Substantial Learning Environments

Wittmann has pointed to the significance of a type of structuring apparatus, the *substantial learning environment*, which he defines in the following terms:

A teaching/learning unit with the following properties:

(1) It represents central objectives, contents and principles of teaching mathematics at a certain level.
(2) It is related to significant mathematical contents, processes and procedures beyond this level, and is a rich source of mathematical activities.
(3) It is flexible and can be adapted to the special conditions of a classroom.
(4) It integrates mathematical, psychological, and pedagogical aspects of teaching mathematics, and so it forms a rich field for empirical research.

(Wittmann, 2001, p. 2)

Wittmann's adaptation of the dialogic cycle model (Figure 22.2), places such environments at the center of the processes of knowledge creation, use, and conversion. He argues that such environments can play an important role for both researchers and teachers, "as common points of reference, as knots in the collective memory, and as stimuli for action" (2001, p. 4).

In effect, Wittmann proposes to recast mathematics education as a "design science" in which the teaching/learning units that he refers to as substantial learning environments serve as boundary-spanning artifacts between the practices of researching and teaching. This, in turn, raises the question of the role of craft knowledge within design research. A recent review examined researcher–teacher interaction within design-research projects (Ormel, Pareja-Roblin, McKenney, Voogt, & Pieters, 2012). The review distinguishes between "collaborative" approaches in which teachers and researchers work closely together on design, and "cooperative" approaches in which a more traditional differentiation of researcher and teacher roles persists. However, perhaps the most important finding is that such interaction is little examined in reports on design research:

> Especially in the small-scale projects, the interaction between [teachers and researchers] is more collaborative than cooperative: when designing together, both contributing from their own expertise and sharing responsibility for the results. In contrast, the studies on larger projects suggest that interaction is more cooperative (researchers are accountable for research tasks, teachers are accountable for teaching tasks) and with less collaborative or shared responsibilities. It must be noted, however, that often very few details are provided about the interaction.
>
> (Ormel et al., 2012, pp. 975–976)

Similarly, analyzing the sources of knowledge referred to in these design-research reports, perhaps the most important finding is the degree to which teaching craft knowledge is overlooked or unacknowledged:

> Most design research projects found in this review use literature and/or project data to inform the design of instructional solutions. Less than half of the reports discuss practical

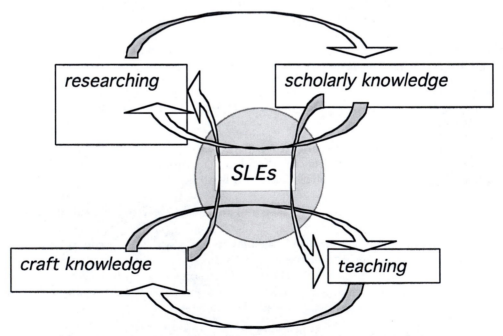

Figure 22.2 Substantial learning environments at the heart of the dialogic cycle (Wittmann, 2001).

knowledge informing the design of instructional solutions. While this suggests that practical knowledge does not necessarily play an important role in these projects, it is also possible that discussion of practical knowledge was strategically omitted, perhaps in an attempt to render articles more attractive to publication in journals that do not value this orientation.

(Ormel et al., 2012, p. 981)

Pursuing Wittmann's proposal, then, to organize the dialogic cycle around substantial learning environments calls for approaches to design research that give more attention to the development and elicitation of craft knowledge underpinning their use.

Developing the Dialogic Cycle: Collaborative Video Analysis of Lesson Sequences

Another development of the dialogic cycle model can be found in Hennessy and Deaney's (2009) approach to collaborative video analysis in developing multimedia representations of teaching practice. This analysis worked towards framing these representations of teaching practice in terms of an "intermediate" theory developed through dialogic interplay between teachers' "practical theories" (the articulate component of craft knowledge) and sociocultural theory (a particular body of scholarly knowledge):

> The study focused on developing understanding and articulating strategies and mechanisms (with the goal of dissemination). . . We were also concerned with theory building, specifically focusing on teacher mediation. [This involved] exposure of teachers to key constructs from sociocultural theory, allowing them to select, appropriate, and apply relevant notions using their own language where desired; supporting initial alignment of all participants in terms of key ideas and subsequent negotiation of a shared analytic account.
> (Hennessy & Deaney, 2009, p. 1769)

Video recordings of lesson sequences taught by participating teachers (and materials associated with them) were subjected to a carefully phased process of analysis and synthesis. A time-coded descriptive summary of the videotaped lesson activities and interactions (with significant utterances transcribed verbatim) was produced to accompany the recording of each lesson sequence. All participating teachers and researchers then used these records to familiarize themselves with the lesson sequence and to reflect on it, recording their impressions in a written commentary, a preliminary selection of critical episodes, and questions for further discussion with the teacher during the subsequent video review meeting.

Prepared in this way, the participants then met together to review each lesson sequence:

> The video review meetings were employed as, and proved to be, a powerful catalyst for teacher introspection. The extensive scheduled discussions of both lesson plans and the various forms of data. . . were intended to create the critical space whereby "craft knowledge can legitimately come under respectful forms of examination comparable to those applied to scholarly knowledge." (Ruthven, 2002. p. 589)
> (Hennessy & Deaney, 2009, p. 1766)

The mathematics case in particular illustrated the strength of this methodology:

> The two teachers encountered various difficulties. . . precluding them from spending much time on written commentary. By contrast, the video review process flagged up numerous points for discussion and questioning during meetings, which helped to fill in the gaps in our understanding and to explicate the underlying rationale for a number of teacher actions and interventions.
> (Hennessy & Deaney, 2009, p. 1777)

In addition, a tentative coding scheme was initiated by the researchers, informed by pedagogical ideas from sociocultural theory. This scheme was refined in the course of analyzing the lesson sequences through fostering dialogue between these sociocultural concepts, as introduced by the researchers, and the ideas used spontaneously by the teacher of the lesson and the other teacher video observers. Once each lesson sequence had been reviewed in its own right, attention turned to refining the coding scheme to acknowledge patterns across the teaching practices recorded in the sequences. This final coding scheme informed decisions about the content and structure of the multimedia representation of the lesson sequences, including the thematic framework developed for each (individual) case and for the associated (multiple) case study across lesson sequences.[1]

The use of video recordings has become increasingly viable and popular as a means of representing teaching practice. Hennessy and Deaney's approach places these (alongside other associated records of teaching practice) at the heart of the dialogic cycle. Significantly, the way in which these records were used goes beyond simply prompting reflection on that practice. This approach seeks both to elicit the craft knowledge underpinning practice in a systematic way and to bring a body of scholarly knowledge to bear on analyzing this practice. It ultimately seeks to develop a new conceptual framework, drawing on, and bridging between, these two resources.

LEARNING STUDY AND COMMUNITIES OF INQUIRY

Learning Study and Communities of Inquiry: Knowledge Growth through Collective Design

In all the examples of dialogue between researching and teaching examined so far, a conventional role differentiation between teacher and researcher has been maintained. We turn now to examine alternatives that challenge these role definitions and differentiation, and examine their relation to the dialogic cycle.

Lesson study is a mode of professional development, designed to facilitate the sharing and development of craft knowledge, that has existed for many decades in Japan (Fernandez, 2002; Lewis, Perry, & Murata, 2006; Stigler & Hiebert, 1999; Watanabe, 2002). Stigler and Hiebert credit lesson study with the development of teaching mathematics in Japan, "the linchpin of the improvement process" (1999, p. 111); they claim that it has made a significant contribution to that country's students' superior performance in international studies of performance in mathematics.

Lesson study typically involves a group of teachers coming together to design a lesson, following which one of the teachers implements the lesson plan while the others in the group observe and take notes. After the lesson the teachers meet to discuss what happened and make changes to the lesson plan, which is usually then implemented by another teacher from the group. In the original Japanese model there does not appear to be any formal mechanism linking the deliberations, experiences, and learning of the group of teachers to a wider body of scholarly knowledge. However, routinely, the group of teachers do produce a report from their activities that might be made more widely available. In this model of professional development, the possibility of learning from and extending the body of teachers' craft knowledge is evident. Implementations of lesson study outside Japan often include a researcher or teacher educator as facilitator; in such instances, successful bridging between craft and scholarly knowledge may occur (Murata, Bofferding, Pother, Taylor, & Wischnia, 2012).

Attempts to develop the lesson study model include a systematic mechanism to connect teachers' craft knowledge with scholarly knowledge and aim to develop both forms of knowledge and teaching practice. We contrast two models of such attempts: "learning study" that takes learning of particular subject content as the point of departure, in particular the relation between the learner and subject; and the development of "communities of inquiry" that focus more explicitly on teaching and learning as forms of participation in cultural practices. Here we focus on two larger developmental research projects, one for each approach, which have comprised teams of researchers and many teachers extended over several years. One is a project based on learning study in Hong Kong, 2000–2003 (Lo, Pong, & Chik, 2005), and the other a project in Norway that set out to develop communities of inquiry, 2004–2007 (Jaworski, Fuglestad, Bjuland, Breiteig, Goodchild, & Grevholm, 2007). We note also reports arising from small-scale studies, including dissertation and award-bearing courses that focus on these developmental approaches. (e.g. Potari, 2013; van Bommel, 2012). We outline the underlying principles of each approach; we then draw attention to their similarities and differences; finally, we briefly describe some of the outcomes and knowledge gains that have been reported.

Learning Study

Learning study (LS) sets out to combine lesson study and design experiments; a specific departure from lesson study is the introduction of a theory of learning. The originators of the LS approach teaching and learning within a theoretical framework referred to as *variation theory*. In this framework, it is argued, concepts are known through their "critical features" that distinguish one concept from another. One learns to recognize and understand a concept by noting the variation of critical features between concepts. The teacher's role is to create a space of learning in which the critical features of a concept are either held constant or varied to enable the learners to apprehend the features and the concept.

> [V]ariation is a critical feature in relation to the way in which the intended learning is brought about, as well as being a critical feature for students' learning. . . . differences in what the students learn is to a large extent a function of what they can possibly learn. What they can possibly learn is a space of learning constituted by that which it is possible to discern.
>
> (Marton, Runesson, & Tsui, 2004, p. 38)

A LS begins by focusing on the "Object of Learning" (OoL): that is, the new knowledge, capability, or beliefs that it is intended learners will appropriate (Marton & Lo, 2007). The OoL is analyzed for its "critical features": these belong to the set ideas, characteristics, and identifying features that uniquely mark the "object." Students are tested before the lesson (pretest) to explore their prior knowledge. Teachers (collaboratively) prepare a lesson that creates a "space of learning" by systematically presenting and varying the critical features, thus providing students with experiences of the OoL consistent with their prior knowledge. A posttest follows the lesson, the results of which are used to inform reflection and a subsequent implementation of the lesson.

Communities of Inquiry

Teaching developmental research that seeks to establish Communities of Inquiry (CoI) claims to draw upon approaches and experiences from lesson study, learning study, action research, design research, and practitioner research (Goodchild, Fuglestad, & Jaworski, 2013; Jaworski, 2004). CoI approaches set out to first establish communities of teachers and researchers/ teacher educators who will collaborate in the design of lessons and activities for students. Teachers' collaborative action in teaching and learning facilitates the sharing of ideas, provides support in meeting new challenges, and opens up opportunities for reflection, discussion, and learning. Inquiry is presented as an approach to learning and practice that will empower students and teachers to face and overcome the challenges of learning and teaching. As with LS and other forms of practitioner research, a cyclical approach is envisaged, proceeding through phases of design and planning for teaching, implementation, and observation of lessons, reflection, reporting, and feeding back into subsequent planning.

Comparing and Contrasting LS and COI

Given their claims to the same antecedents, lesson study and design research, it is not surprising that there is common ground shared by LS and CoI approaches. In both, groups of teachers collaborate with researchers/teacher educators designing for classroom activity. In both, the researcher/teacher educator takes an active part in the design activity, but the design is essentially developed by the teachers and implemented by the teachers with their own classes. Both approaches pay attention to learning or development at three levels: students learning mathematics, teachers learning about teaching and learning mathematics, and researchers testing theory and learning about the developmental processes. Both are concerned with the interaction and exchange of craft and scholarly knowledge. However, there are also significant differences.

An LS focuses on the OoL, and the relation between OoL and the learner. The view of learning is based on phenomenography (Marton, 1981), which is essentially constructivist with its attention to providing a space of learning that structures the learner's experience of the OoL and guides the learner into making the intended sense. LS and variation theory recognize differences between the teachers' intended OoL, the enacted OoL in the lessons implemented, and the lived OoL, which the students experience. A learning study may last 10 to 12 weeks and comprise a sequence of LS events (each including several iterations beginning with analysis of OoL, then through pretest to expose students prior knowledge, lesson design, implementation, posttest to expose knowledge appropriated, and reflection-revised design). Each small group of teachers and their classes included within a LS event form a discrete source of data. The three-year project reported by Lo, Pong, and Chik (2005), for example, comprised 29 separate LSs in several subject areas: a Chinese language (10), English language (1), general studies, (4) and mathematics (14). Each LS event becomes the subject of a separate case study. More than 30 teachers at just two primary schools (grades 1 to 6) were involved. Although this project focused at the primary level, other LSes carried out at secondary levels have reported positive outcomes from the intervention (Marton & Pang, 2006). A key distinguishing feature is the intervention by the researcher/teacher educator who explains the theory of learning (variation theory) and guides the teachers in the application of this theory in their lesson designs.

LSes begin with the explicit development of teachers' craft knowledge. They are established on an a priori—and it is assumed unquestioned—theory of learning that is articulated and explained by researchers and presented to teachers as the basis for lesson design. In the case of LS that regularly incorporate variation theory, the didactical apparatus that structures the activity is framed in terms of the OoL and its critical features. These provide the symbolic, pragmatic, epistemic, and heuristic functions within the teachers' joint planning and implementing activity. Learning study cycles focus on the development of teaching particular content. Nevertheless, the focus on students' prior knowledge in the pretest and planning phase, and later posttest, open up opportunities to explore and refine scholarly knowledge of concept development, although it is not clear in the published literature reviewed that such refinement has resulted from learning studies.

By contrast, CoI is framed within socio-cultural theory, in particular Wenger's Community of Practice (CoP) theory (Wenger, 1998). Learning is theorized as identity formation through participation in a CoP.

The activity of teacher and students engaging with mathematics within an institutional setting can be seen as a practice; teaching itself can be seen as a practice in which teachers engage; similarly, didacticians' engagement in university practices or in working with teachers can be seen as practice. According to Wenger (1998, p. 173 ff.), belonging to a CoP, or having identity within a CoP, involves engagement, imagination, and alignment. Thus, in practices of mathematics learning and teaching, participants engage in their practice alongside their peers, use imagination in interpreting their own roles in the practice, and align themselves with established norms and values. (Goodchild et al., 2013, p. 395).

Jaworski and colleagues (2007) report from a CoI project, Learning Communities in Mathematics, that included teams of at least three teachers from eight schools ranging from primary (grades 1 to 7) through to upper secondary (grades 11 to 13), together with a team of about 12 university based researchers/teacher educators. The project was established on a principle of co-learning in which teachers and university-based participants were both cast as researchers and engaged in professional and practice development. University participants refer to themselves as *didacticians* rather than researchers or teacher educators to mark the distinction between their roles (didacticians were responsible for planning workshops; teachers responsible for planning for their classes) without using a language that presumed greater authority or expertise. All teachers and didacticians within the project came together in workshops, usually three each semester. Workshops included plenary presentations (of scholarly knowledge) by didacticians and teachers' reports from their school-based activity (and craft knowledge). In small groups, didacticians would provide starting points for discussion and the design of tasks and lesson plans, which subsequently would be refined within school teams, implemented, and reported back at a later workshop. Didacticians would often participate in the school-based team planning and observe and record the implementation of the teachers' designs with their classes. The project was set up to pass through three phases, each corresponding to a year of the project's activity: community building, inquiry (in teaching and learning), and goal setting (for sustainability) (Bjuland & Jaworski, 2009). Teachers exerted a strong influence over the activities of the workshops: for example, after the first year they successfully argued for more workshop time within grade-level groups preparing inquiry-based lesson activities that focused more directly on specific curriculum content, rather than developing inquiry approaches using tasks and problems that were not closely identified with rather narrow statements in the curriculum. Events within the project were recorded (video or audio) and the accumulated corpus of recordings and documentary evidence has subsequently been used to construct case studies (e.g. Goodchild et al., 2013; Jaworski, Goodchild, Eriksen, & Daland, 2011).

Learning Communities in Mathematics (LCM) was framed within a developmental research methodology that envisioned and implemented intersecting cycles of theory and teaching development. An exposition of developmental research by Gravemeijer (1994) has been illustrated in the context of LCM (Figure 22.3). A research cycle is depicted as an interaction between

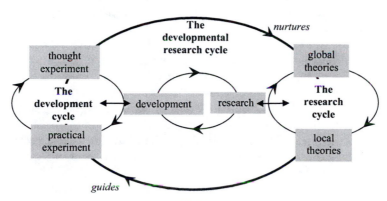

Figure 22.3 Developmental research cycle (Goodchild, 2014).

global and local theories—in LCM these are Community of Practice theory (CPT) and inquiry respectively. The research cycle is informed by the development cycle, that is, from the observations and interpretations following the implementation of inquiry-based teaching. "Inquiry tasks" provide the symbolic, pragmatic, epistemic, and heuristic functions of the didactical apparatus of LCM. Initial ideas of tasks are suggested by didacticians and then adapted and refined by teachers for their classes. Realization of the intersecting cyclical processes is demonstrated in the development of the notion of "critical alignment" (Bjuland & Jaworski, 2009) by the introduction of a local theory of inquiry to Wenger's explanation of alignment in CPT. Theory guides the developmental cycle through task design (Jaworski et al., 2011). Reflection on the developmental activity leads to critical reflection of the theory (Goodchild, 2014).

LS is explicit in presenting variation theory as a productive approach to learning and teaching. By contrast, in the example of LCM the didacticians purposefully do not offer a formula for effective teaching and learning, which are perceived as too complex for didactical formulae or structuring apparatus to be sufficient (Jaworski, 2006). Nevertheless, in CoI, there are principles of inquiry that, like the theory of variation in LS, inform each level of activity: undertaking classroom tasks, designing such tasks, and collaborating in the development of teaching and learning mathematics.

The two approaches also appear to differ in the flow of ideas between craft and scholarship. LS situates the researcher as an expert in a theory of learning, and teachers are led to design lessons that put the theory into practice. The arrangement appears to favor the flow from scholarship to practice. In a CoI, however, the teachers' knowledge and expertise, and their role as researchers are emphasized—even to the point that the teacher educators/researchers refer to themselves as didacticians. In discussions between teachers and didacticians there is the opportunity for an open exchange of ideas, but the CoI emphasizes teachers' agency and empowerment to work on their own practice, utilizing their own resources, with suggestions from didacticians rather than instruction. It thus appears that the relation favors the flow of knowledge from the teachers' practice into scholarship. These differences also appear to be reflected in the results reported from the two approaches.

Reports from LSes are supported by analyses of results from the pre- and posttests, and they demonstrate remarkable consistency in improved performance (Lo et al., 2005). Comparative studies contrasting lesson study and learning study are also reported to favor the latter (Pang & Marton, 2003); however, the design of this comparative research is questionable in that it appears there has been little attempt to match the groups or carefully control the treatments. Reports from CoI developmental research are rather nuanced. The focus on "practice" draws attention to the many constraints from without the classroom that hold the teacher in alignment to a regular practice and thus resist attempts at innovation. The reports from the LCM project offer no hard evidence regarding improvements in students' performance. Moreover, little systematic observation-based evidence of changes in teaching practices is reported. Reports from CoI tend to be descriptive and based upon the interpretation of qualitative data, reports from lessons (Jaworski, et al., 2011), teachers in group discussions (Goodchild et al., 2013), and focus group interviews (Bjuland & Jaworski, 2009). The absence of such evidence emerges directly from the methodology of developmental research and the principle of co-learning framed within communities of inquiry. Assumptions are made about teachers' knowledge of their own classes and didacticians' reluctance to present themselves as experts. The aim is to create a collaborative inquiry in which all participants are cast as researchers, but only the teachers are cast as experts in their classrooms. Furthermore, the socio-cultural and naturalistic roots of the research reject any simplistic relationship between cause and effect that might be made evident through experimental studies. Consequences of engaging in the project are thus based on teachers' reports that their practice has changed (Bjuland & Jaworski, 2009), or that they have developed greater confidence or a language to explain their practice (Jørgensen & Goodchild, 2009). The interpretation of naturally occurring data from recordings made of development and teaching events provides an evidence base for reflecting on teaching and scholarship.

CONCLUSION

This chapter has sought to illustrate how coupling the creation of scholarly knowledge within the practice of researching with the creation of craft knowledge within the practice of teaching can contribute to building a more powerful and systematic knowledge base for teaching. In particular, in one direction, contextualizing and activating scholarly knowledge within teaching and, in the other direction, eliciting and codifying craft knowledge through researching, support knowledge conversion. This helps to define a dialogic cycle through which knowledge creation within the practices of researching and teaching can be coordinated, particularly when the design of boundary-spanning didactical apparatus is placed at the heart of this endeavor. More radical approaches—through collaborative learning study and communities of inquiry—seek to challenge the role differentiation between teacher and researcher that characterizes more traditional approaches. However, depending on their particular formulations of the balance and relations between researching and teaching roles, these alternative approaches tend to privilege particular aspects of knowledge creation and conversion within the dialogic cycle.

NOTE

1. The mathematics case study can be accessed at "Looking at mathematics teaching and learning with projection technology" (http://t-media.educ.cam.ac.uk/T-Media-Mathematics/Maths%20Program%20Files/index.html) The cross-subject case study is available at "Collaborative case studies of teaching and learning with 'interactive' technologies in the secondary classroom" (http://t-media.educ.cam.ac.uk/T-Media-Across-Subjects/Program%20Files/index.html).

REFERENCES

Bjuland, R., & Jaworski, B. (2009). Teachers' perspectives on collaboration with didacticians to create an inquiry community. *Research in Mathematics Education, 11,* 21–38.

Bromme, R., & Tillema, H. (1995). Fusing experience and theory: The structure of professional knowledge. *Learning and Instruction, 5,* 261–267.

Carpenter, T. P., Fennema, E., Peterson, P. L., & Carey, D. A. (1988). Teachers' pedagogical content knowledge of students' problem solving in elementary arithmetic. *Journal for Research in Mathematics Education, 19,* 385–401.

Carpenter, T. P., Fennema, E., Peterson, P. L., Chiang, C.-P., & Loef, M. (1989). Using knowledge of children's mathematics thinking in classroom teaching: An experimental study. *American Educational Research Journal, 26,* 499–531.

Cooper, P., & McIntyre, D. (1996). *Effective teaching and learning: Teachers' and students' perspectives.* Buckingham: Open University Press.

Fennema, E., Carpenter, T. P., Franke, M. L., Levi, L., Jacobs, V. R., & Empson, S. B. (1996). A longitudinal study of learning to use children's thinking in mathematics instruction. *Journal for Research in Mathematics Education, 27,* 403–434.

Fennema, E., & Franke, M. L. (1992). Teachers' knowledge and its impact. In D. Grouws (Ed.), *Handbook of research on mathematics teaching and learning* (pp. 147–164). New York, NY: Macmillan.

Fennema, E., Franke, M. L., Carpenter, T. P., & Carey, D. A. (1993). Using children's mathematical knowledge in instruction. *American Educational Research Journal, 30,* 555–583.

Fernandez, C. (2002). Learning from Japanese approaches to professional development: The case of lesson study. *Journal of Teacher Education, 53,* 393–405.

Goodchild, S. (2014). Mathematics teaching development: Learning from research projects in Southern Norway. *ZDM: The International Journal of Mathematics Education, 46,* 305–316.

Goodchild, S., Fuglestad, A. B., & Jaworski, B. (2013). Critical alignment in inquiry-based practice in developing mathematics teaching. *Educational Studies in Mathematics, 84,* 393–412.

Gravemeijer, K. (1994). Educational development and developmental research in mathematics education. *Journal for Research in Mathematics Education, 25,* 443–471.

Hennessy, S., & Deaney, R. (2009). "Intermediate theory" building: Integrating multiple teacher and researcher perspectives through in-depth video analysis of pedagogic strategies. *Teachers College Record, 111,* 1753–1795.

Huberman, M. (1993). Changing minds: The dissemination of research and its effects on practice and theory. In C. Day, J. Calderhead, & P. Denicolo (Eds.), *Research on teacher thinking: Understanding professional development* (pp. 34–52). London: Falmer.

Jaworski, B. (2004). Grappling with complexity: Co-learning in inquiry communities in mathematics teaching development. In M. Johnsen Høines & A. B. Fuglestad (Eds.) *Proceedings of the 28th Conference of the International Group for the Psychology of Mathematics Education* (Vol. 1, pp. 17–36). Bergen: Bergen University College.

Jaworski, B. (2006). Theory and practice in mathematics teaching development: Critical inquiry as a mode of learning in teaching. *Journal of Mathematics Teacher Education, 9,* 187–211.

Jaworski, B., Fuglestad, A. B., Bjuland, R., Breiteig, T., Goodchild, S., & Grevholm, B. (Eds.) (2007). *Learning communities in mathematics.* Bergen, Norway: Caspar Forlag.

Jaworski, B., Goodchild, S., Eriksen, S., & Daland, E. (2011). Mediating mathematics teaching development and pupils' mathematical learning: The life cycle of a task. In O. Zaslavsky & P. Sullivan (Eds.) *Constructing knowledge for teaching secondary mathematics: Tasks to enhance prospective and practicing teacher learning* (pp. 143–160). London: Springer.

Jørgensen, K. O., & Goodchild, S. (2009). Utvikling av unge elevers relasjonelle forståelse i matematikk (Developing young pupils' relational understanding in mathematics). In J. Fauskanger, & R. Mosvold (Eds.) *Å regne i alle fag* (To calculate in all subjects) (pp. 100–115). Oslo: Universitetsforlaget.

Leinhardt, G. (1988a). Expertise in instructional lessons: An example from fractions. In D. A Grouws & T. Cooney (Eds.) *Effective mathematics teaching* (pp. 47–66). Reston, VA: NCTM/LEA.

Leinhardt, G. (1988b). Situated knowledge and expertise in teaching. In J. Calderhead (Ed.) *Teachers' professional learning* (pp. 146–168). London: Falmer.

Leinhardt, G. (1989). Math lessons: A contrast of novice and expert competence. *Journal for Research in Mathematics Education, 20,* 52–75.

Leinhardt, G., Putnam, T., Stein, M. K., & Baxter, J. (1991). Where subject knowledge matters. *Advances in Research in Teaching, 2,* 87–113.

Lewis, C., Perry, R., & Murata, A. (2006). How should research contribute to instructional improvement? The case of lesson study. *Educational Researcher, 35*(3) 3–14.

Lo, M. L., Pong, W. Y., & Chik, P. P. M. (Eds.) (2005). *For each and everyone: Catering for individual differences through learning studies.* Hong Kong: Hong Kong University Press.

Marton, F. (1981). Phenomenography—describing conceptions of the world around us. *Instructional Science, 10,* 177–200.

Marton, F., & Lo, M. L. (2007). Learning from "The Learning Study." *Journal of Research in Teacher Education, 1,* 31–46.

Marton, F., & Pang, M. F. (2006). On some necessary conditions of learning. *The Journal of the Learning Sciences, 15,* 193–220.

Marton, F., Runesson, U., & Tsui, A. B. M. (2004). The space of learning. In F. Marton, & A. B. M. Tsui (Eds.) *Classroom discourse and the space of learning* (pp. 3–40). Mahwah, NJ: Lawrence Erlbaum Associates.

Murata, A., Bofferding, L., Pother, B. E., Taylor, M. W., & Wischnia, S. (2012). Making connections among student learning, content, and teaching: Teacher talk paths in elementary mathematics lesson study. *Journal for Research in Mathematics Education, 43,* 616–650.

Ormel, B., Pareja-Roblin, N., McKenney, S., Voogt, J., & Pieters, J. (2012). Research-practice interactions as reported in recent design studies: still promising, still hazy. *Educational Technology Research and Development, 60,* 967–986.

Pang, M. F., & Marton, F. (2003). Beyond "lesson study": Comparing two ways of facilitating the grasp of some economic concepts. *Instructional Science, 31,* 175–194.

Peterson, P. L., Fennema, E., & Carpenter, T. P. (1991). Teachers' knowledge of students' mathematics problem-solving knowledge. *Advances in Research on Teaching, 2,* 49–86.

Potari, D. (2013). The relationship of theory and practice in mathematics teacher professional development: an activity theory perspective. *ZDM: The International Journal of Mathematics Education, 45,* 507–519.

Ruthven, K. (2002). Linking researching with teaching: towards synergy of scholarly and craft knowledge. In L. English (Ed.), *Handbook of international research in mathematics education* (pp. 581–598). Mahwah, NJ: Lawrence Erlbaum Associates.

Ruthven, K. (2005). Improving the development and warranting of good practice in teaching. *Cambridge Journal of Education, 35*, 407–426.

Stigler, J.W., & Hiebert, J. (1999). *The teaching gap: Best ideas from the world's teachers for improving education in the classroom.* New York: The Free Press.

van Bommel, J. (2012). *Improving teaching, improving learning, improving as a teacher: Mathematical knowledge for teaching as an object of learning.* Doctoral dissertation, Karlstad University, Sweden.

Watanabe, T. (2002). Learning from Japanese lesson study. *Educational Leadership, 59*, 36–39.

Wenger, E. (1998). *Communities of practice.* Cambridge: Cambridge University Press.

Wittmann, E.C. (2001). Developing mathematics education in a systematic process. *Educational Studies in Mathematics, 48*, 1–20.

Section V

Influences of Advanced Technologies

23 Foundations for the Future
The Potential of Multimodal Technologies for Learning Mathematics

Stephen J. Hegedus

Southern Connecticut State University, United States

David O. Tall

University of Warwick, UK

OVERVIEW

We are entering a new stage of the digital era where certain technologies are becoming ever more ubiquitous in our lives. Such technologies offer immersive experiences for students and fluid forms of interactivity to enhance engagement. Technology is also capturing the affordances of connectivity to enable users to connect with each other, to share their work and favorite media, and to preserve access to such items as they freely roam around a hot-spotted planet through cloud computing. Yet, it is unclear how such ubiquitous and highly usable forms of technology can and will be used in classrooms in mathematically meaningful ways. The warning of Cuban (2001) about the unfulfilled promise of technology as an agent of transformation is still relevant today, and recent national reports in the United States describe the challenging student achievement gaps between ethnic groups in mathematics classrooms, especially in urban settings, with technology still not enhancing access for all.

Ten years ago, much of the technology we are referring to was not available in mainstream classroom. Now, however, research in various countries describe computers and networks as being widely available in even the poorest of schools (U.S. Department of Education, 2007)—even though these established technologies are seldom used for the purpose of meaningful work (Bretscher, in press). Indeed, some researchers have demonstrated that the main issue now is access to quality professional development (Sinclair, Arzarello, Trigueros Gaisman, & Lozano, 2009). This theme also arises in other countries. We situate our work here in recent research funded by the U.S. National Science Foundation that explores the potential benefits of using technologies that embrace multimodal interaction and connectivity in various learning contexts. We outline examples of such technology and use an analytical framework (Tall, 2013) to explain how students can reason and learn mathematically in such environments, and we discuss the potential impact they can have on mathematics education in the future.

LITERATURE REVIEW AND BACKGROUND

Multimodal technologies offer alternative input or combined input/output methods. Common forms of alternative inputs are speech inputs (e.g., voice recognition), touch (e.g., gesture-based interactions), and bodily motion. The latter has rapidly evolved in recent years with the development of multitouch technologies (e.g., tablet PCs, interactive whiteboards, Apple iPads). Combined input/output devices include haptic devices, which integrate visual modes with force-feedback loops, offering the user the ability to feel objects or the results of their interactions with the environment.

As a consequence of new modes of interaction, it becomes possible to integrate new ways of thinking mathematically, taking us beyond textbooks with static pictures, and keyboard input as in the days when Logo was first introduced, by specifying geometric pictures with typed commands. There is now a growing potential based on successful prior research and falling costs to use multimodal technologies in mathematics classrooms to offer students multiple ways to construct meaning using their natural modalities and bodily experiences.

Multimodal interaction has evolved in various research areas and applications including computer vision/visualization, psychology, and artificial intelligence, with increasing use in education—particularly in early learning and developmental psychology. Jaimes and Sebe (2007) offer a survey of many of these disciplines, including methods of face recognition, facial expression analysis, vocal emotion, gesture recognition, human motion analysis, speech recognition, and eye tracking. They outline how multimodal interaction can simply be an environment that responds to inputs in more than one modality or communication channel (e.g., speech, gesture, writing) through perceptual, attentive, or enactive interfaces. Dautenhahn (2000) has developed multimodal interactive learning environments as teaching and learning tools for the rehabilitation of children with autism, which establishes a potential importance for their use in special needs education in general.

Multitouch environments are also evolving. Thompson Avant and Heller (2011) examined the effectiveness of using TouchMath—a multisensory program that uses key signature points on mathematical objects—with students with physical learning disabilities. Using a multiprobe, multiple baseline design, they discovered all students were successful in reaching the criterion in terms of percentages of correct responses to addition problems.

Recent work in mathematics education explores the mathematical affordances of multitouch technologies in that it can help develop number sense in part by virtue of the important role that fingers play in counting, but also because of the multimodal feedback that it offers children (Ladel & Kortenkamp, 2011; Jackiw, 2013; Sinclair & Sedaghat Jou, 2013).

It is of no surprise to us that a lot of work is focused in Special Education and with children with special needs and physical disabilities. A multimodal approach engages other senses with which to investigate and learn. We believe this approach is relevant to all learners, though, especially if the technology can increase access to complex mathematical ideas through various forms of interaction.

Over 10 years ago Chris Dede (2000) also foresaw the profound potential of multimodal technologies but found their cost to be the main impediment for full integration into mainstream schools. This is less problematic today as increasingly affordable multimodal devices flood the market and are being adopted by schools, in particular multitouch devices that incorporate visual and auditory senses with tactile use. A major challenge lies in the dramatic pace of change in technology, which has been so much faster than the changes that can be incorporated into the curriculum in a reasonable time. In addition, we need effective professional development of teachers to rethink their pedagogy with respect to the mathematical affordances and opportunities of such technologies.

In addition to using our senses, utilizing our whole body through motion is another form of mathematizing the world around us. Specific studies in mathematics education have found the use of motion detectors and interactive technologies to be important tools as mediators between students' bodily enactments and more complex mathematical representations such as graphs and functions (Brady, 2013; Nemirovsky, Kelton, & Rhodehamel, 2013; Nemirovsky & Borba, 2003; Radford, Demers, Guzmán, & Cerulli, 2003; Radford, Edwards, & Arzarello, 2009; Radford, Miranda, & Guzmán, 2008; Rasmussen, Nemirovsky, Olszewski, Dost, & Johnson, 2004).

These studies reveal how enactive embodiments can offer a foundation for understanding more subtle mathematical ideas, as indicated by Bruner (1966) in terms of his three successive modes of enactive, iconic, and symbolic operation. More recent studies (e.g. Tomasello, 1999) have shown how humans extend the ability of other primates by not only imitating what others do, but also being able to sense and share the intentions of others, and to use tools, artifacts, and language to build successively more sophisticated levels of thinking. An application of Tomasello's work to mathematics education (Hegedus & Moreno-Armella, 2011) allows us to think about the movement to dynamic, interactive technologies as an illustration of a representational redescription of mathematics in the 21st century. Such redescriptions potentially allow more students access to fundamental ways of mathematical thinking, although we also appreciate that this may also require new ways of thinking in later contexts that the learner may encounter.

A major question is how these enactive embodiments relate to the more subtle mathematical ideas that develop in more sophisticated contexts. Do they provide an embodied form of meaning that supports later developments or are there aspects that can impede later learning? This requires a theoretical framework that studies the detailed development of mathematical thinking in different individuals as they pass through successive stages of sophistication in mathematics.

Other major and related technological advances in mathematics education include the use of dynamic, interactive representations, primarily in the form of software and connectivity through exploiting the use of classroom wireless networks. We offer a brief overview of advances in these domains.

Dynamic Interactive Mathematics

Dynamic interactive mathematics environments such as The Geometer's Sketchpad® and Cabri-Geometre offer tools to construct and interact with mathematical objects and configurations. Interaction is via the executable representations of these mathematical objects. Through this interaction one can *touch* the underlying mathematical structure (Hegedus & Moreno-Armella, 2011). Objects can be selected and dragged by mouse movements in which all user-defined mathematical relationships are preserved. In such environments, students are supported in efforts to formulate conjectures and generalizations by clicking and dragging hotspots on an object, which dynamically redraw and update information on the screen as the user drags the mouse (Drijvers, Kieran, & Mariotti, 2009). In doing so, the user can explore and efficiently test an entire parameter space of equivalent mathematical constructions.

Such environments aim to develop spatial sense and mathematical reasoning by allowing conjectures to be tested, offering "intelligent" tools that constrain users to select, construct, or manipulate objects that obey mathematical rules (Mariotti, 2003) alongside well-developed curriculum activities. The core features are construction and manipulation, allowing constructs to be dynamically reconfigured. Empirical work states how these features can lead to improvement in student achievement (Battista, 1997; Hollebrands, 2002), student engagement through aesthetic motivation (Sinclair, 2001, 2002a, 2002b), student ability to generalize mathematical conjectures (Mariotti, 2000), and student development of theoretical arguments (Laborde, 2000, 2001; Noss & Hoyles, 1996). Actions of pointing, clicking, grabbing, and dragging parts of geometric constructions allows a form of mediation (Falcade, Laborde, & Mariotti, 2007) between the object and the user who is attempting to make sense of, or discover some particular attribute of, the figure or to prove some theorem. This is referred to as *semiotic mediation*, which corresponds to mediation through the use of sign systems and artifacts whose meanings are generated by social construction (Hassan, 1992; Vygotsky, 1980).

Such environments have also been applied to a variety of topics to enable modeling practices (Jackiw & Sinclair, 2007) ranging from applications in the primary grades (Battista, 1997; Sinclair & Crespo, 2006; Sinclair & Moss, 2012) to more advanced applications including analysis

(Cuoco & Goldenberg, 1997), trigonometry (Shaffer, 1995), calculus (Gorini, 1997), physics (Olive, 1997), complex analysis (Jackiw, 2003), non-Euclidean geometry (Dwyer & Pfiefer, 1999; Hegedus & Moreno-Armella 2011), data analysis (Flowers, 2002), and Linear Algebra (Gol Tabaghi & Sinclair, 2013).

Dynamic, interactive environments often are representationally rich, creating multiple perspectives on mathematical ideas. Simulations are used to explore functional relationships (Falcade et al., 2007; Yerulshalmy & Naftaliev, 2011), complex systems (Stroup, 2005), and rate and variation (Hegedus & Roschelle, 2013), to name just a few topics. The affordances of such environment establish a representational infrastructure that provides new ways for students to express, visualize, compute, and interact with mathematical objects (Kaput, Hegedus, & Lesh, 2007). Indeed, many of these topics are currently introduced in the secondary or tertiary grades of mathematics education, but that does not undermine the potential for using multimodal technologies to maximize the use of dynamic representations in the early grades as well. The key idea here is that such technologies offer a representational redescription of the core mathematical structures through executable representations. Such representations can link mathematical attributes to modalities such as touch or force feedback. For us, it is less about the curriculum that as stated should be introduced at various levels but rather the modification of the representational system that such technologies can potentially establish. A graph of a function can be thought of as a static figure and operated on discretely through ordered pairs or represented in tabular format, or it can be redescribed as a continuous object that can be smoothly and fluidly examined dynamically and touched. For example, consider the difference between *feeling* a linear and a quadratic function: How do we sense "linear-ness" or "quadratic-ness"? More profoundly, a student using his or her fingers to manipulate a graph on a tablet can zoom in to *see* how a curved graph (such as a quadratic curve or a circle) magnifies to look "locally straight." Tracing the changing slope of the graph offers an embodied meaning linking to the symbolic processes of differentiation, integration, differential equations, the wider aspects of multidimensional vector calculus, and on to the formal structures of mathematical analysis. In this chapter we posit that multimodal technologies have a role in all grades. Their use with young children plays an essential role in the full range of development from elementary to undergraduate classrooms.

Classroom Connectivity

Classroom connectivity (which generally means networked classroom activities and assessment) has roots in more than a decade of classroom response systems, most notably ClassTalk™ (Abrahamson, 1998, 2000), which enabled instructors to collect, aggregate, and display (often as histograms) student responses to questions, and in so doing create new levels of interaction in large classes in various domains (Burnstein & Lederman, 2001; Crouch & Mazur, 2001; Dufresne, Gerace, Leonard, Mestre, & Wenk, 1996; Hake, 1998; Piazza, 2002) and levels (Hartline, 1997). Roschelle, Abrahamson, and Penuel (2003) show remarkably consistent positive impacts across multiple domains and levels. Some of the new affordances beyond classroom response systems are (1) increased mobility of multiple representations of mathematical objects such as functions, as reflected in the ability to pass these bidirectionally and flexibly between the teacher and students and among students, using multiple device-types; (2) the ability for teachers to arrange, organize, and analyze sets of whole-class contributions at once, and students to make sense of their work in a social context, reasoning, and generalizing about their contribution with respect to their peers' work. Such affordances transform the communication infrastructure of the classroom (Roschelle, Knudsen, & Hegedus, 2010), which extends the normal affordances of social networks by increasing mathematically meaningful participation (Dalton & Hegedus, 2013), offering opportunities for generative activity and investigation space (Stroup, Ares & Hurford, 2005), and establishing comparisons between private and public work (Vahey, Tatar, & Roschelle, 2007). This can all lead to enhanced engagement and learning due to the collaborative nature of the classroom. Such research has primarily been conducted in secondary grades but we believe there is a lot of potential for such work in the primary grades, which often structure classroom activities around small group work or learning stations. It is important to note that in each of these examples it is not just the technology that is the primary agent of change in these classrooms, but rather the integrated nature of the activity design and the technology that structures learning through enhanced discourse. We will return to this key point later.

In summary, there have been many advances in digital technology in mathematics education that are situated, or could be situated, in a wide variety of school classrooms. A technology-enhanced curriculum that combines interactive mathematics software, networked classroom connectivity, and multimodal interaction has the potential to impact learning and enrich mathematical discourse in the future, based on present work and the growing ubiquity of multimodal technologies in society. But we acknowledge that such a claim should be modified by the lack of teacher professional development and preparation that is in Cuban's warning regarding the unfulfilled role of technology in schools (Cuban, 2001). We return to this issue in our concluding remarks.

We will now outline some applications of these ingredients combined in different ways (but focusing on multimodal experiences) before providing an analytical framework for examining how such technologies can provide a platform for mathematical learning.

NEW MATHEMATICAL ACTIVITIES IN A TECHNOLOGY-ENHANCED LEARNING ENVIRONMENT

We have not tried to cover all advances in educational technology relevant to mathematics learning, as we prefer to situate our position in aspects of development that we believe are most promising in taking a mathematical-activity centered approach vs. a technology-centered approach. Technology should not be just a pedagogical prop or a computational aid in instruction or learning (Moreno-Armella & Hegedus, 2009) but rather a transformative device to enhance the discipline of learning between students and teachers. For example we have chosen not to highlight the major relevance of Computer-Aided Instruction or Online Assessment Tutors as a major development in educational technology and computer science in the past 10 years (see Hegedus & Roschelle, 2012 for further details): our focus is primarily on multimodal technologies that allow students to access the beauty and complexity of mathematics in simple ways that engage many aspects of their biological and social self.

Several examples we offer here have been developed at the Kaput Center with support from the National Science Foundation;[1] others are prototypes based on present technological affordances. We focus on several environments that we have explored utilizing various modalities, representationally rich interactive software, and classroom networks where possible. These include (1) force-feedback in concert with 3D visual shapes and surfaces and (2) multitouch technology for exploring mathematical objects and attributes and concepts. The activities serve as exemplars of the types of learning opportunities possible. We can tap into such technological affordances in mathematically meaningful ways that can be generative in the future.

Force Feedback Technology

Sensable's PHANTOM Omni® (www.sensable.com/haptic-phantom-omni.htm)—hereafter referred to as "Omni"—is a desktop haptic device with six degrees of freedom for input (x, y, z, pitch, roll, yaw), and three degrees of output (x, y, z). The Omni's most typical operation is via a stylus-like attachment that includes two buttons (see Figure 23.1). The Omni provides up to three forces of feedback for x, y, and z. It is primarily used in research, with a

Figure 23.1 A student operates the PHANTOM Omni® haptic device.

Figure 23.2 Students' view of the multimodal environment.

significant presence in dentistry and medicine but growing in mathematics education (Hegedus & Moreno-Armella, 2011). In the environment, models of 2D and 3D objects and haptic simulations (e.g., magnetism, friction) are used to create a dynamic, visual-haptic scene (Figure 23.2). User interactions with the models within a scene are graphically displayed through the haptic pointer on the computer screen and physically meditated by the haptic device as the user moves the stylus or presses the buttons on the stylus. For example, one application allows users to move and rotate a cube. In the application, when a user moves the haptic pointer onto the frictional surface of the cube and presses a haptic button, the position and rotation of the cube is synced to those values of the haptic stylus until the button is released.

Multitouch Technology

In collaboration with KCP Technologies, the Kaput Center developed a set of activities for use with Sketchpad®Explorer for the iPad (hereafter referred to as "Explorer"), a viewer application of the widely popular The Geometer's Sketchpad® software (hereafter referred to as "Sketchpad"). This application is available in the Apple Store. Activities were constructed in Sketchpad and then transferred to the iPad through email or other forms of file exchange. All activities are preconfigured for students and teachers to use, as no construction tools are presently available in this version for the iPad. Students directly interact with objects in preconfigured activities including geometric objects (e.g., points), iterative counters through flicking, or buttons that had been configured to perform a set of operations (e.g., reflection of an image).

With multitouch/multi-input devices such as the Apple iPad, the learner can use multiple modes of input and outputs—their natural modes of seeing and feeling—to make sense of a task. The iPad offers a direct (almost zero-interface) mode to touch and directly manipulate mathematical objects (see Figure 23.3). It offers multiple inputs to one mathematical object that are hitherto impossible on a single-input computer with mouse as pointer and selector (see Figure 23.4). In Figure 23.3 you can touch both vertices of the mirror segment at once, which can change the way one thinks about a line of symmetry in a static world. In Figure 23.4, both vertices have to be used simultaneously either with two fingers or by two people, which can change the mathematical experience.

We now present a framework that will enable us to describe how students can use and experience such technologies as a new platform for mathematical learning through a multimodal approach in the future.

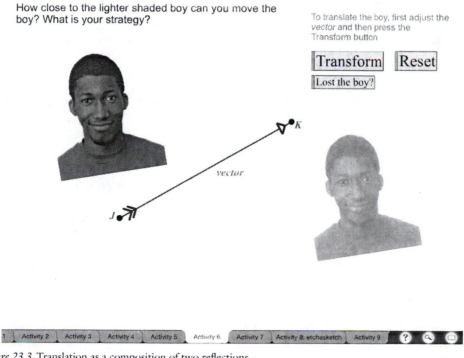

Figure 23.3 Translation as a composition of two reflections.

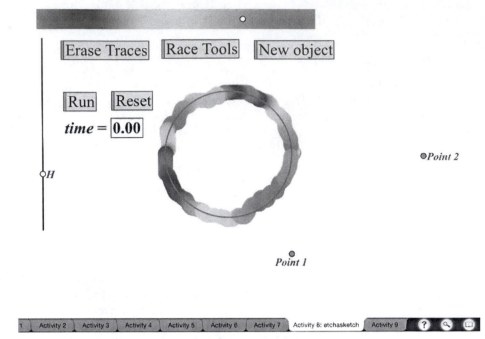

Figure 23.4 Etchasketch—Moving two points simultaneously to obtain a circle.

FRAMEWORK: HOW STUDENTS CAN LEARN MATHEMATICS

To formulate a theoretical framework for the development of mathematical thinking and the use of multimodal technologies, we need to consider not only what individuals may or may not learn at a particular stage of development using various modes of *perception and operation*, but also to consider the increasingly sophisticated forms of *reason* that develops in each individual over the longer term. Contrary to the view that mathematics is a fully coherent system of knowledge, successive mathematical structures involve new meanings that may be supportive in some contexts but problematic in others (Tall, 2013).

For example, the initial stages of counting and number involve physical playing with objects, sorting them, and learning the complex act of counting. Once the child realizes that the number does not change if the objects are placed in different ways, it is possible to focus on the idea that a set of six objects can be seen as four plus two or two plus four, or even three lots of two or two lots of three. This perception of the dynamic layout of the objects can lead to more general ideas, such as the observation that the order of addition or multiplication does not affect the final total. This, in turn, gives mental connections between physical and mental perceptions and operations that Tall (2013) refers to as *embodied compression* from the operation of counting to the concept of number.

When focusing on counting without such an overall conception, however, it is not obvious that 7 + 2 (a short count-on of 2 that can be performed on one hand) is the same as 2 + 7 (a longer count-on of 7 that requires the fingers of both hands). Tall (2013) refers to the focus on counting procedures to build the properties of whole number arithmetic as *symbolic compression*.

The term *embodiment* is used with very different meanings in the literature. For example, Dienes (1960) used the term to describe physical materials such as Dienes' blocks to express the properties of arithmetic of whole numbers, whereas Lakoff & Nunez (2000) use the term more broadly to claim that all human thinking is based on sensori-motor operations that may be expressed metaphorically using language. Here we are interested in the way in which mathematical ideas may be represented and interpreted physically or mentally using multimodal technology.

Embodiments can be supportive and simple in some aspects yet be complicated and even problematic in others. For example, Dienes' blocks are simple embodiments for place value in addition. A unit is a small cube; in base 10, a "long" is ten cubes glued together to represent "10" as a single entity. Adding two collections such as 17 plus 6 is one long with seven units, plus six units. Combining ten of the units to give a new long results in two longs and three units, symbolized as 23. However, when the same embodiment is used for multiplication, additional features arise in which multiplication by 10 replaces ten units with a "long" and ten "longs" with a ten-by-ten "flat" that represents one hundred. So Dienes' blocks are less appropriate for multiplication.

In this case, a new embodiment may offer a more appropriate context for meaning. For instance, in the multiplication of whole numbers, multiplication of decimal numbers by 10 can be embodied by physical operations on the symbols themselves. A simple method is to write three 0s on a piece of paper and cover them with strips of paper with a single digit on the end of the strip (see Figure 23.5). The number 27 is represented by placing a 7 in the units place and a 2 over the first strip in the tens place to represent 27 as two tens and seven units (or 27 units). Multiplying by 10 is embodied by shifting the number one place to the left to get two 100s and seven 10s, or 27 tens, or 270 units. (Tall, 2013, pp. 135–137).

This involves a new physical operation (moving the symbols themselves) that can then be imagined in the mind to "see" digits moving mentally in a more sophisticated way—so the meaning of the symbolic operation can be supported by more sophisticated embodiment. It also offers a much more flexible meaning for symbolism as a basis for multidigit multiplication, in which blocks of digits are moved one place to the left to multiply by 10 or one place to the right to divide by 10, including moving the block of numbers over the decimal point to see that 27 divided by 10 is 2.7, which is 2 units and 7 tenths. (Tall, 2013, pp.135–138).

The development of successive levels of sophistication follows the same broad pattern as new contexts are encountered. New embodiments can support certain aspects of the new situation yet be problematic in others. This occurs at successive stages of the curriculum where previous experience can impede new learning, in the shift from whole numbers to fractions, from unsigned numbers to signed numbers, from fractions to infinite decimals, from arithmetic to algebra. At each stage, properties that were supportive in one context (e.g. multiplication gives a bigger result, subtraction produces a smaller result, and so on) become problematic later on.

The development of new multimedia technology changes the paradigm. The multimodal environment offers the learner a way to operate on objects that behave in a predictable way. This provides the opportunity for the learner to gain insight in an intuitive, embodied way prior to developing algorithms for more sophisticated use. However, the particular embodiment may be supportive at one stage but become problematic in a new context, so there

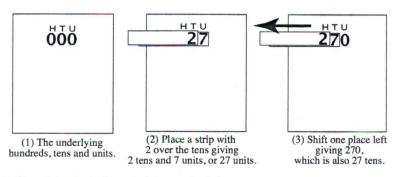

Figure 23.5 Shifting digits physically to the left to multiply by ten.

remains the longer term task of how learning at one stage can impact on later learning. This involves not only the development of the individual child making sense of the fundamental mathematical ideas, but also the social interaction with the technology as a critical factor in their collective sense making.

APPLICATION TO HOW CHILDREN USE MULTIMODAL TECHNOLOGIES

Exemplary Activity 1: Force Feedback

In this activity, we offered students two objects to manipulate: a plane and a 3D shape (e.g. a cone, cube, or pyramid). First the student can use the Omni as a selection device for clicking-and-dragging the objects around the screen and reorienting them through twisting the device handle (see Figure 23.6). Once the plane has been moved to intersect with the 3D shape the device handle becomes a navigation tool for moving the red bug (see Figure 23.6) around the surfaces and intersections, providing feedback through continuous forces. Through iterative design we have found that using magnetism is a useful design principle to enable the user to focus on what part of the shapes the bug is located. This experience locks the bug onto the surface: the device begins to provide continuous force and abrupt changes as you move over a specific discontinuity (e.g. a vertex or edge). In particular, the user also feels "locked-on" or "sucked into" the intersection joints. Navigation is also driven by 3D motions of the device so that as the user moves the Omni handle in real space, it simulates the experience of feeling the pseudo-3D visual shapes on the screen. This design principle and the use of a bug was discovered to be important for children to coordinate their physical motion with the flat-visual space on the screen. It was a way of calibrating the two modalities so that children might begin to talk about both experiences. This had been problematic in previous editions. As we show in the next section, the use of a red bug was not only fun and engaging for the children but became a useful reference point for the children to talk about the experiences. As we will describe, though, children's discourse moved from talking about the bug explicitly (i.e. the results of the bug's actions) to focusing on the specific mathematical attributes of the shapes. The bug had a short life in their exploration. Once the child sensed the relationship between the two situations, it became possible to move on from the specifics of the particular embodiment to reasoning about the underlying mathematical relationships.

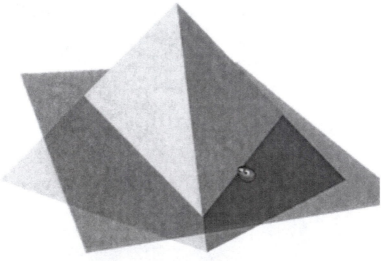

Figure 23.6 Planar intersection with a square-based pyramid.

One variation of this activity was to use a square-based pyramid with the plane. We draw on a case of four 10-year-olds exploring this setup to explain how students make sense of such mathematical configurations through our analytical framework. Our primary goal was to examine the types of discourse that students use to make sense of the configurations.

The children were engaged in the exploration within minutes of introducing them to the environment. Initially, the children were focused on perception, with statements that were a mixture of mathematical observations, metaphors, and behaviors of the elements of the configuration. These are initial observations:

John:	It might be triangle.
Sarah:	Could be.
John:	Could also be a square.
Sarah:	See if it's like a wall.
Peter:	It feels heavy.
Sarah:	Heavy? . . .
Sarah:	The bug is like sucking on it or something.

As the children continued to explore the interplay between visual and haptic modalities it became more evident where their initial visual forms of perceptions were challenged by physical information back from the Omni device:

Sarah:	A triangle it looks like.
Peter:	*[Continues to trace intersection and repeatedly move bug off and back onto intersection.]* When you go up here it's a triangle, *[referring to the shape made between the front facing edge and one part of the intersection]* because that's how it is. But when you go around here *[moves bug beneath blue shape]* it kind of feels like a square.

Several of the children began to focus more on the objects and their properties (Operation) as well as attempting to interpret the effect of their interactions (Reason) and how the plane is perceived of in terms of how it cuts particular parts of the pyramid apart:

Megan:	I think the square is cutting it off *[gestures]* where it's making, because the square it goes like that and it goes like that *[gestures a square with her two hands]*. I think it cuts it off where it goes like that *[gestures one corner of a square with two hands]*.
	Because it's cutting —*[points to screen]* it's just leaving the bottom not the top. *[screen turns black]* What happened? *[comes back]* Oh. It's just —it's not cutting the side of it *[gestures]* where it makes a triangle. It's cutting in the middle, *[gestures]* so it makes a square on the bottom just like the square base pyramid.

The children resolve this conflict by counting sides that they feel and turns that they make. They felt the sharp feedback of moving around a vertex or angle whilst being continually "stuck to" the intersection. The children continue to explore though based on an emerging sense of how this configuration can be extended and a potential understanding of the flexibility of this dynamic intersection. This was not prompted by the interviewer:

Sarah:	I think we can get a five-sided shape.
Interviewer:	Sorry, what? I missed that?
Sarah:	When we felt the triangle if we went on the other side of the square [*the base of the pyramid* [we could get a pentagon.
Peter:	Yeah we could.

Interviewer:	Show me how you can do that using this plane? *[Students pass device down to Sarah]*
Sarah:	*[Sarah adjusts plane to intersect with the base] [Peter is drawing]* It's like that.
Interviewer:	Okay.
Sarah:	*[Traces with bug her intersection, counting sides]* Then you have this side and then it has to go like that. And then you have that side and then you have that. And then that.
Interviewer:	So for a pentagon, how many sides do you want to feel?
Sarah:	Five.

This is an example of embodied compression that could potentially lead to forms of symbolic compression with similar explorations of other polyhedra. Children are focusing on the objects involved in this configuration and can flexibly manipulate the intersection through dynamically (visually) editing the slope of the tangent plane. There is evidence that the faces of the shape are important for the children in trying to reason the classification of the intersection (i.e. by moving the plane into the base of the pyramid) but the faces are not being enumerated at this stage.

At this stage, the young students do not express the idea that the planar intersection of a polyhedron of n faces would be at most an n-gon. However, our work with high school and undergraduate students with a similar activity led to such discoveries being made along with similar forms of reasoning. This suggests that the design and use of multimodal technologies in the future can potentially establish learning environments for students at various age levels and needs. This example and subsequent ones outlines an opportunity space for open-ended and semistructured activities.

Exemplary Activity 2: Multiple Inputs Correspond to Mathematical Variables

In this activity, one student controls the lateral-moving Point 1 and another student controls the vertical-moving Point 2, or one student controls both simultaneously (see Figure 23.7). The goal is for the students to trace a colored blob around the fixed circle. A third student (or

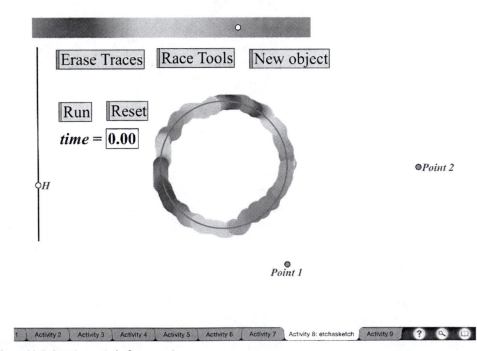

Figure 23.7 Creating a circle from two inputs.

third finger input) can adjust the color of the trace, in order to make a rainbow of color around the circle (point on the spectrum), or the size of the blob (point H).

This activity exemplifies how the technological affordances of multitouch can be adapted in mathematically meaningful ways, hence they could be described as mathematical affordances of the technology. Let us offer a simple example to explain what this means. Consider using an iPad to watch a movie. A pinch gesture can be used to make the movie smaller (or larger if the pinch is reversed outwards). This is a mode of interaction, and an affordance of the operating system and hardware. It allows the user to operate in a particular way. Consider now a geometric shape where the user performs a similar gesture either as a pinch or with two fingers (since the operating system allows such interactions) and the shape is dilated. Here the technological affordances can be made mathematical actions. In a sense, the biological actions are mathematized, putting mathematics at the very tips of students' fingers. Unlike on a desktop computer, here the user can provide two inputs simultaneously to manipulate the sliders (on Points 1 and 2). Point 1 is constrained in order to be moved along an invisible horizontal line segment and Point 2 on a vertical line segment orthogonal to the horizontal one. In this construction we have parameterized two input functions using traditional interactive tools. The two sliders are combined to create one output, hence the input covariates create a single visual output (i.e. the blob), which they need to trace around a fixed circle. Such an input methodology can be conducted by one person with two fingers or by two people with single finger-input strokes. We have found the latter to lead to collaborative problem-solving techniques where each person directs the other to create the desired output. The coordination of such discourse moves can establish mathematical arguments regarding the relationship between the input routines (social/individual) and output (computational/visual).

In our studies, elementary school and undergraduate students rapidly move towards moving the point-sliders separately. This has been completed using single-discrete finger movements of Point 1 followed by Point 2, followed by Point 1 and the Point 2 to create four discrete line segments as the initial trace (i.e. a square). Many groups in our studies have done this both individually and collaboratively. Such initial investigations illustrate perception based on information from actions on base-objects in the learning environment. Following the visual feedback, students realize that they are not meeting the challenge of tracing of a circle and focus more on the effects of their inputs and the properties of these interactive elements controlled by their touch. In one example, two students expressed:

Rob: We need to move point one left and right . . .
Sally: And point two up and down but with a different speed I think.

Given this initial form of reasoning of the essential elements and their potential role in creating a new mathematical object (the blob output point), we highlight this as a form of embodied compression where students focus on the effect of their input operations, in particular the speed of their input as a model for the mathematical variation formerly embedded in this activity. For example, one student in this group said:

Jared: I think we need to move it faster and slower at some points.

Finally, two students in the group move to a form of reasoning that involves the coordination of both inputs:

Rob: Point one is kind of a y-axis. . . And point two is kind of a x-axis.
Sally: Like. . . One person can control . . . like going up-and-down . . . like going on the sides of the circle . . . and the other person can control the . . . top and bottom of the circle.

The combination of such reactions and establishment of properties of the moving inputs and outputs lead to iteratively successful circles. Symbolic compression is at an elementary stage here where the structure of the inputs with respect to the output are informally formulated but the essential properties of such coordination are established: (1) two inputs create one output; (2) the two inputs need to co-vary, i.e. move together in some fashion; (3) the two input-touch motions need to vary in terms of motion to map the circle. This still lacks the formal symbolic clarity of defining how such motions can be described in terms of a phased combination of sinusoidal motions (functions), i.e., $x^2 \times y^2 = (\sin t)^2 = (\cos t)^2 = 1$.

With recent prototypes we have explored a new design space that allows students to share their construction and parameterize their contributions in ways that can lead to mathematically rich discussion in terms of comparison, reasoning, and deduction. Through the affordances of wireless connectivity, students can share their investigations electronically with the teacher, who can display through their device connected to a projector thus providing a public space for discussion. In addition, the activity can be reconfigured at an individual or group level for comparison in this display space, for example, varying the circle diameter or shape, which can lead to a contrast of actions and formulated procedures in a whole-class discussion.

DISCUSSION AND FUTURE PERSPECTIVES

We have looked closely at learners' discourse in terms of their utterances and actions both individually and socially, since they have worked in groups. In particular the role of non-scholastic language in making sense of the properties of mathematical objects or concepts—e.g. the planar intersections of solids, categorizing shapes and surfaces, making sense of geometric transformations or composition of transformations through multitouch, to name a few. We have observed in other work (Güçler, Hegedus, Robidoux, & Jackiw, 2013) that some forms of non-scholastic statements are mathematically meaningful in scaffolding meaning for the group, and some scholastic language can be used in mathematically inaccurate ways (e.g. drawing on prior knowledge of shapes in incorrect ways). Students sometimes experienced cross-modality where one modality (what they see) conflicts with another modality (what they feel).

Using embodied compression, children are focusing on objects and the consequences of their fluid interaction with the environment. They are also engaged in co-action (Moreno-Armella, & Hegedus, 2009) where they are guiding and being guided by their actions within this dynamic, responsive environment, which potentially allows them to "see through" to the underlying mathematical structures inherent in the figures on the screen and the "invisible" forces of the haptic device (Hegedus & Moreno-Armella, 2011). We see the beginning of this in Example 1 where the students realize and rationalize the intersection being a pentagon through visual-haptic arguments and in Example 2 in Jared's comments about the dynamics of his movement (finger actions) in that they need to change speed at some points that give rise to the circularity of the output blob. "Seeing through" can be thought of as potential insights, perceptions into, or metaphors regarding the underlying structure. An underlying structure here might be the formal parametric definition of the circle.

We have observed that it is very difficult to parse out the visual from the haptic experience, but what the child or children perceive is of particular relevance. The real challenge is developing learning environments with sequences of curriculum activities that enable students to transition to forms of symbolic compression. Without a focus, such students might only focus on the embodiment, which could be an impediment to future learning.

These are perennial points for many popular technologies in mathematics education including Logo, Dynamic Geometry, and Spreadsheets. It might be that any aim of moving towards symbolic compression and comprehension (and even application) through the use of such technologies is at odds with providing access to more students: you cannot achieve both. But then, the practice of mathematical thinking is potentially changing because of the transformative role such multimodal technologies have on the distributed cognitive and communicative activities of the classrooms such that the nature of mathematical discourse evolves.

Such technologies can be thought of as *cognitive extensions* of the biological self (i.e. thinking through our fingertips), or the drawing closer of our natural biological senses and the abstraction of mathematical thinking through the mediating effect of multimodal technologies. As Rotman (2000) has suggested:

> [S]uch a transformation of mathematical practice would have a revolutionary impact on how we conceptualize mathematics, on what we imagine a mathematical object to be, on what we consider ourselves to be doing when we carry out mathematical investigations, and persuade ourselves of certain assertions, certain properties and features of mathematical objects, are to be accepted as "true". Indeed the very rules and protocols that control what is and isn't mathematically meaningful, what constitutes a "theorem", for example, would undergo a sea change.
>
> (p. 68–69)

The essential point here is that not only do these technologies allow a shift in the mathematical representational infrastructure but they can also enhance the communication infrastructure of the classroom in the types, and new forms, of mathematical discourse that can arise from such use in the future.

We have explored the affordance of linking mathematical objects or functional relationships through haptic environments. For example, a child can use the haptic device to provide dynamic changes to inputs that are mathematical variables and receive physical feedback that is a dependent variable to the input(s). Here the technological environment co-acts in different ways mathematically to the navigational scenarios described. In the activity illustrated in Figure 23.8, a child can click and drag points A, B, and C (vertices of the triangle) or D (a point to control the translational position of a parallel line which the triangle is constructed on), but the Omni device is programmed to provide resistance (force feedback) that is proportional to the area of the triangle ABC. Moving certain vertices will result in invariant resistance (e.g. C) whereas others will create changing resistance due to the base or height of the triangle being modified.

In our preliminary work, children can attribute the inputs to mathematical variables that result in the output "feeling" and mathematical representation. Whilst children in our studies have not explained this relationship as Area = ½ × base × height, they have described the Area to be related to changes in the base and height, a form of embodied compression. This is also the beginning of symbolic compression. However, more work needs to be done to understand and realize how such experiences can establish such forms of symbolizing.

Multitouch environments such as Explorer allow young learners to interact with simple configurations that involve mathematically meaningful input and outputs. Such modalities allow children to use various modalities to explore configurations and focus on their actions

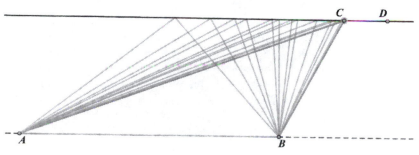

Figure 23.8 Dynamic triangles.

(to develop their perception) and their operations on objects and their iterative responses based on core interactivity design principles. Such forms of co-actions (between multimodal iterations and their output, which further guide actions) can generate learning environments that enable students to focus on the operations that enable an understanding of the mathematical properties and structures being investigated. Tall (2013) aspires towards the "long-term simplification of mathematical ideas"; such infrastructures can offer such opportunities. This notion of *simplification* is both mathematical (where mathematicians and teachers make sense of the mathematical structures by formulating new concepts that can be manipulated as mental entities) and also personal (where learners make sense of the compressed entities in flexible ways). Such flexible thinking can be encouraged at all levels. For example, by building on the prototypical examples described in this chapter students could engage in a multitouch/ input approach to collaboratively create an isosceles triangle or some other classification of 2D triangles through group strategizing. Such actions on the base vertices A or B could establish methods to focus on the steps necessary to create an equiangular shape or similar magnitudes of sides and develop symbolic compression. In addition, with well-configured sketches, many "parent-child" relationships, which preserve mathematical attributes, could be discovered through a multitouch approach. A free triangle with no constraints on the vertices would lead to a collaborative strategy (or an individual one) that focuses on the effect of moving one vertex with respect to the other one; or the effects of moving two vertices with respect to the corresponding sides; or the invariance of such actions on some of the properties of the triangle.

In addition, the potential of such devices in a connected environment can help develop the process of symbolic compression as students individually, collaboratively, and in comparison, externalize the steps that are necessary in coordinating a workspace of procedures and sense-making of mathematical concepts and attributes. The public workspace could be a collaborative arrangement where each student is developing a variation of a set of configurations—e.g. a family of similar triangles—or an aggregative enterprise where children build particular linked pieces of a constructions, knowing how their piece interacts with someone else's product or the whole group construction.

We have attempted to introduce how recent multimodal technologies can create learning environments for students to access the basis for the mathematical properties of shapes, configurations and functional relationships focused on variation and covariation. This can be achieved, and in the future refined, through the combination of various modalities, in particular touch and visual. The primary purpose is to enable access to the embedded mathematical structure in order that a "focus on real-world embodiment can make sense for early learners, giving embodied meaning to symbolic operations." (Tall, 2013, p.173.)

We propose that the long-term development of mathematical thinking can be sustained through the careful use of multimodal technologies and meaningful implementation—careful because of the potential for causing confusion for students in conflicting modal experiences highlighted earlier, and also because of the possibility that formal symbolic compression might not be achieved through such implementation. The opportunity space that we outline here needs to be explored in ways that can create coherent mathematical experiences that not only allow access to mathematical ideas and concepts but also develop into more general symbolic thinking. This might not be possible for the whole spectrum of learners; future work needs to address this critically as more curriculum is developed that integrates such technological affordances in meaningful ways. We have tried to demonstrate here ways of doing this where the physical experience has been preprogrammed to correspond to mathematical attributes or multiple touches (input) correspond to mathematical operations (e.g. transformations). Both of these approaches are time consuming and should be built and tested in a research environment. The alternative is a form of edutainment where the feedback is superfluous to the mathematics of the activity.

Future work also needs to address which populations of students are being addressed and what the significance of the research actually is. In the studies reported here we have worked with traditional populations, but we also see the need to work with multimodal technologies for specific categories of learners, such as those with special educational needs (as outlined at the start of this chapter). Future work needs to focus on pedagogical strategies and the preparation of teachers to implement such strategies.

One of the long-term critical issues for effective implementation of technologies in schools is the professional development of teachers not only to understand how to use the new tools but also the pedagogical implications. Depending on the stage of their careers, teachers might be faced with rethinking how such technologies can enhance the learning environment or even transform the very nature of the classroom in terms of how mathematics is redescribed. If teachers are later in their career this might involve a shift in mindset to how content is conceived of and how it might be effectively introduced through such new technologies. Hennessy, Ruthven, and Brindley (2005) build on Cuban's message by reporting on use of Information and Communications Technology (ICT) in England. They report that teachers in their study might affirm that their practices are changing, but they are not participating actively in technology-based curriculum design and implementation in their schools. Hennessey and colleagues propose five specific aims for successful integration of ICT at the level of departmental policy and planning: (a) providing teachers with "opportunities for long-term collegial interaction involving critical reflection, sharing ideas, and research concerning the use of ICT" (p. 187); (b) integrating ICTs into a structure of work in alignment with the national prescribed curriculum and help in meeting learning objectives with critical and appropriate use; (c) taking into account and enhancing students and teachers' levels of technological expertise; (d) systematically evaluating the affordances of ICT for attainment of specific learning goals; and (e) offering a balance of complementary ICT-based and other learning activities. They claim organizational change processes are important in generating strategies to successful implementation of technology-based instruction and emphasize "shared ownership of plans" (p. 186) at organizational level as a requisite to implement technology into the school instructional practices with a significant impact on student learning. Our work and proposed claims for future development and implementation need to address such aims to have any widespread significance in mathematics classrooms in the future.

In conclusion, the central focus here is on the fundamentals of mathematics and how the latest advances of multimodal technologies can promote learning through the development of mathematically meaningful transformations of technological affordances. This should potentially impact curriculum design, how we teach, and how our children learn in the future.

NOTE

1. This work is based upon work supported by the National Science Foundation under Grant No. REC-0835395. Any opinions, findings, and conclusions or recommendations expressed in this material are those of the authors and do not necessarily reflect the views of the agency.

REFERENCES

Abrahamson, A. L. (1998). *An overview of teaching and learning research with classroom communication systems.* Paper presented at the Samos International Conference on the Teaching of Mathematics, Village of Pythagorion. Samos, Greece.

Abrahamson, A. L. (2000). *A brief history of ClassTalk.* Paper presented at the Teachers Teaching with Technology International Conference. Dallas, TX.

Battista, M. T. (1997). *Shape makers: Developing geometric reasoning with the Geometer's Sketchpad.* Berkeley, CA: Key Curriculum Press.

Brady, C. E (2013). *Perpectives in motion.* Unpublished doctoral dissertation, University of Massachusetts, Dartmouth.

Bretscher, N. (in press). Exploring the quantitative and qualitative gap between expectations and implantation: A survey of English mathematics teachers' use of ICT. In A. Clark-Wilson, O. Robutti, & N. Sinclair (Eds.). *The mathematics teacher in the digital age.* Dordrecht, The Netherlands: Springer.

Bruner, J. S. (1966). *Toward a theory of instruction*. Cambridge, MA: Harvard University Press.

Burnstein, R., & Lederman, L. M. (2001). Using wireless keypads in lecture classes. *Physics Teacher, 39*(8), 8–11.

Crouch, C. H., & Mazur, E. (2001). Peer instruction: Ten years of experience and results. *The Physics Teacher, 69*(9), 970–977.

Cuban, L. (2001). *Oversold and underused: Computers in the classroom*. Cambridge, MA: Harvard University Press.

Cuoco, A., & Goldenberg, P. (1997). Dynamic geometry as a bridge from Euclidean Geometry to analysis. In J. R. King & D. Schattschneider (Eds.), *Geometry turned on!: Dynamic software in learning, teaching and research* (pp. 69–70). Washington, DC: Mathematical Association of America.

Dalton, S., & Hegedus, S. (2013). Learning and motivation in high school classrooms. In S. Hegedus & J. Roschelle (Eds.), *Democratizing access to important mathematics through dynamic representations: Contributions and visions from the SimCalc Research Program*. Berlin: Springer.

Dautenhahn, K. (2000). Design issues on interactive environments for children with autism. In *Proceedings of the 3rd International Conference on Disability, Virtual Reality and Associated Technologies, ICDVRAT* (pp. 153–161). Alghero, Sardinia, Italy.

Dede, C. (2000). Emerging influences of information technology on school curriculum. *Journal of Curriculum Studies, 32*(2), 281–303.

Dienes, Z. P. (1960). *Building up mathematics*. London: Hutchinson.

Drijvers, P., Kieran, C., & Mariotti, M-A. (2009). Integrating technology into mathematics education: Theoretical perspectives. In C. Hoyles & J-B. Lagrange (Eds.), *Mathematics education and technology—rethinking the terrain* (pp. 89–132). New York: Springer.

Dufresne, R. J., Gerace, W. J., Leonard, W. J., Mestre, J. P., & Wenk, L. (1996). Classtalk: A classroom communication system for active learning. *Journal for Computing in Higher Education, 7*(2), 3–47.

Dwyer, M. C., & Pfeifer, R. E. (1999). Exploring hyperbolic geometry with The Geometer's Sketchpad. *Mathematics Teacher, 92*(7), 632–637.

Falcade, R., Laborde, C., & Mariotti, M. A. (2007). Approaching functions: Cabri tools as instruments of semiotic mediation. *Educational Studies in Mathematics, 66*(3), 317–333.

Flowers, L. A. (2002). Developing purposes in college: Differences between freshman and seniors. *College Student Journal, 36*, 478–484.

Gol Tabaghi, S. & Sinclair, N. (2013). Using dynamic geometry software to explore eigenvectors: The emergence of dynamic-synthetic-geometric thinking. *Technology, Knowledge and Learning 18*(3), 149–164.

Gorini, C. A. (1997). Dynamic visualization in calculus. In J. R. King & D. Schattschneider (Eds.), *Geometry turned on!: Dynamic software in learning, teaching and research* (pp. 89–94). Washington, DC: The Mathematical Association of America.

Güçler, B., Hegedus, S., Robidoux, R., & Jackiw, N. (2013). Investigating the mathematical discourse of young learners involved in multi-modal mathematical investigations: The case of haptic technologies. In D. Martinovic, V. Freiman, & Z. Karadag (Eds.), *Visual mathematics cyberlearning* (pp. 97–118). New York: Springer.

Hake, R. R. (1998). Interactive-engagement vs. traditional methods: A six-thousand-student survey of mechanics test data for introductory physics courses. *American Journal of Physics, 66*, 64–74.

Hartline, F. (1997). *Analysis of 1st semester of Classtalk use at MacIntosh elementary school*. Yorktown, VA: Better Education.

Hassan, R. (1992). Speech genre, semiotic mediation and the development of higher mental functions. *Language Sciences, 14*(4), 489–528.

Hegedus, S. J., & Roschelle, J. (2012). Highly adaptive, interactive instruction: Insights for the networked classroom. In C. Dede & J. Richards (Eds.), *Digital teaching platforms* (pp. 103–115). New York: Teachers College Press.

Hegedus, S. J., & Roschelle, J. (2013). (Eds.). *Democratizing access to important mathematics through dynamic representations: Contributions and visions from the SimCalc Research Program*. Berlin: Springer.

Hegedus, S. J., & Moreno-Armella, L. (2011). The emergence of mathematical structures. *Educational Studies in Mathematics, 77*(2–3), 369–388.

Hennessy, S., Ruthven, K., & Brindley, S. (2005). Teacher perspectives on integrating ICT into subject teaching: commitments, constrains, caution, and change. *Journal of Curriculum Studies, 37*(2), 155–192.

Hollebrands, K. (2002). The role of a dynamic software program for geometry in high school students' understandings of geometric transformations. In D. Mewborn, P. Sztajn, D. Y. White, H. G. Wiegel, R. L. Bryant, & K. Nooney (Eds.), *Proceedings of the 24th Annual Meeting of the North American Chapter of the International Group for the Psychology of Mathematics Education* (Vol. 2, pp. 695–705). Columbus, OH: ERIC Clearinghouse on Science, Mathematics and Environmental Education.

Jackiw, N. (2003). Visualizing complex functions with the Geometer's Sketchpad. In T. Triandafillidis & K. Hatzikiriakou (Eds.), *Proceedings of the 6th International Conference on Technology in Mathematics Teaching* (pp. 291–299). Volos, Greece: University of Thessaly.

Jackiw, N. (2013). Touch & multitouch in dynamic geometry: Sketchpad Explorer and "digital" mathematics. *Proceedings of ICTMT12* (pp. 149–155), Bari, Italy.

Jackiw, N., & Sinclair, N. (2007). Dynamic geometry activity design for elementary school mathematics. In C. Hoyles, J.-B. Lagrange, L. H. Sun, & N. Sinclair (Eds.), *Proceedings of the Seventeenth ICMI Study Conference "Technology Revisited"* (pp. 236–245). Paris, France: Hanoi Institute of Technology and Didirem University.

Jaimes, A., & Sebe, N. (2007). Multimodal human computer interaction: A survey. *Computer Vision and Image Understanding, 108*(1–2), 116–134.

Kaput, J., Hegedus, S., & Lesh, R. (2007). Technology becoming infrastructural in mathematics education. In R. Lesh, E. Hamilton, & J. Kaput (Eds.), *Foundations for the future in mathematics and science* (pp. 172–192). Mahwah, NJ: Lawrence Erlbaum Associates.

Laborde, C. (2000). Dynamic geometry environments as a source of rich learning contexts for the complex activity of proving. *Educational Studies in Mathematics (Special edition on proof in dynamic geometry environments), 44*(1–3), 151–161.

Laborde, C. (2001). Integration of technology in the design of geometry tasks with Cabri-Geometre. *International Journal of Computers for Mathematical Learning, 6*, 283–317.

Ladel, S., & Kortenkamp, U. (2011). Implementation of a multitouch-environment supporting finger symbol sets. In M. Pytlak, T. Rowland, & E. Swoboda (Eds.), *Proceedings of the seventh Congress of the European Society for Research in Maths Education* (pp. 1792–1801). University of Rzeszów, Poland.

Lakoff, G., & Nuñez, R. E. (2000). *Where mathematics comes from: How the embodied mind brings mathematics into being*. New York: Basic Books.

Mariotti, M. A. (2000). Introduction to proof: The mediation of a dynamic software environment. *Educational Studies in Mathematics, 44*(1–2), 25–53.

Mariotti, M. A. (2003). The influence of technological advances on students' mathematics learning. In L. D. English (Ed.), *Handbook of international research in mathematics education* (pp. 695–723). Mahwah, NJ: Lawrence Erlbaum Associates.

Moreno-Armella, L., & Hegedus, S. (2009). Co-action with digital technologies. *ZDM: The International Journal on Mathematics Education, Special Issue: Transforming Mathematics Education through the Use of Dynamic Mathematics Technologies, 41*(4), 505–519.

Nemirovsky, R., & Borba, M. (2003). Perceptuo-motor activity and imagination in mathematics learning. In N. Pateman, B. Dougherty, & J. Zilliox (Eds.), *Proceedings of the 27th International Conference for the Psychology of Mathematics* (Vol. 1, pp. 105–136). Honolulu, Hawai'i: Program Committee.

Nemirovsky, R., Kelton, M. L., & Rhodehamel, B. (2013). Playing mathematical instruments: Emerging perceptuomotor integration with an interactive mathematics exhibit. *Journal for Research in Mathematics Education, 44*(2), 372–415.

Noss, R., & Hoyles, C. (1996). *Windows on mathematical meanings: Learning cultures and computers*. Dordrecht, The Netherlands: Kluwer Academic Publishers.

Olive, J. (1997). Creating airfoils from circles: The Jouowski transformation. In J. R. King & D. Schattschneider (Eds.), *Geometry turned on!: Dynamic software in learning, teaching and research* (pp. 169–177). Washington, DC: Mathematical Association of America.

Piazza, S. (2002). *Peer instruction using an electronic response system in large lecture classes*. Presented at the Pennsylvania State University, Center for Educational Technology Services "Teaching with Technology" Series: Departments of Kinesiology, Mechanical Engineering, and Orthopedics and Rehabilitation.

Radford, L., Demers, S., Guzmán, J., & Cerulli, M. (2003). Calculators, graphs, gestures and the production of meaning. In N. A. Pateman, B. J. Dougherty, & J. T. Zilliox (Eds.), *Proceedings of the 27th conference of the International Group for the Psychology of Mathematics Education* (Vol. 4, pp. 55–62). Honolulu, HI: University of Hawaii.

Radford, L., Edwards, L., & Arzarello, F. (2009). Introduction: Beyond words. *Educational Studies in Mathematics, 70*(2), 91–95.

Radford, L., Miranda, I., & Guzmán, J. (2008). *Relative motion, graphs and the heteroglossic transformation of meanings: A semiotic analysis*. Paper presented at the proceedings of the 32nd conference of the International Group for the Psychology of Mathematics Education, Morelia, México.

Rasmussen, C., Nemirovsky, R., Olszewski, J., Dost, K., & Johnson, J. L. (2004). On forms of knowing: The role of bodily activity and tools in mathematical learning. *Educational Studies in Mathematics, 57*(3), 313–316.

Roschelle, J., Abrahamson, A. L., & Penuel, W. (2003). *Catalyst: Toward scientific studies of the pedagogical integration of learning theory and classroom networks*. Menlo Park, CA: SRI International.

Roschelle, J., Knudsen, J., & Hegedus, S. (2010). From new technological infrastructures to curricular activity systems: Advanced designs for teaching and learning. In M. J. Jacobsen & P. Reimann (Eds.), *Designs for learning environments of the future* (pp. 233–262). New York: Springer.

Rotman, B. (2000). *Mathematics as sign*. Palo Alto, CA: Stanford University Press.

Shaffer, D. W. (1995). *Exploring trigonometry with the Geometer's Sketchpad*. Berkeley, CA: Key Curriculum Press.

Sinclair, N. (2001). The aesthetic is relevant. *For the Learning of Mathematics, 21*(1), 25–33.

Sinclair, N. (2002a). Re-constructing a painting with geometric eyes. *For the Learning of Mathematics, 22*(3), 19–23.

Sinclair, N. (2002b). The kissing triangles: The aesthetics of mathematical discovery. *International Journal of Computers for Mathematical Learning, 7*(1), 45–63.

Sinclair, N., Arzarello, F., Trigueros Gaisman, M., & Lozano, M. D. (2009). Implementing digital technologies at a national scale. In C. Hoyles & J. Lagrange (Eds.), *Digital technologies and mathematics teaching and learning: Rethinking the terrain*. Berlin: Springer.

Sinclair, N., & Crespo, S. (2006). Learning mathematics with dynamic computer environments. *Teaching Children Mathematics, 12*(9), 436–444.

Sinclair, N., & Moss, J. (2012). The more it changes, the more it becomes the same: The development of the routine of shape identification in dynamic geometry environments. *International Journal of Education Research, 51&52*, 28–44.

Sinclair, N., & Sedaghat Jou, M. (2013). *Finger counting and adding with TouchCounts*. Presented at CERME 8. Early Mathematics Working Group. Antalya, Turkey.

Stroup, W. (2005). Learning the basics with calculus. *Journal of Computers in Mathematics and Science Teaching, 24*(2), 179–196.

Stroup, W. M., Ares, N. M., & Hurford, A. (2005). A dialectic analysis of generativity: Issues of network supported design in mathematics and science. *Journal of Mathematical Thinking and Learning, 7*(3), 181–206.

Tall, D. O. (2013). *How humans learn to think mathematically: Exploring the three worlds of mathematics*. New York: Cambridge University Press.

Thompson Avant, M. J., & Heller, K. W. (2011). Examining the effectiveness of TouchMath with students with physical disabilities. *Remedial and Special Education, 32*(4), 309–321.

Tomasello, M. (1999). *The Cultural Evolution of Human Cognition*. Cambridge, MA: Harvard University Press.

U.S. Department of Education. (2007). *The nation's report card mathematics 2007: National assessment of educational progress at grades 4 and 8*. Washington, DC.

Vahey, P., Tatar, D., & Roschelle, J. (2007). Using handhelds to link private cognition and public interaction. *Educational Technology, 47*(3), 13–16.

Vygotsky, L. (1980). *Mind in society: The development of the higher psychological processes*. Cambridge, MA: Harvard University Press.

Yerushalmy, M., & Naftaliev, E. (2011). Design of interactive diagrams structured upon generic animations. *Technology, Knowledge and Learning, 16*(3), 221–246.

24 Statistical Software and Mathematics Education
Affordances for Learning

Jane Watson and Noleine Fitzallen

University of Tasmania

Software applications designed for education have become more sophisticated and have the potential to be more than tools employed in the classroom just to make it easier or quicker to perform tasks otherwise completed by hand. By virtue of advances in technology and the complexity of the functionality that is embedded within software applications, the potential of learning *from* computers has shifted to learning *with* computers. This distinction was recognized by Goldenberg (1991) in providing examples of students learning the characteristics of algebraic functions through interacting with a graphing software package by inputting test equations and observing the fit with the correct one. The increase of the use of immersive interactive interfaces has also resulted in many applications that are student-centered; that is, students are able to participate in the learning process by using design features embedded within applications to construct understanding of ideas and concepts within meaningful contexts (Jonassen & Land, 2000; Murray, Blessing, & Ainsworth, 2003). This occurs when students are active participants in the learning process, but it does not occur without support (Land, Hannafin, & Oliver, 2012). The support necessary, in some cases, is offered by the software application itself. Its inherent features, capabilities, and flexibility determine to what extent and the way in which that support is delivered. These characteristics of software applications are affordances, which scaffold and support student learning, and it is the affordances for learning that are the focus of this chapter. What do students learn from using software that they might not learn, or learn as easily, without it? The aim of the chapter is to go beyond what a software application promises to *do* to consider its affordances *for* learning. Further, what are the affordances for teachers in their planning for and assessment of student learning?

AFFORDANCES

Gibson (1977) is credited with developing the Theory of Affordances, which has been extended and applied in many fields (e.g., Jones, 2003; Webb, 2005). For Gibson, *affordance* referred to the perceived usefulness of an object by a potential user. In the context of this chapter, the potential user may be a learner or a teacher, and the object is some facet of software with perceived usefulness by either user. For Gibson, affordances, from the perspective of ecological psychology, were directly related to fitting the organism (in this case the user of the software) to the environment (in this case the software itself). This could be taken to mean that affordances are what the software can *do* for the user. Acknowledging that users must know what the software can do *before* learning can occur, this chapter transfers the focus to the *learning* affordances. Two literatures hence provide a foundation for the chapter. One is based on the affordances of technology (e.g., Bower, 2008). Based on Gibson's definition, Bower is interested in educational affordances, "characteristics of an educational [technology] resource that indicate if and how a particular learning behavior could possibly be enacted within the context," and social affordances, "aspects of the online learning environment that provide social-contextual facilitation relevant to the learner's social interaction" (p. 6). Although social affordances receive some attention in this chapter, the main focus is on educational affordances. With respect to technology generally, Bower goes on to delineate 11 categories of e-learning technology affordances, 10 of which are applicable to the type of software that is the focus of this chapter. These can be interpreted in terms of the characteristics of the software that can be perceived by the user as contributing to its usefulness. They include input/output formats, resizability, accessibility, ability to browse backward and forward, capacity to highlight particular features, ability to combine tools, intuitiveness of features, appearance of the interface, capacity to be used on various platforms, and reliability. The access control affordances related to synchronous and asynchronous collaboration and publication apply to online applications and do not apply to stand-alone software applications.

The second literature is related more specifically to the mathematics that is taught in the classroom and what tasks, problems, demonstrations, and tools are used by the teacher to engage students with the mathematics for learning. Chick (2007) also uses Gibson's (1977) definition of affordances and links it to teachers' pedagogical content knowledge in order to consider *potential* affordances, recognizing the opportunities that are inherent in the "objects" as tasks or tools employed in the classroom. In expanding her exposition, Chick introduces the word *example* to cover the objects that she uses to exemplify the types and range of affordances she analyses. For her, the importance of examples and their potential affordances lies in the learning that takes place. Chick's examples are not embedded in technology use but it is possible to imagine that some of the tasks, demonstrations, and exercises could be so embedded, as similar examples are in the software examples provided in this chapter.

Combining the foundations provided by Chick's (2007) specific concerns about affordances (potential and actual) for mathematics learning and Bower's (2008) focus on the affordances of technology to facilitate learning behavior more generally, this chapter looks at learning and learning behavior based mainly in the statistics part of mathematics curricula using the Tinker-Plots software (Konold & Miller, 2011). The combining of these two perspectives is illustrated by Brown, Stillman, and Herbert (2004) as they attempt to devise an operational definition of affordances that could be used for designing a technology-rich mathematics curriculum. They found it necessary to acknowledge the further contribution of Kennewell (2001) in suggesting that there are also "constraints" to consider, as well as affordances, when judging the usefulness of an object. Kennewell (2001) defines constraints as "the conditions and relationships amongst attributes which provide structure and guidance for the course of actions" (p. 106). He claims that constraints are not the opposite of affordances but complementary to them "and equally necessary for activity to take place" (p. 106) when considering what technology has to offer for particular learning experiences. Brown and her colleagues ask specifically if affordances are positive and constraints negative or are constraints a way of articulating more specifically the affordances that exist in a given situation and if an object affords users to do things in particular ways by constraining them to think or act in a specific way. This chapter furthers the consideration of constraints and their potential as affordances.

BACKGROUND

The context within which the affordances of software for learning are considered is statistics. Content associated with statistics has had a high profile in the mathematics curricula of developed countries since the last decade of the 20th century (e.g., Australian Education Council, 1991; Ministry of Education, 1992; National Council of Teachers of Mathematics, 1989). The objectives of these curricula are intended to meet two needs. One is to prepare students for engaging in serious statistical investigations either in relation to other subjects at school or at higher education levels by completing further study. The second need is for statistically literate citizens who, although not engaging personally in statistical investigations, have the ability to analyze reports and claims made in wider society critically, claims perhaps made by interest groups or the media. Both of these objectives are based on thinking and reasoning statistically. The reasoning skills for both are built around experiencing the stages of a statistical investigation during the school years (Watson, 2006; Watson & Fitzallen, 2010). Over time students ask data-driven questions, collect data to answer the questions, represent the data in some visual form, reduce the data to a summary form, and make a decision related to the question based on the confidence they have in the evidence collected. They also learn about the important relationship between samples and populations in drawing inferences about the latter from the former (Manor, Ben-Zvi, & Aridor, 2014; Saldanha & McAllister, 2014; Watson & Chance, 2012). A challenge for students is to make these decisions acknowledging uncertainty and to develop intuitions in judging levels of certainty (Ainley & Pratt, 2014). Experiencing the process involved in statistical investigations over the school years provides the background for the type of reasoning required for statistical literacy. In social settings where citizens encounter statistical claims, they need to be able to recognize and understand statistical terminology being used, further understand its meaning within the context where it is being applied, and then be able to question claims that are made without proper justification or confirm those that are properly made (Watson, 2006).

The realization two decades ago that visualization through computer graphics could assist learners in learning about algebraic functions (Goldenberg, 1991) was shared in the realm of random phenomena by Weissglass and Cummings (1991). Based on a package called *Hands-On Statistics* (Weissglass, Theis, & Finzer, 1986), they gave examples of a series of programs to complete specific tasks, including flipping coins, lottery draws, sampling means, and comparing means. At that time these could be used by groups of students in computer labs to supplement classroom lectures. These authors recognized early the constructivist perspective in claiming that the advantages (affordances) to students were having control over the choice of parameters when performing experiments, experiencing visual representations of concepts, repeating experiments at will, visualizing results for different sample sizes, and experiencing immediate feedback from experiments. These are supplemented by Goldenberg in relation to graphing more generally with the ability to modify representations, to highlight certain regions, to focus on scale, and to appreciate the importance of using appropriate language to describe the learning experience. These initiatives anticipated the later development of the DataScope package (Konold & Miller, 1994), which allowed many of the same affordances for students in terms of learning.

The software that is the focus of this discussion of affordances for learning statistics is TinkerPlots: Dynamic Data Exploration (Konold & Miller, 2011). Originally created for the middle years of schooling, it is now used much more widely, including at the tertiary level (e.g., Day, 2013; delMas, Garfield, & Zieffler, 2014; Frischemeier; 2014) and in industry (e.g., Hoyles, Bakker, Kent, & Noss, 2007). An earlier version of the software was also the focus of a chapter on software in a previous edition of this *Handbook* (Konold & Lehrer, 2008). Although described in some detail in Konold and Lehrer, a summary of the development of TinkerPlots is necessary here to set the scene for moving from the "doing" affordances of the software to its "learning" affordances for students and their teachers. In describing the rationale for developing the initial version of TinkerPlots (Konold & Miller, 2005) from the earlier package, DataScope (Konold & Miller, 1994), Konold (2007) noted two features that contribute directly to the affordances exhibited in the current chapter. One was the conscious effort to avoid producing a watered-down version of tertiary graphing software that makes assumptions about students' prior knowledge of statistics. The need to know what kind of graph is needed for a particular data set before opening the graphing package means that the software is strictly a tool for "doing" on command, not a tool for "learning" as the student tries various representations. The other feature was positioning TinkerPlots as constructivist software, which fits with the developmental view of the curriculum in today's environment. It is not about telling students definitions and procedures but about guiding them to discover the appropriate ways to display, summarize, compare, and judge data sets to tell the stories behind them. Reflecting a constructivist viewpoint means that students can produce a meaningless representation, realize the story is not seen, delete the plot, and create another from the possibilities available, some of which they may have never seen before (Harradine & Konold, 2006). Students rapidly get used to exploring multiple representations that would take a long time to produce by hand (e.g., Ireland & Watson, 2009).

WHAT TINKERPLOTS OFFERS

To consider the affordances of TinkerPlots for learning it is necessary to explain briefly the structure of the program when one interacts with it. The structure is based on five "objects" that appear in the upper left corner of the window when the program is opened (Figure 24.1). The first two objects, Cards and Table, contain the data that are used in the statistical investigation. The next two objects, Plot and Sampler, provide the major environments within which the activity of the investigation takes place. The final object, Text, provides a box within which text can be entered to report the results of the investigation. TinkerPlots has many other tools and features, which are illustrated in Biehler, Ben-Zvi, Bakker, and Makar (2013) and in Konold and Lehrer (2008).

The Plot is the cornerstone of TinkerPlots. It is used to build graphical representations, which are employed to organize data, making it possible to search for interesting patterns or group differences. Graphical representations are created and manipulated within the Plot using an icon-based click-drag-and-drop function. Changes are quick and fluid, and are viewed as animations. The opportunity to create a large variety of graphical representations arises either by changing the data icon using the drop-down menu at the bottom of the Plot, or by selecting tools from the menu that is added to the TinkerPlots interface at the top of the screen when the Plot window is active (Figure 24.2). Although a stand-alone object, the Plot can be utilized in conjunction with output from the Sampler.

Figure 24.1 The five basic objects in TinkerPlots.

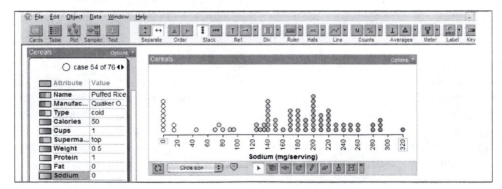

Figure 24.2 Typical Plot with tool bars and associated Cards.

The Sampler is a simulator that can be used to model probabilistic processes and to generate data. It also makes possible the random selection of samples from large finite populations when they are placed in the Sampler. Output from the Sampler can be represented in a Table or a Plot. A Sampler, for example, can be used to simulate tossing two coins, collect data in a Table, and analyze the Table data in a Plot in order to explore questions about the probability of getting two heads. The various devices to use within the Sampler are chosen from a tool bar across the bottom of the object or from drop-down menus within the object. The devices include a Mixer and a Spinner (Figure 24.3). The Mixer shows balls bouncing before one emerges at the top, to be replaced before the next Draw. For the Spinner a pointer is seen to rotate before coming to rest in one section. The Sampler can utilize a combination of individual devices or multiples of devices selected.

These and some of the other features of TinkerPlots are exemplified in the later section on Examples of Affordances of the software. It is also possible to watch the basic demonstration movie for TinkerPlots, as well as other movies, on the Web (www.srri.umass.edu/tinkerplots/overview).

Potential Affordances of TinkerPlots

In order to describe the potential affordances of TinkerPlots it is useful to consider the affordances defined by Bower (2008) within the software context. To do this it is necessary to move from the broad definition of affordances offered by Bower to acknowledging how the relevant affordances are characterized in TinkerPlots. In 2007, Fitzallen conducted an evaluation of TinkerPlots where she outlined the nature of TinkerPlots using a set of organizers called *Enabling Aspects of Software* (Fitzallen & Brown, 2006). The set of six Enabling Aspects were developed by combining three frameworks sourced from the literature: the *Principles for Analysing Visual Representations* (Kidman & Nason, 2000), *Guidelines for Evaluating Software* (Goyne, McDonough, & Padgett, 2000), and the *Model of Learning in EDA Graphing Environments* (Fitzallen, 2006). Although not developed with the notion of affordances in mind, Fitzallen and Brown's *Enabling Aspects of Software* align with Bower's affordances of technology, while focusing directly on TinkerPlots. Fitzallen's (2007) evaluation of Tinker-Plots, highlighting the potential affordances of the software, was based on the original version of TinkerPlots, which featured representing data in graphs. The current version extends the functionality of the software by including the Sampler. Because of its breadth of application, Fitzallen and Brown's framework remains relevant for describing the potential affordances of the current version of TinkerPlots.

 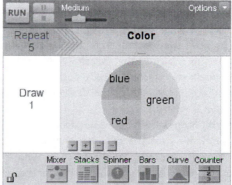

Figure 24.3 Typical Samplers using the Mixer (left) and Spinner (right).

The TinkerPlots interface is accessible and the features are easy to use (Enabling Aspect 1, Fitzallen, 2007). The menus are icon-based and incorporate drop-down menus for accessing additional features. A drop-and-drag functionality is utilized to add Cards, Table, Plot, and Sampler objects to the software interface. This has the potential for students to introduce the different visual representations onto the screen in stages. This is particularly useful when building a Sampler. By adding different elements of the Sampler to the screen in stages, students experience the growing capability of the Sampler as it is constructed.

Data can be displayed in TinkerPlots in multiple forms simultaneously (Enabling Aspect 2). As well as being able to store and record data in sets of data cards and in tables, graphical representations can be used to display the data. Data can also be generated using the Sampler. The way in which the graphical representations are constructed from the data allows learners to transition back and forth and among those various representations easily. This has the potential for students to maintain the connection among the data, the graphical representations constructed, and the data summary tools used to analyze the data, such as the Mean, Mode, Median, and Hat plot. As well as the ability to display data in multiple ways, other information such as text and digital images can be added to the TinkerPlots interface. This has the potential to facilitate the process of translating between mathematical expression and natural language (Enabling Aspect 3) as students add a commentary to a Text box in everyday language to describe and analyze the graphical representations they construct.

TinkerPlots is very flexible. It allows students to build representations that are meaningful to them. They are not confined to using prearranged graph types and they are able to build multiple graphical representations from the one data set. This has the potential for students to draw on the extended memory TinkerPlots offers when organizing and reorganizing data (Enabling Aspect 4). In addition, the Sampler provides an interactive environment that allows multiple entry points for abstraction of concepts (Enabling Aspect 5). The ability to build a Sampler progressively enables students to add complexity and increasing functionality to the object. The capacity then to represent the data generated in graphical representations in the Plot object and use data analysis tools, such as the Ruler, which measures distances between points on a continuous scale, have the potential to allow students to enter the statistical inquiry process from multiple entry points. The visual representations created using the Plot and Sampler objects have the potential to be used for both interpretative and expressive learning activities (Enabling Aspect 6). Fitzallen and Brown's (2006) six Enabling Aspects are evidenced in the studies described in the section, Examples of Affordances.

Affordances of TinkerPlots

The affordances of a graphing software package can be described in terms of its ability to foster students' mathematical learning (Chick, 2007). The capacity to do this is dependent on the characteristics of the software package and the way in which students interact with and access those characteristics. Facilitating this interaction is the way in which teachers incorporate the software package into learning experiences and orchestrate the development of key concepts and ideas. It is important to recognize that software packages alone are not likely to encourage students to build up their capacity to think and reason in particular ways. Learning is facilitated when the teacher artfully combines challenges and scaffolds learning with the resource, in accompaniment with suitable contexts and investigation processes within a larger learning program.

A graphing software package, in this case TinkerPlots, hence has potential affordances when employed by a teacher in a way that gives the opportunity for learning, in this case learning about statistics (and probability). Learning about how to use the software may be a starting point, or happen periodically along the way, but it is not the end game. It may be exciting to see a colorful plot or watch a probability simulation run but the objective is to glean from these an understanding of a context, a question, and the potential answer to the question that one did not have before. In showcasing the affordances of TinkerPlots it is hence necessary to set different scenes, explain the questions, demonstrate the contribution by TinkerPlots, and describe the learning that is facilitated. The following four sections present examples in relation to affordances of TinkerPlots for students' learning statistics, for enhancing teachers' pedagogical content knowledge for teaching statistics, for assessing students' understanding, and for supporting other areas of the mathematics curriculum (as a by-product). In light of the observations of Kennewell (2001), a final section considers constraints in relation to Tinker-Plots and makes suggestions for further enhancement of the affordances.

Examples of Affordances

The affordances of learning that are linked to experiences based in a practical TinkerPlots environment are varied both in content and in the age range of students. In presenting examples of affordances (Chick, 2007), it is understood that they represent specific instances of statistical learning chosen in this case to illustrate or explore the relationship between TinkerPlots and the learning taking place. Four environments are considered in presenting examples of the affordances of TinkerPlots. The most numerous group of examples reflects the main purpose of the software, "Students learning statistics." This generally does not happen without teachers; the second subsection reports on examples relating to "Teachers learning to teach statistics." Associated with teaching is assessing, and the third group of examples of affordances is "Assessing understanding." There are also sometimes spinoffs from using TinkerPlots that are not directly related to statistics. The next subsection provides examples of affordances for "Other mathematics learning." The following subsection, "Constraints," considers affordances in the light of constraints that exist in the structure of TinkerPlots and whether they may have a positive or negative impact on learning.

STUDENTS LEARNING STATISTICS

Paparistodemou and Meletiou-Mavrotheris (2008) provide multiple examples of grade 3 students in Cyprus learning to make arguments based on data they collect from their school on nutrition, health, and safety. The examples are all based on the visualizations that the students create in TinkerPlots with different graphical forms. The affordance of TinkerPlots is based on the freedom it gives students to create unconventional representations that both assist in telling the story students initially want to tell (see also Fitzallen & Watson, 2010), as well as leading them to further argumentation and (at times) generalization (observed by Ben-Zvi & Aridor, 2014; Fitzallen & Watson, 2011).

The affordance provided by TinkerPlots in the open-ended creation of plots is further illustrated when grade 4 students tell the story of their class members each measuring the arm span of one member of the class (Watson & English, 2013a). Some students choose value plots and others choose frequency plots. The interpretations vary greatly, as shown in Figure 24.4, with the value Plot on the top and the stacked dot Plot on the bottom. The value plot is used to identify the mode ("most people thought . . . 142 cm") by comparing the lengths of the value bars, whereas the stacked dot plot shows the mode as the tallest stack.

Among the affordances arising from the use of TinkerPlots by grade 5 students learning about informal inference (Ben-Zvi, 2006) is the ability to personalize icons with labels in small samples. This motivates students to identify errors, interpret plots, and explain irregularities or patterns. For some this leads to searching for the behavior of aggregates of data points in larger samples (further noted by Fitzallen & Watson, 2014). Following the students a year later, Ben-Zvi, Gil, and Apel (2007) report on grade 6 students' developing reasoning about sampling and surveys, where random samples are taken from large collections of surveys collected from grade 6 and 7 students. Students use TinkerPlots to plot and separate data for the

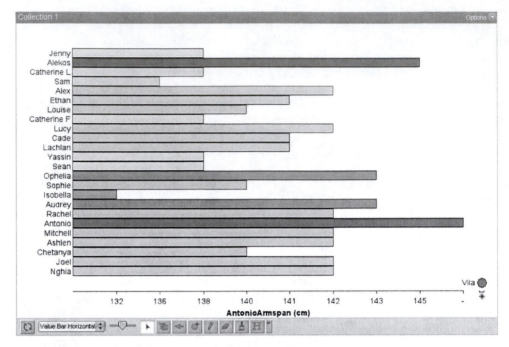

this graph tells me that most people thought that antonioes armspan was142cm.

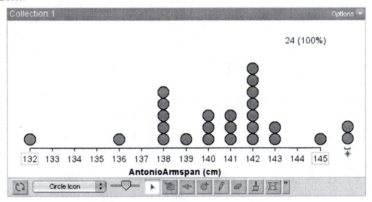

I found that there was mostly people with less than 141cm for Antonio's armspan.This could have been because of that Antonio was tired towards the end,this also could have been because of how people held the Tape measure

This is what my graph shows..

Figure 24.4 Creativity shown in constructing plots in grade 4.

two grades and to discuss and defend their hypotheses about difference or no difference in the attributes considered. The visual presentation and the ability to mark mean values on axes complement the students' understanding of the context and assist the argumentation skills being developed through the unit of work.

Visualization can also be an affordance when studying properties of the mean and median, often thought of mainly as numerical values conceived of as the result of procedural calculations. Yilmaz (2013) presents a well-documented case study highlighting the affordances of TinkerPlots in remediating a grade 6 student's misunderstanding of the mean and median. The student constructs her knowledge through initially displaying her "understanding" of the mean on a Plot with two values and then experiencing conflict when a third or fourth value is added to the Plot and seeing that the mean does not have the value predicted. This leads to reflection on the part of the student who begins to add values to the Plot to confirm her new understanding. The same process occurs for the median. At the end she states several principles involved with the behavior of the mean and median, for example, "If I add a data point greater than the existing mean, the mean will get larger." The affordances of Tinker-Plots are of course dependent on how the teacher uses the software. In this case the teacher sets up a Plot that reflects the student's current understanding, challenges the understanding with new values, and then lets the student reflect and add more values to test and consolidate her understanding. The presence of the mean and median tools in the software avoids tedious calculations so that the visual impact can build the student's intuitions, without relying on procedures.

Going further than Yilmaz (2013), Hudson (2012) introduces the Ruler from TinkerPlots to display visually the differences between data values and the mean. In seeing the mean as the balance point for the data, the sum of the distances from the mean to data values to the left of the mean is the same as the sum of the distances from the mean to data values to the right of the mean. This is confirmed as shown in Figure 24.5 in the lower-left corner of the Plot where "Sum of Diff of 7 cases = 0," recognizing the negative and positive differences on either side of the mean. As well, Hudson (2012) demonstrates the benefit of using the "Drag Value Tool" to move a data value and watch what happens to the mean as its value changes to become larger or smaller. If activities such as these are built into classroom work, there is the potential to consolidate students' understanding of the mean from its introduction.

In a study of grade 6 students' statistical reasoning about center and variation, Bakker, Derry, and Konold (2006) employ the notion of diagrammatic reasoning. This notion suggests three components in the process: making a diagram, experimenting with it, and reflecting on the resulting diagram. Bakker et al. find that TinkerPlots plays a significant role in the first two

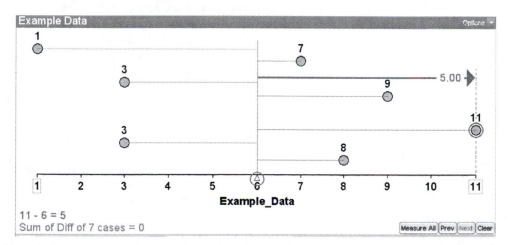

Figure 24.5 Using the Ruler in TinkerPlots to show the sum of distances from data values to their mean is zero.

components, for example, discussing "clumps," producing diagrams, and informally describing center and variation. This leads to reflection in either small or large group classroom discussions. Evidence provided of the affordance of TinkerPlots is shown through examples of the discussion taking place among the students and teacher. Words and phrases such as "bigger clump," "more spread out," "higher values," arise from the initial plots created with the software, and as changes are made to the plots, sophistication grows in the language, for example, "if the mean values are far apart that's how much bigger they are."

The exploratory nature of TinkerPlots affordances are illustrated well by the study of Lehrer, Kim, and Schauble (2007) in having students invent measures (statistics) for variation. The flexibility of plotting options allows students to create ways of measuring the characteristics of distributions of data values. Alternatives include counting repeated values, so that a larger count means less variation, or measuring the distances (without sign) to the mean or median of all values and averaging them, so that a smaller value means less variation. Although beginning with basic plots, students are also introduced to other features of TinkerPlots, such as the Hat plot, to focus on "middles" as a way of describing central variation. In this context, TinkerPlots is allowing students to reflect, create, check, and revise invented statistics.

A more sophisticated affordance of TinkerPlots is the ability to test informal theories that students develop and articulate. Konold, Harradine, and Kazak (2007) illustrate this affordance using the Sampler as a "factory" to create data. In the beginning it is a challenge for students to articulate the attributes that characterize the objects they want to create. Combining the Sampler with the Plot and other features of TinkerPlots, a testing ground is provided to consider the realistic nature of the variation in a "production line." Adjustments can be made to the Sampler and further testing of theories carried out. The instantaneous feedback and possibility for large sample sizes add to the benefits of the software.

Another affordance of TinkerPlots related to 12–14-year-old students' developing understanding of variation, based on either repeated measurements or a repeatable production process, is described by Konold and Harradine (2014). Based on the collection of data from the repeated linear measurement of a single object with two different tools or from the weighing of student-manufactured Play-Doh™ "sausages," the focus is on the identification of "signal" (center) and "noise" (variation) in data sets and the ability to use these to explain differences between data sets. The visualization of the signal and noise in the graphical presentations for concepts that have not been procedurally defined forms an intuitive basis for later development. Konold and Harradine go further to use a modification of the Sampler as employed by Konold et al. (2007) to allow students to simulate chance variation (noise) in a distribution with a fixed center (signal), allowing students to question the absence of systematic variation, which they may conjecture occurs in an actual setting.

Turning to the learning about statistical sampling, one of the main benefits of the Sampler in TinkerPlots is its ability to repeat many probability simulation trials at great speed. Kazak and Konold (2010) use this facility with middle-school students as an affordance for learning about sample size and the approach of the distribution of random trials to a theoretical model as the sample size increases. In this case the affordance of TinkerPlots is immersed in a well-planned and executed teaching sequence. Similarly Ireland and Watson (2009) report on work with a grade 6 class aimed specifically at helping students develop an understanding of the relationship between experimental and theoretical probability through use of the Sampler to generate larger and larger samples of tosses of coins or dice. The Sampler is the important link between the two concepts—experimental and theoretical—as well as consolidating understanding and application of ideas of fairness and equally likely outcomes through creating simulations. Transferring from a chance context to a large finite population that can be placed in the Sampler, Stack and Watson (2013) consider taking samples of size 10 or size 30 from a data set based on Australian convicts. Comparing statistics such as the median for the samples, students are able to observe the decrease in variation of the medians for the larger sample size and in this case actually observe the value for the entire population. In all three contexts it is the Sampler that affords the opportunity for collection of larger samples or many samples to support the learning objectives.

At the tertiary level, Garfield, delMas, and Zieffler (2012) have developed an introductory course to develop statistical modelers and thinkers, using a simulation-based approach to inference requiring "students to create a model with respect to a specific context, repeatedly simulate data from the model, and then use the resulting distribution of a particular computed statistic to draw statistical inferences" (p. 883). This course is in contrast to the traditional statistics course at the tertiary level, which is based on a procedural approach to formal statistical tests, such as the *t*-test and *p*-values. As Garfield et al. (2012) report, this traditional approach has been shown overall to be unsuccessful in achieving the aim of students understanding the meaning of the process taking place and the significance of results. In their course, Garfield et al. (2012) have students use the Sampler in TinkerPlots to set up a model for the context of the problem they are investigating, let the Sampler generate many trials of the model collecting the numerical summary of results, create a Plot of the distribution of the results, and evaluate the initial question from the context. Following the metaphor of Schoenfeld (1998) concerning teaching mathematics so that students can "really cook" with mathematical thinking rather than just "follow a recipe," the authors provide evidence of improved understanding of inference by students in their course compared with students in traditional statistics courses. As TinkerPlots is the basis of the course, combined with the focus on modeling with simulations, its affordance is associated with the documented improved learning outcomes related to inference. Further evidence of the affordance of TinkerPlots for learning is provided in delMas et al. (2014) from interviews with students in the course:

> An interesting observation that emerged was the possible way that the software, TinkerPlots™, facilitated students' thinking and reasoning. When asked to describe how they would answer a question, students seemed to consider how to build the model in TinkerPlots™ and to reason and think through problems using the language of TinkerPlots™.
>
> (pp. 417–418)

Ben-Zvi and Aridor (2014) also have found that a modeling activity using the Sampler and Plot functions in TinkerPlots supports two grade 8 students' reasoning about uncertainty. The activity involves the students developing a data-based model that represents the movement of a toy bird being launched from a catapult. After planning and conducting an experiment with a toy emu, the students model the predicted bird movements in TinkerPlots. They use the Sampler to generate data and subsequently graph the data. The activity promotes several iterations of data collection and graphing in order to make inferences from the data. Generating the graphs in TinkerPlots allows one of the students to make the conjecture that the bird's flight is not linear when different forces are applied. He also suggests that a mathematical formula derived from collecting more data would assist in understanding the toy bird's motion observed during the initial experiment. Although this study only reported on a pair of students, it illustrates the affordance of TinkerPlots as an analytical tool.

The affordance of TinkerPlots as an analytical tool is further evidenced in two other studies of grade 6 students. One involves the use of the Sampler in TinkerPlots to model the distribution of random bunny hops, suggesting that the ability to produce iterations of data when modeling an event supports students' reasoning about distributions (Kazak, Fujita, & Wegerif, 2014). This is further evidenced in the other study in which students use TinkerPlots to model four games that involves selecting a colored chip from each of two bags that contain various combinations of colored chips. By being able to create the simulations to test and revise their conjectures and explanations through multiple iterations of data collection, conflict is created with their original intuitive ideas, which leads to probabilistic thinking (Kazak, Wegerif, & Fujita, 2014).

Turning to the affordances of TinkerPlots as seen by students themselves for their learning, Burgess (2014) reports that students in grades 5 to 8 in New Zealand comment favorably on the time saved when creating graphs for helping answer their investigative questions. Having been introduced to data handling activities through physical cards with data entered on them for relatively small data sets, students quickly recognize the affordance of the software for larger data sets: "Searching little cards takes forever. But when you used TinkerPlots, it just went, went like that!" The features that students particularly like and that are demonstrated in the students' analysis and report of outcomes include stacking, ordering, providing counts or percentages, shifting dividing lines, clicking on dots on a plot to see the corresponding data, and having a text box next to the plot. Burgess concludes from this that a major affordance of TinkerPlots is that it gives students more time to focus on "noticing and analyzing aspects of the investigations," which is demonstrated in student outcomes.

Similar results are described by Allmond and Makar (2014) who are motivated to use TinkerPlots with grade 6 students because of its affordance as a "sense-making tool in statistical investigations." Sense-making involves students making conjectures about a problem, suggesting solutions, monitoring progress, and making adjustments to an investigation through an exploratory process (also a finding of Browning & Smith, 2015). Allmond and Makar's goal is to explore how middle-school students use Hat plots to compare distributions and write justified conclusions. Students' reflections of the benefits of using TinkerPlots reveal three common themes: the removal of computational boundaries allowing for a focus on analysis, the ability to operate accurately and efficiently, and the flexibility offered. Among the examples given, they report that the Hat plot helps them identify where data are skewed, the Plot function averts errors usually made when drawing graphs by hand, and TinkerPlots helps to "make different graphs to support evidence required by changing format turning dot plots into histograms, hat plots or box plots (Lucy)." The students' perceived affordances of TinkerPlots support those identified by researchers in other studies (e.g., Browning & Smith, 2015).

TEACHERS LEARNING TO TEACH STATISTICS

Turning to affordances of TinkerPlots for teachers' learning about statistics, Hall (2008) reports on using TinkerPlots as the vehicle for introducing Census at School, one of Statistics Canada's education programs for schools, a program employing Canadian and international data collected from schoolchildren. Although restricted to a three-hour workshop, Hall tells of positive feedback in evaluations, indicating that teachers find TinkerPlots a fun, user-friendly complement to the Census at School Web site. About half of teachers say "TinkerPlots" or "Everything (all resources)" is the most useful aspect of the workshop. Hall also includes a detailed affordance of TinkerPlots being that it allows the Categorical Attribute values initially listed in a Plot in alphabetical order, to be dragged into whatever order might be more logical for the user. In this context TinkerPlots is a complementary affordance for facilitating an educational goal. Like Hall (2008), Monteiro, Asseker, Carvalho and Campos (2010) use TinkerPlots with adults. They work with preservice teachers to introduce data handling concepts necessary for teaching the Brazilian mathematics curriculum. The affordance of TinkerPlots in this environment is that the preservice teachers can explore different (sometimes unconventional) representations, focusing in on an appropriate approach to use in determining differences in two groups of data.

Similar to Hall (2008), Meletiou-Mavrotheris, Paparistodemou, and Stylianou (2009) report working with in-service teachers, introducing them to TinkerPlots in relation to the mathematics curriculum in Cyprus. They, however, work with the teachers for 15 hours over three weeks, exploring the affordances for teachers' teaching as well as their own understanding of statistics. In answering questions based on a table of data from 12 European countries related to means and comparing the other countries with Cyprus, teachers first work without TinkerPlots. In this mode they produce many correct calculations but none create a visual representation of the data in the table. When given the same data and questions in TinkerPlots, very different strategies emerge with teachers combining visual and numerical strategies in considering entire distributions of the data, making conjectures and observing trends, and using unconventional representations to make comparisons and draw conclusions. These outcomes lead to group discussions of how they would use the software in the classroom and how students would be able to carry out the same types of investigations they have been doing. TinkerPlots is hence an affordance for the teachers' development of understanding beyond paper-and-pencil activities, as well as for providing a platform to plan interventions in their classrooms. The next phase is a potential affordance for their students when they meet Tinker-Plots for analyzing data. Madden (2014) reports similar experiences in working with preservice secondary teachers.

In introducing teachers to features of TinkerPlots, Rubin and Hammerman (2006) describe the affordance of "bins" and "dividers" as allowing the teachers to expose their way of thinking about distributions of data. On the top of Figure 24.6 is a distribution of data across eight bins, rather than on a continuous scale as in the bottom of the figure. When initially providing a dot plot for data with numerical scaled data on an axis, the program splits the data in two bins using the midpoint of the range. Bins as shown at the top of Figure 24.6 occur from dragging an icon to the right. Further dragging produces the continuous distribution. Teachers using the bins generally discuss particular sections of the data rather than the overall distribution. Using dividers with the overall distribution (bottom of Figure 24.6) helps them to make judgments in relation to the entire data set. Using bins, however, is an initial approach that is likely to be

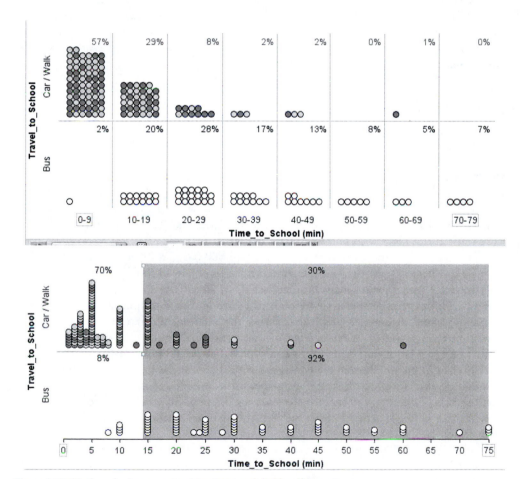

Figure 24.6 Display of a data set using bins (top) and dividers (bottom).

used by students and teachers aware that this is a useful stage that can often be used to draw conclusions in some contexts.

In a statistics course for elementary preservice teachers, TinkerPlots is used to develop these students' understanding of standard deviation (Browning, Goss, & Smith, 2014). The aim is to challenge the students' thinking about measures of variability attained through procedural processes. The students complete a series of tasks that lead to investigation of the mean absolute deviation and, subsequently, standard deviation. In response to a quiz question that requires the students to display a data set using representations of their choosing, seven of the 12 students use either Hat plots, dividers, and/or lines/squares in their descriptions of determining the standard deviation. During interviews conducted at the end of the course, the preservice teachers reflect on their responses to the quiz item. They justify their answers by describing the way in which they use the Hat plot and dividers to think about the spread of the data. One student suggests that the dividers assisted by showing:

> the percentage of points that were within a certain range of the mean, which helped me justify that there was a clump. But then it showed me a percentage of points that were outside of that range which also helped me justify that there was some significant deviation from the mean.

The researchers contend that the visual affordances of TinkerPlots support the preservice teachers to develop conceptual understanding of standard deviation in ways that the procedural knowledge does not. Further to this, Madden (2014) notes that preservice teachers find it difficult to reconcile computational and graphical aspects of standard deviation. Her study suggests that the dynamic nature of TinkerPlots—with the ability to sample, resample, and model statistical ideas using graphical representations—supports development of statistical reasoning skills.

ASSESSING UNDERSTANDING

Fitzallen (2012, 2013) documents research with 12 grades 5 and 6 students over a period of 6 weeks to investigate their development of understanding of covariation. They progress through a learning sequence with two main purposes: to learn about the features of TinkerPlots to equip them with a repertoire of graph types to draw upon when answering questions about data, and to develop an understanding of covariation and the way in which a graphical representation displays covariation. The learning sequence moves from creating and interpreting stacked dot plots with univariate data and small data sets ($n = 12$) to bivariate data, larger data sets, and a variety of graph types (scatterplots, bar graphs, stacked dot plots, and split stacked dot plots). At the end the students are interviewed individually as they work at the computer with an assessment protocol set up as an activity sheet in TinkerPlots. The interview activities require the students both to create and to interpret graphs. One question requires them to create a graph that shows the relationship between two attributes, determining their levels of understanding of covariation. All students are able to identify and describe the relationship evident in a scatterplot that displays bivariate data, identifying clusters of data in the graphs that are consistent with their conclusion and other areas of the graphs that do not comply with their conclusion, including identification of outliers. In this research setting TinkerPlots affords the students the opportunity to display the learning that has taken place through actual interaction with the software, rather than having to transfer to a paper-and-pencil test.

The affordance of TinkerPlots assessment of understanding is further demonstrated as part of a research project exploring students' ability to compare two sets of data and decide which of two groups of children have done better on a spelling test. In this case, two formats

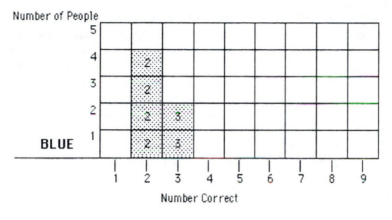

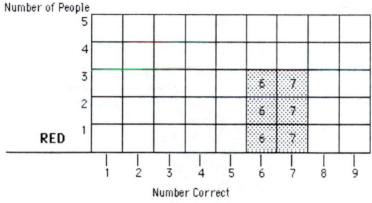

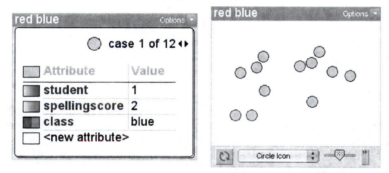

Spelling scores of twelve students in two classes (class red and class blue).

Attribute Description

Student: students are numbered from 1 to 12
Spellingscore: score out of 9 in spelling test
Class: class of each student - red or blue

Question

Which class did better on the spelling test, red or blue?

Figure 24.7 Protocols for Comparing Groups without and with TinkerPlots.

(paper-based or employing TinkerPlots) are used to interview middle school students, with different students in each mode (Watson & Donne, 2009). Of interest here is not how well the students do in comparison with each other but what affordances each mode offers for the students to display their understanding. Students are asked to compare four pairs of graphs with test scores for different classes and decide which class has done better. The students using TinkerPlots have been introduced to the software and completed some lessons in different contexts than the interview. Figure 24.7 shows the presentation of the first (lowest level) comparison to be made in the Comparing Groups protocol for the two settings. The paper-based interviewees view the graphs only, whereas the TinkerPlots students are expected to manipulate the software in a way that will allow them to answer the same question. The question is, What are the affordances offered to students by TinkerPlots in displaying their understanding (i.e., learning) of statistics and how do they compare with affordances in the nonsoftware environments?

For the Comparing Groups protocol TinkerPlots allows students freedom to create various plots to explore the differences in the test scores of the two classes. When comparing groups of equal size, middle-school students have a tendency to compare totals rather than calculate means: this is reflected in the responses of the students viewing the paper protocol. The students using TinkerPlots, however, do not follow this alternative, but most students produce plots where visually they can see the relationships between the two classes in the plots they have created. For the smallest classes (see Figure 24.7), a few students click through the individual data cards to make a decision. For the most difficult part of the protocol—comparing classes of different sizes where the smaller class has the larger proportion of higher scores—students can choose from several representations rather than be fixed on one pair of frequency distributions on paper. Many of the paper-based students continue to use totals and hence choose the wrong group as "better." Although not all TinkerPlots-based students achieve the correct response, they do not use totals for the comparison. The plots in Figure 24.8 show two students' approaches (left and right) in TinkerPlots.

The major affordance offered by TinkerPlots is the flexibility it gives students to create their own representations of the data to display their understanding (see also Fitzallen & Watson, 2010, 2011). The use of bins rather than totally separating the data along an axis, which is what experienced users would be expected to do, illustrates that students can use this characteristic of the software and stop separating the data at whatever point they feel they have enough information to answer the question. The Plot on the left of Figure 24.9 shows the use of four bins to answer the easiest of the four class comparisons, whereas the Plot on the right shows a similar use of bins for the most difficult part. What is interesting is how the student displays emergent intuitive proportional reasoning in explaining her understanding of the story in the Plot (on the right).

> It kinda looks like this one [Black] did better 'cos most of them are up there [5–9] and there is only 4 up there [0–4] . . . Pink could be better because it's got 25 up there and 17 there [comparing 5–9 for Pink and Black] so there is more that has 5, 6, 7, 8, 9 than Black. But Black got less down here [0–4] because it's got less people than this [Pink] class . . . You never know if you have the same [number] in both classes then you might've got a more even thing . . . Black did better actually because this one's [Black] got less people in it but 11 [Pink] got it wrong, got like 1, 2, 3, 4 and only 4 got it here [0–4] [Black] and 17 got it there [5–9] [Black] but 25 got it there [5–9] [Pink] only because there's more in the Pink class.
>
> (Watson & Donne, 2009, p. 15)

Another example of the affordance of flexibility in TinkerPlots is the availability of data in three formats. Students can click through the data Cards (shown in Figure 24.7) in the

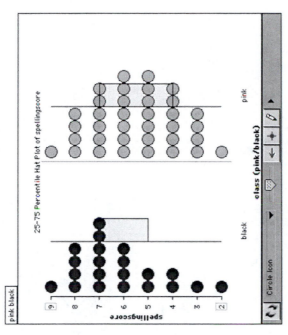

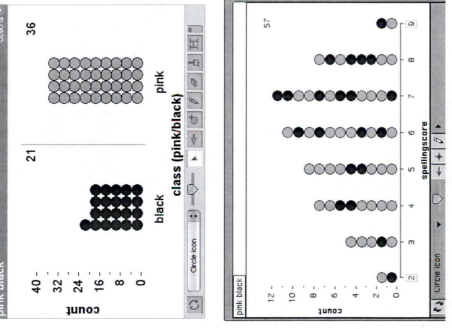

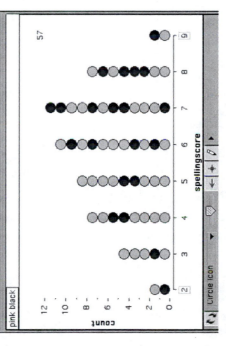

Figure 24.8 Plots created by students for the final part of the Comparing Groups protocol.

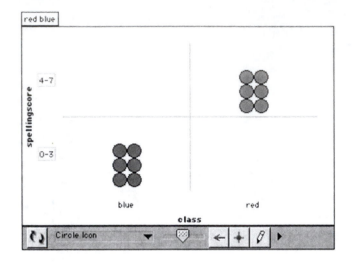

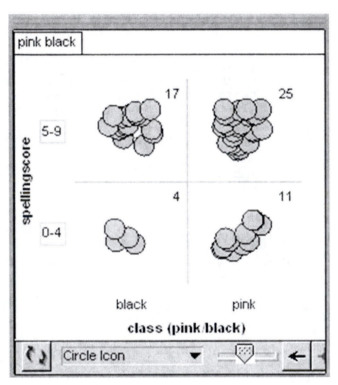

Figure 24.9 Use of bins by students to solve comparison questions.

"stack" one by one, they can drag down a Table with all cases listed in order (not shown in Figure 24.7), or they can click on any icon in the Plot and the associated data Card appears at the top of the stack. Students who answer the paper version of the protocol only have one way to consider the data as presented. Although it is reasonable to assume that all students using TinkerPlots would be familiar with the paper representation from previous classroom experiences, many choose another type of Plot. For a teacher observing and interacting with students in both contexts, much more is learned about the students' creative understanding of the purpose of making a graph in the TinkerPlots setting, rather than just knowing the students can recognize a traditional graph format. This is not to say that all students interviewed with TinkerPlots make appropriate choices between the two classes, just as some of the paper-based similarly do not. The point is that with TinkerPlots there is a good chance of determining the difficulty the students are experiencing.

A further affordance of TinkerPlots for assessment found by Allmond and Makar (2014) grows from focusing on the transition from the Hat plot to the Box plot for explaining variation when comparing two data sets. The Hat plot is unique to TinkerPlots, whereas the Box plot is common in all secondary statistics curricula. As seen in the two plots in Figure 24.10, the Hat plot portrays visually the same information as the Box plot except that the median is missing from the Hat. The associated data are usually visible with the Hat plot (as in the figure) but not in the more common representations of the Box plot (although it is possible to view them in TinkerPlots). Students experience the discussion of variation when comparing two data sets through initially exploring pairs of stacked dot plots, moving to the addition of the Hat plot, following by the Box plot with the data visible, and finally seeing the Box plot without the data. When completing assessment tasks students generally use the software to progress from qualitative to quantitative descriptions of difference with relative ease, demonstrating understanding often not shown by older students introduced directly to the "bare" Box plot (e.g., Bakker, Biehler, & Konold, 2005).

As seen in these examples, the affordances for learning often translate into affordances for assessment. This is particularly true if TinkerPlots itself is used as the setting for carrying out the assessment of learning.

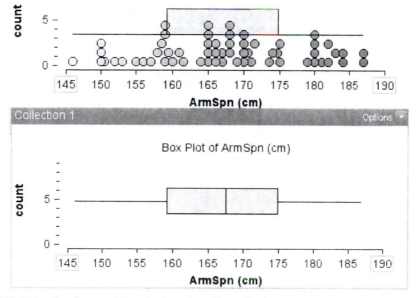

Figure 24.10 A Hat plot showing data and a Box plot without the data.

OTHER MATHEMATICS LEARNING

It is not surprising to find affordances from learning with TinkerPlots that are associated with other areas of the curriculum. An example of this, associated with proportional reasoning, occurs when Watson and English (2013b) are using TinkerPlots to build upon classroom Chance trials with grade 4 students. To introduce the concepts of expectation and variation to the students, there is a discussion of how many heads they would expect to get when tossing a coin 10 times. It is agreed that with a probability of 1/2 of getting a head, they can expect to get five heads. Some however suggest that it might not be exactly five, maybe four or six, showing some acknowledgment of variation. To their surprise, there is quite a lot of variation in their outcomes, with the number varying in one class between three heads and nine heads. The obvious affordance of TinkerPlots in this context, as noted in some earlier examples, is to allow students the opportunity to increase the sample size and simulate large numbers of coin tosses, comparing the variation among the repeated outcomes as the sample size increases. As the students watch the heights in the Plot get closer and closer together, they are learning about the effect of sample size and are able to express this verbally as the "variation gets less" as the Plot shows the heights closer and closer to their expectation of 1/2. In comparing the absolute difference in the number of heads and tails, however, the numbers generally increase with increase in sample size. This is shown in Figure 24.11.

When students attempt to summarize their findings by doing several repetitions of the computer simulations for the same sample size to show how close the number of heads is to half of the number of tosses, they often do so by plotting the "number of heads." Doing this for two different sample sizes, either by hand or in TinkerPlots, and comparing the plots, does not show the difference in variation because the scales on the plots are usually different, as shown in Figure 24.12. The variation, however, is considered the same by students because of the visual impact. The affordance of TinkerPlots in this situation is creating cognitive conflict and showing that the range of variation in the top Plot is five whereas in the bottom Plot, where the variation is supposed to decrease, the range of variation is 12. For a teacher this leads to questioning about *why* the plots look similar and what this has to do with the scales on the plots.

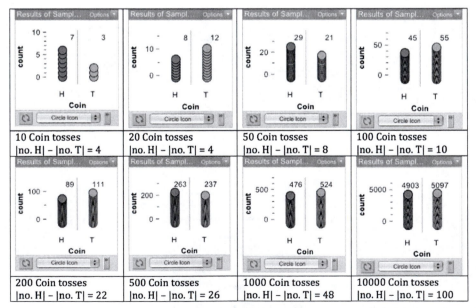

Figure 24.11 The results of simulating tossing a coin an increasing number of times, observing the heights of H and T, and finding the difference between the number of Hs and the number of Ts.

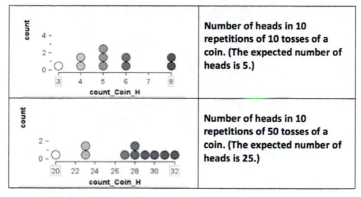

Figure 24.12 Different scales for repetitions of different numbers of coin toss.

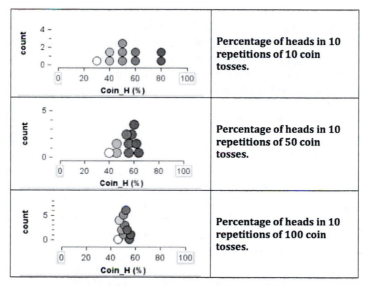

Figure 24.13 Plotting percentage on the same scale to distinguish variation for 10 samples of coin tosses of different sizes.

It is the mathematics of percentage, which represents in one number a part compared to a whole, that is critical to the solving of the dilemma in Figure 24.12. Comparisons can be made across wholes, that is, across different sample sizes of 10 or 50 tosses. The percentages then show on the same scale how close the numbers of heads (the parts), are to half of the total, which is the expected outcome in this case. This is shown in Figure 24.13, where plots on the same scale using percentage show clearly the decrease in variation as the sample size increases.

Rubin and Hammerman (2006) also emphasize the affordance of using proportions in the form of percents to "equalize" groups of unequal size, represented in bins in TinkerPlots acknowledging that for some middle-school students this is a new or unconsolidated idea. Overall, two affordances emerge for focusing attention on students' understanding or misunderstanding of the use of percentage and on the necessity to be aware of scale when comparing two graphs. The solutions to these issues may not appear within the software itself, but the feedback provided by TinkerPlots should provide the teacher with starting points for remediation, either providing clues within the program (Figure 24.13) or working with pencil and paper. These observations are the same as those of Ireland and Watson (2009) when working with grade 6 students.

CONSTRAINTS

Kennewell (2001) thinks of constraints as providing structure and guidance for an activity to occur and learning to take place. When software such as TinkerPlots is employed in the classroom, it is useful to consider whether the constraints support or inhibit other aspects of the software that are considered affordances. Further, it is possible to ask if affordances may also inhibit learning.

One of the constraints imposed on the creation of Plots in TinkerPlots is that when a numerical attribute is placed on an axis, the program automatically introduces an ordered scaling, either in bins or on a continuous scale. This structure forces the student to view data values in an ordered fashion. An example of the difference from what a student might do by hand is seen in Figure 24.14 where a student's hand-created table accurately records measurements of a classmate's arm span but the student does not feel the necessity to order the values, only to show their frequency. Although the data can be entered into TinkerPlots in the same order as seen in the student's table, the Plot—while retaining the frequencies—forces order and displays the shape of the distribution and the outlier. Whether this structural constraint can also be thought of as affordance depends on how the student responds to the representation and perhaps on the teacher's pedagogical content knowledge in reinforcing the experience as one of learning. A related constraint is the initial listing of categorical variables on axes in alphabetical order, as observed by Hall (2008). She notes, however, that the drag-and-drop feature of TinkerPlots means that in this situation the order can be easily changed to suit the requirements of the user.

Another structural constraint of TinkerPlots in relation to creating Plots within the software is the range of types of plots that can be created. This range, including icons (as in Figure 24.14), value bars, value circles, and fused rectangular or circular representations, presents both freedom of choice and the necessity to appreciate what each type can meaningfully represent. On the left of Figure 24.15 are fused representations. The pie chart is shaded from white to very dark to show the increase in arm span length, while the histogram is based on quite large intervals. On the right of Figure 24.15 are two-dimensional representations, using bins to display value icons. The bins result from categorical data (names) or intervals for measurements. In terms of affordances, the range of representation types would appear to provide little opportunity for displaying understanding in the top two plots but provide a creative, less conventional, opportunity to show understanding in the bottom two plots.

The appreciation of the constraints of the Sampler is of particular interest in relation to knowing the models for probability that are common to students. In Figure 24.16, at the top are two Samplers to model the tossing of a single coin twice; at the bottom there are two Samplers to model the tossing of a single die once. On the left, the two Samplers display the elements in the Mixer and they are seen bouncing around the Mixer before one pops out at the top. That element is immediately replaced before another random selection is made. On the right the two probabilities are modelled with Spinners. In the top right, Sampler, heads and tails are no longer equally likely to be chosen, while in the bottom right Sampler each outcome for the die is equally likely. In these cases a Spinner is seen to rotate before coming to rest on a section, which is then the result. The two different Samplers present two different constraints for students. Teachers hence need to be aware of which constraint will lead to meaningful understanding for students and whether there is an affordance in letting students choose their devices within a Sampler and explain how they work to others in the class. The speed of the Sampler is also a constraint. For some students, it may be necessary to continue

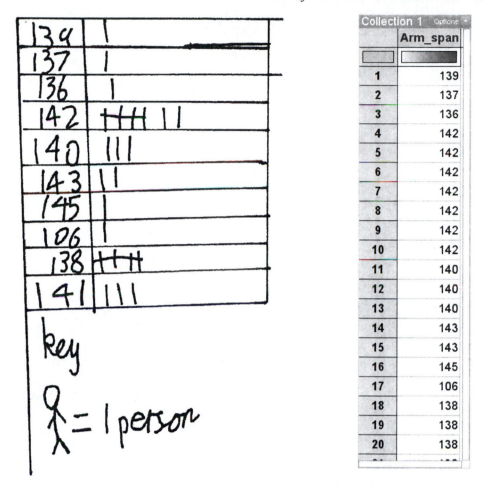

	Arm_span
1	139
2	137
3	136
4	142
5	142
6	142
7	142
8	142
9	142
10	142
11	140
12	140
13	140
14	143
15	143
16	145
17	106
18	138
19	138
20	138

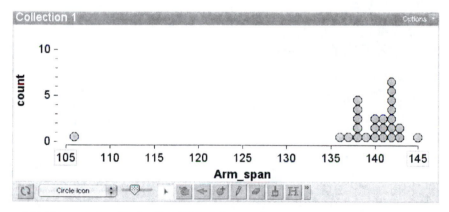

Figure 24.14 A constraint of TinkerPlots is that it forces order on numerical data.

to run the Sampler at a Medium or slower speed in order to reinforce the repeated trials that are occurring. No "action" of the Mixer or Spinner is seen on Fast, and for some students the affordance of understanding the process may be lost.

The structure of TinkerPlots allows a number of ways (constraints) for completing a modelling process with the Sampler. Students given the choice may find greater affordance for

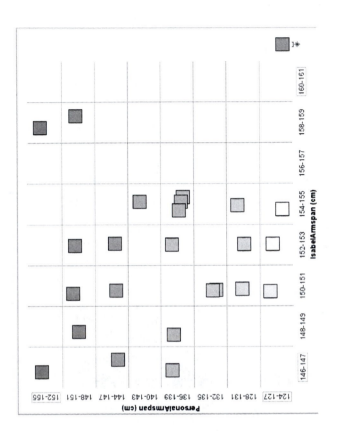

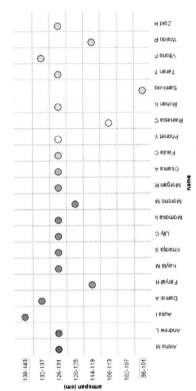

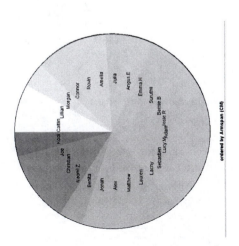

Figure 24.15 Four Plots to show arm-span measurements.

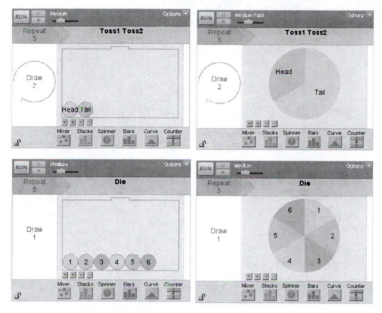

Figure 24.16 Samplers for tossing a coin twice or a die once with a Mixer (left) or Spinner (right).

understanding in one approach than another. The Mixer shown in the upper-left corner of Figure 24.16, for example, models the tossing of one coin twice. What about the tossing of two coins, once each? Can the Sampler be used to model this behavior? Are the outcomes the same? The answers are "yes" but students may not have this advanced understanding. As shown in Figure 24.17, the Sampler has the ability (constraint) to test this conjecture, where on the right a second Mixer is set up in the Sampler and each Mixer tosses one coin once. The Sampler on the left of the figure is set up as in Figure 24.16 but relabeled as "Coin1 Coin2." Figure 24.18 shows the results of running Sampler 1 five times (left) and of running Sampler 2 five times (right). These results are not identical but students have the further opportunity (constraint) to run the two Samplers repeatedly and see if the results become close. Figure 24.19 shows the results of 1,000 trials for each model (Sampler). The different constraints for modeling of the coin become an affordance for building understanding that the two conditions for tossing results are equivalent in the same underlying model.

As the statistical questions become more complex, the constraints for modeling in TinkerPlots become more numerous, creating dilemmas both for students and for teachers. An example of working through constraints is shown in the study of Stack and Watson (2013), where two teachers work with their grade 10 mathematics classes on a five-week unit, leading to using resampling (see also Watson, 2014; Watson & Chance, 2012) as an introduction to informal statistical inference. The teachers in the study, although having used TinkerPlots with younger students in less challenging contexts, have not used the Sampler before or carried out resampling investigations. The students have not used TinkerPlots before. Although the teachers understand the principles involved, they have not had the opportunity to develop the high level of pedagogical content knowledge of the affordances and constraints required to answer students' questions, or in some cases the technical knowledge of the software to retrieve the situation in TinkerPlots when students go astray. Hence in embarking on ambitious goals for employing TinkerPlots, it is necessary for teachers to appreciate the alternative pathways students may take through the constraints.

Over the course of the unit most of the students develop greater mastery within the TinkerPlots constraints, though still under the guidance of the instructions and teacher assistance.

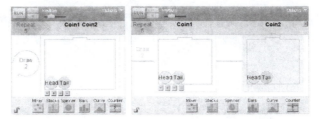

Figure 24.17 Samplers using Mixers to model tossing two coins once.

Figure 24.18 Results from using the Samplers in Figure 24.17.

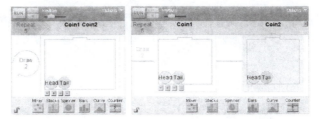

Figure 24.19 Results for 1,000 tosses of two coins using the Samplers in Figure 24.17.

Talk in the classroom shifts from predominantly needing help to fix technical issues or to get help within the constraints, to conversations about the meaning of the data. The teacher is able then to gain a greater insight into the thinking of the students and the students themselves are more engaged in discussing the work. The culminating investigation uses a multistep process of random reallocation of data to determine if experimental data are due to chance alone or a caused result. Many students are able to conduct this investigation without instruction and create a report of their findings explaining what they did and what they found. For some students however, their language lacks sophistication.

One informal inference task is based on data from an experiment with 30 mildly to moderately depressed people taken to the Caribbean for swimming four hours per day for four weeks, half swimming with dolphins and half not (Rossman, 2008). The data in Figure 24.20 show the results for no improvement or improvement for the patients and students are asked if it is reasonable to claim that the treatment was successful. Having gained experience within the structure (constraints) of TinkerPlots using the Sampler in ways related to activities shown in Figures 24.17, 24.18, and 24.19, students are able to work within the constraints of a two-Mixer Sampler that randomly reallocates the results of the experiment to the treatment and control. Redoing this a large number of times makes it possible to estimate how likely it is that the results could have occurred by chance rather than be due to the treatment. The concrete nature of a TinkerPlots experience as complex as this exemplifies the balance of affordances and constraints that leads to understanding of an inferential process not available to grade 10 students through theoretical statistics (e.g., chi-square tests, in this case).

The openness and flexibility constraints of TinkerPlots empower students to create, change, manipulate, and repeat operations in TinkerPlots unimpeded. Although such functionality opens up opportunities for using exploratory data analysis (Tukey, 1977) and active graphing

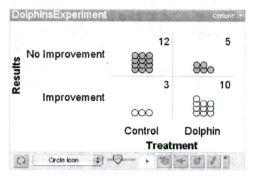

Figure 24.20 Results of Swimming With Dolphins experiment.

strategies (Ainley & Pratt, 2014; Ben-Zvi & Aridor, 2014), for some students, TinkerPlots may open the door too wide. This is evident in some studies that require students to construct simulations or model data in TinkerPlots when using the Sampler and Plot functions with tertiary statistics students (Noll, Gebresenbet, & Glover, 2012), with preservice teachers (Podworny & Biehler, 2014), and with grade 9 students (Saldanha & McAllister, 2014). These studies find that some students experience difficulty imagining how to construct a statistical model and also keeping track of the resampling process. These issues may arise because students do not have the statistical reasoning experience and background necessary to take advantage of the affordance of freedom that TinkerPlots offers. Like Stack and Watson (2013), these researchers note that students are able to develop confidence and engage in statistical reasoning once the statistical model is constructed under instruction.

Podworny and Biehler (2014) support their preservice teachers by utilizing a simulation scheme that involves making them draw diagrams and describe verbally all parts of their simulations. These teachers are able to choose to use the simulation scheme either as a planning tool prior to running the simulation or as a documentation and reflection tool after the simulation. Regardless of when the simulation scheme is used, it helps the students to identify the purpose of each step in the simulation, what can be learned at each step, and how that informs other steps. Saldanha and McAllister (2014) also suggest that students would benefit from activities that require them to identify the processes and objects generated by the resampling process and how they contribute to the graphical distributions produced. They contend that this supports students to establish and maintain robust mental images of the resampling process and its products.

Because of the diversity of the constraints in TinkerPlots it is important for teachers to be aware of their potential either to support or hinder students' developing understanding. Again the pedagogical content knowledge of the teacher is built on knowing well both the affordances and constraints of the software. This will enable them to make the decisions about when and how to scaffold student learning depending on the learning goals and outcomes targeted within learning experiences.

CONCLUSION

The examples of affordances documented in this chapter for TinkerPlots illustrate the *learning* that takes place when students or teachers are using TinkerPlots. There is no intention to claim that TinkerPlots creates the learning experience in isolation from contexts and perhaps prompting from other facilitators. To gain the most from the affordances of TinkerPlots, planning must be put into procedural instructions, scaffolding, provocative questions, reflective questions, and possible extension activities. What is demonstrated here is that research around the world has gone beyond showing what the software can do, to providing evidence that learning takes place in relation to the statistical principles that underpin the makeup of the package. The discussion of constraints, with the potential conflict of meaning with other connotations of the word *constraint*, illustrates the complexity involved when moving from *doing* to *learning*. The structure and guidance provided by the software need to be taken into account in judging the quality of the learning affordance.

TinkerPlots and statistics have been the focus of this chapter on software and mathematics education because there is no equivalent software that provides the range of affordances described here in a form that is accessible to and understandable by school students. Although software applications exist in other areas of the mathematics curriculum, the critical necessity to handle large data sets for meaningful learning within statistics, demands that attention be given to the affordances, in conjunction with the constraints, of TinkerPlots.

Acknowledgment: The authors acknowledge useful conversations with Dr. Sue Stack in preparing this chapter.

REFERENCES

Ainley, J., & Pratt, D. (2014). Expressions of uncertainty when variation is partially determined. In K. Makar, B. deSousa, & R. Gould (Eds.), *Sustainability in statistics education. Proceedings of the 9th International Conference on the Teaching of Statistics.* Flagstaff, AZ, July 13–18. Voorburg, The Netherlands: International Statistical Institute. Retrieved from http://iase-web.org/icots/9/proceedings/pdfs/ICOTS9_9A1_AINLEY.pdf.

Allmond, S., & Makar, K. (2014). From hat plots to box plots in TinkerPlots : Supporting students to write conclusions which account for variability in data. In K. Makar, B. deSousa, & R. Gould (Eds.), *Sustainability in statistics education. Proceedings of the 9th International Conference on the Teaching of Statistics.* Flagstaff, AZ, July 13–18. Voorburg, The Netherlands: International Statistical Institute. Retrieved from http://iase-web.org/icots/9/proceedings/pdfs/ICOTS9_2E1_ALLMOND.pdf.

Australian Education Council. (1991). *A national statement on mathematics for Australian schools.* Melbourne: Author.

Bakker, A., Biehler, R., & Konold, C. (2005). Should young students learn about box plots? In G. Burrill & M. Camden (Eds.), *Curricular development in statistics education. International Association for Statistical Education (IASE) Roundtable, Lund, Sweden, 2004* (pp. 163–173). Voorburg, The Netherlands: International Statistical Institute.

Bakker, A., Derry, J., & Konold, C. (2006). Using technology to support diagrammatic reasoning about center and variation. In A. Rossman & B. Chance (Eds.), *Working cooperatively in statistics education. Proceedings of the 7th International Conference on the Teaching of Statistics.* Salvador, Bahai, Brazil, July 2–7. Voorburg, The Netherlands: International Association for Statistical Education and the International Statistical Institute. Retrieved from http://iase-web.org/documents/papers/icots7/2D4_BAKK.pdf.

Ben-Zvi, D. (2006). Scaffolding students' informal inference and argumentation. In A. Rossman & B. Chance (Eds.), *Working cooperatively in statistics education. Proceedings of the 7th International Conference on the Teaching of Statistics.* Salvador, Bahai, Brazil, July 2–7. Voorburg, The Netherlands: International Association for Statistical Education and the International Statistical Institute. Retrieved from http://iase-web.org/documents/papers/icots7/2D1_BENZ.pdf.

Ben-Zvi, D., & Aridor, K. (2014). Students' emergent roles in developing their reasoning about uncertainty and modeling. In K. Makar, B. deSousa, & R. Gould (Eds.), *Sustainability in statistics education. Proceedings of the 9th International Conference on the Teaching of Statistics.* Flagstaff, AZ, July 13–18. Voorburg, The Netherlands: International Statistical Institute. Retrieved from http://iase-web.org/icots/9/proceedings/pdfs/ICOTS9_9A3_ARIDOR.pdf.

Ben-Zvi, D., Gil, E., & Apel, N. (2007). What is hidden beyond the data? Helping young students to reason and argue about some wider universe. In D. Pratt & J. Ainley (Eds.), *Reasoning about informal inferential statistical reasoning: A collection of current research studies. Proceedings of the Fifth International Research Forum on Statistical Reasoning, Thinking, and Literacy* (SRTL-5). August 11–17. Warwick, UK: University of Warwick.

Biehler, R., Ben-Zvi, D., Bakker, A., & Makar, K. (2013). Technology for enhancing statistical reasoning at the school level. In M.A. Clement, A.J. Bishop, C. Keitel, J. Kilpatrick, & A.Y.L. Leung (Eds.), *Third international handbook on mathematics education* (pp. 643–689). New York: Springer.

Bower, M. (2008). Affordance analysis—matching learning tasks with learning technologies. *Educational Media International, 45*(1), 3–15.

Brown, J., Stillman, G., & Herbert, S. (2004). Can the notion of affordances be of use in the design of a technology enriched mathematics curriculum? In I. Putt, R. Faragher, & M. McLean (Eds.), *Mathematics education for the third millennium: Towards 2010. Proceedings of the 27th Annual Conference of the Mathematics Education Research Group of Australasia* (Vol. 1, pp. 119–124). Sydney, NSW: MERGA.

Browning, C., Goss, J., & Smith, D.O. (2014). Statistical knowledge for teaching: Elementary preservice teachers. In K. Makar, B. deSousa, & R. Gould (Eds.), *Sustainability in statistics education. Proceedings of the 9th International Conference on the Teaching of Statistics.* Flagstaff, AZ, July 13–18. Voorburg, The Netherlands: International Statistical Institute. Retrieved from http://iase-web.org/icots/9/proceedings/pdfs/ICOTS9_2F2_BROWNING.pdf.

Browning, C., & Smith, D.O. (2015). Utilizing technology to engage statistical inquiry in light of the standards for mathematical practice. In D. Polly (Ed.), *Cases of technology integration in mathematics education* (pp. 205–226). Hershey, PA: IGI Global.

Burgess, T. (2014). Student perspectives on being introduced to using *TinkerPlots* for investigations. In K. Makar, B. deSousa, & R. Gould (Eds.), *Sustainability in statistics education. Proceedings of the 9th International Conference on the Teaching of Statistics.* Flagstaff, AZ, July 13–18. Voorburg, The Netherlands: International Statistical Institute. Retrieved from http://iase-web.org/icots/9/proceedings/pdfs/ICOTS9_2B3_BURGESS.pdf.

Chick, H.L. (2007). Teaching and learning by example. In J. Watson & K. Beswick (Eds.), *Essential research, essential practice. Proceedings of the 30th annual conference of the Mathematics Education Research Group of Australasia* (Vol. 1, pp. 3–21). Adelaide, SA: MERGA.

Day, L. (2013). Using statistics to explore cross-curricular and social issues opportunities. *The Australian Mathematics Teacher, 69*(4), 3–7.

delMas, R., Garfield, J., & Zieffler, A. (2014). Using *TinkerPlots* to develop tertiary students' statistical thinking in a modeling-based introductory statistics class. In T. Wassong, D. Frischemeier, P.R. Fischer, R. Hochmuth, & P. Bender (Eds.), *Using tools for learning mathematics and statistics* (pp. 405–420). Heidelberg: Springer Spektrum.

Fitzallen, N. (2006). A model of students' statistical thinking and reasoning about graphs in an ICT environment. In P. Grootenboer, R. Zevenbergen, & M. Chinnappan (Eds.), *Identities, cultures and learning spaces. Proceedings of 29th annual conference of the Mathematics Education Research Group of Australasia* (pp. 203–210). Sydney: MERGA.

Fitzallen, N. (2007). Evaluating data analysis software: The case of *TinkerPlots. Australian Primary Mathematics Classroom, 12*(1), 23–28.

Fitzallen, N. (2012). Interpreting graphs: Students developing an understanding of covariation. In J. Dindyal, L.P. Cheng, & S.F. Ng (Eds.), *Mathematics education: Expanding horizons. Proceedings of the 35th annual conference of the Mathematics Education Research Group of Australasia* (pp. 290–297). Sydney: MERGA.

Fitzallen, N. (2013). Characterising students' interaction with *TinkerPlots. Technology Innovations in Statistics Education, 7*(1), Article 2. Retrieved from www.escholarship.org/uc/item/1074n1dp#.

Fitzallen, N., & Brown, N. (2006). Evaluating data-analysis software: Exploring opportunities for developing statistical thinking and reasoning. In N. Armstrong & C. Sherwood (Eds.), *IT's up here for thinking. Proceedings of the Australian Computers in Education Conference* (CD-ROM). October 2–4. Lesmurdie, WA: Australian Council for Computers in Education.

Fitzallen, N., & Watson, J. (2010). Developing statistical reasoning facilitated by *TinkerPlots.* In C. Reading (Ed.), *Data and context in statistics education: Towards an evidence-based society. Proceedings of the 8th International Conference on the Teaching of Statistics.* Ljubljana, Slovenia, July 11–16. Voorburg, The Netherlands: International Statistical Institute. Retrieved from www.stat.auckland.ac.nz/~iase/publications/icots8/ICOTS8_8A4_FITZALLEN.pdf.

Fitzallen, N., & Watson, J. (2011). Graph creation and interpretation: Putting skills and context together. *Traditions and [new] practices. Proceedings of the joint conference of the Mathematics Education Research Group of Australasia and the Australian Association of Mathematics Teachers* (pp. 203–209). Sydney: MERGA.

Fitzallen, N., & Watson, J. (2014). Extending the curriculum with *TinkerPlots:* Opportunities for early development of informal inference. In K. Makar, B. deSousa, & R. Gould (Eds.), *Sustainability in statistics education. Proceedings of the 9th International Conference on the Teaching of Statistics.* Flagstaff, AZ, July 13–18. Voorburg, The Netherlands: International Statistical Institute. Retrieved from http://iase-web.org/icots/9/proceedings/pdfs/ICOTS9_8D3_FITZALLEN.pdf.

Frischemeier, D. (2014). Comparing groups by using *TinkerPlots* as part of a data analysis task—Tertiary students' strategies and difficulties. In K. Makar, B. deSousa, & R. Gould (Eds.), *Sustainability in statistics education. Proceedings of the 9th International Conference on the Teaching of Statistics.* Flagstaff,

AZ, July 13–18. Voorburg, The Netherlands: International Statistical Institute. Retrieved from http://iase-Web.org/icots/9/proceedings/pdfs/ICOTS9_8J3_FRISCHEMEIER.pdf.

Garfield, J., delMas, R., & Zieffler, A. (2012). Developing statistical modelers and thinkers in an introductory, tertiary-level statistics course. *ZDM: The International Journal on Mathematics Education, 44*, 883–898.

Gibson, J.J. (1977). The theory of affordances. In R. Shaw & J. Bransford (Eds.), *Perceiving, acting, and knowing: Toward an ecological psychology* (pp. 67–82). Hillsdale, NJ: Lawrence Erlbaum Associates.

Goldenberg, E.P. (1991). The difference between graphing software and educational graphing software. In W. Zimmerman & S. Cunningham (Eds.), *Visualization in teaching and learning mathematics* (pp. 77–86). Washington, DC: Mathematical Association of America.

Goyne, J.S., McDonough, S.K., & Padgett, D.D. (2000). Guidelines for evaluating educational software. *The Clearing House, 73*(6), 345–348.

Hall, J. (2008, July). Using Census at School and *TinkerPlots* to support Ontario elementary teachers' statistics teaching and learning. In J. Garfield & M.G. Ottaviani (Chairs), *Topic 6: Building collaboration between mathematics and statistics educators in teacher education*, Joint ICME/IASE Study: Teaching statistics in school mathematics. Challenges for teaching and teacher education, Monterrey, Mexico. Retrieved from www.ugr.es/~icmi/iase_study/Files/Topic6.htm.

Harradine, A., & Konold, C. (2006). How representational medium affects the data displays students make. In A. Rossman & B. Chance (Eds.), *Working cooperatively in statistics education. Proceedings of the 7th International Conference on the Teaching of Statistics* (CD-ROM). Salvador, Bahai, Brazil, July 2–7. Voorburg, The Netherlands: International Statistical Institute and the International Statistical Institute.

Hoyles, C., Bakker, A., Kent, P., & Noss, R. (2007). Attributing meanings to representations of data: The case of statistical process control. *Mathematical Thinking and Learning, 9*, 331–360.

Hudson, R.A. (2012). Finding balance at the elusive mean. *Mathematics Teaching in the Middle School, 18*, 301–306.

Ireland, S., & Watson, J. (2009). Building an understanding of the connection between experimental and theoretical aspects of probability. *International Electronic Journal of Mathematics Education, 4*, 339–370.

Jonassen, D.H., & Land, S.M. (Eds.). (2000). *Theoretical foundations of learning environments*. Mahwah, NJ: Lawrence Erlbaum Associates.

Jones, K.S. (2003). What is an affordance? *Ecological Psychology, 15*(2), 107–114.

Kazak, S., Fujita, T., & Wegerif, R. (2014). Year 6 students' reasoning about random 'bunny hops' through the use of *TinkerPlots* and peer-to-peer dialogic interactions. In K. Makar, B. deSousa, & R. Gould (Eds.), *Sustainability in statistics education. Proceedings of the 9th International Conference on the Teaching of Statistics*. Flagstaff, AZ, July 13–18. Voorburg, The Netherlands: International Statistical Institute. Retrieved from http://iase-web.org/icots/9/proceedings/pdfs/ICOTS9_9F1_KAZAK.pdf.

Kazak, S., & Konold, C. (2010). Development of ideas in data and chance through the use of tools provided by computer-based technology. In C. Reading (Ed.), *Data and context in statistics education: Towards an evidence-based society. Proceedings of the 8th International Conference on the Teaching of Statistics*. Ljubljana, Slovenia, July 11–16. Voorburg, The Netherlands: International Statistical Institute. Retrieved from http://iase-web.org/documents/papers/icots8/ICOTS8_8D2_KAZAK.pdf.

Kazak, S., Wegerif, R., & Fujita, T. (2014). Supporting students' probabilistic reasoning through the use of technology and dialogic talk. In S. Pope (Ed.), *Proceedings of the 8th British Congress of Mathematics Education* (pp. 215–222). Nottingham, UK: British Society for Research into Learning Mathematics.

Kennewell, S. (2001). Using affordances and constraints to evaluate the use of information and communications technology in teaching and learning. *Journal of Information Technology for Teacher Education, 10*(1–2), 101–116.

Kidman, G.C., & Nason, R. (2000). When a visual representation is not worth a thousand words. *Technology in Mathematics Education Conference* (CD-ROM). December 11–14. Auckland: University of Auckland and Auckland University of Technology.

Konold, C. (2007). Designing a data analysis tool for learners. In M.C. Lovett & P. Shah (Eds.), *Thinking with data* (pp. 267–291). New York: Lawrence Erlbaum Associates.

Konold, C., & Harradine, A. (2014). Contexts for highlighting signal and noise. In T. Wassong, D. Frischemeier, P.R. Fischer, R. Hochmuth, & P. Bender (Eds.), *Using tools for learning mathematics and statistics* (pp. 237–250). Heidelberg: Springer Spektrum.

Konold, C., Harradine, A., & Kazak, S. (2007). Understanding distributions by modeling them. *International Journal of Computers for Mathematical Learning, 12*(3), 217–230.

Konold, C., & Lehrer, R. (2008). Technology and mathematics education: An essay in honor of Jim Kaput. In L.D. English (Ed.), *Handbook of International Research in Mathematics Education* (2nd ed., pp. 49–72). New York: Routledge.

Konold, C., & Miller, C. (1994). DataScope. (Computer software). Santa Barbara, CA: Intellimation Library for the Macintosh.

Konold, C., & Miller, C. D. (2005). Tinkerplots: Dynamic data exploration. (Computer software). Emeryville, CA: Key Curriculum Press.

Konold, C. & Miller, C. D. (2011). *TinkerPlots:* Dynamic data exploration. (Computer software, Version 2.0). Emeryville, CA: Key Curriculum Press.

Land, S. M., Hannafin, M. J., & Oliver, K. (2012). Student-centred learning environments: Foundations, assumptions and design. In D. Jonassen & S. Land (Eds.), *Theoretical foundations of learning environments* (2nd Ed., pp. 3–26). Hoboken, NJ: Taylor & Francis.

Lehrer, R., Kim, M. J., & Schauble, L. (2007). Supporting the development of conceptions of statistics by engaging students in measuring and modeling variability. *International Journal of Computers for Mathematical Learning, 12*(3), 195–216.

Madden, S. (2014). Designing technology-rich learning environments for secondary teachers to explore and prepare to teach statistics. In K. Makar, B. deSousa, & R. Gould (Eds.), *Sustainability in statistics education. Proceedings of the 9th International Conference on the Teaching of Statistics.* Flagstaff, AZ, July 13–18. Voorburg, The Netherlands: International Statistical Institute. Retrieved from http://iase-web.org/icots/9/proceedings/pdfs/ICOTS9_9E2_MADDEN.pdf.

Manor, H., Ben-Zvi, D., & Aridor, K. (2014). Students' reasoning about uncertainty while making informal statistical inferences in an "integrated pedagogic approach." In K. Makar, B. deSousa, & R. Gould (Eds.), *Sustainability in statistics education. Proceedings of the 9th International Conference on the Teaching of Statistics.* Flagstaff, AZ, July 13–18. Voorburg, The Netherlands: International Statistical Institute. Retrieved from http://iase-web.org/icots/9/proceedings/pdfs/ICOTS9_8C2_MANOR.pdf.

Meletiou-Mavrotheris, M., Paparistodemou, E., & Stylianou, D. (2009). Enhancing statistics instruction in elementary schools: Integrating technology in professional development. *The Montana Mathematics Enthusiast, 6*(1–2), 57–78.

Ministry of Education. (1992). *Mathematics in the New Zealand curriculum.* Wellington, NZ: Author.

Monteiro, C., Asseker, A., Carvalho, L., & Campos, T. (2010). Student teachers developing their knowledge about data handling using *TinkerPlots.* In C. Reading (Ed.), *Data and context in statistics education: Towards an evidence-based society. Proceedings of the 8th International Conference on the Teaching of Statistics.* Ljubljana, Slovenia, July 11–16. Voorburg, The Netherlands: International Statistical Institute. Retrieved from http://iase-web.org/documents/papers/icots8/ICOTS8_3B1_MONTEIRO.pdf.

Murray, T., Blessing, S., & Ainsworth, S. (Eds.) (2003). *Authoring tools for advanced technology learning environments: Toward cost-effective adaptive, interactive and intelligent educational software.* Dordrecht, The Netherlands: Kluwer Academic Publishers.

National Council of Teachers of Mathematics. (1989). *Curriculum and evaluation standards for school mathematics.* Reston, VA: Author.

Noll, J., Gebresenbet, M., & Glover, E. D. (2012). A modeling and simulation approach to informal inference: Success and challenges. In D. Ben-Zvi & K. Makar (Eds.), *Teaching and learning statistics. Proceedings of the 12th International Congress on Mathematical Education, Topic Study Group 12* (pp. 141–150). Seoul, Korea, July 8–15.

Paparistodemou, E., & Meletiou-Mavrotheris, M. (2008). Developing young students' informal inference skills in data analysis. *Statistics Education Research Journal, 7*(2), 83–106. Retrieved from www.stat.auckland.ac.nz/~iase/serj/SERJ7(2)_Paparistodemou.pdf.

Podworny, S., & Biehler, R. (2014). A learning trajectory on hypothesis testing with *TinkerPlots*—Design and exploratory evaluation. In K. Makar, B. deSousa, & R. Gould (Eds.), *Sustainability in statistics education. Proceedings of the 9th International Conference on the Teaching of Statistics.* Flagstaff, AZ, July 13–18. Voorburg, The Netherlands: International Statistical Institute. Retrieved from http://iase-web.org/icots/9/proceedings/pdfs/ICOTS9_9A2_PODWORNY.pdf.

Rossman, A. J. (2008). Reasoning about informal statistical inference: One statistician's view. *Statistics Education Research Journal, 7*(2), 5–19. Retrieved from www.stat.auckland.ac.nz/serj.

Rubin, A., & Hammerman, J. K. (2006). Understanding data through new software representations. In G. F. Burrill (Ed.), *Thinking and reasoning with data and chance* (pp. 241–256). Reston, VA: National Council of Teachers of Mathematics.

Saldanha, L., & McAllister, M. (2014). Using re-sampling and sampling variability in an applied context as a basis for making statistical inferences with confidence. In K. Makar, B. deSousa, & R. Gould (Eds.), *Sustainability in statistics education. Proceedings of the 9th International Conference on the Teaching of Statistics.* Flagstaff, AZ, July 13–18. Voorburg, The Netherlands: International Statistical Institute. Retrieved from http://iase-web.org/icots/9/proceedings/pdfs/ICOTS9_6C2_SALDANHA.pdf.

Schoenfeld, A. H. (1998). Making mathematics and making pasta: From cookbook procedures to really cooking. In J. G. Greeno & S. V. Goldman (Eds.), *Thinking practices in mathematics and science learning* (pp. 299–320). Mahwah, NJ: Lawrence Erlbaum Associates.

Stack, S., & Watson, J. (2013). Randomness, sample size, imagination and metacognition: Making judgments about differences in data sets. *Australian Mathematics Teacher, 69*(4), 23–30.

Tukey, J.W. (1977). *Exploratory data analysis.* Reading, MA: Addison-Wesley Publishing Company.

Watson, J.M. (2006). *Statistical literacy at school: Growth and goals.* Mahwah, NJ: Lawrence Erlbaum Associates.

Watson, J.M. (2014). *TinkerPlots* as an interactive tool for learning about resampling. In T. Wassong, D. Frischemeier, P.R. Fischer, R. Hochmuth, & P. Bender (Eds.), *Using tools for learning mathematics and statistics* (pp. 421–436). Heidelberg: Springer Spektrum.

Watson, J. M., & Chance, B. (2012). Building intuitions about statistical inference based on resampling. *Australian Senior Mathematics Journal, 26*(1), 6–18.

Watson, J.M., & Donne, J. (2009). *TinkerPlots* as a research tool to explore student understanding. *Technology Innovations in Statistics Education, 3*(1), 1–35.

Watson, J. M., & English, L. D. (2013a). Data and measurement in year 4 of the Australian Curriculum: Mathematics. In S. Herbert, J. Tillyer, & T. Spencer (Eds.), *Mathematics: Launching futures. Proceedings of the 24th biennial conference of the Australian Association of Mathematics Teachers* (pp. 157–165). July 10–13. Adelaide: AAMT.

Watson, J. M., & English, L. D. (2013b). The power of percent. *Australian Primary Mathematics Classroom, 18*(4), 14–18.

Watson, J. M., & Fitzallen, N. (2010). *Development of graph understanding in the mathematics curriculum. Report for the NSW Department of Education and Training.* Sydney: State of New South Wales through the Department of Education and Training. Retrieved from www.curriculumsupport.education.nsw.gov.au/primary/mathematics/assets/pdf/dev_graph_undstdmaths.pdf.

Webb, M.E. (2005). Affordances of ICT in science learning: Implications for an integrated pedagogy. *International Journal of Science Education, 27*(6), 705–735.

Weissglass, J., & Cummings, D. (1991). Dynamic visual experiments with random phenomena. In W. Zimmerman & S. Cunningham (Eds.), *Visualization in teaching and learning mathematics* (pp. 215–223). Washington, DC: Mathematical Association of America.

Weissglass, J., Theis, N., & Finzer, W. (1986). *Hands-on statistics: Explorations with a microcomputer.* Belmont, CA: Wordsworth.

Yilmaz, Z. (2013). Usage of *TinkerPlots* to address and remediate 6th grade students' misconceptions about mean and median. *Anthropologist, 16*(1–2), 21–29.

25 The Use of Digital Technology in Mathematical Practices

Reconciling Traditional and Emerging Approaches

Luis Moreno-Armella and Manuel Santos-Trigo

Cinvestav-IPN, México

INTRODUCTION

The pervasive presence of digital technologies in society, and their transformative powers in this second decade of the 21st century, remind us that we have entered new times full of challenges for educational systems. This is globally true even if one recognizes different levels of economic development of countries around the world. Significant and increasing availability of digital technologies has opened windows for people to explore new social spaces of participation and eventually redefine their own identity. In Mexico, there are about 99 million mobile phones, which means 86 phones per each 100 inhabitants. During a trip in the subway, in Mexico City, one can observe how people become isolated whilst using their phones (basic cell phones and even smartphones) for messaging and playing games. Isolation, however, is apparent as the phones *mediates* their presence in another place. Identity involves presence in social space, but now, social space is extended into a realm of virtual reality, on a permanent basis. The phone is the key to enter and participate in this enlarged infrastructure of society. Friedman (2007) uses the notion of *flatness* to explain and argue that, with the use of technology resources, more people are involved or can directly collaborate in addressing and discussing societal concerns than ever before. He writes: "what the flattening of the world means is that we are now connecting all the knowledge centers on the planet together into a single global network . . . in an amazing era of prosperity, innovation, and collaboration, by companies, communities, and individuals" (p. 8). Digital technologies have transformed and are transforming human relations and human cognitive powers. Friedman's book, among others, provides ample evidence of this fact. At the moment, the use of cognitive technologies (Pea, 1985) could be seen as *amplifiers* of human cognition. For instance, the use of a handheld calculator with Computer Algebra Systems (CAS) can help us solve problems that involve finding the roots of a given polynomial. This is something we could do without the handheld device, but it is faster and convenient to rely on this recourse. Like a magnifying glass, a cognitive technology can improve an ability we already possess. People usually develop this cognitive affordance when they begin representing and exploring tasks through this technology. However, in the long run, this is not quite the only proper role. Like a Trojan horse, a cognitive technology begins working stealthily in our mind and after a while it becomes part of our cognitive resources. This is the case with the technology of writing, for instance. As Donald (2001, p. 302) has explained, literacy skills transform the functional architecture of the brain and have a profound impact on *how literate people perform their cognitive work*. The complex neural components of a literate vocabulary, Donald explains, have to be hammered by years of schooling to rewire the functional organization of our thinking. Similarly, the decimal system (Kaput & Schorr, 2008, p. 212) first enlarged access to computation and eventually paved the way to the Modern Age.

Today, we cannot imagine the world without these technologies. They have become part of our infrastructure—obviously much more than mere amplifiers. That is, they have become essential tools that everyone learns and uses to sustain individual and social activities. They have rewired, as Donald (2001) wrote, the functional organization of individual brains and, at the same time, have become coextensive with our culture. It is the omnipresence of technologies in society that eventually endow them with *invisibility*: they blend into society, as people are increasingly accustomed to their effects.

Thus, technologies eventually become natural and transparent in the social world, the truly human ecology.

We need to develop the critical capabilities to translate scientific and technological developments into our realities, more importantly, into our *educational* realities. Scientific knowledge undergoes tangible transformations before entering into the classroom. One comprehensive framework to guide and understand this translation of scientific knowledge into the knowledge taught in schools is provided by the theory of *didactic transposition* (Chevallard, 1985). Put simply, didactic transposition includes ways to reorganize knowledge so that the new resulting version is available as educational material.

This transposition creates a tension between social expectations, on one side, and what an educational system can deliver and offer to learners on the other. It is important to recognize that a school culture always leaves significant marks on students and teachers' values. As Artigue (2002) has aptly expressed, "these [culture] values were established, through history, in environments poor in technology, and they have only slowly come to terms with the evolution of mathematical practice linked to technological evolution" (p. 245). However, there is a fact that must be singled out: The emergent knowledge produced through the digital media is different from the knowledge emerging from a paper-and-pencil medium, because the mediating artifact is not epistemologically neutral. That is, the nature of the knowledge is inextricably linked to the mediating artifact (Moreno-Armella & Hegedus, 2009, p. 501). We will have an opportunity to discuss this issue broadly, later in this chapter.

It is important to recognize the existence of a natural tension between the past and the future, but it is also possible to resolve it if we realize that the prudent face looks into the past, and the innovative face looks into the future.

Today, our students are increasingly digital natives—and as teachers, we are digital immigrants (Prensky, 2010). Yet, even if we speak (digital) technology with an accent, we need to blend past technologies with the new ones.

In this context, school culture requires a gradual but permanent reorientation of its practices, and of its cognitive and epistemological assumptions, for students to gain access to powerful mathematical ideas. In our view, the classroom should be conceived of as the central nervous system of the educational process. However, that classrooom, as well as the educational system in toto, are open systems and consequently are under the multidimensional influence of its social and cultural environments.

Today, we have new ways to represent and communicate our experiences, in particular, to communicate the knowledge we have acquired. For example, communication technologies facilitate not only direct interaction among research communities, but also the sharing of experiences and results.

Bottino, Artigue, & Noss (2009) present a collaboration project that involves several European research teams discussing goals and ways to frame technology-enhanced learning from different theoretical traditions. But all this is not just about knowledge: it is centrally about *knowing*. As Schmidt and Cohen (2013) pointed out, a computer, in 2025, will be 64 times faster than it is in 2013. This is a huge increase in computational power that should help individuals reorganize their ways of thinking, including their problem solving approaches. We cannot foresee, today, what this would imply for society in general and for education in particular in the next decades.

Mathematics is part of our culture and lives; it is embedded in every digital artifact, phone, computer, eBook, and so on. Eventually, we are compelled to ask: What is the *new* role of mathematics in contemporary societies increasingly saturated by the use of digital artifacts? How can we use available technologies (including smartphones) to foster students' development of sense-making actitivies and reasoning? Thus, we are forced to understand the strategies that teachers follow to appropriate the digital artifacts at their reach. For instance they can use *conveyance technologies* or *mathematical action technologies* (Dick & Hollebrands, 2011). On one hand, the former allow the teacher to present or communicate mathematical ideas in the classroom. Even if these technologies are not mathematics specific (Microsoft Power-Point, LCD projectors, for instance) they are important for integrating the classroom around the discussion of someone's point of view with respect to a mathematical idea. Mathematical action technologies (Dick & Hollebrands, 2011), on the other hand, are used to activate and improve exploration, conjecture formulation, argumentation, and in general, mathematical ways of thinking.

A FOCUS ON MATHEMATICAL TASKS

In the last 10 years we have consistently been involved in several national research projects that aim to analyze and discuss the extent to which the use of digital technologies provide teachers and learners with new avenues to grasp and develop mathematical knowledge (Moreno-Armella & Santos-Trigo, 2008). During the development of those projects we have addressed themes related to teachers' involvement in problem- solving activities that enhance the use of several digital tools, curriculum reforms, and ways to design and implement mathematical tasks in actual learning scenarios (Santos-Trigo & Camacho-Machín, 2009). Our research approach includes working directly with teachers at public institutions through seminars and workshops. There, teachers have an opportunity to identify and discuss international developments around the use of digital technologies such as those published in handbooks and research journals, and ways to frame them in their actual teaching practices. Indeed, several of the tasks used in this chapter to illustrate ways of reasoning that emerge when learners think of and approach the tasks through the tools' affordances came from those projects. That is, tasks play an important role not only in fostering learners' construction of mathematical knowledge, but also in documenting students' ways of reasoning associated with the use of digital technology.

It is a truism that education necessitates the permanent and sustainable transformation of teachers. In Mexico, a country with a population of 112 million, there are 34.8 million students and about 1.8 million teachers. The student population between 15–18 years old represents 12.5% and this is the sector that will grow faster in coming years. There are 286,000 teachers for this sector and 328,000 university teachers. At the university level there are 3.2 million students, which represents 9.1% of the global student population. These updated figures come from the Ministry of Education (SEP) and offer a partial view of the social realities that constitute the environment where teachers work and will develop their professional lives. The tension between local traditions and global transformations, or national and international innovation, is permanent. We need, as educational researchers, to transform ideas that we think are important and spread them along the permanent professional development of teachers. They are our closest colleagues.

GUIDE AND BEING GUIDED BY AN ARTIFACT

Imagine the early encounter of a student with a violin. After the first sessions, the student comes home with pain in her shoulders, neck, and hands. Perhaps the violin is out of tune, but in certain ways the violin is presenting some resistance to the student's efforts to conquer it. These initial obstacles and shortcomings are some of the constraints the artifact imposes on a would-be-violinist. One could say that the student's learning is *being guided* by the structure of the violin. Imagine, now, the same student some 15 years later, as a brilliant professional violinist, in the middle of a concert. No pain in her hands, neck, or shoulders. The music flows smoothly with her performance and now, the violin is *invisible*, meaning that the violinist overcame all those early shortcomings years ago: today, the musician *guides* the violin to express her music and her artistic sensibilities. It is as if the violinist was able to create a distortion of reality *mediated* by the violin (almost) an organic part of her skills. In our view, artifacts and activity influence each other, flow through each other, and even more: the music, the violin, and the artist are coextensive, coterminous. Thus, the subjects' activities are mediated by the use of the artifact, which also influences the subjects' actions.

The long bidirectional process through which the music student *internalizes* the violin, overcoming all its resistances, takes place within a cultural medium. It is within a culture that the musician finds the motives and the concomitant aesthetic values that fill her efforts with meaning.

This short narrative aims to describe the nature of the relationship between a person and an artifact that she/he wants to use for accomplishing a task. There is a deep level of complexity—technical, cultural, and cognitive—implicit in this narrative. We shall try to reveal a significant piece of this complexity in the following pages when we reflect on learning and teaching mathematics with the mediation of digital technologies.

Working with teachers in our graduate program has been an invaluable opportunity to learn how they deal with digital technologies like Geogebra, installed in computers, for instance. The teachers are motivated because they will use this technology when they return to their classrooms. There is a professional commitment as well as an increasing social pressure to gain fluency with these artifacts—we find cell phones in the subway as well as in the schools.

In the first decades of the present century there have been serious efforts to *problematize* the presence of CAS and Dynamic Geometry Software (DGS) in the classroom. Besides having been installed in material artifacts (calculators, computers, smartphones, and so on), CAS and DGS are semiotic artifacts because they *mediate* semiotic tasks when we are, for instance, trying to coordinate several symbolic registers of a mathematical object. We can illustrate this with the analysis of area variation of a family of rectangles with fixed perimeter through a discrete approach (a table), a graphic generated via loci of points, or in terms of an algebraic model.

Teachers need to understand the workings of these artifacts, and their syntactical rules, in order to use them meaningfully as *mediators* of mathematical knowledge. For this to happen, there must be a melody to be played, that is, teachers need a mathematical task. The task is an incentive for teachers to figure out how to integrate in meaningful ways the symbolic artifact to their own intellectual resources in order to solve that task. If a person succeeds in integrating the artifact to his/her cognitive resources to solve a task, then, Verillon and Rabardel (1995) explain that the artifact has become an *instrument*. For instance, when we compute the multiplication of two large numbers our cognitive activity is mediated by the positional system we use to represent numbers. We find it very natural to proceed as we usually do. The positional system in base 10 is more than a cultural artifact: it has become an instrument of our reason to deal with numbers. This is in sheer contrast to computing with numbers written in base, say, seven. In this case we have a cultural artifact that most people have not transformed into an instrument to think in numbers and solve problems.

Let us introduce another example: An architect begins using specific software to design his buildings. Taking profit from the plasticity of the visual images that the software provides, the architect can imagine a new plan, a new design. Gradually he will begin thinking of his design *with* and *through* the software. The architect will incorporate the software as part of his thinking and one day, the software will have *disappeared* as such. Now it is *coextensive* with the architect's thinking whilst solving design tasks. The software has become an instrument and the design activities are *instrumented* activities.

A SYMBOLIC MODE OF EXISTENCE

The drawing of a chair is a representation of the chair, but it is not the actual chair: we cannot sit down on the drawing. We are reminded of the famous René Magritte's painting *The Treachery of Images*: there is the image of a pipe and, below the image, the words: *ceci n'est pas une pipe* (this is not a pipe). Imagine Magritte had drawn a triangle instead of the pipe: this is not a triangle. Knowing that he could smoke with the real pipe *represented* on the canvas, we can ask: Can he bring to the fore a *real* triangle? Obviously, the answer is no. However, if we have a representation of the triangle, what is that "other thing" that is being represented on the canvas? Of course it is not a concrete, material thing, like Magritte's pipe.

We have to look for a different answer. Writing has the power to crystallize an idea and give it a tangible level of objectivity. This is what happens with mathematical notation systems, i.e., symbolic representations. But how does it happen in mathematics? For instance, we have the experience of periodicity (day-night-day again) and we create a periodic function—that is, a conceptual entity—to deal with the diversity of these phenomena. At its early stages, mathematical concepts are born from human perceptions or conceived from activities like building a round object. Later, the symbolic representation that captures our original perception or experience establishes links with other concepts and eventually becomes the initial steps for even further elaboration of mathematical concepts. This is similar to what we find in a dictionary: one looks for the meaning of a word and the dictionary provides a description with other words. Words do not live a full life if they are isolated; they need to live in networks. This happens to mathematical concepts as well. For instance, students can easily search for online sources to explore a concept's meaning and applications, and they can even ask and discuss their peers' views and comprehension of those concepts.

With teachers we have used this example: It is known that the number of atoms in the universe is of the order 10^{85}. Then, what is the meaning of the *number* 10^{400}? Apparently, there are numbers that have no referent but they still are numbers: they are the result, for instance, of arithmetic operations. This problem, simple as it appears to be, opens the door to interesting (epistemological) discussions with teachers. Reference is found not only in the material world, indeed, reference is found in the world of human actions that extend the material world.

So far, we have been trying to depict the conceptual path walked through with teachers. We have been reminded of the importance to invite the teachers to communal reflections and discussions about conceptual difficulties that may be lurking ahead when a student tries to appropriate a piece of mathematics at school.

Saying that a mathematical entity is a cultural object crystallized by symbolic means, from human activity, needs detailed unpacking, especially if one is thinking of education. René Thom, in his plenary lecture at ICME 2, 1972 said: "The real problem that confronts mathematics teaching is not that of rigor but the problem of the development of meaning, of the existence of mathematical objects" (Thom, 1972, p. 202)

One of us remembers a geometry class where students were asked to prove that in a triangle the length of each side is less than the sum of the lengths of the other two sides. A student came to the board with a cord to measure the sum of two sides and verify that the resulting piece of cord was longer than the third side. We had previously discussed that a straight line was *like* a tight cord. The discussion that students engaged (including a discussion about the triangle Earth-Sun-Moon) to prove the theorem, taught the teacher how difficult it was for students to understand that a mathematical object was a conceptual entity and that the only way to access it is through a symbolic representation (Duval, 2006). Even more, one representation is not enough to exhaust all the features of a mathematical entity. In that sense, the mathematical entity is always under construction. It is the lack of ostensive referrals to mathematical entities that generates this sense of elusiveness that students feel, quite often, whilst dealing with mathematical problems. However, it is a matter of levels of abstraction and generality that we have to deal with. Students need to feel they are dealing with something that has a palpable existence (Lakoff & Nuñez, 2000). Indeed, there is evidence that the process of learning a concept is facilitated when the student has the opportunity to work with a rich diversity of symbolic representations of that concept.

To approach these and other delicate matters, we turn to digital media.

VIGNETTES AND EXEMPLARS: GEOMETRY AND CALCULUS.

Like the two faces of Janus that look to the past and to the future, education looks to tradition and innovation. We cannot forget that today's curriculum has deep roots in the ways mathematics has been conceived traditionally with paper and pencil—and we cannot forget, either, the importance of the available digital armamentarium, resources that teachers can incorporate into their teaching practices. But even if digital technologies are not fully integrated within the school mathematical universe, they will gradually erode and transform the mathematical ways of thinking embedded in the traditional system. In Mexico, a government proposal to provide online resources to all elementary schools became important to discuss ways to transform textbooks into interactive materials where students explore mathematical ideas from diverse perspectives.

To consider this dilemma, the tension between tradition and innovation, we explore digital representations of mathematical entities. Doing so will reveal properties of these entities that lie hidden or opaque, to begin with. Our goal is to develop a *transitional way of thinking* more in agreement with the requirements of education today. For instance, simple mathematics objects such as the perpendicular bisector that appears in elementary education are reconceptualized when they are explored dynamically (see the task in the following section). Indeed, this concept becomes crucial for generating and exploring all conic sections studied at the high-school level (Moreno-Armella & Hegedus, 2009; Santos-Trigo & Ortega-Moreno, 2013). At this point, it is crucial that these reflections take place in a classroom with teachers. We cannot conceive of transforming education without the conscientious efforts of the teachers. This is strategic.

Let us begin now presenting some of the aforementioned vignettes and exemplars pertaining to *mathematical ways of thinking* for teachers.

A RECONCEPTUALIZATION OF THE PERPENDICULAR BISECTOR

Of course teachers, could describe this geometric object, but did they *understand* it? Had they used it in meaningful ways? These are questions we wanted to explore. For our work, we decided that *understanding* meant the moment when a cultural artifact (Trouche, 2004) (as the perpendicular bisector) became an instrument integrated with other cognitive instruments. Yet, this was rather restricted, so we searched for the moment the teachers in the classroom were *aware* of the instrument and they could use it to solve a task. This approach did cohere with the possibilities for active exploration within the digital environment. We offered the following task for exploration. Let us consider the segment *AB* and its perpendicular bisector (as shown in Figure 25.1).

At this point the idea was to use the perpendicular bisector as an *organizing principle* to explore conic sections. We suggested the construction of triangles with the third vertex *C* on the perpendicular bisector and then asked teachers to explore the locus of *D* (*D* is the intersection point of the perpendicular bisector of side *BC* and the bisector of angle *CAB*) as *C* travels

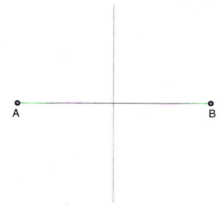

Figure 25.1 Perpendicular bisector.

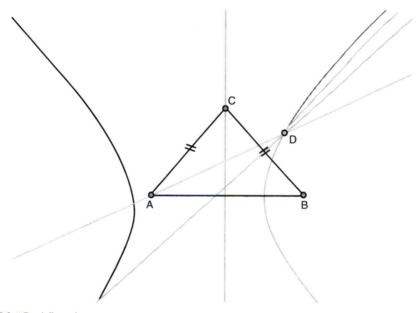

Figure 25.2 "Conic" section.

along the perpendicular bisector of *AB* (see Figure 25.2). Teachers got a locus that looked like a conic section. Now the problem began: Is it a conic section?

The figure does not do justice to what happened next. At that moment teachers were puzzled: The question was unexpected. They had worked with conic sections using the traditional analytic expressions. Now, where were the coordinate axes? After a while a teacher, Victor, realized they could try "to cover" the locus with a conic section passing through five points of the locus. The Geogebra dynamic system provides a command to draw a conic that passes through five points and teachers had used it extensively. Following this idea, teachers understood (after a mediating discussion) that the way to disprove the conjecture was *legitimate*, as they had used something *infrastructural*: the conic section passing through five points. They found the conic that disproved the result by dragging and rotating the vertices and the segments in the figure. This is crucial: they dragged, rotated the figure while *preserving the underlying structure*.

We thought it was more productive to begin with a problem that would find a solution by means of a counterexample. The lesson learned was that dragging is a mediator for exploring.

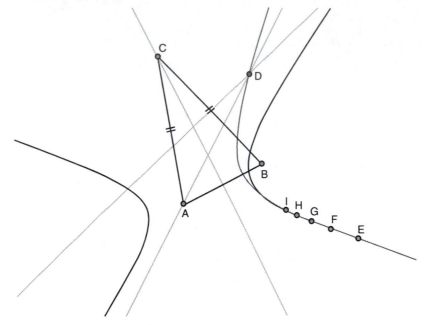

Figure 25.3 Another counterexample.

As a teacher, Laura, said, "If something is true you cannot *destroy it* by dragging it." The window to structure was opened. In the next session, Alvaro came with the construction shown in Figure 25.3.

His five points for the conic were *E, F, G, H,* and *I*. He began playing with the construction by moving Point I along the locus and observing the different conics.

The way to introduce the five-point construction as an infrastructural artifact in the digital medium was establishing the similarity with (i) two points determine one straight line; (iii) three points determine one circle. Then we discussed the fact that mathematics was embedded in the medium.

Discovering the Parabola

Teachers were very enthusiastic about the experience of solving a problem by means of a counterexample. The next time we decided to try a variant of the former exemplar. Instead of taking the bisector of angle *CAB*, we suggested that teachers work with the intersection point of the perpendicular bisector of *CB* and the perpendicular to line *b* at *C* as shown in Figure 25.4.

This time the locus is a parabola and the straight line b is the directrix; the focus is Point B. Teachers had already worked with the definition of the parabola as the locus of points equidistant from a line (the directrix) and a point (the focus). They identified *b* as the directrix and *B* as the focus—but what we did not expect was the fact that, to identify the locus as a parabola, they rotated the figure a right angle to the left, as shown in Figure 25.5.

They hid the segments and points that were not relevant for the original definition of the parabola as a locus. We were wondering why they had to rotate the graph as it was clear that the locus as shown in Figure 25.4 is a parabola. It was clear for us but *not* for them: The definition of parabola *always* comes with this graph (Figure 25.5), so an inertia is created due to the fact that the graphical representation of the conic reflect *our own body*, as when we draw on the slate. There is a sense of vertical and a sense of horizontal that are present when one tries to recognize a shape. It is clear that this event illustrates the *embodiment of knowledge* (Moreno-Armella & Hegedus, 2009).

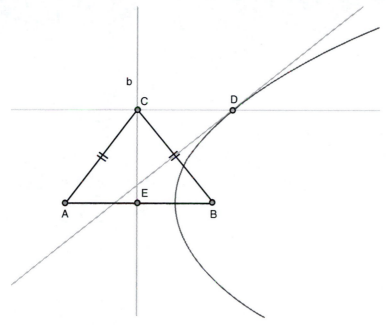

Figure 25.4 The locus of *D* as *C* travels on *b*.

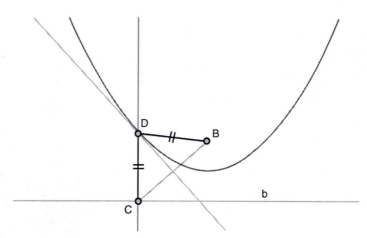

Figure 25.5 Identifying the locus.

Thus, simple mathematical entities such as triangles or circles can be represented digitally and become a platform or departure point to identify and explore more complex entities. This is the case with the following exemplar:

Looking for the Hidden Conics

Draw a circle with center *C*. On the circle we choose Point *E* and draw line *CE*. Then, we select Point *F* on line *CE* and draw the segment *FG*. We take the perpendicular bisector of *FG*. This perpendicular bisector intersects line *CE* at *H* (Figure 25.6).

We asked: What is the locus of Point *H* when Point *E* travels the circle? Figure 25.7 shows that the locus seems to be a hyperbola.

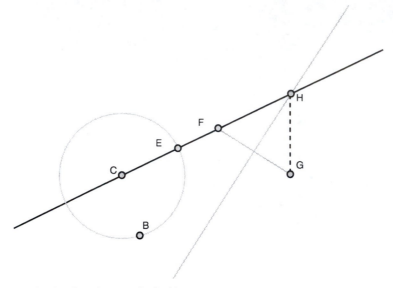

Figure 25.6 Dynamic triangle and perpendicular bisector.

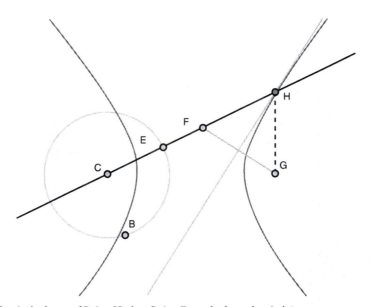

Figure 25.7 What is the locus of Point *H* when Point *E* travels along the circle?

Drawing the locus of H is an infrastructural affordance of the environment. In this context, it is a point-and-click action. Teachers were amazed with the environment's answer. Indeed, the locus *seemed* to be a hyperbola. But was it? At this time, the teachers were almost lost; they could not devise a plan of action. At our suggestion they measured the distances involved and found that the segment *HF* was congruent to segment *HG*. But—and this was Manuel's conclusion—that always happens because *H* is on the perpendicular bisector of *FG*! They drew the segment *HG* and things became clearer. It took another half an hour to write:

It is observed that (for every position of *H*):
$$d(C, H) - d(H, G) = d(C, F)$$
Because $d(H, F) = d(H, G)$. Consequently, the locus is a hyperbola.

We want to emphasize that the ability to drag points and observe the smooth morphing of the locus was instrumental for reaching the right conclusion. In this case the moving point was *F*. That made the teachers propose that *C* and *G* as the foci of the hyperbola. There is no doubt: *Motion is worth a thousand pictures.*

It was visible that by moving Point *G* (this time *F* was fixed) different loci were obtained. We observed that they were moving *G* far from the circle, so we decided to ask: What happens if *G* gets closer to the circle?

We kept quiet for a while as they discovered that *suddenly* the hyperbola morphed into a figure that seemed to be an ellipse.

Teachers found astounding this sudden morphing into an "ellipse" when Point *G* got closer to the circle. They had *proven* after a while playing with the resources provided by the environment that $d(C, H) - d(H, G)$ was a constant equal to $d(C, F)$. Now, the morphed figure seemed to be an ellipse

It was not the difference but the sum: $d(C, H) + d(H, G) = d(C, E)$, a constant for every position of *H* on the perpendicular bisector of segment *FG*.

That made clear for them that the locus was, indeed, an ellipse.

Eventually, teachers came to perceive that the position of *F* on line *CE* has "the key" (their words) to decide if the conic was a hyperbola or an ellipse.

We thought, at that point, that it was time to simplify the construction by identifying Points *E* and *F*. Then we asked the teachers to figure out how to draw a tangent to the ellipse from any Point *C* inside this circle (see Figure 25.9).

We will omit this discussion, which completed a basic *dynamic* analytic geometry course, as we want to share a couple of Calculus examples that we discussed with another group. However, we consider important to offer some reflections based on the previous teaching-teachers experience before the Calculus exemplars.

A Brief Reflection

The Point *F* (see Figures 25.8 and 25.9) is a *hot-point* (Moreno-Armella & Hegedus, 2009) because if we keep fixed all other points, in these constructions, Point *F* controls the underlying structure of conics we can display. What is really central is that the environment provides these points in every construction. Emphasizing this idea made teachers aware that what we have on the screen are not simply dynamic drawings but geometric *structures*. It was the movement that made the structure visible: the structure is hidden behind any particular rendition on the

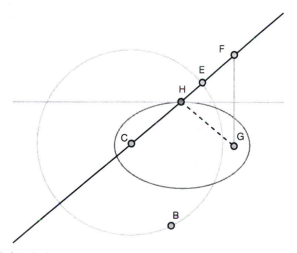

Figure 25.8 Ellipse with foci *C, G.*

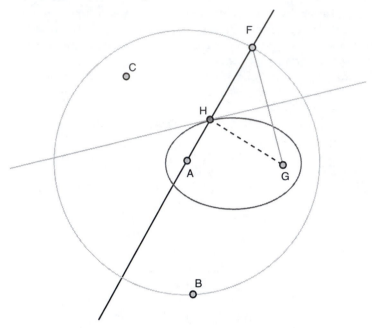

Figure 25.9 The new construction.

screen. One of the teachers, Laura, mentioned that the idea that the structure is visible through movement was similar to camouflaged objects: if a moth is standing still on a tree, then the bird (its predator) cannot see the moth, unless the moth moves. Of course, the similarity ends here as *seeing the structure* is a very complex cognitive process. What one sees, through the digital, executable representation is a conceptual entity (Moreno-Armella & Hegedus, 2009). At this point we pondered over the pertinence of going back to the discussion on the nature of mathematical entities. We found that working in a dynamic environment where learners could drag a figure, and modify the length of a segment, for instance, gave them an opportunity to explore the behavior of a family of objects within the same configuration.

In all the preceding examples, the basic geometric construction has been the perpendicular bisector. This construction is the *organizing principle* for exploring conic sections the way we chose to follow.

Action does not belong (exclusively) to the user and neither does it to the environment; both user and environment are actors and reactors. For instance, if we drag a triangle on the screen, it seems as if we are able to *hold* that figure with our hands and transform it. User and environment are, from the point of view of agency, *coextensive*. Thus, we speak of *coaction* between the user and the environment, not just between the user and the artifact. Coaction is the broader process within which an artifact is being internalized as a cognitive instrument. Yet, in the social space of the classroom there can be a collective actor. One participant can observe how another drives the technology at hand and then incorporate what she observed into her subsequent strategies. At the end participants can act and react to the environment in ways that are essentially different from their initial actions. We can learn *from*, *through*, and *with* the others. So the traditional triangle user-technology-task has to be enlarged: coaction becomes embedded in a social structure. Culture cannot be factorized from the technology appropriation processes, and technology cannot be factorized from culture.

TWO EXEMPLARS FROM CALCULUS

Digital media, with their *executable* representations (Moreno-Armella, Hegedus, & Kaput, 2008, p. 105), have transformed the traditional mathematics of change and accumulation.

There is a profound cognitive difference between applying a geometric transformation, *on paper*, to rotate or dilate a triangle (where all the action takes place in human imagination) and applying that transformation through its executable version and perceiving it on the screen. Thus, variation, change, and accumulation are no longer restricted to the written version of Calculus. However, paper-and-pencil tradition cannot be ignored and left aside. We have to allow its representational redescription in terms of digital representations. In fact, there are many mathematical entities that can be redescribed, translated into digital environments and explored there. In our work with teachers we always intend to take advantage of digital representations for going deeper into the mathematics that we discuss and explore with them. In the next pages we will introduce two exemplars from elementary Calculus that have been the matter of intensive discussions in the classroom.

Area Approximation

Pierre de Fermat (1601–1665) solved, in a very original way, the problem of computing the area under a parabola: $y = x^p$, $p \neq 1$. Fermat began by subdividing the interval $[0, 1]$ into an infinite sequence of subintervals with end-points of the form z^n, with $n = 1,2,3,. . .$ and Z a fixed number $0 < z < 1$. That is, Fermat used an infinite subdivision of the interval by means of a geometric progression as suggested by Figure 25.10.

It takes some work to find a closed expression for the sum of the areas of the rectangles, but Fermat did it. Afterwards, Fermat's reasoning was to eliminate the error, that is, to fill the white triangles over the rectangles. At this point, we decided to stop the narrative (indeed, avoid the computations) and ask the teachers, taking into account their already gained experience with digital environments, how they could *explain* Fermat's result. They had some experience working with sliders; the answer came after a collective and very emotional discussion in the classroom (Vizgin, 2001). Let us see the next figures.

Figure 25.11 on the left shows a fixed value of $Z < 1$, and six rectangles. The slider is used to control the number of rectangles. Figure 25.12 on the right shows six rectangles, but now the value of Z is closer to 1. One can observe that the process of approximation depends not

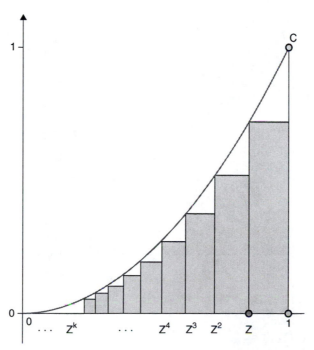

Figure 25.10 Infinite subdivision.

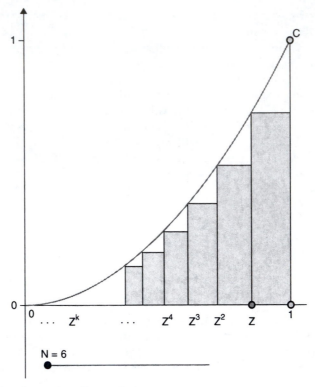

Figure 25.11 Increasing the number of rectangles.

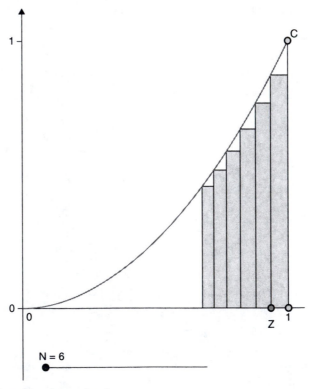

Figure 25.12 Obtaining a better approximation.

only on the number of rectangles (*in principle*, there is an infinite number of rectangles) but on how close to 1 is *Z*. If *Z* is closer to 1, then we need more rectangles.

We certainly believe that the teachers were able to understand the basic idea behind an approximation process, notwithstanding the contextual constraints. We have called these kinds of particular contexts *domains of abstraction*: There is something general "hidden" below the context in question (Moreno-Armella & Sriraman, 2010, pp. 224–225).

It became tangible for the teachers that the environment is full of "treasures" (they used this word), affordances, let us say, that enable the user to express her/his mathematical ideas. There is no neutral artifact, no neutral environment. Each artifact *drives* the actions of the user (individual or collective) and is *driven* by the user in a coextensive process that leaves no one unchanged. As a cognitive agent, the user eventually incorporates the artifact to his/her cognitive resources. That is what we do when add two numbers: we do not *see*, anymore, the decimal notation system that after years of schooling has become incorporated as a cognitive instrument.

Among the treasures the teachers became aware of, sliders and dragging were instrumental for their mathematical thinking: These became instruments to deal with and control continuous and discrete variation.

One of our goals was to help the teachers to develop conceptual and computational fluencies. That is, the tool's affordances are vehicles to represent and explore concept meaning and its uses in problem-solving activities. We believe this is possible if teachers have at their hands the mediation of dynamic, digital environments.

It is important to realize that blending mathematical ideas originally developed in static media with their digital redescriptions has the potential to open windows into a new mathematical culture in the classroom.

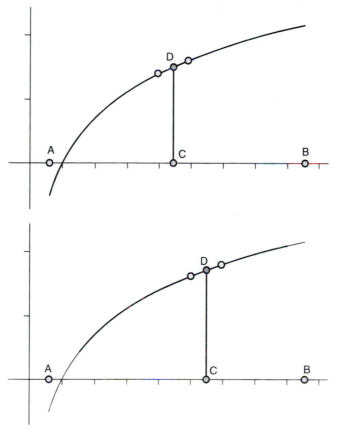

Figure 25.13 A tangent segment.

The Visual Derivative

One of the main obstacles to developing a sound vision of the derivative is *not* being able to conceive of it as a number. Once the derivative has been introduced as the slope of the *tangent line to the graph*, at one point, in most cases this tangent is used to locate maxima or minima of the function. This is done by following a mechanical procedure, almost a mantra: find the derivative; make it equal to zero . . . and so on. But the important step of finding the derivative *and trying to understand what it says about the function globally* is almost never taken. This is the inertial effect we talked about previously. It is part of school culture.

We decided to discuss this issue, taking as a starting point the graph of a function and the tangent line at a point of the graph. Then we took a small segment of the tangent line around the point of tangency as shown in Figure 25.13. The idea we wanted to introduce was that a short—a very short indeed—segment of the tangent line around a point of tangency could generate the graph of the function. Next we dragged the segment (activating the trace for the segment) and we produced the figure on the right in Figure 25.13.

Then a discussion began about the meaning of *close* when we say that the tangent line is the best approximation to the function around a point. After a while we proposed that the teachers discuss the following situation in which we hid the graph of the function but kept visible the tangent segment as in Figure 25.14.

Then, we dragged the segment (with the trace active) and showed that we could recover the curve, the whole curve. Some teachers were amazed, and then one of them essentially asked: "What does the tangent know?" Another replied: "It does not have to know anything, because

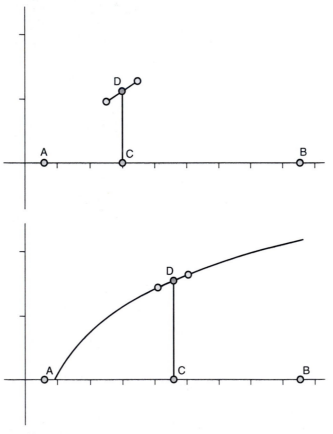

Figure 25.14 Recovering the graph.

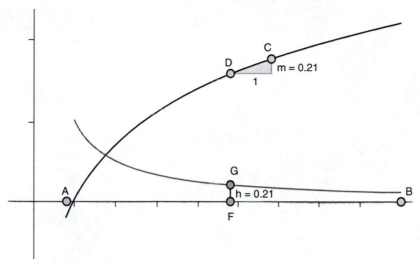

Figure 25.15 Graphing the derivative.

the curve is hidden but not erased." So, in a sense dragging the segment was a way to *uncover* the hidden curve. We thought this discussion was very valuable indeed; something deep was floating in the atmosphere of the classroom. We thought the time was right for making explicit a seed about the fundamental theorem of Calculus. We have simply to extend some ideas that were already under discussion with the teachers. If you have the function then you have the tangent lines—and reciprocally, if you have the tangent lines you can recover the function.

Figure 25.15 illustrates how we tried to animate this discussion.

This time, our emphasis was on establishing that each time you have the function, in fact you have two functions: the one you already have, and the derivative function that maps the behavior of the original function. In these tasks, we were trying to emphasize the conceptual fluency beyond the operational fluency that the teachers were more familiar with.

It has become clear from the vignettes and examples we have previously outlined, that our math intuitions rely in very specific ways on action and motion, and that the digital environment has provided our group of teachers a great service: it has helped them to transform metaphorical thinking on motion and action into sound cognitive instruments.

SIMULATION AND MODELING: ANOTHER EXEMPLAR

The use of digital technology also plays an important role in constructing dynamic models of tasks or situations that involve realistic contexts. For example, Figure 25.16 shows a truck that is approaching a certain underpass where there is a sign indicating the maximum clearance (the height of the bridge). The bridge is located just at the base of a descending roadway (Figure 25.16). What data and conditions do we need to know in order to figure it out whether the truck could clear the bridge? What is the effect of the inclination of the roadway on the height of the truck when passing under the bridge? (A similar task appears in NCTM, 2009 and Santos-Trigo and Barrera-Mora, 2011).

High-school teachers worked on this task. Initially they spent significant time making sense of the task statement and discussing questions regarding dimensions of the truck, wheel positions, height of the bridge, etc. At this stage the goal was to think of a two-dimensional representation of the problem in terms of mathematical objects (lines, rays, angles, rectangles, circles, etc.). Figure 25.17 is a simplified representation of the roadway, the bridge, and the inclination angle of the roadway.

Figure 25.16 The truck entering into an underpass.

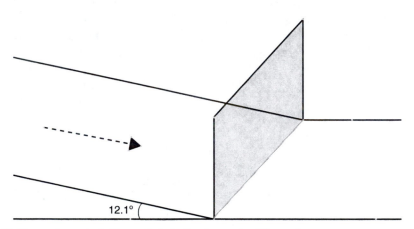

Figure 25.17 The roadway, the bridge, and the inclination angle of the roadway.

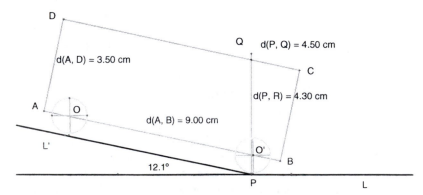

Figure 25.18 A task model constructed through the software.

During the process of constructing a dynamic model of the situation, teachers relied on a set of considerations and assumptions to represent information embedded in the task in terms of mathematical objects. For example, the roadway was represented through two intersecting lines, L and L', the wheels were represented with circles, the truck box with a rectangle, and the height of the bridge with a segment. In addition, when the positions of the wheels were all on the tilted position or on the horizontal position (after the back wheels have crossed the bridge), the sides AB and DC were parallel to line L' and, after the back wheels crossed the bridge, to line L (the roadway; see Figure 25.19). Likewise, it was assumed that the truck's tilting effect, which might produce a shifting load on the truck's wheels, does not distort the height of the truck.

In the model (Figure 25.19), Point M was a mobile or pivot point, Point Q was chosen at a fixed distance equal to 4.5 cm from P (height of the bridge). It is observed that by moving point M along line L, the height of the truck, measured as the distance from Point P (bridge initial point) to Point R, the intersection point of the perpendicular to line L through Point P and the upper side of the rectangle (segment DC) (Figure 25.19) changes depending on the position of Point M. The trace left by Point R when Point M is moved along line L represents the graph of the trunk height variation as a function of the position of Point M. Under these

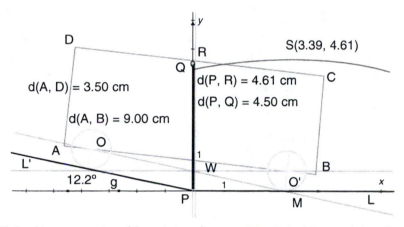

Figure 25.19 Graphic representation of the variation of segment *PR* as Point *M* is moved along line L.

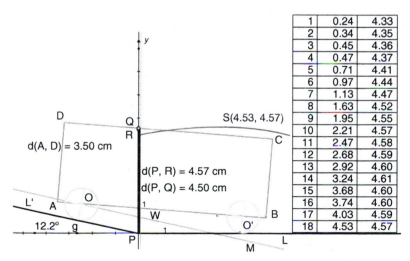

1	0.24	4.33
2	0.34	4.35
3	0.45	4.36
4	0.47	4.37
5	0.71	4.41
6	0.97	4.44
7	1.13	4.47
8	1.63	4.52
9	1.95	4.55
10	2.21	4.57
11	2.47	4.58
12	2.68	4.59
13	2.92	4.60
14	3.24	4.61
15	3.68	4.60
16	3.74	4.60
17	4.03	4.59
18	4.53	4.57

Figure 25.20 Three representations of the problem: the position of the truck, a table showing the variation of the height, and its graphic representation.

conditions, the teachers visualized that there was a position for Point M where the height of the truck reaches a maximum value (Figure 25.19). Thus, a truck with a height of 4.5 meters could not clear the bridge, since at one position of M its height is larger than the clearance under the bridge. In other words, the height of the bridge must be larger than 4.61 meters in order for the truck to clear.

Teachers discussed the fact that the use of the tool does not require expressing symbolically the relation between the position of the truck and its height. It was sufficient to relate the position of the truck's front (Point M) with the corresponding height (Point S) and later the locus of S when Point M is moved along line L (the roadway) generated the graph of the variation of the height. By moving the Point M along the line L, a table including values for different positions of the point and the associated height of the truck can be produced (Figure 25.20).

FINAL THOUGHTS

In 1996, world chess champion Garry Kasparov played a match against Deep Blue, an IBM supercomputer. Kasparov wrote in *TIME* magazine that he could feel, even *smell* a new kind of intelligence across the table.

After almost 17 years, Kasparov's story seems up-to-date; this new intelligence shapes our actions and behaviors. The zeal that let our community to face the challenge of thinking about thinking has been moving indeed. Today, this issue has come to the fore because the presence of digital technologies has made clear that we cannot restrict intelligence to "its confining biological membrane" (Donald, 1991, p. 359).

The *externalization of memory* that inaugurated this momentous stage developed into symbolic technologies. But even if one could feel an intelligence sitting on the page of a novel, that was human intelligence indeed.

Kasparov's feelings had a different source. Societies are already (or will be sooner than later), saturated with the presence of visible and invisible computers. Not all of them play chess but some are able to control the flight of a huge airplane across the Pacific. Others can give us the location of the restaurant we are looking for, or compute a complex mathematical model that we human beings cannot compute with static symbolic technology alone.

If the power of digital technologies is broadly tangible, there is no reason to expect they will not have as well a profound impact at the level of formal education. Educators have to cross that Rubicon and understand that the executable, symbolic, representations are key to making even more tangible the zone of potential development of social, distributed intelligence. Indeed, intelligence is a network phenomenon and we have to conceive of it globally, seamlessly, in a move that includes all kinds of intelligences, such as that Kasparov caught a glimpse of across the table.

What about schools? We might say that old habits die hard—but it is not just a matter of habits, it is more a matter of transformation of cultures. The new classroom with the possibility of sharing an expressive medium, like the digital environment, can help us organize open mathematical discussions and foster a continuous reflection within a social space in permanent evolution. In this space, the meaning of mathematical entities evolves with the opportunities to directly manipulate them.

Mathematical entities, as explained previously, are only indirectly accessible through semiotic representations (Duval, 2006). Consequently, the only way of gaining access to them is using, for instance, words, symbols, expressions, or drawings. But no representation exhausts the represented entity. Nevertheless, any mathematical representation has such a crystallizing impact on how mathematical entities are experienced that when we work with it, we have the feeling of working inside a Platonic mathematical reality. But this is only an illusion that lurks beneath the surface. Mathematical reality is a human reality even if it is a virtual one: one cannot forget that humans have the power to extend their world of experience symbolically.

Closer to our professional interests is the *mode of existence* that teachers have experienced whilst working with the dynamic geometry environment and when they analyzed and discussed a design activity whose goal was to construct a dynamic model involving a truck approaching an underpass. In all these activities, it is made tangible that we can explore and experiment on dynamic representations of mathematical entities as if they were material objects (Santos-Trigo & Reyes-Rodríguez, 2011). In fact, the executable nature of dynamic representations enables the learner to continuously modify those representations while preserving their structural features. This reflects a profound difference from the static representations of traditional mathematics at school. The kind of intelligence living in the executable representations extends human action with digital artifacts into the social space of the classroom. The end result of this process is an instrument loaded with the intelligence shared in the classroom. In practice, it took long weeks for the teachers to master and embody new ways of interacting with the virtual reality of digital entities. No artifact is epistemologically neutral; consequently, there is a disruption in the taken-for-granted aspects of what it means to think mathematically in digital contexts. In this view, an instrument—that is, the internalized artifact—is a template for action. It is relevant here to mention that, with the instrument, the learner can explore new landscapes of mathematical validation. In fact, the notion of *theorem in motion* embodied in the dynamic digital environment comes to the fore; this is how we conceive of it. Then, reconsidering the transformation of static entities through executable representations, we are opening a window to new mathematical entities whose proper ecology is the digital. But it is not the search of the object per se what moves us as researchers, but the search for new ways of thinking.

We expect that the mathematics of change and variations, through their digital embodiments, will contribute to a substantial gain in students' development of conceptual understanding and computational fluency.

ACKNOWLEDGMENTS

The preparation of this chapter was partially funded from two research projects: Conacyt-Mexico, Reference 168543 and Plan Nacional I+D+I del MCIN, Reference EDU2011-29328.

REFERENCES

Artigue, M. (2002). Learning mathematics in a case environment: The genesis of a reflection about instrumentation and the dialectics between technical and conceptual work. *International Journal of Computers for Mathematical Learning, 7*, 245–274, 2002.

Bottino, R. M., Artigue, M., & Noss, R. (2009). Building European collaboration in technology-enhanced learning in mathematics. In N. Balacheff, S. Ludvigsen, T. de Jong, A. Lazonder, & S. Barnes (Eds.), *Technology-enhanced learning: principles and products.* (pp. 73–87). Dordrecht: Springer Netherlands.

Chevallard, Y. (1985). *La transposition didactique—Du savoir savant au savoir enseigne.* Grenoble : La Pensee sauvage.

Dick, T. P. & Hollebrands, K. F. (2011). *Focus in high school mathematics: Technology to support reasoning and sense making.* Reston, VA: National Council of Teachers of Mathematics.

Donald, M. (1991). *Origins of the modern mind: Three stages in the evolution of culture and cognition.* Cambridge, MA: Harvard University Press.

Donald, M. (2001). *A mind so rare.* New York: Norton.

Duval, R. (2006). A cognitive analysis of problem of comprehension in a learning of mathematics. *Educational Studies in Mathematics, 61*, 103–131.

Friedman, T. L. (2007). *The world is flat. A brief history of the twenty-first century* (updated and expanded edition.) New York: Picador/Farrar, Straus and Giroux.

Kaput, J., & Schorr, R. (2008). Changing representational infrastructures changes most everything. The case of SimCalc, Algebra, and Calculus. In G. W. Blume & M. K. Heid (Eds.), *Research on technology and the teaching and learning of mathematics: Vol. 2. Cases and perspectives* (pp. 211–253). Charlotte, NC: Information Age Publishing.

Lakoff, G., & Nuñez, R. E. (2000). *Where mathematics comes form. How the embodied mind brings mathematics into being*. New York: Basic Books.

Moreno-Armella, L., & Hegedus, S. (2009). *Co-action with digital technologies. ZDM: The International Journal of Math Education, 41*, 505–519.

Moreno-Armella, L., Hegedus, S., & Kaput, J. (2008). From static to dynamic mathematics: Historical and representational perspectives. *Educational Studies in Mathematics, 68*(2), 99–112.

Moreno-Armella, L., & Santos-Trigo, M. (2008). Democratic access and use of powerful mathematics in an emerging country. In L. English (Ed.), *Handbook of International Research in Mathematics Education* (2nd ed., pp. 319–351). Routledge, Taylor & Francis.

Moreno-Armella, L., & Sriraman, B. (2010). Symbols and mediation in mathematics education. In B. Sriraman & L. English (Eds.), *Theories of Mathematics Education* (pp. 224–225). Heidelberg: Springer-Verlag.

National Council of Teachers of Mathematics (NCTM). (2009). *Focus in high school mathematics reasoning and sense making*. Reston, VA: Author.

Pea, R. D. (1985). Beyond amplification: Using the computer to reorganize mental functioning. *Educational Psychologist, 20*(4), 167–182.

Prensky, M. (2010). *Teaching digital natives*. Thousand Oaks, CA: Corwin/Sage.

Santos-Trigo, M., & Barrera-Mora, F. (2011). High school teachers' problem solving activities to review and extend their mathematical and didactical knowledge, *PRIMUS, 21*(8), 699–718.

Santos-Trigo, M., & Camacho-Machin, M. (2009). Towards the construction of a framework to deal with routine problems to foster mathematical inquiry. *PRIMUS, 19*(3), 260–279.

Santos-Trigo, M., & Ortega-Moreno, F. (2013). Digit technology, dynamic representations, and mathematical reasoning: extending problem solving frameworks. *International Journal of Learning Technology*, 8:2, pp.186–200.

Santos-Trigo, M., & Reyes-Rodríguez, A. (2011). Teachers' use of computational tools to construct and explore dynamic mathematical models, *International Journal of Mathematical Education in Science and Technology, 42*(3), 313–336.

Schmidt, E. & Cohen, J. (2013). *The new digital area. Reshaping the future of people, nations and business* (eBook edition). New York: Random House and Google.

Thom, R. (1972). Modern mathematics: Does it exist? In A. G. Howson (Ed.), *Developments in mathematics education*. Cambridge: Cambridge University Press.

Trouche, L. (2004). Managing the complexity of human/machine interactions in computerized learning environments: Guiding students' command process through instrumental orchestrations. *International Journal of Computers for Mathematical Learning, 9*, 281–307.

Verillon, P., & Rabardel, P. (1995). Cognition and artifacts: A contribution to the study of thought in relation to instrumented activity. *European Journal of Psychology of Education, 10*(1), 77–101.

Vizgin, V. (2001). On the emotional assumptions without which one could not effectively investigate the laws of nature. *The American Mathematical Monthly, 108*(3): 264–270.

26 Computerized Environments in Mathematics Classrooms
A Research-Design View

Rina Hershkowitz

The Weizmann Institute for Science

Michal Tabach

Tel-Aviv University

Tommy Dreyfus

Tel-Aviv University

INTRODUCTION

Curriculum development is the process of developing a coherent sequence of learning situations, together with appropriate materials, whose implementation has the potential to bring about intended change in learners' knowledge.

The situation is especially complex when the activity of curriculum development is aimed at learning mathematics in an environment in which the benefit from the potential of computerized tools has a central role. In their comprehensive chapter, "Computer-based learning environments in mathematics," Balacheff and Kaput (1996) explained why they think that technology's power is primarily epistemological, and added: "While technology's impact on daily practice has yet to match expectations from two or three decades ago, its epistemological impact is deeper than expected" (p. 469).

Any curriculum development project is embedded in its own socio-cultural context, but there are also many common features between different projects. The CompuMath project was a large-scale mathematics curriculum development, implementation, and research project for a computerized learning environment at the junior high-school level. This project will be used here as a window through which curriculum development is seen as a comprehensive, and theoretically and practically consistent activity. We will focus on research processes that were a central component of the project.

While constrained by the mandatory national syllabus in Israel, the main goal of the project was to design and create a learning environment in which junior high-school students are engaged in meaningful mathematics through the systematic use of computerized tools. By *meaningful mathematics* we mean that students' main concerns are mathematical processes rather than ready-made algorithms. Problem-situations used systematically may provide a natural environment for students' activities of investigating and solving problems, thus avoiding an environment consisting of ritual procedures imposed by the teacher or the textbook. In particular, inductive explorations were conceived as generalizing numerical, geometrical, and structural patterns, making predictions and hypotheses, and explaining, justifying, and proving these hypotheses. Such processes have the potential to be amplified (Lagrange, Artigue,

Laborde, & Trouche, 2003; Pea, 1985) in a technological environment, which can be used as an "inquiry laboratory."

The *CompuMath* project is an example of a curriculum development project in which not only theoretical frameworks and relevant cultural artifacts (such as computerized tools) were taken into account but also lessons learnt from research and from development in previous projects and previous phases of the same project. At the beginning of the project the team leaders did have experience with curriculum development, encouraging investigations and argumentations by students as individuals, groups, and whole class communities—a working inquiry classroom (Artigue and Blomhøj, 2013)—in line with a socio-cultural view about mathematics and its learning. We[1] did not know, however, how this experience would play out in a technology-rich environment. We could only hypothesize the potential of computer tools. That is, we lacked experience with the systematic integration of technological tools and with consistent use of their potential. As designers, we had not yet acquired the needed instrumentation knowledge. Hence, based on our own use and familiarity with computerized tools, we chose to integrate the use of open, general-purpose, technological tools (graphical tools, spreadsheets, dynamic geometry software, and Computer Algebra Systems), and to benefit from their potential in learning mathematics. A discussion about criteria for choosing computerized tools may be found in Hershkowitz et al. (2002).

The development team had to deal with many facets of theory, research, and practice of development and implementation: practices were fed by theory and research, and vice versa. The team functioned as a cell eager to live and develop, whose life was in large part determined by its interaction with an unknown outside world. Through this interaction, the curriculum development activity constantly redefined its own components.

Like many other researchers (e.g., Perret-Clermont, 1993; Yackel & Cobb, 1996), we felt the shortcomings of cognitive theories, methodologies, and tools for describing and interpreting learning and teaching processes in the classroom. We thus adopted activity theory (Engeström, 1987; Kuutti, 1996) as a theoretical frame. The construction of knowledge was analyzed while students were investigating problem-situations in different contexts. Research became a crucial component in the curriculum development activity, in design-research-redesign cycles.

The curriculum development project was a comprehensive process with three stages:

i. The *predesign* stage involving considerations before starting the actual development and research work;
ii. The *initial design-research-redesign* stage consisting of a first design of isolated activities and their implementation in a few classrooms, accompanied by classroom research on learning and teaching practices (observations, data collection, and analysis);
iii. The *expansion* stage comprising the creation of coherent sequences of redesigned activities forming a complete curriculum and its implementation, including the dissemination of the curricular aims and "spirit" on a large scale.

Details on these stages may be found in the first two versions of this chapter, which appeared in earlier editions of the *Handbook*. The current chapter is a follow-up. The chapter by Hershkowitz et al. (2002) in the first edition of this *Handbook* describes and analyzes the stages of the *CompuMath* project, as a paradigm for research-intensive development and implementation of holistic and long-term curricula to be enacted in computerized learning environments. In that chapter, the characteristics of the project are described with particular reference to the use of computerized tools and to design-research-redesign cycles. Narratives representative of the process of curriculum development in functions, geometry, algebra, and statistics are presented. The narratives focus on major issues in curriculum development, on different ways of using open computerized tools, and on different ways in which research interacts with design.

In the version of the chapter that appeared in the second edition of this *Handbook* (Tabach, Hershkowitz, Arcavi, & Dreyfus, 2008), we describe a component of the project that evolved from the teaching and learning of beginning algebra within the *CompuMath* curriculum and uses the paradigm of a computer-intensive environment in which computer tools are available to the students at all times. We discuss its novel characteristics, the design processes, the teaching and learning trials, the accompanying research, and its interaction with the design.

The aim of the present chapter is to highlight the research component of the *CompuMath* project and to discuss its long-term effect, as it continues to influence our and others' work. Three consecutive research strands will be described. The first section concerns the role of research in the development of isolated activities; the second section concerns the research accompanying the development of specific approaches to entire subjects such as geometry or algebra or to certain topics within these subjects; and the third investigates how knowledge is constructed in technological learning environments and how this knowledge develops and shifts in the classroom.

RESEARCH CONCERNING THE DEVELOPMENT OF ISOLATED ACTIVITIES

At the beginning of the project, we needed to acquire experience in how to design activities that would integrate the benefit of open technological tools in an inquiry classroom. Therefore, the first realization in each topic consisted of the design of mathematical activities and the investigation of their impact in trial classrooms. In order to continuously base further design on insights already gained, the activities in each topic were isolated rather than in sequence. These activities were scattered at "key points" along the curriculum. The development was characterized by the dilemmas concerning the translation of the contents prescribed by the mandatory syllabus into trial activities that conform to the project team's emerging standards concerning meaning, investigations, and argumentation, and to their enactment in the classroom. These activities later became the skeleton around which the yearlong course was built in the next development and research cycle.

Hence, the implementation and research concerning the isolated activities had several goals: to learn about the feasibility of such activities in the classroom; to evaluate an effective activity structure; to learn about the orchestration processes of the teacher in such an environment; to study learning processes that emerged during such activities; and to learn about instrumentation processes that took place.

We designed activities comprising several phases based on our previous design experience on one hand, and on our goal to maximize the potential of the technological tool for mathematics learning on the other hand. We also took into account relevant research and design papers (e.g., Kaput, 1992; Balacheff & Kaput, 1996; Pea, 1985).

Isolated activities were structured so as to allow for interaction among students in small groups, as well as interaction between the teacher and students, and between individuals or groups and computerized tools. Our pedagogical standards includes the following:

- Students' work is (often) organized around problem-situations.
- Most of the investigative work with the problem-situation is done in small collaborative groups; computerized tools are available, and students decide when and how to use them.
- Students write group or individual reports, in which they are encouraged to reconstruct, compare, and critique the steps they and others went through.
- The teacher plays several roles, being alternatively a facilitator for individuals and small groups, a modeler, and a coordinator of debates around verbal reports and critiques (syntheses). Such syntheses provide opportunities for students to report, evaluate, and critique their collaborative or individual work in a public forum.

In this section we illustrate the interplay of research and development during the design of an isolated activity by means of a paradigmatic example from the subject of functions. In this isolated inquiry activity students were given a problem-situation in which they were invited to raise hypotheses and then use multirepresentational software to check their hypotheses by using algebraic formulas, drawing graphs, constructing a table of values, and passing from one presentation to another as they investigate the problem-situation. Students were encouraged to decide which representations to use, when and how to link them, and in which medium to work.

The Research on the Overseas Activity

Our paradigmatic example of this research strand is the research accompanying the Overseas activity (Hershkowitz & Schwarz, 1999), which belongs to the functions course for the ninth grade. This activity was purposefully designed to investigate the phases in the structure of an activity, students' ability in making hypotheses, students' awareness of the quality of hypothesizing processes, the nature of different reflective processes in different phases of the activity, and the orchestrating role of the teacher during the activity. Concurrently, the role of the computerized tool in the hypothesizing and problem-solving phases was studied.

The structure of the Overseas activity consists of the following four phases:

Phase 0—Students were given the following homework assignment (Figure 26.1).

Phase 1—Equipped with their eight paper models (their homework from Phase 0) and with graphing calculators, students worked in groups of four on the following worksheet (Figure 26.2).

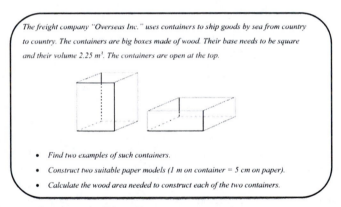

The freight company "Overseas Inc." uses containers to ship goods by sea from country to country. The containers are big boxes made of wood. Their base needs to be square and their volume 2.25 m³. The containers are open at the top.

- *Find two examples of such containers.*
- *Construct two suitable paper models (1 m on container = 5 cm on paper).*
- *Calculate the wood area needed to construct each of the two containers.*

Figure 26.1 The homework assignment (Phase 0).

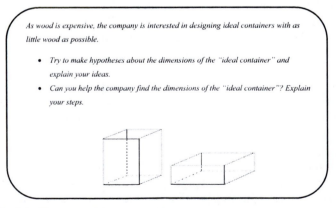

As wood is expensive, the company is interested in designing ideal containers with as little wood as possible.

- *Try to make hypotheses about the dimensions of the "ideal container" and explain your ideas.*
- *Can you help the company find the dimensions of the "ideal container"? Explain your steps.*

Figure 26.2 Phase 1 of the Overseas activity.

Phase 2—Each group was asked to write a common report concerning their ideas and steps of the problem-solving process.

Phase 3—The activity ended with a teacher-led collective reflection.

The various phases of the activity were documented and analyzed in a few ways: For Phase 0, we had the paper models that students brought from home. Phases 1, 2, and 3 were documented by two video cameras; one focused on a focus group or the students' community as a whole and the second focused on the teacher. Three observers who took field notes were present throughout the activity. In addition the group reports from Phase 2 were collected and analyzed.

In the following we discuss each of the main phases in detail.

Phase 1

The declared aim of the developers in this phase was to foster hypothesizing and to challenge the students to find the dimensions of the ideal container. Hypothesizing became a central concern for some groups, whereas other groups moved on quickly to "solve" the problem with the aid of their graphing calculators. The four students in the observed group (Miri, Liat, Osnat, and Hanna) were actively engaged in generating and confronting hypotheses. By doing so for about 40 minutes, they tried to reach a consensus regarding a suitable hypothesis. Only after that did they allow themselves to use an algebraic formula in order to draw the graph with the graphing calculator. They then read off the minimum by "walking" on the graph in no time. To them, the solution process with the graphical calculator was only a way to check the quality of their hypotheses. They began by computing the surfaces of the models they brought from home with the help of their graphical calculators. Then, they relied on the size and shape of the models to start hypothesizing: Osnat raised the first hypothesis (H1) and justified it by intuitive considerations based on two of the models: *Because the height of the container is multiplied by four, the minimum surface is when the height is as small as possible*. From this point on, the four students generated hypotheses that matched the measurements of more than two of their models. Hanna hypothesized H2: *The smaller the height, the bigger the surface*, which she supported using two other model surfaces. While H2 matched two models, it contradicted others and the girls found themselves in a situation of conflict. After some computations of the dimensions of more container models, they moved to a new local hypothesis, H3. In an argumentative process in which all four students participated, the two local hypotheses (H2 and H3) were confronted, numerical computations were used as evidence, and models were compared through manipulations. Hanna declared that H2 and H3 contradict each other and proposed the construction of a table. Liat bridged H2 and H3 by proposing H4: *There must be a segment between 1/2 and 1, maybe it gets smaller there, as if it's not constant, it has to be like that* [gesturing a parabola shape in the air]. Hanna completed the formulation of H4: *Perhaps it's a parabola or something like that*. The dialectic process continued, while the girls constructed an orderly table of values. After raising some more local hypotheses, they confronted H4 with data in the table and interpreted the behavior of the function. This was agreed upon by all four students.

We see in this example that hypothesizing is embedded in argumentative moves. The argumentative process we just described was dialectic in the sense that it consisted of raising hypotheses and refuting them or bridging between them. The hypotheses were formulated on the basis of arguments whose nature varied along the chain of actions: from intuitive arguments, based on visual considerations of the models, via arguments based on data, arguments based on conflicts with data, and arguments based on conflicts between hypotheses, to an argument based on logical considerations, which integrates local hypotheses while encompassing a broad range of data. The final hypothesis was agreed upon by the students only when all of them felt convinced. Then they wrote a correct formula, and used their graphical calculators to obtain the graph and find a numerical answer rather quickly. While the students' motive in Phase 0 was to inquire about relations among dimensions of the open containers, in Phase 1 their common motive was to find the best hypothesis. Solving for the actual dimension of the ideal container served to confirm their choice rather than being an important end in itself.

Phase 2

The group's report generally describes their actions in Phase 1. The requirement to report caused the students to distance themselves in time and perspective from their previous actions and to reflect on their problem-solving process. In this reflective action, they constructed a *purification process* of the actual problem-solving process. Unimportant details were deleted, and parts without progress were skipped (Hershkowitz & Schwarz, 1999, p. 84).

Phase 3

In Phase 3, the teacher initiates a whole-class discussion in which the groups' work is reported, evaluated, and agreed on or refuted with the aim of achieving a synthesis. Hence, a sequence of communicative acts was performed publically and enabled learning from the groups' actions in Phases 1 and 2. The teacher first encouraged a group to report on their hypotheses. This triggered other groups to respond and to extend the discussion, including what makes a good hypothesis. She then asked for students' collective and individual moves performed to check their hypotheses and solve the problem. One of the foci of the discussion relates to the teacher's question: When and how did the students make use of their graphing calculators during Phase 1?

Insights Concerning Isolated Activities

Like the observations on the Overseas activity reported here, members of the *CompuMath* team observed, documented, and analyzed each of the isolated activities that were developed. Similar design-research-redesign cycles were carried out also for activities in other topics in the *CompuMath* project, including geometry (Hadas, Hershkowitz, & Schwarz, 2000), statistics (Ben-Zvi & Arcavi, 2001), and beginning algebra (Tabach, Arcavi, & Hershkowitz, 2008; Tabach, Hershkowitz, & Arcavi, 2008).

The analysis of the observations, and the conclusions the team was able to draw, served as the basis for the design of further activities, as well as for improving the observed activities themselves. In this way, the team accumulated experience concerning the development of learning opportunities through the power of computerized tools, and through inquiry during problem-solving processes. At the same time, changes in classroom practices were noted. These investigations enabled us to outline some conclusions regarding the design and realization of an isolated activity in a computer learning environment.

1. The power of technological tools to deal with a large variety of mathematical data makes rich problem-situations possible; for example, in the Overseas activity students found a local minimum of a function, which is a composition of a rational and quadratic function—a type of task not accessible to ninth graders without a graphical tool (Yerushalmy & Chazan, 2002).
2. Asking students to make hypotheses about possible solutions *before* solving the problem is a valuable didactic technique. Students were able to delay the actual solution and accept hypothesizing as a valuable activity.
3. Students have and use the opportunity to move among representations in order to progress. Students' behavior suggests that in a rich problem-situation within computerized learning environment, inquiry is a natural process.
4. Letting students carry out and report on the inquiry in groups is beneficial, because social interaction in the group can support mathematical argumentation: students complete, oppose and criticize others' proposals, progressing towards consensus among the group.

5. Reflection can be initiated, for example by requiring students to write a group report on their inquiry process, as was done in the Overseas activity, and other isolated activities along the school year (Friedlander & Tabach, 2001).

6. A teacher-led synthesis in a session with the entire class is useful for many reasons. Students can be given an opportunity to report on their work and to practice participation in classroom debates, in which they can criticize and be criticized. The teacher can use their reports to raise criticism and evaluation, as well as for a synthesis of the main processes students went through. The session thus affords another opportunity for reflection. Last, but not least, such a synthesis allows the teacher to define the common knowledge, which she expects the students to have gained as well as socio-mathematical norms she wishes to convey, such as making hypotheses before finding a numerical answer (Tabach, Hershkowitz, & Dreyfus, 2013). In the Overseas activity, for example, she made it clear that the goal is not to present results but to reflect on the process they had gone through, in particular how they had hypothesized possible solutions.

Classroom research thus gave us a large amount of input in an area in which we had little experience from prior cycles of curriculum development: we learned that in computerized learning environments, rich problem-situations (including engaging in functions other than linear and quadratic ones) and extended multiple-phase activities and inquiry are possible, and we learned how to design such activities. We also learned about the teacher's role in inviting students to act differently in each of the phases, so as to have different opportunities for reflection. These model activities later served as models during further curriculum development (see Heid, Sheets, & Matras, 1990, for parallel experiences).

NEW DILEMMAS IN TEACHING "OLD" MATHEMATICAL TOPICS

Design and development of curriculum raise the need to choose a specific approach to each mathematical topic at hand and to generate a coherent sequence of activities to implement this approach. In this section, we exemplify how different studies have supported the decision on and development of such approaches that take into account the potential of computerized learning environments. As paradigmatic examples for this strand of research we briefly describe three studies.

The Linear Equations Example

As a team, we oscillated between two approaches for teaching linear equations: a functional approach and a more static algebraic approach. On one hand, in the technological reality in which students are able to present graphs of many functions and check their intersection points by "walking" on the graph, the notion of "equation" can be invested with additional meaning. In such a learning environment one could choose to describe an equation as the intersection point of two changing phenomena ($f(x) = g(x)$), or as equating a changing phenomenon to a given value ($f(x) = c$). On the other hand, equations in the classical approach were considered as representing a static situation, were a missing (unknown) value needs to be found. Both approaches are important for future mathematics learning of the students.

While the classical approach includes useful algorithms for solving different types of equations in symbolic notation, a functional approach to solving equations provides other advantages. For example, Yerushalmy (2009) claims that:

> Technology, such as graphing calculators or function graphing software, provides students with opportunities to investigate algebraic ideas by linking the symbolic representation of functions and symbolic manipulations with their numeric and graphic representations. Central to such a function-based approach to algebra is the earlier introduction of a particular way of viewing equations—a definition of an equation as a type of comparison of

two functions—and the use of this definition as a primary resource in constructing student understanding of school algebra.

(pp. 56–57)

This raises the question whether the approaches can be combined. In the *CompuMath* project we interweaved the two approaches to solving linear equations and investigated the cognitive effect of our integrated approach. Here we present one research study about this issue: The development of the perceptions of an eighth-grade class of students concerning equations (Stein, 2002). Two focus students, Gila and Noam, were followed along the school year in five activities and three tests. The work of the two students in the activities was recorded, transcribed, and analyzed. Data regarding the three tests were collected from the entire class, to allow the researchers to situate the work of the two students in the class as a whole. The course was designed to start from a functional approach, a natural continuation to the beginning algebra course from seventh grade, for about two months. Next, the algorithm for solving linear equations was studied. Finally, the two approaches were interwoven.

Gila encountered the notion of equation first in its functional context, as comparison between changing phenomena, corresponding with the design and teaching of the topic in class. As the course advanced, Gila was able to work with equations with the functional approach, even without an extra-mathematical situation. Her ability to act with this approach allowed her to also handle nonlinear comparisons in direct analogy to the linear ones. However, while learning to simplify and solve equations according to the conventional approach by adding equivalent expressions to each side, it was notable that Gila found it difficult to connect the symbolic equation and its solution to a graphical representation. From her work at this point in time it was clear that she did not see in the symbolic equation a comparison between two changing phenomena. However, towards the end of the course, she learned to draw the graphs and explain the meaning of their intersection as a point in which the graphs "meet at the same time and place." From this we can conclude that the situation supports the bridging of Gila's ideas of the functional approach and the conventional approach. In addition, it seemed that Gila no longer needed the support of the extra-mathematical situation. We could see that she perceived the equation both as a comparison between two changing phenomena and as an algebraic equation or inequality, and she was able to use a collection of representations and tools to solve equations.

Noam also encountered the notion of equation first in its functional context. She began by perceiving an equation as comparison between changing phenomena. Yet, Noam already knew the algorithm for solving equations by acting on its two sides from the beginning, and she used this algorithm whenever she had to solve an equation. We think that she used the algorithm since she perceived the equation as an "open sentence," under the conventional approach. She was able to provide a (mathematical) situation for a given equation. During the time in which the algorithm for working on both sides of equations was learned in class, Noam had difficulties in connecting it to a graphic representation. Temporarily, she was not able to see the equation as a comparison between two phenomena. However in a further stage of the learning, she was able to perceive equations in both approaches, with the support of a situation or without it.

In addition, it was found that at the end of the school year most students in the class were able to move fluently and flexibly between the two approaches to solving equations.

Multirepresentational Approach to Function

A dilemma related to the development of the functions course was whether and to what extent to include the use of multiple representations in a single problem-situation as classroom practice along the entire course. Our approach to integrate the use of multiple representations as a norm was supported by the literature (e.g., Kaput, 1992; Schwarz & Dreyfus, 1995) and strengthened by Dolev-Cohen's (1996) research within the *CompuMath* project.

Dolev-Cohen (1996) documented and analyzed the work of ninth-grade students during a functions course along the school year. Here we bring one case study from her research. It aimed

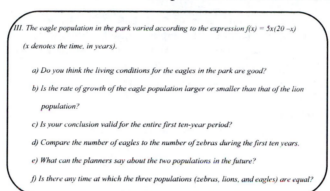

III. The eagle population in the park varied according to the expression $f(x) = 5x(20 - x)$

(x denotes the time, in years).

    a) Do you think the living conditions for the eagles in the park are good?

    b) Is the rate of growth of the eagle population larger or smaller than that of the lion

       population?

    c) Is your conclusion valid for the entire first ten-year period?

    d) Compare the number of eagles to the number of zebras during the first ten years.

    e) What can the planners say about the two populations in the future?

    f) Is there any time at which the three populations (zebras, lions, and eagles) are equal?

Figure 26.3 Part III of the Animal Park problem-situation.

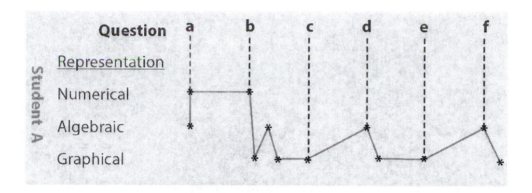

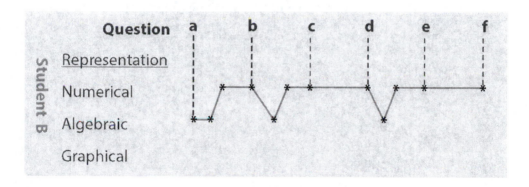

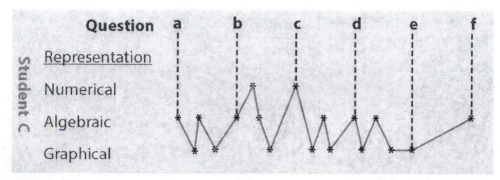

Figure 26.4 Diagrams of representations and moves among them used by each student (Dolev-Cohen, 1996).

to clarify when and how three ninth-grade students pass from one representation to another while dealing with a problem-situation in a computer-based environment. Students were asked to consider three animal populations in a park: zebras, lions, and eagles. The zebra population was described graphically according to $g(x) = 400 - 20x$. The lion population was described verbally according to $h(x) = 60x$. Here we focus on the part of the activity shown in Figure 26.3.

The work of each student on Part III is presented graphically in Figure 26.4. We can see that (a) Students A and B moved between two representations mostly, while Student C moved among the three representations; (b) while Students A and B mostly used a single presentation for answering each task, Student C moved frequently among representations while answering a question. That is, Student C is more flexible in moving among the three representations. In general, Dolev-Cohen (1996) found that students who were flexible enough to change representations within the same task succeeded better in solving functions problem-situations as compared to their peers. Dolev-Cohen's findings encouraged us to incorporate multiple representations in the design of the whole *CompuMath* curriculum.

Note: There are points in between the different questions. These points show the students' transitions between representations within a given question (e.g. Student C makes four transitions in Question c: from numerical to graphical, to algebraic, and back to graphical representations).

The Role of Proof and Proving in Geometry

For mathematicians, proofs play an essential role in establishing the *validity* of a statement and in *enlightening* its meaning (Rota, 1997). Euclidean geometry of triangles, quadrilaterals, and circles forms part of the mandatory curriculum. An analysis of "classical" teaching materials in Euclidean geometry and the research concerning the "classical" strategies of teaching Euclidean geometry indicate that students have many difficulties with proving, that the mathematical and practical importance of proofs in mathematical activities remain hidden, and that students do not feel a need for proving. Hence, it is important to create classroom activities in which the student becomes aware of these aspects of proofs (Zaslavsky, Nickerson, Stylianides, Kidron, & Winicki-Landman, 2012).

Following Hanna (1990) and Hersh (1993), we believed that in school geometry proofs should explain to students *why* the theorem is true, by providing a set of reasons that derive from the phenomenon itself. The advent of dynamic geometry environments in the mathematics classroom raised a dilemma concerning the place of proof in the curriculum, since conviction can be obtained quickly and relatively easily: The dragging operation on a geometrical object enables students to apprehend a whole class of objects in which the conjectured attribute is invariant, and hence to convince themselves of its truth (de Villiers, 1998). The role of design and teaching in this environment is then to also raise and create a need to explain *why* the conjectured attribute is true.

Dreyfus and Hadas (1996) argue that students' appreciation of the roles of proof can be achieved by activities in which the empirical investigations lead to unexpected, surprising situations. Activities of this kind let students experience the need for proof in order to explain the surprising findings, and sometimes even in order to be convinced what the correct conclusions are.

Different kinds of activities were developed in this "spirit" in a research-design way within the *CompuMath* project:

a.   Comprehensive inquiry activities, where the geometrical fact discovered as invariant of a geometrical feature is *surprising*. This surprise is the trigger for the question *why* and for the proof as answer to this question (Dreyfus & Hadas, 1996).
b.   Geometrical constructions under *uncertainty conditions*, where students try to construct a figure satisfying given conditions (Hadas & Hershkowitz, 1998).

c. Activities in which the measurement and graphical options of the dynamic geometry software are used, in order to present the dynamic variations of a geometrical phenomenon in real time, also in the graphical and numerical modes. In such a context, questions and hypotheses raised in one mode may be answered in other modes, and in this way the investigation itself is enriched (Arcavi & Hadas, 2000).

d. Activities in which one cannot find any example for a conjecture one has made. Situations of uncertainty like this lead to the dilemma: Should one continue the empirical search or attempt to understand the impossibility? Hadas and Hershkowitz (1998) argued that, by careful design, based on experimentation and cognitive analysis of students' actions, situations can be constructed in which students will feel the need for proof.

To sum up, in order to cope with students' conviction based on empirical experience only and to create a need for deductive explanations, we developed a collection of innovative activities intended to cause surprise and uncertainty. A more detailed description of this approach to proving in Euclidean geometry was included in the first edition of this *Handbook* (Hershkowitz et al., 2002, pp. 672–678).

PROCESSES OF LEARNING IN THE CLASSROOM

A question that naturally arose at later stages of the project was: What did students learn and consolidate, and how? What mathematical concepts and strategies remain with them? These questions led us to refine the description of the mathematical knowledge we intended to be constructed in the classrooms by the students and to analyze their processes of constructing this knowledge. We found the notion of abstraction to be useful for this purpose. We have been considering not only what abstraction could mean in the framework of this curriculum project, but also how processes of abstraction manifest themselves empirically in the project's classrooms. Hence, our approach to abstraction emerged between two poles: analysis of experimental data and the need to build a theoretical framework.

For this purpose, a theoretical methodological framework—Abstraction in Context (AiC)—was developed. In this section, we present an analysis according to this framework of a pair of beginning algebra students learning about algebra as a tool for justification.

Theoretical Underpinnings of Abstraction in Context

Following Piaget, several mathematics educators have proposed descriptions of the process or mechanism by which students shift their focus from the concrete to the abstract (see Dreyfus, 1991, for a brief review). For most of these educators, abstraction proceeds from a set of mathematical objects (or processes) and consists of focusing on some distinguished properties and relationships of these objects rather than on the objects themselves. This process of abstraction is thus a process of decontextualization—of ignoring the objects—together with some of their features and relations. It is linear, proceeding from the objects to the class or the structure, which may then be considered an object on a higher level.

This classical view of abstraction has raised criticism. For example, van Oers (1998) used the *activity theory* view of context for conceptualizing: "Starting from an assumption that conceives of context as constitutive of meaning, it becomes clear that the notion of 'decontextualization' is a poor concept that provides little explanation for the developmental process toward meaningful abstract thinking" (1998, p. 135). The dependence on contextual elements such as the personal history of the solver, social interactions, and the use of tools conforms to the views of theorists who recognize the importance of context in processes of abstraction.

One way to describe abstraction without reference to decontextualization has been proposed by Davydov (1972/1990). Davydov's theory leads the researchers to a second major difference between the cognitivist and the sociocultural views of abstraction. Davydov (1972/1990) developed an epistemological theory to account for a dialectical connection between abstract and concrete: Abstraction starts from an initial, simple, undeveloped first form, which need not be internally and externally consistent. The development of abstraction proceeds from analysis, at the initial stage of the abstraction, to synthesis. It ends with a consistent and elaborate final form. It does not lead from concrete to abstract but from an undeveloped to a developed form of abstract in which new features of the concrete are emphasized.

The AiC Framework and the RBC+C Model

Our intention to answer the questions raised at the beginning of this section and our related experience in classrooms raised the need for an operational definition of abstraction. We adopted Davydov's approach and translated it to the following operational definition:

> *Abstraction is an activity of vertically reorganizing previously constructed mathematics into a new mathematical structure.*

The term *activity* is to be taken in the sense of activity theory, implying that context needs to be fully taken into account. The phrase *previously constructed mathematics* refers to the outcomes of previous processes of abstraction, which may be used during the current abstraction activity. The phrase *new mathematical structure* relates to the knowledge construct emerging in the current activity. The phrase *reorganizing into a new structure* implies the establishment of hitherto unknown mathematical relationships that requires highly theoretical and empirical thought. Finally, we borrowed the term *vertically* from the Dutch culture of Realistic Mathematics Education (RME), in which researchers speak about vertical mathematization (de Lange, 1996; Treffers & Goffree, 1985) as "an activity in which mathematical elements are put together, structured, organized, developed etc. into other elements, often in more abstract or formal form than the originals" (Hershkowitz, Parzysz, & van Dormolen, 1996, p. 177). The RME approach emphasizes the integrative role of vertical mathematization. It is mainly this integration, which comes about through the establishment of new connections during the process of abstraction, that we point to by means of the term *vertically*. The word *new* in our definition of abstraction is crucial: it expresses that, as a result of abstraction, learners participating in the activity conceptualize something that was previously inaccessible to them.

In order to empirically investigate processes of abstraction we needed to devise a way to make the mental activity of abstraction observable. As activities are composed of actions, and actions are frequently observable, we decided to use *epistemic actions* (Pontecorvo & Girardet, 1993), namely mental actions by means of which knowledge is used or constructed. We consider a specific set of epistemic actions, to be introduced next, because they are characteristic of abstraction. Epistemic actions are often revealed in suitable settings. For example, settings with rich social interactions are good frameworks for observing epistemic actions.

Our definition of *abstraction* served as the theoretical guide to the establishment of an operational model for studying abstraction experimentally. This definition is the result of a dialectical bottom-up approach. The definition is thus a product of oscillating between the researchers' theoretical perspective on abstraction and experimental observations of students' actions, actions the researchers judged to be evidence of abstracting. This oscillation between theoretical principles and empirical data is highly nonlinear.

Hershkowitz, Schwarz, and Dreyfus (2001) defined and described three epistemic actions as constituent of a model. Processes of knowledge construction are expressed in the model through three observable and identifiable epistemic actions: Recognizing, Building-with, and Constructing (RBC). *Recognizing* takes place when the learner recognizes that a specific previous knowledge construct is relevant to the problem he or she is dealing with. *Building-with* is an action comprising the combination of recognized constructs in order to achieve a localized goal, such as the actualization of a strategy or a justification or the solution of a problem. The model suggests *constructing* as the central epistemic action of mathematical abstraction. Constructing consists of assembling and integrating previous constructs by vertical mathematization to produce a new construct. It refers to the first time the new construct is expressed by the learner. It does not refer to the construct becoming freely and flexibly available to the learner; this is part of the construct's *consolidation.*

Recognizing and building-with actions are often nested within constructing actions. Moreover, constructing actions are at times nested within more complex or holistic constructing actions. Therefore the model is called the *nested epistemic actions model of abstraction in context*, or simply the *RBC+C model.* The second C stands for consolidation.

An Example

X	X+2
X+6	X+8

Figure 26.5 The Seals activity.

As an example for this line of theory and research we present a study with dyads of seventh graders at the beginning of an Introduction to Algebra course (Dreyfus, Hershkowitz, & Schwarz, 2001).

The study was conducted in a spreadsheet learning environment. The task was based on number arrays of the form shown in Figure 26.5. The students had never used algebra as a tool for justifying a general statement, nor had they used the extended distributive law $(a + b)(c + d) = ac + ad + bc + bd$, though they had met and used the simple one $a(c + d) = ac + ad$. The students were asked to create a formula for the array using the variable X (see Figure 26.5) in a spreadsheet, to substitute numbers for X, and to suggest as many properties of such arrays as they could find. The students were asked—for one property after the other—whether it always holds, and to justify their claims. Most dyads found many properties. The task then focused on some properties, the most complex of them being the *diagonal product property* (DPP), namely that the difference of the products of the diagonals of an array equals 12. Many dyads were surprised to see, using the spreadsheet, that the DPP holds for each number they substituted for X. The activity design thus led the students to use algebra for justifying a general statement. Most but not all student pairs succeeded in generating components of the equation $(x + 2)(x + 6) - x(x + 8) = 12$, which in turn led them to the need for the extended distributive law (although the law was not expressed in formal terms). Thus, underlying the task design for the study were two mathematical principles: the use of algebra as a tool for justification, and the discovery of the extended distributive law, both previously unknown to the students. From the point of view of the designer, these were two intended new constructs, and the task was designed so as to create a need for these two constructs, to be denoted by C_1 (algebra as a tool for justification) and C_2 (extended distributive law).

The work of two dyads on this activity has been video recorded, transcribed, and analyzed at the micro level by Dreyfus et al. (2001). We illustrate this analysis here with the following transcript excerpt from one of these dyads. They start from the simple distributive law.

Ha	113	So, like, see, X plus 8, X, like, then it is 8X plus XX.
Ne	114	Again?
Ha	115	Wait. X times X plus 8, right? This is XX, like, X, X twice, so it's XX.
Ne	116	Yes.
Ha	117	And X times 8 is 8X.
. . .		
Ha	121	So, like, one does the distributive law.
Ne	122	Ah, yes.
. . .		
Ha	133	And this [pointing to $(x + 2)(x + 6)$] . . .
Ne	134	It's impossible to do the distributive law here. Wait, one can do . . .
Ha	135	This is 6X.
Ne	136	This is 6X times X and 6X times 2.
Ha	137	Wait, first, no . . .
Ne	138	Yes.
Ha	139	No because this is X plus 6, this is not 6X, it's different. Wait. First one does . . . X; then it's XX plus 2X, and here 6X plus 24. Then . . .
. . .		
Ha	152	Ah, it's XX plus 8X, but I don't know, like, how this [pointing to $(x + 2)(x + 6)$] will also be XX plus 8X. Like, it HAS to be.

We then analyzed the students' discourse in terms of the three epistemic actions: In lines 113–121, the students recognize elementary algebraic elements (e.g., 115) and build-with them (e.g., 117) the simple distributive law in the present context (113, 121). In lines 133–134, they find themselves in front of an unknown situation, but, due to the design, they are firmly aware of the simple distributive law. They recognize (135) and build-with (136) algebraic elements, including the simple distributive law (137, 139), to reach a new (to them) result (139). Since this is the first time they have used and verbalized the extended distributive law, the process leading up to line 139, including 133–139, is considered a constructing action, leading to C_2. This constructing action is constituted by the collection of the R and B actions in this excerpt plus the connections between them, which make them into a single whole. It is in this sense that we say that R and B actions are nested within the constructing action. As we can see, the constructing action leading to C_2 is nested within the constructing action, leading to C_2, the use of algebra as a tool for justification.

We assume that a new construct is rather fragile at first, and surmise that when met again, it will progressively become consolidated. Consolidation implies that the student will be able to recognize the construct more easily in further activities and to build-with it with increasing ease and flexibility. Hence we hypothesize that tracing the genesis of an abstraction passes through three stages:

1. A need for a new construct,
2. the emergence of a new construct, a new abstract entity in which recognizing and building-with previous constructs are nested, and
3. the consolidation of the new construct facilitating one's recognizing it with increased ease and building-with it in further activities.

The general mechanism described here outlines the functioning of the RBC+C model. The core of the model relates mainly to the second stage of the model, namely the constructing of a new abstract.

Again this is a paradigmatic example. It shows how students construct new knowledge interactively. This knowledge construction characterizes learning in rich activities and carefully designed learning environments. The model allowed us to study students' constructing of knowledge in small groups. The AiC line of research was further developed within the *Compu-Math* project as well as beyond it, by teams linked to the project and by others (see Schwarz, Dreyfus, & Hershkowitz, 2009; Dreyfus, Hershkowitz, & Schwarz, 2015 for surveys). In the next section we will relate to the latest development of AiC and RBC+C.

DISCUSSION

In this discussion section, we describe the research strands exemplified earlier, from a more holistic point of view.

As mentioned in the section entitled "Research Concerning the Development of Isolated Activities," the initial design-research-redesign stage was characterized by the process of isolated activity development through research, as exemplified by the Overseas activity and the accompanying research study. The process was a dialectic one, during which design and research influenced each other. As was shown in the "Isolated Activities" section, the research on the Overseas activity has led to the insight that hypothesizing is linked to activity in computerized learning environments, which in turn is linked to the establishment of connections between numeric, symbolic, and graphic senses. Similarly, research on other isolated activities yielded other insights. Summing these up, the various aspects considered in the design process include the content, the underlying view of mathematics as a living subject that can be investigated, the intended mathematical thinking processes (generalizing, hypothesizing, reflecting, and justifying), the potential of computer tools, and the classroom organization (including redistribution of learning responsibilities between students and teacher).

The research on isolated activities showed us that several different approaches were possible to many topics, and this necessitated research with a somewhat larger curricular mesh size. In other words, the transition from research on isolated activities to a curricular continuum necessitated decisions on taking specific approaches to specific topics. This was illustrated in the section entitled "New Dilemmas in Teaching 'Old' Mathematical Topics" by research studies on linear equations, on proof in geometry, as well as on multirepresentational environments for functions. The research findings by Stein (2002) informed the team that taking a two-pronged approach to equations—interweaving functional and algebraic considerations—is beneficial for learning: Students become flexible in their understanding of what an equation is and how it may be solved in different technological environments. This was the case even with respect to nonlinear equations, which students had not yet learned to solve (Friedlander & Stein, 2001). The study on geometric proof led to an analogous curricular insight: Interweaving an inquiry approach in a technological environment with a paper-and-pencil environment for proving showed beneficial effects on learning. These studies thus led to the principle that *interweaving several approaches to a topic may be beneficial to learning.*

Similarly, other research studies on approaching other topics have led to other principles, including the following.

The Use of Representations in Computerized Environments

Kaput (1992) pointed out that in the presence of dynamic software environments, notation systems that are static in other environments become dynamic. As a consequence, the gap between a symbolic notation system and others (like numerical and graphical ones) becomes less significant. Adding to this the findings from our research discussed earlier led us to enhance the use of multiple representations in designing further activities and to convey the message that it is legitimate for students to choose their own representation in order to solve a problem. This was done by presenting information about a situation in more than one representation (e.g., Figure 26.3) or by explicitly asking students to start their work by giving several representations for the same phenomenon, and only afterwards asking questions about the phenomenon (e.g., Friedlander & Tabach, 2001; Tabach & Friedlander, 2012). The questions were phrased so as to avoid guiding the solution process towards a specific representation. Also, we incorporated reflective questions that specifically addressed pros and cons of using different representations for the solution process, in order to draw students' attention to these issues. It is worth to note that linking representations is even easier today, due to the development of software packages such as Geogebra, but the guiding principles are the same.

Generalizations and Explanations

We asked students to generalize from numerical patterns, from visual patterns, or from graphical patterns. This was done by first providing several particular cases of a phenomenon, followed by a request to create additional particular cases, and then to express the phenomenon in a more general way, possibly using more than one representation to express the generality (verbal, graphic, and symbolic). Next, students are asked to explain the generalization they have found. Sometimes, several possible generalizations are presented, some correct and some wrong, and students are asked whether they can justify them, possibly with the aid of computerized tools (Tabach, Hershkowitz, & Schwarz, 2006; Tabach & Friedlander, 2012). Hence, the principle of asking students to make generalizations and explain them was given a dominant place in the design of activities.

Raising the Question of Why

One of the critiques raised against the use of dynamic computer software, especially in geometry, is that students are able to see large numbers of examples via the dragging mode of the software, and hence they will no longer experience a need to prove. Indeed, this power of the tools challenged us as curriculum designers. Purposeful task design, in which the learner faces a puzzling phenomenon, may be a key answer for sustaining the need to proof in the computation era, as we elaborated in the "New Dilemmas" section (Hadas et al., 2000; Dreyfus & Hadas, 1996; Prusak, Hershkowitz, & Schwarz, 2012).

Encouraging Students to Become Autonomous Learners

In the topic of statistics in the *CompuMath* project, students carried out their own small-scale projects (Ben-Zvi & Arcavi, 2001; Hershkowitz et al., 2002). This encouraged the team to expand the idea of empowering learners' autonomy in other mathematical topics. At the beginning of this subsection, we reported on students' freedom to choose their preferred representation; this served as an initial step towards more far-reaching student autonomy in learning (see, e.g., Tabach, Hershkowitz, Arcavi and Dreyfus, 2008; Tabach et al., 2013).

After many curricular units were created and implemented according to the principles just discussed, the AiC framework and the RBC+C model emerged as responses to the team's need to investigate in depth what conceptual and structural mathematical knowledge students learn and how they learn it within the *CompuMath* project (see the section entitled "Processes of Learning in the Classroom"). Looking back on our "research journey" with AiC, we observe that we passed from investigating construction of knowledge by individual learners or dyads with an interviewer in a laboratory setting, to investigating focus groups of two to four students in a working classroom. The first phase served to develop the AiC framework and the RBC+C model (Hershkowitz et al., 2001; Dreyfus et al., 2001). In the second phase, we applied the RBC+C model for analyzing students' abstraction processes as they worked in a small group in a classroom (Dreyfus et al., 2015; Hershkowitz, Hadas, Dreyfus, & Schwarz, 2007; Tabach et al., 2006; Schwarz et al., 2009).

It is worth emphasizing that the AiC framework was created while we were struggling to better understand the products and processes of learning in technological environments.

We think that technological tools have an important role to play in processes of abstraction (Kidron & Dreyfus, 2010; Tabach et al., 2006; Weiss & Dreyfus, 2009). They may accelerate students' need for constructing new knowledge. Students' need for constructing new knowledge is the first step in the process of abstraction according to the model. In addition, the ability afforded by technological tools to document—explicitly and at the micro level—students' actions while abstracting may enable researchers to refine their observational and analytical tools, and hence to trace students' processes of abstraction in a more refined way. The micro-level nature of this research provides a tool for investigating and improving curricular micro design.

As mentioned at the end of the "Processes of Learning" section, AiC research is continuing in Israel and elsewhere, concerning learning processes in technological and nontechnological environments. Its most recent development concerns research about constructing and shifting knowledge in classrooms. For this purpose, we coordinated the AiC and RBC+C framework with another theoretical methodology, Documenting Collective Activity (DCA, Rasmussen & Stephan, 2008), to study the ways in which knowledge spreads in the classroom, within and between different social settings: the whole-class community and small groups (Hershkowitz, Tabach, Rasmussen, & Dreyfus, 2014; Tabach, Hershkowitz, Rasmussen, & Dreyfus, 2014). The main findings concern the role of students as knowledge agents in shifts of knowledge between small groups and the whole-class community.

In summary, our research related to the *CompuMath* project started by focusing on cognition, but integrated more and more aspects of classroom practices, socio-mathematical norms (Hershkowitz & Schwarz, 1999), comparison between *CompuMath* classes and other ninth-grade classes (Schwarz & Hershkowitz, 1999) and instrumentation processes (Tabach, Hershkowitz, Arcavi and Dreyfus, 2008) as it progressed. We see this chapter as an example of how operative needs lead to research that has a scope and value transcending the operative needs that triggered it. Such research may initiate new educational activity cycles.

ACKNOWLEDGMENTS

We would like to thank our colleagues who took part directly or indirectly in the journey of the *CompuMath* project and the research that accompanied it. Some of that research and the preparation of this chapter were partially supported by the Israel Science Foundation under grant number 1057/12.

NOTE

1. "We" is used with slightly different interpretations at different places in the chapter: Sometimes it refers to the authors, sometimes to the *CompuMath* team leaders, and at other places to various combinations of team members—see also the acknowledgment at the end of the chapter.

REFERENCES

Arcavi, A., & Hadas, N. (2000). Computer mediated learning: An example of an approach. *International Journal of Computers for Mathematical Learning, 5*, 25–45.

Artigue, M., & Blomhøj, M. (2013). Conceptualizing inquiry-based education in mathematics. *ZDM—The International Journal on Mathematics Education, 45*, 797–810.

Balacheff, N., & Kaput, J. (1996). Computer-based learning environments in mathematics. In A.J. Bishop, K. Clements, C. Keitel, J. Kilpatrick, & C. Laborde (Eds.), *International handbook of mathematics education* (pp. 469–501). Dordrecht, The Netherlands: Kluwer Academic Publishers.

Ben-Zvi, D., & Arcavi, A. (2001). Junior high school students' construction of global views of data and data representations. *Educational Studies in Mathematics, 45*, 35–65.

Davydov, V.V. (1972/1990). *Soviet studies in mathematics education: Vol. 2. Types of generalization in instruction: Logical and psychological problems in the structuring of school curricula* (J. Kilpatrick, Ed., & J. Teller, Trans.). Reston, VA: National Council of Teachers of Mathematics. (Original work published in 1972).

de Lange, J. (1996). Using and applying mathematics in education. In A.J. Bishop, K. Clements, C. Keitel, J. Kilpatrick, & C. Laborde (Eds.), *International handbook of mathematics education* (pp. 49–97). Dordrecht, The Netherlands: Kluwer Academic Publishers.

de Villiers, M. (1998). An alternative approach to proof in dynamic geometry. In R. Lehrer & D. Chazan (Eds.), *Designing learning environment for developing understanding of geometry and space* (pp. 369–393). Hillsdale, NJ: Lawrence Erlbaum Associates.

Dolev-Cohen, O. (1996). *The passage between representations as an action of characterizing student's learning in an interactive computer based environment.* Unpublished MA thesis, The Hebrew University, Jerusalem. [In Hebrew]

Dreyfus, T. (1991). Advanced mathematical thinking processes. In D. Tall (Ed.), *Advanced mathematical thinking* (pp. 25–41). Dordrecht, The Netherlands: Kluwer, Mathematics Education Library.

Dreyfus, T., & Hadas, N. (1996). Proof as answer to the question why. *ZDM—The International Journal on Mathematics Education, 28,* 1–5.

Dreyfus, T., Hershkowitz, R., & Schwarz, B. (2001). Abstraction in Context II: The case of peer interaction. *Cognitive Science Quarterly, 1,* 307–368.

Dreyfus, T., Hershkowitz, R., & Schwarz, B. (2015). The nested epistemic actions model for abstraction in context—Theory as methodological tool and methodological tool as theory. In A. Bikner-Ahsbahs, C. Knipping, & N. Presmeg (Eds.), *Approaches to qualitative research in mathematics education: Examples of methodology and methods.* Dordrecht: Springer, Advances.

Engeström, Y. (1987). *Learning by expanding. An activity-theoretical approach to developmental research.* Helsinki: University of Helsinki.

Friedlander, A., & Stein, H. (2001). Students' choice of tools in solving equations in a technological learning environment. In M. van den Heuvel-Panhuizen (Ed.), *Proceedings of the 25th International Conference for the Psychology of Mathematics Education* (Vol. 2, pp. 441–448). Utrecht, The Netherlands: PME.

Friedlander, A., & Tabach. M. (2001). Promoting multiple representations in algebra. In A.A. Cuoco & F.R. Curcio (Eds.), *The roles of representation in school mathematics* (pp. 173–185). Reston, VA: National Council of Teachers of Mathematics, 63rd Yearbook.

Hadas, N., & Hershkowitz, R. (1998). Proof in geometry as an explanatory and convincing tool. In A. Olivier & K. Newstead (Eds.), *Proceedings of the 22st PME Conference* (Vol. 3, pp. 25–32). Stellenbosch, South Africa: PME.

Hadas, N., Hershkowitz, R., & Schwarz, B.B. (2000). The role of contradiction and uncertainty in promoting the need to prove in dynamic geometry environments. *Educational Studies in Mathematics, 44,* 127–150.

Hanna, G. (1990). Some pedagogical aspects of proof. *Interchange, 21,* 6–13.

Heid, M.K., Sheets, C., & Matras, M.N. (1990). Computer—enhanced algebra: New roles and challenges for teachers and students. In T.J. Cooney & C.R. Hirsh, *Teaching and learning mathematics in the 1990s* (pp. 194–204). Reston, VA: National Council of Teachers of Mathematics, 52nd Yearbook.

Hersh, R. (1993). Proving is convinsing and explaining. *Educational Studies in Mathematics, 24,* 389–399.

Hershkowitz, R., Dreyfus, T., Ben-Zvi, D., Friedlander, A., Hadas, N., Resnick, N., Tabach, M., & Schwarz, B.B. (2002). Mathematics curriculum development for computerized environments: A designer-researcher-learner-activity. In L.D. English (Ed.), *Handbook of international research in mathematics education* (pp. 657–694). Mahwah, NJ: Lawrence Erlbaum Associates.

Hershkowitz, R., Hadas, N., Dreyfus, T., & Schwarz, B.B. (2007). Processes of abstraction, from the diversity of individuals' constructing of knowledge to a group's "shared knowledge." *Mathematics Education Research Journal, 19,* 41–68.

Hershkowitz, R., Parzysz, B., & van Dormolen, J. (1996). Shape and space. In A.J. Bishop, K. Clements, C. Keitel, J. Kilpatrick & C. Laborde (Eds.), *International handbook of mathematics education* (pp. 161–204). Dordrecht, The Netherlands: Kluwer Academic Publishers.

Hershkowitz, R., & Schwarz, B.B. (1999). Reflective processes in a technology-based mathematics classroom. *Cognition and Instruction, 17,* 65–91.

Hershkowitz, R., Schwarz, B.B., & Dreyfus, T. (2001). Abstraction in context: Epistemic actions. *Journal for Research in Mathematics Education, 32,* 195–222.

Hershkowitz, R., Tabach, M., Rasmussen, C., & Dreyfus, T. (2014). Knowledge shifts in a probability classroom—A case study coordinating two methodologies. *ZDM—The International Journal on Mathematics Education, 46,* 363–387.

Kaput, J. (1992). Technology and mathematics education. In D.A. Grouws (Ed.), *Handbook of research on mathematics teaching and learning* (pp. 515–556). Reston, VA: National Council of Teachers of Mathematics.

Kidron, I., & Dreyfus, T. (2010). Interacting parallel constructions of knowledge in a CAS context. *International Journal of Computers for Mathematical Learning, 15,* 129–149.

Kuutti, K. (1996). Activity theory as a potential framework for human-computer interaction research. In B.A. Nardi (Ed.), *Context and consciousness* (pp. 17–44). Cambridge, MA: MIT Press.

Lagrange, J.B., Artigue, M., Laborde, C., & Trouche, L. (2003). Technology and mathematics education: A multidimensional study of the evolution of research and innovation. In A. Bishop, M.A. Clements, C. Keitel, J. Kilpatrick, & F.K.S. Leung (Eds.), *Second international handbook of mathematics education* (pp. 237–269). Dordrecht, The Netherlands: Kluwer Academic Publishers.

Pea, R.D. (1985). Beyond amplification: Using the computer to reorganize mental functioning. *Educational Psychologist, 20*, 167–182.

Perret-Clermont, A.-N. (1993). What is it that develops? *Cognition and Instruction, 11*, 197–205.

Pontecorvo, C., & Girardet, H. (1993). Arguing and reasoning in understanding historical topics. *Cognition and Instruction, 11*, 365–395.

Prusak, N., Hershkowitz, R., & Schwarz, B.B. (2012). From visual reasoning to logical necessity through argumentative design. *Educational Studies in Mathematics, 79*, 19–40. doi:10.1007/s10649-011-9335-0

Rasmussen, C., & Stephan, M. (2008). A methodology for documenting collective activity. In A.E. Kelly, R.A. Lesh, & J.Y. Baek (Eds.), *Handbook of innovative design research in science, technology, engineering, mathematics (STEM) education* (pp. 195–215). New York: Taylor & Francis.

Rota, G.-C. (1997). *Indiscrete thoughts* (pp. 131–135). Boston, MA: Birkhäuser.

Schwarz, B.B., & Dreyfus, T. (1995). New actions upon old objects: A new ontological perspective on functions. *Educational Studies in Mathematics, 29*, 259–291.

Schwarz, B.B., Dreyfus, T., & Hershkowitz, R. (2009). The nested epistemic actions model for abstraction in context. In B.B. Schwarz, T. Dreyfus & R. Hershkowitz (Eds.), *Transformation of knowledge through classroom interaction* (pp. 11–41). London, UK: Routledge.

Schwarz, B.B., & Hershkowitz, R. (1999). Prototypes: Brakes or levers in learning the function concept? The role of computer tools. *Journal for Research in Mathematics Education, 30*, 362–389.

Stein, H. (2002). *Changes in the equation concept and its solution methods in a technological learning environment.* Unpublished MA thesis, the Weizmann Institute of Science, Rehovot. [In Hebrew]

Tabach, M., Arcavi, A., & Hershkowitz, R. (2008). Transitions among different symbolic generalizations by algebra beginners in a computer intensive environment. *Educational Studies in Mathematics, 69*, 53–71.

Tabach, M., & Friedlander, A. (2012). Five considerations in task design—The case of improving grades. *Investigations in Mathematics Learning, 4*, 32–49.

Tabach, M., Hershkowitz, R., & Arcavi, A. (2008). Learning beginning algebra with spreadsheets in a computer intensive environment. *Journal of Mathematical Behavior, 27*, 48–63.

Tabach, M., Hershkowitz, R., Arcavi, A., & Dreyfus, T. (2008). Computerized environments in mathematics classrooms: A research-design view. In L.D. English, M.B. Bussi, G.A. Jones, R.A. Lesh, B. Shriraman, & D. Tirosh (Eds.), *Handbook of international research in mathematics education* (2nd ed., pp. 784–805). New York: Routledge.

Tabach, M., Hershkowitz, R., & Dreyfus, T. (2013). Learning beginning algebra in a computer intensive environment: Design, difficulties, and reality. *ZDM—The International Journal on Mathematics Education, 45*, 377–391. doi:10.1007/s11858-012-0458-2

Tabach, M., Hershkowitz, R., Rasmussen, C., & Dreyfus, T. (2014). Knowledge shifts in the classroom—A case study. *Journal of Mathematics Behavior, 33*, 192–208. doi:10.1016/j.jmathb.2013.12.001

Tabach, M., Hershkowitz, R., & Schwarz, B.B. (2006). Constructing and consolidating of algebraic knowledge within dyadic processes: A case study. *Educational Studies in Mathematics, 63*, 235–258.

Treffers, A., & Goffree, F. (1985). Rational analysis of realistic mathematics education—The Wiskobas program. In L. Streefland (Ed.), *Proceedings of the 9th International Conference for the Psychology of Mathematics Education* (Vol. 2. pp. 97–121). Utrecht, The Netherlands: OW&OC.

van Oers, B. (1998). The fallacy of de-contextualization. *Mind, Culture, and Activity, 5*, 143–153.

Weiss, D., & Dreyfus, T. (2009). Model based construction of fraction comparison. In M. Tzekaki, M. Kaldrimidou & H. Sakonidis (Eds.), *Proceedings of the 33rd Conference of the International Group for the Psychology of Mathematics Education* (Vol. 1, p. 489). Thessaloniki, Greece: PME.

Yackel, E., & Cobb, P. (1996). Socio-mathematical norms, argumentation, and autonomy in mathematics. *Journal for Research in Mathematics Education, 27*, 458–477.

Yerushalmy, M., (2009). Technology-based algebra learning. Epistemological discontinuities and curricular implications. In B.B. Schwarz, T. Dreyfus & R. Hershkowitz (Eds.), *Transformation of knowledge through classroom interaction* (pp. 60–69). London, UK: Routledge.

Yerushalmy, M., & Chazan, D. (2002). Flux in school algebra: Curricular change, graphing technology, and research in students learning and teacher knowledge. In L.D. English (Ed.), *Handbook of international research in mathematics education* (pp. 725–756). Mahwah, NJ: Lawrence Erlbaum Associates.

Zaslavsky, O., Nickerson, S., Stylianides, A., Kidron, I., & Winicki-Landman, G. (2012). The need for proof and proving: Mathematical and pedagogical perspectives. In G. Hanna & M. de Villiers (Eds.), *Proof and proving in mathematics education—the 19th ICMI study* (pp. 215–230). New York: Springer, New ICMI Study series, Vol. 15.

27 E-Textbooks in/for Teaching and Learning Mathematics
A Potentially Transformative Educational Technology

Birgit Pepin

ESoE, Technische Universiteit Eindhoven, The Netherlands

Ghislaine Gueudet

CREAD, University of Brest, France

Michal Yerushalmy

Department of Mathematics Education, University of Haifa, Israel

Luc Trouche

French Institute of Education, École Normale Supérieure de Lyon, France

Daniel I. Chazan

Center for Mathematics Education, University of Maryland, United States

INTRODUCTION

In *The Age of Discontinuity: Guidelines to Our Changing Society* (1992), Professor of Management Peter Drucker lays out ways in which technologies are transforming, and will continue to transform, industries throughout the world economy; for many workers, what characterizes work life now is the continual need to adapt to technological change. Such changes are not limited to the world of work: technology is transforming interactions with media, and this also relates to books. This chapter focuses on one way in which technology may transform educational processes and bring about new educational dynamics. Specifically we examine ways in which e-book technology might influence one genre of book, the (mathematics) textbook.

This chapter's focus on e-textbooks is a little different than the focus of many who do research on technology in mathematics education. For many years, technology in mathematics education has focused on support for student activity in classrooms. While two of the authors have written, in previous editions of this Handbook (Yerushalmy & Chazan, 2002, 2008), about curriculum development and technology, and the impact of various tools and approaches on teaching and learning, we explore in this chapter deep evolutions in the learning, teaching, and professional development processes that digital resources, in particular e-textbooks, may create as they potentially transform current educational practice. We suggest that these potential transformations in teaching and learning require new research perspectives (Gueudet, Pepin, & Trouche, 2012). Further, we suggest that there are interesting opportunities—and even an urgent need—to renew research perspectives on technology and teachers' participation in the design phase of technology tools, in particular on e-textbooks used and designed by teachers. In this chapter, we present a synthesis of research and development studies on e-textbooks, and analyze the crucial evolutions connected with their design and use.

At the same time that our focus on e-textbooks is slightly different than what is often done in the name of technology in mathematics education. This focus is consonant with greater interest in general in the role of textbooks in mathematics education. Textbook conferences in Europe and Asia (e.g. International Conference on School Mathematics Textbooks, East China Normal University, Shanghai, 2011; International Conference on Mathematics Textbook Research and Development, University of Southampton, July 2014) and the recent ICMI Study 22 Conference on Task Design in Mathematics Education" in Oxford (see proceedings: Margolinas, 2013) evidence the renewed interest in textbook research in mathematics education (Fan, Zhu, & Miao, 2013). Recent studies (e.g. *ZDM Special Issue 45*[5]) address new issues and point to new roles for the textbook (e.g. Yerushalmy, 2013), not only as a tool for students and teachers, but also as interface between policy and practice (Pepin, Gueudet, & Trouche, 2013a).

The textbook is commonly seen as the major curriculum resource in the classroom for teachers and students, and many authors claim that the textbook is an important artifact and a major source of provision of educational opportunities (Haggarty & Pepin, 2002, Schmidt, 2012). From the research literature, it is clear that textbooks are a vital ingredient for mathematics teachers' lesson preparations and their pedagogic practice (e.g. Gueudet, Pepin, & Trouche, 2013a). Perhaps as importantly, they may be seen as vehicles and tools for teacher learning and professional development (Brown 2009; Collopy, 2003). At the same time, mathematics textbooks are perceived to reflect the views expressed in national curricular documents, and hence what the country views as appropriate for their students to learn, and how (Schmidt, McKnight, Valverde, Houang, & Wiley, 1997, Valverde, Bianchi, Wolfe, Schmidt, & Houang, 2002). In short, much research has gone into analyzing traditional textbooks and their use in mathematics classrooms (Fan, 2013). The ICMI Study 22 discussion document states that "most teachers use textbooks and/or online packages of materials as their total or main source of tasks" (Margolinas, 2013, p. 11).

It is reasonable to argue that resources such as textbooks/e-textbooks and other materials (also digital materials, e.g. worksheets) are an important part of the context in which pupils and teachers work. In recognition of the central importance of such documents, the framework for the Third International Mathematics and Science Study (TIMSS) included large-scale cross-national analyses of mathematics curricula and textbooks as part of its examination of mathematics education and attainment in almost 50 nations. Concerns have been expressed about the *quality* of textbooks, for example, and about their persuasive influence. It appears that textbook content, and how it is used, are significant influences on students' opportunities to learn and their subsequent achievement (Robitaille & Travers, 1992). It is also commonly assumed that textbooks are one of the main sources for the content covered and the pedagogical styles used in classrooms (Valverde et al., 2002). Teachers often rely heavily on textbooks in their day-to-day teaching when they decide what to teach, how to teach it, and the kinds of tasks and exercises to assign to their students. Hence, it seems sensible to analyze e-/textbooks with respect to their "quality."

It is clear that both content and structure depend on the textbook's design, whether traditional or digital textbooks. In this chapter we investigate textbook design, focusing on its use and developments brought about by digital means, and we examine the ways in which the interfaces (e.g. between teachers, textbook authors and learners) may be different as compared to traditional textbooks. To provide specific examples, with e-textbooks, interfaces may change in terms of the following.

- Interactions amongst teachers: digital means offer opportunities for teachers to easily prepare lessons together, in particular if the necessary tools are provided by the e-textbook—hence more opportunities for collective work.

- Interactions between teachers and textbook authors: if teachers can change the content of the book (e.g. in terms of the sequencing of topic areas, and within topic areas the learning trajectories suggested, or indeed the tasks provided and the digital 'tools' used for particular tasks), these changes may be approved by the textbook author group, and subsequently included in the book—hence teachers become quasi-authors of the text-book, and the authority of the text changes.
- Interactions between teachers and learners: e-textbooks may provide interfaces for teach-ers and pupils to easier communicate, for example in terms of feedback on (written) homework (which may be in or out of class).

Textbooks are now often complemented by digital materials (e.g. files to be projected during the lesson by the teacher; exercises using particular software; etc.). ICMI Study 22 asked the following question:

> How can or should new digital formats influence textbook design: e.g. use of podcasts, twitter, and other social media; implications for design and coherence of materials (either original digital design or transfer from print) if teachers are able to select tasks in varied orders?
>
> (Margolinas, 2013, p. 19)

This question is complex and encompasses several aspects of the evolutions resulting from digital means, in particular the following: digital means provide new opportunities for the structuring of textbooks for their use by teachers, and they open up new possibilities for design and further evolutions. To address this issue we will start by working toward a definition of an e-textbook. To do so, we have to begin with a characterization of the role of textbooks in compulsory schooling. From there, we will move on to examine how e-textbooks have the potential to change both teachers and students' interactions with textbooks. Throughout these sections of the chapter, we will offer periodic "windows" into the use of e-textbooks in teaching and learning. Finally, we will illustrate how the presence of e-textbooks calls for recon-ceptualizations of constructs, such as "quality" and "coherence," which researchers have been using in research on textbooks; thus, one might say that e-textbooks are challenging existing constructs in mathematics education research.

E-TEXTBOOKS: WORKING TOWARDS A DEFINITION

Studying e-textbooks involves being able to identify their nature, to define what an e-textbook is. However, to date there is no clear notion or definition of an e-textbook. We cannot provide a "complete" definition, but we can work toward such a goal. For example, whilst we can claim that a textbook is a book, there is no corresponding claim for e-textbooks. We discuss this next, with both general considerations and examples provided by our research. Developing a deeper understanding of the nature of e-textbooks involves examining their (potential) features and their structure in particular, but also their design modes, and investigating the similarities and differences between paper textbooks and e-textbooks in terms of design.

Textbooks as Artifacts of Compulsory Schooling

Books have been crucial tools for mathematical communication; texts, like Euclid's *Ele-ments*, were at the same time both compendiums of known mathematical knowledge, as well as pedagogical texts that could form the basis for studies (Herbst, 2002) and communicate aspects of mathematical practice (Netz, 1999). More recently, the texts authored by Bourbaki were intended to play a similar role (Guedj, 1985). The French mathematician Cartier, from the Bourbaki School, wrote: "The mathematician belongs to the civilization of the book" (Cartier & Chemla, 2000, p. 166, our translation).

Textbooks, a new kind of mathematical text, came into existence with the advent of compulsory formal schooling and efforts to democratize knowledge (Schubring, 1987). These new kinds of mathematical texts were explicitly designed to communicate at the same time both to pupil and teacher the mathematics (e.g. to supplement texts like Euclid's *Elements*) and the values that the author/s regarded appropriate for common school knowledge. Textbooks now commonly include exposition; worked examples, exercises or questions, images, and more (Love & Pimm, 1996). While at some times and in some places these specialized texts—textbooks—are authored by people whose authority is taken for granted (Kidwell, Ackerberg-Hastings, & Roberts, 2008), in current times, these books are either created by central educational authorities or written by individuals or teams (mathematics teachers, educators, inspectors) to meet guidelines produced by such authorities.

Distinguishing mathematical texts for school from other kinds of mathematical texts is a complex task (Proust, 2012). Moreover, the role they play in schooling is of course crucial. Textbooks are meant to communicate to the teacher what it is that students are supposed to learn and in which order (Westbury, 1990), and something about how it is that students are to do so (Chazan & Yerushalmy, 2014). New electronic means of publishing texts have the potential to change the textbook industry, just as they have changed the publication of other books. When textbooks are published as paper books, they are written at one time and then produced. With this mode of production, the teacher interacts with a final product that is fixed and does not expand as it is used (except under the form of written notes in the margins of the pages). When e-books are published in bits and bytes, they now can potentially be continually edited and supplemented by a large number of people; as books are edited in this way, such changes in mode of publication can reshape the relationships between textbook author or curriculum developer, teacher, and student. In particular, the nature of the authority of the text in the classroom may shift. It is this potential that we seek to explore in our discussion of e-textbooks.

Design of E-Textbooks

Whether in the form of dedicated hardware, tablet PCs, or a software format, digital books have challenged the object we used to refer to as a "book." Clearly, the 21st-century reader will be increasingly reading materials in digital format, and may find them both useful and attractive. For a growing community of readers digital books have already changed the book culture. It did not take too long for the textbook publishing industry to follow these global changes and offer digital textbooks. At first textbook publishers addressed the higher education audience, and recently they have been targeting schools and schoolteachers, both as authors and as users.

The first generation of digital textbooks may be considered "old wine in new wineskin" (Gould, 2011); they were merely digitized versions of their paper counterparts, integrating a given fixed content, and supporting limited interactivity only by means of search and navigation of the digital document. The second generation of digital textbooks bears a noticeable change in the object itself, opening new occasions for interactions, personalization, and evolution of the content: an increasing number of school textbooks are now supplemented by continuously upgraded digital resources that can be found on the Web, such as the ClassroomAid blog (*http://classroom-aid.com/educational-apps*). Textbook publishers are addressing a wide range of expected changes in the affordances of the digital object, including material aspects of weight and cost; the quality and attractiveness of the material; the richness of the modes of presentation; and the opportunities for personalization. Publishers offer teachers the possibility to personalize digital textbooks for their courses, emphasizing flexibility and inexpensive dynamic changes that allow schoolteachers to personalize the textbook by selecting from existing chapters and content, and even individualizing the book for each student. Thus, the change in the object is also associated with an essential change concerning *design, teacher agency*, and *authorship*.

Different Types of E-Textbooks

Working towards a definition, we will introduce three types/models of e-textbooks and describe examples corresponding to each type. Each example describes a complex design but is used to illustrate specific characteristic/s that for us are central dimensions of e-textbooks and their use by teachers or students.

1. The **integrative e-textbook** refers to an "add-on" type model where the digital version of a (traditional) textbook is connected to other learning objects (see Figure 27.1): a digital book that is ideologically similar to a rigid paper textbook; i.e. it is a tradition-ally authored textbook and many users are likely to use it as a digital version of a paper textbook. In that sense, norms of authority, coherence, and quality are not changing. But the integrative e-textbook allows for users (teachers or developers) to add on or link to other learning objects that traditionally are not assumed to be part of a textbook. It is used by educational systems (schools, states, developers) as the core of a Virtual Learning Environment—learning management, course management, authoring tools to add or edit activities (by teachers), etc.

2. The **evolving or "living" e-textbook** refers to an accumulative/developing model where a core community (e.g. of teachers, IT specialists) has authored a digital textbook that is permanently under development due to the input of other practicing members/ teachers (see Window 1 and Figure 27.2). The Sésamath system is an example of a sus-tained project of community-authored resources. The use of such a textbook by teachers who are not contributing is different from the use of the integrative model, because the evolving/"living" e-textbook emphasizes interactivity of "living" resources (and we will show that in the subsequent section).

3. The **interactive e-textbook** refers to a "tool kit" model where the e-textbook (authored to function only as an interactive textbook) is based upon a set of learning objects—tasks and interactives (diagrams and tools)—that can be linked and combined. The VisualMath example (see Window 2) is an example for this type of textbook. It is "traditionally" authored, thus representing the traditional view of external authority. However, different from the other models, (a) the tasks are based on interactives that are an integral part of the textbook (rather than being add-on tools); (b) it is designed to afford object-oriented navigation along mathematical objects and operations that provide mathematical oppor-tunities that can be taught in various orders (like the museum visitors who visit art in different ways.)

The first example (Figure 27.1) refers to the "add-on" model where the digital version of a (traditional) textbook is linked to other learning objects. Korea, considered as one of the leading countries in mathematics and science achievements, became a leading innovator in the area of e-textbooks, especially in school mathematics and science. Korean publishers hold an integrative view in which textbooks remain the central learning resource, surrounded by other types of facilitating media.

Other educational systems are adopting a similar view of the new textbook (Taizan, Bhang, Kurokami, & Kwon, 2012). The Israeli education system requires that each textbook appears in at least one of three formats: a digitized textbook; a digitized textbook that is enriched with external links and multimodal materials; and/or a textbook that is specially designed to work in a digital environment and which includes online tools for authoring, learning, and management.

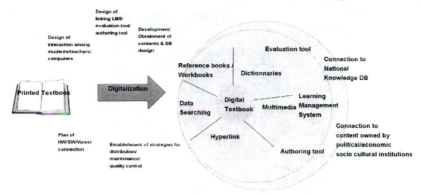

Figure 27.1 The integrated e-textbook. Source: Korea Education and Research Information Service (KERIS), 2007.

Thus, while part of the digital textbook can also function as printed text, the e-textbook integrates functions and uses (by teachers) that traditionally were not part of textbook use, such as grading students' work and organizing their course.

The second example is the Sésamath e-textbook, developed in France (see Window 1). This example refers to a system approach model, where a core group/community (of teachers, IT specialists) has developed a hybrid textbook that is continuously evolving through the input of other practicing members. An e-textbook can be entirely designed by teachers, like in the case of Sésamath. In this case teachers intervened as individual authors of the e-textbook. However, even in the case of commercial publishers and "expert" authors (e.g. "expert teachers", inspectors, teacher educators), teachers are not expected to be passive users of e-textbooks; they are expected to personalize the book (see example in Window 2).

Window 1—Sésamath E-Textbook, a Living Resource System Collaboratively Designed

Sésamath, a French online association of mathematics teachers (most of them teaching in lower secondary school, grades 6–9), started in 2001. Its spirit is summarized on its Web site (www. sesamath.net/) as "Mathematics for all" (Figure 27.2). The association started with a gathering of approximately 20 mathematics teachers who shared their personal Web sites and subsequently designed a "drill-and-practice" software program called *Mathenpoche* (which stands for *mathematics in the pocket)*. Mathenpoche has very quickly become very successful, and it has been used by many teachers and students. The possibilities and opportunities for organizing collaborative work, for offering a set of flexible resources and tools, and for questioning (e.g. through discussions with researchers) its structure and development mode, led Sésamath to become a major reference in the French educational landscape (Trouche, Drijvers, Gueudet, & Sacristan, 2013).

Since, 2005 Sésamath has designed textbooks for grades 6–10 and has now become one of the most popular textbooks in France: 300,000 textbooks have been sold, representing 20% of a very competitive French textbook market (Vieillard-Baron, 2009). Four elements can explain this:

1. The *mode of design* of these textbooks (Sabra & Trouche, 2011) involves a large number of actors. Many teachers (approximately one hundred, for each textbook) have contributed to the design in a *collaborative* and *iterative* way, as "authors of content," or "designers of didactical scenarios," or "testers," or "experimentators" in classes (a single teacher could have several roles, or change roles at different moments).

   The textbook resulting from this process is expected to fit the wishes and needs of a large number of teachers.

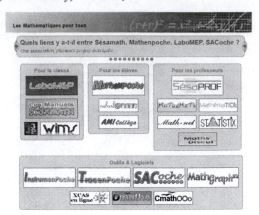

Figure 27.2 The front page of the Sésamath Web site.

2. Far from being a simple textbook, the Sésamath textbooks constitute a *hybrid* system of resources for teaching (i.e., including a classical structure in chapters, online supplements, and animated corrections). Following their development helps to understand this systemic aspect:
    *   the first model of Sésamath textbooks was a *single static book*, available both online (as a. pdf file, but also in. odt format, which allowed teachers to make modifications) and in hard copy, accompanied by separated animations online, a set of Mathenpoche exercises, etc. (i.e. a real *resource system*, see Figure 27.1);
    *   the second model was a *flexible and dynamic digital textbook* that a teacher could organize according to his/her needs, with animation and extra exercises integrated in each chapter;
    *   The third model was both a flexible and dynamic digital textbook *and* a laboratory for collaboratively adjusting the textbook to the needs and projects of the community (school, team of teachers). This laboratory, named *LaboMEP* (which stands for *Laboratory for Mathenpoche*) allows teachers to develop and share their own lessons, but also to differentiate their teaching according to the results of their students (using an application—Pepite—that has been developed through the collaboration of Sésamath with researchers).
3. Sésamath has found an economic model that is well-suited to the world of free software (Vieillard-Baron, 2009): all Sésamath resources, including the textbooks, can be freely downloaded. A printed-paper version can be bought for half the price of other mathematics textbooks in France. The sale of the books allows Sésamath to employ seven teachers, who constitute the technical infrastructure of the association (all authors work without remuneration).
4. Sésamath resources are truly *alive*, as the association itself is *alive* (Gueudet & Trouche, 2009b). Once the textbooks have been produced, they are constantly discussed in the community of users (in discussions lists, forums, etc.), and they are regularly adjusted and "redesigned." For example, the grade 6 Sésamath textbook was comprehensively revised in 2013, and it includes now open-ended problems and more complex tasks than before.

We provide the third example to illustrate the interactive model showing the design of an interactive e-textbook that is based upon a set of independent but conceptually connected learning objects, which address specific content and can be linked and combined to create learning trajectories that reflect different pedagogical ideas (see Window 2).

Window 2—Visual Math Design Process and Structure

VisualMath has been designed to challenge traditional notions of what school mathematics is and how it can be taught and learned (more about the rationale and background can be found in the chapters within the first and second editions of this *Handbook* (Yerushalmy & Chazan, 2002, 2008). The VisualMath Function's based algebra e-textbook is part of a geometry, algebra and calculus curriculum development project that spans more than 25 years. It supports the "what" and the means for the "how" to teach and learn a full school-algebra course based on the concept of function. The tasks and the interactives are all organized around a relatively small number of mathematical objects (functions) and operations (with the functions) represented and interactively manipulated by graphs, sketches, numbers, and symbols. This object-oriented mapping of the curriculum proposes a coherent organization of the algebra curriculum.

The term *VisualMath* indicates the emphasis of the program on mathematical representations and especially on visualization. In this respect, the program is a source for important ideas, as well as methods for students to act on those ideas supported by visual feedback (Chazan & Yerushalmy, 2003). As teachers are expected to guide mathematical inquiry and take a more active role in the ways different resources are used to communicate ideas in their class, a bound book that represents the curriculum plan and assumes a linear progression for all students may not best serve teaching. Thus, the learning units of the e-textbook are designed to support a variety of progressions and sequences. Throughout the development of VisualMath, various formats of printed textbooks and of digital resources were developed and studied.

Paper textbooks were part of the first round of development (1992–2002): digital interactive multiple-representation tools were designed to be part of the work with the textbook, and these were often used (by teachers) for enrichment, rather than as an integral necessary resource. The tasks require making sense of problems, spending longer on analyzing givens, constraints, relationships, and goals. Although problem solving can always be helped by use of appropriate tools, it should be carried out strategically, constructing viable arguments and critiquing the reasoning of others. Expositions were replaced by proposals for hands-on explorations followed by whole group teacher-led discussions.

2. The VisualMath e-textbook was designed anew, based on the printed VisualMath algebra books, as a Web.1 learning environment. (The development by Yerushalmy, Katriel, and Shternberg (2004) is further detailed in Yerushalmy, 2013.) Its design was a joint effort of the teams who developed the tools for explorations and teacher-users groups who participated as developers of the VisualMath tasks. The VisualMath Algebra e-textbook accommodates two objects (functions), the linear and the quadratic, and six operations on/with the objects (represent, modify, transform, analyze, combine, and compare).

The design borrowed images from a "museum setting" and is consistent with the distinction Kress and van Leeuwen (1996) made to describe linear and nonlinear texts. It accommodates two exhibit halls (units): the linear and the quadratic. Entering the hall, the tour leads to various galleries (units) according to the central mathematical operations of functions (on Reals): Modify, Transform, Operate and Compare two functions. Each gallery consists of a central piece that reflects the essence of the mathematical concept at hand. The "art" is located in a few spaces, engaging the visitor in learning a concept in different ways: there are interactive tasks (for problem solving), special-purpose tools (hands-on explorations within limited scope of the gallery), interactive exercises' generators (to improve skills), and an integrative project. As the quantity of the "art" is too vast to be covered in a single course, decisions of choice and sequencing should be made by the teacher. Major design efforts were invested in offering interactive diagrams. An interactive diagram is a relatively small and simple software application (applet) built around a preconstructed example (in contrast to tools). An interactive diagram combines the characteristic features of a static diagram and of a tool.

3. The Algebra VisualMath e-textbook is currently being redesigned attempting to support new teachers' engagements with materials. It is developed to function as Web.2 environment and includes a new set of editing options that allow users to create courses, design their personal version of the e-textbook, redesign the sequences, and rewrite tasks from the authored materials.

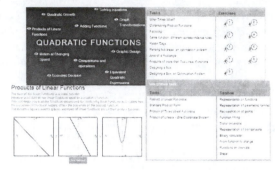

Figure 27.3 The Graph Transformations unit of the VisualMath e- textbook: It offers a tool box; a central piece of exposition; and three working spaces (on the left): Activity Tools, Tasks, and Exercises.

We suggest here that a common feature of e-textbooks is that they constitute networks of digital material that encompass the mathematical content of a traditional textbook, but they also include diverse supplementary tools, in particular those that support the learning of the mathematical content. They can have very different structures, according to the authors, publishers, or national policies. Nevertheless, many e-textbooks seem to offer possibilities for adaptations by teachers, for teacher collaboration, and for building personal paths for students. Hence, we contend that we can *define an e-textbook as an evolving structured set of digital resources, dedicated to teaching, initially designed by different types of authors, but open for redesign by teachers, both individually and collectively.*

The three models and examples presented illustrate these common features and possible differences. Sésamath and VisualMath share a perspective on how students learn mathematics: interactively, meeting various tasks and choosing representations. Both e-textbooks propose different kinds of digital resources, their structure is not linear, and they can be adapted and shaped by teachers according to their particular contexts and teaching objectives. Interestingly, the Sésamath e-textbook was designed solely by teachers; it did not, at least in the early stages, incorporate mathematics education research results (Gueudet et al., 2013a). However, it has been continuously modified according to teacher-users' remarks. VisualMath was designed by experts in the context of a long-term research and development project. In the currently designed version teachers will be able to personalize the text by reordering or rewriting tasks and adding new tasks and live resources. It will be important to study patterns of use, such as choosing a path within the offered original materials, creating a "personal book" from the given materials, or adding and dropping tasks and live resources. It will also be important to observe whether the inserted changes and personalization will serve only the teachers in their classrooms, or whether teachers will attempt to share their work in online communities, as is happening with Sésamath.

We develop these examples further in subsequent sections, to investigate the evolutions developing from the digital format, and moreover to examine not only the features/designs of e-textbooks, but also their use by students or teachers.

USE OF E-TEXTBOOKS BY STUDENTS AND TEACHERS

Most authors agree that mathematics textbooks address both the teacher and the learner (Love & Pimm, 1996). Rezat (2006), who challenges this dichotomy, suggests four triangular connections related to the use of any textbook: student-textbook-mathematical knowledge; student-teacher-textbook; teacher-textbook-mathematical knowledge (didactical); and student-teacher-mathematical knowledge (represented by the textbook and mediated by the teacher). A recent typology for analyzing digital programs in mathematics by Choppin and colleagues (2014) offers three themes corresponding to the compound relations of resources, learning, and teaching: students' interactions with the program, curriculum uses and adaptation, and assessment. In this section we approach general issues illustrated by two examples: the first focuses on student-text-knowledge, and the second on the student-teacher-textbook triad specifically related to digital interactive textbooks (supported by recent limited research results).

E-Textbooks and Changes in the Relationship Between Students and Textbooks

Whilst indeed a textbook is most commonly conceptualized as an artifact that is mediated and used primarily by the teacher, some recent studies analyze student-textbook-mathematical knowledge relations. Engagement with mathematics is a critical component when designing learning experiences with e-textbooks. As it is a too large an issue to be addressed in one section, we choose one aspect of engagement of students' problem solving with e-textbooks: learning with interactive visuals. Offering qualitative observations, Rezat (2013) describes how students choose tasks for practicing on their own by identifying three utilization schemes, amongst them visual appearance similarity. Diagrams are core visual elements of mathematics textbooks and increasingly more dominant in reform textbooks (Love & Pimm, 1996). Yerushalmy's (2005) review of studies involving students' engagement with diagrams in mathematical text stresses that diagrams (intending to present information) are likely to implicitly engage the viewer in meaningful interpretations. Research of problem solving by students suggests that diagrams can support structuring students' ideas by making them meaningfully visible and concrete, and they may focus students on core aspects of the problem and engagement in their own sense-making process (Murata, 2008). Engagement with diagrams has also been studied by Bremigan (2005) who found that the modification of given diagrams or the construction of new diagrams in students' solutions are related to success in problem-solving. Naftaliev and Yerushalmy (2013) studied structures of design and affordances of interactive diagrams and analyzed students' problem solving experiences with e-textbooks. Window 3 (below) offers an example:

Window 3—Students' Engagements With Interactive Tasks
of the VisualMath E-Textbook

Yaniv, Lior, and Daniel, 13–14-year-old algebra students, were observed while solving an unfamiliar task in the Linear Function modeling unit. The task aims at understanding properties of linear graphs that are mathematical models of animated motion. The diagram consists of two representations of motion by seven cars: a simulation, and a hot-linked position-time graph. The graph and the simulation are only partially linked: motion occurs simultaneously on the simulation and on the graph but there is no color match, so the identification process requires extracting data from the simulation and the graph in order to link them.

Students began their work by activating the animation and observing the motion of the cars (which they called "dots") as well as the related animated dots on the graphs. They ran through the entire race several times, then identified a conflict between the two animated representations: one "car" out of the six dots does not move, but all seven dots on the graphs are in motion! They stopped the animation and attempted to retell the story of the motion by

Figure 27.4 A student working on the Linear Function modeling unit.

viewing the given static components and identified the constant function graph that describes the static state.

Yaniv: Time doesn't pass for it [for the dot].

Lior: Time is constant—doesn't move.

Yaniv: Time passed for the dot but it [the dot] doesn't use it because it doesn't have speed.

Lior: No, the time does move. The dot doesn't move during that time. . . For all of them. . . time is passing but it [points at a dot along the path] simply doesn't move during that time.

Daniel: Maybe. It doesn't run. Time always changes but there is a common starting point and then time starts. And it is impossible to say that because it doesn't move its time stops.

Lior: Ah! I know, because in. . . wait a minute. . . in this dimension, the dimension of the time it is impossible to control.

Daniel: You can't control because it is the x-axis and here time always moves and can't stand still. Only on the y-axis can you change [the position].

In the discussion the students started to treat the graph as a description of a process taking place over time. They discussed the graph in the static state and began interpreting it. They reached a conclusion about time as an independent variable: time always changes and it cannot be stopped, and the passage of time cannot be controlled. The work they performed was mental: formulating hypotheses and reaching conclusions.

Next, they activated the animation to verify the hypotheses and to choose the appropriate graph for the dot that does not move. Although they reached the right conclusion and seemed to understand the situation, they were still surprised when they identified a constant function line as the graph that matched the static dot. They continued to explain the correct albeit peculiar result they arrived at regarding the static point, and continued to explore relations between motion and distance-time graphs. By imagining rather than executing motion they learned the two central pieces of knowledge concerning motion: rate of change and directional motion.

While it was expected that students would engage more due to the animation, and would experiment and try out different answers, a noteworthy finding in the demonstrated problem-solving process is the unusually extensive mental work, encompassing an entire cycle of logical argumentation (raising assumptions, deriving conclusions through conjectures and refutations), which eventually led to the solution. Our evidence suggests that interactive tasks offer engaging reading by providing readers with explicit options for manipulating given examples and especially diagrams (Naftaliev & Yerushalmy, 2013). Although characteristics of problem-solving processes of complex challenges cannot be attributed to a single factor, we were able to elicit the central role of the boundaries, designed into interactive tasks, in the processes of interactive learning. Whilst live-learning resources are often empowered by attractive video clips and animation-based demonstrations, we found that important fine tuning should be considered in the design of e-textbook tasks to include 1) a well-planned interactive example that presents the necessary repertoire of examples that would provide cognitive support (such as the conflicting animations in the example above) rather than cognitive load; 2) partial control and partial links between representations that help to capture interesting "views," but also a balance between the experimentations and the analytic phases. More generally, students' interactive learning of algebra occurred whilst reading and solving tasks of interactive text that we studied in a long-term research project. The interactive tasks offered experimentation with multiple-linked-representations that reflect back the student's actions. We have evidence that these tasks led to processes of personalization of the text and to the development of main mathematical ideas within the boundaries designed in the interactive diagrams. The design of the diagrams organized and directed the process of development of the students' knowledge, but the students controlled the task, produced the given presentation of the task, and formulated new questions.

Beyond the challenging problem solving, other interactive scenarios that e-textbooks are often designed to support are *dynamic expositions* (as the one described in Window 4) and *exercises* for practice. Dynamic exposition is designed to present an example and to afford limited user control: for example, dragging a given figure or running a video or simulation are frequent elements used in either teachers' illustrations or students' own first exploration of a new term. Dynamic exposition contributes to the learner's awareness of which features (of an object) make it a specific example, and which features can be varied to form a class of similar or related examples. The widespread use of examples in mathematics textbooks serves as a means of communication and mediation between learners and ideas. If examples are well selected, the variations between examples are the means by which students can distinguish between essential and redundant features (Goldenberg & Mason, 2008, Watson & Shipman, 2008). One of the unique features of the computerized environment lies in the possibility for systematically creating multiple related examples. In contrast, the design assumption in regard to exercises is that they are performed after students have constructed correct (though not necessarily complete) concept images and concept definitions (Tall & Vinner, 1981). The strength of technology in this phase of learning includes the large quantity of exercises generated semi-randomly (random within constraints) for practice, and the different types of feedback that can be designed to support skills practice with understanding, even in domains that traditionally offer rote exercises. The self-generation and analysis of examples and practice with understanding are two central topics currently within the scope of the design of assessment systems that could be embedded within interactive e-textbooks (but are beyond the scope of this chapter).

E-Textbooks and Changes in the Relationship Between Teachers and Textbooks

In the previous section, we discussed ways in which e-textbooks may change students' work. Now, we will consider potential changes to the role of the teacher, and student-teacher interactions, in class and out of class.

We adhere to the theoretical perspective of the documentational approach (Gueudet & Trouche, 2009a). This means that we focus on the interactions between teachers and the resources that they use in/for their teaching. Learning from Pepin & Gueudet (2013) and amending their categories for our use, we categorize teacher e-resources in the following way:

- e-text resources: e.g. e-textbooks, online teacher curricular guidelines, Web sites, and online student worksheets;
- e-based "material" resources: e.g. interactive whiteboards, computer software, applets;
- e-based works and exchanges: e.g. mail exchanges with colleagues, pupils, and parents; pupil work submitted electronically (such as online homework).

According to Adler (2000), a resource is anything likely to *re-source* the work of the teacher. Teachers search for resources, retain some resources and discard others, modify them, associate them, set them up in class—and as they perform this documentational work, they develop a structured *resource system* (Gueudet & Trouche, 2009a).

Understanding the modifications resulting from the e-textbook means understanding how a teacher's integration and appropriation of the e-textbook in the teacher's resource system modifies this system, and the implications for the teacher's work and professional development.

Window 4—Vera's Use of Sésamath E-Textbook

Vera teaches mathematics at a middle school. She uses the Sésamath e-textbook (Window 1), amongst other textbooks, for all her classes. With the video projector, she shows extracts of the e-textbook in class, including lesson texts, animations with Dynamic Geometry software, and interactive exercises.

Figure 27.5 Solving an interactive exercise in class.

Vera also programs exercise sessions on LaboMEP (Window 1 and Window 5), which the students can do in class, but mostly complete as homework. She has access to the individual and collective summary of their activity, and uses it to plan remedial activities for selected students.

Her grade 6 students have the Sésamath paper textbook as their common text. However, for this class Vera does not follow the curriculum plan of the Sésamath textbook (which is directly transferred from the official national curriculum). She has her own textbook, *Helice* (English translation: helix), and follows its spiral progression, hence deepening pupils' understanding by revisiting particular topics (Gueudet et al., 2013b).

In a teacher's resource system, e-textbooks are associated with other resources: resources linked with the projection in class (the computer and video projector in the classroom, the screen, sometimes an interactive whiteboard, Dynamic Geometry software); resources linked with the preparation of worksheets to be handed out to students (files on the teacher's computer that are printed out and handed to students). Other resources are linked with out-of-class work: specific sessions that can be programmed for the students, and a Virtual Learning Environment. Considering these changes in the teacher's resource system evidences changes in the teacher's activity and proposes potential further changes (which would require further investigation).

Designing worksheets for students with a summary of the main properties, and "holes" to be filled in (in class) is certainly common practice. This practice can be supported if the teacher has access to the textbook's. doc or. odt files. Similarly, the use of projection devices is frequent, which can also be fostered by the use of an e-textbook, which constitutes, both for the teacher and the students, a shared reference easy to project. The collective solving of exercises by the whole class, and managed by the teacher, does not require an e-textbook. However, students seem more motivated when an interactive exercise is displayed (see Figure 27.5). In terms of out-of-class work, e-textbooks can offer possibilities, for example, for differentiation (attending to individual pupils' needs) and checking work. With particular programs linked to e-textbooks, homework can be checked by the teacher out of class (see Figure 27.6, the summary provided for each pupil by LaboMEP), and the results and formative assessments communicated to individual pupils. Supplementary work can be provided in differentiated form and different homework can be provided to individual students. Moreover, students seem more motivated to work on interactive exercises, and may be more engaged in related homework—at least in the present context of relative novelty of this kind of digital material. Taking into account the needs of individual students, or particular student groups can be

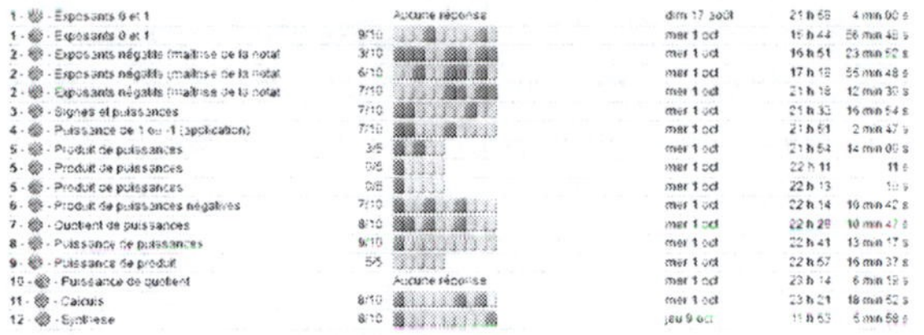

Figure 27.6 Following the work of a student in LaboMEP.

considered an important dimension for the quality of mathematics teaching and management of pupil/teacher work. Whilst we do not claim here that these possibilities are actually used by many teachers—this would require further investigation—the e-textbook certainly offers interesting possibilities in this respect. Nevertheless, in the cases we studied (Gueudet & Trouche, 2009a, Gueudet et al., 2013a), we noticed that the use of the e-textbook was linked to the provision of differentiated tasks. In the perspective of documentational genesis we propose that this can be interpreted as knowledge development: using the e-textbook fosters the development of professional knowledge about the management of tasks in a heterogeneous class.

We also observed, in the case of an e-textbook being designed by a group of teachers (e.g. Sésamath), that the users/teachers were able to introduce/suggest modifications to the content, and in this way participate in the design process of the e-textbook. Evidently, not all suggestions by users yield modifications to the content (shared by the Sésamath authors)—in particular because not all the suggestions are relevant, but also because continuous modifications are time-consuming for the authors (Trgalovà & Jahn, 2013). Considering various potential contributions and contributors to the e-textbook, how can the quality and the coherence of an e-textbook be examined and defined? We discuss this in the next section.

E-TEXTBOOKS AND CHANGING RESEARCH CATEGORIES: TOWARDS A RECONCEPTUALIZATION OF TEXTBOOK QUALITY AND COHERENCE

In this chapter we have described the design of e-textbooks, developed a working definition of e-textbooks, and identified three different types/models of e-textbooks. We have also described their use by teachers and students. We have provided evidence that an e-textbook can be collaboratively designed, and that its content can be coauthored, in terms of modifications, by its users. These developments imply major evolutions in how textbooks operate in schools and raise questions about how (a) the "quality"; and (b) the "coherence" of textbooks change as textbooks become e-textbooks. What does mathematical quality/coherence mean, if the teacher can change the e-textbook elements? It is clear that these evolutions require serious consideration, and possibly a reconceptualization of the notions of "quality" and "coherence" with respect to e-textbooks.

A Reconceptualization of Quality

Quality of Textbooks

The quality of textbooks has been the subject of many studies, not least because they play a vital role in educational practice and curricula provide a "crucial link between standards and accountability measures" (Confrey & Stohl, 2004). Evaluation studies can provide information on how effective a particular curriculum is, and for whom and under what conditions. In the United States a National Research Council committee (2004) examined a large array of evaluation studies. The committee did not evaluate the curriculum materials directly (or indeed rank particular programs), neither did it provide criteria for evaluating textbooks, but it identified four types of evaluation studies: (1) content analyses (examining the content of curriculum materials: e.g. accuracy, depth of coverage, logical sequencing of topics, etc.); (2) comparative studies (comparing two or more curricula and their effects on student learning); (3) case studies (documenting how programs and components of curricula of a particular curriculum play out in classrooms); and (4) synthesis studies (summarizing several evaluation studies across a particular curriculum). This work highlights the importance of the quality of curriculum materials.

Concerning more specific studies for the examination of the notion of "quality," selected authors consider a macro level and analyze quality with a more "global" appreciation; e.g. Charalambous, Delaney, Hsu, and Mesa (2010) propose a "horizontal" analysis of the textbook where the textbook "is examined as a whole, as part of technology in the educational system" (p. 119). Studies on this level include those that focus on general textbook characteristics (e.g. Schmidt et al., 1997, Stevenson & Bartsch, 1992).

Other studies consider a micro level; they analyze textbooks for quality, according to their particular aims (e.g. Oesterholm & Bergqvist, 2013). Often, in these studies a single mathematical concept is examined (e.g. Li, 2000, Mesa, 2010), viewing the textbook as an "environment for construction of knowledge" (Herbst, 1995, p. 3). Charalambous and colleagues (2010) would call this a "vertical analysis." They developed a three-layered framework to analyze textbooks (from three countries) to investigate the learning opportunities offered by textbooks. In our view, learning opportunities are closely linked to "knowledge construction" and to "learning mathematics with understanding." During the past decades there has been much concern and discussion about learning opportunities linked to students' conceptual understanding and with respect to students' developing expertise in terms of mathematical thinking, reasoning, and problem-solving (e.g. National Research Council, 1989, Hiebert & Carpenter, 1992, Hiebert et al., 1997).

Quality of Online Resources

Assessing the quality of online resources is a complex issue. Several research works have considered the issue of quality of online resources in mathematics and in science, in particular with a focus on their potential for investigation. The Intergeo project (Kortenkamp et al., 2009) concerns resources using Dynamic Geometry, and the research introduces nine dimensions for studying the quality of such a resource for inquiry: metadata (names of the authors, theme, date etc.), technical aspect, mathematical content, instrumental content, added-value of dynamic geometry, didactical implementation (learning objectives, adaptation to different kinds of pupils etc.), pedagogical implementation (organization in the class, management of different parts etc.), integration in a teaching sequence, and ergonomic aspects (ease of identification of the different texts, links etc.). Moreover, considering the importance of a resource's adequacy with respect to the users' needs, Intergeo has designed an assessment of quality by the users themselves (Trgalovà, Jahn, & Soury-Lavergne, 2009). This assessment can potentially lead to a further design of the resource, by and involving the users. Drawing on this work and on other studies in science education, Bueno-Ravel et al. (2009) propose seven dimensions for assessing the quality of an online resource for inquiry-based science learning and teaching: scientific aspects, scaffolding inquiry aspects, possible customization, ergonomics, choice of media, possible involvement of the users in the resource design, and possibilities offered for collective work.

In line with the move from traditional curriculum resources to online resources, the notion of "resource evaluation" has been replaced by the notion of "resource quality" (see Pepin et al., 2013b). Recent research about the quality of online resources for the teaching and learning of mathematics (Trouche et al., 2013) stresses in particular the importance of the ease of *appropriation* of the resource by the user. The involvement of users in the resource design, more generally the possibility of communication between the designers and the users of an online resource, can thus be retained as an important dimension for quality. This dimension can be related with the issue of connectivity (Hoyles et al., 2010), which encompasses in particular the potential for creating virtual communities. We draw on this idea to propose a reconceptualization of quality, in the case of e-textbooks.

Quality of E-Textbooks

It can be assumed that e-textbooks combine the features of textbooks and of online resources. We thus suggest studying the quality of e-textbooks by combining the two perspectives evoked earlier.

Connectivity is certainly an important dimension for the quality of an e-textbook. The potential to create virtual communities, connecting users and users (both teachers and students), as well as users and designers, can be considered as *connectivity at a macro level*. Moreover, at this macro level, the connectivity of the e-textbook can also mean that it actually interacts with other resources via Web links, or on a platform for example (see Window 5). More generally, this **macro level** for connectivity could include the following criteria, which we group under two headings, in order to assess the quality of an e-textbook:

EXISTING CONNECTIONS

- Connections between resources provided by the e-textbook;
- Connections to other resources outside the e-textbook (e.g. Geogebra);
- Connections across grades;
- Connections to the national curriculum.

POTENTIAL CONNECTIONS AFFORDED BY THE E-TEXTBOOK

- Connections between e-textbook and teacher resource system (for synergistic effects);
- Connections in terms of teacher collective work, e.g. connecting teacher resource system in a school, or professional community (see LaboMEP in Window 5);
- Connections between teacher and students;
- Connections to "larger" teacher needs/relevance (e.g. e-textbook as a means to prepare lessons) or pupils (e.g. revision for tests)
- Connections between teachers using the textbook and the authors of the textbook.

Moreover, connectivity can also be considered at a **micro level** concerning specific mathematics content. At this level, it means that the e-textbook offers different kinds of articulated materials, and offers connections and links between different features. We consider these at two levels:

EXISTING CONNECTIONS

- Connections between different topic areas;
- Connections between different semiotic representations (text, figures, static and dynamic), in order to develop a flexible awareness of the different facets of the mathematical content);
- Connections between different software for carrying out the same task, in order to develop a flexible use of technology.

POTENTIAL CONNECTIONS AFFORDED BY THE E-TEXTBOOK

- Connecting different concepts of a same conceptual field (Vergnaud, 1996);
- Connecting different strategies for problem solving;
- Connecting different moments of appropriating a given concept (e.g. spiral progression).

In Window 5 we show selected connections in the case of the Sésamath textbook.

Window 5—Sésamath Textbook Connectivity

SÉSAMATH TEXTBOOKS, CONNECTIVITY AT THE MICRO LEVEL

Each exercise in the Sésamath e-textbooks is connected with "complements." These complements can include, for example, Dynamic Geometry constructions to be done by the students, or with interactive helps (dynamic presentations of a solving method). Thus, we can claim that the Sésamath textbooks offer a lot of possible connections between representations.

At the same time, in previous works (Gueudet et al., 2013b) analyzing the Sésamath grade 6 textbook we have observed that the primary-secondary transition was not really taken into account, since the authors were not familiar with primary school curriculum—and this is an important missing connection, a criterion to retain in assessing quality. We have also noticed that the organization of the book, according to the official curriculum entries, does not favor connections between mathematical topics.

SÉSAMATH TEXTBOOK WITHIN LABOMEP, CONNECTIVITY AT THE MACRO LEVEL

The Sésamath e-textbooks are part of a wider Virtual Learning Environment, LaboMEP (see Window 1). Once connected in LaboMEP, the teacher has access to all Sésamath resources (left column, Figure 27.7), including the e-textbooks. The teacher can choose extracts of the e-textbook such as lessons or exercises and insert them into a personal session she/he is building (central column). All his/her sessions are recorded and saved in his/her personal space (right column). Each session can include extracts from the textbook and also online exercises, geometric constructions with Dynamic Geometry software, or even external Web links. Thus the Sésamath textbooks are connected, via LaboMEP, to a very large set of potential resources. The teacher can also share his/her sessions with other colleagues, groups of colleagues can design *a shared resources repertoire* that appears as shared resources in the left column; s/he

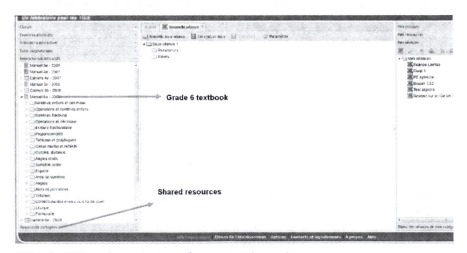

Figure 27.7 LaboMEP, teacher environment for programming sessions.

can also communicate with Sésamath members. But LaboMEP is above all a communication tool between the teacher and his/her students, via the sessions programmed by the teacher for them.

Connectivity is considered here as a feature of digital content. Nevertheless, in particular at the micro level, it suggests the possibility of defining a new, more general notion of connectivity. Hiebert et al. (1997) argue that "learning mathematics with understanding" is linked to "making connections." "Connectedness" is not a new idea in the field of education, or indeed in mathematics education. Hiebert and Carpenter (1992), for example, believe that it is essential to make connections in mathematics if one intends to develop mathematical understanding. They emphasize the importance of learning with and for understanding. According to them, understanding can be defined as:

> [T]he way information is represented and structured. A mathematical idea or fact is understood if its mental representation is part of a network of representations. The degree of understanding is determined by the number and strength of the connections.
>
> (Hiebert & Carpenter, 1992, p. 67)

The digital means can be used, within an e-textbook, to provide a network of representations. Nevertheless, such possibilities also exist in traditional textbooks. These textbooks can also foster the development of connections by the students, by offering rich mathematical tasks. It is indeed important that students have "frequent opportunities to engage in dynamic mathematical activity that is grounded in rich, worthwhile mathematical tasks" (Henningsen & Stein, 1997, p. 525), and it is argued that this is an essential component for understanding in order for connections to be made by the learner (Hiebert et al., 1997). Thus, we suggest that the idea of connectivity at the micro level could be extended beyond the case of digital textbooks, to define a kind of "mathematical connectivity," which could be an essential feature for quality of any textbook. This requires nevertheless further studies, complementing this chapter.

Coherence of the Design and Coherence for Use

Similar to our considerations earlier, we propose to reconsider/conceptualize the notion of "coherence." The coherence of a textbook can encompass many different aspects, as pointed out in Gueudet et al. (2013a): correctness of the mathematical content; consistency with the national curriculum; correctness of the sequencing of notions, of the articulation between the course and the exercises; etc. Yerushalmy and Chazan (2008), drawing on Tall (2002), propose that coherence involves how the character of the objects of study is handled.

We want to emphasize here three specific dimensions of e-textbooks that should be taken into account to evaluate their coherence.

1. *Initial design coherence*: In contrast to traditional textbooks that are often designed by a small number/team of experts (e.g. a coordinate designer chooses a number of "acquainted" colleagues; see Gueudet et al., 2013b), e-textbooks are commonly designed by a larger collective (e.g. by teachers working together, or teachers and inspectors/ teacher educators working together). In the case of a small expert teams, these typically meet on a regular basis to insure the coherence of the process of design, whereas a large team of designers (as in the Sésamath case), not chosen but volunteered, is not likely to ever meet as a whole, but divides the design into compartmentalized tasks for each subteam (e.g. division according to topic areas). Hence the strategies for "insuring coherence" become crucial for e-textbooks with large designer teams. In this case, coherence can also mean that "the individual mathematical intentions of the individual authors, their epistemological stances, are well coordinated" (Gueudet et al., 2013a, p. 328). Assessing the coherence of such a textbook requires identifying these intentions

and stances to evaluate their coordination, the production, during the design process, of a shared intention shaping the choices of content.

2. *Product coherence* (strongly linked to quality): Yerushalmy and Chazan (2008) show how technological tools (e.g. graphing tools, symbol manipulators, spreadsheets) carry with them particular orientations toward the representations of function used in algebra classrooms. Using the notion of "discontinuities" (Tall, 2002), Yerushalmy and Chazan suggest that algebra curricula must negotiate the discontinuities between these symbol systems. Thus, the rollout of students' use of technological tools can be in conflict with or support textbook expositions. This is a different sense of "coherence" (sequencing of topics and uses of technology) compared to ones used with traditional print curricula: for example, graphing tools can offer different affordances in terms of different views of equations that may or may not be in tension with textbook exposition. Linking to this, it can be argued that e-textbooks (which are supported by and designed for particular technological tools) can provide a particular/different coherence, combining different views and practices (for a particular topic area), different sequencing of ideas within that topic area, and making accessible (through technology) to learners different ideas, perhaps by using different representations and hence different views or notions. Perhaps the integrated design of software and exposition in e-textbook environments has the potential to lead to greater coherence.

3. *Coherence-in-use*: In terms of implications for learning, the most important issue linked to coherence is likely to be the "coherence" of what teachers propose to their students, drawing on the textbook/curriculum materials (Pepin, 2012). As several authors point out (e.g. Shield & Dole, 2013, Lloyd, 2009) analyzing textbooks and other curriculum materials (e.g. in professional development activities) provide only limited support for the development of teachers' pedagogic practice, and coherence-in-use is dependent on how teachers actually use the resources. In many cases "teacher guides" provide guidelines of how authors/designer teams consider the use of the textbooks, and these guidelines link to the designers' pedagogical intentions.

We explain and exemplify the three dimensions in Window 6. The *initial design coherence* might be studied drawing on texts actually inserted in the book, or associated with it, which present the authors' stance and their didactical objectives.

Window 6—Sésamath Textbook Coherence, the Authors Didactical Choices

The Sésamath e-textbook for grade 6 starts with a classical table of contents complemented by the line of buttons above the text, labeled by the chapter numbers, and displaying the title of the chapter when the mouse is on the button. Then two pages present choices of structure (Figure 27.8), in terms of nature of activities proposed. Two other pages present the numerical complement present on each page. Three pages propose advice to the pupils, for the use of the textbook. Thus, we contend that an autonomous use of the textbook by pupils seems to be one objective of the authors.

The chapters correspond to the titles of the official curriculum (e.g. fractions, symmetry), except for two chapters dedicated to the articulation with primary school (N0 about integers and G0 about geometry), and one "synthesis chapter" that proposes more elaborate problems (for example "complex tasks," as required by the official curriculum). There is also a dictionary (*lexique*) at the "end" of the book: pupils can refer to it, if they meet an expression or word they do not know. This is particularly useful for mathematical language/expressions. The organization of each chapter is classical (except for the synthesis chapter): introductory activities, course, direct application exercises, exercises, multiple choice (self-testing) and mathematical games. A very important choice of the authors (also aligned with the institutional

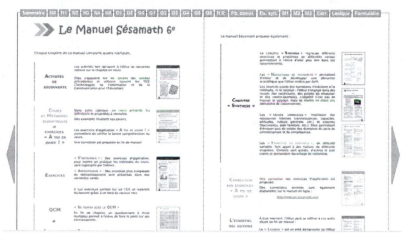

Figure 27.8 Sésamath grade 6 e-textbook, explanations about the structure of the textbook.

expectations) is an important use of information and communications technology (ICT), in the introductory activities and in exercises (identified by a special color).

E-textbooks can also be analyzed by studying the design process itself and following the choices of content and structure: see Sabra & Trouche (2011), or Gueudet, Sabra, Pepin & Trouche (in press). However, such studies would require specific design and data collection strategies. One way to study the design of an e-textbook would be to use design-based methods, because the e-text will be a document that is constantly changing based on an iterative process. Further, the coherence of the design can be studied by analyzing (a) the book's content, searching for didactic choices common to different sections and different components of the book; and (b) the "e-traces" left by authors/author team: e.g. traces of the design process and traces of the "design contract" (what did the designer team do to ensure the coherence of the e-textbook?) At this macro level, assessing coherence requires to consider a collection of tasks/text, typically a whole textbook for a given grade. Leaning on the works of the 22nd ICMI study on task design (Margolinas, 2013, Theme C), coherence of such published collections is related to "the overall philosophy of the collection . . . beliefs about the nature of mathematics and what it means to do or learn mathematics vary and are manifested in the nature of the texts and tasks" (p. 13).

Product coherence and *coherence-in-use* are closely connected. Whilst an analysis in terms of *product coherence* may show the e-textbook's affordances, for example, to favor a particular learning path (e.g. a hyperlink proposes another notion of the hyperlinked word), the final use of the e-textbook also depends on the teachers' choices (e.g. of tasks in the book). Coherence clearly depends on these two connected factors: the affordances of the book (e.g. the learning paths/trajectories) and the teacher's particular use. In the recent research literature (e.g. Cohen, Raudenbush, & Loewenberg Ball, 2003, Charalambous et al., 2010, Cai, Wang, & Ding, 2014) the term *coherence* is often linked to the *coherence of instruction* (e.g. Hiebert et al., 2003, Stigler & Hiebert, 1999), which was seen more prominently in Japanese lessons, for example, than in U.S. classroom instruction—this links to our notion of coherence-in-use. Moreover, and linking coherence-in-use to product coherence, coherence of curriculum resources/materials and textbooks, as we see it, is related to sequencing of topics (for instructional purposes), for example learning trajectory/ies (e.g. "curriculum coherence," Schmidt & Huang, 2012), to instructional issues. Hence, in our discussion of coherence, we refer more particularly to coherence of e-textbooks with respect to sequencing of topics, learning trajectories, and instructional issues.

Recently, Cai et al. (2014) conducted a study in which they investigated Chinese and U.S. mathematics teachers' views about instructional coherence. They distinguish between "surface" (e.g. designed in advance of the lesson) and "real" coherence (achieved in the lesson) in instruction (as would apply for traditional as well as e-textbooks). Interestingly, studying textbooks and student thinking for lesson preparation were two of the most-mentioned approaches by Chinese teachers in order to achieve coherence at the lesson design stage. Whilst emerging classroom events may disrupt this surface coherence, it is still part of the development of real coherence. The study points to two kinds of instructional coherence: "predesigned"; and "emerging"/"situational," and teachers are said to need both for real coherence. This view goes hand-in-hand with our understandings of coherence in e-textbooks, which is linked to instructional issues, and it suggests to reconceptualize coherence from a "dynamic, co-constructive and situational perspective" (Cai et al., 2014, p. 25).

CONCLUSION

In this chapter, we worked towards a definition of e-textbooks, identified and described three different model types, and analyzed their design and use. Moreover, we have argued that these new technological artifacts have the potential to change traditional relationships between student and textbook, teacher and textbook, and between students and teachers, as well as categories used by educational researchers. The e-textbooks' affordances offer new possibilities for student and teacher agency. This raises questions about differences and similarities of student/teacher agency, and how they play out at different levels/stages of mathematics learning. At the university level, teachers (and perhaps students) have the ability—and in many countries the possibility—to develop their own teaching/learning paths through the topic area, and they are likely to benefit from the collaboration opportunities offered by e-textbooks. The situation may be very different at the primary school level, as primary-school teachers are often not specialized in mathematics and are more likely to rely on the textbook (e.g. to be "assured" that their teaching is in line with governmental guidance, in order to provide an "accepted" coherence in their learning paths/opportunities for pupils). We propose this first limitation of the potential impact of e-textbooks: exploiting their potential requires a certain level of expertise, and the provision of specific professional development programs to support the development of this expertise.

In his article, Friesen (2013) leans on Kuhn (1962) to consider that textbooks, in line with their traditional pedagogic and didactic function, tend to present accumulation of knowledge rather than shifts of paradigms. Friesen (2013) asks: "What is it that textbooks provide pedagogically and epistemologically, besides a reminder of the past?" (p. 498). Textbooks cannot provide access to the process of production of the scientific knowledge/concepts they present. However, students and teachers can—collectively or individually—work and elaborate on e-textbook contents. This certainly changes the relationships between students, teachers, and textbooks. But does it really affect the teaching and learning processes, the educational institution at large? Friesen (2013) sees the textbook as "an evolving pedagogical form," and considers that its components changed "not so much through technological innovation as in synchrony with larger cultural and epistemological developments" (p. 498). With reference to e-textbooks, this begs the question whether the e-textbook changes the user, or the user's intentions/epistemological beliefs change the e-textbook. In line with our research results, we consider that any change happens *in interaction* between user/s and the book (see Yerushalmy & Chazan, 2002, 2008; Gueudet et al., 2012), hence our phrasing of "design-in-use" (Pepin et al., 2013a).

At the same time we concur with Friesen (2013) that textbook features "provide an indispensable animating didactic function," and that textbooks are an "evolving pedagogical form," to point to the synergy between e-textbooks and users. Having said that, we consider that we have contributed to an understanding of e-textbooks by comparing "old" and "new" designs of e-textbooks: for the moment we investigate new designs of e-textbooks as compared to previous designs. That means that we view the developments as stages of evolution rather than revolution. We consider that we do not yet have sufficient examples of research studies that have examined the teaching, learning, and designs of e-textbook communities, and hence the new ideas and concepts, including terminologies, are still vague. However, we have attempted to provide reconceptualizations of categories and concepts that we propose here for researchers, practitioners, and policy makers: from static quality to dynamic quality; from design (and implementation) to design-in-use; from teachers making connections (for their students), to e-textbooks making/providing connections for teachers (also amongst teachers/colleagues/principals) and students (and parents); from static coherence to coherence-in-use; from individual design and use to collective design and use—all due to the affordances of a changing digital environment and the accompanying (potentially) changing practices and mindsets.

If teachers become more engaged in the development of e-textbooks, they will develop, and redevelop, their own categories for the change/development of the e-textbook, and more generally for the design of their teaching. Hence, we consider that a new paradigm in terms of teaching is accompanied by, and necessitates, the development/design of new books, tools, and pedagogically innovative ideas.

However, the existence of new artifacts is not enough. Technology had always created excessive expectations in the field of education, but technology alone has not yet produced sustained changes in education. There are, however, several examples where a material change in object resulted in the development of new paradigms. This is what happened to the picture album when it was transformed into a digital folder, causing pictures to play a completely new visual, social, semiotic role. Music (as text), after it was converted to digital formats, changed from a passive market commodity into a creative, engaged process. Even if at present the only noticeable benefit of digital textbooks is the fact that the object is cheap, efficient, and easy to use anywhere, the examples reviewed in this chapter (see for example the Sésamath experience) suggest that more substantial challenges are just around the corner, opening new ways for teacher collaboration and creativity.

REFERENCES

Adler, J. (2000). Conceptualising resources as a theme for teacher education. *Journal of Mathematics Teacher Education, 3*, 205–224.

Bremigan, E. G. (2005). An analysis of diagram modification and construction in students' solutions to applied calculus problems. *Journal for Research in Mathematics Education, 36*(3), 248–277.

Brown, M. (2009). The teacher-tool relationship: theorising the design and use of curriculum materials. In J. Remillard, G. Lloyd, & B. Herbel-Eisenmann (Eds.), *Mathematics teachers at work: connecting curriculum materials and classroom instruction* (pp. 17–36). New York: Routledge.

Bueno-Ravel, L., Ferrière, H., Forest, D., Gueudet, G., Laubé, S., Kuster, Y., & Sensevy, G. (2009). Technologies, resources, and inquiry-based science teaching. A literature review. *Deliverable 5.1, Mind the Gap FP7 project 217725* (p. 32). Retrieved from www.migaproject.eu.

Cai, J., Wang, T., & Ding, M. (2014). How do exemplary Chinese and US Mathematics teachers view instructional coherence? *Educational Studies in Mathematics, 85*, 265–280.

Cartier, P. , & Chemla, K. (2000). La création des noms mathématiques: l'exemple de Bourbaki. In D. Rousseau, & M. Morvan (Eds.), *La dénomination, le Temps des savoirs* (Vol. 1, pp. 153–170). Paris: IHES.

Charalambous, C. Y., Delaney, S., Hsu, H. Y., & Mesa, V. (2010). A comparative analysis of the addition and subtraction of fractions in textbooks from three countries. *Mathematical Thinking and Learning, 12*, 117–151.

Chazan, D., & Yerushalmy, M. (2003). On appreciating the cognitive complexity of school algebra: Research on algebra learning and directions of curricular change. In J. Kilpatrick, D. Schifter, & G. Martin (Eds.), *A Research Companion to the Principles and Standards for School Mathematics*. Reston, VA: National Council of Teachers of Mathematics.

Chazan, D., & Yerushalmy, M. (2014). The future of mathematics textbooks: ramifications of technological change. In M. Stochetti (Ed.), *Media and Education in the Digital Age: a critical introduction.* New York: Peter Lang.

Choppin, J., Carson, C., Borys, Z., Cerosaletti, C., & Gillis, R. (2014). A typology for analyzing digital curricula in mathematics education. *International Journal of Education in Mathematics, Science and Technology, 2*(1), 11–25.

Cohen, D. K., Raudenbush, S. W., & Loewenberg Ball, D. (2003). Resources, instruction and research. *Educational Evaluation and Policy Analysis, 25*(2), 119–142.

Collopy, R.M.B. (2003). Curriculum materials as a professional development tool: How a mathematics textbook affected two teachers' learning. *Elementary School Journal, 103*(3), 287–311.

Confrey, J., & Stohl, V. (Eds.) (2004). *On evaluating curricular effectiveness: Judging the quality of K–12 mathematics evaluations.* Washington, DC: National Academies Press.

Drucker, P. (1992). *The age of discontinuity: Guidelines to our changing society.* New York: Harper & Row.

Fan, L. (2013). Textbook research as scientific research: towards a common ground on issues and methods of research on mathematics textbooks. *ZDM—The International Journal on Mathematics Education, 45*(5), 765–777.

Fan, L., Zhu, Y., & Miao, Z. (2013). Textbook research in mathematics education: development status and directions. *ZDM—The International Journal on Mathematics Education, 45*(5), 633–646.

Friesen, N. (2013). The past and likely future of an educational form: A textbook case. *Educational researcher, 42,* 498–508.

Goldenberg, P., & Mason, J. (2008). Spreading light on and with example spaces. *Educational Studies in Mathematics, 69*(2) 183–194.

Gould, P. (2011). *Electronic mathematics textbooks: Old wine in new skins?* Paper presented at APEC-Tsukuba International Conference V (Tsukuba Session), Japan. Retrieved from www.criced.tsukuba.ac.jp/math/apec/apec2011/19-20/02_PeterGould-paper.pdf.

Guedj, D. (1985). Nicholas Bourbaki, collective mathematician an interview with Claude Chevalley. *The Mathematical Intelligencer, 7*(2), 18–22.

Gueudet, G., Pepin, B., & Trouche, L. (Eds.) (2012). *From text to 'lived' resources: Mathematics curriculum materials and teacher development.* New York: Springer.

Gueudet, G., Pepin, B., & Trouche, L. (2013a). Textbook design and digital resources. In C. Margolinas (Ed.), *Designing and using tasks for learning mathematics,* 22nd ICMI Study. Retrieved from http://hal.archives-ouvertes.fr/docs/00/83/74/88/PDF/ICMI_STudy_22_proceedings_2013-FINAL_V2.pdf.

Gueudet, G., Pepin, B., & Trouche, L. (2013b). Collective work with resources: an essential dimension for teacher documentation. *ZDM—The International Journal on Mathematics Education, 45*(7), 1003–1016.

Gueudet, G., Sabra, H., Pepin, B., & Trouche, L. (in press). Resources, task design and mathematics teachers' collective engagement: towards e-textbooks as shared living resources. *Journal of Mathematics Teacher Education.*

Gueudet, G., & Trouche, L. (2009a). Towards new documentation systems for mathematics teachers? *Educational Studies in Mathematics, 71*(3), 199–218.

Gueudet, G., & Trouche, L. (2009b). Conception et usages de ressources pour et par les professeurs: Développement associatif et développement professionnel. *Dossiers De l'Ingénierie Éducative, 65,* 78–82.

Haggarty, L., & Pepin, B. (2002). An investigation of mathematics textbooks and their use in English, French and German Classrooms: Who gets an opportunity to learn what? *British Educational Research Journal, 28*(4), 567–590.

Henningsen, M., & Stein, M. (1997). Mathematical tasks and student's cognition: Classroom-based factors that support and inhibit high-level mathematical thinking and reasoning. *Journal for Research in Mathematics Education, 28,* 524–94.9.

Herbst, P. (1995). *The construction of the real number system in textbooks: a contribution to the analysis of discoursive practices in mathematics.* Unpublished master's thesis, University of Georgia, Athens.

Herbst, P. (2002). Establishing a custom of proving in American school geometry: evolution of the two-column proof in the early twentieth century. *Educational Studies in Mathematics, 49*(3), 283–312.

Hiebert, J., & Carpenter, T. (1992). Learning and teaching with understanding. In D.A. Grouws (Ed.), *Handbook of research on mathematics teaching and learning* (pp. 65–97). New York: Macmillan.

Hiebert, J., Carpenter, T., Fennema, E., Fuson, K., Wearne, D., Human, P. , Murray, H., & Olivier, A. (1997). *Making sense: teaching and learning mathematics with understanding.* Portsmouth, NH: Heinemann.

Hiebert, J., Gallimore, R., Garnier, H., Giwin, K. B., Hollingsworth, H., Jacobs, J., & Stigler, J. (2003). *Teaching mathematics in seven countries: results from the TIMSS video study.* Washington, DC: U.S. Department of Education, National Center for Educational Statistics.

Hoyles, C., Kalas, I., Trouche, L., Hivon, L., Noss, R., & Wilensky, U. (2010). Connectivity and virtual networks for learning. In C. Hoyles, & J.-B. Lagrange, *Mathematics education and technology-rethinking the terrain* (pp. 439–462). New York: Springer.

Kidwell, P. A., Ackerberg-Hastings, A., & Roberts, D. L. (2008). *Tools of American mathematics teaching, 1800–2000.* Baltimore, MD: The Johns Hopkins University Press.

Korea Education and Research Information Service (KERIS). (2007). Concept map of digital textbook. Retrieved from https://en.wikipedia.org/wiki/File:Concept_of_dt.PNG.

Kortenkamp, U., Blessing, A. M., Dohrmann, C., Kreis, Y., Libbrecht, P., & Mercat, C. (2009). Interoperable interactive geometry for Europe: First technological and educational results and future challenges of the Intergeo project. In V. Durand-Guerrier, S. Soury-Lavergne, & F. Arzarello (Eds.), *Proceedings of the Sixth European Conference on Research on Mathematics Education* (pp. 1150–1160). Lyon: INRP. Retrieved from www.inrp.fr/editions/cerme6.

Kress, G., & van Leeuwen, T. (1996). *Reading images—The grammar of visual design.* London: Routledge.

Kuhn, T. (1962). *The structure of scientific revolutions.* Chicago, IL: University of Chicago Press.

Li, Y. (2000). A comparison of problems that follow selected content presentations in American and Chinese mathematics textbooks. *Journal for Research in Mathematics Education, 31,* 234–241.

Lloyd, G. M. (2009). School mathematics curriculum materials for teachers' learning: future elementary teachers' interactions with curriculum materials in a mathematics course in the United States. *ZDM—The International Journal on Mathematics Education, 41,* 763–775.

Love, E., & Pimm, D. (1996). This is so: a text on texts. In A. Bishop, K. Clements, C. Keitel, J. Kilpatrick, & C. Laborde (Eds.), *International handbook of mathematics education* (Vol. 1, pp. 371–409). New York: Springer.

Margolinas, C. (Ed.). (2013). *Task design in mathematics education.* Proceedings of ICMI Study 22. Oxford. Retrieved from http://hal.archives-ouvertes.fr/docs/00/83/74/88/PDF/ICMI_STudy_22_proceedings_2013-FINAL_V2.pdf.

Mesa, V. (2010). Strategies for controlling the work in mathematics textbooks for introductory calculus. *Research in Collegiate Mathematics Education, 16,* 235–265.

Murata, A. (2008). Mathematics teaching and learning as a mediating process: The case of tape diagrams. *Mathematical Thinking and Learning, 10*(4), 374–406.

Naftaliev, E., & Yerushalmy, M. (2013). Guiding explorations: Design principles and functions of interactive diagrams. *Computers in the Schools, 30*(1–2), 61–75.

National Research Council (1989). *Everybody counts: A report to the nation on the future of mathematics education.* Washington, DC: National Academy Press.

National Research Council. (2004). J. Confrey & V. Stohl (Eds.). *On evaluating curricular effectiveness: Judging the quality of K–12 mathematics evaluations.* Washington, DC: National Academy Press.

Netz, R. (1999). *The shaping of deduction in Greek mathematics: A study in cognitive history.* Cambridge: Cambridge University Press.

Oesterholm, M., & Bergqvist, E. (2013). What is so special about mathematical texts? Analyses of common claims in research literature and of properties of textbooks. *ZDM—The International Journal on Mathematics Education, 45*(5), 751–763.

Pepin, B. (2012). Working with teachers on curriculum materials to develop mathematical knowledge in/for teaching: Task analysis as 'catalytic tool' for feedback and teacher learning. In G. Gueudet, B. Pepin, & L. Trouche (Eds.) *From text to 'lived' resources: Mathematics curriculum material and teacher development* (pp. 123–142). New York: Springer.

Pepin, B., & Gueudet, G. (2013). Curricular resources and textbooks. In S. Lerman (Ed.), *Encyclopedia of mathematics education* (pp 132–135). New York: Springer.

Pepin, B., Gueudet, G., & Trouche, L. (2013a). Investigating textbooks as crucial interfaces between culture, policy and teacher curricular practice: two contrasted case studies in France and Norway. *ZDM—The International Journal on Mathematics Education, 45* (5), 685–698.

Pepin, B., Gueudet, G., & Trouche, L. (2013b). Re-sourcing teachers' work and interactions: a collective perspective on resources, their use and transformation. *ZDM—The International Journal on Mathematics Education, 45*(7), 929–944.

Proust, C. (2012). Masters' writings and students' writings: School material in Mesopotamia. In G. Gueudet, B. Pepin, & L. Trouche (Eds.) *From text to 'lived' resources: Mathematics curriculum material and teacher Development* (pp. 161–180). New York: Springer.

Rezat, S. (2006). A model of textbook use. In J. Novotná, H. Moraová, M. Krátká & N. a. Stehlíko vá (Eds.), *Proceedings of the 30th Conference of the International Group for the Psychology of Mathematics Education* (Vol. 4, pp. 409–416). Prague: Charles University, Faculty of Education.

Rezat, S. (2013). The textbook-in-use: Students' utilization schemes of mathematics textbooks related to self-regulated practicing. *ZDM—The International Journal on Mathematics Education, 45*(5), 659–670.

Robitaille, D., & Travers, K. (1992). International studies of achievement in mathematics. In D. Grouws (Ed.) *Handbook of research on mathematics education* (pp. 687–709). New York: Macmillan Publishing Company.

Sabra, H., & Trouche, L. (2011). Collective design of an online math textbook: when individual and collective documentation works meet. In M. Pytlak, T. Rowland, & E. Swoboda (Eds.), *Proceedings of the Seventh European Conference on Research on Mathematics Education* (pp. 2356–2366). February 9–13, Rzesów, Poland.

Schmidt, W. H. (2012). Measuring content through textbooks: The cumulative effect of middle-school tracking. In G. Gueudet, B. Pepin, & L. Trouche (Eds.) *From text to 'lived' resources: Mathematics curriculum material and teacher development* (pp. 143–160). New York: Springer.

Schmidt, W. H., & Huang, R. T. (2012). Curricular coherence and the Common Core State Standards for Mathematics. *Educational Researcher, 41,* 294–308.

Schmidt, W. H., McKnight, C. C., Valverde, G., Houang, R. T., & Wiley, D. E. (1997). *Many visions, many aims: A cross-national investigation of curricular intentions in school mathematics.* Dordrecht, The Netherlands: Kluwer.

Schubring, G. (1987). On the methodology of analysing historical textbooks: Lacroix as textbook author. *For the Learning of Mathematics, 7*(3), 41–51.

Shield, M., & Dole, S. (2013). Assessing the potential of mathematics textbooks to promote deep learning. *ZDM—The International Journal on Mathematics Education, 45*(5), 183–199.

Stevenson, H.W., & Bartsch, K. (1992). An analysis of Japanese and American textbooks in mathematics. In R. Leetsma, & H. Walberg (Eds.) *Japanese educational productivity* (pp. 103–133). Ann Arbor: Center for Japanese Studies, University of Michigan.

Stigler, J., & Hiebert, J. (1999). *The teaching gap.* New York: Free Press.

Taizan, Y., Bhang, S., Kurokami, H., & Kwon, S. (2012). A comparison of functions and the effect of digital textbook in Japan and Korea. *International Journal for Educational Media and Technology, 6*(1), 85–93.

Tall, D. (2002). Continuities and discontinuities in long-term learning schemas. In D. Tall & M. Thomas (Eds.), *Intelligence, learning and understanding—A tribute to Richard Skemp* (pp. 151–177). Flaxton, Australia: PostPressed.

Tall, D., & Vinner, S. (1981). Concept image and concept definition in mathematics with particular reference to limits and continuity. *Educational Studies in Mathematics, 12*(2), 151–169.

Trgalovà, J., & Jahn, A. P. (2013). Quality issue in the design and use of resources by mathematics teachers. *ZDM—The International Journal on Mathematics Education,45*(7), 973–986.

Trgalovà, J., Jahn, A. P. , & Soury-Lavergne, S. (2009). Quality process for dynamic geometry resources: The Intergeo project. In V. Durand-Guerrier, S. Soury-Lavergne, & F. Arzarello (Eds.), *Proceedings of the Sixth European Conference on Research on Mathematics Education* (pp. 1161–1170). Lyon: INRP. Retrieved from www.inrp. fr/editions/cerme6.

Trouche, L., Drijvers, P., Gueudet, G., & Sacristan, A. I. (2013). Technology-driven developments and policy implications for mathematics education. In A. J. Bishop, M. A. Clements, C. Keitel, J. Kilpatrick, & F.K.S. Leung (Eds.), *Third international handbook of mathematics education* (pp. 753–790). New York: Springer.

Valverde, G. A., Bianchi, L. J., Wolfe, R. G., Schmidt, W. H., & Houang, R. T. (2002). *According to the book—Using TIMSS to investigate the translation of policy into practice through the world of textbooks.* Dordrecht, The Netherlands: Kluwer Academic Publishers.

Vergnaud, G. (1996). The theory of conceptual fields. In L. P. Steffe, P. Nesher, P. Cobb, G.A. Goldin, & B. Greer (Eds.), *Theories of mathematical learning* (pp. 219–239). Mahwah, NJ: Lawrence Erlbaum Associates.

Vieillard-Baron, E. (2009). Sesamath, un modèle de mutualisation et de diffusion gratuite de ressources mathématiques. In *Séminaire international thématique ePrep*, Institut Henri Poincaré, Paris. Retrieved from www.eprep.org/seminaires/seminaire09/comm_sem09/ePrep09_Sesamath_descriptif.pdf.

Watson, A., & Shipman, S. (2008). Using learner-generated examples to introduce new concepts. *Educational Studies in Mathematics, 69*(2), 97–109.

Westbury, I. (1990). Textbooks, textbook publishers, and the quality of schooling. In D. Elliott & A. Woodward (Eds.), *Textbooks and schooling in the United States: 89th yearbook of the National Society for the Study of Education* (Part 1, pp. 1–22). Chicago: University of Chicago.

Yerushalmy, M. (2005). Function of interactive visual representations in interactive mathematical textbooks. *International Journal of Computers for Mathematical learning, 10*(3), 217–249.

Yerushalmy, M. (2013). Designing for inquiry in school mathematics. *Educational Designer, 2*(6). Retrieved from www.educationaldesigner.org/ed/volume2/issue6/article22/.

Yerushalmy, M., & Chazan, D. (2002). Flux in school algebra: Curricular change, graphing technology, and research on student learning and teacher knowledge. In L. English (Ed.) *Handbook of international research in mathematics education* (pp. 725–756). Hillsdale, NJ: Lawrence Erlbaum Associates.

Yerushalmy, M., & Chazan, D. (2008). Technology and curriculum design: The ordering of discontinuities in school algebra. In L. English (Ed.) *Handbook of international research in mathematics education* (2nd ed., pp. 806–837). London: Routledge.

Yerushalmy, M., Katriel, H., & Shternberg, B. (2004). VisualMath: Function. Interactive mathematics text. Ramat-Aviv: The Centre of Educational Technology. Retrieved from www.cet.ac.il/math/function/english.

28 Digital Technologies in the Early Primary School Classroom

Nathalie Sinclair

Simone Fraser University (Canada)

Anna Baccaglini-Frank

University of Modena and Reggio Emilia (Italy)

INTRODUCTION

Papert's (1980) work with Turtle Geometry offered an early and provocative vision of how digital technologies could be used with young learners. Since then, research on digital technology use has focused on the middle- and high-school levels (notable exceptions include Sarama & Clements, 2002; Hoyles, Noss, & Adamson, 2002). Given the increasing diversity of digital technologies, and their varied underlying pedagogical goals and design choices, Clements' (2002) claim that "there is no single effect of the computer on mathematics achievement" (p. 174) is as true now as it was a decade ago. However, many advances have been made in better articulating the range of design choices that are possible, their potential effect on the cognitive and affective dimensions on mathematics learning, and their varying demands on the teacher. The aim of this chapter is to summarize the research literature on the use of digital technologies in the teaching and learning of mathematics at the K–2 level. In particular, we focus on literature that contributes to our understanding of *how* the use of digital technologies affects and changes the teaching and learning of mathematics—that is, how different affordances and design choices impact on the way teachers and learners interact and express themselves mathematically. By digital technologies we refer to a range of tools including multipurpose computer-based software programs, Web-based applets, virtual manipulatives, programming languages, CD-ROMs, games, calculators, touch-screen applications, and interactive whiteboards. The distinction between these various types is not always evident[1] and, indeed, one goal of this chapter is to provide useful distinguishing features of these various technologies in order to help educators better evaluate and choose amongst them.

We begin by outlining some of the major theoretical developments that are shaping the way researchers are studying the use of digital technologies; we hope that some of these developments, which originate in research conducted for the middle and high school grades, can inform research at the younger grade levels, thus building on decades-old insights and constructs. We then present an overview of research related first to two content areas of the primary school curriculum—number sense and geometry—and then to a mix of content areas approached through the use of programming languages. Where possible, we try to describe the particular affordances of the digital technology involved—that is, the kinds of interactions that can be performed—acknowledging that intended affordances may not always be perceived as possible by users.[2] We are also aware of the fact that many of the tools we describe may quickly disappear, to be replaced by new interpretations or available on new platforms. We have thus tried to focus attention on the design principles that may have relevance beyond specific examples. At the end of the chapter we discuss several themes that emerge from our survey of the literature and recommend future research directions.

HISTORICAL AND THEORETICAL PERSPECTIVES

The use of digital technologies in the early grades has traditionally encountered opposition by those concerned that children at this age need tactile, concrete experiences. Indeed, the K–2 classroom has long featured the use of physical manipulatives, with both researchers and teachers acknowledging their importance (Sowell, 1989). This presence of a rich set of resources in the classroom may in fact make it easier for digital technologies to be integrated, in comparison to the higher grades where the technologies of paper-and-pencil usually prevail. Indeed, over the past decade, several researchers have argued for the appropriateness and benefit of using "virtual manipulatives" (VMs) in the early grades, which build on the familiarity of physical ones, but which may also provide a range of added affordances (Bolyard & Moyer-Packenham, 2012; Moyer-Packenham & Suh, 2012; Moyer-Packenham, Salkind, Bolyard, & Suh, 2013). These researchers have questioned the assumption that "concrete" tools are more appropriate for young children and have argued that physical manipulatives are limited in their ability to promote both mathematical actions and reflections on these actions (Sarama & Clements, 2009). Sarama and Clements point specifically to a VM's potential for supporting the development of *integrated-concrete* knowledge, which interconnects knowledge of physical objects, actions on these objects and symbolic representations of these objects and actions. They offer seven hypothesized, interrelated affordances that have been ratified by an admittedly small amount of existing research: bringing mathematical ideas and action to conscious awareness; encouraging and facilitating complete, precise explanations; supporting mental "actions on objects"; changing the very nature of the manipulative; symbolizing mathematical concepts; linking the concrete and the symbolic with feedback; and recording and replaying student actions. Thus, one way to approach the design and evaluation of particular tools is to see whether these affordances are present in the tool in a way that is relevant to the mathematical concept under investigation and accessible to both teachers and learners. We will use these affordances as a way of describing and contrasting the various VMs presented in the next sections.

These affordances, of course, are not unique to VMs and offer a compelling set of macro-level goals for digital technology design. However, they say little about the forms of interaction that different digital technologies might offer. Sedig and Sumner (2006) propose a framework that distinguishes three forms of interaction that are "based on three fundamental, root metaphors derived from the way in which humans use their bodies to interact with the external world" (p. 9): conversing, manipulating, and navigating. Conversing interactions are ones in which learners issue an input action—which can be done through, for example, procedure-based programming languages, text-based menus, and pen-based gestures. *Conversing* interactions are usually *discrete* in that there is a separation between the learner's actions and the computer-based reaction. For example, clicking a button on the screen that rotates a shape is an example of a discrete conversing interaction. *Manipulating* interactions involve touching, handling, or grasping element(s) on a screen through selecting, dragging, and moving. Such interactions are usually considered more tangible than conversing ones in that learners can "reach their hand" into the screen to handle the objects. They are often *continuous* in contrast to *discrete*, as exemplified by the interaction of a learner dragging the vertex of a shape to rotate it, so that cause and effect are observed simultaneously.[3] *Navigating* interactions involve moving on, over, or through the screen. The majority of digital technologies researched at the K–2 level focus primarily on manipulating and conversing interactions. This may be in part due to the number-focused nature of most of these technologies, since navigating interactions are more associated with spatial reasoning. All three interactions can have either a *direct* or *indirect* "focus," this distinction being based on whether the learner is directly interacting with a screen object or interacting with it through an intermediary representation. When a learner is rotating a triangle by dragging one of its vertices, the interaction is direct, but if the learner is dragging a dial in order to rotate the triangle, the interaction is indirect.

Goodwin and Highfield (2013) offer a somewhat different characterization of digital technologies, which focuses more on their constraints and underlying pedagogy: instructive, manipulable, and constructive. *Instructive* digital technologies tend to promote procedural learning, relying on evaluative feedback and repetitive interactions with imposed representations. *Manipulable* digital technologies enable the imposed representations to be manipulated so as to engage students in discovery and experimentation. There is much overlap between this category and Sedig and Sumner's manipulating form of interaction, though the former carries with it particular pedagogical goals that the latter does not assume. Finally, *constructive* digital technologies are ones in which learners create their own representations, which are often the goal of the activity, thereby promoting mathematical modeling and what Noss and Hoyles (1996) characterize as expressive uses of technology. Goodwin and Highfield argue that while instructive technologies may be well-suited for procedural learning, manipulable and constructive technologies better support conceptual learning.

While some digital technologies fit neatly into one particular category (of each of these tripartite characterizations), many will belong to more than one category. However, each characterization provides a way of comparing the constraints and affordances of different digital technologies, which may guide the choice of a specific digital technology for a particular topic and/or grade level. However, educators must also make larger-scale decisions that involve choosing appropriate digital technologies for a wide range of topics across several grade levels. Is it preferable to promote one category of digital technology or to have a mix of forms of interactions (conversing, manipulating, and navigating) and of constraints (instructive, manipulable and constructive)? Although the research has little to say about such a question, Goldenberg (2000) has argued for the "fluency principle," which states that "[l]earning a few good tools well enough to use them knowledgeably, intelligently, mathematically, confidently, and appropriately in solving otherwise difficult problems makes a genuine contribution to a student's mathematical education" (p. 7). A "good" tool might offer a variety of forms of interactions and even enable different kinds of constraints, while also having a consistency that more easily enables teachers and learners to perceive important affordances. Unfortunately, no longitudinal research exploring the effect of long-term use of particular "good" technologies currently exists.

While Sedig and Sumner's framework says very little about *how* mathematical learning happens, several other theories in mathematics education have been proposed with that purpose in mind. These include the *instrumental genesis* approach, which is primarily concerned with the process of how a computer tool becomes for learners an instrument to learn and do mathematics with (Artigue, 2002); it attends to the way affordances are perceived both through increased experience with the tool and through the problems that the tool enables solving. This theory is specifically devoted to studying technology-based interactions and does not get used by researchers working outside this domain. Very few studies at the primary school level draw on this theory, perhaps because of the nature of computer tools at this age level, which do not require a significant instrumentation process because of their ease of use. However, the expanded notions of instrumental orchestration (Trouche, 2004; Drijvers, 2012) and documentational genesis (Gueudet & Trouche, 2008), both of which focus on the work of the teacher in a computer-based classroom, have been used to show, for example, the specific strategies (known as *orchestration types*) that kindergarten teachers use to manage heterogeneity and lack of reading ability at this school level (Gueudet, Bueno-Ravel, & Poisard, 2013).

Another important theoretical approach is that of *semiotic mediation* (Bartolini Bussi & Mariotti, 2008), which has its roots in Vygotsky's work approach and attends to the specific ways in which tools (including digital ones) are transformed by learners into mathematical concepts through a process of internalization. Although focused on tool use, and developed by researchers working with digital technologies, this theory also concerns mathematical learning more generally. This approach enables researchers to focus on the specific actions that certain tools enable (such as dragging and tracing), and on the types of signs they can give rise to. Similar in its Vygotskian origins, activity theory has also been used in the context of research on technology-based teaching and learning. Ladel and Kortenkamp (2013) propose a specific version of it, which they call artifact-centric activity theory (ACAT), and which they developed specifically for the primary school level, with touch-screen technologies in mind. This approach, more than the others, emphasizes how tools radically change the way learners act and think, thus moving away from a view that tools are discardable crutches that merely scaffold the learning of mathematics. Ladel and Kortenkamp also use it in the very design process of their touch-screen digital technologies.

Another Vygotsky-inspired framework that has been used to investigate technology-based student learning is Sfard's communicational approach, which takes thinking to be communicating and thus learning to be a change in one's discourse (Sfard, 2008). Changes in discourse can involve different uses of particular words and gestures; they can also be based on or produce different visual mediators and different "routines" for identifying shapes or describing quantity. Due to their highly visual and often temporal nature, digital technologies quite frequently offer unique visual mediators, thus inviting different ways of describing and comparing mathematical objects and relationships. They also give rise to new ways of thinking that may conflict with the established discourse of formal mathematics (which tends to be static and alphanumeric); Sfard's approach can help draw attention to the potential communication conflicts that may thus arise, especially as teachers attempt to transition between digital and text-based resources (see Sinclair & Yurita, 2008).

Much of the research on the use of digital technologies has also been informed by theories of embodied cognition. Papert's notion of "body syntonicity" can be seen as an early precursor to the now widely shared recognition of the important role that the body plays in mathematical meaning-making. While there are a range of assumptions about the relationship between the body and the mind—with dualist perspectives seeing the body as an important and sometimes necessary scaffolding for the development of mathematical schemas and concept and the monist perspective seeing the body itself as doing the knowing—there is growing consensus that particular kinds of bodily engagement can support mathematics learning. Research focused on the particular ways in which digital technologies can enable and promote bodily engagement highlights the precise and temporal actions that these technologies afford, which enable learners to move in mathematically relevant ways (Nemirovsky, Kelton, & Rhodehamel, 2013; Robutti, 2006; Sinclair, de Freitas, & Ferrara, 2013). Indeed, the three basic metaphors mentioned earlier—conversing, manipulating, and navigating—provide ways for the speaking, hearing, touching, and seeing body to interact with mathematical objects. This multimodal kind of interaction seems particularly important at the primary school level, where children's communication is much less language based. We return to this point in our discussion of new, touch-screen technologies.

More recently, research focused on learning with media (such as television or videos) suggests that joint engagement—which involves parental mediation—can provide powerful additional affordances for learning beyond what is found with technology use alone (Moorthy et al., 2013; Stevens & Penuel, 2010). This work has been extended to the context of digital games as well, but they are often less suitable for joint engagements because of the demands they make in terms of attention and rapid cognitive and physical responses. This research may be highly relevant to mathematics education settings, especially if teacher mediation is taken into account. It suggests that there may be advantages to designing environments in which teacher-student(s) conversation can be built into the technology-based activities. This may be easier to accomplish with open-ended environments in which the teacher is involved in proposing tasks or responding to students' actions, in contrast to level-driven and highly instructive environments where the parent or the teacher has little role to play.

DIGITAL TECHNOLOGIES FOCUSING ON NUMBER SENSE

In this section we report on studies involving digital technologies designed to support the teaching and learning of number sense,[4] a fundamental aspect of early mathematical learning. As mentioned earlier, a wide range of digital technologies have been developed and studied, including desktop computer software, Internet-based applets, touch-screen applications and, of course, calculators.[5] Some studies report on the "effectiveness," while others describe design features, or particular aspects of the "usability," that are hypothesized to support student learning. We report first on studies that involved VMs, focusing specifically on the constraints imposed, and then offer that contrast with the associated physical manipulative. We next consider a variety of digital tools used for different aspects of number sense while not being virtual instantiations of physical manipulatives. Finally, we present three new touch-screen applications and discuss their unique potential with respect to the development of children's number sense.

From Physical to Virtual Manipulatives

Children whose learning occurs in rich environments that include (virtual) manipulatives tend to learn better and reach higher levels of academic achievement (see for example, Steen, Brookes, & Lyon, 2006). However, it is not the simple presence of the (physical or virtual) manipulatives that makes the difference, but how these manipulatives are designed and used (for example, Goodwin & Highfield, 2013). Despite the abundant availability of VMs for the early years, little research has been carried out on their effectiveness and use in the classroom. VMs are, for the most part, manipulable digital technologies, both in Sedig and Sumner's sense as well as in Goodwin and Highfield's—this is not surprising given their connection to physical manipulatives. For the most part, the benefits of virtual manipulatives are seen as augmenting those of physical ones by providing more precision and more feedback that is mathematically relevant, and by demanding more mathematical forms of expression (through numbers, symbols, or actions).

Some recent research focuses on studying the way teachers can or could orchestrate the use of VMs.[6] As a first example, we consider the *e-pascaline*, a virtual version of the mathematical machine known as the *pascaline* (Maschietto & Soury-Lavergne, 2013). In the studies reported by these authors, this VM is used after students have interacted extensively with the physical pascaline, a mathematical machine used in many Italian primary school classrooms to foster the learning of place value (Bartolini Bussi, 2011), thereby leading to the notion of a "duo of artefacts" in which *both* physical and virtual manipulatives feature in a mathematics lessons. The e-pascaline has the main constitutive elements (and even colors) as the physical manipulative; however, its implementation involves additional design decisions that lead to new affordances (see Figure 28.1). First, all tasks are made explicit within the VM, whereas the physical pascaline does not include any instructions or directions. Second, the e-pascaline's

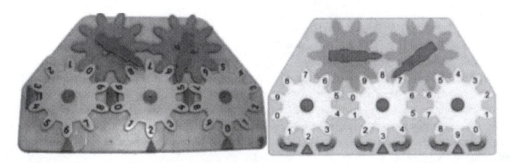

Figure 28.1 (a) A physical pascaline; (b) the e-pascaline.

buttons can be hidden or shown, which affords bringing mathematical ideas and action to conscious awareness. For example, to count by 1s the 10s button and the 100s button may be hidden or grayed out. Third, the wheels are turned by clicking arrows that indicate clockwise or counterclockwise rotations, thereby affording a discrete, indirect interaction that differs from the direct, continuous one of the physical pascaline. The authors explain the rationale for this decision (as opposed to, say, "click and drag to the left or right") in terms of helping children attend to the number of moves of a wheel—thus affording Sarama and Clements' sense of bringing mathematical ideas and action to conscious awareness. The authors thus make a theoretical argument that using the e-pascaline will help children develop a mathematical awareness that may only be left implicit with the physical counterpart. More research on how children move from these machines to paper-and-pencil forms of expressing place value may be needed in order to better understand how the pascaline and the e-pascaline function as models or analogies in children's thinking.

A second example of a VM is base-10 blocks, for which many applets have been designed. We highlight two specific affordances of these VMs that distinguish them from their associated physical manipulatives. The first involves the automatic transformation of a 10-block into 10 individual unit blocks when moved from a 10s column into a 1s column (see Base Blocks from the National Library of Virtual Manipulatives' [NLVM0 collection, at http://nlvm.usu.edu/en/nav/topic_t_1.html). This conversing interaction enables learners to see how the column location affects the meaning of the block while also affording Sarama and Clements' mental actions on objects. Although no empirical evidence for the effect of such a design choice has been reported, its presence in other VMs, such as Kortenkamp's Place Value[7] (an app for the Apple iPad and iPhone), indicates some consensus about its desirability. Second, most of these VMs also show and update the numerical value of the tokens, blocks, or chips placed in the different areas, thereby providing symbolic feedback and reducing the need for learners to count and calculate. This seems to be an important affordance not specifically identified by Sarama and Clements (2009) but potentially significant in shifting the attention of both the learner and the teacher away from computation.

Another example we include in this section is Numberbonds[8] (also developed for the iPad[9]), which aims to strengthen continuous and relational representations of numbers. Introducing numbers through this kind of representation emphasizes *relations* between them (a form of ordinality) as opposed to their *absolute denotation* of sets of objects (cardinality). Such an approach has been adopted, for example, in a mathematics curriculum developed by Gattegno (1970); moreover, some neuroscientific studies suggest that a more explicit and early emphasis on ordinality may be the key to learning early number (Lyons & Beilock, 2011). Numberbonds has a Tetris-like setup in which a Cuisinaire-like rod falls in an area with a set length and the player has to quickly choose a rod from the ones displayed on the right that together with the one that has fallen completes the set base length (see Figure 28.2). At each level the game offers different sets of rods—until a total of 10 are displayed—to choose from to complete the reference length. Research from the fields of neuroscience and cognitive psychology conducted with students showing weak number sense highlights some advantages of this virtual adaptation of the manipulatives (Butterworth, 2011; Butterworth & Laurillard, 2010): timing of the falling allows for some "training" to occur; the changeability of the rod color; and the replacement of the rod's color by a numerical value, which affords the symbolizing of mathematical concepts as well as the linking of the concrete and the symbolic through feedback. Moreover, the learning environment provides guided feedback, which enables learners to adjust their actions in relation to the goal, rather than rely on help from a teacher. Unlike the previous two examples, which replicate most of the manipulative possibilities of the associated physical manipulatives, Numberbonds addresses only one small component of the activities enabled by Cuisinaire rods; it also has a more *instructive* design, though the feedback from the environment may provide some of the mediation that features in joint engagement with media.

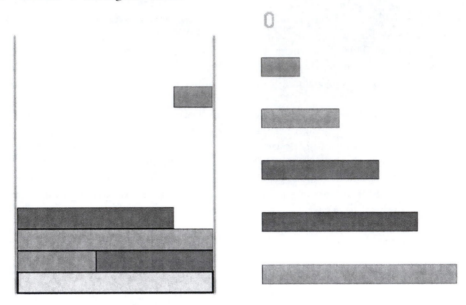

Figure 28.2 Part-whole number sense with Numberbonds.

As a last example, we discuss some possible instantiations of the number line in order to introduce a more general issue of feedback. Consider a number line such as the one in Motion Math-Fractions[10] for the iPad, an *instructive* digital manipulative that focuses on fraction estimation. Within this environment a number line appears on the ground together with a ball that can bounce (completely elastically) and that can be controlled by the gravity accelerator of the iPad. The ball contains a fraction that has to be placed correctly on the line. Positive feedback is given for a correct placement while a hint is offered for an incorrect placement. Although this type of feedback loop may improve fraction estimation skills (Riconscente, 2013), it does not provide opportunities for learners to manipulate or express new mathematical meanings. Such possibility can be provided only through an educator's mediation (see, for example, Bartolini, Baccaglini-Frank, & Ramploud, 2014). Indeed, in her study of children 5–8 years old, Goodwin (2009) found that using manipulable digital technologies to learn about fractions resulted in the production of the "most developed and advanced representations," in comparison with those using an instructive digital technology (cited in Goodwin & Highfield, 2013, p. 208). Further, these researchers note that children working with the instructive digital technology were more focused on receiving positive feedback than on discussing or reflecting on the embedded mathematical concept—as would be predicted by the joint engagement with media literature.

Other Digital Tools for Learning Number

We now report on studies involving digital tools that focus on different aspects of number sense while not being what we have referred to as VMs. We begin with Building Blocks, which is a preschool mathematics program that includes a set of different digital tools, each associated with specific concepts in the curriculum and designed to meet benchmarks in a hypothesized learning trajectories (see Clements & Sarama, 2004). For example, the early levels of one of the on-computer activity sets, which are more *instructive* than *manipulative*, use a cookie-baking scenario to teach matching collections and various counting skills; at higher levels, children add. For example, a character may hide two, then one more chip under a napkin, and the child is asked to make the second cookie have the same number of chips—thus aiming at the

Non-Verbal Addition level (Clements & Sarama, 2004, p. 183). This task could also proposed without the support of technology, but that technology provides enables the teacher (or student) to control the length of exposure of the items hidden and added; further, the system can repeat the task a large number of times, adjusting its difficulty to the input given each time by the student and recording the performance (speed and accuracy) each time. Various other software applications have been developed to propose this kind of task, including How Many Under the Shell?[11] from the National Council of Teachers of Mathematics (NCTM). Although Clements and Sarama do not report on the gains or effects particularly related to this computer-based activity, they have shown that the curriculum as a whole increases children's development of number sense in comparison with other curricula.

In addition to classroom-oriented software programs, several remedial interventions have also been designed. For young children with difficulties with numbers.[12] studies of *adaptive* and *instructive* software games such as The Number Race (Wilson, Revkin, Cohen, Cohen, & Dehaene, 2006, Wilson & Dehaene, 2007), Grapho-Game Maths (Räsänen Salminen, Wilson, Aunio, & Dehaene, 2009), Numberbonds, and Dots2Track[13] (Butterworth & Laurillard, 2010; Butterworth, 2011) have been undertaken. Dots2Track, developed within the Digital Interventions for Dyscalculia and Low Numeracy project (Butterworth & Laurillard, 2010; see http://low-numeracy.ning.com/ and http://number-sense.co.uk/), is based on a very simple kind of interaction in which a set of dots (or other objects) is shown on the screen and children type the corresponding number in Arabic digits, or in letters. The dots given are in fixed arrangements (for example three dots are in a top-left to lower-right diagonal in the stimulus area, Figure 28.3).

The software registers the response time and immediately provides corrective feedback. Preliminary results are reported as being encouraging. In the near future, the authors expect neuroimaging to be part of summative evaluation of intervention for dyscalculia. Number Race is another adaptive software program designed to target the inherited approximate numerosity system in the intraparietal sulcus (Feigenson, Dehaene, & Spelke, 2004) that may support early arithmetic, by presenting comparison tasks of small magnitudes presented in analogical and symbolic forms. For example, two sets of dots can appear simultaneously (and stay on the screen until the child answers, or disappear after a short time) and the child has to select the set with greater numerosity (Figure 28.4a). Wilson and colleagues (Wilson, Dehaene, Pinel, Revkin, Cohen, & Cohen, 2006) show how the software is designed to create a multidimensional model of the evolution of a learner's "knowledge space" along three variables and time (Figure 28.4b). After five weeks, experimental subjects showed greater improvement in their number sense with respect to the control group (Wilson & Dehaene, 2007).

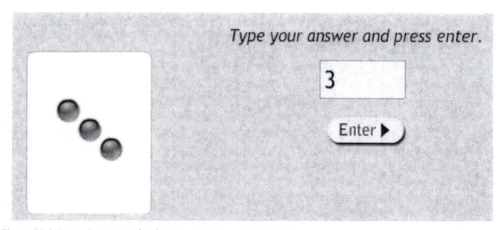

Figure 28.3 Dots given are in fixed arrangements in Dots2Track.

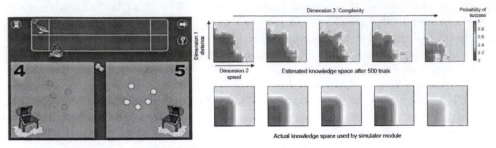

Figure 28.4 (a) Screenshot from the Number Race; the child has chosen the set with greater numerosity. On the right (b) a multidimensional model of the evolution of a learner's "knowledge space."

Potentials of Multitouch Technology

The previous examples in this section have been designed for the mouse and keyboard inputs available with desktop and laptop computers. The main interaction is through clicking (rather than typing) discrete objects, with one child working with the software at a time. In contrast, the following three examples are prototypical in exploiting various potentials of multitouch technology with respect to number sense learning. With multitouch technology, the interaction becomes more immediate, as the fingers contact the screen directly, either through tapping or a wide variety of gestures. Further, the screen can be touched by multiple users simultaneously, which invites different types of activity structures than the computer or laptop. We have devoted a section to these new technologies because of the close link between their main interaction mode (through the fingers) and the emerging neuroscientific literature pointing to the importance of fingers in the development of number sense (e.g., Butterworth, 1999a, 1999b; 2005; Penner-Wilger et al., 2007; Gracia-Bafalluy, 2008; Andres, Seron, & Olivier 2007; Sato, Cattaneo, Rizzolatti, & Gallese, 2007; Thompson, Abbott, Wheaton, Syngeniotis, & Puce, 2004). Basic component abilities that can be powerfully mediated through multitouch technology are: 1) subitizing; 2) one-to-one correspondence between numerosities in analogical form and fingers placed on screen/raised simultaneously/counting with fingers, and in general finger gnosia; 3) fine motor abilities; and 4) the part-whole concept. While the examples we discuss here may quickly be replaced with newer versions, they allow us to identify particular design decisions that will be relevant to new applications as well.

Our first example is an *instructive, conversing* digital technology called Fingu[14] (Barendregt, Lindstrom, Rietz-Leppanen, Holgersson, & Ottosson, 2012), an iPad application in which the stimuli are given as fixed arrangements of floating objects (see Figure 28.5a). Users must place the corresponding number of fingers on the screen simultaneously. Each touch produces a fingerprint, thus providing visual feedback and rapid closure to the *conversation* (see Figure 28.5b), which ends with an additional yes/no feedback (auditory signal as well as visual cues: happy animations for correct responses and sad animations for incorrect ones). The game is timed. At each of the seven levels the number of objects that appear increases while the time to respond decreases. Very little opportunity for joint engagement is offered.

The necessity for simultaneous rather than sequential input further encourages subitizing. The choice of floating groups of objects (where the disposition of each group remains invariant) differs from the fixed arrays typically offered in other environments, providing a different type of stimulus for the solver's object tracking system (Fayol & Seron, 2005; van Herwegen, Ansari, Xu, & Karmiloff-Smith, 2008; Cantlon Safford & Brannon, 2010), a system upon which the ability to subitize supposedly relies (Piazza, 2010). In an exploratory micro-longitudinal pilot study with 5–6-year-old students, researchers found that children playing the game for a three-week period (with guidance from the teacher) would score significantly lower in higher levels of the game, but overall would increase their percentage of right

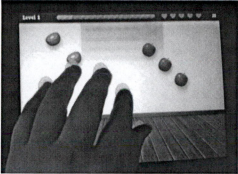

Figure 28.5 (a) Different sets of fruit have appeared on the screen until (b) the player places the corresponding number of fingers, simultaneously, on the screen.

answers (Barendregt et al., 2012). The researchers also identified some indicators (counting all, counting from smallest, counting from largest, counting fingers to five, counting fingers over five, manipulating fingers with other hand, problem pressing down) that could contribute to understanding different learning trajectories in Fingu that may lead to improvement of children's mathematical abilities. This is claimed as one of the goals of an ongoing study (Barendregt et al., 2012, p. 4).

Ladel and Kortenkamp (2011) report on an open-ended, *manipulable, constructive* multitouch environment developed to foster children's development of the *part-whole concept*[15] (as proposed, for example, by Resnick, Bill, Lesgold, & Leer, 1991) and of *finger symbols sets.* These are thought to foster flexible calculation strategies, such as composing and decomposing numbers with respect to 5 and 10 (Brissiaud, 1992). The environment consists of a table connected to a computer that recognizes multitouch inputs. Children can create and move tokens simultaneously (through multitouch but also multiuser). Tokens can also be "fused together" (for example, 3 and 5 to make 8) and the environment will give symbolic feedback (3 + 5 = 8) on the action. It is also possible to give tasks in symbolic form (e.g. "3 + 4 = _" or "3 + _ = 7"), which the children are asked to express with tokens. Ladel and Kortenkamp (2013) report on a different task in this environment designed for children aged 5–7, in which a certain number of virtual tokens must be placed on the table "all at once," thus focusing on the shift from sequential, ordinal counting to holistic cardinal count.[16] The researchers describe the different ways in which the children attempted to solve the task, stressing how the environment enabled the children to exteriorize their thinking about number, and noting the important role of the teacher in interpreting and responding to the children's actions.

TouchCounts (Sinclair & Jackiw, 2011) is made up of two constructive microworlds involving *manipulable, constructive* interactions: ("1, 2, 3,. . .") and ("1 + 2 + 3 +. . ."). Audio feedback can be given in English, Italian, or French. In the "1, 2, 3,. . ." microworld, the mode "with gravity" presents a "shelf" on the screen (Figure 28.6a). As a finger is placed on the screen, a colored circle containing an Arabic numeral appears on the screen and the number is also spoken orally. When the finger is lifted from the screen the numbered object falls, unless it is dragged so that it "sits" on the shelf (see Figure 28.6b). When more fingers are placed on the screen, the counting continues on from the last number reached with the previous touch. If the child interacts through successive touches using a single finger, or different fingers placed on the screen sequentially, TouchCounts will end up "counting" for the child, so it may strengthen her or his recollection of the number words (in sequence) and possibly fine motor abilities. If multiple fingers touch the screen, the same number of numbered objects appears but only the last number is given orally—this enables, for example, counting by twos. In the "no gravity" mode, the numbered objects do not fall, so that placing five fingers on the screen (sequentially or simultaneously) will produce something similar to Figure 28.6c.

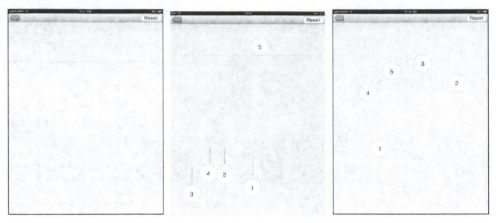

Figure 28.6 (a) Counting (initial state); (b) after four taps below the shelf and a fifth tap above the shelf (arrows indicate falling numbered shapes); (c) the effect of five fingers placed on the screen simultaneously.

This type of interaction involves various number sense component abilities such as subitizing and fine motor skills (simultaneous touch to generate the proper enumeration and dragging of a selected finger to place the circle on the line), but the environment may also help lay foundations for counting principles and for the transition from ordinal to cardinal counting. This is because it can foster the development of awareness of the one-to-one correspondence between fingers and numerosities, or between numbers and successive touch-actions on the screen (one-to-one correspondence principle); it may foster memorization of the sequence of number-words to recite when counting (stable order principle); in the modality without gravity, the last word heard through the audio feedback corresponds to the total number of circles on the screen (cardinality principle); and finally in the gravity mode the possibility of marking certain numbers by dragging them on the line may favor a process of reification (Sfard, 2008) of the number, necessary for operating on numbers.

In the "1 + 2 + 3. . ." microworld, touching the screen with several fingers simultaneously generates sets of circles, of a same random color, enclosed in a numbered circle indicating its magnitude (Figure 28.7a, b). Through the "pinch" gesture (Figure 28.7c) it is possible to act on the cardinal numbers, in this case, adding them together. This gesture constitutes a fundamental metaphor of addition, that of "grouping together" (Lakoff & Núñez, 2000). The gesture can be performed prior to any formal instruction about addition, of course, but may help children develop a metaphoric meaning for addition, as well as a sense of the symmetry of this operation (and thus the commutative property). The result of pinching two groups together is a larger group in which the colors of the addend circles have been preserved in order to leave a trace of the action (Figure 28.7d).

Pilot studies indicate that with the use of certain tasks, children 5–6 years old can learn to shift from thinking of number in terms of the process of counting to thinking of them as reified objects (Sinclair & Heyd-Metzuyanim, 2014). Further, with even younger children (3–4 years old), pilot research has shown that the task of placing fingers all-at-once on the screen can help develop their "gestural subitizing" (Sinclair, 2013). These studies show how a

Figure 28.7 (a) Creating a herd of digital counters; (b) the rearranged herd; (c) pinching two herds together; (d) the sum of two herds.

Table 28.1 Summary of the basic features of multitouch technology that can be used to foster the development of number-based concepts and abilities.

Concepts and abilities	Technology features
Subitizing	• Numerosities can be shown on the screen for very brief amounts of time; • immediate feedback; • the objects to be considered may appear still and randomly placed on the screen or in given arrangements (for example like dots on dice), they can move all together or one with respect to the other; • input is accepted in the form of a touch gesture (e.g. "lasso/capture").
One-to-one correspondence between numerosities in analogical form and numbers of fingers, and in general finger gnosia	• Input is accepted in the form of a number of fingers placed simultaneously on the screen, of a number of sequential taps (possibly on items in the stimulus); • accurate timing of the user's performance; • possible manipulation of virtual hands.
Fine-motor abilities	• Detecting and differentiating rapid sequences of inputs from different areas of the screen; • keeping sequential track of areas of the screen touched (trace mark); • recording of different gestures as separate inputs (swipe with 1 finger, swipe with two fingers, lasso, pinch, un-pinch/enlarge. . .).
Part-whole concept	• Detecting as different inputs the simultaneous presence at a given time (or small interval of time) of two or more fingers; • possible manipulation of virtual objects through gestures.

rich *manipulative* and *constructive* environment can be also be *instructive*, thus fostering the development of both procedures and associated concepts.

While research is in its early phases with respect to new touch-screen and multitouch environments, we propose the following summary of the basic features of multitouch technology that can be used to foster the development of number-based concepts and abilities.

As has been the case with other significantly new digital technologies, we also expect to see some changes in the way number sense concepts themselves may develop—along with the order and pace by which these concepts are learned—as children interact not only through alphanumeric means but through touch, sound, and image as well. While the affordances seem to be clearly geared to supporting young children's learning, more research is needed into how these touch-screen devices might affect children's interactions with physical tasks involving number sense, including the still pervasive pencil-and-paper media of the mathematics classroom.

DIGITAL TECHNOLOGIES FOCUSED ON GEOMETRY

The goals of geometry learning at the K–2 level are to develop a better understanding of objects in relation to their shape and position, and to attend to the geometric properties (parallelism, congruence, symmetry) and behaviors (invariance, sameness) of these objects. Since similar goals pertain also to higher elementary and middle school geometry, some of the research already conducted at these later grades using digital technologies is relevant to this chapter.[17] Dynamic geometry environments (DGEs) have been the most widely researched geometry technologies. Researchers have shown how they help foster conjecturing, enable learners to interact with a larger number of examples, and help learners attend to invariances (see Baccaglini-Frank & Mariotti, 2010; Laborde, Kynigos, Hollebrands, & Sträßer, 2006; Mariotti, 2006; Sinclair & Robutti, 2013) in a wide range of geometry-related topics. Many of these findings relate to the dragging tool available in DGEs, which enables direct, continuous manipulation (and this form of interaction is now also available in some Web-based applets and VMs aimed at young children). For example, Battista (2007) has shown that the dragging tool, used to transform constructed quadrilaterals enabled children in grades 4 and 5 to attend to the invariant properties of the different quadrilaterals and even identify certain quadrilaterals (rectangles) as subclasses of others (parallelograms). At the high-school level, Hollebrands (2003) has shown that the use of dragging can help students develop a functional understanding of transformations (reflections and rotations) since dragging one object continuously on the screen changes the position of another associated object.

Example From the Building Blocks Curriculum

In addition to the Building Block VMs mentioned earlier, Sarama and Clements (2002) describe a geometric *manipulable* and *constructive* digital technology called *Piece Puzzler*. It was intentionally designed to contain screen versions of pattern blocks and tangram shapes, which children can manipulate to create or duplicate larger composite shapes. The authors report research results on the effect of the curriculum as a whole (Clements & Sarama, 2007), but not on the specific use of the virtual manipulative. However, the principles used for its design are of interest for several reasons. One such principle stipulates that the virtual manipulative, along with the specific tasks, be designed in terms of a hypothetical learning trajectory. In this case, the authors propose seven levels along this trajectory, each of which is accompanied by a specific task aimed at achieving the particular level, with the final level aiming at having children be able to iteratively compose composite shapes to tile the plane. For example, the goal of Level 4 (Shape Composer) is for children to choose and manipulate, through turning and flipping, given shapes to completely fill a region. The given regions are multiply cornered so that children have to attend to angles in the shapes as well as in the region.[18] In Level 6, the children can use shapes to create a composite objects in the shape of a toy (like a rocket ship), which they can then duplicate by pressing the "do it again" tools, thus creating iteratively composite units. In the final Level 7, children create superordinate units of tetrominoes and use them to tile the plane.

In their early reporting on the use of the Building Blocks program, Sarama and Clements (2002) report that the "use of the tools encourages children to become explicitly aware of the actions they perform on the shapes" (p. 103) since, unlike physical pattern blocks and tangram shapes, children cannot just pick up and move the pieces with their hands. Further, the children are able to create designs that are more precisely assembled than if they were working with physical objects since, as Moyer, Niezgoda, and Stanley (2005) have also pointed out in their study of the NLVM Pattern Block, the shapes can be "snapped" into position and stay fixed. This description of the software hides many design choices that are central in determining how children use it and what they learn as they use it. Sarama and Clements (2002) acknowledge that their pilot testing raised questions about whether unexpected outcomes should lead to changes in the software design or changes in the learning trajectory. This should not be surprising if one acknowledges how tools mediate learning, which is in keeping with Clements and Sarama's general Vygotskian approach.

In terms of design, Clements and Sarama briefly discuss decisions made around how turning would be handled by the software. They tested four possible choices (tool, button, direct manipulation with continuous motion, and direct manipulation with discrete units). Their ultimate choice of a tool interface that is discrete and direct was motivated by the fact that 3–4-year-old children found this interface easier to learn and to use. However, it requires the designer to choose a default turn angle, which means that children's turn actions are actually "turn-by-30-degrees" actions (for the pattern blocks, and 15 degrees for the tangrams), thereby highly constraining the example space of turn (not to mention the fact that the center of rotation is always in the middle of the shape). Similarly, for the flip tool the designers decided that the line of reflection would be horizontal and immediately under the shape being flipped.

Given the intended learning trajectory, these constraints on reflecting and rotating may not be too problematic. However, they are the kinds of constraints that may no longer be needed with touch-screen interfaces, where children can act on objects with their fingers instead of through the intermediary of a mouse. Indeed, in the next section, we describe a learning environment in which the turn interface chosen is that of direct manipulation with continuous motion.

An example that focuses on very similar mathematical ideas, but that differs both in the design of the interface and the accompanying task, comes from a project involving the use of Cabri Elem, which is a multipurpose dynamic geometry environment that can be used to design microworlds suitable for primary school learners. The "Tiling" microworld, which is both *manipulable* and *constructive*, involves the composition of shapes into tiling patterns. Children can manipulate eight different shapes directly by sliding, turning, or flipping. Laborde and Marcheteau (2009) report on a study conducted with grade 3 children who were asked to work in pairs to create tilings involving at least two different shapes. They then described their pattern to another pair who would try to recreate the pattern. While all 14 pairs successfully created tilings, only three were able to describe these tilings in terms of a repeating unit. Given the success of Clements and Sarama's Piece Puzzler, as well as the NLVM Pattern Block used by both Moyer et al. (2005) and Highfield and Mulligan (2007) with younger children, the "cloning" affordance through which a user can duplicate an existing set of shapes seems instrumental in promoting thinking in terms of repeating units.

Example of Whole Classroom Dynamic Geometry

In the third example, we offer a cluster of examples that focus on different aspects of geometry at the K–2 level, and that involve a plenary mode of interaction in the classroom with a DGE being projected on a wall or an interactive whiteboard. The first example concerns Sinclair and Moss's (2012) study involving kindergarten children (4–5 years old) and triangle identification in which Sketchpad is used as a *conversing* and *manipulable* as well as a *constructive* technology. In this study—which used Sfard's communicational approach in which learning is conceptualized as a change in discourse—children moved relatively quickly from a first van Hiele level (in communicational terms, a discourse about the physical reality around us where shapes are identified as the same if they match) to a second one (in communicational terms, a discourse that treats level one things as objects and where shapes are identified as the same if they can be transformed one into the other), with some even moving to a third van Hiele level (in communicational terms, a reified one, where shapes are identified as the same by comparing verbal descriptions of the shape). In particular, the children initially used the word *triangle* much like a proper name corresponding to an equilateral triangle and identified shapes as triangles if they looked like an equilateral triangle. When these children were shown a triangle with its vertex pointing down, which was constructed using the segment tool in Sketchpad, they either said that it was an "upside down triangle" or that they could see it as a triangle if they turned themselves upside down. After the teacher dragged one of the vertices of the triangle on the screen, all but one child began to speak of triangle as a family name that describes a larger set of triangles than just equilateral ones. They identified these nonequilateral triangles using a routine of transformation in which a shape was a triangle because you could "stretch it out." A few children even began describing the triangles on the screen in definitional ways, stating that "[e]very triangle could be, um, a different shape but it just has three corners" (Sinclair & Moss, 2012, p. 36). The children were given the opportunity to create their own triangles using the teacher's computer and made a variety of triangle shapes, including long and pointy ones and upside-down ones. When the teacher shifted to squares instead of triangles, some of the children immediately used a discourse of transformation when talking about a square that was sitting on its vertex, while others insisted that this shape was a diamond. This suggests that the children had not all succeeded in shifting discourse, but this is not surprising given the short intervention (30 minutes).

A more extended intervention described in Sinclair and Kaur (2011) involves introducing young children (kindergarten and grade 1) to the concept of angle, this time using Sketchpad in a *manipulative/manipulable* manner. While angle is typically not formally included in the curriculum at this age, the researchers deemed it both possible and desirable to introduce it in a visual and dynamic way rather than a measurement-based one (which involves learning about degrees and using relatively large numbers like 180 degrees). The goal of the study was to determine whether focusing on the metaphor angle-as-turn might enable young children to develop understandings about angle and help address common errors that students make (as identified in the literature), such as assuming that an angle with longer arms is bigger than an angle with shorter arms. The initial task in the intervention focuses on developing benchmark angles. This is done by offering children clockwise and counterclockwise turning options of ¼, ½, ¾, and 1: when one of these buttons are pressed, the arrow turns dynamically and leaves a trace of the swept-out angle (see Figure 28.8). The teacher prompts the children to arrive at a given destination using a smaller or bigger angle so that the word *angle* comes to be associated with the turning motion. Then, children are invited to use the sketch shown in Figure 28.8 with the task of getting the car to the gas station. By dragging the angle labeled "dial," children determine the amount by which the car will turn. This requires children to coordinate the turning of the dial with the turning of the car, which is challenging when the car is not facing up, like the vertical arm of the angle dial. The disassociation of the car form the angle dial is thus crucial to the design of the sketch.

The researchers found that the children had no difficulty using benchmark angles to describe the position of objects in the screen. Further, although the children initially struggled with the angle dial, they were eventually able to use it to get the car to the gas station as well as to solve more complicated, multistep trips. Follow-up computer-based as well as paper-and-pencil based tasks showed that the children, when asked to compare angles (with distracting features such as differently sized arms and different orientations), focused on the amount of turn rather than the size of the arms. Further, when working on tasks involving triangles, the children were as likely to focus on the number and size of the angles than on the sides. The dynamic nature of the software, along with the immediate, nonevaluative feedback, enables children to see the turning action and experiment with the effect of different sizes of turns, while the teacher's questions and interactions help the children associate the word *angle* to this turning action. This research offers initial evidence to support the claim that angles could be effectively introduced earlier in the geometry curriculum, which would have implications for the way other topics are taught.

The final example involves reflectional symmetry. Ng and Sinclair (2015) describe a three-lesson intervention involving both computer-based and paper-and-pencil based activities aimed at helping children attend to the geometric properties of reflectional symmetry. In the

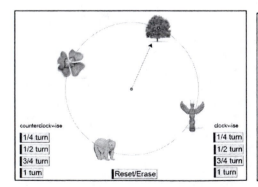
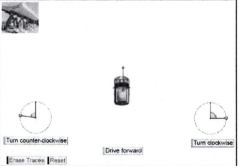

Figure 28.8 (a) Focusing on benchmark angles; (b) using angle-as-turn to navigate the screen.

first lesson, the children explore the *manipulative/manipulable* "symmetry machine" through direct, discrete interaction by dragging one of the squares on the screen and observing the resulting motion of the associated square (see Figure 29.9a, b). The discrete motion of the square is meant to draw students' attention to how the movement of the square and its image are related. After initial exploration, the children are shown various designs and asked whether they could be created using the symmetry machine. If so, the students recreate the design, with the environment providing self-checking feedback; and if cannot, they are invited to explain why. The children can also interact through direct, continuous dragging with the line of symmetry in order to reproduce designs that have horizontal or oblique, as well as vertical symmetry (see Figure 29.9c). In the second lesson, children are shown a broken symmetry machine containing squares only on one side of the line of symmetry and they are asked to fix the other side to make it symmetric. On the third lesson, the children use the continuous symmetry machine, which involves direct, continuous dragging of a traced point, as does a symmetric point. The children are asked to create certain shapes using this continuous symmetry machine (butterfly, a square, a house, etc.).

The researchers found that the children developed new and embodied ways of thinking about symmetry and its properties. Further, the children moved from a static conception of symmetry to a functional and dynamic one, focusing on the symmetric relation between

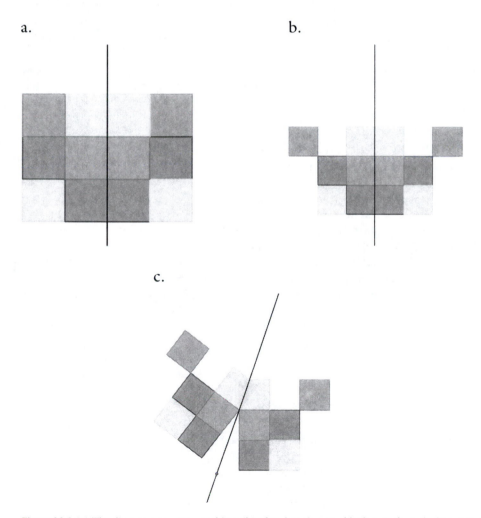

Figure 28.9 (a) The discrete symmetry machine; (b) after dragging one block away from the line; (c) after rotating the line of symmetry.

a shape and its image rather than on the static property of being symmetric. This shift was occasioned by the processes of semiotic mediation in which the dragging and tracing tool, as well as the language and gestures of the teacher, became signs that enabled communication about central features of reflectional symmetry including the way in which one side of a symmetric design is the same as the other, the way in which one component of a symmetric design is the same distance away from the line of symmetry as its corresponding image, the way in which a pre-imagine component and its image have to be on the same line relative to the line of symmetry, and, the way in which a pre-image and an image gives rise to parity.

LEARNING MATHEMATICS THROUGH PROGRAMMING

Programming is an important topic that some countries, such as Italy and the UK,[19] even included explicitly in the curriculum indications for preschool or primary school.[20] However, after the research on Logo, little research has been published on the teaching and learning of mathematics through computer programming. Currently, a variety of programmable toys (such as Bee-bot, Probot, and Lego NXT) are being used in classrooms around the world, as may be seen by the number of activities available (especially for Bee-Bot) on Web sites from different countries. In addition, the use of such toys is proposed in textbooks for college courses for Italian preservice teachers (see Baccaglini-Frank, Ramploud, & Bartolini Bussi, 2012) or in special documents for Australian in-service teachers.[21] However as reported by Highfield and Mulligan (2008), "The consequence of young children's immersion in these technologies has not been adequately investigated and the potential advantages and disadvantages for mathematics education need to be examined" (p. 1). In a study aimed at comparing mathematical processes that preschool children might encounter whilst "playing" with different forms of technology, including the Bee-Bot, the researchers report that it remains "unclear how mathematical processes are explored, understood or assimilated by young learners" (Highfield & Mulligan, 2008, p. 6), and teacher assistance and guidance are heavily needed. A similar finding is reported by Pekárová (2008), who notes that "some children clearly demonstrated deep comprehension of principles of Bee-Bot's control" (p. 120). These findings resonate with what is reported in theses of graduate students at the Department of Education and Human Sciences at the University of Modena and Reggio Emilia (Italy) who have carried out a number of preschool and early elementary school interventions using the Bee-Bot (e.g. Bartolini Bussi & Baccaglini-Frank, 2015). Other studies propose the use of robotic toys to foster problem solving, mapping, and measurement activities (Highfield, 2010; Highfield, 2009; Highfield & Mulligan, 2009).

One of the few published studies involving the use of a programming environment at the K–2 level is that of Yelland (2002), who developed a microworld based on the use of Geo Logo, which encouraged young children (with a mean age of 7 years and 4 months) to explore concepts of length measurement. The microworld enabled the children to move different turtles, each of which took a different length of step. The children worked in pairs and had to decide how to coordinate the length of each step with the number of steps in order to reach a destination. Yelland (2002) found that the computer-based environment was more conducive to interactions between the pairs of children "which forced them to use number and compare numbers in new and dynamic ways" (p. 86). She further opined that the environment "facilitated playing with units of measurement in ways that were not possible without the technology" (p. 91). These findings are consistent with research conducted at the higher grade levels (see, for example, Clements & Battista, 1989). It also suggests that children at this age are capable of more sophisticated reasoning with measurement—in terms of covarying the length of the step and the number of steps—than current curricula assume (also see Goodwin & Highfield, 2013; English & Mulligan, 2013).

DISCUSSION

The rate of proliferation of new digital media far outpaces the amount of research that can be conducted. This is in part due to the ever-changing developments in hardware and software, and also to the gap between the kinds of environments valued by researchers and those produced by software design companies. Indeed, several of the examples we have analyzed have been designed by the researchers themselves, who generally favor more open-ended environments that support both conceptual and procedural aspects of concept development. However, funding for such software development can be scarce, and support for ongoing maintenance even more so. Software is not like textbooks—it needs continuous debugging, upgrading, and adaptation to new operating systems and hardware affordances. Although it is likely that many of the environments discussed here will be superseded in the years to come, our analyses should be understood from a broader perspective, and a reader should appreciate how they will remain the same regardless of the "game" or "interface." To that end, we have highlighted some of the different design decisions that are relevant to mathematics learning at the K–2 grades.

Multitouch devices seem to have particularly strong potential in children's development of number sense, in large part because of the important role that fingers play in this development and also because of the direct mediation enabled by this technology. Other computer-based programs, including VMs, have also been shown to be effective, especially when the feedback—either from the computer or a teacher—can help children reflect on the mathematically relevant aspects of their actions. We expect that many of these VMs will soon be available on multitouch platforms as well. The specific ways in which they are implemented—in terms of the kinds of interactions that are made possible—will be important in determining their effectiveness. In terms of geometry, a large portion of the studies have focused on microworlds that have been built within dynamic geometry environments. The ease with which young children can see and explore a wide variety of continuously changing shapes, as well as relationships between shapes, seems to make them highly suitable for the K–2 level, particularly with appropriate teacher mediation. We expect to see more stand-alone microworlds developed for multitouch platforms, which will lead to interesting research questions about the different activity structures that would enable several children at once to interact with shapes, perhaps working together to compose a set of polygons.

Clearly, much more research on the effects of digital technologies on K–2 teaching and learning is needed. Although there exists an abundance of digital tools for researchers and teachers to choose from, especially in terms of Internet applets and touch-screens apps, we know very little about how particular design choices might affect children's learning—as well as children's use of physical materials in the classroom. We would like to draw attention to specific themes that we think are and will become significant in this area of research, including choosing between discrete and continuous flow of interaction, accounting for the affective dimension of learning, acknowledging the impact of different types of feedback, and attending to constraints.

While earlier software programs often chose more discrete modes of interaction (as in Clements and Sarama's discrete angle interface and the NVLM's discrete number line applets), there may be a move toward more continuous models both because of the new forms of interactions afforded by dynamic and touch-screen technologies and because of changes in our assumptions about what mathematical objects children should be exposed to. In terms of the latter, if prior technologies privileged whole numbers (Cuisinaire rods, base-10 blocks, and even discrete number lines), new technologies enable and sometimes require children to work with real numbers (Sinclair & Crespo, 2006), which presents interesting challenges for VMs as well as, more generally, for orchestrations of digital and physical classroom resources. We are reminded of Papert's promotion of the Mathland learning environment: much like living in a foreign country, Mathland does not limit forms of participation and interaction to the novice's basic vocabulary.

Many of the research studies we read, as well as reports in professional journals, highlight the higher level of engagement that children seem to experience when working with digital technologies. Although we assume this is not universally true, it is also part of the anecdotal evidence surrounding digital technology use at the high grades. Cognizant of the negative effects that too much "screen time" can have on young children (see Public Health England, 2013), more research on the nature and function of that engagement is warranted. It is not always clear from research reports whether the enjoyment stems from a simple change in environment, from the tighter feedback loop that the digital tool provides, or from the kind of curiosity, pride, and intellectual engagement that is typically associated with self-directed and deep mathematical learning. This would require theoretical and methodological tools that enable analyses that do not dichotomize the cognitive, affect, and aesthetic dimensions of learning.

One of the frequently mentioned strengths of digital technologies is their ability to provide instantaneous, customized feedback, which is very challenging for a classroom teacher to do. However, as we have signaled throughout the chapter, there are a wide variety of forms of feedback, each potentially functioning very differently both cognitively and affectively for children. More work is needed to understand how young children process and use these different forms of feedback.[22] For example, given the extensive research showing that evaluative, corrective teacher feedback (of the yes/no form) in the classroom has negative effects on student learning, developing and using digital technologies that only have this kind of feedback must have a strong counterrationale. At the same time, for teachers and research opting for more guided forms of feedback (responding through hints, for example), research that studies the way that children use—and what they learn from—this feedback would be very helpful. In addition, the exteriorization of thinking offered by digital technologies (which Noss & Hoyles, 1996 refer to as a "window on mathematical meanings") can be extremely helpful to teachers. This implies that more research is needed on how teachers make sense of and use feedback in working with and assessing their students.

We offered two different frameworks for distinguishing various digital technologies, both of which provided comparative power, but neither of which helps designers, researchers, and teachers attend to the way particular constraints can affect the development of mathematical meanings. Some constraints are determined by the technology (as in Clements and Sarama's choice of a discrete interaction) while others are the result of didactic goals. Constraints can be used purposefully to restrict and focus a learner's interactions, as discussed by Ladel and Kortenkamp (2011, 2013) and by Manches, O'Malley, and Benford (2010). For example, a constraint in TouchCounts is that numbered objects cannot be moved once they are placed on the screen; this constraint aims to restrict the children's externalizing actions in order to the internalization of the one-to-one-to-one correspondence between touch, objects, and number. In order to fully understand the potential of digital technologies, and their impact on student learning, the nature and consequence of these constraints needs to be taken into account. This will require better communication between designers, researchers and teachers in future research. Further, methodological choices for research need to reflect the way in which the learning environment as a whole, including the teacher and the tasks used in concert with the digital technology, functions to affect mathematical learning. To this end, we find persuasive Stylianides and Stylianides' (2013) argument in favor of teaching experiment (or classroom-based interventions) methodologies, which can increase the likelihood that the results of research are applicable while also shedding light on how and why certain situations work.

NOTES

1. For example, dynamic geometry environments (such as The Geometer's Sketchpad and Cabri-Elem) can be used to create microworlds that may function as virtual manipulatives or used on interactive whiteboards (with Sketchpad also available for the Apple iPad).
2. Sedig & Sumner (2006) distinguish between "real" and "perceived" affordances as a way of underscoring the fact that users do not always use digital technologies in the ways intended by their designers. This fact is central to the theory of *instrumental genesis*, which is discussed in the next section.
3. Sedig and Sumner (2006) point out that such interactions are often seen as reducing the cognitive load on learners, especially if they do not have to plan their actions in advance, which they might be more inclined to do in discrete, conversing interactions. The choice of a manipulating interaction over a conversing one will depend on the goal of the tool/task/concept.
4. We acknowledge that there are some major differences between the ways in which number sense is defined in the mathematical cognition literature and its definition in the literature in mathematics education (see, for example, Berch, 2005). Here we will refer to the literature in both fields, assuming that the more specific meaning within the former field is a necessary stepping stone towards its vaster, much more complex and multifaceted connotation proposed in the latter.
5. There is extensive literature showing the value of using calculators in the early years (Groves & Stacey, 1998) However, there seems to be much less enthusiasm for them amongst teachers and researchers, perhaps in part because they do not offer the visual forms of interaction that other digital technologies at this early age now do.
6. Research on the use of digital technologies with younger learners seems to have coincided with a new focus on the role of the teacher in technology-based classroom environments—this focus having been prompted by the realization that despite high levels of accessibility and institutional support, as well as supporting research, the use of digital technologies in the mathematics classroom remains relatively low (see Laborde, 2008).
7. Available on iTunes at https://itunes.apple.com/us/app/place-value-chart/id568750442?mt=8.
8. To play the game, visit http://number-sense.co.uk/numberbonds/.
9. Available on iTunes at https://itunes.apple.com/us/app/number-bonds-by-thinkout/id494521339?mt=8.
10. Available on the Apple App store at www.appstore.com/motionmathhd.
11. To play the game, visit http://illuminations.nctm.org/Activity.aspx?id=3566.
12. These children may be referred to in the literature as being affected by *dyscalculia* (Butterworth, 2005).
13. To play the game, visit http://number-sense.co.uk/dots2track/.
14. Available on iTunes at https://itunes.apple.com/it/app/fingu/id449815506?mt=8.
15. Something analogous to the part-whole concept is present in the Chinese mathematics education tradition in its presentation of "variation problems" (Sun, 2011).
16. Indeed, they are also relevant for topics other than geometry. However, it would seem that geometric environments such as DGEs have been more amenable to stretched across the grade levels.
17. Indeed, they are also relevant for topics other than geometry. However, it would seem that geometric environments such as dynamic geometry environments (DGEs) have been more amenable to stretched across the grade levels.
18. In a study focused more specifically on children's patterning, Moyer *et al.* (2005) also studied the use of a Pattern Block VM with kindergarten children and found that the patterns they created were more creative, complex and prolific when using the VM than when using concrete materials. Similarly, Highfield and Mulligan (2007) report that preschool children using a Pattern Block VM as well as a drawing tool called *Kidpix* experimented with more patterns, created more precise patterns and made more use of transformations than children who worked only with physical materials. The authors do caution that the children found the use of the mouse challenging—again, this is a hardware limitation that touch-screen technology can mitigate—and the additional affordances of *Kidpix* sometimes distracting.
19. For example, in Italy, the national curriculum stipulates that by grade three, when possible, students should be introduced to some programming languages that are simple and versatile in order to develop a taste for the planning and realization of projects and in order to understand the relation between coding language and its visual output. In the UK national curriculum, children are expected to develop competence in two or more programming languages by the age of eleven.

20. We highlight several new programming languages are specifically been developed for young children, such as *Squeak, ToonTalk* and Giorgi & Baccaglini-Frank's (2011) *Mak-Trace* app for the iPad.
21. See http://elresources.skola.edu.mt/wp-content/uploads/2010/06/doc_669_2468_beebotguide A4v2.pdf.
22. It seems like not all children do this in the same way. See Goodwin and Highfield (2013, p. 214).

REFERENCES

Andres, M., Seron, X., & Oliver, E. (2007). Contribution of hand motor circuits to counting. *Journal of Cognitive Neuroscience, 19*, 563–576.

Artigue, M. (2002). Learning mathematics in a CAS environment: The genesis of a reflection about instrumentation and the dialectics between technical and conceptual work. *International Journal of Computers for Mathematical Learning, 7*(3), 245–274.

Baccaglini-Frank, A., & Mariotti, M. A. (2010) Generating conjectures in dynamic geometry: The maintaining dragging model. *International Journal of Computers for Mathematical Learning, 15*(3), 225–253.

Baccaglini-Frank, A., Ramploud, A., & Bartolini Bussi, M. G. (2012). *Informatica Zero: Un percorso formativo per insegnanti di scuola dell'infanzia e primaria*. Fano, Italy: EduTouch.

Bafalluy, M. G. & Noël, M. P. (2008). Does finger training increase young children's numerical performance? *Cortex, 44*(4), 368–375. Retrieved from www.sciencedirect.com/science/article/pii/S0010945207000780.

Barendregt, W., Lindstrom, B., Rietz-Leppanen, E., Holgersson, I., & Ottosson, T. (2012). Development and evaluation of Fingu: A mathematics iPad game using multitouch interaction. *IDC 2012* (pp. 1–4). June 12–15, Bremen, Germany.

Bartolini Bussi, M. G. (2011). Artefacts and utilization schemes in mathematics teacher education: place value in early childhood education. *Journal of Mathematics Teacher Education, 14*(2), 93–112.

Bartolini Bussi, M. G. & Baccaglini-Frank, A. (2015). Geometry in early years: sowing the seeds towards a mathematical definition of squares and rectangles. *ZDM—The International Journal on Mathematics Education*. doi:10.1007/s11858-014-0636-5

Bartolini, M. G., Baccaglini-Frank, A., & Ramploud, A. (2014). Intercultural dialogue and the geography and history of thought. *For the Learning of Mathematics, 34*(1), 31–33.

Bartolini Bussi, M. G., & Mariotti, M. A. (2008). Semiotic mediation in the mathematics classroom: Artifacts and signs after a Vygotskian perspective. In L. English, M. Bartolini Bussi, G. Jones, R. Lesh, & D. Tirosh (Eds.), *Handbook of international research in mathematics education* (2nd ed.). Mahwah, NJ: Lawrence Erlbaum Associates.

Battista, M. T. (2007). The development of geometric and spatial thinking. In F. Lester (Ed.), *Second handbook of research on mathematics teaching and learning* (pp. 843–908). Reston, VA: National Council of Teachers of Mathematics.

Berch, D. B. (2005). Making sense of number sense: Implications for children with mathematical disabilities. *Journal of Learning Disabilities, 38*(4), 333–339.

Bolyard, J., & Moyer-Packenham, P. S. (2012). Making sense of integer arithmetic: The effect of using virtual manipulatives on students' representational fluency. *Journal of Computers in Mathematics and Science Teaching, 31*(2), 93–113.

Brissiaud, R. (1992). A toll for number construction: Finger symbol sets. In J. Bidaud, C. Meljac & J.-P. Fischer (eds.). *Pathways to number. Children's Developing Numerical Abilities*. Mahwah, NJ: Lawrence Erlbaum Associates.

Butterworth, B. (1999a). *What counts—how every brain is hardwired for math*. New York: The Free Press.

Butterworth, B. (1999b). *The mathematical brain*. London: Macmillan.

Butterworth, B. (2005). The development of arithmetical abilities. *Journal of Child Psychology and Psychiatry, 46*, 3–18.

Butterworth, B. (2011). Dyscalculia: From brain to education. *Science, 332*, 1049–1053.

Butterworth, B., & Laurillard, D. (2010). Low numeracy and dyscaclulia: Identification and intervention. *ZDM—The International Journal on Mathematics Education, 42*, 527–539.

Cantlon, J., Safford, K., & Brannon, E. (2010). Spontaneous analog number representations in 3-year-old children. *Developmental Science, 13*, 289–297.

Clements, D. H. (2002). Computers in Early Childhood Mathematics. *Contemporary Issues in Early Childhood, 3*(2), 160–181.

Clements, D. H., & Battista, M. T. (1989). Learning of geometric concepts in a Logo environment. *Journal of Research in Mathematics Education, 20*, 450–467.

Clements, D. H., & Sarama, J. (2004). Building Blocks for early childhood mathematics. *Early Childhood Research Quarterly, 19*, 181–189.

Clements, D. H., & Sarama, J. (2007). Effects of a preschool mathematics curriculum: Summary research on the *building blocks* project. *Journal for Research in Mathematics Education, 38*, 136–163.

Drijvers, P. (2012). Teachers transforming resources into orchestrations. In Gueudet, G., Pepin, B., & Trouche, L. *From textbooks to 'lived' resources: Mathematics curriculum materials and teacher documentation* (pp. 265–281), New York: Springer.

English L. D., & Mulligan J. (2013). *Advances in Mathematics Education: Vol. 8. Reconceptualizing early mathematics learning*. New York: Springer.

Fayol, M., & Seron, X. (2005). About numerical representations: Insights from neuropsychological, experimental, and developmental studies. In J.I.D. Campbell (Ed.), *Handbook of mathematical cognition*. New York: Psychology Press.

Feigenson, L., Dehaene, S., & Spelke, E., (2004). Core systems of number. *Trends in Cognitive Science, 8*(7), 307–314.

Gattegno, C. (1970). *Gattegno mathematics textbook 1*. New York: Educational Solution Worldwide.

Giorgi, G., & Baccaglini-Frank, A. (2011). Mak-Trace. Free application downloadable from Apple iTunes: http://itunes.apple.com/it/app/maktrace/id467939313?m t=8.

Goldenberg, P. (2000). *Thinking (and talking) about technology in math classrooms*. Educational Development Center. Retrieved from www2.edc.org/mcc/pdf/iss_tech.pdf.

Goodwin, K. (2009). *Impact and affordances of interactive multimedia*. Unpublished PhD thesis. Macquarie University, Sydney.

Goodwin, K., & Highfield, K. (2013). A framework for examining technologies and early mathematics learning. In L.D. English and J.T. Mulligan (Eds.), *Reconceptualizing early mathematics learning (pp 205–226)*. New York: Springer.

Gracia-Bafalluy, M., & Noel, M. (2008). Does finger training increase young children's numerical performance? *Cortex, 44*(4), 368–375.

Groves, S., & Stacey, K. (1998). Calculators in primary mathematics: Exploring number before teaching algorithms. *The Teaching and Learning of Algorithms in School Mathematics: 1998 Yearbook of the National Council of Teachers of Mathematics* (pp. 120–129, Reston, VA: National Council of Teachers of Mathematics.

Gueudet, G., Bueno-Ravel, L., & Poisard, C. (2013). Teaching mathematics with technology at the kindergarten level: Resources and orchestrations. In A. Clark-Wilson, O. Robutti, & N. Sinclair (Eds.), *The mathematics teacher in the digital era: An international perspective on technology focused professional development*. Dordrecht: Springer.

Gueudet, G., & Trouche, L. (2008). Towards new documentation systems for mathematics teachers? *Educational Studies in Mathematics, 71*(3), 199–218.

Highfield, K. (2009). Mapping, measurement and robotics. *Reflections, Journal of the Mathematical Association of New South Wales, 34*(1), 52–55.

Highfield, K. (2010). Robotic toys as a catalyst for mathematical problem solving. *Australian Primary Mathematics Classroom, 15*, 22–27.

Highfield, K., & Mulligan, J. (2007). The role of dynamic interactive technological tools in preschoolers' mathematical patterning. In J. Watson & K. Beswick (Eds.), *Proceedings of the 30th annual conference of the Mathematics Education Research Group of Australasia* (pp. 372–381). MERGA. Adelaide, Australia.

Highfield, K., & Mulligan, J.T. (2008). *Young children's engagement with technological tools: The impact on mathematics education*. Paper presented to the International Congress of Mathematical Education (ICME 11). Discussion Group 27: How is technology challenging us to re-think the fundamentals of mathematics education? Retrieved from http://dg.icme11.org/tsg/show/28.

Highfield, K., & Mulligan, J.T. (2009). Young children's embodied action in problem-solving tasks using robotic toys. In M. Tzekaki, M. Kaldrimidou, & H. Sakonidis (Eds.), *Proceedings of the 33rd conference of the International Group for the Psychology of Mathematics Education* (Vol. 2, pp. 273–280). Thessaloniki, Greece: PME.

Hollebrands, K. (2003). High school students' understandings of geometric transformations in the context of a technological environment. *Journal of Mathematical Behavior, 22*, 55–72.

Hoyles, C., Noss, R., & Adamson, R. (2002). Rethinking the microworld idea. *Journal of Educational Computing Research, 27*(1–2), 29–53.

Laborde, C. (2008). Technology as an instrument for teachers. In *Proceedings of the international commission for mathematics instruction centennial symposium*. Rome, Italy. Retrieved from www.unige.ch/math/EnsMath/ Rome2008/partWG4.html.

Laborde, C., Kynigos, C., Hollebrands, K., & Sträßer, R. (2006). Teaching and learning geometry with technology. In A. Gutiérrez & P. Boero (Eds.), *Handbook of research on the psychology of mathematics education: Past, present and future* (pp. 275–304). Rotterdam, The Netherlands: Sense Publishers.

Laborde, C., & Marcheteau, A. (2009). L'incontro tra reale e virtuale in Cabri Elem per attività matematiche nella scuola primaria, *La matematica e la sua didattica, 23*(1), 19–34.

Ladel, S., & Kortenkamp, U. (2011). Implementation of a multitouch-environment supporting finger symbol sets. In *Proceedings of the Seventh Congress of the European Society for Research in Mathematics Education*. Rzeszow, Poland: CERME.

Ladel, S., & Kortenkamp, U. (2013). An activity-theoretic approach to multi-touch tools in early maths learning. *The International Journal for Technology in Mathematics Education, 20*(1), 3–8.

Lakoff, G., & Núñez, R. (2000). *Where mathematics comes from: How the embodied mind brings mathematics into being*. New York: Basic Books.

Lyons, I., & Beilock, S. (2011). Numerical ordering ability mediates the relation between number-sense and arithmetic competence. *Cognition, 121*, 256–261.

Manches, A., O'Malley, C., & Benford, S. (2010). The role of physical representations in solving number problems: A comparison of young children's use of physical and virtual materials. *Computers & Education, 54*(3), 622–640.

Mariotti, M. A. (2006). Proof and proving in mathematics education. In A. Guttiérrez & P. Boero (Eds.), *Handbook of research on the psychology of mathematics education: Past, present and future* (pp. 173–204). Rotterdam, The Netherlands: Sense Publishing.

Maschietto, M., & Soury-Lavergne, S. (2013). The beginning of the adventure with pascaline and e-pascaline. In E. Faggiano & A. Montone (Eds.), *Proceedings of the 11th international conference on technology in mathematics teaching* (ICTMT 11; pp. 195–199). Bari: Università degli Studi di Bari.

Moorthy, S., Dominguez, X., Llorente, C., Pinkerton, L., Christiano, E., & Lesk, H. (2013). *Joint engagement with media that supports early science learning*. Paper presented at the Annual Meeting of the American Educational Research Association (AERA). San Francisco, CA.

Moyer, P., Niezgoda, D., & Stanley, J. (2005). Young children's use of virtual manipulatives and other forms of mathematical representations. In W. Masalski & P.C. Elliott (Eds.), *Technology-supported mathematics learning environments: 67th yearbook* (pp. 17–34). Reston, VA: National Council of Teachers of Mathematics.

Moyer-Packenham, P., Salkind, G.W., Bolyard, J., & Suh, J.M. (2013). Effective choices and practices: Knowledgeable and experienced teachers' uses of manipulatives to teach mathematics. *Online Journal of Education Research, 2*(2), 18–33. Retrieved from www.onlineresearchjournals.org/IJER/cont/2013/apr.htm.

Moyer-Packenham, P.S., & Suh, J.M. (2012). Learning mathematics with technology: The influence of virtual manipulatives on different achievement groups. *Journal of Computers in Mathematics and Science Teaching, 31*(1), 39–59.

Nemirovksy, R., Kelton, M. & Rhodehamel, B. (2013). Playing mathematical instruments: Emerging perceptuomotor integration with an interactive mathematics exhibit. *Journal for Research in Mathematics Education, 44*(2), 372–415.

Ng, O., & Sinclair, N. (2015). "They are getting married!" Towards a dynamic, functional understanding of symmetry in primary school. *ZDM—The International Journal on Mathematics Education*.

Noss, R., & Hoyles, C. (1996). *Windows on mathematical meanings*. Dordrecht, The Netherlands: Kluwer Academic Publishers.

Papert, S. (1980). *Mindstorms: Children, computers and powerful ideas*. New York: Basic Books.

Pekárová, J. (2008). Using a programmable toy at preschool age: Why and how? In *Proceedings of the international conference on simulation, modeling and programming for autonomous robots* (pp. 112–121). Heidelberg: Springer.

Penner-Wilger, M., Fast, L., LeFevre, J. A., Smith-Chant, B. L., Skwarchuk, S. L, Kamawar, D., & Bisanz, J. (2007). The foundations of numeracy: Subitizing, finger gnosis, and fine motor ability. In D.S. McNamara & J.G. Trafton (Eds.), *Proceedings of the 29th annual conference of the cognitive science society* (pp. 1385–1390). Austin, TX: Cognitive Science Society.

Piazza, M. (2010). Neurocognitive start-up tools for symbolic number representations. *Trends in Cognitive Sciences, 14*(12), 542–551.

Public Health England. (2013). *How healthy behaviour supports children's well-being*. PHE Publications gateway number: 2013146. Retrieved from www.gov.uk/government/publications/how-healthy-behaviour-supports-childrens-wellbeing.

Räsänen, P., Salminen, J., Wilson, A. J., Aunio, P., & Dehaene, S. (2009). Computer-assisted intervention for children with low numeracy skills. *Cognitive Development 24*(4), 450–472.

Riconscente, M. (2013). *Mobile learning game improves 5th graders' knowledge and attitudes*. Los Angeles: GameDesk Institute. Retrieved from www.gamedesk.org/projects/motion-math-in-class/.

Robutti, O. (2006). Motion, technology, gesture in interpreting graphs. *The International Journal for Technology In Mathematics Education, 13*(3), 117–126.

Resnick, L. B., Bill, V., Lesgold, S., & Leer, M. (1991). Thinking in arithmetic class. In B. Means, C. Chelemer, & M. S. Knapp (ed.). *Teaching advanced skills to at-risk students: Views from research and practice* (pp. 27–53). San Francisco: Jossey-Bass.

Sarama, J., & Clements, D. H. (2002). Building blocks for young children's mathematical development. *Journal of Educational Computing Research, 27*(1–2), 93–110.

Sarama, J., & Clements, D. H. (2009). "Concrete" computer manipulatives in mathematics education. *Child Development Perspectives, 3*(3), 145–150.

Sato, M., Cattaneo L., Rizzolatti, G., & Gallese, V. (2007). Numbers within our hands: Modulation of corticospinal excitability of hand muscles during numerical judgment. *Journal of Cognitive Neuroscience, 19*(4), 684–693.

Sedig, K., & Sumner, M. (2006). Characterizing interaction with visual mathematical representations. *International Journal of Computers for Mathematical Learning, 11*(1), 1–55.

Sfard, A. (2008). *Thinking as communicating: Human development, the growth of discourses, and mathematizing.* New York: Cambridge University Press.

Sinclair, N. (2013). TouchCounts: An embodied, digital approach to learning number. *Proceedings of the International Conference of Technology in Mathematics Teaching 11.* Bari, Italy: Università degli Studi di Bari.

Sinclair, N., & Crespo, S. (2006). Learning mathematics with dynamic computer environments. *Teaching Children Mathematics 12*(9), 436–444.

Sinclair, N., de Freitas, E., & Ferrara, F. (2013). Virtual encounters: The murky and furtive world of mathematical inventiveness. *ZDM—The International Journal on Mathematics Education, 45*(2), 239–252.

Sinclair, N., & Heyd-Metzayunim, E. (2014). Learning number with TouchCounts: The role of emotions and the body in mathematical communication. *Technology, Knowledge and Learning.*

Sinclair, N., & Jackiw, N. (2011). TouchCounts. Free application downloadable on the App Store, https://itunes.apple.com/ca/app/touchcounts/id897302197?mt=8.

Sinclair, N., & Kaur, H. (2011). Young children's understanding of reflection symmetry in a dynamic geometry environment. *Proceedings of the 35th conference of the international group for the psychology of mathematics education.* Ankara, Turkey: PME.

Sinclair, N. & Moss, J. (2012). The more it changes, the more it becomes the same: The development of the routine of shape identification in dynamic geometry environments. *International Journal of Education Research, 51&52*(3), 28–44.

Sinclair, N., & Robutti, O. (2013). Technology and the role of proof: The case of dynamic geometry. In A. J. Bishop, M. A. Clements, C. Keitel, & F. Leung (Eds.), *Third international handbook of mathematics education.* Dordrecht, The Netherlands: Kluwer Academic Publishers.

Sinclair, N., & Yurita, V. (2008). To be or to become: How dynamic geometry changes discourse. *Research in Mathematics Education, 10*(2), 135–150.

Sowell, E. J. (1989). Effects of manipulative materials in mathematics instruction. *Journal of Research in Mathematics Education, 20*(5), 498–505.

Steen, K., Brookes, D., & Lyon, T. (2006). The impact of virtual manipulatives on first grade geometry instruction and learning. *Journal of Computers in Mathematics and Science Teaching, 25*(4), 373–391.

Stevens, R., & Penuel, W. R. (2010, October). *Studying and fostering learning through joint media engagement.* Paper presented at the Principal Investigators Meeting of the National Science Foundation's Science of Learning Centers, Arlington, VA.

Stylianides, A. J., & Stylianides, G. J. (2013). Seeking research-grounded solutions to problems of practice: Classroom-based interventions in mathematics education. *ZDM—The International Journal on Mathematics Education, 45*(3), 333–340.

Sun, X. (2011). "Variation problems" and their roles in the topic of fraction division in Chinese mathematics textbook examples. *Educational Studies in Mathematics, 76*(1), 65–85.

Thompson J. C., Abbott, D. F., Wheaton, K. J., Syngeniotis, A., & Puce. A. (2004). Digit representation is more than just hand waving. *Cognitive Brain Research, 21*, 412–17.

Trouche, L. (2004). Managing complexity of human/machine interactions in computerized learning environments: Guiding students' command process through instrumental orchestrations. *International Journal of Computers for Mathematical Learning, 9*, 281–307.

Yelland, N. (2002). Creating microworlds for exploring mathematical understandings in the early years of school. *Journal of Educational Computing Research, 27*(1–2), 77–92.

van Herwegen, J., Ansari, D., Xu, F., & Karmiloff-Smith, A. (2008). Small and large number processing in infants and toddlers with Williams syndrome. *Developmental Science, 11*, 637–643.

Wilson, A., Revkin, S., Cohen, D., Cohen, L., & Dehaene, S. (2006). An open trial assessment of "The Number Race," an adaptive computer game for remediation of dyscalculia. *Behavioral and Brain Functions, 2*(20).

Wilson, A. J., Dehaene, S., Pinel, P., Revkin, S. K., Cohen, L., & Cohen, D. (2006). Principles underlying the design of "The Number Race," an adaptive computer game for remediation of dyscalculia. *Behavioral and Brain Functions, 2*(19). doi:10.1186/1744-9081-2-19

Wilson, A., & Dehaene, S. (2007). Number sense and developmental dyscalculia. In D. Coch, G. Dawson, & K. Fischer (Eds.), *Human behavior, learning, and the developing brain: Atypical development* (pp. 212–238). New York: Guilford Press.

Final Comment

29 Mathematics Education Research
A Strategic View

Hugh Burkhardt

Shell Centre, University of Nottingham and the University of California, Berkeley

INTRODUCTION

The previous chapters in this handbook have brought together a huge amount of research by the community of scholars in mathematics education, integrated and summarized in each chapter by some of the leaders in the field. Here I am going to look at research in mathematics education from a strategic point of view[1]—as a collective enterprise that aims to serve various communities. In doing so I respect the scholars who assert their traditional academic right to plough their own furrow, wherever it may lead; this chapter is not for them. However, I believe that most researchers in education are motivated by the thought that their work will benefit others, notably but not exclusively students at various stages in their education.

Yet, the influence of our work on what happens in classrooms at large usually travels a long path where any causal effect is far from clear (Burkhardt & Schoenfeld, 2003). What are the reasons that underlie this limited impact? It is certainly not that the research is irrelevant—far from it.

This question is reflected in many of the earlier chapters. While impact "at scale" is not their main focus, its absence is recognized as a concern. I'll mention just two examples. Cobb, Jackson, and Dunlap (Chapter 20), at the end of their luminous chapter on design research, put it thus:

> A third major weakness concerns the frequent failure of researchers conducting classroom and PD design studies to design for scale when preparing for studies, thereby limiting the potential pragmatic payoff and relevance of their work beyond the research community.
>
> (p. 498)

This points to a neglect of *teacher* variables in the study of *teaching*. The attitude of Charalambous and Pitta-Pantazi (Chapter 2) is perhaps more typical. They end their review of the impact of teaching on learning:

> In this respect, working on unpacking and understanding this complex relationship creates an arena for forging fruitful and productive collaborations between researchers, policy makers, and practitioners—which comprises a still unfulfilled demand.
>
> (p. 44)

From this perspective, the role of research is to provide insights; how the "unfulfilled demand" is to be met is left for others to work out.

Accordingly, this chapter addresses the specific questions: Can the research community do better in turning insights into impact on policy and practice—and how?

Levels of Research and Development

I find it useful to distinguish four levels, focused respectively on learning, teaching, teachers and their professional development, and school system change. Research gets more difficult as one moves up the size scale in a way summarized in Table 29.1 (Burkhardt, 2001, 2013). Each level embraces those above. Successful large-scale high-quality improvement requires coherent alignment throughout the levels, which is itself a system-level challenge.

Table 29.1 Four levels of R&D

	Focal variables	*Typical Research and Development Foci*
Learning (L)	Student Task	R: Concepts, skills, strategies, metacognition, beliefs D: Learning situations, probes, data capture
Teaching (T)	Instruction Student Task	R: Teaching strategies and tactics, nature of student learning D: Classroom materials that are OK for some teachers
Typical Teachers (RT)	Teacher Instruction Student Task	R: Performance of representative teachers with realistic support. Basic studies of teacher knowledge and competency. D: Classroom materials that "work" for most teachers
System Change (SC)	System School Teacher Instruction Student Task	R: System change D: Tools for change—i.e., materials for classrooms, assessment, professional development, community relations

The great majority of research in mathematics education reflected in this *Handbook* has studied learning and/or teaching. This preponderance is particularly true of solution-focused research that goes beyond "diagnosis" in the direction of developing more effective "treatments." This is not only understandable but, in some ways, right. What happens in the classroom is what school systems are all about. City, Elmore, Fiarman, and Teitel (2009) have emphasized that any initiative is only successful insofar as it supports improvement in this "zone of instruction." However, marvelous things that emerge in classrooms working closely with a research project may not be directly accessible to representative teachers. In any skilled activity—and mathematics teaching is surely that—there will be a wide range of expertise.[2] But instead of extending the research to this third level in the table, by addressing teacher variables, there is a tendency simply to end a research paper with a call for more and better professional development—a highly desirable goal, but one that inevitably needs R&D at the fourth system level. Though the research in this *Handbook* looks at mathematics education from a variety of perspectives, there are no chapters (other than this one) that focus on the third or fourth level in Table 29.1—for example, on the processes of professional development of representative teachers, various ways in which that has been supported, and the outcomes, or on the dynamics of change at system level. This is a reflection of the balance of current effort across the research community.

It is worth noting that the standards of evaluation are different at each level in Table 29.1, reflecting the number of variables and the difficulty in controlling them. Whereas learning studies can reliably report specific phenomena, system studies must inevitably work with distributions. However, they need to focus on what is important, notably what happens in classrooms with teachers and students at various stages of development throughout the processes of systemic change.

The Research Community

I will take the viewpoint, implicit in any handbook like this, that research is a community enterprise. The research community itself is a system, where our influence on others is evidenced by the references in their papers—sometimes with comments and responses in the text. Teachers who are active in action research in their own classrooms build on the work of others and spread the insights they have gained. But how well does the design of this collective enterprise help the communities it aims to serve?

Of course, I am adopting a contrary perspective: the pattern of work in the research community is not *designed*. Individual researchers, mostly university staff and their graduate students, make autonomous decisions as to what to work on next. But these decisions are influenced by a variety of pressures and opportunities. A graduate student's choice of dissertation topic is usually guided by his or her supervisor—and rightly so, since choosing a topic with the right balance of challenge and feasibility requires insight and experience. This influence continues: some fresh PhDs who follow an academic career go on working on extensions of their dissertation, sometimes for many years. The availability of research grants may give a researcher the opportunity to build a team so that more ground can be covered, but such research leverage comes at a price: fitting your proposal to the priorities of the funding agency. Finally, there is "fashion." Some types of research are more in vogue than others.

Fashions, of course, change with time—otherwise they would not be fashions. For example, over the last 30 years the balance of highly regarded research in mathematics education has swung from quantitative methods that yield statistically reliable answers to (inevitably) simple questions towards qualitative studies that look in depth at (inevitably) small samples. *Design research*—a term first coined by Anne Brown (1992) though the style of research is much older (see e.g. Swan, 1980; Swan et al., 1984; Birks, 1987)—has moved from being seen as "not really research" to achieving some academic respectability. Engineering research in education (Burkhardt, 2006), where improved products and processes for use in practice are as important as the insights underlying them, still hovers on the edge—though it is well-supported by those funding agencies whose priority is impact on what happens in classrooms.

Three Different Traditions

There are profound variations in the view of research and scholarship that coexist in the education community. They arise from very different traditions, reflecting respectively the humanities, science, and engineering (Burkhardt, 2001, 2006).

The humanities tradition, widely used across the social sciences, is based on richly informed observation and analysis, distilled into commentary. It does not demand empirical testing of assertions, but places emphasis on the plausibility of the arguments and the quality of the writing. These priorities help to make this the approach that has most influence with policy makers, partly at least because it is an implicit invitation for anyone to play—an invitation that politicians are often happy to accept. Their "common sense"[3] thinking is plausible, to them and some of their constituents at least, and they are often skilled with language—their stock in trade. As well as the lack of empirical testing, a key weakness of this approach is that so many plausible ideas in education turn out not to work well in practice. For example, "no social promotion"—a favorite in the United States that makes students repeat a year they did not "pass"—is superficially plausible and politically attractive as showing a determination to "raise standards."

Next, there is the *science* tradition. It is based on empirical investigation: the study of phenomena and the creation and careful testing of hypotheses. Not surprisingly, as the other chapters in this *Handbook* show, it dominates within the research communities in science education and, mostly,[4] in mathematics education. More surprisingly, most of it has little impact on policy makers or, directly, on practice. For example, the evidence on repeating a year shows that few students do better the second time and many drop out of mathematics, or leave school altogether. Why is the large body of research evidence like this not taken more seriously[5] and what could be done about it? That is the theme of this chapter.

An exception is survey work. Trends in Mathematics and Science Study (TIMSS), the Programme for International Student Assessment (PISA), the U.S. National Assessment of

Educational Progress (NAEP), and a host of smaller-scale surveys can provide useful diagnostic information. They are often taken seriously by policy makers—perhaps too seriously, because they rarely offer reliable *formative* evidence on what to do about the challenges they reveal. Cultural backgrounds, reviewed here by Appelbaum and Stathopoulou (Chapter 13), are critically important. Frederick Leung (2001, 2006), for example, has argued that East Asian culture (which is not readily transferred to "Western" countries) plays a central role in the high performance of East Asian countries in mathematics tests.[6]

Last, and least in number of researchers, there is the engineering approach to research in education (Burkhardt, 2006). Its priority is impact on practice. It uses insights from prior research, design skills, and research methods of development to create improved products and processes, as well as deeper insights into design principles.[7] It goes beyond most design research, as described here by Cobb, Jackson, and Dunlap (Chapter 20), in carrying the development process through iterative trialing and revision until intentions and outcomes converge—i.e. the products are made widely available and work well in the hands of specified target groups of teachers and students.

These distinctions are symbiotically linked to variations in the academic value system, the set of criteria by which the quality of research in education is judged—both driven by it and reinforcing it. I'll look at this critical issue in more detail next.

RESEARCH FOR WHOM?

In this section, I will look at the way research currently serves three different communities: graduate students as aspiring members of the research community, the research community itself, and education systems as a whole with a particular focus on their students. These are issues of *strategic design* (Burkhardt, 2009). In describing this concept, which addresses those aspects of design that relate to the system that the design aims to serve, I noted that, while excellence in an educational product or process depends on the quality of its structural and technical design, including the details, the failure of an educational initiative to have impact often arises from inadequate strategic design—insufficient design attention to its interface with the system.

I found no shortage of examples of initiatives with unintended consequences that were entirely predictable—and often predicted. In a nutshell, these initiatives had "doom written all over them" as to their intended purpose. A familiar example is the introduction of new learning goals backed by high-stakes tests without the proven support that would enable teachers to meet the new challenges. More generally, the fact that a successful initiative depends on having a well-engineered balance of pressure and support matched to a digestible pace of change, has not been widely taken on board—perhaps because pressure is relatively cheap, while effective support for long-term professional and system development is not.

Sometimes, though initiatives failed to come close to their declared goals, there were beneficial side effects. For example, some curriculum projects that had none of the hoped-for large-scale impact have provided invaluable professional growth for those involved in and with the project. Often, they have also created high-quality exemplars for others to use or to build on. Equally, discontent with attempts to improve teaching through crude evaluations dominated by narrow tests (pressure without support again) have led to deeper research on what is good mathematics teaching (e.g. Schoenfeld, 2014) and how it might be evaluated in real classrooms, for formative guidance in professional development and/or summative evaluation for accountability.

Serving the Graduate Student

Universities see the research training of graduate students as one of their main responsibilities. What this means in practice, indeed the very meaning of the term *graduate student,* varies from country to country. In some the graduate student is in the anteroom of an academic career; in others, the PhD is also an entry qualification for a variety of professions within education, including assessment and various leadership or administrative roles in the public or private sectors. This affects the kind of support that is provided—for example, the balance of knowledge transmission and research experience. In this handbook on research, I shall focus on the support for aspiring researchers—those who hope to pursue an academic career.

Though few graduate schools have all the qualities set out here by Kilpatrick and Spangler (Chapter 11), the story is basically one of success, at least in the Anglophone countries I know best. There is a steady demand for access to graduate study. Students move through their courses, whether for masters or doctoral degrees, and most graduate within the expected time. Indeed, signs of slow progress lead to criticisms of the institution that are taken seriously. The PhD gives access to academic or other high-level careers, with the most prestigious universities recruiting those who do best, as judged by peer review of their dissertations and publications, and their supervisor's recommendation and reputation. Those who don't pursue academic careers can usually find interesting and well-paid jobs in education or other fields.

There are ideas for developing graduate education further. For example, should research training become part of every teacher's trajectory of professional development, in order to promote reflective practice in the classroom and help bridge the gap between research and practice? Should more teachers become active partners in design research and engineering research projects? One such approach, through the dialogic interaction between the teachers and researchers described here by Ruthven and Goodchild (Chapter 22), seems enormously rich as professional development. However, it and other research-based models of teaching place design loads on the teacher-partners that may not work well on a large-scale, in just the way that Cobb, Jackson, and Dunlap (Chapter 20) noted. But ideas like this are another sign of a healthy, lively graduate education scene.

There are some concerns: for example, the issue of "market demand." In a steady state, where the average faculty member holds on to a tenured job for 25 years, s/he should produce only one or two PhDs for "replacement purposes." Is graduate training paying enough attention to preparing graduate students for other professional roles? Would a broader education in research methods from across the social sciences help?

Serving the Research Community

At first sight, and not surprisingly, we seem to do rather well in serving our own community. Worldwide, there are tens of thousands of people working in educational research. In the United States alone, around 20,000 find resources to attend the annual conferences of the American Educational Research Association, which has thriving special interest groups in mathematics education and other specialties. The salaries of the academics involved represent a huge investment in research, currently larger than all other sources combined.

The processes within our research community work smoothly. Papers get written and published in journals with wide circulation and impeccable systems of peer review. Major results are brought together in handbooks such as this. Professors get appointed, are given tenure, and promoted on criteria that emphasize research quality in a way that satisfies the community. Research grants are awarded on similar criteria, enabling researchers to expand their contribution, yielding more papers and reports that meet the funder's accountability needs. All this provides grounds for pride. What, if any, are the grounds for concern?

Academic posts have other major demands, notably for teaching and administration. While that diversity of roles is within the tradition of academic research in all fields, research time in education is often particularly squeezed by these other, more immediate demands. Research is also constrained by other pressures, notably time scale and resources—a flow of journal papers must be sustained year-by-year, each produced within the research time available in practice.

It is notable how few people are employed in full-time research in education, within universities and outside, when compared with established research-based fields, whether "pure" or "applied." This reflects the scale of direct outside funding of research. In the UK, for example, the Economic and Social Research Council, which covers all the social sciences[8] including education, receives only about 5% of the total research council budget—and education gets a small fraction of this. This certainly does not reflect the relative importance of education in policy makers' eyes; it does reflect the lowly position of educational research in the public eye and on the academic totem pole. Is there a missed opportunity here?

What can be learned from other fields? At the "pure" end, physics in wealthy countries is funded through research-funding structures that support the many postdoctoral researchers who form a large proportion of the research manpower needed to tackle major challenges. International consortia are formed in order to match human capital to the scale of each problem. The two main experimental groups at CERN's Large Hadron Collider each involve thousands of postdoctoral scientists, full- and part-time, many of whom have been working on the project for half an academic lifetime. This is an extreme example, and many physicists do not want to work this way, preferring small-scale studies on smaller problems amenable to that approach; its relevance here is that tackling big problems of real importance effectively may require big team efforts, and that research communities can, over time, organize themselves in this way to meet such challenges. How has this scale of research funding become established? Highly visible past achievements of physicists (radar, operations research, the bomb and nuclear power, the World Wide Web, and so on) have led the public to believe that physics research has long-term payoffs for them, and so deserves respect and substantial funding.[9]

Society sees education as an "applied" field, with children's learning the prime measure of success. Are there useful comparisons there? At the applied end of well-established research-based fields, engineering has a centuries-old history of systematic research and development, so that it now rests on a solid theoretical foundation. As a research community, it has a base of full-time researchers in universities, supported by funding agencies, and others working in industry. Together they gather insights into engineering problems, often involving physics and other fundamental sciences. These insights help them to invent new devices and develop them into prototypes, often in collaboration with companies. These will do the later systematic development and refinement that turns prototypes into robust products and processes that work well in the hands of the intended users. The relevance of this example is that it highlights the near absence of a research-based industry in education; currently, if a research group wants its ideas to become robust products that work well in practice, it has to carry through the development and testing itself—hence the nature of engineering research in education. I will argue that a key factor behind the lack of a research-based industry is the lack of serious *evaluation in depth* of educational products—not only "What works?" but "What happens, to whom, under what circumstances, and how can we make it better?"

Medicine is probably the field from which education can learn most. A century ago medicine was largely a "craft-based" field in which the main source of wisdom was experienced practitioners, sharing their insights in person and through writing. Though much was known about human anatomy, and something about physiology, most research was regarded as "academic" and had little impact on the work of doctors and surgeons.[10] Since then, triggered in the United States by the Flexner (1910) report, the situation has been gradually transformed. The human body and its pathologies still contain many basic mysteries, presenting important unsolved problems. But systematic empirical work has gone hand-in-hand with theoretical analysis of the results and subsequent development of products and processes in collaboration with industry, yielding a gradual transformation of the field. Medical practice is now heavily theory-based, with empirical R&D used mainly for refining treatments at the many points where theory is insufficient. In the UK for example, the National Institute for Health and Care Excellence (NICE) produces evidence-based evaluations of treatments, using the best research evidence available along with specific criteria for both effectiveness and, more controversially, cost effectiveness.[11] Internationally, the Cochrane Collaboration is a large group of researchers who work together to distil and integrate the results of the many separate studies in important areas. Though progress has happened on nearly all fronts,[12] I shall mention just two significant examples that have different, but equally important, lessons for us, if education is to move forward to becoming a more research-based field of practice.

The discovery of penicillin by Alexander Fleming led to an explosion of research and development on antibiotics that necessarily involved academic-industry collaboration and the major impact on health care we all know. Its main significance here is the effect on public perceptions of research. As with the high-impact developments in physics, this was something that the public could see and value for themselves, ensuring support for the subsequent major increases in funding for medical research.

The second example is the discovery in 1952 of the structure of DNA by Crick and Watson. This fundamental discovery, though it has led to useful inventions like "DNA fingerprinting," has yet to have an impact on large-scale health care comparable with antibiotics. Yet its *perceived potential* is such that a huge effort, both collaborative and competitive, has gone into its development. The first sequencing of a human genome took an international collaboration a decade and cost about $3 billion. Twenty years later, refinement and automation have reduced the cost to a few thousand dollars, offering the prospect of treatments that are tailored to an individual's DNA. This shows how large-scale collaborative enterprises that offer convincing *prospects* for societal good, even decades later, can attract major support.

These "proof of concept" examples show how research communities can organize themselves to become more respected, better supported, and more influential within society.[13] They show how either highly visible impact on society or perceived potential can lead to major support. Next I outline how research in mathematics education can move in these directions.

Serving Students in Schools

There is general agreement across the world that the education of most students in mathematics needs to improve, substantially and in many dimensions. The broad goals set out by PISA, TIMSS, the U.S. National Council of Teachers of Mathematics (NCTM) Standards, the recent Common Core State Standards in the United States, and briefer specifications from other countries have much in common with each other and reflect a broad consensus across the international mathematics education community, at least on performance goals. So does the dissatisfaction with the status quo. Summarizing this for an international review of mathematics curricula, I wrote:

> Around the world people seem to have much the same goals for the outcomes of a mathematics education. Students should emerge with a reliable command of a wide range of mathematical skills, a deep understanding of the concepts that underlie them, and an ability to use them, flexibly and effectively, to tackle problems that arise—within mathematics and in life and work beyond the classroom. Students should, as far as possible, find learning and using mathematics interesting and enjoyable.
>
> (Burkhardt, 2014, p. 14)

But I also described groups of people with different *priorities* and different *beliefs* about how to reach these goals. The effect is usually to narrow the goals from the broad set that I outlined. So "basic skills people" believe that tackling nonroutine problems, though important, should wait until students have "a solid foundation in skills"—a stage that is, in practice, never reached by most students. They discount the ability of young children to think through real-world problems using (inevitably) simple mathematics as "trivial." In contrast, "mathematical literacy people" see this last activity as central; they give lower priority to students' acquiring knowledge of more advanced mathematics that they can only reproduce in imitative exercises, if at all—the position of most adults for all the mathematics they were first taught in secondary school.

However, the focus of this chapter is largely independent of the performance goals that are chosen. Rather, it is on how research could better help school systems to enable students to achieve these goals. It is often true that narrower goals may be easier to achieve, but here I will stay with the broad widely accepted goals that I outlined—goals that have been achieved in *many* classrooms but not, as far as I know, across *most* of the classrooms in any school system worldwide. Elsewhere, I've analyzed why this is so (Burkhardt, 2014); here I focus on the roles (actual and potential) of the research community in enabling school systems to rise to this well-recognized challenge.

Given the relatively healthy picture of research in mathematics education outlined in this *Handbook,* why is the research community not the first port of call when policy makers seek improvement? It is not for want of advice—but that advice, even when sought, is often treated as merely opinion, of no greater validity than the politicians' own "views." Why is this so, when it is very different in the well-established research-based applied fields discussed earlier?

Among the factors behind this impotence are the apparent conflicts of opinion among "the experts" (basic skills vs. problem solving; "phonics" vs. mixed reading; technology throughout vs. light and late, and so on) that are often really matters of emphasis and of strategic design. But I believe it goes deeper, lying in an academic value system that meets the internal needs and constraints of the research community in ways that, incidentally but inevitably, limit its impact on policy and practice.

Theory: For Whom and for What?

Here I want to take a somewhat deeper look at the relationships in the value system that drives and constrains research in education: between the analytic and the creative aspects of research, including theory, exemplification, and design. The academy has traditionally stuck to the analytic. In the humanities tradition insights are expressed in critical commentary, with internal and external plausibility and originality among the key criteria of quality. Professors' novels or plays, however good, were "small change" academically. In academic music depart-ments, playing and even composing were slightly beside the central point: analysis in the form of music theory and history. Academic engineering, too, was usually about theory rather than design in both research and teaching. Over recent decades this has begun to change. Painters and musicians are appointed as professors, as are engineers with original design achievements. Design research (Brown, 1992) and engineering research in education (Burkhardt, 2006) are increasingly recognized as academically legitimate, though such research is still often judged more on the journal papers than on the influence of the products on practice.

What about science, the ultimate insight-focused academic pursuit? As I have noted, its paradigms dominate research in mathematics education, though not in education more widely. Science is all about theory building, so a closer comparison with education is worthwhile. First, the ultimate prize in both fields is a grand theory, concisely explained, that describes a huge range of phenomena—the wider the better. Newton's laws of motion and gravitation epito-mize this: a towering edifice of simple mathematical rules that accurately describe and predict a huge range of phenomena, from motion in the solar system to roller coasters—a range with well-understood limits at very small and very large distances. Though some theoretical physi-cists spend their whole careers as *Newtons-manqué,* most scientists do not work in this way. The overwhelming majority of theory building in scientific research is much more modest, phe-nomenological, and collective. In the architectural metaphor, people add bricks to a growing building of theory or—occasionally if they are very good and lucky—begin a new wing. Always the value of their contribution to the whole structure is the key criterion, guided and judged by agreement of theoretical predictions with experiment. The design of an airplane, for example, depends on combining a *global theory*—Newton's laws of motion—with a massive amount of experimentally based *local phenomenological theory* on the properties of materials, from metals to air. For example, it is crucial to know not only how much a metal stretches when stressed, but when it will break—and to know it reliably. Even there, where theory is strong enough to design on a computer a prototype that will fly, careful development with rich and detailed feedback from testing is an essential part of aeronautical engineering.

Where do theories in education stand from this perspective? David Kirshner (Chapter 4) brings out the enormous variety of ways in which researchers look at teaching and learning. There are grand theories: behaviorism and the various flavors of constructivism are obvious examples. From a scientific viewpoint these are not *theories* but *effects*: true but incomplete and, often, with no well-established boundaries of validity (Burkhardt, 1988). When they are used in the design of products and processes, their too-enthusiastic proponents often cause harm to students' education by ignoring the limitations of the theory in relation to broader learning goals: mathematics curricula designed entirely on behaviorist lines are a well-recognized example. Other theoretical contributions provide valuable insights into specific phenomena; however, they often seem to overlap, differing in nuance and language rather than fundamentals—fine as commentary but perhaps unhelpful for building coherent theory.

There *are* well-founded phenomenological theories in education but they, too, tend to be oversold, gaining local success by ignoring the bigger picture of the global goals. For example, practice alone *can* enable students to "master" the procedures of arithmetic and algebra. However, retaining these skills requires either conceptual understanding of why they work or continual further practice—and life is too short and the different skills of mathematics too many for that. Nonetheless that approach is still widely used in classrooms around the world. Equally, the effectiveness of phonics teaching in enabling children to decode text into sounds is well established, but phonics-dominated reading schemes can delay reading for comprehension and enjoyment—the global goals.

Complementing these theories, global and more local, there are very many small-scale empirical studies in depth of learning and teaching that provide intriguing insights but with no warrants for their wider validity beyond their plausibility. As Alan Schoenfeld put it in a previous *Handbook:*

> A very large percentage of educational studies are of the type, "here is a perspective, phenomenon, or interpretation worth attending to," and that their ultimate value is both heuristic ("one should pay attention to this aspect of reality") and as catalysts for further investigation.
>
> (Schoenfeld, 2002, Section 4, p. 470)

Schoenfeld traces this remarkably—and deservedly—modest level of confidence in the products of the research enterprise to three dimensions of efficacy:

Trustworthiness: How well substantiated are the claims?
Generalizability: How wide a range of phenomena does the evidence cover?
Importance: How much should we care?

(Schoenfeld, 2002, Section 4, pp. 466–467)

Within given resources of time and effort, there is a trade-off between these. A study has to score high on perceived trustworthiness to get published. Thus there is often insufficient time and resources to get empirical evidence of generalizability, which requires studying an adequate variety of circumstances that spans a well-defined range in each of the important variables. Issues of importance are often irreducible to the scale of a study that fits a researcher's constraints of time and resources.[14]

This multiplicity of overlapping theories, though each may provide useful insights, is a weakness; theoretical power comes from a small amount of theory, preferably simply expressed, that describes the essential features of a specific range of phenomena. "Reductive" is a pejorative term in education, and rightly so for both phenomena and analytical commentary on them. However, powerful theory is essentially reductive. The challenge is not to throw out the baby with the bathwater, keeping all the essentials for the phenomena concerned, but only those. Thus Newton's analysis of planetary motion treats each planet as a point mass—fine for this purpose but not for, say, weather forecasting.

The use of terms is equally profligate. Lyn English and Julie Gainsburg begin Chapter 12 by pointing to the diversity of meanings of "problem solving," noted decades ago by Jeremy Kilpatrick (1981), that are still in use. They remark that "traditionally, problems have been defined as tasks in which the solver does not know how to arrive at an answer" (p. 314), then examine the multiplicity of other ways "problems and problem solving" have been and are used, before going on to the important issues of substance: relating problem solving to the demands of the 21st-century world. There has been occasional modest progress in reaching general agreement on terms. The 1989 NCTM Standards used *evaluation* in its many possible meanings. I and others pushed for a more refined lexicon: *assessment* in relation to student performance; *appraisal* for the performance of teachers and other professionals; and *evaluation* for projects and programs of various sorts—only the first has been widely adopted.[15]

This profligacy of terms and theories does not help the development of a firm foundation on which to move forward and build a coherent structure that could be commended to designers as reliable, or to policy makers as sound. Though every student, teacher, and classroom is unique, there is a great deal of commonality across the phenomena observed in mathematics classrooms. Even a very perceptive observer might hope for some consolidation of the body of theory and the use of terms. This can only be done as a community enterprise—one for which there currently seems neither mechanism nor appetite.

The Academic Value System

Where does this pattern of research come from? I have noted that the educational research community reflects traditions with very different views of research and scholarship—roughly those of the humanities, sciences, and engineering—and, particularly, the constraints of time and resources under which most researchers operate. Emerging from this has been a set of values as to what is "good research" that might be summarized in a list of academic priorities, which favor:

- new investigations *over* replication and extension
- new ideas *over* results that can be relied on
- disputation *over* consensus building
- trustworthiness *over* generalizability
- first author *over* team member
- personal research *over* team research
- small studies *over* major programs
- journal papers *over* products and processes

These priorities are the reverse of what is needed to provide a reliable basis for the design of tools and processes that will improve policy and practice. These values encourage the reworking, remarked on earlier, of familiar concepts in different terms, leading to the multiplicity of closely related theoretical viewpoints. They reward new perspectives over the consolidation of theory.

These conventions in educational research reflect and perpetuate a priority for small-scale work. Other fields show that it doesn't have to be this way. They recognize that "personal research" usually means either small problems or little testing of evidence. Giving priority to "first author" in genuine team research is usually invidious—if the others have not made essential contributions they should not be authors. In physics, where papers may have many authors, the convention is to list the names of the team alphabetically; those who need to find out who did what in the collective enterprise can inquire.

The payoff from disputation inhibits the consolidation of theory. Researchers, particularly those from the different traditions, often disagree in their judgments of quality. In a recent attempt to agree on common standards for research quality across a large school of education, a group of senior professors each rank-ordered six well-regarded papers of different kinds. There was no agreement; indeed some of the rank orders were the reverse of others, reflecting the different priorities referred to above—between quality of imagination and writing *versus* empirical evidence, for example.

In this light it is little wonder that the collective impact of the educational research communities on practice is limited, indeed much less than the sum of its parts, with contradictory perspectives at the global level along with less data-driven fine-grained phenomenological work that addresses high-level learning goals. In the next section, I will look at ways in which some of the great skills in the research community might be redirected to change this, and the huge total effort made more influential.

However, there is a growing body of research that moves beyond these stereotypes, at once less and more ambitious. It exemplifies what can be done—and could be done more widely in developing solid phenomenology and good engineering within a global vision and a broad set of goals for learning. That work provides the basis for the more constructive sections that follow.

HOW MIGHT WE SERVE STUDENTS BETTER?

I now want to outline ways in which the research community in mathematics education can move to increase the impact of its work on practice—ultimately, in the improvement of the learning experiences of students in classrooms, and the lives of the adults they become. I believe that, largely as the result of the last 40 years' work across the field of mathematics education, we know how to enable typical teachers to guide their students to learn much better mathematics much better—but that it won't happen unless the kind of things outlined in this section are in place.

A decade ago, Alan Schoenfeld and I (Burkhardt & Schoenfeld, 2003) described six features that characterize fields where practice is symbiotically informed and improved by research:

1. Robust mechanisms for taking ideas from laboratory scale to widely used practice.
2. Norms for research methods and reporting that are rigorous and consistent, resulting in a set of insights and/or prototype tools on which designers can rely.
3. A reasonably stable theoretical base, with a minimum of faddishness and a clear view of the reliable range of each aspect of the theory.
4. Teams of adequate size to grapple with large tasks, over the relatively long timescales required for sound work of major importance in both research and development.
5. Sustained funding to support the research-practice process on realistic timescales.
6. Individual and group accountability for ideas and products. Do they work as claimed, in the range of circumstances claimed?

Some limited progress has been made in education in some of these areas. Here I want to look at specific ways in which we can move forward more rapidly in the future. The common theme is collaboration: building a community of researchers in education that constructs programs that match the scale of major challenges they identify as worth the effort, and building and consolidating theory that is a reliable basis for design and development. Mathematics education is well placed to take the lead for education.

I shall discuss mechanisms that can advance the overall enterprise. Central to this is building high-power collaborative research and development programs that can gradually come to guide policy and practice—"Big Education" learning from "Big Science."

Build a Body of Accepted Knowledge

All research fields have areas of controversy. Usually these are confined to the leading edge of current research. At the core of each field is a body of results that are accepted as true, each based on evidence accumulated from a range of complementary studies that also serve to define the boundaries of their validity.

In education things are complicated by some lack of agreement on the various phenomena of interest, compounded by the many overlapping theoretical perspectives. Focusing on performance goals—the main concern of society at large—reduces the problem but does not eliminate it. For example, I noted that the goals summarized in the quote in the last section are not universally accepted. The "body of accepted knowledge" is thus conditional on a well-defined range of phenomena and goals. Two linked elements are needed: agreement on what counts, and a body of facts that are important in that context.

In science, for the most part, phenomena of interest in each area are agreed upon, after which one can build a body of knowledge. Across mathematics education, there is still controversy over the definition of mathematical proficiency: the various "standards" aren't fully accepted; indeed, much of the infighting over recent decades has been because people have differing views of proficiency. So work has to be conditional. If you stipulate that mathematical understanding includes problem solving, reasoning, and modeling, then you can work to build a body of related knowledge. If, in contrast, you view proficiency only as being able to reproduce procedures that you've been shown, then a different, narrower body of knowledge is relevant. Similarly, there are issues of grain size: you may believe that teaching can be studied by focusing on the teacher's moves or that it must necessarily involve studying the students as well. However, the central points remain: building such knowledge requires a coherent body of work, including replication and systematic investigation of the boundaries of validity; such work is not encouraged by the academic value system sketched earlier.

Such a body of results is a social construct of the research community, built through the familiar processes of hypothesis generation and testing, replication, and peer review. Without such a solid foundation, research results on important issues will continue to be seen as opinion—more or less plausible, but still just opinion.

Climate change is a vivid current example of research in a complex area of phenomena. There are some unquestioned basic facts, such as the warming effect of CO_2 in the atmosphere, and a wide range of intensely-tested models that bring together the complex amalgam of factors that affect the climate. Everything has been questioned, replicated, and reanalyzed in various ways. A host of alternative explanations were sought, modeled, and similarly confronted with the data. The community conclusion is that human causes of global warming are almost certainly important, and the consequences potentially dire. This was a research community enterprise.

Building such a body of accepted results in mathematics education has, to put it mildly, not been a priority. For the reasons set out earlier, the academic value system does not encourage or reward it. My guess is that most of us could write down our own modest list—though few of us do. But that is not the point: only as a research community consensus, built on a coherent body of well-tested evidence, would such a list have power.

Recently, the National Centre for Excellence in the Teaching of Mathematics in the UK brought together a group of researchers and practitioners to distil and set of design principles for effective teaching (NCETM, 2012). Table 29.2 is the summary that the NCETM

Table 29.2 Principles for effective mathematics teaching. Source: NCETM (2012).

Teaching is more effective when it:

- **Builds on the knowledge learners already have**
  This means developing formative assessment techniques and adapting our teaching to accommodate individual learning needs.

- **Exposes and discusses common misconceptions and other surprising phenomena**
  Learning activities should expose current thinking, create "tensions" by confronting learners with inconsistencies and surprises, and allow opportunities for resolution through discussion.

- **Uses higher-order questions**
  Questioning is more effective when it promotes explanation, application, and synthesis rather than mere recall.

- **Makes appropriate use of whole class interactive teaching, individual work and cooperative small group work.**
  Collaborative group work is more effective after learners have been given an opportunity for individual reflection. Activities are more effective when they encourage critical, constructive discussion, rather than argumentation or uncritical acceptance. Shared goals and group accountability are important.

- **Encourages reasoning rather than "answer getting"**
  Often, learners are more concerned with what they have "done" than with what they have learned. It is better to aim for depth than for superficial "coverage."

- **Uses rich, collaborative tasks**
  The tasks we use should be accessible, extendable, encourage decision making, promote discussion, encourage creativity, encourage "what if" and "what if not?" questions.

- **Creates connections between topics both within and beyond mathematics and with the real world**
  Learners often find it difficult to generalize and transfer their learning to other topics and contexts. Relate concepts remain unconnected. Effective teachers build bridges between ideas.

- **Uses resources, including technology, in creative and appropriate ways**
  Information and communications technology (ICT) offers new ways to engage with mathematics. At its best it is dynamic and visual: relationships become more tangible. ICT can provide feedback on actions and enhance interactivity and learner autonomy. Through its connectivity, ICT offers the means to access and share resources and—even more powerfully—the means by which learners can share their ideas within and across classrooms.

- **Confronts difficulties rather than seeks to avoid or preempt them**
  Effective teaching challenges learners and has high expectations of them. It does not seek to "smooth the path" but creates realistic obstacles to be overcome. Confidence, persistence, and learning are not attained through repeating successes, but by struggling with difficulties.

- **Develops mathematical language through communicative activities**
  Mathematics is a language that enables us to describe and model situations, think logically, frame and sustain arguments and communicate ideas with precision. Learners do not know mathematics until they can "speak" it. Effective teaching therefore focuses on the communicative aspects of mathematics by developing oral and written mathematical language.

- **Recognizes both what has been learned and also how it has been learned**
  What is to be learned cannot always be stated prior to the learning experience. After a learning event, however, it is important to reflect on the learning that has taken place, making this as explicit and memorable as possible. Effective teachers will also reflect on the ways in which learning has taken place, so that learners develop their own capacity to learn.

---

produced. The point is not that this list is "correct," let alone unique. But it does have the following essential properties from a scientific research perspective:

- It is reasonably specific, in this case effectively embodying a set of design principles.
- Each statement is testable[16] —further research and development can establish its range of validity, if any.

Since this way of teaching is qualitatively different from that in the great majority of mathematics classrooms around the world, where the "3X model" (explanation, worked examples, practice exercises) predominates, it is societally important to establish its range of validity, and to refine it, while embarking on the massive effort that will be needed to equip and empower teachers to work in this way.[17]

There have been some other efforts of this kind. A European group, the Committee of Education of the European Mathematical Society, has begun to tackle this problem, producing a series of reports on "solid findings in mathematics education"(EMS, 2011–13), intended for the broad mathematical community.

Testing Theoretical Models

Testing such propositions can be done effectively only through building substantial coherent collaborations within the research community, each studying specific questions across a well-planned range of the important variables: students, teachers, topics, etc. I shall describe one example, one among not too many. Over the last 35 years Alan Bell, Malcolm Swan, and members of the Shell Centre team have undertaken a coherent sequence of studies of "diagnostic teaching," which embodies many of the principles[18] in Table 29.2. They first explored in small scale studies the validity across three key variables: students, mathematical topics, and different designers of the experimental teaching materials (see e.g. Swan 1980; Birks 1987; Bell 1993). Later teacher variables were included in a broader sequence of studies, described with extensive references in Swan (2006).

This "diagnostic teaching" program, when compared with the standard direct instruction approach of the time, showed a common pattern of much improved *long-term learning* illustrated by Figure 29.1.

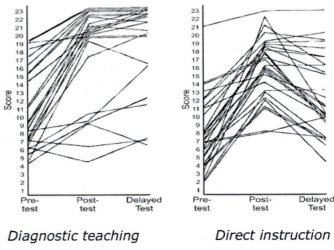

Diagnostic teaching   *Direct instruction*

Figure 29.1 Mean scores on pre-, post-, and delayed post-tests (Birks, 1987).

The key point: Only such common patterns, emerging from exploring a hypothesis over the range of relevant variables in a coherent program, can test and establish a principle. Separate small-scale studies without this coherence, however trustworthy they may be individually, do not establish any warrants for generalizability. They are studies of specific treatments not design principles.

Note in the right-hand graph the subsequent loss, so familiar to teachers, of most of the gains made during the teaching of the unit; this does not occur with the diagnostic teaching approach. This key result was stable across the various "parallel" studies.

There is no suggestion, of course, that such a program will establish a *unique* set of principles—in this case for the design of teaching—but simply one that is soundly based in both research and practice, with well-researched outcomes and boundaries of established validity. Similar studies based on other sets of principles can then give a sound basis for comparisons.

There are other examples of such coherent sequences of research and development studies, usually spread over several decades, that led to phenomenological theories, expressed as design principles. They include:

- The Freudenthal Institute team's development of "realistic mathematics education," building concept development on students looking at concrete situations in increasingly abstract ways. (See e.g. van den Heuvel-Panhuizen, 1998.)

- The work of Glenda Lappan, Elizabeth Phillips, and others on middle-grade mathematics through their Middle Grade Mathematics Program and, ultimately, *Connected Mathematics*. (See e.g. Lappan & Phillips, 2009.)
- CGI: Cognitively Guided Instruction, a research-based approach to improving teaching through a specific style of professional development, was developed through a program of research at the University of Wisconsin. (See e.g., Carpenter, Fennema, Peterson, Chiang, & Loef, 1989.)
- The research linking curriculum change, assessment, teaching and systematic professional development by Kaye Stacey and colleagues in and around the University of Melbourne is assisting the state mathematics curriculum and high stakes examinations to embrace the capabilities offered by mathematically able calculators and computers. (See Pierce & Stacey, 2010; Pierce, Stacey, Wander, & Ball, 2011.)

However, in all these cases the work has largely been carried through by a single team. Independent probing through replication and critique are as rare as they are important in establishing a body of knowledge that is generally accepted across the research community.

Such a collective enterprise requires agreed goals, focus, and methodology. The diagnostic teaching studies are, in truth, a pitifully small-scale example of what is needed, limited by the familiar constraints of the academic environment discussed earlier.

Make Evaluation-in-Depth Central

"If you're so smart, how come you ain't rich?" as the old saying goes. Why have such well-engineered materials, though they have had significant impact, not become the norm in most classrooms? "Evaluation by inspection," though far from the only factor, is a sufficient explanation.

Evaluative *evidence*, even when it is available, is neither sought nor valued in choosing materials, or in policy making more widely. The opinion-based humanities approach still dominates. New teaching materials are reviewed in educational publications like novels or plays. "Will 500 words be OK? Can you let us have it in three weeks?" How different from trials of new medicines. Equally, in the United States, for example, the coverage of textbooks is mandated by committees that, in practice, require so many "good things" (fluent skills, problem solving, real-world applications, and so on) that the total is far too much[19] to be teachable in the time allocated—many times the number of pages in the corresponding Japanese textbooks. So teachers choose the things they are most comfortable with, taking into account other pressures they face: any professional development they may encounter, district plans, and, particularly, the tasks in any high-stakes tests on which they and their students will be judged. Clearly, solid information on what happens in classrooms when the materials are used is not expected. Acquiring that would cost money and take time. Yet large amounts of money are spent by school systems on materials chosen on the basis of such "reviews by inspection."

How can we do better? I see four avenues for improvement. First, the fundamental responsibility for evaluation lies with those who design and develop new products and processes. It is, or should be, an integral part of the development process, providing formative feedback to guide revisions. Innovations that do not come with this information should be labeled as untested. Second, since people are rightly suspicious of "seller's reassurances," the design and collection of such information should be independently monitored, paid for by the funders of the development; too often, evaluation is peripheral to the main enterprise, satisfying a need for funder accountability but coming too late and without enough detail to help improve the product. Third, we need larger, longer-term evaluative studies of products and processes that are societally important—either because they are widely used or potentially very powerful. Finally, we need the research community to build a consensus around the importance and validity of these processes, and the results they produce.

The skills of evaluation needed for parallel studies or for summative evaluation have developed much greater depth over recent years, and this expertise is now widely available in the mathematics education research community. Yet it is not used in so many areas where it could and should be central. Most evaluations should be fundamentally formative. This body of research should guide the next round of design and development, building refinements of both the design principles and the design tactics that turn the principles into effective and absorbing tools and processes for teaching and learning, professional development, or system improvement.

Use a Common Set of Instruments

For the results of collective research to be of value, they need to look at similar things in similar, or at least overlapping, ways. Equally important, the instruments need to cover *all* the elements that are considered significant by members of the collaboration and/or the designers of the treatment. If you have a unit that is focused on teaching nonroutine problem solving, or critiquing reasoned arguments, there is no point in relying on a short-item test where only answers count.[20]

The negotiation of the instruments is a key set of decisions for a collaboration. Cost-effectiveness is important. Does this feedback give us something important in terms of the goals? This negotiation should include the designers of the treatments, since they know what they are aiming for in more detail, and perhaps more depth, than the evaluative researchers. Of course, once the studies get going, the designers should remain at a distance, as (very) interested friends.

As results begin to emerge, it makes sense to discuss them with the design team—particularly if there seem to be important implications for design. In any case, the designers will have questions that will be worth thinking about.

As always NIH—the "not invented here" syndrome—will appear. None of the candidate instruments will be "quite what we want." The development of new instruments is a worthy contribution, but only if they become widely used. Common, and commonly understood, instruments are key to communication and convincing the research community. Unless the collaboration is large, it may be wise to regard a new instrument as an extra design and development element, rather than an established instrument.

Use Focal Exemplars

The central strategic design challenge for such a collective program of focused research is to control the degree of variation between the parallel studies. On the one hand, it is essential to explore the space of important variables including mathematical focus, students, teachers, teacher preparation and support, and the treatments that are being investigated—both their design principles and the detailed realizations. (In design, the details matter.) On the other hand, to be useful, comparison demands a substantial degree of commonality between parallel studies.

This starts with straight replication—a core phase in scientific research where the goal is to check out any study on which interesting claims are based. For this to work, we need to know what was actually done; in education the lack of such information in enough detail often prevents replication.[21] For example, how often could another researcher replicate a treatment in the research referenced in other chapters here? Is the description specific enough, and available? Does it pass "the gold card test"?[22]

This problem can be mitigated by identifying and using specific exemplar treatments. They should be based on well-specified design principles, imaginatively designed and carefully developed across a well-defined range of circumstances, *and published*. These tools are then readily available to researchers for further study in depth—the variations in their use and outcomes being important issues for the research—and for informing the next phase of design. Sets of a few such focal exemplars of each kind, variations on a theme, would allow a community of researchers gradually to build an understanding of what is general and what is variable, even idiosyncratic, in the outcomes observed with students and teachers of various levels of experience and support.

What kinds of exemplar do I have in mind? In the 1990s the NSF spent around $100 million funding the development of teaching materials for 13 multiyear curricula, all based on a broad set of principles that were informed by research and set out in the NCTM *Curriculum and Evaluation Standards* (1989). The five middle grades curricula, for example, spanned a variety of approaches within this common framework. A coherent program of collective research in depth on sample units from some of these curricula, and traditional alternatives, would inform the next round of design and development, spinning off not just research papers but variants of the units concerned. To do this well needed funding comparable to the original investment—a common ratio in product development. It has not been forthcoming.

A more recent example on a smaller scale is the set of 100 formative assessment lessons for sixth grade and up developed by the Shell Centre team as part of the Gates Foundation's College and Career Readiness program.[23] This Mathematics Assessment Project is, effectively, the latest phase of the "diagnostic teaching" program described earlier. These "Classroom Challenges" are based on design principles (Swan & Burkhardt, 2014), similar to those in Table 29.2. Designed in Nottingham, each "classroom challenge" went through two rounds of trials in a few U.S. classrooms, closely observed and reported on by skilled observers using a well-defined protocol. This research base was focused on improving the materials, but new insights also emerged.

There is much more to be learned about learning and teaching of this kind from further study in depth of such focal exemplars, across a wider range of variables. For example, one such study (Evans & Swan, 2014) has looked at the effects of various ways of selecting and using "sample student work" on the subsequent group and class discussions.

The space of focal exemplars that could underpin useful research is, of course, much wider than design principles for teaching materials. For example, on one hand, Alan Schoenfeld's classic studies of the key dimensions in problem solving (Schoenfeld, 1985) have been followed and largely confirmed by others' research and development, including research-based teaching materials (e.g., Swan et al., 1984, 1985). These confirm and extend his findings—for example, that Polya's strategies are insufficiently specific to be much help to novice problem solvers. The latter need to learn tactical instantiations of these strategies for specific types of problem as part of developing a pervasive culture of doing mathematics which has problem solving at its heart.

On the other hand, his team's sequence of studies of teacher behavior (Schoenfeld, 2010) led him to claim that to understand a teacher's "moves" in the classroom, you need to understand in detail only three things: the teacher's *knowledge, goals,* and *beliefs* (or *orientations*). This work was based on an intense study of just three very different lessons, taught by three different teachers. To reduce mathematics teaching to three essential dimensions is an important, even startling, claim—and an impressive example of a consolidation of theory. It has practical implications for teaching and professional development. It deserves to be tested much more fully.

The choice of focal exemplars for study is, along with the instruments to be used, a key decision for any collaboration. To summarize, to justify the effort needed for such research, treatments to be studied in depth should be:

- innovative,
- make important claims,
- well-specified,
- available.

WHAT EFFORT IS NEEDED WHERE?

What is the balance of effort that seems to be needed to achieve maximum impact in this vision of a research community that serves teachers and their students more effectively?

Classroom Level

Research on the "zone of instruction," which includes both Learning and Teaching levels in Table 29.1, is all-important. However, from the strategic perspective of this chapter, this is the least problematic level. Perhaps this is not surprising, given the huge preponderance of R&D effort that has gone into learning and teaching, described in the other chapters of this *Handbook*. Again, I think it fair to say that:

- We know how to teach much better mathematics much better than is current in most classrooms.
- We have a variety of well-engineered tools that have been shown to enable typical teachers to make this a reality in their classrooms.

The uses of calculators and computers in mathematics education provide a vivid illustration of the challenges of turning knowledge at classroom level into large-scale practice. First, the mismatch between the way mathematics is done in most school classrooms and in the world outside is qualitative—and scandalous. A huge amount of research over the last 35 years has shown that students can learn traditional mathematics, along with many rich new things, more easily and more deeply with appropriate uses of technology. In this *Handbook*, Hegedus and Tall (Chapter 23) review the potential of multimodal technologies whereas, looking more broadly, Moreno-Armella and Santos-Trigo (Chapter 25) stress the need to develop the critical capabilities to translate scientific and technological developments into *educational* realities. Why do so many school systems still keep technology out of mathematics classrooms or, when it is let in, exploit its potential so poorly—often, for example, just replacing drill and practice exercises on pencil and paper with computer game versions? The answers all involve the third and fourth levels of R&D. Technology gives teachers and students huge flexibility in structuring rich learning activities—but most mathematics teachers are used to teaching with detailed guidance from a published scheme of work. Why then are there no comprehensive schemes that exploit technology? Because it is a moving target—the decade timescale of developing rich robust curriculum materials is mismatched with the few-year timescale of change in the technology. For which platform should we design, when it will inevitably be out of date before we finish? The situation may be stabilizing now with "tablets for all" but, when you try to go beyond the existing pool of fine enrichment materials towards a comprehensive technology-aware curriculum, the design and development challenge remains formidable.[24]

Since the problems at other levels are much more challenging, I shall leave it at that.

Teacher Level

The path of professional development that teachers follow has received less attention. Various stages are well recognized: survival in the classroom; delivering the curriculum that is set out in the chosen teaching materials; enriching the curriculum with stimulating activities that the teacher chooses; acquiring "adaptive expertise" (Hatano & Inagaki, 1986), in which the teacher continually modifies each lesson to make use of feedback from the students on their thinking.

The challenge of reaching this last stage is often underestimated: it represents a qualitative change in the pedagogical and mathematical skills that a teacher needs, in the roles played by the teacher and the students, and in the classroom culture—the set of mutual expectations that Brousseau (1997) called the "didactic contract." Yet higher-level mathematical practices, such as nonroutine problem solving or constructing and critiquing mathematical reasoning, can be developed only in such classrooms. Unfortunately, but unsurprisingly, they remain relatively rare.

What approaches have been developed that effectively help teachers climb the steep slope to adaptive expertise? Some teaching materials, including those referred to earlier, are supportive, structuring lessons to promote "productive struggle," the resolution of conceptual conflicts through discussion, and student reflection and explanation. This reduces the *design load* on the teacher and, as the developmental research shows, enables typical teachers to make the style shifts that are essential. Still unclear is how much well-supported experience of this kind is needed for teachers to begin constructively to generalize the principles involved, and to incorporate these style elements into all their teaching.

This is an established area of research that, ironically, still seems at a relatively early stage. There are serious methodological issues. Professional development programs have traditionally been evaluated through the participants' reactions, essentially: Did you find this valuable? This reflects an attitude that sees teachers as fellow professionals whose judgments are not to be questioned. However, if the aim is to modify teachers' behavior in the classroom, adding to their repertoire of strategies and skills, direct evidence is surely important; yet professional development studies that are built around structured before-after observation of teachers at work in their classrooms are still rare. (Observation is, of course, much more expensive than using questionnaires.[25])

One of the challenges that this area of R&D has to sort out is what constitutes "a good lesson." In the context of materials development, this is defined by the principles behind the design, embodied in the lesson plan; the core focus of observation is how well the lesson reflects this, in particular avoiding what Anne Brown called "lethal mutations." However, a more general framework is needed such as that provided by the Teaching for Robust Understanding scheme and its various tools (Schoenfeld, 2014). This claims that the essential quality of a mathematics lesson can be understood in just five dimensions: the mathematics, cognitive demand, access, agency and authority, and formative assessment elements. Like any such claim, this needs to be tested and probed independently.

Any such scheme needs to incorporate a coherent set of tools for use at different levels: by teachers and students in the classroom, in professional development activities, and at system level for defining and monitoring improvement objectives.

System Level: The Case for "Big Education"

I shall argue that our most intractable challenges lie at system level so, in the spirit of focusing on the most important problems, much more effort is needed there. This chapter has reviewed many of the factors that have limited the impact of research on practice and, particularly, on the policy decisions within which any improvement effort has to operate. In summary, these limiting factors include:

- The absence of any solid body of research findings accepted across the mathematics education research community and publicly articulated by its leaders. This lowers the prestige of educational research—and effectively legitimizes politicians' own opinions in the eyes of the public.
- The scale of research programs needed to remedy this situation, reflecting the many variables involved in a classroom—and the many more in a school system.
- The timescale mismatch between the few years between elections in politics and the decade timescale of educational improvement.

In order to make progress with these challenges, I see no credible alternative to large-scale research collaborations, conducted in the kind of collegial spirit that is reflected in this *Handbook* but not yet in the work of the research community at large.

Building and Funding Collaborative Research

How do we get there from here? How can those researchers who would like their work to have impact on improving practice across the education system work together to make it happen? How can they, together, counter the values that are currently prevalent—be it single-author papers or evaluations based on inspection alone? There are no established answers but many hopeful signs.

First, it can be done and has been done in other fields. As we have seen, big problems in science, engineering, and medicine have led to big teams with big programs. Big Science arose from researchers seeing the need to join the big teams needed to make real progress with big problems. For the same reasons, we need some Big Education programs.

There are already some modest examples of collaboration in mathematics education, and signs of more. The Strategic Education Research Partnership (SERP; http://serpinstitute.org/) partners with U.S. school districts and researchers to address long-term problems over sustained periods of partnership. However, SERP is not consistently funded and has to be entrepreneurial to obtain ongoing funding. In 2014 the Core Practice Consortium (see, e.g., McDonald, Kazemi, & Kavanagh, 2013), a multi-university U.S. collaboration, presented a live-streamed session on enriching research and innovation through the specification of professional practice in various subjects. These are hopeful signs, still on a small scale; we await evidence of impact.

Specific funding will be needed but a major resource is in place: the research time of the university staff and graduate students, funded through their academic salaries. Further, Big Education will cost much less than Big Science because it does not need equipment on the same scale—facilities like the space telescopes and the Large Hadron Collider cost billions. The major costs in large-scale impact-focused education research are:

- the time of skilled people, academics working with full-time researchers;
- a reasonable amount of computing power and information handling support;
- the costs of collaboration: planning and reporting meetings, and leadership support.

These things are within the budgets of research funders, particularly in the United States where the National Science Foundation (NSF) and various private foundations fund substantial programs. The NSF, in particular, has moved away from further direct support of materials development to support projects with a research focus that have the prospect of payoff. Thus I believe a case along the lines outlined in this chapter has a good chance of significant support.

The potential prize is enormous. I wrote earlier of the highly visible research breakthroughs in the last century that led to the current high levels of public respect and financial support for research in science and medicine. We know how to achieve the necessary qualitative improvements in the performance and attitude of students in mathematics, but it needs to be realized "at scale" in typical classrooms and supported by a solid body of evaluative evidence. A research and development effort that led to this has the potential to unlock a similar change in respect and financial support—and to protect students from the "common sense" of our political masters.

The real challenge is to the research community. Do enough of us give impact on policy and practice enough priority to channel our research efforts in this way? Who will come forward to lead such enterprises?

NOTES

1. In developing this approach to research design, I have benefited enormously from discussions over the years with friends and colleagues, notably Phil Daro, Mark St John, Alan Schoenfeld, and Kaye Stacey.

2. On one hand, though some professions adopt the posture that being qualified is all that matters, no one likes to think that their doctor or lawyer (or teacher) is "borderline"—though some inevitably are. On the other, everyone recognizes that there is a qualitative difference in skill between Yo Yo Ma and the average conservatory graduate cellist.

3. "Common sense" provides a cornucopia of contradictions. You may, for example, choose "A stitch in time saves nine" or "Haste makes waste" according to your view of the specific case.

4. There are still plausible speculators who have influence, many of them research mathematicians. They come from a field where logic alone is enough. Most know that learning is not that simple but think that how they (think they) learned mathematics is empirical evidence enough.

5. Burkhardt and Schoenfeld (2003) give examples of the long trail of indirect influence that sometimes occurs.

6. One should also not overlook the learning of a non-phonetic form of writing as early experience in abstract representations.

7. This has links to a fourth, more recent approach—the *fine arts* tradition.

8. A former minister of education insisted on removing the word "science" from the title of the then Social Science Research Council, leading to ESRC.

9. In the 1930s, the famous Cavendish Laboratory at Cambridge, led by the nuclear science pioneer Ernest Rutherford, is said to have had a research budget of about £3,500—about $6,000—a year, equivalent to about $200,000 today, when the budget is two orders of magnitude larger.

10. Asepsis is a notable earlier exception, the work of Pasteur and others gradually changing hospital practice, with surgeons washing their hands before as well as after surgery.

11. In the United States such bodies have sometimes been described as "death panels," a role traditionally filled there by insurance companies.

12. The organization of health-care systems often being, at least until recently, an exception.

13. Battista and Clements (2000) have made related arguments.

14. João Pedro da Ponte and Olive Chapman give a similar analysis in the context of teaching in Chapter 10.

15. There is an interesting contrast between mathematics and physics in choosing formal technical definitions. The mathematics community tends to coin new words: describing "essentially the same" as *isomorphic*, for example (though *catastrophe theory* and *fiber bundles* are among recent counterexamples). Physics tends to use familiar words in a technical sense: Work = Force × Distance, so however hard you push against a solid wall, you are technically doing no Work—though clearly working hard. (My proposal that words used technically should always have a capital letter has, of course, got nowhere. For those who may be tempted to take up this cause, "May the Force be with you.")

16. The great physicist Wolfgang Pauli, never the kindest of critics, was asked to comment on a research paper: "It's not even wrong." We have too much of that in education.

17. In an ideal world this would be done prior to large-scale implementation—but education is too impatient to "sacrifice a generation of students" in this way. Regard it as using drugs that are not fully tested in lethal epidemics.

18. Not coincidentally, these principles are similar to those of formative assessment for learning, as set out by Paul Black and Dylan Wiliam (1998).

19. Informed rough estimates suggest it would take about three years to teach the whole content of a typical grade's state-approved U.S. textbook.

20. A lot of effort in the evaluation of the NSF curricula was of this kind, using state tests—perhaps necessary for political purposes but uninformative on key goals of the NCTM Standards (NCTM 1989) that the curricula were funded and designed to support.

21. Alan Schoenfeld (1980, 1994) has made a particular point of researchers ensuring that the raw material and detailed analysis in their studies are available for others to investigate—a trend now becoming common in scientific research. The Web now offers essentially free and unlimited space for researchers to make available the treatments they used and the subsequent analysis.

22. Dick Fletcher coined this phrase for long-promised software that continued to be elusive. It means: "Can I go into a shop and buy it yet?" (Private communication.)

23. They may be downloaded from http://map.mathshell.org/materials, free for noncommercial use.

24. There is a movement away from comprehensive published schemes of work towards "curriculum curation": a process of informed selection of high-quality resources from the large pool available on the Web. It will not be easy to do this well!

25. Malcolm Swan developed an approach (Swan. 2006) that gives the teacher and the students parallel questionnaires. He collected evidence that the inferences correlate well with direct observation.

REFERENCES

Battista, M. T., & Clements, D. H. (2000). Mathematics curriculum development as a scientific endeavor. In A. Kelly & R. Lesh (Eds.), *Handbook of research design in mathematics and science education* (pp. 737–760). Mahwah, NJ: Lawrence Erlbaum Associates.

Bell, A. (1993). Some experiments in diagnostic teaching. *Educational Studies in Mathematics, 24*(1), 115–137.

Birks, D. (1987). *Reflections: A diagnostic teaching experiment.* Nottingham, UK: University of Nottingham.

Black, P. J., & Wiliam, D. (1998). Assessment and classroom learning. *Assessment in Education*, 5, 7–74.

Brousseau, G. (1997). *Theory of didactical situations in mathematics: Didactique des mathematiques,* 1970–1990. Dordrecht: Kluwer.

Brown, A. (1992). Design experiments: Theoretical and methodological challenges in creating complex interventions in classroom settings. *Journal of the Learning Sciences, 2*(2), 141–178.

Burkhardt, H. (1988). The roles of theory in a "systems" approach to mathematical education, article in honor of prof. Hans-Georg Steiner's 60th birthday. *International Reviews on Mathematical Education, ZDM—The International Journal on Mathematics Education,* 5, 174–177.

Burkhardt, H. (2001). *Where next? Some comments on implementation.* Concluding remarks at the ICMI Algebra Study Conference, University of Melbourne.

Burkhardt, H. (2006). From design research to large-scale impact: Engineering research in education. In J. Van den Akker, K. Gravemeijer, S. McKenney, & N. Nieveen (Eds.), *Educational design research.* London: Routledge.

Burkhardt, H. (2009). On strategic design. *Educational Designer, 1*(3). Retrieved from http://www.educationaldesigner.org/ed/volume1/issue3/article9.

Burkhardt, H. (2013). Methodological issues in research and development. In Y. Li & J. N. Moschkovich (Eds.), *Proficiency and beliefs in learning and teaching mathematics—Learning from Alan Schoenfeld and Günter Törner.* Rotterdam: Sense Publishers.

Burkhardt, H. (2014). Curriculum design and systemic change. In Y. Li & G. Lappan (Eds.), *Mathematics curriculum in school education.* Heidelberg: Springer.

Burkhardt, H., & Schoenfeld, A. H. (2003). Improving educational research: Towards a more useful, more influential and better funded enterprise. *Educational Researcher, 32,* 3–14.

Carpenter, T. P., Fennema, E., Peterson, P. L., Chiang, C. P., & Loef, M. (1989). Using knowledge of children's mathematics thinking in classroom teaching: An experimental study *American Educational Research Journal, 26,* 499–531.

City, E. A., Elmore, R. F. Fiarman, S. E., & Teitel, L. (2009). *Instructional rounds in education: A network approach.* Cambridge, MA: Harvard Education Press.

EMS (2011–13). EMS Committee of Education (Eds.) "Solid Findings" in mathematics education. *EMS Newsletter* Vol. 81, 46–49, Vol. 82, 46–50, Vol. 83, 46–50, Vol. 84, 53–55, Vol. 87, 42–44.

Evans, S., & Swan, M. (2014). Developing students' strategies for problem solving: The role of pre-designed "Sample Student Work," *Educational Designer, 2*(7). Retrieved from http://www.educationaldesigner.org/ed/volume2/issue7/article25.

Flexner, A. (1910). *Medical education in the United States and Canada: A report to the Carnegie Foundation for the Advancement of Teaching* (Bulletin No. 4). New York: Carnegie Foundation for the Advancement of Teaching.

Hatano, G., & Inagaki, K. (1986). Two courses of expertise. In H. W. Stevenson, H. Azuma, & K. Hakuta (Eds.), *Child development and education in Japan* (pp. 262–272). New York: W H Freeman/Times Books/ Henry Holt & Co.

Kilpatrick, J. (1981). One point of view: Stop the bandwagon I want off. *Arithmetic Teacher, 28*(8), 2.

Lappan, G., & Phillips, E. (2009). A designer speaks. *Educational Designer, 1*(3). Retrieved from http://www.educationaldesigner.org/ed/volume1/issue3/article11.

Leung, F.K.S. (2001). In search of an East Asian identity in mathematics education. *Educational Studies in Mathematics, 47,* 35–52.

Leung, F.K.S. (2006). Mathematics education in East Asia and the West: Does culture matter? In F.K.S. Leung, K-D. Graf, & F. J. Lopez-Real (Eds.), *Mathematics education in different cultural traditions: A comparative study of East Asia and the West, the 13th ICMI study* (pp. 21–46). New York: Springer.

McDonald, M., Kazemi, E. Kavanagh, S. S. (2013). Core Practices and Pedagogies of Teacher Education: A Call for a Common Language and Collective Activity, *Journal of Teacher Education,* 64 (5).

NCETM. (2012). *Mathematics matters.* Sheffield: National Centre for Excellence in Teaching Mathematics. Retrieved from https://www.ncetm.org.uk/public/files/309231/Mathematics+Matters+Final+Report.pdf.

NCTM. (1989). *Curriculum and evaluation standards for school mathematics.* Reston, VA: National Council of Teachers of Mathematics.

Pierce, R. & Stacey, K. (2010). Mapping pedagogical opportunities provided by mathematics analysis software. *International Journal of Computers for Mathematical Learning, 15*(1) 1–20. doi:10.1007/s10758-010-9158-6.

Pierce, R., Stacey, K., Wander, R., & Ball, L. (2011). Principles for design of lessons that use multiple representations in mathematically able integrated document systems. *Technology, Pedagogy and Education, 20*(1), 95–112.

Schoenfeld, A. H. (1980). On useful research reports. *Journal for Research in Mathematics Education, 11*(5), 34–57.

Schoenfeld, A. H. (1985). *Mathematical problem solving.* Orlando, FL: Academic Press.

Schoenfeld, A. H. (1994). A discourse on methods. *Journal for Research in Mathematics Education, 25,* 697–710.

Schoenfeld, A. H. (2002). Research methods in (mathematics) education. In L. English (Ed.), *Handbook of international research in mathematics education* (pp. 435–488). Mahwah, NJ: Lawrence Erlbaum Associates.

Schoenfeld, A. H. (2010). *How we think: A theory of goal-oriented decision making and its educational applications.* London: Routledge.

Schoenfeld, A. H. (2014). What makes for powerful classrooms, and how can we support teachers in creating them? A story of research and practice, productively intertwined. *Educational Researcher, 43*(8), 404–412.

Swan, M. (1980). *The language of graphs.* Nottingham: Shell Centre for Mathematical Education.

Swan, M. (2006). *Collaborative learning in mathematics: A challenge to our beliefs and practices.* London: National Institute for Advanced and Continuing Education (NIACE) for the National Research and Development Centre for Adult Literacy and Numeracy (NRDC).

Swan, M., & Burkhardt, H. (2014). Lesson design for formative assessment. *Educational Designer, 2*(7). Retrieved from http://www.educationaldesigner.org/ed/volume2/issue7/article24/.

Swan, M., Pitts, J., Fraser, R., & Burkhardt, H., and the Shell Centre Team. (1984). *Problems with patterns and numbers.* Manchester, UK: Joint Matriculation Board and Shell Centre for Mathematical Education. Retrieved from http://www.nationalstemcentre.org.uk/elibrary/maths/resource/349/problems-with-patterns-and-numbers.

Swan, M., Pitts, J., Fraser, R., Burkhardt, H, and the Shell Centre Team. (1985). *The Language of Functions and Graphs,* Manchester, UK: Joint Matriculation Board and Shell Centre for Mathematical Education. Retrieved from http://www.nationalstemcentre.org.uk/elibrary/maths/resource/350/language-of-functions-and-graphs.

van den Heuvel-Panhuizen, M. (1998). *Realistic mathematics education.* Retrieved from http://www.fi.uu.nl/en/rme/.

Index

Note: Page number in *italics* followed by *f* indicate figures and by *t* indicate tables

CPSIA information can be obtained
at www.ICGtesting.com
Printed in the USA
LVOW09s2114260517

535981LV00005B/163/P